Collins
ESSENTIAL ROAD ATLAS
BRITAIN

Collins

Published by Collins
An imprint of HarperCollins Publishers
Westerhill Road, Bishopbriggs, Glasgow G64 2QT

www.harpercollins.co.uk

Copyright © HarperCollins Publishers Ltd 2016
Collins® is a registered trademark of HarperCollins Publishers Limited

Mapping generated from CollinsBartholomew digital databases

Contains Ordnance Survey data © Crown copyright and database right (2015)

The grid on this map is the National Grid taken from the Ordnance Survey map with the permission of the Controller of Her Majesty's Stationery Office.

Printed in China by RR Donnelley APS Co Ltd

ISBN 978 0 00 815856 9   10 9 8 7 6 5 4 3 2 1

e-mail: roadcheck@harpercollins.co.uk   facebook.com/collinsmaps   @collinsmaps

© Natural England copyright. Contains Ordnance Survey data © Crown copyright and database right (2015)

Information for the alignment of the Wales Coast Path provided by © Natural Resources Wales. All rights reserved. Contains Ordnance Survey Data. Ordnance Survey Licence number 100019741. Crown Copyright and Database Right (2013).

Information for the alignment of several Long Distance Trails in Scotland provided by © walkhighlands

Information on fixed speed camera locations provided by PocketGPSWorld.com

With thanks to the Wine Guild of the United Kingdom for help with researching vineyards.

Information regarding blue flag beach awards is current as of summer 2009. For latest information please visit www.blueflag.org.uk

Conten[ts]

Route planning

Route planning map	
Restricted motorway	viii-ix
Motorway services information	x-xi
Orbital motorway maps - M25 & Birmingham	xii-xiii
Risk rating of Britain's motorways and A roads	xiv-xv
Distance chart	xvi

Urban approach maps (1 mile to 1 inch)   1-32

Symbols used on maps / Locator map	1
Plymouth	2
Bournemouth	3
Southampton & Portsmouth	4-5
Swansea	6
Cardiff & Newport	7
Bristol	8
Milton Keynes	9
London	10-13
West Midlands	14-15
Coventry	16
Leicester	17
Derby & Nottingham	18-19
Stoke-on-Trent	20
Sheffield	21
Merseyside	22-23
Greater Manchester	24-25
Leeds & Bradford	26-27
Newcastle upon Tyne & Sunderland	28
Middlesbrough	29
Glasgow	30-31
Edinburgh	32

Street maps   33-91

Symbols used on maps / Locator map	33	Hastings	75
Birmingham	34-35	Hereford	75
Edinburgh	36-37	Hull	76
Glasgow	38-39	Inverness	76
Leeds	40-41	Leicester	77
Liverpool	42-43	Lincoln	77
London	44-45	Middlesbrough	78
Manchester	46-47	Milton Keynes	78
Birmingham index	48	Newcastle upon Tyne	79
Edinburgh index	49	Norwich	79
Glasgow index	51	Nottingham	80
Leeds index	52	Oxford	80
Liverpool index	54	Perth	81
London index	56	Plymouth	81
Manchester index	60	Portsmouth	82
Aberdeen	63	Reading	82
Bath	63	Salisbury	83
Blackpool	64	Scarborough	83
Bournemouth	64	Sheffield	84
Bradford	65	Southampton	84
Brighton	65	Stoke-on-Trent	85
Bristol	66	Stratford-upon-Avon	85
Cambridge	66	Sunderland	86
Canterbury	67	Swansea	86
Cardiff	67	Swindon	87
Carlisle	68	Torquay	87
Cheltenham	68	Watford	88
Chester	69	Weston-super-Mare	88
Coventry	69	Winchester	89
Derby	70	Windsor	89
Dover	70	Worcester	90
Dundee	71	York	90
Durham	71		
Eastbourne	72	**Airport plans**	
Exeter	72	Birmingham International	91
Folkestone	73	Gatwick	91
Gloucester	73	Glasgow	91
Guildford	74	Heathrow	91
Harrogate	74	Manchester	91
		Stansted	91

Road maps   92-279

Symbols used on maps & key to map pages	92-93
England, Wales & Southern Scotland (3.2 miles to 1 inch)	94-253
Northern Scotland (4.2 miles to 1 inch)	254-279

Index   280-318

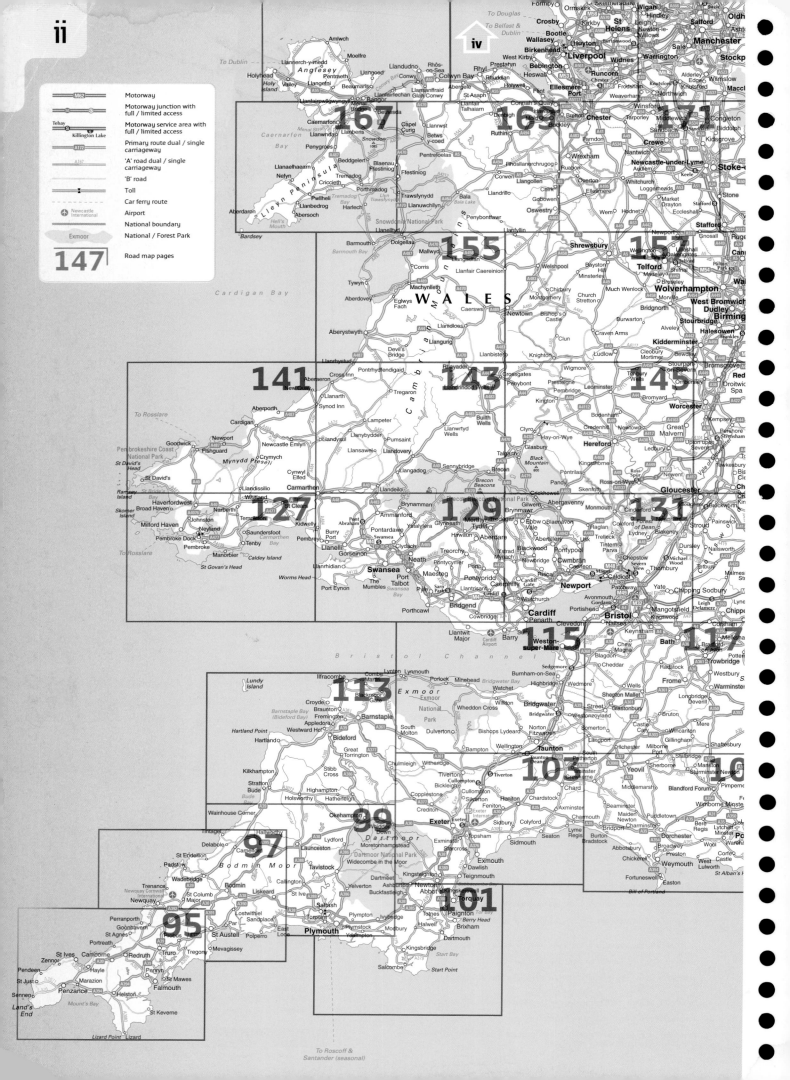

Motorway

Motorway junction with full / limited access

Motorway service area with full / limited access

Primary route dual / single carriageway

'A' road dual / single carriageway

'B' road

Toll

Car ferry route

Airport

National boundary

National / Forest Park

Road map pages

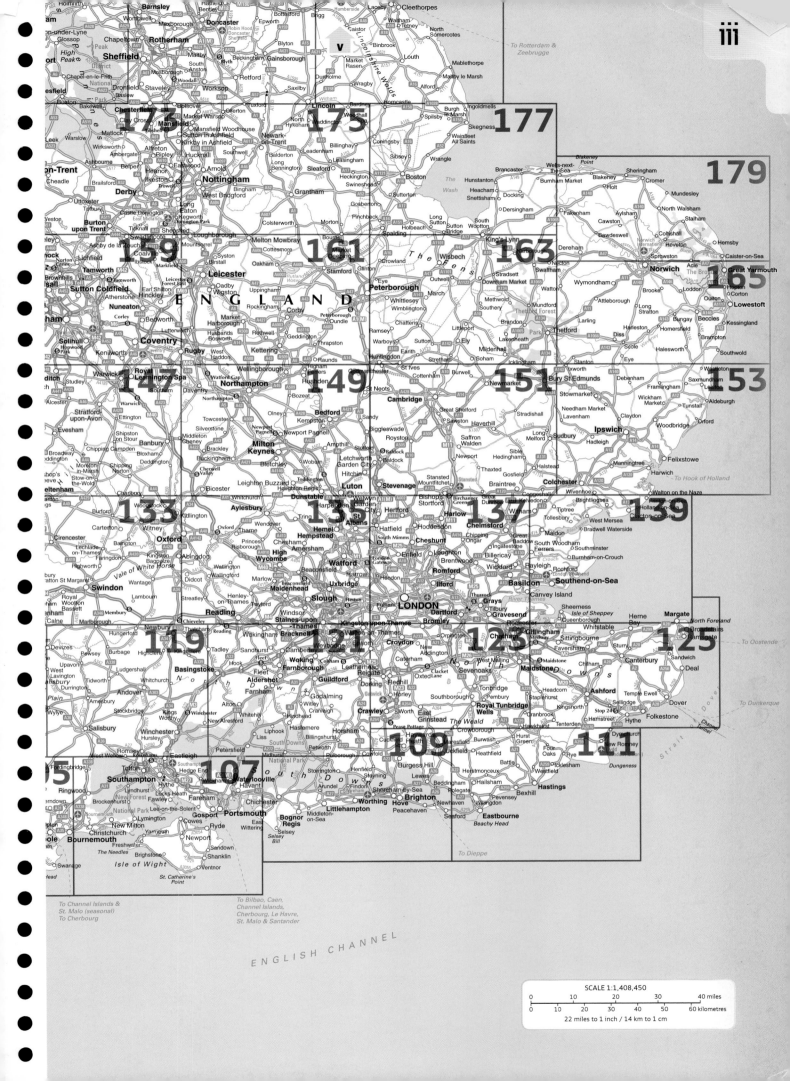

SCALE 1:1,408,450

0   10   20   30   40 miles

0 10   20   30   40   50   60 kilometres

22 miles to 1 inch / 14 km to 1 cm

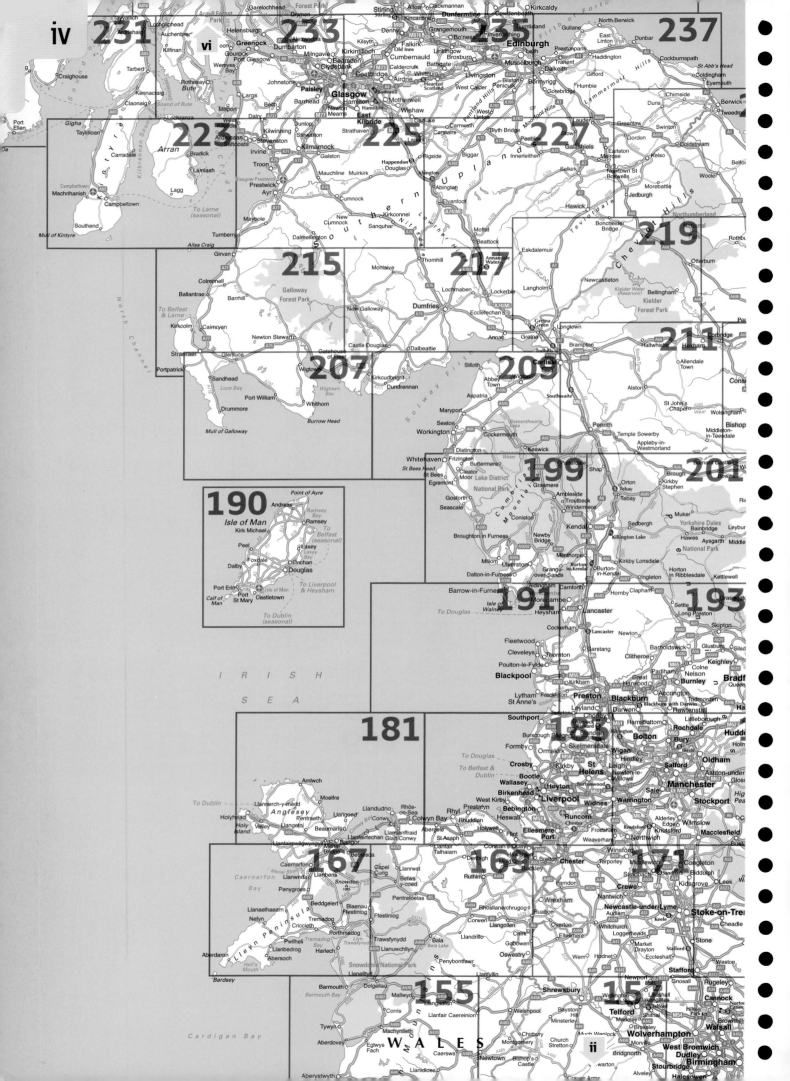

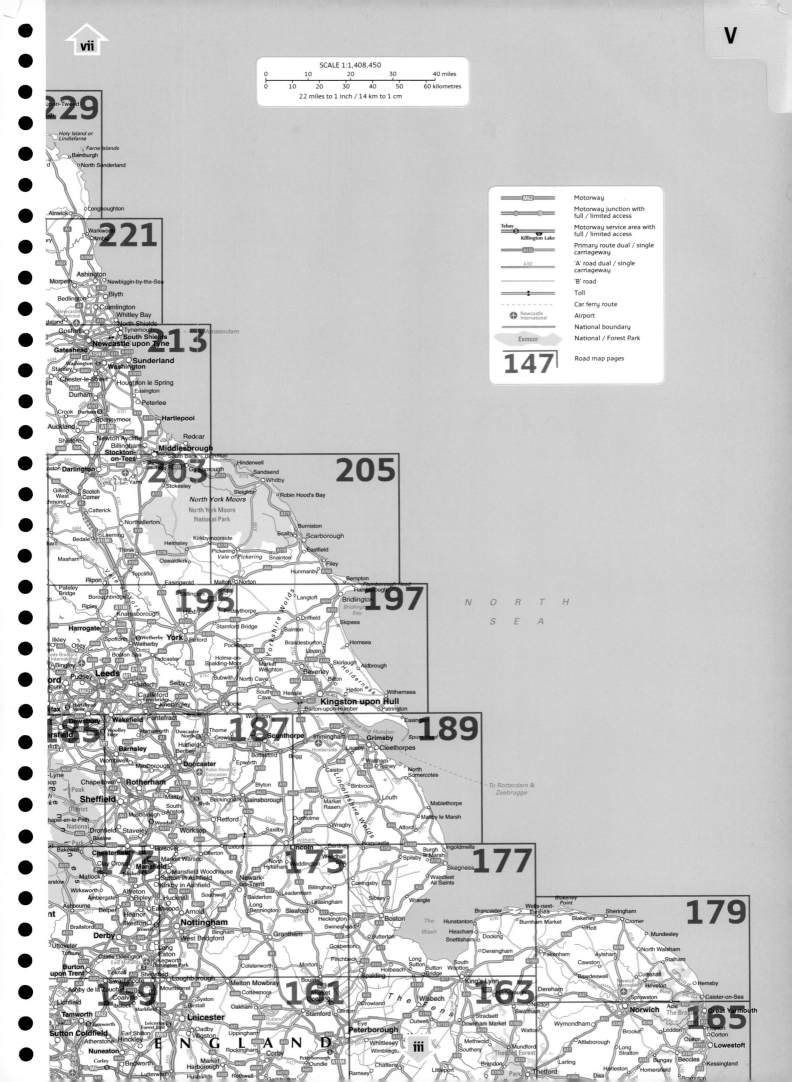

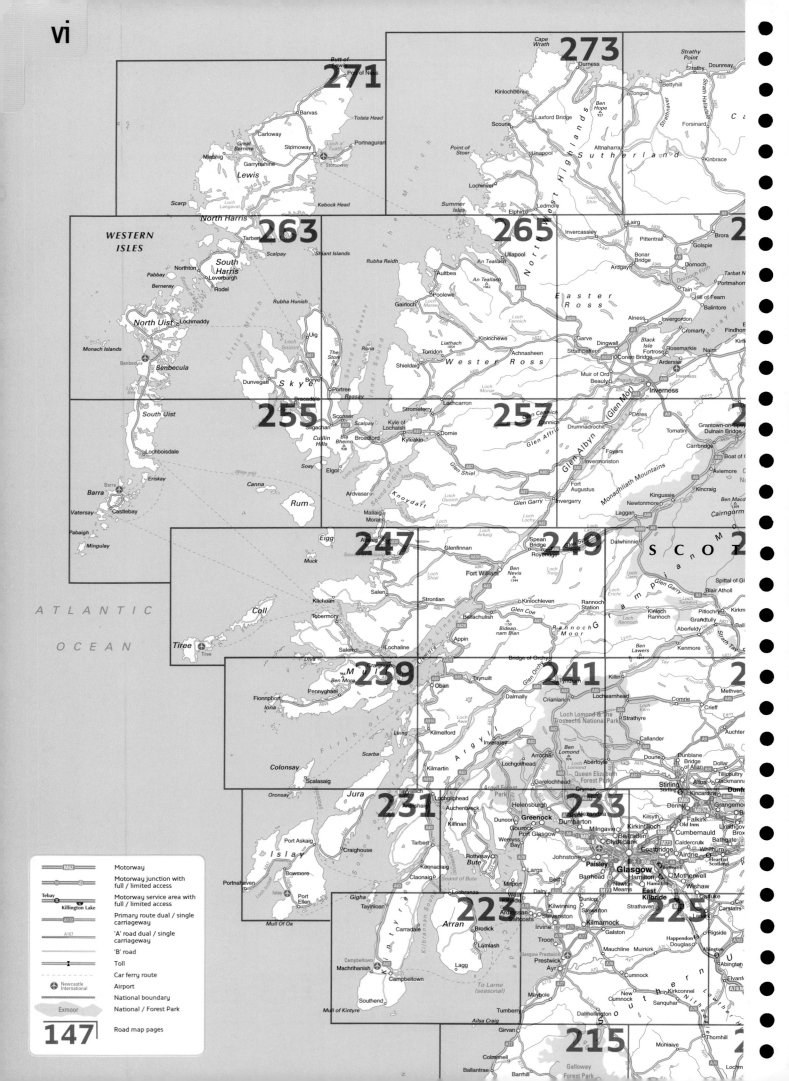

		Motorway
		Motorway junction with full / limited access
Tebay, Killington Lake		Motorway service area with full / limited access
A172		Primary route dual / single carriageway
A167		'A' road dual / single carriageway
		'B' road
		Toll
		Car ferry route
Newcastle International		Airport
		National boundary
Exmoor		National / Forest Park
147		Road map pages

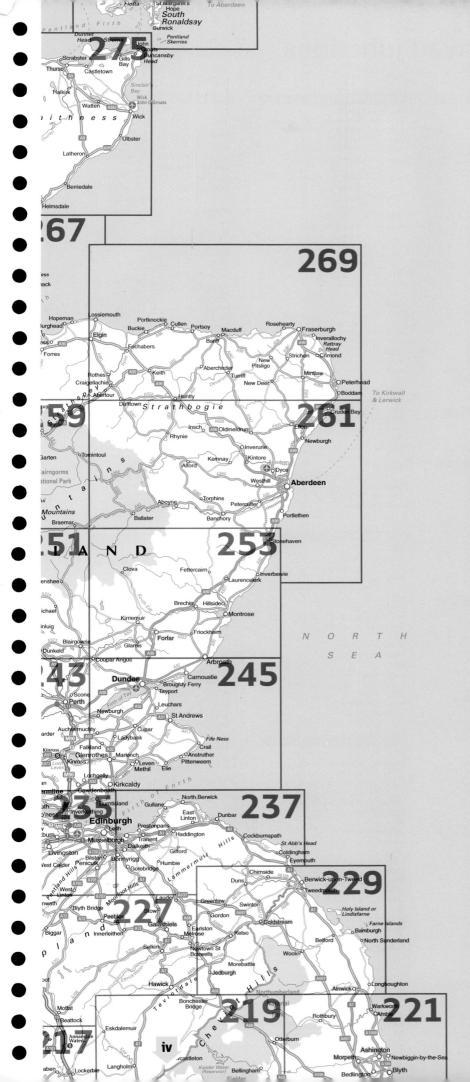

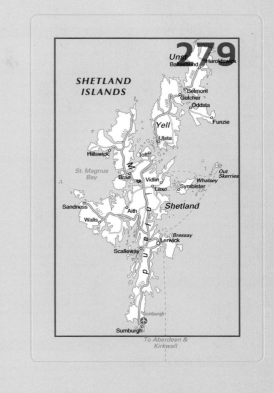

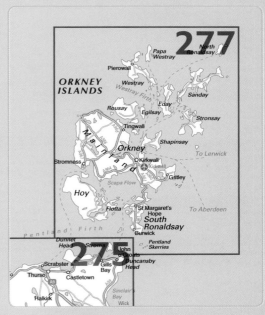

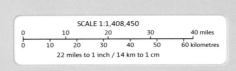

SCALE 1:1,408,450

0   10   20   30   40 miles

0   10   20   30   40   50   60 kilometres

22 miles to 1 inch / 14 km to 1 cm

Restricted motorway junctions

A1(M) LONDON TO NEWCASTLE

(2)
Northbound : No access
Southbound : No exit

(3)
Southbound : No access

(5)
Northbound : No exit
Southbound : No access
: No exit

(41)
Northbound : No exit to M62 Eastbound

(43)
Northbound : No exit to M1 Westbound

Dishforth
Southbound : No access from A168 Eastbound

(57)
Northbound : No access
: Exit only to A66(M) Northbound
Southbound : Access only from A66(M) Southbound
: No exit

(65)
Northbound : No access from A1
Southbound : No exit to A1

A3(M) PORTSMOUTH

(1)
Northbound : No exit
Southbound : No access

(4)
Northbound : No access
Southbound : No exit

A38(M) BIRMINGHAM

Victoria Road
Northbound : No exit
Southbound : No access

A48(M) CARDIFF

Junction with M4
Westbound : No access from M4 (29) Eastbound
Eastbound : No exit to M4 (29) Westbound

(29A)
Westbound : No exit to A48 Eastbound
Eastbound : No access from A48 Westbound

A57(M) MANCHESTER

Brook Street
Westbound : No exit
Eastbound : No access

A58(M) LEEDS

Westgate
Southbound : No access
Woodhouse Lane
Westbound : No exit

A64(M) LEEDS

Claypit Lane
Eastbound : No access

A66(M) DARLINGTON

Junction with A1(M)
Northbound : No access from A1(M) Southbound
: No exit
Southbound : No access
: No exit to A1(M) Northbound

A74(M) LOCKERBIE

(18)
Northbound : No access
Southbound : No exit

A167(M) NEWCASTLE

Campden Street
Northbound : No exit
Southbound : No access
: No exit

M1 LONDON TO LEEDS

(2)
Northbound : No exit
Southbound : No access

(4)
Northbound : No exit
Southbound : No access

(6A)
Northbound : Access only from M25 (21)
: No exit
Southbound : No access
: Exit only to M25 (21)

(7)
Northbound : Access only from A414
: No exit
Southbound : No access
: Exit only to A414

M1 LONDON TO LEEDS (continued)

(17)
Northbound : No access
: Exit only to M45
Southbound : Access only from M45
: No exit

(19)
Northbound : Exit only to M6
Southbound : Access only from M6

(21A)
Northbound : No access
Southbound : No exit

(23A)
Northbound : No access from A453
Southbound : No exit to A453

(24A)
Northbound : No exit
Southbound : No access

(35A)
Northbound : No access
Southbound : No exit

(43)
Northbound : No access
: Exit only to M621
Southbound : No exit
: Access only from M621

(48)
Northbound : No exit to A1(M) Southbound
: Access only from A1(M) Northbound
Southbound : Exit only to A1(M) Southbound
: No access

M2 ROCHESTER TO CANTERBURY

(1)
Westbound : No exit to A2 Eastbound
Eastbound : No access from A2 Westbound

M3 LONDON TO WINCHESTER

(8)
Westbound : No access
Eastbound : No exit

(10)
Northbound : No access
Southbound : No exit

(13)
Southbound : No exit to A335 Eastbound
: No access

(14)
Westbound : No access
Eastbound : No exit

M4 LONDON TO SWANSEA

(1)
Westbound : No access from A4 Eastbound
Eastbound : No exit to A4 Westbound

(2)
Westbound : No access from A4 Eastbound
: No exit to A4 Eastbound
Eastbound : No access from A4 Westbound
: No exit to A4 Westbound

(21)
Westbound : No access from M48 Eastbound
Eastbound : No exit to M48 Westbound

(23)
Westbound : No exit to M48 Eastbound
Eastbound : No access from M48 Westbound

(25)
Westbound : No access
Eastbound : No exit

(25A)
Westbound : No access
Eastbound : No exit

(29)
Westbound : No access
: Exit only to A48(M)
Eastbound : Access only from A48(M) Eastbound
: No exit

(38)
Westbound : No access

(39)
Westbound : No exit
Eastbound : No access
: No exit

(41)
Westbound : No exit
Eastbound : No access

(42)
Westbound : No exit to A48
Eastbound : No access from A48

M5 BIRMINGHAM TO EXETER

(10)
Northbound : No exit
Southbound : No access

(11A)
Northbound : No access from A417 Eastbound
Southbound : No exit to A417 Westbound

M6 COVENTRY TO CARLISLE

Junction with M1
Northbound : No access from M1 (19) Southbound
Southbound : No exit to M1 (19) Northbound

(3A)
Northbound : No access from M6 Toll
Southbound : No exit to M6 Toll

(4)
Northbound : No exit to M42 Northbound
: No access from M42 Southbound
Southbound : No exit to M42
: No access from M42 Southbound

(4A)
Northbound : No access from M42 (8)
Northbound
: No exit
Southbound : No access
: Exit only to M42 (8)

(5)
Northbound : No access
Southbound : No exit

(10A)
Northbound : No access
: Exit only to M54
Southbound : Access only from M54
: No exit

(11A)
Northbound : No exit to M6 Toll
Southbound : No access from M6 Toll

(24)
Northbound : No exit
Southbound : No access

(25)
Northbound : No access
Southbound : No exit

(30)
Northbound : Access only from M61 Northbound
: No exit
Southbound : No access
: Exit only to M61 Southbound

(31A)
Northbound : No access
Southbound : No exit

M6 Toll BIRMINGHAM

(T1)
Northbound : Exit only to M42
: Access only from A4097
Southbound : No exit
: Access only from M42 Southbound

(T2)
Northbound : No exit
: No access
Southbound : No access

(T5)
Northbound : No exit
Southbound : No access

(T7)
Northbound : No access
Southbound : No exit

(T8)
Northbound : No access
Southbound : No exit

M8 EDINBURGH TO GLASGOW

(8)
Westbound : No access from M73 (2)
Southbound
: No access from A8 Eastbound
: No access from A89 Eastbound
Eastbound : No access from A89 Westbound
: No exit to M73 (2) Northbound

(9)
Westbound : No exit
Eastbound : No access

(13)
Westbound : Access only from M80
Eastbound : Exit only to M80

(14)
Westbound : No exit
Eastbound : No access

(16)
Westbound : No exit
Eastbound : No access

(17)
Eastbound : Access only from A82,
not central Glasgow
: Exit only to A82,
not central Glasgow

(18)
Westbound : No access
Eastbound : No access

(19)
Westbound : Access only from A814 Eastbound
Eastbound : Exit only to A814 Westbound,
not central Glasgow

M8 EDINBURGH TO GLASGOW (cont)

(20)
Westbound : No access
Eastbound : No exit

(21)
Westbound : No exit
Eastbound : No access

(22)
Westbound : No access
: Exit only to M77 Southbound
Eastbound : Access only from M77 Northbound
: No exit

(23)
Westbound : No access
Eastbound : No exit

(25A)
Eastbound : No exit
Westbound : No access

(28)
Westbound : No access
Eastbound : No exit

(28A)
Westbound : No access
Eastbound : No exit

M9 EDINBURGH TO STIRLING

(2)
Westbound : No exit
Eastbound : No access

(3)
Westbound : No access
Eastbound : No exit

(6)
Westbound : No exit
Eastbound : No access

(8)
Westbound : No exit
Eastbound : No exit

M11 LONDON TO CAMBRIDGE

(4)
Northbound : No access from A1400 Westbound
: No exit
Southbound : No access
: No exit to A1400 Eastbound

(5)
Northbound : No access
Southbound : No exit

(8A)
Northbound : No access
Southbound : No exit

(9)
Northbound : No access
Southbound : No exit

(13)
Northbound : No access
Southbound : No exit

(14)
Northbound : No access from A428 Eastbound
: No exit to A428 Westbound
: No exit to A1307
Southbound : No access from A428 Eastbound
: No access from A1307
: No exit

M20 LONDON TO FOLKESTONE

(2)
Westbound : No exit
Eastbound : No access

(3)
Westbound : No access
: Exit only to M26 Westbound
Eastbound : Access only from M26 Eastbound
: No exit

(11A)
Westbound : No exit
Eastbound : No access

M23 LONDON TO CRAWLEY

(7)
Northbound : No exit to A23 Southbound
Southbound : No access from A23 Northbound

(10A)
Southbound : No access from B2036
Northbound : No exit to B2036

Restricted motorway junctions are shown on the maps as:

M25 LONDON ORBITAL MOTORWAY

(1B)
Clockwise : No access
Anticlockwise : No exit

(5)
Clockwise : No exit to M26 Eastbound
Anticlockwise : No access from M26 Westbound

Spur of M25 (5)
Clockwise : No access from M26 Westbound
Anticlockwise : No exit to M26 Eastbound

(19)
Clockwise : No access
Anticlockwise : No exit

(21)
Clockwise : No access from M1 (6A)
Northbound
: No exit to M1 (6A) Southbound
Anticlockwise : No access from M1 (6A)
Northbound
: No exit to M1 (6A) Southbound

(31)
Clockwise : No exit
Anticlockwise : No access

M26 SEVENOAKS

Junction with M25 (5)
Westbound : No exit to M25 Anticlockwise
: No exit to M25 spur
Eastbound : No access from M25 Clockwise
: No access from M25 spur

Junction with M20
Westbound : No access from M20 (3)
Eastbound
Eastbound : No exit to M20 (3) Westbound

M27 SOUTHAMPTON TO PORTSMOUTH

(4) West
Westbound : No exit
Eastbound : No access

(4) East
Westbound : No access
Eastbound : No exit

(10)
Westbound : No access
Eastbound : No exit

(12) West
Westbound : No exit
Eastbound : No access

(12) East
Westbound : No access from A3
Eastbound : No exit

M40 LONDON TO BIRMINGHAM

(3)
Westbound : No access
Eastbound : No exit

(7)
Eastbound : No exit

(8)
Northbound : No access
Southbound : No exit

(13)
Northbound : No access
Southbound : No exit

(14)
Northbound : No exit
Southbound : No access

(16)
Northbound : No access
Southbound : No exit

M42 BIRMINGHAM

(1)
Northbound : No exit
Southbound : No access

(7)
Northbound : No access
: Exit only to M6 Northbound
Southbound : Access only from M6 Northbound
: No exit

(7A)
Northbound : No access
: Exit only to M6 Eastbound
Southbound : No access
: No exit

(8)
Northbound : Access only from M6 Southbound
: No exit
Southbound : Access only from M6 Southbound
: Exit only to M6 Northbound

M45 COVENTRY

Junction with M1
Westbound : No access from M1 (17) Southbound
Eastbound : No exit to M1 (17) Northbound

Junction with A45
Westbound : No exit
Eastbound : No access

M48 CHEPSTOW

M4
Westbound : No exit to M4 Eastbound
Eastbound : No access from M4 Westbound

M49 BRISTOL

(18A)
Northbound : No access from M5 Southbound
Southbound : No access from M5 Northbound

M53 BIRKENHEAD TO CHESTER

(11)
Northbound : No access from M56 (15) Eastbound
: No exit to M56 (15) Westbound
Southbound : No access from M56 (15) Eastbound
: No exit to M56 (15) Westbound

M54 WOLVERHAMPTON TO TELFORD

Junction with M6
Westbound : No access from M6 (10A)
Southbound
Eastbound : No exit to M6 (10A) Northbound

M56 STOCKPORT TO CHESTER

(1)
Westbound : No access from M60 Eastbound
: No access from A34 Northbound
Eastbound : No exit to M60 Westbound
: No exit to A34 Southbound

(2)
Westbound : No access
Eastbound : No exit

(3)
Westbound : No exit
Eastbound : No access

(4)
Westbound : No access
Eastbound : No exit

(7)
Westbound : No access
Eastbound : No exit

(8)
Westbound : No exit
Eastbound : No access

(9)
Westbound : No exit to M6 Southbound
Eastbound : No access from M6 Northbound

(15)
Westbound : No access
: No access from M53 (11)
Eastbound : No exit
: No exit to M53 (11)

M57 LIVERPOOL

(3)
Northbound : No exit
Southbound : No access

(5)
Northbound : Access only from A580 Westbound
: No exit
Southbound : No access
: Exit only to A580 Eastbound

M58 LIVERPOOL TO WIGAN

(1)
Westbound : No access
Eastbound : No exit

M60 MANCHESTER

(2)
Westbound : No exit
Eastbound : No access

(3)
Westbound : No access from M56 (1)
: No access from A34 Southbound
: No exit to A34 Northbound
Eastbound : No access from A34 Southbound
: No exit to M56 (1)
: No exit to A34 Northbound

(4)
Westbound : No access
Eastbound : No exit to M56

M60 MANCHESTER (continued)

(5)
Westbound : No access from A5103 Southbound
: No exit to A5103 Southbound
Eastbound : No access from A5103 Northbound
: No exit to A5103 Northbound

(14)
Westbound : No access from A580
: No exit to A580 Eastbound
Eastbound : No access from A580 Westbound
: No exit to A580

(16)
Westbound : No access
Eastbound : No exit

(20)
Westbound : No access
Eastbound : No exit

(22)
Westbound : No access

(25)
Westbound : No access

(26)
Eastbound : No access
: No exit

(27)
Westbound : No exit
Eastbound : No access

M61 MANCHESTER TO PRESTON

(2)
Northbound : No access from A580 Eastbound
: No access from A666
Southbound : No exit to A580 Westbound

(3)
Northbound : No access from A580 Eastbound
: No access from A666
Southbound : No exit to A580 Westbound

Junction with M6
Northbound : No exit to M6 (30) Southbound
Southbound : No access from M6 (30) Northbound

M62 LIVERPOOL TO HULL

(23)
Westbound : No exit
Eastbound : No access

(32A)
Westbound : No exit to A1(M) Southbound

M65 BURNLEY

(9)
Westbound : No exit
Eastbound : No access

(11)
Westbound : No access
Eastbound : No exit

M66 MANCHESTER TO EDENFIELD

(1)
Northbound : No access
Southbound : No exit

Junction with A56
Northbound : Exit only to A56 Northbound
Southbound : Access only from A56 Southbound

M67 MANCHESTER

(1)
Westbound : No exit
Eastbound : No access

(2)
Westbound : No access
Eastbound : No exit

M69 COVENTRY TO LEICESTER

(2)
Northbound : No exit
Southbound : No access

M73 GLASGOW

(1)
Northbound : No access from A721 Eastbound
Southbound : No exit to A721 Eastbound

(2)
Northbound : No access from M8 (8)
Eastbound
Southbound : No exit to M8 (8) Westbound

M74 GLASGOW

(1A)
Westbound : No exit to M8 Kingston Bridge
Eastbound : No access from M8 Kingston Bridge

(3)
Westbound : No access
Eastbound : No exit

(3A)
Westbound : No exit
Eastbound : No access

M74 GLASGOW (continued)

(7)
Northbound : No exit
Southbound : No access

(9)
Northbound : No access
: No exit
Southbound : No access

(10)
Southbound : No exit

(11)
Northbound : No exit
Southbound : No access

(12)
Northbound : Access only from A70 Northbound
Southbound : Exit only to A70 Southbound

M77 GLASGOW

Junction with M8
Northbound : No exit to M8 (22) Westbound
Southbound : No access from M8 (22)
Eastbound

(4)
Northbound : No exit
Southbound : No access

(6)
Northbound : No exit to A77
Southbound : No access from A77

(7)
Northbound : No access
: No exit

(8)
Northbound : No access
Southbound : No access

M80 STIRLING

(4A)
Northbound : No access
Southbound : No exit

(6A)
Northbound : No exit
Southbound : No access

(8)
Northbound : No access from M876
Southbound : No exit to M876

M90 EDINBURGH TO PERTH

(2A)
Northbound : No access
Southbound : No exit

(7)
Northbound : No exit
Southbound : No access

(8)
Northbound : No access
Southbound : No exit

(10)
Northbound : No access from A912
: No exit to A912 Southbound
Southbound : No access from A912 Northbound
: No exit to A912

M180 SCUNTHORPE

(1)
Westbound : No exit
Eastbound : No access

M606 BRADFORD

Straithgate Lane
Northbound : No access

M621 LEEDS

(2A)
Northbound : No exit
Southbound : No access

(5)
Northbound : No access
Southbound : No exit

(6)
Northbound : No exit
Southbound : No access

M876 FALKIRK

Junction with M80
Westbound : No exit to M80 (8) Northbound
Eastbound : No access from M80 (8) Southbound

Junction with M9
Westbound : No access
Eastbound : No exit

Motorway services information

All motorway service areas have fuel, food, toilets, disabled facilities and free short-term parking

For further information on motorway services providers:
Moto www.moto-way.com
Euro Garages www.eurogarages.com
RoadChef www.roadchef.com
Extra www.extraservices.co.uk
Welcome Break www.welcomebreak.co.uk
Westmorland www.westmorland.com

Motorway	Junction	Service provider	Service name	Fuel supplier	Information	Accommodation	Conference facilities	Showers	M&S Simply Food	Costa Coffee	Starbucks	Burger King	KFC	McDonalds	Wimpy
A1(M)	1	Welcome Break	South Mimms	BP	●	●	●	●		●		●	●	●	
	10	Extra	Baldock	Shell		●	●		●			●	●	●	
	17	Extra	Peterborough	Shell		●	●		●	●			●	●	
	34	Moto	Blyth	Esso		●		●	●	●		●			
	46	Moto	Wetherby	BP		●	●			●	●				
	61	RoadChef	Durham	Total		●	●	●		●				●	
	64	Moto	Washington	BP		●	●								
A74(M)	16	RoadChef	Annandale Water	BP		●	●			●					
	22	Welcome Break	Gretna Green	BP		●	●			●	●	●			
M1	2-4	Welcome Break	London Gateway	Shell	●	●	●	●		●	●				
	11-12	Moto	Toddington	BP		●		●	●	●	●				
	14-15	Welcome Break	Newport Pagnell	Shell	●	●			●	●	●				
	15A	RoadChef	Northampton	BP	●				●				●		
	16-17	RoadChef	Watford Gap	BP	●	●			●				●		
	21-21A	Welcome Break	Leicester Forest East	BP	●	●	●	●		●	●	●			
	22	Euro Garages	Markfield	BP	●	●			●						
	23A	Moto	Donington Park	BP	●	●	●	●	●	●					
	25-26	Moto	Trowell	BP	●	●		●	●	●					
	28-29	RoadChef	Tibshelf	Shell	●	●	●		●				●		
	30-31	Welcome Break	Woodall	Shell	●	●				●	●	●	●	●	
	38-39	Moto	Woolley Edge	BP	●	●		●	●	●	●				
M2	4-5	Moto	Medway	BP		●		●	●	●		●			
M3	4A-5	Welcome Break	Fleet	Shell	●	●	●	●		●	●	●			
	8-9	Moto	Winchester	Shell	●	●			●	●		●			
M4	3	Moto	Heston	BP	●	●	●	●		●		●			
	11-12	Moto	Reading	BP	●	●	●	●		●		●			
	13	Moto	Chieveley	BP		●			●	●		●			
	14-15	Welcome Break	Membury	BP	●	●	●			●	●	●			
	17-18	Moto	Leigh Delamere	BP	●	●	●	●	●	●		●			
	23A	RoadChef	Magor	Esso	●	●			●				●		
	30	Welcome Break	Cardiff Gate	Total		●				●	●				
	33	Moto	Cardiff West	Esso	●	●			●	●					
	36	Welcome Break	Sarn Park	Shell		●			●			●	●		
	47	Moto	Swansea	BP	●	●				●					
	49	RoadChef	Pont Abraham	Texaco					●						
M5	3-4	Moto	Frankley	BP	●	●	●	●	●	●					
	8	RoadChef	Strensham (South)	BP	●				●				●		
	8	RoadChef	Strensham (North)	Texaco	●	●			●						
	11-12	Westmorland	Gloucester	Texaco					●						
	13-14	Welcome Break	Michaelwood	BP	●	●		●		●	●	●			
	19	Welcome Break	Gordano	Shell	●	●	●	●		●	●	●			
	21-22	RoadChef	Sedgemoor (South)	Total	●			●	●						
	21-22	Welcome Break	Sedgemoor (North)	Shell	●	●	●	●		●	●				
	24	Moto	Bridgwater	BP		●		●	●	●					
	25-26	RoadChef	Taunton Deane	Shell	●	●			●						
	27	Moto	Tiverton	Shell	●	●									
	28	Extra	Cullompton	Shell	●			●	●	●			●		
	29-30	Moto	Exeter	BP	●	●		●	●	●					
M6 Toll	T6-T7	RoadChef	Norton Canes	BP	●	●			●						

Motorway	Junction	Service provider	Service name	Fuel supplier	Information	Accommodation	Conference facilities	Showers	M&S Simply Food	Costa Coffee	Starbucks	Burger King	KFC	McDonalds	Wimpy
M6	3-4	Welcome Break	Corley	Shell	●	●				●	●	●	●	●	
	10-11	Moto	Hilton Park	BP	●	●		●	●	●	●				
	14-15	RoadChef	Stafford (South)	Esso	●	●	●	●		●			●		
	14-15	Moto	Stafford (North)	BP	●	●		●	●	●					
	15-16	Welcome Break	Keele	Shell	●	●			●	●	●	●			
	16-17	RoadChef	Sandbach	Esso	●	●			●				●		
	18-19	Moto	Knutsford	BP	●	●			●	●	●	●			
	27-28	Welcome Break	Charnock Richard	Shell	●	●				●	●	●			
	32-33	Moto	Lancaster	BP	●	●			●	●	●				
	35A-36	Moto	Burton-in-Kendal (N)	BP		●			●	●					
	36-37	RoadChef	Killington Lake (S)	BP	●	●			●						
	38-39	Westmorland	Tebay	Total	●	●	●								
	41-42	Moto	Southwaite	BP	●	●		●	●	●	●				
	44-45	Moto	Todhills	BP/Shell											
M8	4-5	BP	Heart of Scotland	BP				●	●	●					
M9	9	Moto	Stirling	BP	●	●		●		●		●			
M11	8	Welcome Break	Birchanger Green	Shell	●	●	●	●			●	●	●		
M18	5	Moto	Doncaster North	BP	●	●	●	●		●		●			
M20	8	RoadChef	Maidstone	Esso	●	●			●					●	
	11	Stop 24	Stop 24	Shell	●			●					●	●	
M23	11	Moto	Pease Pottage	BP				●	●	●	●	●			
M25	5-6	RoadChef	Clacket Lane	Total	●	●			●	●			●		
	9-10	Extra	Cobham	Shell		●	●		●	●		●	●	●	
	23	Welcome Break	South Mimms	BP	●	●	●			●	●	●			
	30	Moto	Thurrock	Esso	●	●		●	●	●		●			
M27	3-4	RoadChef	Rownhams	Esso	●	●			●				●		
M40	2	Extra	Beaconsfield	Shell	●	●		●	●	●		●	●	●	
	8	Welcome Break	Oxford	BP	●	●		●		●		●			
	10	Moto	Cherwell Valley	Esso	●	●		●	●	●					
	12-13	Welcome Break	Warwick	BP	●	●	●	●		●	●	●			
M42	2	Welcome Break	Hopwood Park	Shell	●			●		●		●	●	●	
	10	Moto	Tamworth	Esso	●	●		●	●	●	●	●			
M48	1	Moto	Severn View	BP		●		●	●		●		●		
M54	4	Welcome Break	Telford	Shell	●	●		●							
M56	14	RoadChef	Chester	Shell	●	●			●					●	
M61	6-7	Euro Garages	Rivington	BP	●			●		●		●	●		
M62	7-9	Welcome Break	Burtonwood	Shell	●			●			●	●			
	18-19	Moto	Birch	BP	●	●	●	●	●	●		●			
	25-26	Welcome Break	Hartshead Moor	Shell	●	●	●			●	●	●			
	33	Moto	Ferrybridge	Esso	●	●		●	●	●		●			
M65	4	Extra	Blackburn with Darwen	Shell	●	●	●	●		●				●	
M74	4-5	RoadChef	Bothwell (South)	BP	●		●	●		●					
	5-6	RoadChef	Hamilton (North)	BP	●	●	●	●		●					
	11-12	Cairn Lodge	Happendon	Shell	●	●			●	●					
	12-13	Welcome Break	Abington	Shell	●	●	●			●	●	●			
M80	6-7	Shell	Old Inns	Shell											
M90	6	Moto	Kinross	BP	●	●		●		●		●			

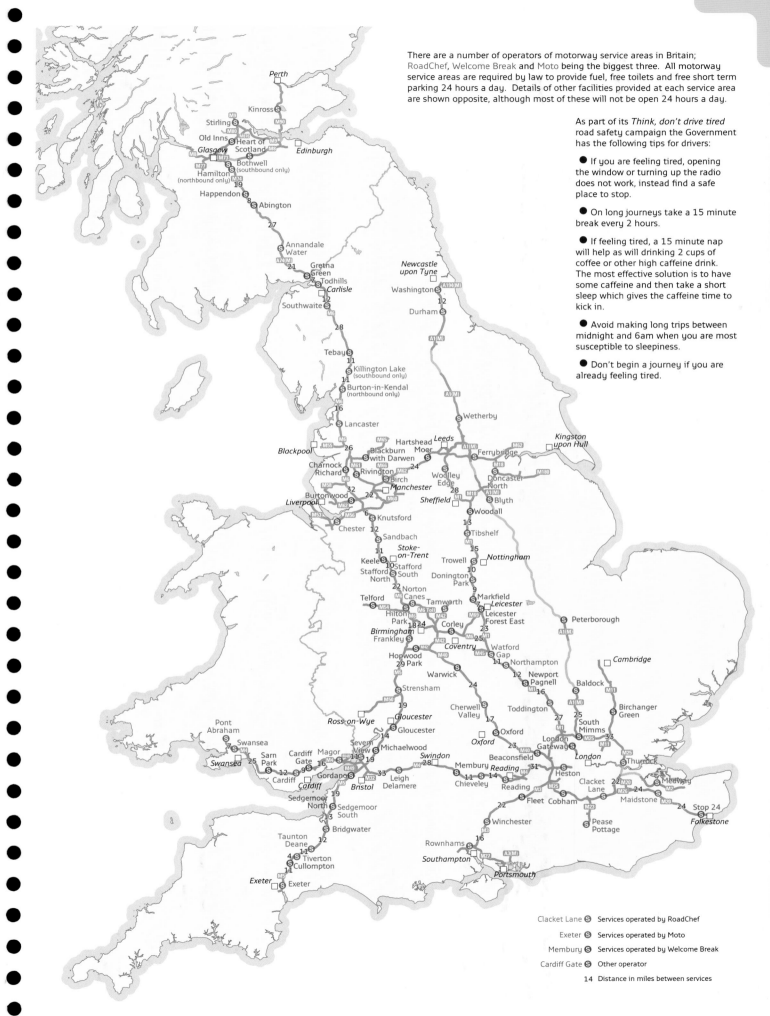

There are a number of operators of motorway service areas in Britain; RoadChef, Welcome Break and Moto being the biggest three. All motorway service areas are required by law to provide fuel, free toilets and free short term parking 24 hours a day. Details of other facilities provided at each service area are shown opposite, although most of these will not be open 24 hours a day.

As part of its *Think, don't drive tired* road safety campaign the Government has the following tips for drivers:

● If you are feeling tired, opening the window or turning up the radio does not work, instead find a safe place to stop.

● On long journeys take a 15 minute break every 2 hours.

● If feeling tired, a 15 minute nap will help as will drinking 2 cups of coffee or other high caffeine drink. The most effective solution is to have some caffeine and then take a short sleep which gives the caffeine time to kick in.

● Avoid making long trips between midnight and 6am when you are most susceptible to sleepiness.

● Don't begin a journey if you are already feeling tired.

Clacket Lane Ⓢ   Services operated by RoadChef

Exeter Ⓢ   Services operated by Moto

Membury Ⓢ   Services operated by Welcome Break

Cardiff Gate Ⓢ   Other operator

14   Distance in miles between services

M25 orbital map

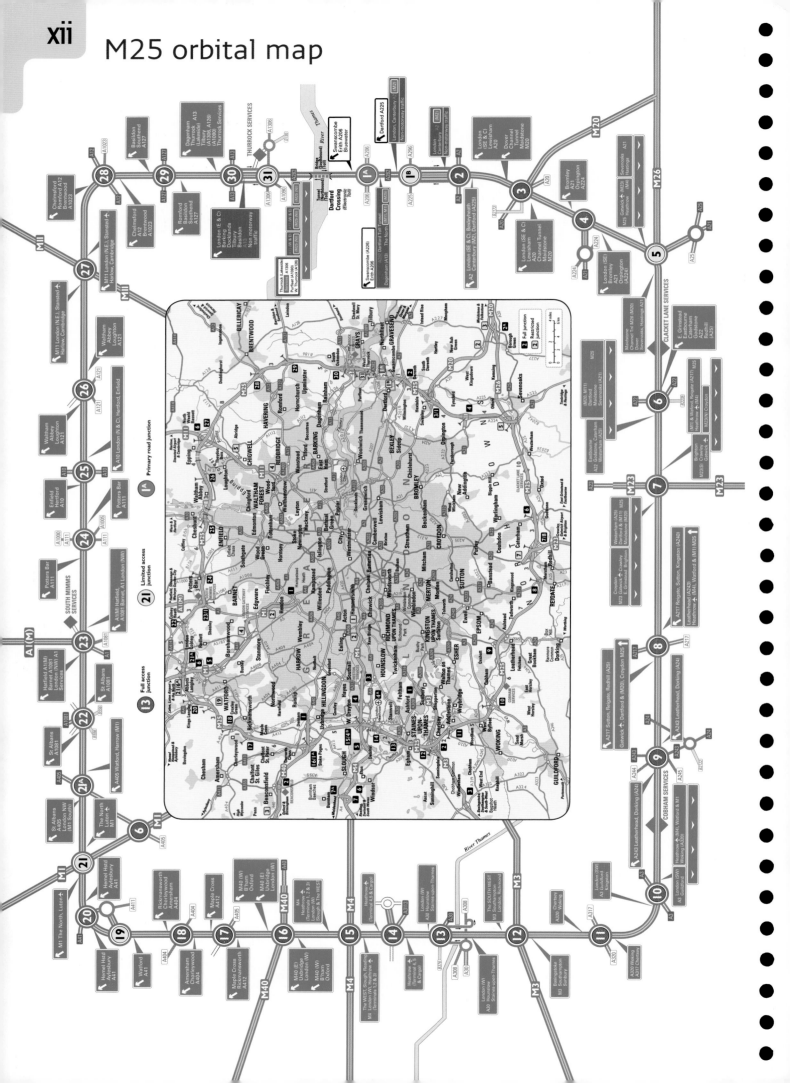

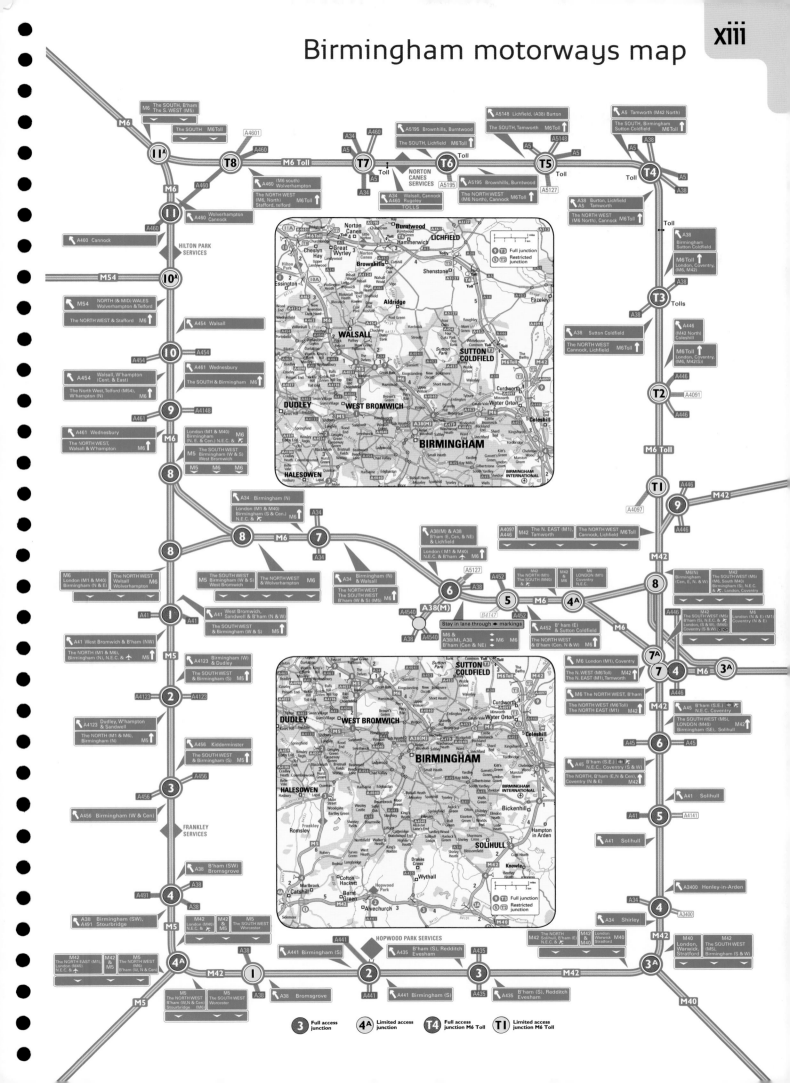

Risk rating of Britain's motorways and A roads

EuroRAP

This map shows the statistical risk of death or serious injury occurring on Britain's motorway and A road network for 2011-2013. Covering 44,500km in total, the British EuroRAP network represents just 10% of Britain's road network but carries 56% of the traffic and half of Britain's road fatalities.

The risk is calculated by comparing the frequency of road crashes resulting in death and serious injury on every stretch of road with how much traffic each road is carrying. For example, if there are 20 crashes on a road carrying 10,000 vehicles a day, the risk is 10 times higher than if the road has the same number of crashes but carries 100,000 vehicles.

Some of the roads shown have had improvements made to them recently, but during the survey period the risk of a fatal or serious injury crash on the black road sections was 23 times higher than on the safest (green) roads.

For more information on the Road Safety Foundation go to **www.roadsafetyfoundation.org.**

For more information on the statistical background to this research, visit the EuroRAP website at **www.eurorap.org.**

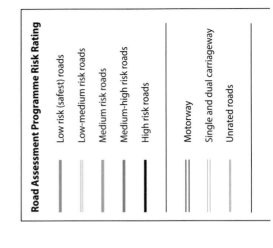

Road Assessment Programme Risk Rating

Low risk (safest) roads

Low-medium risk roads

Medium risk roads

Medium-high risk roads

High risk roads

Motorway

Single and dual carriageway

Unrated roads

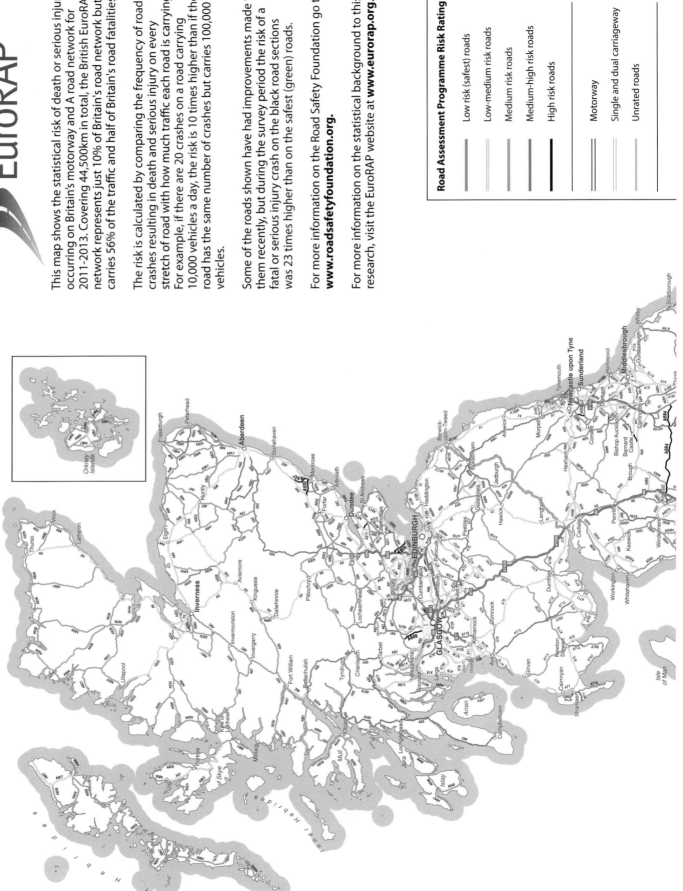

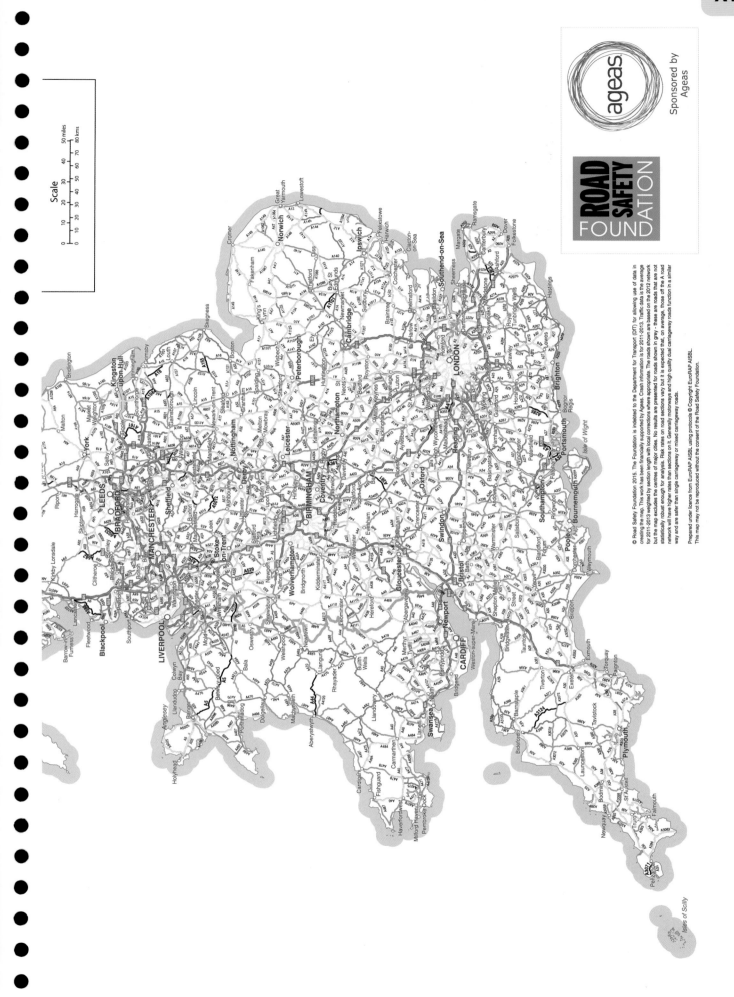

Distance chart

Distances between two selected towns in this table are shown in miles and kilometres.
In general, distances are based on the shortest routes by classified roads.

Distance in kilometres

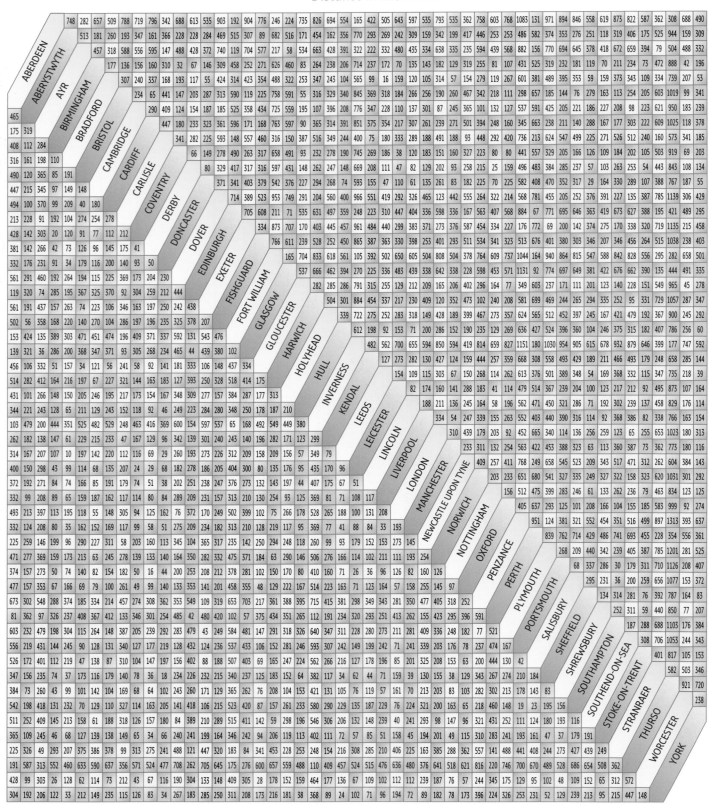

Distance in miles

Symbols used on the map

Blue place of interest symbols e.g ★ are listed on page 93

Motorway junction with full / limited access	
Motorway service area	
Toll motorway	
Primary route dual / single carriageway / junction / service area	
'A' road dual / single carriageway	
'B' road dual / single carriageway	
Minor road dual / single carriageway	
Restricted access road	
Road proposed or under construction	
Road tunnel	
Roundabout	
Toll / One way street	

Level crossing

National Trail / Long Distance Route

Fixed safety camera / fixed average-speed safety camera. Speed shown by number within camera, a V indicates a variable limit.

Park and Ride site operated by bus / rail (runs at least 5 days a week)

Car ferry with destination

Foot ferry with destination

Airport

Railway line / Railway tunnel / Light railway line

Railway station / Light rail station

London Underground / London Overground stations

Glasgow Subway station

Extent of London congestion charging zone

Notable building

Hospital

Spot height (in metres) / Lighthouse

Built up area

Woodland / Park

National Park

Heritage Coast

County / Unitary Authority boundary and name

Area covered by street map

Locator map

Urban approach maps	
Birmingham	14-15
Bournemouth	3
Bradford	26-27
Bristol	8
Cardiff	7
Coventry	16
Derby	18-19
Edinburgh	32
Glasgow	30-31
Greater Manchester	24-25
Leeds	26-27
Leicester	17
Liverpool	22-23
London	10-13
Manchester	24-25
Merseyside	22-23
Middlesbrough	29
Milton Keynes	9
Newcastle upon Tyne	28-29
Newport	7
Nottingham	18-19
Plymouth	2
Portsmouth	4-5
Sheffield	21
Southampton	4-5
Stoke-on-Trent	20
Sunderland	28-29
Swansea	6
West Midlands	14-15

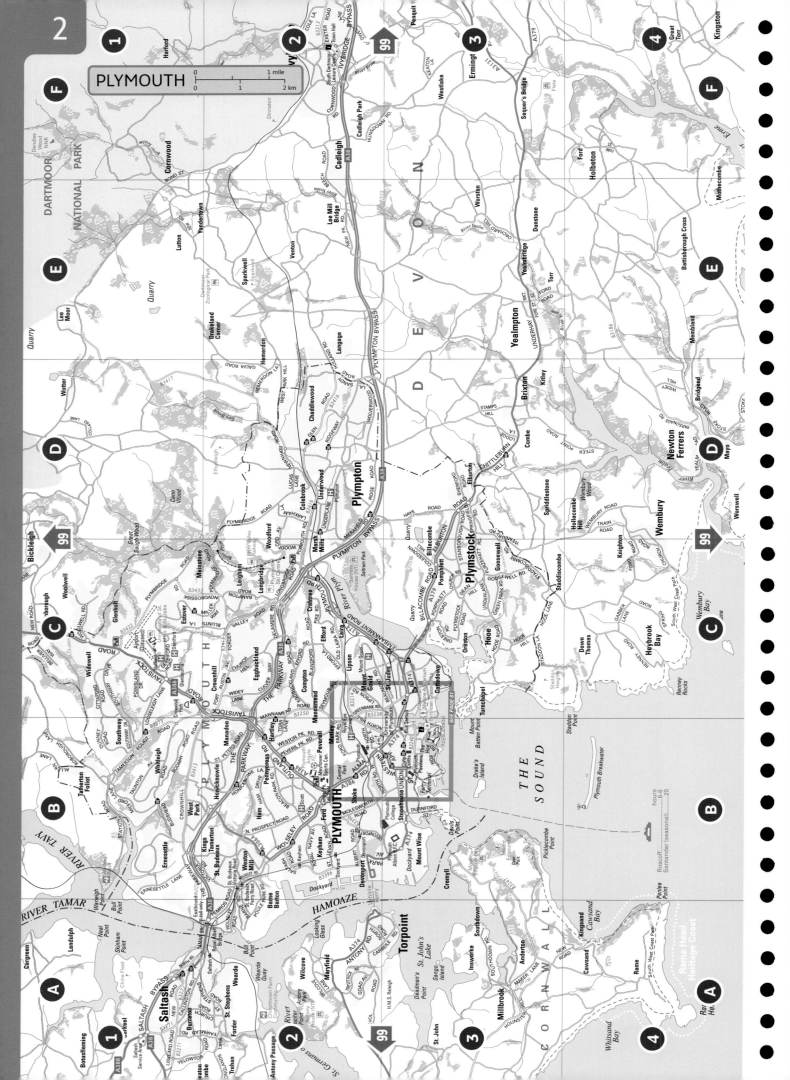

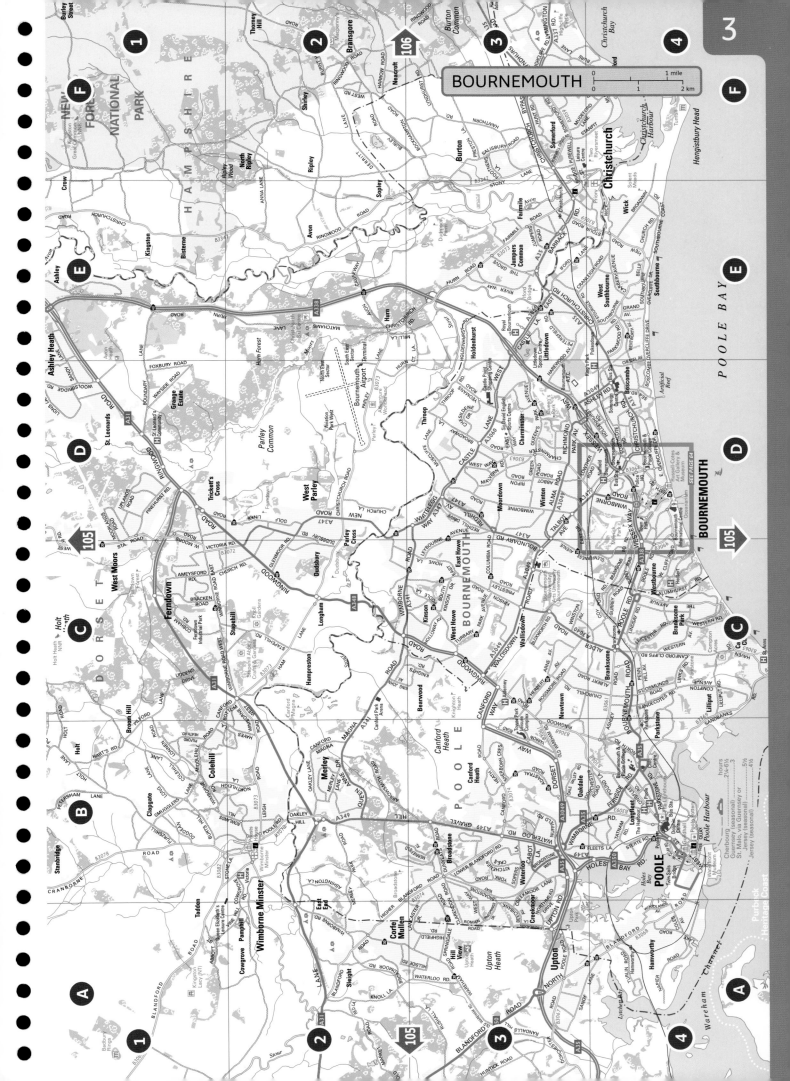

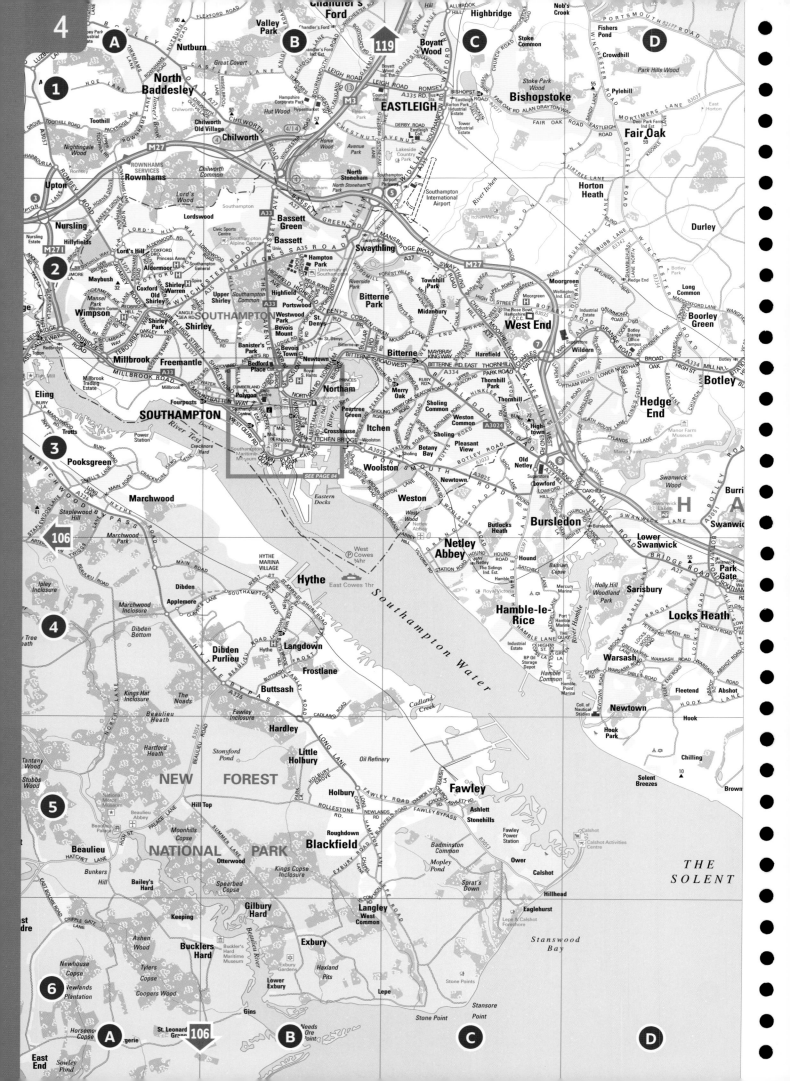

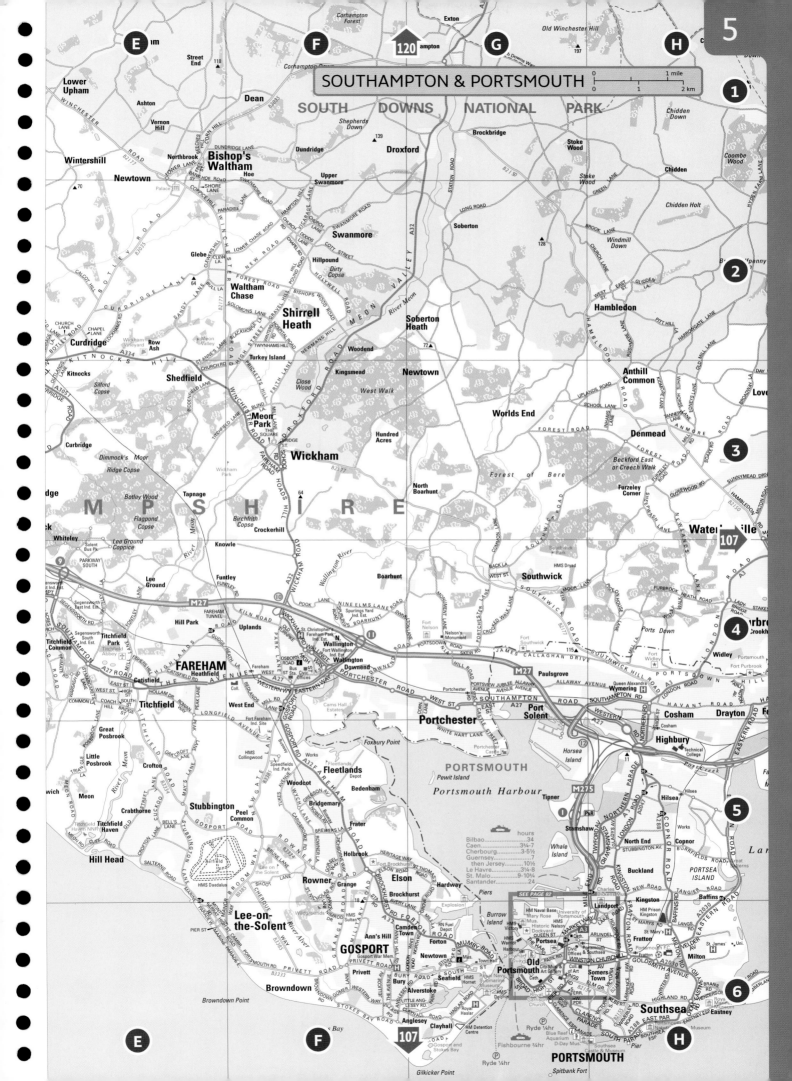

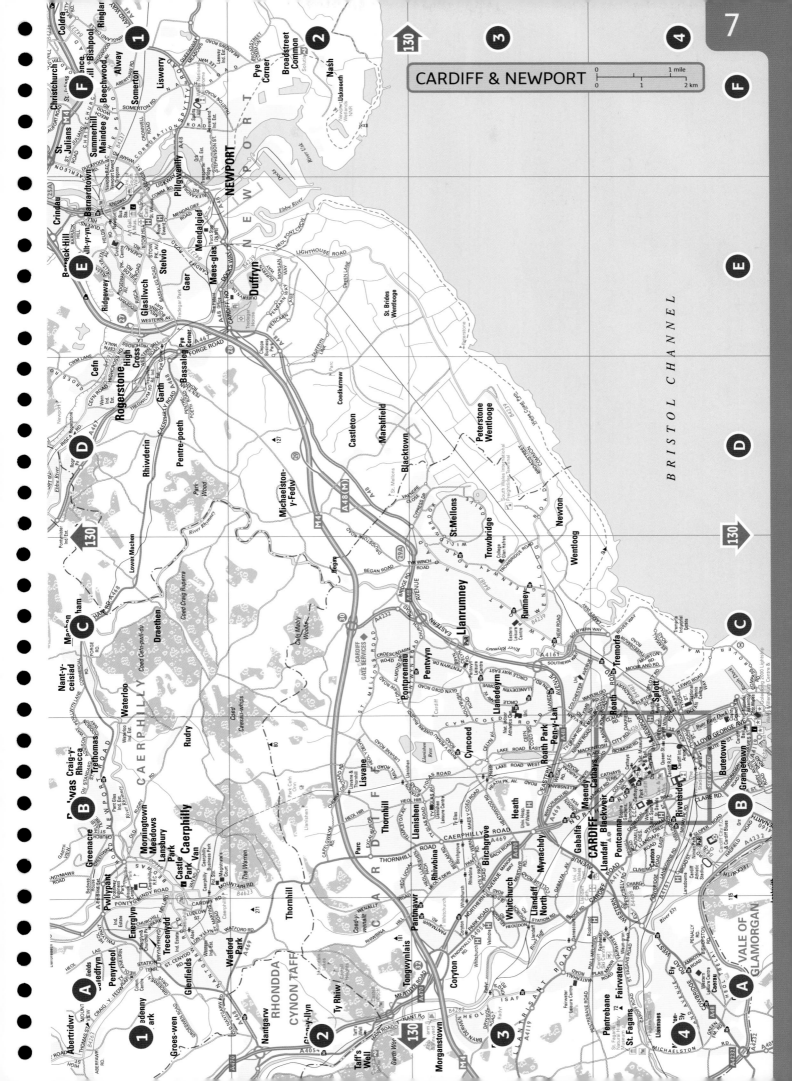

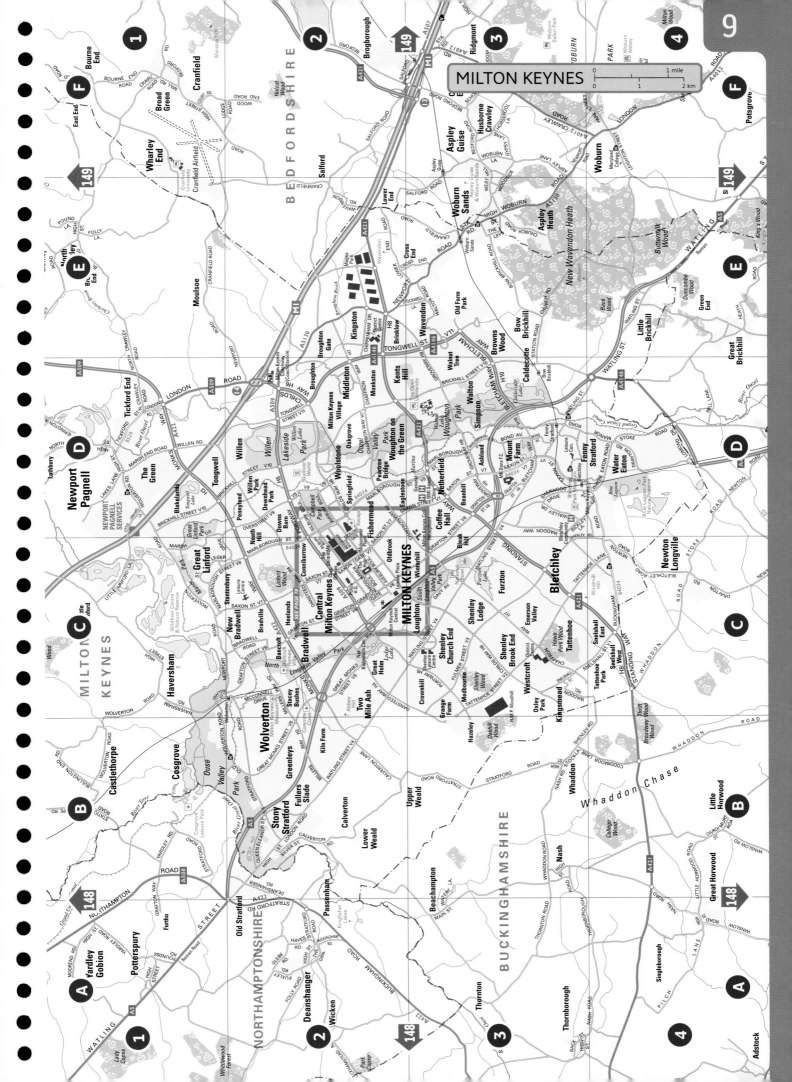

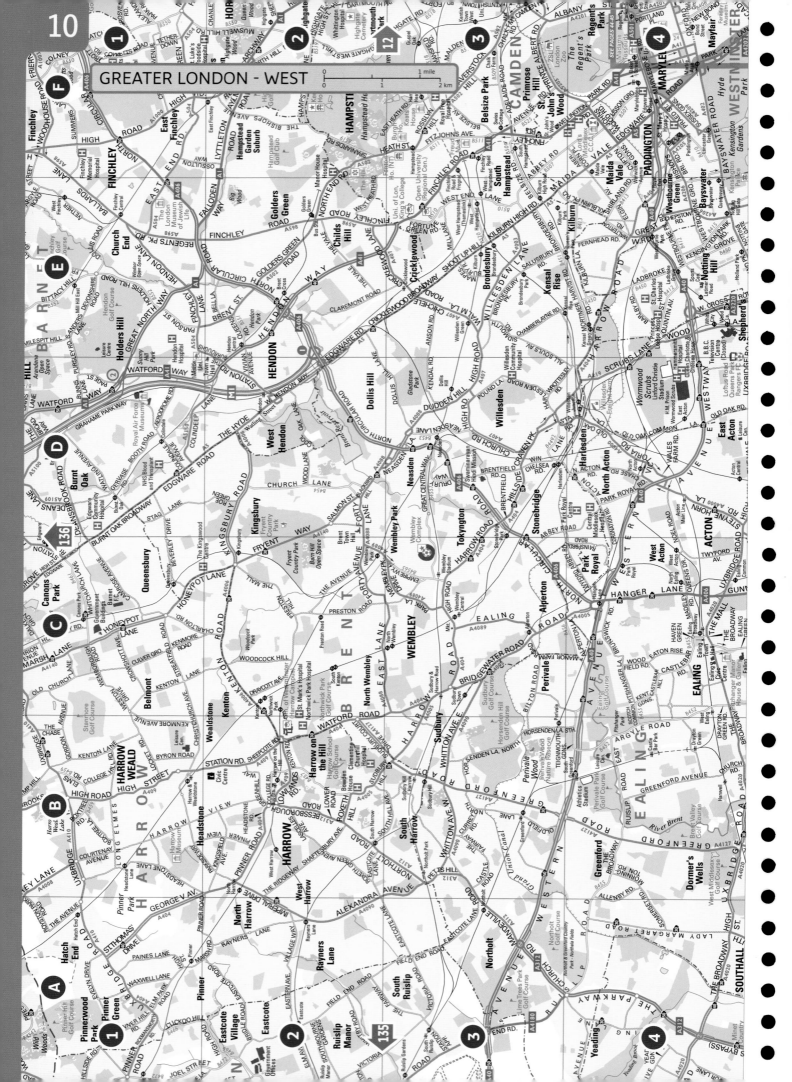

GREATER LONDON - WEST

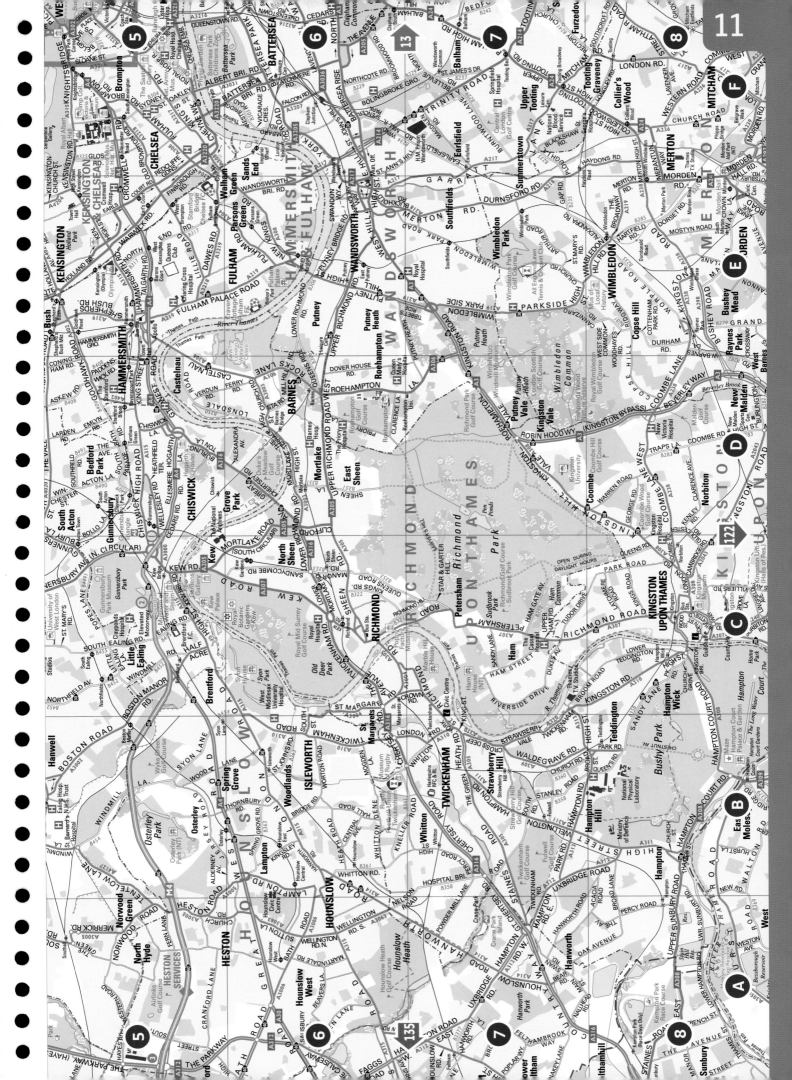

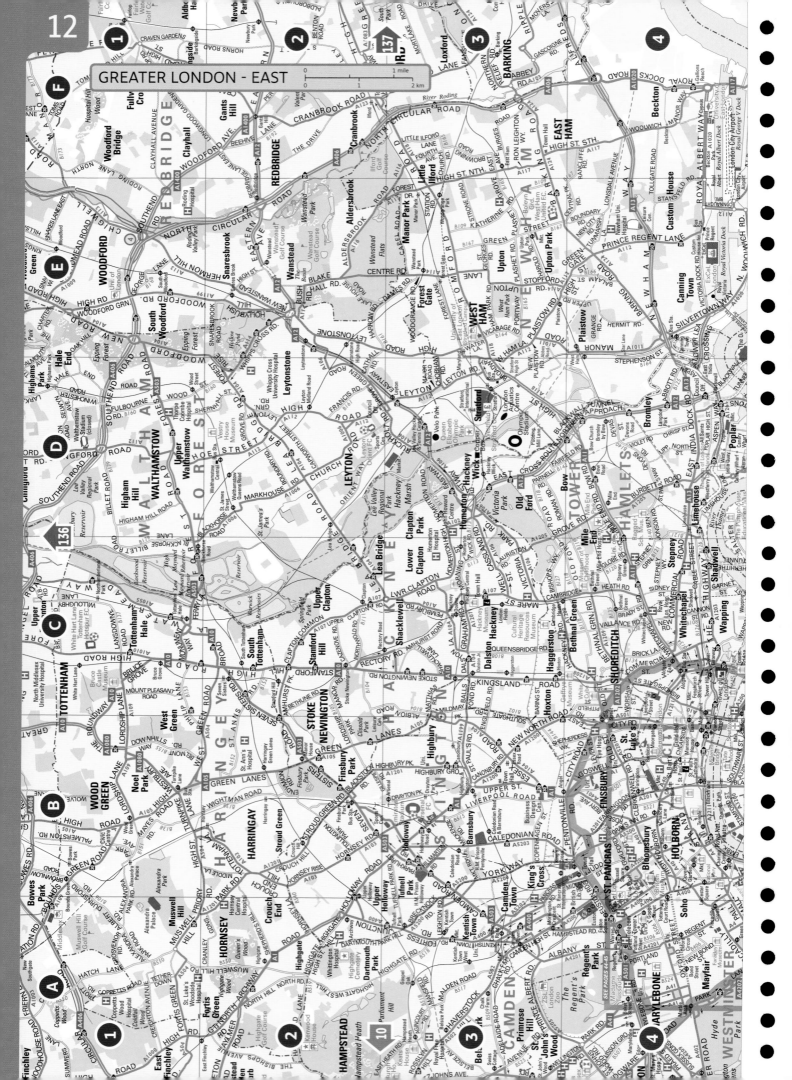

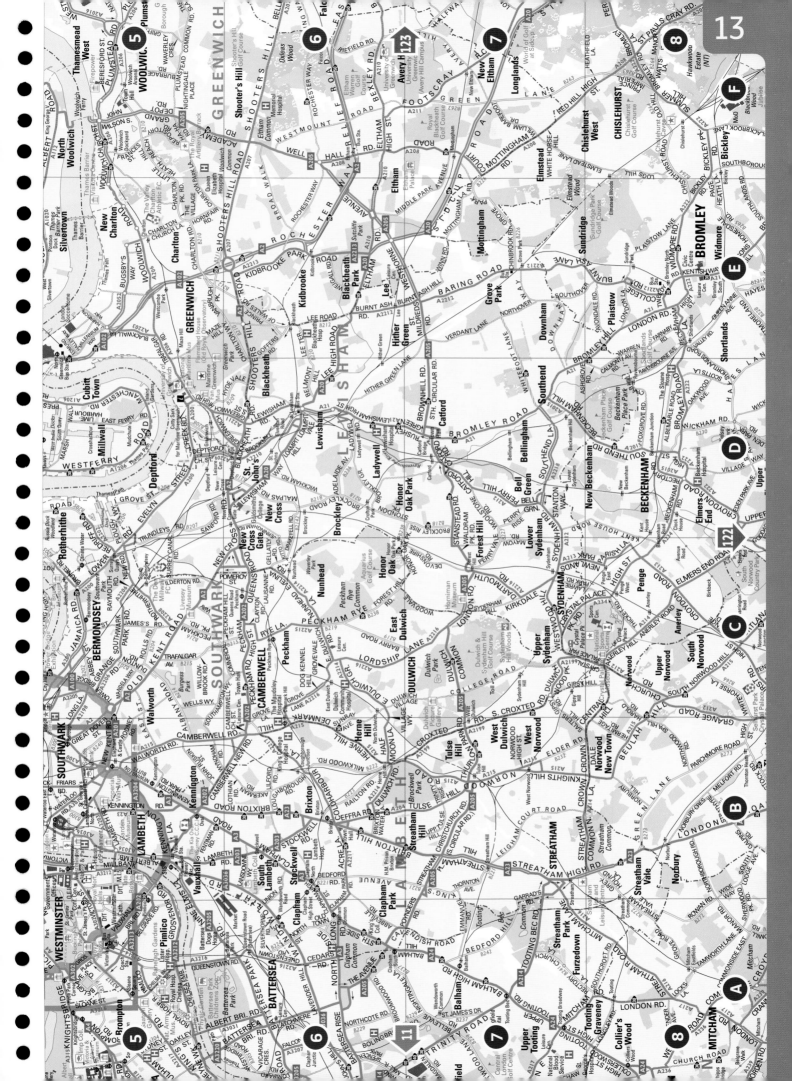

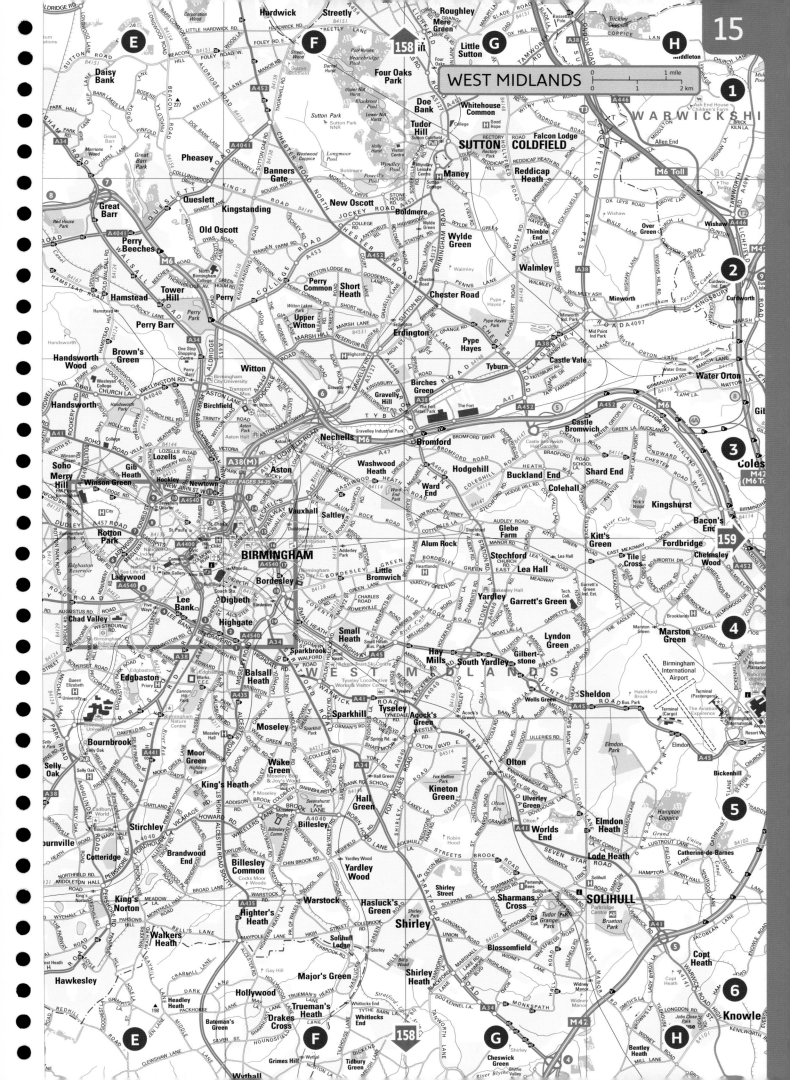

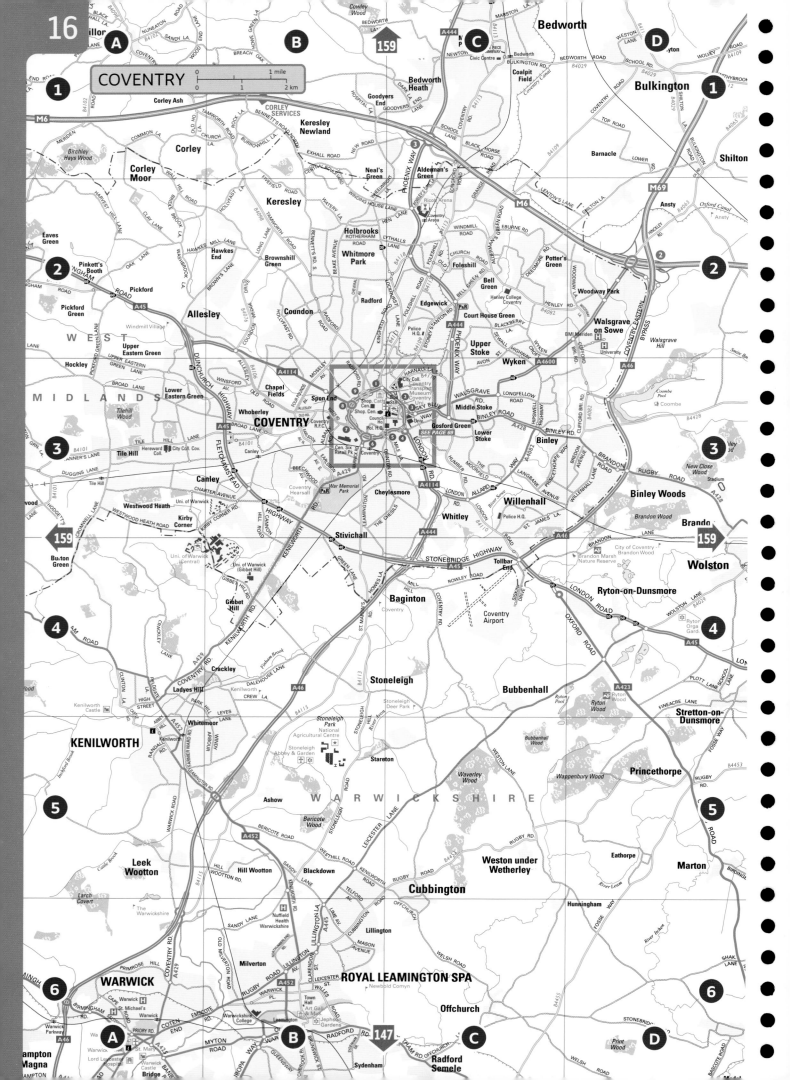

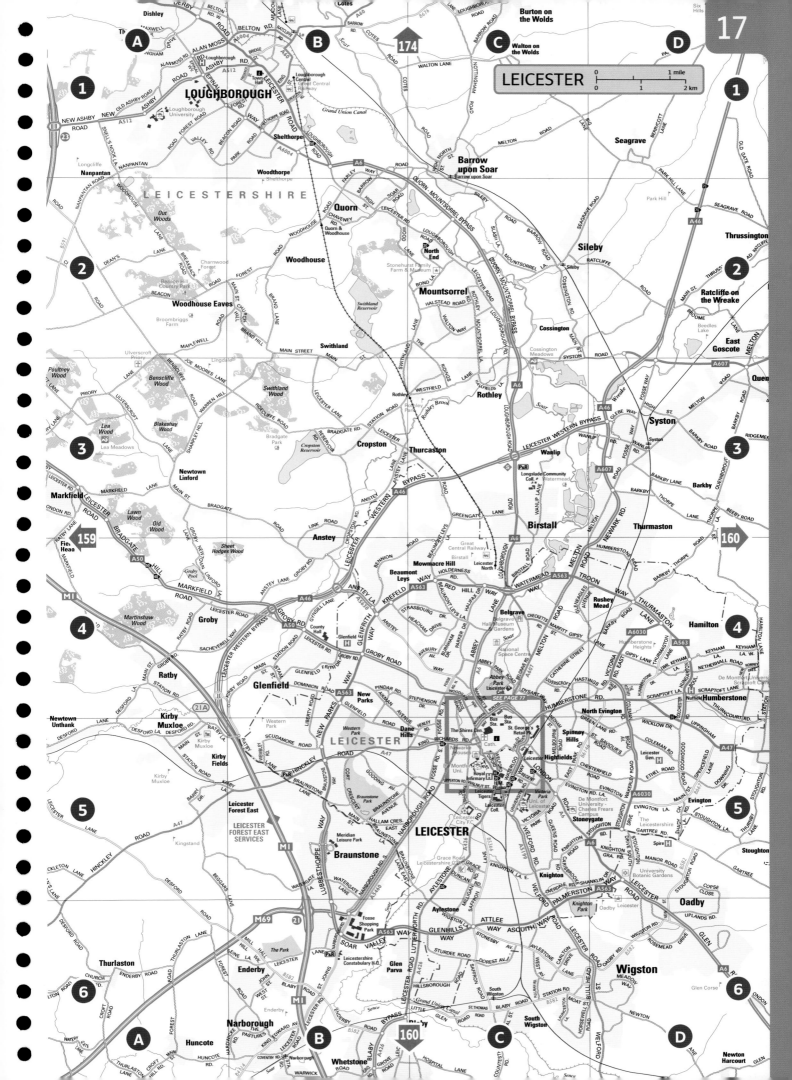

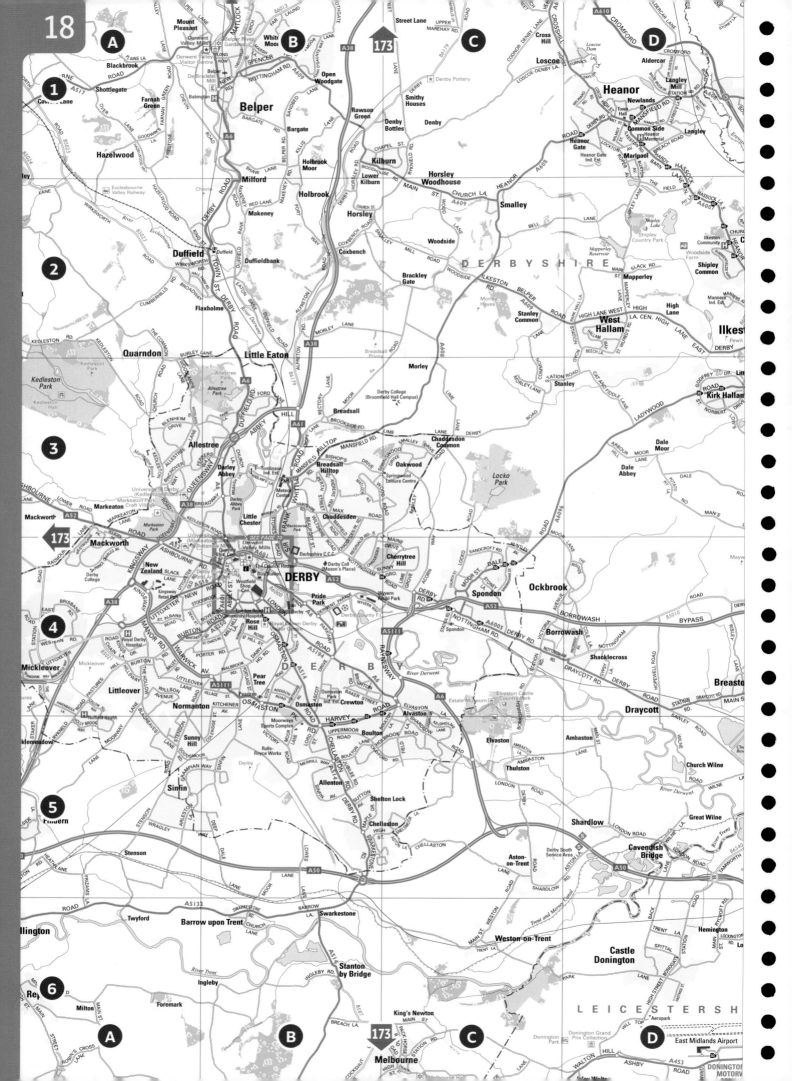

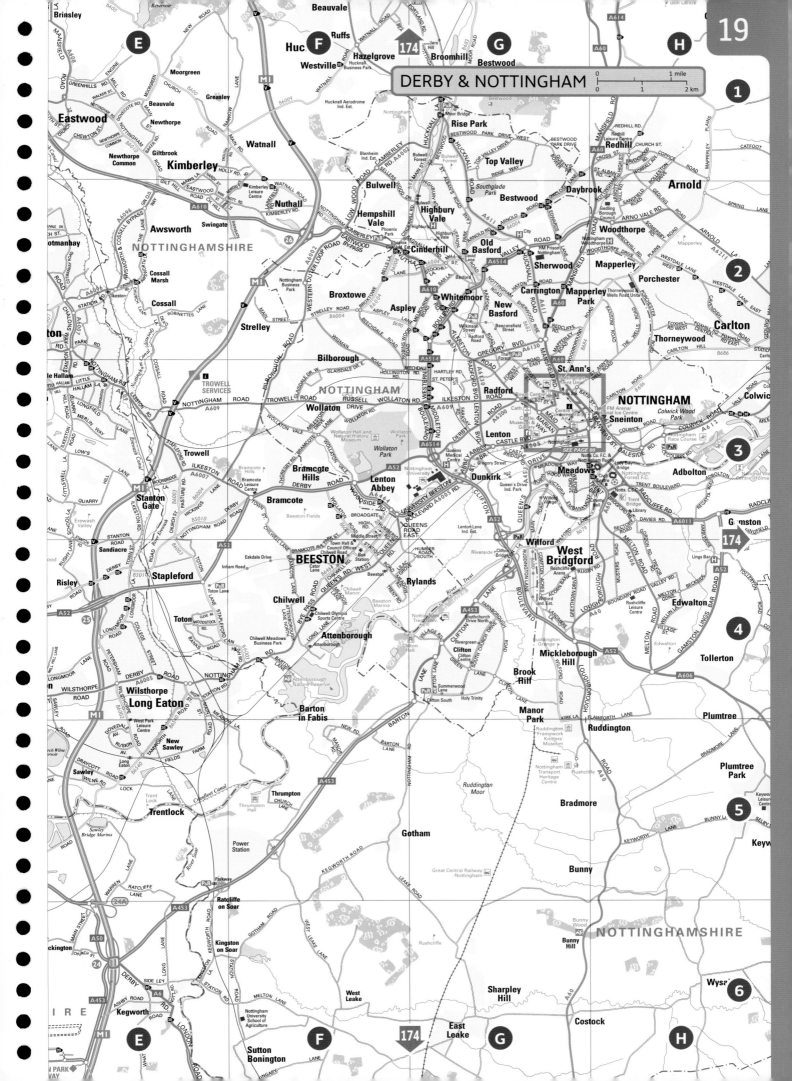

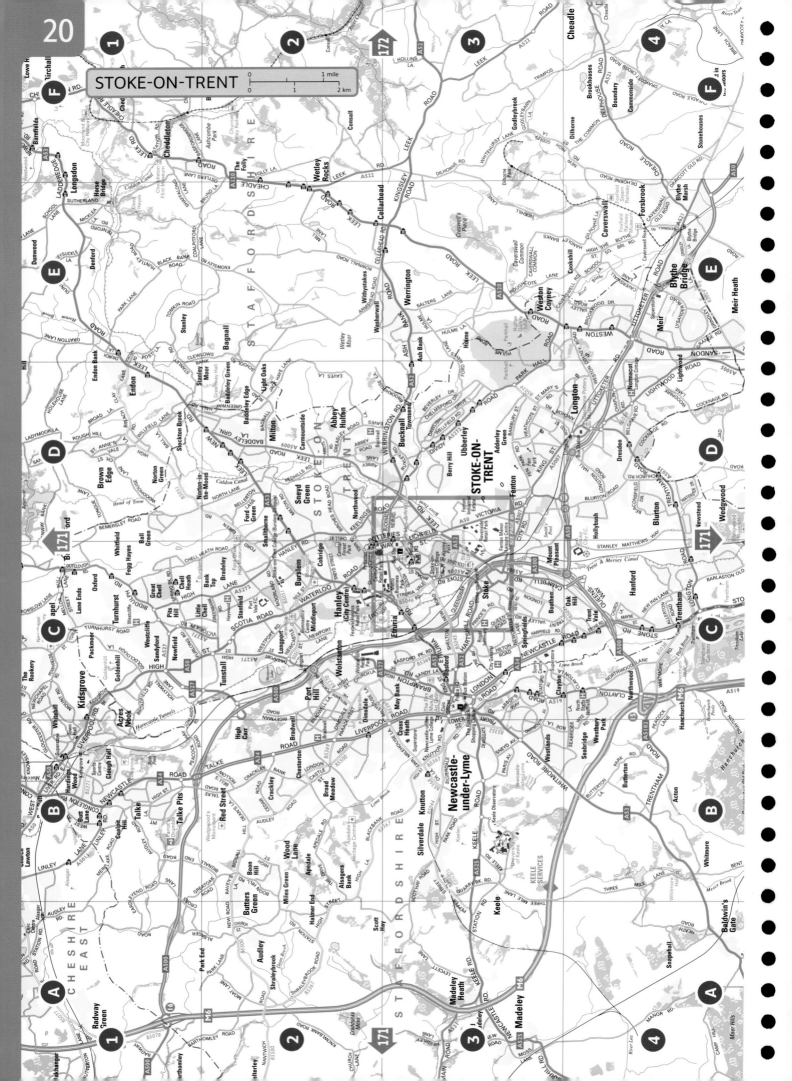

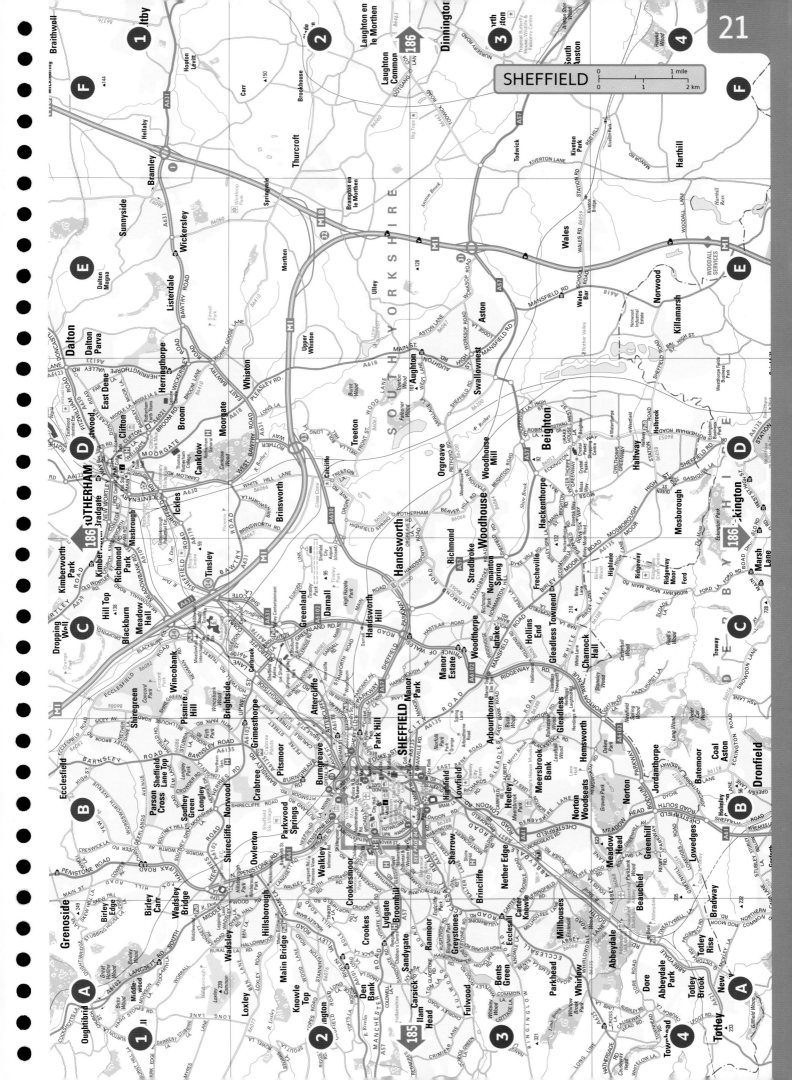

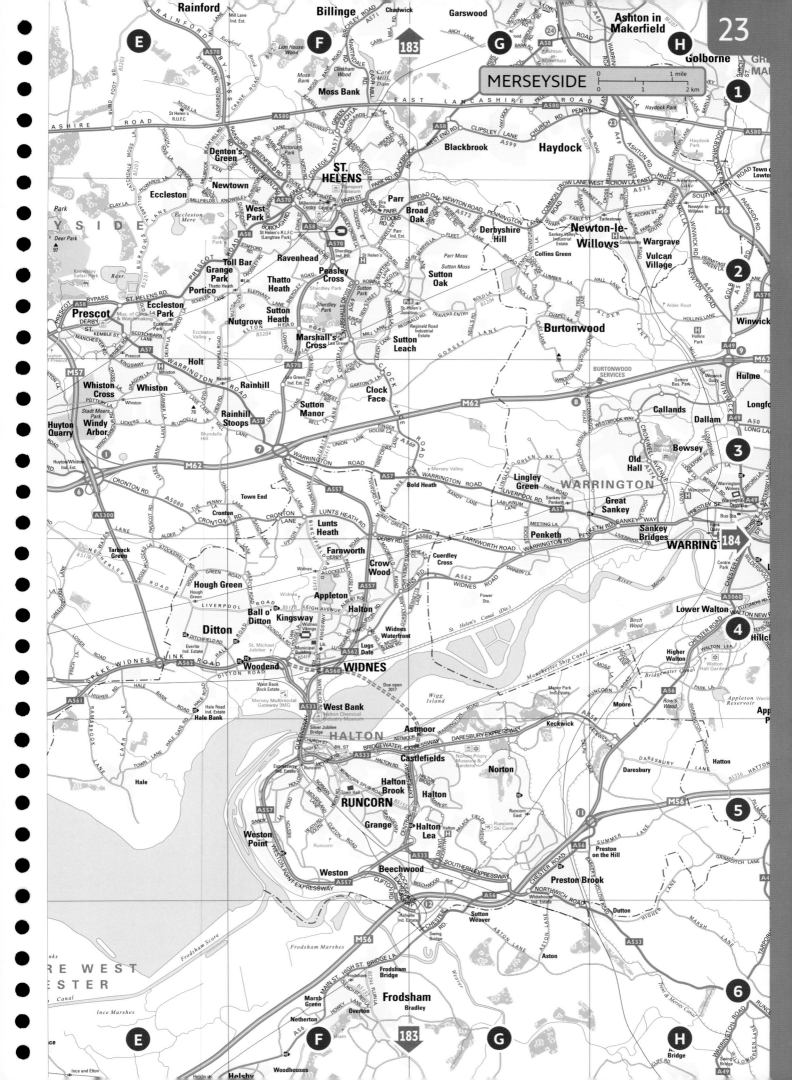

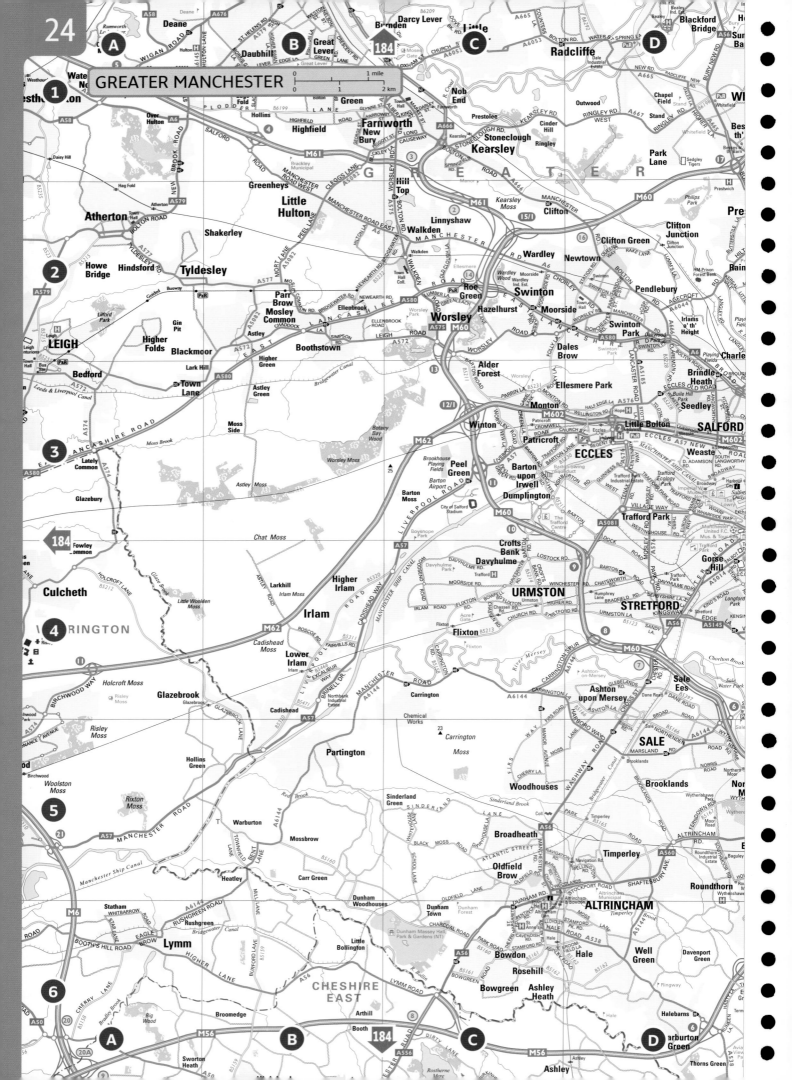

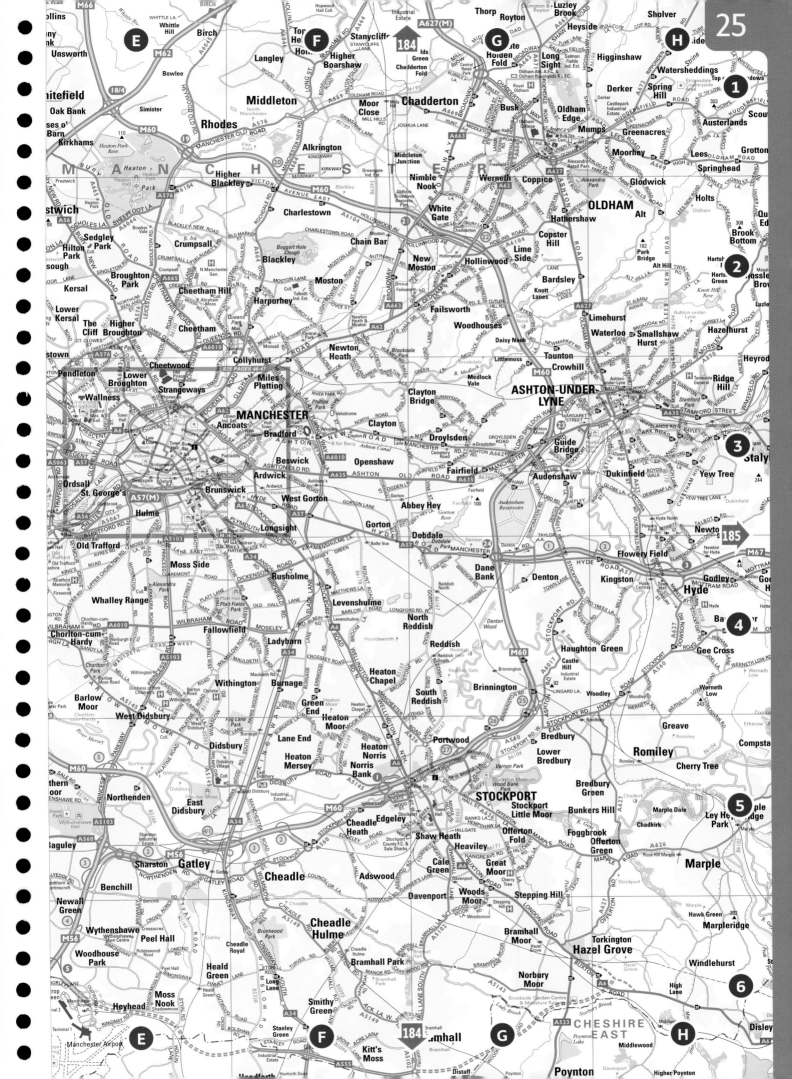

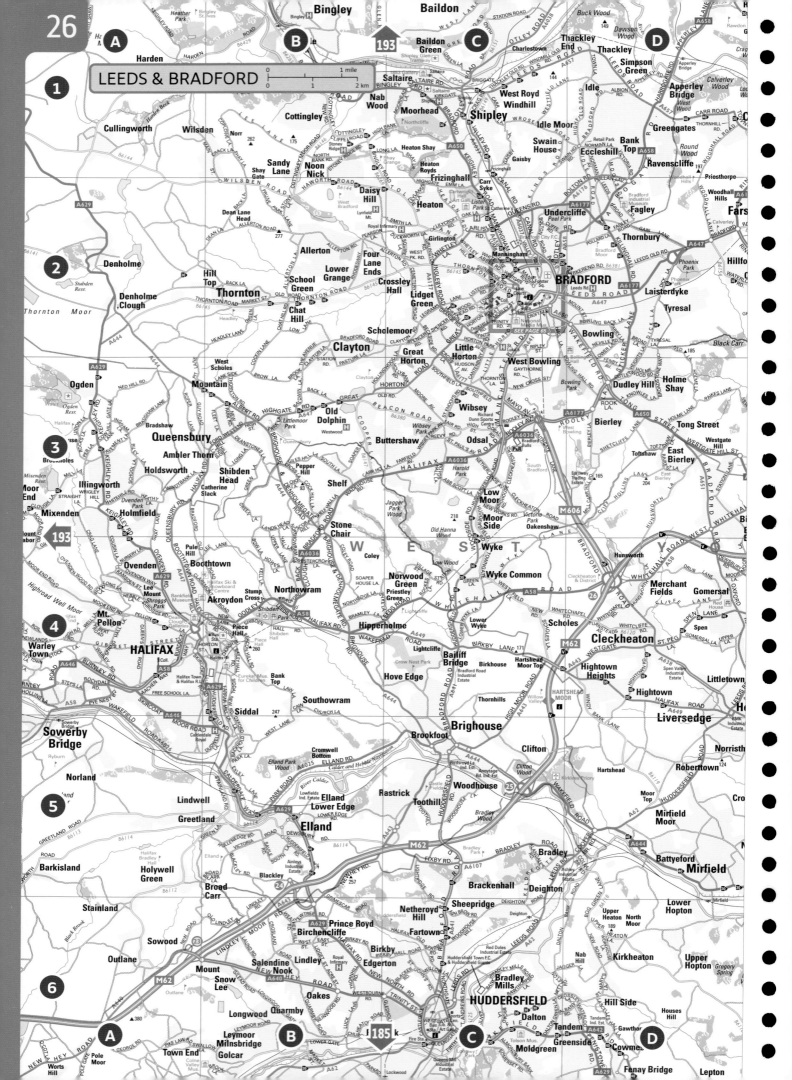

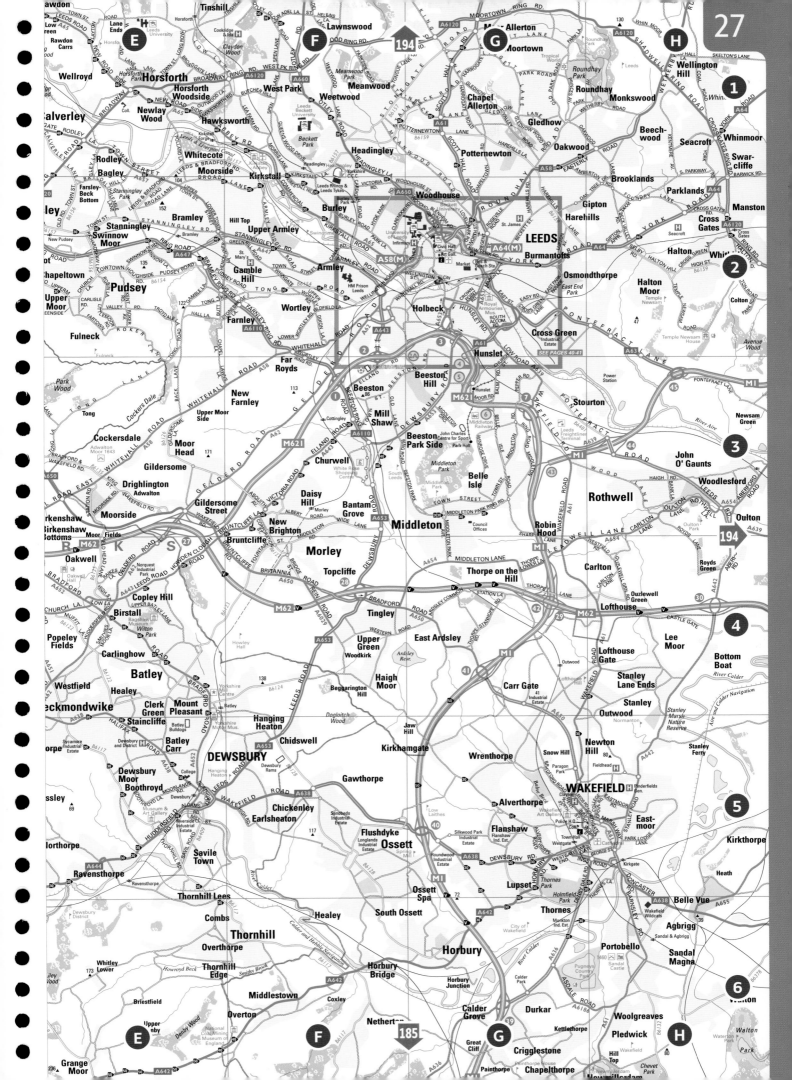

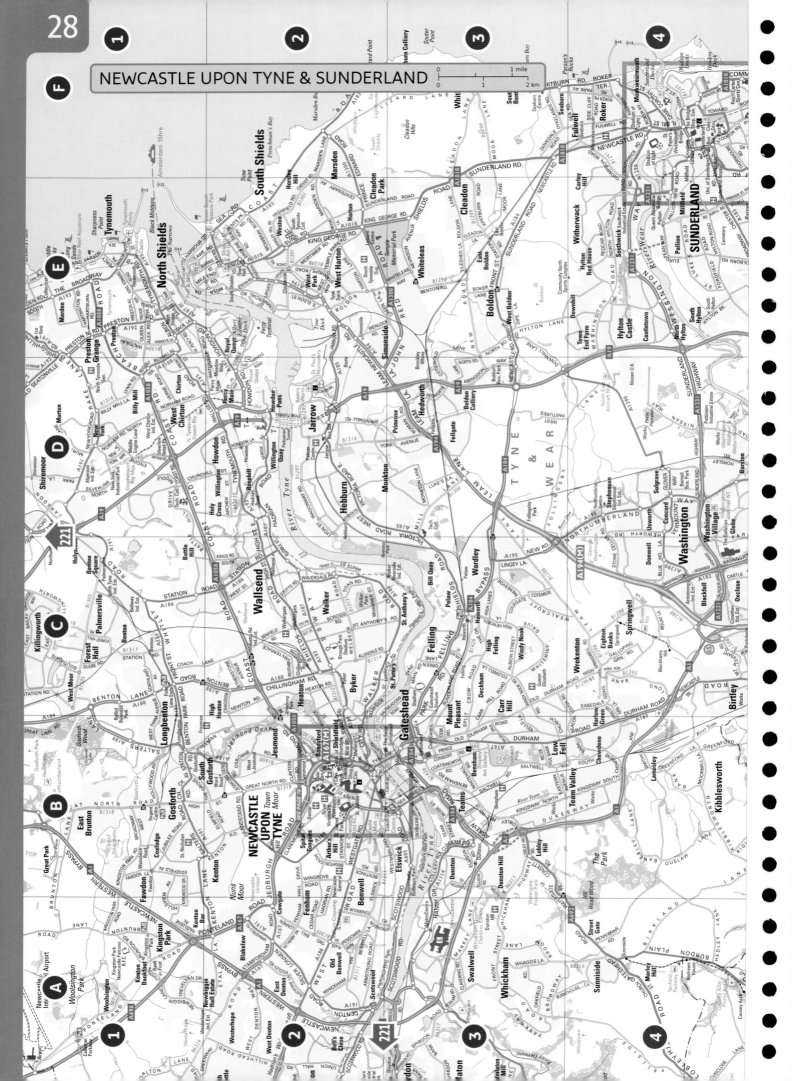

NEWCASTLE UPON TYNE & SUNDERLAND

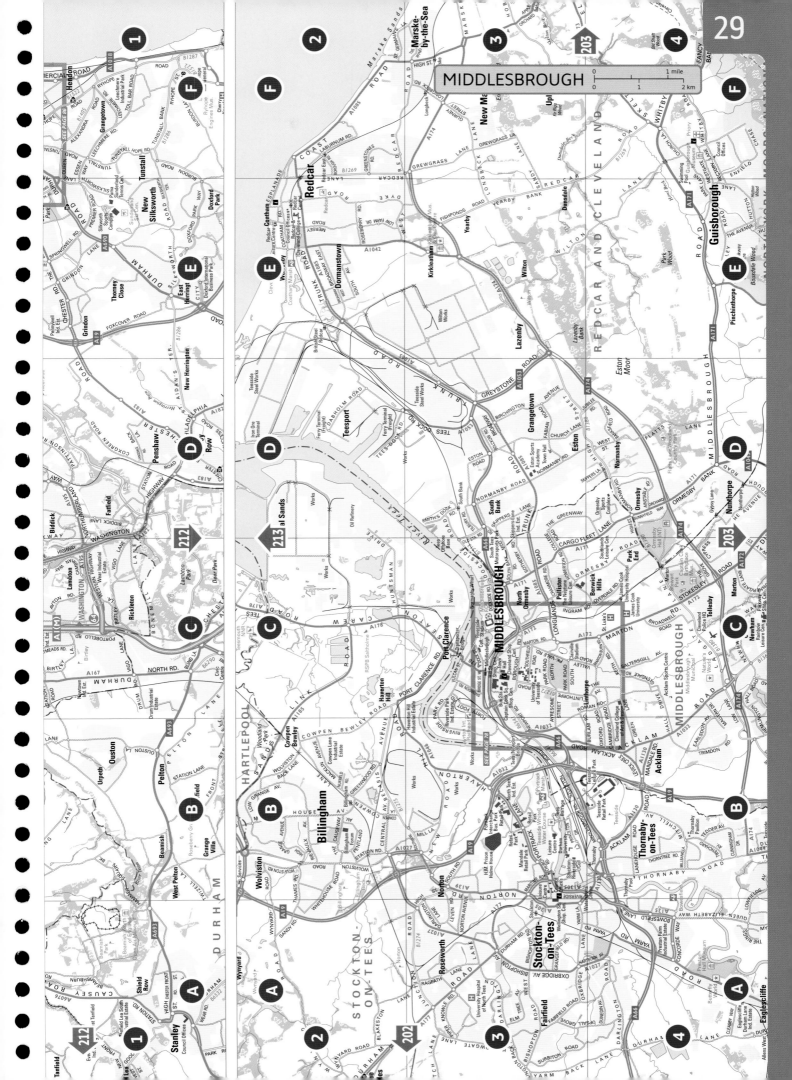

MIDDLESBROUGH

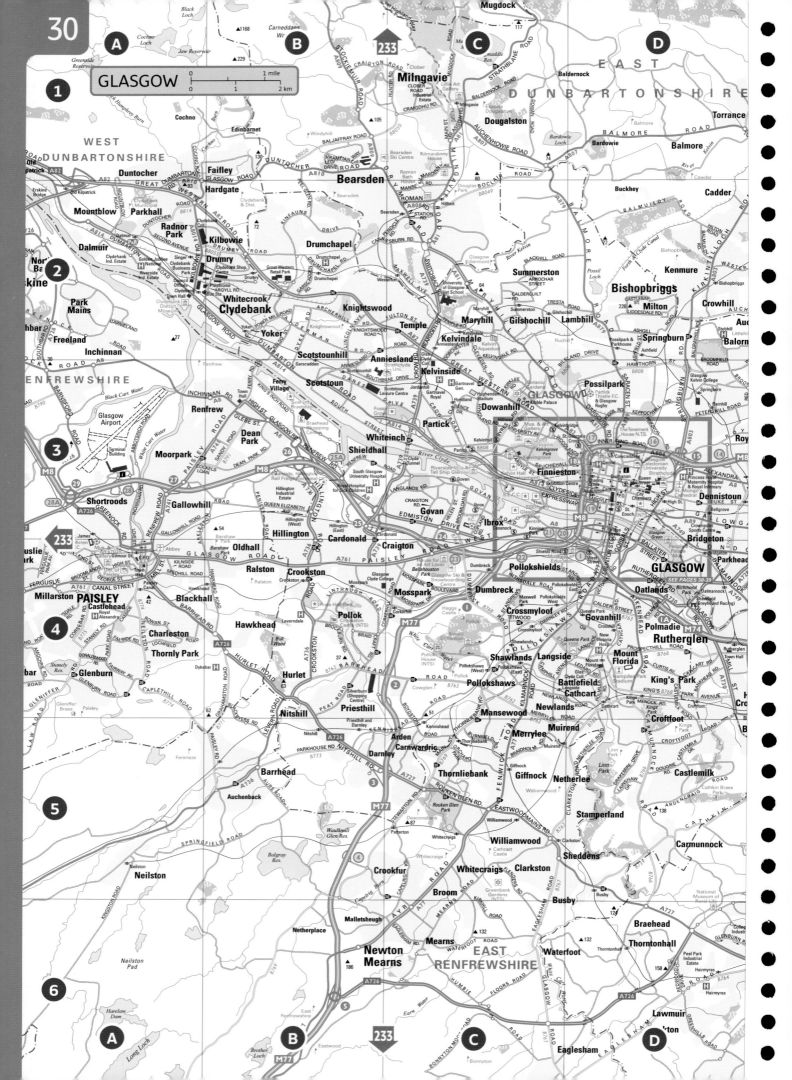

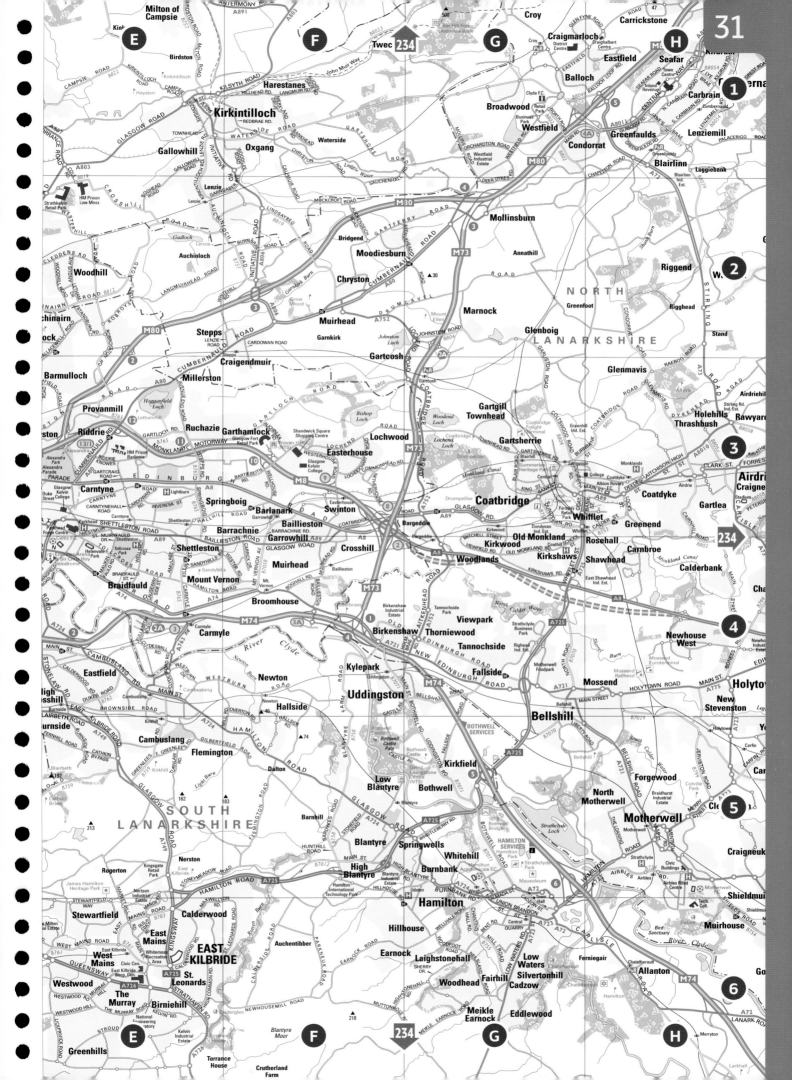

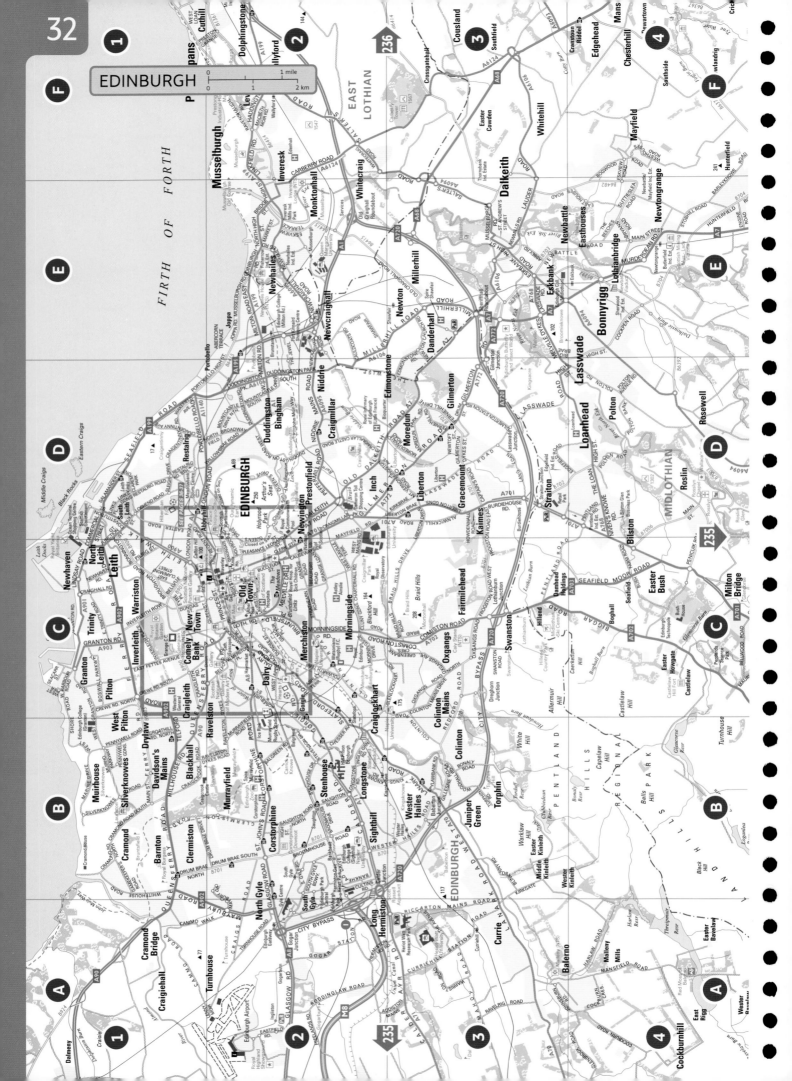

Symbols used on the map

M8	Motorway
A4 ❶	Primary route dual / single carriageway / Junction
A40	'A' road dual / single carriageway
B507	'B' road dual / single carriageway
Toll	Other road dual / single carriageway / Toll
→ ══7══	One way street / Orbital route
	Access restriction
	Pedestrian street
	Street market
	Minor road / Track
FB	Footpath / Footbridge
	Road under construction
🚉	Main / other National Rail station
	London Underground / Overground station
Ⓐ	Light Rail / Station

Bus / Coach station	
P&R	Park and Ride site - rail operated (runs at least 5 days a week)
	Extent of London congestion charging zone
Dublin 8hrs	Vehicle / Pedestrian ferry
P P	Car park
Ⓤ	Theatre
	Major hotel
	Public House
Pol	Police station
Lib	Library
PO	Post Office
ⓘ ⓘ	Visitor information centre (open all year / seasonally)
🚻	Toilet

⌐JAPAN	Embassy
🎥 🎥	Cinema
✚ +	Cathedral / Church
☾ ☼ ■ Mormon	Mosque / Synagogue / Other place of worship
	Leisure & tourism
	Shopping
	Administration & law
	Health & welfare
	Education
	Industry / Office
	Other notable building
	Park / Garden / Sports ground
↑↑↑↑	Cemetery

Locator map

Street maps

Aberdeen	63	Leeds index	52
Bath	63	Leicester	77
Birmingham	34-35	Lincoln	77
Birmingham index	48	Liverpool	42-43
Blackpool	64	Liverpool index	54
Bournemouth	64	London	44-45
Bradford	65	London index	56
Brighton	65	Manchester	46-47
Bristol	66	Manchester index	60
Cambridge	66	Middlesbrough	78
Canterbury	67	Milton Keynes	78
Cardiff	67	Newcastle upon Tyne	79
Carlisle	68	Norwich	79
Cheltenham	68	Nottingham	80
Chester	69	Oxford	80
Coventry	69	Perth	81
Derby	70	Plymouth	81
Dover	70	Portsmouth	82
Dundee	71	Reading	82
Durham	71	Salisbury	83
Eastbourne	72	Scarborough	83
Edinburgh	36-37	Sheffield	84
Edinburgh index	49	Southampton	84
Exeter	72	Stoke-on-Trent	85
Folkestone	73	Stratford-upon-Avon	85
Glasgow	38-39	Sunderland	86
Glasgow index	51	Swansea	86
Gloucester	73	Swindon	87
Guildford	74	Torquay	87
Harrogate	74	Watford	88
Hastings	75	Weston-super-Mare	88
Hereford	75	Winchester	89
Hull (Kingston upon Hull)	76	Windsor	89
Inverness	76	Worcester	90
Leeds	40-41	York	90

Airport plans

Birmingham International	91
Gatwick	91
Glasgow	91
Heathrow	91
Manchester	91
Stansted	91

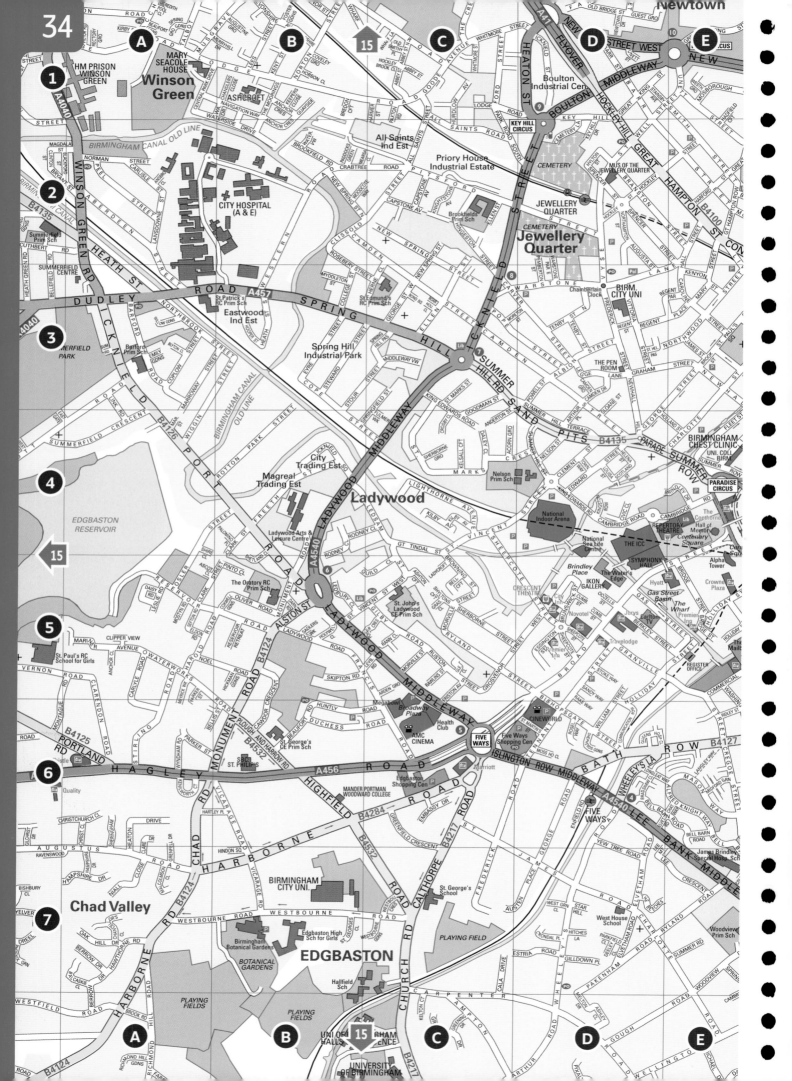

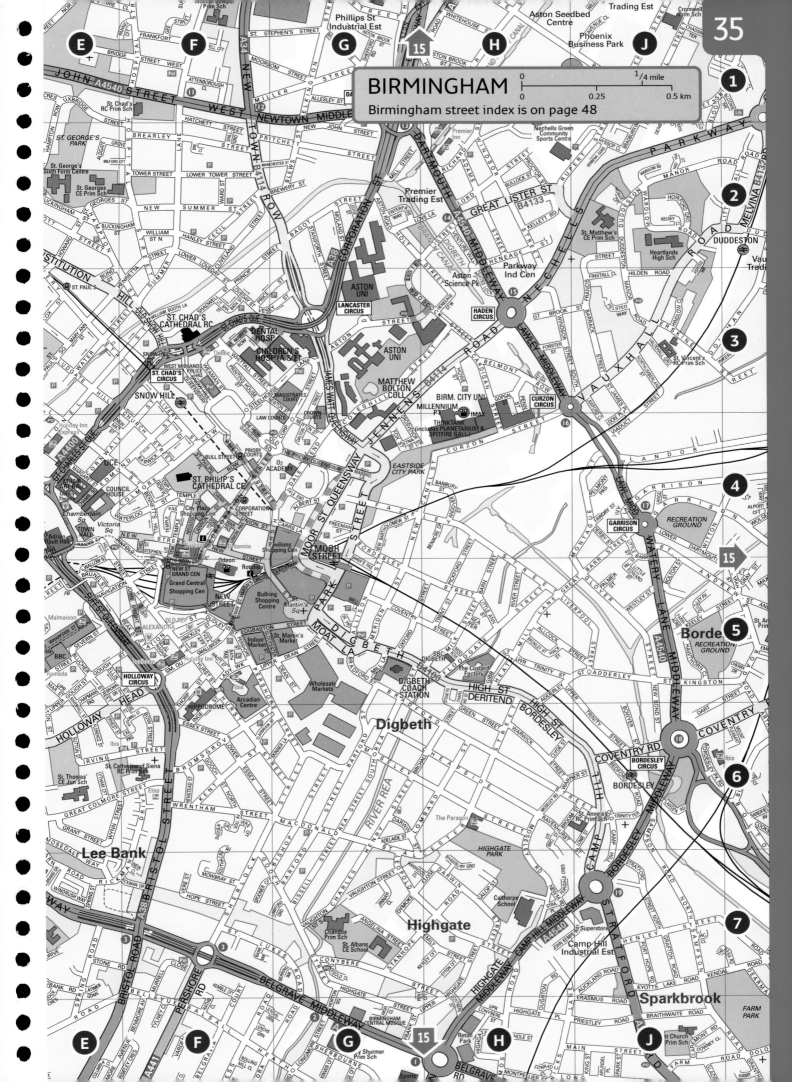

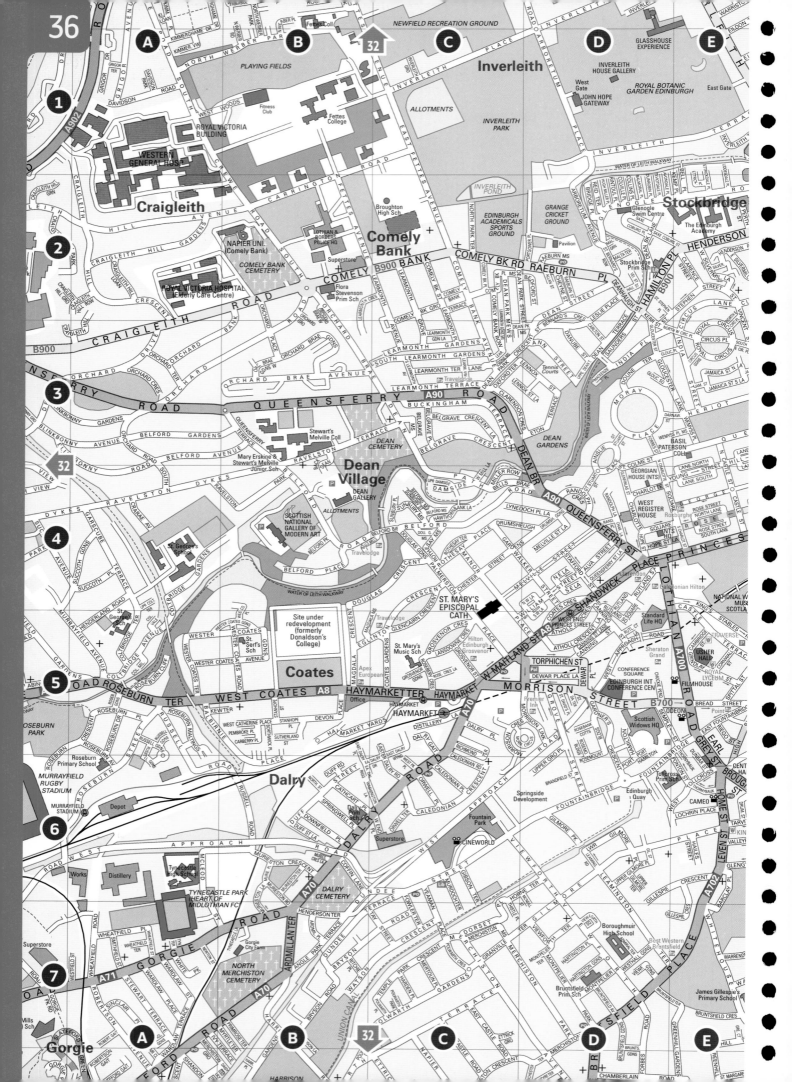

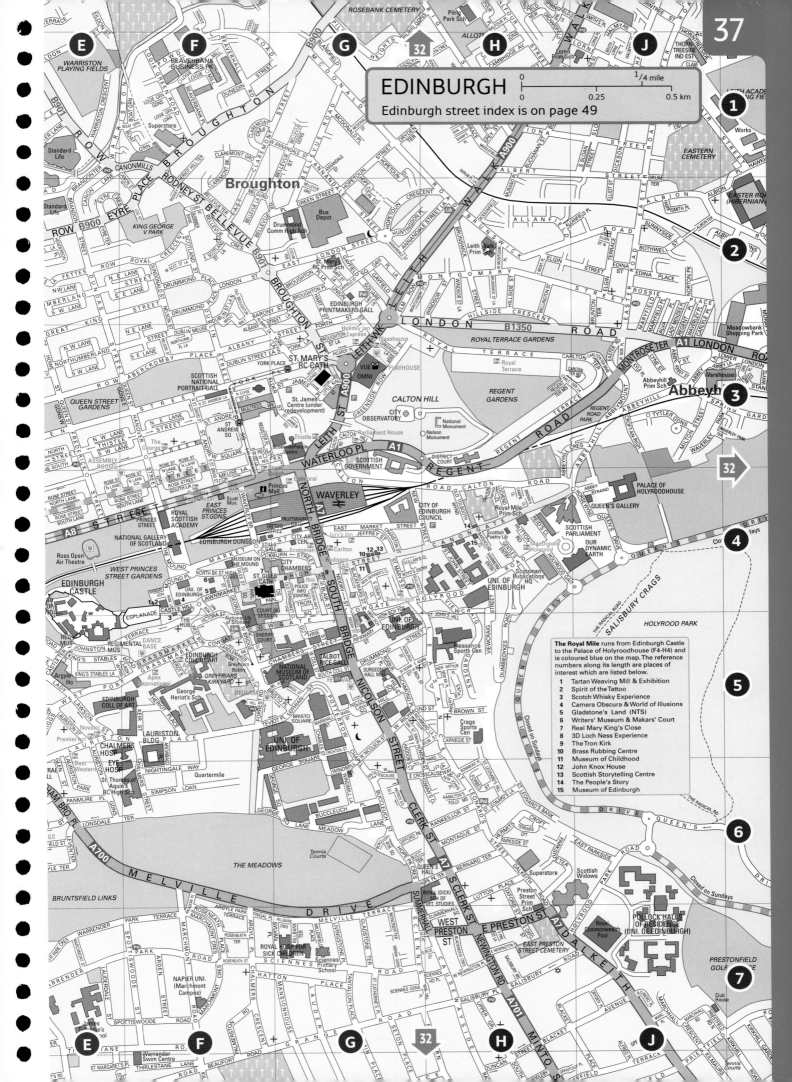

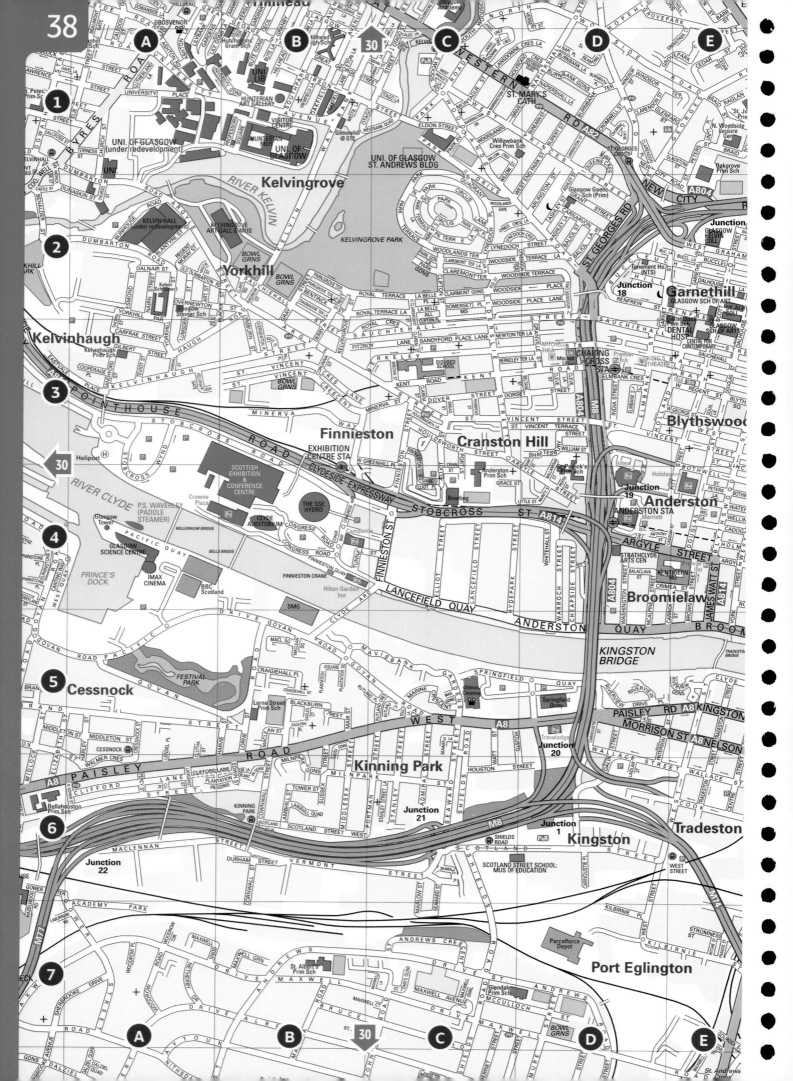

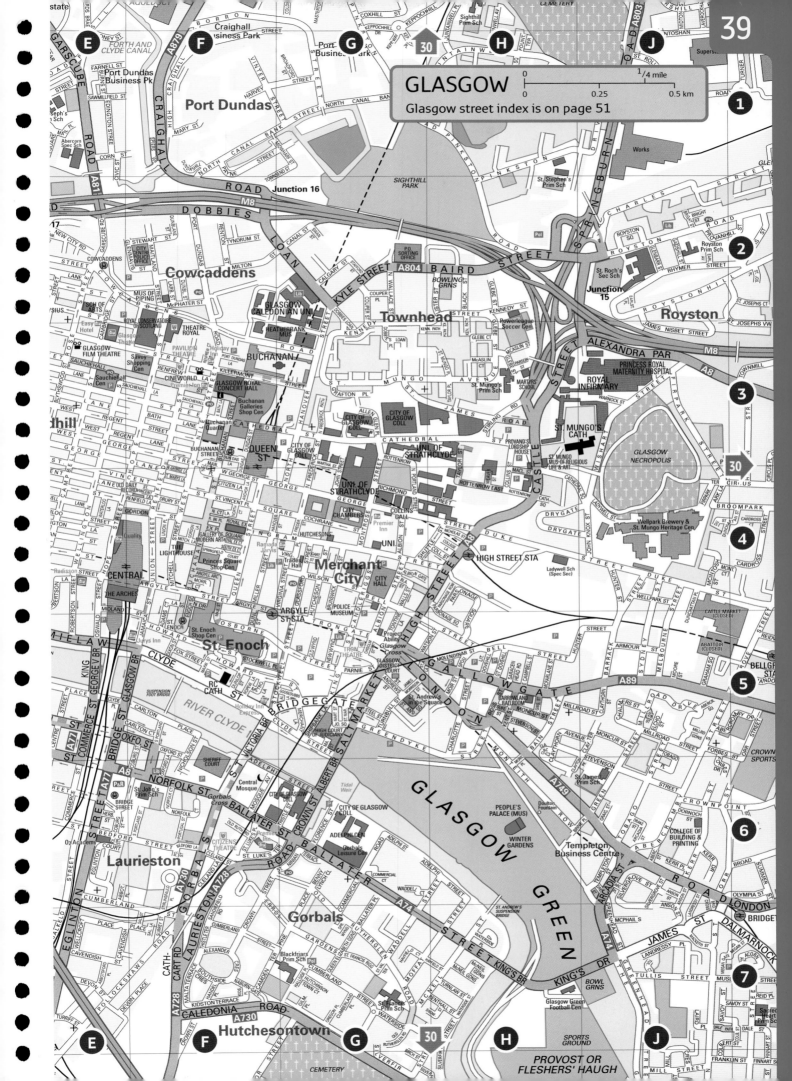

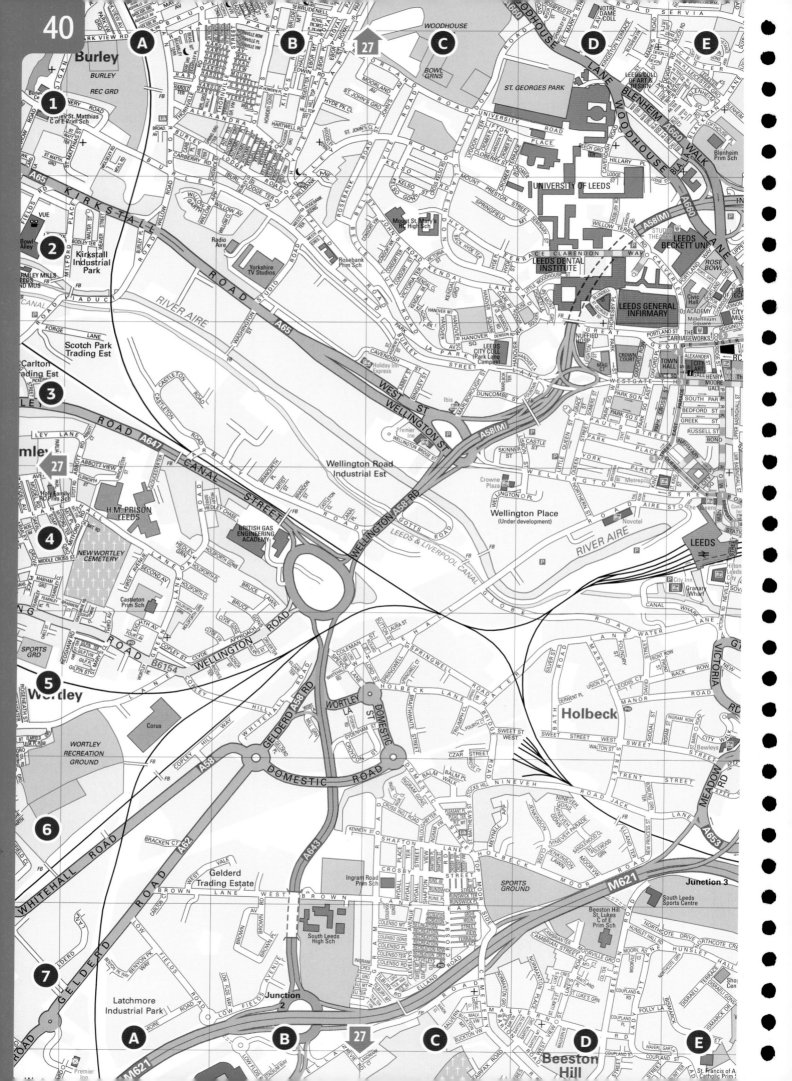

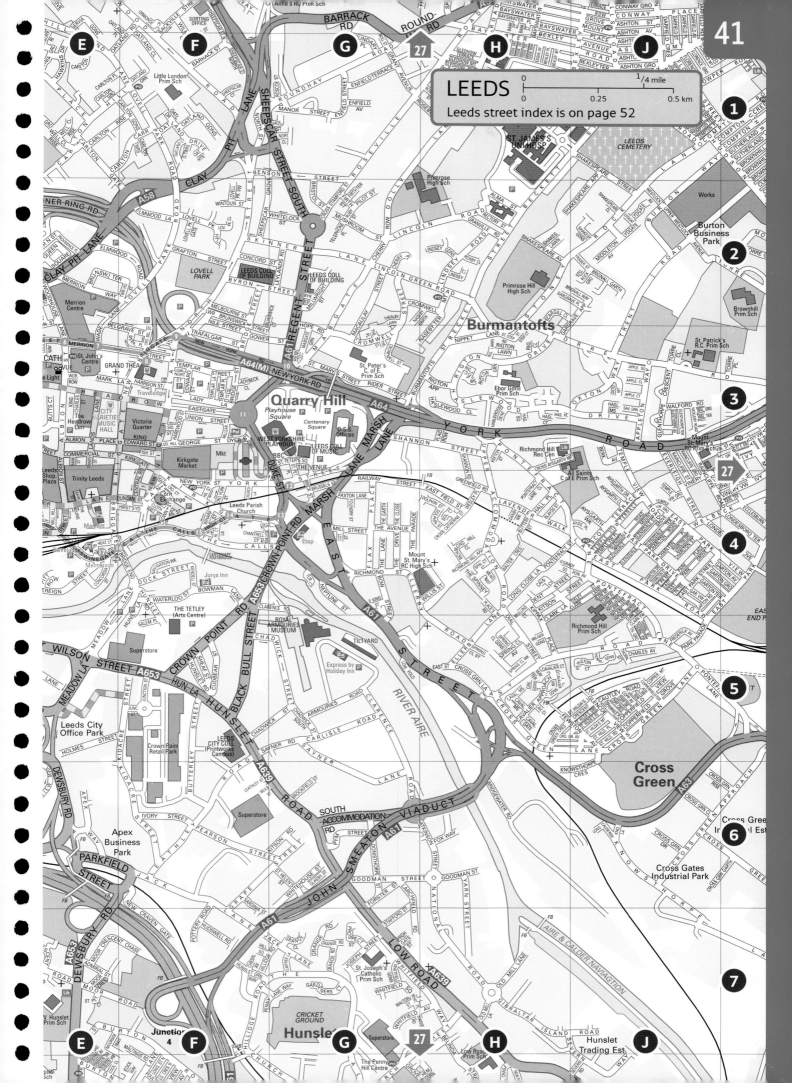

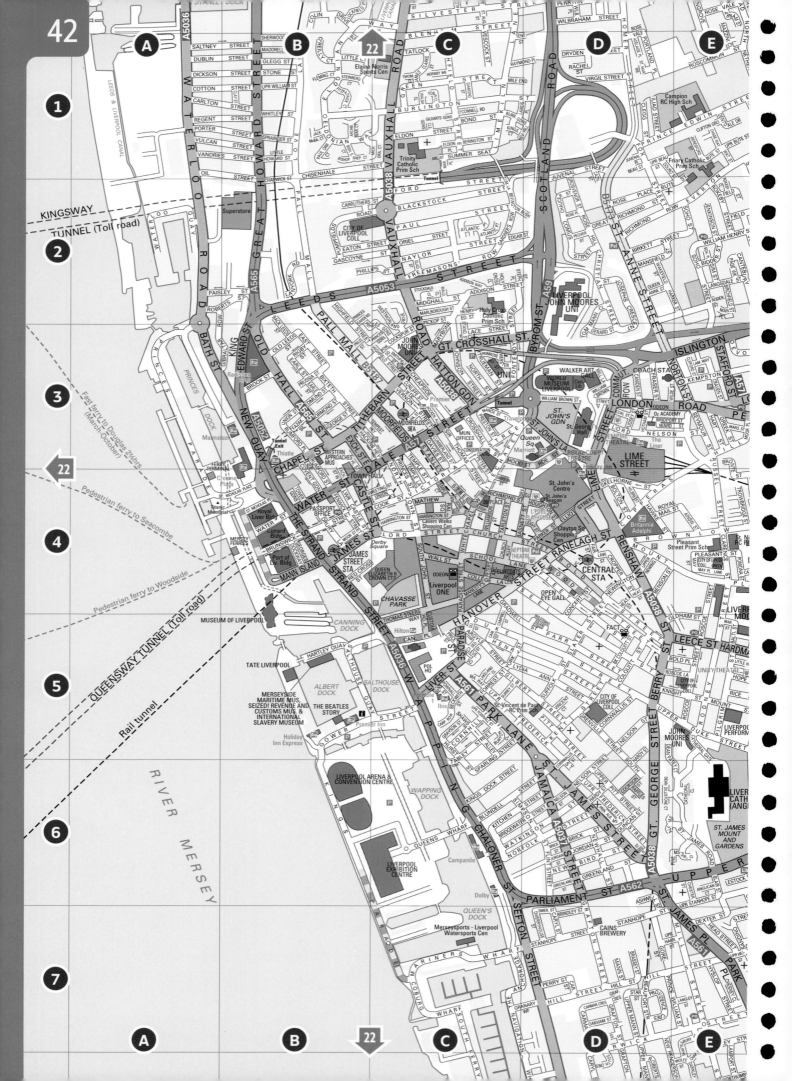

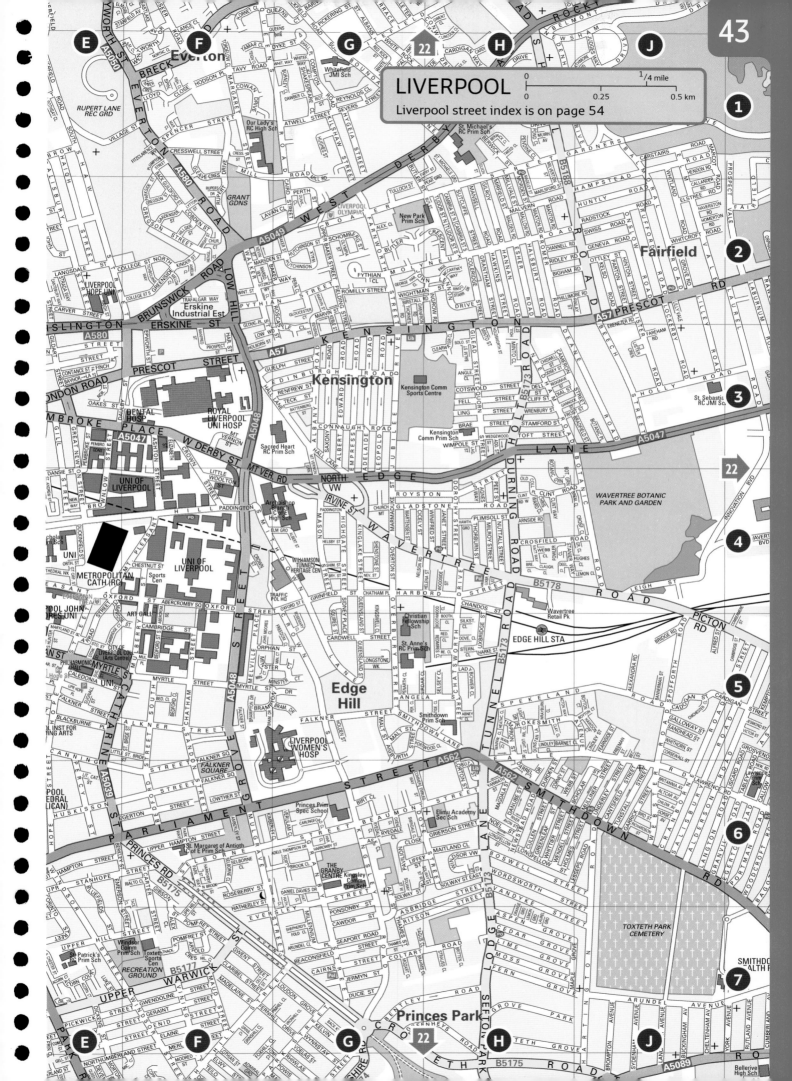

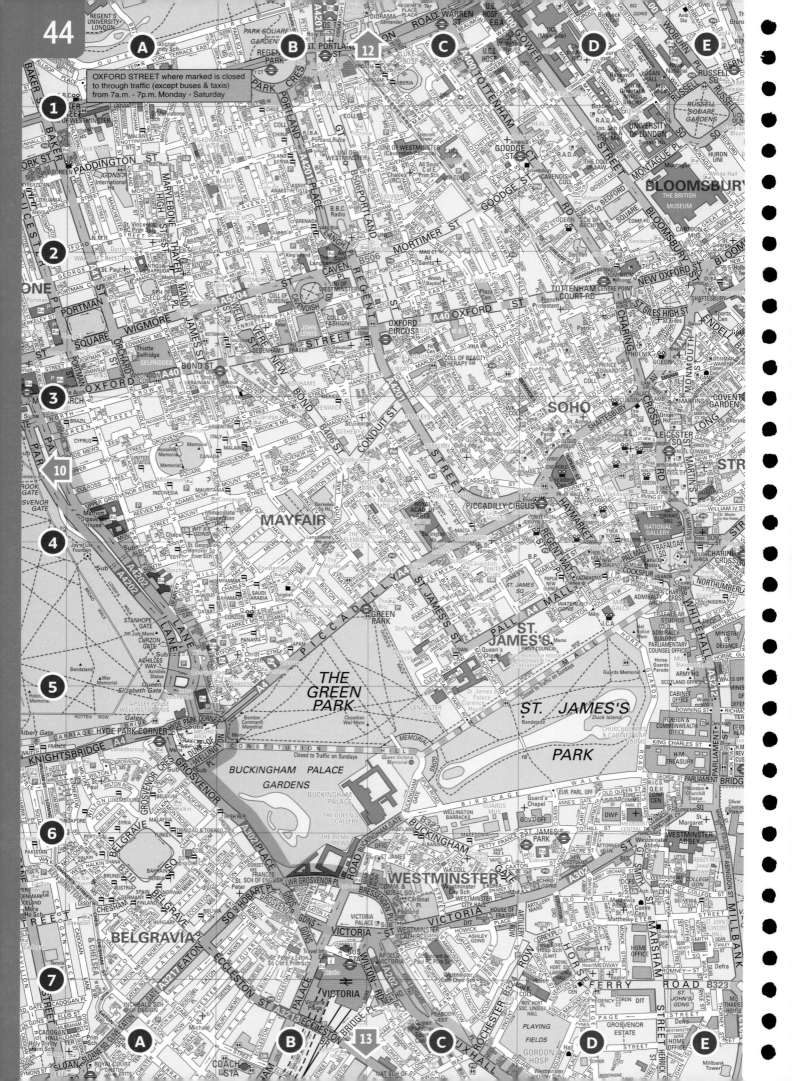

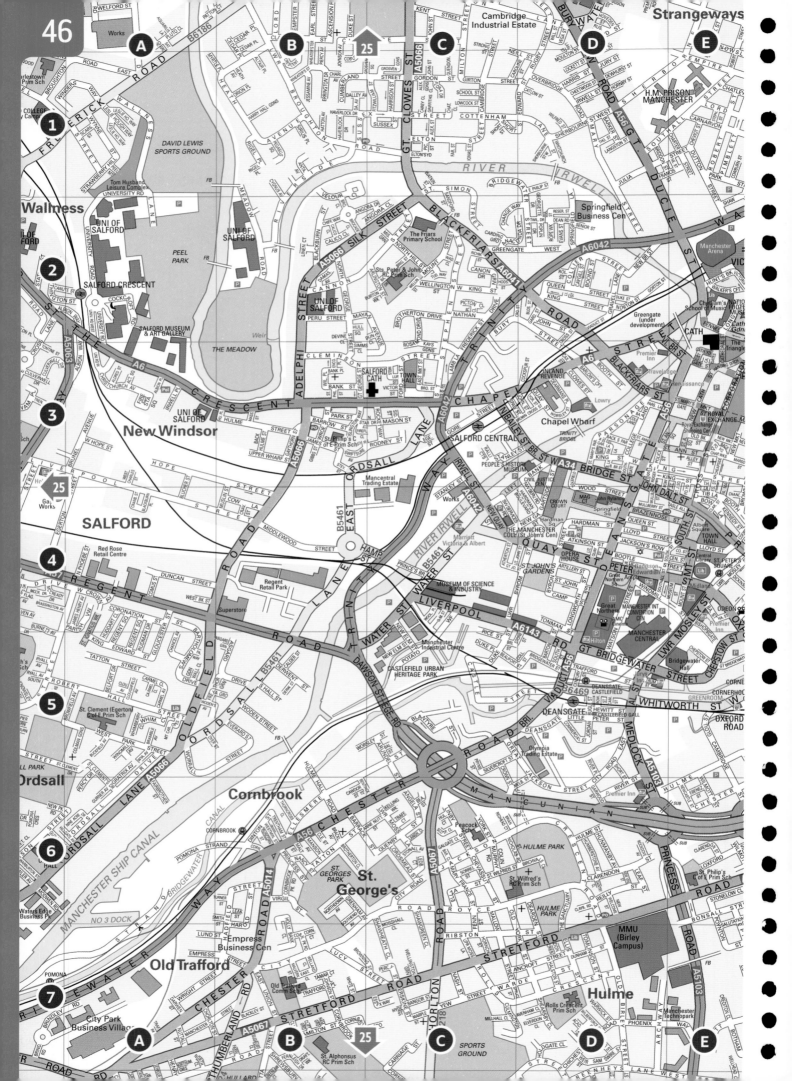

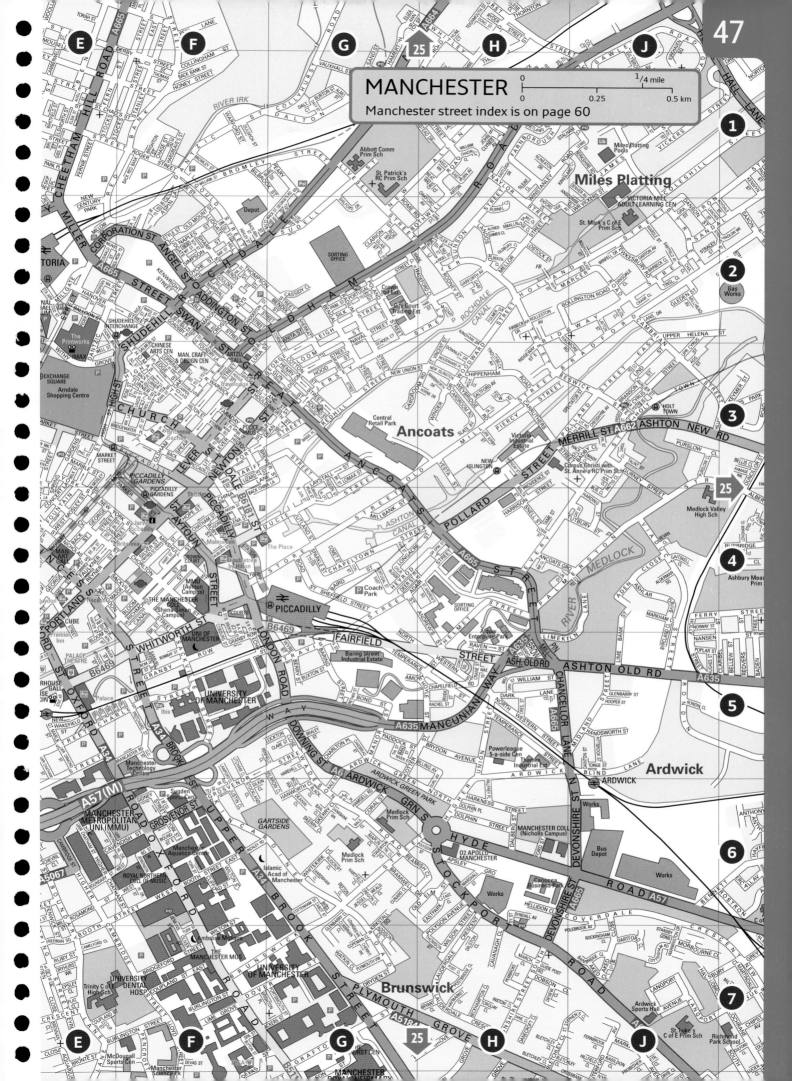

Indexes to street maps

General abbreviations

All	Alley	Chyd	Churchyard	Embk	Embankment	La	Lane	Pl	Place	W	West		
App	Approach	Circ	Circus	Est	Estate	Lo	Lodge	Rd	Road	Wf	Wharf		
Arc	Arcade	Clo	Close	Flds	Fields	Mans	Mansions	Ri	Rise	Wk	Walk		
Av/Ave	Avenue	Cor	Corner	Gdn	Garden	Mkt/Mkts	Market/Markets	S	South	Yd	Yard		
Bdy	Broadway	Cres	Crescent	Gdns	Gardens	Ms	Mews	Sq	Square				
Bldgs	Buildings	Ct	Court	Grd	Ground	N	North	St	Street				
Br/Bri	Bridge	Ctyd	Courtyard	Grn	Green	Par	Parade	St.	Saint				
Cen	Central, Centre	Dr	Drive	Gro	Grove	Pas	Passage	Ter	Terrace				
Ch	Church	E	East	Ho	House	Pk	Park	Twr	Tower				

Place names are shown in bold type

Birmingham street index

A
Abbey St 34 C1
Abbey St N 34 C1
Aberdeen St 34 A2
Acorn Gro 34 C4
Adams St 35 H2
Adderley St 35 H5
Adelaide St 35 G6
Albert St 35 G4
Albion St 34 D3
Alcester St 35 G7
Aldgate Gro 35 E2
Alfred Knight Way 34 E6
Allcock St 35 H5
Allesley St 35 G1
Allison St 35 G5
All Saints Rd 34 C1
All Saints St 34 C2
Alston St 34 B5
Anchor Cl 34 A5
Anchor Cres 34 B1
Anderton St 34 C4
Angelina St 35 G7
Ansbro Cl 34 A2
Arden Gro 34 C5
Arthur Pl 34 D4
Ascot Cl 34 A5
Ashted Lock 35 H3
Ashted Wk 35 J2
Ashton Cft 34 C5
Aston 35 H1
Aston Br 35 G1
Aston Brook St 35 G1
Aston Brook St E 35 H1
Aston Expressway 35 G2
Aston Rd 35 H1
Aston St 35 G3
Attenborough Cl 35 F1
Auckland Rd 35 J7
Augusta St 34 D2
Augustine Gro 34 B1
Austen Pl 34 C7
Autumn Gro 34 E1
Avenue Cl 35 J1
Avenue Rd 35 H1
B
Bacchus Rd 34 A1
Bagot St 35 G2
Balcaskie Cl 34 A7
Banbury St 35 G4
Barford Rd 34 A3
Barford St 35 G6
Barn St 35 H5
Barrack St 35 J3
Barrow Wk 35 F7
Barr St 34 D1
Bartholomew Row 35 G4
Bartholomew St 35 G4
Barwick St 35 F4
Bath Pas 35 F5
Bath Row 34 D6
Bath St 35 F3
Beak St 35 F5
Beaufort Gdns 34 A1
Beaufort Rd 34 B6
Bedford Rd 35 J6
Beeches, The 34 D7
Belgrave Middleway 35 F7
Bell Barn Rd 34 D6
Bellcroft 34 C5
Bellevue 35 F7
Bellis St 34 A6
Belmont Pas 35 J4
Belmont Row 35 H3
Benacre Dr 35 H4
Bennett's Hill 35 F4
Benson Rd 34 A1
Berkley St 34 D5
Berrington Wk 35 G7
Birchall St 35 G6
Bishopsgate St 34 D5
Bishop St 35 G7
Bissell St 35 G7
Blews St 35 G2
Bloomsbury St 35 J2
Blucher St 35 E5
Blyton Cl 34 A3
Boar Hound Cl 34 C3
Bodmin Gro 35 J1
Bolton St 35 J5
Bond Sq 34 C3
Bond St 35 E3
Bordesley 35 J5
Bordesley Circ 35 J6
Bordesley Middleway 35 J7
Bordesley Pk Rd 35 J6
Bordesley St 35 G4
Boulton Middleway 34 D1
Bow St 35 F6
Bowyer St 35 J6
Bracebridge St 35 G1
Bradburn Way 35 J2
Bradford St 35 G5
Branston St 34 D2
Brearley Cl 35 F2
Brearley St 35 F2
Bredon Cft 34 B1
Brewery St 35 G2
Bridge St 34 E5
Bridge St W 35 E1
Brindley Dr 34 D4
Brindley Pl 34 D5
Bristol St 35 F7
Broad St 34 D6
Broadway Plaza 34 C6
Bromley St 35 H5
Bromsgrove St 35 F6
Brookfield Rd 34 B2
Brook St 34 E3
Brook Vw Cl 34 E1
Broom St 35 H6
Brough Cl 35 J1
Browning St 34 C5
Brownsea Dr 35 E5
Brunel St 35 E5
Brunswick St 34 D5
Buckingham St 35 E2
Bullock St 35 H2
Bull St 35 F4
C
Cala Dr 34 C7
Calthorpe Rd 34 C7
Cambridge Rd 34 D4
Camden Dr 34 D3
Camden Gro 34 D3
Camden St 34 B2
Camp Hill 35 J7
Camp Hill Middleway 35 H7
Cannon St 35 F4
Capstone Av 34 C2
Cardigan St 35 H3
Carlisle St 34 A2
Carlyle Rd 34 A5
Caroline St 34 E3
Carpenter Rd 34 C7
Carrs La 35 G4
Carver St 34 C3
Cawdor Cres 34 B6
Cecil St 35 F2
Cemetery La 34 D2
Centenary Sq 34 E4
Central Pk Dr 34 A1
Central Sq 34 E5
Chad Rd 34 A7
Chadsmoor Ter 35 J1
Chad Valley 34 A7
Chamberlain Sq 35 E4
Chancellor's Cl 34 A7
Chandlers Cl 34 B1
Chapel Ho St 35 H5
Chapmans Pas 35 E5
Charles Henry St 35 G7
Charlotte Rd 34 D7
Charlotte St 34 E4
Chatsworth Way 34 E6
Cheapside 35 G6
Cherry St 35 F4
Chester St 35 H1
Chilwell Cft 35 F1
Christchurch Cl 34 A6
Church Rd 34 C7
Church St 35 F3
Civic Cl 34 D4
Clare Dr 34 A7
Clarendon Rd 34 A5
Clark St 34 A5
Claybrook St 35 F6
Clement St 34 D4
Clipper Vw 34 A5
Clissold Cl 35 G7
Clissold St 34 B2
Cliveland St 35 F3
Clyde St 35 H6
Colbrand Gro 35 E7
Coleshill St 35 G4
College St 34 B3
Colmore Circ 35 F3
Colmore Row 35 F4
Commercial St 34 E5
Communication Row 34 D6
Constitution Hill 34 E2
Conybere St 35 G7
Cope St 34 B3
Coplow St 34 A3
Cornwall St 35 E4
Corporation St 35 F4
Coveley Gro 34 B1
Coventry Rd 35 J6
Coventry St 35 G5
Cox St 35 E3
Coxwell Gdns 34 B5
Crabtree Rd 34 B2
Cregoe St 34 E6
Crescent, The 34 C1
Crescent Av 34 C1
Cromwell St 35 J1
Crondal Pl 34 D7
Crosby Cl 34 C4
Cumberland St 34 D5
Curzon Circ 35 H3
Curzon St 35 H4
D
Daisy Rd 34 A5
Dale End 35 G4
Daley Cl 34 C4
Dalton St 35 G4
Darnley Rd 34 B5
Dartmouth Circ 35 G1
Dartmouth Middleway 35 G2
Dart St 35 J6
Darwin St 35 G6
Dean St 35 G5
Deeley Cl 34 D7
Denby Cl 35 J2
Derby St 35 J4
Devonshire Av 34 B1
Devonshire St 34 B1
Digbeth 35 G6
Digbeth 35 G5
Dollman St 35 J3
Dover St 34 B1
Duchess Rd 34 B6
Duddeston Manor Rd 35 J2
Dudley St 35 F5
Dymoke Cl 35 G7
E
Edgbaston 34 B7
Edgbaston St 35 F5
Edmund St 35 E4
Edward St 34 D4
Eldon Rd 34 A5
Elkington St 35 G1
Ellen St 34 C3
Ellis St 35 E5
Elvetham Rd 34 D7
Embassy Dr 34 C6
Emily Gdns 34 A3
Emily St 35 G7
Enfield Rd 34 D6
Enterprise Way 35 G2
Ernest St 35 E6
Erskine St 35 J3
Essex St 35 F6
Essington St 34 D5
Estria Rd 34 C7
Ethel St 35 F4
Exeter Pas 35 F6
Exeter St 35 F6
Eyre St 34 B3
Eyton Cft 35 H7
F
Farmacre 35 J5
Farm Cft 34 D1
Farm St 34 D1
Fawdry St 35 J4
Fazeley St 35 G4
Felsted Way 35 J3
Ferndale Cres 35 H7
Finstall Cl 35 J3
Five Ways 34 C6
Fleet St 34 E4
Floodgate St 35 H5
Florence St 35 E6
Ford St 34 C1
Fore St 35 F4
Forster St 35 H3
Foster Gdns 34 B1
Fox St 35 G4
Francis Rd 34 B5
Francis St 35 J3
Frankfort St 35 F1
Frederick Rd 34 C7
Frederick St 34 D3
Freeman St 35 G4
Freeth St 34 B4
Friston Av 34 C6
Fulmer Wk 34 C4
G
Garrison Circ 35 J4
Garrison La 35 J4
Garrison St 35 J4
Gas St 34 D5
Gas St Basin 34 E5
Geach St 35 F1
Gee St 35 F1
George Rd 34 D7
George St 34 D4
George St W 34 C3
Gibb St 35 H5
Gilby Rd 34 C5
Gilldown Pl 34 D7
Glebeland Cl 34 C5
Gloucester St 35 F5
Glover St 35 J5
Gooch St 35 F7
Gooch St N 35 F6
Goode Av 34 C1
Goodman St 34 C4
Gopsal St 35 H3
Gough St 35 E5
Grafton Rd 35 J7
Graham St 34 D3
Grant St 35 E6
Granville St 34 D5
Graston Cl 34 C5
Great Barr St 35 H5
Great Brook St 35 H3
Great Charles St Queensway 35 E4
Great Colmore St 34 E6
Great Hampton Row 34 E2
Great Hampton St 34 D2
Great King St 34 D1
Great King St N 34 E1
Great Lister St 35 H2
Great Tindal St 34 C4
Greenfield Cres 34 C6
Green St 35 H6
Grenfell Dr 34 A7
Grosvenor St 35 G4
Grosvenor St W 34 C5
Guest Gro 34 D1
Guild Cl 34 B5
Guild Cft 35 F1
Guthrie Cl 35 E1
H
Hack St 35 H5
Hadfield Cft 34 E2
Hagley Rd 34 A6
Hall St 34 E3
Hampshire Dr 34 A7
Hampton St 35 E2
Hanley St 35 F2
Hanwood Cl 35 G7
Harborne Rd 34 A7
Harford St 34 E2
Harmer St 34 C2
Harold Rd 34 A5
Hartley Pl 34 A6
Hatchett St 35 F1
Hawthorn Cl 35 J5
Hawthorne Rd 34 A7
Heath Mill La 35 H5
Heath St S 34 B3
Heaton Dr 34 A7
Heaton St 34 D1
Helena St 34 D4
Heneage St 35 H2
Heneage St W 35 H3
Henley St 35 J7
Henrietta St 35 F3
Henstead St 35 F6
Herne Cl 34 C3
Hickman Gdns 34 B5
Highfield Rd 34 B6
Highgate 35 H7
Highgate St 35 G7
High St 35 G4
Hilden Rd 35 J3
Hill St 35 E4
Hinckley St 35 F5
Hindlow Cl 35 J3
Hindon Sq 34 B7
Hingeston St 34 C2
Hitches La 34 D7
Hobart Cft 35 J2
Hobson Cl 34 B1
Hockley Brook Cl 34 B1
Hockley Cl 35 F1
Hockley Hill 34 D1
Hockley St 34 D2
Holland St 34 D4
Holliday Pas 34 E5
Holliday St 34 E5
Holloway Circ 35 F5
Holloway Head 35 E6
Holt St 35 G2
Holywell Cl 34 B5
Hooper St 34 B3
Hope St 35 F7
Hospital St 35 F1
Howard St 35 E2
Howe St 35 H3
Howford Gro 35 J2
Hubert St 35 H1
Hunter's Vale 34 D1
Huntly Rd 34 B6
Hurdlow Av 34 C2
Hurst St 35 F5
Hylton St 34 D2
Hyssop Cl 35 J2
I
Icknield Port Rd 34 A3
Icknield Sq 34 B4
Icknield St 34 C3
Inge St 35 F6
Inkerman St 35 J3
Irving St 35 E6
Islington Row Middleway 34 C6
Ivy La 35 J4
J
Jackson Cl 35 J7
James St 34 E3
James Watt Queensway 35 G3
Jennens Rd 35 G4
Jewellery Quarter 34 D2
Jinnah Cl 35 G7
John Bright St 35 F5
John Kempe Way 35 H7
K
Keeley St 35 J5
Keepers Cl 34 B1
Kellett Rd 35 H2
Kelsall Cft 34 C4
Kelsey Cl 35 J2
Kemble Cft 35 F7
Kendal Rd 35 J7
Kenilworth Ct 34 A6
Kent St 35 F6
Kent St N 34 B1
Kenyon St 34 E3
Ketley Cft 35 G7
Key Hill 34 D2
Key Hill Dr 34 D2
Kilby Av 34 C4
King Edwards Rd 34 D4
Kingston Rd 35 J5
Kingston Row 34 D4
Kirby Rd 34 A1
Knightstone Av 34 C2
Kyotts Lake Rd 35 J7
L
Ladycroft 34 C5
Ladywell Wk 35 F5
Ladywood 34 C4
Ladywood Middleway 34 B5
Ladywood Rd 34 B5
Lancaster Circ 35 G3
Landor St 35 J4
Langdon St 35 J4
Lansdowne St 34 A2
Latimer Gdns 35 E7
Lawden Rd 35 J6
Lawford Cl 35 J3
Lawford Gro 35 G7
Lawley Middleway 35 H3
Ledbury Cl 34 B5
Ledsam St 34 C4
Lee Bk 35 E7
Lee Bk Middleway 34 D6
Lee Cres 34 D7
Lee Mt 34 D7
Lees St 34 B1
Legge La 34 D3
Legge St 35 G2
Lennox St 35 E1
Leopold St 35 G7
Leslie Rd 34 A5
Leyburn Rd 34 C5
Lighthorne Av 34 C4
Link Rd 34 A3
Lionel St 34 E4
Lister St 35 G3
Little Ann St 35 H5
Little Barr St 35 J4
Little Broom St 35 H6
Little Edward St 35 J5
Little Francis Grn 35 J2
Little Shadwell St 35 F3
Liverpool St 35 H5
Livery St 35 F3
Locke Pl 35 J4
Lodge Rd 34 A1
Lombard St 35 G6
Longleat Way 34 D6
Lord St 35 H2
Louisa St 34 D4
Loveday St 35 F3
Love La 35 G2
Lower Dartmouth St 35 J4
Lower Essex St 35 F6
Lower Loveday St 35 F2
Lower Severn St 35 F5
Lower Temple St 35 F4

Lower Twr St	35 F2	New Canal St	35 G4
Lower Trinity St	35 H5	Newhall Hill	34 D3
Lowe St	35 J6	Newhall St	34 E3
Ludgate Hill	35 E3	Newhope Cl	35 F7
Lytham Cft	35 E6	New John St	35 G2
		New John St W	34 E1
M		New Mkt St	34 E4
Macdonald St	35 G6	New Moseley Rd	35 H7
Malcolmson Cl	34 A7	New Spring St	34 C2
Manchester St	35 F2	New Spring St N	34 B2
Margaret St	35 E4	New St	35 F4
Mariner Av	34 A5	New Summer St	35 F2
Marroway St	34 A3	Newton St	35 G4
Marshall St	35 E5	**Newtown**	34 E1
Mary Ann St	35 E3	Newtown Dr	34 D1
Mary St	34 E3	Newtown Middleway	35 F1
Mason Way	34 E6	New Town Row	35 F1
Masshouse La	35 G4	Niall Cl	34 A7
Mearse Cl	34 C2	Noel Rd	34 A5
Melton Dr	34 D7	Norman St	34 A2
Meredith Pool Cl	34 A1	Northampton St	34 D2
Meriden St	35 G5	Northbrook St	34 A3
Merryhill Dr	34 A1	Northumberland St	35 J3
Meyrick Wk	34 A6	Northwood St	34 D3
Middleway Vw	34 C3	Norton St	34 B1
Midford Grn	34 E6	Nova Scotia St	35 G4
Milford Cft	35 E2	Nursery Rd	34 D1
Milk St	35 H5		
Miller St	35 F1	**O**	
Mill La	35 G5	Oak Hill Dr	34 A7
Mill St	35 G2	Old Br St	34 D1
Milton St	35 F1	Old Camp Hill	35 J6
Moat La	35 G5	Old Smithy Pl	34 C1
Moland St	35 G2	Old Snow Hill	35 F3
Montague St	35 J4	Old Sq	35 F4
Monument Rd	34 B6	Oliver Rd	34 B5
Moore's Row	35 H5	Oliver St	35 J1
Moorings, The	34 B1	Oozells St	34 D5
Moorsom St	35 F1	Orchid Dr	35 E1
Moor St Queensway	35 G4	Orwell Pas	35 G5
Moreton St	34 C3	Osler St	34 A5
Morville St	34 C5	Oxford St	35 G5
Mosborough Cres	34 E1		
Mosedale Way	35 E6	**P**	
Moseley Rd	35 H6	Paddocks Grn	34 B2
Moseley St	35 G6	Pakenham Rd	34 D7
Moss Ho Cl	34 D6	Palmer St	35 J5
Mostyn Rd	34 A5	Palomino Pl	34 B4
Mott St	34 E2	Pannel Cft	35 F1
Mowbray St	35 F7	Parade	34 D4
Murrell Cl	35 F7	Paradise Circ	34 E4
Musgrave Rd	34 A1	Paradise St	35 E4
Myddleton St	34 B3	Parker St	34 A6
		Parkfield Cl	34 D7
N		Park Rd	34 C1
Navigation St	35 E5	Park Rd S	34 C1
Navigation Way	34 B1	Park St	35 G5
Nechells Parkway	35 H3	Paxton Rd	34 C2
Needless All	35 F4	Peel St	34 A2
Nelson St	34 D4	Pemberton St	34 D2
New Bartholomew St	35 G4	Penn St	35 H3
Newbold Cft	35 J1	Pershore St	35 F5
New Bond St	35 J5	Pickford St	35 H5

Pinfold St	35 E4	St. Lukes Rd	35 F7
Pinto Cl	34 B5	St. Marks Cres	34 C4
Pitsford St	34 C2	St. Marks St	34 C3
Pitt St	35 H3	St. Martin's Circ	
Plough & Harrow Rd	34 B6	Queensway	35 F5
Pool St	35 G1	St. Martin's Sq	35 G5
Pope St	34 C3	St. Martin's St	34 D6
Port Hope Rd	35 J7	St. Mary's Row	35 F3
Powell St	34 D3	St. Paul's Sq	34 E3
Power Cres	34 C5	St. Phillips Pl	35 F4
Price St	35 F3	St. Stephen's St	35 F1
Princip St	35 F3	St. Vincent St	34 C4
Printing Ho St	35 F3	St. Vincent St W	34 B5
Priory		Salop St	35 H7
Queensway, The	35 G4	Sampson Rd	35 J7
Pritchett St	35 F2	Sampson Rd N	35 J6
Proctor St	35 H2	Sand Pits	34 C3
		Sandy Way	34 D5
Q		Scotland St	34 D4
Quayside	34 B1	Sefton Rd	34 A5
Queens Hosp Cl	34 D6	Severn St	35 E5
Quigley Av	35 J5	Shadwell St	35 F3
		Shawbury Gro	35 H7
R		Shaw's Pas	35 G5
Radnor St	34 B1	Sheepcote St	34 C4
Radshaw Cl	34 D6	Shefford Rd	35 G1
Rake Way	34 D5	Shepherds Gdns	34 D6
Rann Cl	34 C5	Sherborne Gro	34 C4
Ravenhurst St	35 H6	Sherborne St	34 C5
Rawlins St	34 C5	Sheringham	34 A6
Rea St	35 G6	Sherlock St	35 F7
Rea St S	35 G6	Shetland Cl	34 B5
Rea Ter	35 H5	Shillcock Gro	35 F2
Rectory Gro	34 A1	Shire Cl	34 A4
Regent Par	34 D3	Shyltons Cft	34 C5
Regent Pl	34 D3	Skinner La	35 G6
Regent St	34 D3	Skipton Rd	34 B5
Reservoir Retreat	34 B5	Sloane St	34 D4
Reservoir Rd	34 A5	Smallbrook	
Richard St	35 H2	Queensway	35 F5
Rickman Dr	35 E7	Smith St	34 E1
Ridley St	34 E6	Snow Hill Queensway	35 F3
River St	35 H5	Soho Pool Way	34 B1
Rocky La	35 J1	Southacre Av	35 F7
Rodney Cl	34 B4	South Rd	35 J7
Rosebery St	34 B2	Spencer St	34 D2
Roseland Way	34 D6	Spooner Cft	35 F7
Rotton Pk St	34 B4	Springbank Rd	34 E7
Rupert St	35 H2	Springfield St	34 B4
Ruston St	34 C5	Spring Gro Gdns	34 A1
Ryland Rd	34 D7	Spring Hill	34 B3
Ryland St	34 C5	Spring Hill Pas	34 C3
		Spring St	35 E7
S		Stainsby Av	34 D1
Sadlers Wk	34 B5	Stanhope Rd	35 G7
St. Andrew's Rd	35 J4	Staniforth St	35 G2
St. Chad's Queensway	35 F3	Star Hill	34 D7
St. Georges Cl	34 B7	Station St	35 F5
St. Georges St	34 E2	Steelhouse La	35 F5
St. Helen's Pas	34 D3	Stephenson Pl	35 F5
St. James Pl	35 J3	Stephenson St	35 F4
St. James Rd	34 C6	Steward St	34 B3
St. Jude's Pas	35 F5	Stirling Rd	34 A6

Stoke Way	35 F7	Vittoria St	34 D3
Stone Rd	34 C4	Vyse St	34 D3
Stone Yd	34 C3		
Stour St	34 B3	**W**	
Stratford Pl	35 H7	Walter St	35 J1
Stratford Rd	35 J7	Wardlow Rd	35 J2
Stratford St N	35 J7	Ward St	35 F2
Suffolk St		Warner St	35 H6
Queensway	35 E5	Warstone La	34 C3
Sugden Gro	35 F6	Warstone Par E	34 D2
Summer Cft	35 F1	Warwick Pas	35 F4
Summerfield Rd	34 A3	Warwick St	35 H6
Summer Hill Rd	34 C3	Washington St	34 E5
Summer Hill St	34 D4	Waterloo St	35 E4
Summer Hill Ter	34 D3	Waterside Dr	34 A1
Summer La	35 F3	Waterside Vw	34 B2
Summer Rd	34 E7	Water St	35 E3
Summer Row	34 E4	Waterworks Rd	34 A5
Sutton St	35 E6	Watery La Middleway	35 J4
Swallow St	35 E5	Weaman St	35 F3
		Well La	35 G5
T		Well St	34 D2
Talbot St	34 A1	Westbourne Cres	34 C7
Temple Pas	35 F4	Westbourne Gdns	34 B7
Temple Row	35 F4	Westbourne Rd	34 A7
Temple Row W	35 F4	Western Rd	34 B3
Temple St	35 F4	West Grn Cl	34 D7
Tenby St	34 D3	Westhorpe Gro	34 E1
Tenby St N	34 D3	Westley St	35 J5
Tennant St	34 D6	Wharf, The	34 E5
Theatre App	35 F5	Wharf La	34 C1
Theresa Rd	35 J7	Wharfside St	35 E5
Thomas St	35 G1	Wharf St	34 B1
Thorp St	35 F6	Wheeler St	35 E1
Tower St	35 F2	Wheeley's La	34 D6
Townsend Way	34 D4	Whitehouse St	35 H1
Trent St	35 H5	Whitmore St	34 C1
Trinity Ter	35 J6	Whittall St	35 F3
		Wiggin St	34 A4
U		William Booth La	35 F3
Unett St	34 E1	William Henry St	35 J1
Union Pas	35 F4	William St	34 D6
Union St	35 F4	William St N	35 F2
Upper Dean St	35 F5	Willow Gdns	34 A3
Upper Gough St	35 E6	Windmill St	35 F6
Upper Marshall St	35 E5	Windrush Way	35 E7
Upper Trinity St	35 H5	Windsor St	35 H2
Uxbridge St	35 E1	Windsor St S	35 H3
		Winson Grn	34 A1
V		Witton St	35 J4
Vaughton St	35 G7	Woodcock St	35 G3
Vaughton St S	35 G7	Woodcote Way	34 B2
Vauxhall Gro	35 J3	Woodview Dr	34 E7
Vauxhall Rd	35 J3	Wrentham St	35 F6
Venture Way	35 H2	Wrottesley St	35 F5
Verbena Gdns	35 J2	Wyndham Rd	34 A6
Vere St	35 F7	Wynn St	35 E6
Vernolds Cft	35 F6		
Vesey St	35 F3	**Y**	
Viaduct St	35 J4	Yew Tree Rd	34 D6
Vicarage Rd	34 B6		
Victoria Sq	35 E4		
Victor Rd	34 A1		

Edinburgh street index

A		Archibald Pl	37 F6
Abbeyhill	37 J3	Arden St	37 F7
Abbeyhill	37 J3	Ardmillan Pl	36 B7
Abbeyhill Cres	37 H4	Ardmillan Ter	36 B7
Abbey La	37 J3	Argyle Pk Ter	37 F7
Abbeymount	37 J3	Argyle Pl	37 F7
Abbey Strand	37 J4	Arthur St	37 H1
Abbey St	37 J3	Arthur St La	37 H1
Abercromby Pl	37 F3	Atholl Cres	36 D5
Admiral Ter	36 D7	Atholl Cres La	36 D5
Ainslie Pl	36 D3	Avondale Pl	36 D1
Albany La	37 F2		
Albany St	37 F3	**B**	
Albany St La	37 F3	Back Dean	36 B4
Albert St	37 H1	Bakehouse Cl	37 H4
Albion Gdns	37 J2	Balbirnie Pl	36 A5
Albion Pl	37 J2	Balmoral Pl	36 D2
Albion Rd	37 J2	Bank St	37 F4
Albion Ter	37 J2	Barclay Pl	36 E7
Alfred Pl	37 J7	Barony St	37 F2
Allanfield	37 H2	Beaverbank Pl	37 F1
Allanfield Pl	37 H2	Beaverhall Rd	37 F1
Allan St	36 D2	Bedford St	36 D2
Alva Pl	37 J3	Belford Av	36 A3
Alva St	36 D4	Belford Br	36 C4
Angle Pk Ter	36 B7	Belford Gdns	36 A3
Annandale St	37 G1	Belford Ms	36 C4
Annandale St La	37 G2	Belford Pk	36 B4
Ann St	36 D3	Belford Pl	36 B4
Arboretum Av	36 D2	Belford Rd	36 B4
Arboretum Pl	36 D1	Belgrave Cres	36 C3

Belgrave Cres La	36 C3	Brandon Ter	37 E2
Belgrave Ms	36 C3	Bread St	36 E5
Belgrave Pl	36 C3	Bridge St	36 D2
Bellevue	37 F2	Briery Bauks	37 H5
Bellevue Cres	37 F2	Brighton St	37 G5
Bellevue Gdns	37 G1	Bristo Pl	37 F5
Bellevue Gro	37 G2	Bristo Port	37 F5
Bellevue La	37 F2	Brougham Pl	37 E6
Bellevue Pl	37 F2	Brougham St	36 E6
Bellevue Rd	37 G2	**Broughton**	37 F1
Bellevue St	37 G2	Broughton Mkt	37 F3
Bellevue Ter	37 F2	Broughton Pl	37 G2
Bell Pl	36 E1	Broughton Pl La	37 G2
Bells Brae	36 C4	Broughton Rd	37 F1
Bell's Mills	36 B4	Broughton St	37 G2
Bernard Ter	37 H6	Broughton St La	37 G3
Blacket Av	37 H7	Brown's Cl	37 H4
Blacket Pl	37 H7	Brown St	37 H5
Blackfriars St	37 G5	Brunswick Rd	37 H2
Blackwood Cres	37 H7	Brunswick St	37 H2
Blair St	37 G4	Brunswick St La	37 H2
Blandfield	37 G1	Brunton Ter	37 J3
Boat Grn	37 F1	Bruntsfield Av	36 D7
Boroughloch	37 G6	Bruntsfield Cres	36 E7
Boroughloch Sq	37 G6	Bruntsfield Gdns	36 D7
Borthwick Pl	36 B5	Bruntsfield Ter	36 D7
Bothwell St	37 J2	Bryson Rd	36 B7
Bowmont Pl	37 H6	Buccleuch Pl	37 G6
Boyd's Entry	37 G4	Buccleuch St	37 G6
Brandfield St	36 D6	Buccleuch Ter	37 G6
Brandon St	37 E2	Buchanan St	37 H1

Buckingham Ter	36 C3	Castle Ter	36 E4
		Cathcart Pl	36 B6
C		Cathedral La	37 G3
Caledonian Cres	36 C6	Causewayside	37 H7
Caledonian Pl	36 C6	Chalmers Cres	37 F7
Caledonian Rd	36 C6	Chalmers St	37 F5
Calton Hill	37 G3	Chambers St	37 G5
Calton Rd	37 G3	Chapel St	37 G5
Cambridge Av	37 H1	Charles St	37 G5
Cambridge Gdns	37 H1	Charlotte La	36 D4
Cambridge St	36 E5	Charlotte Sq	36 D4
Campbell's Cl	37 H4	Chester St	36 C4
Candlemaker Row	37 F5	Cheyne St	36 D2
Canning St	36 D5	Chuckie Pend	36 D5
Canning St La	36 D5	Circus Gdns	36 E3
Canongate	37 G4	Circus La	36 E3
Canon La	37 E2	Circus Pl	36 E3
Canonmills	37 E1	Claremont Bk	37 F2
Canon St	37 E1	Claremont Cres	37 F1
Carberry Pl	36 B5	Claremont Gro	37 F1
Carlton St	36 D3	Clarence St	36 E2
Carlton Ter	37 H3	Clarendon Cres	36 C3
Carlton Ter Brae	37 J3	Clerk St	37 G6
Carlton Ter La	37 H3	**Coates**	36 B5
Carlton Ter Ms	37 H3	Coates Cres	36 D5
Carlton Wynd	37 H4	Coates Gdns	36 C5
Carlyle Pl	37 J3	Cochran Ter	37 G2
Carnegie St	37 H5	Cockburn St	37 F4
Carrington Rd	36 B2	Coffin La	36 B6
Castle Hill	37 F4	Collins Pl	36 D2
Castle St	36 E4	Coltbridge Av	36 A5

Street	Ref
Coltbridge Gdns	36 A5
Coltbridge Millside	36 A5
Coltbridge Ter	36 A5
Coltbridge Vale	36 A5
Colville Pl	36 D2
Comely Bk	36 C2
Comely Bk	36 B2
Comely Bk Av	36 C2
Comely Bk Gro	36 C3
Comely Bk Pl	36 C2
Comely Bk Pl Ms	36 C2
Comely Bk Rd	36 C2
Comely Bk Row	36 C2
Comely Bk St	36 C5
Comely Bk Ter	36 C2
Conference Sq	36 D5
Cornwallis Pl	37 F2
Cornwall St	36 E5
Cowan's Cl	37 G6
Cowgate	37 F5
Cowgatehead	37 F5
Craigleith	36 A2
Craigleith Hill Cres	36 A2
Craigleith Hill Gdns	36 A2
Craigleith Hill Ln	36 A2
Craigleith Hill Row	36 A2
Cranston St	37 G4
Crarae Av	36 A4
Crewe Rd S	36 A1
Crichton St	37 G5
Croft-an-Righ	37 J3
Cumberland St	36 E2
Cumberland St N E La	37 E2
Cumberland St N W La	37 E2
Cumberland St S E La	37 E2
Cumberland St S W La	37 E2
Cumin Pl	37 G7
D	
Dalkeith Rd	37 H6
Dalmeny St	37 H1
Dalry	36 B6
Dalry Gait	36 C5
Dalry Pl	36 C5
Dalry Rd	36 B7
Damside	36 C4
Danube St	36 D3
Darnaway St	36 D3
Davidson Pk	36 A1
Davidson Rd	36 A1
Davie St	37 G5
Dean Bk La	36 D2
Dean Br	36 C3
Deanhaugh St	36 D2
Dean Pk Cres	36 C3
Dean Pk Ms	36 C2
Dean Pk St	36 C2
Dean Path	36 C3
Dean St	36 D3
Dean Ter	36 D3
Dean Village	36 B4
Devon Pl	36 B5
Dewar Pl	36 D5
Dewar Pl La	36 D5
Dicksonfield	37 H2
Dickson St	37 J1
Distillery La	36 C5
Dorset Pl	36 C7
Douglas Cres	36 B4
Douglas Gdns	36 C4
Douglas Gdns Ms	36 C4
Doune Ter	36 D3
Downfield Pl	36 B6
Drumdryan St	36 E6
Drummond Pl	37 F2
Drummond St	37 G5
Drumsheugh Gdns	36 C4
Drum Ter	37 J2
Dryden Gait	37 G1
Dryden Gdns	37 G1
Dryden Pl	37 J7
Dryden St	37 G1
Dryden Ter	37 G1
Dublin Meuse	37 F3
Dublin St	37 F2
Dublin St La N	37 F2
Dublin St La S	37 F3
Duff Rd	36 B6
Duff St	36 B6
Duff St La	36 B6
Dumbiedykes Rd	37 H5
Dundas St	36 E2
Dundee St	36 B7
Dundee Ter	36 B7
Dundonald St	37 F2
Dunedin St	37 F1
Dunrobin Pl	36 D2
E	
Earl Grey St	36 E5
East Adam St	37 G5
East Castle Rd	36 C7
East Claremont St	37 F2
East Crosscauseway	37 G6
Easter Dalry Dr	36 B6
Easter Dalry Pl	36 B5
Easter Dalry Rigg	36 B6
Easter Dalry Rd	36 C5
Easter Dalry Wynd	36 C6
Easter Rd	37 J3
East Fettes Av	36 C1
East Fountainbridge	36 E5
East London St	37 G2
East Mkt St	37 G4
East Montgomery Pl	37 H2
East Newington Pl	37 H7
East Parkside	37 H6
East Preston St	37 H7
East Preston St La	37 H7
East Sciennes St	37 G7
East Scotland St La	37 F2
East Silvermills La	36 E2
Edina Pl	37 J2
Edina St	37 J2
Edinburgh Quay	36 D6
Eglinton Cres	36 B5
Eildon St	36 E1
Eildon Ter	36 E1
Elder St	37 F3
Elgin Pl	37 H2
Elgin St	37 J2
Elgin St N	37 J2
Elgin Ter	37 J2
Elliot St	37 J2
Elm Row	37 G2
Eton Ter	36 D3
Ettrickdale Pl	36 E1
Ettrick Gro	36 C7
Eyre Cres	37 E2
Eyre Pl	37 E2
Eyre Ter	37 E2
F	
Fettes Av	36 B2
Fettes Row	37 E2
Findhorn Pl	37 G7
Fingal Pl	37 F7
Forbes St	37 H6
Forres St	36 D3
Forrest Hill	37 F5
Forrest Rd	37 F5
Forth St	37 G3
Fountainbridge	36 D6
Fowler Ter	36 C6
Frederick St	37 E3
G	
Gardner's Cres	36 D5
Garscube Ter	36 A4
Gayfield La	37 G2
Gayfield Pl La	37 G2
Gayfield Sq	37 G2
Gayfield St	37 G2
Gayfield St La	37 G2
Gentle's Entry	37 H4
George IV Br	37 F4
George Sq	37 F6
George Sq La	37 F6
George St	36 E4
Gibson Ter	36 C6
Gifford Pk	37 G6
Gillespie Cres	36 D6
Gillespie St	36 D6
Gilmore Pk	36 D6
Gilmore Pl	36 D7
Gilmour St	37 G5
Gladstone Ter	37 G7
Glencairn Cres	36 C5
Glenfinlas St	36 D4
Glengyle Ter	36 E6
Glenogle Rd	36 D2
Glen St	37 E5
Gloucester La	36 D3
Gloucester Pl	36 D3
Gloucester Sq	36 D3
Gloucester St	36 D3
Gorgie Rd	36 A7
Grange Rd	37 F7
Granville Ter	36 C7
Grassmarket	37 F5
Great King St	37 E3
Great Stuart St	36 D4
Greenhill Ct	36 E7
Greenhill Gdns	36 E7
Greenhill Pl	36 E7
Greenhill Ter	36 E7
Greenside La	37 G3
Greenside Row	37 G3
Green St	37 G2
Greyfriars Pl	37 F5
Grigor Av	36 A1
Grigor Dr	36 A1
Grigor Gdns	36 A1
Grigor Ter	36 A1
Grindlay St	36 E5
Grosvenor Cres	36 C5
Grosvenor Gdns	36 C5
Grosvenor St	36 C5
Grove St	36 D5
Gullan's Cl	37 G4
Guthrie St	37 G5
H	
Haddon's Ct	37 G5
Hailes St	36 E6
Halmyre St	37 J1
Hamilton Pl	36 D2
Hamilton's Folly Ms	37 H6
Hammermen's Entry	37 H4
Hanover St	37 F3
Harden Pl	36 C7
Hardwell Cl	37 H6
Harrismith Pl	37 J2
Harrison La	36 B7
Harrison Rd	36 B7
Hartington Gdns	36 D7
Hartington Pl	36 D7
Hart St	37 G2
Hatton Pl	37 F7
Haugh St	36 D2
Hawthornbank La	36 C4
Hawthornden Pl	37 H1
Haymarket	36 C5
Haymarket Ter	36 B5
Haymarket Yards	36 B5
Henderland Rd	36 A5
Henderson Pl	37 E2
Henderson Pl La	37 E2
Henderson Row	36 E2
Henderson Ter	36 B7
Heriot Br	37 F5
Heriot Hill Ter	37 F2
Heriot Pl	37 F5
Heriot Row	36 E3
Hermits Cft	37 H6
High Riggs	36 E5
High Sch Wynd	37 G4
High Sch Yards	37 G5
High St	37 F4
Hill Pl	37 G5
Hillside Cres	37 H2
Hillside St	37 H2
Hill Sq	37 G5
Hill St	36 E3
Hill St La N	36 E3
Hill St La S	36 E4
Holyrood Gait	37 H4
Holyrood Pk Rd	37 H7
Holyrood Rd	37 G4
Home St	36 E6
Hope Pk Cres	37 G6
Hope Pk Ter	37 G6
Hope St	36 D4
Hope St La	36 D4
Hopetoun Cres	37 G2
Hopetoun St	37 G2
Horne Ter	36 C6
Horse Wynd	37 J4
Howden St	37 G5
Howe St	37 E3
Hugh Miller Pl	36 D2
Hunter Sq	37 G4
Huntingdon Pl	37 G2
Hutton Rd	37 H4
I	
India Pl	36 D3
India St	36 E3
Infirmary St	37 G5
Inverleith	36 C1
Inverleith Gro	36 C1
Inverleith Pl	36 C1
Inverleith Ter	36 D1
Inverleith Ter La	36 E1
Iona St	37 H1
Ivy Ter	36 A7
J	
Jamaica St	36 E3
Jamaica St N La	36 E3
Jamaica St S La	36 E3
Jameson Pl	37 H1
Jeffrey St	37 G4
Johnston Ter	37 E5
K	
Keir St	37 F5
Kemp Pl	36 D1
Kerr St	36 D2
Kew Ter	36 A5
Kimmerghame Dr	36 A1
Kimmerghame Vw	36 A1
King's Stables La	37 E5
King's Stables Rd	36 E4
Kirkhill Rd	37 J7
Kyle Pl	37 J3
L	
Lady Lawson St	37 E5
Lady Menzies Pl	37 J3
Lady Wynd	37 F5
Lamb's Cl	37 H6
Lansdowne Cres	36 C5
Lauderdale St	37 E7
Lauder Rd	37 G7
Lauriston Gdns	37 E5
Lauriston Pk	37 E5
Lauriston Pl	37 E6
Lauriston St	37 F4
Lawnmarket	37 F4
Leamington Rd	36 D6
Leamington Ter	36 D6
Learmonth Av	36 B2
Learmonth Cres	36 B3
Learmonth Gdn La	36 C3
Learmonth Gdns	36 C3
Learmonth Gdns Ms	36 C3
Learmonth Gro	36 C2
Learmonth Pl	36 C2
Learmonth Ter	36 C3
Learmonth Ter La	36 C3
Learmonth Vw	36 C3
Leith St	37 G3
Leith Wk	37 G3
Lennox St	36 C3
Lennox St La	36 C3
Leslie Pl	36 D3
Leven St	36 E6
Leven Ter	36 E6
Liddesdale Pl	36 E1
Little King St	37 G3
Livingstone Pl	37 G7
Lochend Cl	37 H4
Lochrin Pl	36 E6
Logan St	37 F2
Logie Grn Gdns	37 F1
Logie Grn Ln	37 F1
Logie Grn Rd	37 F1
Logie Mill	37 F1
London Rd	37 J3
London St	37 F2
Lonsdale Ter	37 E6
Lorne Pl	37 J1
Lorne Sq	37 J1
Lorne St	37 J1
Lothian Rd	36 D4
Lothian St	37 G5
Lower Gilmore Pl	36 D6
Lower London Rd	37 J3
Lutton Pl	37 H6
Lynedoch Pl La	36 C4
Lyne St	37 J3
M	
McDonald Pl	37 G1
McDonald Rd	37 G1
McDonald St	37 G1
Mackenzie Pl	36 D3
McLeod St	36 A6
McNeill St	36 D6
Magdala Cres	36 B5
Magdala Ms	36 B5
Malta Grn	36 D2
Malta Ter	36 D2
Manor Pl	36 C4
Mansionhouse Rd	37 G7
Marchhall Cres	37 J7
Marchhall Pl	37 J7
Marchhall Rd	37 J7
Marchmont Cres	37 F7
Marchmont Rd	37 F6
Marchmont St	37 E7
Market St	37 F4
Marshall's Ct	37 G3
Marshall St	37 G5
Maryfield	37 J3
Maryfield Pl	37 J3
Meadow La	37 G6
Meadow Pl	37 F7
Melgund Ter	37 F2
Melville Dr	37 E6
Melville St	36 C4
Melville St La	36 D4
Melville Ter	37 G7
Merchant St	37 F5
Merchiston Av	36 C7
Merchiston Gro	36 A7
Merchiston Ms	36 C7
Merchiston Pk	36 C7
Mertoun Pl	36 C7
Meuse La	37 F4
Middlefield	37 H1
Millerfield Pl	37 G7
Miller Row	36 C4
Milton St	37 J3
Minto St	37 H7
Moncrieff Ter	37 G7
Montague St	37 H6
Montgomery St	37 G2
Montgomery St La	37 H2
Montpelier	36 D7
Montpelier Pk	36 D7
Montpelier Ter	36 D7
Montrose Ter	37 J3
Moray Pl	36 D3
Morrison Circ	36 C5
Morrison Cres	36 D5
Morrison Link	36 D5
Morrison St	36 C5
Mound, The	37 F4
Mound Pl	37 F4
Multrees Wk	37 F3
Murano Pl	37 H2
Murdoch Ter	36 C6
Murieston Cres	36 B6
Murieston Cres La	36 B6
Murieston La	36 B7
Murieston Pl	36 B6
Murieston Rd	36 B6
Murieston Ter	36 B6
Myrtle Ter	36 B7
N	
Napier Rd	36 C7
Nelson St	37 F2
New Arthur Pl	37 H5
Newington Rd	37 H7
New John's Pl	37 H6
New Skinner's Cl	37 G4
New St	37 G4
Newton St	36 A7
Nicolson Sq	37 G5
Nicolson St	37 G5
Niddry St	37 G4
Niddry St S	37 G5
Nightingale Way	37 G7
North Bk St	37 F4
North Br	37 G4
North Castle St	36 E3
North Charlotte St	36 D3
North Clyde St La	37 F3
Northcote St	36 B6
North E Circ Pl	36 E3
North Pk Ter	36 C2
North Richmond St	37 G5
North St. Andrew La	37 F3
North St. Andrew St	37 F3
North St. David St	37 F3
Northumberland Pl La	37 F3
Northumberland St	37 E3
Northumberland St N E La	37 F3
Northumberland St N W La	37 E3
Northumberland St S E La	37 F3
Northumberland St S W La	37 E3
North Werber Pk	36 A1
North Werber Pl	36 B1
North W Circ Pl	36 D3
Norton Pk	37 J2
O	
Old Broughton	37 F2
Old Fishmarket Cl	37 G4
Old Tolbooth Wynd	37 H4
Orchard Bk	36 A3
Orchard Brae	36 B2
Orchard Brae Av	36 B3
Orchard Brae Gdns	36 B3
Orchard Brae Gdns W	36 B3
Orchard Brae W	36 B2
Orchard Cres	36 A3
Orchard Dr	36 A3
Orchard Gro	36 B2
Orchard Pl	36 B2
Orchard Rd	36 A3
Orchard Rd S	36 A3
Orchard Ter	36 A3
Orwell Pl	36 C6
Orwell Ter	36 C6
Oxford St	37 H6
Oxford Ter	36 C3
P	
Palmerston Pl	36 C4
Panmure Pl	37 E6
Papermill Wynd	37 G1
Parkside St	37 H6
Parkside Ter	37 H6
Parliament Sq	37 F4
Pembroke Pl	36 B5
Perth St	36 E2
Picardy Pl	37 G3
Pilrig Gdns	37 G1
Pilrig Glebe	37 H1
Pleasance	37 G5
Polwarth Cres	36 C7
Polwarth Gdns	36 C7
Polwarth Pk	36 C7
Polwarth Pl	36 C7
Ponton St	36 D6
Portgower Pl	36 D2
Port Hamilton	36 D6
Potterrow	37 G5
Powderhall Rd	37 F1
Priestfield Rd N	37 J7
Primrose Ter	36 B7
Princes St	36 D4
Q	
Queen's Dr	37 H5
Queensferry Rd	36 B3
Queensferry St	36 D4
Queensferry St La	36 D4
Queensferry Ter	36 B3
Queen St	36 E3
Queen St Gdns E	37 F3
Queen St Gdns W	37 E3
R	
Raeburn Ms	36 D2
Raeburn Pl	36 D2
Raeburn St	36 D2
Ramsay Gdn	37 F4
Ramsay La	37 F4
Randolph Cres	36 D4
Randolph La	36 D4
Randolph Pl	36 D4
Rankeillor St	37 H6
Ravelston Dykes	36 A4
Ravelston Pk	36 A4
Ravelston Ter	36 B4
Regent Pl	37 J3
Regent Rd	37 G3
Regent Ter	37 H3
Regent Ter Ms	37 H3
Register Pl	37 F3
Reid's Cl	37 H4
Reid Ter	36 D2
Richmond La	37 G5
Richmond Pl	37 G5
Richmond Ter	36 C5
Riego St	36 E5
Rillbank Cres	37 G7
Rillbank Ter	37 G7
Rintoul Pl	36 D2
Ritchie Pl	36 B7
Robertson Av	36 A7
Robertson Gait	36 A7
Robertson's Cl	37 G5
Rodney Pl	37 F2
Rodney St	37 F1
Romero Pl	37 J7
Rosebank Cotts	36 D5
Rosebery Cres	36 C5
Rosebery Cres La	36 C5
Roseburn Av	36 A5
Roseburn Cliff	36 A5
Roseburn Dr	36 A5
Roseburn Gdns	36 A5
Roseburn Maltings	36 A5
Roseburn Pl	36 A5
Roseburn Ter	36 A5
Rosemount Bldgs	36 D6
Roseneath Pl	37 F7
Roseneath St	37 F7
Roseneath Ter	37 F7
Rose St	36 E4
Rose St N La	36 E4
Rose St S La	36 E4
Rossie Pl	37 J2
Rosslyn Cres	37 G1
Rosslyn Ter	37 H1
Rothesay Ms	36 C4
Rothesay Pl	36 C4
Rothesay Ter	36 C4
Roxburgh Pl	37 G5
Roxburgh St	37 G5
Royal Cir	36 E3
Royal Cres	37 F2
Royal Ter	37 G3
Russell Gdns	36 A5
Russell Rd	36 A5
Rutland Ct La	36 D5
Rutland Sq	36 D4
Rutland St	36 D4
S	
St. Andrew Sq	37 F3
St. Bernard's Cres	36 D3
St. Bernard's Row	36 D2
St. Catherine's Pl	37 G7
St. Clair Av	37 J1
St. Clair Pl	37 J1
St. Clair Rd	37 J1
St. Clair St	37 J1
St. Colme St	36 D4
St. David's Pl	36 D5
St. David's Ter	36 D5
St. Giles St	37 F4

Street	Ref	Street	Ref	Street	Ref
St. James Pl	37 G3	Silvermills	36 E2	Stevenlaw's Cl	37 G4
St. James Sq	37 G3	Simon Sq	37 G5	Stewart Ter	36 A7
St. John's Hill	37 H5	Simpson Loan	37 F6	Stockbridge	36 E2
St. John St	37 H4	Sinclair Cl	36 A7	Succoth Gdns	36 A4
St. Leonard's Bk	37 H6	Sinclair Gdns	36 A7	Succoth Pl	36 A4
St. Leonard's Hill	37 H6	Sinclair Pl	36 A7	Summer Bk	37 F2
St. Leonard's La	37 H6	Sloan St	37 J1	Summerhall	37 G6
St. Leonard's St	37 H6	Smithfield St	36 A7	Summerhall Sq	37 H7
St. Mary's St	37 G4	South Br	37 G4	Sunbury Ms	36 C4
St. Patrick Sq	37 G6	South Charlotte St	36 E4	Sunbury Pl	36 C4
St. Stephen Pl	36 D2	South Clerk St	37 H6	Sunbury St	36 C4
St. Stephen St	36 D3	South Coll St	37 G5	Sunnyside	37 J2
St. Vincent St	36 E2	South E Circ Pl	36 E3	Sutherland St	36 B5
Salisbury Ms	37 H7	South Gray's Cl	37 G4	Sylvan Pl	37 G7
Salisbury Pl	37 H7	South Learmonth Av	36 C3		
Salisbury Rd	37 H7	South Learmonth Gdns	36 C3	**T**	
Saunders St	36 D3	South Lorne Pl	37 J1	Tantallon Pl	37 G7
Saxe Coburg Pl	36 D2	South Oxford St	37 H7	Tarvit St	36 E6
Saxe Coburg St	36 D2	South St. Andrew St	37 F3	Tay St	36 C7
Sciennes	37 G7	South St. David St	37 F3	Temple Pk Cres	36 C7
Sciennes Gdns	37 G7	South Sloan St	37 J1	Terrars Cft	37 H6
Sciennes Hill Pl	37 G7	Spence St	37 J7	Teviotdale Pl	36 D1
Sciennes Ho Pl	37 G7	Spey St	37 H1	Teviot Pl	37 F5
Sciennes Pl	37 G7	Spey St La	37 H1	Thirlestane Rd	37 E7
Sciennes Rd	37 F7	Spey Ter	37 H1	Thistle Pl	36 C7
Scotland St	37 F2	Spittal St	36 E5	Thistle St	37 E3
Semple St	36 D5	Spottiswoode Rd	37 E7	Thistle St N E La	37 F3
Seton Pl	37 G7	Spottiswoode St	37 F7	Thistle St N W La	37 E3
Shandwick Pl	36 D5	Spring Gdns	37 J3	Thistle St S W La	37 E3
Shaw's Pl	37 H1	Springwell Pl	36 B6	Thornybauk	36 E6
Shaw's St	37 H1	Stafford St	36 D4	Torphichen St	36 D5
Shaw's Ter	37 H1	Stanhope Pl	36 D5	Tron Sq	37 G4
Shrub Pl La	37 H1	Stanhope St	36 B5	Tynecastle La	36 B7
Sienna Gdns	37 G7			Tynecastle Ter	36 A7

Street	Ref	Street	Ref	Street	Ref
Tytler Gdns	37 J3	Waterloo Pl	37 G3	West Port	37 E5
		Watson Cres	36 B7	West Preston St	37 H7
U		Waverley Br	37 F4	West Register St	37 F3
Union St	37 G2	Waverley Pk	37 J3	West Register St La	37 F3
Upper Bow	37 F4	Waverley Pk Ter	37 J3	West Richmond St	37 G5
Upper Coltbridge Ter	36 A4	Waverley Pl	37 J3	West Scotland St La	37 F3
Upper Damside	36 C4	Wellington St	37 H2	West Silvermills La	36 E2
Upper Dean Ter	36 D3	Wemyss Pl	36 E3	West Tollcross	36 E6
Upper Gilmore Pl	36 D6	Wemyss Pl Ms	36 D3	West Wds	36 A1
Upper Gilmore Ter	36 D6	West Adam St	37 G5	Wheatfield Pl	36 A7
Upper Gray St	37 H7	West Annandale St	37 F1	Wheatfield Rd	36 A7
Upper Gro Pl	36 D6	West App Rd	36 D5	Wheatfield St	36 A7
		West Bow	37 F5	Wheatfield Ter	36 A7
V		West Bryson Rd	36 B7	Whitehouse Ln	36 E7
Valleyfield St	36 E6	West Castle Rd	36 C7	White Pk	36 A7
Veitch's Sq	36 D2	West Catherine Pl	36 B5	William St	36 C5
Victoria St	37 F5	West Coates	36 A5	William St N E La	36 D4
Viewcraig Gdns	37 H4	West Coll St	37 G5	William St N W La	36 D4
Viewcraig St	37 H5	West Crosscauseway	37 G6	William St S E La	36 D4
Viewforth	36 C6	West End Pl	36 C6	William St S W La	36 D5
Viewforth Gdns	36 D7	Wester Coates Av	36 A5	Windmill La	37 G6
Viewforth Sq	36 D7	Wester Coates Gdns	36 A5	Windmill St	37 G6
Viewforth Ter	36 D7	Wester Coates Pl	36 B5	Windsor St	37 H2
		Wester Coates Rd	36 B5	Windsor St La	37 H2
W		Wester Coates Ter	36 A5		
Walker St	36 C4	Westfield St	36 A7	**Y**	
Wardlaw Pl	36 A7	Westhall Gdns	36 D7	Yeaman Pl	36 C6
Wardlaw St	36 A7	West Maitland St	36 C5	York La	37 G3
Warrender Pk Cres	36 E7	West Mill La	36 C4	York Pl	37 F3
Warrender Pk Rd	36 E7	West Montgomery Pl	37 H2	Young St	36 D4
Warrender Pk Ter	37 E7	West Newington Pl	37 H7	Young St La N	36 E4
Warriston Cres	37 E1	West Nicolson St	37 G5	Young St La S	36 E4
Warriston Rd	37 E1	West Norton Pl	37 J3		
Washington La	36 B6	West Pk Pl	36 C6		

Glasgow street index

Street	Ref	Street	Ref	Street	Ref
A		Binnie Pl	39 H6	Castle St	39 H4
Abbotsford Pl	39 E7	Bishop St	38 D4	Cathcart Rd	39 F7
Abercromby Dr	39 J5	Blackburn St	38 B5	Cathedral Sq	39 H4
Abercromby Sq	39 J5	Blackfriars St	39 G4	Cathedral St	39 F3
Abercromby St	39 J6	Blackie St	38 B3	Cavendish Pl	39 E7
Academy Pk	38 A7	Black St	39 H2	Cavendish St	39 E7
Adams Ct La	39 F5	Blantyre St	38 A2	Cecil St	38 B1
Adelphi St	39 F6	**Blythswoodhill**	38 E3	Cedar Ct	38 E1
Admiral St	38 C6	Blythswood Sq	38 E3	Cedar St	38 E1
Aird's La	39 G5	Blythswood St	38 E4	Centre St	38 E6
Albert Br	39 G6	Bothwell La	38 E4	**Cessnock**	38 A5
Albert Dr	38 B7	Bothwell La (Hillhead)	38 C1	Chalmers St	39 J5
Albion Gate	39 G4	Bothwell St	38 E4	Charles St	39 J2
Albion St	39 G5	Braid Sq	38 E1	Charlotte St	39 H5
Alexander Cres	39 F7	Braid St	38 E1	Cheapside St	38 D5
Alexandra Par	39 J3	Breadalbane St	38 C3	Chisolm St	39 G5
Allen Glen Pl	39 G3	Brechin St	38 C3	Church St	38 A2
Anchor La	39 F4	Bridgegate	39 F5	Circus Dr	39 J4
Anderston	38 E4	Bridge St	39 E6	Citizen La	39 F4
Anderston Quay	38 C5	Bridgeton Cross	39 J6	Civic St	39 F2
Anson St	39 J7	Bright St	39 J2	Clairmont Gdns	38 C2
Anthony St	38 D4	Broadford St	39 G1	Claremont Pl	38 C2
Arcadia Pl	39 J6	Broomielaw	38 E5	Claremont St	38 C3
Arcadia St	39 J6	Broompark Dr	39 J4	Claremont Ter	38 C2
Argyle St	39 F4	Brown St	38 E5	Claremont Ter La	38 C2
Argyll Arc	39 F4	Bruce Rd	38 B7	Clarendon Pl	38 D1
Ark La	39 J4	Brunswick St	39 G4	Clarendon St	38 D1
Arlington St	38 D2	Buccleuch La	38 E2	Clayslaps Rd	38 B2
Armour St	39 J5	Buccleuch St	38 D2	Claythorn Av	39 H6
Arthur St	38 A2	Buchanan St	39 F4	Claythorn Circ	39 H5
Ashley La	38 D2	Bunhouse Rd	38 A2	Claythorn Pk	39 H6
Ashley St	38 D2	Burnbank Gdns	38 D1	Claythorn St	39 J5
Ashton La	38 A1	Burnbank La	38 D1	Claythorn Ter	39 J5
Ashton Rd	38 A1	Burnbank Pl	38 D1	Cleland La	39 F6
Auchentoshan Ter	39 J1	Burnbank Ter	38 D1	Cleland St	39 F6
		Burns St	39 E1	Cleveland La	38 D3
B		Bute Gdns	38 B1	Cleveland St	38 D3
Bain St	39 H5	Bute La	38 B1	Clifford La	38 A6
Baird St	39 H2			Clifford Pl	38 A6
Balaclava St	38 D4	**C**		Clifford St	38 A6
Baliol La	38 D2	Cadogan St	38 E4	Cliff Rd	38 C1
Baliol St	38 D2	Cadzow St	38 D4	Clifton Pl	38 C3
Ballantrae Ct	38 D4	Caledonian Cres	38 C1	Clifton St	38 C2
Ballater Pl	39 G7	Caledonia Rd	39 F7	Clutha St	38 A6
Ballater St	39 F6	Caledon La	38 A1	Clyde Arc	38 B5
Bank St	38 B1	Caledon St	38 A1	Clyde Pl	38 D5
Barrack St	39 J5	Calgary St	39 G2	Clydeside Expressway	38 B4
Barrington Dr	38 C1	Cambridge St	39 E3	Clyde St	39 F5
Bath La	38 D3	Camden Ter	39 F7	Cobden Rd	39 J1
Bath St	38 D3	Canal St	39 G2	Coburg St	39 E6
Beaumont Gate	38 A1	Candleriggs	39 G5	Cochrane St	39 G4
Bedford La	39 F6	Cardwell St	38 E7	College La	39 H4
Bedford St	39 E6	Carfrae St	38 A3	College St	39 G4
Bell St	39 G4	Carlton Ct	39 F5	Collins St	39 H4
Beltane St	38 D3	Carlton Pl	39 F5	Commerce St	39 E5
Benny Lynch Ct	39 G6	Carnarvon St	38 D2	Commercial Ct	39 G6
Benthall St	39 G7	Carnoustie Pl	38 D6	Commercial Rd	39 G7
Bentinck St	38 B2	Carnoustie St	38 D6	Congress Rd	38 B4
Berkeley St	38 C3	Carrick St	38 E5	Congress Way	38 B4
Berkeley Ter La	38 C3	Carrington St	38 D1	Cook St	38 E6

Street	Ref	Street	Ref	Street	Ref
Cooperage Pl	38 A3	Eaglesham Pl	38 B5	Glasgow Br	39 F5
Corn St	39 E1	Eagle St	39 F1	Glassford St	39 G4
Cornwall St S	38 B7	Earlston Av	39 J2	Glebe Ct	39 H3
Corunna St	38 B3	Earlston Pl	39 J2	Glebe St	39 H2
Couper Pl	39 G2	East Bath La	39 F3	Glenbarr St	39 J2
Couper St	39 G2	East Campbell St	39 H5	Glenfarg St	38 D1
Cowan La	38 C1	Edington St	39 E1	Glenmavis St	39 E2
Cowan St	38 B1	Edwin St	38 B1	Gloucester St	38 D6
Cowcaddens	38 E6	Eglinton Ct	39 F6	Goosedubbs	39 G5
Cowcaddens Rd	39 F2	Elcho St	39 J5	**Gorbals**	39 G7
Cownwall St	38 B6	Elderslie St	38 C2	Gorbals St	39 F7
Cragmaddie Ter La	38 B2	Eldon St	38 C1	Gordon La	39 F4
Craighall Rd	39 F1	Elie St	38 A1	Gordon St	39 E4
Craigiehall Pl	38 B5	Elliot Pl	38 C4	Gourock St	38 E7
Craigiehall St	38 B5	Elliot St	38 C4	Govan Rd	38 A5
Cranston Hill	38 C3	Elmbank Cres	38 D3	Grace St	38 C4
Cranston St	38 C4	Elmbank St	38 D3	Grafton Pl	39 G3
Cressnock St	38 A5	Elmbank St La	38 D3	Graham Sq	39 J5
Crimea St	38 D4	Errol Gdns	39 F6	Graignestock St	39 J6
Cromwell La	38 D1	Esmond St	38 A2	Granby La	38 B1
Cromwell St	38 D1	Eton La	38 B1	Grant St	38 D2
Crownpoint Rd	39 J6	Exchange Pl	39 F4	Granville St	38 D3
Crown St	39 F7			Gray St	38 B3
Cumberland Pl	39 G7	**F**		Great Dovehill	39 H5
Cumberland St	39 E6	Falfield St	38 E7	Great George St	38 B1
		Farnell St	39 E1	Green, The	39 J7
D		**Finnieston**	38 B3	Greendyke St	39 G5
Dale Path	39 J7	Finnieston Quay	38 B4	Greenhead St	39 J6
Dalhouse St	38 E3	Finnieston Sq	38 C3	Green St	39 J6
Dalhousie La	38 E2	Finnieston St	38 C4	Grovepark Ct	38 D1
Dalintober St	38 D6	Firpark St	39 J3	Grovepark Gdns	38 D1
Dalmarnock Rd	39 J7	Firpark Ter	39 J4		
Dalnair St	38 A2	Fitzroy La	38 B3	**H**	
Derby St	38 B3	Florence St	39 G6	Hallside Pl	39 G7
Devon Pl	39 E7	Forbes Dr	39 J6	Handel Pl	39 F7
Devon St	39 E7	Forbes St	39 J5	Hanover St	39 F4
Dixon St	39 F5	Fountainwell Av	39 H1	Harley St	38 A6
Dobbies Ln	39 F2	Fountainwell Dr	39 H1	Harvey St	39 F1
Dobbie's Ln Pl	39 G3	Fountainwell Pl	39 H1	Harvie St	38 B5
Dornoch St	39 J6	Fountainwell Rd	39 H1	Hastie St	38 A2
Dorset St	38 C3	Fountainwell Sq	39 H1	Haugh Rd	38 A3
Douglas La	38 E3	Fountainwell Ter	39 H1	Hayfield Ct	39 G7
Douglas St	38 E4	Fox St	39 F5	Hayfield St	39 G7
Dover St	38 C3	Francis St	38 E7	Herbertson St	39 E6
Drake St	39 J6			High Craighall Rd	39 F1
Drury St	39 F4	**G**		High St	39 G5
Drygate	39 H4	Gadshill St	39 J2	Hillhead St	38 B1
Duke St	39 H4	Gallowgate	39 H5	Hill St	38 D2
Dunblane St	39 F2	**Garnethill**	38 E2	Holland St	38 D3
Dunchattan Pl	39 J3	Garnethill St	38 E2	Holm St	38 E4
Dunchattan St	39 J4	Garnet St	38 D3	Holyrood Cres	38 C1
Dundashill	39 F1	Garscube Rd	39 F1	Holyrood Quad	38 D1
Dundas La	39 F3	Garth St	39 G4	Hopehill Rd	38 D1
Dundas St	39 F3	George Sq	39 F4	Hope St	39 E4
Dunearn St	38 D1	George St	39 G4	Houldsworth La	38 C3
Dunlop St	39 F5	Gibson St	39 H5	Houldsworth St	38 C3
Durham St	38 B6	Gibson St (Hillhead)	38 B1	Houston Pl	38 C5
		Gilbert St	38 A3	Houston St	38 C6
E		Gilmour Pl	39 G7	Howard St	39 F5
Eaglesham Ct	38 B5	Gladstone St	38 D1	Hunter St	39 H5

Street	Ref		Street	Ref		Street	Ref
Huntingdon Rd	39 H1		Lynedoch Pl	38 C2		Napiershall St	38 D1
Huntingdon Sq	39 H1		Lynedoch St	38 C2		Nelson Mandela Pl	39 F4
Hutcheson St	39 G5		Lynedoch Ter	38 D2		Nelson St	38 E5
Hutchesontown	39 G7					Netherby Dr	38 A7
Hutchinson Town Ct	39 G7		**M**			New City Rd	38 D2
Hydepark St	38 C5		Mcalpine St	38 D5		Newton St	38 D2
			McAslin Ct	39 H3		Newton Ter La	38 C3
I			Mcaslin St	39 H3		New Wynd	39 G5
India St	38 D3		McCulloch St	38 C7		Nicholas St	39 H4
Ingram St	39 G4		Mcfarlane St	39 H5		Nicholson St	39 F6
			McIntosh Ct	39 J4		Norfolk Ct	39 F6
J			McIntosh St	39 J4		Norfolk St	39 F6
Jamaica St	39 F5		Mcintyre St	38 D4		North Canal Bk	39 G1
James Morrison St	39 G5		MacKeith St	39 J7		North Canal Bk St	39 F1
James Nisbet St	39 J3		MacKinlay St	39 E7		North Claremount St	38 C2
James St	39 J7		Maclean Sq	38 B5		North Ct	39 F4
James Watt St	38 E5		Maclean St	38 B5		North Ct La	39 F4
Jocelyn Sq	39 G5		Maclennan St	38 A6		North Dr	39 F4
John Knox St	39 J4		Macleod St	39 H4		North Frederick Path	39 G3
John St	39 G4		McNeil Gdns	39 H7		North Frederick St	39 G4
			McNeil St	39 G7		North Gower St	38 A6
K			McPhail St	39 J7		North Hanover St	39 G4
Kelvingrove	38 B2		McPhater St	39 F2		North Portland St	39 G4
Kelvingrove St	38 B3		Mair St	38 B5		North St	38 D2
Kelvinhaugh	38 A3		Maitland St	39 F2		North Wallace St	39 G2
Kelvinhaugh Gate	38 A3		Malta Ter	39 F7			
Kelvinhaugh Pl	38 B3		Manresa Pl	39 E1		**O**	
Kelvinhaugh St	38 A3		Marine Cres	38 C5		Oakfield Av	38 B1
Kelvin Way	38 B2		Marine Gdns	38 C5		Oakfield La	38 B1
Kennedy Path	39 G3		Marlow St	38 C7		Oak St	38 D4
Kennedy St	39 G3		Martha St	39 G3		Old Dumbarton Rd	38 A2
Kent Rd	38 C3		Mart St	39 G5		Old Rutherglen Rd	39 G6
Kent St	39 H5		Mary St	39 F1		Old Wynd	39 G5
Keppochhill Pl	39 G1		Mauchline St	38 E7		Oregon Pl	39 G7
Keppochhill Way	39 G1		Mavisbank Gdns	38 B5		Orr St	39 J6
Kerr Dr	39 J6		Maxwell Av	38 C7		Osborne St	39 F5
Kerr Pl	39 J6		Maxwell Ct	38 B7		Oswald St	39 E5
Kerr St	39 J6		Maxwell Dr	38 B7		Otago La	38 C1
Kidston Pl	39 F7		Maxwell Gdns	38 A7		Otago La N	38 C1
Kidston Ter	39 F7		Maxwell Grn	38 B7		Otago St	38 B1
Kilbarchan St	39 E6		Maxwell La	38 C7		Overnewton Pl	38 B3
Kilbirnie Pl	38 D7		Maxwell Oval	38 C7		Overnewton Sq	38 A3
Kilbirnie St	38 D7		Maxwell Rd	38 C7		Overnewton St	38 A2
Killermont St	39 F3		Maxwell St	39 F5		Oxford La	39 F5
King George V Br	39 E5		Megan Gate	39 J7		Oxford St	39 E5
King's Br	39 H7		Megan St	39 J7			
King's Dr	39 H7		Melbourne St	39 J5		**P**	
Kingston	38 D6		Melrose St	38 D1		Pacific Dr	38 A5
Kingston St	38 E5		**Merchant City**	39 G4		Pacific Quay	38 A4
King St	39 G5		Merchant La	39 G5		Paisley Rd	38 D5
Kinning Pk	38 B6		Metropole La	39 F5		Paisley Rd W	38 C5
Kinning St	38 D6		Middlesex Gdns	38 B6		Palmerston Pl	38 B3
Kyle St	39 G2		Middlesex St	38 B6		Parnie St	39 G5
			Middleton St	38 A5		Park Av	38 C1
L			Midland St	39 E4		Park Circ	38 C2
La Belle Allee	38 C2		Midwharf St	39 F1		Park Circ La	38 C2
La Belle Pl	38 C2		Miller St	39 F4		Park Circ Pl	38 C2
Ladywell St	39 J4		Millroad Dr	39 J5		Park Dr	38 C1
Laidlaw St	38 D6		Millroad Gdns	39 J5		Park Gdns	38 C2
Laird Pl	39 J7		Millroad St	39 H5		Park Gdns La	38 C2
Lambhill Quad	38 B6		Milnpark Gdns	38 B6		Park Gate	38 C2
Lambhill St	38 B6		Milnpark St	38 B6		Parkgrove Ter	38 B2
Lanark St	39 H5		Milton St	39 F2		Parkgrove Ter La	38 B2
Lancefield Quay	38 C4		Minerva St	38 B3		Park Quad	38 C2
Lancefield St	38 C4		Minerva Way	38 B3		Park Rd	38 C1
Landressy Pl	39 J7		Mitchell La	39 F4		Park St S	38 C2
Landressy St	39 J7		Mitchell St	39 F4		Park Ter	38 C2
Langshot St	38 A6		Moffat St	39 G7		Park Ter E La	38 C2
Lansdowne Cres	38 C1		Moir St	39 H5		Park Terrrace La	38 C2
Lansdowne Cres La	38 C1		Molendinar St	39 H5		Parsonage Row	39 H4
Larbert St	39 F2		Moncur St	39 H5		Parsonage Sq	39 H4
Laurieston	39 F6		Montague St	38 C1		Parson St	39 H3
Laurieston Rd	39 F7		Monteith Pl	39 H6		Paterson St	38 D6
Lendel Pl	38 A6		Monteith Row	39 H5		Payne St	39 F1
Lilybank Gdns	38 A1		Montrose St	39 G4		Pembroke St	38 C3
Lilybank Gdns La	38 A1		Moore St	39 J5		Percy St	38 A6
Lilybank Ter	38 B1		Morrison Ct	39 F4		Perth St	38 D4
Lister St	39 H2		Morrison St	38 D5		Piccadilly St	38 D4
Little Dovehill	39 H5		Mosque Av	39 F6		Pine Pl	39 G7
Little St	38 C4		Muslin St	39 J7		Pinkston Dr	39 H2
London Rd	39 G5					Pinkston Rd	39 H1
Lorne St	38 B5		**N**			Pitt St	38 E4
Lumsden St	38 A3		Naburn Gate	39 F7		Plantation Pk Gdns	38 A6
Lymburn St	38 B2		Nairn St	38 A2		Plantation Sq	38 B5
Lynedoch Cres	38 C2		Napiershall La	38 D1		**Port Dundas**	38 D1
Lynedoch Cres La	38 C2		Napiershall Pl	38 D1		Port Dundas La	39 F3

Street	Ref		Street	Ref		Street	Ref
Port Dundas Rd	39 F2		Salisbury La	39 F7		Tureen St	39 J5
Port Eglington	38 D7		Salisbury St	39 F7		Turnbull St	39 G5
Portman St	38 C6		Salkeld St	38 E7		Turnlaw St	39 H7
Port St	38 C3		Saltmarket	39 G5		Turriff St	39 E7
Portugal St	39 F6		Sandiefield Rd	39 F7		Tyndrum St	39 F2
Possil Rd	39 E1		Sandyford Pl La	38 C3			
Professors Sq	38 B1		Sandyford St	38 A3		**U**	
Provanhill St	39 J2		Saracen Head Rd	39 H5		Union Pl	39 F4
			Sauchiehall La	38 E3		Union St	39 F4
Q			Sauchiehall St	38 B2		Unity Pl	38 E1
Queen Elizabeth Gdns	39 G7		Savoy St	39 J7		University Av	38 A1
Queens Cres	38 D1		Sawmillfield St	39 E1		University Gdns	38 A1
Queen St	39 F4		Scotland St	38 C6		University Pl	38 A1
			Scotland St W	38 B6			
R			Scott St	38 E3		**V**	
Radnor St	38 B2		Seamore St	38 D1		Vermont St	38 B6
Raglan St	38 E1		Seaward La	38 C5		Victoria Br	39 F5
Regent Moray St	38 A2		Seaward Pl	38 C6		Viewfield La	38 B1
Renfield La	38 E4		Seaward St	38 C6		Vinter St	39 F1
Renfield St	39 F4		Shaftesbury St	38 D3		Virginia Pl	39 G4
Renfrew Ct	39 F3		Shamrock St	38 E2		Virginia St	39 G4
Renfrew La	39 F3		Shields Rd	38 C6			
Renfrew St	38 D2		Shipbank La	39 G5		**W**	
Renton St	39 F2		Shuttle St	39 G4		Waddell Ct	39 G6
Rhymer St	39 J2		**Sighthill**	39 H1		Waddell St	39 G7
Richmond St	39 G4		Silverfir St	39 G7		Wallace St	38 D5
Ritchie St	38 E7		Silvergrove St	39 J6		Walls St	39 G4
Riverview Dr	38 D5		Snowdon St	39 G7		Walmer Cres	38 A6
Riverview Gdns	38 E5		Somerset Pl Ms	38 C2		Warnock St	39 J3
Riverview Pl	38 D5		South Ex Ct	39 F4		Warroch St	38 D5
Robertson La	38 E4		South Frederick St	39 G4		Washington St	38 D5
Robertson St	38 E5		Southpark Av	38 B1		Waterloo La	39 E4
Rodney St	39 E1		Southpark La	38 B1		Waterloo St	38 E4
Ropework La	39 F5		South Portland St	39 F5		Waterside Pl	39 H7
Rose St	38 E3		Southside Cres	39 F7		Waterside St	39 G7
Ross St	39 H5		South Woodside Rd	38 C1		Watson St	39 G5
Rottenrow	39 G3		Spiers Wf	39 F1		Watt St	38 C6
Rottenrow E	39 H4		Spoutmouth	39 H5		Weaver St	39 H4
Royal Bk Pl	39 F4		Springburn Rd	39 J2		Wellcroft Pl	39 E7
Royal Cres	38 B3		Springfield Ct	39 F4		Wellington La	38 E4
Royal Ex Ct	39 F4		Springfield Quay	38 C5		Wellington St	38 E4
Royal Ex Sq	39 F4		Spring Wynd	39 G7		Wellpark St	39 J4
Royal Ter	38 B2		Stafford St	39 G2		Westbank La	38 B1
Royal Ter La	38 B2		Stanley St	38 C6		Westbank Quad	38 B1
Royston	39 J2		Stanley St La	38 C6		West Campbell St	38 E4
Roystonhill	39 J2		Steel St	39 G5		West End Pk St	38 C2
Royston Rd	39 J2		Stevenson St	39 J6		West George La	38 E3
Royston Sq	39 J2		Stewart St	39 F2		West George St	39 E3
Rupert St	38 D1		Stirlingfauld Pl	39 F7		West Graham St	38 E2
Rutland Ct	38 C5		Stirling Rd	39 H3		West Greenhill Pl	38 B3
Rutland Cres	38 C5		Stobcross Rd	38 A3		West Nile St	39 F4
Rutland Pl	38 B5		Stobcross St	38 C4		West Prince's La	38 C1
			Stobcross Wynd	38 A3		West Princes St	38 C1
S			Stockwell Pl	39 F5		West Regent La	39 E3
St. Andrews Cres	38 C7		Stockwell St	39 F5		West Regent St	39 E3
St. Andrew's La	39 G5		Stromness St	38 E7		West St	38 D7
St. Andrews Rd	38 C7		Suffolk St	39 H5		Whitehall St	38 D4
St. Andrews Sq	39 G5		Surrey St	39 F7		William St	38 D3
St. Andrews St	39 G5		Sussex St	38 B6		Willowbank Cres	38 C1
St. Clair St	38 D1		Sutherland La	38 A1		Willowbank St	38 C2
St. Enoch	39 F5		Swan St	39 G2		Wilson St	39 G4
St. Enoch Sq	39 F4		Sydney St	39 J5		Windsor St	38 D1
St. Francis Rigg	39 G7					Windsor Ter	38 D1
St. Georges Rd	38 D2		**T**			Wishart St	39 J4
St. Georges Rd	38 D2		Taylor Pl	39 H3		Woodlands Dr	38 C1
St. James Rd	39 G3		Taylor St	39 H4		Woodlands Gate	38 C2
St. John's Ct	38 B7		Templeton St	39 J6		Woodlands Rd	38 C1
St. John's Quad	38 C7		Teviot St	38 A3		Woodlands Ter	38 C2
St. Josephs Vw	39 J2		Thistle St	39 G6		Woodrow Circ	38 A7
St. Luke's Pl	39 F6		Thistle Ter	39 F7		Woodrow Pl	38 A7
St. Luke's Ter	39 F6		Thornbank St	38 A3		Woodrow Rd	38 A7
St. Margaret's Pl	39 G5		Thurso St	38 A2		Woodside Cres	38 D2
St. Marys La	39 F4		Tobago Pl	39 J5		Woodside Pl	38 C2
St. Mungo Av	39 G3		Tobago St	39 J6		Woodside Pl La	38 C2
St. Mungo Pl	39 H3		Toll La	38 C5		Woodside Ter	38 C2
St. Ninian Ter	39 F6		Tontine La	39 G5		Woodside Ter La	38 C2
St. Peters La	38 E4		Torness St	38 A1			
St. Peters St	38 E2		Tower St	38 B6		**Y**	
St. Rollox Brae	39 J1		**Townhead**	39 G2		**Yorkhill**	38 B2
St. Valentine Ter	39 G7		Townsend St	39 F2		Yorkhill Par	38 A2
St. Vincent Cres	38 B3		**Tradeston**	38 E6		Yorkhill St	38 A3
St. Vincent Cres La	38 B3		Tradeston St	38 E6		York St	38 E5
St. Vincent La	38 E3		Trongate	39 G5			
St. Vincent Pl	39 F4		Tullis Ct	39 J7			
St. Vincent St	38 C3		Tullis St	39 J7			
St. Vincent Ter	38 C3		Tunnel St	38 B4			

Leeds street index

Street	Ref		Street	Ref		Street	Ref
A			Albion St	41 E3		Apex Way	41 E6
Abbey St	40 C3		Alexander St	40 E3		Appleton Cl	41 J3
Abbott Ct	40 A3		Alexandra Gro	40 B1		Appleton Ct	41 J3
Abbott Rd	40 A4		Alexandra Rd	40 A1		Appleton Sq	41 J3
Abbott Vw	40 A3		Alma St	41 H2		Appleton Way	41 J3
Admiral St	41 E7		Anderson Av	41 H1		Archery Pl	40 D1
Aire St	40 D4		Anderson Mt	41 H1		Archery Rd	40 D1
Albion Pl	41 E3		Apex Vw	40 E6		Archery St	40 E1

Street	Ref		Street	Ref		Street	Ref
Archery Ter	40 E1		Ashton Av	41 J1		Atkinson St	41 G6
Armley Rd	40 A3		Ashton Gro	41 J1		Autumn Av	40 B1
Armouries Rd	41 G5		Ashton Mt	41 J1		Autumn Gro	40 B1
Artist St	40 B4		Ashton Pl	41 J1		Autumn Pl	40 B1
Ascot Ter	41 J4		Ashton Ter	41 J1		Autumn St	40 B1
Ashley Av	41 J1		Ashton Vw	41 J1		Autumn Ter	40 B1
Ashley Rd	41 J1		Ashville Vw	40 A1		Avenue, The	41 G4
Ashley Ter	41 J1		Assembly St	41 F4		Aysgarth Cl	41 J4

Aysgarth Dr 41 J4
Aysgarth Pl 41 J4
Aysgarth Wk 41 J4

B
Back Ashville Av 40 A1
Back Hyde Ter 40 C2
Back Row 40 E5
Balm Pl 40 C6
Balm Wk 40 C6
Bank St 41 E4
Baron Cl 40 C7
Barrack St 41 F1
Barran Ct 41 H1
Barton Gro 40 D7
Barton Mt 40 D7
Barton Pl 40 C7
Barton Rd 40 C7
Barton Ter 40 D7
Barton Vw 40 C7
Bath Rd 40 D5
Bayswater Vw 41 H1
Beamsley Gro 40 A1
Beamsley Mt 40 A1
Beamsley Pl 40 A1
Beamsley Ter 40 A1
Beckett St 41 H3
Bedford St 40 E3
Beech Gro Ter 40 D1
Belgrave St 41 E3
Belinda St 41 H7
Belle Vue Rd 40 B2
Bell St 41 G3
Belmont Gro 40 D2
Benson St 41 F1
Benyon Pk Way 40 A7
Berking Av 41 J3
Bertrand St 40 C6
Bexley Av 41 H1
Bexley Gro 41 J1
Bexley Mt 41 H1
Bexley Pl 41 H1
Bexley Rd 41 J1
Bexley Ter 41 J1
Bingley St 40 C3
Bishopgate St 40 E4
Bismarck Dr 40 E7
Bismarck St 40 E7
Black Bull St 41 F5
Blackman La 40 E1
Blandford Gdns 40 D1
Blandford Gro 40 D1
Blayds St 41 H4
Blayd's Yd 41 E4
Blenheim Av 40 E1
Blenheim Ct 40 E1
Blenheim Cres 40 E1
Blenheim Gro 40 E1
Blenheim Sq 40 E1
Blenheim Vw 40 D1
Blenheim Wk 40 D1
Blundell St 40 D2
Boar La 40 E4
Bodley Ter 40 A2
Bond St 40 E3
Boundary Pl 41 G1
Boundary St 41 G1
Bourse, The 41 E4
Bowling Grn Ter 40 D6
Bowman La 41 F4
Bow St 41 G4
Bracken Ct 40 A6
Braithwaite St 40 C5
Brancepeth Pl 40 B4
Brandon Rd 40 C2
Brandon St 40 B4
Branksome Pl 40 B1
Brick St 41 G4
Bridge Ct 40 C5
Bridge End 41 E4
Bridge Rd 40 C5
Bridge St 41 F3
Bridgewater Rd 41 H6
Briggate 41 E4
Brignall Garth 41 J2
Brignall Way 41 H2
Bristol St 41 G2
Britannia St 40 D4
Broadway Av 40 A1
Brookfield St 41 G6
Brown Av 40 B7
Brown La E 40 B6
Brown La W 40 A6
Brown Pl 40 B7
Brown Rd 40 B7
Bruce Gdns 40 B4
Bruce Lawn 40 B4
Brunswick Ct 41 F3
Brunswick Ter 41 E2
Brussels St 41 G4
Buckton Cl 40 C7
Buckton Mt 40 C7
Buckton Vw 40 C7
Burley 40 A1

Burley Lo Pl 40 B2
Burley Lo Rd 40 A1
Burley Lo St 40 B2
Burley Lo Ter 40 B1
Burley Pl 40 A2
Burley Rd 40 A1
Burley St 40 C3
Burmantofts 41 H3
Burmantofts St 41 G3
Burton Row 41 E7
Burton St 41 E7
Burton Way 41 J2
Butterfield St 41 H4
Butterley St 41 F6
Butts Ct 41 E3
Byron St 41 F2

C
Cain Cl 41 H4
Call La 41 F4
Calls, The 41 F4
Calverley St 40 D2
Cambrian St 40 D7
Cambrian Ter 40 D7
Canal Pl 40 B4
Canal St 40 A3
Canal Wf 40 D4
Carberry Pl 40 A1
Carberry Rd 40 A1
Carberry Ter 40 A1
Carlisle Rd 41 G5
Carlton Carr 41 E1
Carlton Ct 40 A7
Carlton Gdns 41 E1
Carlton Gate 41 E1
Carlton Gro 41 E1
Carlton Hill 41 E1
Carlton Pl 41 E1
Carlton Ri 41 E1
Carlton Twrs 41 F1
Carlton Vw 41 E1
Castle St 40 D3
Castleton Cl 40 B4
Castleton Rd 40 A3
Cautley Rd 41 J5
Cavalier App 41 H5
Cavalier Cl 41 H5
Cavalier Gdns 41 H5
Cavalier Gate 41 H5
Cavalier Ms 41 H5
Cavalier Vw 41 H5
Cavendish Rd 40 D1
Cavendish St 40 C3
Cemetery Rd 40 C7
Central Rd 41 F4
Central St 40 D3
Chadwick St 41 F5
Chadwick St S 41 G5
Chantrell Ct 41 F4
Charles Av 41 J5
Charlton Gro 41 J4
Charlton Pl 41 J4
Charlton Rd 41 J4
Charlton St 41 J4
Cherry Pl 41 G2
Cherry Row 41 G2
Chesney Av 41 F7
Chiswick St 40 A2
Chorley La 40 D2
Churchill Gdns 40 E1
Church La 41 F4
City Sq 40 E4
City Wk 40 E5
Claremont Av 40 C2
Claremont Gro 40 C2
Claremont Vw 40 C2
Clarence Rd 41 G5
Clarendon Pl 40 C1
Clarendon Rd 40 C1
Clarendon Way 40 D2
Clark Av 41 J4
Clark Cres 41 J4
Clark Gro 41 J5
Clark La 41 H5
Clark Mt 41 J4
Clark Rd 41 J5
Clark Row 41 J5
Clark Ter 41 J4
Clark Vw 41 J5
Clay Pit La 41 E2
Cleveleys Av 40 C7
Cleveleys Mt 40 C7
Cleveleys Rd 40 C7
Cleveleys St 40 C7
Cleveleys Ter 40 C7
Cloberry St 40 C1
Close, The 41 G4
Cloth Hall St 41 F4
Clyde App 40 A5
Clyde Gdns 40 B5
Clyde Vw 40 A5
Coleman St 40 C4
Colenso Gdns 40 C7

Colenso Mt 40 C7
Colenso Pl 40 C7
Colenso Rd 40 C7
Colenso Ter 40 C7
Colville Ter 40 D7
Commercial St 41 E3
Compton Av 41 J1
Compton Cres 41 J1
Compton Gro 41 J1
Compton Mt 41 J1
Compton Pl 41 J1
Compton Rd 41 J1
Compton St 41 J1
Compton Ter 41 J1
Compton Vw 41 J1
Concordia St 41 E4
Concord St 41 F2
Consort St 40 C2
Consort Ter 40 C2
Consort Vw 40 B2
Consort Wk 40 C2
Constance Gdns 40 E1
Constance Way 40 E1
Cookridge St 40 E3
Copley Hill 40 A5
Copley Hill Way 40 A6
Copley Pl 40 A5
Copley St 40 A5
Copperfield Av 41 J5
Copperfield Cres 41 J5
Copperfield Gro 41 J5
Copperfield Mt 41 J5
Copperfield Pl 41 J5
Copperfield Row 41 J5
Copperfield Ter 41 J5
Copperfield Vw 41 J5
Copperfield Wk 41 J5
Copperfiield Dr 41 J5
Cotton St 41 G4
Coupland Pl 40 D7
Coupland Rd 40 D7
Cowper Av 41 J1
Cowper Cres 41 J1
Cowper Rd 41 J1
Cromer Pl 40 C1
Cromer Rd 40 C1
Cromer St 40 C1
Cromer Ter 40 C2
Cromwell Mt 41 G2
Cromwell St 41 G3
Crosby Pl 40 C6
Crosby Rd 40 C7
Crosby Ter 40 C6
Crosby Vw 40 C6
Cross Aysgarth Mt 41 H4
Cross Belgrave St 41 F3
Cross Catherine St 41 H4
Cross Grn App 41 J6
Cross Grn Av 41 H5
Cross Grn Cl 41 J6
Cross Grn Cres 41 H5
Cross Grn Dr 41 J6
Cross Grn Garth 41 J6
Cross Grn La 41 H5
Cross Grn Ri 41 J6
Cross Grn Way 41 J6
Cross Ingram Rd 40 C6
Cross Kelso Rd 40 C2
Cross Mitford Rd 40 A4
Cross Stamford St 41 G2
Cross York St 41 F4
Crown Ct 41 F4
Crown Pt Rd 41 F5
Crown St 41 F4
Croydon St 40 B5
Cudbear St 41 F5
Czar St 40 C5

D
Danby Wk 41 H4
David St 40 D5
Dene Ho Ct 40 E1
Denison Rd 40 C3
Dent St 41 H4
Derwent Pl 40 D5
Devon Cl 40 D1
Devon Rd 40 D1
Dewsbury Rd 41 E6
Dial St 41 H5
Disraeli Gdns 40 E7
Disraeli Ter 40 E7
Dock St 41 F4
Dolly La 41 H2
Dolphin Ct 41 H4
Dolphin St 41 H4
Domestic Rd 40 B6
Domestic St 40 C5
Donisthorpe St 41 G6
Drive, The 41 G4
Driver Ter 40 B5
Dudley Way 40 A5
Duke St 41 F4
Duncan St 40 C7

Duncombe St 40 C3
Duxbury Ri 40 E1
Dyer St 41 F3

E
East Fld St 41 H4
Eastgate 41 F3
East King St 41 G4
East Par 40 E3
East Pk Dr 41 J4
East Pk Gro 41 J4
East Pk Mt 41 J4
East Pk Par 41 J4
East Pk Pl 41 J4
East Pk Rd 41 J4
East Pk St 41 J4
East Pk Ter 41 J4
East Pk Vw 41 J4
East St 41 G4
Easy Rd 41 H5
Ebor Mt 40 B1
Ebor Pl 40 B1
Ebor St 40 B1
Edgware Av 41 H1
Edgware Gro 41 H1
Edgware Mt 41 H1
Edgware Pl 41 H1
Edgware Row 41 H1
Edgware St 41 H1
Edgware Ter 41 H1
Edgware Vw 41 H1
Edward St 41 F3
Edwin Rd 40 B1
Eighth Av 40 A5
Elland Rd 40 C7
Elland Ter 40 D6
Ellerby La 41 H5
Ellerby Rd 41 G4
Elmtree La 41 G7
Elmwood La 41 F2
Elmwood Rd 41 E2
Elsworth St 40 A4
Enfield Av 41 G1
Enfield St 41 G1
Enfield Ter 41 G1
Euston Gro 40 B7
Euston Mt 40 B7
Euston Ter 40 B7
Everleigh St 41 J3

F
Far Cft Ter 40 A5
Fewston Av 41 H5
Fewston Ct 41 J5
Finsbury Rd 40 D2
First Av 40 A4
Firth St 41 G2
Firth Ter 41 G2
Fish St 41 F3
Flax Pl 41 G4
Florence Av 41 J1
Florence Gro 41 J1
Florence Mt 41 J1
Florence Pl 41 J1
Florence St 41 J1
Folly La 40 D7
Forster St 41 G6
Foundry St (Holbeck) 40 C2
Foundry St (Quarry Hill) 41 G4
Fountain St 40 D3
Fourteenth Av 40 A5
Fourth Ct 40 C5
Fox Way 41 F4
Fraser St 40 B5
Frederick Av 41 F5
Front Row 40 D5
Front St 40 D5

G
Gardeners Ct 41 G7
Gargrave App 41 H3
Gargrave Pl 41 H2
Garth, The 41 G4
Garton Av 41 J4
Garton Gro 41 J4
Garton Rd 41 J4
Garton Ter 41 J4
Garton Vw 41 J4
Gelderd Pl 40 B5
Gelderd Rd 40 A7
George St 41 F3
Gibraltar Island Rd 41 H7
Gilpin Pl 40 A5
Gilpin St 40 A5
Gilpin Ter 40 A5
Gilpin Vw 40 A5
Glasshouse St 41 G6
Gledhow Mt 41 H1
Gledhow Pl 41 H1
Gledhow Rd 41 H1
Gledhow Ter 41 H1

Glencoe Vw 41 J5
Glensdale Gro 41 J4
Glensdale Mt 41 J4
Glensdale Rd 41 J4
Glensdale Ter 41 J4
Glenthorpe Av 41 J3
Glenthorpe Cres 41 J3
Glenthorpe Ter 41 J3
Globe Rd 40 C4
Gloucester Ter 40 A4
Goodman St 41 G6
Gotts Rd 40 C4
Gower St 41 F3
Grace St 40 D3
Grafton St 41 F2
Grange Cl 41 G7
Grange Rd 41 G7
Grant Av 41 G1
Granville Rd 41 H2
Grape St 41 F7
Grasmere Cl 40 A5
Grassmere Rd 40 A5
Great George St 40 D3
Great Wilson St 40 E5
Greek St 40 E3
Greenfield Rd 41 H4
Green La 40 A5
Grosvenor Hill 41 E1

H
Hall Gro 40 B1
Hall La 40 A4
Hall Pl 41 H4
Hanover Av 40 C2
Hanover La 40 D3
Hanover Mt 40 C2
Hanover Sq 40 C2
Hanover Wk 40 C3
Harewood St 41 F3
Harold Av 40 A1
Harold Gro 40 A1
Harold Mt 40 A1
Harold Pl 40 A1
Harold Rd 40 A1
Harold St 40 A1
Harold Ter 40 A1
Harold Vw 40 A1
Harold Wk 40 A1
Harper St 41 F4
Harrison St 41 F3
Hartwell Rd 40 B1
Haslewood Cl 41 H3
Haslewood Ct 41 H3
Haslewood Dene 41 H3
Haslewood Dr 41 H3
Haslewood Ms 41 J3
Haslewood Pl 41 H3
Haslewood Sq 41 H3
Hawkins Dr 41 E1
Headrow, The 40 D3
Heaton's Ct 41 E4
Hedley Chase 40 A4
Hedley Gdns 40 A4
Hedley Grn 40 A4
High 40 D7
High Ct 41 G6
High Ct La 41 F4
Hillary Pl 40 D1
Hillidge Rd 41 F7
Hillidge Sq 41 F7
Hill Top Pl 40 B1
Hill Top St 40 B1
Hirst's Yd 41 F4
Holbeck 41 H6
Holbeck La 40 C5
Holbeck Moor Rd 40 C6
Holdforth Cl 40 A4
Holdforth Gdns 40 A4
Holdforth Grn 40 A4
Holdforth Pl 40 A4
Holmes St 41 E5
Holroyd St 41 G1
Hope Rd 41 G3
Howden Gdns 40 B1
Howden Pl 40 B1
Hudson Rd 41 J1
Hudswell Rd 41 F7
Hunslet 41 G7
Hunslet Grn Way 41 F7
Hunslet Hall Rd 40 E7
Hunslet La 41 F5
Hunslet Rd 41 F4
Hyde Pk Cl 40 B1
Hyde Pk Rd 40 B1
Hyde Pl 40 C2
Hyde St 40 C2
Hyde Ter 40 C2

I
Infirmary St 40 E3
Ingram Cl 40 C6
Ingram Cres 40 B7

Ingram Gdns 40 C6
Ingram Rd 40 C7
Ingram Row 40 E5
Ingram St 40 E5
Ingram Vw 40 C6
Inner Ring Rd 40 E2
Ivory St 41 F6

J
Jack La 40 D6
Jenkinson Cl 40 D6
Jenkinson Lawn 40 D6
John Smeaton Viaduct 41 G6
Joseph St 41 G7
Junction St 41 F5

K
Keeton St 41 H3
Kelsall Av 40 B1
Kelsall Gro 40 B2
Kelsall Pl 40 B1
Kelsall Rd 40 B1
Kelsall Ter 40 B1
Kelso Gdns 40 C1
Kelso Rd 40 C1
Kelso St 40 C2
Kendal Bk 40 C2
Kendal Cl 40 C2
Kendal Gro 40 C2
Kendal La 40 C2
Kendell St 41 F4
Kenneth St 40 B6
Kepler Gro 41 H1
Kepler Mt 41 H1
Kepler Ter 41 H1
Kidacre St 41 F5
Kildare Ter 40 B5
King Charles St 41 E3
King Edward St 41 F3
Kings Av 40 B2
King's Rd 40 B1
Kingston Ter 40 D1
King St 40 D4
Kippax Pl 41 H4
Kirkgate 41 F4
Kirkstall Rd 40 A2
Kitson Rd 41 G6
Kitson St 41 H4
Knowsthorpe Cres 41 H5
Knowsthorpe La 41 J6

L
Ladybeck Cl 41 F3
Lady La 41 F3
Lady Pit La 40 D7
Lands La 41 E3
Lane, The 41 G4
Larchfield Rd 41 G6
Latchmore Rd 40 A7
Laura St 40 C5
Lavender Wk 41 H4
Leathley Rd 41 F6
Leathley St 41 F6
Leicester Cl 40 E1
Leicester Gro 40 E1
Leicester Pl 40 D1
Leighton St 40 D3
Leodis Ct 41 G2
Leylands Rd 41 G2
Lifton Pl 40 C1
Lincoln Grn Rd 41 G2
Lincoln Rd 41 G2
Lindsey Ct 41 H2
Lindsey Gdns 41 H2
Lindsey Rd 41 H2
Lisbon St 40 D3
Little King St 40 E4
Little Queen St 40 D4
Little Woodhouse St 40 D2
Livinia Gro 40 E1
Lodge St 40 D1
Lofthouse Pl 40 E1
Londesboro Gro 41 J4
Long Causeway 41 H6
Long Cl La 41 H4
Lord St 40 C5
Lord Ter 40 B5
Lovell Pk Cl 41 F2
Lovell Pk Gate 41 F2
Lovell Pk Hill 41 F2
Lovell Pk Rd 41 F2
Lovell Pk Vw 41 F2
Lower Basinghall St 40 E3
Lower Brunswick St 41 F2
Low Flds Av 40 B7
Low Flds Rd 40 A7
Low Flds Way 40 B7
Low Fold 41 G5
Low Rd 41 G7
Low Whitehouse Row 41 G6
Ludgate Hill 41 F3
Lyddon Ter 40 C1
Lydgate 41 J2

Street	Ref
Lydia St	41 F3
M	
Mabgate	41 G3
Mabgate Grn	41 G3
Macaulay St	41 G3
Maitland Pl	40 D7
Maltings Rd	41 F7
Malvern Gro	40 D7
Malvern Ri	40 D7
Malvern Rd	40 C7
Malvern St	40 C7
Malvern Vw	40 C7
Manor Rd	40 D5
Manor St	41 G1
Mark La	41 E3
Marlborough Gdns	40 D1
Marlborough Gro	40 D1
Marlborough St	40 C3
Marlborough Twrs	40 C3
Marshall St	40 D5
Marsh La	41 G4
Maude St	41 F4
May Ter	41 H5
Meadowcroft Ms	41 H4
Meadow La	41 E5
Meadow Rd	40 E6
Melbourne St	41 F2
Merrion Pl	41 F3
Merrion St	41 E3
Merrion Way	41 E2
Meynell App	40 C6
Middleton Av	41 J2
Milford Pl	40 A2
Millgarth St	41 F3
Mill Grn	40 B5
Mill Hill	41 E4
Mill St	41 G4
Millwright St	41 G2
Milner Gdns	41 H5
Milnes St	40 B5
Mitford Rd	40 A4
Mitford Vw	40 A4
Moor Cres	41 E7
Moor Cres Chase	41 E7
Moorland Av	40 B1
Moorland Rd	40 B1
Moor Rd	41 E7
Moorside Maltings	41 E7
Moor Vw	40 D6
Moorvile Cl	40 D7
Moorville Ct	40 D7
Moorville Gro	40 D7
Moorville Rd	40 D7
Mount Preston St	40 C2
Mulberry St	41 F6
Mullins Ct	41 H5
Mushroom St	41 G2
N	
Naseby Garth	41 G2
Naseby Ter	41 H3
National Rd	41 H6
Navigation Wk	41 F4
Neptune St	41 G4
Neville St	40 E4
New Briggate	41 F3
New Craven Gate	41 F6
New La	40 E5
New Mkt St	41 F4
New Princess St	40 D6
New Sta St	40 E4
New York Rd	41 G3
New York St	41 F4
Nickleby Rd	41 J3
Nile St	41 F3
Nineveh Gdns	40 D6
Nineveh Par	40 D6
Nineveh Rd	40 C6
Nippet La	41 H3
Nortech Cl	41 G1
Normanton Gro	40 C7
Normanton Pl	40 D7
Northcote Cres	40 E7
Northcote Dr	40 D7
Northcote Grn	40 D7
North Ct	41 F3
Northern St	40 D4
North St	41 F3
O	
Oak Rd	40 A4
Oatland Cl	41 F1
Oatland Ct	41 F1
Oatland Dr	41 F1
Oatland Gdns	41 F1
Oatland Grn	41 F1
Oatland Hts	41 F1
Oatland La	41 E1
Oatland Rd	41 E1
Oatland Twrs	41 F1
O'Grady Sq	41 H4
Old Mill La	41 H7
Oval, The	41 G7
Oxford Pl	40 D3
Oxford Row	40 D3
Oxley St	41 J4
Oxton Mt	41 J3
Oxton Way	41 J3
P	
Parade, The	41 G4
Park Cross St	40 D3
Parkfield St	41 E6
Park La	40 C3
Park Par	41 J5
Park Pl	40 D3
Park Row	40 E3
Park Sq E	40 D3
Park Sq N	40 D3
Park Sq S	40 D3
Park Sq W	40 D3
Park St	40 D3
Park Vw Rd	40 A1
Pearson St	41 F6
Penny La Way	41 F7
Pilot St	41 G2
Pitt Row	41 E4
Place's Rd	41 H4
Plaid Row	41 H3
Playhouse Sq	41 G3
Pleasant Mt	40 C6
Pleasant Pl	40 C6
Pleasant Ter	40 C6
Pontefract Av	41 J4
Pontefract La	41 H3
Pontefract La Cl	41 H4
Pontefract St	41 H4
Portland Cres	40 E2
Portland Gate	40 E2
Portland St	40 D3
Portland Way	40 E2
Pottery Rd	41 F7
Prosper St	41 G7
Providence Pl	41 E2
Pym St	41 G6
Q	
Quarry Hill	41 G3
Quebec St	40 D3
Queen Sq	41 E2
Queens Rd	40 B1
Queen St	40 D4
R	
Radnor St	40 B5
Railway St	41 G4
Raincliffe Gro	41 J3
Raincliffe Rd	41 J3
Raincliffe St	41 J3
Recreation Cres	40 C7
Recreation Gro	40 C7
Recreation Mt	40 C7
Recreation Pl	40 C7
Recreation Row	40 C7
Recreation St	40 C7
Recreation Ter	40 C7
Recreation Vw	40 C7
Rectory St	41 H2
Redshaw Rd	40 A5
Regent St	41 G3
Regent Ter	40 B1
Rhodes Ter	40 A5
Richmond Hill App	41 H4
Richmond Hill Cl	41 H4
Richmond St	41 G4
Rickard St	40 C5
Rider St	41 G3
Rigton App	41 H3
Rigton Cl	41 H3
Rigton Dr	41 H3
Rigton Grn	41 H3
Rigton Lawn	41 H3
Rigton Ms	41 H3
Rillbank La	40 B2
Roscoe St	41 G1
Rosebank Gdns	40 B2
Rosebank Rd	40 B2
Rosebud Wk	41 G1
Roseville Rd	41 G1
Roseville St	41 H1
Rossington St	40 E3
Roundhay Rd	41 G1
Roxby Cl	41 H2
Royal Pk Av	40 B1
Royal Pk Gro	40 B1
Royal Pk Rd	40 A1
Royal Pk Ter	40 B1
Ruby St	41 G2
Runswick Av	40 C6
Runswick Pl	40 C6
Runswick St	40 C6
Runswick Ter	40 C6
Russell St	40 E3
Rydall Pl	40 C6
Rydall St	40 C6
Rydall Ter	40 C6
S	
Sackville St	41 F1
St. Andrew's St	40 C3
St. Barnabas Rd	40 E5
St. Georges Rd	40 D2
St. Helen's St	41 G6
St. Hilda's Av	41 J5
St. Hilda's Cres	41 H5
St. Hilda's Gro	41 J5
St. Hilda's Mt	41 J5
St. Hilda's Pl	41 J5
St. Hilda's Rd	41 J5
St. John's Av	40 C1
St. John's Cl	40 B1
St. John's Gro	40 B1
St. John's Rd	40 B2
St. Luke's Cescent	40 D7
St. Luke's Cres	40 D7
St. Luke's Grn	40 D7
St. Luke's Rd	40 D7
St. Luke's Ter	40 D7
St. Mark's Av	40 D1
St. Mark's Rd	40 D1
St. Mark's St	40 D1
St. Mary's Cl	40 A5
St. Mary's St	41 G3
St. Matthew's St	40 C6
St. Matthias St	40 A1
St. Matthias Ter	40 A1
St. Paul's St	40 D3
St. Peter's Ct	41 E7
St. Peter's Pl	41 G3
St. Peter's Sq	41 G3
St. Stephen's Ct	41 H3
St. Stephen's Rd	41 H3
Salem Pl	41 F5
Sandlewood Cl	40 D6
Sandlewood Grn	40 D6
Sardinia St	41 F6
Saville Grn	41 J3
Saxton La	41 G4
Sayner La	41 G5
Sayner Rd	41 F5
Scargill Cl	41 H2
Scarth Av	41 J1
Second Av	40 A4
Seminary St	40 D2
Severn Way	41 H7
Shafton La	40 C6
Shafton Pl	40 C6
Shafton St	40 C6
Shafton Vw	40 C6
Shakespeare App	41 H2
Shakespeare Av	41 H2
Shakespeare Cl	41 J2
Shakespeare Gdns	41 J2
Shakespeare Lawn	41 H2
Shakespeare St	41 J1
Shannon Rd	41 H3
Shannon St	41 G3
Sheaf St	41 F5
Sheepscar Ct	41 F1
Sheepscar Gro	41 F2
Sheepscar St N	41 F1
Sheepscar St S	41 F1
Siddal St	40 D5
Sidney St	41 F3
Silver St	40 D5
Skinner La	41 F2
Skinner St	40 C3
Somers St	40 D3
South Accommodation Rd	41 G6
South Par	40 E3
Sovereign St	40 E4
Spence La	40 B5
Spenceley St	40 D1
Spinney, The	41 H4
Spinneyfield Ct	41 H4
Spring Cl Av	41 H5
Spring Cl Gdns	41 H5
Spring Cl St	41 H5
Spring Cl Wk	41 H5
Springfield Mt	40 C2
Spring Gro Ter	40 A1
Spring Gro Vw	40 B1
Spring Gro Wk	40 A1
Springwell Ct	40 C5
Springwell Rd	40 C5
Springwell St	40 C5
Springwell Vw	40 C5
Stafford St	41 G7
Stanley Av	41 J1
Stanley Pl	41 J1
Stanley Rd	41 J1
Stanley Ter	41 J1
Stocks Hill	40 C6
Stoney Rock Gro	41 J2
Stoney Rock La	41 H2
Stott Rd	40 A4
Studio Rd	40 B2
Sutton St	40 C5
Sweet St	40 D5
Sweet St W	40 C5
Swinegate	41 E4
Sydenham Rd	40 B5
Sydenham St	40 B5
T	
Telephone Pl	41 G2
Templar La	41 F3
Templar Pl	41 F3
Templar St	41 F3
Temple Vw Gro	41 J4
Temple Vw Pl	41 J4
Temple Vw Rd	41 J3
Temple Vw Ter	41 J4
Thealby Cl	41 G3
Thealby Lawn	41 G2
Thealby Pl	41 G3
Third Av	40 A5
Thirsk Row	40 D4
Thoresby Pl	40 D3
Thornleigh Gdns	41 J5
Thornleigh Gro	41 J5
Thornleigh Mt	41 J5
Thornleigh St	41 J5
Thornleigh Vw	41 J5
Thornville Pl	40 B1
Thornville Rd	40 A1
Thornville Row	40 B1
Thornville St	40 B1
Thornville Vw	40 B1
Tilbury Av	40 C7
Tilbury Gro	40 C7
Tilbury Mt	40 C7
Tilbury Par	40 C7
Tilbury Rd	40 C7
Tilbury Ter	40 C7
Tilbury Vw	40 C7
Tong Rd	40 A5
Top Moor Side	40 C6
Torre Cl	41 J3
Torre Dr	41 J2
Torre Rd	41 H3
Tower Ho St	41 F2
Trafalgar St	41 F3
Trent Rd	41 J3
Trent St	40 D6
Trinity St	41 E3
Triumph Cl	40 C5
Turlow Ct	41 G4
U	
Union Pl	40 D5
Union St	41 F3
University Rd	40 C1
Upper Accommodation Rd	41 H3
Upper Basinghall St	40 E3
Upper N St	40 E2
Upper Westlock Av	41 J2
V	
Vernon Rd	40 D2
Vernon St	40 E2
Vicar La	41 F3
Victoria Rd	40 E5
Victoria Sq	40 D3
Victoria St	40 C2
Victoria Ter	40 C2
Village Ter	40 A1
Vinery Mt	41 J4
Vinery Pl	41 J4
Vinery St	41 J3
Vinery Ter	41 J4
W	
Wade La	41 E3
Walford Gro	41 J3
Walford Rd	41 J3
Walford Ter	41 J3
Walter Cres	41 H4
Walter St	40 A2
Walton St	40 D5
Washington St	40 B3
Water La	40 C5
Waterloo Rd	41 G7
Waterloo St	41 F4
Waverley Garth	40 D7
Weaver St	40 A2
Welbeck Rd	41 J4
Well Cl Ri	41 E1
Wellington Br St	40 C3
Wellington Pl	40 C4
Wellington Rd	40 B4
Wellington St	40 D4
Wesley Pl	41 H4
Westfield Cres	40 B2
Westfield Rd	40 B2
Westfield Ter	40 B2
Westgate	40 D3
Westlock Av	41 J2
West St	40 C3
West Vale	40 A6
Wharf St	41 F4
Whitehall Rd	40 B5
Whitehouse St	41 G7
Whitelock St	41 F2
Whitfield Av	41 G7
Whitfield Gdns	41 G7
Whitfield Pl	41 G7
Whitfield Sq	41 G7
Whitfield Way	41 G7
Willis St	41 H4
Willoughby Ter	40 C6
Willow App	40 A2
Willow Av	40 A2
Willow Cl	40 B2
Willow Garth	40 A2
Willow Rd	40 A2
Willow Ter Rd	40 D2
Wilmington St	41 F1
Winchester St	40 A4
Winfield Gro	40 E1
Winfield Pl	40 E1
Winfield Ter	40 E1
Wintoun St	41 F2
Wolseley Rd	40 A1
Woodhouse La	40 D1
Woodhouse Sq	40 D3
Woodsley Grn	40 B1
Woodsley Rd	40 B2
Wormald Row	41 E3
Wortley La	40 B5
Wortley Pk	40 A5
Y	
Yarn St	41 H6
York Pl	40 D3
York Rd	41 H3
York St	41 F4

Liverpool street index

Street	Ref
A	
Abercromby Sq	43 F4
Abney Cl	43 H5
Acorn Ct	43 E7
Acton Way	43 H5
Adderley St	43 H3
Addison St	42 C2
Addison Way	42 C2
Adelaide Pl	42 D1
Adelaide Rd	43 G4
Adele Thompson Dr	43 F6
Agnes Way	43 H4
Aigburth St	43 G5
Ainsworth St	42 E4
Albany Rd	43 G3
Albert Edward Rd	43 G3
Albert St	43 G4
Alderson Rd	43 J6
Alexandra Cl	43 G2
Alexandra Rd	43 J5
Alex Cl	43 F7
Alfred Ms	42 D6
Alfred St	43 J5
Altcar Av	43 J6
Alt St	43 G6
Amberley St	43 F6
Amelia Cl	43 F2
Amethyst Cl	43 G1
Anchorage, The	42 C7
Angela St	43 G5
Anglezark Cl	43 H3
Anglican Ct	42 E6
Archbishop Warlock Ct	42 B1
Argyle St	42 C5
Arley St	42 C1
Arnold Cres	43 F7
Arnside Rd	43 H4
Arrad St	43 E5
Arundel Av	43 J7
Arundel Cl	43 G7
Asbridge St	43 G7
Ashton St	43 F3
Ashwell St	42 D6
Askham Cl	43 G6
Aspen Gro	43 H7
Atlantic Pt	42 C2
Atwell St	43 G1
B	
Back Colquitt St	42 D5
Back Guildford St	43 F1
Back Kelvin Gro	43 G7
Back Leeds St	42 B2
Baker St	43 G2
Baker Way	43 F2
Balmoral Rd	43 J1
Balm St	43 H3
Baltimore St	42 E5
Bannerman St	43 J5
Barnet Cl	42 C4
Basnett St	42 C4
Bath St	42 A3
Battenberg St	43 G3
Bayhorse La	43 E3
Beaconsfield St	43 G7
Beaufort St	42 D7
Beaumont St	43 G6
Beau St	42 D1
Beckwith St	42 C5
Bective St	43 J5
Bedford Cl	43 F5
Bedford St S	43 F6
Beech St	43 J3
Benson St	42 D4
Bentley Rd	43 G7
Beresford St	42 E1
Berington St	42 C1
Berkley St	43 E6
Berry St	42 D5
Berwick Cl	43 H1
Berwick St	43 H1
Bevington Bush	42 C2
Bevington Hill	42 C1
Bidder St	42 E2
Bigham Rd	43 H2
Birchfield St	42 E2
Bird St	43 J6
Birkett St	42 D2
Birstall Rd	43 G2
Birt Cl	43 G6
Bishop Sheppard Ct	42 B1
Bixteth St	42 B3
Blackburne Pl	43 E5
Blackstock St	42 C2
Blair St	42 E6
Blenheim St	42 C1
Bluefields St	43 E6
Blundell St	42 C6
Boaler St	43 G2
Bold Pl	42 D5
Bold St	42 D4
Bolton St	42 D4
Bond St	42 C1
Boothwood Cl	43 H5
Boswell St	43 H6
Botanic Grn	43 H3
Botanic Pl	43 J3
Botanic Rd	43 J3
Boundary La	43 G1
Boyton Ct	43 J5
Bradfield St	43 H3
Brae St	43 H3

Brahms Cl 43 G7
Brampton Dr 43 F5
Brassey St 42 D7
Breames Cl 43 H4
Breck Rd 43 F1
Bremner Cl 43 H4
Brick St 42 D6
Bridge Rd 43 J5
Bridgewater St 42 C6
Bridport St 42 D3
Bright St 43 F2
Brindley St 42 D7
Britannia Av 43 J6
Britten Cl 43 H7
Bronte St 42 E3
Brook St 42 B3
Brownlow Hill 42 D4
Brownlow St 43 E4
Brow Side 43 E1
Brunswick Rd 43 F3
Brunswick St 42 B4
Bryges St 43 G4
Brythen St 42 C4
Burlington St 42 C1
Burnley Cl 43 G1
Burroughs Gdns 42 C1
Burrows Ct 42 B1
Burton Cl 42 C5
Bute St 42 D2
Bute St (Edge Hill) 43 H6
Butler Cres 43 G2
Butler St 43 G1
Button St 42 C4
Byrom St 42 D3

C

Cadogan St 43 J5
Caird St 43 G2
Cairns St 43 G7
Caledonia St 43 E5
Callander Rd 43 J2
Cambria St N 43 H2
Cambria St S 43 H2
Cambridge Ct 43 E5
Cambridge St 43 E4
Camden St 42 D3
Cameo Cl 43 G1
Cameron St 43 H3
Campbell St 42 C5
Canada Boul 42 B4
Canning Pl 42 C4
Canning St 43 E5
Cantebury St 42 E2
Cantebury Way 43 E2
Cantsfield St 43 J6
Cardigan St 43 J5
Cardigan Way 43 H1
Cardwell St 43 G5
Carlingford Cl 43 G6
Carlton St 42 A1
Carmarthen Cres 42 D7
Carpenters Row 42 C5
Carruthers St 42 B2
Carstairs Rd 43 J1
Carter St 43 F6
Carver St 43 E2
Caryl St 42 D7
Castle St 42 B4
Catharine St 43 F5
Cathedral Cl 42 E6
Cathedral Gate 42 E5
Cathedral Wk 42 E4
Cawdor St 43 G7
Cazneau St 42 D1
Cedar Gro 43 H7
Celtic St 43 F7
Chadwick St 42 B2
Chaloner St 42 C6
Chandos St 43 H4
Channell Rd 43 H2
Chapel St 42 B4
Chase Way 42 E1
Chatham Pl 43 G4
Chatham St 43 F5
Chatsworth Dr 43 H5
Chaucer St 42 D2
Cheapside 42 C3
Chesney Cl 42 E7
Chesterfield St 42 E6
Chester St 42 E7
Chestnut St 43 F4
Chichester Cl 43 J5
Childwall Av 43 J6
Chisenhale St 42 B1
Chiswell St 43 H3
Christian St 42 D2
Chris Ward Cl 43 H4
Church All 42 C4
Church Mt 43 G4
Church St 42 C4
Churton Ct 43 F2
Cicely St 43 G4
Clarence St 42 E4
Claribel St 43 F7
Claughton Cl 43 H4
Claypole Cl 43 H5
Clay St 42 B1
Clearwater Cl 43 H3
Clegg St 42 D1
Clement Gdns 42 C1
Cleveland Sq 42 C5
Clifford St 42 E3
Cliff St 43 H3
Clifton Gro 42 E1
Clint Rd 43 H4
Clint Rd W 43 H4
Clint Way 43 H4
Coal St 42 D3
Cobden St 43 F2
Coburg Wf 42 C7
Cockspur St 42 C3
Coleridge St 43 H2
College La 42 C4
College St N 43 E2
College St S 43 F2
Colquitt St 42 D5
Coltart Rd 43 G7
Comberme St 43 E7
Commerce Way 43 G6
Commutation Row 42 D3
Compton Rd 43 G1
Comus St 42 D2
Concert St 42 D5
Connaught Rd 43 G3
Contance St 43 E3
Cookson St 42 D6
Cook St 42 C4
Copperas Hill 42 D4
Corinto St 42 E6
Corney St 43 H6
Cornhill 42 C5
Cornwallis St 42 D5
Corsewall St 43 J5
Cotswold St 43 H3
Cotton St 42 A1
Covent Gdn 42 B3
Cowan Dr 43 F1
Cranborne Rd 43 J6
Craven St 42 E3
Cresswell St 43 F1
Cropper St 42 D4
Crosfield Cl 43 J4
Crosfield Rd 43 H4
Crosshall St 42 C3
Crown St 43 F3
Croxteth Gro 43 H7
Croxteth Rd 43 G7
Crump St 42 D6
Cullen St 43 H6
Cumberland St 42 C3
Cunliffe St 42 C3
Custom Ho Pl 42 C5

D

Dale St 42 B4
Daniel Davies Dr 43 G6
Dansie St 43 E4
Danube St 43 H6
Darrel Dr 43 H6
Daulby St 43 F3
Davies St 42 C3
Dawber Cl 43 G1
Dawson St 42 C4
Dean Dillistone Ct 42 D6
Deane Rd 43 H3
Dean Patey Ct 42 D5
Deeley Cl 43 H4
Dell St 43 H3
Denham Dr 43 H1
Denham Way 43 H1
Dentdale Dr 42 E1
Devon St 42 E3
Dexter St 42 E7
Dial St 43 H3
Diamond St 42 C1
Dickens St 43 E7
Dickson St 42 A1
Dombey St 43 E7
Dorothy St 43 H4
Dorrit St 43 E7
Dorset Av 43 J6
Douro St 42 D1
Dovestone Cl 43 H5
Dove St 43 G6
Drury La 42 B4
Dryden St 42 D1
Dublin St 42 A1
Ducie St 43 G7
Duckinfield St 43 E4
Duke St 42 C5
Duncan St 42 D6
Dunkeld Cl 43 G2
Dunstan La 43 H5
Durden St 43 H6
Durning Rd 43 H3
Dwerryhouse St 42 D7
Dyke St 43 F1

E

Earle Rd 43 H6
Earle St 42 B3
East St 42 B3
Eaton St 42 B2
Ebenezer Rd 43 J3
Eden St 43 H6
Edgar St 42 C2
Edge Hill 43 G5
Edge La 43 G4
Edinburgh Rd 43 G3
Edmund St 42 B3
Egerton St 43 E6
Elaine St 43 F7
Eldonian Way 42 B1
Eldon Pl 42 C1
Eldon St 42 C1
Elizabeth St 43 F3
Elliot St 42 D4
Elm Gro 43 F4
Elm Vale 43 J1
Elstree Rd 43 J2
Ember Cres 43 F1
Embledon St 43 G6
Emerson St 43 E6
Empress Rd 43 G4
Enid St 43 F7
Epworth St 43 F3
Erin Cl 42 E7
Erskine St 43 F3
Esher Rd 43 H2
Eversley St 43 F7
Everton Brow 42 E2
Everton Rd 43 F1
Every St 43 G1
Exchange St E 42 B3
Exchange St W 42 B3

F

Fairclough St 42 D4
Fairfield 43 J2
Falkland St 43 E3
Falkner Sq 43 F6
Falkner St 43 E5
Fareham Rd 43 J3
Farnworth St 43 G2
Fazakerley St 42 B3
Fearnside St 43 J5
Fell St 43 H3
Fenwick St 42 B4
Fern Gro 43 H7
Fernhill Dr 43 F7
Fielding St 43 G2
Field St 42 E2
Finch Pl 43 E3
Finlay St 43 H2
Fishguard Cl 43 F1
Fitzclarence Way 43 F1
Fitzpatrick Ct 42 B1
Fitzroy Way 43 F2
Fleet St 42 D4
Fleming Ct 42 B1
Flint St 42 D6
Fontenoy St 42 C3
Ford St 42 C2
Forrest St 42 C5
Fowler Cl 43 H4
Foxhill Cl 43 F7
Fox St 42 D1
Fraser St 42 D3
Freedom Cl 43 G5
Freeman St 43 J5
Freemasons' Row 42 C2
Frost St 43 H3

G

Galloway St 43 J5
Gannock St 43 H3
Gardenside St 43 F2
Gardners Dr 43 H1
Gardner's Row 42 C2
Garrick St 43 J6
Gascoyne St 42 B2
Geneva Rd 43 J2
George Harrison Cl 43 G2
Georges Dockway 42 B4
George St 42 B3
Geraint St 43 F7
Gerard St 42 D3
Gibraltar Row 42 B3
Gibson St 43 F6
Gilbert St 42 C5
Gildarts Gdns 42 C1
Gildart St 43 E3
Gilead St 43 H3
Gill St 43 E3
Gilroy Rd 43 H2
Gladstone Rd 43 G4
Gladstone St 42 C2
Gleave Cres 43 F1
Glegg St 42 B1
Gloucester Ct 43 G2
Gloucester Pl 43 F3
Gore St 42 D7
Gower St 42 B5
Gradwell St 42 C4
Grafton Cres 42 D7
Grafton St 42 D6
Granary Wf 42 C7
Granby St 43 G6
Grantham St 43 H2
Granville Rd 43 J6
Grayson St 42 C5
Great Crosshall St 42 C3
Great George Pl 42 D6
Great George St 42 D6
Great Howard St 42 B2
Great Nelson St 42 D1
Great Newton St 43 E3
Great Orford St 43 E4
Great Richmond St 42 D2
Greek St 42 E3
Greenheys Rd 43 G7
Greenland St 42 D6
Green La 42 E4
Greenleaf St 43 H6
Greenside 43 F2
Green St 42 C1
Gregson St 43 F2
Grenville St S 42 D5
Gresley Cl 43 J4
Grierson St 43 H6
Grinfield St 43 G4
Grinshill Cl 43 F7
Grosvenor St 42 D1
Grove Pk 43 H7
Grove Rd 43 J2
Grove St 43 F6
Guelph St 43 F3
Guion St 43 H1
Gwendoline St 43 F7
Gwenfron Rd 43 G2
Gwent St 43 F7

H

Hackins Hey 42 B3
Haigh St 43 E1
Hale St 42 C3
Hall La 43 F3
Halsbury Rd 43 H2
Hampstead Rd 43 J2
Hampton St 43 E6
Hannan Rd 43 H2
Hanover St 42 C5
Harbord St 43 G4
Hardman St 42 E5
Hardy St 42 D6
Harewood St 43 G1
Harker St 42 D2
Harke St 43 H5
Harper St 43 F3
Harrington St 42 C4
Harrowby Cl 43 G6
Harrowby St 43 F6
Hartley Quay 42 B5
Hart St 42 E3
Hatherley Cl 43 G6
Hatherley St 43 F7
Hatton Gdn 42 C3
Haverston Rd 43 J2
Hawdon Ct 43 J5
Hawke St 42 D4
Hawkins St 43 H2
Hawthorn Gro 43 H4
Head St 42 E7
Heathcote Cl 43 H5
Heathfield St 42 D4
Helena St 43 H4
Helsby St 43 G4
Hendon Rd 43 J1
Henglers Cl 43 F2
Henry Edward St 42 C2
Henry St 42 C5
Hewitts Pl 42 C3
Highfield St 42 B2
Highgate St 43 G4
High St 42 B3
Hilbre St 42 D4
Hillaby Cl 43 F7
Hillside St 43 F2
Hill St 42 D7
Hinton St 43 J2
Hockenhall All 42 C3
Hodson Pl 43 F1
Holborn St 43 F3
Holden St 43 G5
Holdsworth St 43 H3
Holly Rd 43 J3
Holmes St 43 H6
Holt Rd 43 H3
Holy Cross Cl 42 C2
Homerton Rd 43 J2
Hood St 42 C3
Hope Pl 42 E5
Hope St 43 E6
Hornby Wk 42 C1
Hotham St 42 D3
Houghton St 42 D4
Houlton St 43 H3
Hughes Cl 43 J4
Hughes St 43 G1
Huntly Rd 43 J2
Hurst St 42 C5
Huskisson St 43 E6
Hutchinson St 43 G2
Hutchinson Wk 43 G2
Hygeia St 43 G1
Hyslop St 42 E7

I

Iliad St 42 D1
Ingrow Rd 43 H2
Innovation Bvd 43 K4
Irvine St 43 G4
Islington 42 E3
Ivatt Way 43 H4

J

Jack McBain Ct 42 B1
Jade Rd 43 H1
Jamaica St 42 D6
James Clarke St 42 C1
James St 42 B4
Janet St 43 H4
Jasmine Cl 43 E1
Jenkinson St 42 E2
Jermyn St 43 G7
Jet Cl 43 H1
John Lennon Dr 43 G2
John Moores Cl 43 F5
Johnson St 42 C3
John St 42 E2
Jordan St 42 D6
Jubilee Dr 43 G3
Judges Dr 43 J1
Judges Way 43 J1
Juvenal Pl 42 D1
Juvenal St 42 D2

K

Keble St 43 G2
Kelso Rd 43 J2
Kelvin Gro 43 G7
Kempston St 42 E3
Kenley Cl 43 H1
Kensington 43 G3
Kensington 43 G3
Kensington St 43 G2
Kent St 42 D5
Kilshaw St 43 G1
Kimberley Cl 43 F6
Kinder St 43 F2
King Edward St 42 B3
Kinglake St 43 G4
Kings Dock St 42 C6
Kingsley Rd 43 G6
Kings Par 42 B5
Kingsway Ct 42 C1
Kingswell Cl 43 G4
Kitchen St 42 C6
Knight St 42 D5

L

Lace St 42 C3
Ladybower Cl 43 H5
Laggan St 43 H3
Lairds Pl 42 C1
Lakeland Cl 42 C5
Lambert Way 42 E3
Lamport St 42 E7
Lance Cl 43 F1
Langley St 42 E7
Langsdale St 42 E2
Langton Rd 43 J6
Lanyork Rd 42 B2
Laurel Gro 43 H7
Lavan Cl 43 F2
Lawrence Rd 43 J6
Lawton St 42 D4
Laxey St 42 E7
Leece St 42 E5
Leeds St 42 B2
Leigh St 42 C4
Leigh St (Edge Hill) 43 J4
Lemon Cl 43 J4
Lemon Gro 43 H7
Leopold Rd 43 G4
Lesseps Rd 43 H6
Lestock St 42 E6
Liffey St 43 G6
Lightwood Dr 43 H5
Lightwood St 43 H5
Lilley Rd 43 J2
Lilly Vale 43 J2
Lime Gro 43 H7
Limekiln La 42 C1
Lime St 42 D4
Lincoln Cl 43 H1
Lindley Cl 43 H5
Lindley St 43 J5
Ling St 43 H3
Lister Cres 43 J3
Lister Rd 43 J2
Little Catherine St 43 E6
Little Ct 42 B1
Little Hardman St 42 E5
Little Howard St 42 B1
Little St. Bride St 43 E5
Little Woolton St 43 F4
Liver St 42 C5
Lloyd Cl 43 F1
Lockerby Rd 43 J2
Lodge La 43 H7
London Rd 42 D3
Longfellow St 43 H6
Longstone Wk 43 G5
Lord Nelson St 42 D3
Lord St 42 C4
Lorton St 43 H6
Lothian St 43 F7
Loudon Gro 43 G7
Love La 42 B1
Lower Castle St 42 B4
Low Hill 43 F2
Lowther St 43 F6
Low Wd St 43 F3
Luke St 43 E7
Lyceum Pl 42 D4
Lydia Ann St 42 C5
Lytton St 43 F2

M

Maddrell St 42 B1
Madelaine St 43 F7
Madeley St 43 H1
Magdala St 43 H6
Maitland Cl 43 H6
Malden Rd 43 H2
Mallow Rd 43 H2
Malt St 43 G5
Malvern Rd 43 H2
Manchester St 42 C3
Manesty's La 42 C4
Manfred St 43 F3
Mann Island 42 B4
Mann St 42 D7
Mansell Rd 43 H2
Mansfield St 42 D2
Manton Rd 43 H2
Maple Gro 43 H7
Marathon Cl 43 F1
Marcot Rd 43 J1
Margaret St 43 F1
Mariners Wf 42 C7
Maritime Pl 42 E2
Maritime Way 42 C5
Marlborough St 42 C2
Marlsford St 43 H2
Marmaduke St 43 G4
Marquis St 42 E3
Marsden St 43 F2
Marsden Way 43 F2
Marshall Pl 42 C1
Martensen St 43 G4
Marvin St 43 G2
Marybone 42 C3
Maryland St 43 E5
Mason St 43 G4
Mathew St 42 C4
Maud St 43 F7
Maxton Rd 43 H2
Mayfair Cl 43 H1
May Pl 42 E4
May St 42 E4
Melda Cl 43 F2
Melville Pl 43 F5
Merlin St 43 F7
Michael Dragonette Ct 42 C1
Midghall St 42 C2
Mile End 42 C1
Millennium Pl 43 G7
Mill La 42 D3
Mill Rd 43 F1
Mill St 42 E7
Millvale St 43 H1
Milroy St 43 H4
Milverton St 43 H1
Minshull St 43 F4
Minster Ct 43 F5
Minto Cl 43 H3
Minto St 43 H3
Mirfield St 43 H2
Molyneux Rd 43 G2
Montgomery Way 43 H1
Moorfields 42 C3
Moor Pl 42 E3
Moor St 42 B4
Morden St 43 H1
Moss Gro 43 H7
Mount Pleasant 42 D4
Mount St 42 E5

Mount Vernon Grn 43 G3
Mount Vernon Rd 43 F4
Mount Vernon St 43 F3
Mozart Cl 43 G7
Muirhead Av 43 H1
Mulberry Pl 43 F5
Mulberry St 43 F5
Mulgrave St 43 F6
Mulliner St 43 J6
Myrtle St 43 E5

N
Navigation Wf 42 C7
Naylor St 42 C2
Needham Rd 43 H3
Nelson Rd 43 G4
Nelson St 42 D6
Netherfield Rd S 42 E1
Nevin St 43 F2
Nevison St 43 G4
New Bird St 42 D6
New Grey Rock Cl 43 G1
Newhall St 42 D6
New Henderson St 42 D7
Newington 42 D4
New Quay 42 B3
New Red Rock Vw 43 G1
Newsham Dr 43 H1
Newstead Rd 43 H6
Newton Way 43 E4
Noel St 43 H6
Norfolk St 42 C6
Norman St 43 E3
Northbrook Cl 43 G6
North Brook St 43 F6
Northcote Cl 43 F1
North John St 42 C3
North St 42 C3
North Vw 43 G4
Norton St 42 D3
Norwood Gro 43 H1
Nuttall St 43 H4

O
Oakes St 43 E3
Oakham St 42 D7
O'Connell Rd 42 C1
Odsey St 43 H3
Oil St 42 A1
Old Coll Pl 43 H4
Old Hall St 42 B3
Oldham St 42 D5
Old Leeds St 42 B3
Olympia St 43 G2
Onslow Rd 43 J2
Opal Cl 43 G1
Orange Gro 43 H7
O'Reilly Ct 42 B1
Oriel Steet 42 C2
Ormond St 42 B3
Orphan St 43 F5
Orthes St 43 E4
Ottley St 43 J2
Overbury St 43 G4
Overton St 43 G4
Oxendale Cl 43 G6
Oxford St 43 E4
Oxford St E 43 G4

P
Paddington 43 F4
Page Wk 42 E2
Paisley St 42 A2
Pall Mall 42 B2
Paradise St 42 C5

Parker St 42 D4
Park La 42 C5
Park Pl 42 E7
Park Rd 43 E7
Parkside St 43 F2
Park Way 43 F6
Parliament Cl 42 E6
Parliament St 42 D6
Parr St 42 D5
Parton St 43 J2
Paul McCartney Way 43 H2
Paul Orr Ct 42 B1
Paul St 42 C2
Pavilion Cl 43 G6
Pear Gro 43 H2
Pearl Way 43 G1
Peet St 43 H4
Pembroke Gdns 43 E3
Pembroke Pl 42 E3
Pembroke St 43 E4
Penarth Cl 43 G5
Pendine Cl 43 H1
Penlinken Dr 43 H1
Penvalley Cres 43 H1
Peover St 42 D2
Pera Cl 43 G2
Percy St 43 E6
Perrygate Cl 43 G5
Perry St 42 D7
Perth St 43 G2
Peter's Arcade 42 C4
Peter St 42 C3
Phillimore Rd 43 H2
Pickop St 42 C3
Pickwick St 43 E7
Picton Rd 43 J5
Pilgrim St 42 E5
Pimhill Cl 43 G7
Pine Ms 42 E6
Pinetop Cl 43 H1
Pitt St 42 D5
Pleasant St 42 E4
Plimsoll St 43 H4
Plumpton St 43 F1
Pomfret St 43 F7
Pomona St 42 E4
Pond Cl 43 H1
Ponsonby St 43 G7
Porter St 42 A1
Portland Pl 42 D1
Portwood Cl 43 G5
Pownall Sq 42 C3
Pownall St 42 C5
Prescot Rd 43 J2
Prescot St 43 F3
Preston St 42 C3
Price St 42 C5
Primrose Hill 42 C3
Prince Albert Ms 42 D6
Prince Edwin St 42 D1
Princes Av 43 F6
Princes Gdns 42 B2
Princes Par 42 A3
Princes Pk 43 G7
Princes Rd 43 F6
Princes St 42 C3
Prince William St 42 D7
Prospect St 43 F3
Providence Cres 42 D7
Prussia St 42 B3
Pudsey St 42 D3
Pumpfields Rd 42 B2
Pythian Cl 43 G2
Pythian St 43 F2

Q
Queen Anne St 42 D2
Queensland St 43 G4
Queens Sq 42 D3
Queens Wf 42 C6
Quorn St 43 H3

R
Rachel St 42 D1
Radstock Rd 43 J2
Raffles St 42 D6
Rainford Gdns 42 C4
Rainford Sq 42 C4
Ranelagh St 42 D4
Raven Cl 43 F2
Raymond Pl 42 C1
Red Cross St 42 B4
Redgrave St 43 H3
Redmires Cl 43 H5
Red Rock St 43 G1
Regent St 42 A1
Renfrew St 43 G3
Renshaw St 42 D4
Reservoir St 43 F1
Reynolds Cl 43 G1
Rialto Cl 43 F6
Rice St 42 E5
Richardson St 43 J6
Richmond Row 42 D2
Richmond St 42 C4
Ridley Rd 43 H2
Rigby St 42 B3
Ringo Starr Dr 43 H2
Ritson St 43 G7
River Avon St 43 H6
Roberts St 42 A2
Roderick St 42 E2
Rodney St 42 E5
Roe St 42 D3
Rokeby Cl 42 E2
Rokeby St 42 E2
Rokesmith Av 43 H5
Romer Rd 43 H2
Romilly St 43 G2
Roscastle Cl 43 G2
Roscoe La 42 D5
Roscoe St 42 E5
Roscommon St 42 D1
Roseberry St 43 F6
Rose Hill 42 D2
Rosemary Cl 43 G4
Rose Pl 42 D2
Rothsay Cl 42 E1
Rothwell St 43 G1
Royal Mail St 42 D4
Royston St 43 G4
Rufford Rd 43 J2
Rumford Pl 42 B3
Rumford St 42 B3
Rupert Dr 43 F2
Russel St 42 E3
Ryedale Cl 43 G6

S
St. Andrew St 42 E4
St. Anne St 42 D2
St. Bride St 43 F5
St. James Pl 42 D6
St. James Rd 42 E6
St. James St 42 D6
St. John's La 42 D3
St. Josephs Cres 42 D2
St. Martins Ms 42 D1
St. Michaels Gro 43 H1
St. Nicholas Pl 42 A4

St. Stephen's Pl 42 C2
Salisbury Rd 43 J6
Salisbury St 42 E1
Salthouse Quay 42 B5
Saltney St 42 A1
Sandhead St 43 J5
Sandino St 42 E7
Sandon St 43 F5
Saxon Cl 43 G1
Saxony Rd 43 G3
Scholar St 43 J6
Schomberg St 43 G2
School La 42 C4
Scotland Rd 42 D2
Seaport Rd 43 G7
Seddon St 42 C5
Seel St 42 C4
Sefton Pk Rd 43 H7
Sefton St 42 C6
Selborne Cl 43 F6
Selborne St 43 F6
Selsey Cl 43 H5
Severs St 43 G1
Seymour St 42 E3
Shakespeare Cl 43 G1
Shallcross Pl 43 G1
Shaws All 42 C5
Shaw St 43 E1
Sheil Rd 43 H1
Shenstone St 43 G4
Shepherd's Fold Cl 43 G7
Sherwood St 42 B1
Shimmin St 43 G4
Sidney Pl 43 G4
Silkstone Cl 43 H5
Simpson St 42 C6
Sim St 42 E2
Sirdar Cl 43 H5
Sir Thomas St 42 C3
Skelhorne St 42 D4
Slater St 42 D5
Smithdown La 43 F4
Smithdown Rd 43 H6
Smithfield St 42 C3
Soho Pl 42 E2
Soho St 42 E2
Solomon St 43 H3
Solway St E 43 H6
Solway St W 43 G6
South Chester St 43 G7
Southern Cres 42 D7
South Ferry Quay 42 C7
South Hunter St 42 E5
South John St 42 C4
Sparling St 42 C6
Spekeland Rd 43 H5
Spencer St 43 F1
Spindle Cl 43 F1
Spofforth Rd 43 J5
Sprainger St 42 B1
Springfield 42 D2
Squires St 43 G4
Stafford St 42 E3
Stamford St 43 H3
Standish St 42 C3
Stanhope St 42 D7
Stanier Way 43 H4
Stanley St 42 C3
Star St 42 D7
Steinberg Ct 42 B1
Sterndale Cl 43 H5
Stockdale Cl 42 C2
Stone St 42 B1
Stowell St 42 E5
Strada Way 43 E2
Strand, The 42 B4

Strand St 42 B4
Strathmore Rd 43 H1
Strauss Cl 43 H7
Suffolk St 42 D5
Sugnall St 43 E5
Summer Seat 42 C1
Surrey St 42 C5
Sutcliffe St 43 H2
Sweeting St 42 B4
Swindale Cl 43 G6
Swiss Rd 43 J2

T
Tabley St 42 C6
Tace Cl 43 F6
Tagus St 43 G7
Tamar Cl 43 F1
Tarleton St 42 C4
Tatlock St 42 C1
Tavy Rd 43 F1
Teck St 43 G3
Teign Cl 43 F1
Tempest Hey 42 B3
Temple Ct 42 C4
Temple La 42 C3
Temple St 42 C3
Tenterden St 42 C1
Thackeray Pl 43 F7
Thames St 43 G7
Thomas St Way 42 C5
Thorburn St 43 H4
Thornes Rd 43 G2
Tichbourne Way 43 F2
Tideswell Cl 43 H5
Timpron St 43 H5
Titchfield St 42 C1
Tithebarn St 42 B3
Tobin Cl 42 C1
Toft St 43 H3
Tom Mann Cl 42 D3
Tordelow Cl 43 F1
Tower Gdns 42 B4
Trafalgar Way 43 F2
Trowbridge St 42 E4
Trueman St 42 C3
Tudor St N 43 H2
Tudor St S 43 H2
Tulloch St 43 G2
Tunnel Rd 43 H5
Tunstall St 43 J6
Tweed Cl 43 H1
Twomey Cl 42 C1

U
Underley St 43 J6
Union Ct 42 C4
Union St 42 B3
Upper Baker St 43 G2
Upper Beau St 42 D1
Upper Bute St 42 E1
Upper Duke St 42 D5
Upper Frederick St 42 C5
Upper Hampton St 43 F6
Upper Harrington St 42 D7
Upper Hill St 43 E7
Upper Hope Pl 43 E5
Upper Mann St 42 D7
Upper Mason St 43 G4
Upper Newington 42 D4
Upper Parliament St 42 D6
Upper Pitt St 42 D6
Upper Pownall St 42 C5
Upper Stanhope St 43 E6
Upper Warwick St 43 E7
Upper William St 42 B1
Uxbridge St 43 H5

V
Vandries St 42 A1
Vandyke St 43 H6
Vauxhall Rd 42 C2
Vernon St 42 C3
Verulam Cl 43 G6
Victoria St 42 C4
Village St 43 E1
Vincent Ct 42 D5
Vining St 43 F7
Virgil St 42 D1
Voelas St 43 G7
Vronhill Cl 43 G7
Vulcan St 42 A1

W
Wainwright Cl 43 H5
Wakefield St 42 D2
Waldron Cl 42 C2
Walker St 43 F2
Wall St 42 C1
Walsh Cl 42 C5
Wapping 42 C5
Ward St 42 D3
Warwick St 42 E7
Waterloo Quay 42 A2
Water St 42 B4
Watkinson St 42 C6
Watmough St 42 E1
Wavertree Bvd 43 K4
Wavertree Rd 43 G4
Webb Cl 43 H4
Webb St 43 H6
Webster Rd 43 J6
Webster St 42 C3
Wedgewood St 43 H3
Wendell St 43 H6
Wentworth Dr 43 F1
West Derby Rd 43 G2
West Derby St 43 F3
Westmorland Dr 42 C2
Whitcroft Rd 43 J2
Whitechapel 42 C4
Whitefield Rd 43 G1
Whitefield Way 43 G1
White Rock Ct 43 G1
White Rock St 43 G1
Whithorn St 43 J5
Whitland Rd 43 J1
Whitley St 42 B1
Whittier St 43 H6
Wightman St 43 G2
Wilde St 42 D3
Wilfer Cl 43 H5
William Brown St 42 D3
William Henry St 42 E2
Williamson St 42 C4
Wimpole St 43 H3
Windsor St 43 E6
Windsor Vw 43 H6
Winifred St 43 H4
Winter St 43 F2
Wolstenholme Sq 42 D5
Woodside St 43 H4
Wood St 42 D4
Wordsworth St 43 H6
Wrayburn Cl 43 H5
Wrenbury St 43 H3
Wynnstay St 43 G7

Y
Yanwath St 43 H6
York St 42 C5

London street index

A
Abbey Orchard St SW1 44 D6
Abingdon St SW1 44 E6
Achilles Way W1 44 A5
Adam & Eve Ct W1 44 C2
Adams Row W1 44 A4
Adam St WC2 45 E4
Addington St SE1 45 F6
Addle Hill EC4 45 H3
Adelaide St WC2 44 E4
Adeline Pl WC1 44 D2
Adelphi Ter WC2 45 E4
Agar St WC2 44 E4
Air St W1 44 C4
Alaska St SE1 45 G5
Albany W1 44 C4
Albany Ctyd W1 44 C4

Albemarle St W1 44 B4
Albemarle Way EC1 45 H1
Albert Barnes Ho SE1 45 J7
Albion Pl EC1 45 H1
Albion Way EC1 45 J2
Aldburgh Ms W1 44 A2
Aldermanbury EC2 45 J2
Aldermanbury Sq EC2 45 J2
Aldersgate St EC1 45 J2
Aldford St W1 44 A4
Aldwych WC2 45 F3
Alfred Ms W1 44 D1
Alfred Pl WC1 44 D1
Allington St SW1 44 C7
All Souls Pl W1 44 B1
Ambassador's Ct SW1 44 C5
Ambrosden Av SW1 44 C7
Amen Cor EC4 45 H3

Amen Ct EC4 45 H2
America St SE1 45 J5
Andrew Borde St WC2 44 D2
Andrewes Ho EC2 45 J2
Andrews Crosse WC2 45 G3
Angel Ct SW1 44 C5
Angel Ct EC1 45 J2
Apothecary St EC4 45 H3
Apple Tree Yd SW1 44 C4
Apsley Way W1 44 A5
Aquinas St SE1 45 G4
Archer St W1 44 D3
Arches, The WC2 45 E4
Archibald Ms W1 44 A4
Arch St SE1 45 J7
Argyll St W1 44 C2
Aria Ho WC2 45 E2
Arlington St SW1 44 C4

Arne St WC2 45 E3
Arneway St SW1 44 D7
Arrol Ho SE1 45 J7
Artillery Mans SW1 44 D6
Artillery Pl SW1 44 D7
Artillery Row SW1 44 D7
Arundel Gt Ct WC2 45 F3
Arundel St WC2 45 F3
Ashenden SE17 45 J7
Ashentree Ct EC4 45 G3
Ashland Pl W1 44 A1
Ashley Gdns SW1 44 C7
Ashley Pl SW1 44 C7
Astbury Ho SE11 45 G7
Audley Sq W1 44 A4
Austral St SE11 45 H7
Ave Maria La EC4 45 H3
Avery Row W1 44 B3

Avonmouth St SE1 45 J6
Avon Pl SE1 45 J6
Aybrook St W1 44 A2
Aylesbury St EC1 45 H1
Ayres St SE1 45 J5

B
Babmaes St SW1 44 D4
Back Hill EC1 45 G1
Bainbridge St WC1 44 D2
Baker's Ms W1 44 A2
Baker's Row EC1 45 G1
Baker's Yd EC1 45 G1
Balderton St W1 44 A3
Baldwin's Gdns EC1 45 G1
Balfour Ms W1 44 A4
Balfour Pl W1 44 A4
Baltic St E EC1 45 J1

Baltic St W EC1 45 J1
Banbury Ct WC2 44 E3
Bank End SE1 45 J4
Banks Ho SE1 45 J7
Bankside SE1 45 J4
Bankside Lofts SE1 45 H4
Banner St EC1 45 J1
Barbican EC2 45 J2
Barbican, The EC2 45 J1
Barbon Cl WC1 45 E1
Barge Ho St SE1 45 G4
Barkham Ter SE1 45 H6
Barley Mow Pas EC1 45 H2
Barlow Pl W1 44 B4
Barnard's Inn EC1 45 G2
Barons Pl SE1 45 G6
Barrett St W1 44 A3
Barter St WC1 45 E2

Bartholomew Cl EC1 45 J2
Bartholomew Pl EC1 45 J2
Bartlett Ct EC4 45 G2
Bartletts Pas EC4 45 G2
Barton St SW1 44 E6
Bastion Highwalk EC2 45 J2
Bateman's Bldgs W1 44 D3
Bateman St W1 44 D3
Bath Ct EC1 45 G1
Bath Ter SE1 45 J7
Bayley St WC1 44 D2
Baylis Rd SE1 45 G6
Beak St W1 44 C3
Bear All EC4 45 H2
Bear Gdns SE1 45 J4
Bear La SE1 45 H4
Bear St WC2 44 D3
Beauchamp St EC1 45 G2
Beaumont Ms W1 44 A1
Beaumont St W1 44 A1
Bedford Av WC1 44 D2
Bedfordbury WC2 44 E3
Bedford Ct WC2 44 E4
Bedford Pl WC1 44 E1
Bedford Row WC1 45 F1
Bedford Sq WC1 44 D2
Bedford St WC2 44 E3
Bedford Way WC1 44 D1
Bedlam Ms SE11 45 G7
Beech St EC2 45 J1
Beeston Pl SW1 44 B7
Belgrave Ms N SW1 44 A6
Belgrave Ms S SW1 44 A6
Belgrave Ms W SW1 44 A6
Belgrave Pl SW1 44 A6
Belgrave Sq SW1 44 A6
Belgrave Yd SW1 44 B7
Belgravia SW1 44 A7
Bell Wf La EC4 45 J4
Bell Yd WC2 45 G2
Belvedere Bldgs SE1 45 H6
Belvedere Pl SE1 45 H6
Belvedere Rd SE1 45 F5
Benjamin St EC1 45 H1
Bennet's Hill EC4 45 H3
Bennet St SW1 44 C4
Bennetts Yd SW1 44 D7
Bentinck Ms W1 44 A2
Bentinck St W1 44 A2
Berkeley Sq W1 44 B4
Berkeley St W1 44 B4
Bernard St WC1 44 E1
Berners Ms W1 44 C2
Berners Pl W1 44 C2
Berners St W1 44 C2
Berwick St W1 44 D3
Betterton St WC2 44 E3
Bingham Pl W1 44 A1
Binney St W1 44 A3
Birdcage Wk SW1 44 C6
Bird St W1 44 A3
Bishop's Ct EC4 45 H2
Bishop's Ct WC2 45 G2
Bishops Ter SE11 45 G7
Bittern St SE1 45 J6
Blackburne's Ms W1 44 A3
Blackfriars Br EC4 45 H3
Blackfriars Br SE1 45 H3
Blackfriars Ct EC4 45 H3
Black Friars La EC4 45 H3
Blackfriars Pas EC4 45 H3
Blackfriars Rd SE1 45 H6
Bleeding Heart Yd EC1 45 G2
Blenheim St W1 44 B3
Bloomfield Pl W1 44 B3
Bloomsbury WC1 44 D2
Bloomsbury Ct WC1 45 E2
Bloomsbury Pl WC1 45 E1
Bloomsbury Sq WC1 45 E2
Bloomsbury St WC1 44 D2
Bloomsbury Way WC1 44 E2
Blore Ct W1 44 D3
Blue Ball Yd SW1 44 C5
Bolsover St W1 44 B1
Bolt Ct EC4 45 G3
Bolton St W1 44 B4
Book Ms WC2 44 D3
Booth La EC4 45 J3
Booth's Pl W1 44 C2
Borough, The SE1 45 J6
Borough High St SE1 45 J6
Borough Rd SE1 45 H6
Borough Sq SE1 45 J6
Boscobel Pl SW1 44 A7
Boswell Ct WC1 45 E1
Boswell St WC1 45 E1
Boundary Row SE1 45 H5
Bourchier St W1 44 D3
Bourdon Pl W1 44 B3
Bourdon St W1 44 B3
Bourlet Cl W1 44 C2
Bourne Est EC1 45 G1
Bouverie St EC4 45 G3
Bow Chyd EC4 45 J3
Bow La EC4 45 J3
Bow St WC2 45 E3
Boyce St SE1 45 F5
Boyfield St SE1 45 H6
Boyle St W1 44 C3
Brackley St EC1 45 J1
Brad St SE1 45 G5
Bread St EC4 45 J3
Bream's Bldgs EC4 45 G2
Bressenden Pl SW1 44 B6
Brewer's Grn SW1 44 D6
Brewers Hall Gdns EC2 45 J2
Brewer St W1 44 C3
Briant Est SE1 45 G7
Briant Ho SE1 45 F7
Brick Ct EC4 45 G3
Brick St W1 44 B5
Bride Ct EC4 45 H3
Bride La EC4 45 H3
Bridewell Pl EC4 45 H3
Bridford Ms W1 44 B1
Bridge Pl SW1 44 B7
Bridge St SW1 44 E6
Bridgewater Sq EC2 45 J1
Bridgewater St EC2 45 J1
Bridle La W1 44 C3
Brinton Wk SE1 45 H5
Briset St EC1 45 H1
Britton St EC1 45 H1
Broadbent St W1 44 B3
Broad Ct WC2 45 E3
Broad Sanctuary SW1 44 D6
Broadstone Pl W1 44 A2
Broad Wk W1 44 A4
Broadwall SE1 45 G4
Broadway SW1 44 D6
Broadwick St W1 44 C3
Broad Yd EC1 45 H1
Brockham St SE1 45 J6
Broken Wf EC4 45 J3
Bromley Pl W1 44 C1
Brook Dr SE11 45 G7
Brooke's Ct EC1 45 G1
Brookes Mkt EC1 45 G1
Brooke St EC1 45 G2
Brook's Ms W1 44 B3
Brook St W1 44 A3
Brown Hart Gdns W1 44 A3
Browning Ms W1 44 B2
Brownlow Ms WC1 45 F1
Brownlow St WC1 45 F2
Brunswick Sq WC1 45 E1
Bruton La W1 44 B4
Bruton Pl W1 44 B4
Bruton St W1 44 B4
Brydges Pl WC2 44 E4
Buckingham Arc WC2 45 E4
Buckingham Gate SW1 44 C6
Buckingham Ms SW1 44 C6
Buckingham Pl SW1 44 C6
Buckingham St WC2 45 E4
Buckley St SE1 45 G5
Bucknall St WC2 44 D2
Bull Inn Ct WC2 45 E4
Bulstrode Pl W1 44 A2
Bulstrode St W1 44 A2
Burdett St SE1 45 G6
Burgon St EC4 45 H3
Burleigh St WC2 45 F3
Burlington Arc W1 44 C4
Burlington Gdns W1 44 C4
Burrell St SE1 45 H4
Burrows Ms SE1 45 H5
Bury Pl WC1 44 E2
Bury St SW1 44 C4
Butler Pl SW1 44 D6
Byng Pl WC1 44 D1
Bywell Pl W1 44 C2

C

Cadogan La SW1 44 A7
Cahill St EC1 45 J1
Caleb St SE1 45 J5
Cambridge Circ WC2 44 D3
Candover St W1 44 C2
Cannon St EC4 45 J3
Canon Row SW1 44 E6
Canterbury Ho SE1 45 F6
Canvey St SE1 45 H4
Capener's Cl SW1 44 A6
Capper St WC1 44 C1
Carburton St W1 44 B1
Carey La EC2 45 J2
Carey St WC2 45 F3
Carlisle La SE1 45 F7
Carlisle Pl SW1 44 C7
Carlisle St W1 44 D3
Carlos Pl W1 44 A4
Carlton Gdns SW1 44 D5
Carlton Ho Ter SW1 44 D5
Carlton St SW1 44 D4
Carmelite St EC4 45 G3
Carnaby St W1 44 C3
Carpenter St W1 44 B4
Carrington St W1 44 B5
Carteret St SW1 44 D6
Carter La EC4 45 H3
Carthusian St EC1 45 J1
Carting La WC2 45 E4
Castle Baynard St EC4 45 H3
Castlebrook Cl SE11 45 H7
Castle La SW1 44 C6
Castle Yd SE1 45 H4
Cathedral Piazza SW1 44 C7
Cathedral Wk SW1 44 C6
Catherine Pl SW1 44 C6
Catherine St WC2 45 F3
Catherine Wheel Yd SW1 44 C5
Catton St WC1 45 F2
Cavendish Ms N W1 44 B1
Cavendish Ms S W1 44 B2
Cavendish Pl W1 44 B2
Cavendish Sq W1 44 B2
Caxton St SW1 44 C6
Cecil Ct WC2 44 D4
Centaur St SE1 45 F6
Centrepoint WC1 44 D2
Chadwick St SW1 44 D7
Chancel St SE1 45 H4
Chancery La WC2 45 G2
Chandos Pl WC2 44 E4
Chandos St W1 44 B2
Chapel Pl W1 44 B3
Chapel St SW1 44 A6
Chaplin Cl SE1 45 G5
Chapone Pl W1 44 D3
Chapter Ho Ct EC4 45 J3
Charing Cross SW1 44 D4
Charing Cross Rd WC2 44 D2
Charles II St SW1 44 D4
Charles St W1 44 B4
Charlotte Ms W1 44 C1
Charlotte Pl W1 44 C2
Charlotte St W1 44 C1
Charterhouse, The EC1 45 H1
Charterhouse Bldgs EC1 45 H1
Charterhouse Ms EC1 45 H1
Charterhouse Sq EC1 45 H1
Charterhouse St EC1 45 G2
Cheapside EC2 45 J3
Chenies Ms WC1 44 D1
Chenies St WC1 44 D1
Chequer St EC1 45 J1
Cherry Tree Wk EC1 45 J1
Chesham Cl SW1 44 A7
Chesham Ms SW1 44 A6
Chesham Pl SW1 44 A7
Chesham St SW1 44 A7
Cheshire Ct EC4 45 G3
Chester Cl SW1 44 A6
Chesterfield Gdns W1 44 B4
Chesterfield Hill W1 44 B4
Chesterfield St W1 44 B4
Chester Ms SW1 44 B6
Chester Sq SW1 44 B7
Chester Sq Ms SW1 44 B7
Chester St SW1 44 A6
Chicheley St SE1 45 F5
Chichester Rents WC2 45 G2
Chiltern St W1 44 A1
Ching Ct WC2 44 E3
Chiswell St EC1 45 J1
Chitty St W1 44 C1
Christ Ch Pas EC1 45 H2
Church Entry EC4 45 H3
Church Pl SW1 44 C4
Churchyard Row SE11 45 H7
Clare Mkt WC2 45 F3
Clarges Ms W1 44 B4
Clarges St W1 44 B4
Clarke's Ms W1 44 A1
Clement's Inn WC2 45 F3
Clement's Inn Pas WC2 45 F3
Clennam St SE1 45 J5
Clerkenwell EC1 45 H1
Clerkenwell Grn EC1 45 G1
Clerkenwell Rd EC1 45 G1
Cleveland Ms W1 44 C1
Cleveland Pl SW1 44 C4
Cleveland Row SW1 44 C5
Cleveland St W1 44 C1
Clifford's Inn Pas EC4 45 G3
Clifford St W1 44 C4
Clink St SE1 45 J4
Clipstone Ms W1 44 C1
Clipstone St W1 44 B1
Cliveden Pl SW1 44 A7
Cloak La EC4 45 J3
Cloth Ct EC1 45 H2
Cloth Fair EC1 45 H2
Cloth St EC1 45 J1
Coach & Horses Yd W1 44 B3
Coburg Cl SW1 44 C7
Cock La EC1 45 H2
Cockpit Steps SW1 44 D6
Cockpit Yd WC1 45 F1
Cockspur Ct SW1 44 D4
Cockspur St SW1 44 D4
Coin St SE1 45 G4
Cole St SE1 45 J6
Coley St WC1 45 F1
College Hill EC4 45 J3
College Ms SW1 44 E6
College St EC4 45 J3
Collinson St SE1 45 J6
Collinson Wk SE1 45 J6
Colnbrook St SE1 45 H7
Colombo St SE1 45 H5
Colonnade WC1 44 E1
Colville Pl W1 44 C2
Computer Pass EC2 45 J2
Concert Hall App SE1 45 F5
Conduit Ct WC2 44 E3
Conduit St W1 44 B3
Cons St SE1 45 G5
Constitution Hill SW1 44 B5
Conway Ms W1 44 C1
Conway St W1 44 C1
Cooper Cl SE1 45 G6
Copeland Ho SE11 45 F7
Copperfield St SE1 45 H5
Coptic St WC1 44 E2
Coral St SE1 45 G6
Coram St WC1 44 E1
Cork St W1 44 C4
Cork St Ms W1 44 C4
Corner Ho St WC2 44 E4
Cornwall Rd SE1 45 G4
Cosmo Pl WC1 45 E1
Cosser St SE1 45 G6
Cottesloe Ms SE1 45 G6
County St SE1 45 J7
Covent Gdn WC2 45 E3
Covent Gdn Mkt WC2 45 E3
Coventry St W1 44 D4
Cowcross St EC1 45 H1
Cowley St SW1 44 E6
Craigs Ct SW1 44 E4
Cramer St W1 44 A2
Cranbourn St WC2 44 D3
Crane Ct EC4 45 G3
Cranfield Row SE1 45 G6
Craven Pas WC2 44 E4
Craven St WC2 44 E4
Crawford Pas EC1 45 G1
Creed La EC4 45 H3
Crescent Row EC1 45 J1
Cripplegate St EC2 45 J1
Cromwell Twr EC2 45 J1
Cross Keys Cl W1 44 A2
Cross Keys Sq EC1 45 J2
Crown Ct EC2 45 J3
Crown Ct WC2 45 E3
Crown Office Row EC4 45 G3
Crown Pas SW1 44 C5
Cubitts Yd WC2 45 E3
Cuddington SE17 45 J7
Culross St W1 44 A4
Cursitor St EC4 45 G2
Curzon Gate W1 44 A5
Curzon Sq W1 44 A5
Curzon St W1 44 A5
Cut, The SE1 45 G5
Cypress Pl W1 44 C1

D

Dacre St SW1 44 D6
Dane St WC1 45 F2
Dansey Pl W1 44 D3
Dante Pl SE11 45 H7
Dante Rd SE11 45 H7
D'Arblay St W1 44 C3
Dartmouth St SW1 44 D6
Davidge St SE1 45 H6
Davies Ms W1 44 B3
Davies St W1 44 B3
Deacon Way SE17 45 J7
Dean Bradley St SW1 44 E7
Deanery Ms W1 44 A4
Deanery St W1 44 A4
Dean Farrar St SW1 44 D6
Dean Ryle St SW1 44 E7
Deans Ct EC4 45 H3
Deans Ms W1 44 B2
Dean Stanley St SW1 44 E7
Dean St W1 44 D2
Dean's Yd SW1 44 D6
Dean Trench St SW1 44 E7
Denman St W1 44 D4
Denmark Pl WC2 44 D2
Denmark St WC2 44 D3
Derby Gate SW1 44 E5
Derby St W1 44 A5
Dering St W1 44 B3
Devereux Ct WC2 45 G3
Devonshire Cl W1 44 B1
Devonshire Ms N W1 44 B1
Devonshire Ms S W1 44 B1
Devonshire Ms W W1 44 B1
Devonshire Pl W1 44 A1
Devonshire Pl Ms W1 44 A1
Devonshire Row Ms W1 44 B1
Devonshire St W1 44 A1
De Walden St W1 44 A2
Diadem Ct W1 44 D3
Dickens Ms EC1 45 H1
Dickens Sq SE1 45 J6
Disney Pl SE1 45 J5
Disney St SE1 45 J5
Distaff La EC4 45 J3
Doby Ct EC4 45 J3
Dodson St SE1 45 G6
Dolben St SE1 45 H5
Dombey St WC1 45 F1
Doon St SE1 45 G5
Dorrington St EC1 45 G1
Dorrit St SE1 45 J5
Dorset Bldgs EC4 45 H3
Dorset Ms SW1 44 B6
Dorset Ri EC4 45 H3
Doughty Ms WC1 45 F1
Dover St W1 44 B4
Dover Yd W1 44 B4
Downing St SW1 44 E5
Down St W1 44 B5
Down St Ms W1 44 B5
Doyce St SE1 45 J5
D'Oyley St SW1 44 A7
Drake St WC1 45 F2
Draper Ho SE1 45 H7
Drury La WC2 45 E3
Dryden St WC2 45 E3
Duchess Ms W1 44 B2
Duchess St W1 44 B2
Duchy Pl SE1 45 G4
Duchy St SE1 45 G4
Duck La W1 44 D3
Dufferin St EC1 45 J1
Dufour's Pl W1 44 C3
Dugard Way SE11 45 H7
Duke of Wellington Pl SW1 44 A5
Duke of York St SW1 44 C4
Duke's Ms W1 44 A2
Duke St SW1 44 C4
Duke St W1 44 A2
Duke's Yd W1 44 A3
Duncannon St WC2 44 E4
Dunns Pas WC1 45 E2
Dunstable Ms W1 44 A1
Durham Ho St WC2 45 E4
Dyer's Bldgs EC1 45 G2
Dyott St WC1 44 E2

E

Eagle Ct EC1 45 H1
Eagle Pl SW1 44 C4
Eagle St WC1 45 F2
Earlham St WC2 44 D3
Earnshaw St WC2 44 D2
Easley's Ms W1 44 A2
Eastcastle St W1 44 C2
East Harding St EC4 45 G2
East Pas EC1 45 H1
East Poultry Av EC1 45 H2
Eaton Gate SW1 44 A7
Eaton La SW1 44 B7
Eaton Ms N SW1 44 A7
Eaton Ms S SW1 44 A7
Eaton Ms W SW1 44 A7
Eaton Pl SW1 44 A7
Eaton Row SW1 44 B6
Eaton Sq SW1 44 B6
Eaton Ter SW1 44 A7
Eaton Ter Ms SW1 44 A7
Ebury Ms SW1 44 A7
Ebury Ms E SW1 44 B7
Ebury St SW1 44 B7
Eccleston Br SW1 44 B7
Eccleston Ms SW1 44 A7
Eccleston Pl SW1 44 B7
Eccleston St SW1 44 B7
Edwards Ms W1 44 A3
Elba Pl SE17 45 J7
Elephant & Castle SE1 45 H7
Elephant Rd SE17 45 J7
Elizabeth Ct SW1 44 D7
Elizabeth St SW1 44 A7
Ellington Ho SE1 45 J6
Elliotts Row SE11 45 H7
Elm Ct EC4 45 G3
Elm St WC1 45 F1
Elverton St SW1 44 D7
Ely Ct EC1 45 G2
Ely Pl EC1 45 G2
Embankment Pier WC2 45 F4
Embankment Pl WC2 45 E4
Emerald St WC1 45 F1
Emerson St SE1 45 J4
Emery Hill St SW1 44 C7
Emery St SE1 45 G6
Endell St WC2 44 E2
Errol St EC1 45 J1
Essex Ct EC4 45 G3
Essex St WC2 45 G3
Euston Rd NW1 44 B1
Evelyn Yd W1 44 D2
Ewer St SE1 45 J5
Excel Ct WC2 44 D4
Exchange Ct WC2 45 E4
Exeter St WC2 45 E3
Exton St SE1 45 G5
Eyre St Hill EC1 45 G1

F

Falconberg Ct W1 44 D2
Falconberg Ms W1 44 D2
Falcon Ct EC4 45 G3
Falmouth Rd SE1 45 J6
Fann St EC1 45 J1
Fann St EC2 45 J1
Fareham St W1 44 D2
Farm St W1 44 B4
Farnham Pl SE1 45 H5
Farringdon La EC1 45 G1
Farringdon St EC4 45 H2
Faulkner's All EC1 45 H1
Ferrybridge Ho SE11 45 F7
Fetter La EC4 45 G3
Field Ct WC1 45 F2
Fisher St WC1 45 E2
Fitzalan St SE11 45 G7
Fitzhardinge St W1 44 A2
Fitzmaurice Pl W1 44 B4
Fitzroy Ct W1 44 C1
Fitzroy Ms W1 44 C1
Fitzroy Sq W1 44 C1
Fitzroy St W1 44 C1
Fives Ct SE11 45 H7
Flaxman Ct W1 44 D3
Fleet St EC4 45 G3
Flitcroft St WC2 44 D2
Floral St WC2 44 E3
Florin Ct EC1 45 J1
Foley St W1 44 C2
Fore St EC2 45 J2
Fortune St EC1 45 J1
Forum Magnum Sq SE1 45 F5
Foster La EC2 45 J2
Foubert's Pl W1 44 C3
Fountain Ct EC4 45 G3
Fountain Sq SW1 44 B7
Fox & Knot St EC1 45 H1
Francis St SW1 44 C7
Frazier St SE1 45 G6
Friars Cl SE1 45 H5
Friar St EC4 45 H3
Friary Ct SW1 44 C5
Friday St EC4 45 J3
Frith St W1 44 D3
Fulwood Pl WC1 45 F2
Furnival St EC4 45 G2
Fynes St SW1 44 D7

G

Gabriel's Wf SE1 45 G4
Gage St WC1 45 E1
Galen Pl WC1 45 E2
Gambia St SE1 45 H5
Ganton St W1 44 C3
Garbutt Pl W1 44 A1
Garden Row SE1 45 H7
Gardners La EC4 45 J3
Garlick Hill EC4 45 J3
Garrick St WC2 44 E3
Garrick Yd WC2 44 E3
Gate Ho Sq SE1 45 J4
Gate St WC2 45 F2
Gaunt St SE1 45 H6
Gayfere St SW1 44 E7
Gaywood Est SE1 45 H7
Gaywood St SE1 45 H7
Gees Ct W1 44 A3
George Ct WC2 45 E4
George Mathers Rd SE11 45 H7
George Yd W1 44 A3
Geraldine St SE11 45 H7
Gerald Ms SW1 44 A7
Gerald Rd SW1 44 A7
Gerrard Pl W1 44 D3

Gerrard St W1   44 D3
Gerridge St SE1   45 G6
Gilbert Pl WC1   44 E2
Gilbert St W1   44 A3
Gildea St W1   44 B2
Gillingham Row SW1   44 C7
Gillingham St SW1   44 B7
Giltspur St EC1   45 H2
Gladstone St SE1   45 H6
Glasshill St SE1   45 H5
Glasshouse St W1   44 C4
Glasshouse Yd EC1   45 J1
Globe St SE1   45 J6
Globe Yd W1   44 B3
Godliman St EC4   45 J3
Golden Jubilee Br SE1   45 F5
Golden Jubilee Br
  WC2   45 E4
Golden La EC1   45 J1
Golden La East EC1   45 J1
Golden Sq W1   44 C3
Goodge Pl W1   44 C2
Goodge St W1   44 C2
Goodwins Ct WC2   44 E3
Gordon Sq W1   44 D1
Gosfield St W1   44 C1
Goslett Yd WC2   44 D3
Goswell Rd EC1   45 J1
Gough Sq EC4   45 G2
Gower Ms WC1   44 D2
Grafton Ms W1   44 C1
Grafton St W1   44 B4
Grafton Way W1   44 C1
Grafton Way WC1   44 C1
Granby Pl SE1   45 G6
Grand Av EC1   45 H1
Grange Ct WC2   45 F3
Grantham Pl W1   44 B5
Granville Pl W1   44 A3
Grape St WC2   44 E2
Gray's Inn WC1   45 F1
Gray's Inn Pl WC1   45 F2
Gray's Inn Sq WC1   45 G1
Gray St SE1   45 G6
Gray's Yd W1   44 A3
Great Arthur Ho EC1   45 J1
Great Castle St W1   44 B2
Great Chapel St W1   44 D2
Great Coll St SW1   44 E6
Great Dover St SE1   45 J6
Great George St SW1   44 D6
Great Guildford St
  SE1   45 J4
Great James St WC1   45 F1
Great Marlborough St
  W1   44 C3
Great New St EC4   45 G2
Great Ormond St
  WC1   45 E1
Great Peter St SW1   44 D7
Great Portland St W1   44 B1
Great Pulteney St W1   44 C3
Great Queen St WC2   45 E3
Great Russell St WC1   44 D2
Great St. Thomas
  Apostle EC4   45 J3
Great Scotland Yd
  SW1   44 E5
Great Smith St SW1   44 D6
Great Suffolk St SE1   45 H5
Great Sutton St EC1   45 H1
Great Titchfield St W1   44 C2
Great Trinity La EC4   45 J3
Great Turnstile WC1   45 F2
Great Windmill St W1   44 D3
Greek Ct W1   44 D3
Greek St W1   44 D3
Green Arbour Ct EC1   45 H2
Greencoat Pl SW1   44 C7
Greencoat Row SW1   44 C7
Greenham Cl SE1   45 G6
Greenhill's Rents EC1   45 H1
Green's Ct W1   44 D3
Greenwell St W1   44 B1
Greet St SE1   45 G5
Grenville St WC1   45 E1
Gresham St EC2   45 J2
Gresse St W1   44 D2
Greville St EC1   45 G2
Greycoat Pl SW1   44 D7
Greycoat St SW1   44 D7
Greyfriars Pas EC1   45 H2
Greystoke Pl EC4   45 G2
Grindal St SE1   45 G6
Groom Pl SW1   44 A6
Grosvenor Cotts SW1   44 A7
Grosvenor Cres SW1   44 A6
Grosvenor Cres Ms
  SW1   44 A6
Grosvenor Est SW1   44 D7
Grosvenor Gdns SW1   44 B6
Grosvenor Gdns Ms E
  SW1   44 B6

Grosvenor Gdns Ms N
  SW1   44 B7
Grosvenor Gdns Ms S
  SW1   44 B7
Grosvenor Hill W1   44 B3
Grosvenor Pl SW1   44 A6
Grosvenor Sq W1   44 A3
Grosvenor St W1   44 B3
Grotto Pas W1   44 A1
Groveland Ct EC4   45 J3
Guildhall Yd EC2   45 J2
Guildhouse St SW1   44 C7
Guilford Pl WC1   45 F1
Guilford St WC1   45 E1
Gunpowder Sq EC4   45 G2
Gutter La EC2   45 J2

H

Half Moon Ct EC1   45 J2
Half Moon St W1   44 B4
Halkin Arc SW1   44 A6
Halkin Ms SW1   44 A6
Halkin Pl SW1   44 A6
Halkin St SW1   44 A6
Hallam Ms W1   44 B1
Hallam St W1   44 B1
Hamilton Ms W1   44 C1
Hamilton Pl W1   44 A5
Ham Yd W1   44 D3
Hand Ct WC1   45 F2
Hanging Sword All
  EC4   45 G3
Hanover Pl WC2   45 E3
Hanover Sq W1   44 B3
Hanover St W1   44 B3
Hanson St W1   44 C1
Hanway Pl W1   44 D2
Hanway St W1   44 D2
Hare Ct EC4   45 G3
Hare Pl EC4   45 G3
Harewood Pl W1   44 B3
Harley Pl W1   44 B2
Harley St W1   44 B2
Harmsworth Ms SE11   45 H7
Harp All EC4   45 H2
Harper Rd SE1   45 J6
Harpur Ms WC1   45 F1
Harpur St WC1   45 F1
Hat & Mitre Ct EC1   45 H1
Hatfields SE1   45 G4
Hatton Gdn EC1   45 G1
Hatton Pl EC1   45 G1
Hatton Wall EC1   45 G1
Haunch of Venison Yd
  W1   44 B3
Hay Hill W1   44 B4
Hayles St SE11   45 H7
Haymarket SW1   44 D4
Haymarket Arc SW1   44 D4
Hayne St EC1   45 H1
Hay's Ms W1   44 B4
Hayward's Pl EC1   45 H1
Headfort Pl SW1   44 A6
Heddon St W1   44 C3
Hedger St SE11   45 H7
Hen & Chicken Ct
  EC4   45 G3
Henrietta Pl W1   44 B3
Henrietta St WC2   45 E3
Herald's Pl SE11   45 H7
Herbal Hill EC1   45 G1
Hercules Rd SE1   45 F7
Herrick St SW1   44 D7
Hertford St W1   44 B4
High Holborn WC1   45 E2
High Timber St EC4   45 J3
Hills Pl W1   44 C3
Hill St W1   44 A4
Hind Ct EC4   45 G3
Hinde St W1   44 A2
Hindon Ct SW1   44 C7
Hobart Pl SW1   44 B6
Holborn WC2   45 F2
Holborn Circ EC1   45 G2
Holborn Pl WC1   45 F2
Holborn Viaduct EC1   45 G2
Holland St SE1   45 H4
Hollen St W1   44 D2
Holles St W1   44 B2
Holmes Ter SE1   45 G5
Holsworthy Sq WC1   45 F1
Holyoak Rd SE11   45 H7
Honey La EC2   45 J3
Hood Ct EC4   45 G3
Hop Gdns WC2   44 E4
Hopkins St W1   44 C3
Hopton's Gdns SE1   45 H4
Hopton St SE1   45 H4
Horse & Dolphin Yd
  W1   44 D3
Horseferry Rd SW1   44 D7
Horse Guards Av SW1   44 E5

Horse Guards Rd SW1   44 D5
Horsemongers Ms
  SE1   45 J6
Horse Ride SW1   44 D5
Hosier La EC1   45 H2
Houghton St WC2   45 F3
Howick Pl SW1   44 C7
Howland Ms E W1   44 C1
Howland St W1   44 C1
Hudson's Pl SW1   44 B7
Huggin Ct EC4   45 J3
Huggin Hill EC4   45 J3
Hulme Pl SE1   45 J6
Hungerford Br SE1   45 E4
Hungerford Br WC2   45 E4
Hungerford La WC2   44 E4
Huntley St WC1   44 C1
Hunt's Ct WC2   44 D4
Hutton St EC4   45 G3
Hyde Pk Cor W1   44 A5

I

India Pl WC2   45 F3
Ingestre Pl W1   44 C3
Ingram Cl SE11   45 F7
Inigo Pl WC2   45 E3
Inner Temple La EC4   45 G3
Invicta Plaza SE1   45 H4
Ireland Yd EC4   45 H3
Irving St WC2   44 D4
Isaac Way SE1   45 J5
Isabella St SE1   45 H5
Ivybridge La WC2   45 E4

J

Jacob's Well Ms W1   44 A2
James St W1   44 A2
James St WC2   45 E3
Jermyn St SW1   44 C4
Jerusalem Pas EC1   45 H1
Jervis Ct W1   44 B3
Joan St SE1   45 H5
Jockey's Flds WC1   45 F1
Johanna St SE1   45 G6
John Adam St WC2   45 E4
John Carpenter St
  EC4   45 H3
John Milton Pass EC2   45 J3
John Princes St W1   44 B2
John's Ms WC1   45 F1
John St WC1   45 F1
Jones St W1   44 B4
Jubilee Mkt Hall WC2   45 E3
Juxon St SE11   45 F7

K

Kean St WC2   45 F3
Keeley St WC2   45 F3
Kell St SE1   45 H6
Kemble St WC2   45 F3
Kemp's Ct W1   44 C3
Kendall Pl W1   44 A2
Kennet Wf La EC4   45 J3
Kennington Rd SE1   45 G6
Kennington Rd SE11   45 G7
Kenrick Pl W1   44 A1
Keppel Row SE1   45 J5
Keppel St WC1   44 D1
Keyworth Pl SE1   45 H6
Keyworth St SE1   45 H6
King Charles St SW1   44 D5
King Edward St EC1   45 J2
King Edward Wk SE1   45 G6
Kinghorn St EC1   45 J2
King James Ct SE1   45 H6
King James St SE1   45 H6
Kingly Ct W1   44 C3
Kingly St W1   44 C3
Kings Bench St SE1   45 H5
Kings Bench Wk EC4   45 G3
Kingscote St EC4   45 H3
King's Ms WC1   45 F1
Kings Pl SE1   45 J6
King's Reach Twr SE1   45 G4
King's Scholars' Pas
  SW1   44 C7
King St EC2   45 J3
King St SW1   44 C5
King St WC2   45 E3
Kingsway WC2   45 F2
Kinnerton St SW1   44 A6
Kirby St EC1   45 G1
Kirkman Pl W1   44 D2
Kirk St WC1   45 F1
Knightrider St EC4   45 J3

L

Lambeth SE1   45 F7
Lambeth Br SE1   45 E7
Lambeth Br SW1   45 E7
Lambeth Hill EC4   45 J3
Lambeth Palace Rd
  SE1   45 F7
Lambeth Pier SE1   45 E7

Lambeth Rd SE1   45 F7
Lambeth Rd SE11   45 F7
Lambeth Twrs SE11   45 G7
Lambeth Wk SE1   45 F7
Lambeth Wk SE11   45 F7
Lambs Conduit Pas
  WC1   45 F1
Lamb's Conduit St
  WC1   45 F1
Lamlash St SE11   45 H7
Lamp Office Ct WC1   45 F1
Lancashire Ct W1   44 B3
Lancaster Pl WC2   45 F3
Lancaster St SE1   45 H6
Lanesborough Pl
  SW1   44 A5
Langham Pl W1   44 B2
Langham St W1   44 B2
Langley Ct WC2   44 E3
Langley St WC2   44 E3
Lansdowne Row W1   44 B4
Lansdowne Ter WC1   45 E1
Lant St SE1   45 J5
Lauderdale Twr EC2   45 J1
Launcelot St SE1   45 G6
Lavington St SE1   45 H5
Lawrence La EC2   45 J3
Laystall St EC1   45 G1
Layton's Bldgs SE1   45 J5
Lazenby Ct WC2   44 E3
Leake St SE1   45 F5
Leather La EC1   45 G2
Lees Pl W1   44 A3
Leicester Ct WC2   44 D3
Leicester Pl WC2   44 D3
Leicester Sq WC2   44 D4
Leicester St WC2   44 D3
Leigh Hunt St SE1   45 J5
Leigh Pl EC1   45 G1
Leopards Ct EC1   45 G1
Leo Yd EC1   45 H1
Lewisham St SW1   44 D6
Lexington St W1   44 C3
Library St SE1   45 H6
Lily Pl EC1   45 G1
Limeburner La EC4   45 H3
Lincoln's Inn WC2   45 F2
Lincoln's Inn Flds
  WC2   45 F2
Lindsey St EC1   45 H1
Lisle St WC2   44 D3
Litchfield St WC2   44 D3
Little Argyll St W1   44 C3
Little Britain EC1   45 J2
Little Chester St SW1   44 A6
Little Coll St SW1   44 E6
Little Dean's Yd SW1   44 E6
Little Dorrit Ct SE1   45 J5
Little Essex St WC2   45 G3
Little George St SW1   44 E6
Little Newport St WC2   44 D3
Little New St EC4   45 G2
Little Portland St W1   44 C2
Little Russell St WC1   44 E2
Little St. James's St
  SW1   44 C5
Little Sanctuary SW1   44 D6
Little Smith St SW1   44 D6
Little Titchfield St W1   44 C2
Little Trinity La EC4   45 J3
Little Turnstile WC1   45 F2
Livonia St W1   44 C3
Lollard St SE11   45 F7
Loman St SE1   45 H5
Lombard La EC4   45 G3
London Cen Mkts
  EC1   45 H1
London Rd SE1   45 H6
London Silver Vaults
  WC2   45 G2
London Trocadero,
  The W1   44 D4
London Wall EC2   45 J2
Long Acre WC2   44 E3
Long La EC1   45 H1
Longridge Ho SE1   45 J7
Long's Ct WC2   44 D3
Longstone Ct SE1   45 J6
Longville Rd SE11   45 H7
Long Yd WC1   45 F1
Lord N St SW1   44 E7
Love La EC2   45 J2
Lover's Wk W1   44 A4
Lower Belgrave St
  SW1   44 B7
Lower Grosvenor Pl
  SW1   44 B6
Lower James St W1   44 C3
Lower John St W1   44 C3
Lower Marsh SE1   45 G6
Lower Rd SE1   45 G5
Lowndes Cl SW1   44 A7
Lowndes Ct W1   44 C3
Lowndes Pl SW1   44 A7

Ludgate Bdy EC4   45 H3
Ludgate Circ EC4   45 H3
Ludgate Hill EC4   45 H3
Ludgate Sq EC4   45 H3
Lumley Ct WC2   45 E4
Lumley St W1   44 A3
Luxborough St W1   44 A1
Lyall Ms SW1   44 A7
Lyall Ms W SW1   44 A7
Lyall St SW1   44 A7
Lygon Pl SW1   44 B7

M

McAuley Cl SE1   45 G6
Macclesfield St W1   44 D3
McCoid Way SE1   45 J6
Macfarren Pl NW1   44 A1
Macklin St WC2   45 E2
Mac's Pl EC4   45 G2
Maddox St W1   44 B3
Magpie All EC4   45 G3
Maiden La SE1   45 J4
Maiden La WC2   45 E4
Maidstone Bldgs Ms
  SE1   45 J5
Malet Pl WC1   44 D1
Malet St WC1   44 D1
Mall, The SW1   44 C5
Maltravers St WC2   45 F3
Manchester Ms W1   44 A2
Manchester Sq W1   44 A2
Manchester St W1   44 A2
Mandeville Pl W1   44 A2
Manette St W1   44 D3
Mansfield Ms W1   44 B2
Mansfield St W1   44 B2
Maple Pl W1   44 C1
Maple St W1   44 C1
Margaret Ct W1   44 C2
Margaret St W1   44 B2
Marigold All SE1   45 H4
Market Ct EC1   44 C2
Market Ms W1   44 B5
Market Pl W1   44 C2
Marlborough Ct W1   44 C3
Marlborough Rd SW1   44 C5
Marshall St W1   44 C3
Marshalsea Rd SE1   45 J5
Marsham St SW1   44 D7
Martin Ho SE1   45 J7
Martlett Ct WC2   45 E3
Marylebone High St
  W1   44 A1
Marylebone La W1   44 A3
Marylebone Ms W1   44 B2
Marylebone Pas W1   44 C2
Marylebone St W1   44 A2
Masons Arms Ms W1   44 B3
Mason's Yd SW1   44 C4
Matthew Parker St
  SW1   44 D6
Matthews Yd WC2   44 E3
Maunsel St SW1   44 D7
Mayfair W1   44 B4
Mayfair Pl W1   44 B4
Mays Ct WC2   44 E4
Meadow Row SE1   45 J7
Mead Row SE1   45 G6
Meard St W1   44 D3
Medway St SW1   44 D7
Melbourne Pl WC2   45 F3
Memel Ct EC1   45 J1
Memel St EC1   45 J1
Mepham St SE1   45 F5
Mercer St WC2   44 E3
Merrick Sq SE1   45 J6
Metro Cen Hts SE1   45 J7
Meymott St SE1   45 H5
Middlesex Pas EC1   45 H2
Middle St EC1   45 J1
Middle Temple EC4   45 G3
Middle Temple La
  EC4   45 G3
Middleton Pl W1   44 C2
Midford Pl W1   44 C1
Milcote St SE1   45 H6
Milford La WC2   45 F3
Milk St EC2   45 J3
Millbank SW1   44 E7
Millbank Ct SW1   44 E7
Millennium Br EC4   45 J3
Millennium Br SE1   45 J3
Miller Wk SE1   45 G5
Millman Ms WC1   45 F1
Millman St WC1   45 F1
Mill St W1   44 B3
Milroy Wk SE1   45 H4
Minera Ms SW1   44 A7
Mint St SE1   45 J5
Mitre Ct EC2   45 J2
Mitre Rd SE1   45 G5
Monck St SW1   44 D7
Monkton St SE11   45 G7
Monkwell Sq EC2   45 J2

Monmouth St WC2   44 E3
Montague Pl WC1   44 D1
Montague St EC1   45 J2
Montague St WC1   44 E1
Montreal Pl WC2   45 F3
Montrose Pl SW1   44 A6
Moor St W1   44 D3
Morley St SE1   45 G6
Morpeth Ter SW1   44 C7
Mortimer Mkt WC1   44 C1
Mortimer St W1   44 C2
Morton Pl SE1   45 G7
Morwell St WC1   44 D2
Mount Pleasant WC1   45 F1
Mount Row W1   44 B4
Mount St W1   44 A4
Mount St Ms W1   44 B4
Moxon St W1   44 A2
Munton Rd SE17   45 J7
Murphy St SE1   45 G6
Museum St WC1   44 E2

N

Nag's Head Ct EC1   45 J1
Nassau St W1   44 C2
Neal St WC2   44 E3
Neal's Yd WC2   44 E3
Neathouse Pl SW1   44 C7
Nelson Sq SE1   45 H5
Newall Ho SE1   45 J6
New Bond St W1   44 B3
New Br St EC4   45 H3
Newburgh St W1   44 C3
New Burlington Ms
  W1   44 C3
New Burlington Pl
  W1   44 C3
New Burlington St
  W1   44 C3
Newbury St EC1   45 J2
Newcastle Cl EC4   45 H2
New Cavendish St W1   44 B1
New Change EC4   45 J3
New Compton St
  WC2   44 D3
New Fetter La EC4   45 G2
Newgate St EC1   45 H2
New Globe Wk SE1   45 J4
Newington SE1   45 J7
Newington Causeway
  SE1   45 H7
New Inn Pas WC2   45 F3
New Kent Rd SE1   45 J7
Newman Pas W1   44 C2
Newman's Row WC2   45 F2
Newman St W1   44 C2
Newman Yd W1   44 C2
Newnham Ter SE1   45 G6
New N St WC1   45 F1
New Oxford St WC1   44 D2
Newport Ct WC2   44 D3
Newport Pl WC2   44 D3
New Row WC2   44 E3
New Sq WC2   45 F2
New St Sq EC4   45 G2
Newton St WC2   45 E2
New Turnstile WC1   45 F2
Nicholson St SE1   45 H5
Nightingale Ms SE11   45 G7
Noble St EC2   45 J2
Noel St W1   44 C3
Norfolk Row SE1   45 F7
Norris St SW1   44 D4
North Audley St W1   44 A3
North Cres WC1   44 D1
Northington St WC1   45 F1
North Ms WC1   45 F1
Northumberland Av
  WC2   44 E4
Northumberland St
  WC2   44 E4
Norwich St EC4   45 G2
Nottingham Ct WC2   44 E3
Nottingham Pl W1   44 A1
Nottingham St W1   44 A1
Nottingham Ter NW1   44 A1

O

Oakden St SE11   45 G7
Oakey La SE1   45 G6
Oat La EC2   45 J2
Odhams Wk WC2   45 E3
Ogle St W1   44 C1
Old Bailey EC4   45 H3
Old Barrack Yd SW1   44 A5
Old Bond St W1   44 C4
Old Brewers Yd WC2   44 E3
Old Bldgs WC2   45 G2
Old Burlington St W1   44 C3
Oldbury Pl W1   44 A1
Old Cavendish St W1   44 B2
Old Compton St W1   44 D3
Old Fish St Hill EC4   45 J3
Old Fleet La EC4   45 H2

Old Gloucester St WC1 45 E1
Old Mitre Ct EC4 45 G3
Old N St WC1 45 F1
Old Palace Yd SW1 44 E6
Old Paradise St SE11 45 F7
Old Pk La W1 44 A5
Old Pye St SW1 44 D6
Old Queen St SW1 44 D6
Old Seacoal La EC4 45 H2
Old Sq WC2 45 F2
O'Meara St SE1 45 J5
Onslow St EC1 45 G1
Ontario St SE1 45 H7
Orange St WC2 44 D4
Orange Yd W1 44 D3
Orchard St W1 44 A3
Orde Hall St WC1 45 F1
Orient St SE11 45 H7
Ormond Cl WC1 45 E1
Ormond Ms WC1 45 E1
Ormond Yd SW1 44 C4
Osnaburgh St NW1 44 B1
Ossington Bldgs W1 44 A1
Oswin St SE11 45 H7
Outer Circle NW1 44 A1
Oxendon St SW1 44 D4
Oxford Circ Av W1 44 C3
Oxford St W1 44 C2
Oxo Twr Wf SE1 45 G4

P

Paddington St W1 44 A1
Pageantmaster Ct EC4 45 H3
Page St SW1 44 D7
Palace Pl SW1 44 C6
Palace St SW1 44 C6
Pall Mall SW1 44 C5
Pall Mall E SW1 44 D4
Palmer St SW1 44 D6
Pancras La EC4 45 J3
Panton St SW1 44 D4
Panyer All EC4 45 J3
Paris Gdn SE1 45 H4
Park Cres W1 44 B1
Park Cres Ms E W1 44 B1
Park Cres Ms W W1 44 B1
Parker Ms WC2 45 E2
Parker St WC2 45 E2
Park La W1 44 A5
Park Pl SW1 44 C5
Park Sq Ms NW1 44 B1
Park St SE1 45 J4
Park St W1 44 A3
Parliament Sq SW1 44 E6
Parliament St SW1 44 E6
Parliament Vw Apts SE1 45 F7
Passing All EC1 45 H1
Pastor St SE11 45 H7
Paternoster Row EC4 45 J3
Paternoster Sq EC4 45 H3
Paul's Wk EC4 45 H3
Peabody Est EC1 45 J1
Peabody Est SE1 45 G5
Peabody Est SW1 44 C7
Peabody Sq SE1 45 H6
Peabody Trust SE1 45 J5
Pearman St SE1 45 G6
Pear Pl SE1 45 G5
Pear Tree Ct EC1 45 G1
Pemberton Row EC4 45 G2
Pembroke Cl SW1 44 A6
Penhurst Pl SE1 45 F7
Pepper St SE1 45 J5
Percy Ms W1 44 D2
Percy Pas W1 44 C2
Percy St W1 44 D2
Perkin's Rents SW1 44 D6
Perkins Sq SE1 45 J4
Perrys Pl W1 44 D2
Peters Hill EC4 45 J3
Peter's La EC1 45 H1
Peter St W1 44 C3
Petty France SW1 44 C6
Phipp's Ms SW1 44 B7
Phoenix St WC2 44 D3
Piccadilly W1 44 B5
Piccadilly Arc SW1 44 C4
Piccadilly Circ W1 44 D4
Piccadilly Pl W1 44 C4
Pickering Pl SW1 44 C5
Pickwick St SE1 45 J6
Picton Pl W1 44 A3
Pilgrim St EC4 45 H3
Pineapple Ct SW1 44 C6
Pitt's Head Ms W1 44 A5
Playhouse Yd EC4 45 H3
Plaza Shop Cen, The W1 44 C2
Pleydell Ct EC4 45 G3
Pleydell St EC4 45 G3
Plough Pl EC4 45 G2
Plumtree Ct EC4 45 G2
Pocock St SE1 45 H5
Poland St W1 44 C3
Pollen St W1 44 B3
Polperro Ms SE11 45 G7
Pontypool Pl SE1 45 H5
Pooles Bldgs EC1 45 G1
Poppins Ct EC4 45 H3
Porter St SE1 45 J4
Portland Ms W1 44 C3
Portland Pl W1 44 B1
Portman Ms S W1 44 A3
Portman St W1 44 A3
Portpool La EC1 45 G1
Portsmouth St WC2 45 F3
Portugal St WC2 45 F3
Powis Pl WC1 45 E1
Pratt Wk SE11 45 F7
Price's St SE1 45 H5
Priest Ct EC2 45 J2
Primrose Hill EC4 45 G3
Prince's Arc SW1 44 C4
Princes Pl SW1 44 C4
Princess St SE1 45 H7
Princes St W1 44 B3
Princeton St WC1 45 F1
Printers Inn Ct EC4 45 G2
Printer St EC4 45 G2
Procter St WC1 45 F2
Providence Ct W1 44 A3
Prudent Pas EC2 45 J2
Puddle Dock EC4 45 H3

Q

Quadrant Arc W1 44 C4
Quality Ct WC2 45 G2
Queen Anne Ms W1 44 B2
Queen Anne's Gate SW1 44 D6
Queen Anne St W1 44 B2
Queenhithe EC4 45 J3
Queen's Head Pas EC4 45 J2
Queen Sq WC1 45 E1
Queen Sq Pl WC1 45 E1
Queen St EC4 45 J3
Queen St W1 44 B4
Queen St Pl EC4 45 J4
Queen's Wk SW1 44 C5
Queen's Wk, The SE1 45 F5
Queens Yd WC1 44 C1
Queen Victoria St EC4 45 H3
Quilp St SE1 45 J5

R

Ramillies Pl W1 44 C3
Ramillies St W1 44 C3
Rathbone Pl W1 44 D2
Rathbone St W1 44 C2
Raymond Bldgs WC1 45 F1
Ray St EC1 45 G1
Ray St Br EC1 45 G1
Redcross Way SE1 45 J5
Red Lion Ct EC4 45 G2
Red Lion Sq WC1 45 F2
Red Lion St WC1 45 F1
Red Lion Yd W1 44 A4
Red Pl W1 44 A3
Reeves Ms W1 44 A4
Regency Pl SW1 44 D7
Regency St SW1 44 D7
Regent Pl W1 44 C3
Regent St SW1 44 D4
Regent St W1 44 B2
Remnant St WC2 45 F2
Renfrew Rd SE11 45 H7
Rennie St SE1 45 H4
Rex Pl W1 44 A4
Richardson's Ms W1 44 C1
Richbell Pl WC1 45 F1
Richmond Bldgs W1 44 D3
Richmond Ms W1 44 D3
Richmond Ter SW1 44 E5
Ridgmount Gdns WC1 44 D1
Ridgmount Pl WC1 44 D1
Ridgmount St WC1 44 D1
Riding Ho St W1 44 C2
Risborough St SE1 45 H5
Rising Sun Ct EC1 45 H2
River Ct SE1 45 H4
Robert Adam St W1 44 A2
Roberts Ms SW1 44 A7
Robert St WC2 45 E4
Rochester Row SW1 44 C7
Rochester St SW1 44 D7
Rockingham Est SE1 45 J7
Rockingham St SE1 45 J7
Rodney Pl SE17 45 J7
Rodney Rd SE17 45 J7
Roger St WC1 45 F1
Rolls Bldgs EC4 45 G2
Rolls Pas EC4 45 G2
Romilly St W1 44 D3
Romney Ms W1 44 A1
Romney St SW1 44 D7
Roscoe St EC1 45 J1
Rose All SE1 45 J4
Rose & Crown Ct EC2 45 J2
Rose & Crown Yd SW1 44 C4
Rosebery Av EC1 45 G1
Rosebery Sq EC1 45 G1
Rose St EC4 45 H2
Rose St WC2 44 E3
Rotary St SE1 45 H6
Rotherham Wk SE1 45 H5
Rotten Row SW1 44 A5
Roupell St SE1 45 G5
Royal Arc W1 44 C4
Royal Ms, The SW1 44 B6
Royal Opera Arc SW1 44 D4
Royal St SE1 45 F6
Royalty Ms W1 44 D3
Rugby St WC1 45 F1
Rupert Ct W1 44 D3
Rupert St W1 44 D3
Rushworth St SE1 45 H5
Russell Ct SW1 44 C5
Russell Sq WC1 44 E1
Russell St WC2 45 E3
Russia Row EC2 45 J3
Rutherford St SW1 44 D7
Rutland Pl EC1 45 J1
Ryder Ct SW1 44 C4
Ryder St SW1 44 C4
Ryder Yd SW1 44 C4

S

Sackville St W1 44 C4
Saddle Yd W1 44 B4
Saffron Hill EC1 45 G1
Saffron St EC1 45 G1
Sail St SE11 45 F7
St. Albans Ct EC2 45 J2
St. Albans St SW1 44 D4
St. Alphage Gdns EC2 45 J2
St. Andrew's Hill EC4 45 H3
St. Andrew St EC4 45 G2
St. Anne's Ct W1 44 D3
St. Ann's La SW1 44 D6
St. Ann's St SW1 44 D6
St. Anselm's Pl W1 44 B3
St. Brides Av EC4 45 H3
St. Bride St EC4 45 H2
St. Christopher's Pl W1 44 A2
St. Clement's La WC2 45 F3
St. Cross St EC1 45 G1
St. Ermin's Hill SW1 44 D6
St. Georges Circ SE1 45 H6
St. Georges Ct EC4 45 H2
St. Georges Ms SE1 45 G6
St. Georges Rd SE1 45 G6
St. George St W1 44 B3
St. Giles High St WC2 44 D2
St. Giles Pas WC2 44 D3
St. James's SW1 44 D5
St. James's Ct SW1 44 C6
St. James's Mkt SW1 44 D4
St. James's Palace SW1 44 C5
St. James's Pk SW1 44 D5
St. James's Pl SW1 44 C5
St. James's Sq SW1 44 C4
St. James's St SW1 44 C4
St. John's La EC1 45 H1
St. John's Path EC1 45 H1
St. John's Pl EC1 45 H1
St. John's Sq EC1 45 H1
St. John St EC1 45 H1
St. Margaret's Ct SE1 45 J5
St. Margaret's St SW1 44 E6
St. Martin's La WC2 44 E3
St. Martin's-le-Grand EC1 45 J2
St. Martin's Ms WC2 44 E4
St. Martin's Pl WC2 44 E4
St. Martin's St WC2 44 D4
St. Mary's Gdns SE11 45 G7
St. Mary's Wk SE11 45 G7
St. Matthew St SW1 44 D7
St. Olaves Gdns SE11 45 G7
St. Paul's Chyd EC4 45 H3
St. Vincent St W1 44 A2
Salisbury Ct EC4 45 H3
Salisbury Sq EC4 45 G3
Sanctuary, The SW1 44 D6
Sanctuary St SE1 45 J6
Sandell St SE1 45 G5
Sandland St WC1 45 F2
Saperton Wk SE11 45 F7
Sardinia St WC2 45 F3
Savile Row W1 44 C3
Savoy Bldgs WC2 45 F4
Savoy Ct WC2 45 E4
Savoy Hill WC2 45 F4
Savoy Pl WC2 45 E4
Savoy Row WC2 45 F3
Savoy St WC2 45 F3
Savoy Way WC2 45 F4
Sawyer St SE1 45 J5
Scala St W1 44 C1
Scoresby St SE1 45 H5
Scotland Pl SW1 44 E4
Scovell Cres SE1 45 J6
Scovell Rd SE1 45 J6
Secker St SE1 45 G5
Sedding St SW1 44 A7
Sedley Pl W1 44 B3
Sekforde St EC1 45 H1
Serjeants Inn EC4 45 G3
Serle St WC2 45 F2
Sermon La EC4 45 J3
Seymour Ms W1 44 A2
Shaftesbury Av W1 44 D3
Shaftesbury Av WC2 44 D3
Shakespeare Twr EC2 45 J1
Shavers Pl SW1 44 D4
Sheffield St WC2 45 F3
Shelton St WC2 44 E3
Shepherd Mkt W1 44 B4
Shepherd's Pl W1 44 A3
Shepherd St W1 44 B5
Sheraton St W1 44 D3
Sherlock Ms W1 44 A1
Sherwood St W1 44 C3
Shoe La EC4 45 G2
Shorts Gdns WC2 44 E3
Short St SE1 45 G5
Shropshire Pl WC1 44 C1
Sicilian Av WC1 45 E2
Sidford Pl SE1 45 F7
Silex St SE1 45 H6
Silk St EC2 45 J1
Silver Pl W1 44 C3
Silvester St SE1 45 J6
Skinners La EC4 45 J3
Slingsby Pl WC2 44 E3
Smart's Pl WC2 45 E2
Smeaton Ct SE1 45 J7
Smithfield St EC1 45 H2
Smith's Ct W1 44 C3
Smith Sq SW1 44 E7
Smokehouse Yd EC1 45 H1
Snow Hill EC1 45 H2
Snow Hill Ct EC1 45 H2
Soho W1 44 C3
Soho Sq W1 44 D2
Soho St W1 44 D2
Southampton Bldgs WC2 45 G2
Southampton Pl WC1 45 E2
Southampton Row WC1 45 E1
Southampton St WC2 45 E3
South Audley St W1 44 A4
South Cres WC1 44 D2
South Eaton Pl SW1 44 A7
South Molton La W1 44 B3
South Molton St W1 44 B3
South Sq WC1 45 G2
South St W1 44 A4
Southwark SE1 45 H5
Southwark Br EC4 45 J4
Southwark Br SE1 45 J4
Southwark Br Rd SE1 45 H6
Southwark St SE1 45 H4
Spanish Pl W1 44 A2
Spenser St SW1 44 C6
Spring Gdns SW1 44 D4
Spur Rd SE1 45 G5
Spur Rd SW1 44 C6
Stable Yd SW1 44 C5
Stable Yd Rd SW1 44 C5
Stacey St WC2 44 D3
Stafford Pl SW1 44 C6
Stafford St W1 44 C4
Staining La EC2 45 J2
Stamford St SE1 45 G5
Stangate SE1 45 F6
Stanhope Gate W1 44 A4
Stanhope Row W1 44 B5
Staple Inn WC1 45 G2
Staple Inn Bldgs WC1 45 G2
Star Yd WC2 45 G2
Station App SE1 45 F5
Stedham Pl WC1 44 E2
Stephen Ms W1 44 D2
Stephen St W1 44 D2
Stew La EC4 45 J3
Stillington St SW1 44 C7
Stone Bldgs WC2 45 F2
Stonecutter St EC4 45 H2
Stones End St SE1 45 J6
Store St WC1 44 D2
Storey's Gate SW1 44 D6
Strand WC2 44 E4
Strand WC2 44 E4
Strand La WC2 45 F3
Stratford Pl W1 44 B3
Stratton St W1 44 B4
Streatham St WC1 44 D2
Strutton Grd SW1 44 D6
Stukeley St WC1 45 E2
Stukeley St WC2 45 E2
Sturge St SE1 45 J5
Sudrey St SE1 45 J6
Suffolk Pl SW1 44 D4
Suffolk St SW1 44 D4
Sullivan Rd SE11 45 G7
Summers St EC1 45 G1
Sumner St SE1 45 H4
Surrey Row SE1 45 H5
Surrey St WC2 45 F3
Sutton La EC1 45 H1
Sutton Row W1 44 D2
Sutton's Way EC1 45 J1
Sutton Wk SE1 45 F5
Swallow Pl W1 44 B3
Swallow St W1 44 C4
Swan St SE1 45 J6
Swiss Ct W1 44 D4
Sycamore St EC1 45 J1

T

Tachbrook Ms SW1 44 C7
Tallis St EC4 45 G3
Tanswell Est SE1 45 G6
Tanswell St SE1 45 G6
Tarn St SE1 45 J7
Tavistock St WC2 45 E3
Telford Ho SE1 45 J7
Temple Av EC4 45 G3
Temple La EC4 45 G3
Temple Pl WC2 45 F3
Temple W Ms SE11 45 H7
Tenison Ct W1 44 C3
Tenison Way SE1 45 G5
Tenterden St W1 44 B3
Terminus Pl SW1 44 B7
Thavies Inn EC1 45 G2
Thayer St W1 44 A2
Theed St SE1 45 G5
Theobald's Rd WC1 45 F1
Thirleby Rd SW1 44 C7
Thomas Doyle St SE1 45 H6
Thorney St SW1 44 E7
Thornhaugh Ms WC1 44 D1
Thornhaugh St WC1 44 D1
Thrale St SE1 45 J5
Three Barrels Wk EC4 45 J4
Three Cups Yd WC1 45 F2
Three Kings Yd W1 44 B3
Tilney St W1 44 A4
Tiverton St SE1 45 J7
Took's Ct EC4 45 G2
Torrington Pl WC1 44 C1
Torrington Sq WC1 44 D1
Tothill St SW1 44 D6
Tottenham Ct Rd W1 44 C1
Tottenham Ms W1 44 C1
Tottenham St W1 44 C2
Toulmin St SE1 45 J6
Tower Ct WC2 44 E3
Tower Royal EC4 45 J3
Tower St WC2 44 D3
Trafalgar Sq SW1 44 D4
Trafalgar Sq WC2 44 D4
Trebeck St W1 44 B4
Treveris St SE1 45 H5
Trig La EC4 45 J3
Trinity Ch Sq SE1 45 J6
Trinity St SE1 45 J6
Trio Pl SE1 45 J6
Trump St EC2 45 J3
Trundle St SE1 45 J5
Tudor St EC4 45 G3
Tufton St SW1 44 D6
Turk's Head Yd EC1 45 H1
Turnagain La EC4 45 H2
Turnmill St EC1 45 G1
Tweezer's All WC2 45 G3
Twyford Pl WC2 45 F2
Tyler's Ct W1 44 D3

U

Ufford St SE1 45 G5
Ulster Pl NW1 44 B1
Ulster Ter NW1 44 B1
Union Jack Club SE1 45 G5
Union St SE1 45 H5
University St WC1 44 C1
Upper Belgrave St SW1 44 A6
Upper Brook St W1 44 A4
Upper Grosvenor St W1 44 A4
Upper Grd SE1 45 G4
Upper James St W1 44 C3
Upper John St W1 44 C3
Upper Marsh SE1 45 F6
Upper St. Martin's La WC2 44 E3
Upper Tachbrook St SW1 44 C7
Upper Thames St EC4 45 H3
Upper Wimpole St W1 44 B1

V

Valentine Pl SE1 45 H5
Valentine Row SE1 45 H6
Vandon Pas SW1 44 C6
Vandon St SW1 44 C6
Vane St SW1 44 C7
Vauxhall Br Rd SW1 44 C7
Vere St W1 44 B3
Vernon Pl WC1 45 E2
Verulam Bldgs WC1 45 F1
Verulam St WC1 45 G1
Vesage Ct EC1 45 G2
Victoria Embk EC4 45 F4
Victoria Embk SW1 45 E5
Victoria Embk WC2 45 F4
Victoria Pl SW1 44 B7
Victoria Sq SW1 44 B6
Victoria Sta SW1 44 B7
Victoria St SW1 44 C7
Vigo St W1 44 C4
Villiers St WC2 44 E4
Vincent Sq SW1 44 C7
Vincent St SW1 44 D7
Vine Hill EC1 45 G1
Vine St W1 44 C4
Vine St Br EC1 45 G1
Vine Yd SE1 45 J5
Vintners Ct EC4 45 J3
Virgil St SE1 45 F6
Viscount St EC1 45 J1

W

Waithman St EC4 45 H3
Walcot Sq SE11 45 G7
Walcott St SW1 44 C7
Walkers Ct W1 44 D3
Wallis All SE1 45 J5
Wallside EC2 45 J2
Walnut Tree Wk SE11 45 G7
Walworth Rd SE1 45 J7
Walworth Rd SE17 45 J7
Wardens Gro SE1 45 J5
Wardour Ms W1 44 C3
Wardour St W1 44 D3
Wardrobe Ter EC4 45 H3
Warner St EC1 45 G1
Warner Yd EC1 45 G1
Warren Ms W1 44 C1
Warren St W1 44 B1
Warwick Ct WC1 45 F2
Warwick Ho St SW1 44 D4
Warwick La EC4 45 H3
Warwick Pas EC4 45 H2
Warwick Row SW1 44 B6
Warwick Sq EC4 45 H2
Warwick St W1 44 C3
Warwick Yd EC1 45 J1
Watergate EC4 45 H3
Watergate Wk WC2 45 E4
Waterhouse Sq EC1 45 G2
Waterloo Br SE1 45 F4
Waterloo Br WC2 45 F4
Waterloo Pl SW1 44 D4
Waterloo Rd SE1 45 G5
Waterloo Sta SE1 45 G5
Water St WC2 45 F3
Watling Ct EC4 45 J3
Watling St EC4 45 J3
Waverton St W1 44 A4
Webber Row SE1 45 G6
Webber St SE1 45 G5
Wedgwood Ho SE11 45 G7
Wedgwood Ms W1 44 D3
Weighhouse St W1 44 A3
Welbeck St W1 44 B2
Welbeck Way W1 44 B2
Well Ct EC4 45 J3
Weller St SE1 45 J5
Wellington St WC2 45 E3
Wells Ms W1 44 C2
Wells St W1 44 C2
Wesley St W1 44 A2
West Cen St WC1 44 E2
West Eaton Pl SW1 44 A7
West Eaton Pl Ms SW1 44 A7
West Halkin St SW1 44 A6
West Harding St EC4 45 G2
Westminster SW1 44 C6
Westminster Br SE1 45 E6
Westminster Br SW1 45 E6
Westminster Br Rd SE1 45 F6
Westminster Gdns SW1 44 E7
Westmoreland St W1 44 A2

West One Shop Cen W1 44 A3
West Poultry Av EC1 45 H2
West Smithfield EC1 45 H2
West Sq SE11 45 H7
West St WC2 44 D3
Weymouth Ms W1 44 B1
Weymouth St W1 44 A2
Wheatley St W1 44 A2
Whetstone Pk WC2 45 F2
Whichcote St SE1 45 G5
Whitcomb St WC2 44 D4
Whitefriars St EC4 45 G3

Whitehall SW1 44 E4
Whitehall Ct SW1 44 E5
Whitehall Gdns SW1 44 E5
Whitehall Pl SW1 44 E5
White Hart St EC4 45 H2
White Horse All EC1 45 H1
White Horse Ms SE1 45 G6
White Horse St W1 44 B5
White Lion Hill EC4 45 H3
White Lyon Ct EC2 45 J1
Whitfield Pl W1 44 C1
Whitfield St W1 44 D2
Whitgift St SE11 45 F7

Whittlesey St SE1 45 G5
Whitworth Ho SE1 45 J7
Wicksteed Ho SE1 45 J7
Wigmore Pl W1 44 B2
Wigmore St W1 44 A3
Wilcox Pl SW1 44 C7
Wild Ct WC2 45 F2
Wild St WC2 45 E3
Wilfred St SW1 44 C6
William IV St WC2 44 E4
Willoughby St WC1 45 E1
Willow Pl SW1 44 C7
Wilton Cres SW1 44 A6

Wilton Ms SW1 44 A6
Wilton Pl SW1 44 A6
Wilton Rd SW1 44 B7
Wilton Row SW1 44 A6
Wilton St SW1 44 B6
Wilton Ter SW1 44 A6
Wimpole Ms W1 44 B1
Wimpole St W1 44 B2
Wincott St SE11 45 G7
Windmill St W1 44 D2
Windmill Wk SE1 45 G5
Windsor Pl SW1 44 C7
Wine Office Ct EC4 45 G2

Winnett St W1 44 D3
Winsley St W1 44 C2
Woburn Sq WC1 44 D1
Wollaston Cl SE1 45 J7
Woodstock Ms W1 44 A2
Woodstock St W1 44 B3
Wood St EC2 45 J3
Wootton St SE1 45 G5

Y
Yarmouth Pl W1 44 B5
York Bldgs WC2 45 E4
York Gate NW1 44 A1

York Pl WC2 45 E4
York Rd SE1 45 F5
Yorkshire Grey Yd WC1 45 F2
York Ter E NW1 44 A1
York Ter W NW1 44 A1

Z
Zoar St SE1 45 J4

Manchester street index

A
Abingdon St 47 E4
Academy Wk 46 D7
Ackers St 47 F7
Acton Sq 46 A3
Adair St 47 G4
Addington St 47 F2
Addison Cl 47 G7
Adelphi St 46 B3
Aden Cl 47 J4
Adlington St 47 H5
Adstone Cl 47 J3
Adswood St 47 J3
Airton Cl 47 H1
Aked Cl 47 J7
Albion Pl 46 A3
Albion St 46 D5
Albion Way 46 A3
Alderman Sq 47 J4
Aldred St 46 A3
Alexander Gdns 46 C1
Alexandra St 46 C1
Alfred James Cl 47 H2
Alker Rd 47 J2
Alley St 46 E3
Almond St 47 G1
Altair Pl 46 B1
Amory St 47 G5
Anaconda Dr 46 C2
Ancoats 47 G3
Ancoats Gro 47 H4
Ancroft St 46 C7
Angela St 46 C6
Angel St 47 F2
Angora Cl 46 B2
Angora Dr 46 B2
Anita St 47 G3
Anne Nuttall St 46 B6
Anscombe Cl 47 H1
Antares Av 46 B1
Apsley Gro 47 H6
Aquarius St 47 E7
Archway 46 D7
Ardwick 47 J5
Ardwick Grn N 47 G5
Ardwick Grn S 47 G5
Arlington St 46 C2
Arnott Cres 46 E7
Artillery St 46 D4
Arundel St 46 C5
Asgard Dr 46 B5
Asgard Grn 46 B5
Ashlar Dr 47 J4
Ashley St 47 F2
Ashton New Rd 47 J3
Ashton Old Rd 47 H5
Aspin La 47 F2
Atherton St 46 C4
Atkinson St 46 D4
Atwood St 47 E5
Auburn St 47 F4
Audlem Cl 47 J2
Augustus St 47 E1
Avenham Cl 46 D7
Aytoun St 47 F4

B
Back Acton St 47 F4
Back Ashley St 47 F2
Back Bk St 47 F1
Back Br St 46 D3
Back China La 47 F4
Back Coll Land 46 D3
Back George St 47 E4
Back Hampson St 47 H1
Back Hulme St 46 B3
Back Junct St 47 G4
Back Piccadilly 47 F3
Back Pool Fold 46 E3
Back Red Bk 47 F1
Back St. George's Rd 47 G2
Back S Par 46 D3
Back Thomas St 47 F3

Back Turner St 47 F3
Badby Cl 47 J3
Bainbridge Cl 47 J7
Baird St 47 G4
Bale St 46 E4
Balloon St 47 E2
Balmforth St 46 C5
Balsam Cl 47 G6
Bangor St 46 C7
Bankmill Cl 47 G6
Bank Pl 46 B3
Bank St 46 B3
Baptist St 47 F2
Barbeck Cl 47 J2
Baring St 47 G5
Barker St 46 D1
Barlow Pl 47 G6
Barlow's Cft 46 D3
Barnett Dr 46 C2
Barrack St 46 B6
Barrhill Cl 46 C6
Barrow St 46 B3
Barton St 46 D5
Basildon Cl 47 J7
Beamish Cl 47 G6
Beattock St 46 C6
Beaufort St 46 C5
Beaver St 47 E5
Beckhampton Cl 47 H7
Bednal Av 47 J1
Beechcroft Cl 47 H2
Belfort Dr 46 A5
Bendix St 47 F2
Bengal St 47 G2
Bennett St 47 J6
Bentinck St 46 B6
Bent St 47 E1
Berkshire Rd 47 J1
Berry St 47 G5
Beswick Row 47 E2
Beswick St 47 H3
Betley St 47 G4
Bevan Cl 47 J4
Bilbrook St 47 F1
Billing Av 47 G5
Binns Pl 47 G3
Birchin La 47 F3
Birchvale Cl 46 D6
Birt St 47 H1
Bishopsgate 46 E4
Blackburn Pl 46 A4
Blackburn St 46 B2
Blackfriars Rd 46 C2
Blackfriars St 46 D3
Blackhill Cl 47 G6
Blackley St 46 B7
Blacklock St 46 E1
Blantyre St 46 C5
Bletchley Cl 47 H7
Blind La 47 J5
Blisworth Cl 47 J3
Bloom St 47 F4
Blossom St 46 D2
Blossom St (Ancoats) 47 G3
Blucher St 46 A4
Blyton St 47 F7
Boad St 47 G4
Bollington Rd 47 H2
Bombay St 47 F5
Bond St 47 G5
Bonsall St 46 E7
Boond St 46 E4
Booth St 46 E4
Booth St (Salford) 46 D3
Booth St E 47 F7
Booth St W 47 E7
Bootle St 46 D4
Botham Cl 47 F7
Bothwell Rd 47 G2
Boundary La 47 E6
Boundary St E 47 F6
Boundary St W 47 E6
Bourdon St 47 J2

Bow La 46 E4
Bow St 46 D4
Brackley Av 46 B6
Bradford Rd 47 H3
Bradleys Ct 47 F3
Braley St 47 G5
Bramble Av 46 A5
Bramwell Dr 47 G6
Brancaster Rd 47 F5
Branson St 47 J3
Brazennose St 46 D4
Brazil St 47 F5
Brennan Cl 47 E7
Brewer St 47 F3
Brian Redhead Ct 46 C6
Brickley St 47 E1
Brick St 47 F3
Briddon St 46 D1
Bridgeford St 47 F7
Bridge St 46 D3
Bridge St W 46 D3
Bridgewater Pl 47 E3
Bridgewater St 46 D5
Bridgewater St (Salford) 46 C1
Bridgewater Viaduct 46 D5
Briggs St 46 C2
Brighton Pl 47 F7
Brighton St 47 F1
Brindle Pl 47 E7
Brocade Cl 46 B2
Brock St 47 G3
Bromley St 47 F1
Bronte St 47 E7
Brook St 47 F5
Brotherton Cl 46 B6
Brotherton Dr 46 C2
Browfield Av 46 A5
Brown Cross St 46 C3
Browning St 46 B7
Browning St (Salford) 46 C3
Brown St 46 E4
Brunel Av 46 A3
Brunswick 47 G7
Brunswick St 47 F7
Bryant Cl 47 H7
Brydon Av 47 H5
Buckfield Av 46 A5
Bugle St 46 D5
Bunsen St 47 F3
Burlington St 47 E7
Burnell Cl 47 H2
Burstock St 47 F1
Burton St 47 G1
Burton Wk 46 B2
Bury St 46 C2
Butler La 47 H2
Butler St 47 H2
Butter La 46 D3
Buxton St 47 G5
Byrcland Cl 47 J5
Byron St 46 D4

C
Cable St 47 F2
Cabot St 47 G6
Cakebread St 47 G5
Calder St 46 B5
Calico Cl 46 B2
Camberwell St 47 E1
Cambrian St 47 J2
Cambridge St 46 E5
Cambridge St (Salford) 46 C1
Camelford Cl 47 E7
Cameron St 46 D5
Canal St 47 F4
Cannon St 46 E3
Canon Ct 46 E3
Canon Grn Dr 46 C2
Carding Gro 46 C2
Cardroom Rd 47 G3
Carey Cl 46 C1

Carib St 46 D7
Carmel Av 46 A5
Carmel Cl 46 A5
Carnarvon St 46 E1
Caroline St 46 C1
Carpenters La 47 F3
Carriage St 46 C7
Carruthers St 47 H3
Cassidy Cl 47 G2
Castle St 46 C5
Caterham St 47 J4
Cathedral Gates 46 E3
Cathedral St 46 E3
Cathedral Yd 46 E3
Catlow La 47 F3
Catlow St 46 D1
Cavalier St 47 J3
Cavanagh Cl 47 H7
Cavell St 47 F3
Cavendish St 46 E6
Cawdor St 46 B6
Caxton St 46 D3
Caygill St 46 D2
Cedar Pl 46 B1
Central St 46 E4
Century St 46 D5
Chadderton St 47 F2
Chain St 47 E4
Chancel Av 46 A5
Chancellor La 47 H5
Chancery La 46 E4
Change Way 46 C2
Chapelfield Rd 47 H5
Chapel St 46 C3
Chapeltown St 47 G4
Chapel Walks 46 E3
Charles St 47 E5
Charley Av 46 B1
Charlotte St 46 E4
Charlton Pl 47 G5
Charlton Cl 47 J2
Charnley Cl 47 J2
Charter St 46 D1
Chase St 46 E1
Chatford Cl 46 C1
Chatham St 47 F4
Chatley St 46 E1
Cheapside 46 E3
Cheetham Hill Rd 47 E2
Cheetwood St 46 D1
Chepstow St 46 E5
Cherryton Wk 47 G7
Chesshyre Av 47 J3
Chester Rd 46 B6
Chester St 46 E6
Chevassut St 46 C6
Cheviot St 46 E1
Chevril Cl 47 E6
Chichester Rd 46 D7
Chiffon Way 46 B2
China La 47 F4
Chippenham Rd 47 H3
Chorlton Rd 46 C7
Chorlton St 46 E5
Chorlton St (Old Trafford) 46 A7
Christchurch Av 46 A3
Churchgate Bldgs 47 G4
Church St 47 F3
Cinder St 47 G2
Cipher St 47 G2
City Rd 46 B7
City Rd E 46 D6
Clarence St 46 E4
Clarendon St 46 D6
Clare St 47 G5
Clarion St 47 G2
Clayburn Rd 46 D6
Cleminson St 46 B3
Cleworth St 46 B6
Clifford St 47 F6
Clifton Gro 46 B7
Clifton St 46 B7
Clive St 47 F2

Cloak St 47 F5
Cloughfield Av 46 A5
Clowes St 46 D3
Cobourg St 47 F4
Coburg Av 46 B1
Cockcroft Rd 46 A2
Cockspur St 46 D3
Coleshill St 47 J1
Colin Murphy Rd 46 C6
Collier St 46 D5
Collier St (Salford) 46 D2
Collingham St 46 E1
Collyhurst Rd 47 G1
Colman Gdns 46 A5
Comet St 47 G4
Commercial St 46 D5
Comus St 46 A4
Concert La 47 E4
Congou St 47 G4
Cooper St 46 E4
Coop St 47 F3
Copeman Cl 47 G7
Copperas St 47 F3
Coral St 47 G6
Cork St 47 J4
Cornbrook 46 B6
Cornbrook Ct 46 B7
Cornbrook Gro 46 B7
Cornbrook Pk Rd 46 B6
Cornbrook St 46 B7
Cornell St 47 G2
Coronation Sq 47 H5
Coronation St 46 A4
Corporation St 46 E3
Cottenham La 46 C1
Cottenham St 47 G6
Cotter St 47 G5
Cottingham Rd 47 J7
Cotton St 47 G3
County St 46 E4
Coupland St 47 E7
Coupland St E 47 F7
Coverdale Cres 47 H6
Cowan St 47 J3
Cowburn St 46 E1
Cow La 46 B4
Crabbe St 47 F1
Cranbourne St 46 A4
Crane St 47 H5
Cranfield Cl 47 J2
Craven St 46 B4
Crediton Cl 46 E7
Cresbury St 47 H5
Crescent, The 46 A2
Cross Keys St 47 F2
Crossley Ct 47 J3
Cross St 46 E4
Cross St (Salford) 46 D3
Crown La 47 F2
Crown St 46 C5
Crown St (Salford) 46 C2
Culmington Cl 46 C7
Cumberland St 46 B1
Cumbrian Cl 47 G6
Cunard Cl 47 G6
Cygnus Av 46 B1
Cyrus St 47 J3

D
Dainton St 47 J5
Daintry Cl 46 D6
Dalberg St 47 H6
Dale St 47 F3
Dalley Av 46 B1
Dalton Ct 47 G1
Dalton St 47 G1
Damask Av 46 B2
Danebank Wk 47 G6
Danecroft Cl 47 H7
Danson St 47 J2
Dantzic St 47 E3

Dark La 47 H5
Dartford Cl 47 J7
Darton Av 47 J2
Darwen St 46 A7
Davy St 47 G1
Dawson St 46 B5
Dean Rd 46 D2
Deansgate 46 D4
Dean St 47 F3
Deanwater Cl 47 G6
Dearden St 46 D6
Dearmans Pl 46 D3
Deer St 47 G4
Denewell Cl 47 H7
Denver Av 47 J1
Derby St 47 E1
Derwent St 46 B5
Devas St 47 F7
Devine Cl 46 B2
Devonshire St 47 H7
Devonshire St N 47 J6
Devonshire St S 47 H7
Dewhurst St 46 D1
Dickinson St 46 E4
Dilston Cl 47 H7
Dinsdale Cl 47 J2
Dinton St 46 B6
Dobson Cl 47 H7
Dolefield 46 D3
Dolphin Pl 47 H6
Dolphin St 47 H6
Donald St 47 F5
Dorsey St 47 F3
Dover St 47 F7
Downing St 47 G5
Downley Dr 47 H3
Drayton Wk 46 B7
Droitwich Rd 47 H1
Dryden St 47 G7
Dryhurst Wk 47 E7
Ducie St 47 F4
Duke Pl 46 C5
Duke St 46 C5
Duke St (Salford) 46 D2
Dulwich St 47 F1
Duncan St 46 A4
Dun Cl 46 B3
Dunham St 46 D7
Dunlop St 46 D3
Durant St 47 F2
Durling Av 47 H6
Dutton St 46 E1
Dyche St 47 F2
Dyer St 46 A5

E
Eagle St 47 F2
Eastburn Av 47 H1
Eastfield Av 47 J2
Eastleigh Dr 47 H1
East Mkt St 46 C3
East Newton St 47 H2
Eastnor Cl 46 B7
East Ordsall La 46 B4
Eastpark Cl 47 H6
East Philip St 46 D1
East Union St 46 B7
Ebden St 47 F4
Ebenezer St 47 E6
Echo St 47 F5
Eden Cl 46 E7
Edgehill St 47 F3
Edge St 47 F3
Edward St 46 D1
Egerton Rd 46 C5
Egerton St 46 C3
Elbe St 47 H5
Eliza St 46 C6
Ellesmere St 46 B6
Ellis St 46 D7
Elsworth St 47 E1
Elton St 46 C1
Elton's Yd 46 C1

Street	Ref	Street	Ref	Street	Ref
Elverdon Cl	46 D7	Great Marlborough St	47 E5	Hunt's Bk	46 E2
Empire St	46 E1	Greek St	47 F6	Hyde Gro	47 G7
Empress St	46 A7	Greengate W	46 C2	Hyde Pl	47 H7
Encombe Pl	46 B3	Grenham Av	46 B6	Hyde Rd	47 H6
Epping St	46 E6	Griffiths Cl	46 C1	Hyde St	46 C7
Epsley Cl	47 E7	Groom St	47 F6		
Epworth St	47 H4	Grosvenor Gdns	46 C1	**I**	
Errington Dr	46 B1	Grosvenor Sq	46 C1	Inchley Rd	47 F6
Erskine St	46 C7	Grosvenor St	47 F6	Instow Cl	47 H7
Essex St	46 E4	Guide Post Sq	47 H7	Ionas St	46 C1
Essex Way	46 C7	Gunson St	47 H2	Irk St	47 F1
Etruria Cl	47 J7	Gun St	47 G3	Iron St	47 J2
Evans St	46 D2	Gurner Av	46 A6	Irwell Pl	46 A3
Everard St	46 B5	Gurney St	47 J3	Irwell St	46 D1
Every St	47 H4			Irwell St (Salford)	46 C3
Exford Cl	47 H2	**H**		Islington Way	46 B3
Eyre St	47 E7	Hackleton Cl	47 J3		
		Hadfield St	46 B7	**J**	
F		Half St	46 D2	Jackson Cres	46 C6
Fairbrother St	46 A6	Hall St	46 E4	Jackson's Row	46 D4
Fairfield St	47 G5	Halmore Rd	47 H2	James Henry Av	46 A4
Fair St	47 G4	Halsbury Cl	47 J7	James St	47 J1
Falkland Av	47 J1	Halston St	46 D7	James St (Salford)	46 B3
Faraday St	47 F3	Hamerton Rd	47 G1	Jenkinson St	47 F6
Farnborough Rd	47 H1	Hamilton Gro	46 B7	Jersey St	47 G3
Farrell St	46 C1	Hamilton St	46 B7	Jerusalem Pl	46 D4
Farwood Cl	46 B7	Hampson St	47 H1	Jessamine Av	46 B1
Faulkner St	47 E4	Hamsell St	47 G6	Jessel Cl	47 G6
Federation St	47 E2	Handsworth St	47 J5	Joddrell St	46 D4
Fennel St	46 E2	Hanging Ditch	46 E3	John Clynes Av	47 H1
Fenn St	46 C7	Hanover St	47 E2	John Dalton St	46 D3
Fenwick St	46 E6	Hanworth Cl	47 G6	Johnson Sq	47 H1
Ferdinan St	47 H1	Harding St	47 J4	Johnson St	46 B7
Fernbrook Cl	47 J7	Harding St (Salford)	46 C3	Johnson St (Salford)	46 C3
Fernie St	47 E1	Hardman Sq	46 D4	John St	47 F3
Fernleigh Dr	46 B7	Hardman St	46 D4	John St (Lower Broughton)	46 C1
Fern St	47 E1	Hardshaw Cl	47 G6	John St (Salford)	46 D2
Ferry St	47 J4	Harehill Cl	47 G5	Joiner St	46 E3
Filby Wk	47 J1	Hare St	47 F3	Jordan St	46 D5
Firbeck Dr	47 H2	Hargreave's St	47 F1	Joynson Av	46 B1
Firefly Cl	46 B3	Harkness St	47 H6	Julia St	46 D1
Fire Sta Sq	46 A3	Harold St	46 B7	Jury St	46 D1
Fir St	47 H1	Harriett St	47 H2	Justin Cl	47 F6
Fitzwilliam St	46 C1	Harrison St	47 H4	Jutland St	47 G4
Flatley Cl	47 E7	Harrison St (Salford)	46 C1		
Flora Dr	46 C1	Harris St	46 D1	**K**	
Ford St	47 H6	Harry Hall Gdns	46 B1	Kale St	47 G6
Ford St (Salford)	46 C3	Harter St	47 E4	Kays Gdns	46 C3
Foundry La	47 F3	Hartfield Cl	47 G6	Keele Wk	47 H1
Fountain St	47 E4	Hart St	47 F4	Kelling Wk	46 C6
Four Yards	46 E4	Hatter St	47 F2	Kelvin St	47 F3
Frances St	47 G6	Hatton Av	46 B1	Kennedy St	46 E4
Francis St	46 D1	Haverlock Dr	46 B1	Kenwright St	47 F2
Frederick St	46 C3	Haymarket Cl	47 H7	Kincardine Rd	47 F6
Freeman Sq	47 E7	Heath Av	46 B1	King Edward St	46 A5
Freya Gro	46 A5	Helga St	47 H1	Kingham Dr	47 H2
Frobisher Cl	47 J7	Hellidon Cl	47 H6	Kingsfold Av	47 H1
Frost St	47 J3	Helmet St	47 H5	Kingsland Cl	47 H1
Fulmer Dr	47 H2	Henry St	47 G3	King St	46 D3
		Henry St (Old Trafford)	46 A7	King St (Salford)	46 D2
G		Hewitt St	46 D5	King St W	46 D3
Gaitskell Cl	47 J4	Heyrod St	47 G4	Kirkgate St	47 H2
Galgate Cl	46 C6	Higher Ardwick	47 H2	Kirkhaven Sq	47 J1
Garden La	46 D3	Higher Cambridge St	47 E6	Kirkstall Sq	47 G7
Garden St	46 D2	Higher Chatham St	47 E6	Kirkwood Dr	47 H1
Garden Wall Cl	46 A5	Higher Ormond St	47 F6		
Garforth Av	47 H2	Higher Oswald St	47 F2	**L**	
Gartside St	46 D4	Higher York St	47 F6	Lackford Dr	47 H1
Garwood St	46 D6	High St	47 E3	Lamb La	46 C3
Gateaton St	46 E3	Hillcourt St	47 F6	Lamport Cl	47 F5
Gaythorn St	46 B3	Hillfield Cl	47 J7	Lanchester St	47 J2
George Leigh St	47 F3	Hillkirk St	47 J3	Landos Rd	47 H2
George St	47 E4	Hilton St	47 F3	Langholme Cl	46 C6
Georgette Dr	46 D2	Hinton St	47 G2	Langport Av	47 J7
Gibbs St	46 B3	Hodson St	46 C2	Langston St	46 D1
Gibson Pl	47 E1	Holdgate Cl	46 D7	Lanstead Dr	47 J2
Girton St	46 C1	Holkham Cl	47 H3	Lauderdale Cres	47 H7
Glasshouse St	47 G2	Holland St	47 H2	Laystall St	47 G3
Gleden St	47 J2	Holly Bk Cl	46 B6	Layton St	47 J2
Glenbarry Cl	47 G7	Holly St	47 J4	Leaf St	46 D6
Glenbarry St	47 J5	Holt Town	47 J3	Leak St	46 B6
Gloucester St	46 E5	Honey St	47 F1	Ledburn Ct	46 C6
Gloucester St (Salford)	46 A5	Hood St	47 G3	Left Bk	46 C4
Goadsby St	47 F2	Hooper St	47 J5	Lena St	47 F4
Gold St	47 F4	Hope St	47 F4	Leslie Hough Way	46 A1
Gordon St	46 C1	Hope St (Salford)	46 A3	Lever St	47 F3
Gore St	47 F4	Hornby St	46 D1	Lewis St	47 J1
Gore St (Salford)	46 C3	Hornchurch St	46 C7	Leycroft St	47 G4
Gorton St	46 D2	Horne Dr	47 H3	Lidbrook Wk	47 J7
Goulden St	47 F1	Houldsworth St	47 F3	Lime Bk St	47 J5
Gould St	47 F1	Hoyle St	47 H5	Lime Gro	47 F7
Grafton St	47 G7	Huddart Cl	46 A5	Limekiln La	47 H5
Granby Row	47 F5	Hughes St	47 J5	Linby St	46 C6
Granshaw St	47 J2	Hull Sq	46 B2	Lind St	47 J3
Gratrix Av	46 A6	**Hulme**	46 D7	Linen Ct	46 B2
Gravell La	46 D2	Hulme Ct	46 C6	Linsley St	46 D2
Grear Ducie St	46 E2	Hulme Hall Rd	46 B5	Linton Cl	47 H4
Great Ancoats St	47 F3	Hulme Pl	46 B3	Litcham Cl	47 F5
Great Bridgewater St	46 D5	Hulme St	46 D6	Little Ancoats St	47 F3
Great Clowes St	46 C1	Hulme St (Salford)	46 B2	Little Holme St	47 J3
Great Ducie St	46 D1	Humberstone Av	47 D6	Little John St	46 C4
Great George St	46 B3	Hunmanby Av	46 D6	Little Lever St	47 F3
Great Jackson St	46 C5			Little Nelson St	47 F2
Great John St	46 C4				

Street	Ref	Street	Ref	Street	Ref
Little Peter St	46 D5	Mozart Cl	47 H2	Pattishall Cl	47 J4
Little Pit St	47 G3	Mulberry St	46 D4	Peak St	47 G3
Little Quay St	46 D4	Munday St	47 H3	Peary St	47 G1
Liverpool Rd	46 C4	Munster St	47 E2	Peel Mt	46 A1
Livesey St	47 G1	Murrey St	47 G3	Pegasus Sq	46 B1
Lizard St	47 F3	Museum St	46 E4	Pembroke Cl	47 H7
Lloyd St	46 D4	Muslin St	46 B4	Pencroft Way	47 F7
Lloyd St N	47 F7	Myrtle Pl	46 A1	Penfield Cl	47 F5
Lockett St	46 D1			Percy Dr	46 A6
Lockton Cl	47 G5	**N**		Percy St	46 C7
Lomax St	47 F1	Nancy St	46 B6	Peru St	46 B2
London Rd	47 F4	Nansen St	47 J5	Peter St	46 D4
Longacre St	47 G4	Naples St	47 F2	Phoenix St	47 E3
Long Millgate	46 E2	Nash St	46 C7	Phoenix Way	46 D7
Longworth St	46 D4	Nathan Dr	46 C2	Piccadilly	47 F3
Loom St	47 G3	Naval St	47 G3	Pickford St	47 G3
Lordsmead St	46 C6	Naylor St	47 H1	Picton Cl	46 C2
Lord St	46 E1	Neild St	47 G5	Picton St	46 C1
Lostock St	47 H2	Neill St	46 C1	Piercy Av	46 B1
Lowcock St	46 C1	Nelson St	46 C1	Piercy St	47 H3
Lower Byrom St	46 C4	Nether St	47 G5	Pigeon St	47 G3
Lower Chatham St	47 E6	New Allen St	47 G2	Pimblett St	46 E1
Lower Mosley St	46 D5	Newbeck St	47 F2	Pine St	47 E4
Lower Moss La	46 C6	New Br St	46 D2	Pin Mill Brow	47 H5
Lower Ormond St	47 E5	Newcastle St	46 E6	Pittbrook St	47 J5
Lower Vickers St	47 J2	New Cath St	46 E3	Plymouth Gro	47 G7
Lowndes Wk	47 G6	New Century Park	47 E2	Plymouth Vw	47 G7
Loxford St	46 E6	Newcombe St	46 E1	Pochin St	47 J1
Lucy St	46 B7	New Elm St	46 C4	Poland St	47 G2
Ludgate Hill	47 F2	New Gartside St	46 D4	Polebrook Av	47 H7
Ludgate St	47 F2	New Islington	47 H3	Police St	46 D3
Luna street	47 F3	New Mkt	46 E3	Pollard St	47 H4
Lund St	46 A7	New Mkt St	46 E3	Pollard St E	47 H3
Lupton St	46 C3	New Mt St	47 F2	Polygon Av	47 H7
Lyceum Pl	47 E6	New Quay St	46 C4	Polygon St	47 G6
		Newton St	47 F3	Pomona Strand	46 A6
M		New Union St	47 G3	Poplar St	47 J5
Maidford Cl	47 J3	New Vine St	46 D6	Poplin Dr	46 D2
Major St	47 E4	New Wakefield St	47 E5	Portland St	47 E5
Makin St	47 E5	New Welcome St	46 D6	Portsmouth St	47 G7
Mallard St	47 E5	**New Windsor**	46 A3	Port St	47 F3
Mallow St	46 C6	New York St	47 E4	Portugal St	47 G2
Malta St	47 H3	Nicholas St	47 E4	Portugal St E	47 G4
Malt St	46 B6	Nine Acre Dr	46 A6	Postal St	47 G3
Malvern St	46 B7	Niven St	47 G5	Postbridge Cl	47 H7
Manchester St	46 A7	North Bailey St	46 C3	Potato Wf	46 C5
Mancunian Way	46 C6	Northdown Av	46 B6	Poynton St	46 E6
Mangle St Street	47 F3	North George St	46 B2	Price St	47 J3
Manor St	47 G5	North Hill St	46 C2	Primrose St	47 G2
Manson Av	46 B6	North Phoebe St	46 A4	Prince's Br	46 C4
Maplin Cl	47 G6	North Star Dr	46 B3	Princess Rd	46 D6
Marble St	47 E3	Northumberland Cl	46 A7	Princess St	46 E4
Marchmont Cl	47 H7	Northumberland Cres	46 A7	Princess St (Cornbrook)	46 B6
Market St	46 E3	North Western St	47 G5	Pritchard St	47 F5
Markfield Av	47 J7	North W Services Rd	47 G5	Providence St	47 H4
Markham Cl	47 J4	Norton St	46 D2	Pryme St	46 C5
Marple St	46 C7	Norway St	47 J4	Purslow Cl	47 J3
Marsden St	46 E3	Nuneaton Dr	47 H1		
Marshall St	47 F2	Nuttall St	46 A7	**Q**	
Marshall St (Ardwick)	47 H6			Quay St	46 C4
Marsworth Dr	47 H3	**O**		Quay St (Salford)	46 D3
Mary France St	46 C6	Oakford Av	47 G1	Queen St	46 D4
Mary St	46 D1	Oak St	47 F3	Queen St (Salford)	46 D2
Mason St	47 F2	Old Bk St	46 E3	Quenby St	46 C6
Mason St (Salford)	46 C3	Old Birley St	46 D7	Quendon Av	46 C1
Massey St	46 B3	Oldbury Cl	47 H2		
Mayan Av	46 B2	Old Elm St	47 G6	**R**	
Mayes St	46 E2	Oldfield Rd	46 A5	Rachel St	47 H5
Mayo St	47 H5	Oldham Rd	47 F3	Radium St	47 G2
Mayor St	47 F2	Oldham St	47 F2	Ralli Cts	46 C3
Meadow Rd	46 B1	Old Medlock St	46 C4	Randerson St	47 G5
Medlock St	46 D5	Old Mill St	47 G3	Rankin Cl	46 D7
Melbourne St	46 C6	Old Mt St	47 F2	Raven St	47 H5
Mellor St	47 H2	**Old Trafford**	46 A7	Reather Wk	47 H1
Melville St	46 C3	Old York St	46 C6	Red Bk	46 E2
Merrill St	47 H3	Oliver St	47 F7	Redfern St	47 E2
Middlewood St	46 B4	Ordsall Dr	46 A6	Redhill St	47 G3
Midland St	47 J5	Ordsall La	46 A5	Red Lion St	47 F3
Miles Platting	47 J1	Oregon Cl	47 G6	Regent Sq	46 A5
Millbank St	47 G4	Orion Pl	46 B1	Reilly St	46 D6
Millbeck St	47 E6	Ormsgill St	46 D7	Reservoir St	46 D2
Miller St	47 F2	Orsett Cl	47 H1	Reyner St	47 E4
Mill Grn St	47 H5	Osborne St	47 G1	Rial Pl	46 E7
Millhall Cl	46 C7	Oswald St	47 E2	Ribston St	46 C7
Millhead Av	47 J2	Oswald St (Ancoats)	47 H4	Rice St	46 C5
Millow St	47 E2	Overbridge Rd	46 D1	Richmond St	47 F4
Milnrow Cl	47 F5	Oxford Rd	47 E5	Richmond St (Salford)	46 C2
Mincing St	47 F2	Oxford St	46 E4	Ridgefield	46 D3
Minshull St	47 F4			Ridgeway St E	47 H3
Minshull St S	47 F4	**P**		Ridgway St	47 H3
Mistletoe Grn	46 C2	Paddock St	47 G5	Riga St	47 F2
Moorhead St	47 G2	Palfrey Pl	47 H6	Rigel Pl	46 B1
Morbourne Cl	47 J7	Pall Mall	46 E4	Rigel St	47 H2
Mosley St	47 E4	Palmerston St	47 H4	Rimworth Dr	47 H1
Mosscott Wk	47 G5	Parish Vw	46 A4	Ringstead Dr	47 G1
Mosshall Cl	46 C7	Parker St	47 F3	Ripley Cl	47 H4
Moulton St	46 D1	Park Pl	47 E1	River Pl	46 D5
Mouncey St	47 E5	Park St	46 E1	Riverside	46 B2
Mount Carmel Cres	46 A5	Park St (Salford)	46 B3	River St	46 D6
Mount St	46 E4	Parsonage	46 D3	River St (Ardwick)	47 H5
Mount St (Salford)	46 C2	Parsonage La	46 D3	Robert St	46 E1
		Parsonage Way	46 A5	Roby St	47 F4
		Paton St	47 F4		

Street	Ref	Street	Ref	Street	Ref	Street	Ref
Rochdale Rd	47 F2	Skerry Cl	47 G6	Trafford Bk Rd	46 A7	Windmill St	46 D4
Rockdove Av	46 D6	Skip Pl	47 E1	Trafford Ct	46 C6	Winfell Dr	47 J2
Rocket Way	46 C3	Slate Av	47 H3	Trafford Pl	46 B7	Winscombe Dr	47 H1
Rockingham Cl	47 J7	Sleaford Cl	47 H1	Trafford St	46 D5	Winser St	47 E5
Rodney St	47 H2	Smallridge Cl	47 H2	Travis St	47 G5	Winstanley Rd	47 H2
Rodney St (Salford)	46 C3	Smith St	46 A6	Trentham St	46 B6	Withy Gro	47 E3
Roe St	47 G2	Smithy La	46 D3	Trinity Way	46 B5	Woden's Av	46 A5
Roger St	47 F1	Snell St	47 H4	Tristam Cl	47 G6	Woden St	46 B5
Rolla St	46 D2	Soar St	47 F3	Troutbeck Av	47 H3	Woodlark Cl	46 B3
Rolleston Av	47 H2	Sorrel St	46 C6	Trumpet St	46 D5	Wood St	46 D4
Rolls Cres	46 C7	Southall St	46 D4	Tudbury Way	46 C2	Woodward Pl	47 H3
Roman St	47 F3	Southall St		Tuer St	47 F7	Woodward St	47 H3
Rome Rd	47 G2	(Strangeways)	46 D1	Turner St	47 F3	Woollam Pl	46 C4
Rondin Cl	47 J5	Southend Av	46 B7	Turner St		Worrall St	46 A5
Rondin Rd	47 J5	Southern St	46 D5	(Old Trafford)	46 A6	Worsley St	46 B5
Rope Wk	46 D2	Southgate	46 D3	Tutbury St	47 H4	Worsley St (Salford)	46 D3
Rosamond Dr	46 C3	South Hall St	46 B5	Twillbrook Dr	46 D2	Wright St	46 A7
Rosamond St W	47 E6	South King St	46 D3			Wroe St	46 B3
Rosewell Cl	47 J1	Southmill St	46 E4	**U**		Wyatt Av	46 A5
Rostron Av	47 J6	South Pump St	47 F4	Union St	47 F3	Wynne St	46 A1
Rowendale St	46 D5	South W Services Rd	46 C4	Union St (Ardwick)	47 H5	Wyre St	47 G5
Royce Rd	46 C6	Sparkle St	47 G4	University Rd	46 A2		
Roydale St	47 J2	Spa St	47 F7	University Rd W	46 A2	**Y**	
Royds Cl	47 J7	Spaw St	46 C3	Upper Brook St	47 F6	Yew St	46 C7
Ruby St	47 E7	Spear St	47 F3	Upper Cyrus St	47 J3	Yorkshire St	46 D3
Rudcroft Cl	47 G6	Spectator St	47 H3	Upper Helena St	47 J2	York St	47 E3
Rudman Dr	46 A5	Springfield La	46 D2	Upper Kirby St	47 H3	York St (Hulme)	46 C6
Rugby St	46 D1	Springfield Sq	46 D4	Upper Moss La	46 C7	York St (off Charles	
Runcorn St	46 B6	Spring Gdns	47 E4	Upper Wf St	46 B3	Street)	47 E5
		Spruce St	46 C7			York St E	47 F6
S		Stalham Cl	47 H1	**V**			
Sackville St	47 E4	Stanley Rd	46 B7	Varley St	47 J1	**Z**	
Sagar St	46 D1	Stanley St	47 F1	Vauxhall St	47 G1	Zion Cres	46 D7
St. Andrew's Sq	47 H4	Stanley St (Salford)	46 C4	Velour Cl	46 B1		
St. Andrew's St	47 G4	Stansby Gdns	47 J7	Vesta St	47 H3		
St. Ann's Sq	46 D3	Station App (for		Viaduct St	47 J4		
St. Ann St	46 D3	Oxford Road		Viaduct St (Salford)	46 D2		
St. Bartholomew's Dr	46 A4	Station)	47 E5	Vickers St	47 J1		
St. Chad's St	47 E1	Station App (for		Victoria Br St	46 D3		
St. Clement's Dr	46 A5	Piccadilly Station)	47 F4	Victoria Sta App	46 E2		
St. George's	46 B6	Staverton Cl	47 G6	Victor St	47 G1		
St. Ignatius Wk	46 A5	Stephen St	46 E1	Victor St (Salford)	46 C3		
St. James's Sq	46 E4	Stevenson Pl	47 F3	Virgil St	46 B6		
St. James St	47 E4	Stevenson Sq	47 F3				
St. John St	46 D4	Stevenson St	46 B3	**W**			
St. Mary's Gate	46 E3	Stockland Cl	47 F6	Wadeford Cl	47 G2		
St. Mary's		Stockport Rd	47 H6	Wadeson Rd	47 G5		
Parsonage	46 D3	Stocks St	47 E1	Wadlow Cl	46 C2		
St. Mary's St	46 C3	Stocks St E	47 E1	Walker's Cft	46 E2		
St. Nicholas Rd	46 C6	Stonall Av	46 C6	**Wallness**	46 A1		
St. Philip's St	46 B3	Stonelow Cl	46 E6	Wallness La	46 A1		
St. Simon St	46 C1	Stone St	46 C5	Warde St	46 C7		
St. Stephen's Cl	47 H7	Store St	47 F4	Wardle St	47 J2		
St. Stephen St	46 C3	Stracey St	47 J2	Warford St	47 F1		
St. Thomas St	47 F1	Strawberry Hill	46 A1	Warmington Dr	47 J7		
St. Vincent St	47 H3	Stretford Rd	46 B7	Warwick St	47 F3		
St. Wilfrids St	46 C6	Style St	47 F2	Warwick St (Hulme)	46 D7		
Salford	46 A4	Sudbury Cl	46 B7	Waterloo St	47 E4		
Salmon St	47 F3	Sudell St	47 G2	Water St	46 B5		
Saltford Av	47 H3	Sussex St	46 B1	Water St (Ardwick)	47 H5		
Salutation St	46 E7	Swan St	47 F2	Watkin Cl	47 G7		
Samouth Cl	47 H2	Swiftsure Av	46 B3	Watkin St	46 C1		
Sam Swire St	46 D7	Syndall Av	47 H6	Watson St	46 D5		
Samuel Ogden St	47 F5	Syndall St	47 H6	Weald Cl	47 G6		
Sanctuary, The	46 D7			Weir St	46 D7		
Sandal St	47 J2	**T**		Welland Cl	46 B7		
Sandford St	46 C1	Talgarth Rd	47 G1	Wellhead Cl	46 E7		
Sand St	47 G1	Tamar Ct	46 B7	Wellington Grn	46 C7		
Sawley Rd	47 J1	Tame St	47 H4	Wellington St	46 C2		
Scarsdale St	46 A1	Tariff St	47 F3	Well St	47 E3		
School Ct	47 G3	Tasle All	46 D4	West Bk St	46 A4		
School St	47 F2	Tatton St	46 B6	West Charles St	46 A3		
School St (Salford)	46 C1	Tatton St (Salford)	46 A5	West Crown Av	46 A4		
Scotporth Cl	46 C6	Taunton St	47 J3	West Hope St	46 A3		
Sefton Cl	47 G6	Tavery Cl	47 H3	West King St	46 C2		
Senior St	46 D2	Tebutt St	47 G2	Westminster St	46 B6		
Seymour Cl	46 A7	Teer St	47 J3	West Mosley St	47 E4		
Sharp St	47 F2	Temperance St	47 G5	Weston St	47 J3		
Shaw Cres	46 E2	Tewkesbury Rd	47 J2	West Pk St	46 A5		
Shawgreen Cl	46 C6	Thirsk St	47 G5	Weybridge Rd	47 H3		
Shawheath Cl	46 C6	Thomas St	47 F3	Whalley St	47 H2		
Shearsby Cl	46 D7	Thompson St	47 F2	Wheater's Cres	46 B1		
Sheffield St	47 G4	Thompson St		Wheater's St	46 B1		
Sherborne St	46 D1	(Strangeways)	46 D1	Wheater's Ter	46 B1		
Sherbourne St W	46 D1	Thomson St	47 H7	Whimberry Cl	46 A5		
Sherratt St	47 G2	Thor Grn	46 B5	Whitchurch St	46 D1		
Shetland Rd	47 H1	Thornage Dr	47 H1	Whitekirk Cl	47 G6		
Shilford Dr	47 G2	Thorncross Cl	46 B6	White St	46 B7		
Shortcroft St	46 D5	Thornden Rd	47 J1	Whitfield St	47 E1		
Short St	47 F3	Thornley Brow	47 E2	Whittle's Cft	47 G4		
Short St (Salford)	46 C1	Thornton St	47 H1	Whittle St	47 F3		
Shrewsbury St	46 B7	Tib La	46 E4	Whitworth St	47 F5		
Shudehill	47 F3	Tib St	47 F3	Whitworth St W	46 D5		
Sidney St	47 F6	Tideswell Av	47 H2	Wilberforce Cl	46 D7		
Sidney St (Salford)	46 C3	Tidworth Av	47 H3	Wilfred St	46 D1		
Silkin Cl	47 F6	Tinsley Cl	47 J2	William Chadwick Cl	47 H1		
Silk St	47 G2	Tivoli St	46 D4	Williamson St	47 F1		
Silk St (Salford)	46 B2	Todd St	47 E2	William St	47 H5		
Silvercroft St	46 C5	Tomlinson St	46 D7	Wilmott St	46 E6		
Silver St	47 F4	Tonge St	47 J5	Wilson St	47 H7		
Simeon St	47 F2	Tonman St	46 D4	Wilton Pl	46 B3		
Simms Cl	46 B3	Torquay Cl	47 H7	Wilton St	47 F6		
Simpson St	47 F2	Towcester Cl	47 J3	Winder Dr	47 H3		
Sirius Pl	46 B1	Town Hall La	46 E3	Windmill Av	46 A5		

Aberdeen

Tourist Information Centre: 23 Union Street
Tel: 01224 269180

Albert Quay	C3	Hutcheon Street	B2
Albert Street	B2	Justice Mill Lane	B3
Albury Road	B3	King's Crescent	C1
Albyn Place	A3	King Street	C1
Argyll Place	A2	Langstane Place	B3
Ashgrove Road	A1	Leadside Road	B2
Ashgrove Road West	A1	Leslie Terrace	B1
Ash-hill Drive	A1	Links Road	C2
Ashley Road	A3	Linksfield Road	C1
Back Hilton Road	A1	Loch Street	B2
Baker Street	B2	Maberly Street	B2
Beach Boulevard	C2	Market Street	C3
Bedford Place	B1	Menzies Road	C3
Bedford Road	B1	Merkland Road East	C1
Beechgrove Terrace	A2	Mid Stocket Road	A2
Belgrave Terrace	A2	Mile-end Avenue	A2
Berryden Road	B1	Miller Street	C2
Blaikie's Quay	C3	Mount Street	B2
Bon-Accord Street	B3	Nelson Street	C2
Bonnymuir Place	A2	North Esplanade East	C3
Bridge Street	B2	North Esplanade West	C3
Brighton Place	A3	Orchard Street	C1
Cairncry Road	A1	Osborne Place	A3
Canal Road	B1	Palmerston Road	C3
Carden Place	A3	Park Road	C1
Carlton Place	A3	Park Street	C2
Cattofield Place	A1	Pittodrie Place	C1
Causewayend	B2	Pittodrie Street	C1
Chapel Street	B2	Powis Place	B1
Claremont Street	A3	Powis Terrace	B1
Clifton Road	A1	Queens Road	A3
College Bounds	B1	Queens Terrace	A3
College Street	C3	Regent Quay	C2
Commerce Street	C2	Rosehill Crescent	A1
Commercial Quay	C3	Rosehill Drive	A1
Constitution Street	C2	Rosemount Place	A2
Cornhill Drive	A1	Rose Street	B2
Cornhill Road	A1	Rubislaw Terrace	B3
Cornhill Terrace	A1	St. Swithin Street	A3
Cotton Street	C2	Schoolhill	B2
Cromwell Road	A3	Seaforth Road	C1
Desswood Place	A3	Sinclair Road	C3
Devonshire Road	A3	Skene Square	B2
Elmbank Terrace	B1	Skene Street	B2
Esslemont Avenue	B2	South Crown Street	B3
Ferryhill Road	B3	South Esplanade West	C3
Fonthill Road	B3	Spital	C1
Forest Road	A3	Springbank Terrace	B3
Forest Avenue	A3	Spring Gardens	B2
Fountainhall Road	A2	Stanley Street	A3
Froghall Terrace	B1	Sunnybank Road	B1
Gallowgate	C2	Sunnyside Road	B1
George Street	B1	Union Glen	B3
Gillespie Crescent	A1	Union Grove	A3
Gladstone Place	A3	Union Street	B2
Golf Road	C1	Urquhart Road	C2
Gordondale Road	A2	Victoria Bridge	C3
Great Southern Road	B3	Victoria Road	C3
Great Western Road	A3	Walker Road	C3
Guild Street	C3	Waterloo Quay	C2
Hamilton Place	A2	Waverley Place	B3
Hardgate	B3	Well Place	C3
Hilton Drive	A1	Westburn Drive	A1
Hilton Place	A1	Westburn Road	A2
Hilton Street	A1	West North Street	C2
Holburn Road	B3	Whitehall Place	A2
Holburn Street	B3	Whitehall Road	A2
Holland Street	B1	Willowbank Road	B3

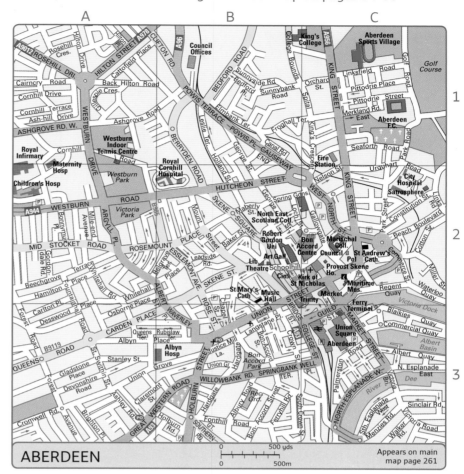

ABERDEEN

0 — 500 yds
0 — 500m

Appears on main
map page 261

Bath

Tourist Information Centre: Abbey Chambers, Abbey Churchyard
Tel: 0906 711 2000

Ambury	A3	Pierrepont Street	B3
Archway Street	C3	Pulteney Gardens	C3
Argyle Street	B2	Pulteney Mews	C1
Avon Street	A2	Pulteney Road	C2
Barton Street	A2	Queen Street	A2
Bath Street	B2	Quiet Street	A1
Bathwick Hill	C1	Rossiter Road	B3
Beau Street	B2	Royal Crescent	A1
Bennett Street	A1	St. James's Parade	A2
Bridge Street	B2	St. John's Road	B1
Broad Quay	A3	St. Marks Road	B3
Broad Street	B1	Sawclose	A2
Broadway	C3	Southgate Street	B3
Brock Street	A1	Spring Crescent	C3
Chapel Row	A2	Stall Street	B2
Charles Street	A2	Sutton Street	C1
Charlotte Street	A1	Sydney Place	C1
Cheap Street	B2	The Circus	A1
Claverton Street	B3	Union Street	B2
Corn Street	A3	Upper Borough Walls	A2
Daniel Street	C1	Walcot Street	B1
Darlington Street	C1	Wells Road	A3
Dorchester Street	B3	Westgate Buildings	A2
Edward Street	C1	Westgate Street	A2
Excelsior Street	C3	Wood Street	A1
Ferry Lane	C2	York Street	B2
Gay Street	A1		
George Street	A1		
Grand Parade	B2		
Great Pulteney Street	C1		
Green Park Road	A2		
Green Street	B1		
Grove Street	B2		
Henrietta Gardens	C1		
Henrietta Mews	C1		
Henrietta Road	B1		
Henrietta Street	B1		
Henry Street	B2		
High Street	B2		
Holloway	A3		
James Street West	A2		
John Street	A1		
Kingsmead East	A2		
Kingsmead Square	A2		
Lansdown Road	B1		
Laura Place	B1		
Lime Grove	C2		
Lime Grove Gardens	C2		
Lower Borough Walls	B2		
Lower Bristol Road	A3		
Magdalen Avenue	A3		
Manvers Street	B3		
Milk Street	A2		
Milsom Street	B1		
Monmouth Place	A1		
Monmouth Street	A2		
Newark Street	B3		
New Bond Street	B2		
New King Street	A2		
New Orchard Street	B2		
New Street	A2		
North Parade	B2		
North Parade Road	C2		
Old King Street	A1		
Orange Grove	B2		
Paragon	B1		

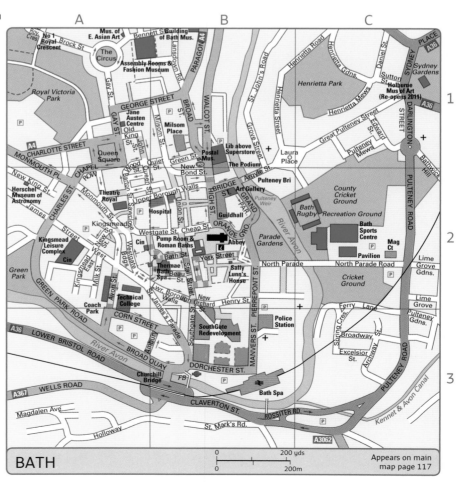

BATH

0 — 200 yds
0 — 200m

Appears on main
map page 117

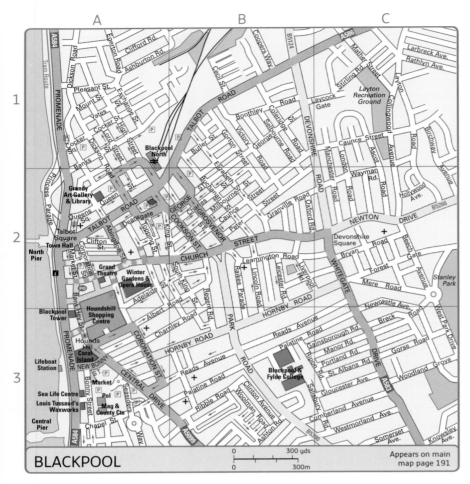

BLACKPOOL

Tourist Information Centre: Festival House, Promenade
Tel: 01253 478222

Abingdon Street	A2	Manor Road	C3
Adelaide Street	A3	Market Street	A2
Albert Road	A3	Mather Street	C1
Ascot Road	C1	Mere Road	C2
Ashburton Road	A1	Milbourne Street	B2
Ashton Road	B3	Mount Street	A1
Bank Hey Street	A2	New Bonny Street	A3
Banks Street	A1	Newcastle Avenue	C2
Beech Avenue	C2	Newton Drive	C2
Birchway Avenue	C1	Oxford Road	B2
Bonny Street	A3	Palatine Road	B3
Boothley Road	B1	Park Road	B3
Breck Road	C3	Peter Street	B2
Bryan Road	C2	Pleasant Street	A1
Buchanan Street	B2	Portland Road	C3
Butler Street	B1	Princess Parade	A2
Caunce Street	B2/C1	Promenade	A1
Cecil Street	B1	Queens Square	A2
Central Drive	A3	Queen Street	A2
Chapel Street	A3	Rathlyn Avenue	C1
Charles Street	B2	Reads Avenue	B3
Charnley Road	A3	Regent Road	B2
Church Street	B2	Ribble Road	B3
Clifford Road	A1	Ripon Road	B3
Clifton Street	A2	St. Albans Road	C3
Clinton Avenue	B3	Salisbury Road	C3
Cocker Square	A1	Seasiders Way	A3
Cocker Street	A1	Selbourne Road	B1
Coleridge Road	B1	Somerset Avenue	C3
Collingwood Avenue	C1	South King Street	B2
Cookson Street	B2	Stirling Road	C1
Coopers Way	B1	Talbot Road	A2/B1
Coronation Street	A3	Talbot Square	A2
Corporation Street	A2	Topping Street	A2
Cumberland Avenue	C3	Victory Road	B1
Deansgate	A2	Wayman Road	C2
Devonshire Road	B1	Westmorland Avenue	C3
Devonshire Square	C2	West Park Drive	C2
Dickson Road	A1	Whitegate Drive	C2/C3
Egerton Road	A1	Woodland Grove	C3
Elizabeth Street	B1	Woolman Road	B3
Exchange Street	A1	Yates Street	A1
Forest Gate	C2		
Gainsborough Road	B3		
George Street	B2/B1		
Gloucester Avenue	C3		
Gorse Road	C3		
Gorton Street	B1		
Granville Road	B2		
Grosvenor Street	B2		
High Street	A1		
Hollywood Avenue	C2		
Hornby Road	A3		
Hounds Hill	A3		
King Street	A2		
Knowsley Avenue	C3		
Larbreck Avenue	C1		
Laycock Gate	C1		
Layton Road	C1		
Leamington Road	B2		
Leicester Road	B2		
Lincoln Road	B2		
Liverpool Road	B2		
London Road	C1		
Lord Street	A1		
Manchester Road	C1		

Appears on main
map page 191

0 300 yds / 0 300m

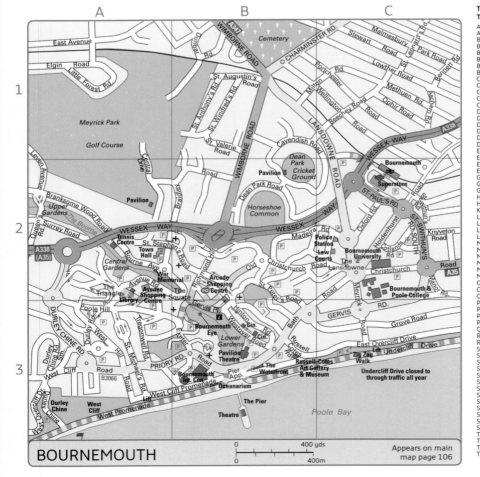

BOURNEMOUTH

Tourist Information Centre: Westover Road
Tel: 0845 05 11 700

Ascham Road	C1	Undercliff Drive	C3
Avenue Road	A2	Wellington Road	C1
Bath Road	B3	Wessex Way	A2/C1
Beechey Road	C1	West Cliff Promenade	A3
Bennett Road	C1	West Cliff Road	A3
Bourne Avenue	A2	West Hill Road	A3
Braidley Road	B2	West Overcliff Drive	A3
Branksome Wood Road	A2	West Promenade	A3
Cavendish Road	B1	Westover Road	B3
Central Drive	A1	Wimborne Road	B2
Charminster Road	B1		
Christchurch Road	C2		
Cotlands	C2		
Dean Park Road	B2		
Dunbar Road	B1		
Durley Chine	A3		
Durley Chine Road	A3		
Durley Chine Road South	A3		
Durley Road	A3		
East Avenue	A1		
East Overcliff Drive	C3		
Elgin Road	A1		
Exeter Road	B3		
Gervis Place	B3		
Gervis Road	C3		
Grove Road	C3		
Hinton Road	B3		
Holdenhurst Road	C2		
Knyveton Road	C2		
Lansdowne Road	B1		
Leven Avenue	A1		
Little Forest Road	C1		
Lowther Road	C1		
Madeira Road	B2		
Malmesbury Park Road	C1		
Manor Road	C1		
Methuen Road	C2		
Meyrick Road	C2		
Milton Road	B1		
Old Christchurch Road	B2		
Ophir Road	C1		
Oxford Road	C2		
Pier Approach	B3		
Poole Hill	A3		
Portchester Road	C1		
Priory Road	A3		
Queen's Road	A2		
Richmond Hill	B2		
Russell Cotes Road	B3		
St. Augustin's Road	B1		
St. Anthony's Road	B1		
St. Leonard's Road	C1		
St. Michael's Road	A3		
St. Pauls' Road	C2		
St. Peter's Road	B2		
St. Stephen's Road	A2		
St. Swithun's Road	C2		
St. Swithun's Road South	C2		
St. Valerie Road	B1		
St. Winifred's Road	B1		
Stewart Road	C1		
Surrey Road	A2		
The Lansdowne	C2		
The Square	B2		
The Triangle	A2		
Tregonwell Road	A3		

Appears on main
map page 106

0 400 yds / 0 400m

BRADFORD

Tourist Information Centre: Britannia House, Broadway
Tel: 01274 433678

Akam Road	A1	John Street	A2
Ann Place	A3	Kirkgate	B2
Ashgrove	A3	Leeds Road	C2
Balme Street	B1	Little Horton Lane	A3
Bank Street	B2	Lower Kirkgate	B2
Baptist Place	A1	Lumb Lane	A1
Barkerend Road	C1	Manchester Road	B3
Barry Street	A2	Manningham Lane	A1
Bolling Road	C3	Mannville Terrace	A3
Bolton Road	C1	Manor Row	B1
Brearton Street	A1	Melbourne Place	A3
Bridge Street	B2	Midland Road	B1
Britannia Street	B3	Moody Street	C3
Broadway	B2	Morley Street	A3
Burnett Street	C2	Neal Street	A3
Caledonia Street	B3	Nelson Street	B3
Canal Road	B1	North Parade	B1
Captain Street	C1	North Street	C1
Carlton Street	A2	North Wing	C1
Carter Street	C3	Nuttall Road	C1
Centenary Square	B2	Otley Road	C1
Chain Street	A1	Paradise Street	A1
Channing Way	B2	Park Road	B3
Chapel Street	C2	Peckover Street	C2
Charles Street	B2	Prince's Way	B2
Cheapside	B2	Prospect Street	C3
Chester Street	A3	Radwell Drive	A3
Churchbank	C2	Rawson Place	B1
Claremont	C1	Rawson Road	A1
Croft Street	B3	Rebecca Street	A1
Darfield Street	A1	Rouse Fold	C3
Darley Street	B1	Russell Street	A3
Drake Street	B2	Salem Street	B1
Drewton Road	A1	Sawrey Place	A3
Dryden Street	C3	Sedgwick Close	A1
Duke Street	B1	Sharpe Street	B3
Dyson Street	A1	Shipley Airedale Road	C1
East Parade	C2	Simes Street	A1
Edmund Street	A3	Snowden Street	A1
Edward Street	C3	Sunbridge Road	A1
Eldon Place	A1	Sylhet Close	A1
Fairfax Street	C3	Ternhill Grove	B3
Filey Street	C3	Tetley Street	A2
Fitzwilliam Street	C3	The Tyrls	B2
Fountain Street	A1	Thornton Road	A2
George Street	C2	Trafalgar Street	A1
Godwin Street	B2	Trinity Road	A3
Gracechurch Street	A1	Tumbling Hill Street	A2
Grafton Street	A3	Valley Road	B1
Grattan Road	A2	Vaughan Street	A1
Great Horton Road	A3	Vicar Lane	C2
Grove Terrace	A3	Vincent Street	A2
Guy Street	C3	Wakefield Road	C3
Hall Ings	B2	Wapping Road	C1
Hall Lane	C3	Water Lane	A2
Hallfield Road	A1	Westgate	A1
Hamm Strasse	B1	Wigan Street	A2
Hammerton Street	C2		
Hanover Square	A1		
Harris Street	C2		
Heap Lane	C1		
Houghton Place	A1		
Howard Street	A3		
Hustlergate	B2		
Ivegate	B2		
James Street	B2		

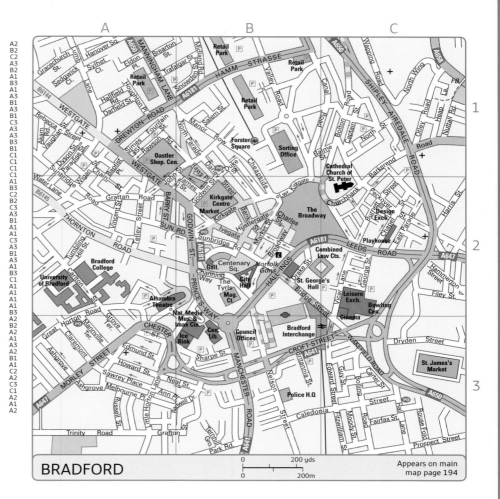

BRADFORD — 200 yds / 200m — Appears on main map page 194

BRIGHTON

Tourist Information Centre: Royal Pavilion Shop,
4-5 Pavilion Buildings Tel: 01273 290337

Addison Road	A1	Southover Street	C2
Albion Hill	C2	Springfield Road	B1
Beaconsfield Road	B1	Stafford Road	A1
Brunswick Square	A2	Stanford Road	B1
Buckingham Place	B1	Sussex Street	C2
Buckingham Road	B2	Terminus Road	B2
Carlton Hill	C2	The Lanes	B3
Cheapside	B2	The Upper Drive	A1
Church Street	B2	Trafalgar Street	B2
Churchill Square	B3	Union Road	C1
Clifton Hill	A2	Upper Lewes Road	C1
Clyde Road	B1	Upper North Street	A2
Davigdor Road	A1	Upper Rock Gardens	C3
Ditchling Rise	B1	Viaduct Road	B1
Ditchling Road	C1	Victoria Road	A2
Dyke Road	B2	Waterloo Street	A2
Dyke Road Drive	B1	Wellington Road	C1
Eastern Road	C3	West Drive	C2
Edward Street	C3	West Street	B3
Elm Grove	C1	Western Road	A2
Fleet Street	B2	Wilbury Crescent	A1
Florence Road	B1	York Avenue	A2
Freshfield Road	C3	York Place	C2
Furze Hill	A2		
Gloucester Road	B2		
Grand Junction Road	B3		
Hamilton Road	B1		
Hanover Street	C2		
Highdown Road	A1		
Holland Road	A2		
Hollingdean Road	C1		
Howard Place	B1		
Islingword Road	C1		
John Street	C2		
King's Road	A3		
Lansdowne Road	A2		
Lewes Road	C1		
London Road	B1		
Lyndhurst Road	A1		
Madeira Drive	C3		
Marine Parade	C3		
Montefiore Road	A1		
Montpelier Road	A2		
New England Road	B1		
New England Street	B1		
Nizells Avenue	A1		
Norfolk Terrace	A2		
North Road	B2		
North Street	B2		
Old Shoreham Road	A1		
Old Steine	C3		
Park Crescent Terrace	C1		
Park Street	C2		
Port Hall Road	A1		
Preston Circus	B1		
Preston Road	B1		
Preston Street	A3		
Prince's Crescent	C1		
Queen's Park Road	C2		
Queen's Road	B2		
Richmond Place	C2		
Richmond Road	C1		
Richmond Street	C2		
Richmond Terrace	C2		
St. James's Street	C3		
Somerhill Road	A2		

BRIGHTON — 200 yds / 200m — Appears on main map page 109

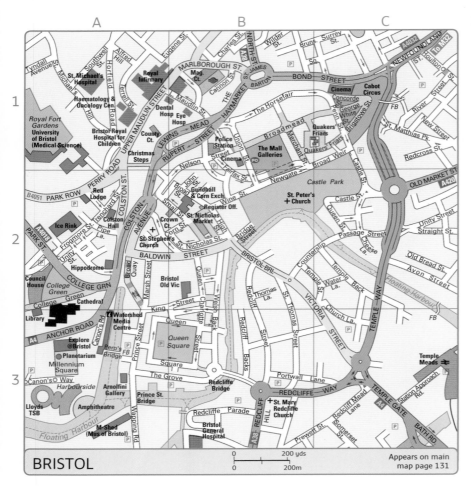

BRISTOL

Appears on main
map page 131

Tourist Information Centre: E Shed 1, Canons Road
Tel: 0906 711 2191

Alfred Hill	A1	Redcliffe Bridge	B3
Anchor Road	A3	Redcliffe Parade	B3
Avon Street	C2	Redcliff Hill	B3
Baldwin Street	A2	Redcliff Mead Lane	C3
Bath Road	C3	Redcliff Street	B2
Bond Street	B1	Redcross Street	C1
Bridge Street	B2	River Street	C1
Brigstowe Street	C1	Rupert Street	A1
Bristol Bridge	B2	St. James Barton	B1
Broadmead	B1	St. Matthias Park	C1
Broad Quay	A2	St. Michael's Hill	A1
Broad Street	B2	St. Nicholas Street	B2
Broad Weir	B1	St. Thomas Street	B2
Brunswick Square	B1	Small Street	A2
Cannon Street	B1	Somerset Street	C3
Canon's Road	A3	Southwell Street	A1
Canon's Way	A3	Station Approach Road	C3
Castle Street	C2	Straight Street	C2
Charles Street	B1	Surrey Street	C1
Cheese Lane	C2	Temple Back	C2
Christmas Steps	A1	Temple Gate	C3
Church Lane	C2	Temple Street	B2
College Green	A2	Temple Way	C3
Colston Avenue	A2	Terrell Street	A1
Colston Street	A2	The Grove	A3
Concorde Street	C1	The Haymarket	B1
Corn Street	C1	The Horsefair	B1
Countership	B2	Thomas Lane	B2
Eugene Street	A1	Trenchard Street	A2
Fairfax Street	B1	Tyndall Avenue	A1
Frogmore Street	A2	Union Street	B1
George White Street	C1	Unity Street	A2
High Street	B2	Unity Street	C2
Horfield Road	A1	Upper Maudlin Street	A1
Houlton Street	C1	Victoria Street	B2
John Street	B2	Wapping Road	A3
King Street	A2	Water Lane	C2
Lewins Mead	A1	Welsh Back	B2
Lower Castle Street	C1	Wilder Street	B1
Lower Maudlin Street	B1	Wine Street	B2
Marlborough Street	B1		
Marsh Street	A2		
Merchant Street	B1		
Nelson Street	B1		
Newfoundland Street	C1		
Newgate	B2		
New Street	C1		
North Street	B1		
Old Bread Street	C2		
Old Market Street	C2		
Park Row	A2		
Park Street	A2		
Passage Street	C2		
Penn Street	C1		
Pero's Bridge	A3		
Perry Road	A2		
Pipe Lane	A2		
Portwall Lane	B3		
Prewett Street	B3		
Prince Street	A3		
Prince Street Bridge	C1		
Quakers' Friars	B1		
Queen Charlotte Street	B2		
Queen Square	A3		
Queen Street	C2		
Redcliff Backs	B3		

CAMBRIDGE

Appears on main
map page 150

Tourist Information Centre: Wheeler Street
Tel: 0871 226 8006

Adam and Eve Street	C2	Tenison Road	C3
Alpha Road	B1	Tennis Court Road	B2
Aylestone Road	C1	Trinity Street	B2
Barton Road	A3	Trumpington Road	B3
Bateman Street	B3	Trumpington Street	B3
Belvior Road	C1	Union Road	B3
Brookside	B3	Victoria Avenue	B1
Burleigh Street	C2	Victoria Road	B1
Carlyle Road	B1	West Road	A2
Castle Street	A1		
Chesterton Lane	B1		
Chesterton Road	B1		
Clarendon Street	C2		
De Freville Avenue	C1		
Devonshire Road	C3		
Downing Street	B2		
East Road	C2		
Eden Street	C2		
Elizabeth Way	C1		
Emmanuel Road	B2		
Fen Causeway, The	A3		
Glisson Road	C3		
Gonville Place	C3		
Granchester Street	A3		
Grange Road	A3		
Gresham Road	C3		
Hamilton Road	C1		
Harvey Road	C3		
Hills Road	C3		
Humberstone Road	C1		
Huntingdon Road	A1		
Jesus Lane	B2		
King's Parade	B2		
King Street	B2		
Lensfield Road	B3		
Madingley Road	A1		
Magdalene Bridge Street	B1		
Maids Causeway	C2		
Market Street	B2		
Mawson Road	C3		
Millington Road	A3		
Mill Road	C3		
Montague Road	C1		
Newmarket Road	C2		
Newnham Road	A3		
Norfolk Street	C2		
Panton Street	B3		
Parker Street	B2		
Park Parade	B1		
Parkside	C2		
Park Terrace	B2		
Pembroke Street	B2		
Queen's Road	A2		
Regent Street	B2		
Regent Terrace	B2		
St. Andrew's Street	B2		
St. Barnabas Road	C3		
St. John's Street	B2		
St. Matthew's Street	C2		
St. Paul's Road	C3		
Searce Street	A1		
Sidgwick Avenue	A3		
Sidney Street	B2		
Silver Street	A3		
Station Road	C3		
Storey's Way	A1		

Tourist Information Centre: 18 The High Street
Tel: 01227 862162

Best Lane	B2	Watling Street	B2
Borough Northgate	B1	Whitehall Gardens	A2
Broad Street	C1	Whitehall Road	A2
Burgate	B2	Wincheap	A3
Castle Row	A3	York Road	A3
Castle Street	A3		
College Road	C1		
Cossington Road	C3		
Craddock Road	C1		
Dover Street	C2		
Edgar Road	C1		
Ersham Road	C3		
Forty Acres Road	A1		
Gordon Road	A3		
Havelock Street	C1		
Hawk's Lane	B2		
High Street	B2		
Ivy Lane	C2		
King Street	B1		
Kirby's Lane	A1		
Lansdown Road	B3		
Longport	C2		
Lower Bridge Street	C2		
Lower Chantry Lane	C2		
Marlowe Avenue	B3		
Martyrs' Field Road	A3		
Mead Way	A2		
Military Road	C1		
Monastery Street	C2		
New Dover Road	C3		
North Holmes Road	C1		
North Lane	A1		
Nunnery Fields	C3		
Oaten Hill	C3		
Old Dover Road	C3		
Orchard Street	A1		
Oxford Road	B3		
Palace Street	B2		
Pin Hill	A3		
Pound Lane	A1		
Puckle Lane	C3		
Rheims Way	A2		
Rhodaus Town	B3		
Roper Road	A1		
Rose Lane	B2		
St. Dunstan's Street	A1		
St. George's Lane	B2		
St. George's Place	C2		
St. George's Street	B2		
St. Gregory's Road	C1		
St. Margarets Street	B2		
St. Peter's Lane	B1		
St. Peter's Place	A2		
St. Peter's Street	A1		
St. Radigund's Street	B1		
St. Stephen's Road	B1		
Simmonds Road	A3		
Station Road East	A3		
Station Road West	A1		
Stour Street	A2		
The Causeway	B1		
The Friar's	B2		
Tourtel Road	C1		
Tudor Road	A3		
Union Street	C1		
Upper Bridge Street	B3		

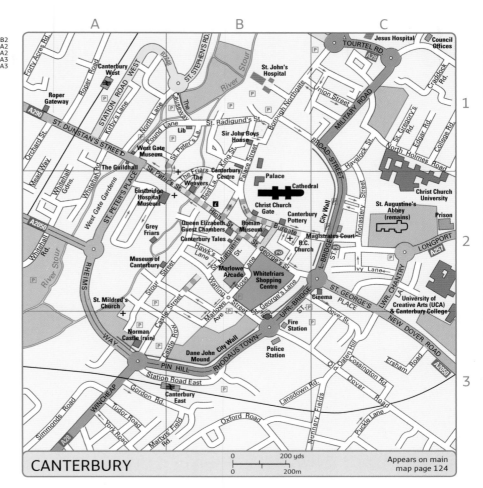

CANTERBURY

0   200 yds
0   200m

Appears on main map page 124

Tourist Information Centre: The Old Library, Trinity Street
Tel: 029 2087 3573

Adam Street	C3	Moira Terrace	C2
Albany Road	C1	Moy Road	C1
Allerton Street	A3	Museum Avenue	B1
Arran Place	C1	Neville Street	A2
Arran Street	C1	Newport Road	C2
Basil Place	B1	Newport Road Lane	C2
Bedford Street	C1	Ninian Park Road	A3
Boulevard de Nantes	B2	North Road	A1
Bridge Street	B3	Oxford Lane	C2
Brook Street	A3	Park Grove	B2
Bute Street	B3	Park Place	B1
Bute Terrace	B3	Park Street	B3
Castle Street	A2	Partridge Road	C1
Cathays Terrace	B1	Penarth Road	B3
Cathedral Road	A2	Pendyris Street	A3
Celerity Drive	C3	Pitman Street	A2
Central Link	C3	Planet Street	C2
Charles Street	B2	Queen Street	B2
Churchill Way	C2	Rhymney Street	B1
City Road	C1	Richard Street	B1
Clare Road	A3	Richmond Road	C1
Clare Street	A2	Ryder Street	A2
Claude Road	C1	St. Mary Street	B3
Coburn Street	B1	St. Peters Street	C2
College Road	B2	Salisbury Road	B1
Colum Road	A1	Schooner Way	C3
Corbett Road	B1	Senghennydd Road	B1
Cornwall Street	A3	Stafford Road	A3
Cottrell Road	C1	Strathnairn Street	C1
Cowbridge Road East	A2	Stuttgarter Strasse	B2
Craddock Street	A3	Taffs Mead Embankment	B3
Craiglee Drive	C3	Talbot Street	A2
Croft Street	C1	Thesiger Street	B1
Crwys Road	B1	The Parade	C2
Cyfartha Street	C1	The Walk	C1
De Burgh Street	A2	Tudor Street	A3
Despenser Street	A3	Tyndall Street	C3
Duke Street	B2	Wedmore Road	A3
Dumfries Place	C2	Wells Street	A3
Ellen Street	C3	West Grove	C2
Elm Street	C1	Westgate Street	B2
Fanny Street	B1	Windsor Place	B2
Fitzhamon Embankment	A3	Windsor Road	C2
Flora Street	B1	Wood Street	B3
Glossop Road	C2	Woodville Road	B1
Gordon Road	C1	Wordsworth Avenue	C2
Greyfriars Road	B2	Working Street	B2
Hamilton Street	A2	Wyeverne Road	B1
Harriet Street	B1		
Herbert Street	C3		
High Street	B2		
Hirwain Street	B1		
Keppoch Street	C1		
Kingsway	B2		
Lewis Street	A2		
Longcross Street	C2		
Maindy Road	A1		
Mardy Street	A3		
Mark Street	A2		
Merches Gardens	A3		
Merthyr Street	B1		
Meteor Street	C2		
Mill Lane	B3		
Minny Street	B1		
Miskin Street	B1		
Moira Place	C2		

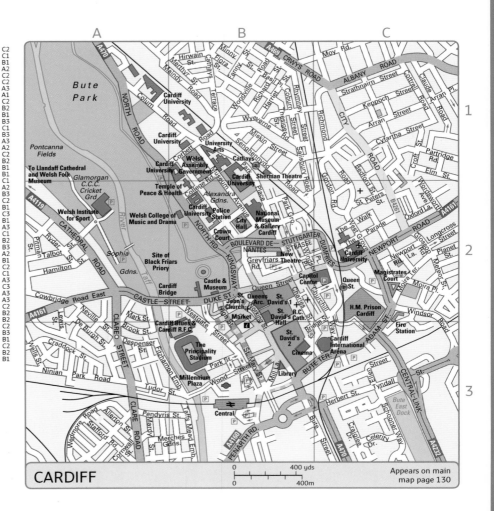

CARDIFF

0   400 yds
0   400m

Appears on main map page 130

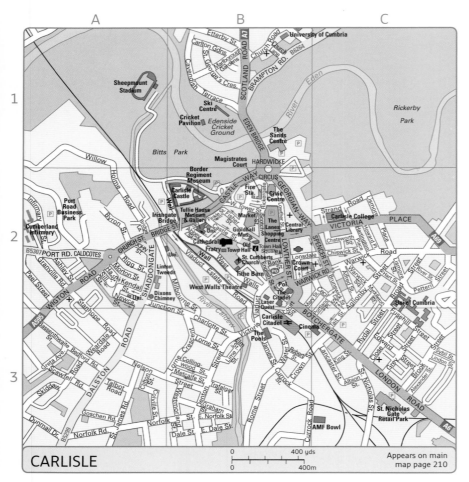

CARLISLE

Scale: 0 — 400 yds / 0 — 400m

Appears on main map page 210

Tourist Information Centre: Old Town Hall, Green Market
Tel: 01228 598596

Street	Grid	Street	Grid
Abbey Street	B2	Lancaster Street	C3
Aglionby Street	C2	Lime Street	B3
Albion Street	C3	Lindon Street	C3
Alexander Street	C3	Lismore Place	C2
Alfred Street	C2	Lismore Street	C2
Ashley Street	A2	London Road	C3
Bank Street	B2	Lonsdale	B2
Bassenthwaite Street	A3	Lorne Crescent	B3
Bedford Road	A3	Lorne Street	B3
Botchergate	B3	Lowther Street	B2
Brampton Road	B1	Marlborough Gardens	B1
Bridge Lane	A2	Mary Street	B2
Bridge Street	A2	Metcalfe Street	B3
Broad Street	C2	Milbourne Street	B2
Brook Street	C3	Morton Street	A2
Brunswick Street	C2	Muddleton Street	C2
Byron Street	A2	Nelson Street	A3
Caldcotes	A2	Newcastle Street	A2
Carlton Gardens	B1	Norfolk Road	A3
Castle Street	B2	Norfolk Street	A3
Castle Way	B2	Peel Street	A2
Cavendish Terrace	B1	Petteril Street	C2
Cecil Street	C2	Port Road	A2
Charlotte Street	B3	Portland Place	C3
Chatsworth Square	C2	Rickergate	B2
Chiswick Street	C2	Rigg Street	A2
Church Lane	B1	River Street	C2
Church Road	B1	Robert Street	B3
Church Street	A2	Rome Street	B3
Clifton Street	A3	Rydal Street	C3
Close Street	C3	St. George's Crescent	B1
Collingwood Street	B3	St. James Road	A3
Colville Street	A3	St. Nicholas Street	C3
Crown Street	B3	Scawfell Road	A3
Currock Road	B3	Scotch Street	B2
Currock Street	B3	Scotland Road	B1
Dale Street	B3	Shaddongate	A2
Denton Street	B3	Silloth Street	A2
Dunmail Drive	A3	Skiddaw Road	A3
East Dale Street	B3	Spencer Street	C2
East Norfolk Street	B3	Stanhope Road	A2
Eden Bridge	B1	Strand Road	C2
Edward Street	C3	Sybil Street	C3
Elm Street	B3	Tait Street	C3
English Street	B2	Talbot Road	A3
Etterby Street	B1	Trafalgar Street	B3
Finkle Street	B2	Viaduct Estate Road	B2
Fisher Street	B2	Victoria Place	C2
Fusehill Street	C3	Victoria Viaduct	B3
Georgian Way	B2	Warwick Road	B2
Goschen Road	A3	Warwick Square	C2
Graham Street	B3	Water Street	B3
Granville Road	A2	Weardale Road	A3
Greta Avenue	A3	West Tower Street	B2
Grey Street	C3	West Walls	B2
Hardwicke Circus	B1	Westmorland Street	B3
Hart Street	C2	Wigton Road	A2
Hartington Place	C2	Willow Holme Road	A1
Hawick Street	A2		
Howard Place	C2		
Infirmary Street	A2		
James Street	B3		
John Street	A2		
Junction Street	A2		
Kendal Street	A2		
King Street	C3		

CHELTENHAM

Scale: 0 — 300 yds / 0 — 300m

Appears on main map page 146

Tourist Information Centre: 77 Promenade
Tel: 01242 522878

Street	Grid	Street	Grid
Albany Road	A3	Portland Street	B2
Albert Road	C1	Prestbury Road	C1
Albion Street	B2	Princes Road	A3
All Saints Road	C2	Priory Street	C3
Andover Road	A3	Promenade	B2
Arle Avenue	A1	Rodney Road	B2
Ashford Road	A3	Rosehill Street	C3
Bath Parade	B2	Royal Well Road	B2
Bath Road	B3	St. George's Place	B2
Bayshill Road	A2	St. George's Road	A2
Berkeley Street	B2	St. James Street	B2
Brunswick Street	B1	St. Johns Avenue	B2
Carlton Street	C2	St. Margaret's Road	B1
Central Cross Drive	C1	St. Paul's Road	B1
Christchurch Road	A2	St. Paul's Street North	B1
Churchill Drive	C3	St. Paul's Street South	B1
Clarence Road	B1	St. Stephen's Road	A3
College Lawn	B3	Sandford Mill Road	C3
College Road	B3	Sandford Road	B3
Cranham Road	C3	Sherborne Street	C2
Douro Road	A2	Southgate Drive	C3
Dunalley Street	B1	Strickland Road	C3
Eldon Road	C2	Suffolk Road	A3
Evesham Road	C1	Suffolk Square	A3
Fairview Road	C2	Sun Street	A1
Folly Lane	B1	Swindon Road	A1
Gloucester Road	A2	Sydenham Road	C2
Grafton Road	A3	Sydenham Villas Road	C3
Hales Road	C3	Tewkesbury Road	A1
Hanover Street	B1	Thirlestaine Road	B3
Hayward's Road	C3	Tivoli Road	A3
Henrietta Street	B2	Townsend Street	A1
Hewlett Road	C2	Vittoria Walk	B3
High Street	B1	Wellington Road	C1
Honeybourne Way	A1	West Drive	B1
Hudson Street	B1	Western Road	A2
Imperial Square	B2	Whaddon Road	C1
Keynsham Road	B3	Winchcombe Street	B2
King Alfred Way	C3	Windsor Street	C1
King's Road	C2		
Lansdown Crescent	A3		
Lansdown Road	A3		
London Road	C3		
Lypiatt Road	A3		
Malvern Road	A2		
Market Street	A1		
Marle Hill Parade	B1		
Marle Hill Road	B1		
Millbrook Street	A1		
Montpellier Spa Road	B3		
Montpellier Street	A3		
Montpellier Terrace	A3		
Montpellier Walk	A3		
New Street	A2		
North Place	B2		
North Street	B2		
Old Bath Road	C3		
Oriel Road	B2		
Overton Road	A2		
Painswick Road	A2		
Parabola Road	A2		
Park Place	A3		
Park Street	A1		
Pittville Circus	C1		
Pittville Circus Road	C2		
Pittville Lawn	C1		

Tourist Information Centre: Town Hall, Northgate Street
Tel: 0845 647 7868

Bath Street	C2	Queen's Park Road	B3
Bedward Row	A2	Queen's Road	C1
Black Diamond Street	B1	Queen Street	B2
Black Friars	A3	Raymond Street	A1
Bold Square	B2	Russel Street	A1
Boughton	C2	St. Anne Street	B1
Bouverie Street	A1	St. George's Crescent	C3
Bridge Street	B2	St. John's Road	C3
Brook Street	B1	St. John Street	A1
Canal Street	A1	St. Martins Way	A1
Castle Drive	A3	St. Oswalds Way	B1
Charles Street	B1	St. Werburgh Street	B2
Cheyney Road	A1	Seller Street	C2
Chichester Street	A1	Sibell Street	C1
City Road	C2	Souter's Lane	B3
City Walls Road	A2	Stanley Street	A2
Commonhall Street	A2	Station Road	C1
Cornwall Street	B1	Steam Mill Road	C1
Crewe Street	C1	Talbot Street	B1
Cuppin Street	A3	The Bars	C2
Dee Hills Park	C2	The Groves	B3
Dee Lane	C2	Trafford Street	B1
Deva Terrace	C2	Union Street	B2
Duke Street	B3	Upper Northgate Street	A1
Eastgate Street	B2	Vicar's Lane	B2
Edinburgh Way	C3	Victoria Crescent	C3
Egerton Street	B1	Victoria Place	B2
Elizabeth Crescent	C3	Victoria Road	A1
Foregate Street	B2	Walker Street	C1
Forest Street	B2	Walpole Street	A1
Francis Street	C1	Walter Street	B1
Frodsham Street	B2	Watergate Street	A2
Garden Lane	A1	Water Tower Street	A2
George Street	B1	Weaver Street	A2
Gloucester Street	B1	White Friars	A3
Grey Friars	A3	York Street	B2
Grosvenor Park Terrace	C2		
Grosvenor Road	A3		
Grosvenor Street	A3		
Handbridge	B3		
Hoole Road	B1		
Hoole Way	B1		
Hunter Street	A2		
King Street	A2		
Leadworks Lane	C2		
Lightfoot Street	C1		
Louise Street	A1		
Love Street	B2		
Lower Bridge Street	B3		
Lower Park Road	C3		
Mill Street	C2		
Milton Street	B1		
Newgate Street	B2		
Nicholas Street	A2		
Nicholas Street Mews	A2		
Northern Pathway	C3		
Northgate Avenue	A2		
Northgate Street	A2		
Nun's Road	A3		
Old Dee Bridge	B3		
Pepper Street	B3		
Phillip Street	C1		
Prince's Avenue	C1		
Princess Street	A2		
Queen's Avenue	C1		
Queen's Drive	C3		

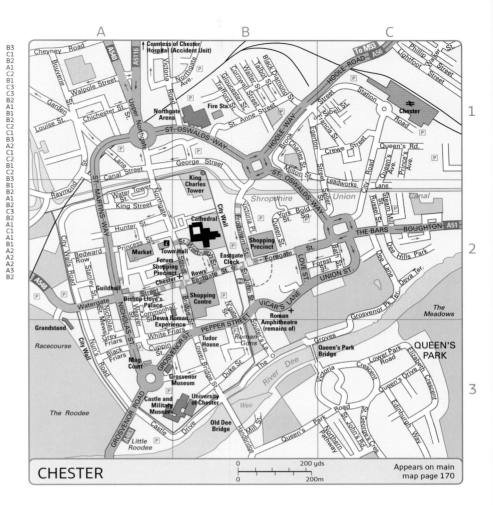

CHESTER

0   200 yds
0   200m

Appears on main
map page 170

Tourist Information Centre: St. Michael's Tower, Coventry
Cathedral   Tel: 024 7622 5616

Abbott's Lane	A1	New Union Street	B2
Acacia Avenue	C3	Norfolk Street	A2
Albany Road	A3	Oxford Street	C2
Alma Street	C2	Park Road	B3
Asthill Grove	B3	Parkside	B3
Barker's Butts Lane	A1	Primrose Hill Street	C1
Barras Lane	A2	Priory Street	B2
Berry Street	C1	Puma Way	B3
Bishop Street	B1	Quarryfield Lane	C3
Blythe Road	C1	Queen's Road	A3
Bond Street	A2	Queen Street	C1
Bramble Street	C2	Queen Victoria Road	A2
Bretts Close	C1	Quinton Road	B3
Broadway	A3	Radford Road	A1
Burges	B2	Raglan Street	C2
Butts Road	A2	Regent Street	A3
Cambridge Street	C1	Ringway Hill Cross	A2
Canterbury Street	C1	Ringway Queens	A2
Clifton Street	C1	Ringway Rudge	A2
Colchester Street	C1	A2	
Cornwall Street	C3	Ringway St. Johns	B3
Corporation Street	B2	Ringway St. Nicholas	B1
Coundon Road	A1	Ringway St. Patricks	B3
Coundon Street	A1	Ringway Swanswell	B1
Cox Street	C2	B2	
Croft Road	A2	Ringway Whitefriars	C2
Drapers Fields	B1	St. Nicholas Street	B1
Earl Street	B2	Sandy Lane	B1
East Street	C2	Seagrave Road	C3
Eaton Road	B3	Silver Street	B1
Fairfax Street	B2	Sky Blue Way	C2
Far Gosford Street	C2	South Street	C2
Foleshill Road	B1	Spencer Avenue	A3
Fowler Road	A1	Spon Street	A2
Gordon Street	A3	Srathmore Avenue	C3
Gosford Street	C2	Stoney Road	B3
Greyfriars Road	A2	Stoney Stanton Road	B1
Gulson Road	C2	Swanswell Street	B1
Hales Street	B2	The Precinct	B2
Harnall Lane East	C1	Tomson Avenue	A1
Harnall Lane West	B1	Trinity Street	B2
Harper Road	C2	Upper Hill Street	A2
Harper Street	B2	Upper Well Street	B2
Hertford Street	B2	Vauxhall Street	C2
Hewitt Avenue	A1	Vecqueray Street	C2
High Street	B2	Victoria Street	C1
Hill Street	A2	Vine Street	C1
Holyhead Road	A2	Warwick Road	A3
Hood Street	C2	Waveley Road	A2
Howard Street	B1	Westminster Road	A3
Jordan Well	B2	White Street	B1
King William Street	C1	Windsor Street	A2
Lamb Street	B2	Wright Street	C1
Leicester Row	B1		
Leigh Street	C1		
Little Park Street	B3		
London Road	C3		
Lower Ford Street	C2		
Market Way	B2		
Meadow Street	A2		
Michaelmas Road	A3		
Middleborough Road	A1		
Mile Lane	B3		
Mill Street	A1		
Minster Road	A2		
Much Park Street	B2		

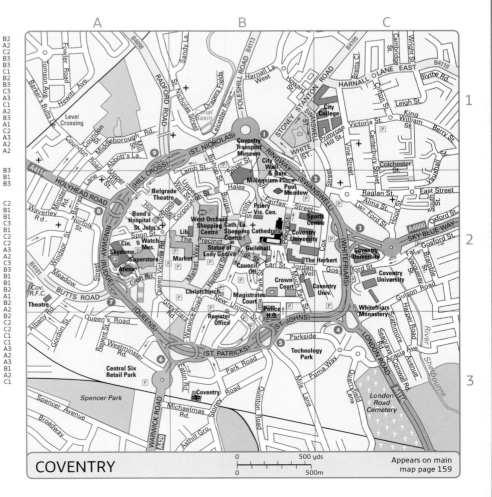

COVENTRY

0   500 yds
0   500m

Appears on main
map page 159

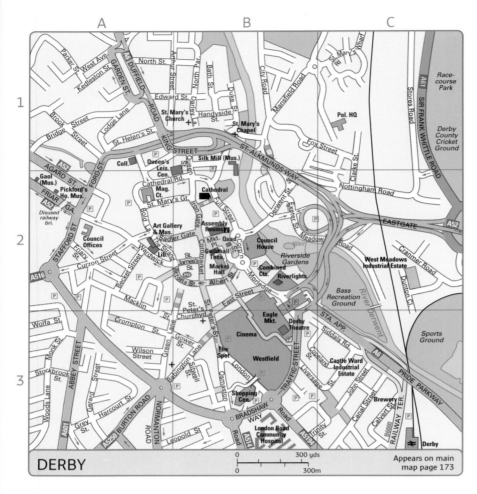

Tourist Information Centre: Assembly Rooms, Market Place
Tel: 01332 643411

Abbey Street	A3	Railway Terrace	C3
Agard Street	A1	Sadler Gate	B2
Albert Street	B2	St. Alkmunds Way	B1
Arthur Street	A1	St. Helen's Street	A1
Babington Lane	A3	St. James Street	B2
Bath Street	B1	St. Mary's Gate	A2
Becket Street	A2	St. Mary's Wharf Road	C1
Bold Lane	A2	St. Peter's Churchyard	B3
Bradshaw Way	B3	St. Peter's Street	B2
Bridge Street	A1	Siddals Road	C3
Brook Street	A1	Sir Frank Whittle Road	C1
Burton Road	A3	Sitwell Street	B3
Calvert Street	C3	Stafford Street	A2
Canal Street	C3	Station Approach	C2
Cathedral Road	A2	Stockbrook Street	A3
City Road	B1	Stores Road	C1
Clarke Street	C2	The Strand	A2
Copeland Street	B3	Traffic Street	B3
Cornmarket	B2	Trinity Street	B3
Corporation Street	B2	Victoria Street	A2
Cranmer Road	C2	Wardwick	A2
Crompton Street	A3	West Avenue	A1
Curzon Street	A2	Wilson Street	A3
Darley Lane	B1	Wolfa Street	A3
Derwent Street	B2	Woods Lane	A3
Duffield Road	A1		
Duke Street	B1		
Dunton Close	C2		
Eastgate	C2		
East Street	B2		
Edward Street	A1		
Exeter Street	B2		
Ford Street	A2		
Fox Street	B1		
Friar Gate	A2		
Friary Street	A2		
Full Street	B2		
Garden Street	A1		
Gerard Street	A3		
Gower Street	B3		
Green Lane	A3		
Grey Street	A3		
Handyside Street	B1		
Harcourt Street	A3		
Iron Gate	B2		
John Street	C3		
Kedleston Street	A1		
King Street	A1		
Leopold Street	A3		
Liversage Street	B3		
Lodge Lane	A1		
London Road	B3		
Macklin Street	A2		
Mansfield Road	B1		
Market Place	B2		
Meadow Road	B2		
Monk Street	A3		
Morledge	B2		
Normanton Road	A3		
North Parade	B1		
North Street	A1		
Nottingham Road	C2		
Osmaston Road	B3		
Parker Street	A1		
Pride Parkway	C3		
Queen Street	B1		

Appears on main
map page 173

DERBY

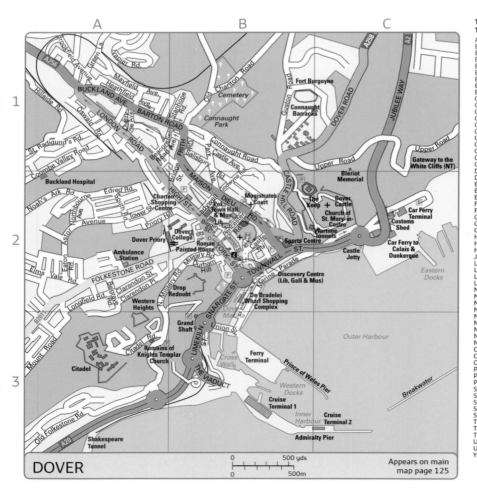

Tourist Information Centre: Dover Museum, Market Square
Tel: 01304 201066

Astor Avenue	A2
Barton Road	A1
Beaconsfield Avenue	A1
Beaconsfield Road	A1
Belgrave Road	A2
Biggin Street	B2
Bridge Street	B2
Brookfield Avenue	A1
Buckland Avenue	A1
Cannon Street	B2
Canons Gate Road	B2
Castle Avenue	B1
Castle Hill Road	B2
Castle Street	B2
Cherry Tree Avenue	A1
Citadel Road	A3
Clarendon Place	A2
Clarendon Street	A2
Connaught Road	B1
Coombe Valley Road	A2
Dover Road	C1
Durham Hill	B2
Eaton Road	A2
Edred Road	A2
Elms Vale Road	A2
Folkestone Road	A2
Frith Road	B1
Godwyne Road	B2
Green Lane	A1
Guston Road	B1
Heathfield Avenue	A1
High Street	B2
Hillside Road	A1
Jubilee Way	C1
Ladywell	B2
Limekiln Street	B3
London Road	A1
Longfield Road	A2
Maison Dieu Road	B2
Marine Parade	B2
Mayfield Avenue	A1
Military Road	B2
Mount Road	A3
Napier Road	A1
Noah's Ark Road	A2
Northbourne Avenue	A2
North Military Road	A2
Old Charlton Road	B1
Old Folkestone Road	A3
Oswald Road	A1
Park Avenue	B1
Pencester Road	B2
Priory Hill	A2
St. Radigund's Road	A1
Salisbury Road	B1
Snargate Street	B3
South Road	A2
Stanhope Road	B1
The Viaduct	B3
Tower Street	A2
Townwall Street	B2
Union Street	B3
Upper Road	C1
York Street	B2

Appears on main
map page 125

DOVER

Tourist Information Centre: 16 City Square
Tel: 01382 527527

Adelaide Place	A1	South Marketgait	B3
Albany Terrace	A1	South Tay Street	A3
Albert Street	C2	Strathmartine Road	B1
Alexander Street	B1	Tannadice Street	B1
Ann Street	B2	Tay Road Bridge	B3
Arbroath Road	C2	Trades Lane	B2
Arklay Street	C1	Upper Constitution Street	A1
Arklay Terrace	C1	Victoria Road	B2
Arthurstone Terrace	C2	Victoria Street	C2
Barrack Road	A2	Ward Road	A2
Blackness Road	A2	West Marketgait	A2
Blinshall Street	A2	West Port	A2
Brewery Lane	A2	William Street	C2
Brook Street	A2		
Broughty Ferry Road	C2		
Brown Street	A2		
Bruce Street	A1		
Byron Street	A1		
Canning Street	B1		
City Square	B3		
Clepington Road	C1		
Constitution Road	B2		
Constitution Street	B1		
Court Street	C1		
Cowgate Street	B2		
Dens Road	B1		
Douglas Street	A2		
Dudhope Street	A1		
Dudhope Terrace	C1		
Dundonald Street	C1		
Dura Street	C2		
East Dock Street	C2		
East Marketgait	B2		
Fairbairn Street	B1		
Greenmarket	B3		
Guthrie Street	A2		
Hawkhill	A2		
High Street	B3		
Hill Street	B1		
Hilltown	B1		
Kenmore Terrace	A1		
Killin Avenue	A1		
Kinghorne Road	A1		
King Street	B2		
Larch Street	A2		
Law Crescent	A1		
Lawside Avenue	A1		
Law Street	A1		
Leng Street	A1		
Lochee Road	A2		
Lower Princes Street	C2		
Mains Road	B1		
Main Street	B1		
Meadowside	B2		
Morgan Street	C2		
Murraygate	B2		
Nelson Street	B2		
Nethergate	A3		
North Marketgait	A2		
Perth Road	A3		
Polepark Road	A2		
Princes Street	C2		
Riverside Drive	A3		
Roseangle	A3		
Rosebank Road	B2		
Seagate	B2		

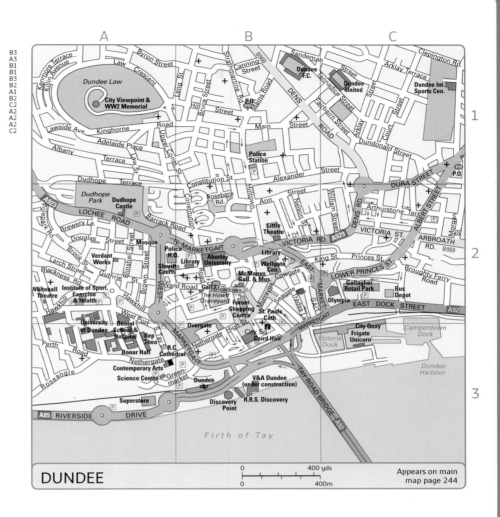

Tourist Information Centre: 2 Millennium Place
Tel: 0191 384 3720

Aykley Heads	A1
Church Street	B3
Clay Lane	A3
Claypath	B2
Crossgate	B2
Crossgate Peth	A3
Darlington Road	A3
Dryburn Road	A1
Durham Road	A1
Fieldhouse Lane	A1
Framwelgate	B2
Framwelgate Peth	B1
Framwelgate Waterside	B2
Gilesgate	C2
Great North Road	A1
Green Lane	C2
Grove Street	B3
Hallgarth Street	C3
Hawthorn Terrace	A2
Leazes Road	B2
Margery Lane	B3
Market Place	B2
Millburngate Bridge	B2
Newcastle Road	A1
New Elvet	B2
North Bailey	B2
North End	A1
North Road	B2
Old Elvet	C2
Pity Me Bypass	A1
Potters Bank	A3
Quarryheads Lane	B3
Providence Row	B2
Redhills Lane	A2
St. Monica Grove	A2
Sidegate	B2
Silver Street	B2
South Bailey	B3
South Road	B3
South Street	B3
Southfield Way	A1
Stockton Road	B3
Sutton Street	B2
The Avenue	A3
Toll House Road	A2
Western Hill	A2
Whinney Hill	C3
Whitesmocks	A1

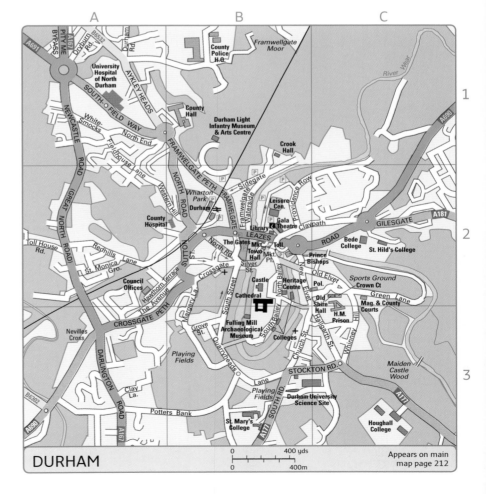

Eastbourne   Exeter

Edinburgh street map on pages 36-37

EASTBOURNE

0   200 yds
0   200m

Appears on main
map page 110

Tourist Information Centre: 3 Cornfield Road
Tel: 01323 415415

Street	Grid
Arlington Road	A2
Arundel Road	B1
Ashford Road	B2/C2
Avondale Road	C1
Bedfordwell Road	B1
Belmore Road	C1
Blackwater Road	B3
Borough Lane	A1
Bourne Street	C2
Carew Road	A1/B1
Carlisle Road	A3
Cavendish Avenue	C1
Cavendish Place	C2
College Road	B3
Commercial Road	B2
Compton Place Road	A2
Compton Street	B3
Cornfield Terrace	B2
Denton Road	A3
Devonshire Place	B2
Dittons Road	A2
Dursley Road	C2
Enys Road	B1
Eversfield Road	B1
Fairfield Road	A3
Firle Road	C1
Furness Road	B3
Gaudick Road	A3
Gilbert Road	C1
Gildredge Road	B2
Gorringe Road	A2
Grand Parade	C3
Grange Road	B3
Grassington Road	B3
Grove Road	B2
Hartfield Road	B1
Hartington Place	C2
High Street	A1
Hyde Gardens	B2
King Edward's Parade	B3
Langney Road	C2
Lewes Road	B1
Marine Parade	C2
Mark Lane	B2
Meads Road	A3
Melbourne Road	C1
Mill Gap Road	A1
Mill Road	A1
Moat Croft Road	A1
Moy Avenue	C1
Ratton Road	A1
Royal Parade	C2
Saffrons Park	A3
Saffrons Road	A2
St. Anne's Road	A1
St. Leonard's Road	B2
Seaside	C2
Seaside Road	C2
Selwyn Road	A1
Silverdale Road	B3
South Street	B2
Southfields Road	A2
Station Parade	B2
Susan's Road	C2
Sydney Road	C2
Terminus Road	B2
The Avenue	B2
The Goffs	A1
Trinity Trees	C2
Upper Avenue	B1
Upperton Lane	B2
Upperton Road	A1
Watts Lane	A1
Whitley Road	A1
Willingdon Road	A1
Winchcombe Road	C1

EXETER

0   400 yds
0   400m

Appears on main
map page 102

Tourist Information Centre: Dix's Field
Tel: 01392 665700

Street	Grid
Albion Street	A3
Alphington Street	A3
Barnfield Road	B2
Bartholomew Street West	A2
Bedford Street	B2
Belmont Road	C1
Blackboy Road	C1
Blackall Road	B1
Bonhay Road	A2
Buller Road	A3
Church Road	A3
Clifton Hill	C1
Clifton Road	C2
Clifton Street	C2
College Road	C2
Commercial Road	B3
Cowick Street	A3
Cowley Bridge Road	A1
Danes Road	B1
Denmark Road	C2
Devonshire Place	C1
Dix's Field	B2
East Grove Road	C3
Elmside	C1
Exe Street	A2
Fore Street	B2
Haldon Road	A2
Haven Road	B3
Heavitree Road	C2
Hele Road	A1
High Street	B2
Holloway Street	B3
Hoopern Street	B1
Howell Road	B1
Iddesleigh Road	C1
Iron Bridge	A2
Isca Road	B3
Jesmond Road	C1
Longbrook Street	B1
Looe Road	A1
Lyndhurst Road	C3
Magdalen Road	C2
Magdalen Street	B3
Marlborough Road	C3
Matford Avenue	C3
Matford Lane	C3
Mount Pleasant Road	C1
New Bridge Street	A3
New North Road	A1/B1
North Street	B2
Okehampton Road	A3
Okehampton Street	A3
Old Tiverton Road	C1
Oxford Road	C1
Paris Street	B2
Paul Street	B2
Pennsylvania Road	B1
Portland Street	C2
Prince of Wales Road	A1
Princesshay	B2
Prospect Park	C1
Queen's Road	A3
Queen Street	B2
Radford Road	C3
Richmond Road	A2
St. David's Hill	A1
St. James' Road	C1
St. Leonard's Road	C3
Sidwell Street	B2
Southernhay East	B2
South Street	B2
Spicer Road	C2
Station Road	A1
Streatham Drive	A1
Streatham Rise	A1
The Quay	B3
Thornton Hill	B1
Topsham Road	B3
Velwell Road	A1
Victoria Street	C1
Water Lane	B3
Well Street	C1
West Avenue	B1
Western Road	A2
Western Way	C2
Wonford Road	C3
York Road	B1

Tourist Information Centre: Discover Folkestone, 20 Bouverie Place. Tel: 01303 258594

Alder Road	B2
Archer Road	C2
Bathurst Road	A2
Beatty Road	C1
Black Bull Road	B2
Bournemouth Road	B2
Bouverie Road West	A3
Bradstone Road	B2
Broadfield Road	A2
Broadmead Road	B2
Brockman Road	B2
Canterbury Road	C1
Castle Hill Avenue	B3
Cheriton Gardens	B3
Cheriton Road	A2/B2
Cherry Garden Avenue	A1
Christ Church Road	B3
Churchill Avenue	B1
Clifton Crescent	A3
Coniston Road	A1
Coolinge Road	B2
Cornwallis Avenue	A2
Dawson Road	B2
Dixwell Road	A3
Dolphins Road	B1
Dover Hill	C1
Dover Road	C1
Downs Road	B1
Earles Avenue	A3
Foord Road	B2
Godwyn Road	A3
Grimston Avenue	A3
Grimston Gardens	A3
Guildhall Street	B2
Guildhall Street North	B2
Harbour Way	C2
Hill Road	C1
Ivy Way	C1
Joyes Road	C1
Linden Crescent	B2
Links Way	A1
Lower Sandgate Road	A3
Lucy Avenue	A1
Manor Road	B3
Marine Parade	B3
Marshall Street	C1
Mead Road	B2
Old High Street	C3
Park Farm Road	B1
Pavilion Road	B2
Radnor Bridge Road	C2
Radnor Park Avenue	A2
Radnor Park Road	B2
Radnor Park West	A2
Sandgate Hill	A3
Sandgate Road	B3
Shorncliffe Road	A2
Sidney Street	C2
The Leas	B3
The Stade	C3
The Tram Road	C2
Tontine Street	C2
Turketel Road	A3
Tyson Road	C1
Wear Bay Crescent	C2
Wear Bay Road	C1

Westbourne Gardens	A3
Wingate Road	B1
Wood Avenue	C1
Wilton Road	A2

FOLKESTONE

0 — 200 yds
0 — 200m

Appears on main map page 125

Tourist Information Centre: 28 Southgate Street Tel: 01452 396572

Adelaide Street	B3
Alexandra Road	B1
Alfred Street	C2
Alma Place	A3
Alvin Street	B1
Archdeacon Street	A1
Argyll Road	C1
Askwith Road	C3
Barnwood Road	C1
Barton Street	B2
Black Dog Way	B1
Bristol Road	A3
Brunswick Road	B2
Bruton Way	B2
Calton Road	B3
Castle Meads Way	A1
Cecil Road	A3
Cheltenham Road	C1
Churchill Road	A3
Clifton Road	A3
Conduit Street	B3
Coney Hill Road	C3
Dean's Way	B1
Denmark Road	B1
Derby Road	B2
Estcourt Road	B1
Eastern Avenue	C3
Eastgate Street	B2
Frampton Road	A3
Gouda Way	A1
Great Western Road	B2
Greyfriars	B2
Hatherley Road	B3
Heathville Road	B1
Hempsted Lane	A2
Henry Road	B1
High Street	B3
Hopewell Street	B3
Horton Road	C2
Howard Street	B3
India Road	C2
King Edward's Avenue	B3
Kingsholm Road	B1
Lansdown Road	B1
Linden Road	A3
Llanthony Road	A2
London Road	B1
Lower Westgate Street	A1
Marlborough Road	C3
Merevale Road	C1
Metz Way	B2
Midland Road	B3
Millbrook Street	B2
Myers Road	C2
Northgate Street	B2
Oxford Road	B1
Oxstalls Lane	C1
Painswick Road	C3
Park Road	B2
Parkend Road	B3
Pitt Street	B1
Quay Street	A2
Regent Street	B3
Robinson Road	A3
Ryecroft Street	B3
St. Ann Way	A3

St. Oswald's Road	A1
Secunda Way	A3
Severn Road	A2
Seymour Road	A3
Southgate Street	A2
Spa Road	A2
Stanley Road	B3
Station Road	B2
Stroud Road	A3
The Quay	A2
Tredworth Road	B3
Trier Way	A3
Upton Street	B3
Vicarage Road	C3
Victoria Street	B2
Wellington Street	B2
Westgate Street	A1
Weston Road	A3
Wheatstone Road	B3
Willow Avenue	C3
Worcester Street	B1

GLOUCESTER

0 — 500 yds
0 — 500m

Appears on main map page 132

GUILDFORD

Scale: 0 — 200 yds / 0 — 200m

Appears on main map page 121

Tourist Information Centre: 155 High Street
Tel: 01483 444333

Abbot Road	C3	Portsmouth Road	B3
Artillery Road	B1	Poyle Road	C3
Artillery Terrace	B1	Quarry Street	B2
Bedford Road	B1	Queens Road	C1
Bridge Street	B2	Rookwood Court	A3
Bright Hill	C2	Rupert Road	A2
Brodie Road	C2	Sand Terrace	B1
Bury Fields	B3	Semaphore Road	C3
Bury Street	B3	South Hill	C2
Castle Hill	C3	Springfield Road	C1
Castle Square	C2	Station Approach	C1
Castle Street	B2	Station View	A1
Chertsey Street	C1	Stoke Road	C1
Cheselden Road	C2	Swan Lane	B2
Commercial Road	B2	Sydenham Road	C2
Dapdune Court	B1	Testard Road	A2
Dapdune Road	B1	The Bars	B2
Dapdune Wharf	B1	The Mount	A3
Dene Road	C1	Tunsgate	C2
Denmark Road	C1	Upperton Road	A2
Denzil Road	A2	Victoria Road	C1
Drummond Road	B1	Walnut Tree Close	A1
Eagle Road	C1	Warwicks	C3
Eastgate Gardens	C1	Wharf Road	B1
Falcon Road	C1	Wherwell Road	A2
Farnham Road	A2	William Road	B1
Flower Walk	B3	Wodeland Avenue	A3
Fort Road	C3	Woodbridge Road	B1
Foxenden Road	C1	York Road	B1
Friary Bridge	B2		
Friary Street	B2		
Genyn Road	A2		
George Road	B1		
Great Quarry	C3		
Guildford Park Avenue	A1		
Guildford Park Road	A2		
Harvey Road	C2		
Haydon Place	B1		
High Pewley	C3		
High Street	B2/C2		
Laundry Road	B1		
Lawn Road	B3		
Leap Lane	B2		
Leas Road	B1		
Ludlow Road	A2		
Mareschal Road	A3		
Margaret Road	B1		
Market Street	B2		
Martyr Road	B2		
Mary Road	B1		
Millbrook	B3		
Millmead	B2		
Millmead Terrace	B3		
Mount Pleasant	A3		
Mountside	A3		
Nether Mount	A3		
Nightingale Road	C1		
North Place	B1		
North Street	B2		
Onslow Road	C1		
Onslow Street	B2		
Oxford Road	C2		
Pannells Court	C2		
Park Road	B1		
Park Street	B2		
Pewley Hill	C2		

HARROGATE

Scale: 0 — 150 yds / 0 — 150m

Appears on main map page 194

Tourist Information Centre: Royal Baths, Crescent Road
Tel: 01423 537300

Ainsty Road	C1	Regent Grove	C1
Albert Street	B2	Regent Parade	C1
Alexandra Road	B1	Regent Street	C1
Arthington Avenue	B2	Regent Terrace	C1
Beech Grove	A3	Ripon Road	A1
Belford Road	B2	Robert Street	B3
Bower Road	B1	St. James Drive	C3
Bower Street	B2	St. Mary's Walk	A3
Cambridge Street	B2	Skipton Road	C1
Cavendish Avenue	C3	South Park Road	B3
Chelmsford Road	B2	Springfield Avenue	A1
Cheltenham Mount	B1	Spring Grove	A1
Chudleigh Road	C1	Spring Mount	A1
Clarence Drive	A2	Station Avenue	B2
Claro Road	C1	Station Parade	B2
Cold Bath Road	A3	Stray Rein	B3
Commercial Street	B1	Stray Walk	C3
Coppice Drive	A1	Studley Road	B1
Cornwall Road	A2	Swan Road	A2
Crescent Gardens	A2	The Grove	C1
Dragon Avenue	B1	Tower Street	B3
Dragon Parade	B1	Trinity Road	B3
Dragon Road	B1	Valley Drive	A2
Duchy Road	A1	Victoria Avenue	B2
East Parade	B2	Victoria Road	A3
East Park Road	B2	West End Avenue	A3
Franklin Mount	B1	West Park	B2
Franklin Road	B1	Woodside	B2
Gascoigne Crescent	C1	York Place	B3
Glebe Avenue	A2	York Road	A2
Glebe Road	A3		
Grove Park Terrace	C1		
Grove Road	B1		
Harcourt Drive	C2		
Harcourt Road	C1		
Heywood Road	A3		
Hollins Road	A1		
Homestead Road	B2		
James Street	B2		
Kent Road	A1		
King's Road	A2		
Knaresborough Road	C2		
Lancaster Road	A3		
Leeds Road	B3		
Lime Grove	C1		
Lime Street	C1		
Mayfield Grove	B1		
Montpellier Hill	A2		
Montpellier Street	A2		
Mowbray Square	C1		
North Park Road	C2		
Oatlands Drive	C3		
Otley Road	A3		
Oxford Street	B2		
Park Chase	C1		
Park Drive	B3		
Park Parade	C2		
Park Road	A3		
Park View	B2		
Parliament Street	A2		
Princes Villa Road	B2		
Providence Terrace	B1		
Queen Parade	C2		
Queen's Road	A3		
Raglan Street	B2		
Regent Avenue	C1		

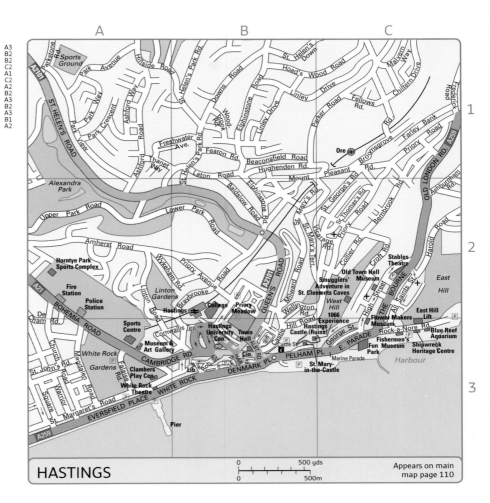

HASTINGS

Tourist Information Centre: Aquila House, 2 Breeds Place
Tel: 01424 451111

Street	Grid
Albert Road	B3
All Saints Street	C2
Amherst Road	A2
Ashburnham Road	C2
Ashford Road	A1
Ashford Way	A1
Baldslow Road	B2
Beaconsfield Road	B1
Bembrook Road	C2
Bohemia Road	A2
Braybrooke Road	B2
Broomsgrove Road	C1
Cambridge Road	A3
Castle Hill Road	B3
Castle Street	B3
Chiltern Drive	C1
Church Road	A3
Collier Road	C2
Cornwallis Terrace	A3
Croft Road	C2
De Cham Road	A3
Denmark Place	B3
Downs Road	B1
East Parade	C3
Elphinstone Road	B1
Eversfield Place	A3
Falaise Road	A3
Farley Bank	C1
Fearon Road	B1
Fellows Road	C1
Frederick Road	C1
Freshwater Avenue	A1
George Street	C3
Harold Place	B3
Harold Road	C2
High Street	C2
Hillside Road	A1
Hoad's Wood Road	B1
Hughenden Road	B1
Laton Road	B1
Linley Drive	B1
Linton Road	A2
Lower Park Road	A2
Magdalen Road	A3
Malvern Way	C1
Marine Parade	C3
Milward Road	B2
Mount Pleasant Road	B1
Old London Road	C2
Park Avenue	A1
Park Crescent	A1
Park View	A1
Park Way	A1
Parker Road	B1
Parkstone Road	A1
Pelham Place	B3
Priory Avenue	B2
Priory Road	C2
Queen's Road	B2
Robertson Street	B3
Rock-a-Nore Road	C3
St. George's Road	C2
St. Helen's Down	B1
St. Helen's Park Road	B2
St. Helen's Road	A1
St. John's Road	A3
St. Margaret's Road	A3
St. Mary's Road	B2
St. Mary's Terrace	B2
St. Thomas's Road	C2
Thanet Way	A1
The Bourne	C2
Upper Park Road	A2
Vicarage Road	B2
Warrior Square	A3
Wellington Road	B2
White Rock	A3
Woodbrook Road	B1
Wykeham Road	A2

HEREFORD

Tourist Information Centre: Town Hall, St. Owen Street
Tel: 01432 268430

Street	Grid
Aubrey Street	B2
Barrs Court Road	C1
Barton Road	A2
Barton Yard	A2
Bath Street	C2
Belmont Avenue	A3
Berrington Street	B2
Bewell Street	B2
Blackfriars Street	B1
Blueschool Street	B1
Brewers Passage	B2
Bridge Street	B2
Broad Street	B2
Canonmoor Street	A1
Cantilupe Street	C2
Castle Street	B2
Catherine Street	B1
Central Avenue	C2
Church Street	B2
Commercial Road	C1
Commercial Street	B2
Coningsby Street	B1
East Street	B2
Edgar Street	B1
Eign Gate	B2
Eign Street	A2
Ferrers Street	B2
Friars Street	A2
Gaol Street	C2
Green Street	C3
Grenfell Road	A3
Greyfriars Avenue	A3
Greyfriars Bridge	B2
Grove Road	C3
Harold Street	C3
High Street	B2
High Town	B2
King Street	B2
Kyrle Street	C2
Maylord Street	B2
Mill Street	C3
Monkmoor Street	C1
Moorfield Street	A1
Moor Street	B1
Mostyn Street	A1
Nelson Street	C3
Newmarket Street	B1
Park Street	C3
Penhaligon Way	A1
Plough Lane	A1
Portland Street	A1
Quay Street	B2
Ryeland Street	A2
St. Guthiac Street	C2
St. James Road	C3
St. Martin's Avenue	B3
St. Martin's Street	B3
St. Owen Street	C2
Station Approach	C1
Station Road	A2
Stonebow Road	C1
Symonds Street	C2
The Atrium	B1
Turner Street	C3
Union Street	B2
Union Walk	C1
Vaughan Street	C2
Victoria Street	A2
West Street	B2
Widemarsh Street	B2
Wye Street	B3

Appears on main map page 110

Appears on main map page 145

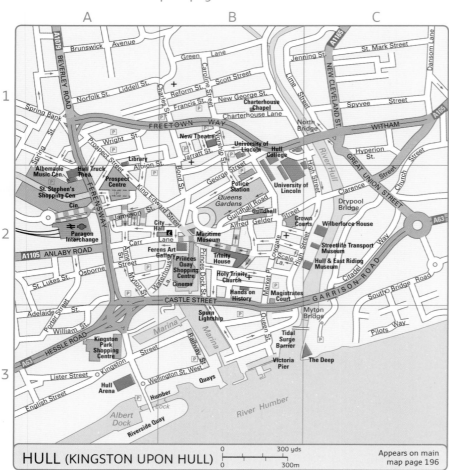

A   B   C

HULL (KINGSTON UPON HULL)

| | 300 yds |
| | 300m |

Appears on main map page 196

Tourist Information Centre: 1 Paragon Street
Tel: 01482 300300

Adelaide Street	A3
Albion Street	A2
Alfred Gelder Street	B2
Anlaby Road	A2
Anne Street	A2
Beverley Road	A1
Bond Street	B2
Brunswick Avenue	A1
Caroline Street	B1
Carr Lane	A2
Castle Street	B2
Charles Street	B1
Charterhouse Lane	B1
Church Street	C2
Citadel Way	C2
Clarence Street	C2
Cleveland Street	C1
Dansom Lane	C1
English Street	A3
Ferensway	A2
Francis Street	B1
Freetown Way	A1
Garrison Road	C2
George Street	B2
Great Union Street	C1
Green Lane	B1
Guildhall Road	B2
Hessle Road	A3
High Street	C1
Hyperion Street	C1
Jameson Street	A2
Jarratt Street	B1
Jenning Street	B1
King Edward Street	A2
Kingston Street	A3
Liddell Street	A1
Lime Street	B1
Lister Street	A3
Lowgate	B2
Market Place	B2
Myton Street	A2
New Cleveland Street	C1
New George Street	B1
Norfolk Street	A1
North Bridge	B1
Osborne Street	A2
Pilots Way	C3
Porter Street	A3
Princes Dock Street	B2
Prospect Street	A1
Queen Street	B3
Reform Street	B1
St. Lukes Street	A2
St. Mark Street	C1
Scale Lane	B2
Scott Street	B1
Scott Street Bridge	B1
South Bridge Road	C2
Spring Bank	A1
Spring Street	A2
Spyvee Street	C1
Waterhouse Lane	A2
Wellington Street West	A3
William Street	A3
Witham	C1
Worship Street	B1
Wright Street	A1

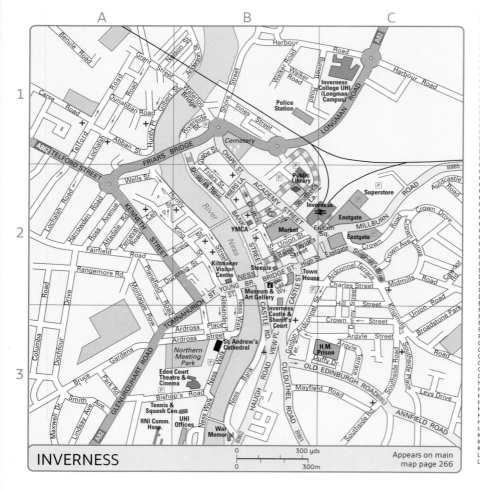

A   B   C

INVERNESS

| | 300 yds |
| | 300m |

Appears on main map page 266

Tourist Information Centre: Castle Wynd
Tel: 01463 252401

Abban Street	A1	Lochalsh Road	A1
Academy Street	B2	Longman Road	C1
Alexander Place	B2	Maxwell Drive	A3
Anderson Street	B1	Mayfield Road	B3
Ardconnel Street	B3	Midmills Road	C2
Ardconnel Terrace	C2	Millburn Road	C2
Ardross Place	B3	Montague Row	A2
Ardross Street	B3	Muirfield Road	C3
Argyle Street	C3	Nelson Street	A1
Argyle Terrace	C3	Ness Bank	B3
Attadale Road	A2	Ness Bridge	B2
Auldcastle Road	C2	Ness Walk	B3
Bank Street	B2	Old Edinburgh Road	B3
Baron Taylor's Street	B2	Park Road	A3
Benula Road	A1	Perceval Road	A2
Bishop's Road	A3	Planefield Road	A2
Bridge Street	B2	Queensgate	B2
Broadstone Park	C3	Rangemore Road	A2
Bruce Gardens	A3	Riverside Street	B1
Burnett Road	C1	Ross Avenue	A2
Carse Road	A1	Shore Street	B1
Castle Road	B2	Smith Avenue	A3
Castle Street	B2	Southside Place	C3
Castle Wynd	B2	Southside Road	C3
Cawdor Road	C2	Stephen's Brae	C2
Celt Street	A2	Strother's Lane	B2
Chapel Street	B1	Telford Road	A1
Charles Street	C2	Telford Street	A1
Church Street	B2	Tomnahurich Street	A3
Columba Road	A3	Union Road	C3
Crown Avenue	C2	Union Street	B2
Crown Circus	C2	View Place	B3
Crown Drive	C2	Walker Road	B1
Crown Road	C2	Waterloo Bridge	B1
Crown Street	C3	Wells Street	A2
Culduthel Road	B3	Young Street	B2
Denny Street	C3		
Dochfour Drive	A3		
Douglas Row	B1		
Duffy Drive	B3		
Duncraig Street	A2		
Eastgate	C2		
Fairfield Road	A2		
Falcon Square	B2		
Friars Bridge	A1		
Friars Lane	B2		
Friars Street	B2		
Gilbert Street	A1		
Glebe Street	B1		
Glen Urquhart Road	A3		
Gordon Terrace	B3		
Grant Street	A1		
Greig Street	A2		
Harbour Road	B1		
Harrowden Road	A2		
Haugh Road	B3		
High Street	B2		
Hill Street	C2		
Hontly Place	A1		
Huntly Street	A2		
Innes Street	B1		
Kenneth Street	A2		
Kingsmills Road	C2		
King Street	A2		
Leys Drive	C3		
Lindsay Avenue	A3		

Liverpool street map on pages 42-43, London street map on pages 44-45

Tourist Information Centre: 7-9 Every Street, Town Hall Square
Tel: 0844 888 5181

Street	Ref	Street	Ref
Abbey Street	B1	Market Place South	B2
Albion Street	B2	Market Street	B2
All Saints Road	A2	Mill Lane	A3
Aylestone Road	B3	Millstone Lane	B2
Bassett Street	A1	Montreal Road	C1
Bath Lane	A2	Morledge Street	C2
Bedford Street North	C1	Narborough Road	A3
Belgrave Gate	B1	Narborough Road North	A2
Bell Lane	C1	Nelson Street	C3
Belvoir Street	B2	Newarke Close	A3
Braunstone Gate	A2	Newarke Street	B2
Burgess Street	B1	Northgate Street	A1
Burleys Way	B1	Ottawa Road	C1
Byron Street	B1	Oxford Street	B2
Cank Street	B2	Pasture Lane	A1
Castle Street	A2	Peacock Lane	B2
Charles Street	C2	Pocklingtons Walk	B2
Christow Street	C1	Prebend Street	C3
Church Gate	B1	Princess Road East	C3
Clarence Street	B1	Pringle Street	A1
Clyde Street	C1	Queen Street	C2
College Street	C2	Regent Road	B3
Colton Street	C2	Regent Street	C3
Conduit Street	C2	Repton Street	A1
Crafton Street East	C1	Rutland Street	C2
Cravan Street	A1	Samuel Street	C2
De Montfort Street	C3	Sanvey Gate	A1
Deacon Street	B3	Saxby Street	C3
Dryden Street	B1	Slater Street	A1
Duns Lane	A2	Soar Lane	A1
Dunton Street	A1	South Albion Street	C2
Eastern Boulevard	A3	Southampton Street	C2
Friar Lane	B2	Sparkenhoe Street	C2
Friday Street	B1	St. George Street	C2
Frog Island	A1	St. George's Way	C2
Gallowtree Gate	B2	St. John's Street	B1
Gaul Street	A3	St. Margaret's Way	A1
Glebe Street	C2	St. Matthew's Way	C1
Gotham Street	C3	St. Nicholas Circle	A2
Granby Street	B2	Swain Street	C2
Grange Lane	B3	Swan Street	A1
Grasmere Street	A3	Taylor Road	C1
Great Central Street	A1	Thames Street	B1
Halford Street	B2	The Gateway	A3
Havelock Street	B3	The Newarke	A2
Haymarket	B1	Tigers Way	B3
High Street	B2	Tower Street	B3
Highcross Street	A1	Tudor Road	A1
Hobart Street	C2	Ullswater Street	A3
Horsfair Street	B2	University Road	C3
Humberstone Gate	B2	Upperton Road	A3
Humberstone Road	C1	Vaughan Way	A1
Infirmary Road	B3	Vestry Street	C2
Jarrom Street	A3	Walnut Street	A3
Jarvis Street	A2	Waterloo Way	C3
Kamloops Crescent	C1	Welford Road	B2
Kent Street	C1	Wellington Street	B2
King Richard's Road	A2	West Street	B3
King Street	B2	Western Boulevard	A3
Lancaster Road	B3	Western Road	A3
Lee Street	B1	Wharf Street North	C1
Lincoln Street	C2	Wharf Street South	C1
London Road	C3	Wilberforce Road	A3
Loseby Lane	B2	Windermere Street	A3
Lower Brown Street	B2	Woodboy Street	C1
Manitoba Road	C1	Yeoman Street	B2
Mansfield Street	B1	York Road	B2

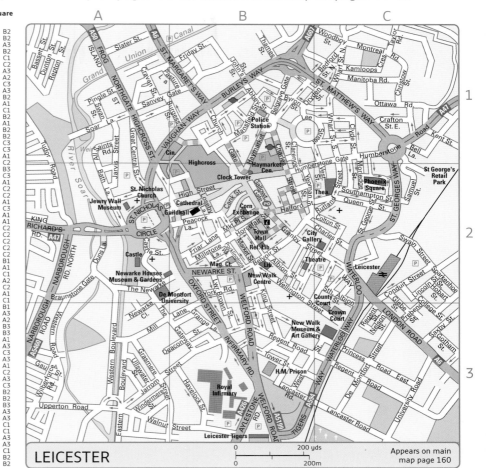

LEICESTER

0   200 yds
0   200m

Appears on main
map page 160

Tourist Information Centre: 9 Castle Hill
Tel: 01522 545458

Street	Ref	Street	Ref
Alexandra Terrace	A2	Spa Road	C3
Bagholme Road	C2	St. Anne's Road	C2
Bailgate	B1	St. Giles Avenue	C1
Beaumont Fee	B2	St. Mark Street	B3
Beevor Street	A3	St. Mary's Street	B3
Brayford Way	A3	St. Rumbold Street	B2
Brayford Wharf North	A2	Stamp End	C3
Broadgate	B2	Steep Hill	B2
Broadway	B1	The Avenue	A2
Bruce Road	C1	Tritton Road	A3
Burton Road	A1	Union Row	B2
Canwick Road	B3	Upper Lindum Street	C2
Carholme Road	A2	Upper Long Leys Road	A1
Carline Road	A1	Vere Street	B1
Carr Street	A2	Vine Street	C2
Cheviot Street	C1	Waterside North	B3
Church Lane	B1	Waterside South	B3
Clasketgate	B2	West Parade	A2
Croft Street	B2	Westgate	B1
Cross Street	B3	Wigford Way	B2
Curle Avenue	C1	Wilson Street	A1
Drury Lane	B2	Winn Street	C2
East Gate	B2	Wragby Road	C2
Firth Road	A3	Yarborough Road	A1
George Street	C3		
Great Northern Terrace	B3		
Greetwell Close	C1		
Greetwell Road	C2		
Gresham Street	A2		
Hampton Street	A2		
Harvey Street	A2		
High Street	B3		
John Street	C2		
Langworthgate	B1		
Lee Road	C1		
Lindum Road	B2		
Lindum Terrace	C2		
Long Leys Road	A1		
Mainwaring Road	C1		
Mill Road	A1		
Milman Road	C2		
Monks Road	C2		
Monson Street	B3		
Moor Street	A2		
Mount Street	A1		
Nettleham Road	B1		
Newland	A2		
Newland Street West	A2		
Newport	B1		
Northgate	B1		
Orchard Street	A2		
Pelham Bridge	B3		
Portland Street	B3		
Portland Street	B3		
Pottergate	B2		
Queensway	C1		
Rasen Lane	B1		
Richmond Road	A2		
Ripon Street	B3		
Rope Walk	A3		
Rosemary Lane	B2		
Ruskin Avenue	C1		
Saltergate	B2		
Sewell Road	C2		
Silver Street	B2		
Sincil Bank	B3		

LINCOLN

0   200 yds
0   200m

Appears on main
map page 187

Middlesbrough   Milton Keynes

Manchester street map on pages 46-47

MIDDLESBROUGH

Tourist Information Centre: Town Hall, Albert Road
Tel: 01642 729700

Abingdon Road	B2	Roman Road	A3
Aire Street	A2	Roseberry Road	C2
Albert Road	B1	Saltwells Road	C2
Ayresome Green Lane	A2	Scotts Road	C1
Ayresome Street	A2	Sheperdson Way	C1
Beech Grove Road	B3	Snowdon Road	B1
Belle Vue Grove	C3	Southfield Road	B2
Bishopton Road	B3	Southwell Road	B3
Borough Road	B1/C3	St. Barnabas Road	A2
Breckon Hill Road	C2	Surrey Street	A2
Bridge Street East	B1	Sycamore Road	B3
Bridge Street West	B1	The Avenue	A3
Burlam Road	A3	The Crescent	A3
Cambridge Road	A3	The Vale	B3
Cannon Park Way	A1	Thornfield Road	A3
Cannon Street	A1	Union Street	A2
Cargo Fleet Road	C1	Valley Road	B3
Chipchase Road	A3	Victoria Road	B2
Clairville Road	B2	Victoria Street	A1
Clive Road	A2	Westbourne Grove	C2
Corporation Road	B1	Westbourne Road	A3
Crescent Road	A2	Westminster Road	B3
Cumberland Road	B3	Wilson Street	B1
Deepdale Avenue	B3	Woodlands Road	B2
Derwent Street	A1		
Dockside Road	B1/C1		
Douglas Street	C2		
Eastbourne Road	B3		
Emerson Avenue	B3		
Forty Foot Road	A1		
Grange Road	B1		
Granville Road	B2		
Gresham Road	A2		
Harford Street	A2		
Harrow Road	A3		
Hartington Road	A1		
Heywood Street	A2		
Highfield Road	C3		
Holwick Road	A1		
Hudson Quay	C1		
Hutton Road	C2		
Ingram Road	C2		
Keith Road	B3		
Lansdowne Road	C2		
Linthorpe Road	B3		
Longford Street	A2		
Longlands Road	C2		
Marsh Street	A1		
Marton Burn Road	B3		
Marton Road	C2/C3		
Newport Road	A1/B1		
North Ormesby Road	C1		
Nut Lane	C2		
Orchard Road	A3		
Overdale Road	C3		
Oxford Road	A3		
Park Lane	B2		
Park Road North	B2		
Park Road South	B2		
Park Vale Road	B2		
Parliament Road	A2		
Portman Street	B2		
Princes Road	A2		
Reeth Road	A3		
Riverside Park Road	A1		
Rockcliffe Road	A3		

Appears on main map page 213

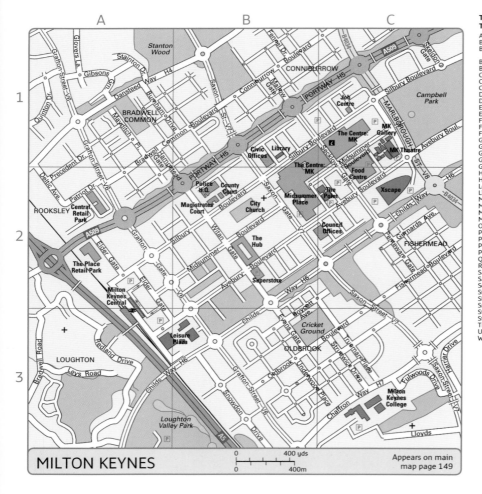

MILTON KEYNES

Tourist Information Centre: Silbury Arcade
Tel: 01908 688293

Avebury Boulevard	B2/C1
Boycott Avenue	B3
Bradwell Common Boulevard	A1
Bradwell Road	A3
Burnham Drive	A1
Chaffron Way	C3
Childs Way	A3/C2
Conniburrow Boulevard	B1
Dansteed Way	A1
Deltic Avenue	A2
Elder Gate	A2
Evans Gate	B3
Fennel Drive	B1
Fishermead Boulevard	C2
Fulwoods Drive	C3
Gibsons Green	A1
Glovers Lane	A1
Grafton Gate	A2
Grafton Street	A1/B3
Gurnards Avenue	C2
Hampstead Gate	A1
Harrier Drive	C3
Leys Road	A3
Lloyds	C3
Mallow Gate	B1
Marlborough Street	C1
Mayditch Place	A1
Midsummer Boulevard	B2/C1
Oldbrook Boulevard	B3
Patriot Drive	A2
Pentewan Gate	C2
Portway	B2/C1
Precedent Drive	A2
Quinton Drive	A1
Redland Drive	A3
Saxon Gate	B2
Saxon Street	B1/C3
Secklow Gate	C1
Silbury Boulevard	B2/C1
Skeldon Gate	C1
Snowdon Drive	B3
Stainton Drive	A1
Strudwick Drive	C3
Trueman Place	C3
Underwood Place	B3
Witan Gate	B2

Appears on main map page 149

Newcastle upon Tyne

Tourist Information Centre: 8-9 Central Arcade
Tel: 0191 277 8000

Albert Street	C2
Ancrum Street	A1
Argyle Street	C2
Askew Road	C3
Barrack Road	A1
Barras Bridge	B1
Bath Lane	A2
Bigg Market	B2
Blackett Street	B2
Byron Street	C1
Chester Street	C1
City Road	C2
Claremont Road	B1
Clarence Street	C2
Clayton Street	B2
Clayton Street West	A3
Corporation Street	A2
Coulthards Lane	C3
Crawhall Road	C2
Dean Street	B2
Diana Street	A2
Elswick East Terrace	A3
Eskdale Terrace	C1
Essex Close	A3
Falconar Street	C1
Forth Banks	B3
Forth Street	A3
Gallowgate	A2
Gateshead Highway	C3
George Street	A3
Gibson Street	C2
Grainger Street	B2
Grantham Road	C1
Grey Street	B2
Hanover Street	B3
Hawks Road	C3
Helmsley Road	C1
High Street	C3
Hillgate	C3
Howard Street	C2
Hunters Road	A1
Ivy Close	A3
Jesmond Road	C1
Jesmond Road West	B1
John Dobson Street	B2
Kelvin Grove	C1
Kyle Close	A3
Lambton Street	C3
Mansfield Street	A2
Maple Street	A3
Maple Terrace	A3
Market Street	B2
Melbourne Street	C2
Mill Road	C3
Neville Street	A3
New Bridge Street	C2
Newgate Street	B2
Northumberland Road	B2
Northumberland Street	B1
Oakwellgate	C3
Orchard Street	B3
Oxnam Crescent	A1
Park Terrace	B1
Percy Street	B2
Pilgrim Street	B2
Pipewellgate	B3
Pitt Street	A2
Portland Road	C1
Portland Terrace	C1
Pottery Lane	A3
Quarryfield Road	C3
Quayside	B2
Queen Victoria Road	B1
Railway Street	A3
Redheugh Bridge	A3
Richardson Road	A1
Rye Hill	A3
St. James Boulevard	A3
St. Mary's Place	B1
St. Thomas Street	B1
Sandyford Road	B1/C1
Scotswood Road	A3
Skinnerburn Road	B3
South Shore Road	C3
Stanhope Street	A2
Starbeck Avenue	C1
Stodart Street	C1
Stowell Street	A2
Strawberry Place	A2
Summerhill Grove	A2
Swing Bridge	B3
The Close	B3
Tyne Bridge	C3
Union Street	C2
Warwick Street	C1
Wellington Street	A2
West Street	C3
Westgate Road	A2
Westmorland Road	A3
Windsor Terrace	B1
York Street	A2

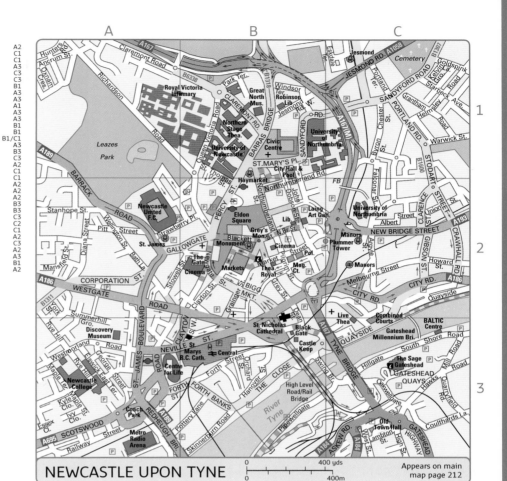

NEWCASTLE UPON TYNE

Appears on main map page 212

Norwich

Tourist Information Centre: The Forum, Millennium Plain
Tel: 01603 213999

Albion Way	C3
All Saints Green	B3
Ashby Street	B3
Bakers Road	A1
Bank Plain	B2
Barker Street	A1
Barn Road	A2
Barrack Street	B1
Bedford Street	B2
Ber Street	B3
Bethel Street	A2
Bishopbridge Road	C2
Bishopgate	C2
Botolph Street	B1
Brazen Gate	B3
Britannia Road	C1
Brunswick Road	A3
Bullclose Road	B1
Canary Way	C3
Carrow Hill	C3
Carrow Road	C3
Castle Meadow	B2
Chapel Field Road	A2
Chapelfield North	A2
City Road	B3
Clarence Road	C3
Colegate	B1
Coslany Street	A2
Cowgate	B1
Dereham Road	A2
Duke Street	B1
Earlham Road	A2
Edward Street	B1
Elm Hill	B2
Fishergate	B1
Gas Hill	C1
Grapes Hill	A2
Grove Avenue	A3
Grove Road	A3
Grove Walk	A3
Gurney Road	C1
Hall Road	B3
Hardy Road	C3
Heathgate	C1
Heigham Street	A1
Horns Lane	B3
Ipswich Road	A3
Ketts Hill	C1
King Street	B3
Koblenz Avenue	C3
Lothian Street	A1
Lower Clarence Road	C2
Magdalen Street	B1
Magpie Road	B1
Market Avenue	B2
Marlborough Road	B1
Mountergate	B2
Mousehold Street	C1
Newmarket Road	A3
Newmarket Street	A3
Oak Street	A1
Orchard Street	A1
Palace Street	B2
Pitt Street	B1
Pottergate	A2
Prince of Wales Road	B2
Queens Road	B3
Rampant Horse Street	B2
Recorder Road	C2
Red Lion Street	B2
Riverside	C3
Riverside Road	C2
Rosary Road	C2
Rose Lane	B2
Rouen Road	B3
Rupert Street	A3
Russell Street	A1
St. Andrew's Street	B2
St. Augustine's Street	A1
St. Benedict's Street	A2
St. Crispin's Road	A1
St. Faiths Lane	B2
St. George's Street	B1
St. Giles Street	A2
St. James Close	C1
St. Leonards Road	C2
St. Martin's Road	A1
St. Stephen's Road	A3
St. Stephen's Street	B3
Silver Road	B1
Silver Street	B1
Southwell Road	B3
Surrey Street	B3
Sussex Street	A1
Theatre Street	A2
Thorn Lane	B3
Thorpe Road	C2
Tombland	B2
Trinity Street	A3
Troy Street	A2
Union Street	A3
Unthank Road	A3
Vauxhall Street	A3
Victoria Street	A3
Wensum Street	B1
Wessex Street	A3
Westwick Street	A1
Wherry Road	C3
Whitefriars	B1
Wodehouse Street	B1
York Street	A3

NORWICH

Appears on main map page 178

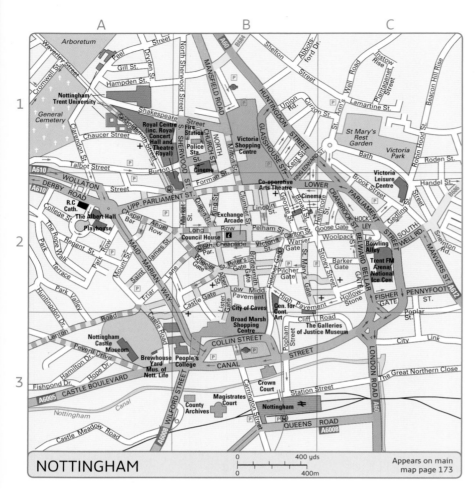

NOTTINGHAM

Scale: 0 – 400 yds / 0 – 400m

Appears on main map page 173

Tourist Information Centre: 1-4 Smithy Row
Tel: 08444 77 56 78

Abbotsford Drive	B1	Maid Marian Way	A2
Albert Street	B2	Mansfield Road	B1
Angel Row	A2	Manvers Street	C2
Barker Gate	C2	Market Street	B2
Bath Street	C1	Middle Pavement	B2
Beacon Hill Rise	C1	Milton Street	B1
Bellar Gate	C2	Mount Street	A2
Belward Street	C2	North Church Street	B1
Bridlesmith Gate	B2	North Sherwood Street	B1
Broad Street	B2	Park Row	A2
Brook Street	C1	Park Terrace	A2
Burton Street	A1	Park Valley	A2
Canal Street	B3	Peel Street	A1
Carlton Street	B2	Pelham Street	B2
Carrington Street	B3	Pennyfoot Street	C2
Castle Boulevard	A3	Peveril Drive	A3
Castle Gate	B2	Pilcher Gate	B2
Castle Meadow Road	A3	Plantagenet Street	C1
Castle Road	A3	Popham Street	B3
Chapel Bar	A2	Poplar Street	C2
Chaucer Street	A1	Queens Road	B3
Cheapside	B2	Queen Street	B2
City Link	C3	Regent Street	A2
Clarendon Street	A1	Robin Hood Street	C1
Cliff Road	B3	Roden Street	C1
Clumber Street	B2	St. Ann's Well Road	C1
College Street	A2	St. James Street	A2
Collin Street	B3	St. Mary's Gate	B2
Cranbrook Street	C2	St. Peter's Gate	B2
Cromwell Street	A1	Shakespeare Street	B1
Curzon Street	B1	Shelton Street	B1
Derby Road	A2	Sneinton Road	C2
Dryden Street	A1	South Parade	B2
Fisher Gate	C2	South Sherwood Street	B1
Fishpond Drive	A3	Southwell Road	C2
Fletcher Gate	B2	Station Street	B3
Forman Street	B2	Stoney Street	C2
Friar Lane	A2	Talbot Street	A1
Gedling Street	C2	The Great Northern Close	C3
George Street	B2	The Rope Walk	A2
Gill Street	A1	Union Road	B1
Glasshouse Street	B1	Upper Parliament Street	A2
Goldsmith Street	A1	Victoria Street	B2
Goose Gate	C2	Warser Gate	B2
Hamilton Drive	A3	Waverley Street	A1
Hampden Street	A1	Wheeler Gate	B2
Handel Street	C2	Wilford Street	A3
Heathcote Street	B2	Wollaton Street	A2
High Pavement	B2	Woolpack Lane	C2
Hockley	C2		
Hollowstone	C2		
Hope Drive	A3		
Huntingdon Drive	A2		
Huntingdon Street	B1		
Instow Rise	C1		
Kent Street	B1		
King Edward Street	B2		
King Street	B2		
Lamartine Street	C1		
Lenton Road	A3		
Lincoln Street	B2		
Lister Gate	B2		
London Road	C3		
Long Row	B2		
Low Pavement	B2		
Lower Parliament Street	B2		

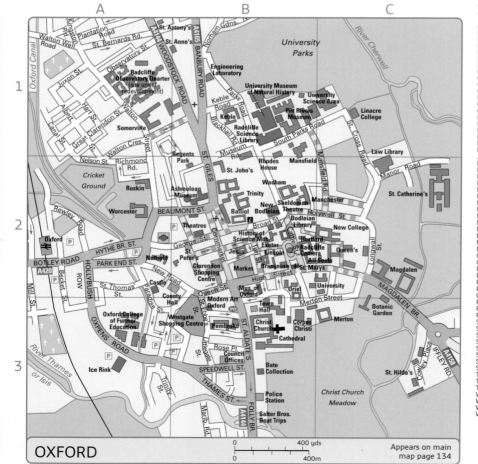

OXFORD

Scale: 0 – 400 yds / 0 – 400m

Appears on main map page 134

Tourist Information Centre: 15-16 Broad Street
Tel: 01865 686430

Albert Street	A1
Banbury Road	B1
Beaumont Street	A2
Becket Street	A2
Blackhall Road	B1
Botley Road	A2
Broad Street	B2
Canal Street	A1
Cattle Street	B2
Cornmarket	B2
Cowley Place	C3
Folly Bridge	B3
George Street	A2
Great Clarendon Street	A1
Hart Street	A1
High Street	B2
Hollybush Row	A2
Holywell Street	A2
Hythe Bridge Street	A2
Iffley Road	C3
Juxon Street	A1
Keble Road	B1
Kingston Road	A1
Littlegate Street	B3
Longwall Street	C2
Magdalen Bridge	C2
Manor Road	C2
Mansfield Road	C1
Marlborough Road	B3
Merton Street	B3
Mill Street	A2
Museum Road	B1
Nelson Street	A2
New Road	A2
Norham Gardens	B1
Observatory Street	A1
Oxpens Road	A3
Paradise Street	A2
Park End Street	A2
Parks Road	B1
Plantation Road	A1
Queen Street	B2
Rewley Road	A2
Richmond Road	A2
Rose Place	B3
St. Aldate's	B3
St. Bernards Road	A1
St. Cross Road	C1
St. Ebbe's Street	B3
St. Giles	B1
St. Thomas' Street	A2
South Parks Road	B1
Speedwell Street	B3
Thames Street	B3
Trinity Street	A3
Turl Street	B2
Walton Crescent	A1
Walton Street	A1
Walton Well Road	A1
Woodstock Road	A1

PERTH

Abbot Crescent	A3	Shore Road	C3
Abbot Street	A3	South Methven Street	B2
Albany Terrace	A1	South Street	B2
Atholl Street	B1	Strathmore Street	C1
Balhousie Street	B1	Stuart Avenue	A3
Barossa Place	B1	Tay Street	C2
Barossa Street	B1	Victoria Street	B2
Barrack Street	B1	Watergate	C2
Bowerswell Road	C2	Whitefriars Crescent	A2
Caledonian Road	B2	Whitefriars Street	A2
Canal Street	B2	William Street	B2
Cavendish Avenue	A3	Wilson Street	A3
Charlotte Street	B1	Young Street	A3
Clyde Place	A3	York Place	A2
Darnhall Drive	A3		
Dundee Road	C2		
Dunkeld Road	A1		
Edinburgh Road	B3		
Feus Road	A1		
Friar Street	A3		
George Street	C2		
Glasgow Road	A2		
Glover Street	A2		
Gowrie Street	C1		
Gray Street	A2		
Graybank Road	A2		
Hay Street	B1		
High Street	B2		
Isla Road	C1		
Jeanfield Road	A2		
King's Place	B3		
King James Place	B3		
King Street	B2		
Kinnoull Street	B1		
Kinnoull Terrace	C2		
Knowelea Place	A3		
Leonard Street	B2		
Lochie Brae	C1		
Long Causeway	A1		
Main Street	C1		
Manse Road	C2		
Marshall Place	B3		
Melville Street	B1		
Mill Street	B2		
Milne Street	B2		
Murray Crescent	A3		
Needless Road	A3		
New Row	B2		
North Methven Street	B1		
Park Place	A3		
Perth Bridge	C1		
Pickletullum Road	A2		
Pitcullen Terrace	C1		
Pitheavlis Crescent	A3		
Princes Street	C3		
Priory Place	B3		
Queen Street	A3		
Queens Bridge	C2		
Raeburn Park	A3		
Riggs Road	A2		
Rose Crescent	A2		
Rose Terrace	B1		
St. Catherines Road	A1		
St. John Street	C2		
St. Leonard's Bank	B3		
Scott Street	B2		

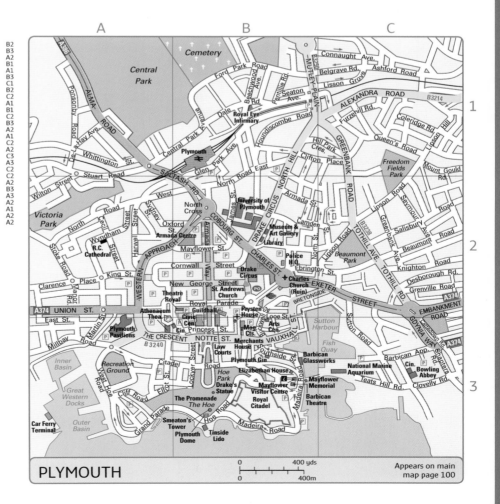

PERTH

0 — 300 yds
0 — 300m

Appears on main map page 243

PLYMOUTH

Alexandra Road	C1	North Street	B2
Alma Road	A1	Notte Street	B3
Armada Street	B2	Oxford Street	A2
Armada Way	B2	Pentillie Road	B1
Ashford Road	C1	Ponsonby Road	A1
Barbican Approach	C3	Princess Street	B3
Beaumont Road	C2	Queen's Road	C1
Beechwood Avenue	B1	Royal Parade	B2
Belgrave Road	C1	Salisbury Road	C2
Bretonside	B2	Saltash Road	A1
Buckwell Street	B3	Seaton Avenue	B1
Camden Street	B2	Seymour Avenue	C2
Cattledown Road	C3	Southside Street	B3
Cecil Street	A2	Stoke Road	A2
Central Park Avenue	A1	Stuart Road	A1
Charles Street	B2	Sutton Road	C2
Citadel Road	A3	Sydney Street	A2
Clarence Place	A2	Teats Hill Road	C3
Cliff Road	A3	The Crescent	A3
Clifton Place	B1	Tothill Avenue	C2
Clovelly Road	C3	Tothill Road	C2
Cobourg Street	B2	Union Street	A2
Coleridge Road	C1	Vauxhall Street	B3
Connaught Avenue	C1	West Hoe Road	A3
Cornwall Street	B2	Western Approach	A2
Dale Road	B1	Whittington Street	A1
De-La-Hay Avenue	A1	Wilton Street	A2
Desborough Road	C2	Wyndham Street	A2
Drake Circus	B2		
East Street	A3		
Ebrington Street	B2		
Elliot Street	A3		
Embankment Road	C2		
Exeter Street	B2		
Ford Park Road	B1		
Furzehill Road	C1		
Gdynia Way	C3		
Glen Park Avenue	B1		
Grand Parade	A3		
Greenbank Avenue	C2		
Greenbank Road	C2		
Grenville Road	C2		
Harwell Street	A2		
Hill Park Crescent	B1		
Hoe Road	B3		
Houndiscombe Road	B1		
James Street	B2		
King Street	A2		
Knighton Road	C2		
Lipson Hill	C1		
Lipson Road	C2		
Lisson Grove	C1		
Lockyer Street	B3		
Looe Street	B2		
Madeira Road	B3		
Manor Road	A2		
Martin Street	A3		
Mayflower Street	B2		
Millbay Road	A3		
Mount Gould Road	C1		
Mutley Plain	B1		
New George Street	B2		
North Cross	B2		
North Hill	B2		
North Road East	B2		
North Road West	A2		

PLYMOUTH

0 — 400 yds
0 — 400m

Appears on main map page 100

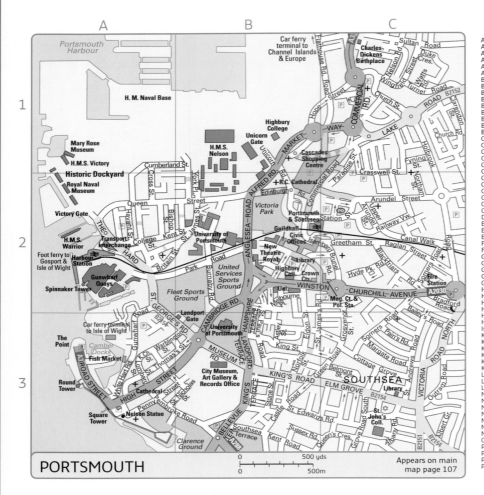

PORTSMOUTH

Appears on main map page 107

Albany Road	C3	Penny Street	A3
Albert Grove	C3	Queen's Crescent	C3
Alfred Road	B2	Queen Street	A2
Anglesea Road	B2	Raglan Street	C2
Arundel Street	C2	Railway View	C2
Astley Street	B3	St. Andrews Road	C3
Bailey's Road	C2	St. Edward's Road	B3
Bellevue Terrace	B3	St. George's Road	A2
Belmont Street	C3	St. James Road	B3
Bishop Street	A1	St. James Street	B2
Blackfriars Road	C2	St. Paul's Road	B3
Bradford Road	C2	St. Thomas's Street	A3
Britain Street	A2	Somers Road	C2
Broad Street	A3	Southsea Terrace	B3
Burnaby Road	B2	Station Street	C2
Cambridge Road	B3	Stone Street	B3
Canal Walk	C2	Sultan Road	C1
Castle Road	B3	Sussex Street	B3
Church Road	C1	The Hard	A2
Church Street	C1	Turner Road	C1
Clarendon Street	C1	Unicorn Road	B1
College Street	A2	Upper Arundel Street	C2
Commercial Road	B2	Victoria Road North	C3
Cottage Grove	C3	Warblington Street	A3
Crasswell Street	C1	Watts Road	C1
Cross Street	A1	White Hart Road	A3
Cumberland Street	A1	Wingfield Street	C2
Duke Crescent	C1	Winston Churchill Avenue	B2
Edinburgh Road	B2	York Place	B2
Eldon Street	B3		
Elm Grove	C3		
Flathouse Road	C1		
Fyning Street	C1		
Green Road	B3		
Greetham Street	C2		
Grosvenor Street	C3		
Grove Road South	C3		
Gunwharf Road	A3		
Hampshire Terrace	B3		
Havant Street	A2		
High Street	A3		
Holbrook Road	C1		
Hope Street	B1		
Hyde Park Road	C2		
Isambard Brunel Road	B2		
Kent Road	B3		
Kent Street	A1		
King Charles Street	A3		
King's Road	B3		
King's Terrace	B3		
King Street	B3		
Lake Road	C1		
Landport Terrace	B3		
Lombard Street	A3		
Margate Road	C3		
Market Way	B1		
Melbourne Place	B2		
Museum Road	B3		
Nelson Road	C1		
Norfolk Street	B3		
Northam Street	C2		
Outram Road	C3		
Pain's Road	C2		
Paradise Street	C2		
Park Road	B2		
Pembroke Road	A3		

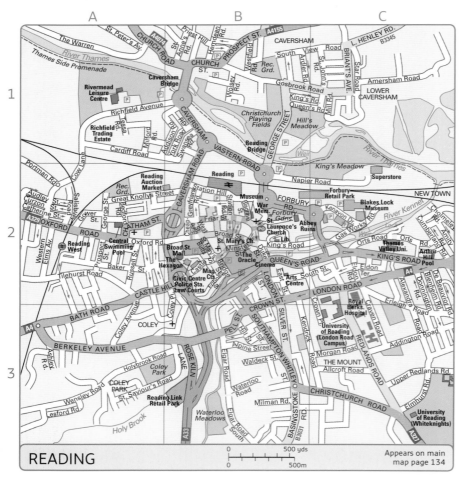

READING

Appears on main map page 134

Addington Road	C3	Lesford Road	A3
Addison Road	A1	London Road	C2
Alexandra Road	C2	London Street	B2
Allcroft Road	C3	Lower Henley Road	C1
Alpine Street	B3	Mill Road	C1
Amersham Road	C1	Milford Road	A1
Amity Road	A2	Milman Road	B3
Ardler Road	B1	Minster Street	B2
Ashley Road	A3	Morgan Road	C3
Audley Street	A2	Napier Road	B2
Baker Street	A2	Orts Road	C2
Basingstoke Road	B3	Oxford Road	A2
Bath Road	A3	Pell Street	B3
Bedford Road	A2	Portman Road	A1
Berkeley Avenue	A3	Priest Hill	B1
Blagrave Street	B2	Prospect Street Caversham	B1
Blenheim Road	C2	Prospect Street Reading	B1
Briant's Avenue	C1	Queen's Road Caversham	B1
Bridge Street	B2	Queen's Road Reading	B2
Broad Street	B2	Richfield Avenue	A1
Cardiff Road	A1	Rose Kiln Lane	B3
Castle Hill	A2	Russell Street	A2
Castle Street	B2	St. Anne's Road	B1
Catherine Street	A2	St. John's Road	C1
Caversham Road	B2	St. Mary's Butts	B2
Chatham Street	A2	St. Peters Avenue	A1
Cheapside	B2	St. Saviours Road	A3
Cholmeley Road	C2	Silver Street	B3
Christchurch Road	C3	South Street	B2
Church Road	A1	Southampton Street	B3
Church Street	B1	South View Road	B1
Coley Avenue	A3	Star Road	C1
Coley Place	B2	Station Hill	B2
Cow Lane	A2	Station Road	B2
Craven Road	C3	Swansea Road	B1
Crown Place	C2	Tessa Road	A1
Crown Street	B3	The Warren	A1
Cumberland Road	C2	Tilehurst Road	A2
Curzon Street	A2	Upper Redlands Road	C3
De Beauvoir Road	C2	Vastern Road	B1
Donnington Road	C2	Waldek Street	B3
Duke Street	B2	Waterloo Road	B3
East Street	B2	Wensley Road	A3
Eldon Road	C2	Western Elms Avenue	A2
Eldon Terrace	C2	Westfield Road	B1
Elgar Road	B3	West Street	B2
Elgar Road South	B3	Whitley Street	B3
Elmhurst Road	C3	Wolsey Road	B1
Erleigh Road	C3	York Road	B1
Fobney Street	B2		
Forbury Road	B2		
Friar Street	B2		
Gas Work Road	B2		
George Street Caversham	B1		
George Street Reading	A2		
Gosbrook Road	B1		
Gower Street	A2		
Great Knollys Street	A2		
Greyfriars Road	B2		
Hemdean Road	B1		
Hill Street	B3		
Holybrook Road	A3		
Kenavon Drive	C2		
Kendrick Road	B3		
King's Road Caversham	B1		
King's Road Reading	B2		

Tourist Information Centre: Fish Row
Tel: 01722 342860

Albany Road	B1
Ashley Road	A1
Avon Terrace	A1
Barnard Street	C2
Bedwin Street	B1
Belle Vue Road	B1
Bishops Walk	B3
Blackfriars Way	C3
Blue Boar Row	B2
Bourne Avenue	C1
Bourne Hill	C1
Bridge Street	B2
Brown Street	B2
Butcher Row	B2
Carmelite Way	B3
Castle Street	B1
Catherine Street	B2
Chipper Lane	B2
Churchfields Road	A2
Churchill Way East	C2
Churchill Way North	B1
Churchill Way South	C3
Churchill Way West	A1
Clifton Road	A1
College Street	C1
Crane Bridge Road	A2
Crane Street	B2
De Vaux Place	B3
Devizes Road	A1
Elm Grove Road	C2
Endless Street	B1
Estcourt Road	C1
Exeter Street	B3
Fairview Road	C1
Fisherton Street	A2
Fowlers Hill	C2
Fowlers Road	C2
Friary Lane	C3
Gas Lane	A1
Gigant Street	C2
Greencroft Street	C1
Hamilton Road	B1
High Street	B2
Ivy Street	B2
Kelsey Road	C1
Laverstock Road	C2
Manor Road	C1
Marsh Lane	A1
Meadow Road	A1
Milford Hill	C2
Milford Street	B2
Mill Road	A2
Millstream Approach	B1
Minster Street	B2
New Canal	B2
New Street	B2
North Walk	B3
Park Street	C1
Pennyfarthing Street	B2
Queens Road	B1
Rampart Road	C2
Rollestone Street	B1
St. Ann Street	C3
St. John's Street	B2
St. Marks Road	C1
St. Paul's Road	A1
Salt Lane	B2
Scots Lane	B2
Silver Street	B2
Southampton Road	C3
Swaynes Close	B1
Tollgate Road	C2
Trinity Street	C2
Wain-a-long Road	C1
West Walk	B3
Wilton Road	A1
Winchester Street	B2
Windsor Road	A2
Wyndham Road	B1
York Road	A1

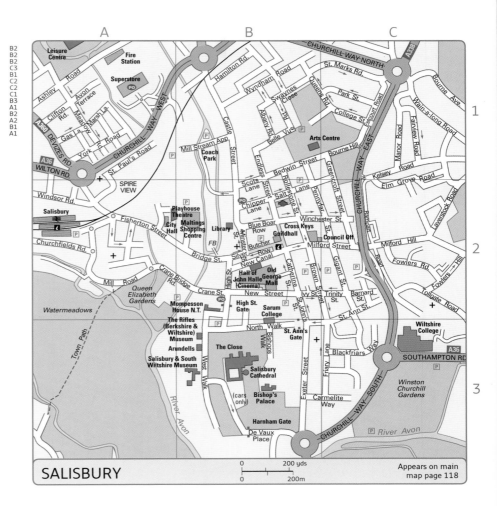

SALISBURY — 0 200 yds / 0 200m — Appears on main map page 118

Tourist Information Centre: Brunswick Shopping Centre, Unit 15a, Westborough Tel: 01723 383636

Aberdeen Walk	B2
Albion Road	B3
Ashville Avenue	A2
Avenue Road	A3
Belmont Road	B3
Candler Street	A2
Castle Road	B2
Chatsworth Gardens	A1
Columbus Ravine	A2
Commercial Street	A3
Cross Street	B2
Dean Road	A2
Eastborough	B2
Esplanade	B3
Falconers Rd	B2
Falsgrave Road	A3
Foreshore Road	B2
Franklin Street	A2
Friargate	B2
Friarsway	B2
Garfield Road	A2
Gladstone Road	A2
Gladstone Street	A2
Gordon Street	A2
Grosvenor Road	B3
Highfield	A3
Hoxton Road	A2
Longwestgate	C2
Manor Road	A2
Marine Drive	C1
Mayville Avenue	A2
Moorland Road	A1
New Queen Street	B1
Newborough	B2
North Marine Road	B1
North Street	B2
Northstead Manor Drive	A1
Northway	A2
Norwood Street	A2
Oak Road	A3
Peasholm Crescent	A1
Peasholm Drive	A1
Peasholm Road	A1
Prince Of Wales Terrace	B3
Princess Street	C2
Prospect Road	A2
Queen Street	B2
Queen's Parade	B1
Raleigh Street	A2
Ramshill Road	B3
Roscoe Street	A3
Rothbury Street	A2
Royal Albert Drive	B1
Royal Avenue	B3
Sandside	C2
Seamer Road	A3
St. James Road	A3
St. John's Avenue	A3
St. John's Road	A3
St. Thomas Street	B2
Tollergate	B1
Trafalgar Road	A1
Trafalgar Square	B1
Trafalgar Street West	A2
Trinity Road	A3
Valley Bridge Parade	B3
Valley Bridge Road	B2
Valley Road	A3
Vernon Road	B2
Victoria Park Mount	A1
Victoria Road	A3
Victoria Street	B2
West Street	B3
Westborough	A3
Westbourne Grove	B3
Westover Road	A3
Westwood	B3
Westwood Road	A3
Weydale Avenue	A1
Wykeham Street	A3

SCARBOROUGH — 0 400 yds / 0 400m — Appears on main map page 204

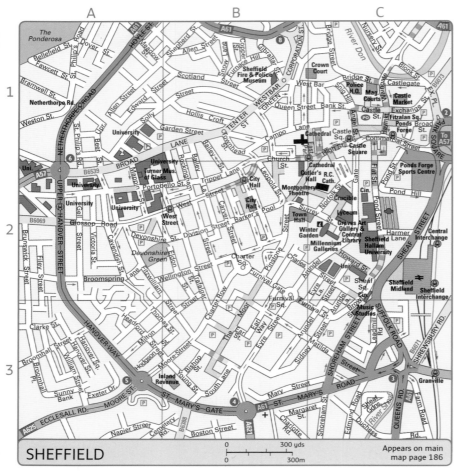

SHEFFIELD

Appears on main map page 186

Tourist Information Centre: Winter Garden, 90 Surrey Street
Tel: 0114 221 1900

Allen Street	B1	Hanover Square	A3
Angel Street	C1	Hanover Street	A3
Arundel Gate	B2	Hanover Way	A3
Arundel Lane	C3	Harmer Lane	C2
Arundel Street	B3	Haymarket	C1
Bailey Lane	B1	Headford Street	A3
Bailey Street	B1	High Street	C1
Bank Street	C1	Hodgson Street	A3
Barker's Pool	B2	Hollis Croft	B1
Beet Street	A1	Howard Street	C2
Bellefield Street	A1	Hoyle Street	A1
Bishop Street	B3	Leadmill Road	C3
Blonk Street	C1	Leopold Street	B2
Boston Street	B3	Mappin Street	A2
Bower Street	B1	Margaret Street	B3
Bramwell Street	A1	Mary Street	B3
Bridge Street	C1	Matilda Street	C3
Broad Lane	A2	Meadow Street	A1
Broad Street	C1	Milton Street	A3
Broomhall Street	A3	Moore Street	A3
Broomhall Place	A3	Napier Street	A3
Broomspring Lane	A2	Netherthorpe Road	A1
Brown Street	C3	Norfolk Street	C2
Brunswick Street	A2	Nursery Street	C1
Campo Lane	B1	Pinstone Street	B2
Carver Street	B2	Pond Hill	C2
Castle Square	C1	Pond Hill	C2
Castle Street	C1	Pond Street	C2
Castlegate	C1	Portobello Street	A2
Cavendish Street	A2	Queen Street	B1
Cemetery Road	A3	Queens Road	C3
Charles Street	B2/C2	Rockingham Street	B2
Charlotte Road	B3	St. Mary's Gate	B3
Charter Row	B3	St. Mary's Road	B3
Charter Square	B2	St. Philip's Road	A1
Church Street	B1	Scotland Street	B1
Clarke Street	A3	Sheaf Gardens	C3
Commercial Street	C1	Sheaf Square	C2
Copper Street	B1	Sheaf Street	C2
Corporation Street	B1	Shepherd Street	B1
Devonshire Street	A2	Shoreham Street	C3
Division Street	B2	Shrewsbury Road	C3
Dover Street	A1	Sidney Street	B3
Duchess Road	C3	Snig Hill	C1
Earl Street	B3	Snow Lane	B1
Earl Way	B3	Solly Street	A1
East Parade	C1	South Lane	B3
Ecclesall Road	A3	Spring Street	B1
Edmund Road	C3	Suffolk Road	C3
Edward Street	A1	Sunny Bank	A3
Eldon Street	B2	Surrey Street	B2
Exchange Street	C1	Tenter Street	B1
Exeter Drive	A3	The Moor	B3
Eyre Lane	C2	Thomas Street	A3
Eyre Street	B3	Townhead Street	B1
Farm Road	C3	Trafalgar Street	B2
Fawcett Street	A1	Trippet Lane	B2
Filey Street	A2	Upper Allen Street	A1
Fitzwilliam Street	A2	Upper Hanover Street	A2
Flat Street	C1	Victoria Street	A2
Furnace Hill	B1	Waingate	C1
Furnival Gate	B2	Wellington Street	B1
Furnival Square	B2	West Bar	B2
Furnival Street	B2	West Street	B1
Garden Street	A1	Westbar Green	B1
Gell Street	A2	Weston Street	A1
Gibraltar Street	B1	William Street	A3
Glossop Road	A2	Young Street	B3

SOUTHAMPTON

Appears on main map page 106

Tourist Information Centre: 9 Civic Centre Road
Tel: 023 8083 3333

Above Bar Street	B2	Queensway	B3
Albert Road North	C3	Radcliffe Road	C1
Argyle Road	B1	Roberts Road	A1
Bedford Place	A1	St. Andrews Road	B1
Belvidere Road	C2	St. Mary's Road	B1
Bernard Street	B3	St. Mary Street	B2
Brintons Road	B1	Shirley Road	A1
Britannia Road	C1	Solent Road	A2
Briton Street	B3	Southern Road	A2
Burlington Road	A1	South Front	B2
Canute Road	B3	Terminus Terrace	B3
Castle Way	B2	Town Quay	A3
Central Bridge	B3	Trafalgar Road	B3
Central Road	B3	West Quay Road	A2
Chapel Road	B2	West Road	B3
Civic Centre Road	A2	Western Esplanade	A2
Clovelly Road	B1	Wilton Avenue	A1
Commercial Road	A1		
Cranbury Avenue	B1		
Cumberland Place	A1		
Denzil Avenue	B1		
Derby Road	C1		
Devonshire Road	A1		
Dorset Street	B1		
East Park Terrace	B1		
East Street	B2		
Endle Street	C2		
European Way	B3		
Golden Grove	B2		
Graham Road	B1		
Harbour Parade	A2		
Hartington Road	C1		
Henstead Road	A1		
Herbert Walker Avenue	A2		
High Street	B2		
Hill Lane	A1		
Howard Road	A1		
James Street	B2		
Kent Road	C1		
Kingsway	B2		
Landguard Road	A1		
London Road	B1		
Lyon Street	B1		
Marine Parade	C2		
Marsh Lane	B2		
Melbourne Street	C2		
Millbank Street	C1		
Milton Road	A1		
Morris Road	A1		
Mount Pleasant Road	B1		
Newcombe Road	A1		
New Road	B2		
Northam Road	C1		
North Front	B2		
Northumberland Road	C1		
Ocean Way	B3		
Onslow Road	B1		
Orchard Lane	B3		
Oxford Avenue	B1		
Oxford Street	B3		
Palmerston Road	B2		
Peel Street	C1		
Platform Road	B3		
Portland Terrace	A2		
Pound Tree Road	B2		
Princes Street	C1		

Tourist Information Centre: The Potteries Museum & Art Gallery, Bethesda Street Tel: 01782 236000

Albion Street	B1	Snow Hill	B2
Ashford Street	B2	Stafford Street	B1
Avenue Road	B2	Station Road	B3
Aynsley Road	B2	Stoke	B3
Bedford Road	B2	Stoke Road	B3
Bedford Street	A2	Stone Street	A3
Belmont Road	A1	Stuart Road	C2
Beresford Street	B2	Sun Street	B1
Berry Hill Road	C2	The Parkway	B2
Boon Avenue	A3	Trentmill Road	C2
Botteslow Street	C1	Victoria Road	C2
Boughey Road	B3	Warner Street	B1
Broad Street	B1	Waterloo Street	C1
Bucknall New Road	C1	Wellesley Street	B2
Bucknall Old Road	C1	Wellington Road	C1
Cauldon Road	B2	West Avenue	A3
Cemetery Road	A2	Westland Street	A3
Church Street	B3	Yoxall Avenue	A3
Clough Street	B1		
College Road	B2		
Commercial Road	C1		
Copeland Street	B3		
Dewsbury Road	C3		
Eagle Street	C1		
Eastwood Road	C1		
Elenora Street	B3		
Etruria Road	A1		
Etruria Vale Road	A1		
Etruscan Street	A2		
Festival Way	A1		
Forge Lane	A1		
Garner Street	A2		
Glebe Street	B3		
Greatbatch Avenue	A3		
Hanley	B1		
Hartshill Road	A3		
Hill Street	A3		
Honeywall	A3		
Howard Place	B2		
Ivy House Road	C1		
Leek Road	B3		
Lichfield Street	C1		
Liverpool Road	B3		
Lordship Lane	B3		
Lytton Street	B3		
Manor Street	C3		
Marsh Street	B1		
Newlands Street	B2		
North Street	A2		
Old Hall Street	B1		
Oxford Street	A3		
Parliament Row	B1		
Potteries Way	B1		
Potters Way	C1		
Prince's Road	A3		
Quarry Avenue	A3		
Quarry Road	A3		
Queen's Road	A3		
Queensway	A2		
Rectory Road	B2		
Regent Road	B2		
Richmond Street	A3		
Ridgway Road	B2		
Seaford Street	B2		
Shelton New Road	A2		
Shelton Old Road	A3		

STOKE-ON-TRENT

0   500 yds
0   500m

Appears on main
map page 171

**Tourist Information Centre: Bridgefoot
Tel: 01789 264293**

Albany Road	A2	Swan's Nest Lane	C2
Alcester Road	A1	The Waterways	A1
Arden Street	A1	Tiddington Road	C2
Avonside	B3	Trinity Street	B3
Banbury Road	C2	Tyler Street	B1
Bancroft Place	C2	Union Street	B2
Birmingham Road	A1	Warwick Court	B1
Brewery Street	B1	Warwick Crescent	C1
Bridgefoot	C2	Warwick Road	C1
Bridge Street	B2	Waterside	B2
Bridgeway	C2	Welcombe Road	C1
Bridgetown Road	C3	Westbourne Grove	A2
Broad Street	A3	Western Road	A1
Broad Walk	A3	West Street	A3
Bull Street	A3	Wharf Road	A1
Chapel Lane	B2	Windsor Street	B2
Chapel Street	B2	Wood Street	B2
Cherry Orchard	A3		
Chestnut Walk	A2		
Church Street	B2		
Clopton Bridge	C2		
Clopton Road	B1		
College Lane	B3		
College Street	B3		
Ely Street	B2		
Evesham Place	A3		
Evesham Road	A3		
Great William Street	B1		
Greenhill Street	A2		
Grove Road	A2		
Guild Street	B1		
Henley Street	B1		
High Street	B2		
Holtom Street	A3		
John Street	B1		
Kendall Avenue	B1		
Maidenhead Road	B1		
Mansell Street	A1		
Meer Street	B2		
Mill Lane	B3		
Mulberry Street	B1		
Narrow Lane	A3		
New Street	B3		
Old Town	A3		
Old Town Square	A3		
Old Tramway Walk	C3		
Orchard Way	A3		
Payton Street	B1		
Red Lion Court	B1		
Rother Street	A2		
Ryland Street	B3		
St. Andrews Crescent	A2		
St. Gregory's Road	B1		
Sanctus Drive	A3		
Sanctus Road	A3		
Sanctus Street	A3		
Sandfield Road	A3		
Scholar's Lane	A2		
Seven Meadow Road	A3		
Shakespeare Street	B1		
Sheep Street	B2		
Shipston Road	C3		
Shottery Road	A2		
Shrieve's Walk	B2		
Southern Lane	B3		
Station Road	A1		

STRATFORD-UPON-AVON

0   500 yds
0   500m

Appears on main
map page 147

SUNDERLAND

0   400 yds
0   400m

Appears on main
map page 212

Tourist Information Centre: 50 Fawcett Street
Tel: 0191 553 2000

Abbotsford Grove	B3	Lime Street	A2
Addison Street	C3	Livingstone Road	B2
Aiskell Street	A2	Lumley Road	A2
Argyle Street	B3	Matamba Terrace	A2
Ashwood Street	A3	Milburn Street	A2
Azalea Terace South	B3	Millennium Way	B1
Barnes Park Road	A3	Moor Terrace	C2
Barrack Street	C1	Mount Road	A3
Beach Street	A2	Mowbray Road	B3
Beechwood Terrace	A3	New Durham Road	A3
Belvedere Road	B3	Newcastle Road	B1
Black Road	B1	North Bridge Street	B2
Borough Road	B2/C2	Otto Terrace	A3
Bramwell Road	C3	Pallion New Road	A2
Brougham Street	B2	Park Lane	B2
Burdon Road	B3	Park Road	B3
Burn Park Road	A3	Peel Street	B3
Burnaby Street	A3	Prospect Row	C2
Burnville Road	A3	Queens Road	A1
Carol Street	A2	Raby Road	A2
Chatsworth Street	A3	Railway Row	A2
Chaytor Grove	C2	Roker Avenue	B1/C1
Chester Road	A2	Rosalie Terrace	C3
Chester Street	A2	Ryhope Road	B3
Church Street East	C2	St. Albans Street	C3
Church Street North	B1	St. Leonards Street	C3
Cleveland Road	A3	St. Marks Road	A2
Commercial Road	C3	St. Mary's Way	B2
Cooper Street	C1	St. Michaels Way	B2
Coronation Street	C2	St. Peter's Way	C1
Corporation Road	C3	Salem Road	C3
Cousin Street	C2	Salem Street	C3
Cromwell Street	A2	Salisbury Street	B2
Crozier Street	B1	Sans Street	C2
Dame Dorothy Street	B1	Selbourne Street	B1
Deptford Road	A2	Silksworth Row	A2
Deptford Terrace	A1	Sorley Street	A2
Durham Road	A3	Southwick Road	A1
Easington Street	B1	Southwick Road	B1
Eden House Road	A3	Stewart Street	A3
Eglinton Street	B1	Stockton Road	B3
Enderby Road	A2	Suffolk Street	C3
Farringdon Row	A1	Sunderland Road	A1
Forster Street	C1	Swan Street	B1
Fox Street	A3	Tatham Street	C2
Fulwell Road	B1	The Cedars	B3
General Graham Street	A3	The Cloisters	B3
Gladstone Street	B1	The Parade	C3
Gray Road	B3/C3	The Quadrant	C2
Hanover Place	A1	The Royalty	A2
Hartington Street	C1	Thornhill Park	B3
Hartley Street	C2	Thornhill Terrace	B3
Hastings Street	C3	Thornholme Road	A3
Hay Street	B1	Toward Road	B2/C3
Hendon Road	C2	Tower Street	C3
Hendon Valley Road	C3	Tower Street West	C3
High Street East	C2	Trimdon Street	A2
High Street West	B2	Tunstall Road	B3
Holmeside	B2	Tunstall Vale	B3
Horatio Street	C1	Vaux Brewery Way	B1
Hurstwood Road	A3	Villette Road	C3
Hutton Street	A3	Vine Place	B2
Hylton Road	A2	Wallace Street	B1
Hylton Street	A2	West Lawn	B3
Jackson Street	A3	West Wear Street	B2
James William Street	C2	Western Hill	A2
Kenton Grove	B1	Wharncliffe Street	A2
Kier Hardy Way	A1	White House Road	C3
King's Place	A2	Woodbine Street	C2
Lawrence Street	C2	Wreath Quay Road	B1

SWANSEA

0   500 yds
0   500m

Appears on main
map page 128

Tourist Information Centre: Plymouth Street
Tel: 01792 468321

Aberdyberthi Street	C1	Mount Pleasant	B2
Albert Row	B3	Mumbles Road	A3
Alexandra Road	B2	Neath Road	C1
Argyle Street	A3	Nelson Street	B3
Baptist Well Place	B1	New Cut Road	C2
Baptist Well Street	B1	New Orchard Street	B1
Beach Street	A3	Nicander Parade	A2
Belgrave Lane	A2	Norfolk Street	A2
Belle Vue Way	B2	North Hill Road	B1
Berw Road	A1	Orchard Street	B2
Berwick Terrace	B1	Oxford Street	A3
Bond Street	A3	Oystermouth Road	A3
Brooklands Terrace	A2	Page Street	B2
Brunswick Street	A3	Pant-y-Celyn Road	A2
Brynymor Crescent	A3	Park Terrace	B1
Brynymor Road	A3	Pedrog Terrace	A1
Burrows Place	C3	Penlan Crescent	A2
Cambrian Place	C3	Pentre Guinea Road	C1
Carig Crescent	A1	Pen-y-Craig Road	A1
Carlton Terrace	B2	Picton Terrace	B2
Carmarthen Road	B1	Powys Avenue	A1
Castle Street	B2	Princess Way	B2
Clarence Terrace	B3	Quay Parade	C2
Colbourne Terrace	B1	Rhondda Street	A2
Constitution Hill	A2	Rose Hill	A2
Creidiol Road	A1	St. Elmo Avenue	C1
Cromwell Street	A2	St. Helen's Avenue	A3
Cwm Road	C1	St. Helen's Road	A3
De La Beche Street	B2	St. Mary Street	B2
Delhi Street	C2	Singleton Street	B3
Dillwyn Street	B3	Somerset Place	C3
Dyfatty Street	B1	South Guildhall Road	A3
Dyfed Avenue	A2	Strand	C2
Earl Street	C1	Taliesyn Road	A2
East Burrows Road	C3	Tan-y-Marian Road	A2
Eigen Crescent	A1	Tegid Road	A1
Emlyn Road	A1	Teilo Crescent	A1
Fabian Way	C2	Terrace Road	A2
Fairfield Terrace	A2	The Kingsway	B2
Ffynone Drive	A2	Townhill Road	A1
Ffynone Road	A2	Trawler Road	B3
Foxhole Road	C1	Villiers Street	C1
Glamorgan Street	B3	Vincent Street	B3
Gors Avenue	A1	Walter Road	A3
Granagwen Road	B1	Watkin Street	B2
Grove Place	B2	Waun-Wen Road	B1
Gwent Road	A1	Wellington Street	B3
Gwili Terrace	A1	West Way	B3
Hanover Street	A2	Westbury Street	A3
Heathfield	B2	Western Street	A3
Hewson Street	A2	William Street	B3
High Street	B2	Windmill Terrace	C1
High View	B1	York Street	C3
Islwyn Road	A1		
Kilvey Road	C1		
Kilvey Terrace	C2		
King Edward's Road	A3		
King's Road	C2		
Llangyfelach Road	B1		
Long Ridge	B1		
Mackworth Street	C2		
Maesteg Street	C1		
Mansel Street	A2		
Mayhill Road	A1		
Milton Terrace	B2		
Morris Lane	C2		

SWINDON

Tourist Information Centre: Central Library, Regent Circus
Tel: 01793 466454

Albion Street	A3
Bath Road	B3
Beatrice Street	B1
Beckhampton Street	C2
Birch Street	A2
Bridge Street	B2
Broad Street	C1
Canal Walk	B2
Caulfield Road	C1
Church Place	A2
Cirencester Way	C1
Clifton Street	B3
Commercial Road	B2
County Road	C1
Cricklade Street	C3
Curtis Street	B2
Dean Street	A2
Drove Road	C3
Eastcott Hill	B3
Edmund Street	B2
Elmina Road	C1
Euclid Street	C2
Faringdon Road	A2
Farnsby Street	B2
Fleet Street	B2
Fleming Way	B2
Gladstone Street	C1
Goddard Avenue	B3
Great Western Way	A1
Grosvenor Road	A3
Groundwell Way	C2
Hawksworth Way	A1
High Street	C3
Holbrook Way	B2
Hythe Road	B3
Islington Street	B2
Jennings Street	A2
Kemble Drive	A1
Kent Road	B3
Kingshill Street	A3
Lansdown Road	B3
Manchester Road	B1
Market Street	B2
Milford Street	B2
Milton Road	B2
Morris Street	A1
Newburn Crescent	A2
Newcombe Drive	A1
North Star Avenue	B1
Ocotal Way	C1
Okus Road	A3
Park Lane	A2
Penzance Drive	A2
Plymouth Street	C2
Princes Street	C2
Queen Street	B2
Radnor Street	A3
Redcliffe Street	A2
Regent Street	B2
Rodbourne Road	A1
Roseberry Street	C1
Spring Gardens	C2
Stafford Street	B3
Station Road	B1
Swindon Road	B3
The Parade	B2
Upham Road	C3
Victoria Road	C2
Westcott Place	A3
Western Street	C3
William Street	A3
York Road	C2

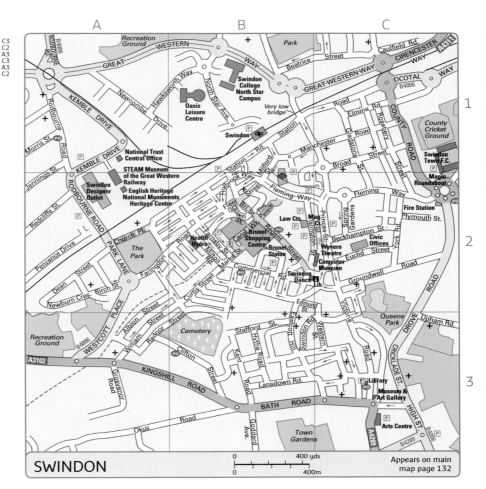

SWINDON

0   400 yds
0   400m

Appears on main map page 132

TORQUAY

Tourist Information Centre: 5 Vaughan Parade
Tel: 01803 211211

Abbey Road	B2
Ash Hill Road	B1
Avenue Road	A2
Bampfylde Road	A2
Barton Road	A1
Belgrave Road	A2
Belmont Road	C1
Braddons Hill Road East	C2
Bridge Road	A2
Bronshill Road	B1
Brunswick Square	B1
Carlton Road	C1
Cary Parade	C3
Cedars Road	C2
Chestnut Avenue	A2
Cockington Lane	A3
Croft Road	B2
Crownhill Park	A1
Dunmere Road	C1
East Street	A1
Ellacombe Church Road	C1
Ellacombe Road	B1
Falkland Road	A2
Falkland Road	A2
Fleet Street	B2
Forest Road	B1
Goshen Road	A2
Hatfield Road	B1
Hennapyn Road	A3
Higher Warberry Road	C2
Hillesdon Road	C2
Kenwyn Road	C1
Lower Warberry Road	C2
Lucius Street	A2
Lymington Road	B1
Mallock Road	A2
Market Street	B2
Marnham Road	C1
Meadfoot Lane	C3
Meadfoot Road	C3
Middle Warberry Road	C2
Mill Lane	A2
Newton Road	A1
Old Mill Road	A2
Old Mill Road	A3
Parkfield Road	B1
Parkhill Road	C3
Prince's Road	C2
Princes Road East	C2
Quinta Road	C1
Rathmore Road	A3
Reddenhill Road	C1
Rosehill Road	C2
Sanford Road	A2
Seaway Lane	A3
Shedden Hill	B2
Sherwell Lane	A2
Solsbro Road	A3
South Street	A2
St. Lukes Road	B2
St. Marychurch Road	B2
St. Michael's Road	A1
Stitchill Road	C2
Strand	C3
Teignmouth Road	A1
The King's Drive	A2
Thurlow Road	B1
Tor Hill Road	B2
Torbay Road	A3
Torwood Gardens Road	C3
Torwood Street	C3
Union Street	B2
Upton Hill	B1
Upton Road	A1
Vanehill Road	C3
Victoria Parade	C3
Walnut Road	A3
Warbro Road	C1
Warren Road	B2
Windsor Road	C1

TORQUAY

0   400 yds
0   400m

Appears on main map page 101

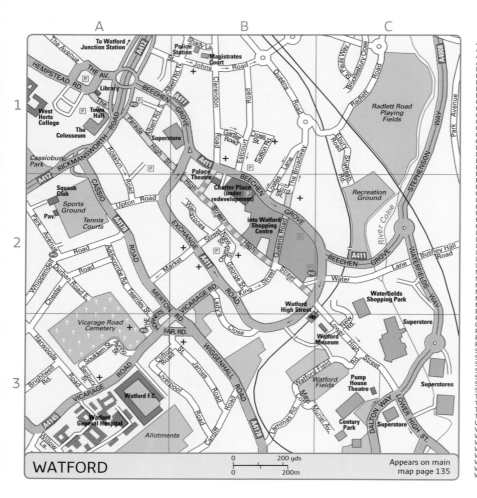

WATFORD

Scale: 0 — 200 yds / 0 — 200m

Appears on main map page 135

Street	Grid
Addiscombe Road	A2
Albert Road North	A1
Albert Road South	A1
Aynho Street	A3
Banbury Street	A3
Beechen Grove	A1/C2
Brightwell Road	A3
Brocklesbury Close	C1
Bushey Hall Road	C2
Cardiff Road	B3
Cassio Road	A2
Chester Road	A2
Church Street	B2
Clarendon Road	B1
Clifton Road	A3
Cross Street	B1
Dalton Way	C3
Durban Road East	A2
Ebury Road	C1
Estcourt Road	B1
Exchange Road	A2
Farraline Road	A3
Fearnley Street	A2
Garlet Road	B1
George Street	B2
Harwoods Road	A3
Hempsted Road	A1
High Street	A1/B2
King Street	B2
Lady's Close	B2
Lammas Road	B3
Liverpool Road	A3
Loates Lane	B2
Lord Street	B2
Lower High Street	C3
Market Street	A2
May Cottages	B3
Merton Road	A2
Muriel Avenue	B3
New Road	C3
New Street	B2
Park Avenue	C1
Park Avenue	A2
Queens Road	B1/B2
Radlett Road	C1
Rickmansworth Road	A2
Rosslyn Road	A1
Shaftesbury Road	C1
Souldern Street	A3
St. James Road	B3
St. Johns Road	A1
St. Pauls Way	C1
Stephenson Way	C2
Sutton Road	B1
The Avenue	A1
The Broadway	B2
The Hornets	A3
The Parade	A1
Upton Road	A2
Vicarage Road	A3/B2
Water Lane	C2
Waterfields Way	C2
Watford Field Road	B3
Wellstones	B2
Whippendell Road	A2
Wiggenhall Road	B3
Willow Lane	A3

WESTON-SUPER-MARE

Scale: 0 — 400 yds / 0 — 400m

Appears on main map page 115

Tourist Information Centre: Winter Gardens, Royal Parade
Tel: 01934 417117

Street	Grid	Street	Grid
Addicott Road	B3	Stafford Road	C2
Albert Avenue	B3	Station Road	B2
Alexandra Parade	B2	Sunnyside Road	B3
Alfred Street	B2	Swiss Road	C2
All Saints Road	B1	The Centre	B2
Amberey Road	C3	Trewartha Park	C1
Arundell Road	B1	Upper Church Road	A1
Ashcombe Gardens	C1	Walliscote Road	B3
Ashcombe Road	C2	Waterloo Street	B2
Atlantic Road	A1	Whitecross Road	B3
Baker Street	B2	Winterstoke Road	C3
Beach Road	B3		
Beaconsfield Road	B2		
Birnbeck Road	A1		
Boulevard	B2		
Brendon Avenue	C1		
Bridge Road	C2		
Brighton Road	B3		
Bristol Road	B1		
Carlton Street	B2		
Cecil Road	B1		
Clarence Road North	B3		
Clarendon Road	C2		
Clevedon Road	B3		
Clifton Road	B3		
Drove Road	C3		
Earlham Grove	C2		
Ellenborough Park North	B3		
Ellenborough Park South	B3		
Exeter Road	B3		
George Street	B2		
Gerard Road	B1		
Grove Park Road	B1		
High Street	B2		
Highbury Road	A1		
Hildesheim Bridge	B2		
Hill Road	C1		
Jubilee Road	B2		
Kenn Close	C3		
Kensington Road	C3		
Knightstone Road	A1		
Langford Road	C3		
Lewisham Grove	C2		
Locking Road	C2		
Lower Bristol Road	C1		
Lower Church Road	A1		
Manor Road	C1		
Marchfields Way	C3		
Marine Parade	B3		
Meadow Street	B2		
Milton Road	C2		
Montpelier	B1		
Neva Road	B2		
Norfolk Road	C3		
Oxford Street	B2		
Queen's Road	B1		
Rectors Way	C3		
Regent Street	B2		
Ridgeway Avenue	B3		
Royal Crescent	A1		
St. Paul's Road	B3		
Sandford Road	C2		
Severn Road	B3		
Shrubbery Road	A1		
South Road	A1		
Southside	B1		

Tourist Information Centre: Guildhall, High Street
Tel: 01962 840500

Alison Way	A1	St. Peter Street	B2
Andover Road	A1	St. Swithun Street	B3
Archery Lane	A2	St. Thomas Street	B3
Bar End Road	C3	Saxon Road	B1
Barfield Close	C3	Silver Hill	B2
Beaufort Road	A3	Southgate Street	A3
Beggar's Lane	C2	Staple Gardens	B2
Blue Ball Hill	C2	Station Road	A1
Bridge Stret	C2	Step Terrace	A2
Broadway	B2	Stockbridge Road	A1
Canon Street	B3	Sussex Street	A2
Chesil Street	C3	Swan Lane	B1
Christchurch Road	A3	Symond's Street	B3
City Road	A1	Tanner Street	B2
Clifton Hill	A2	The Square	B2
Clifton Road	A1	Tower Street	A2
Clifton Terrace	A2	Union Street	C2
Colebrook Street	B2	Upper Brook Street	B2
College Street	B3	Upper High Street	A2
College Walk	B3	Wales Street	C2
Compton Road	A3	Water Lane	C2
Cranworth Road	A1	Wharf Hill	C3
Culver Road	B3	Worthy Lane	A1
Domum Road	C3		
Durngate	C2		
East Hill	C3		
Eastgate Street	C2		
Easton Lane	C1		
Ebden Road	C1		
Edgar Road	A3		
Elm Road	A1		
Fairfield Road	A1		
Friarsgate	B2		
Gordon Road	B1		
Great Minster Street	B2		
Hatherley Road	A1		
High Street	B2		
Hyde Abbey Road	B1		
Hyde Close	B1		
Hyde Street	B1		
Jewry Street	B2		
King Alfred Place	B1		
Kingsgate Street	B3		
Little Minster Street	B2		
Lower Brook Street	B2		
Magdalen Hill	C2		
Market Lane	B2		
Middle Brook Street	B2		
Middle Road	A2		
Milland Road	C3		
North Walls	A1		
Parchment Street	B2		
Park Avenue	B1		
Peninsula Square	A2		
Portal Road	C3		
Quarry Road	C3		
Romans' Road	A3		
Romsey Road	A2		
St. Catherine's Road	C3		
St. Cross Road	A3		
St. George's Street	B2		
St. James Lane	A2		
St. James Villas	A3		
St. John's Street	C2		
St. Michael's Road	A3		
St. Paul's Hill	A1		

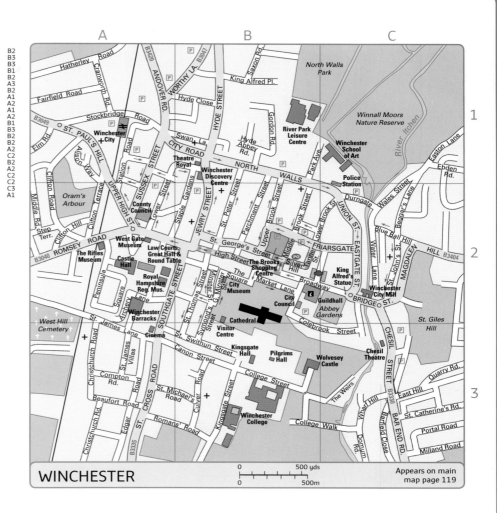

Tourist Information Centre: Old Booking Hall, Central Station
Tel: 01753 743900

Adelaide Square	C3
Albert Street	A2
Alexandra Road	B3
Alma Road	B2/B3
Arthur Road	B2
Barry Avenue	B1
Bexley Street	B2
Bolton Avenue	B3
Bolton Crescent	B3
Bolton Road	B3
Bulkeley Avenue	A3
Castle Hill	C2
Charles Street	B2
Clarence Crescent	B2
Clarence Road	A2
College Crescent	A3
Dagmar Road	B2
Datchet Road	C1
Frances Road	B3
Goslar Way	A2
Goswell Road	B2
Green Lane	A2
Grove Road	B2
Helston Lane	A2
High Street (Eton)	B1
High Street (Windsor)	C2
Imperial Road	A3
King Edward VII Avenue	C1
Kings Road	C3
Meadow Lane	B1
Mill Lane	A1
Osborne Road	B3
Oxford Road	B2
Park Street	C2
Parsonage Lane	A2
Peascod Street	B2
Peel Close	A3
Princess Avenue	A3
Romney Lock Road	C1
St. Leonards Road	B3
St. Marks Road	B2
Sheet Street	C2
South Meadow Lane	B1
Springfield Road	A3
Stovell Road	A1
Thames Street	C1
The Long Walk	C3
Upcroft	A3
Vansittart Road	B2
Victoria Street	B2
Victor Road	B3
Westmead	A3
Windsor & Eton Relief Road	A2
York Avenue	A3
York Road	A3

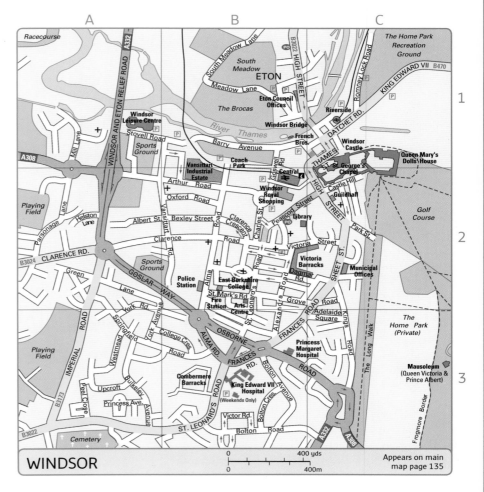

Worcester York

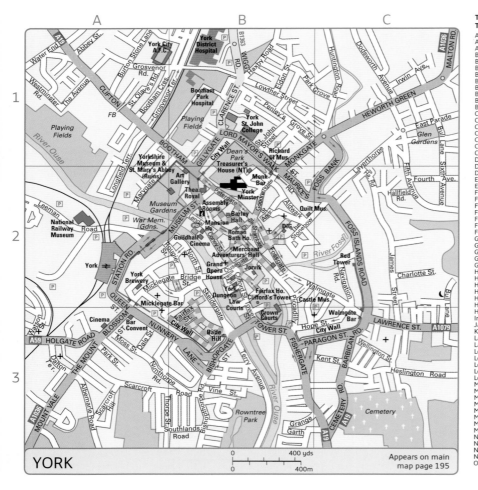

WORCESTER

A A430
UPPER TYTHING
Albany Terrace
Swimming Pool
Chestnut Street
Lansdowne Crescent
Lansdowne Walk
B4550
Chestnut Walk
RAINBOW HILL
St. Oswalds Rd.
Washington St.
Arboretum Rd.
Westbury St.
B4637
Police Sta. & Mag. Court
Shire Hall Crown Courts
Vesta Tilley Centre
LOWESMOOR PL.
TOLLADINE ROAD
Sherriff St.
Shrub Hill
Swan Theatre
Library, Art Gallery & Museum
Foregate Street
Shrub Hill Road
B4636
To Worcestershire Royal Hospital
Racecourse
City Council Offices
Worcestershire Library & History Centre
Shrub Hill Retail Park
Coach & Lorry Park
Corn Market
Reindeer Court Shopping Centre
MIDLAND ROAD
Crowngate Shopping Centre
Crowngate Shopping Centre
The Shambles
Guildhall
Charles St.
Vincent Rd.
Stanley Rd.
Countess of Huntingdon Hall
Copenhagen St.
Pump St.
The Greyfriars
Carden St.
Compton Rd.
B4205
College of Technology
Cathedral Plaza Shopping Centre
Kleve Walk
Wyld's Lane
Cole Hill
Cripplegate Park
NEW ROAD
COLLEGE ST.
Richmond Hill
County Cricket Ground
Cathedral
Commandery Museum
Fort Royal Park
Royal Worcester Porcelain
LONDON RD.
Fort Royal Hill
Park St.

Appears on main map page 146

Tourist Information Centre: The Guildhall, High Street
Tel: 01905 726311

Albany Terrace	A1	Sherriff Street	C1
Albert Road	C3	Shrub Hill	C2
Angel Place	A2	Shrub Hill Road	C2
Angel Street	B2	Sidbury	B3
Arboretum Road	B1	Southfield Street	B1
Back Lane South	A1	Spring Hill	C2
Bath Road	B3	Stanley Road	C3
Bridge Street	A2	Tallow Hill	C2
Britannia Road	A1	Tennis Walk	A1
Britannia Square	A1	The Butts	A2
Broad Street	A2	The Cross	B2
Carden Street	B3	The Moors	A1
Castle Street	A2	The Shambles	B2
Charles Street	B3	The Tything	A1
Chestnut Street	B1	Tolladine Road	C1
Chestnut Walk	B1	Trinity Street	B2
City Walls Road	B2	Upper Tything	A1
Cole Hill	C3	Vincent Road	C3
College Street	B3	Washington Street	B1
Compton Road	C3	Westbury Street	B1
Copenhagen Street	A3	Wyld's Lane	C3
Croft Road	A2		
Deansway	A2		
Dent Close	C3		
Dolday	A2		
Farrier Street	A2		
Foregate Street	B2		
Fort Royal Hill	C3		
Foundry Street	B3		
Friar Street	B3		
George Street	C2		
Grand Stand Road	A2		
High Street	B2		
Hill Street	C2		
Hylton Road	A2		
Infirmary Walk	A2		
Kleve Walk	B3		
Lansdowne Crescent	B1		
Lansdowne Walk	C1		
London Road	B3		
Loves Grove	A1		
Lowesmoor	B2		
Lowesmoor Place	B2		
Midland Road	C3		
Moor Street	A1		
Newport Street	A2		
New Road	A3		
New Street	B2		
Northfield Street	B1		
North Quay	A2		
Padmore Street	B2		
Park Street	B3		
Park Street	C3		
Pheasant Street	B2		
Pump Street	B3		
Rainbow Hill	B1		
Richmond Hill	C3		
St. Martin's Gate	B2		
St. Mary's Street	A1		
St. Oswalds Road	A1		
St. Paul's Street	B2		
Sansome Street	B2		
Sansome Walk	B1		
Severn Street	B3		
Severn Terrace	A1		
Shaw Street	A2		

YORK

A19
A1036
MALTON RD.
Abbey St.
York City A.F.C.
York District Hospital
B1363
WIGGINTON RD.
Water End
Grosvenor Rd.
Hexby Road
Dodsworth Avenue
Irwin Ave.
CLIFTON
St. Olave's Rd.
Bootham Crcs.
Bootham Park Hospital
Park Grove
HEWORTH GREEN
Playing Fields
FB
York St. John College
Penley's Grove St.
East Parade
Glen Gardens
River Ouse
Yorkshire Museum & St. Mary's Abbey (Ruins)
Art Gallery
Dean's Park Treasurer's House (NT)
Monk Bar
Hallfield Rd.
Fourth Avenue
Fifth Avenue
Sixth Avenue
National Railway Museum
Museum Gardens
War Mem. Gdns.
Thea. Royal
York Minster
Quilt Mus.
Assembly Rooms
Mansion Ho.
DIG
Guildhall
Cinema
Roman Bath Ho.
Merchant Adventurers' Hall
Red Tower
York Brewery
Grand Opera House
Jorvik
Charlotte St.
York Dungeon
York Law Courts
Fairfax Ho.
Clifford's Tower
Castle Mus.
Micklegate Bar
Crown Courts
Walmgate Bar
Cinema
Bar Convent
City Wall
Baile Hill
City Wall
LAWRENCE ST.
A1079
HOLGATE ROAD
A59
NUNNERY LANE
BISHOPGATE
TOWER ST.
PARAGON ST.
Kent St.
Heslington Road
THE MOUNT
Scarcroft
Rowntree Park
Cemetery
Grange Garth
A19
CEMETERY RD.
Southlands Road
MOUNT VALE
A1036

Appears on main map page 195

Tourist Information Centre: 1 Museum Street
Tel: 01904 550099

Abbey Street	A1	Paragon Street	B3
Albermarle Road	A3	Park Grove	B1
Aldwark	B2	Park Street	A3
Barbican Road	C3	Penley's Grove Street	B1
Bishopthorpe Road	B3	Petergate	B2
Bishopgate Street	B3	Piccadilly	B2
Blossom Street	A3	Queen Street	A2
Bootham	A1	Rougier Street	A2
Bootham Crescent	A1	St. Andrewgate	B2
Bridge Street	B2	St. John Street	B1
Bull Lane	C1/C2	St. Maurice's Road	B2
Burton Stone Lane	A1	St. Olave's Road	A1
Cemetery Road	C3	Scarcroft Hill	A3
Charlotte Street	C2	Scarcroft Road	A3
Church Street	B2	Shambles	B2
Clarence Street	B1	Sixth Avenue	C1
Clifford Street	B2	Skeldergate	B2
Clifton	A1	Southlands Road	A3
Coney Street	B2	Station Road	A2
Dale Street	A3	Terry Avenue	B3
Dalton Terrace	A3	The Avenue	A1
Dodsworth Avenue	C1	The Mount	A3
East Parade	C1	The Stonebow	B2
Eldon Street	B1	Thorpe Street	A3
Fairfax Street	B3	Tower Street	B2
Fifth Avenue	C1	Vine Street	B3
Fishergate	B3	Walmgate	B2
Foss Bank	C2	Water End	A1
Fossgate	B2	Watson Street	A3
Foss Islands Road	C2	Wellington Street	C3
Fourth Avenue	C2	Westminster Road	A1
Gillygate	B1	Wigginton Road	B1
Goodramgate	B2		
Grange Garth	B3		
Grosvenor Road	A1		
Grosvenor Terrace	A1		
Hallfield Road	C2		
Haxby Road	B1		
Heslington Road	C3		
Heworth Green	C1		
Holgate Road	A3		
Hope Street	B3		
Huntington Road	C1		
Irwin Avenue	C1		
James Street	B2		
Kent Street	C3		
Lawrence Street	C3		
Layerthorpe	C2		
Leeman Road	A2		
Lendal	B2		
Longfield Terrace	A2		
Lord Mayor's Walk	B1		
Lowther Street	B1		
Malton Road	C1		
Marygate	A2		
Maurices Road	B2		
Micklegate	A2		
Monkgate	B1		
Moss Street	A3		
Mount Vale	A3		
Museum Street	B2		
Navigation Road	C2		
North Street	B2		
Nunnery Lane	A3		
Nunthorpe Road	A3		
Ousegate	B2		

Key to map symbols

P Short stay car park   P Mid stay car park   P Long stay car park   P Other car park   ▭ Airport terminal building

BIRMINGHAM INTERNATIONAL (BHX)

Appears on main map page 159

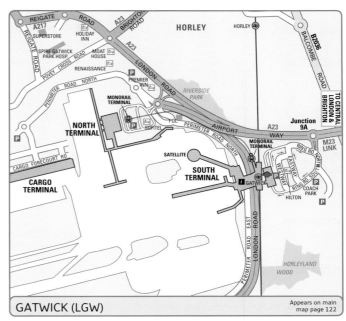

GATWICK (LGW)

Appears on main map page 122

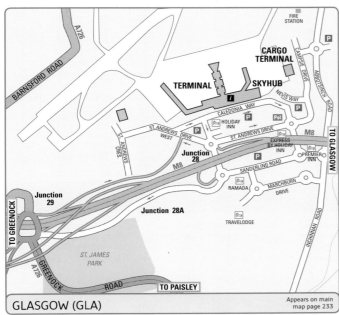

GLASGOW (GLA)

Appears on main map page 233

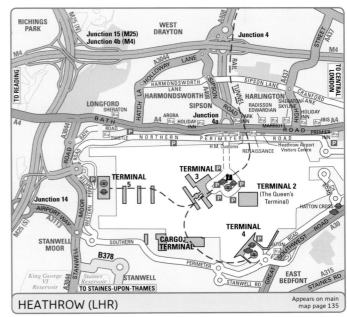

HEATHROW (LHR)

Appears on main map page 135

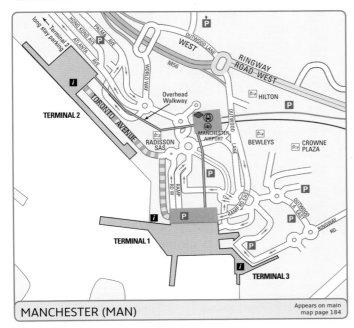

MANCHESTER (MAN)

Appears on main map page 184

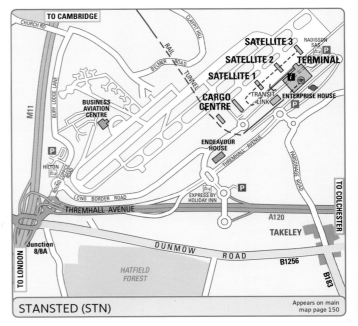

STANSTED (STN)

Appears on main map page 150

Symbols used on the map

M5 Motorway

M6Toll Toll motorway

8 9 Motorway junction with full / limited access (in congested areas there is just a numbered symbol)

Maidstone Birch Sarn Motorway service area with off road / full / limited access

A556 Primary route dual / single carriageway

$ 24 hour service area on primary route

Peterhead Primary route destination
Primary route destinations are places of major traffic importance linked by the primary route network. They are shown on a green background on direction signs.

A30 'A' road dual / single carriageway

B1403 'B' road dual / single carriageway

Minor road

Road with restricted access

Roads with passing places

Road proposed or under construction

33 Multi-level junction with full / limited access (with junction number)

Roundabout

4 Road distance in miles between markers

Road tunnel

Steep hill (arrows point downhill)

Toll Level crossing /Toll

St. Malo 8hrs Car ferry route with journey times

Railway line /station / tunnel

Wales Coast Path National Trail / Long Distance Route

---

30 **V** Fixed safety camera
Speed limit shown by a number within the camera, a V indicates a variable limit.

30 30 Fixed average-speed safety camera
Speed limit shown by a number within the camera.

✈ ✈ Airport with / without scheduled services

H Heliport

P&R P&R Park and Ride site operated by bus / rail (runs at least 5 days a week)

Built up area

□ □ □ Town / Village / Other settlement

Hythe Seaside destination

National boundary

KENT County / Unitary Authority boundary and name

0	150	300	500	700	900	metres
water 0	490	985	1640	2295	2950	feet

Heritage Coast

National Park

Regional / Forest Park boundary

Woodland

Danger Zone Military range

468 ▲941 Spot / Summit height (in metres)

Lake / Dam / River / Waterfall

Canal / Dry canal / Canal tunnel

Beach / Lighthouse

SEE PAGE 3 Area covered by urban area map

Land height reference bar

Reading our maps

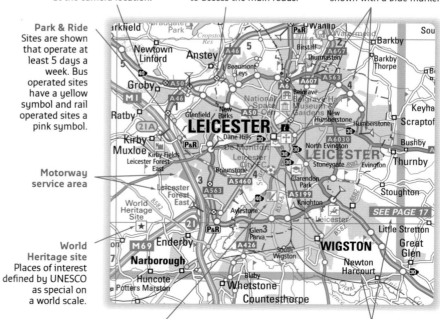

Safety Camera
The number inside the camera shows the speed limit at the camera location.

Multi-level junctions
Non-motorway junctions where slip roads are used to access the main roads.

Distances
Blue numbers give distances in miles between junctions shown with a blue marker.

Park & Ride
Sites are shown that operate at least 5 days a week. Bus operated sites have a yellow symbol and rail operated sites a pink symbol.

Motorway service area

World Heritage site
Places of interest defined by UNESCO as special on a world scale.

Places of interest
Blue symbols indicate places of interest. See the section at the bottom of the page for the different types of feature represented on the map.

More detailed maps
Green boxes indicate busy built-up-areas. More detailed mapping is available.

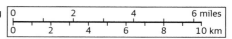

Places of interest

A selection of tourist detail is shown on the mapping. It is advisable to check with the local tourist information centre regarding opening times and facilities available.

Any of the following symbols may appear on the map in maroon ⭐ which indicates that the site has World Heritage status.

🅸	Tourist information centre (open all year)
ⓘ	Tourist information centre (open seasonally)
m̄	Ancient monument
🐠	Aquarium
🏛	Aqueduct / Viaduct
🍁	Arboretum
⚔ 1643	Battlefield
⚑	Blue flag beach
Å 🚐	Camp site / Caravan site
🏰	Castle
⌂	Cave
🌳	Country park
🏏	County cricket ground
🍶	Distillery
✝	Ecclesiastical feature
🎪	Event venue
🐄	Farm park
❀	Garden
⛳	Golf course
🏛	Historic house
⛵	Historic ship
⚽	Major football club
£	Major shopping centre / Outlet village
🏟	Major sports venue
🏁	Motor racing circuit
🚵	Mountain bike trail
🏛	Museum / Art gallery
➤	Nature reserve (NNR indicates a National Nature Reserve)
🏇	Racecourse
🚂	Rail Freight Terminal
⛷ 🎿	Ski slope (artificial / natural)
🐾	Spotlight nature reserve (Best sites for access to nature)
🚂━━	Steam railway centre / preserved railway
🏄	Surfing beach
🎢	Theme park
🎓	University
🍇	Vineyard
🐘	Wildlife park / Zoo
🦋	Wildlife Trust nature reserve
⭐	Other interesting feature
(NT) (NTS)	National Trust / National Trust for Scotland property

Map scale

A scale bar appears at the bottom of every page to help with distances.

```
0          2          4      6 miles
|━━━━━━━━━━━━━━━━━━━━━━━━━━━━━━━━━|
0     2     4     6     8    10 km
```

England, Wales & Southern Scotland are at a scale of 1:200,000 or 3.2 miles to 1 inch
Northern Scotland is at a scale of 1:263,158 or 4.2 miles to 1 inch.

Map pages

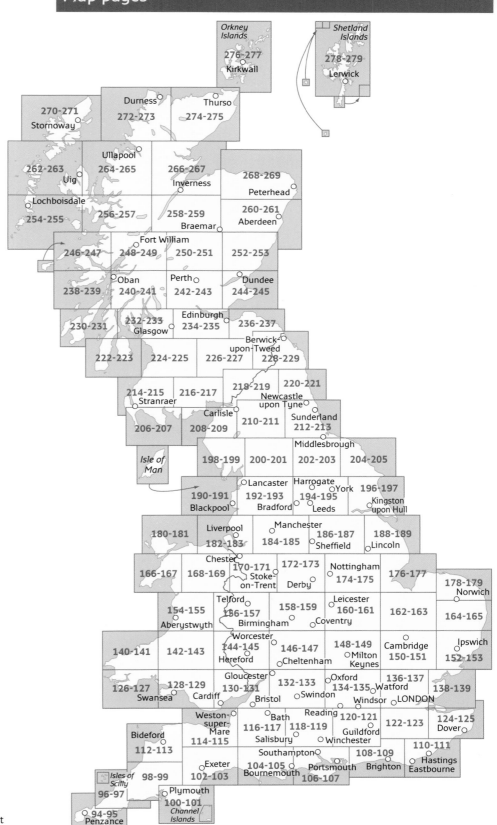

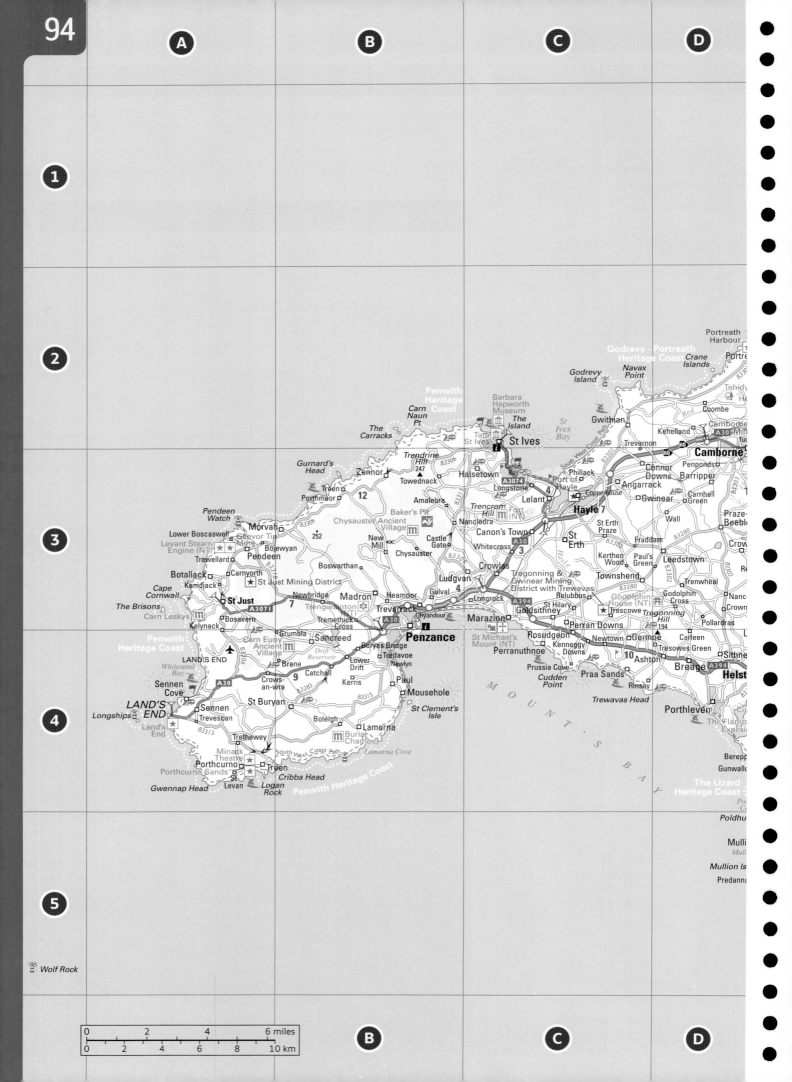

A B C D

1

2

3

4

5

Portreath
Harbour
Godrevy - Portreath
Heritage Coast
Crane
Islands
Portre
Godrevy
Island
Navax
Point
Tehidy
Penwith
Heritage
Coast
Carn
Naun
Pt
Barbara
Hepworth
Museum
St
Ives
Bay
Gwithian
Coombe
Red
Camborne
The
Carracks
Tate
St Ives
The
Island
St Ives
Kehelland
A30
Trevarnon
60
Camborne
Gurnard's
Head
Trendrine
Hill
247
B3306
Carbis
Bay
Connor
Downs
Penponds
Barripper
Zennor
Halsetown
Phillack
Port of
Hayle
Longstone
Copperhouse
60
Towednack
Amalebra
Lelant
Gwinear
Wall
Praze-
Beeble
Treen
Porthmeor
12
Trencrom
Hill
Hayle 7
Carnhell
Green
Pendeen
Watch
Chysauster Ancient
Village
Baker's Pit
Nancledra
Fort
(NT)
St Erth
Praze
Crow
Lower Boscaswell
Levant Steam
Engine (NT)
252
New
Mill
Canon's Town
A30
St
Erth
Fraddam
B3280
Leedstown
Morvah
Castle
Gate
Whitecross
3
Kerthen
Wood
Paul's
Green
R
Bojewyan
Chysauster
Crowlas
B3302
Trenwheal
Trewellard
Boswarthan
B330
Townshend
Pendeen
Ludgvan
Tregonning &
Gwinear Mining
District with Trewavas
B3280
Godolphin
Cross
Nanc
Botallack
Carnyorth
St Just Mining District
Gulval
4
Relubbus
Godolphin
House (NT)
Crown
Kenidjack
Cape
Cornwall
Heamoor
Longrock
A394
St Hilary
Trescowe
Tregonning
Hill
194
Pollardras
The Brisons
Carn Leskys
St Just
A3071
7
Newbridge
Madron
Trengwainton
(NT)
Trevarrack
A30
Chyandour
Marazion
Goldsithney
Perran Downs
Crown
Kelynack
Bosavern
Tremethick
Cross
Penzance
St Michael's
Mount (NT)
Rosudgeon
Kenneggy
Downs
Newtown
Germoe
Carleen
Sithne
Penwith
Heritage Coast
Carn Euny
Ancient Village
Sancreed
Grumbla
Buryas Bridge
Tredavoe
Newlyn
Perranuthnoe
Prussia Cove
10
Ashton
Tresowes Green
Breage
A394
Helst
LAND'S END
Brane
Lower
Drift
Paul
Cudden
Point
Praa Sands
Rinsey
Whitesand
Bay
Crows-
an-wra
9
Catchall
Kerris
Mousehole
Trewavas Head
Porthleven
Sennen
Cove
7
A30
St Buryan
Boleigh
St Clement's
Isle
M
O
U
N
T
'
S
Bereppi
LAND'S
END
Sennen
Trevescan
Lamorna
Burial
Chamber
B
A
Y
Gunwallo
Longships
Land's
End
Trethewey
B3315
Lamorna Cove
The Lizard
Heritage Coast
Minack
Theatre
South West Coast Path
Poldhu
Porthcurno
Porthcurno Sands
Treen
St
Levan
Cribba Head
Poldhu
Gwennap Head
Logan
Rock
Penwith Heritage Coast
Mulli
Mull
Mullion Is
Predanna

Wolf Rock

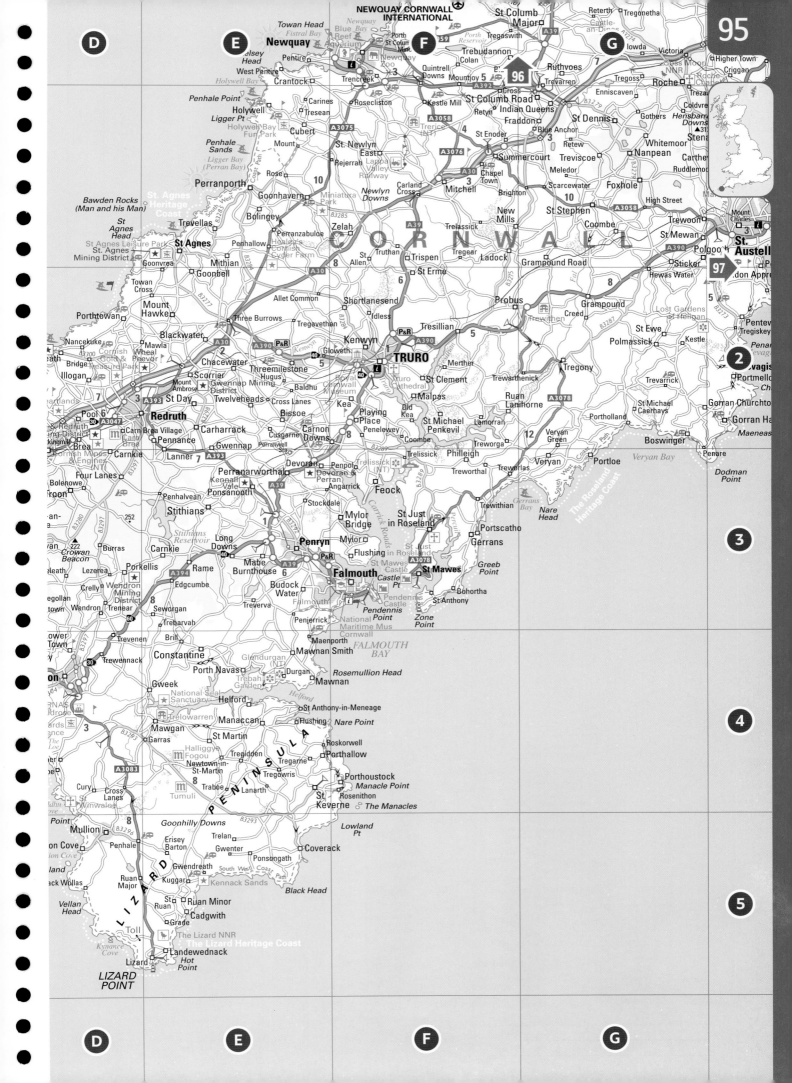

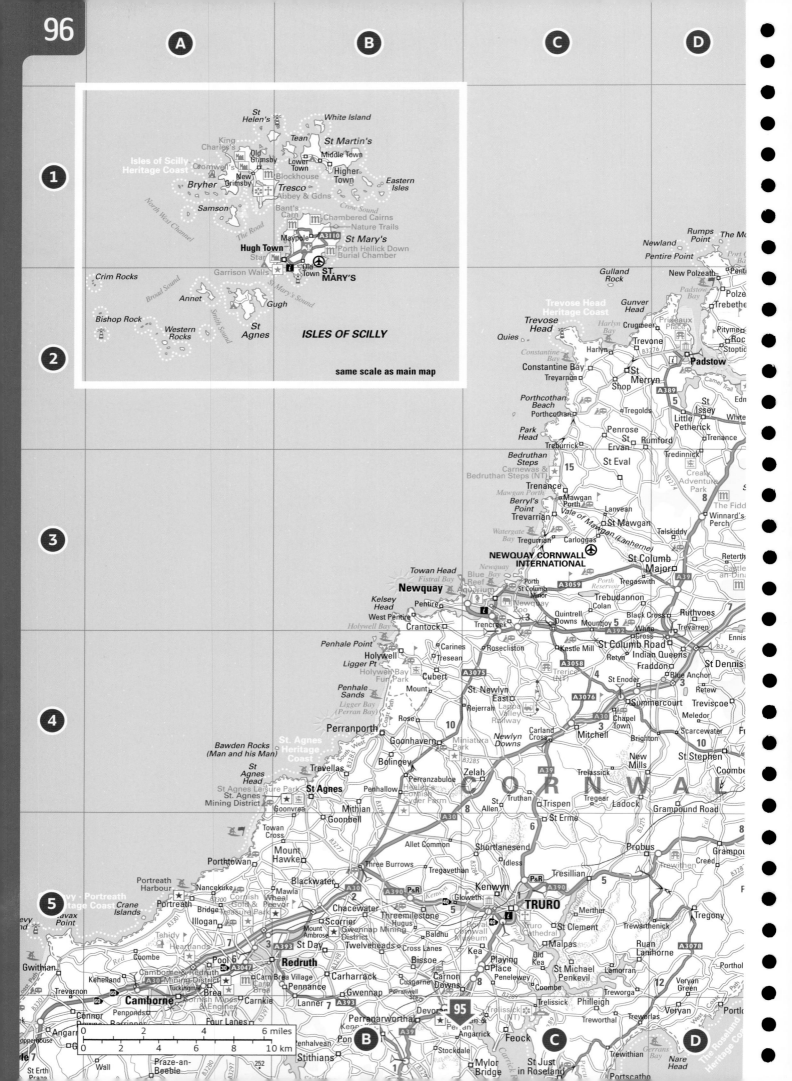

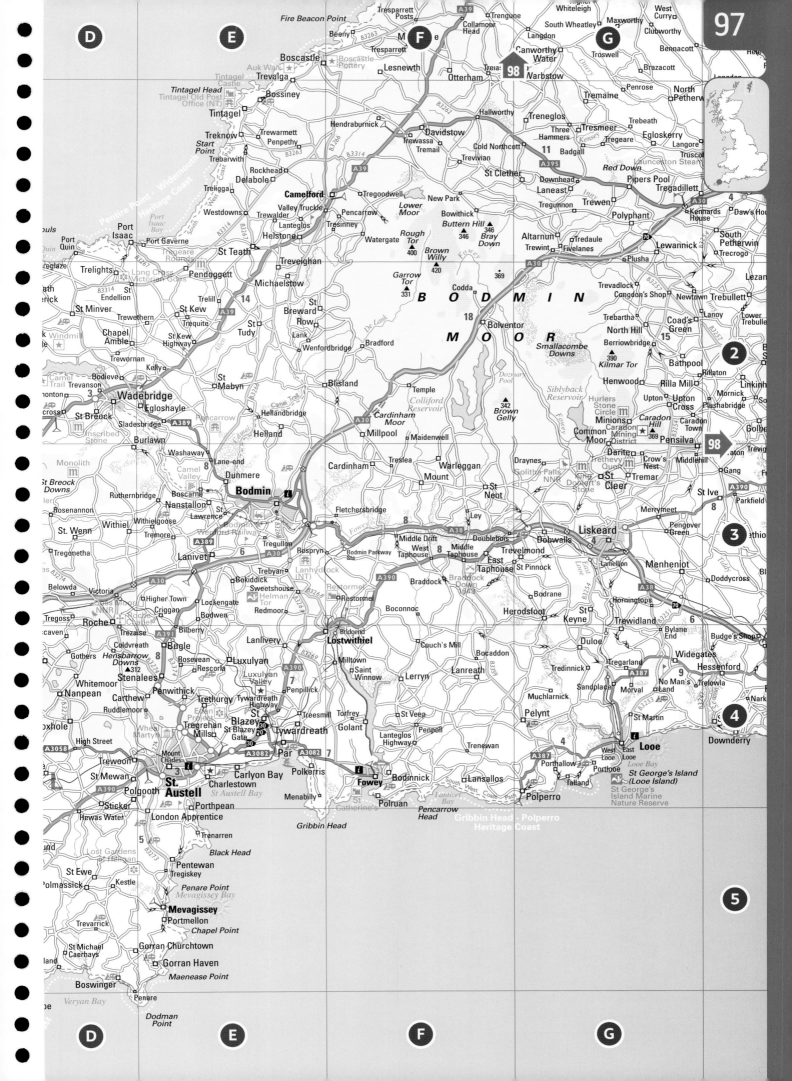

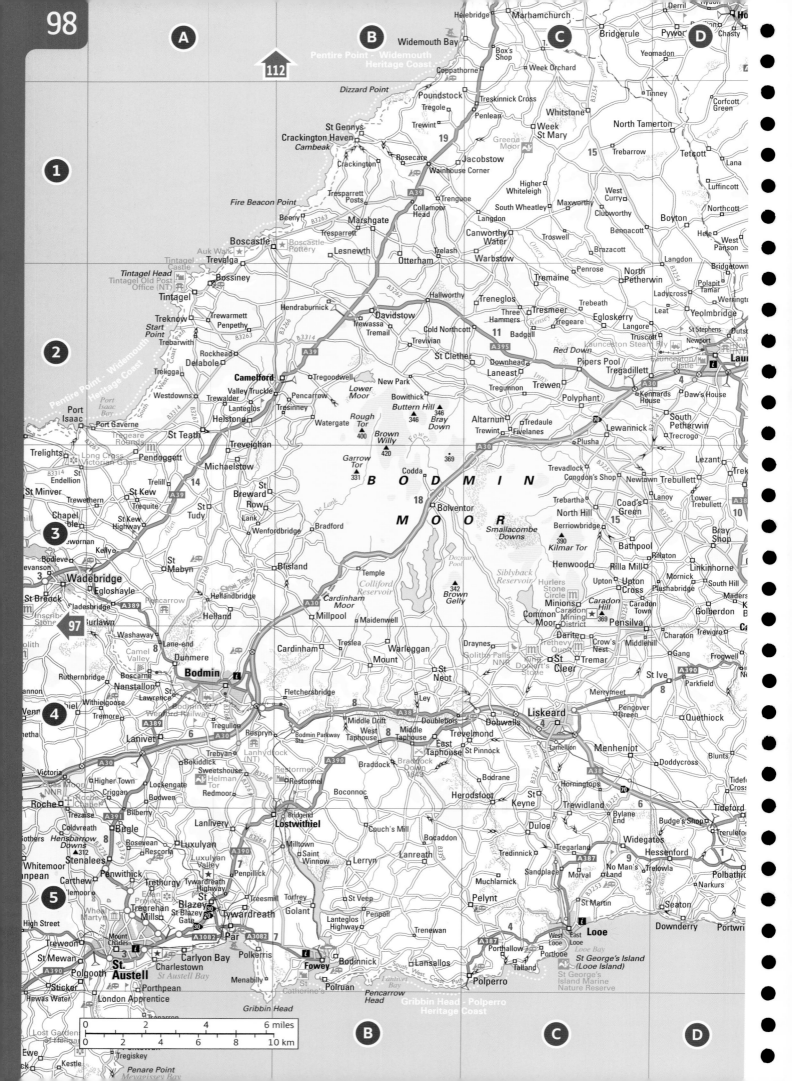

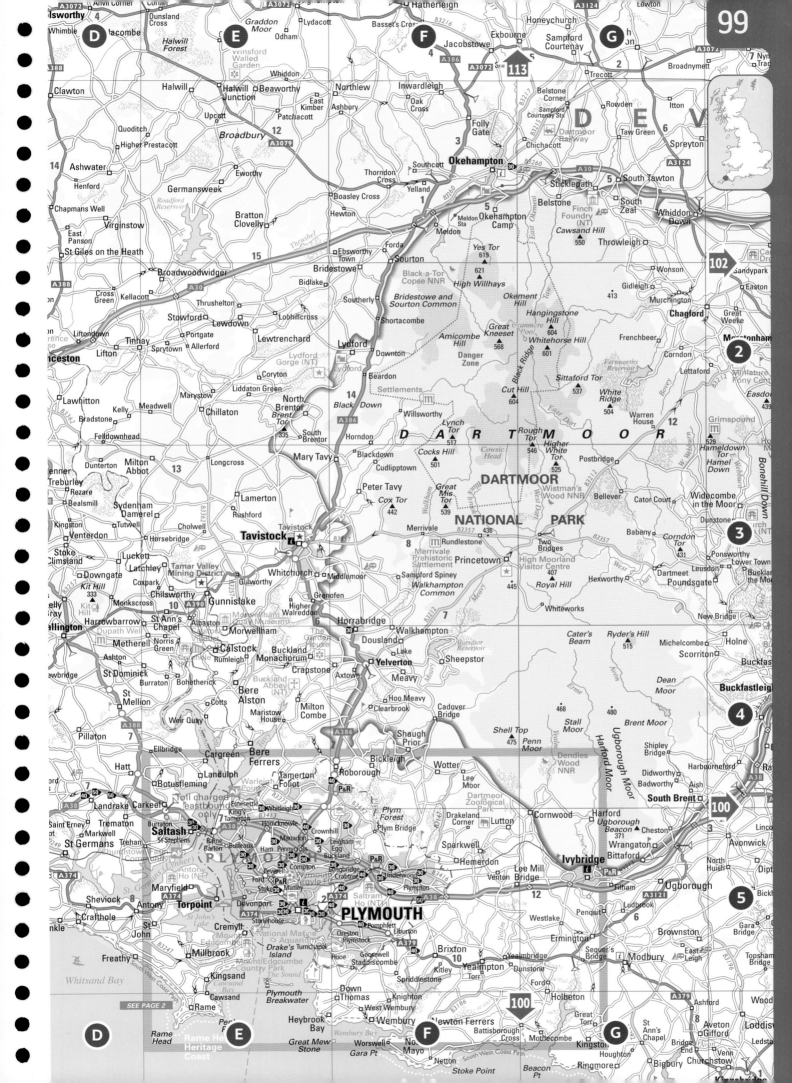

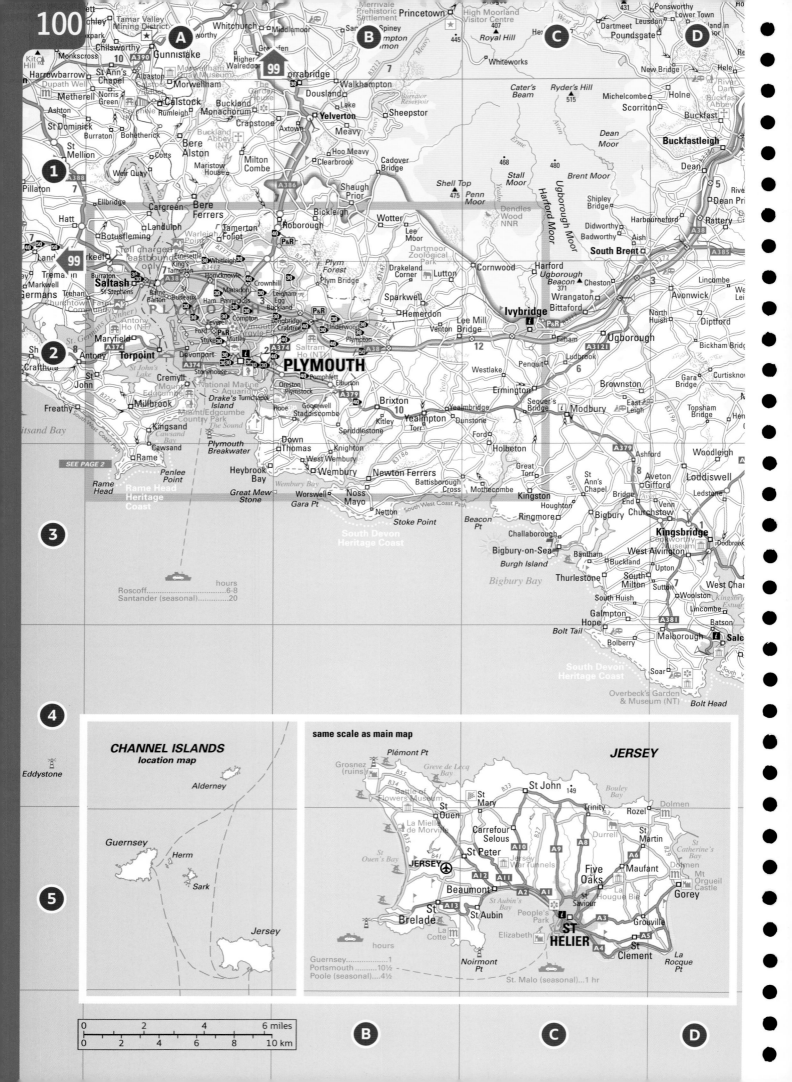

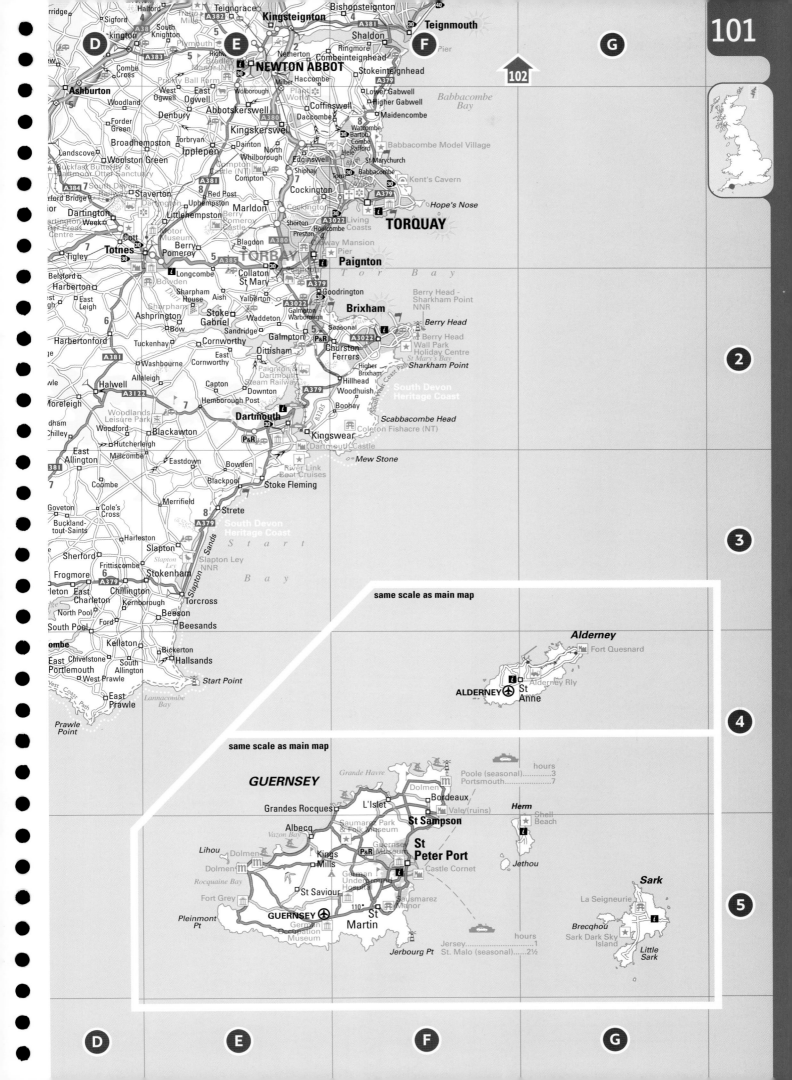

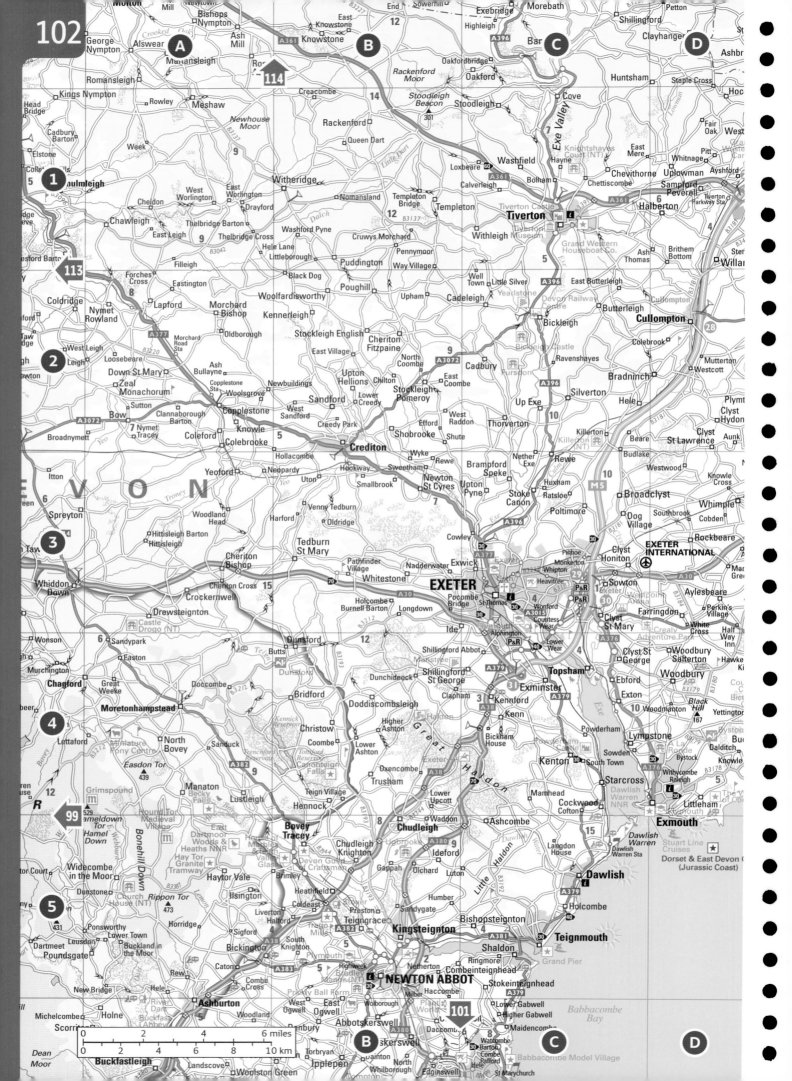

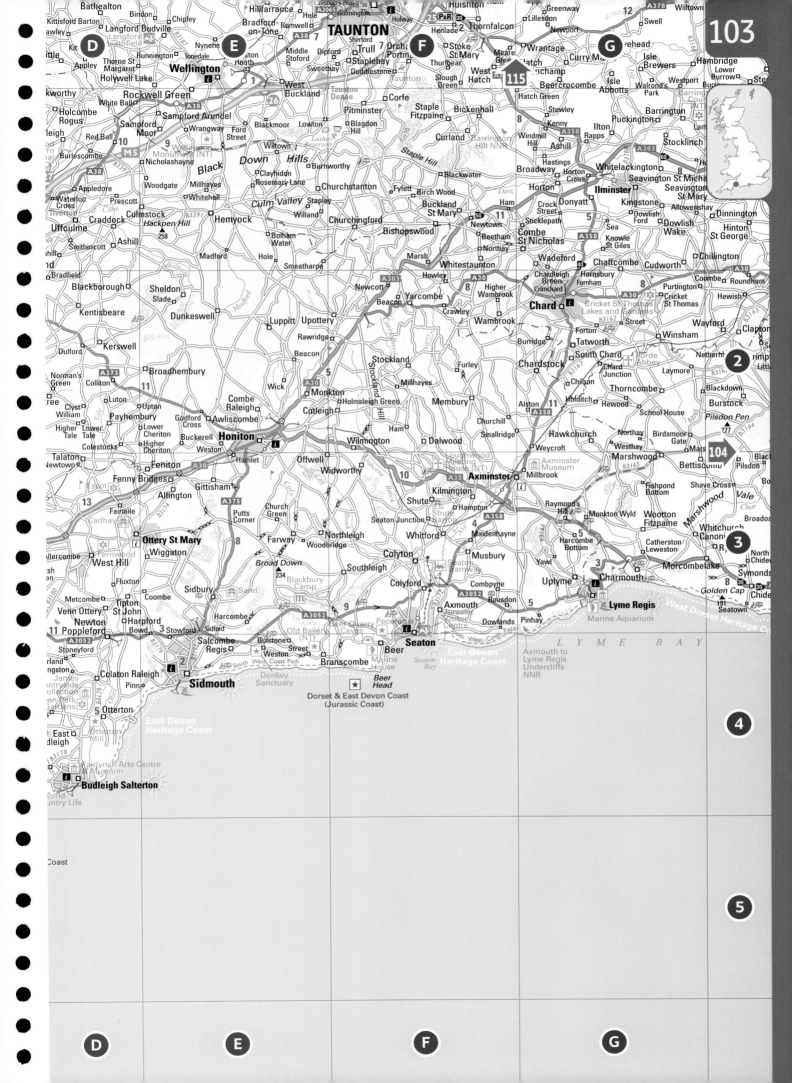

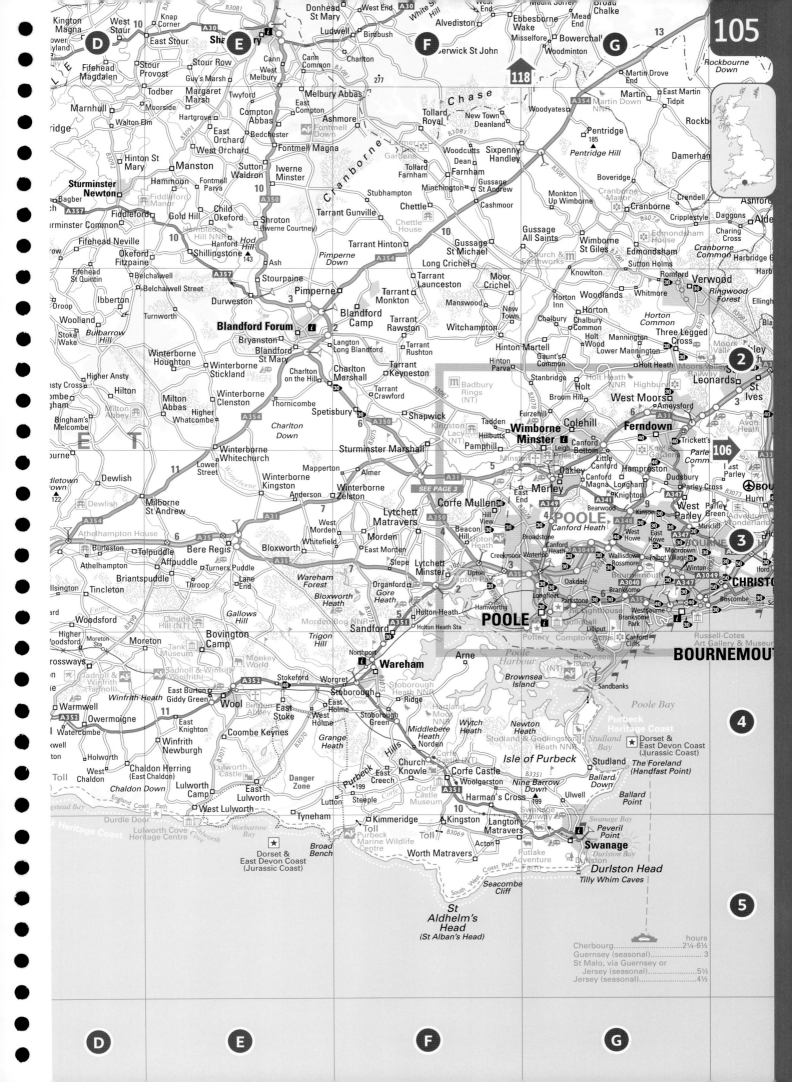

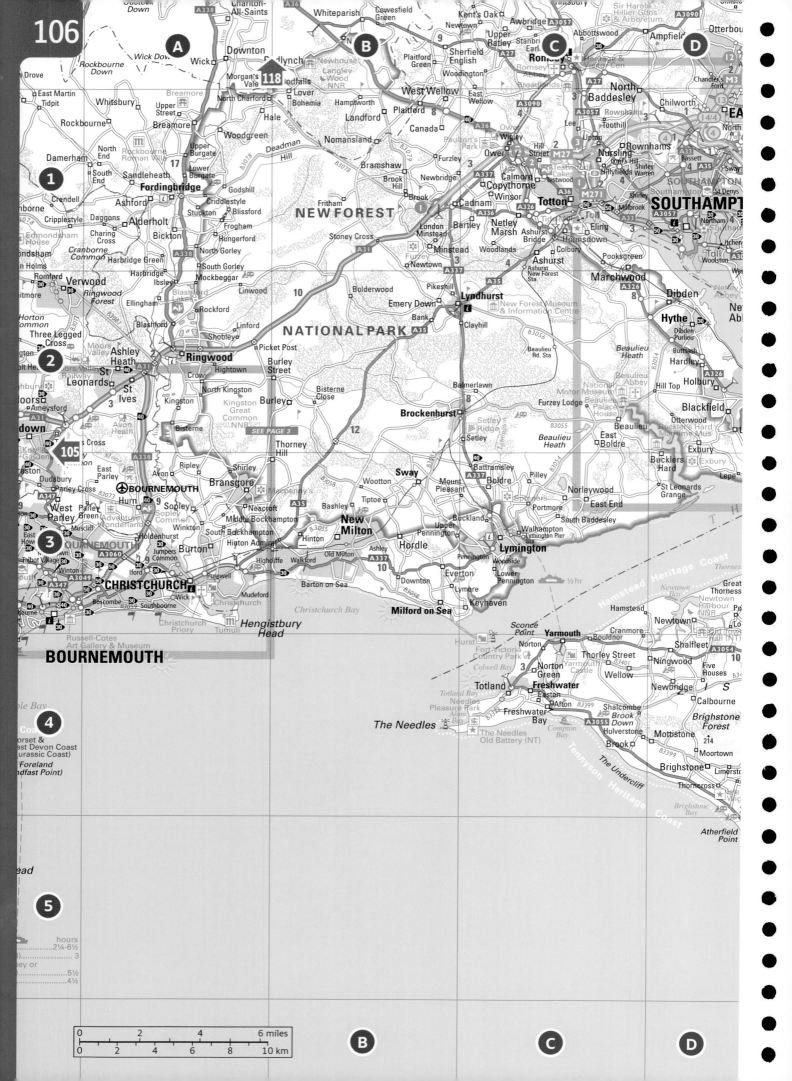

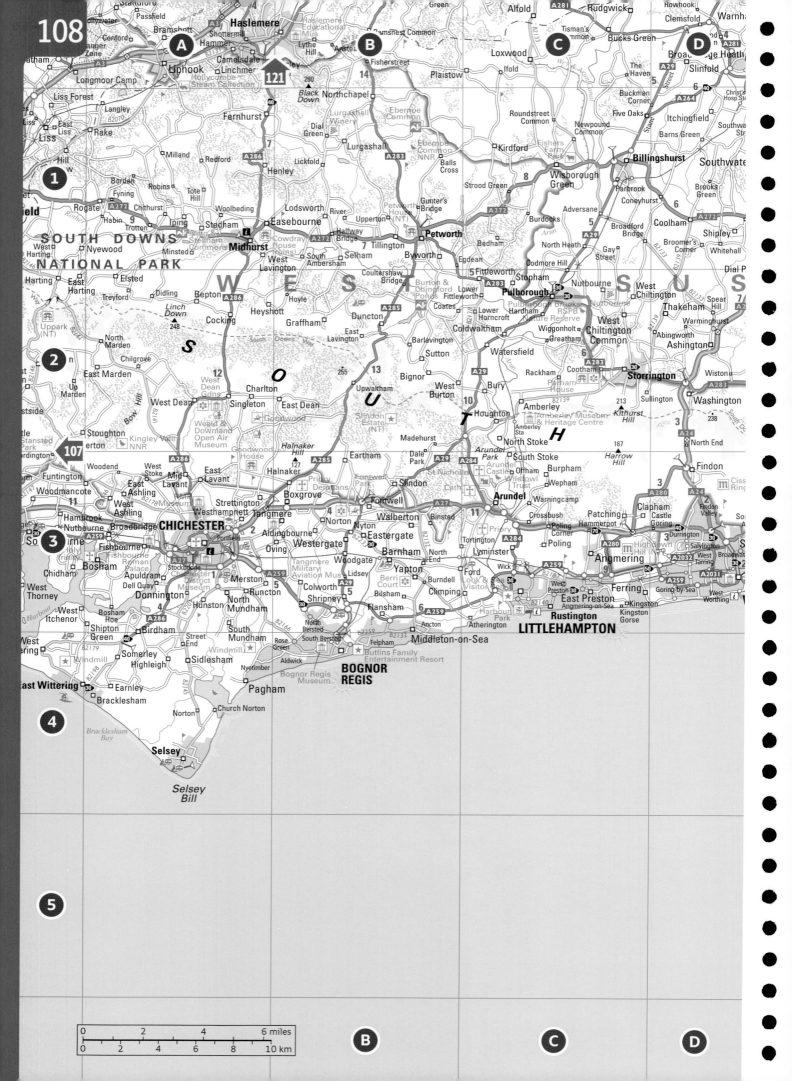

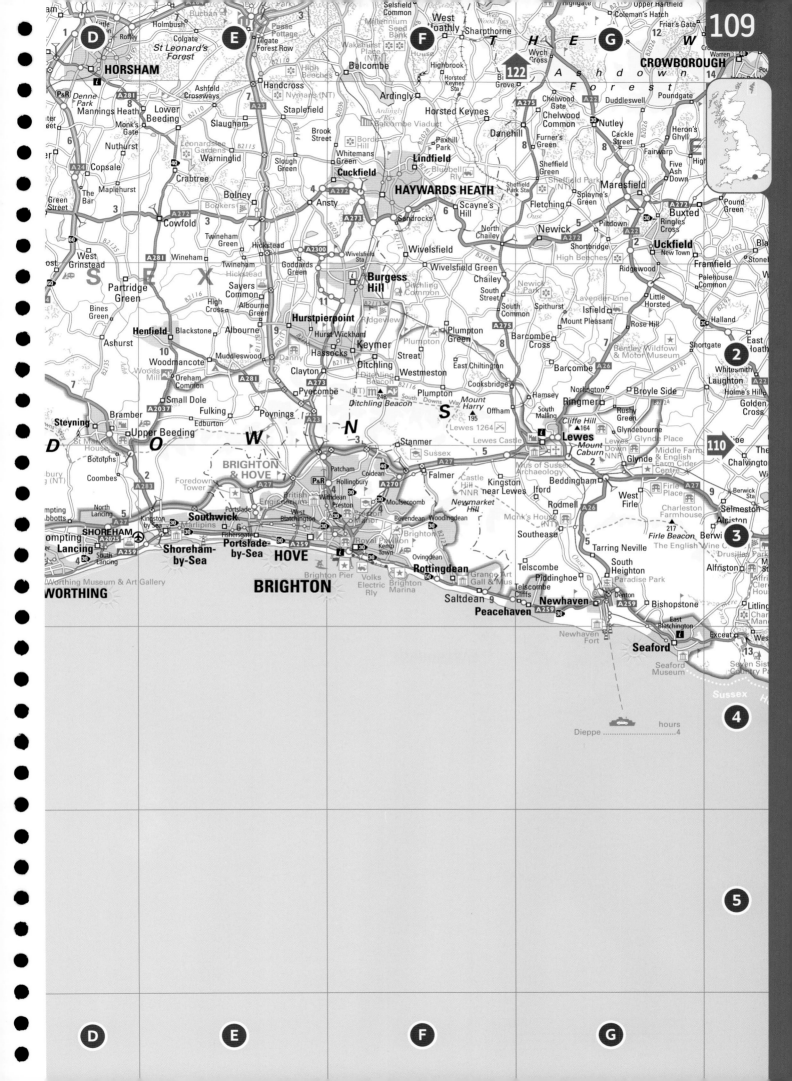

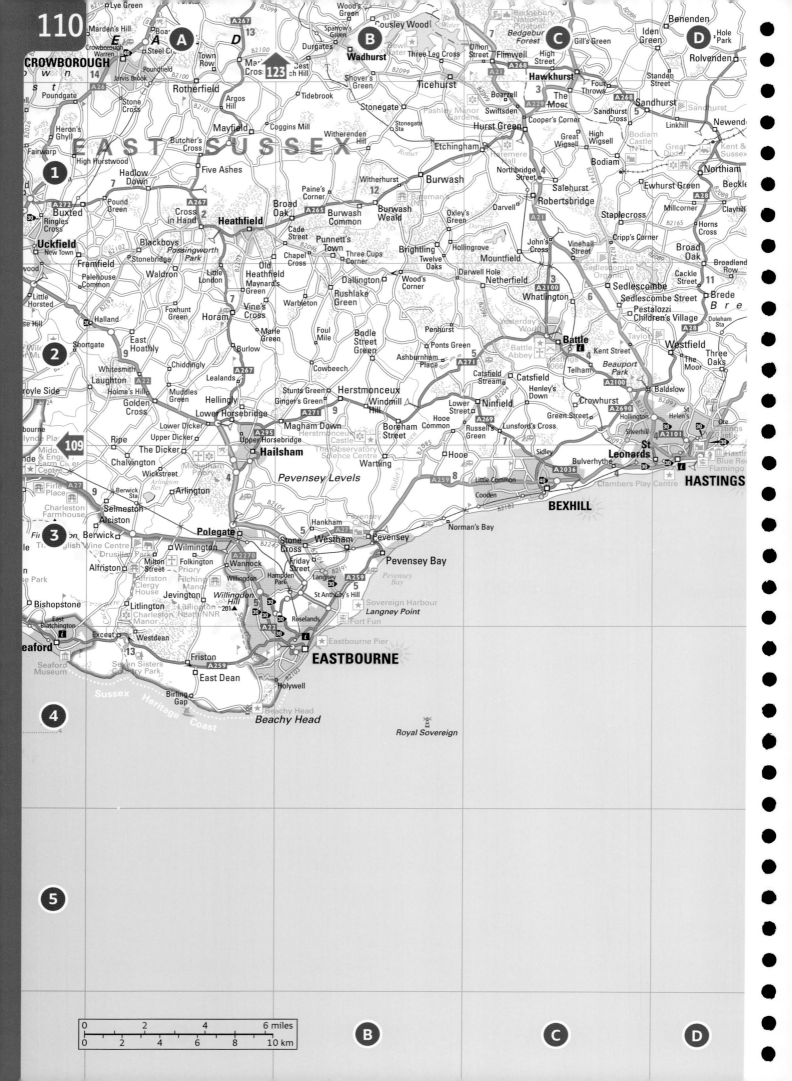

Channel Tunnel terminal maps

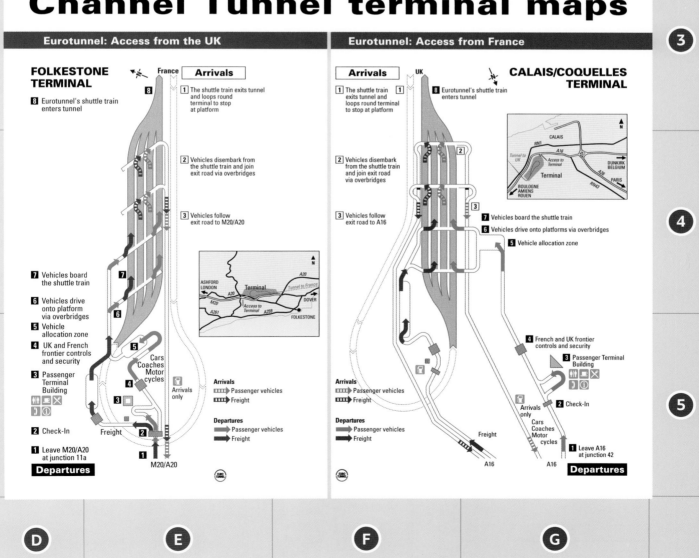

Eurotunnel: Access from the UK

FOLKESTONE TERMINAL

Arrivals

8 Eurotunnel's shuttle train enters tunnel

1 The shuttle train exits tunnel and loops round terminal to stop at platform

2 Vehicles disembark from the shuttle train and join exit road via overbridges

3 Vehicles follow exit road to M20/A20

7 Vehicles board the shuttle train

6 Vehicles drive onto platform via overbridges

5 Vehicle allocation zone

4 UK and French frontier controls and security

3 Passenger Terminal Building

2 Check-In

1 Leave M20/A20 at junction 11a

Departures

Arrivals
Passenger vehicles
Freight

Departures
Passenger vehicles
Freight

Cars Coaches Motor cycles

Arrivals only

ASHFORD LONDON — Terminal — Tunnel to France — DOVER
A20 M20 A261 Access to Terminal A259 FOLKESTONE

Freight

M20/A20

Eurotunnel: Access from France

Arrivals

1 The shuttle train exits tunnel and loops round terminal to stop at platform

2 Vehicles disembark from the shuttle train and join exit road via overbridges

3 Vehicles follow exit road to A16

8 Eurotunnel's shuttle train enters tunnel

CALAIS/COQUELLES TERMINAL

CALAIS
RN1 A16
Tunnel to UK — Access to Terminal — DUNKIRK BELGIUM
Terminal A26 RN42 PARIS
BOULOGNE AMIENS ROUEN

7 Vehicles board the shuttle train

6 Vehicles drive onto platforms via overbridges

5 Vehicle allocation zone

4 French and UK frontier controls and security

3 Passenger Terminal Building

2 Check-In

1 Leave A16 at junction 42

Departures

Arrivals
Passenger vehicles
Freight

Departures
Passenger vehicles
Freight

Arrivals only

Cars Coaches Motor cycles

Freight

A16

A16

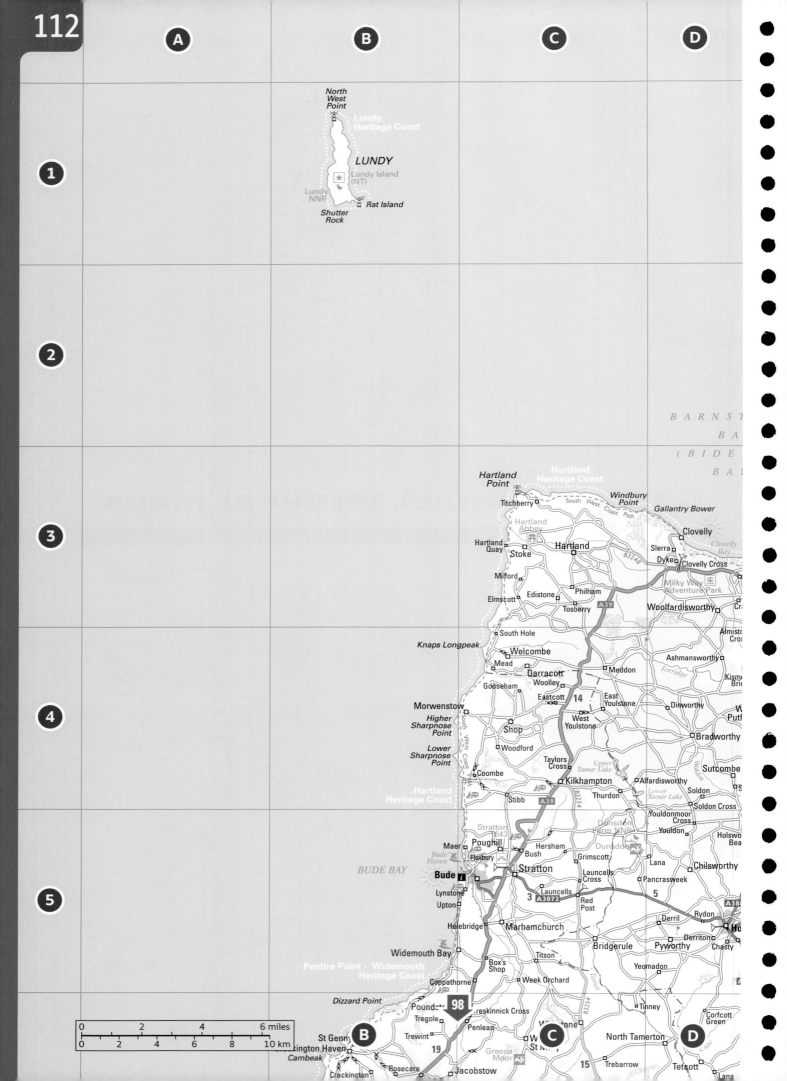

A   B   C   D

1

2

3

4

5

North
West
Point
Lundy
Heritage Coast

LUNDY
Lundy Island
(NT)
Lundy
NNR
Rat Island
Shutter
Rock

BARNST
BA
(BIDE
BAY

Hartland
Point
Hartland
Heritage Coast
Titchberry
South West Coast Path
Windbury
Point
Gallantry Bower
Clovelly
Clovelly
Bay
Hartland
Abbey
Hartland
Quay
Stoke
Hartland
Slerra
Dyke
B3248
Clovelly Cross
Milford
Milky Way
Adventure Park
Edistone
Philham
A39
Woolfardisworthy
Cra
Elmscott
Tosberry
Almisto
Cros

South Hole
Knaps Longpeak
Welcombe
Ashmansworthy
Torridge
Mead
Darracott
Meddon
Kismi
Bri
Gooseham
Woolley
Morwenstow
Eastcott
14
East
Youlstone
Dinworthy
W
Putf
Higher
Sharpnose
Point
Shop
West
Youlstone
Bradworthy
Woodford
Lower
Sharpnose
Point
Taylors
Cross
Upper
Tamar Lake
Sutcombe
Coombe
Kilkhampton
Alfardisworthy
Soldon
Hartland
Heritage Coast
Stibb
A39
B3254
Thurdon
Lower
Tamar Lake
Soldon Cross
Youldonmoor
Cross
Youldon
Holsw
Bea
Stratton
643
Dunsdon
Farm NNR
Maer
Poughill
Hersham
Bush
Grimscott
Dunsdon
Lana
Chilsworthy
Bude
Haven
Flexbury
Stratton
Launcells
Cross
Pancrasweek
BUDE BAY
Bude i
3
Launcells
A3072
Red
Post
5
A38
Lynstone
Derril
Rydon
H
Upton
Marhamchurch
Derriton
Chasty
Helebridge
Bridgerule
Pyworthy
Widemouth Bay
Titson
Yeomadon
Pentire Point - Widemouth
Heritage Coast
Box's
Shop
Week Orchard
Tamar
Dizzard Point
Coppathorne
Tinney
Corfcott
Green
Poundst
98
reskinnick Cross
W
stone
B3254
Tregole
Penlean
North Tamerton
St Genn
B
Trewint
19
C
W
St M
15
Trebarrow
Tetcott
kington Haven
Greena
Moor
D
Cambeak
Rosecare
Jacobstow
Lana

0   2   4   6 miles
0   2   4   6   8   10 km

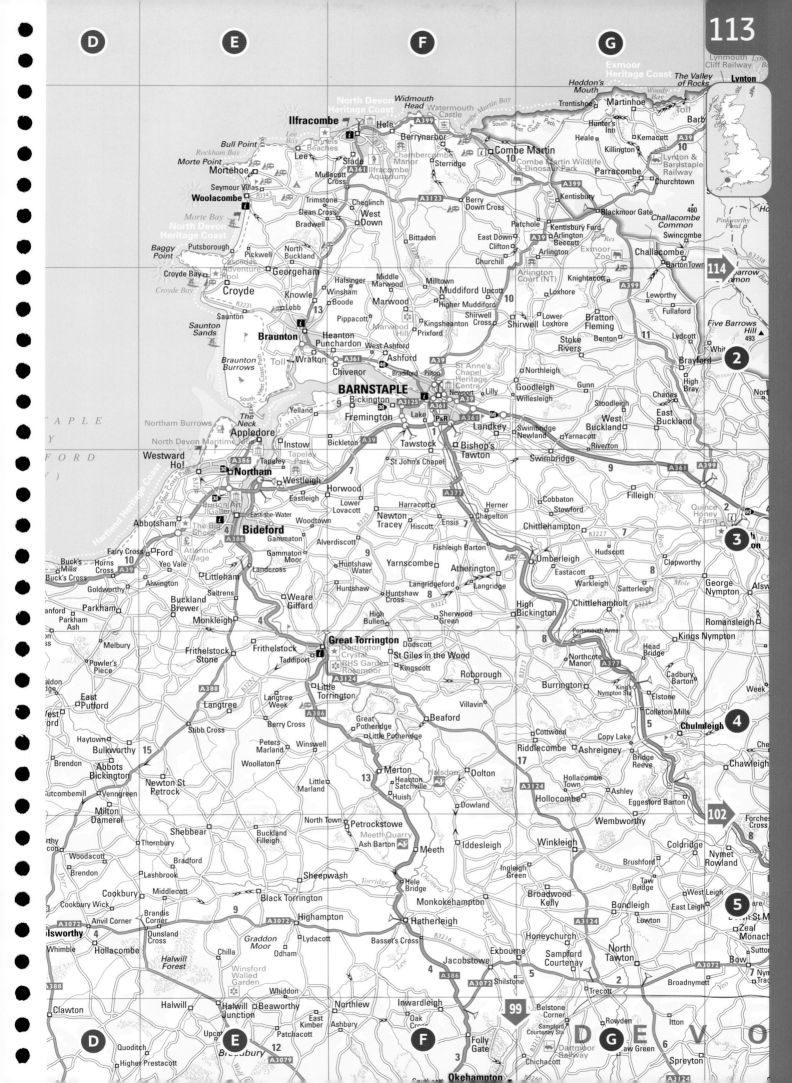

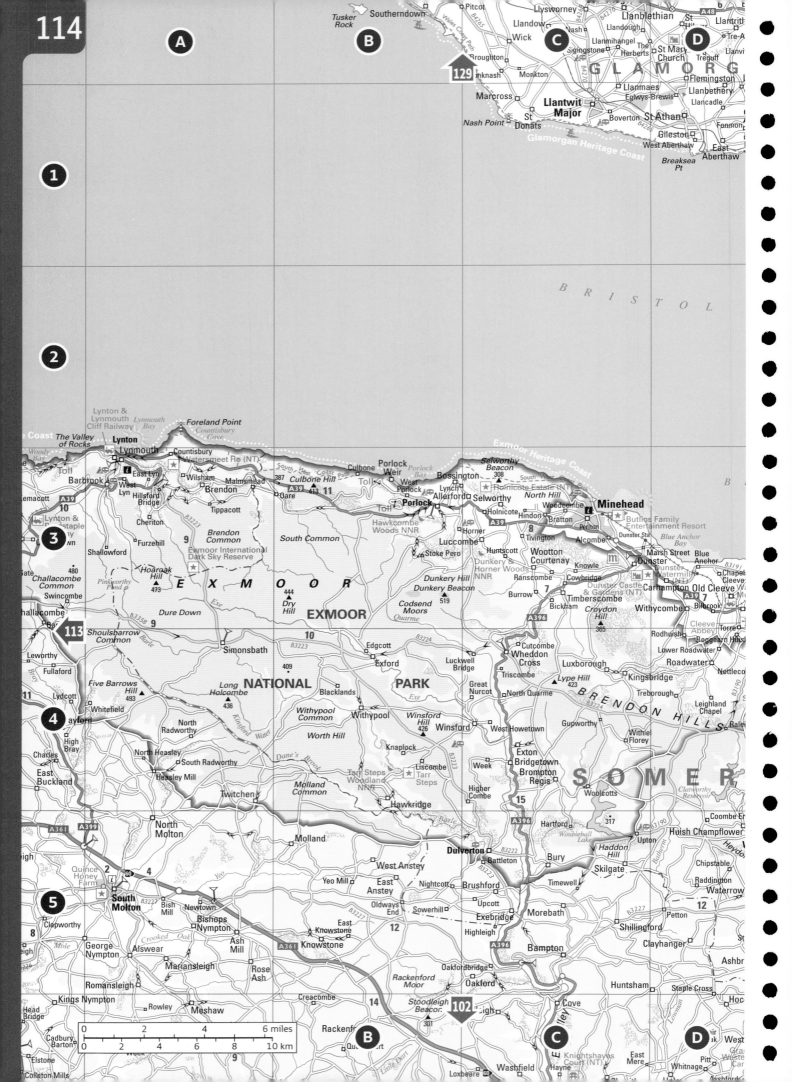

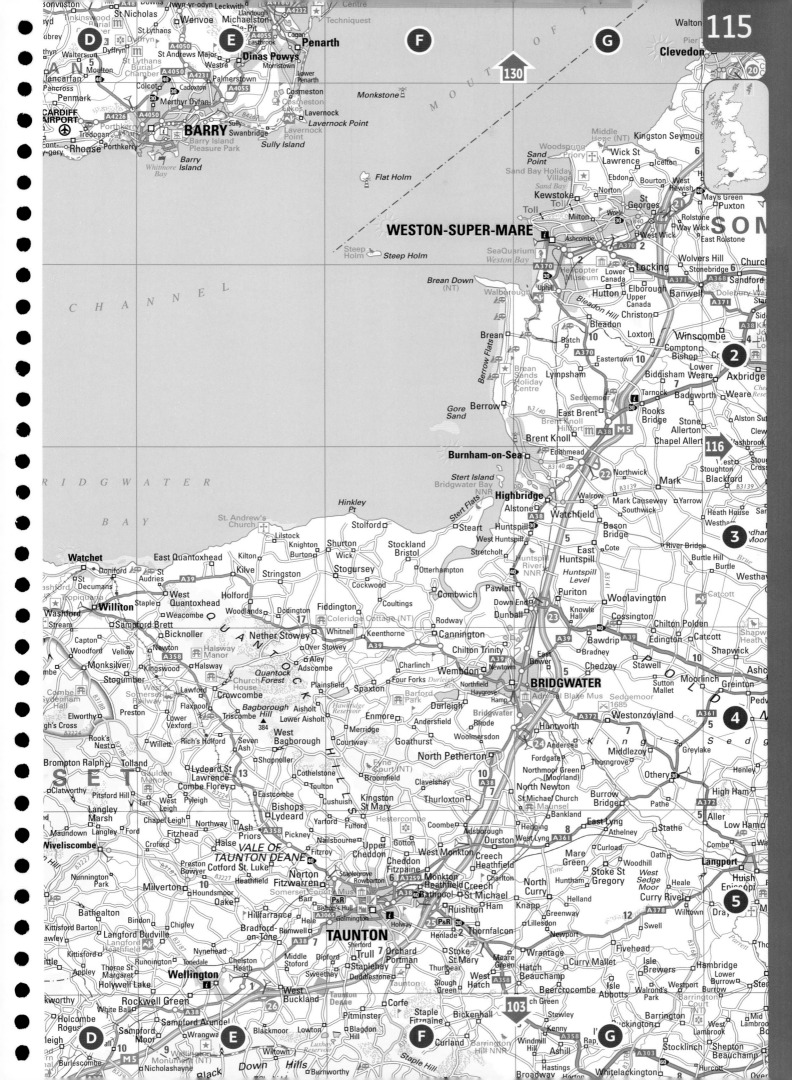

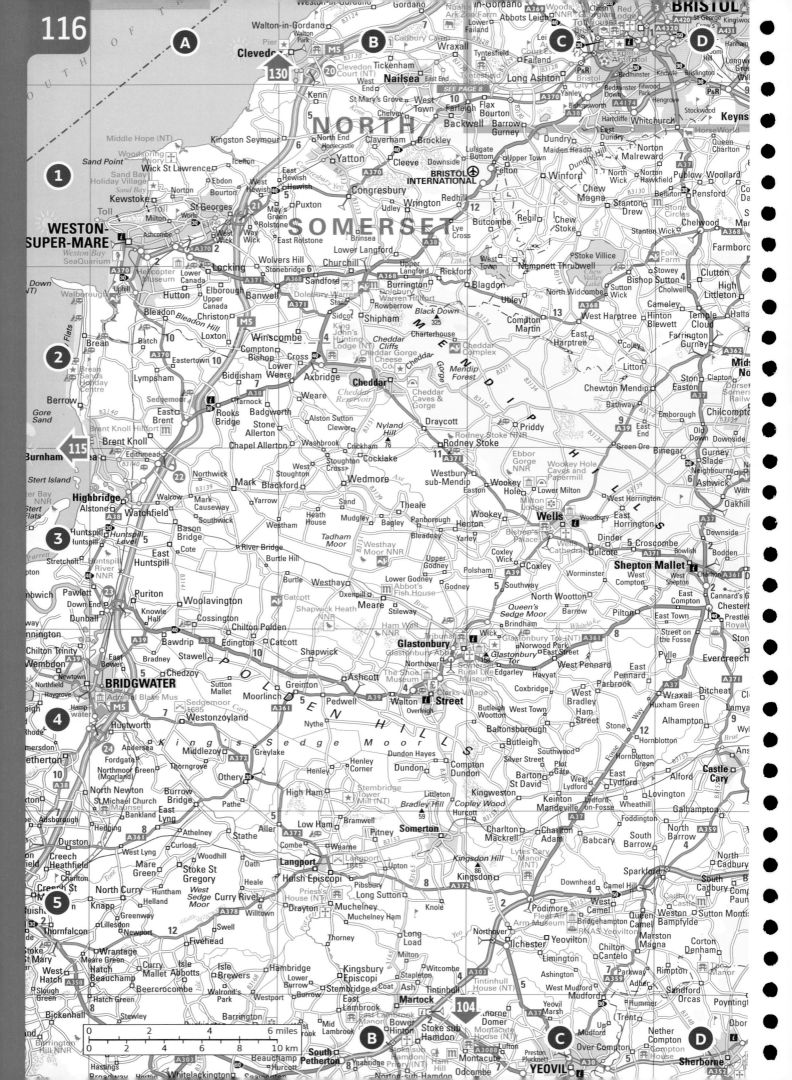

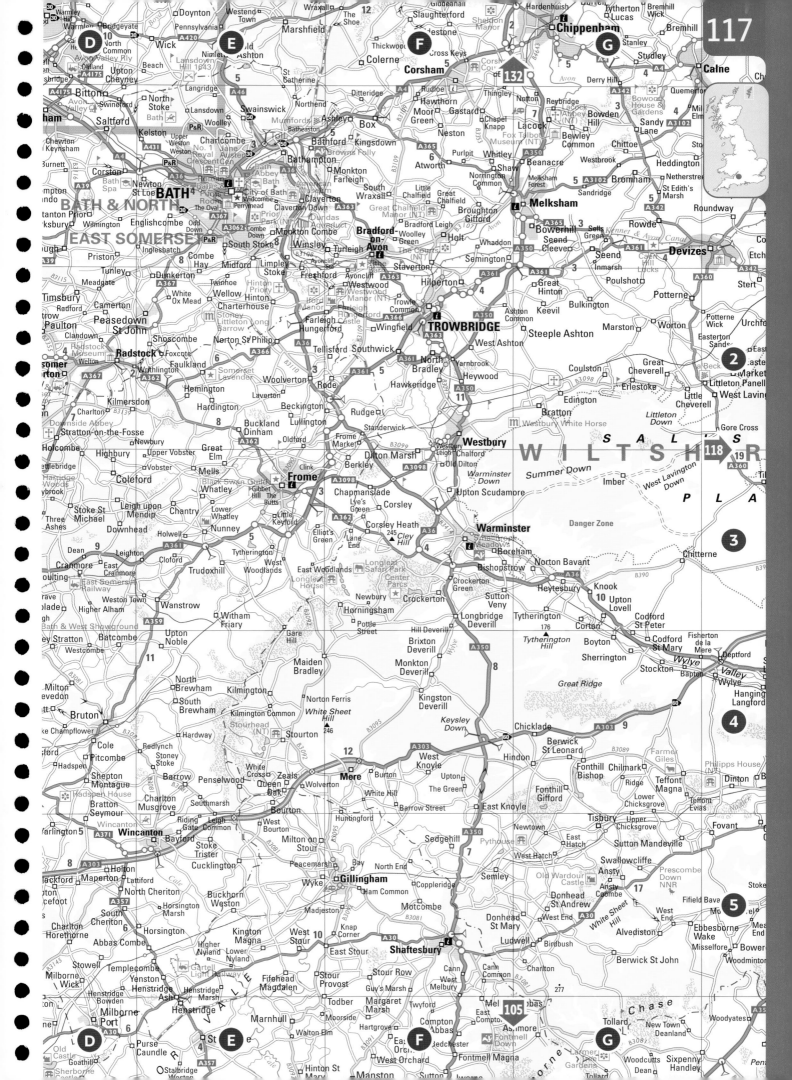

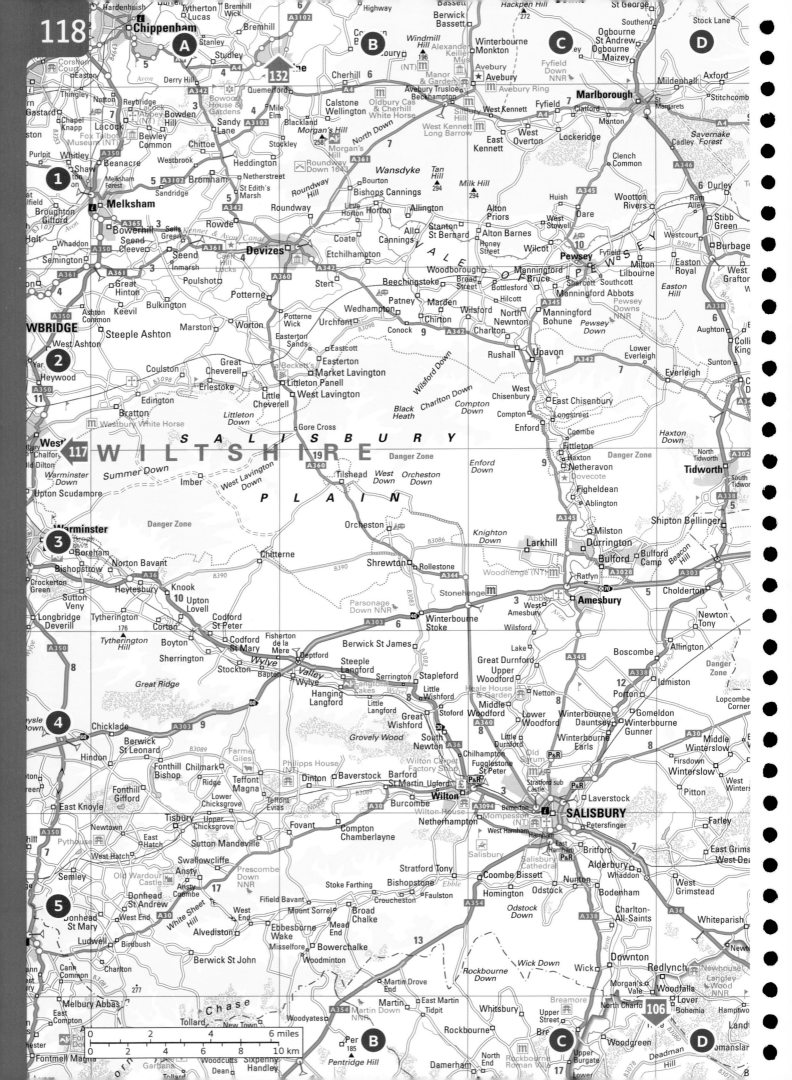

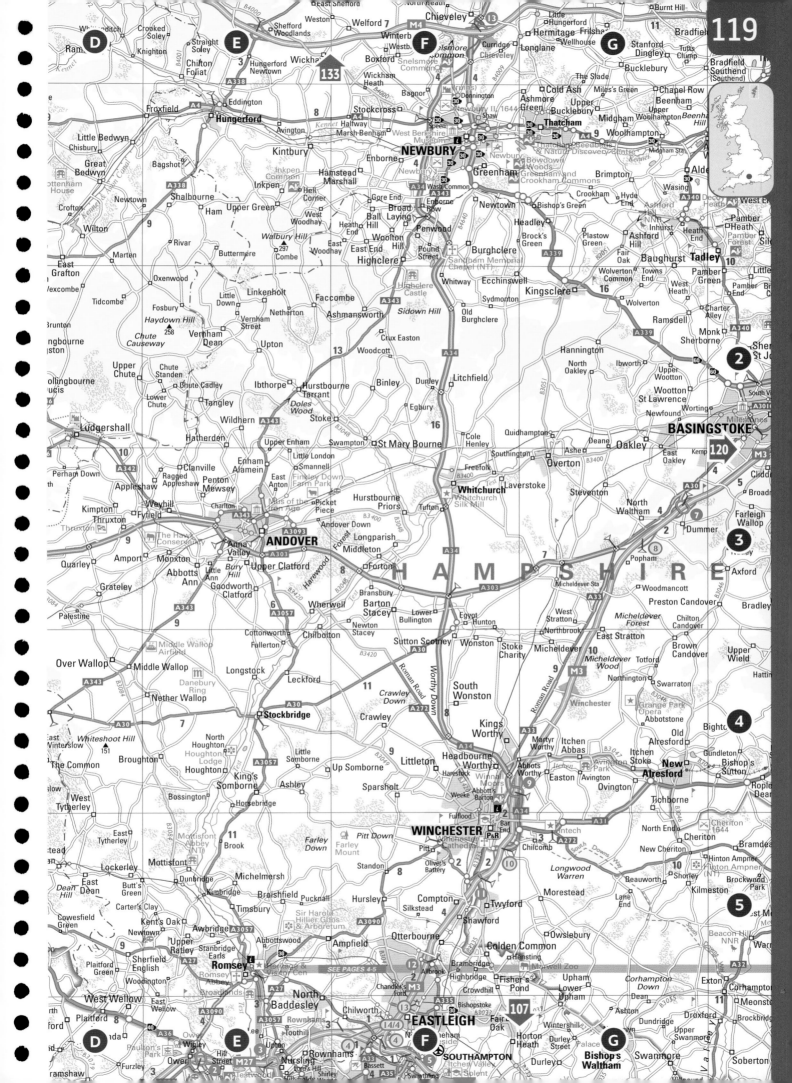

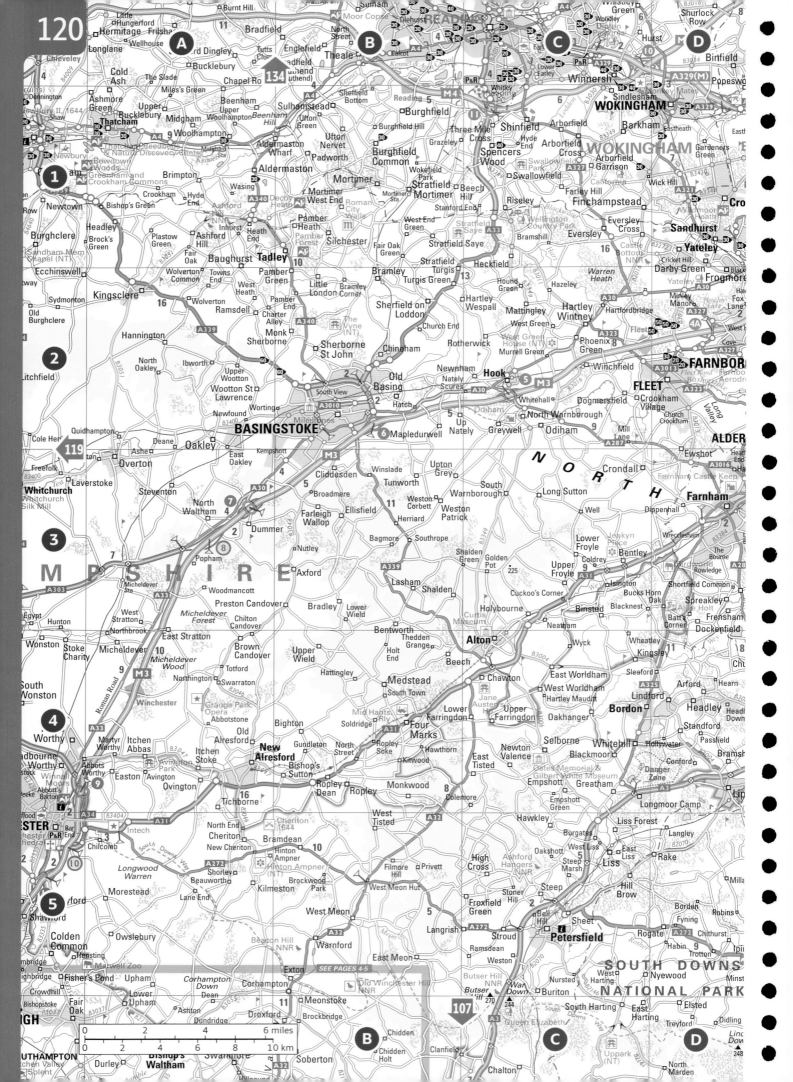

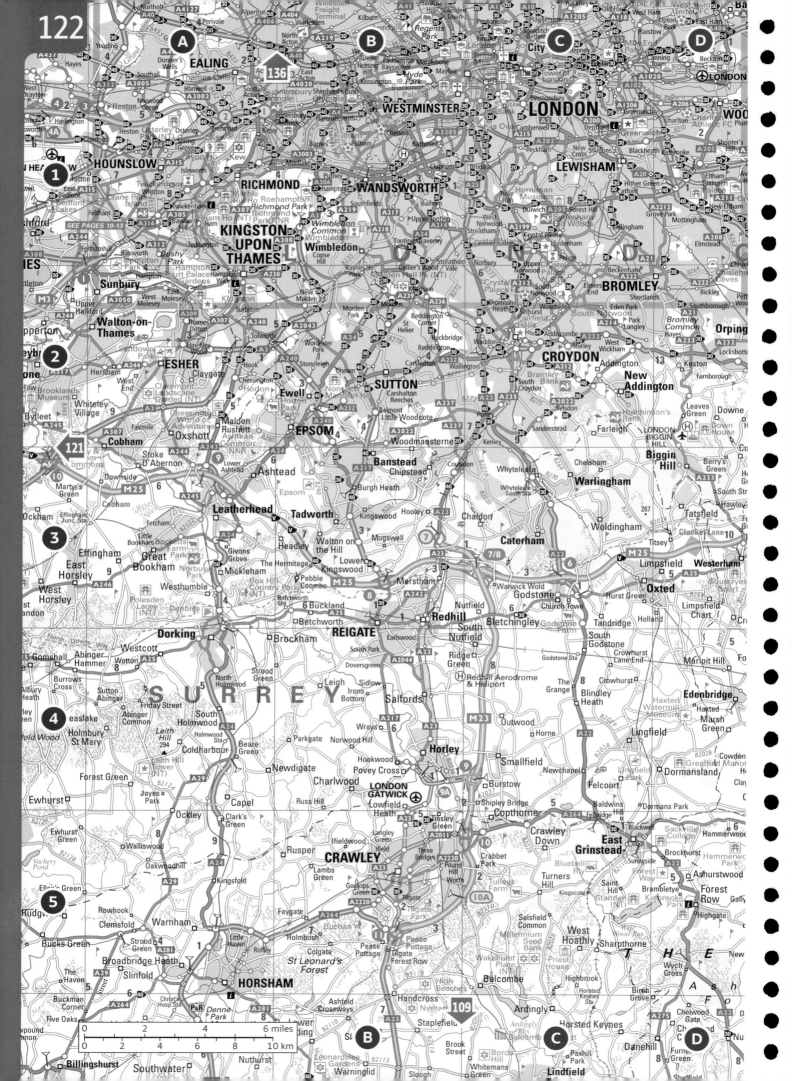

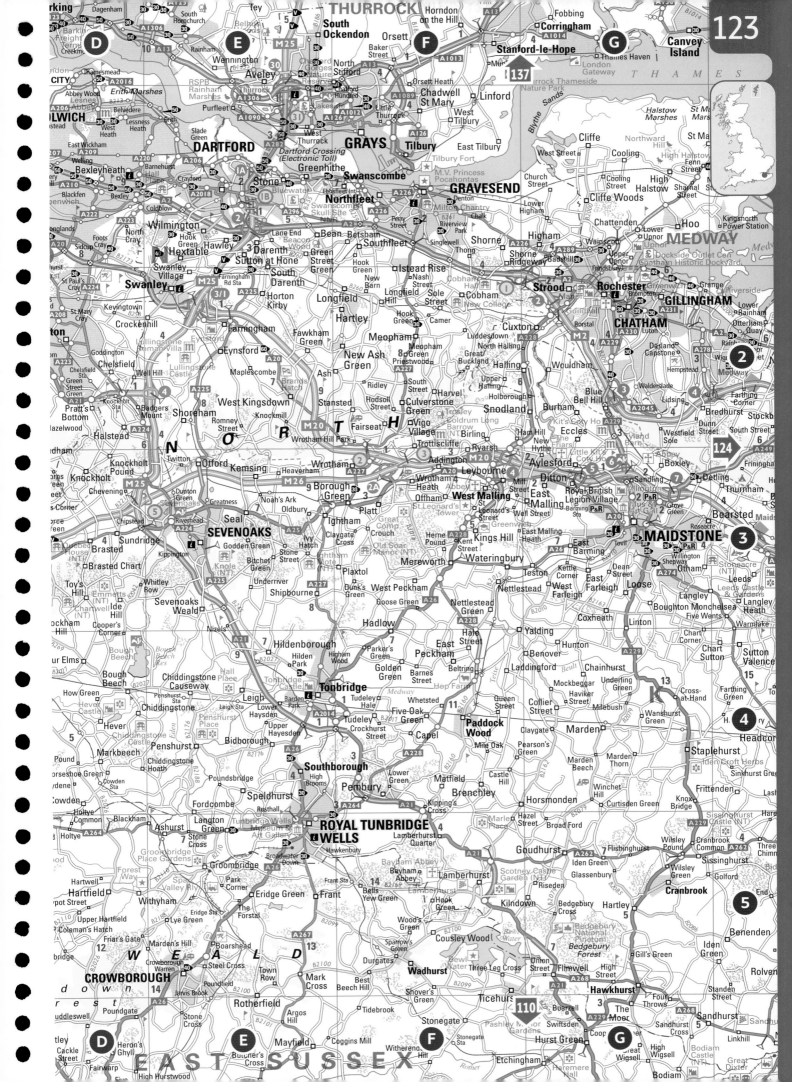

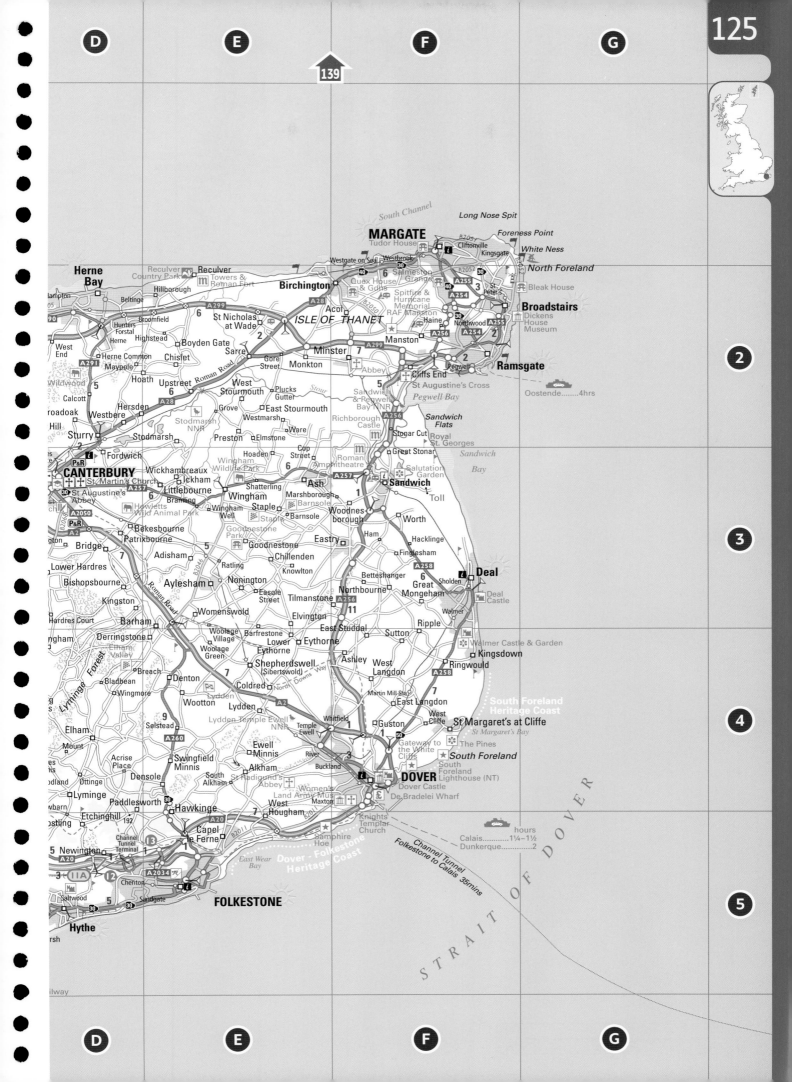

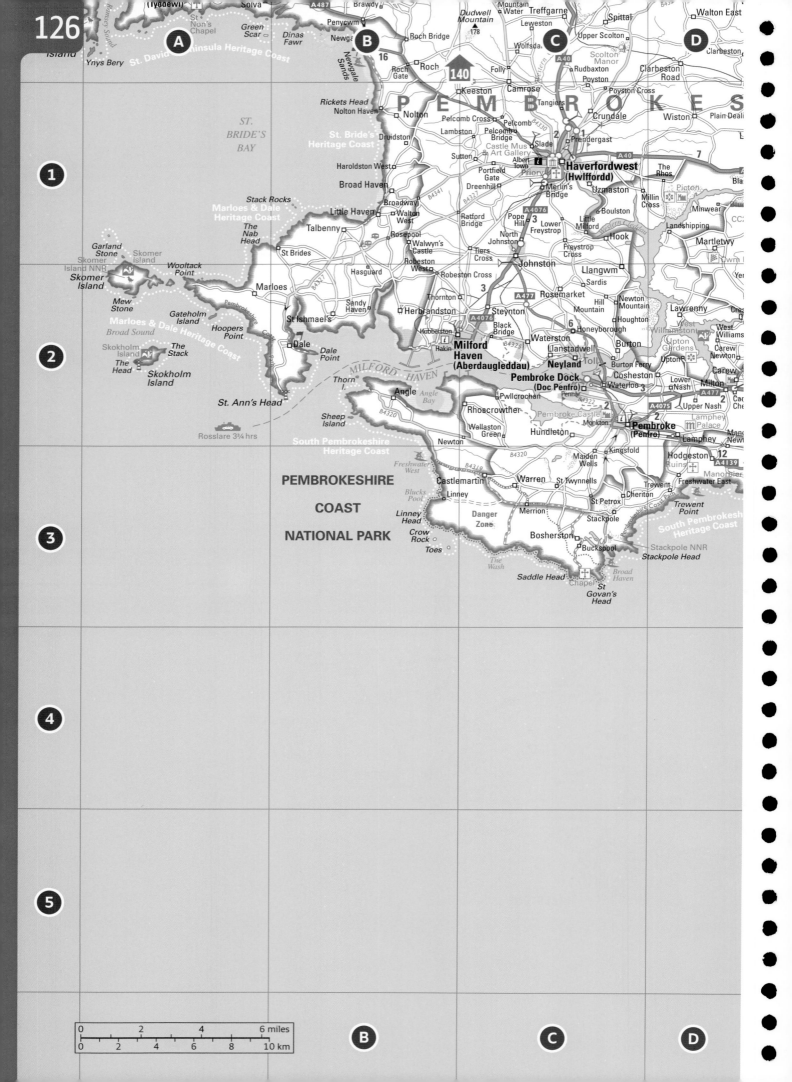

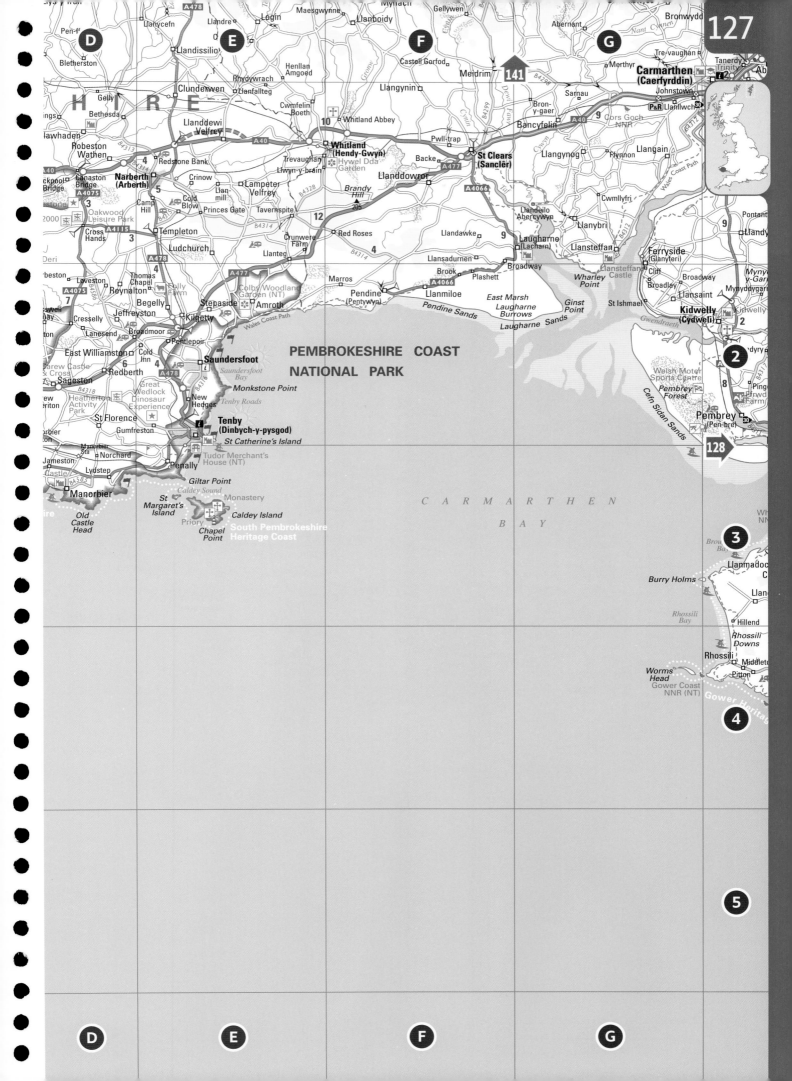

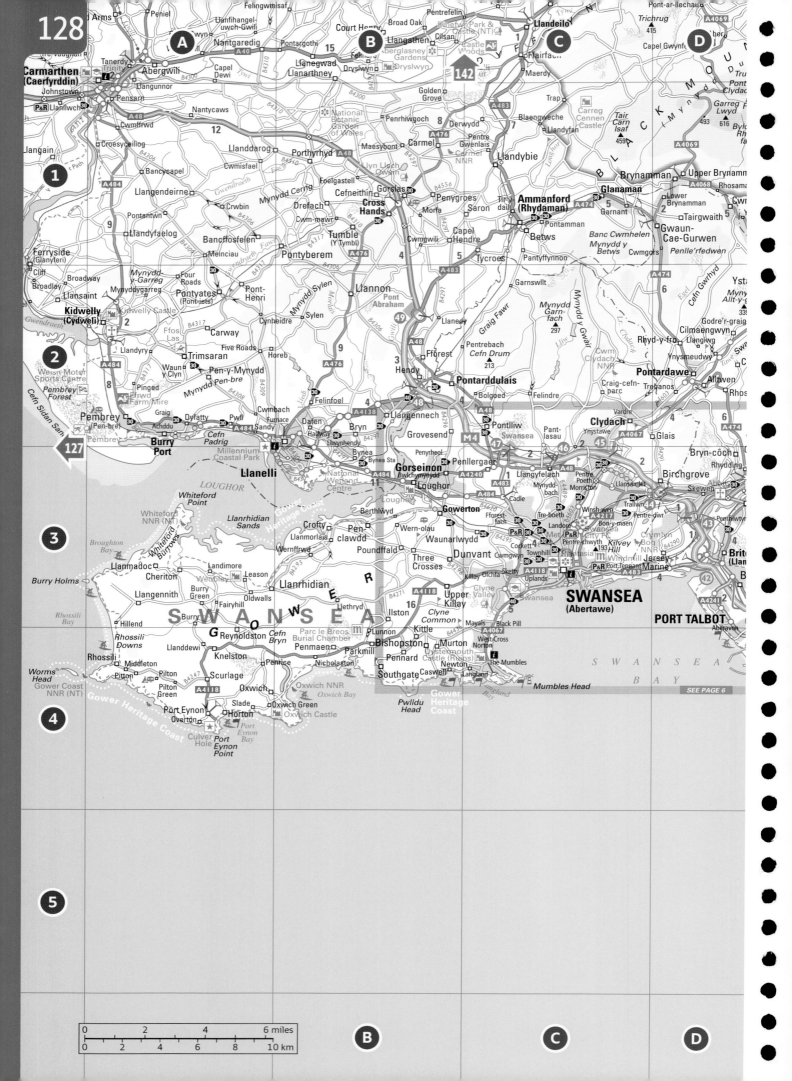

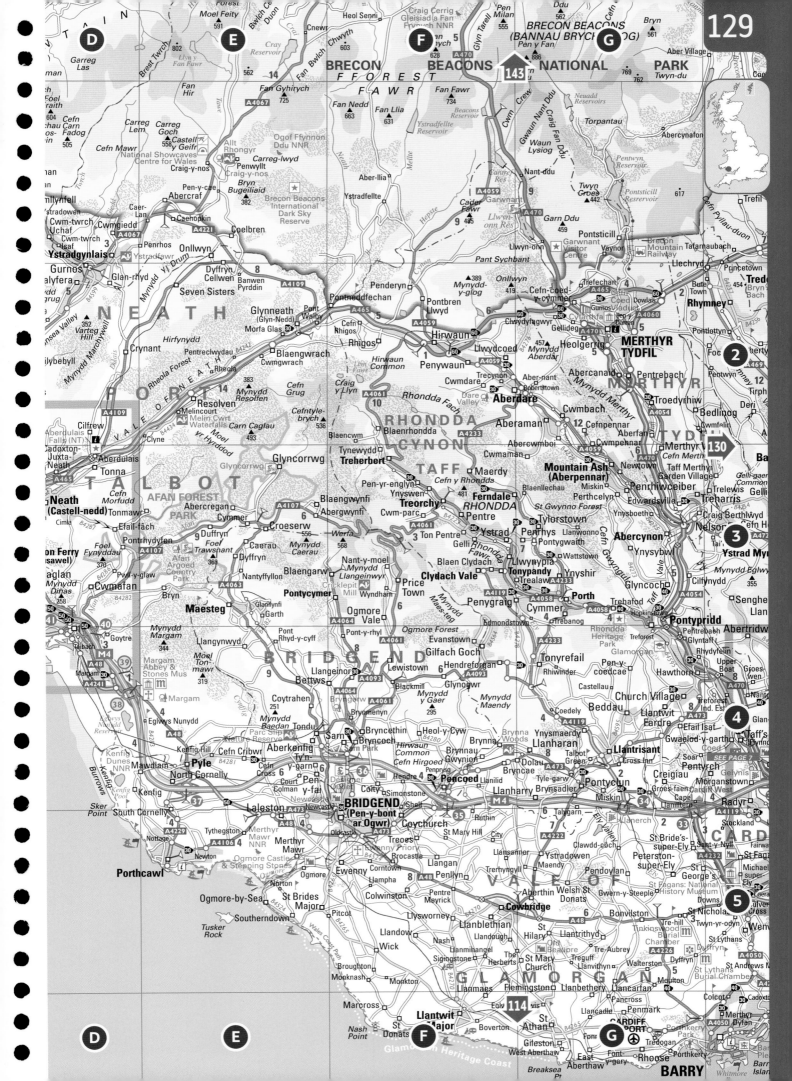

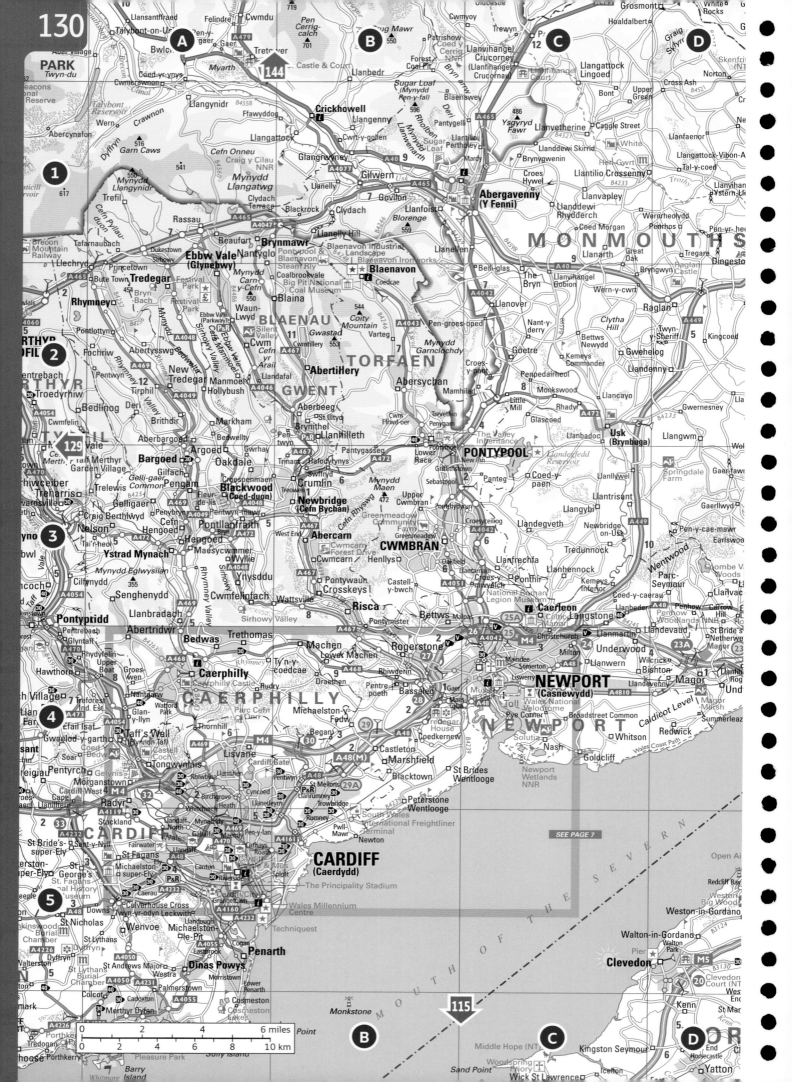

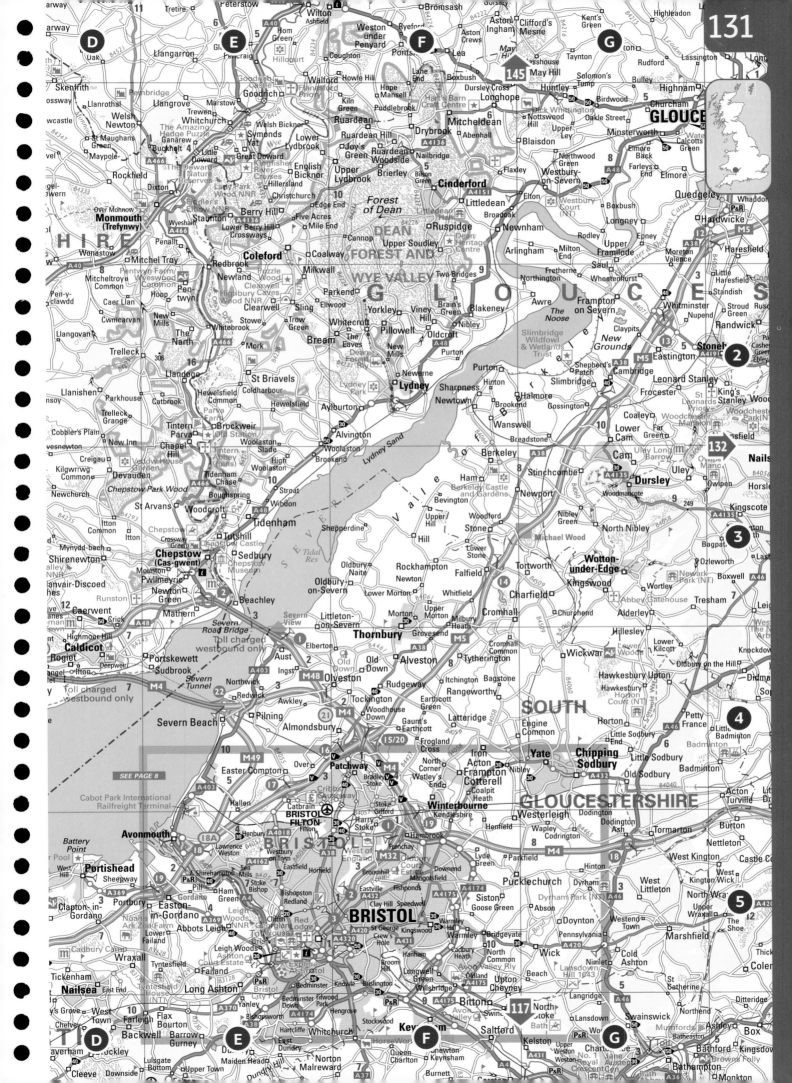

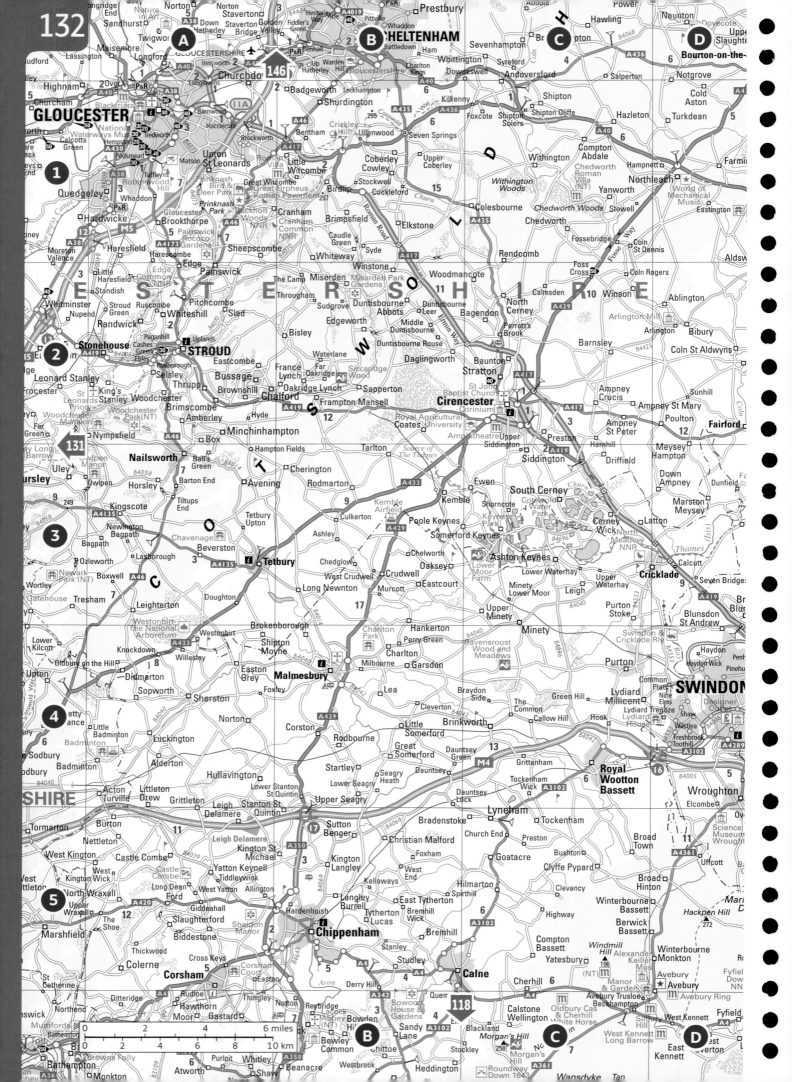

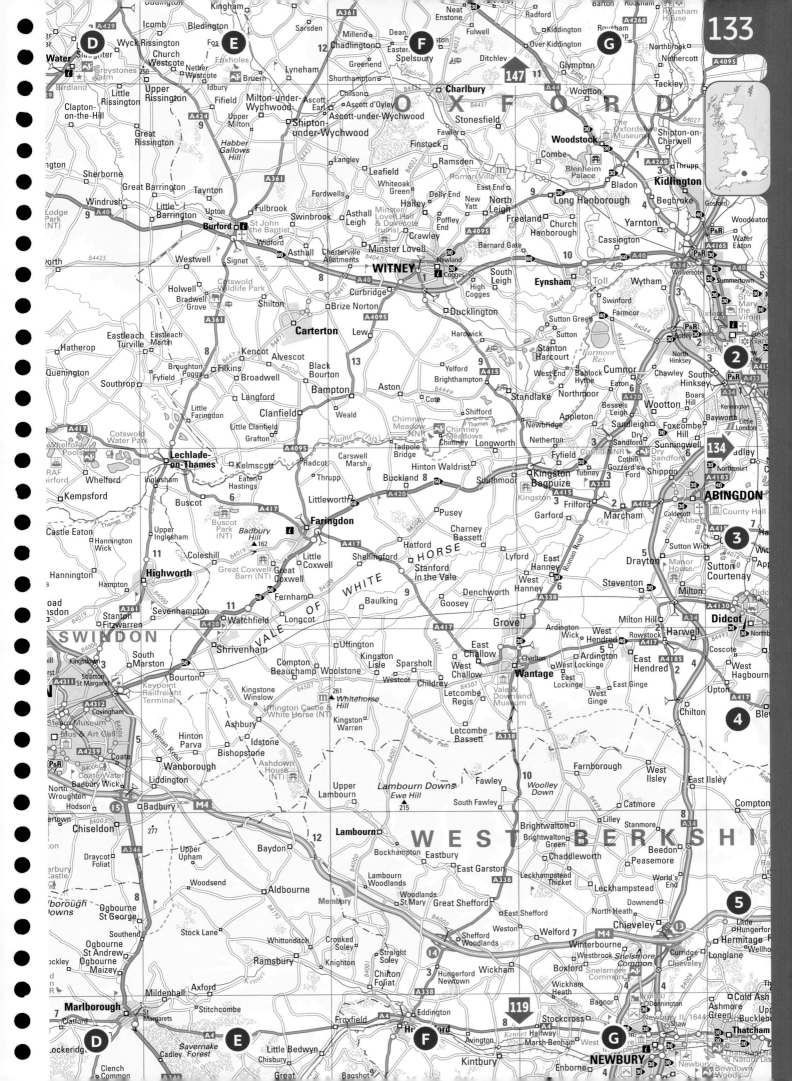

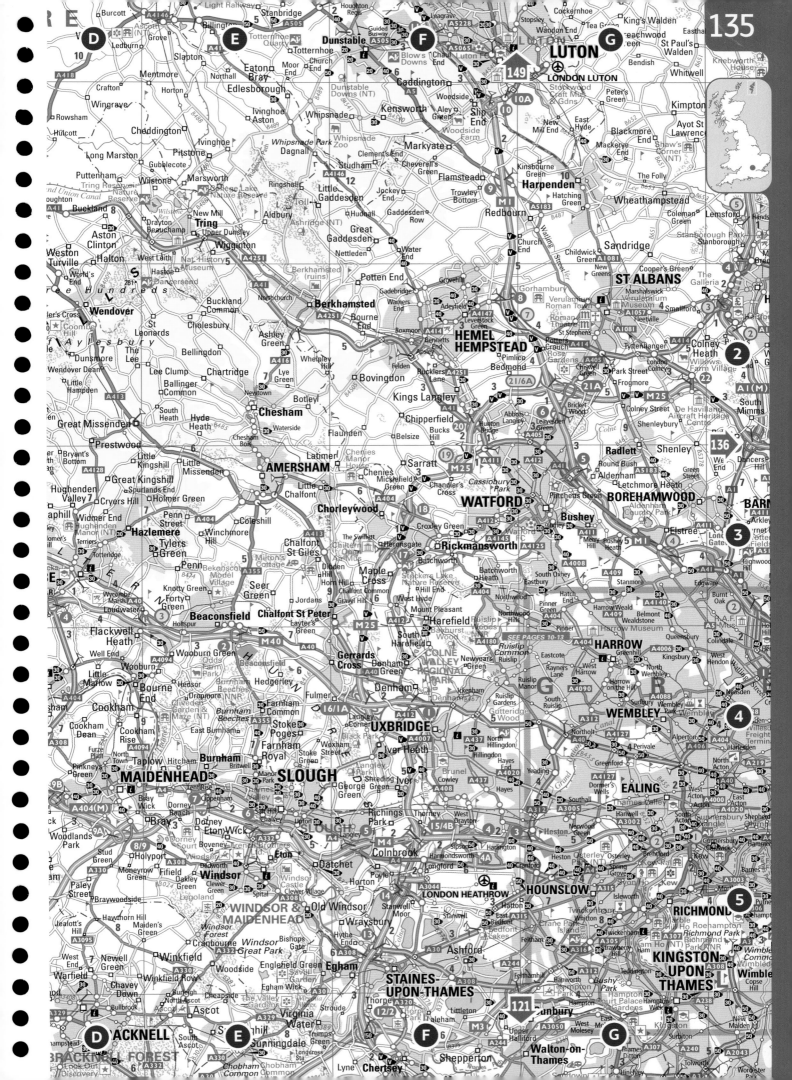

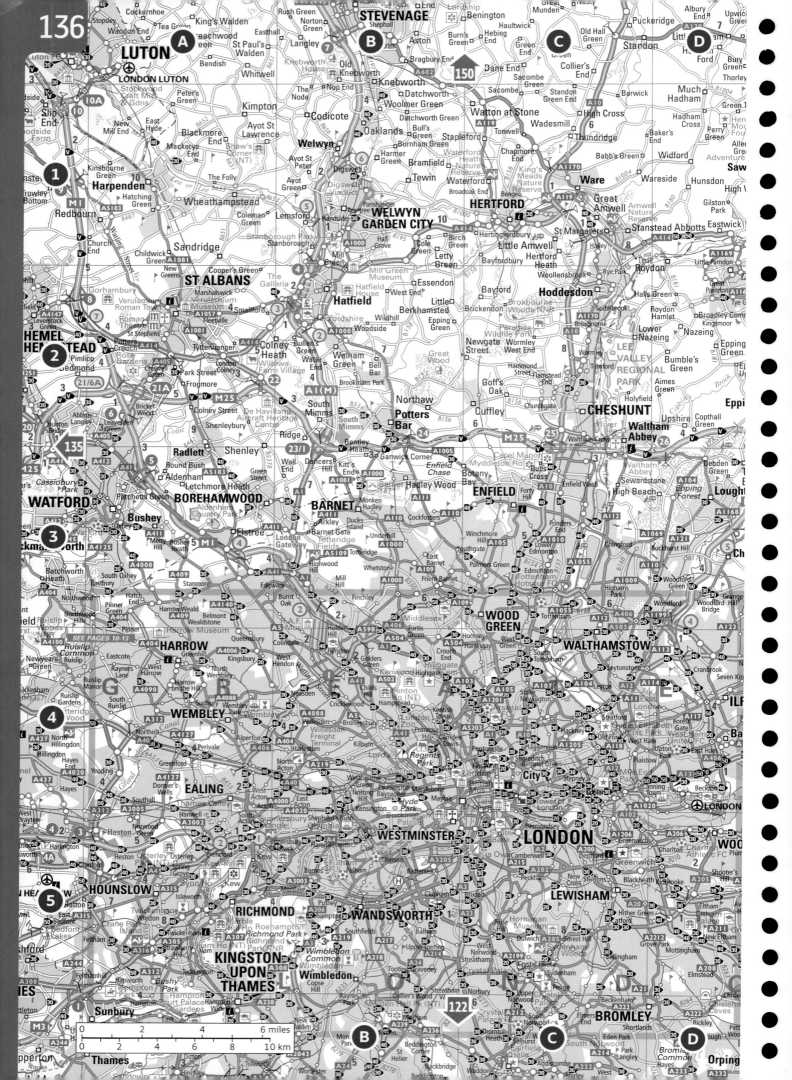

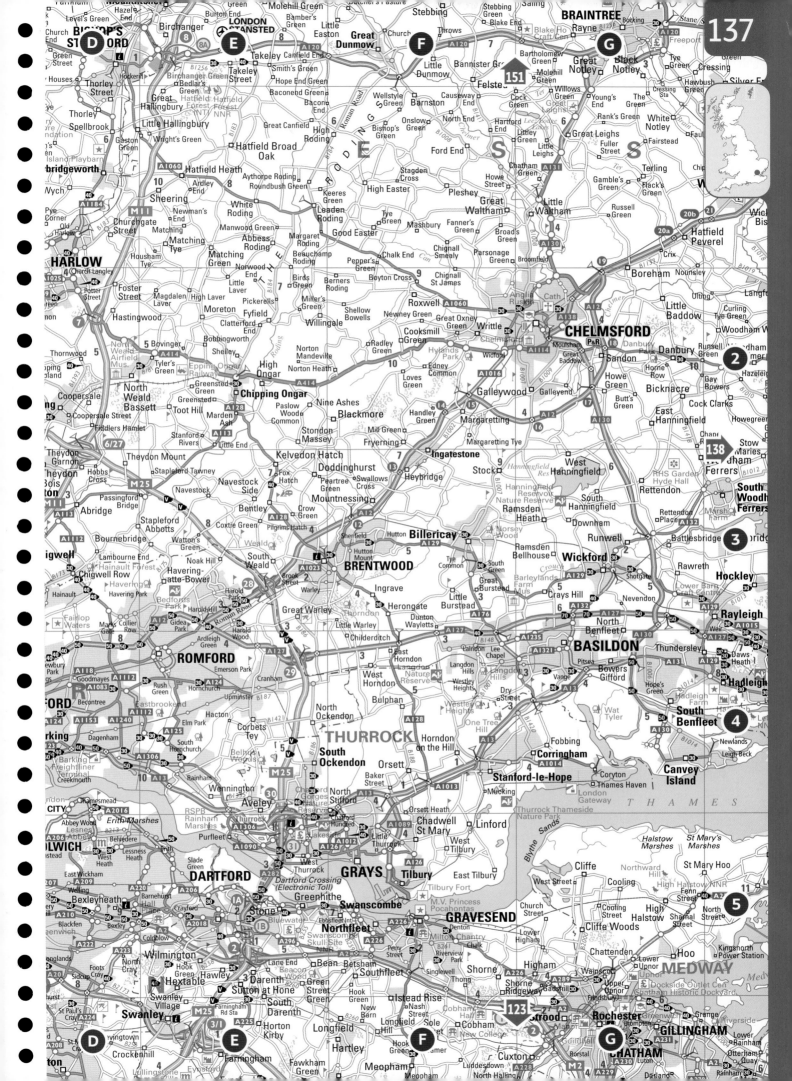

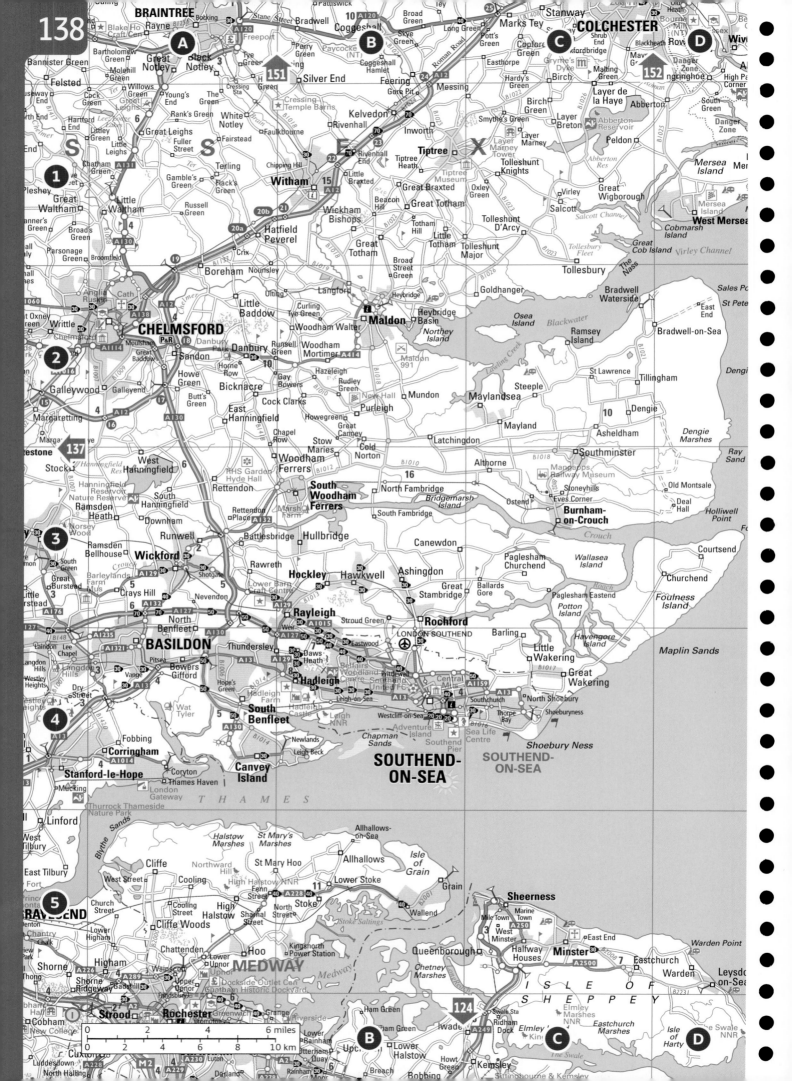

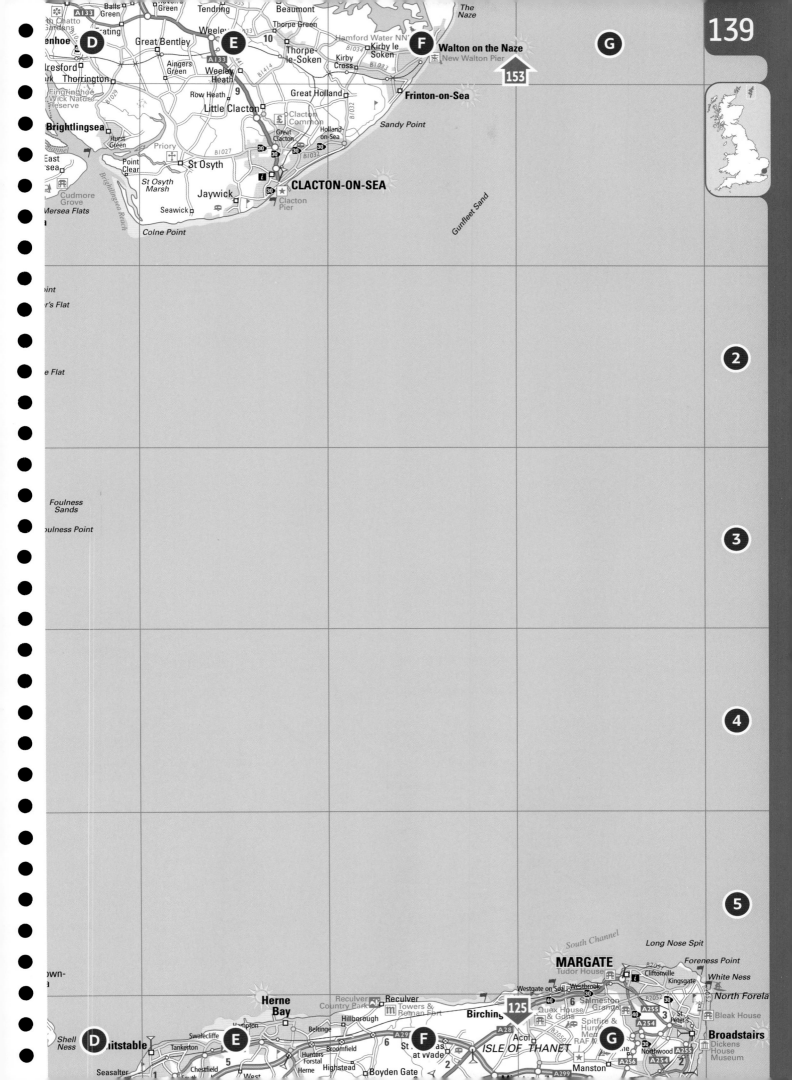

North Chatto Gardens
A133
Balls Green
enhoe
D
Tendring
Beaumont
Great Bentley
Weeley
E
10
Thorpe Green
Thorpe-le-Soken
The Naze
Hamford Water NNR
Kirby le Soken
Kirby Cross
Walton on the Naze
F
G
Aingers Green
A133
Weeley Heath
B1414
B1033
New Walton Pier
153
resford
Thorrington
Fingringhoe Wick Nature Reserve
Row Heath
9
Great Holland
B1032
Frinton-on-Sea
Brightlingsea
Little Clacton
Clacton Common
Holland-on-Sea
Sandy Point
East sea
Priory
B1027
Great Clacton
30
30
B1034
Hurst Green
30
Point Clear
St Osyth
30
CLACTON-ON-SEA
St Osyth Marsh
Jaywick
30
i
Clacton Pier
Cudmore Grove
Seawick
30
Mersea Flats
Colne Point
Gunfleet Sand
Brightlingsea Reach

oint
r's Flat
2

e Flat

Foulness Sands
oulness Point
3

4

5

South Channel
Long Nose Spit
MARGATE
Tudor House
Foreness Point
Cliftonville
Kingsgate
White Ness
North Forela
Westgate on Sea
Westbrook
B205
A255
own-
a
Herne Bay
Reculver Country Park
Reculver
Towers & Roman Fort
Birching
125
6
Salmeston Grange
A254
Quex House & Gdns
Spitfire & Hurr Mem RAF M
A255
3
St Peter's
Bleak House
Shell Ness
D
iitstable
Hampton
E
Hillborough
Beltinge
St as at vvade
A29
F
6
ISLE OF THANET
A28
Acot
B205
G
Dickens House Museum
Broadstairs
Swalecliffe
Tankerton
Broomfield
Hunters Forstal
A256
Northwood
A254
A255
2
Seasalter
Chestfield
West
Herne
Highstead
Boyden Gate
Manston
A299
Shell Ness
5
1

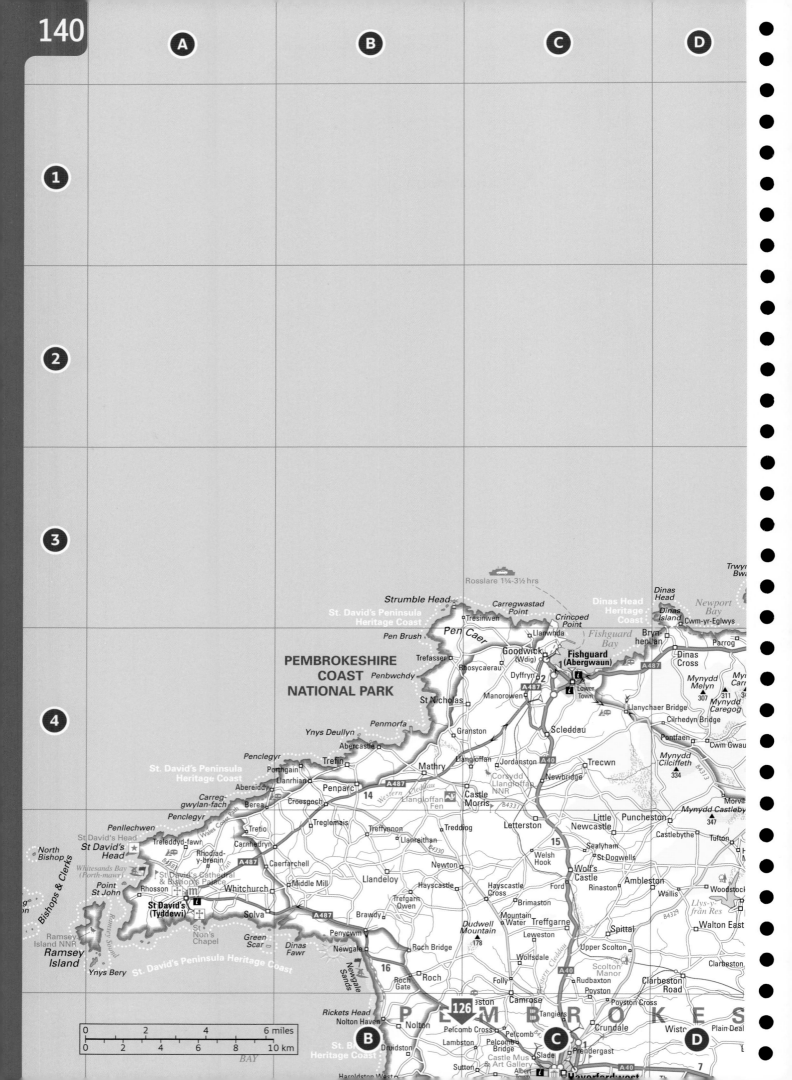

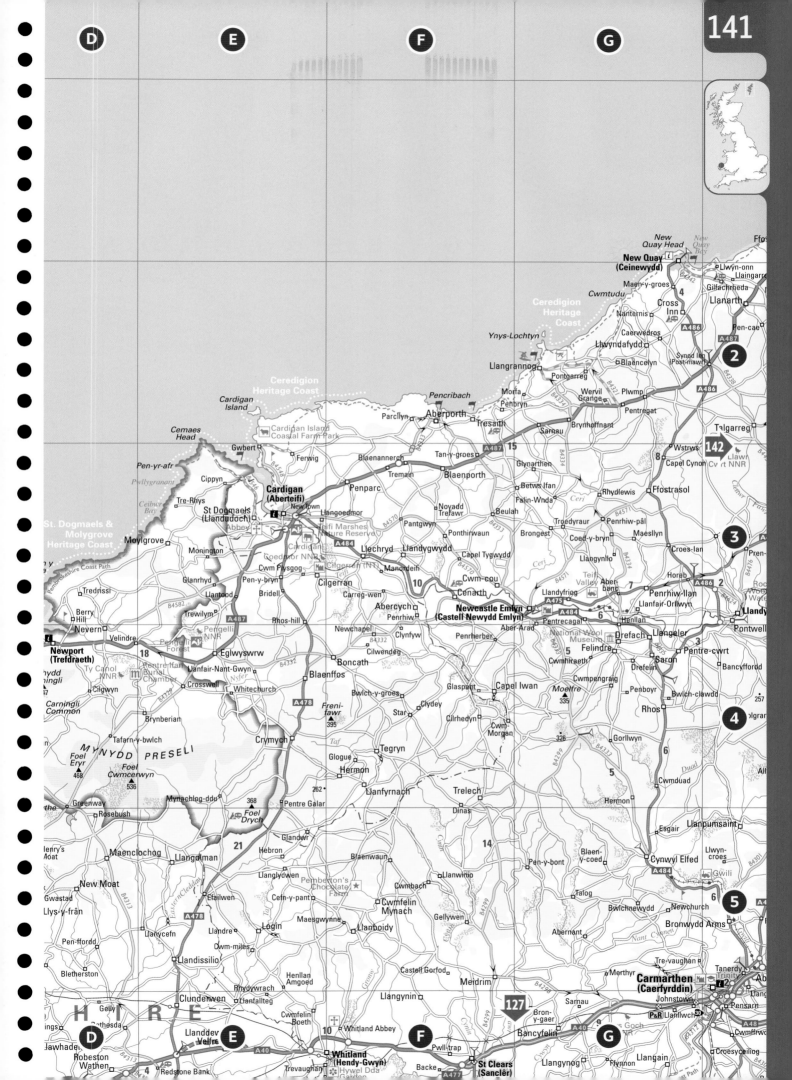

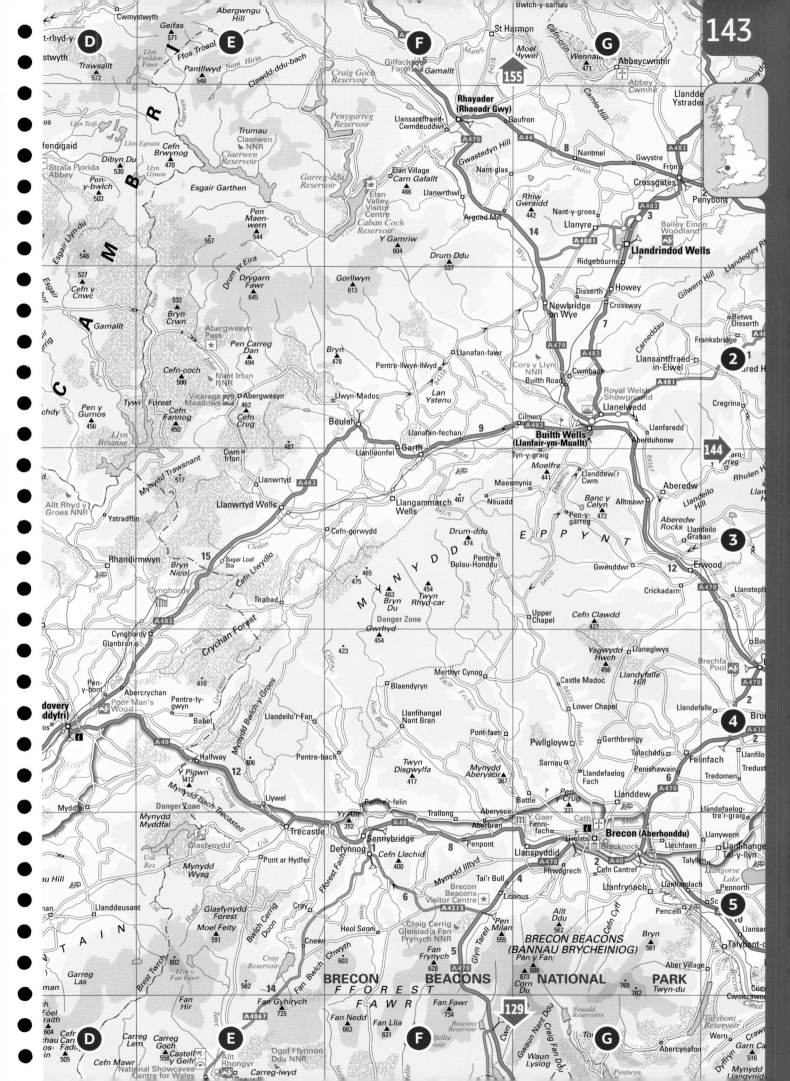

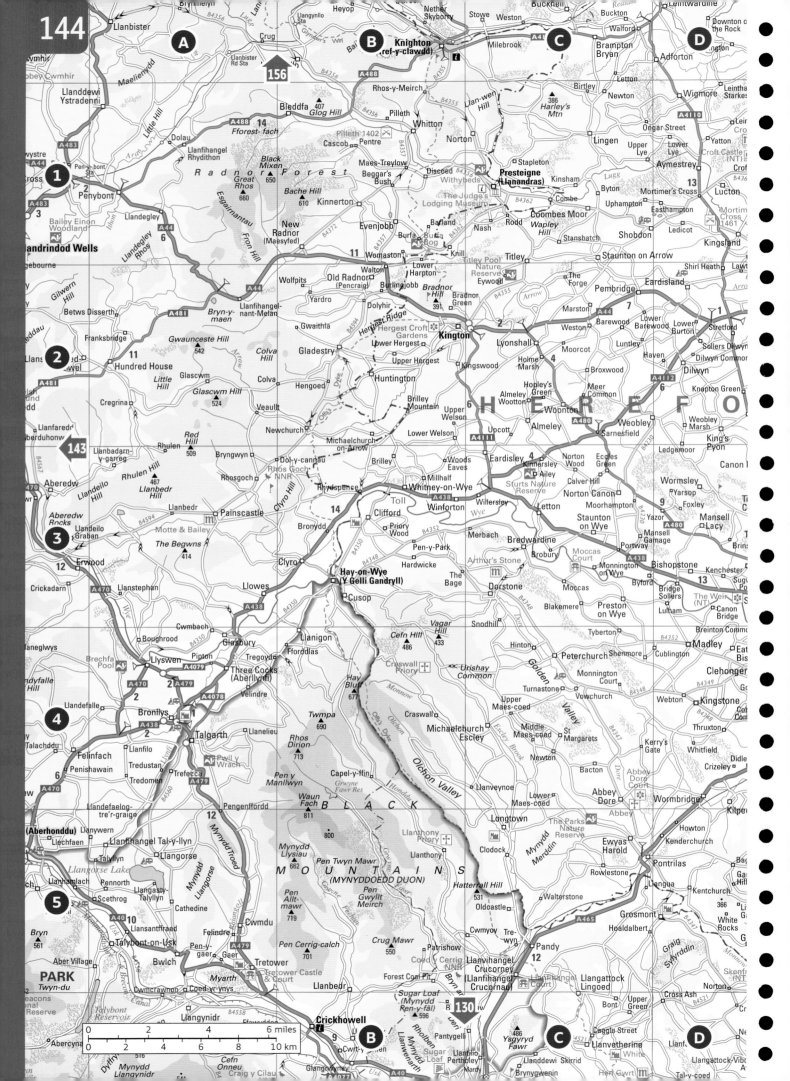

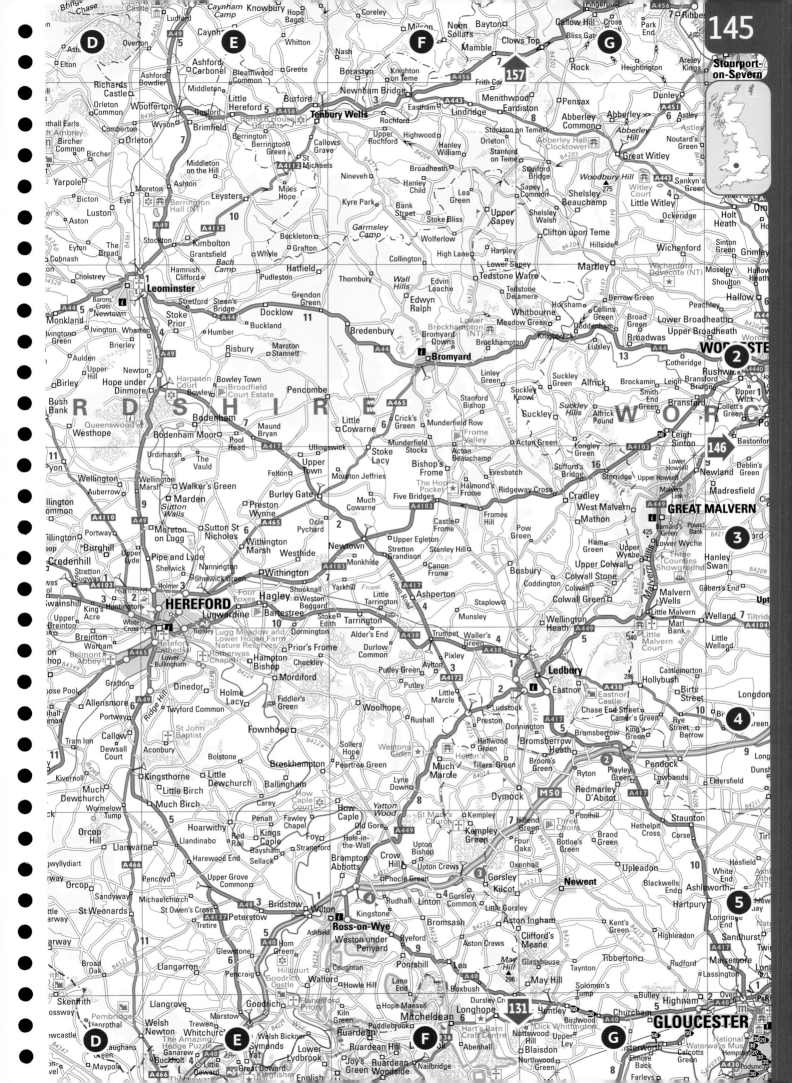

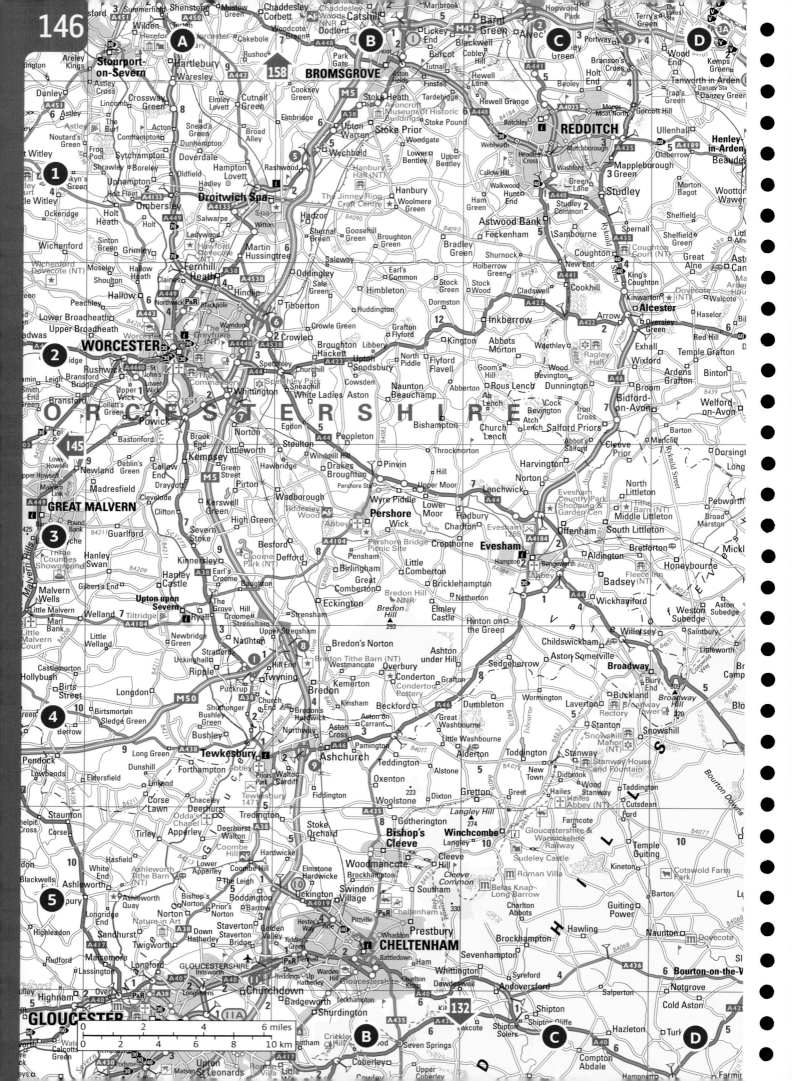

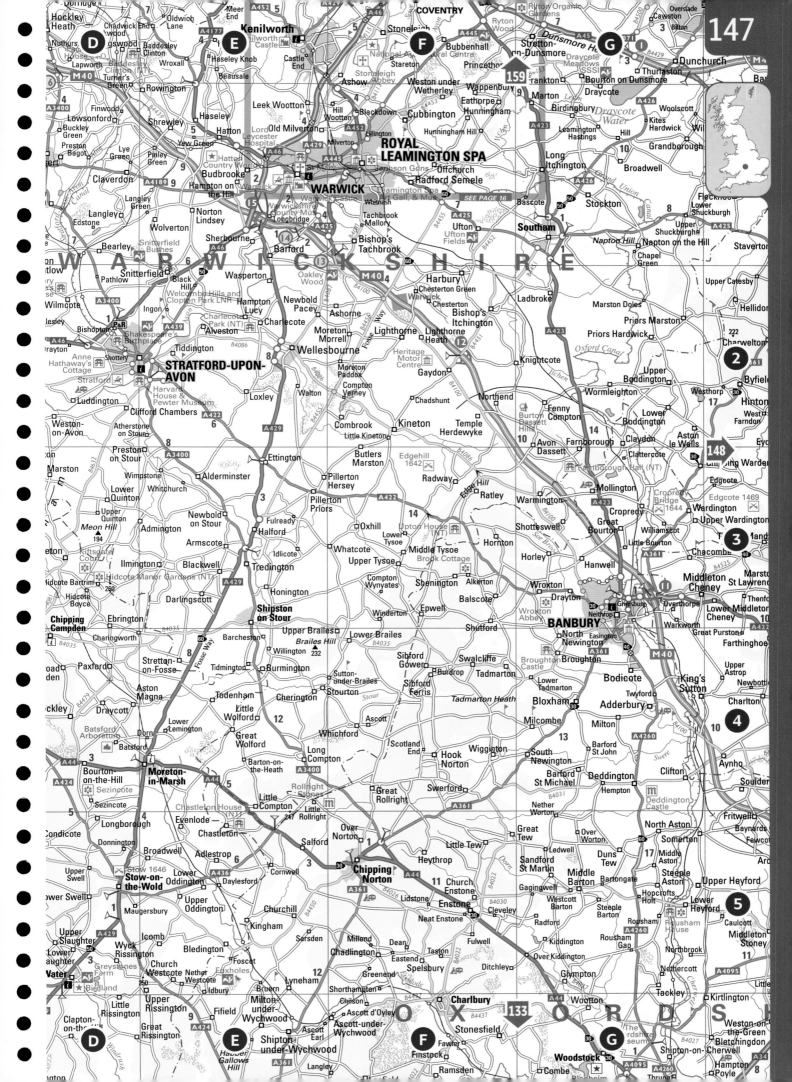

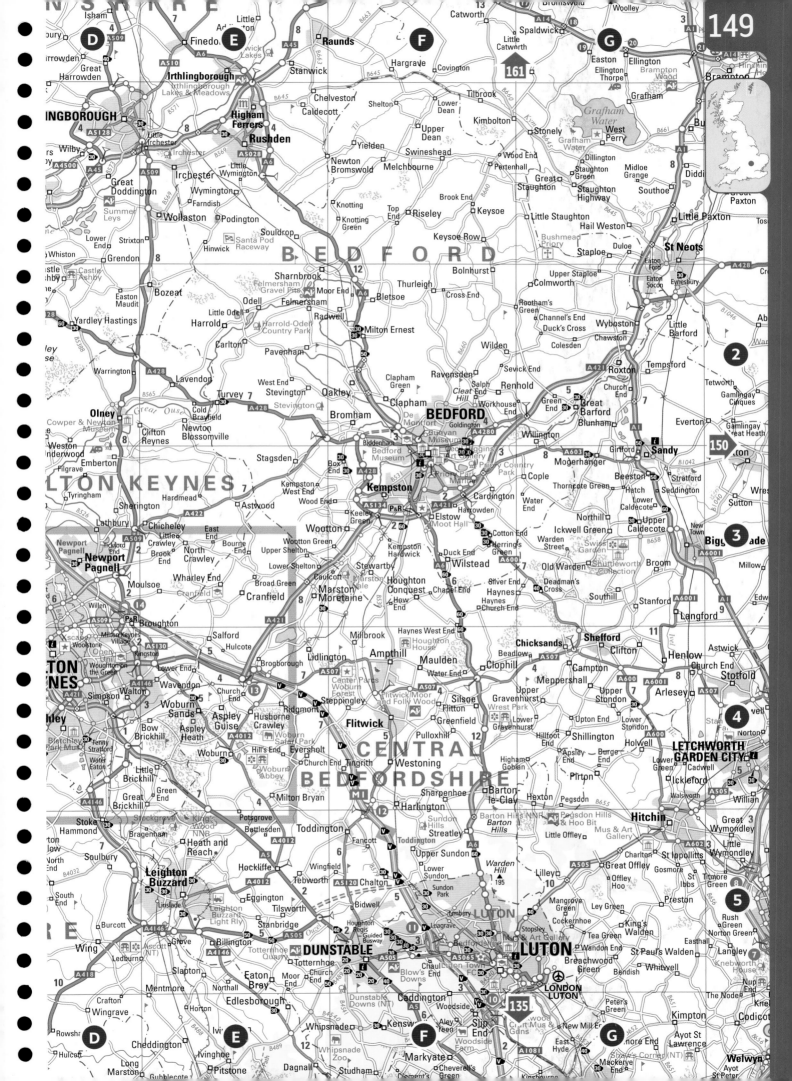

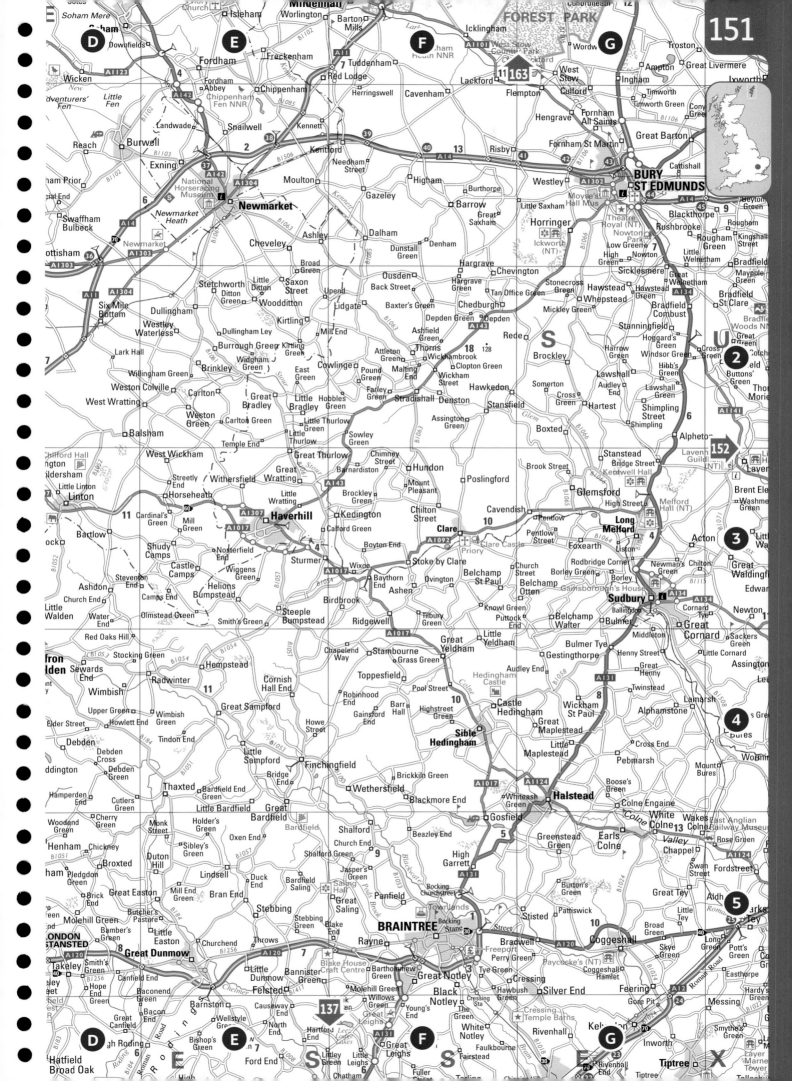

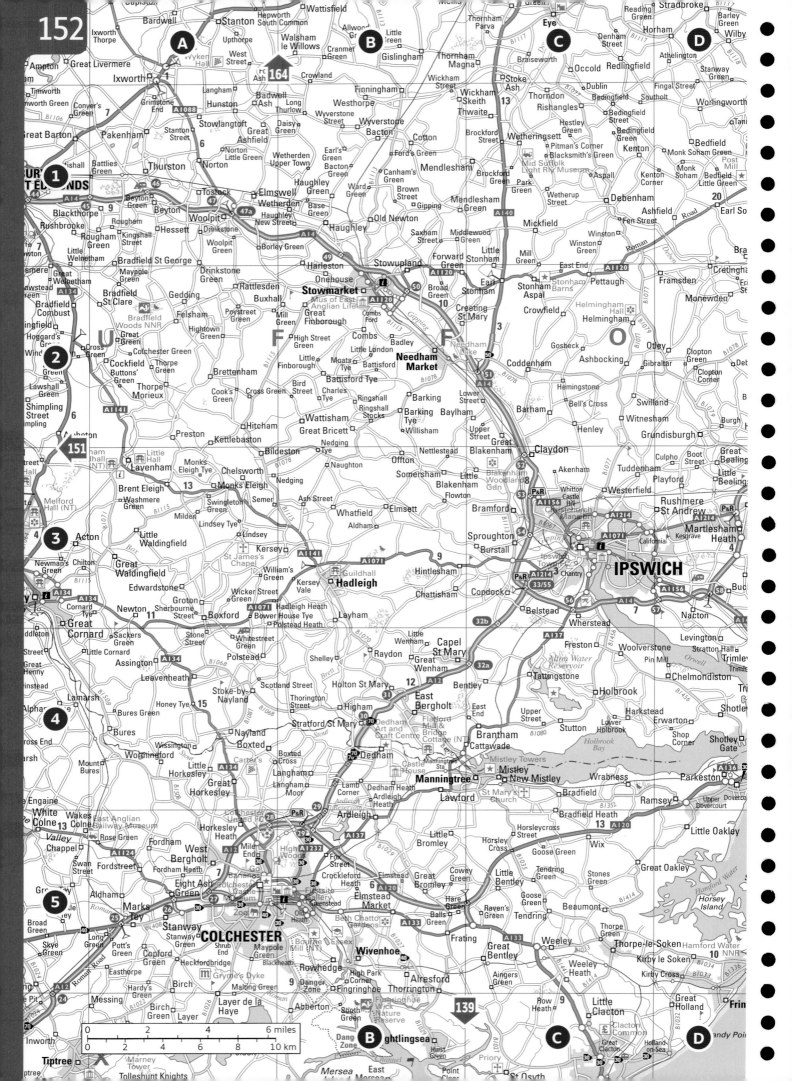

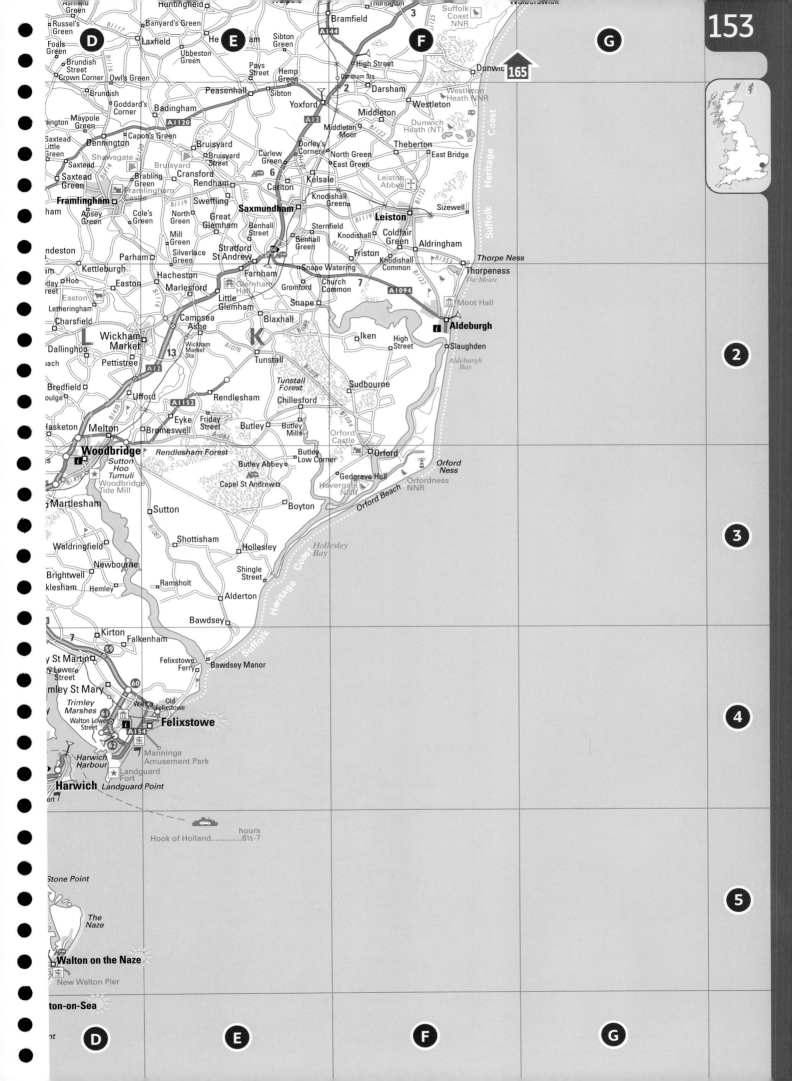

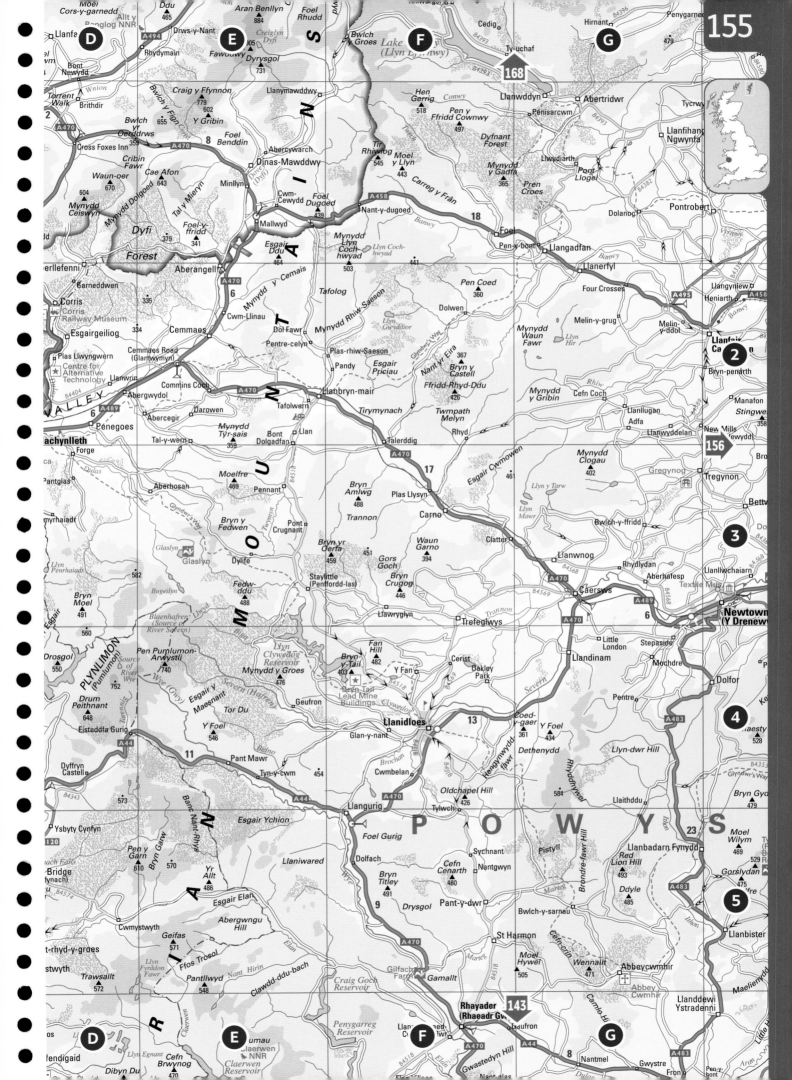

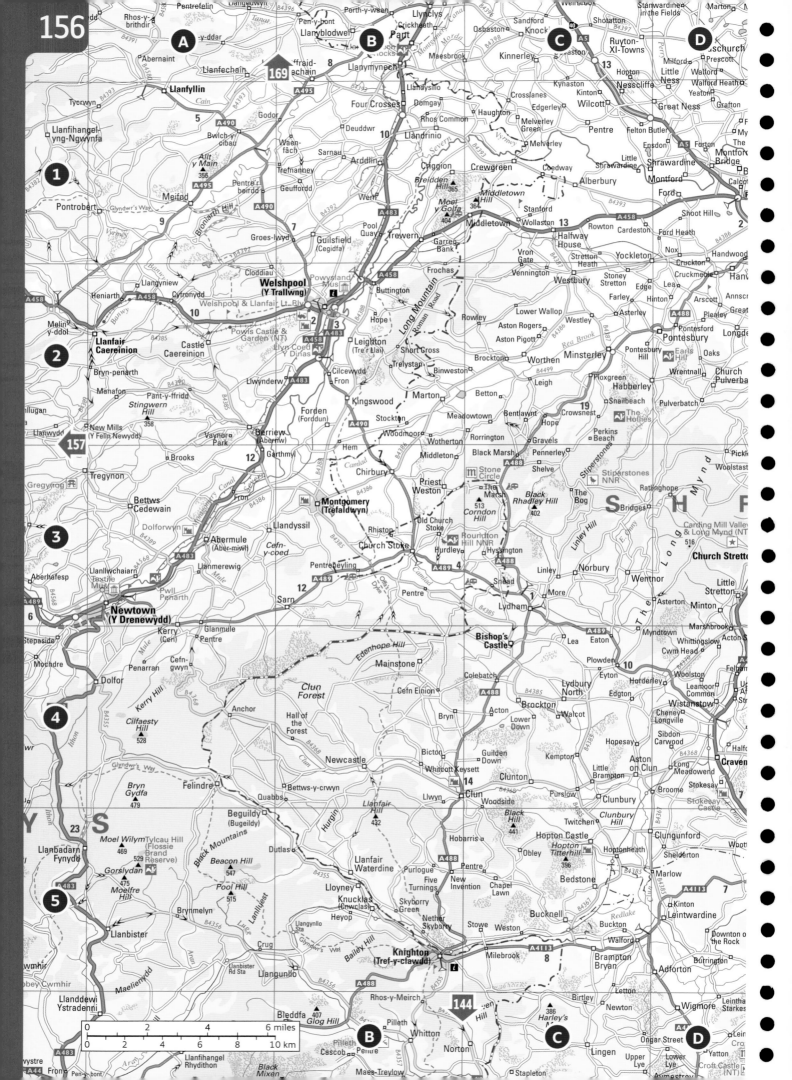

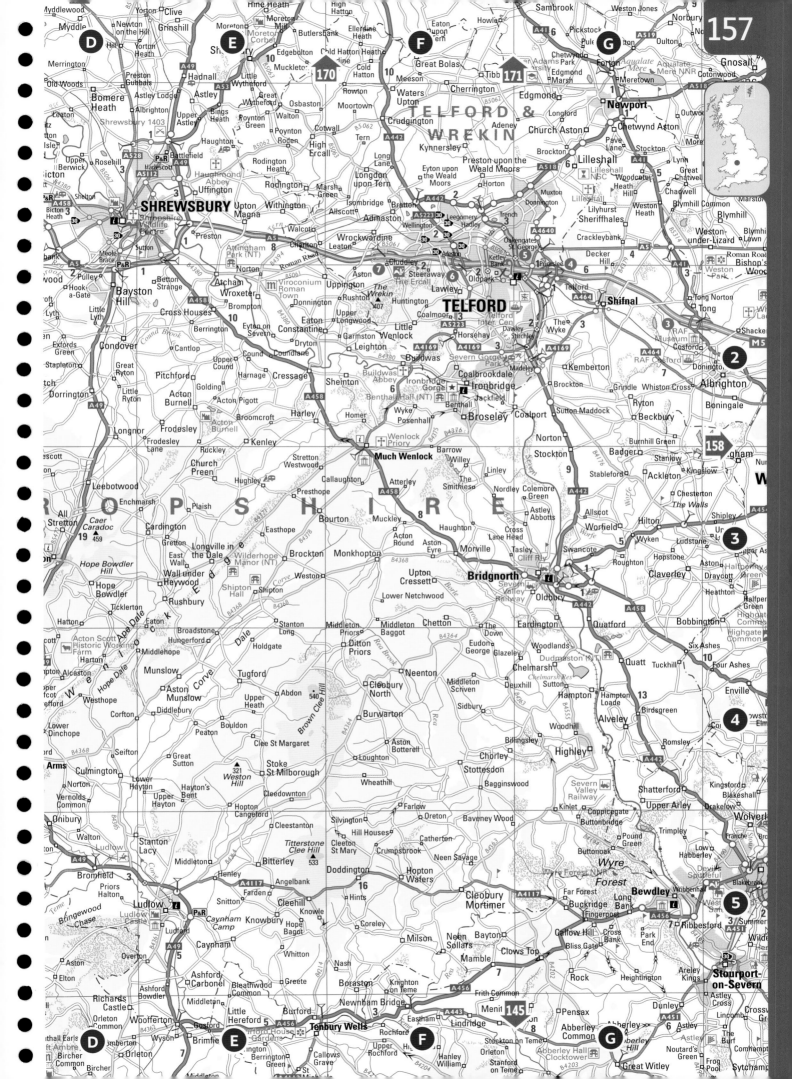

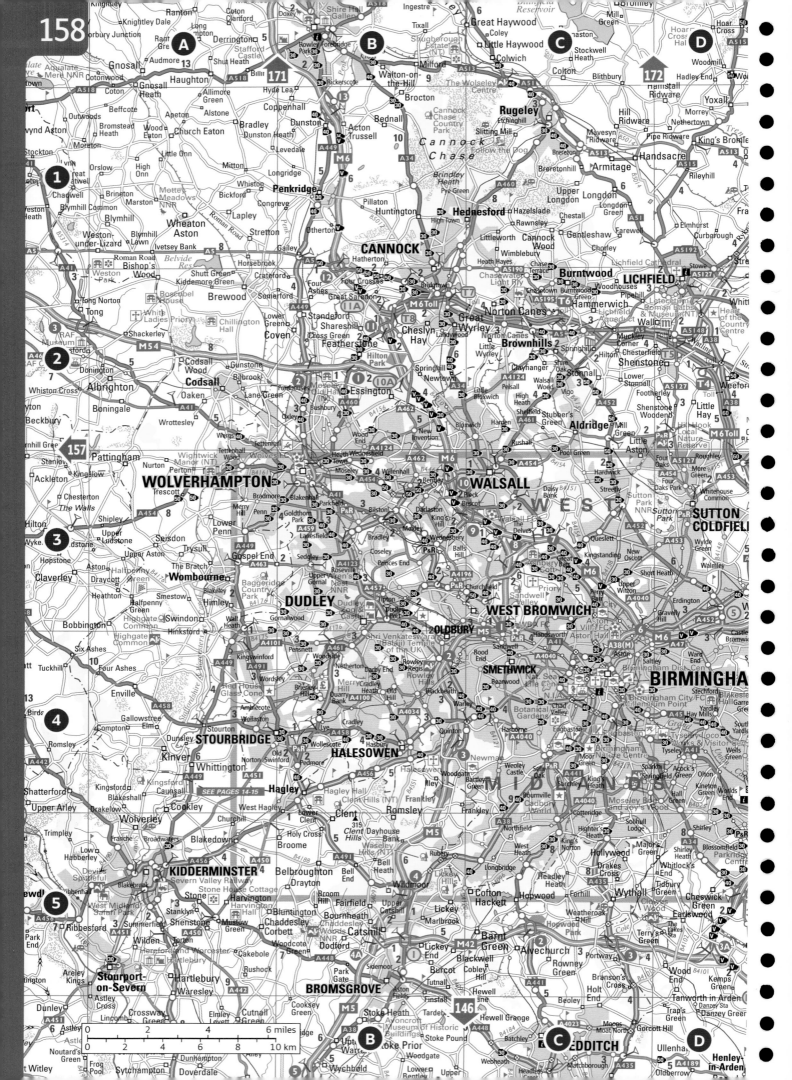

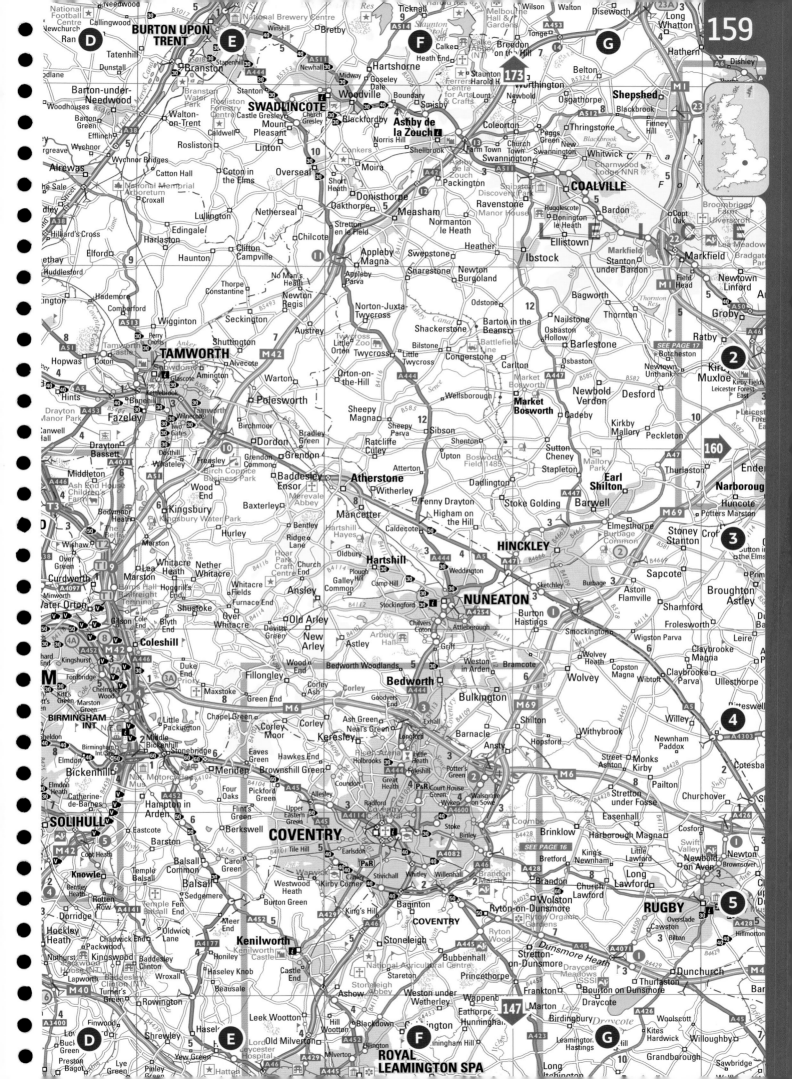

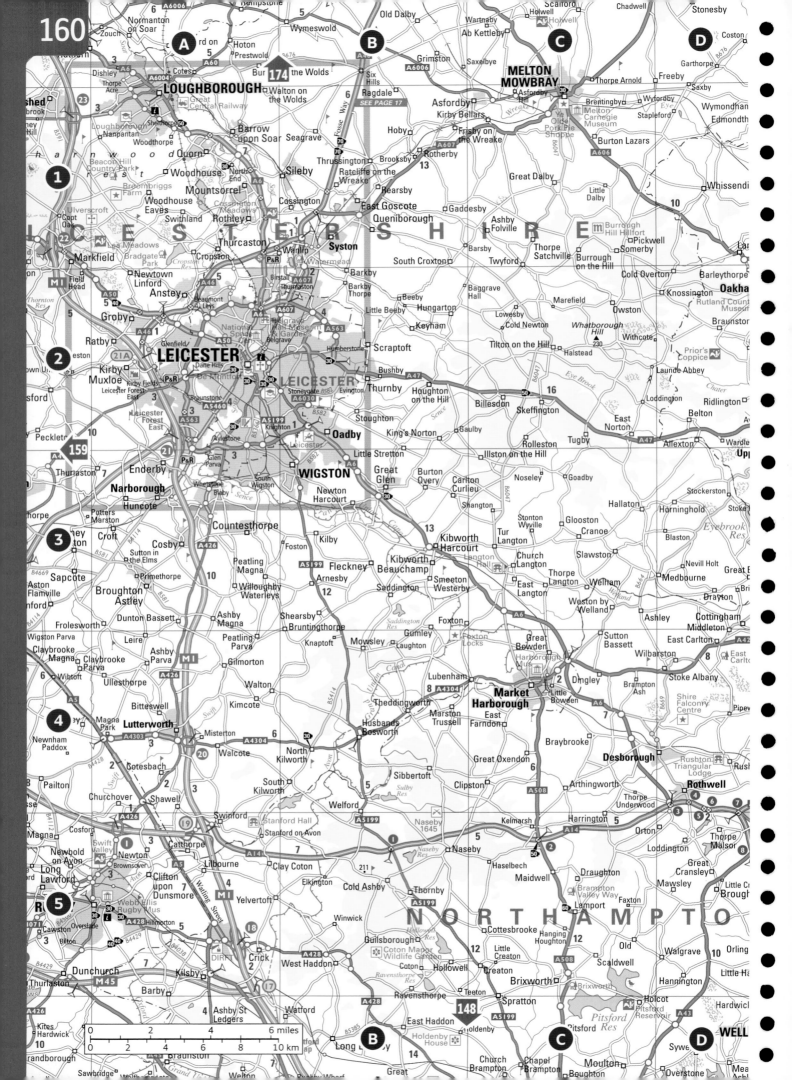

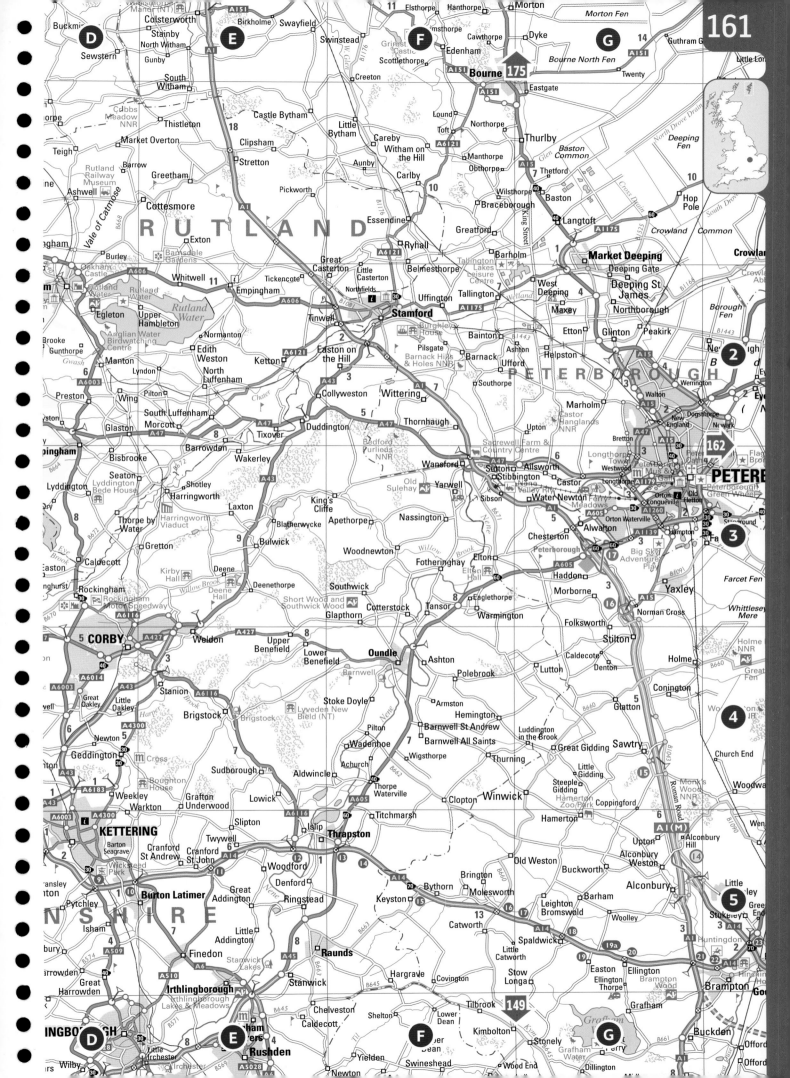

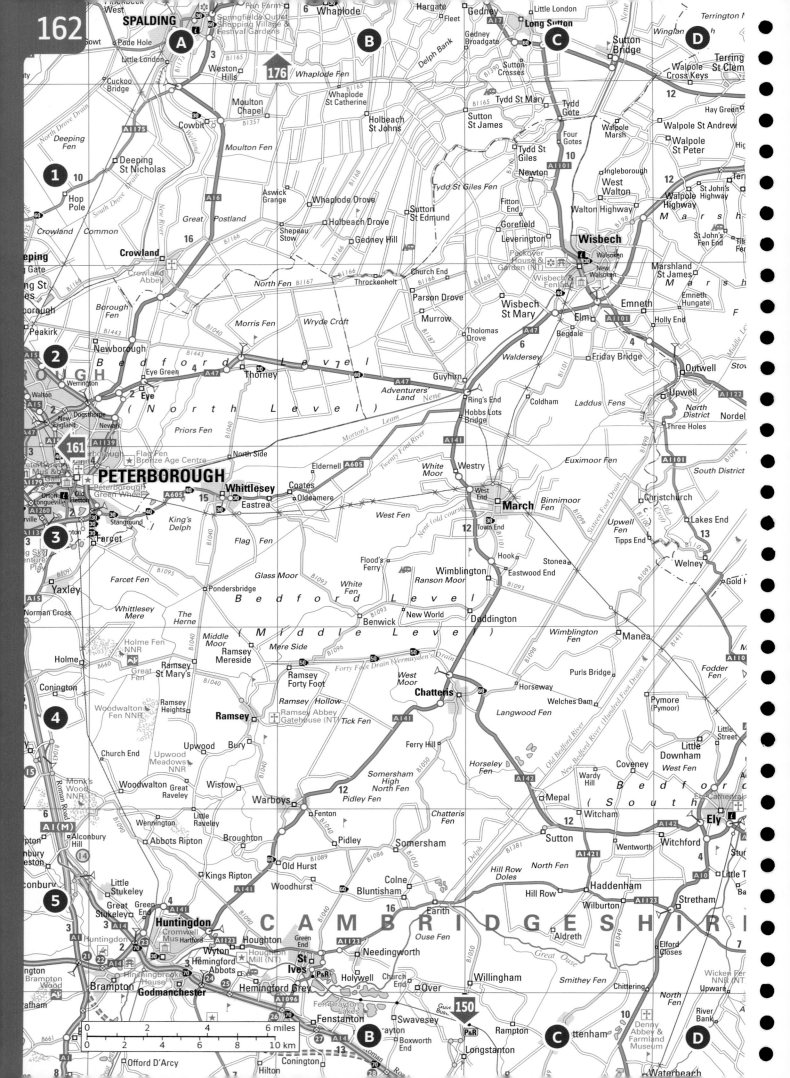

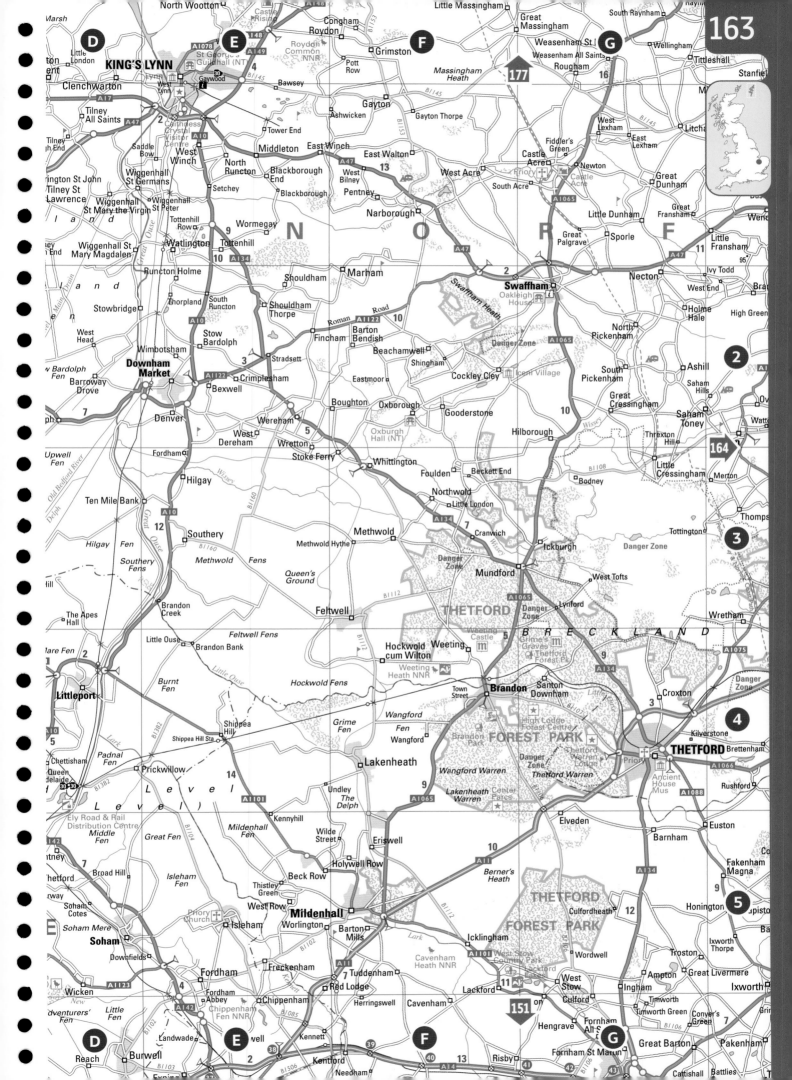

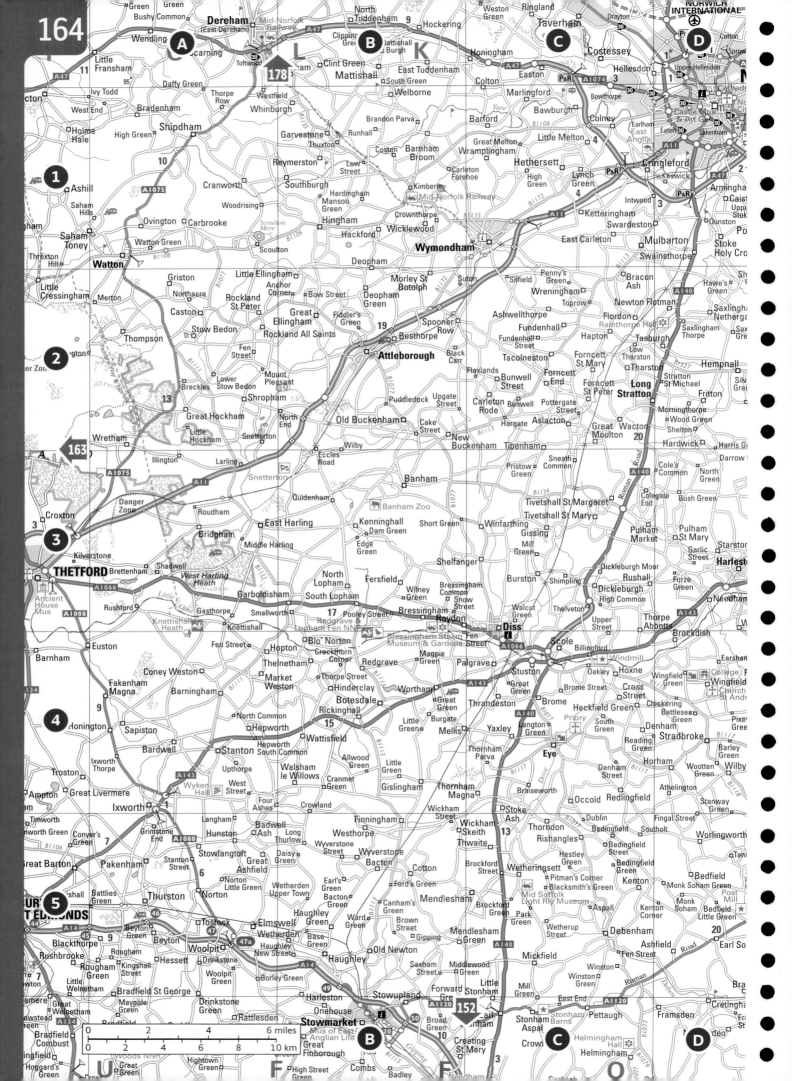

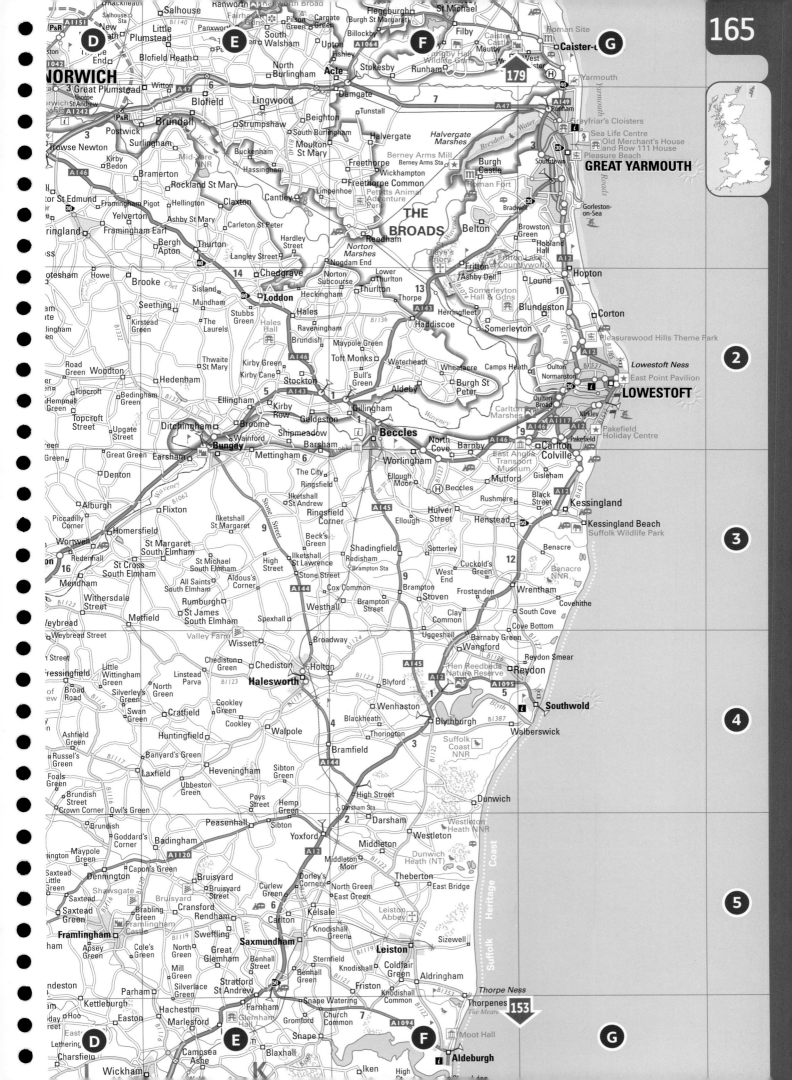

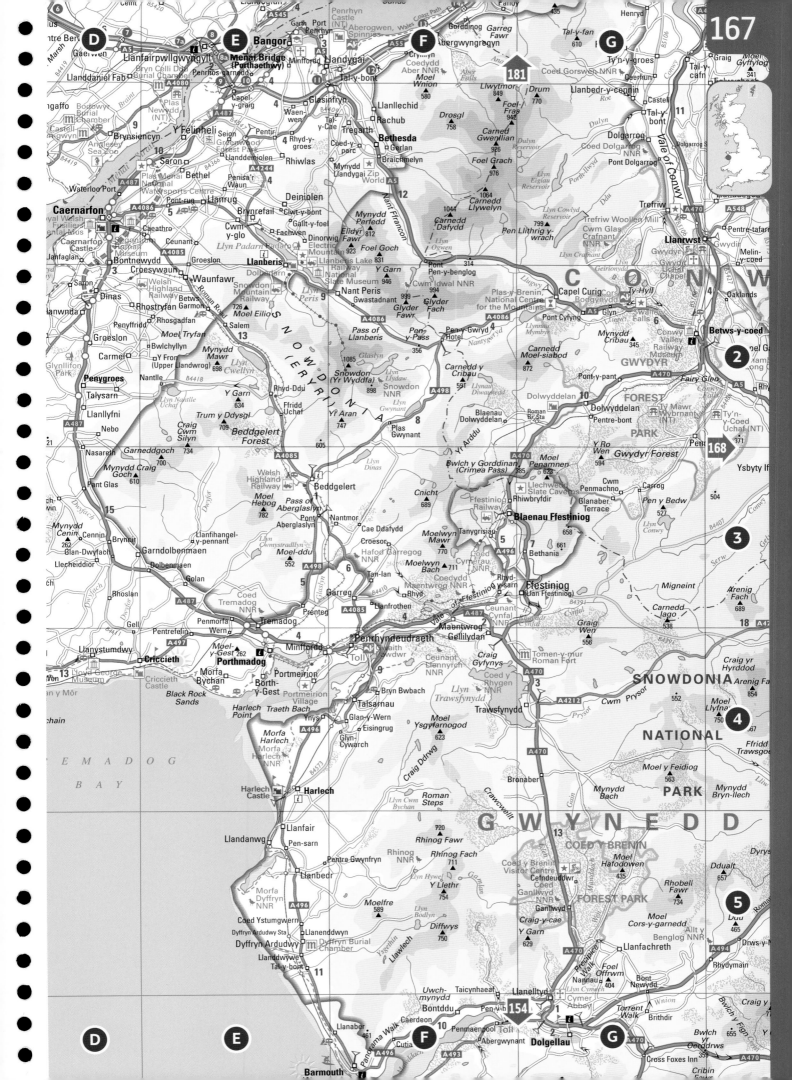

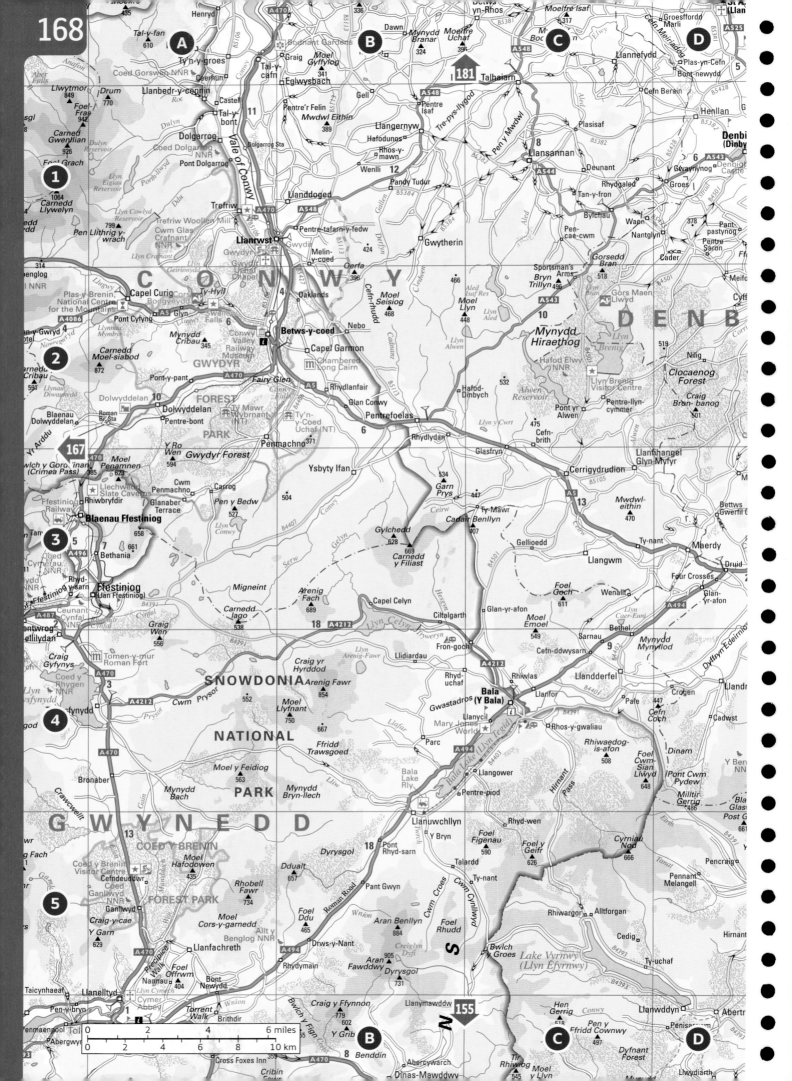

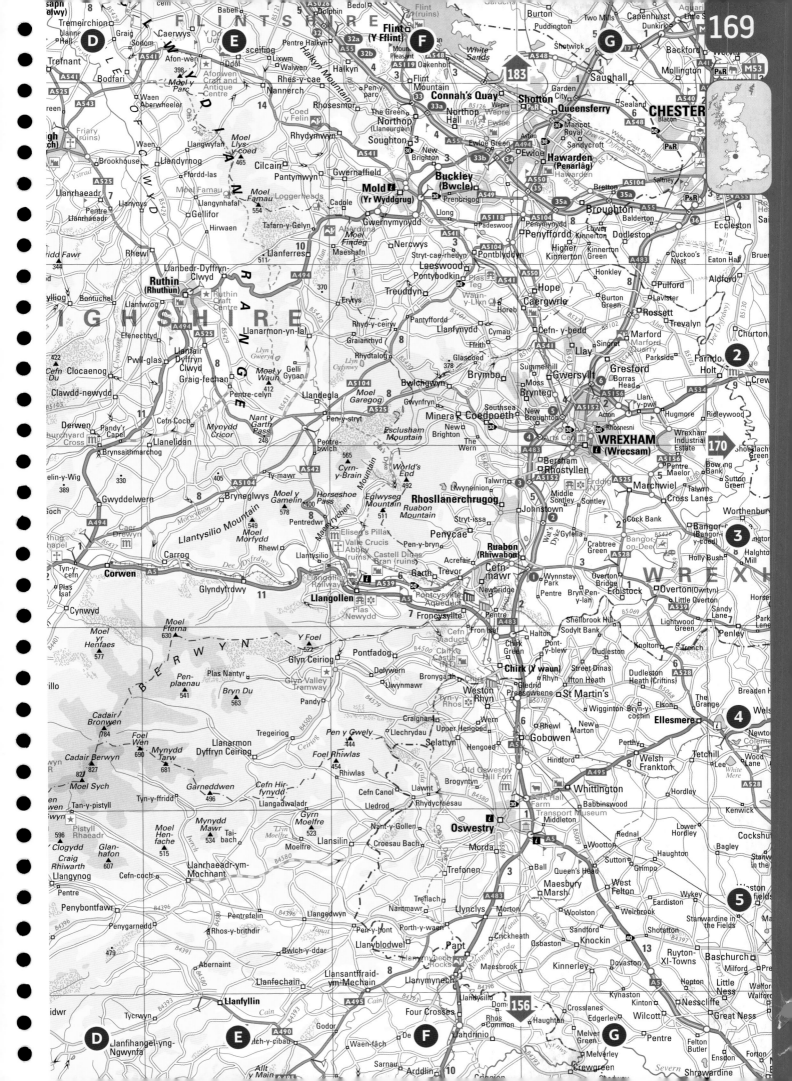

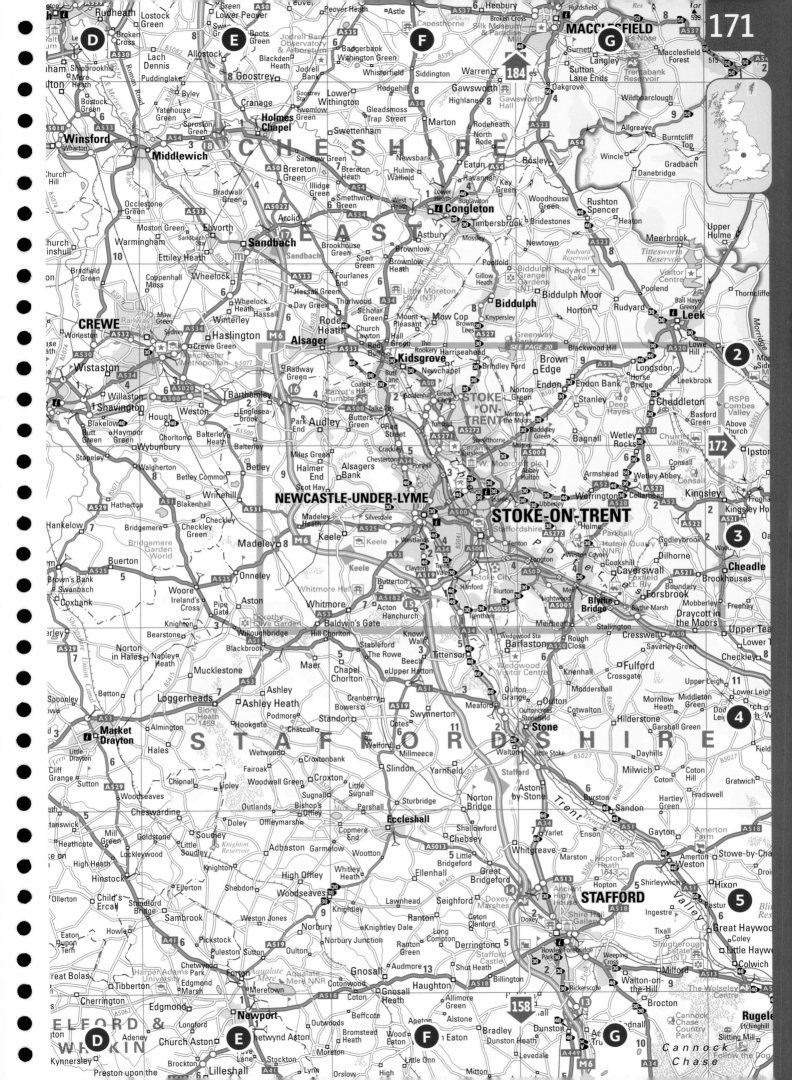

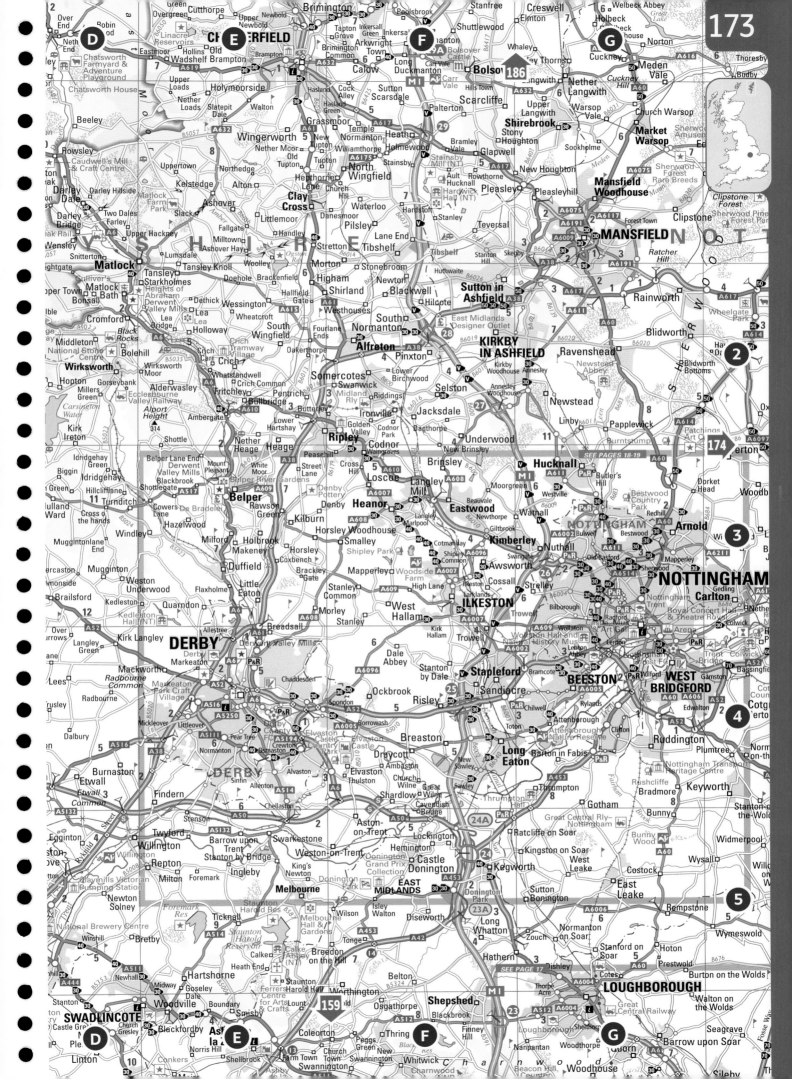

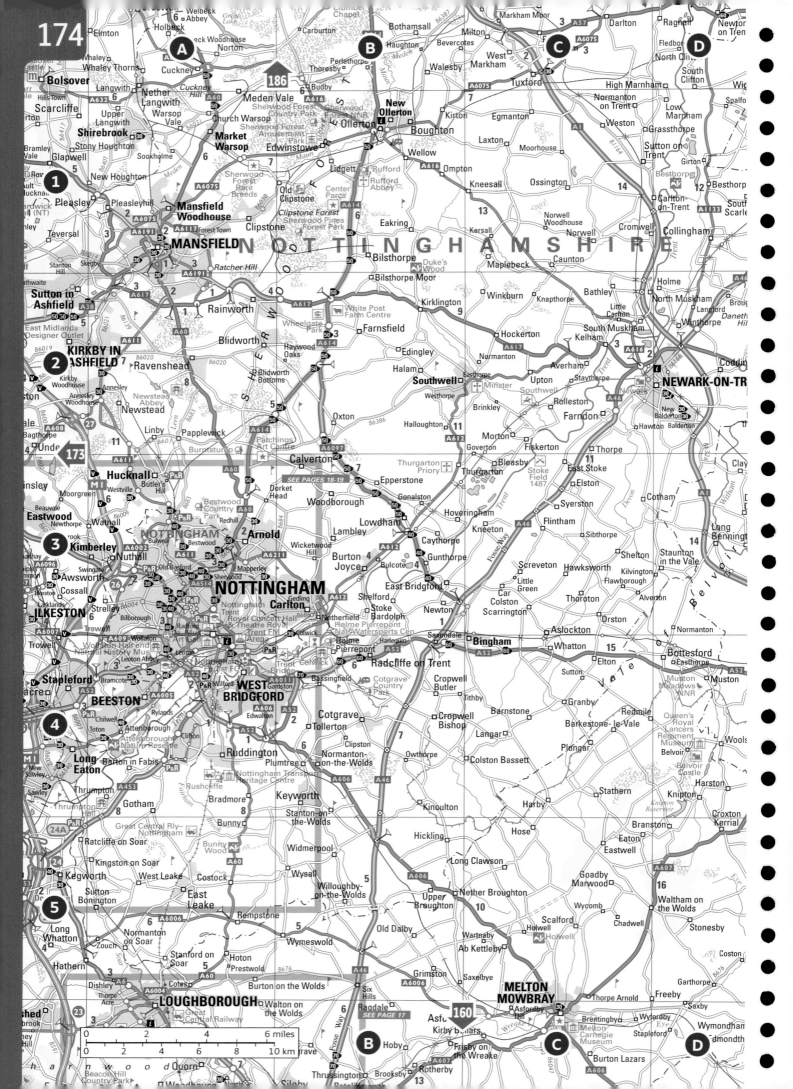

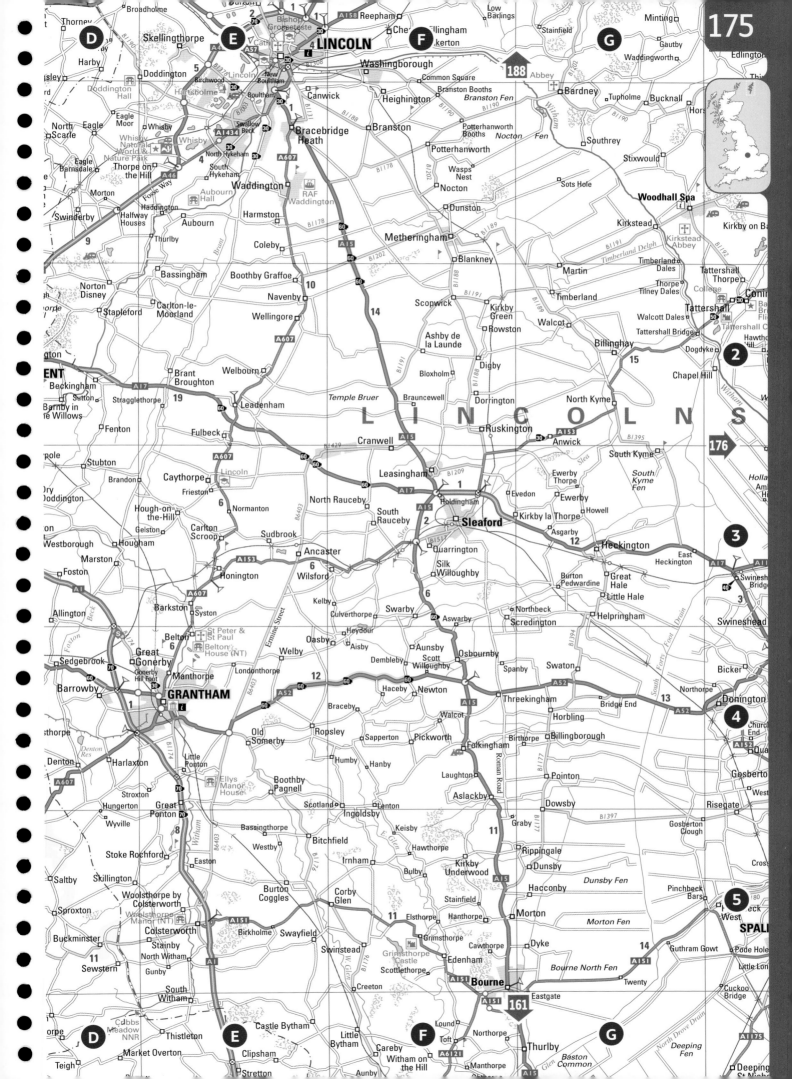

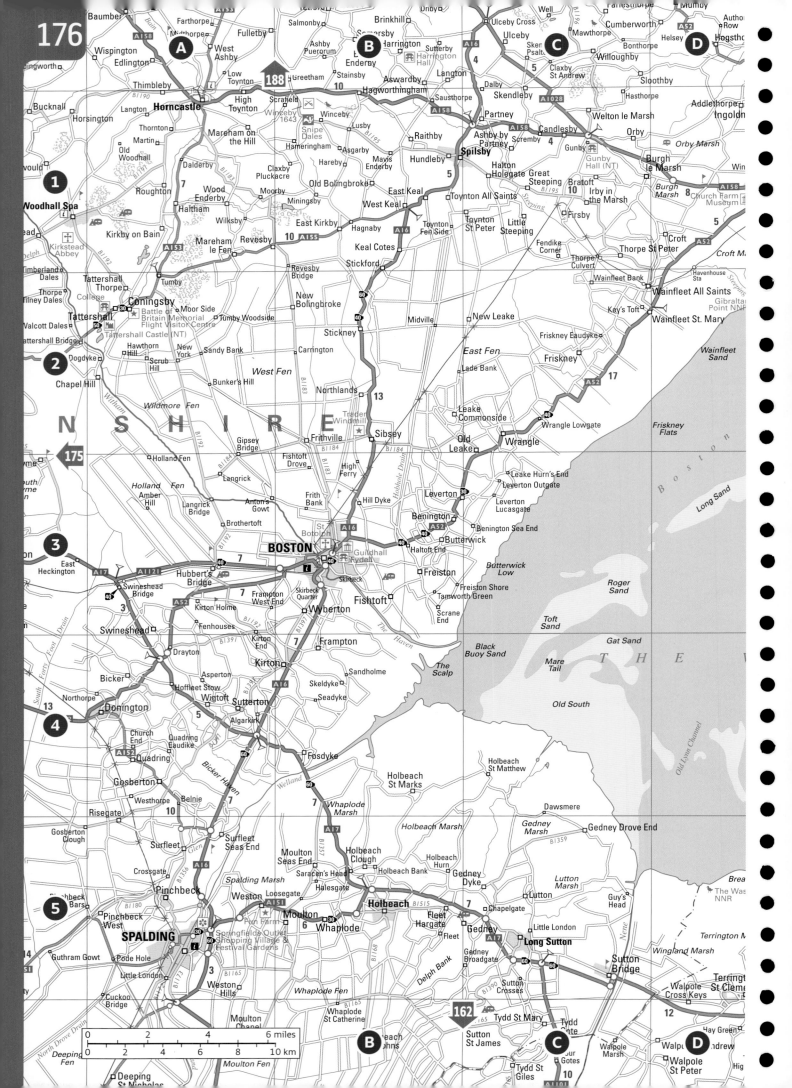

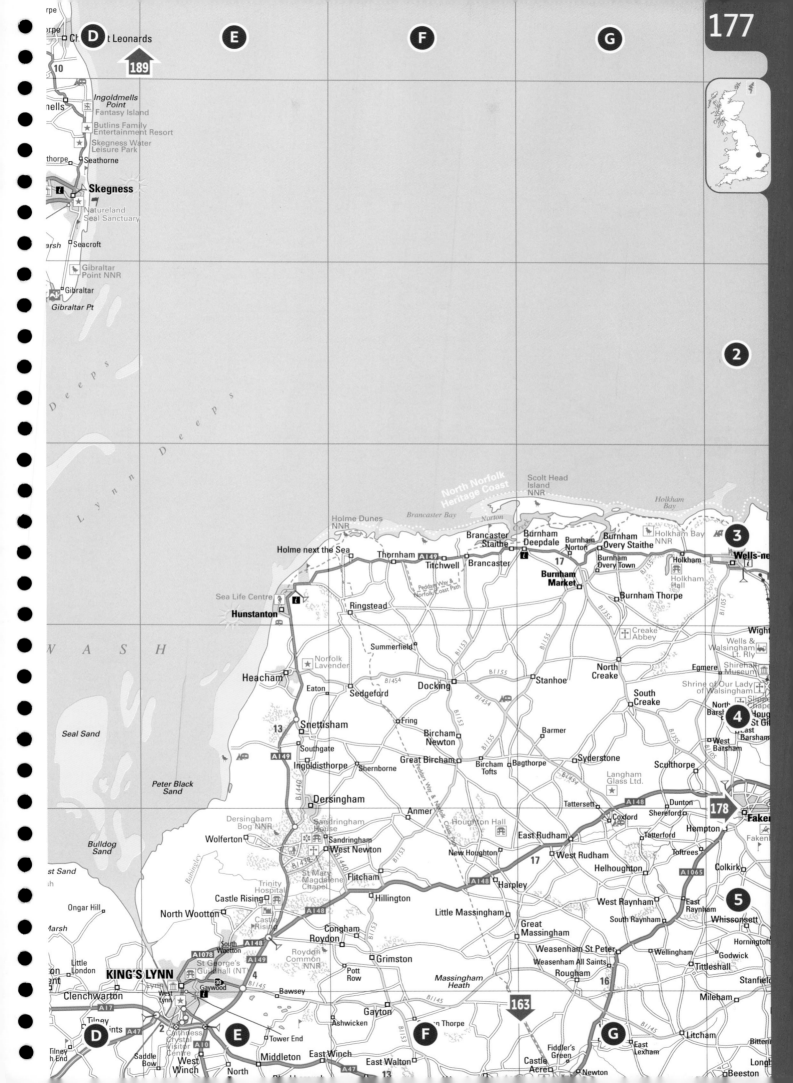

D E F G

t Leonards

189

Ingoldmells
Point
Fantasy Island
Butlins Family
Entertainment Resort
Skegness Water
Leisure Park

Seathorne

Skegness

Natureland
Seal Sanctuary

Seacroft

Gibraltar
Point NNR

Gibraltar

Gibraltar Pt

2

Deeps

Lynn Deeps

North Norfolk
Heritage Coast

Scolt Head
Island
NNR

Holkham
Bay

Brancaster Bay

Norton

Holme Dunes
NNR

Brancaster
Staithe

Burnham
Deepdale

Burnham
Norton

Burnham
Overy Staithe

Holkham
NNR

3

Holme next the Sea

Thornham A149

Titchwell

Brancaster

17

Burnham
Overy Town

Burnham
Market

Holkham

Wells-ne

Sea Life Centre

Ringstead

Burnham Thorpe

Hunstanton

Creake
Abbey

Wight

W A S H

Summerfield

B1153

North
Creake

Wells &
Walsingham
Lt. Rly

Norfolk
Lavender

Egmere

Shirehall
Museum

Heacham

Docking

Stanhoe

South
Creake

Shrine of Our Lady
of Walsingham

B1454

Eaton

Sedgeford

B1155

North
Barsh

4

Hough
St Gi

Fring

Bircham
Newton

Barmer

Syderstone

Sculthorpe

East
Barsham

Snettisham

13

Southgate

A149

Great Bircham

Bircham
Tofts

Bagthorpe

West
Barsham

Ingoldisthorpe

Shernborne

Langham
Glass Ltd.

Seal Sand

B1440

Dersingham

Anmer

Tattersett

A148

Coxford

Dunton

178

Fake

Peter Black
Sand

Dersingham
Bog NNR

Sandringham
House

Houghton Hall

East Rudham

Shereford

Hempton

Fakenn

Bulldog
Sand

Wolferton

Sandringham

West Newton

New Houghton

West Rudham

17

Tatterford

Toftrees

Colkirk

t Sand

Trinity
Hospital

St Mary
Magdalene
Chapel

Flitcham

Harpley

Helhoughton

A1065

Marsh

Castle Rising

Hillington

Little Massingham

West Raynham

East
Raynham

5

North Wootton

Castle
Rising

A148

Great
Massingham

South Raynham

Whissonsett

Ongar Hill

Congham

Roydon

Roydon
Common
NNR

Weasenham St Peter

Wellingham

Hornington

Little
London

A1078

South
Wootton

A148

Grimston

Weasenham All Saints

Godwick

KING'S LYNN

A149

Pott
Row

Rougham

16

Tittleshall

Clenchwarton

Lynn

West
Lynn

Gaywood

Caithness
Crystal
Visitor
Centre

A10

Bawsey

B1145

Massingham
Heath

163

Stanfield

Mileham

Tilney
ints

A47

Tower End

Gayton

Ashwicken

B1153

Fiddler's
Green

East
Lexham

Litcham

Tilney
h End

Saddle
Bow

West
Winch

Middleton

East Winch

East Walton

Castle
Acre

Newton

Longh

Beeston

A47

13

D E F G

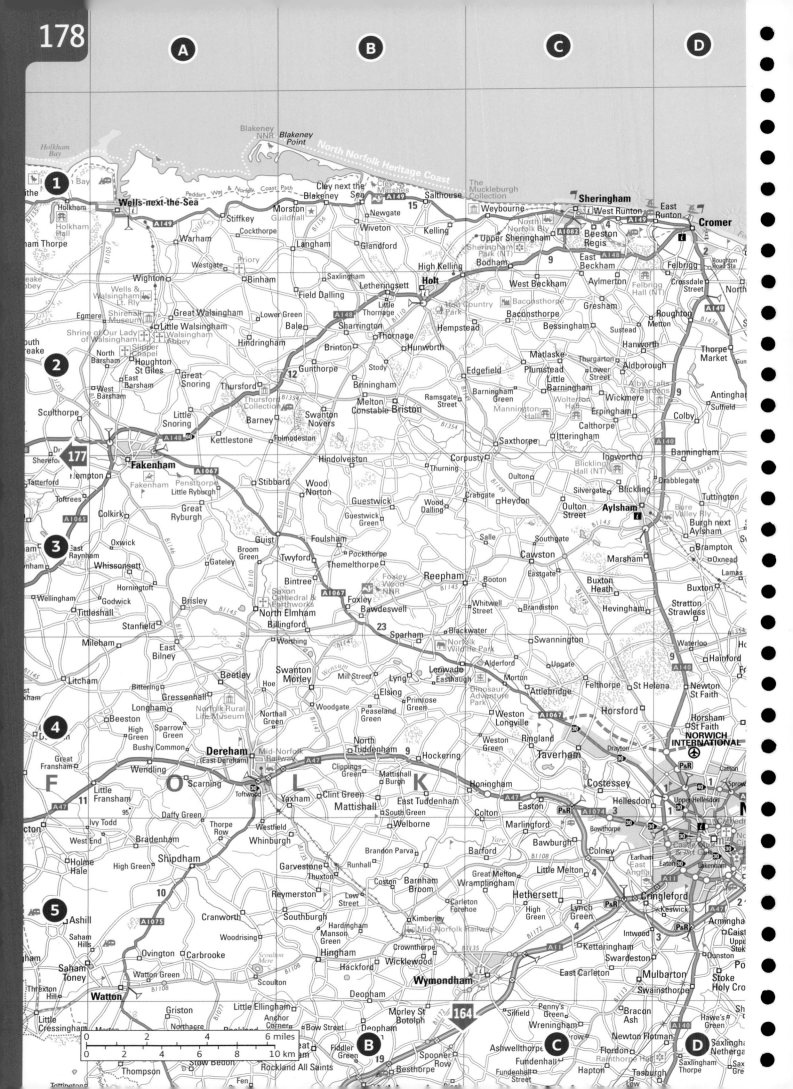

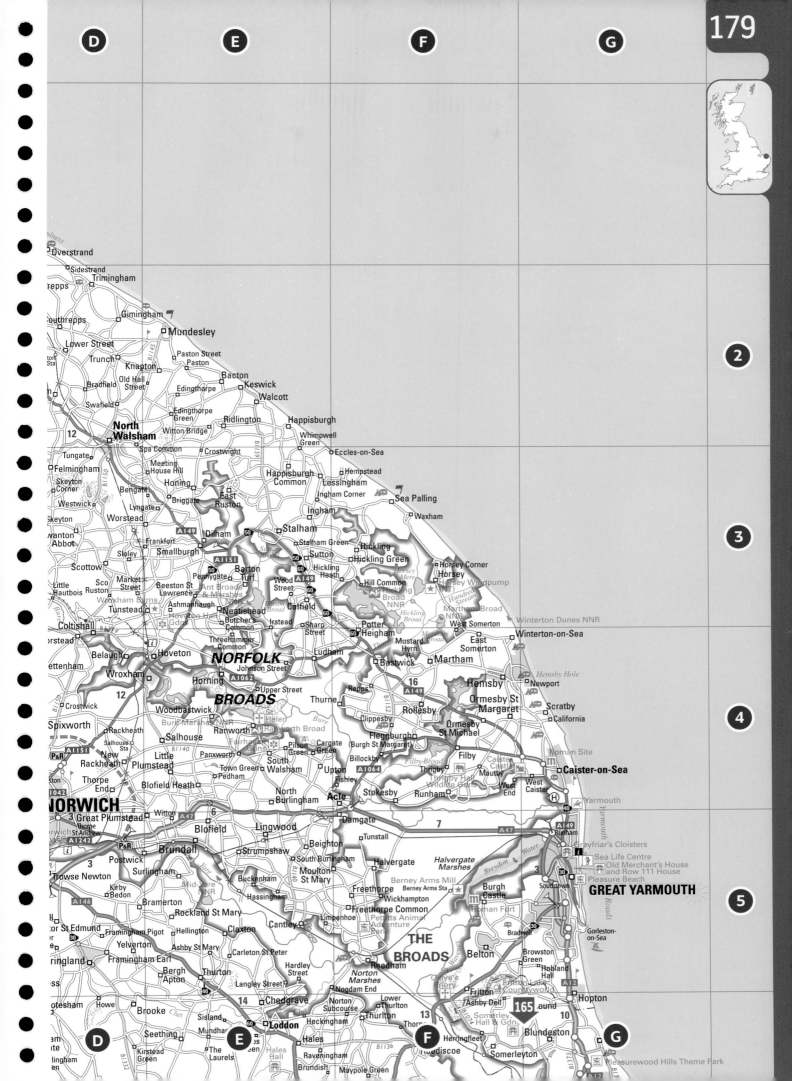

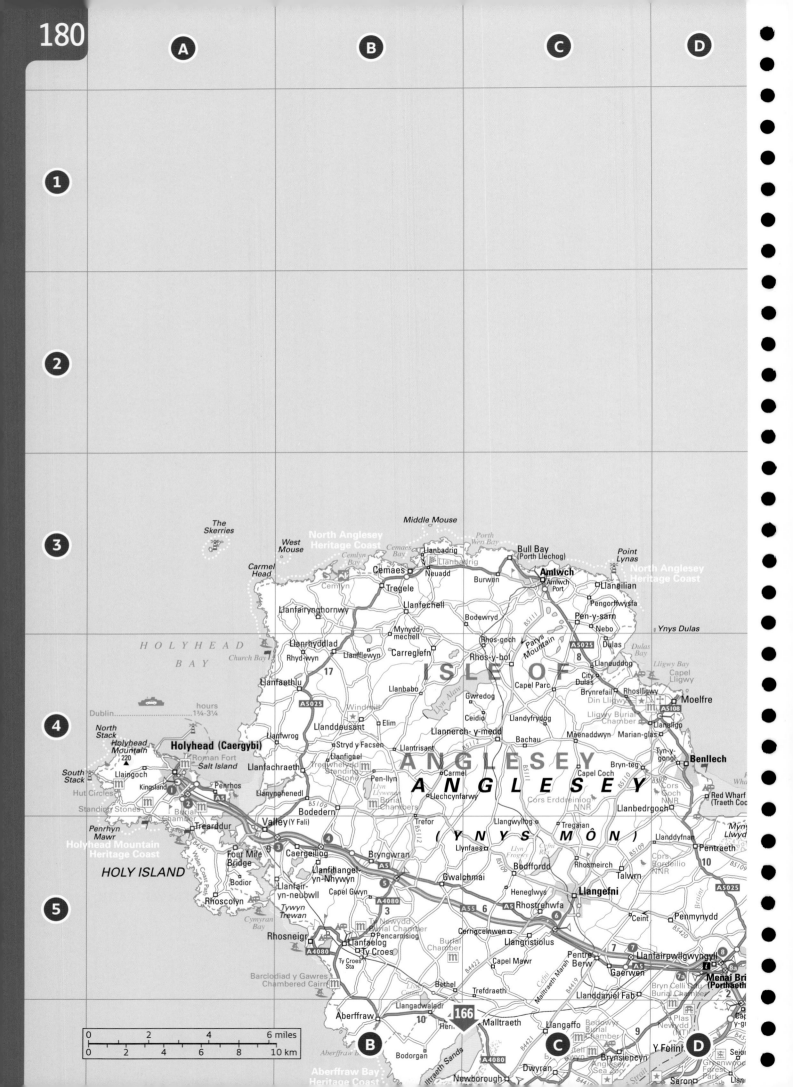

A   B   C   D

1

2

The Skerries

North Anglesey Heritage Coast

Middle Mouse

West Mouse

Porth Wen Bay

Bull Bay (Porth Llechog)

Point Lynas

3

Carmel Head

Cemlyn Bay

Cemaes Bay

Llanbadrig

Llanbadrig

Amlwch

North Anglesey Heritage Coast

Cemlyn

Cemaes

Neuadd

Amlwch Port

Llaneilian

Tregele

Llanfechell

Burwen

Pengorffwysfa

Llanfairynghornwy

Bodewryd

Pen-y-sarn

Mynydd mechell

Parys Mountain

Rhos-goch

Nebo

Ynys Dulas

HOLYHEAD BAY

Llanrhyddlad

Rhyd-wyn

Llanfflewyn

Carreglefn

Rhos-y-bol

A5025

Dulas

Dulas Bay

Church Bay

Llanfaethlu

17

Llanbabo

Gwredog

Capel Parc

City Dulas

Llaneuddog

Lligwy Bay

Capel Lligwy

Ceidio

ISLE OF

Brynrefail

Rhoslligwy

Din Lligwy

Moelfre

Windmill

Llanddeusant

Elim

Llannerch-y-medd

Llandyfrydog

Lligwy Burial Chamber

A5108

Llanaligo

hours 1¾-3¼

Dublin

North Stack

Holyhead Mountain 220

Holyhead (Caergybi)

Roman Fort Salt Island

Llanfwrog

Stryd y Facsen

Llanfigael

Llantrisant

Bachau

ANGLESEY

Maenaddwyn

Marian-glas

Tyn-y-gongl

South Stack

Llaingoch

Kingsland

Penrhos

Llanfachraeth

Tregwehelydd Standing Stone

Pen-llyn

Llyn Llywenan

ANGLESEY

Capel Coch

Bryn-teg

Benllech

Hut Circles

Standing Stones

A5

Burial Chamber

Bodedern

Llynnon Burial Chambers

Llechcynfarwy

Cors Erddreiniog NNR

Llanbedrgoch

Red Wharf (Traeth Coch

Penrhyn Mawr

Trearddur

B4545

Wales Coast Path

Valley (Y Fali)

Trefor

Llangwyllog

Tregaian

Llanddyfnan

Cors Goch NNR

Holyhead Mountain Heritage Coast

HOLY ISLAND

Four Mile Bridge

Bodior

Caergeiliog

Bryngwran

A5

(YNYS MÔN)

Llynfaes

Llyn Frogwy

Cefni Res

Bodffordd

Rhosmeirch

Cors Bodeilio NNR

10

Pentraeth

Mynyd Llwyd

Rhoscolyn

Llanfairyn-neubwll

Llanfihangel-yn-Nhywyn

Capel Gwyn

Gwalchmai

Heneglwys

A55

A5

Rhostrehwfa

Llangefni

Talwrn

A5025

5

Cymyran Bay

Tywyn Trewan

4080

3

Newydd Burial Chamber

Pencarnisiog

Cerrigceinwen

Llangristiolus

7

Llanfairpwllgwyngyll

Rhosneigr

Llanfaelog

Ty Croes

Burial Chamber

A5

Pentre Berw

Gaerwen

Menai Bri (Porthaeth

Ty Croes Sta

B4422

Capel Mawr

Malltraeth Marsh

Bethel

Plas Newydd (NT)

Barclodiad y Gawres Chambered Cairn

Bryn Celli Ddu Burial Chamber

Aberffraw

Llangadwaladr

10

166

Malltraeth

Llangaffo

Bodowyr Burial Chamber

9

Y Felin

Aberffraw Bay Heritage Coast

Bodorgan

Illtraeth Sands

A4080

Dwyran

Brynsiencyn

Anglesey Sea Zoo

Newborough

Greenwood Forest Park

Saron

B   C   D

0   2   4   6 miles
0   2   4   6   8   10 km

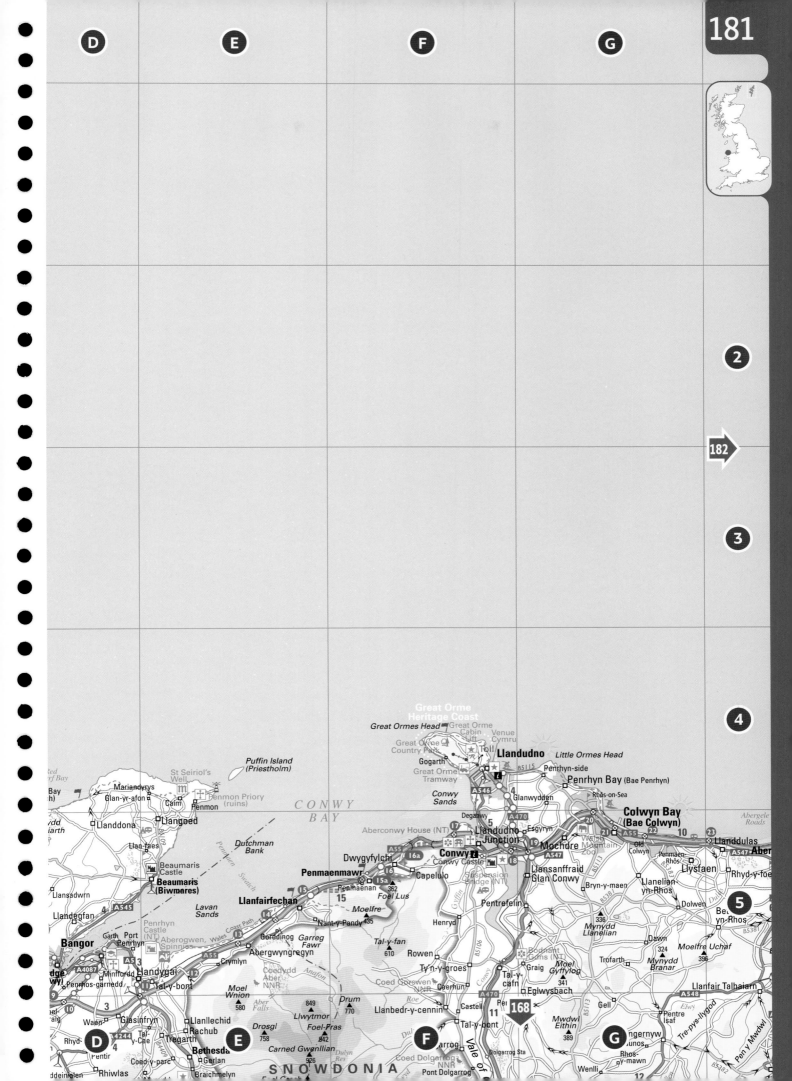

182

168

2

3

4

5

D E F G

Great Orme
Heritage Coast
Great Ormes Head Great Orme
Cabin
Lift
Great Orme Venue
Country Park Cymru
Gogarth Toll Llandudno
Great Orme Little Ormes Head
Tramway B5115
Conwy Penrhyn-side
Sands Penrhyn Bay (Bae Penrhyn)
A546 Rhos-on-Sea
Glanwydden
Degannwy Colwyn Bay
Aberconwy House (NT) Llandudno 5 A470 (Bae Colwyn)
Junction Esgyryn 20 Abergele
CONWY Conwy Mochdre Roads
BAY 16a Welsh 21 A55 22 10 23
Dwygyfylchi Conwy Mountain Old Llanddulas
Conwy Castle 18 Zoo Colwyn Penmaen A547 Aber
Penmaenmawr 16 Capelulo Llansanffraid Rhôs Llysfaen
15a Suspension Glan Conwy Bryn-y-maen Llanelian- Rhyd-y-foel
Penmaen 362 Bridge (NT) B5383 yn-Rhos
15 Foel Lus Pentrefelin Dolwen Be
Llanfairfechan Moelfre y 336 Moelfre Uchaf yn-Rhos 5
14 Nant-y-Pandy 435 Henryd Mynydd Dawn 324 396 B5381
Lavan 13 Gorddinog Garreg Tal-y-fan Llanelian 341 Llanfair Talhaiarn
Sands Fawr 610 Rowen Graig Moel Trofarth
Bangor Garth Port Abergwyngregyn Ty'n-y-groes Gyffylog Mynydd Pentre
Penrhyn Crymlyn Coed Gorswen Bodnant Branar Isaf
A4087 Castle Aberogwen NNR Caerhun Gdns (NT) Gell Tre-pys-llygod
(NT) Spinnies Coed Tal-y- Eglwysbach A548
dge Minffordd Llandygai Aber cafn Per 324 Mwdwl ngernyw Pen y
wy Penrhos-garnedd Tal-y-bont NNR A470 11 Castell Eithin unos Rhos-
9 Moel Aber Drum 770 Llanbedr-y-cennin Tal-y-bont 389 y-mawn Wenlli
10 Wnion Falls 849 168 Dolgarrog Sta 12
D 580 Llwytmor Roe Dul arrog Vale of
Rhyd Tal- Llanllechid Drosgl Foel-Pras E Coed Dolgarrog F G
Pentir y-Cae Rachub 758 Carned Gwenllian Dulyn Pont Dolgarrog
Coed-y-parc Tregarth 926 Res
ddeiniolen Rhiwlas Bethesda Gerlan SNOWDONIA
Braichmelyn

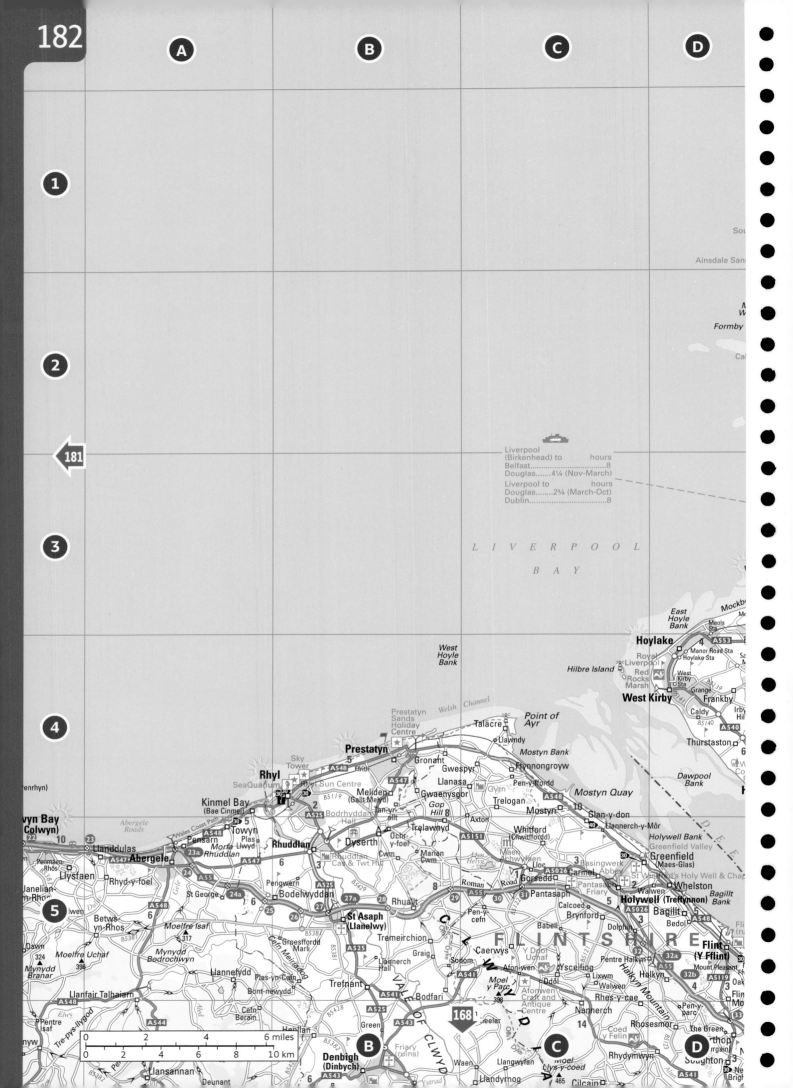

A B C D

1

2

181

3

Liverpool
(Birkenhead) to   hours
Belfast...................................8
Douglas.......4¼ (Nov-March)
Liverpool to   hours
Douglas........2¾ (March-Oct)
Dublin..................................8

L I V E R P O O L

B A Y

West
Hoyle
Bank

East
Hoyle
Bank

Mockb

Meols Sta

Hoylake 4 A553

Manor Road Sta
Hoylake Sta

Royal
Liverpool

Hilbre Island

Red
Rocks
Marsh

West
Kirby
Sta

Grange
B5139

A540

West Kirby Caldy
B5140

Frankby

Irby
Hil

Thurstaston

4

Prestatyn
Sands
Holiday
Centre

Welsh Channel

Talacre

Point of
Ayr

Prestatyn

Sky
Tower

5 7

Gronant

Gwespyr

Mostyn Bank

Ffynnongroyw

Dawpool
Bank

H

Rhyl

SeaQuarium

Rhyl Sun Centre

30 B5119

A548 Ffrith

2

Llanasa

Pen-y-ffordd

Gyrn

Mostyn Quay

Kinmel Bay
(Bae Cinmel)

Meliden
(Gallt Melyd)

Gwaenysgor

Trelogan

Mostyn 18

Glan-y-don

A548

5

Bodrhyddan
Hall

A525

Tan-yr-
allt

Gop
Hill 8

Axton

40

Llannerch-y-Môr

wyn Bay
(Colwyn)

22

10

*Abergele
Roads*

Towyn

Wales Coast Path

30 5

Plas
Llwyd

Pensarn

Rhuddlan

Dyserth

Ochr-
y-foel

Trelawnyd

Whitford
(Chwitffordd)

Maen
Achwyfaen

A5151

Holywell Bank

Greenfield Valley

30

Llanddulas

23

Plas
Rhuddlan

6

Rhuddlan
Cas & Twt Hil

3

Cwm

Marian
Cwm

Lloc

A5026

Gorsedd

Basingwerk
Abbey

3

Greenfield
(Maes-Glas)

D

Abergele

A547

23a

24

Rhyd-y-foel

St George

Bodelwyddan

24a

28

Rhuallt

Roman
Road

A55

Carmel

Pantasaph
Friary

St Winefride's Holy Well & Chap

Whelston

Penmaen
Rhôs

A55

27a

29

Calcoed

31 Pantasaph

Walwen

Bagillt
Bank

Llysfaen

Llanelian-
-yn-Rhos

lwen

5

Betws
yn-Rhos

6

26

27

St Asaph
(Llanelwy)

Pen-y-
cefn

30

Babell

Brynford

Dolphin

5

Holywell (Treffynnon)

A5026

2

Bagillt

Bedol

A548

Fli

Dawn

B5381

Moelfre Isaf

317

Pengwern

Tremeirchion

Graig

Caerwys

Y Dŵol
Uchaf

Ysceifiog

Lixwm

Pentre Halkyn

32

32a

A55

Mount Pleasant

Flint
(Y Fflint)

Moelfre Uchaf

Mynydd
Branar

396

Mynydd
Bodrochwyn

Cefn Meiriadog

Llannerch
Hall

Sodom

Afon-wen

Halkyn

32b

B5119

Oak

Llannefydd

Plas-yn-Cefn

Trefnant

Bodfari

A541

Moel
y Parc

Afonwen
Craft and
Antique
Centre

398

Walwen

Rhes-y-cae

Nannerch

4

3

Fli
Mo

33

Llanfair Talhaiarn

Bont-newydd

A525

A543

168

reeler

14

Coed
y Felin

B5123

Rhosesmor

The Green
thop

Pen-y-
parc

urgain

ntre
af

A544

Cefn
Berain

Henllan

B5428

Green

B

Denbigh
(Dinbych)

Friary
(ruins)

Waen

C

Moel
Llys-y-coed

465

D

Sughton

A541

30

Bri

nyw

B5382

Llansannan

Deunant

Llandyrnog

Cilcain

0   2   4   6 miles
0 2 4 6 8 10 km

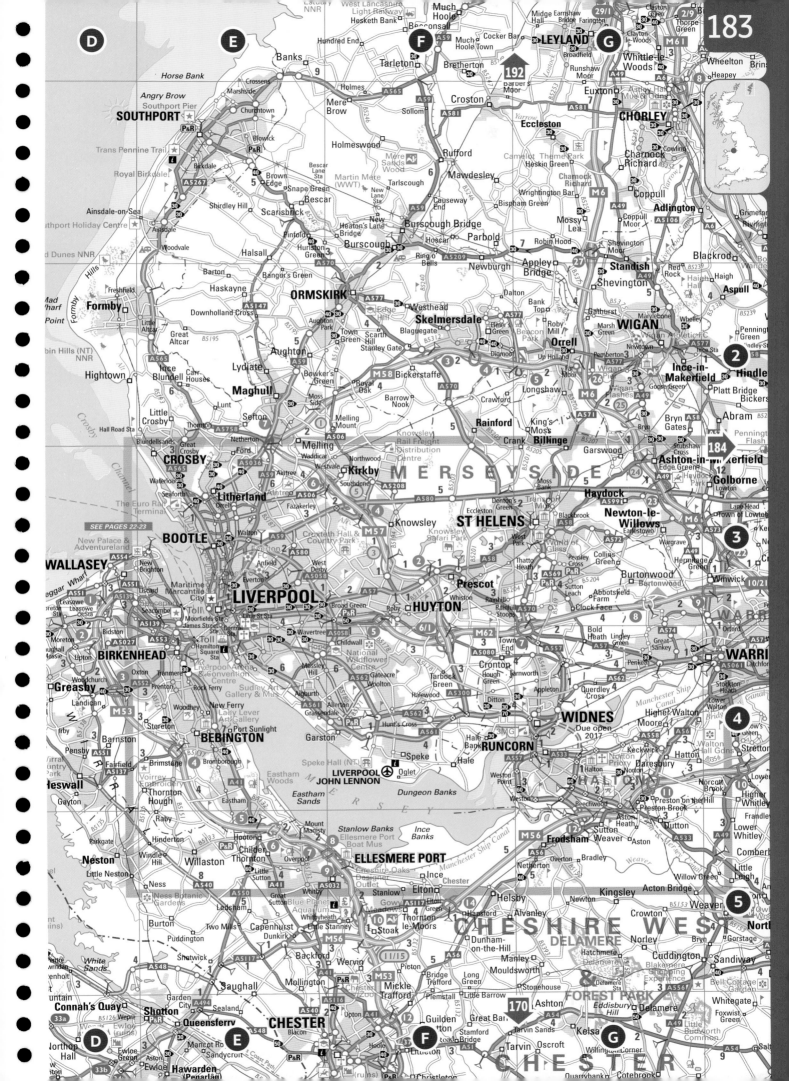

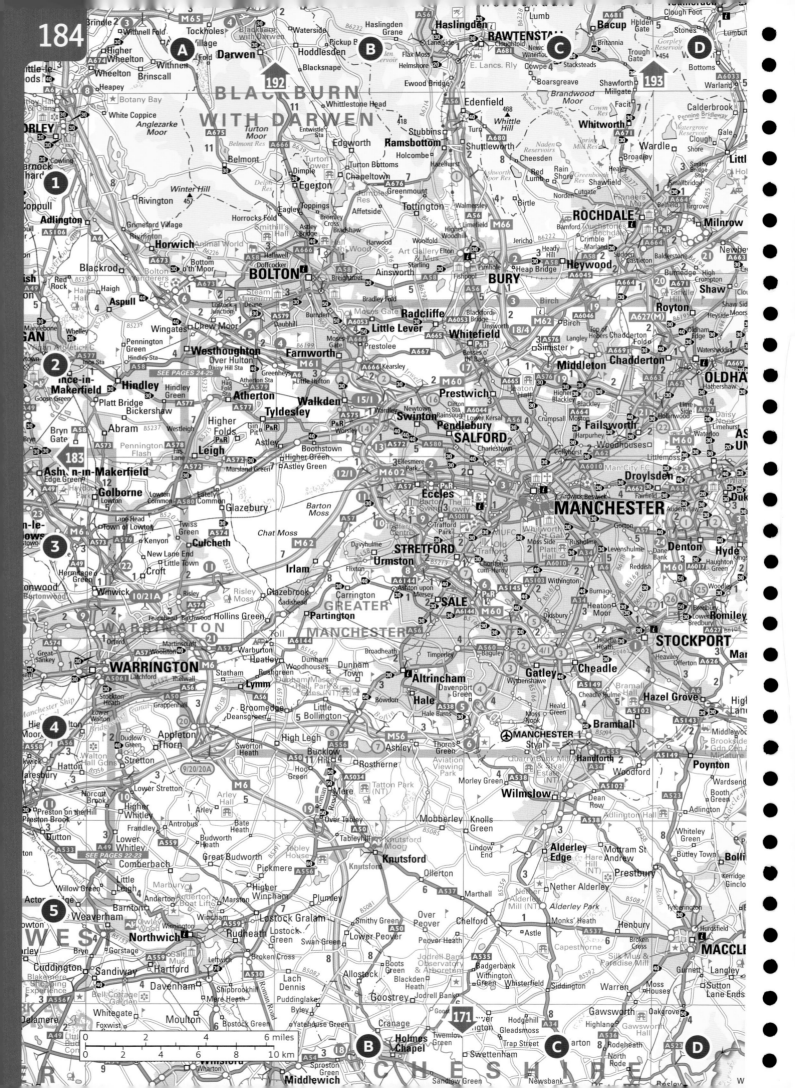

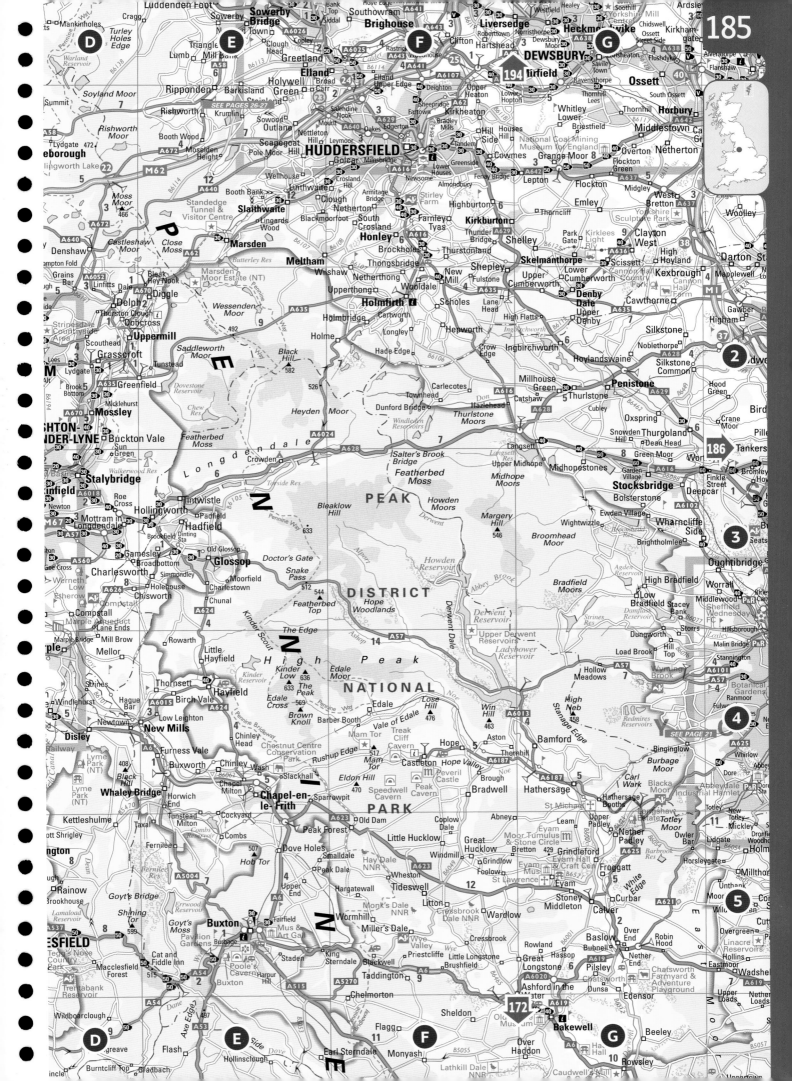

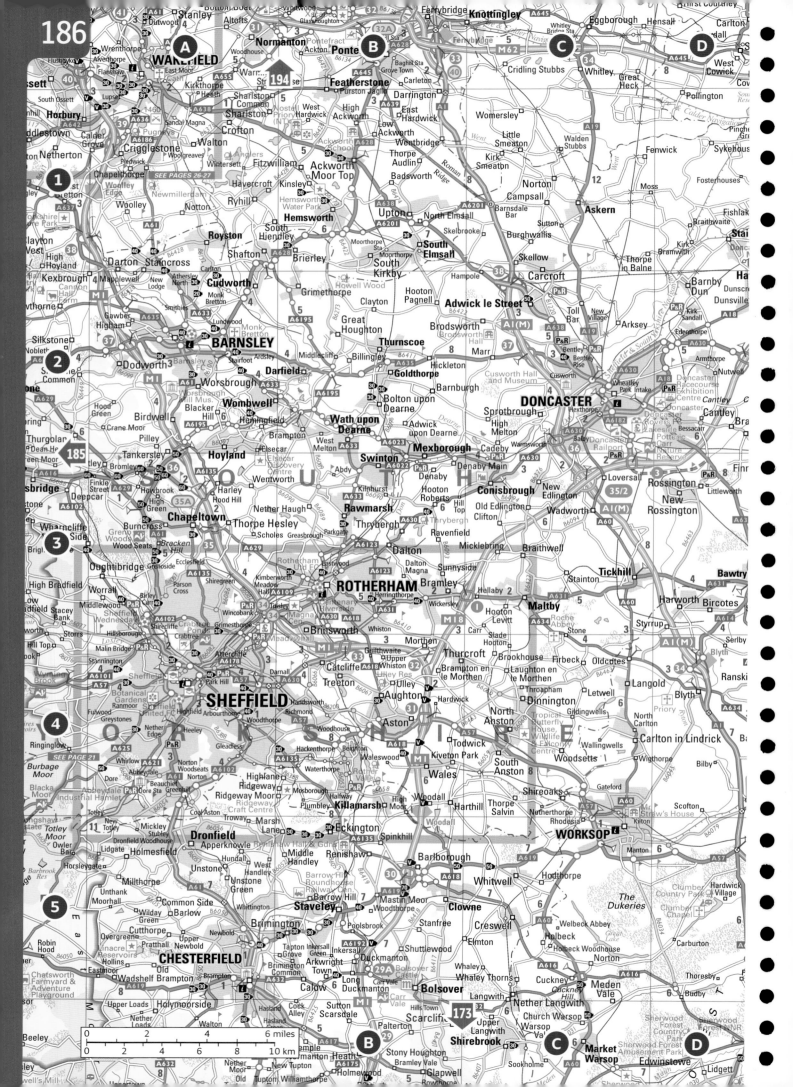

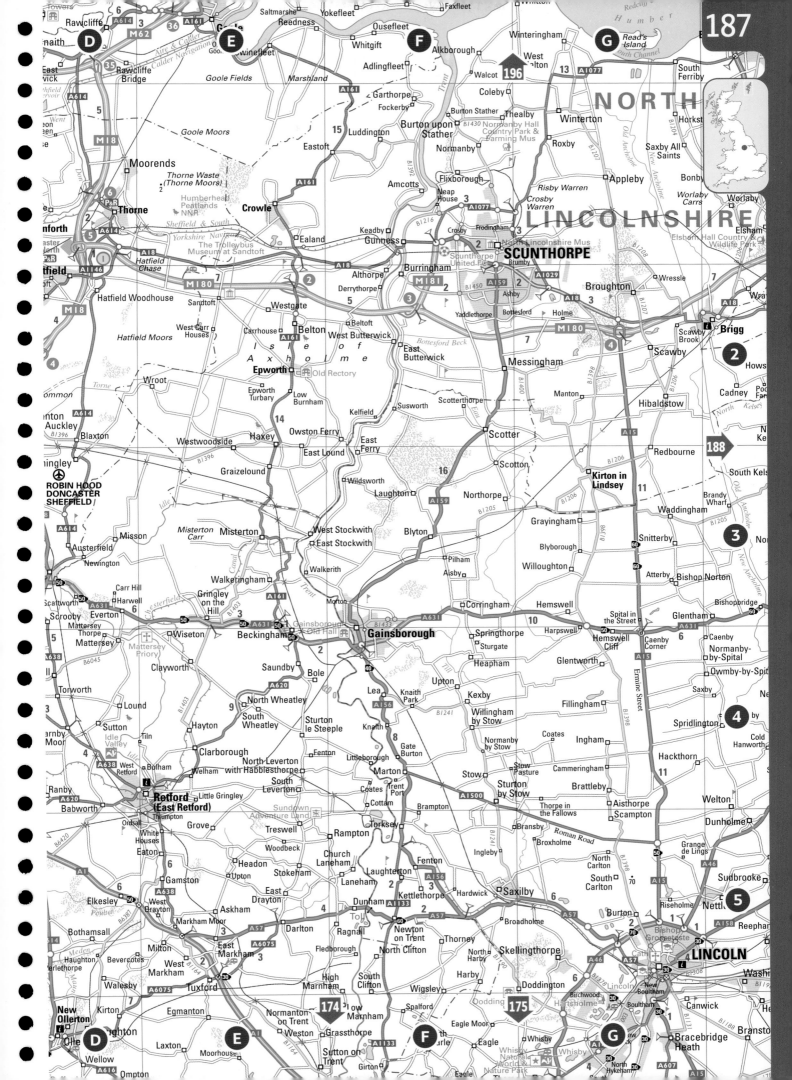

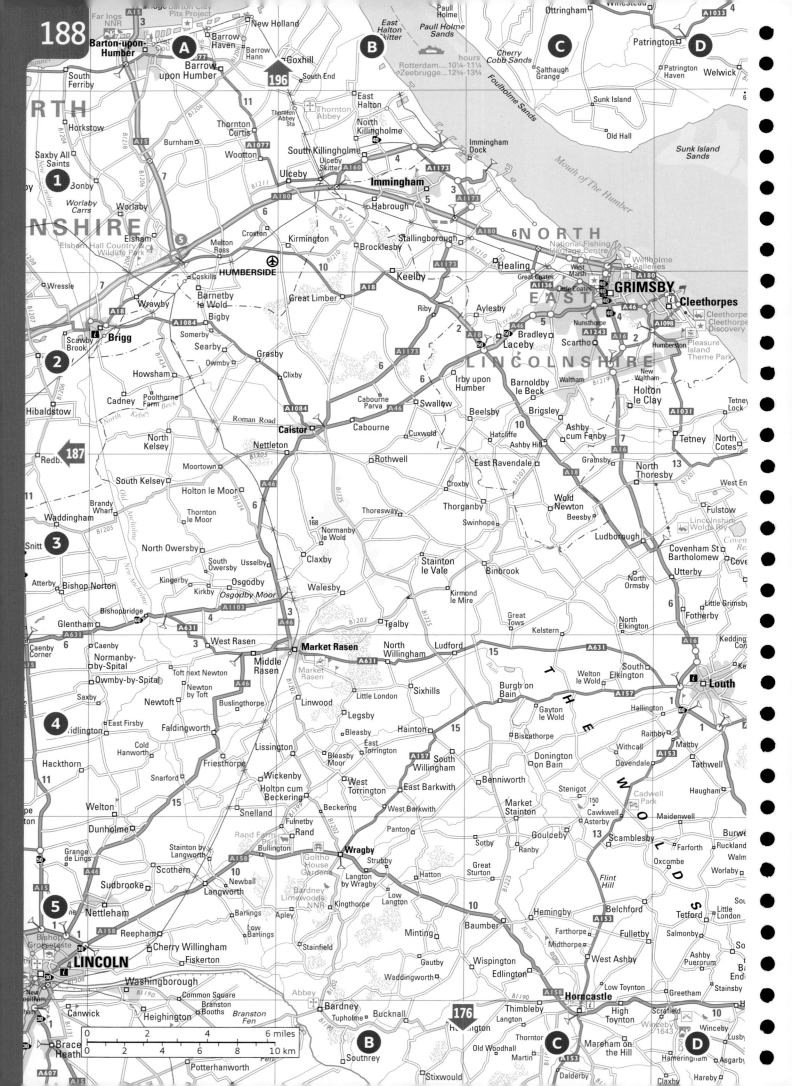

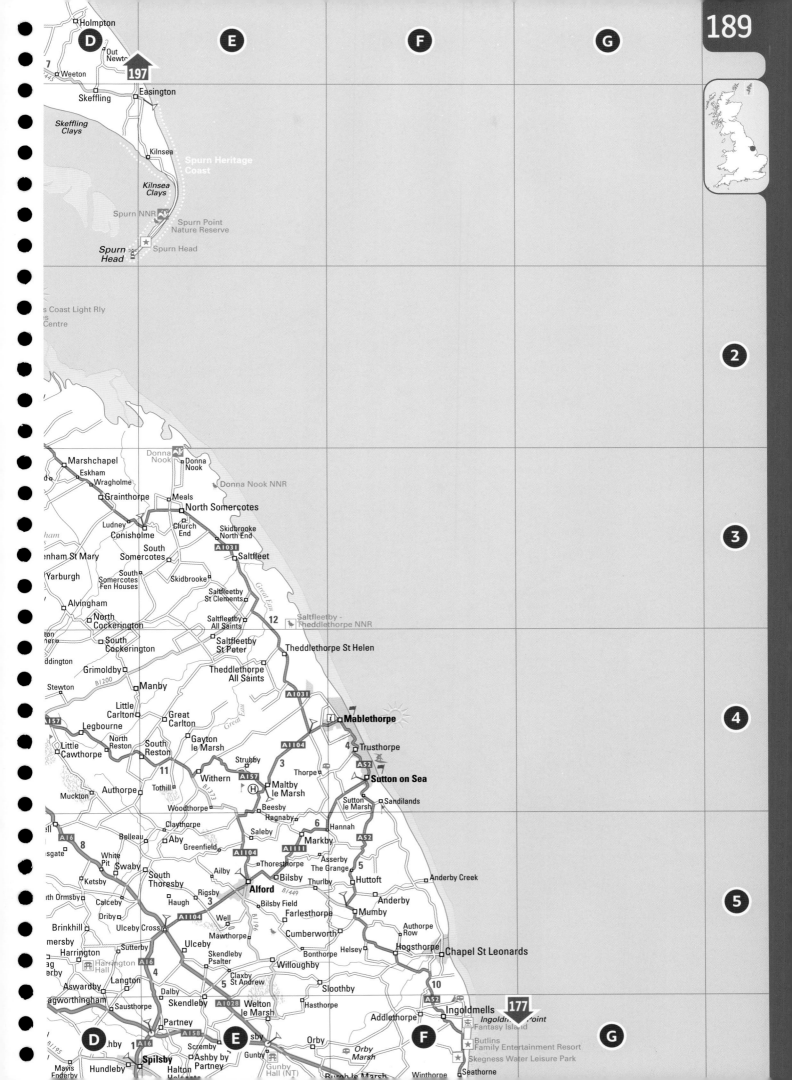

D
E
F
G

Holmpton
Out Newton
7
Weeton
197
Easington
Skeffling

Skeffling Clays

Kilnsea

Spurn Heritage Coast

Kilnsea Clays

Spurn NNR

Spurn Point Nature Reserve

Spurn Head
Spurn Head

2

s Coast Light Rly
Centre

Marshchapel
Donna Nook
Donna Nook
Eskham
Wragholme
Donna Nook NNR
Grainthorpe
Meals
North Somercotes
Ludney
Church End
Skidbrooke North End
Conisholme
3
nham St Mary
South Somercotes
A1031
Saltfleet
Yarburgh
South Somercotes Fen Houses
Skidbrooke
Alvingham
Saltfleetby St Clements
North Cockerington
Saltfleetby All Saints
12
Saltfleetby - Theddlethorpe NNR
ddington
South Cockerington
Saltfleetby St Peter
Grimoldby
Theddlethorpe St Helen
Stewton
B1200
Manby
Theddlethorpe All Saints
Little Carlton
A1031
Legbourne
Great Carlton
A157
Gayton le Marsh
i **Mablethorpe**
4
Little Cawthorpe
North Reston
South Reston
4
Trusthorpe
Strubby
11
3
Thorpe
A52
Muckton
Authorpe
Withern
A157
Sutton on Sea
Tothill
Maltby le Marsh
H
Woodthorpe
Beesby
Sutton le Marsh
Sandilands
Claythorpe
Ragnaby
ll
A16
Belleau
Aby
Saleby
6
Hannah
8
White Pit
Greenfield
A1104
Markby
A52
sgate
Swaby
A1111
Asserby
5
Ketsby
South Thoresby
Ailby
Thoresthorpe
The Grange
Huttoft
Anderby Creek
h Ormsby
Rigsby
Bilsby
Thurlby
5
Calceby
Alford
B1449
Anderby
Driby
Haugh
3
Bilsby Field
Mumby
Brinkhill
A1104
Well
Farlesthorpe
Authorpe Row
mersby
Ulceby Cross
Mawthorpe
Cumberworth
Hogsthorpe
Harrington
Sutterby
Ulceby
Helsey
Chapel St Leonards
erby
Harrington Hall
A16
Skendleby Psalter
Bonthorpe
Langton
Willoughby
Aswardby
4
Claxby St Andrew
Sloothby
10
gworthingham
Sausthorpe
Dalby
5
A52
Skendleby
A1028
Welton le Marsh
Hasthorpe
177
Partney
Ingoldmells
Ingoldmells Point
Addlethorpe
Fantasy Island
D
.hby
1
A16
A158
sby
Scremby
Orby
Butlins Family Entertainment Resort
Spilsby
Ashby by Partney
Gunby
Skegness Water Leisure Park
Hundleby
Halton
Gunby Hall (NT)
Orby Marsh
Burgh le Marsh
Winthorpe
Seathorne

E
F
G

Mavis Enderby

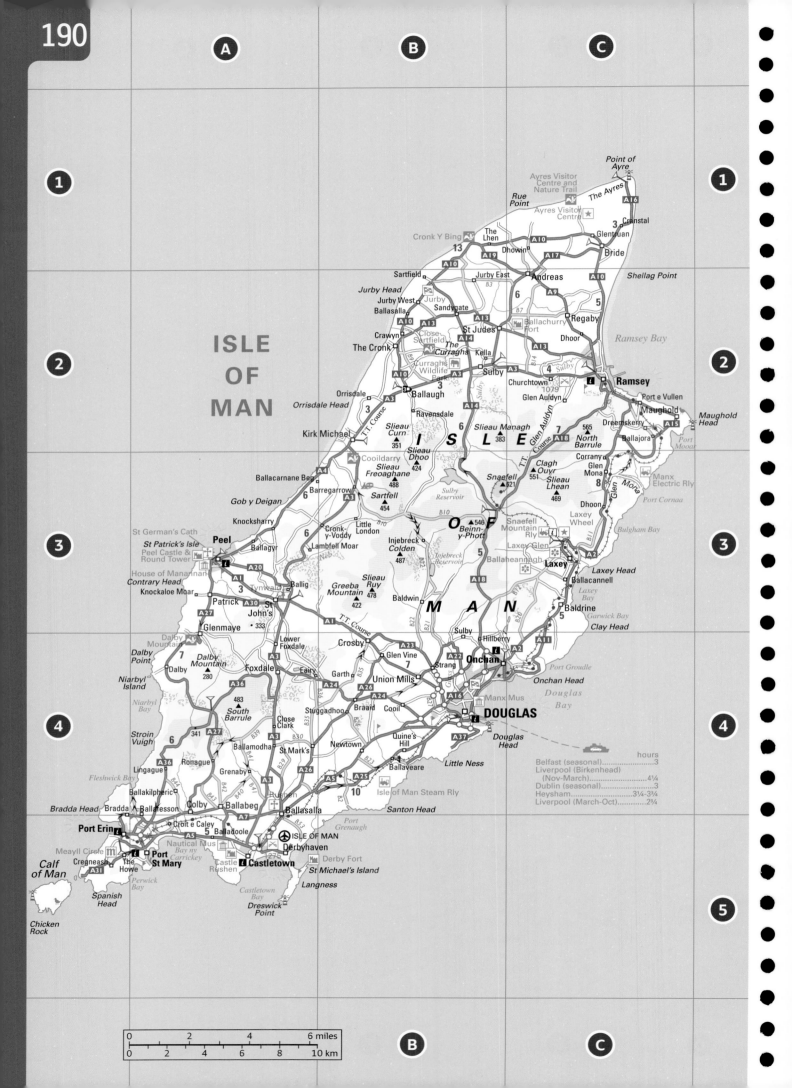

D E F G

199

MORECAMBE BAY

Humphrey Head Point

Great Urswick
Little Urswick
Bardsea
Dalton-in-Furness
Stainton with Adgarl
Newtor
Scales
9 Baycliff
Hawcoat
North Walney NNR
Gleaston
Aldingh
Furness
Abbey
Newbarns
Furness
Mns
A5087
Dendron
A590
North Scale
Roose
Leece
Cartmel Wharf
Dock Museum
Roosecote
Newbiggin
Vickerstown
BARROW-IN-FURNESS
A590
Tummer
Hill Scar
Roosebeck
Lancaster Sound
Biggar
Rampside
Mort
Bank
Sandylands
3
Whi
Oxclif
Isle of
Walney
Roa Island
Foulney Island
Yeoman
Wharf
Heysham
Sheep
Island
Piel
South End
Piel Island
Heysh
Moss
South
Walney
Piel Bar
Middleton
Hilpsford Point

2

Douglas 3¼-3¾hrs

Sunderland
Bank

Sunderland
2
Low
Upp
Cockersand
Abbey
Bernard
Wharf

North
Wharf
Pilling Lane
192
22
Rossall
Point
Lad
Hi
Fisher's Row
Knott End-
on-Sea
Stake Pool
Fleetwood
Pilling
Scronkey
Freeport
Stalmine
Eagland
3
Moor End
A587
A585
Hale Nook
Out Rawcliffe
Rat
Rov
Burn
Naze
Staynall
Cold
Row
Sower Carr
7
Trunnah
Stanah
Hambleton
Larbreck
Toll
Grea
Cleveleys
Thornton
Little
Thornton
Whin Lane End
Little Bispham
Skippool
2
Little
Singleton
Little
Eccleston
Copp
Norbreck
Carleton
A586
A584
A587
Singleton
Bispham
Warbreck
Poulton-
le-Fylde
Thistleton
Elswi
North Shore
Normoss
4
BLACKPOOL
Hardhorn
Newton
Greenhalgh
Esprick
BLACKPOOL
Layton
Staining
Wha
Blackpool Zoo
Weeton
3
Blackpool Tower
Sea Life Centre
Great
Marton
Mythop
Mereside
dlar
Moor
South Shore
South Pier
Blackpool
Great
Plumpton
Wesham
4
Common
Edge
Little
Plumpton
Great
Plumpton
Blackpool Pleasure Beach
Squires
Gate
Westby
Kir
Peel
Lower
Ballam
Wrea Green
Higher
Ballam
Moss
Side
Bryning
Hall Cross
St Anne's
LYTHAM ST ANNE'S
Hey Houses
Ansdell
Saltcotes
Warton
Fairhaven
Lytham
Salter's
Bank
Royal Lytham
& St. Anne's
A584
10
Warton
Bank
Ribble

5
Banks Sands
Ribble
Estuary
NNR
5
Wes
Lancash
Light Ran
Hesketh Ba
Hundred End
Banks
9
Tar
Horse Bank
Crossens
Marshside
y Brow
Mere
Brow
183
Churchtown
SOUTHPORT
P&R
Blowick
Holmeswood
P&R
Trans Pennine Trail
Birkdale
Bescar

D E F G

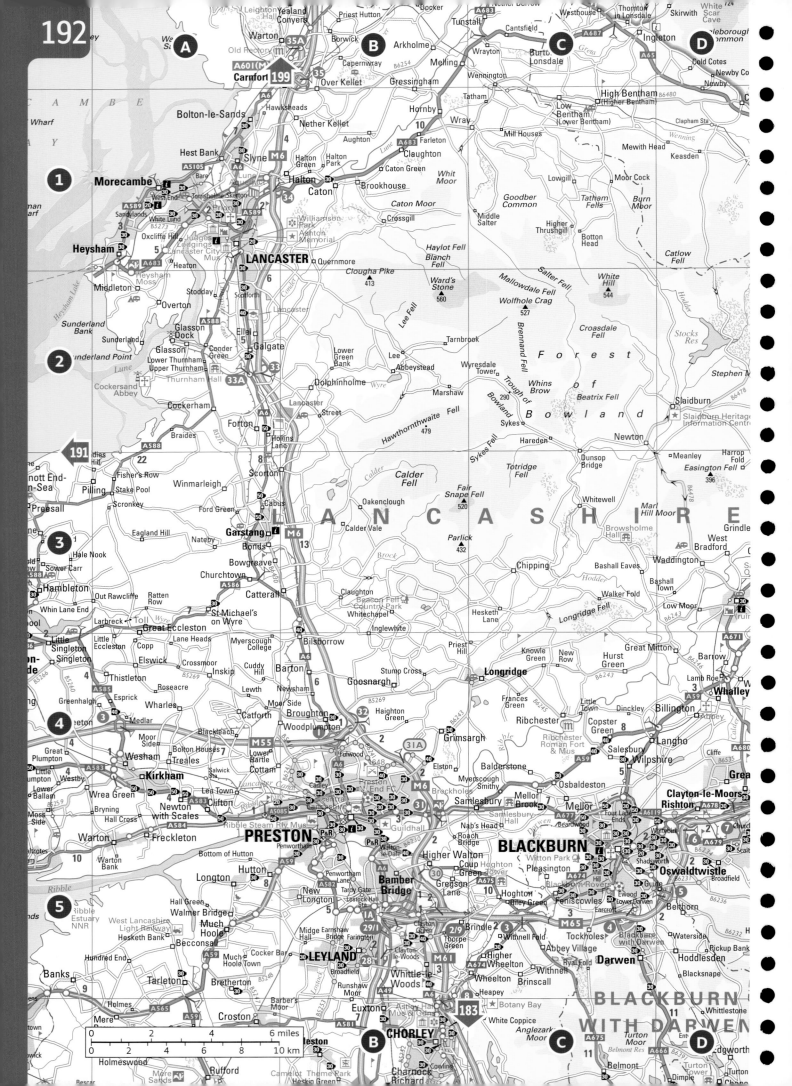

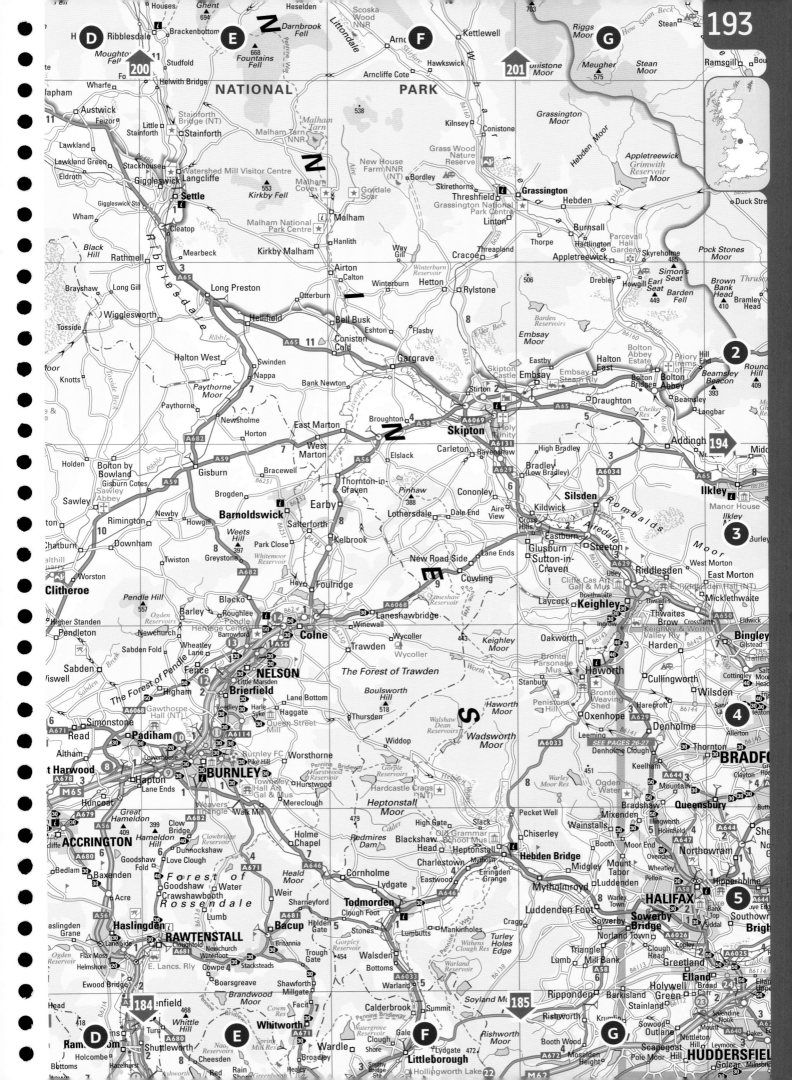

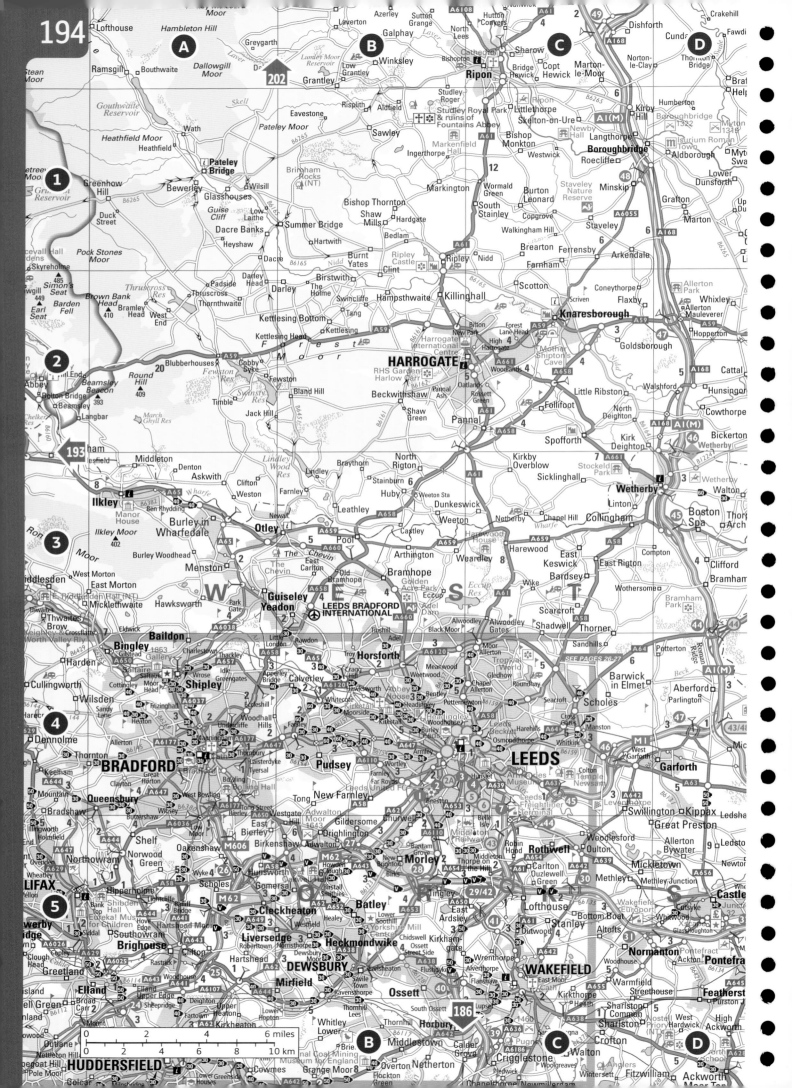

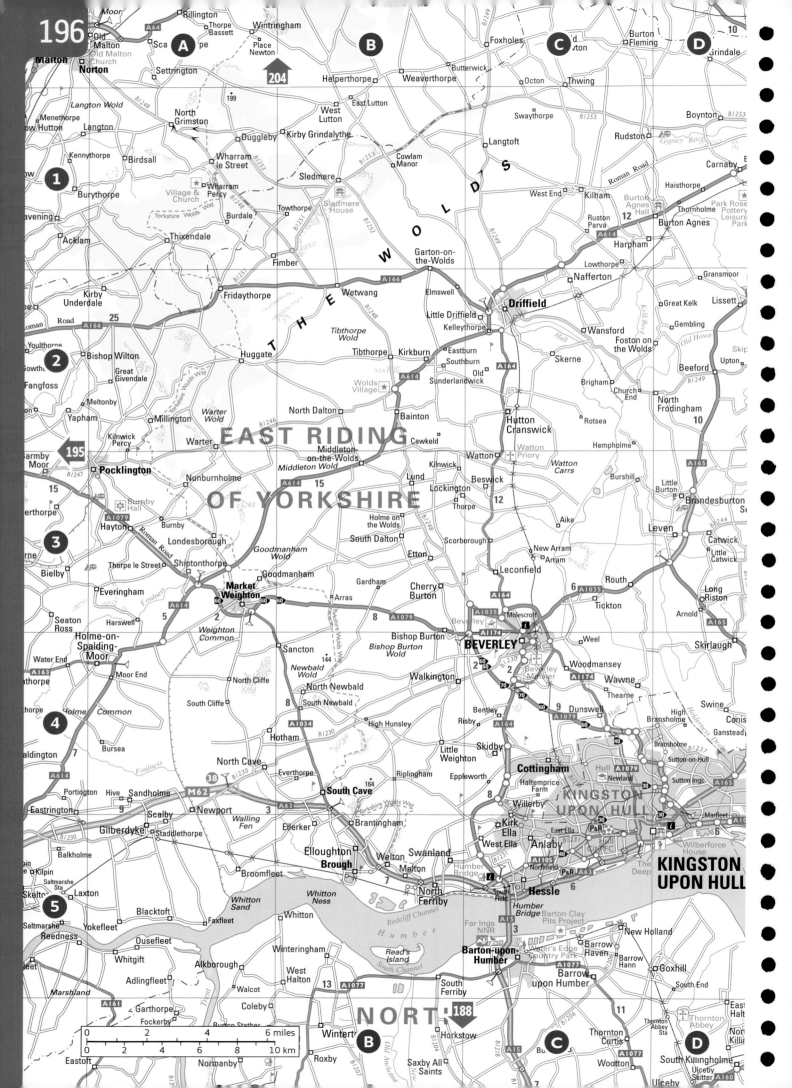

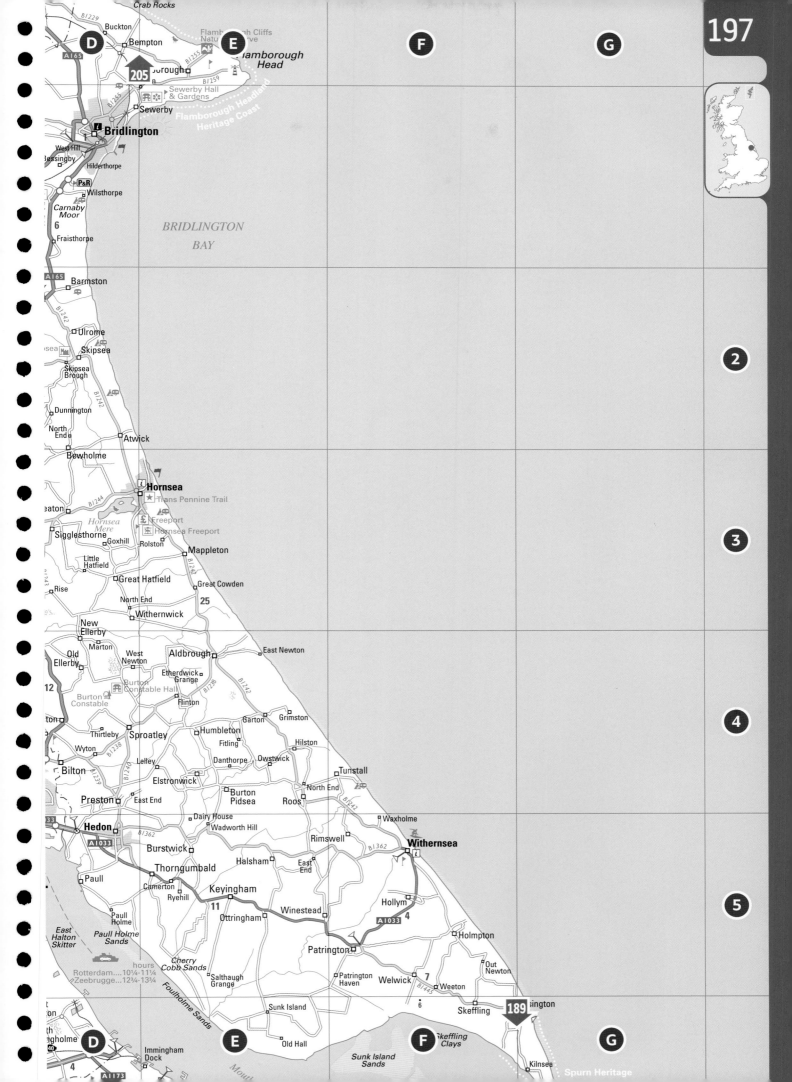

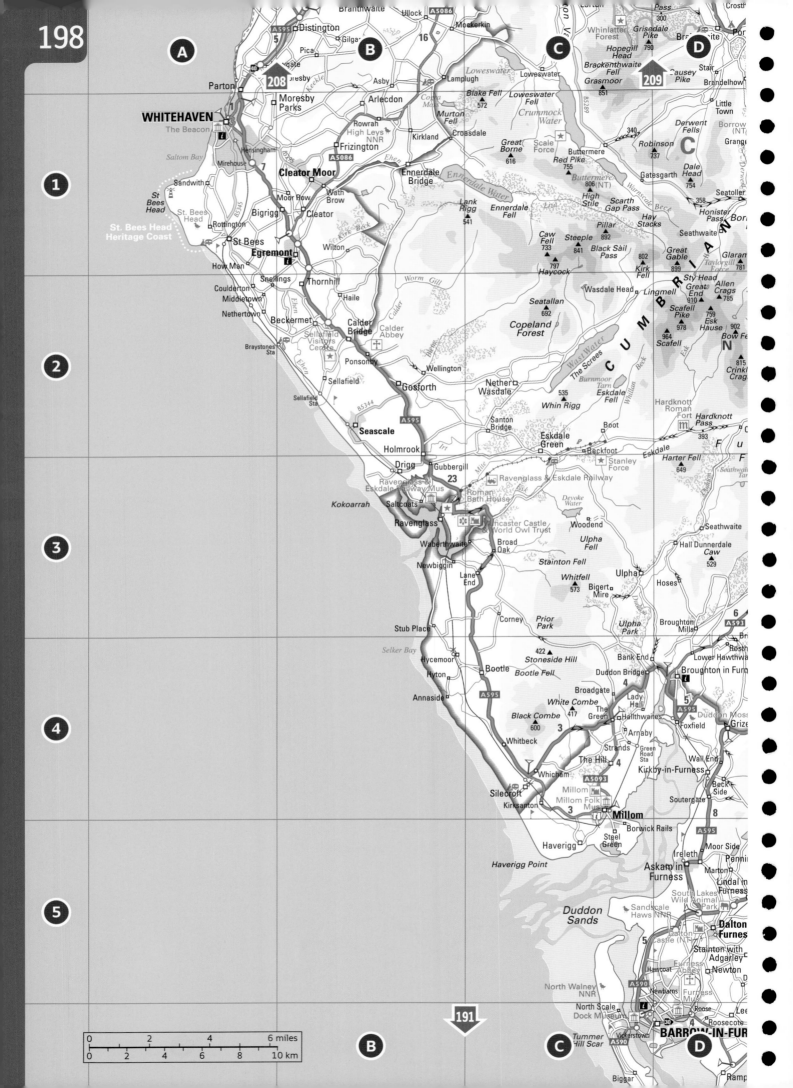

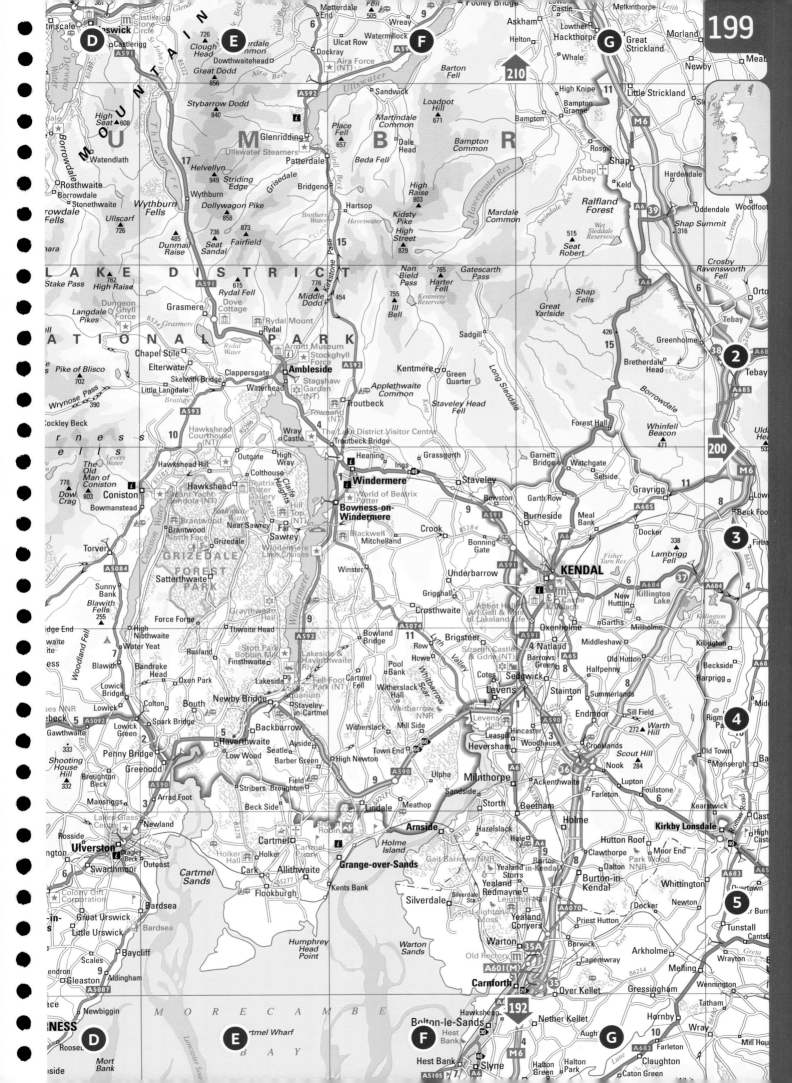

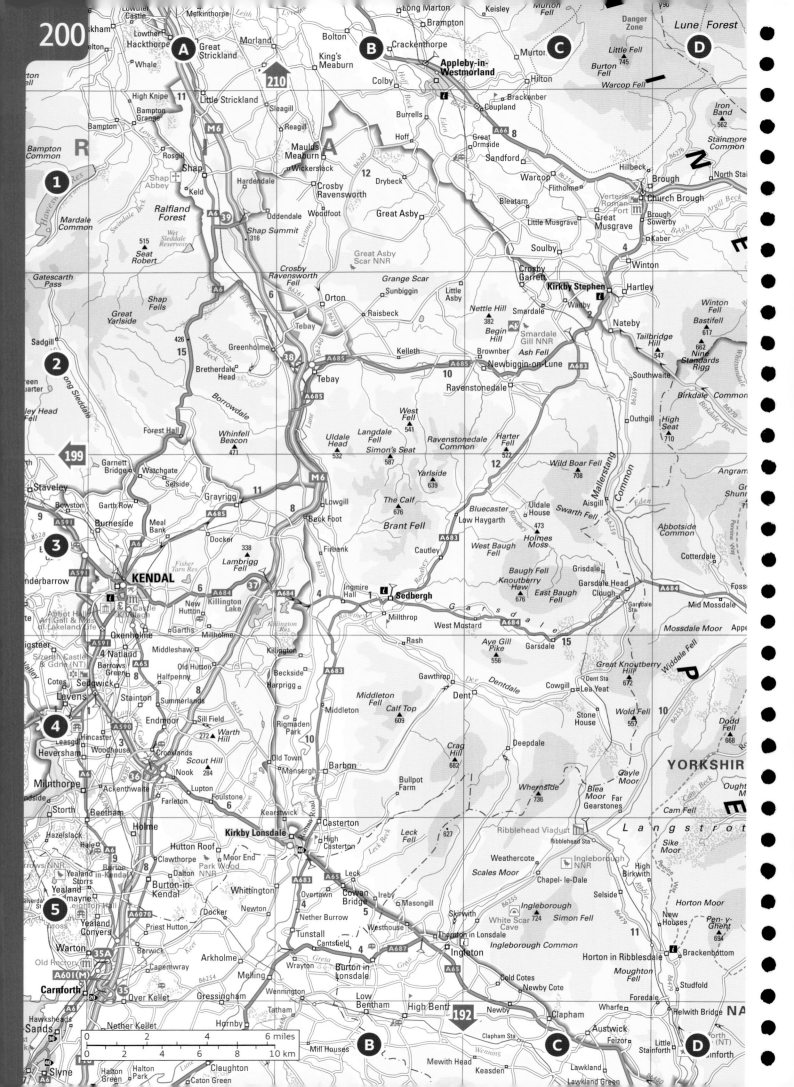

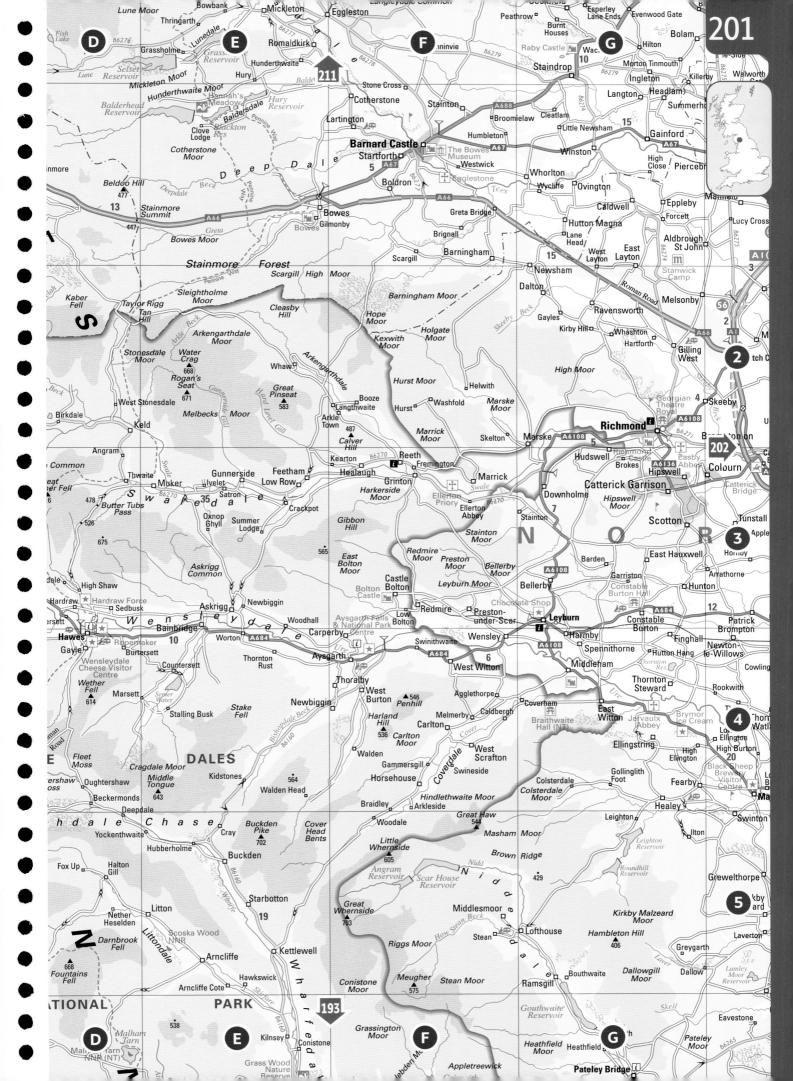

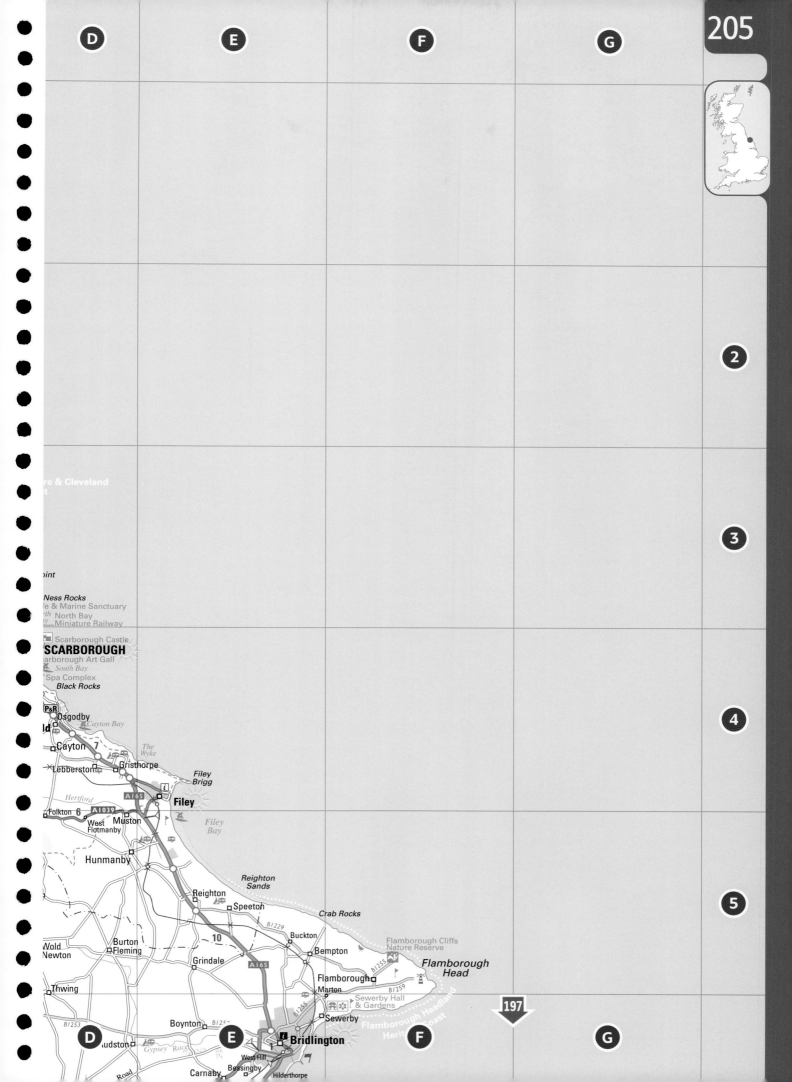

2

3

& Cleveland

point

Ness Rocks
fe & Marine Sanctuary
th North Bay
y Miniature Railway

Scarborough Castle
SCARBOROUGH
arborough Art Gall
South Bay
Spa Complex
Black Rocks

P&R
Osgodby
ld   Cayton Bay
Cayton   7
Lebberston   Gristhorpe
                          Filey
                          Brigg
Hertford   i
A165   i   **Filey**
Folkton 6   A1039
West   Muston
Flotmanby   Filey
                        Bay
Hunmanby

                        Reighton
                        Sands
        Reighton
                Speeton   Crab Rocks
Wold   B1229
Newton   Burton   Buckton
          Fleming   Flamborough Cliffs
    10   Nature Reserve
          Grindale   B1255
          A165   **Flamborough**
Thwing   Flamborough   Head
                    Marton   B1259
                              Sewerby Hall
                              & Gardens
Boynton B1253
B1253   Sewerby
                                        Flamborough Headland
                                        Heri   Coast
dudston   Gypsey Race   197
                    Bridlington
        West Hill
Road   Carnaby Bessingby
                  Hilderthorpe

4

5

197

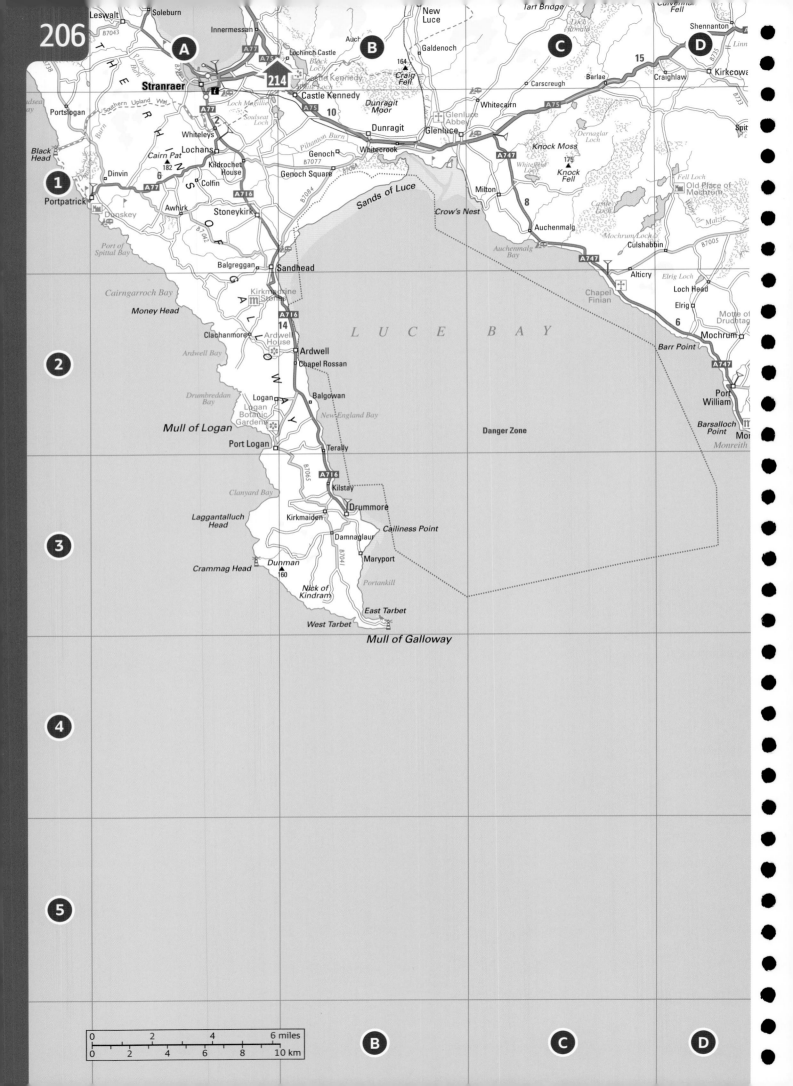

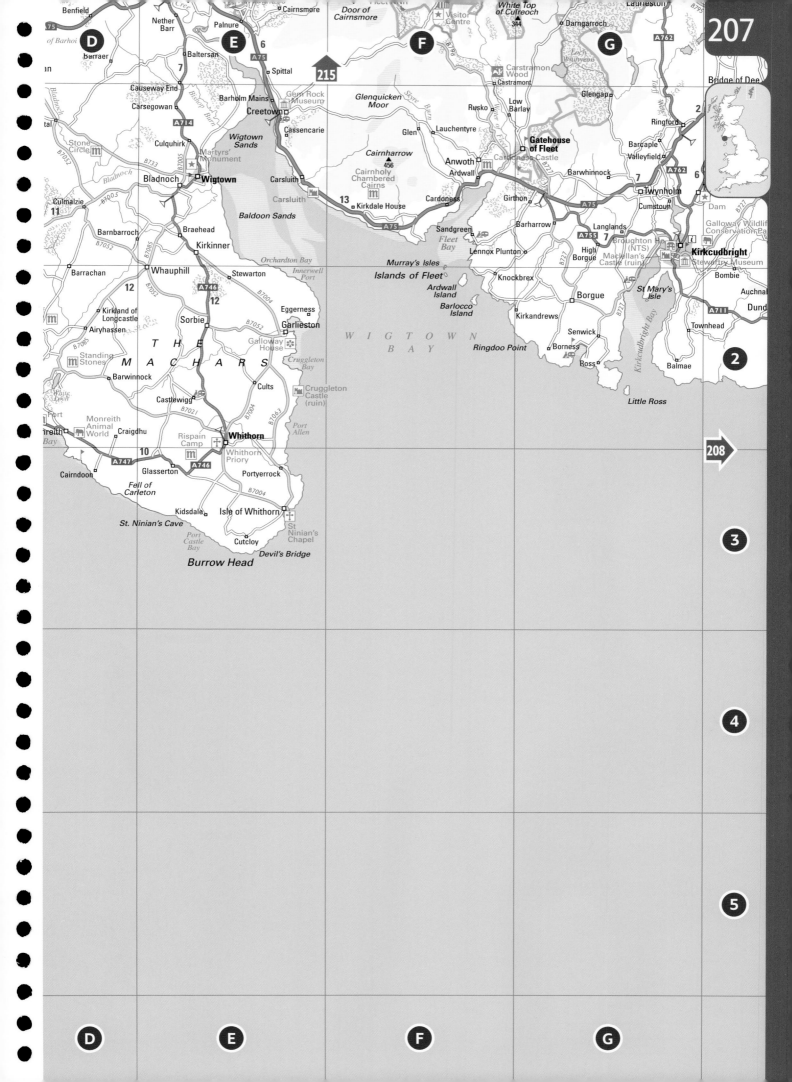

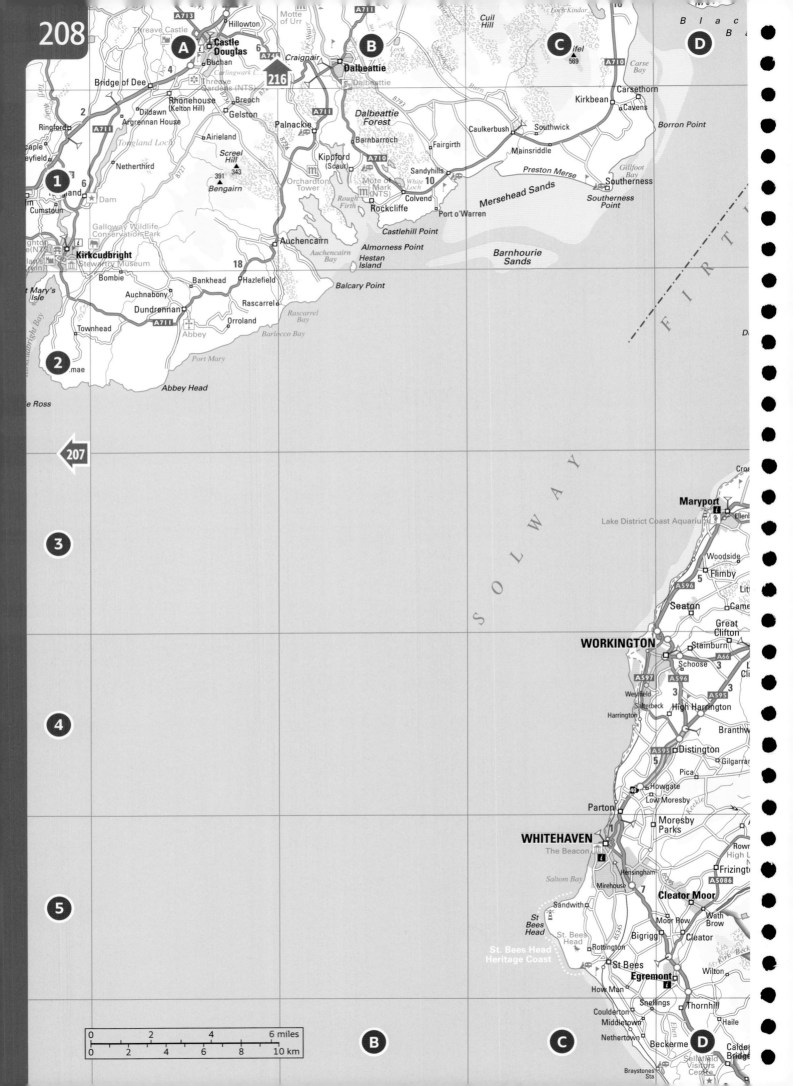

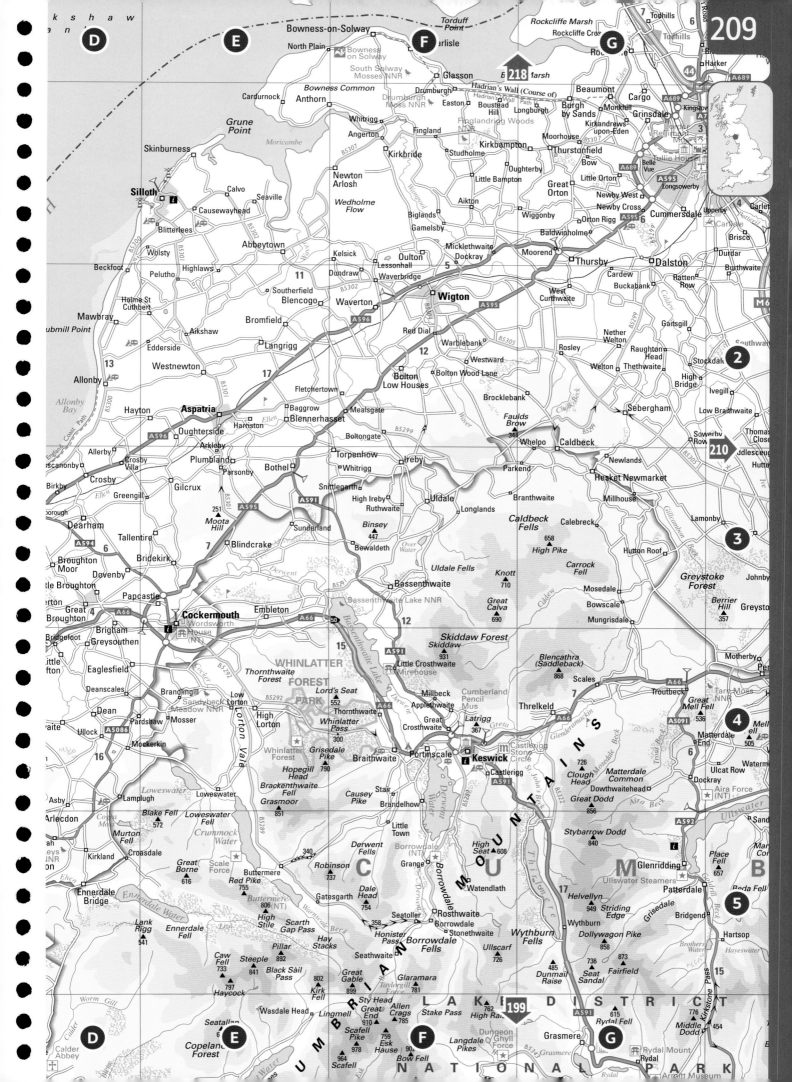

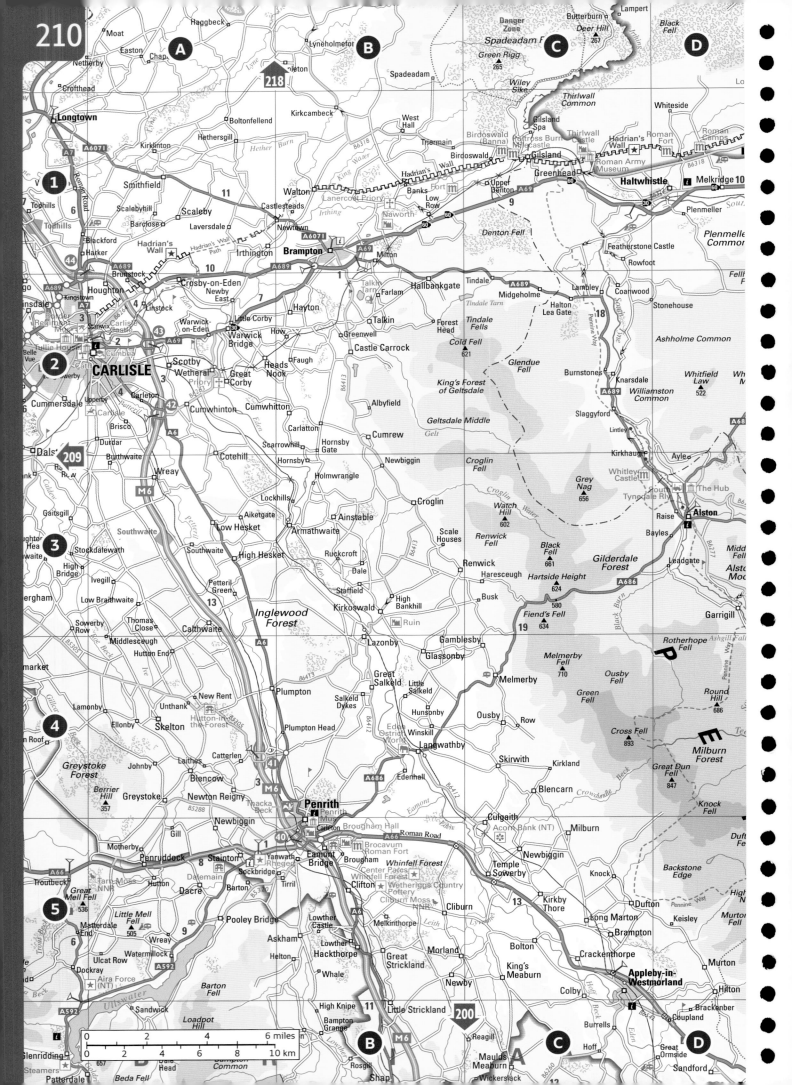

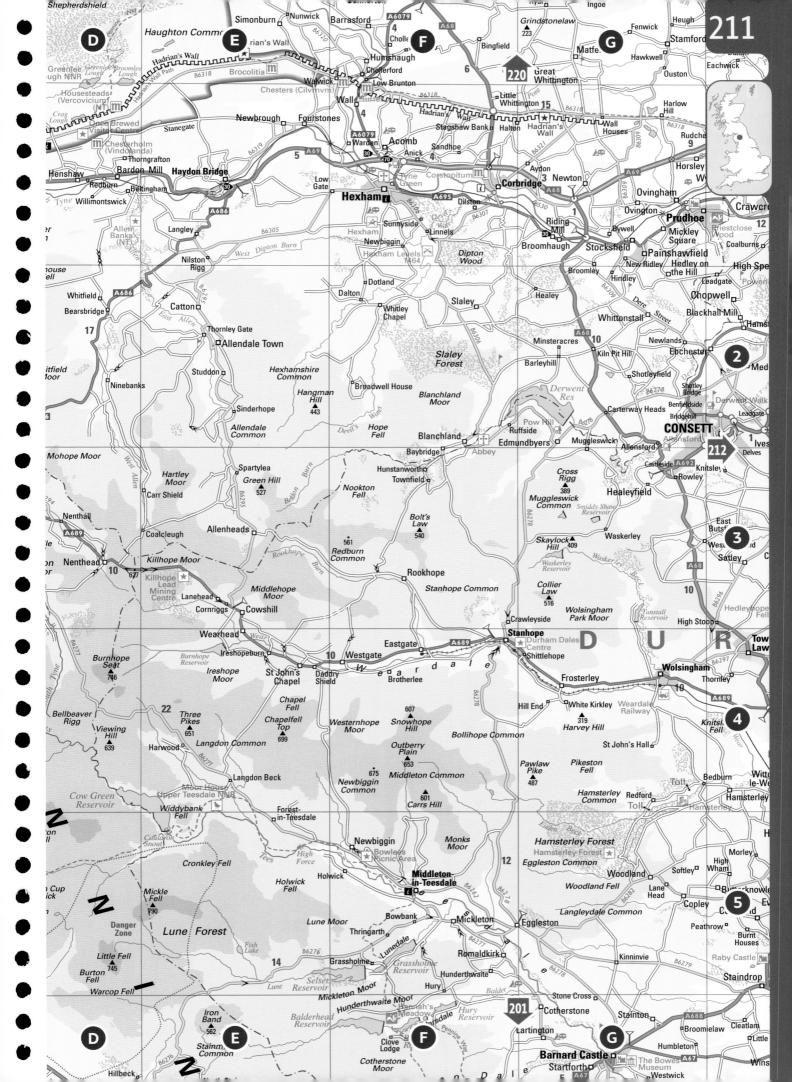

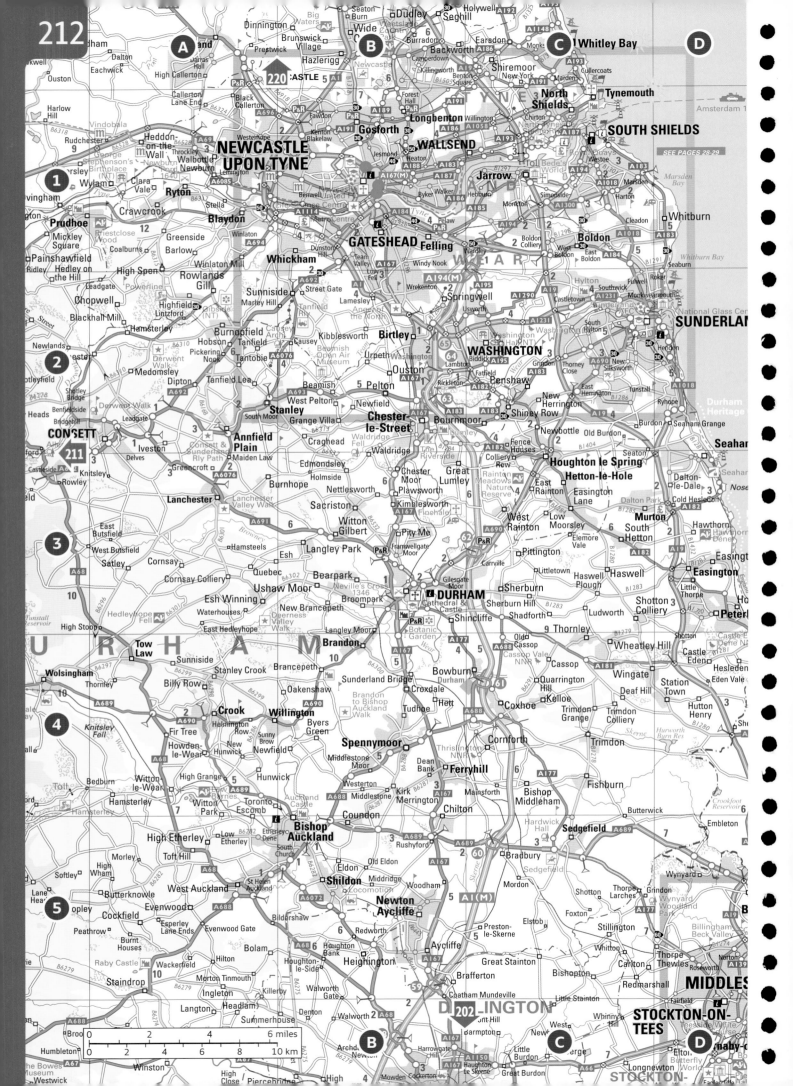

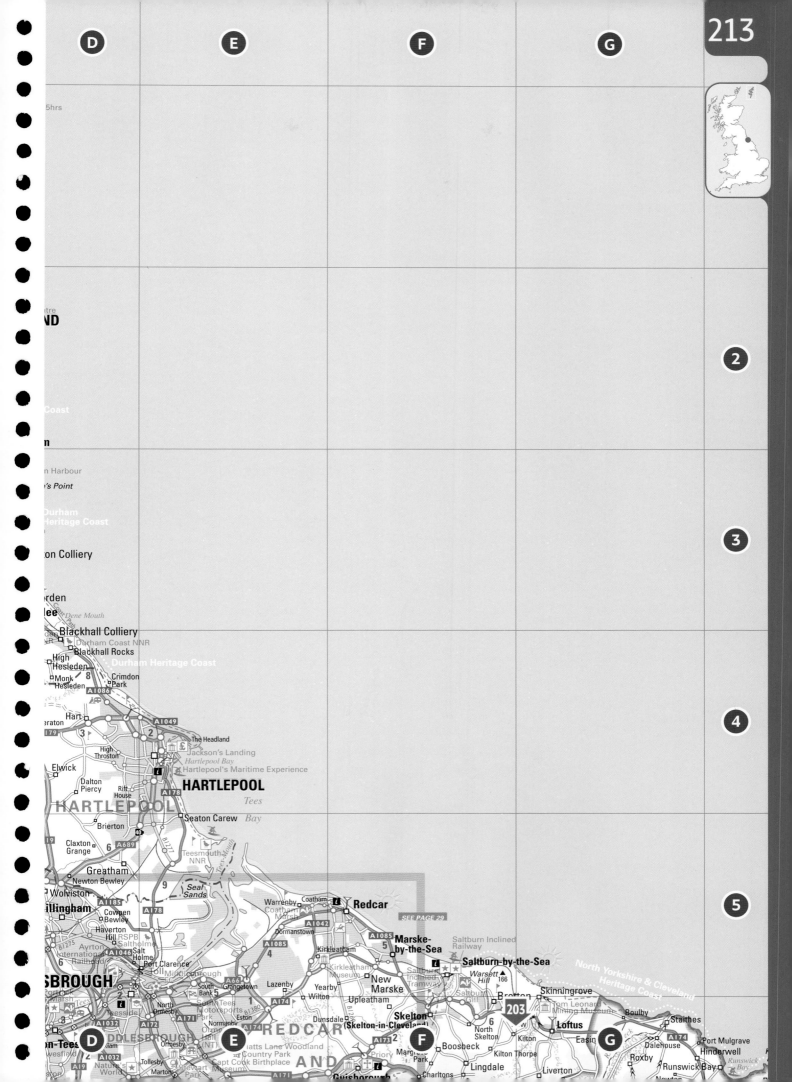

D E F G

2

3

4

5

5hrs

...ND

...Coast

...on

...n Harbour
...e's Point

...Durham
...Heritage Coast

...on Colliery

...rden
...lee

Dene Mouth

Blackhall Colliery
Durham Coast NNR
Blackhall Rocks

High
Hesleden

Monk
Hesleden

Crimdon
Park

Durham Heritage Coast

A1086

Hart

A1049

eraton

A179

3

High
Throston

2

The Headland

Jackson's Landing

Hartlepool Bay

Hartlepool's Maritime Experience

Elwick

Dalton
Piercy

Rift
House

A178

HARTLEPOOL

Tees

HARTLEPOOL

Seaton Carew

Bay

Brierton

A19

40

B1277

Claxton
Grange

6

A689

Greatham

Teesmouth
NNR

Newton Bewley

Wolviston

9

Seal
Sands

A1185

Cowpen
Bewley

A178

Warrenby Coatham

Coatham

Redcar

illingham

Haverton
Hill RSPB

A1042

Coatham
Marsh

B1275

Ayrton

A1046

Salt
Holme

Port Clarence

Dormanstown

A1085

Marske-
by-the-Sea

Saltburn Inclined
Railway

6

Railroad

Middlesbrough

A66

Lazenby

A1085

5

Kirkleatham

Saltburn Inclined
Tramway

Saltburn-by-the-Sea

North Yorkshire & Cleveland
Heritage Coast

SBROUGH

Marsh

Tees

North
Ormesby

A171

A174

Wilton

New
Marske

Warsett
Hill

166

Saltburn
Gill

Skinningrove

Grangetown

4

Yearby

Upleatham

Brotton

203

Tom Leonard
Mining Museum

Boulby

Staithes

D

Eston

B1380

A174

Skelton

North
Skelton

Loftus

G

on-Tees

DDLESBROUGH

am

Normanby

Orme

Hall

E

REDCAR

Dunsdale

Margrove
Park

Skelton
(Skelton-in-Cleveland)

6

F

Boosbeck

Kilton

Kilton Thorpe

Easin

A174

Dalehouse

Port Mulgrave

Hinderwell

vesfield

A1032

Nature's
World

Marton

Tollesby

Watts Lane Woodland
Country Park

Capt Cook Birthplace
Museum

AND

Priory

A171

Charltons

Lingdale

Liverton

Roxby

Runswick Bay

Runswick
Bay

Guisborough

Newton

SEE PAGE 29

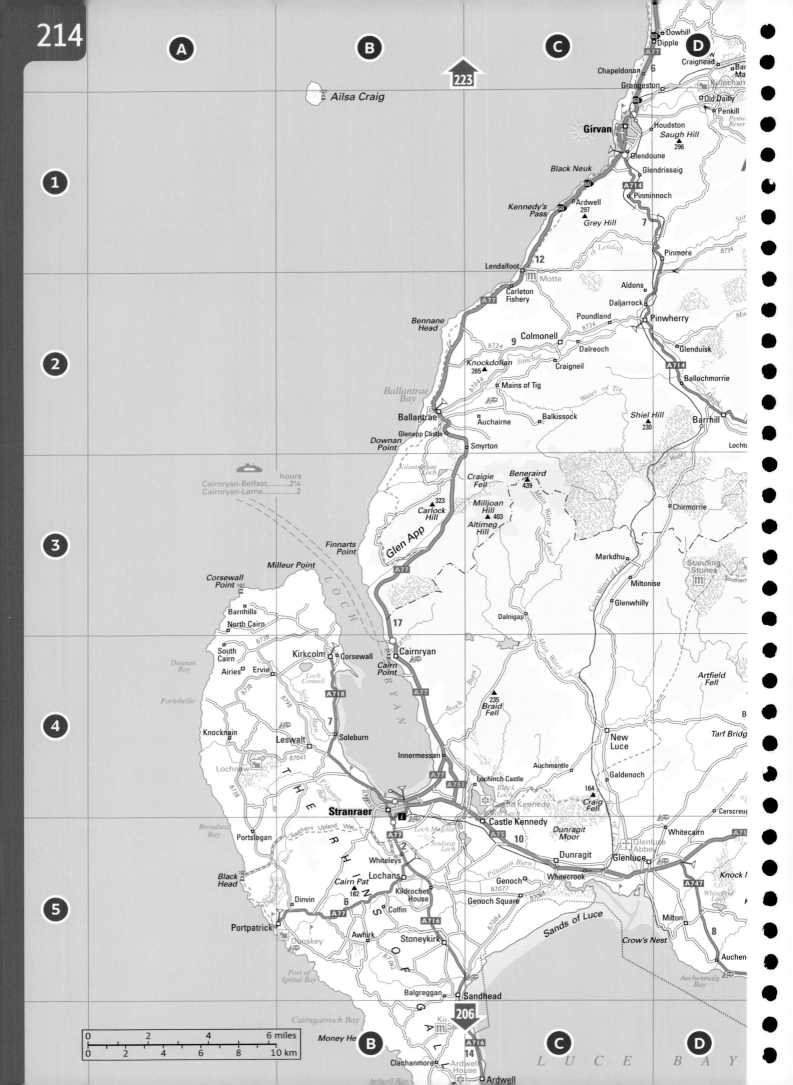

A B C D

223

Ailsa Craig

Chapeldonan
Grangeston
Dowhill
Dipple
Craighead
Old Daily
Penkill

Girvan
Houdston
Saugh Hill
296

Black Neuk
Glendoune
Glendrissaig

Kennedy's
Pass
Ardwell
297
Grey Hill

Pinminnoch

Pinmore

Lendalfoot
12
Motte

Carleton
Fishery
Aldons
Daljarrock

Poundland
Pinwherry
Bennane
Head

Colmonell
9
Dalreoch
Glenduisk

Knockdolian
265
Craigneil
Ballochmorrie

Ballantrae
Bay
Mains of Tig

Ballantrae
Auchairne
Balkissock
Shiel Hill
230
Barrhill

Glenapp Castle
Downan
Point
Smyrton

Craigie
Fell
Beneraird
439

Kilantringan
Loch

Carlock
Hill
323

Milljoan
Hill
403
Altimeg
Hill

Chirmorrie

hours
Cairnryan-Belfast..........2¼
Cairnryan-Larne.................2

Finnarts
Point

Glen App

Markdhu

Standing
Stones

Milleur Point
A77

Miltonise

Glenwhilly

Corsewall
Point
Barnhills
North Cairn

17

Dalnigap

South
Cairn
Airies
Ervie

Kirkcolm
Corsewall

Cairnryan
Cairn
Point

Artfield
Fell

Dounan
Bay

Loch
Connell

A718

235
Braid
Fell

Tarf Bridg

Portobello
B798

7
Soleburn

Knocknain

Leswalt
B7043

Innermessan

New
Luce

Auchmantle

Galdenoch

Lochnaw

Lochinch Castle

164
Craig
Fell

Carscreug

Castle Kennedy

Stranraer

A751
Black
Loch

White Loch

Castle Kennedy
Dunragit
Moor
Whitecairn
A75

Broadsea
Bay
Portslogan

Southern Upland Way

A77
Loch Magillie
Soulseat
Loch
A75
10
Dunragit
Glenluce Abbey
Glenluce

Whiteleys
Lochans
Genoch
Whitecrook
Knock
A747

Black
Head
Dinvin

Cairn Pat
182
6
Kildrochet
House
Colfin

Genoch Square
B7077
B7084
Milton

Sands of Luce
Whitefield
Loch
8

Portpatrick
Dunskey
Awhirk
Stoneykirk
A716

Crow's Nest

Port of
Spittal Bay

Balgreggan
Sandhead

Cairngarroch Bay
206

Auchenmalg
Bay

Money He
B
A716
14
C
D

Clachanmore
Ardwell
House
Ardwell

L U C E   B A Y

0   2   4   6 miles
0   2   4   6   8   10 km

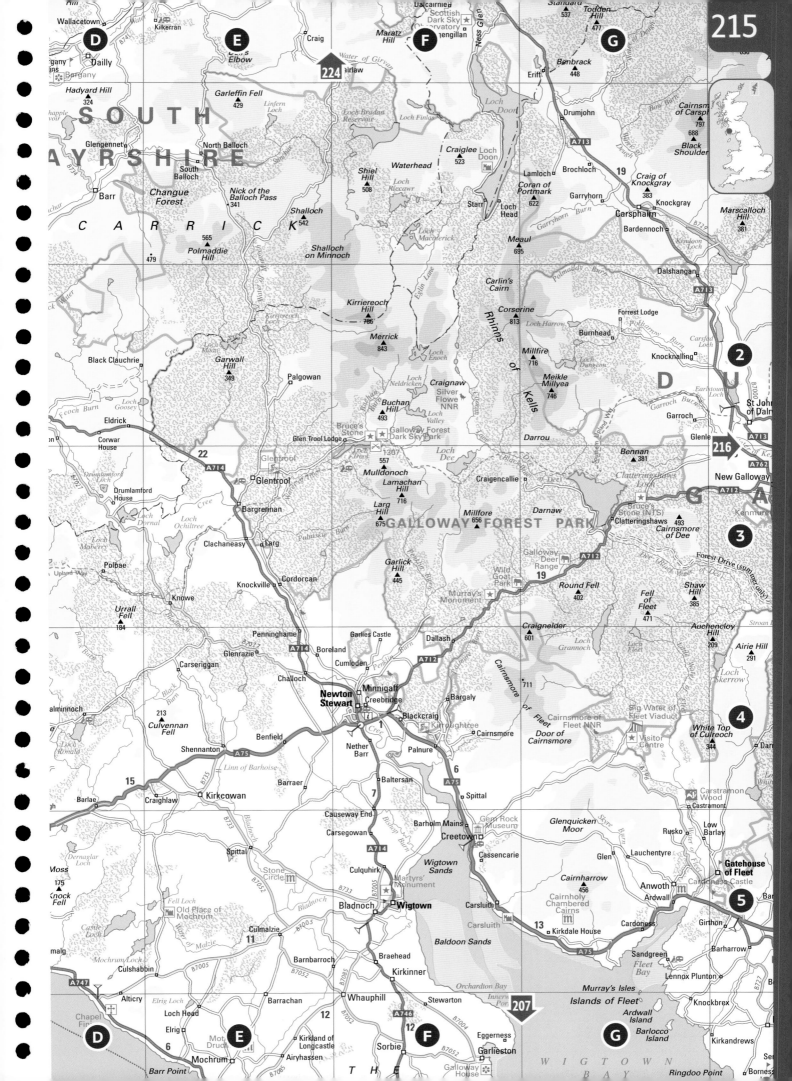

D
Wallacetown
Kilkerran
Craig
B741

E
Dell's Elbow
Craig

F
Dalcairnie
Scottish Dark Sky Observatory
Chengillan
Maratz Hill
★

G
Standard 537
Todden Hill 477
Benbrack 448
Erift
224

Dailly
Bargany

Garleffin Fell 429
Linfern Loch
Fairlaw
irlaw

Water of Girvan

Loch Doon
Drumjohn
A713
Cairnsm of Carspi 797
688 Black Shoulder
650

Hadyard Hill 324

S O U T H

Loch Bradan Reservoir

Waterhead

Craiglee 523
Loch Doon
Lamloch
Brochloch
Coran of Portmark 622
Garryhorn
Craig of Knockgray 383
19
Knockgray
Marscalloch Hill 381

A Y R S H I R E

Glengennet
North Balloch
South Balloch
Loch Finlas
Shiel Hill 508
Loch Riecawr
Starr
Loch Head
Meaul 695
Garryhorn Burn
Carsphairn
Bardennoch
Keldoon Loch

Barr
Changue Forest
Nick of the Balloch Pass 341
Shalloch 542

C A R R I C K

Polmaddie Hill 565
479
Shalloch on Minnoch
Loch Macaterick
Carlin's Cairn
Polmaddy Burn
Dalshangan
A713

Kirriereoch Hill 766
Corserine 813
Loch Harrow
Forest Lodge
Polharrow Burn
Carsfad Loch

Merrick 843
Loch Enoch
Millfire 716
Burnhead
Loch Dungeon
Knocknalling
2

Rhinns of Kells

Black Clauchrie
Garwall Hill 349
Loch Moan
Loch Neldricken
Craignaw Silver Flowe NNR
Meikle Millyea 746
Earlstoun Loch
B7000
St Joh of Daln

Cree
Palgowan
Buchan Hill 493
Loch Valley
Darrou
Garroch Burn
Garroch
Glenle
A713

Eldrick
Feoch Burn
Loch Goosey
Bruce's Stone ★
Galloway Forest Dark Sky Park
Loch Dee
Bennan 381
Clatteringshaws Loch
A762
A713
216

Corwar House
Glen Trool Lodge
1307
557
Loch Trool
Loch Dee
Bruce's Stone (NTS)
New Galloway

22
A714
Glentrool
Mulldonoch
Loch Dee
Craigencallie
493
Clatteringshaws
Cairnsmore of Dee
Kenmure
G A

Drumlamford House
Bargrennan
Lamachan Hill 716
A712
Darnaw
3

Loch Dornal
Loch Ochiltree
Larg Hill 675
Millfore 656
GALLOWAY FOREST PARK
Galloway Deer Range
19
Clatteringshaws
Round Fell 402
Fell of Fleet 471
Shaw Hill 385
Forest Drive (summer only)

Loch Maberry
Polbae
Clachaneasy
Larg
Garlick Hill 445
Murray's Monument ★
A712
Craignelder 601
Loch Grannoch
Loch Fleet
Auchencloy Hill 209
Airie Hill 291
Stroan

Upland Way
Knockville
Wild Goat Park
Loch Skerrow

Urrall Fell 184
Knowe
Penninghame
Garlies Castle
Dallash
A712
711
Cairnsmore of Fleet
Big Water of Fleet Viaduct
4

Black Burn
Glenrazie
Boreland
Cumloden
Pendicle Burn
Bargaly
Cairnsmore of Fleet NNR
Visitor Centre
White Top of Culreoch 344

alminnoch
Carseriggan
Challoch
Minnigaff
Creebridge
Blackcraig
Door of Cairnsmore
B796
Dar

Culvennan Fell 213
Newton Stewart
Kirroughtree
Cairnsmore
Carstramon Wood
Castramont

Benfield
Nether Barr
Palnure
i 1
6

Shennanton
A75
Cree
A75
Spittal
15

Barlae
Craighlaw
Linn of Barhoise
Barraer
Baltersan
7
Spittal
Carstramon Wood

Kirkcowan
B735
Bladnoch
Causeway End
Barholm Mains
Gem Rock Museum
Glenquicken Moor
Rusko
Low Barlay
5

Moss
Dernaglar Loch 175
Spittal
Carsegowan
Creetown
Cassencarie
Glen
Lauchentyre
Gatehouse of Fleet
Cardness Castle

Knock Fell
B7027
Stone Circle **m**
Culquhirk
Martyrs' Monument ★
Wigtown Sands
Cairnharrow 456
Anwoth
Ardwall
Cardoness
m

Old Place of Mochrum
Bladnoch
Bladnoch
Wigtown
Carsluith
Cairnholy Chambered Cairns
13
Kirkdale House
Girthon
Barharrow
B727

Castle Loch
Culshabbin
B7005
Culmalzie
11
Baldoon Sands
Carsluith
Cardoness
Sandgreen
Fleet Bay
Lennox Plunton

malg
A747
Culshabbin
Mochrum Loch
Barnbarroch
Braehead
Kirkinner
Orchardton Bay
Murray's Isles
Ardwall Island
Knockbrex

Chapel Fin
Alticry
Elrig Loch
Barrachan
Whauphill
Stewarton
B7004
207
Islands of Fleet
Barlocco Island
Kirkandrews

D
Loch Head
E
Mot Druid
Kirkland of Longcastle
F
Sorbie
A746
12
Galloway House ✦
Garlieston
G
Ringdoo Point
Borness
Sen

Barr Point
Mochrum
Elrig
6
Airyhassen
Eggerness
B7052
WIGTOWN BAY

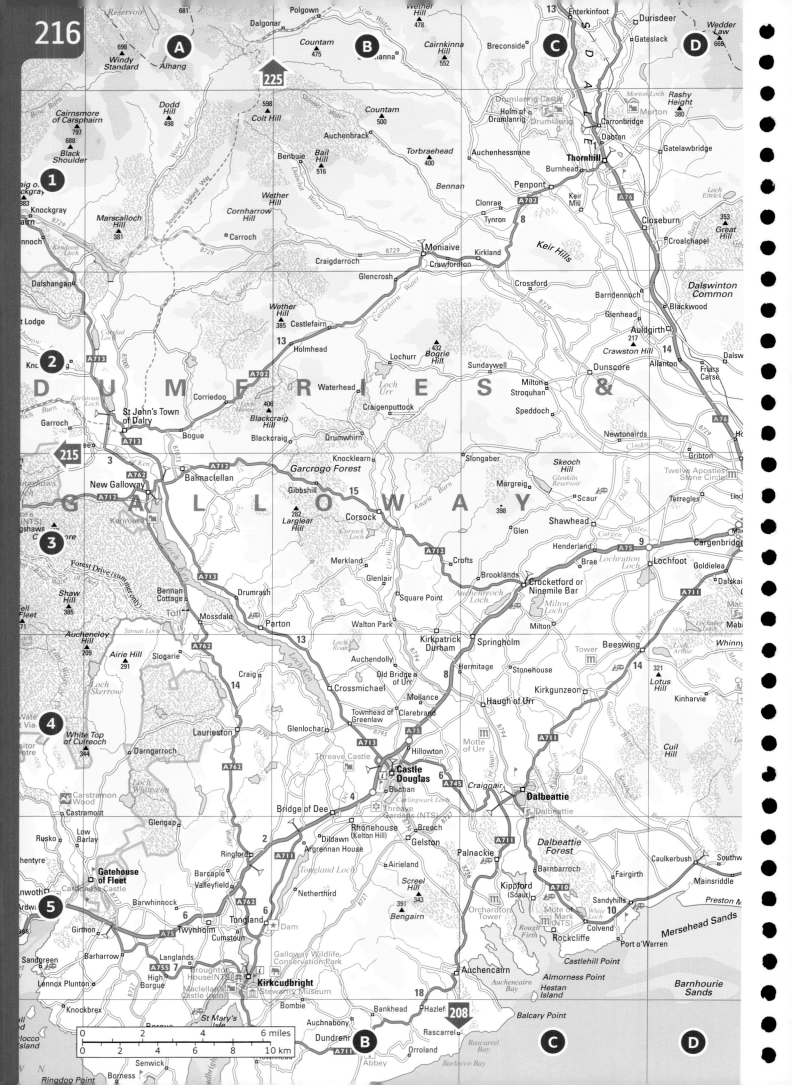

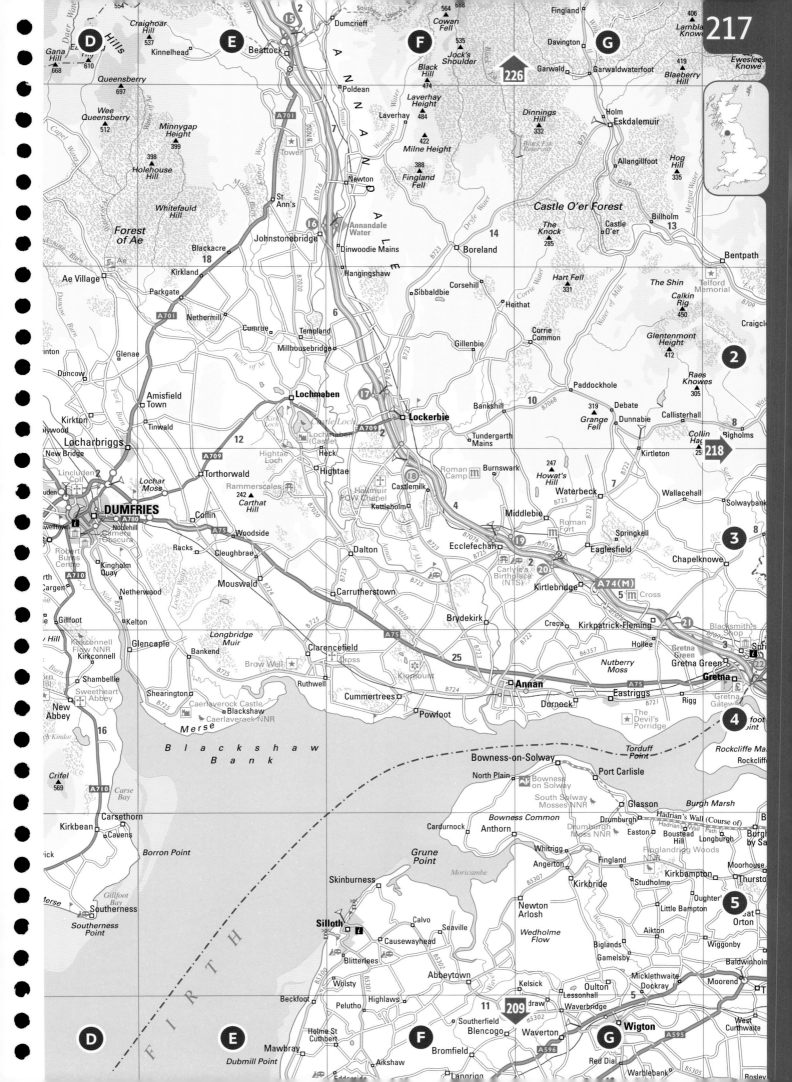

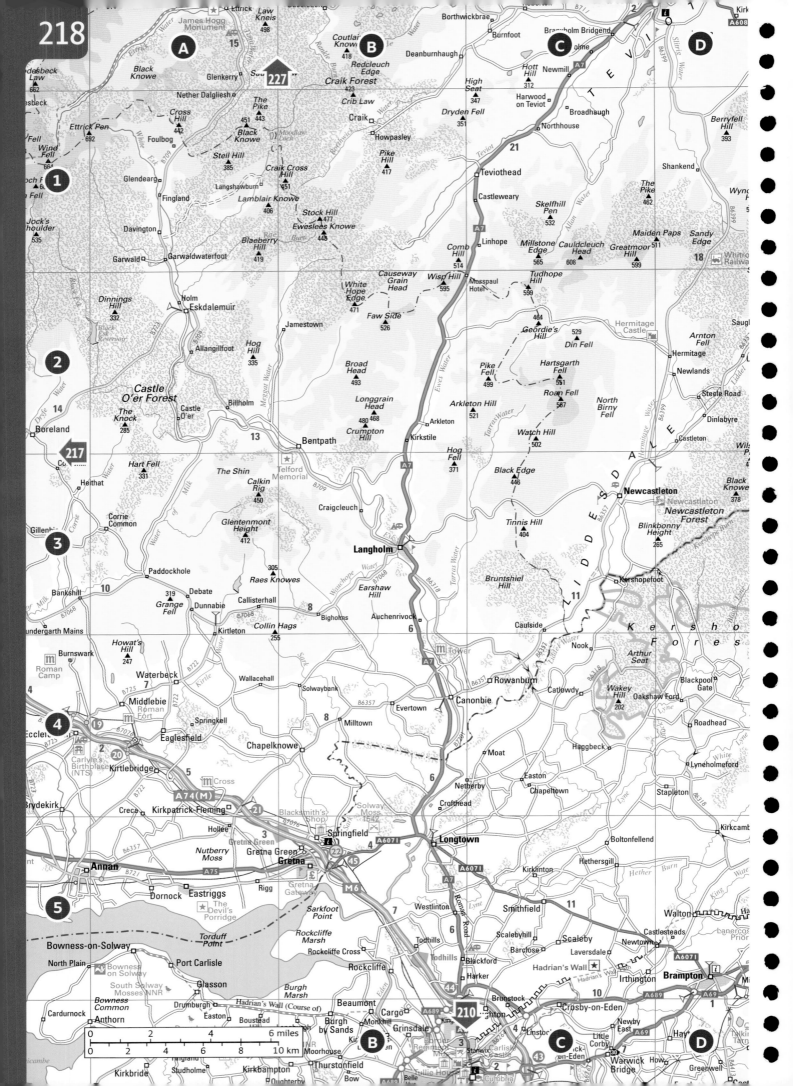

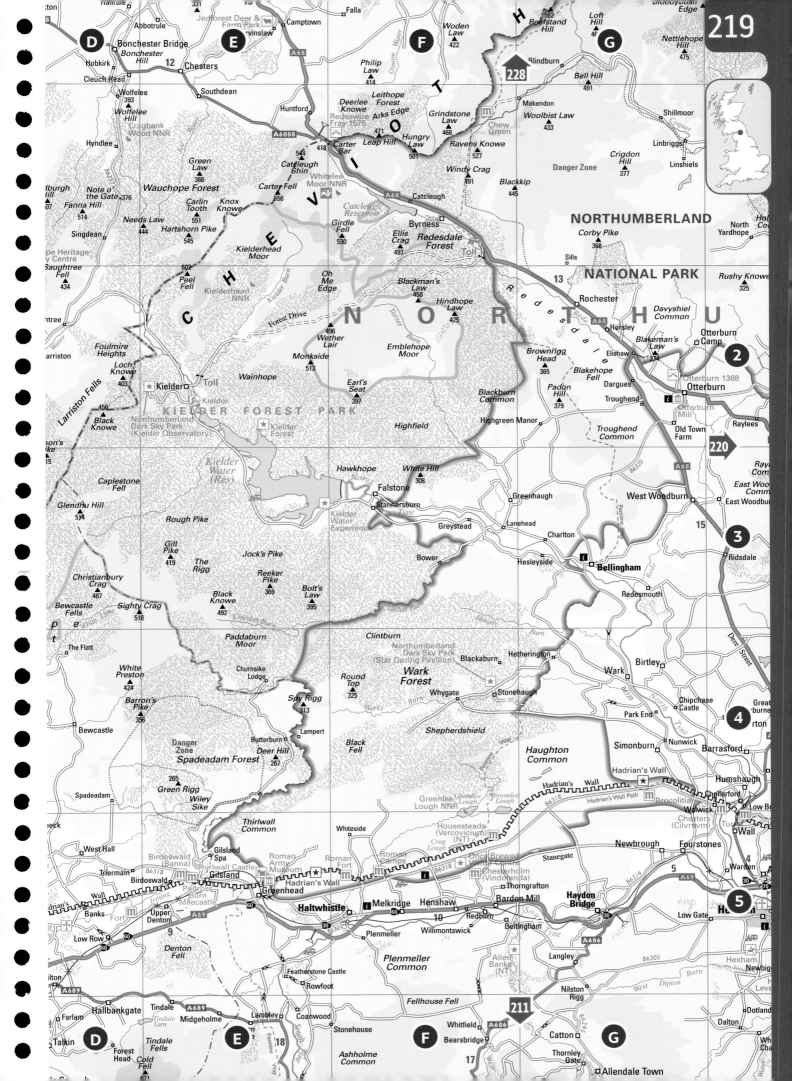

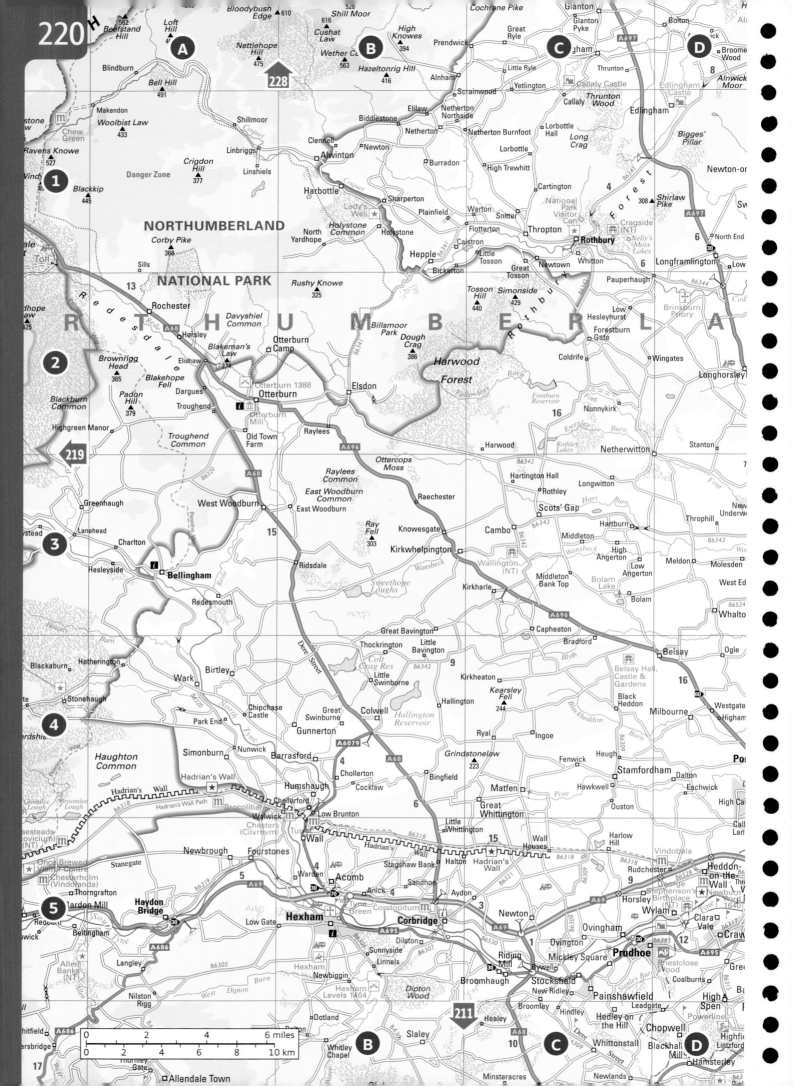

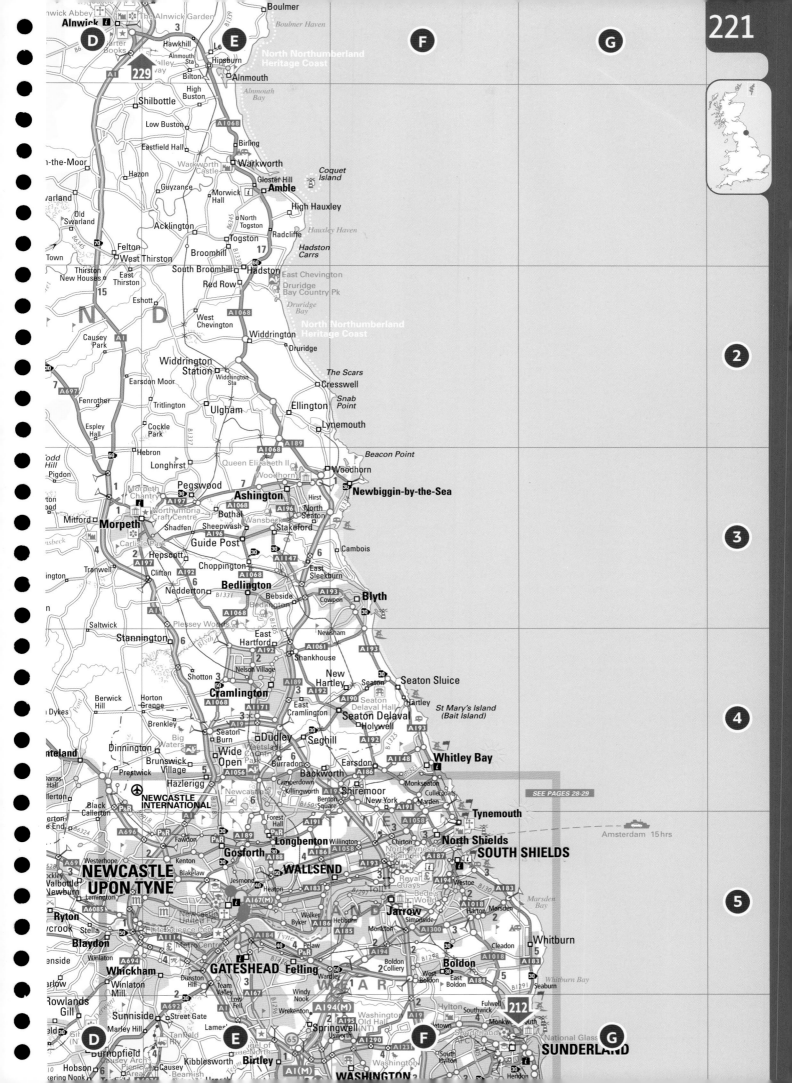

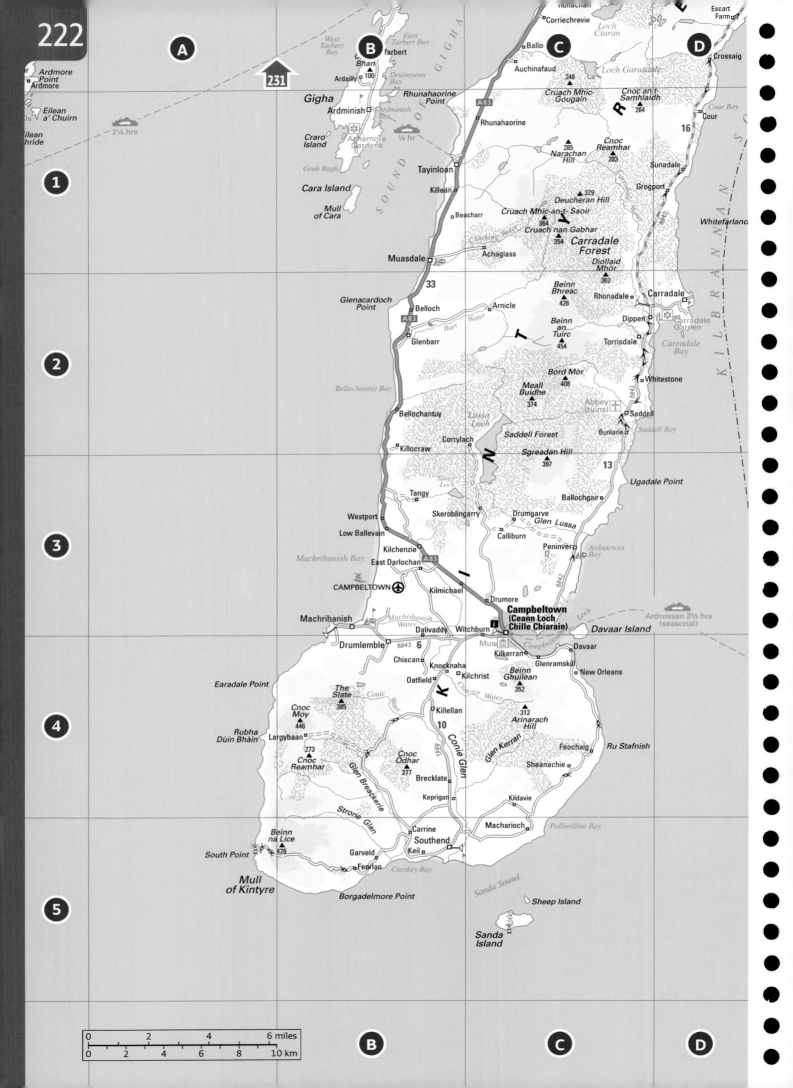

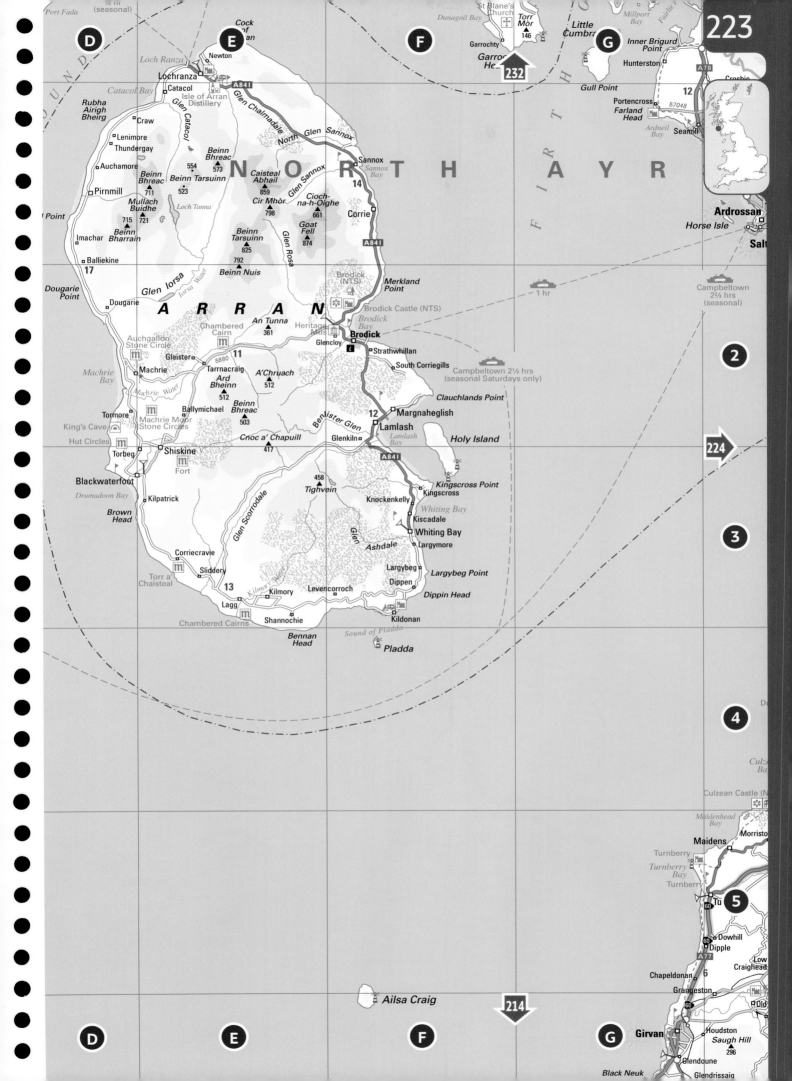

D

E

F

G

A78

12

B7048

Port Fada
(seasonal)

St Blane's Church

Dunagoil Bay

Torr
Mòr
146

Little
Cumbrae

Millport
Bay

Fairlie

Garrochty

Inner Brigurd
Point

Hunterston

Cock
of
an

Newton

Garroch
He...

Gull Point

Croshie

Loch Ranza

Portencross
Farland
Head

Seamill

Ardneil
Bay

Lochranza

Catacol Bay

Catacol

Isle of Arran
Distillery

A841

Glen Chalmadale

Rubha
Airigh
Bheirg

Craw

Lenimore

Thundergay

Auchamore

Beinn
Bhreac

Beinn Bhreac

554
573

Caisteal
Abhail

North Glen Sannox

Glen Sannox

Sannox

Sannox
Bay

N O R T H   A Y R

Pirnmill

711

Beinn Tarsuinn

523

859

Cir Mhòr

798

661

Cioch-
na-h-Oighe

Mullach
Buidhe

Loch Tanna

Corrie

715   721

Beinn
Bharrain

Goat
Fell
874

Imachar

Beinn
Tarsuinn
825

Ardrossan

Balliekine

17

792

Beinn Nuis

Brodick
(NTS)

Merkland
Point

Horse Isle

Salt

Dougarie
Point

Glen Iorsa

Dougarie

A R R A N

Brodick Castle (NTS)

Brodick
Bay

1 hr

Campbeltown
2⅔ hrs
(seasonal)

Chambered
Cairn

An Tunna
361

Heritage
Mus

Brodick

2

Auchgallon
Stone Circle

11

Glencloy

Strathwhillan

Glaister

B880

Tarrnacraig

A'Chruach
512

South Corriegills

Campbeltown 2⅓ hrs
(seasonal Saturdays only)

Machrie
Bay

Machrie

Ard
Bheinn
512

Machrie Water

Ballymichael

Beinn
Bhreac
503

Clauchlands Point

Tormore

King's Cave

Machrie Moor
Stone Circles

Cnoc a' Chapuill
417

12

Margnaheglish

Lamlash

224

Hut Circles

Torbeg

Shiskine

Glenkiln

Lamlash
Bay

Holy Island

Blackwaterfoot

Fort

Benlister Glen

A841

Drumadoon Bay

Kilpatrick

458
Tighvein

Kingscross Point

Kingscross

Brown
Head

Knockenkelly

Whiting Bay

Corriecravie

Sliddery

Glen Scorrodale

Kiscadale

Whiting Bay

3

Largymore

Torr a'
Chaisteal

13

Kilmory

Glen
Ashdale

Largybeg

Largybeg Point

Kilmory Water

Levencorroch

Dippen

Dippin Head

Lagg

Chambered Cairns

Shannochie

Kildonan

4

Bennan
Head

Sound of Pladda

Pladda

Culze...
Bay

Culzean Castle (N

Maidenhead
Bay

Maidens

Morristo

Turnberry

Turnberry
Bay
Turnberry

5

A77

Tu

A77

Dowhill
Dipple

Low
Craighead

Chapeldonan

Ailsa Craig

Grangeston

Old...

60

60

Girvan

Houdston
Saugh Hill
296

Glendoune

Black Neuk

Glendrissaig

D

E

F

G

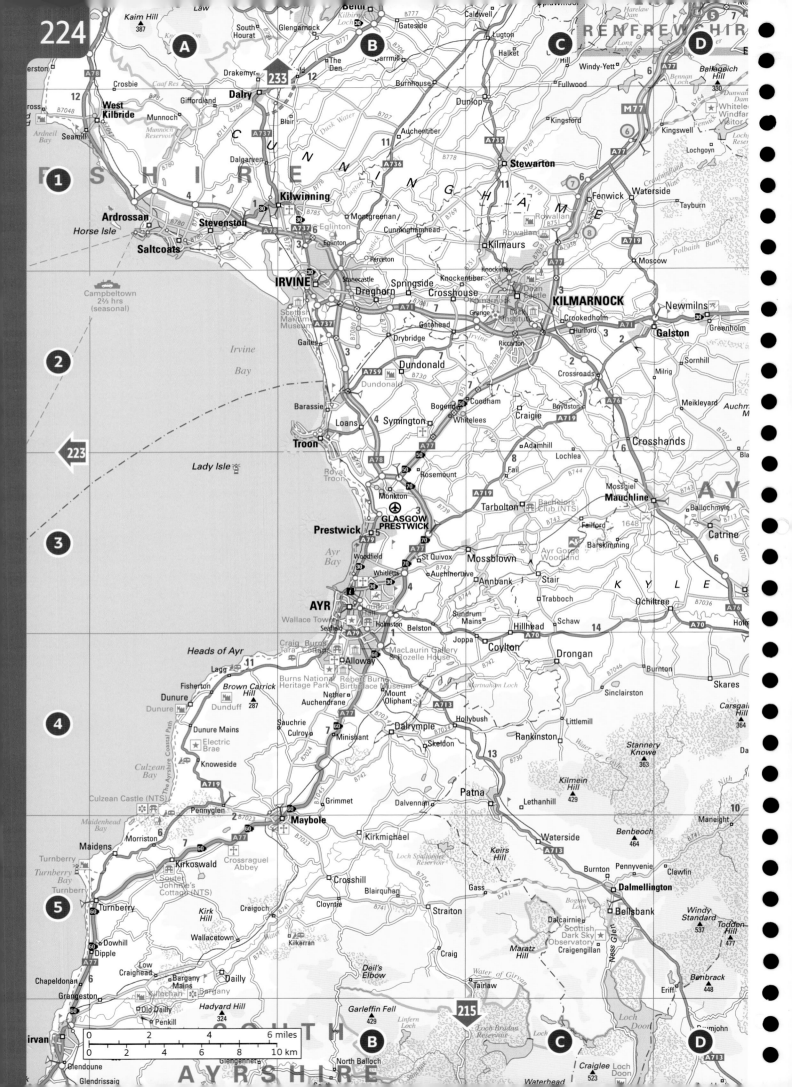

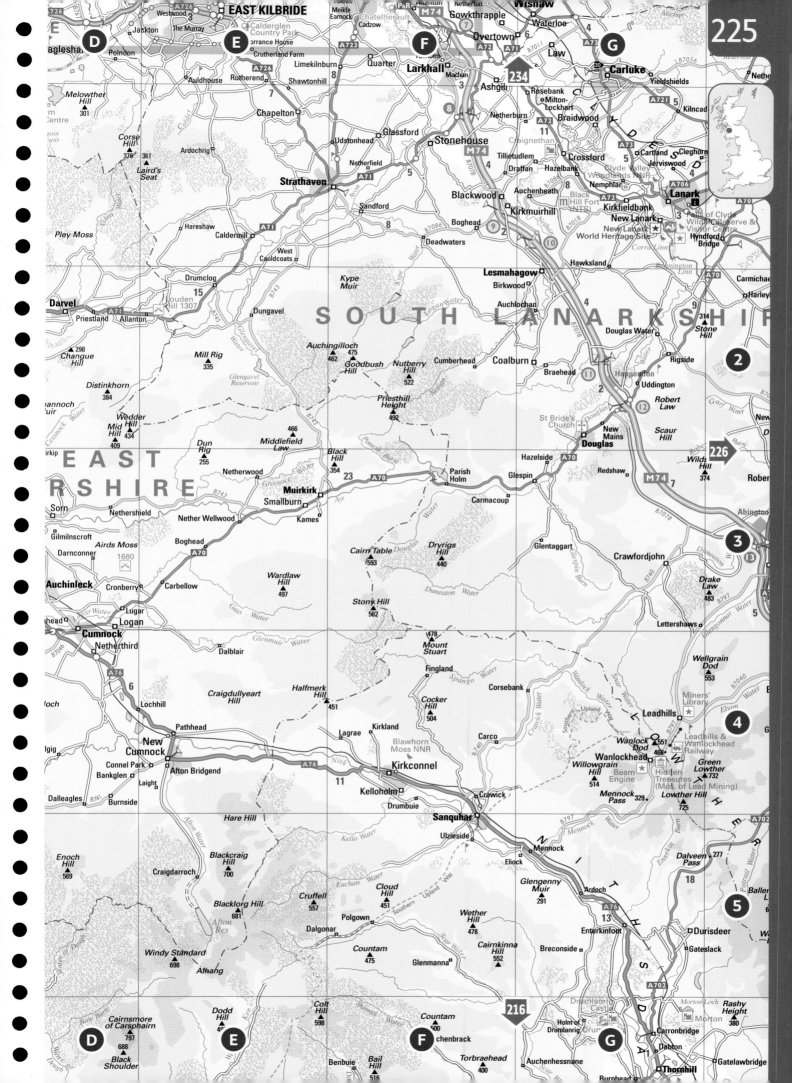

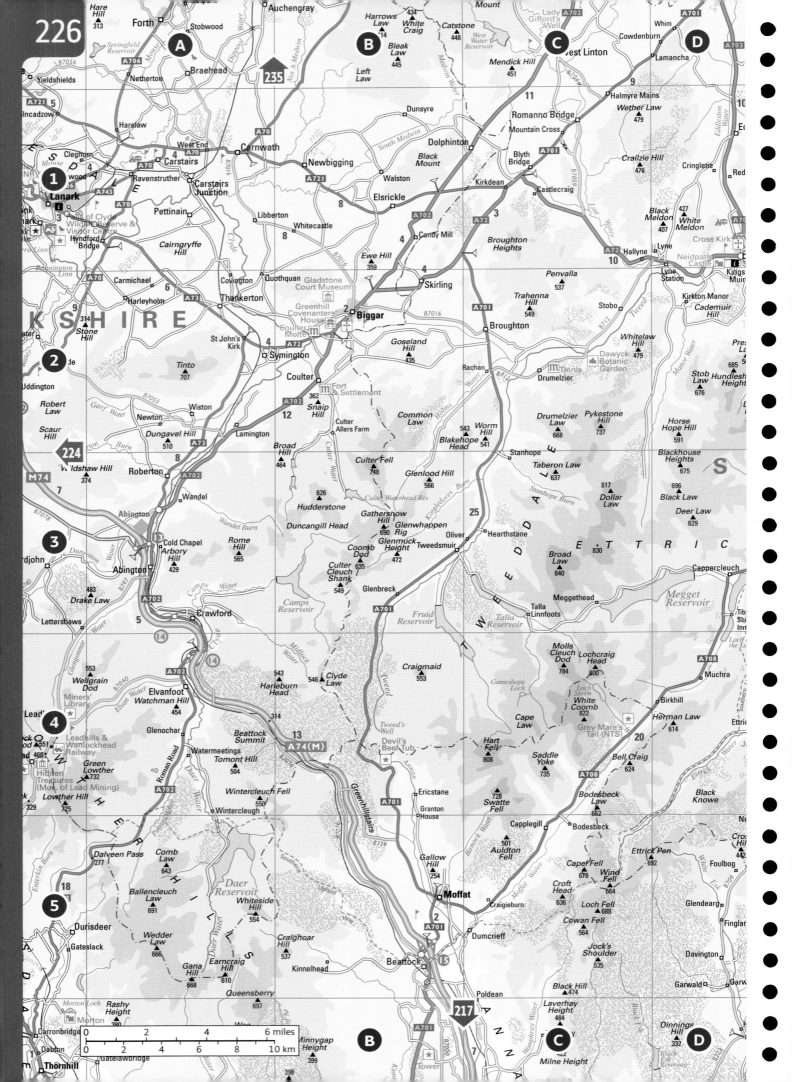

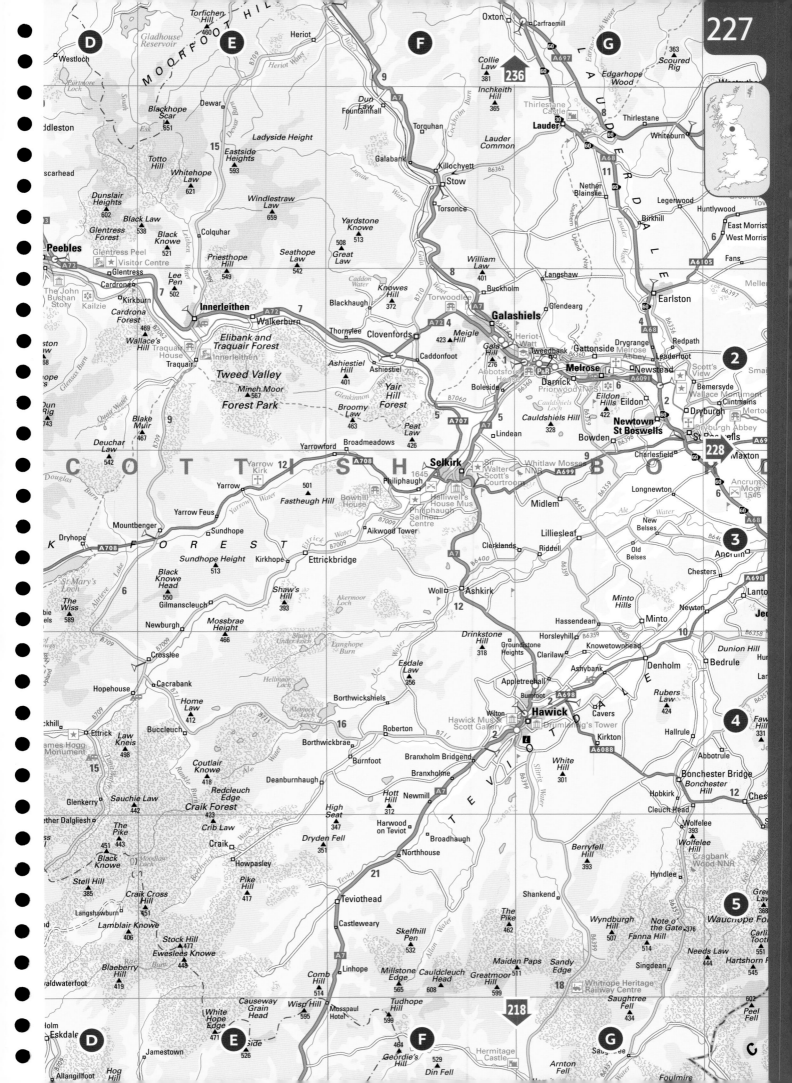

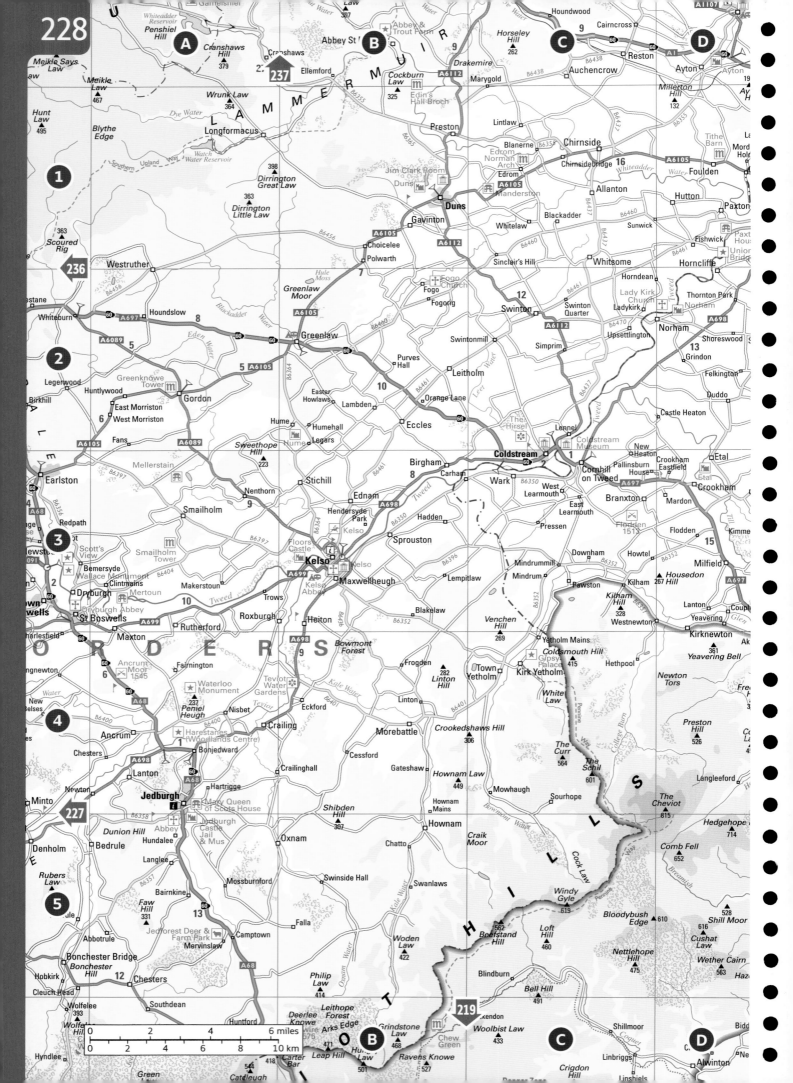

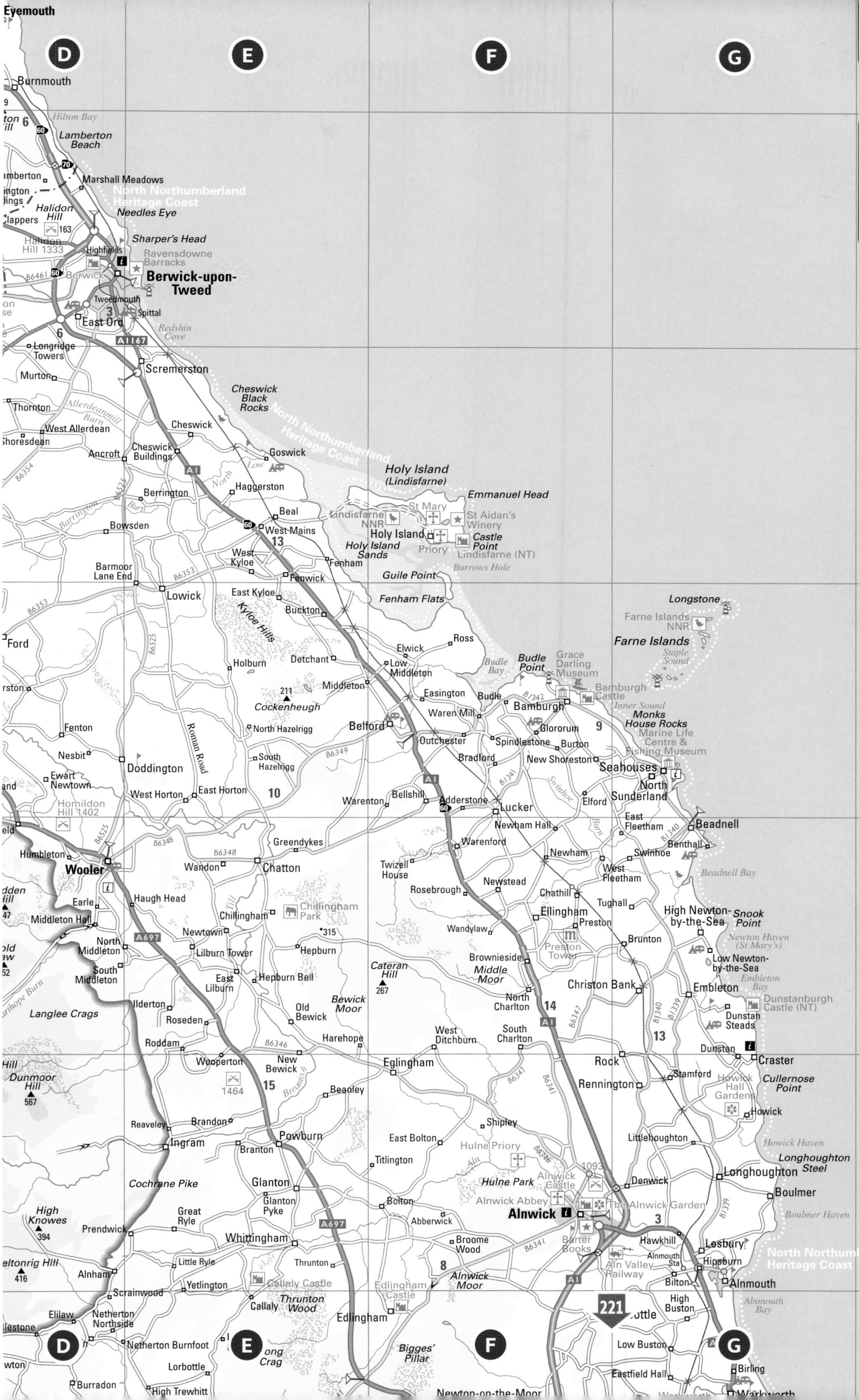

Eyemouth

D E F G

Burnmouth
Hilton Bay
Lamberton Beach
Marshall Meadows
Needles Eye
Halidon Hill
North Northumberland Heritage Coast
Sharper's Head
163
Halidon Hill 1333
Highfields
Ravensdowne Barracks
Berwick-upon-Tweed
B6461 60 Berwick
Tweedmouth
East Ord
Spittal
Redshin Cove
A1167
Longridge Towers
Murton
Scremerston
Cheswick Black Rocks
Thornton
Allerdeanmill Burn
West Allerdean
Cheswick
Shoresdean
Ancroft
Cheswick Buildings
Goswick
North Northumberland Heritage Coast
B6354
Berrington
Haggerston
Holy Island (Lindisfarne)
Emmanuel Head
Bowsden
Beal
West Mains
St Mary
Lindisfarne NNR
St Aidan's Winery
13
West Kyloe
Fenwick
Fenham
Holy Island
Priory
Castle Point
Lindisfarne (NT)
Barmoor Lane End
Holy Island Sands
Guile Point
Burrows Hole
B6353
Lowick
East Kyloe
Buckton
Fenham Flats
Ford
Kyloe Hills
Ross
Longstone
Holburn
Elwick
Farne Islands NNR
B6525
Detchant
Low Middleton
Budle Bay
Budle Point
Grace Darling Museum
Farne Islands
Staple Sound
Fenton
211
Cockenheugh
Middleton
Easington
Budle
Bamburgh
Bamburgh Castle
Inner Sound
Monks House Rocks
Marine Life Centre & Fishing Museum
Nesbit
North Hazelrigg
Belford
Waren Mill
Glororum
Burton
9
Ewart Newtown
South Hazelrigg
B6349
Outchester
Bradford
Spindlestone
New Shoreston
Seahouses
Doddington
Roman Road
West Horton
East Horton
10
Warenton
Bellshill
Adderstone
Lucker
Elford
North Sunderland
Homildon Hill 1402
Greendykes
Newham Hall
Warenford
Newham
East Fleetham
Beadnell
Humbleton
B6525
B6348
B6348
Wandon
Chatton
Twizell House
Rosebrough
Newstead
Chathill
West Fleetham
Swinhoe
Benthall
Beadnell Bay
Wooler
Haugh Head
Chillingham Park
Ellingham
Tughall
High Newton-by-the-Sea
Snook Point
Earle
Newtown
Wandylaw
Preston
Brunton
Newton Haven (St Mary's)
Middleton Hall
Chillingham
Hepburn
Brownieside
Middle Moor
Chathill
Preston Tower
Low Newton-by-the-Sea
North Middleton
A697
Lilburn Tower
Christon Bank
Embleton
Embleton Bay
South Middleton
East Lilburn
Hepburn Bell
Cateran Hill
267
North Charlton
14
B6347
Dunstanburgh Castle (NT)
Langlee Crags
Ilderton
Old Bewick
Bewick Moor
Dunstan Steads
Roddam
B6346
Harehope
West Ditchburn
South Charlton
B1340
13
Dunstan
Craster
Dunmoor Hill 567
Wooperton
New Bewick
Eglingham
Rock
Stamford
Cullernose Point
1464
15
Beanley
B6341
Rennington
Howick Hall Gardens
Reaveley
Brandon
Shipley
Littlehoughton
Howick
Howick Haven
Ingram
Branton
Powburn
East Bolton
Hulne Priory
Longhoughton
Longhoughton Steel
High Knowes 394
Glanton
Titlington
Denwick
Boulmer
Cochrane Pike
Glanton Pyke
Bolton
Hulne Park
Alnwick Castle
1093
The Alnwick Garden
Boulmer Haven
North Northumberland Heritage Coast
Prendwick
Great Ryle
Whittingham
Abberwick
Alnwick Abbey
Alnwick
Barter Books
Hawkhill
Lesbury
Little Ryle
Thrunton
Broome Wood
B6341
3
Hipsburn
Alnham
Yetlington
8
Alnwick Moor
Aln Valley Railway
Bilton
Alnmouth
Scrainwood
Callaly Castle
Edlingham Castle
221
High Buston
Alnmouth Bay
Elilaw
Netherton Northside
Thrunton Wood
Low Buston
Birling
Netherton Burnfoot
Callaly
Edlingham
Bigges' Pillar
Eastfield Hall
Lorbottle
ong Crag
Newton-on-the-Moor
Warkworth
Burradon
High Trewhitt

D E F G

2 3 4 5

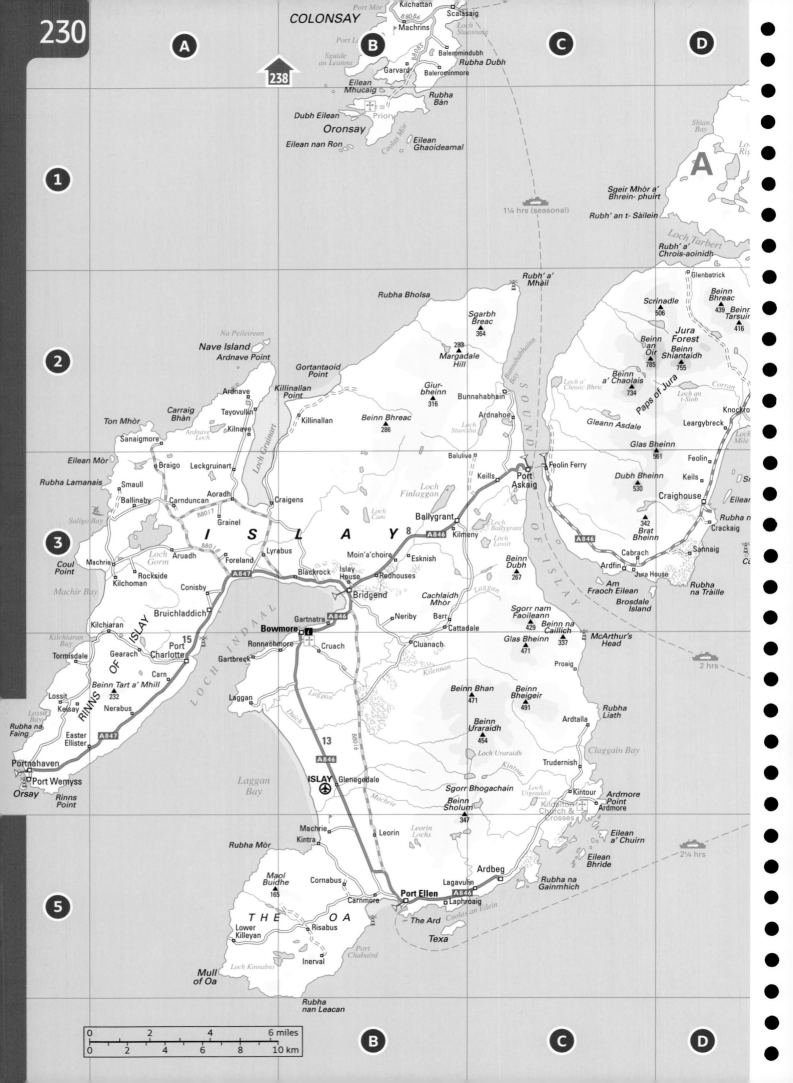

COLONSAY

Port Mòr
Kilchattan
Scalasaig
Machrins
B80.86
Loch
Staosnaig
Balerominduhh
Sguide
an Leanna
Garvard
Rubha Dubh
Balerominmore
Eilean
Mhucaig
Rubha
Bàn
Dubh Eilean
Oronsay
Priory
Rubha
Shian
Bay
Eilean nan Ron
Caolas Mòr
Eilean
Ghaoideamal

A

Loch
Rigg

1

1¼ hrs (seasonal)

Sgeir Mhòr a'
Bhrein- phuirt
Rubh' an t- Sàilein
Loch Tarbert
Rubh' a'
Chrois-aoinidh

Rubh' a'
Mhàil
Glenbatrick
Rubha Bholsa
Scrinadle
506
Beinn
Bhreac
439
Beinn
Tarsuir
416
Sgarbh
Breac
364
Jura
Forest
283
Margadale
Hill
Beinn
an
Oir
785
Beinn
Shiantaidh
755
Na Peileirean
Nave Island
Ardnave Point
Giur-
bheinn
316
Bunnahabhain
Bunnahabhainn Bay
Loch a'
Chnuic Bhric
Beinn
a' Chaolais
734
Paps of Jura
Loch an
t-Siob
Gortantaoid
Point
Beinn Bhreac
286
Loch
Staoisha
Ardnahoe
Gleann Asdale
Leargybreck
Knockro
Loch
Mile
Ardnave
Killinallan
Point
Tayovullin
Kilnave
Killinallan
Balulive
Keills
Glas Bheinn
561
Feolin
Keils
Carraig
Bhàn
Sanaigmore
Ardnave
Loch
Port
Askaig
Feolin Ferry
Dubh Bheinn
530
Eilean Mòr
Braigo
Leckgruinart
Ballygrant
Craighouse
Eilea
Rubha Lamanais
Smaull
Ballinaby
Carnduncan
Aoradh
Grainel
Craigens
Loch
Finlaggan
Loch
Cam
8
A846
Kilmeny
Loch
Ballygrant
Loch
Lossit
342
Brat
Bheinn
Cabrach
Sannaig
Saligo Bay
I S L A Y
B8017
Moin'a'choire
Esknish
Beinn
Dubh
267
Ardfin
Jura House
Rubha na
Crackaig
Coul
Point
Machrie
Aruadh
B8018
Lyrabus
Foreland
Blackrock
Islay
House
Redhouses
Am
Fraoch Eilean
Brosdale
Island
Rubha
na Tràille
Loch
Gorm
A847
Kilchoman
Rockside
Conisby
Bridgend
Cachlaidh
Mhòr
Machir Bay
Bruichladdich
Gartnatra
A846
Neriby
Barr
Sgorr nam
Faoileann
429
Beinn na
Caillich
McArthur's
Head
Kilchiaran
Port
Charlotte
15
Bowmore
Ronnachmore
Cruach
Cluanach
Cattadale
Glas Bheinn
471
337
Kilchiaran
Bay
Gartbreck
Proaig
2 hrs
Tormisdale
Gearach
Carn
RINNS
Laggan
Beinn Bhan
471
Beinn
Bheigeir
491
Rubha
Liath
Beinn Tart a' Mhill
232
OF
Laggan
Dutch
Loch
Kilennan
Beinn
Uraraidh
454
Ardtalla
Lossit
Kelsay
Nerabus
ISLAY
A847
Laggan
Loch Uraraidh
Trudernish
Claggain Bay
Rubha na
Faing
13
A846
Kintour
Portnahaven
Port Wemyss
Laggan
Bay
ISLAY
Glenegedale
Sgorr Bhogachain
Beinn
Sholum
347
Loch
Uigeadail
Kintour
Ardmore
Point
Ardmore
Orsay
Rinns
Point
Machrie
Kintra
Leorin
Leorin
Lochs
Kildalton
Church &
Crosses
Rubha Mòr
B8016
Eilean
a' Chuirn
2¼ hrs
Maol
Buidhe
165
Cornabus
Carnmore
Ardbeg
Lagavulin
Rubha na
Gainmhich
Eilean
Bhrìde

5

THE
OA
Risabus
Port Ellen
Laphroaig
A846
Lower
Killeyan
The Ard
Texa
Mull
of Oa
Inerval
Loch Kinnabus
Port
Chubaird
Caolas an Eilein

Rubha
nan Leacan

0   2   4   6 miles
0 2 4 6 8 10 km

A   B   C   D

B   C   D

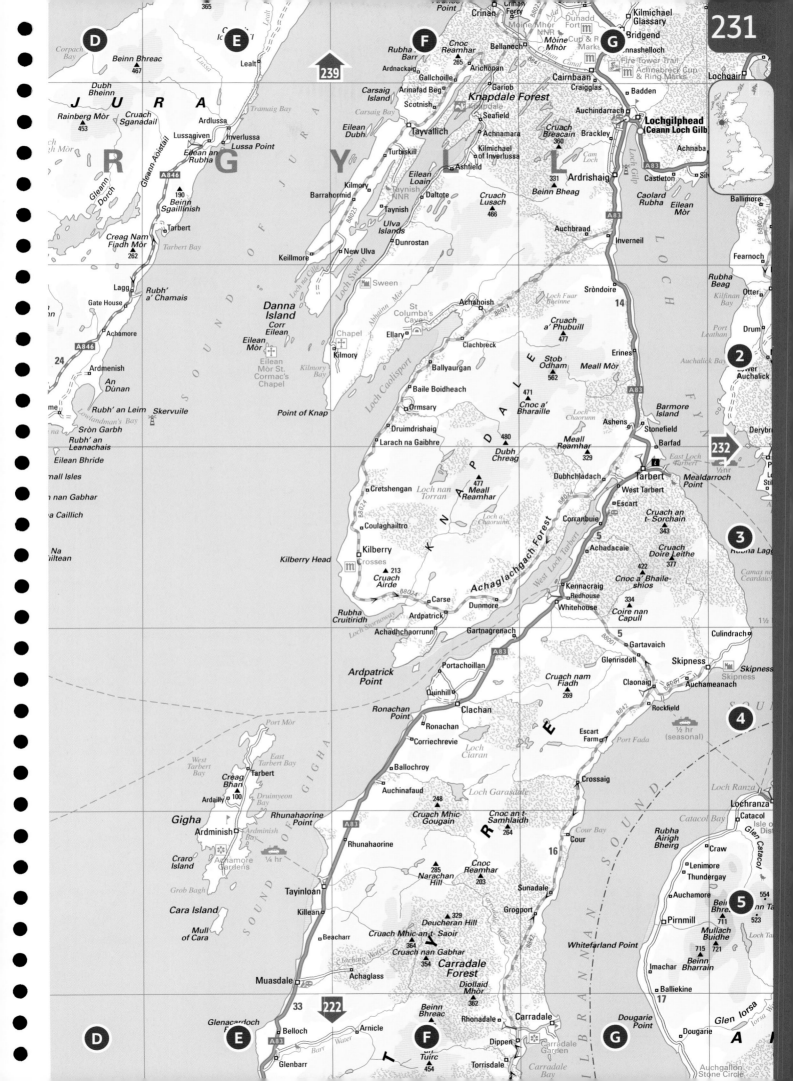

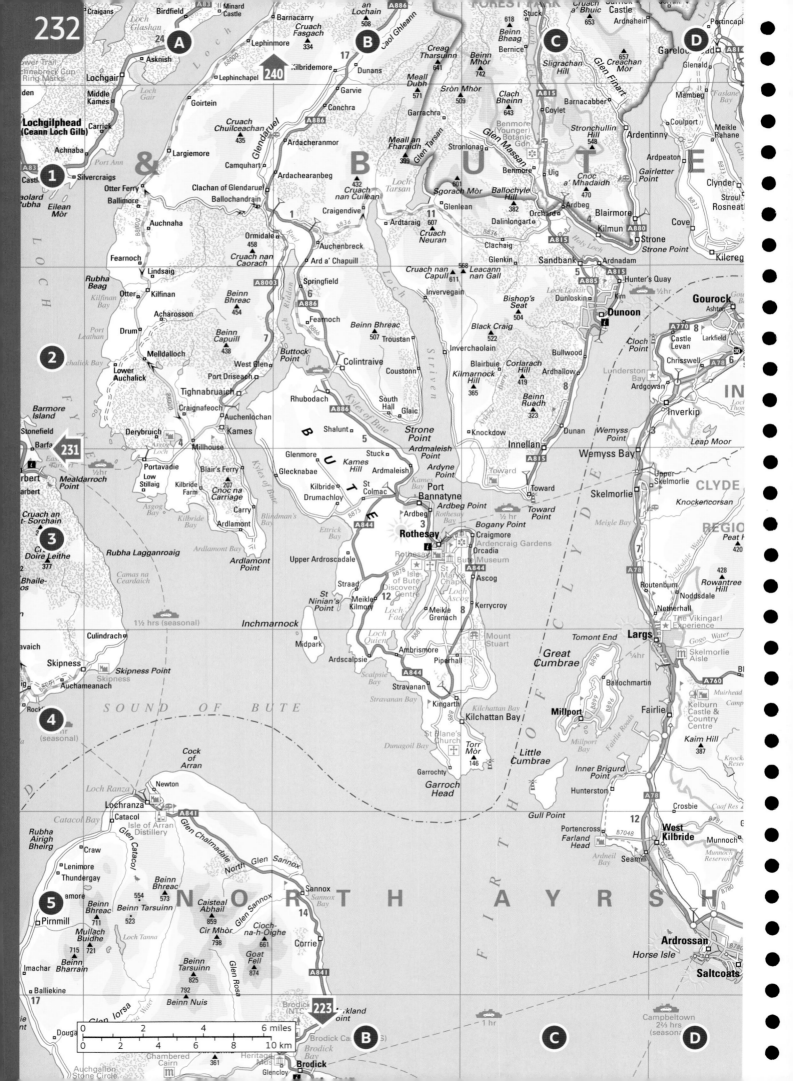

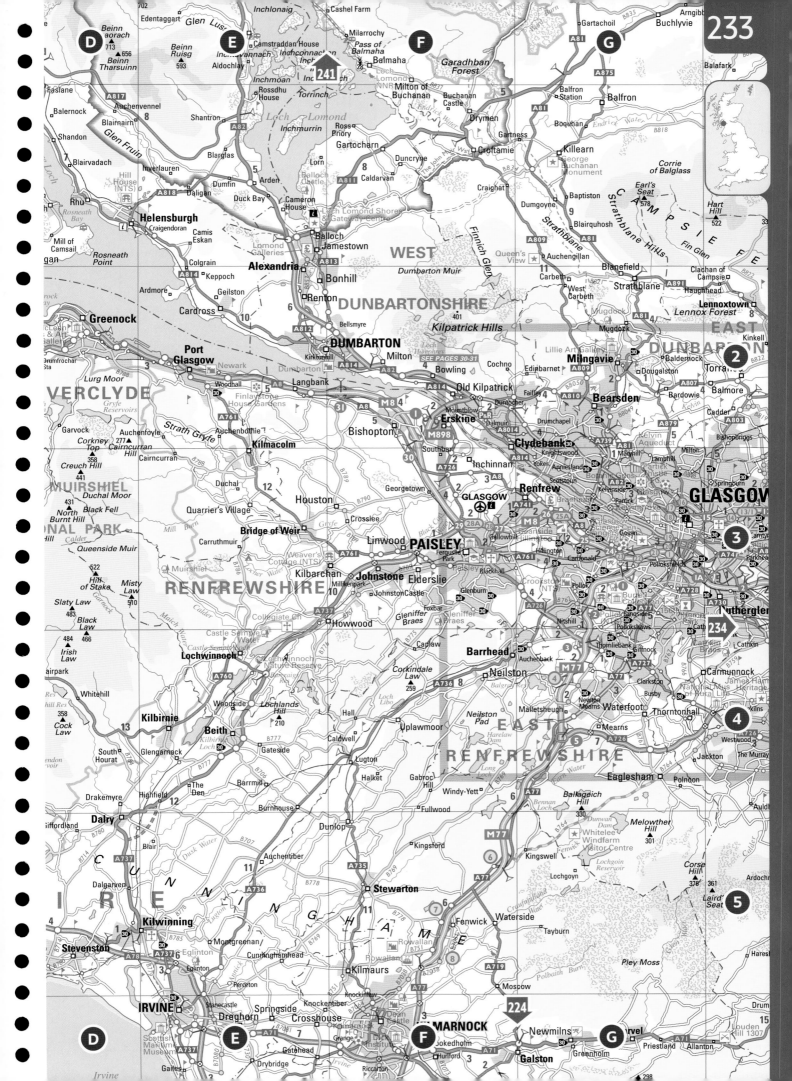

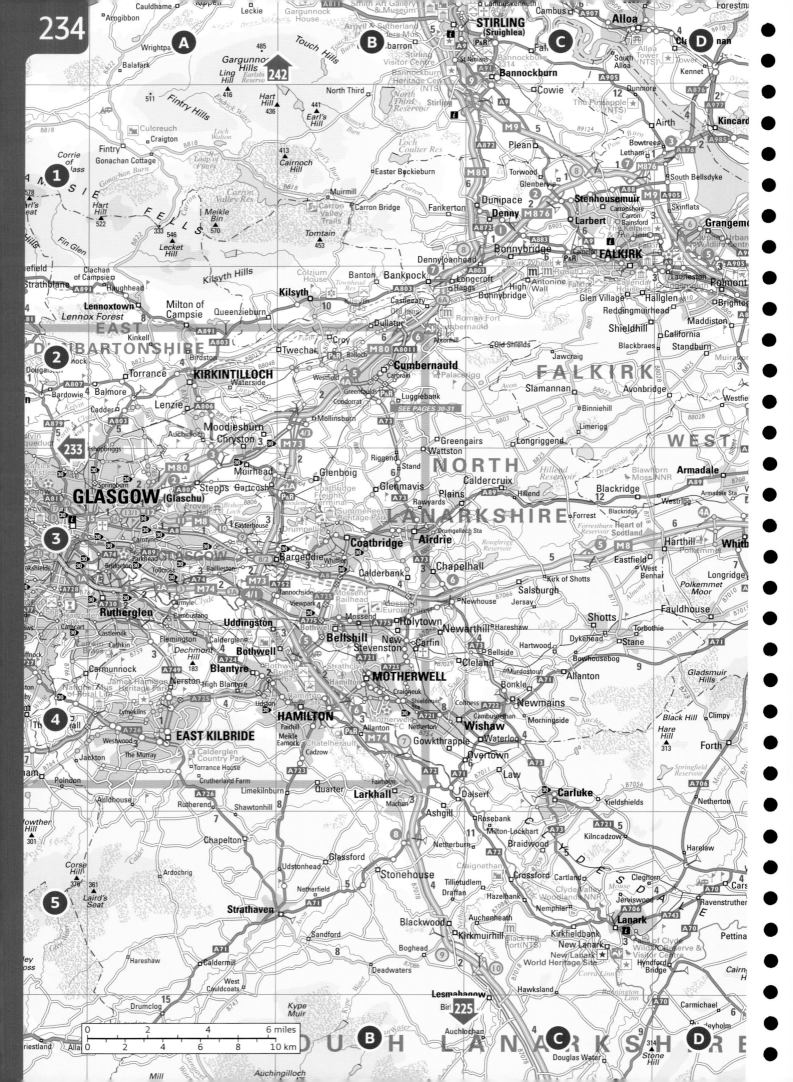

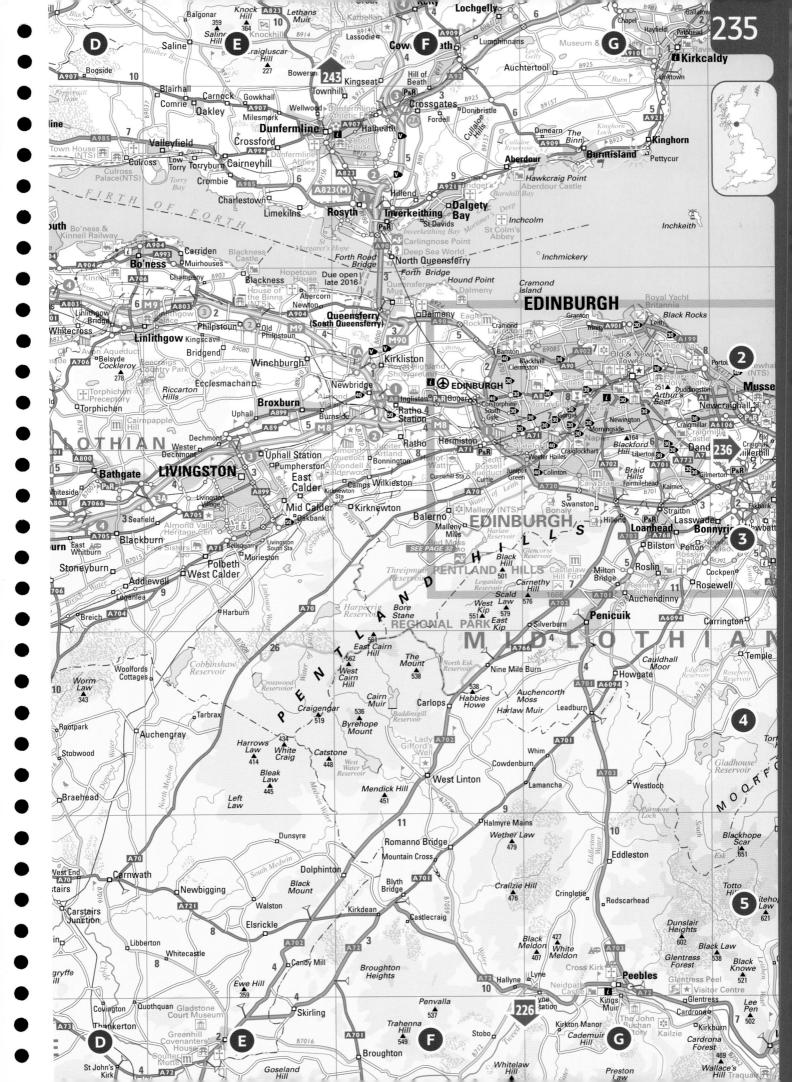

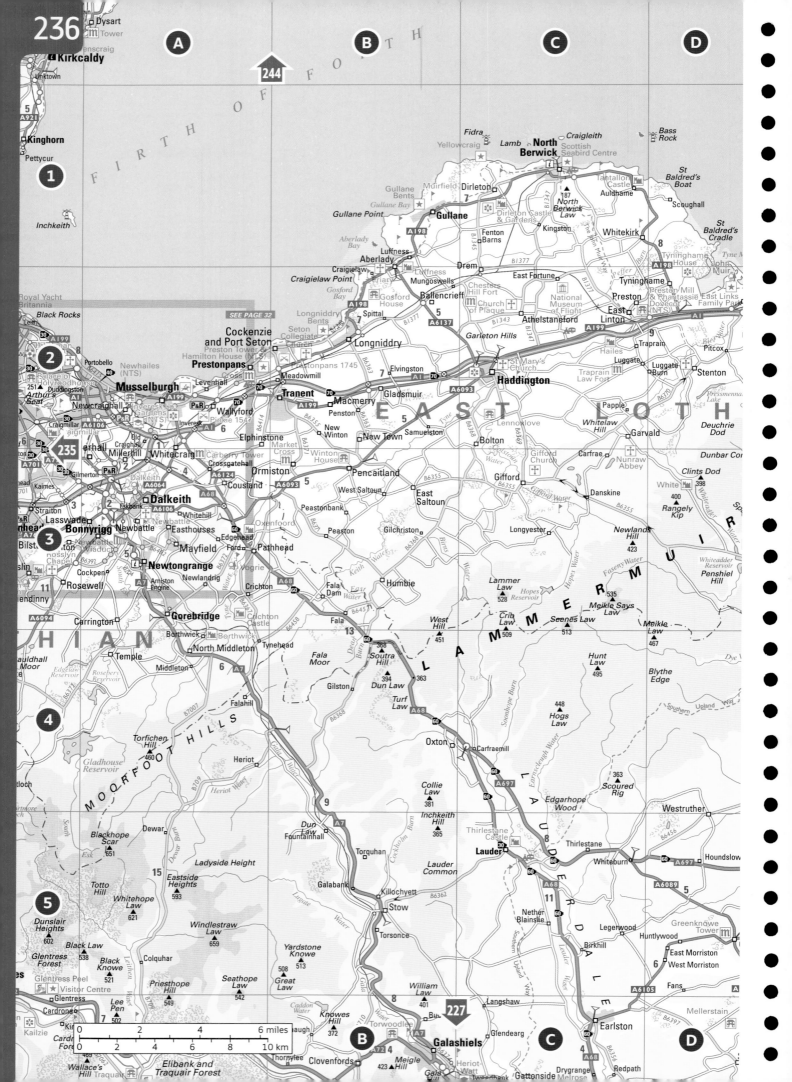

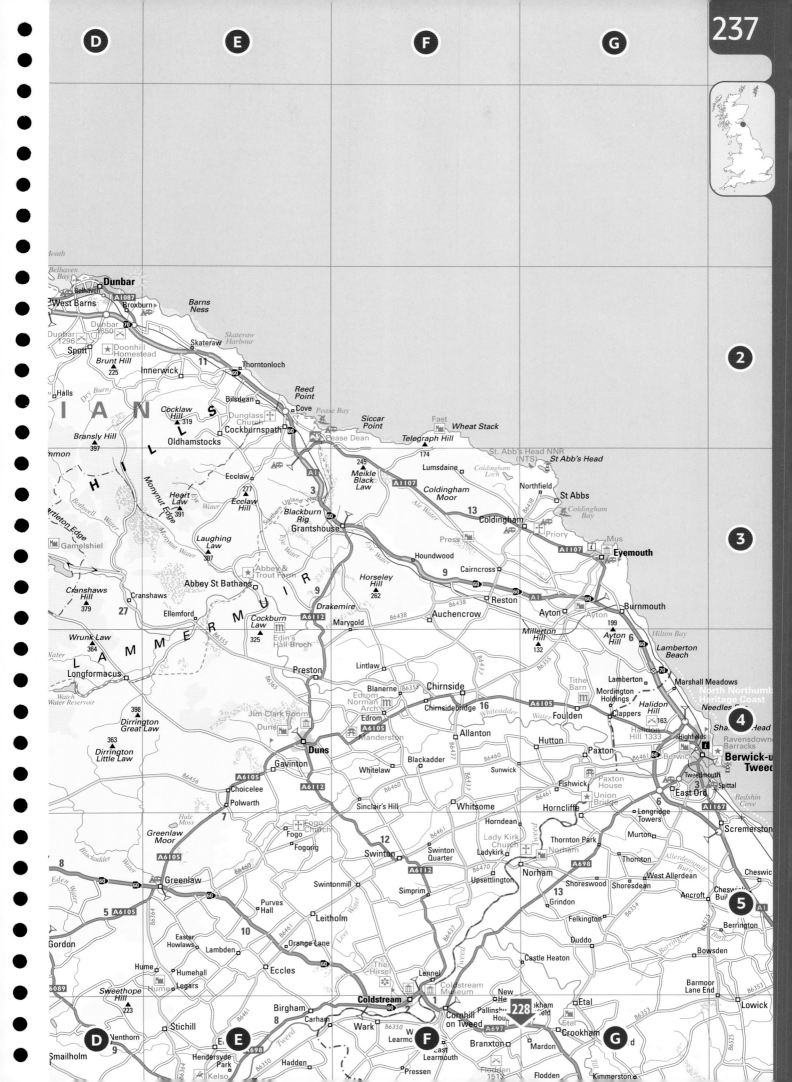

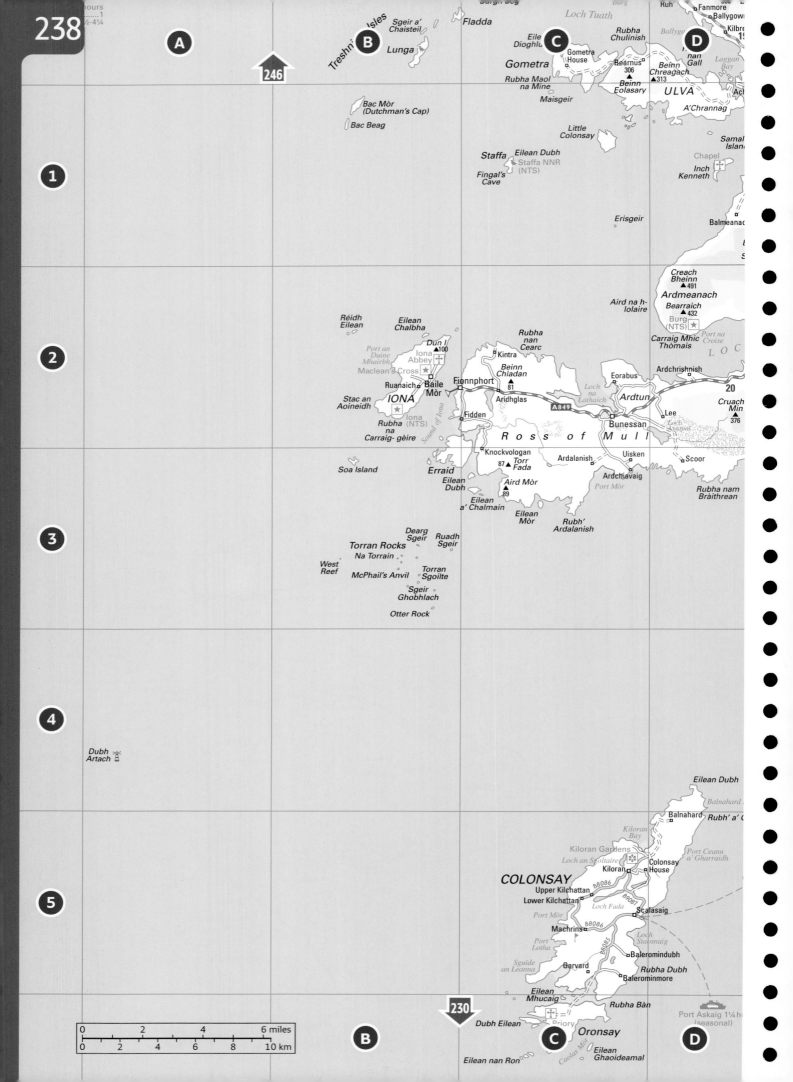

A

B

C

D

1

2

3

4

5

Treshn' Isles
Sgeir a' Chaisteil
Fladda
Lunga
Burgh Bog
Loch Tuath
Burg
Ruh
Fanmore
Ballygown
Kilbre
19

Eile Dioghlu
Gometra House
Rubha Chulinish
Bearnus 306
Beinn Chreagach ▲313
nan Gall
Ballygo
Laggan Bay
Ach

Gometra
Rubha Maol na Mine
Beinn Eolasary
ULVA
A'Chrannag

Bac Mòr (Dutchman's Cap)
Bac Beag
Maisgeir
Little Colonsay
Samal Islan

Staffa
Eilean Dubh
Staffa NNR (NTS)
Inch Kenneth
Chapel

Fingal's Cave

Erisgeir
Balmeanac

Creach Bheinn ▲491
Ardmeanach
Aird na h-Iolaire
Bearraich ▲432
Burg (NTS)
Port na Croise

Réidh Eilean
Eilean Chalbha
Rubha nan Cearc
Carraig Mhic Thòmais
LOC

Port an Duine Mhairbh
Dùn I ▲100
Iona Abbey
Kintra
Beinn Chladan ▲ 81
Eorabus
Ardchrishnish

Maclean's Cross
Ruanaich
Baile Mòr
Fionnphort
Aridhglas
Loch na Lathaich
Ardtun
20

Stac an Aoineidh
IONA
Fidden
A849
Bunessan
Lee
Cruach Min ▲ 376

Rubha na Carraig- gèire
Iona (NTS)
Sound of Iona
R o s s   o f   M u l l
Loch Assapol

Soa Island
Erraid
Eilean Dubh
Knockvologan
Torr Fada 87 ▲
Ardalanish
Uisken
Scoor

Aird Mòr 89 ▲
Port Mòr
Ardchiavaig
Rubha nam Bràithrean

Eilean a' Chalmain
Eilean Mòr
Rubh' Ardalanish

Dearg Sgeir
Ruadh Sgeir

Torran Rocks
Na Torrain

West Reef
McPhail's Anvil
Torran Sgoilte

Sgeir Ghobhlach

Otter Rock

Dubh Artach

Eilean Dubh

Balnahard
Balnahard
Rubh' a' C

Kiloran Bay
Port Ceann a' Gharraidh

Kiloran Gardens
Loch an Sgoltaire
Kiloran
Colonsay House

COLONSAY
Upper Kilchattan
B8086
Lower Kilchattan
B8087
Loch Fada
Scalasaig

Port Mòr
B8086

Machrins
Loch Staosnaig

Port Lotha
B8085
Baleromindubh

Sguide an Leanna
Garvard
Rubha Dubh
Balerominmore

Eilean Mhucaig
Rubha Bàn
Port Askaig 1¼ hi (seasonal)

Priory
Dubh Eilean
Oronsay

Eilean nan Ron
Caolas Mòr
Eilean Ghaoideamal

246

230

0   2   4   6 miles
0   2   4   6   8   10 km

hours
......1
½-4¼

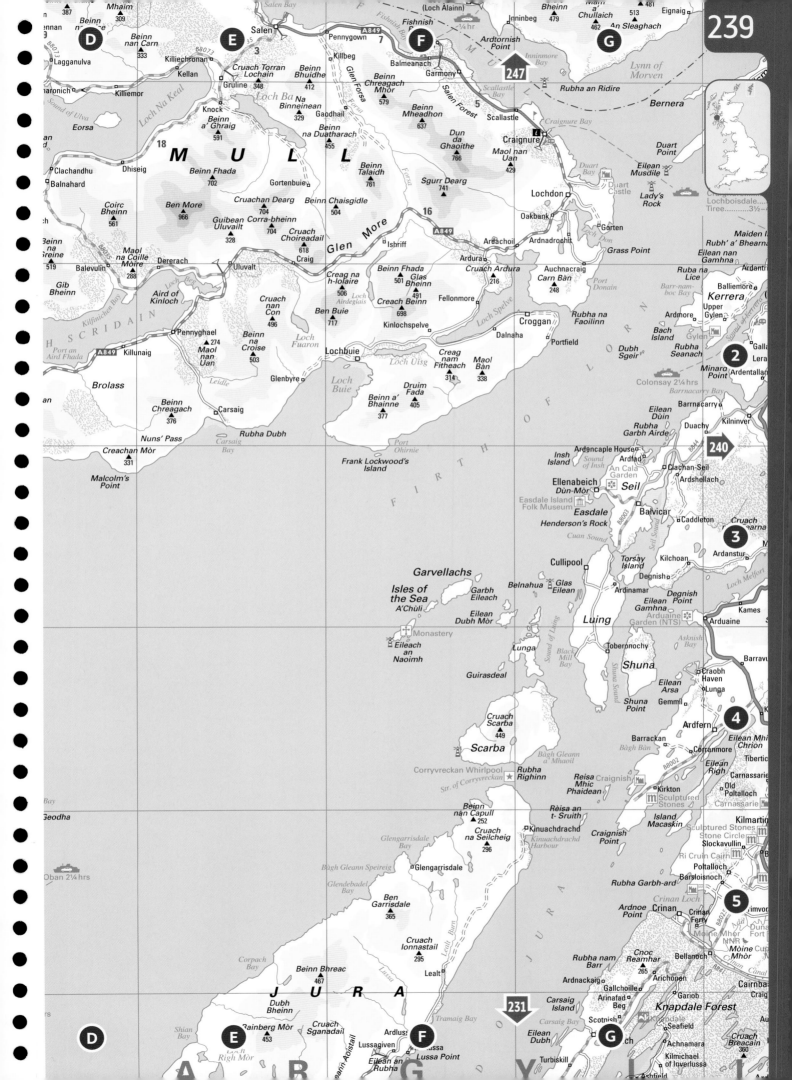

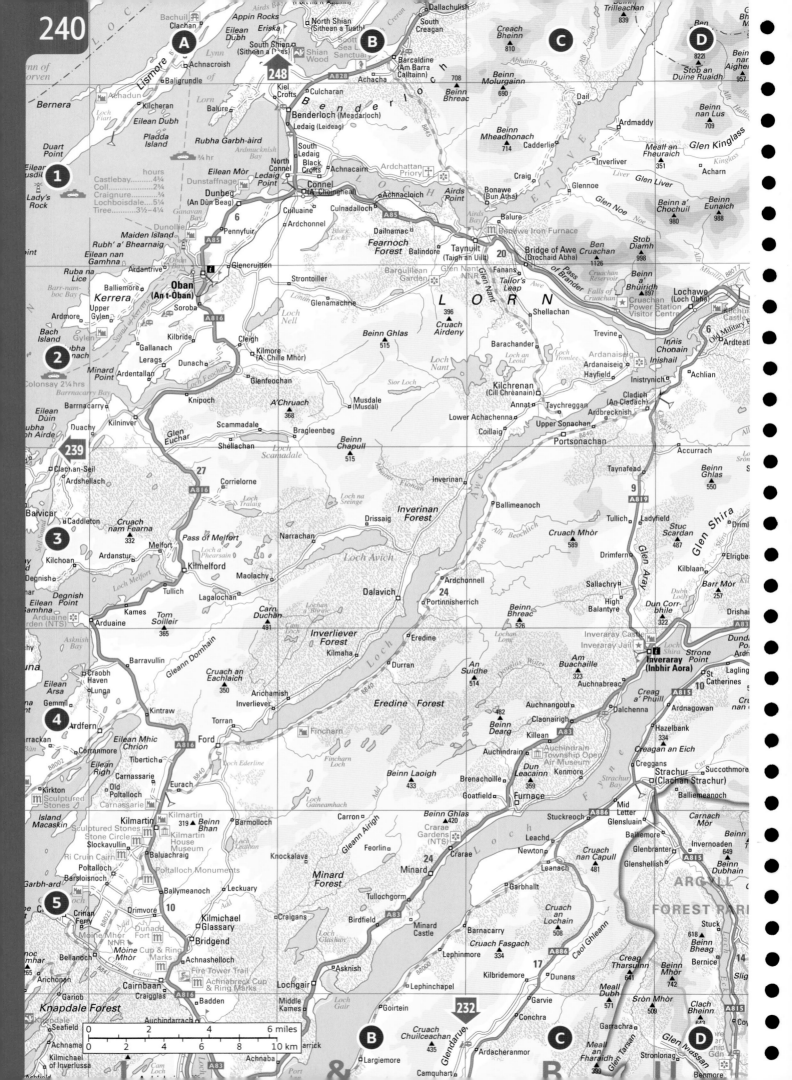

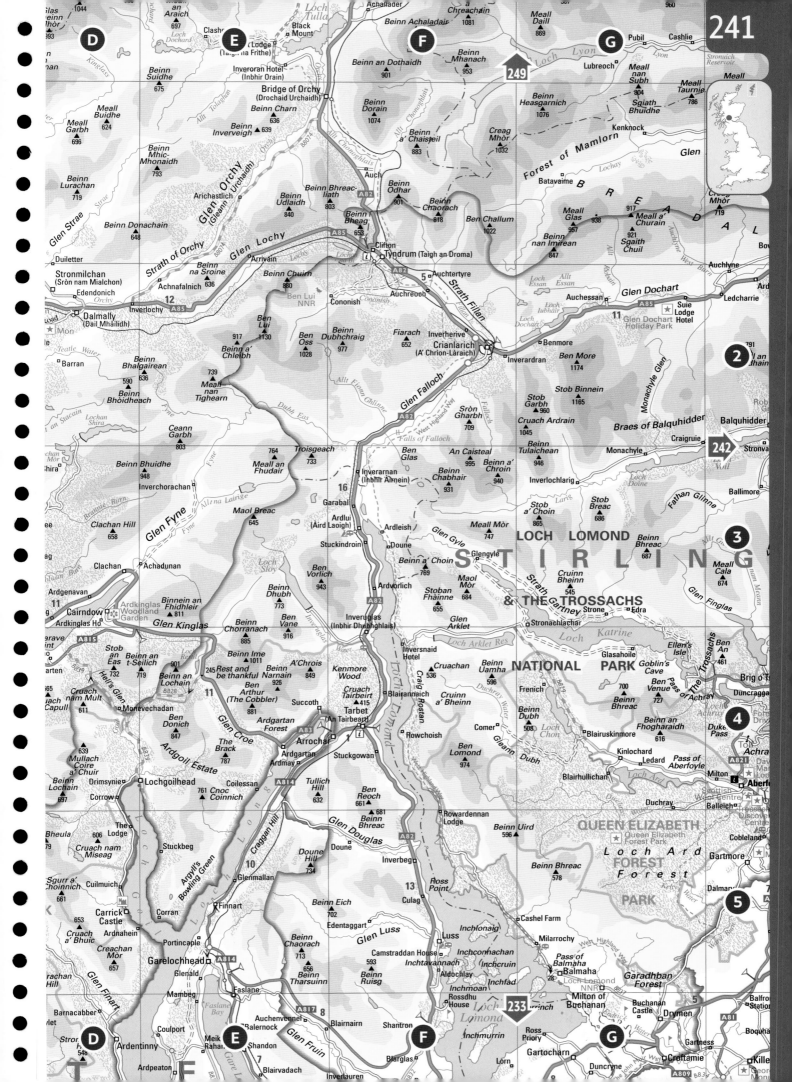

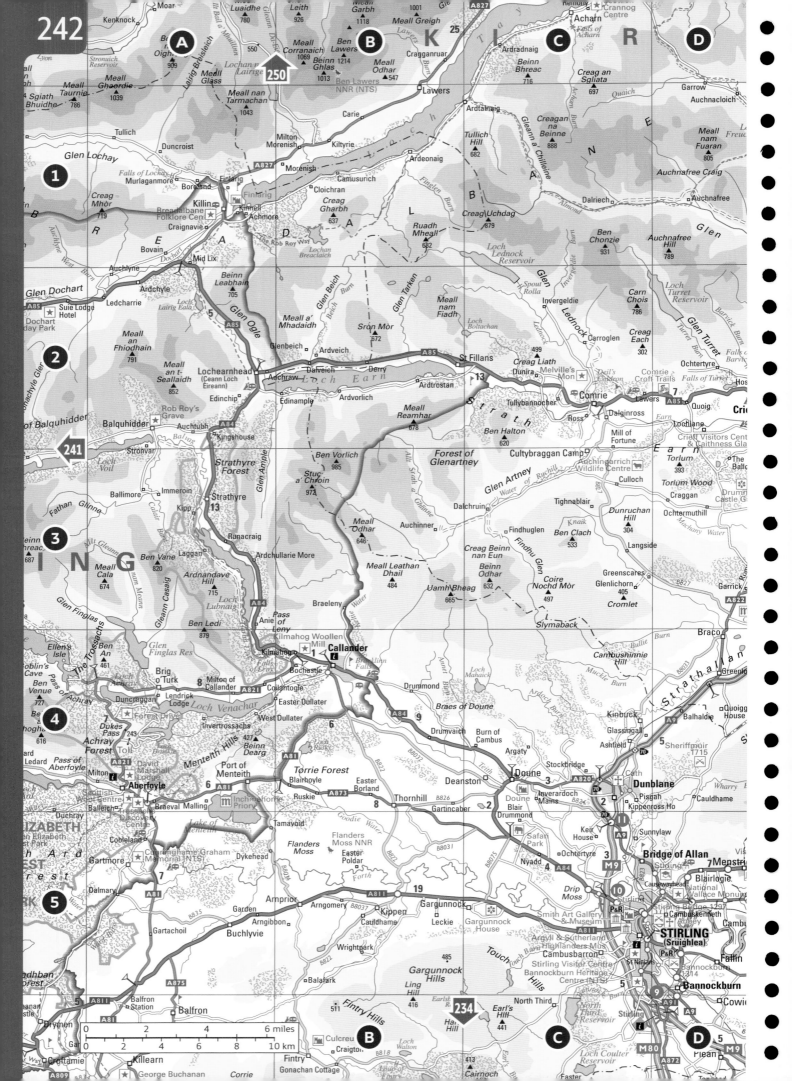

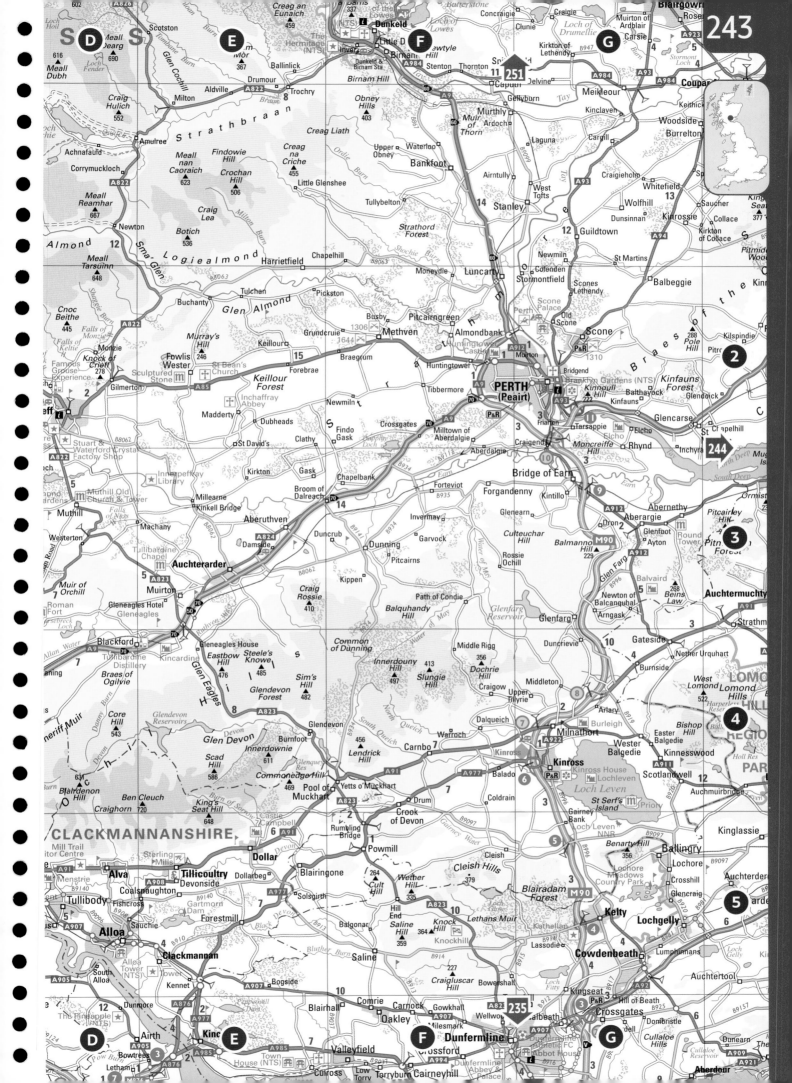

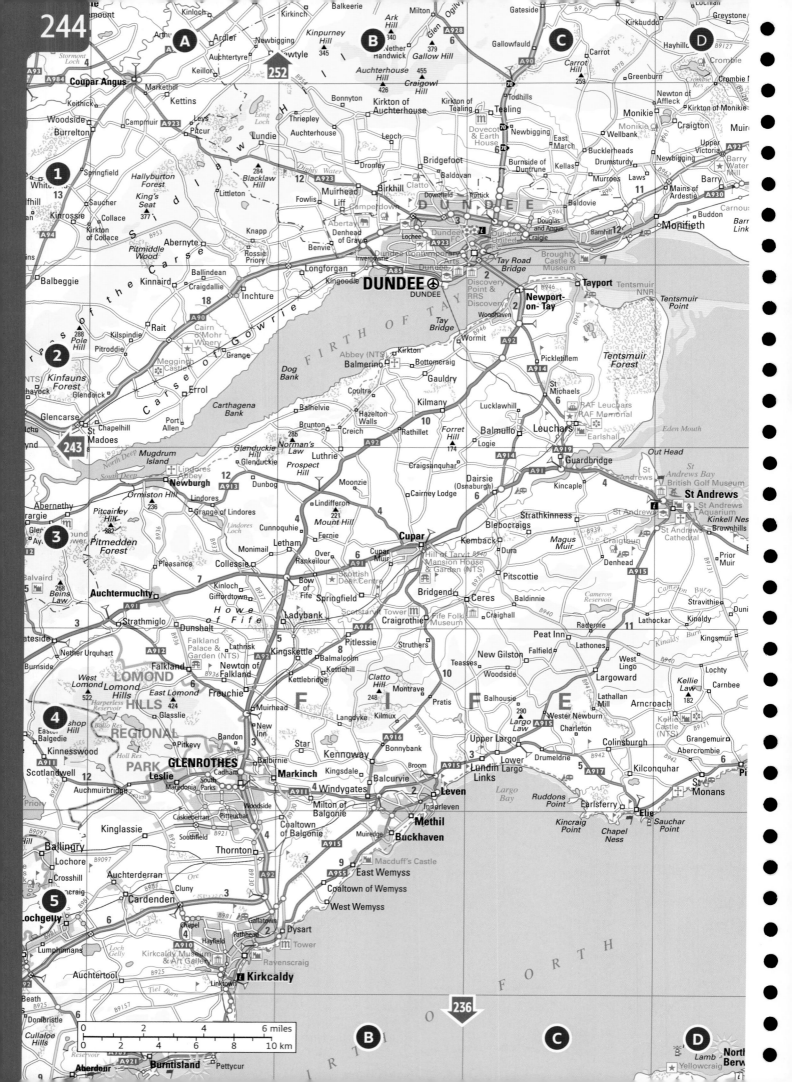

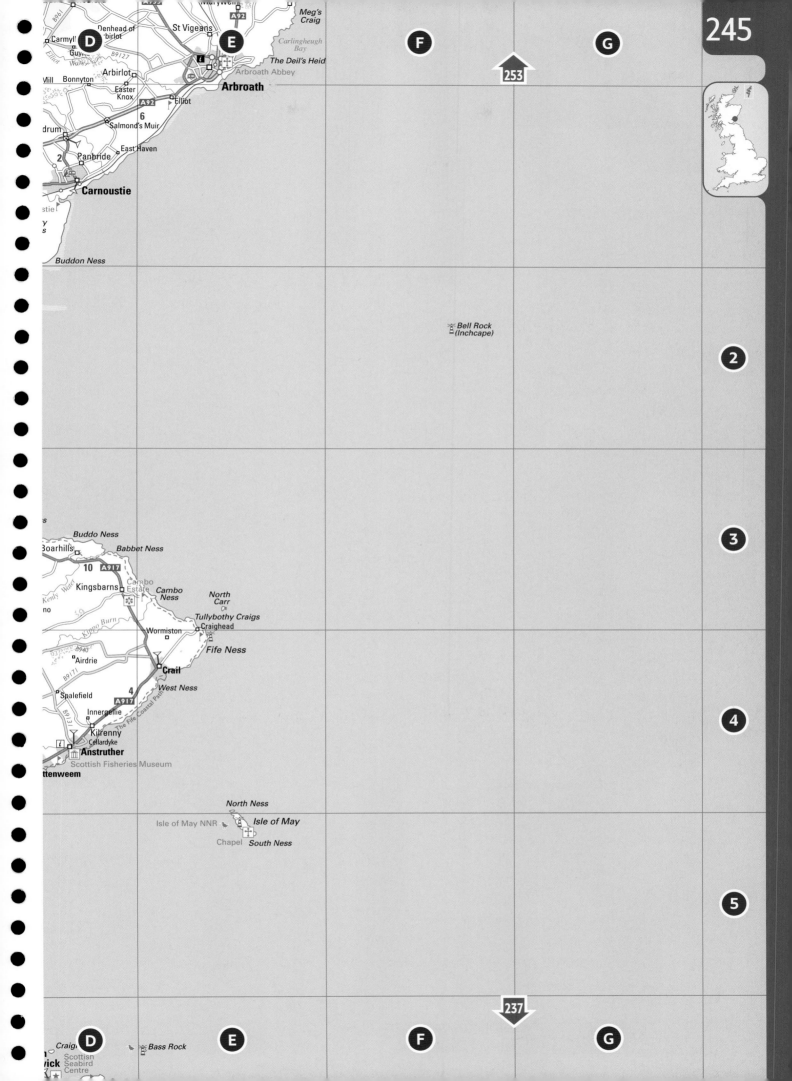

D
E
F
G

Meg's
Craig

St Vigeans

Carlingheugh
Bay

Denhead of
birlot

Carmyll

Guy

The Deil's Heid

Arbroath Abbey

Arbirlot

Bonnyton

Easter
Knox

Mill

Arbroath

Elliot

drum

Salmond's Muir

6

East Haven

Panbride

2

Carnoustie

stie

s

Buddon Ness

Bell Rock
(Inchcape)

2

Buddo Ness

Babbet Ness

Boarhills

3

10   A917

Kingsbarns

Cambo
Estate

Cambo
Ness

North
Carr

Tullybothy Craigs

Wormiston

Craighead

no

Kinpo Burn

Airdrie

Fife Ness

Crail

West Ness

Spalefield

4   A917

Innergellie

The Fife Coastal Path

4

Kilrenny

Cellardyke

Anstruther

Scottish Fisheries Museum

ttenweem

North Ness

Isle of May NNR

Isle of May

Chapel

South Ness

5

253

237

D
E
F
G

Craig

Bass Rock

Scottish
Seabird
Centre

rick

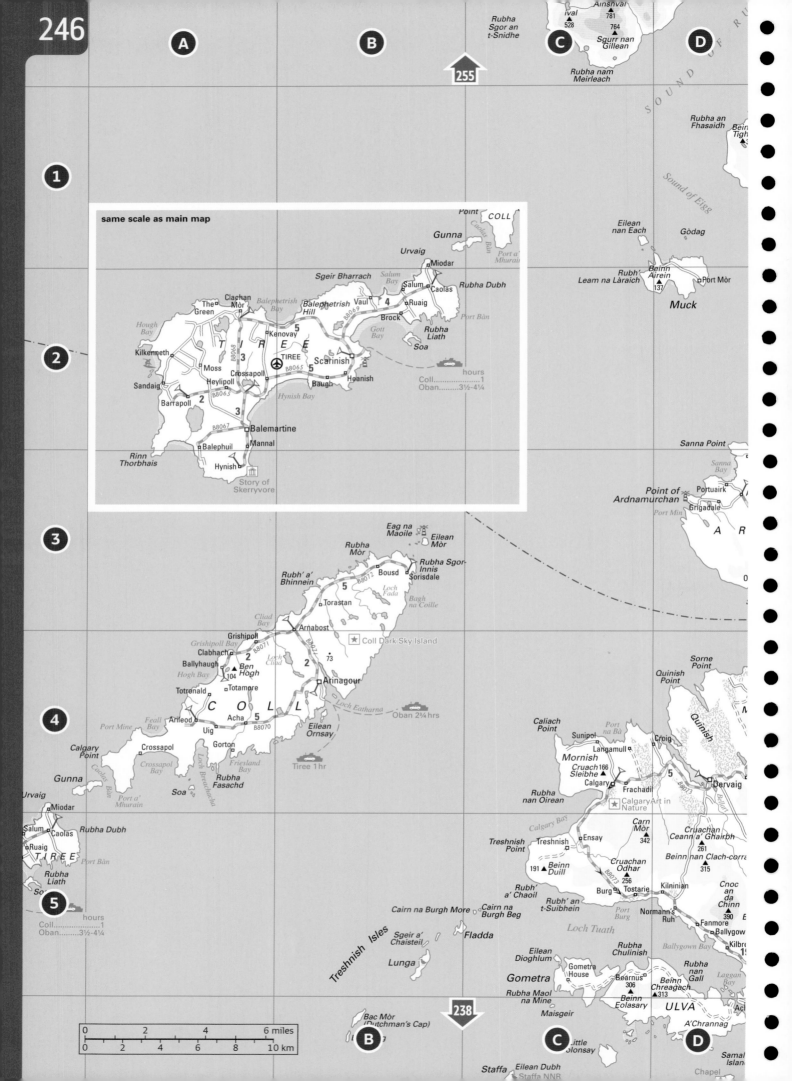

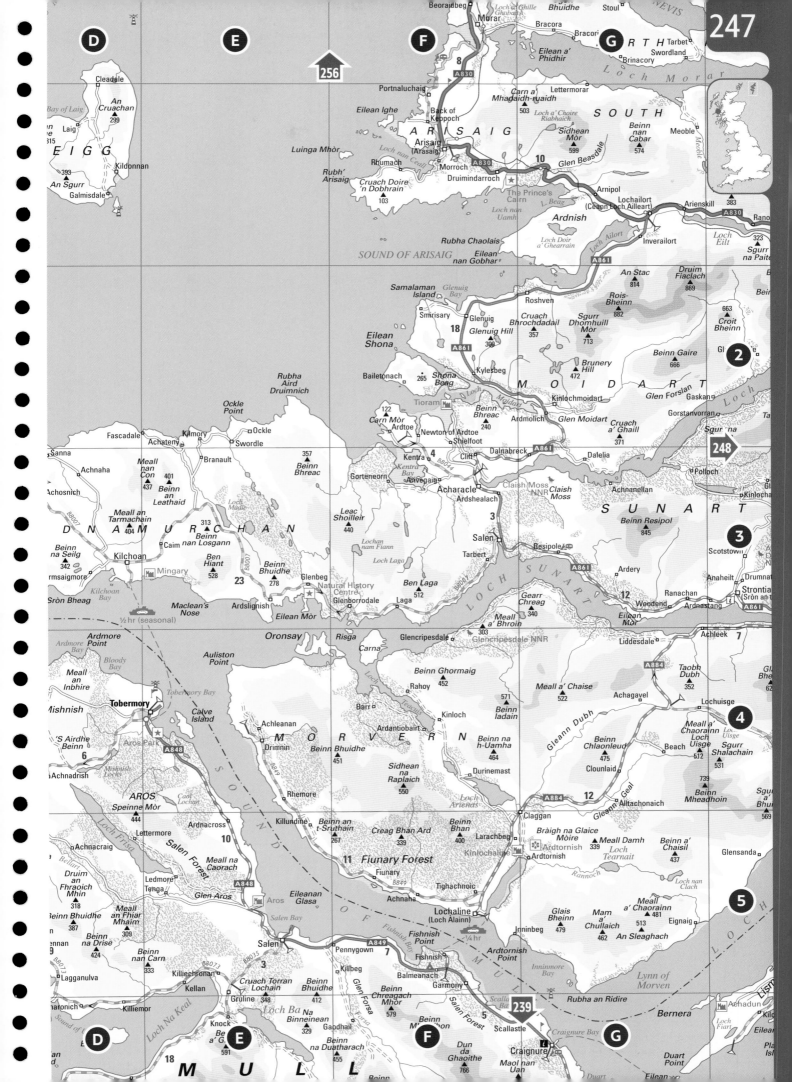

MORAR

A B C D

Kylesknoydart
Kylesmorar
Kinlochmorar
Swordland
Kinlochmorar

Sgurr na h-Aide 859
Sgurr B
Carn Mor
Glen Dessarry
Upper Glendessarry
Glendessarry Murlaggan
Strathan 470
Kinlocharkaig

256

Glen Pean Pean
Glen Finnan

Mullach Choire nan Geur- oirean 727
Locheil Forest
Gleann Camgharaidh
Glen Mallie
Inver Mallie

An Stac 718
Druim a' Chùirn
MORAR
Meith Bheinn 710
Meoble
Loch Beoraid

Sgurr an Ursainn 817
Sgurr nan Coireachan 956
Sgurr Thuilm 963
Streap 909
Stob Coire nan Cearc 887
Braigh nan Uamhachan
Gulvain 987
765
962
Meall a' Phubuill 774
Druim Gleann Laoigh 698
Beinn Bhan 796
771

Sròn Thoraraidh 383
Kinlochbeoraid
Glas-charn 633
Sgurr an Utha 796
Beinn an Tuim 810
Na h-Uamhachan
Gleann Dubh Lighe 691
Gleann Fionnlighe
Gleann Suileag
Coille Mhòr 635
729
Stob a' Ghrianain 744
Strone

1

Arienskill
Ranochan
Sgurr a' Mhuidhe
A830
Glen Loy
Druim Fada

14

Inverailort
Loch Eilt
323
Sgurr na Paite
Glenfinnan Viaduct
Glenfinnan (Gleann Fhionnainn)
Glenfinnan Monument (NTS)
A830
Kinlocheil
Corribeg Fassfern
Loch Eil Outward Bound
Meall Bhanabhie 326
Torcastle

Druim Fiaclach 869
Beinn Odhar Mhòr 870
Beinn Odhar Bheag 882
Meall a' Bhainne 559
Drumfern
Locheilside Sta
Loch Eil
11
Corpach (A' Chorpaich)
Neptune's Staircase
Banavie (Banbhaidh)

663
Croit Bheinn
Glenaladale
Sgorr Craobh a' Chaorainn 775
849
Sgurr Ghiubhsachain
Meall nan Damh 723
Garvan
Glen Garvan
Sròn an t- Sluichd
Duisky
Blaich
A861
Achaphubuil
Caol
Old Inverlochy

2

247

Croit
Glen Forslan
Gaskan
Glenaladale
Scamodale
Meall Mòr 759
Sgurr an Tarmachain 756
Resourie
Meall an Fheidh 423
367
Meall an Doire Shleaghaich 407
Stob Coire a' Chearcaill 770
Ceann Caol 488
467
Meall an t- Slamain
Camusnagaul
Trislaig
West Highland Line
Fort William (An Gearasdan)
West Highland Museum
Claggan (An Claig
T431 &

Sgurr na Greine 497
Gorstanvorran
Carn na Nathrach 786
Stob Mhic Bheathain 721
Corrlarach
Cona Glen
722
Sgurr an Lubhair
Goirtean a' Chladaich
21
Druimarbin
Bidhein Bad na h-Iolaire
Nevis Forest
Blarmachfoldach
Achintee Ho (Achadh an t-
Glen Nevis (Gleann Nibheis)

3

Pollach
Glenhurich
Kinlochan
Glen Hurich
Druim Garbh
Sgurr Dhomhnuill 888
Druim Leathad nam Fias
Glen Scaddle
Tighnacomaire
Creagbheitheachain
Sgorr a' Chaorainn 477
ARDGOUR
Glen Gour
Sgurr na h- Eanchainne 730
Aryhoulan
Inverscaddle Bay
A861
Corrychurrachan
Lundavra
Beinn na Gucaig 616
9
Polldubh
Achriabhach
Blar a' Chaorainn 939
Mullach nan Coirean
West Highland

Resipol 845
Scotstown
Arundle Oakwood NNR
Sgurr nan Cnamh 701
Sallachan
Clovullin
Corran (Ardgour)
Keppanach
Inchree
Doire Ban 566
Glenrigh Forest
Lairigmor
Mam na Gualainn 796
B863

Anaheilt
Drumnatorran
Strontian (Sròn an t-Sithein)
A861
Garbh Bheinn 885
Beinn Leamhain 502
7
Corran Narrows
Onich (Omhanaich)
3
North Ballachulish (Baile a' Chaolais a Tuath)

Ranachan
Ardnastang
woodend
Achnalea
Glen Tarbert
6
Gearradh
Rubh' a' Bhaid Bheithe
A82
Loch Leven
Caolasn

Achleek
7
Meall a' Choirein Luachraich 539
Inversanda
Inversanda Bay
South Ballachulish (Baile a' Chaolais a Deas)
Glencoe (A' Charnaich)
Ballachulish (Baile a' Chaolais)
Glencoe Visitor Centre (NTS)
Pap of Glencoe 742
Sgorr nam Fiannaidh 966
Ao.

A884
Taobh Dubh 352
Glas Bheinn 620
Creach Bheinn 853
Fuar Bheinn 765
Meall nan Each 591
Kilmalieu
Rubha Mòr
Cuil Bay
Kentallen (Ceann an t-Sàilein)
Auchindarroch
A828
Sgorr Dhonuil 1001
Sgorr Dhearg 1024
Bheithir
Sgorr a' Choise 663
Meall Mòr 676
1692
Ossian's Cave

4

Lochuisge
Beinn Na Cille 651
13
Eilean Balnagowan
Keil
Dalnatrat (Dail na Tràghad)
Glenduror Forest
Glen Duror
Beinn a' Bheithir
Laroch
Bidean nam Bian 1150

Meall a' Chaorainn Loch Uisge
Beach
512
Sgurr Shalachain 531
739
Glengalmadale
Camasnacroise
Rubha na h-Airde Uinnsinn
Achvlair
Salachan Glen
Fraochaidh 879
Salachail
Meall an Aodainn 679
Meall Lighiche 772
Sgor na h-Ulaidh 994
Beinn Maol Chaluim 847

Beinn Mheadhoin
Sgurr a' Bhuic 569
Ceanna Mòr
Loch a' Choire
Lurignich
Bealach
Meall Ban Mhic na Ceisich 655
627
Elleric (Eilearig)
Barnamuc
Beinn Fhionnlaidh 959
Invercharnan

Beinn a' Chaisil 437
Glensanda
Shuna Island
Appin House
North Dallens
Polanach
Fasnacloich
Invercreran
Glenure
Glen Ure
Beinn Sgulaird 932
Gualachulain

5

Loch nan Clach
Eilean Loch Oscair
Eilean Ramsay
Port Ramsay
Stalker
Ardtur
Appin (An Apainn)
Port Appin (Port na h-Againn)
Kinlochlaich
Portnacroish (Port na Croise)
Creagan
Inver
Druimavuic
Glasdrum Wood NNR
Glasdrum
Taraphocain
Creach Bheinn 810
Beinn Trilleachan 839
Kinlochetive
Eignaig 481
ghach

Bachuil
Clachan
Appin Rocks
Eilean Dubh
Eriska
North Shian (Sithean a Tuath)
South Shian (Sithean a Deas)
Seabank
Shian Wood
Scottish Sea Life Sanctuary
Dallachulish
South Creagan
Barcaldine (Am Barra Calltainn)
Achacha
Ben Starav 1078
822
Stob an Duine Ruaidh 957

Bernera
Duart Point
Eilean
Achadun
Kilcheran
Balure
Baligrundle
Lismore
Lynn of Lorn
8
Achnacroish
Kiel Crofts
Culcharan
A828
240
Benderloch (Meadarloch)
Meadaig (Leideag)
708
Beinn Molurgainn 690
Dail
Beinn us
Ardmaddy
Beinn Mheadhonach 714
Cadderlie
Meall an Fheuraich
Glen Kinglass

0 2 4 6 miles
0 2 4 6 8 10 km

B C D

Duart
Eilean
Ledaig Black
Ardmucknish Bay
North
Inverliver

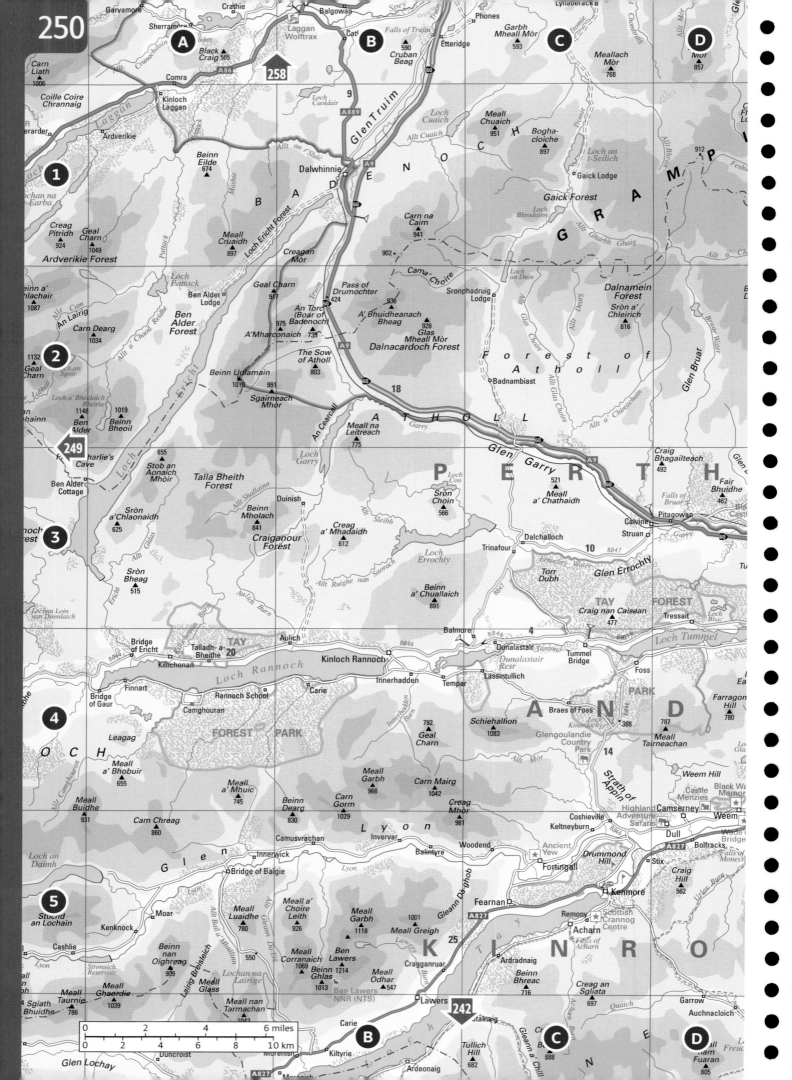

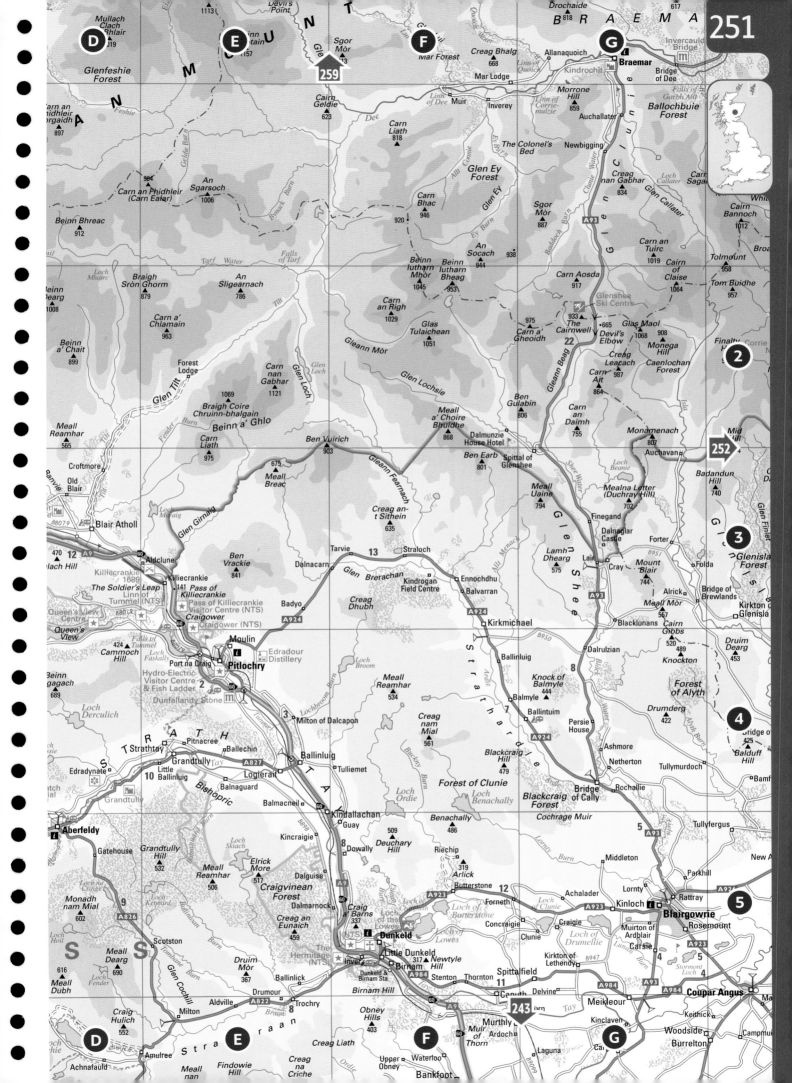

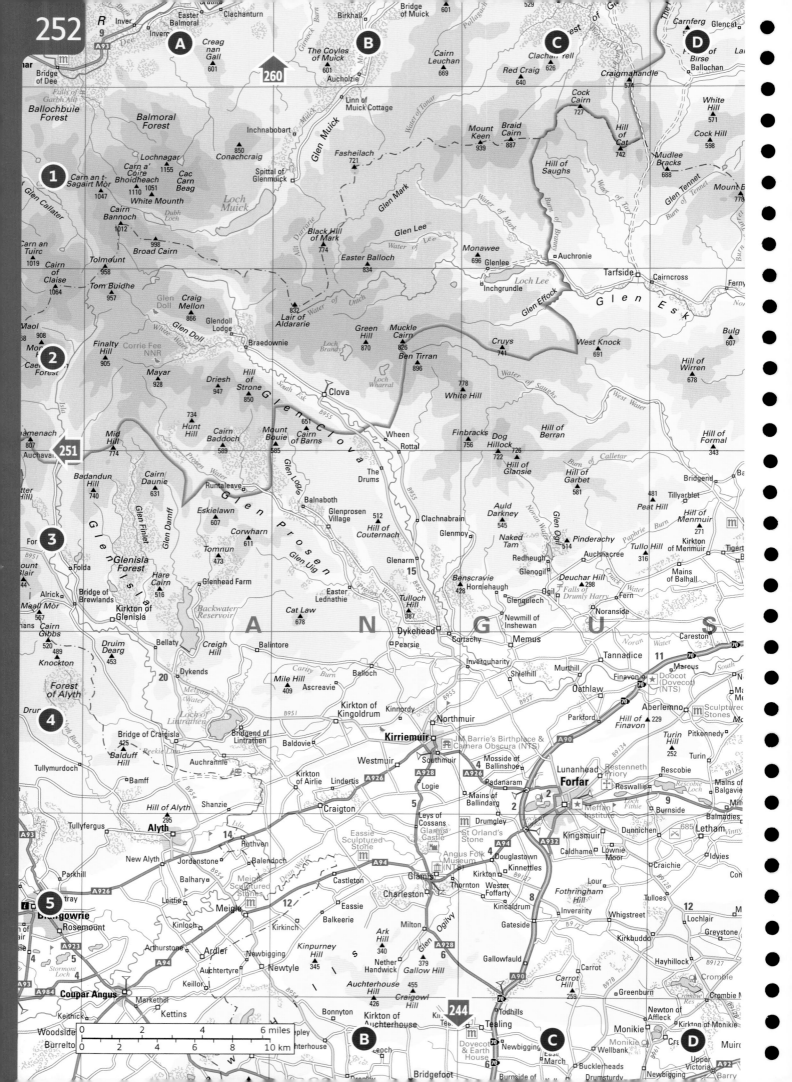

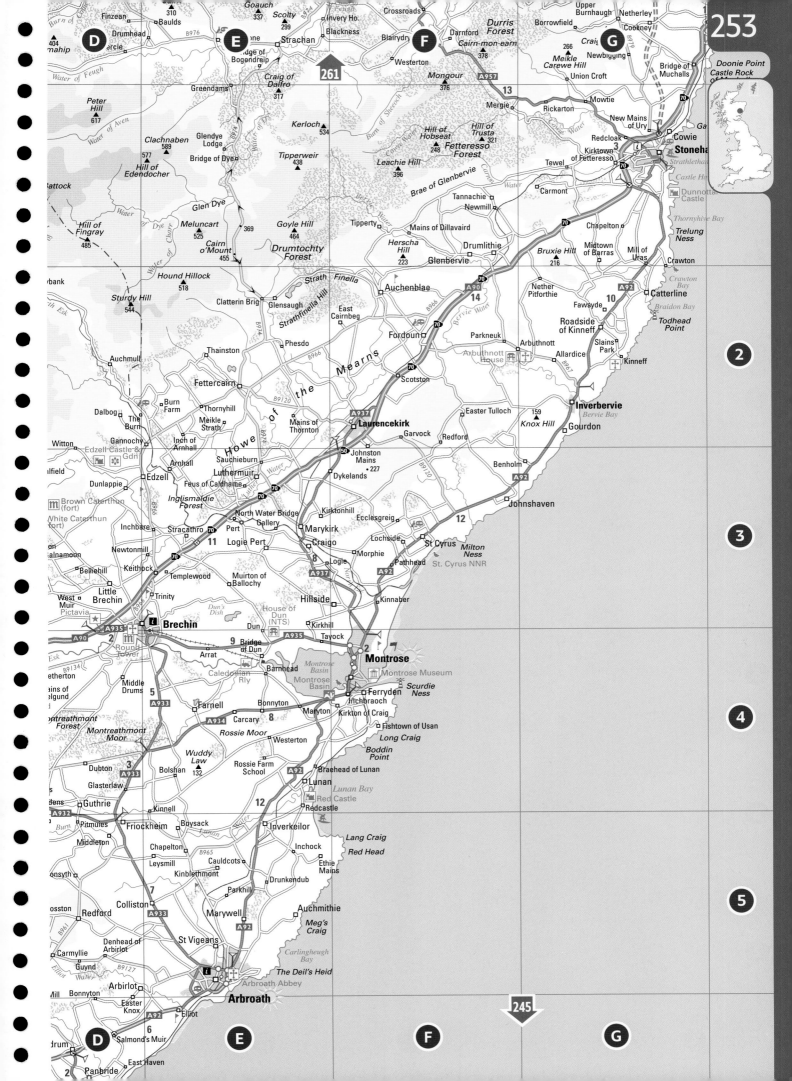

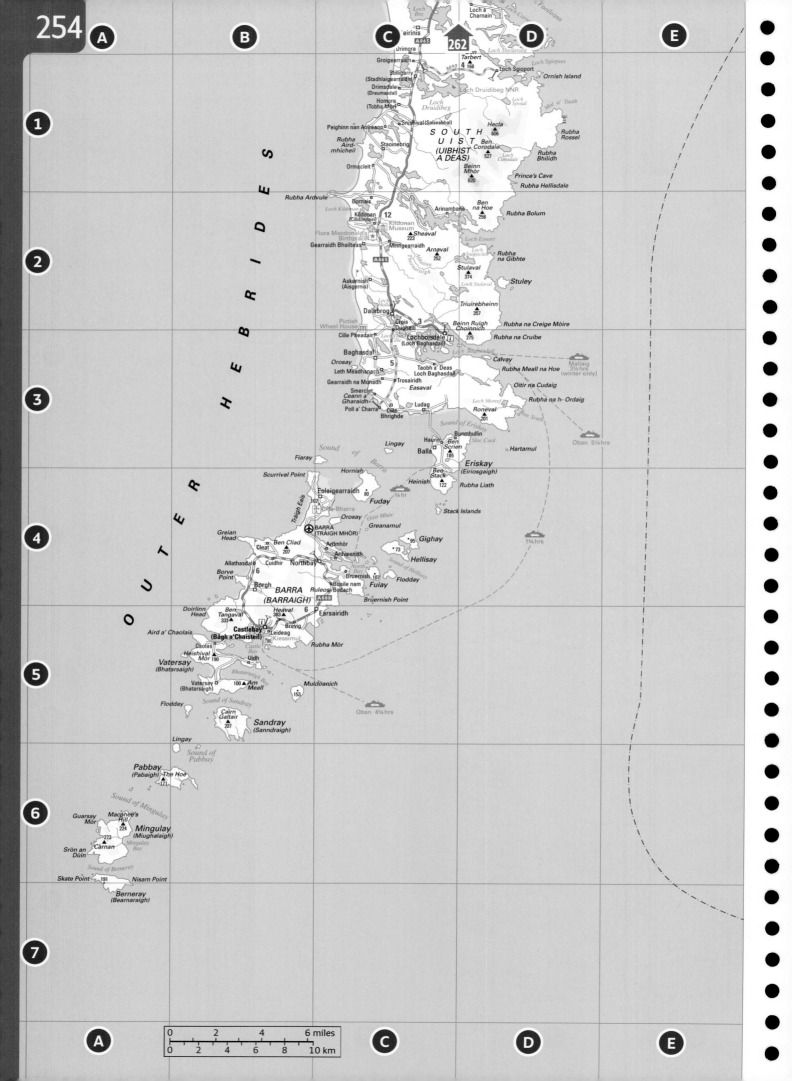

SOUTH UIST (UIBHIST A DEAS)

OUTER HEBRIDES

BARRA (BARRAIGH)

Vatersay (Bhatarsaigh)

Sandray (Sanndraigh)

Pabbay (Pabaigh)

Mingulay (Miughalaigh)

Berneray (Bearnaraigh)

| 0 | 2 | 4 | 6 miles |
| 0 | 2 4 6 8 | 10 km |

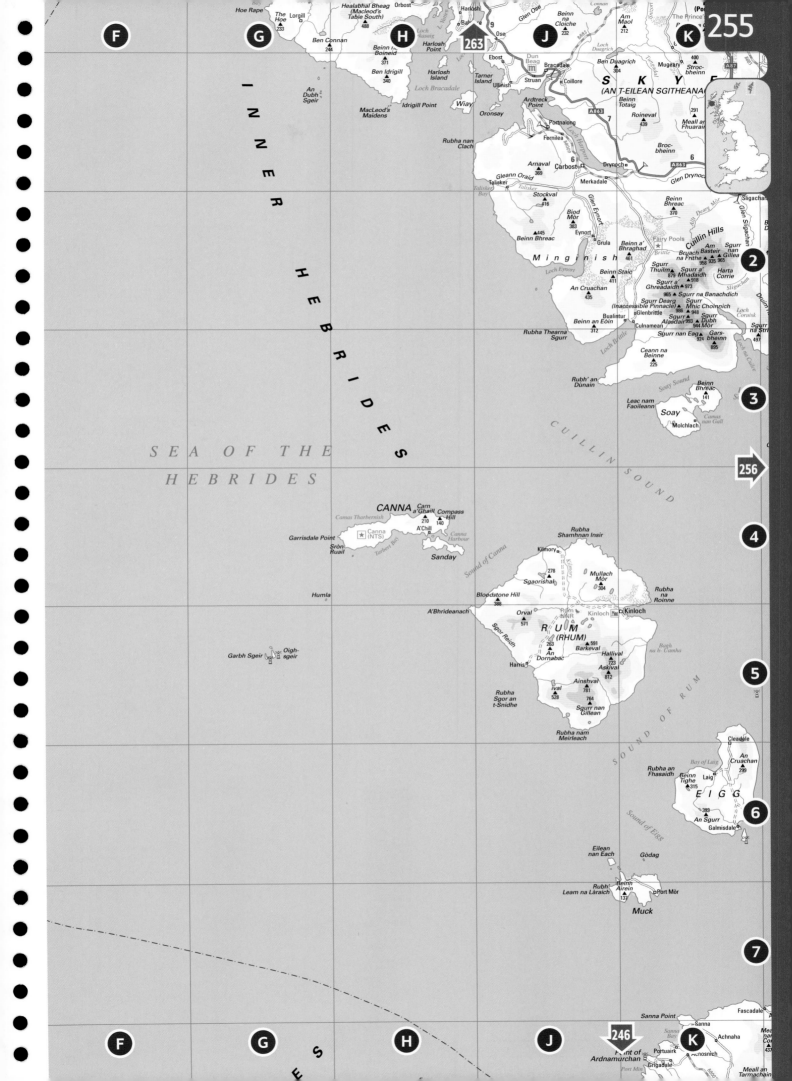

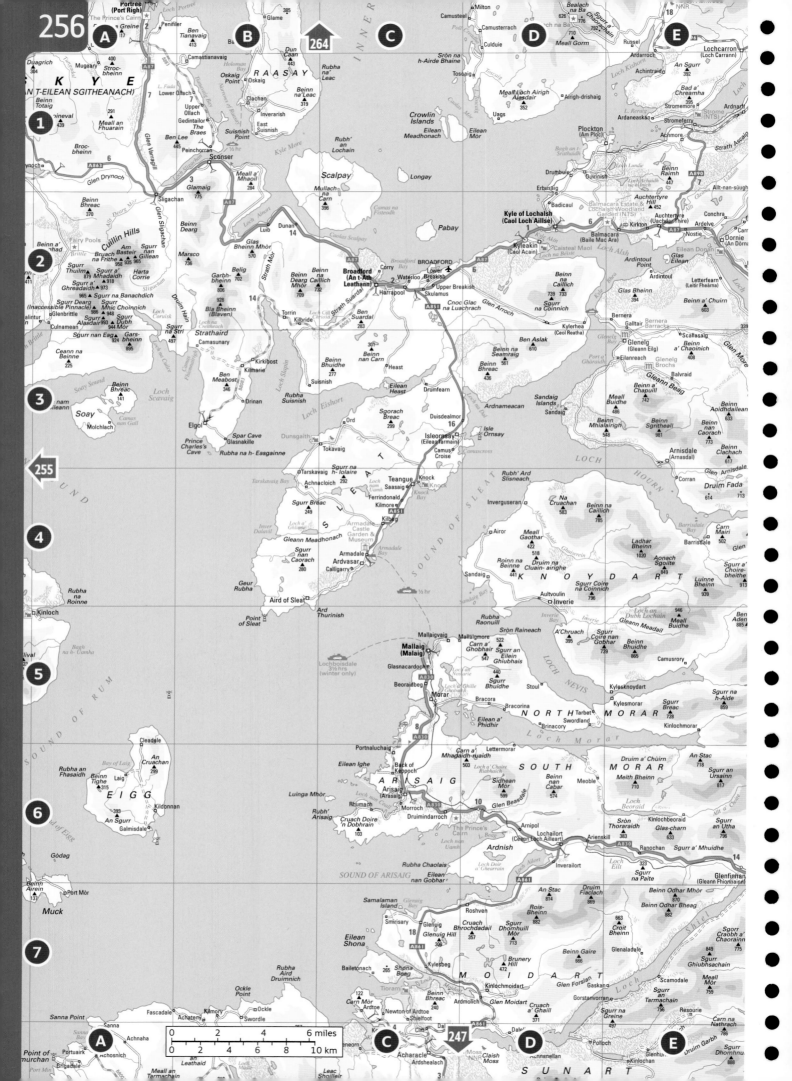

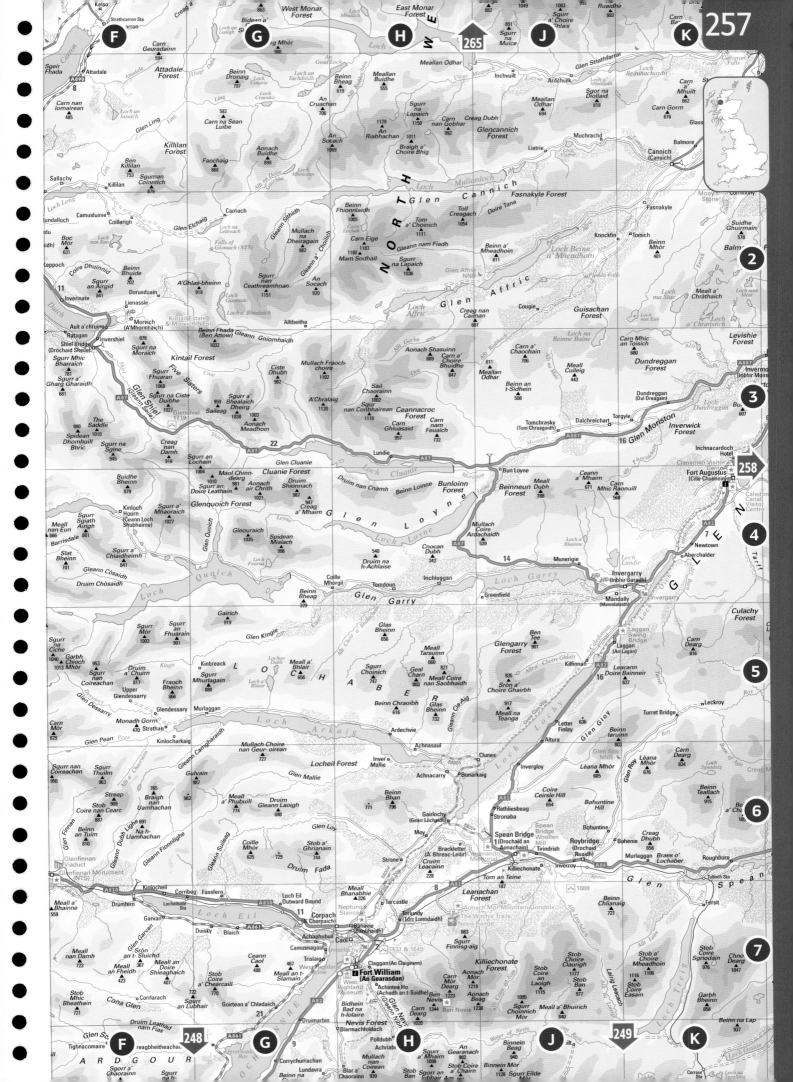

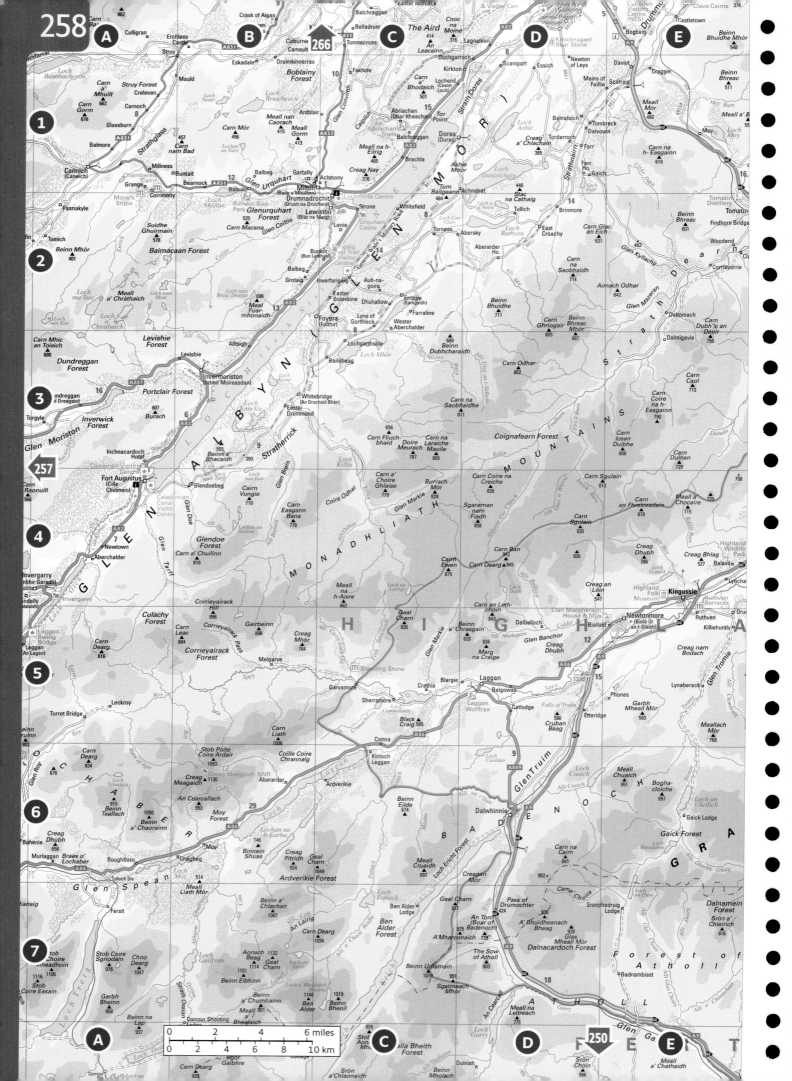

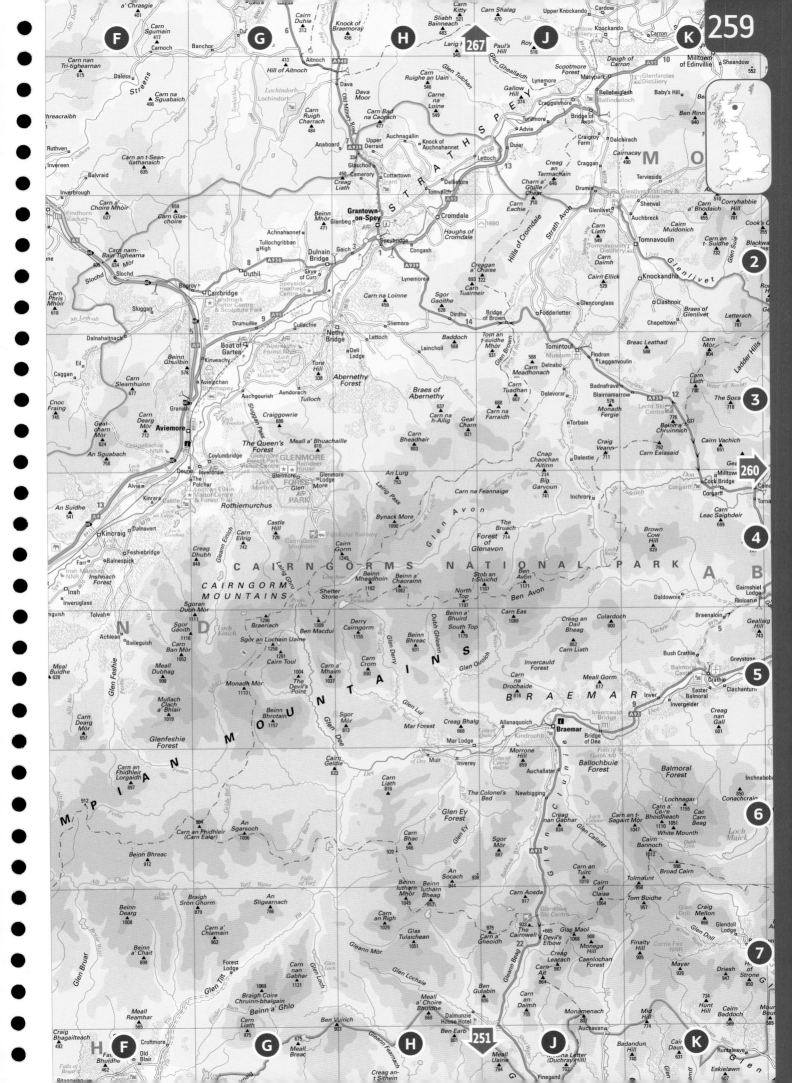

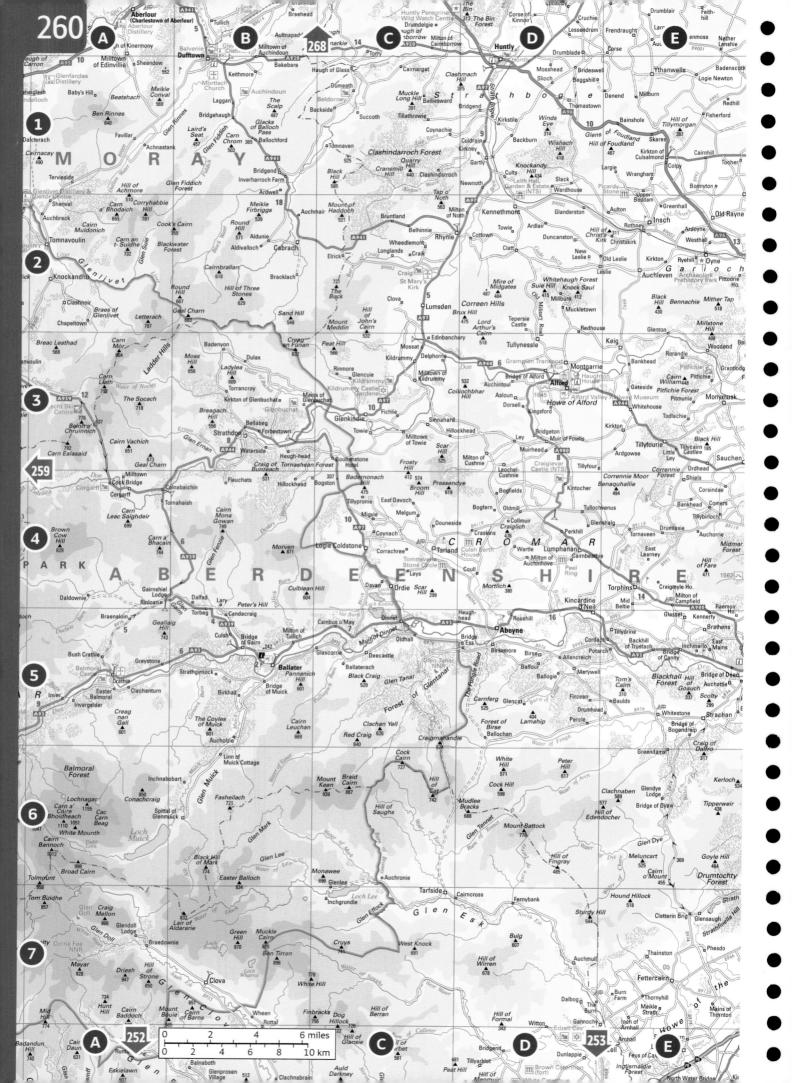

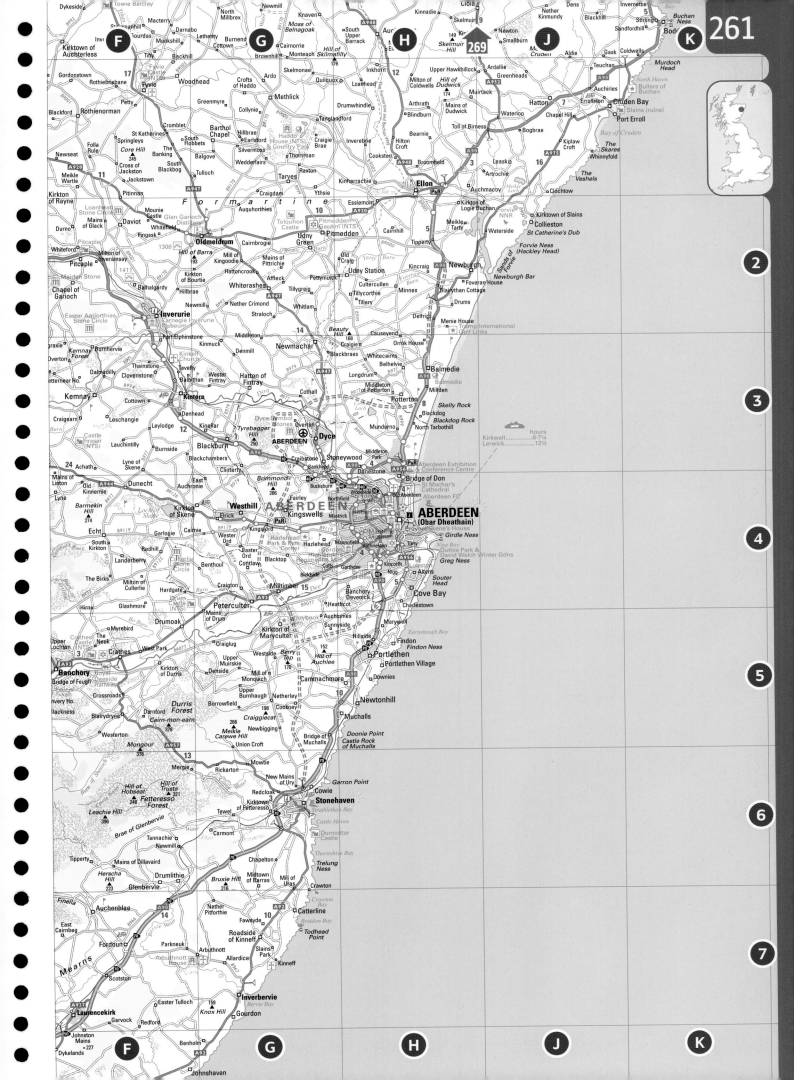

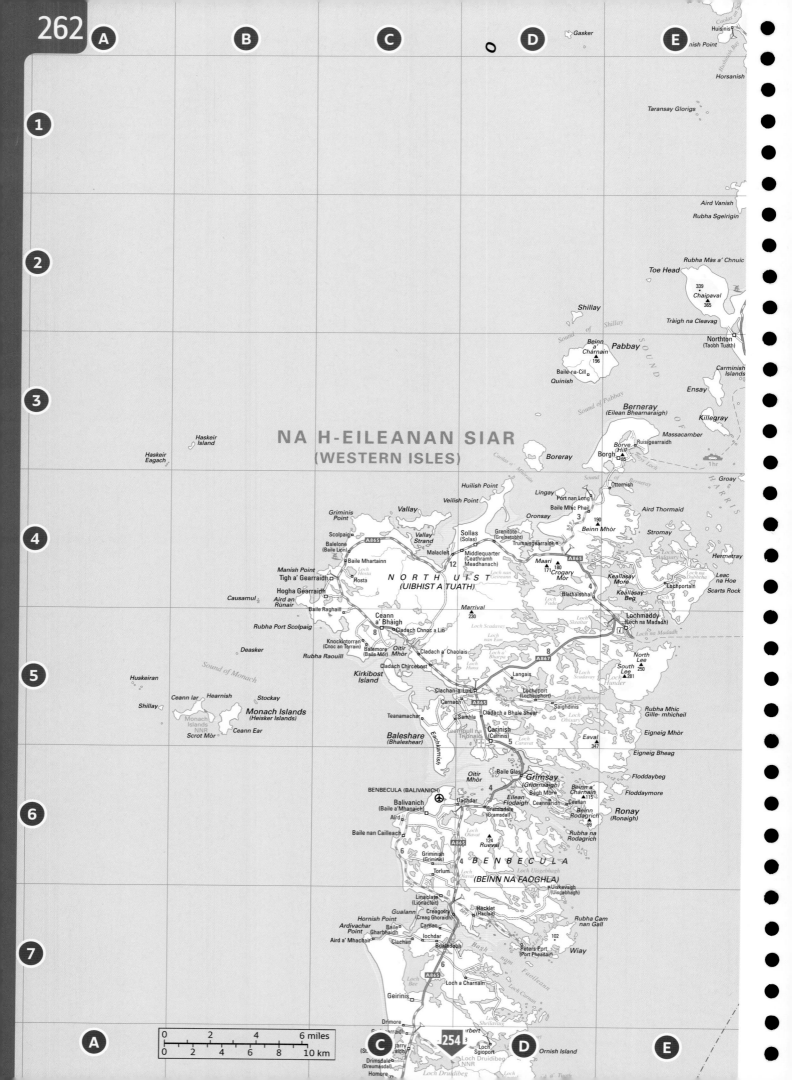

NA H-EILEANAN SIAR
(WESTERN ISLES)

NORTH UIST
(UIBHIST A TUATH)

BENBECULA
(BEINN NA FAOGHLA)

BENBECULA (BALIVANICH)

Monach Islands
(Heisker Islands)

Sound of Monach

Pabbay

Berneray
(Eilean Bhearnaraigh)

Killegray

Ensay

Northton
(Taobh Tuath)

Toe Head

Chaipaval
365
339

Tràigh na Cleavag

Rubha Màs a' Chnuic

Rubha Sgeirigin

Aird Vanish

Taransay Glorigs

Horsanish

Huisinis

Gasker

Carminish
Islands

Massacamber

Groay

Gray

Lochportain

Scarts Rock

Leac
na Hoe

Hermetray

Stromay

Aird Thormaid

Keallasay
More

Keallasay
Beg

Lochmaddy
(Loch na Madadh)

North
Lee

South
Lee
281

Rubha Mhic
Gille- mhicheil

Eigneig Mhòr

Eigneig Bheag

Eaval
347

Ronay
(Ronaigh)

Rubha na
Rodagrich

Beinn
Rodagrich
99

Beinn
a' Chàrnain
115

Floddaybeg

Floddaymore

Rubha Cam
nan Gall

Wiay

Peters Port
(Port Pheadair)
102

Saighdinis

Langais

Locheport
(Lochephort)

Clachan-a-Luib

Carnach

Cladach a Bhale Shear

Samhla

Teanamachar

Baleshare
(Bhaleshear)

Carinish
(Cairinis)

Grimsay
(Griomsaigh)

Bàgh Mòr

Baile Glas

Oitir
Mhòr

Eilean
Flodaigh

Ceannaridh

Ceallan

Gramisdale
(Gramsdal)

Uachdar

Balivanich
(Baile a'Mhanaich)

Aird

Baile nan Cailleach

Griminish
(Griminis)

Torlum

Rueval
124

Linaclate
(Lionacleit)

Creagofry
(Creag Ghoraidh)

Hacklet
(Haclait)

Uiskevagh
(Uisgebhagh)

Gualann

Hornish Point

Ardivachar
Point

Baile
Gharbhaidh

Carnan

Iochdar

Clachan

Bualadobh

Aird a' Machair

Geirinis

Drimore

Loch a Charnain

Loch
Bee

Gearraidh
(St.

Garry
raidh)

Drimsdale
(Dreumasdal)

Hombre

Ornish Island

Loch Druidibeg
NNR

Loch Sgioport

Loch
Druidibeg

Huskeiran

Shillay

Ceann Iar

Hearnish

Stockay

Ceann Ear

Scrot Mòr

Monach
Islands
NNR

Kirkibost
Island

Cladach Chircebost

Oitir
Mhòr

Batemore
(Baile-Mòr)

Knockintorran
(Cnoc an Torrain)

Deasker

Rubha Raouill

Ceann
a' Bhàigh

Cladach Chnoc a Lìn

Cladach a' Chaolais

Rubha Port Scolpaig

Causamul

Aird an
Rùnair

Baile Raghaill

Hogha Gearraidh

Tigh a' Gearraidh

Manish Point

Hosta

Baile Mhartainn

Balelone
(Baile Lìon)

Scolpaig

Griminis
Point

Valley

Valley
Strand

Malaclet

Sollas
(Solas)

Middlequarter
(Ceathramh
Meadhanach)

Veilish Point

Huilish Point

Grenitote
(Greinetobht)

Trumaisgearraidh

Oronsay

Lingay

Port nan Long

Baile Mhic Phail

Beinn Mhòr
190

Maari
180
171

Crogary
Mòr

Blathaisbhal

Marrival
230

Otternish

Borve
Hill

Borgh

Ruisigearraidh

Baile-na-Cill

Quinish

Beinn
a'
Chàrnain
196

Shillay

Haskeir
Island

Haskeir
Eagach

Loch
Hunder

Loch
Scadavay

Loch
Scadavay

Loch
Fada

Loch
Euphoirt

Loch
Obisary

1hr

254

A865

A867

A865

A865

12

8

8

8

4

4

5

5

6

6

3

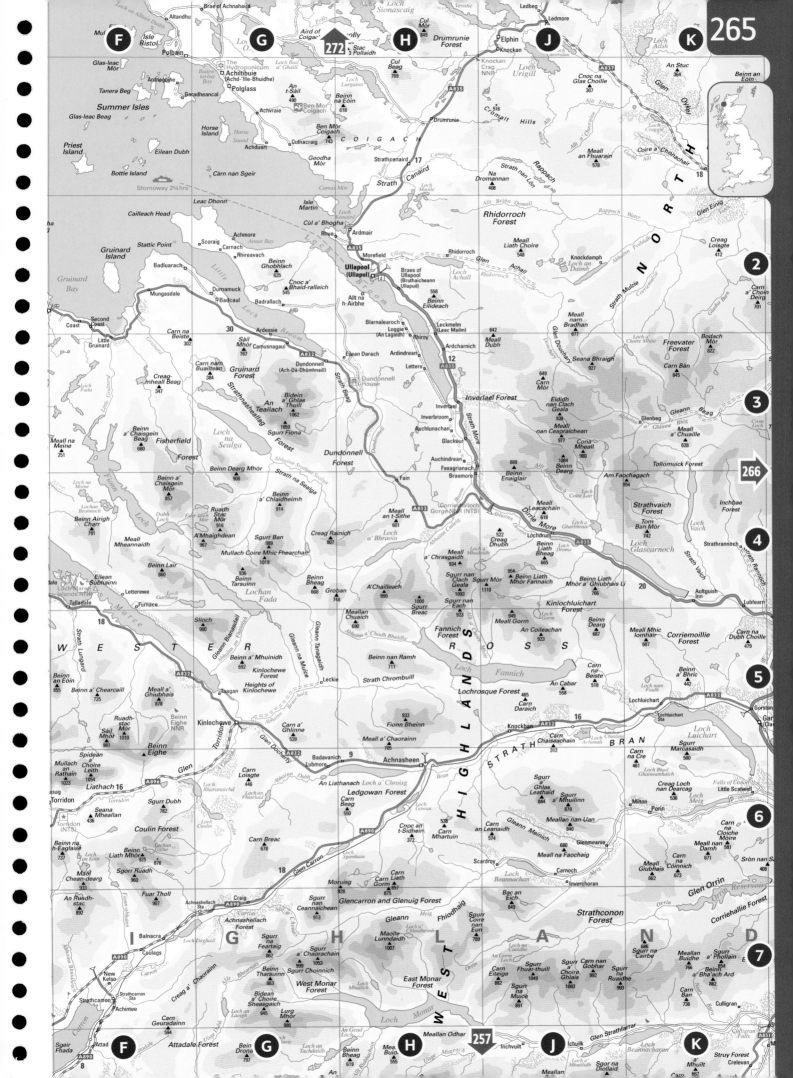

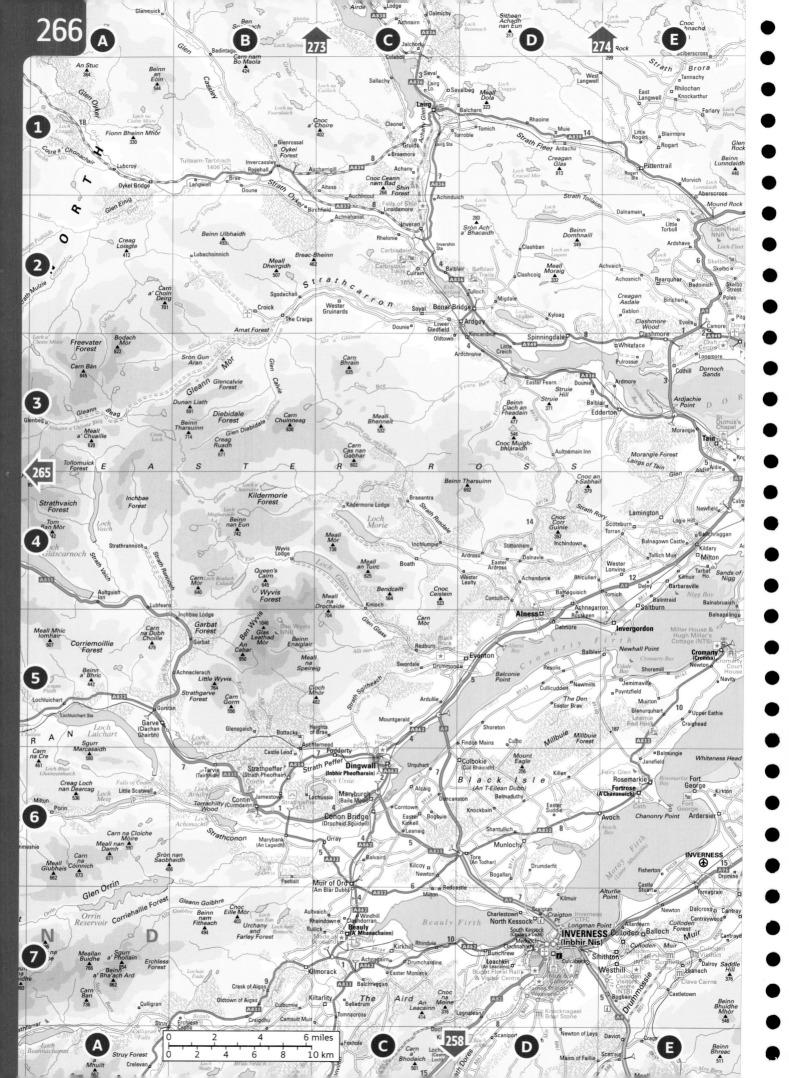

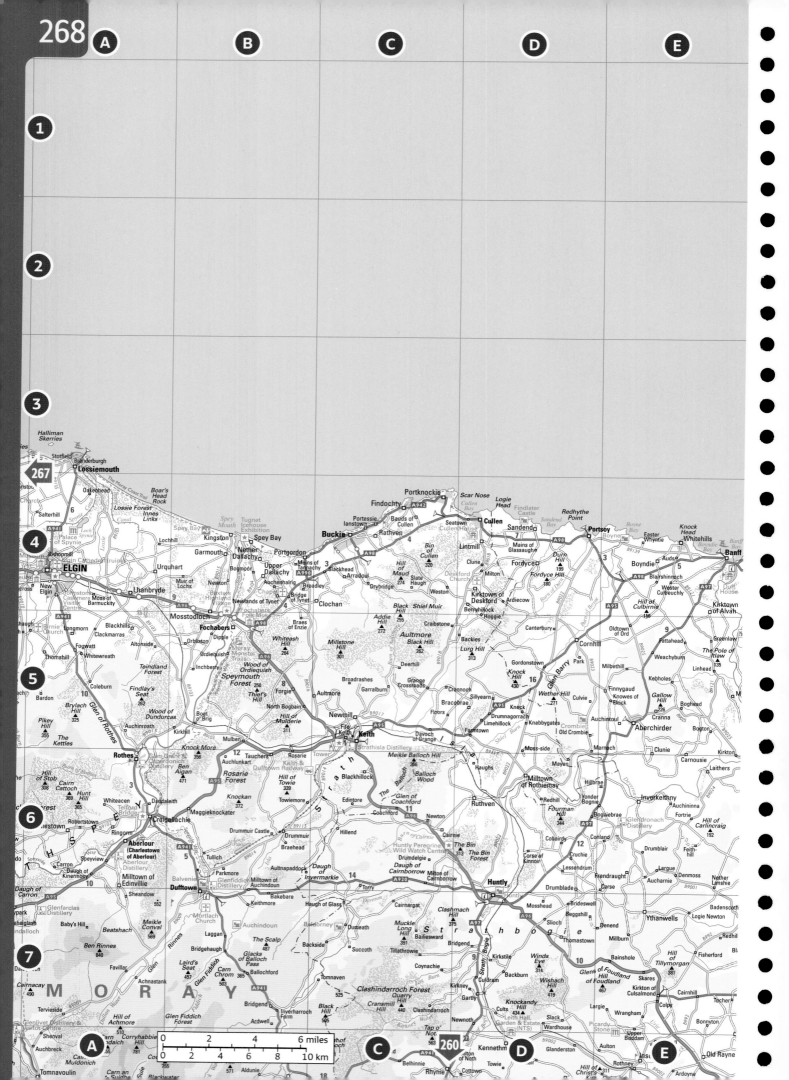

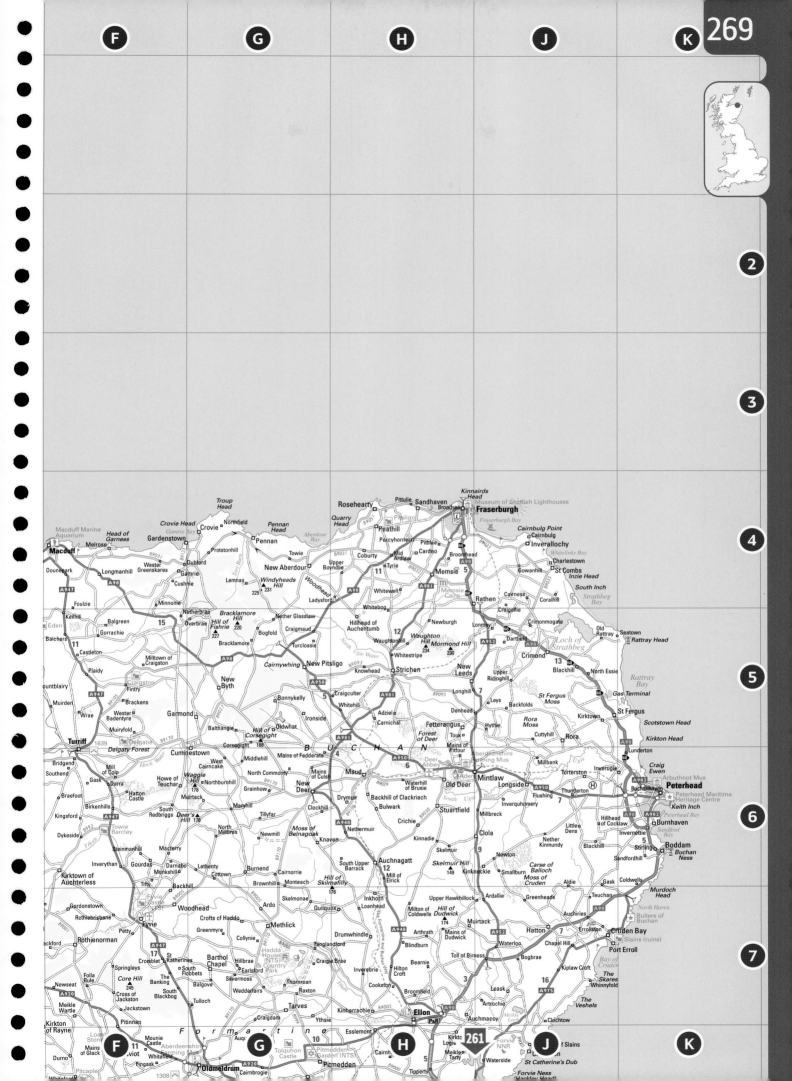

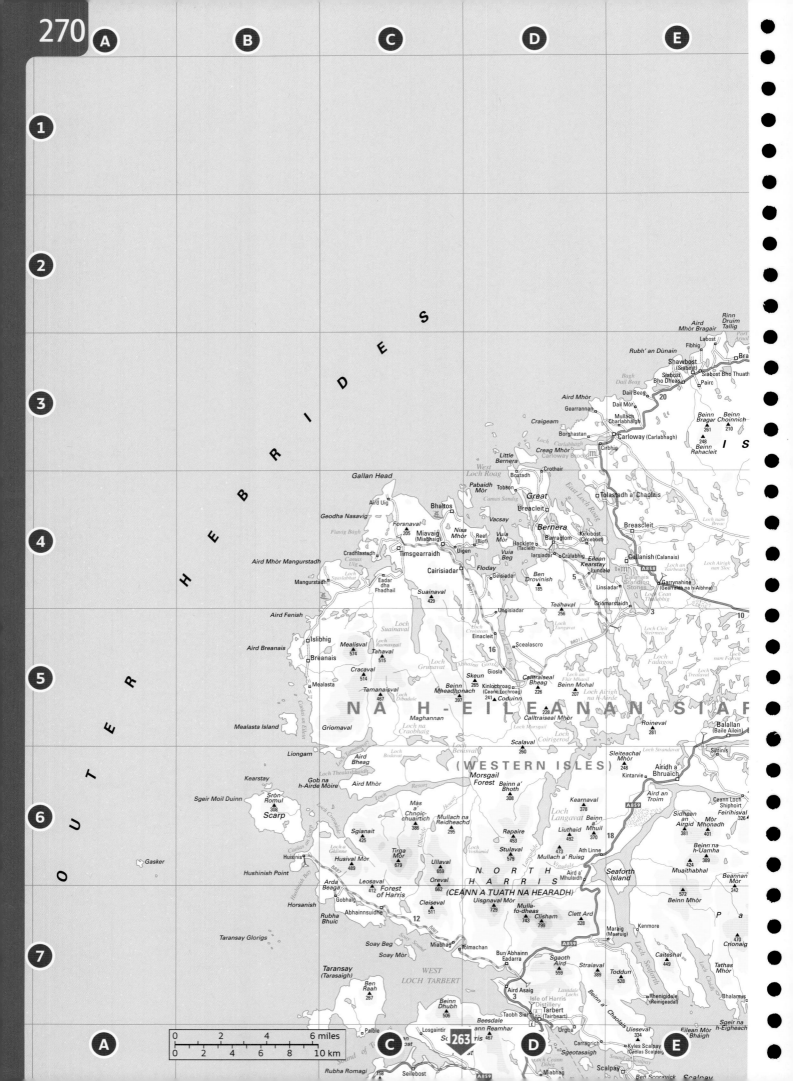

OUTER HEBRIDES

NA H-EILEANAN SIAR

(WESTERN ISLES)

NORTH HARRIS
(CEANN A TUATH NA HEARADH)

Forest of Harris

WEST LOCH TARBERT

Isle of Harris Distillery
Tarbert (Tairbeart)

Morsgail Forest

Loch Langavat

Seaforth Island

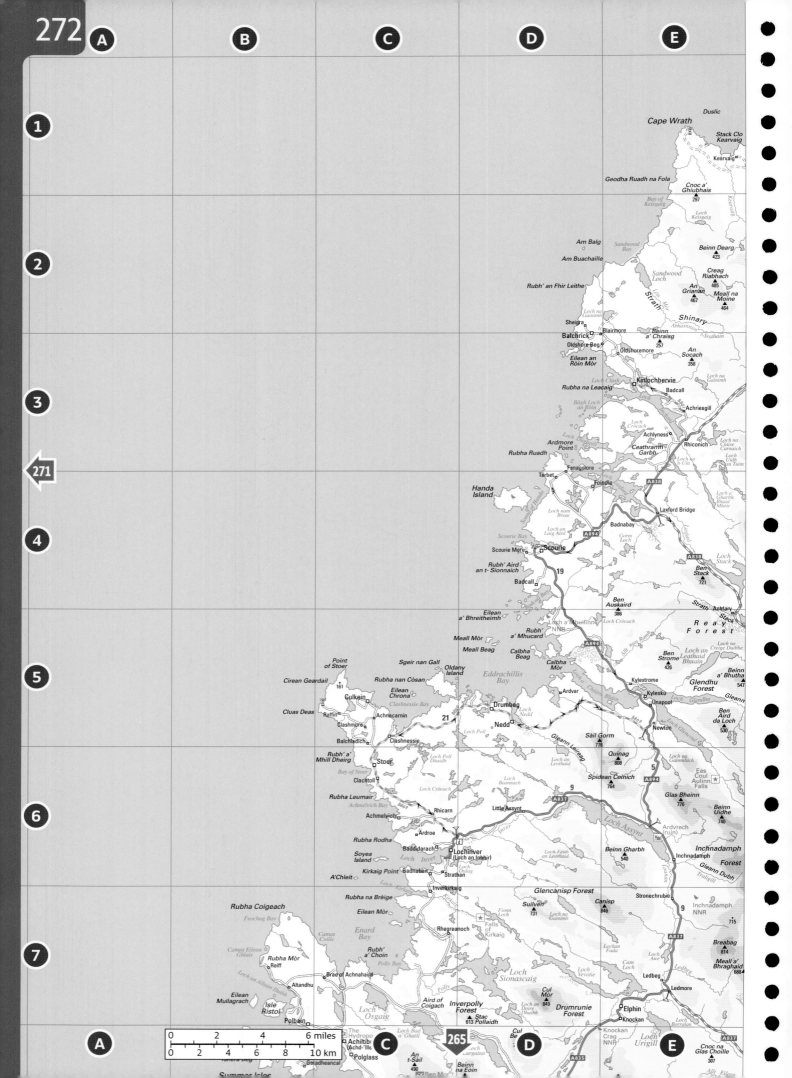

A B C D E

1

Cape Wrath
Duslic
Stack Clo
Kearvaig
Kearvaig
Geodha Ruadh na Fola
Cnoc a'
Ghiubhais
297
Bay of
Keisgaig
Loch
Keisgaig

2
Am Balg
Sandwood Bay
Beinn Dearg
423
Am Buachaille
Sandwood
Loch
Creag
Riabhach
485
Rubh' an Fhir Leithe
An
Grianan
467
Meall na
Moine
464
Strath
Shinary
Sheigra
Blairmore
Beinn
a' Chraisg
257
Balchrick
Oldshore Beg
Oldshoremore
An
Socach
358
Eilean an
Ròin Mòr
Loch Clash
Kinlochbervie
Rubha na Leacaig
Badcall

3
Achriesgill
Bàgh Loch
an Ròin
Achlyness
Loch
Cròcach
Ardmore
Point
Ceathramh
Garbh
Rhiconich
Loch na
Claise
Carnaich
Rubha Ruadh
Fanagmore
Loch
Uidh
an Tuim

271
Tàrbet
Foindle
A838
Loch a'
Gharbh
Bhaid Mhòr
Handa
Island
Laxford Bridge
Sound of Handa
Loch nam
Breac
Badnabay
A894
Loch an
Laig Aird

4
Scourie Bay
Scourie More
Scourie
A838
Gorm
Loch
Loch
Stack
Ben
Stack
721
Rubh' Aird
an t- Sionnaich
19
Strath
Achfary
Reay
Forest
Badcall
Ben
Auskaird
386
Loch na
Creige Duibhe

5
Eilean
a' Bhreitheimh
Loch a' Mbuilinn
NNR
Loch Cròcach
Ben
Strome
426
Loch an
Leathaid
Bhuain
Rubh'
a' Mhucard
Meall Mòr
Calbha
Beag
Beinn
a' Bhutha
547
Meall Beag
Calbha
Mòr
Kylestrome
Glendhu
Forest
Point
of Stoer
Sgeir nan Gall
Oldany
Island
Eddrachillis
Bay
Loch Chùrn Bhàin
Kylesku
Gleann
Cirean Geardail
161
Rubha nan Còsan
Eilean
Chròna
Ardvar
Unapool
Ben
Aird
da Loch
530
Culkein
Clashnessie Bay
Drumbeg
Loch
Nedd
Newton
Cluas Deas
Raffin
Achnacarnin
21
Nedd
Clashmore
Balchladich
Clashnessie
Loch Poll
Sàil Gorm
776
Loch
Poll
Gleann Leireag

6
Rubh' a'
Mhill Dheirg
Stoer
Loch Poll
Dhaidh
Quinag
808
Loch na
Gainmhich
Bay of Stoer
Clachtoll
Loch Beannach
Loch an
Leathaid
Spidean Coinich
764
5
A894
Eas
Coul
Aulinn
Falls
Rubha Leumair
Loch Cròcach
9
A837
Glas Bheinn
776
Achmelvich Bay
B869
Rhicarn
Little Assynt
Inver
Loch Assynt
Ardvreck
(ruin)
Beinn
Uidhe
740
Achmelvich
Rubha Rodha
Ardroe
Beinn Gharbh
540
Inchnadamph
Inchnadamph
Forest
Baddidarach
Lochinver
(Loch an Inbhir)
Loch Fèith
an Leothaid
Gleann Dubh
Traligill
Soyea
Island
Loch Inver
Badnaban
Strathan
Kirkaig Point
A'Chleit
Glencanisp Forest
Stronechrubie
Inverkirkaig
Rubha na Brèige
Suilven
731
Canisp
846
9
Inchnadamph
NNR
Rubha Coigeach
Eilean Mòr
Kirkaig
Fionn
Loch
Loch na
Gainmhich
715
Feochag Bay
Rhegreanoch
Falls
of
Kirkaig
A837

7
Camas
Coille
Rubh'
a' Choin
Breabag
814
Camas Eilean
Ghlais
Polly Bay
Enard
Bay
Loch
Sionascaig
Lochan
Fada
Meall a'
Bhraghaid
688
Rubha Mòr
Reiff
Loch
Veyatie
Cam
Loch
Loch
Awe
Ledbeg
Altandhu
Brae of Achnahaird
Loch un Altain Dubh
Cùl
Mòr
849
Ledmore
Eilean
Mullagrach
Isle
Ristol
Aird of
Coigach
Loch na
Doire
Dhuibh
Drumrunie
Forest
Elphin
Polbain
Loch Polly
Inverpolly
Forest
Stac
613 Pollaidh
Knockan
Loch
Borralan
A835

A
The
Hydropo
Achiltib
(Achd- Ille)
Polglass
0 2 4 6 miles
0 2 4 6 8 10 km
Loch
Osgaig
C
Loch Bad
a' Ghaill
An
t-Sàil
265
Cùl
Be
D
Knockan
Crag
NNR
Knockan
Cargainn
A835
Loch
Urigill
E
Cnoc na
Glas Choille
307
Tanera Beg
Garadheancal
An
490
Summer Isles
Ben Mor
na Eoin
Allt Eileag

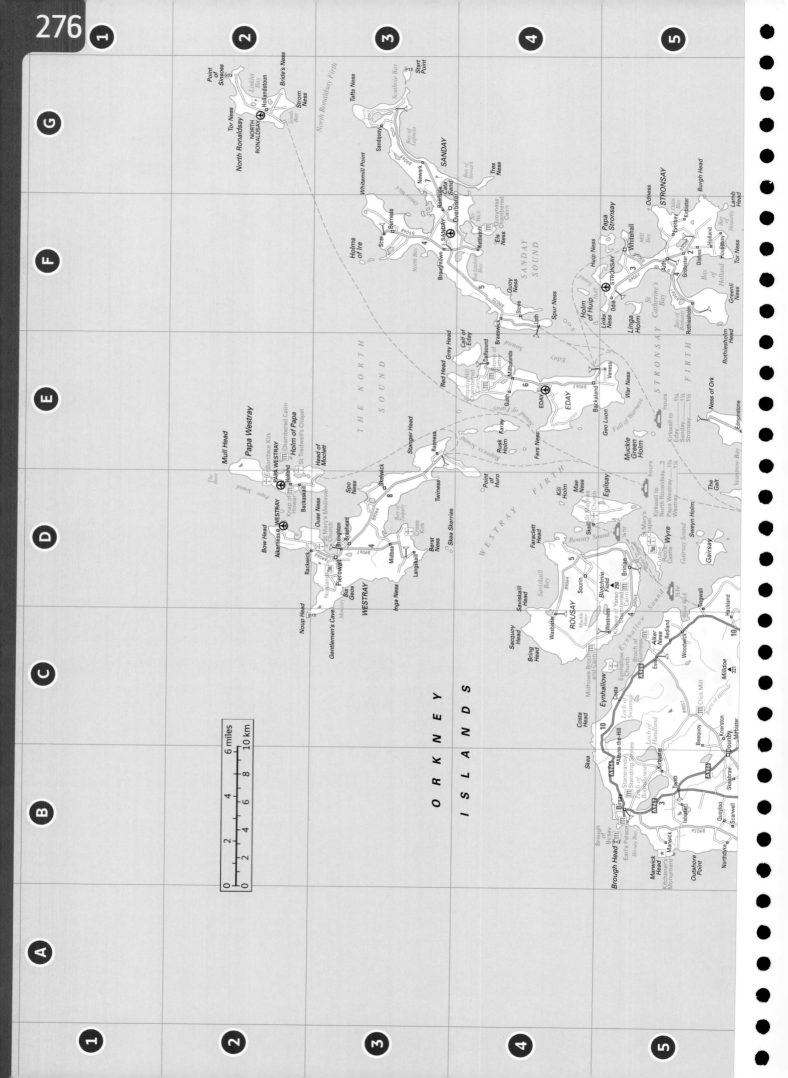

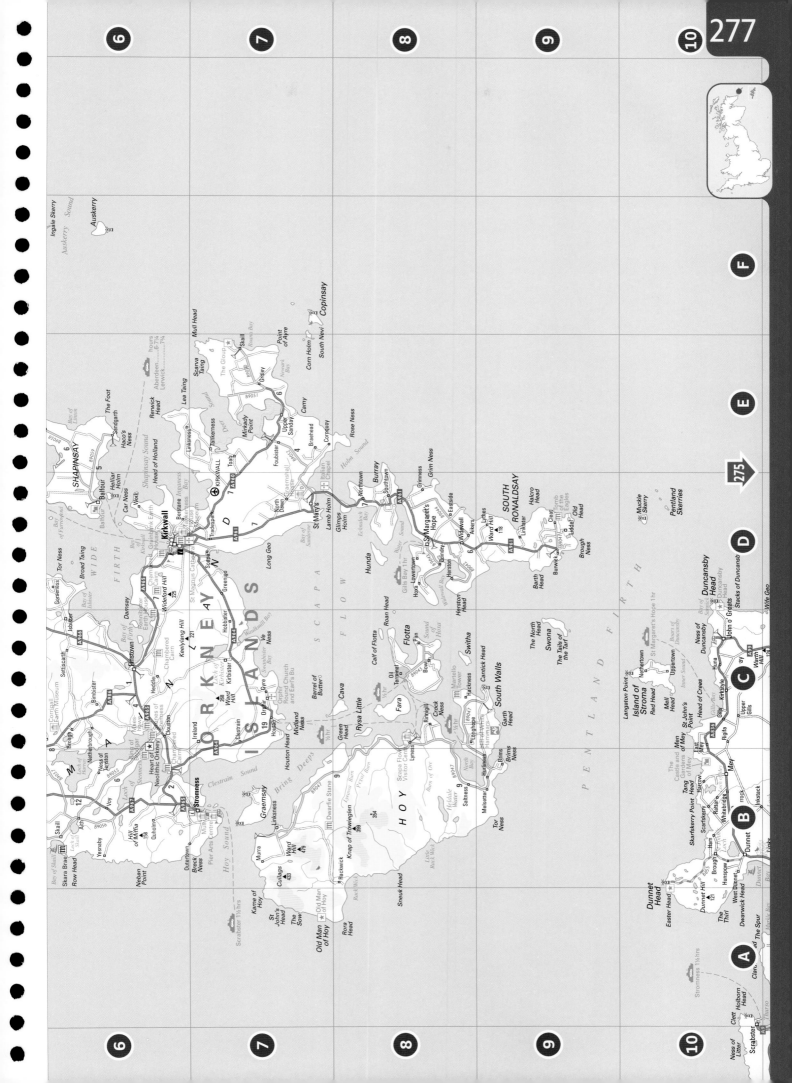

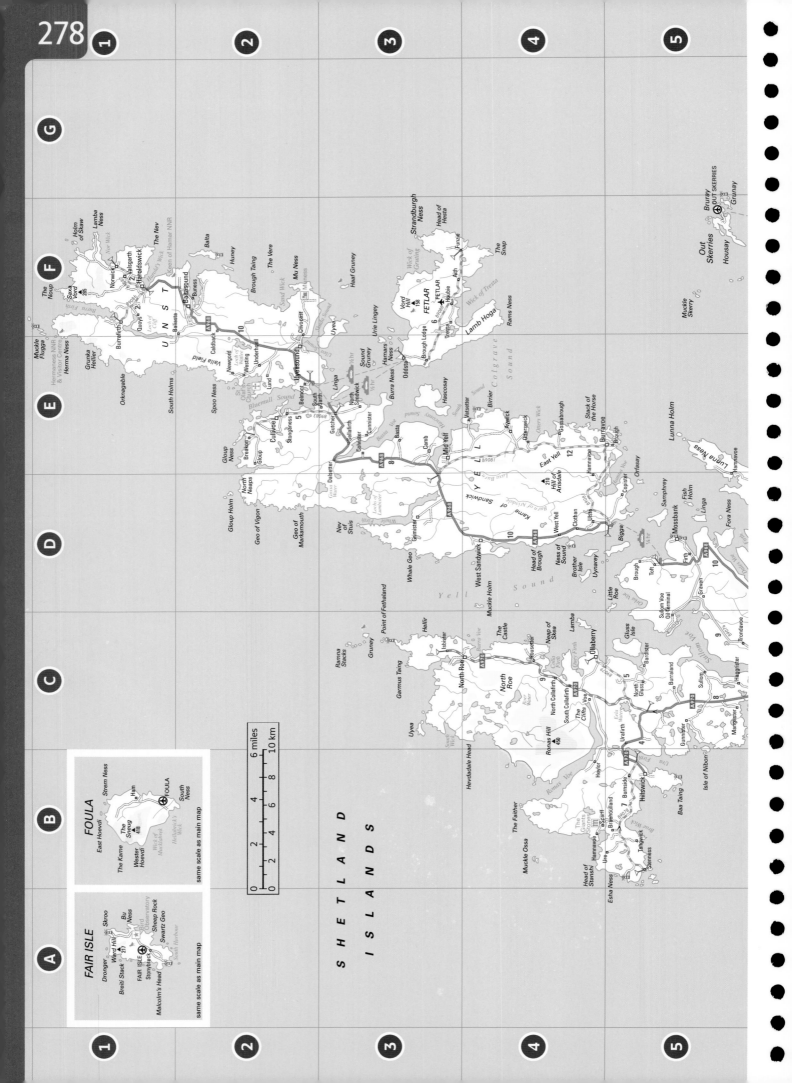

SHETLAND ISLANDS

FAIR ISLE

Dronger
Skroo
Ward Hill
217
Breiti Stack
FAIR ISLE
Bird Observatory
Stonybrack
Sheep Rock
Swartz Geo
Malcolm's Head
South Harbour
Bu Ness

same scale as main map

FOULA

East Hoevdi
Stremm Ness
Ham
The Kame
The Sneug
418
Wester Hoevdi
FOULA
South Ness
Hellabrek's Wick
Wick of Mucklaberb

same scale as main map

miles
0 2 4 6
0 2 4 6 8 10 km

UNST

The Noup
Burra Firth
Muckle Flugga
Hermaness NNR & Visitor Centre
Herma Ness
Grunka Hellier
Orknagable
South Holms
Holm of Skaw
Lamba Ness
Norwick
Valsgarth
Saxa Vord
285
Haroldswick
A968
Quoys
Loch of Cliff
Burrafirth
Baliasta
Caldback
Newgord
Loch of Watlee
Westing
Underhull
Valla Field
Lund
St Olaf's Church
Spoo Ness
Uyeasound
A968
10
Balta
Huney
The Vere
Brough Taing
Mu Ness
Sand Wick
Uyea
Keen of Hamar NNR
Baltasound
Buness
Clivocast
Muness
South Unst Sound

FETLAR

Wick of Gruting
Strandburgh Ness
Head of Hesta
Urie Lingey
Haaf Gruney
Vord Hill
158
FETLAR
Brough Lodge
Tresta
Lamb Hoga
Wick of Tresta
Rams Ness
The Snap
Aith
Funzie
½ hr

YELL

Gloup Ness
Breakon
Gloup
Gloup Holm
North Neaps
Geo of Vigon
Geo of Markamouth
Nev of Stuis
Whale Geo
Cullivoe
Stonganess
5
B9081
Gutcher
Cullivoe
Sellafirth
Kirkabister
Gossa Water
Dalsetter
A968
8
Basta
Camb
Mid Yell
Burra Voe
Basta Voe
Linga
North Sandwick
Sound Gruney
Hamars Ness
Oddsta
Burra Ness
½ hr
Hascosay
Vatsetter
Birrier
Aywick
Otterswick
Otters Wick
B9081
East Yell
Colgrave Sound
South Sound
Gossaborough
Stack of the Horse
Burravoe
Brough
½ hr
Hill of Arisdale
270
Loch of Lumbister
Loch of Lumbister
Kame of Flouravoug
Burn of Arisdale
Windhouse
Whale Firth
West Sandwick
Ness of Sound
Head of Brough
Brother Isle
Clothan
West Yell
Uynarey
A968
10
Ulsta
Bigga
A968
½ hr
Hamnavoe
Copister
Orfasay

Point of Fethaland
Ramna Stacks
Gruney
Uyea
Garmus Taing
Hevdadale Head
The Faither
Muckle Ossa
Head of Stanshi
Hamnavoe
Ure
Esha Ness
Stenness
Hellir
Isbister
North Roe
North Roe
North Collafirth
South Collafirth
The Cliffs
Ronas Hill
450
Ronas Voe
Heylor
The Giants Stones
Brehoulland
Tangwick
Baa Taing
Breer Wick
B9078
Burnside
Hillswick
Urafirth
Sullom
The Castle
Neap of Skea
Lamba
Housetter
Firths Voe
Ollaberry
Gluss Isle
North Glussa
Burraland
Gluss
Gunnister
Isle of Nibon
Mossbank
Samphrey
Fish Holm
Linga
Fora Ness
Little Roe
Muckle Holm
Yell Sound
Lunna Ness
Lunna Holm
Hamnavoe
Toft
Brough
Sullom Voe Oil Terminal
Graven
Firth
Trondavoe
Haggrister
Mangaster
Gluss Voe
Sullom Voe
B9071
A970
9
A970
5
A970
8
A970
4
A970
7
A970
A968
10
Swinister

Out Skerries
Bruray
Out Skerries
Grunay
Housay
Muckle Skerry
Rams Ness

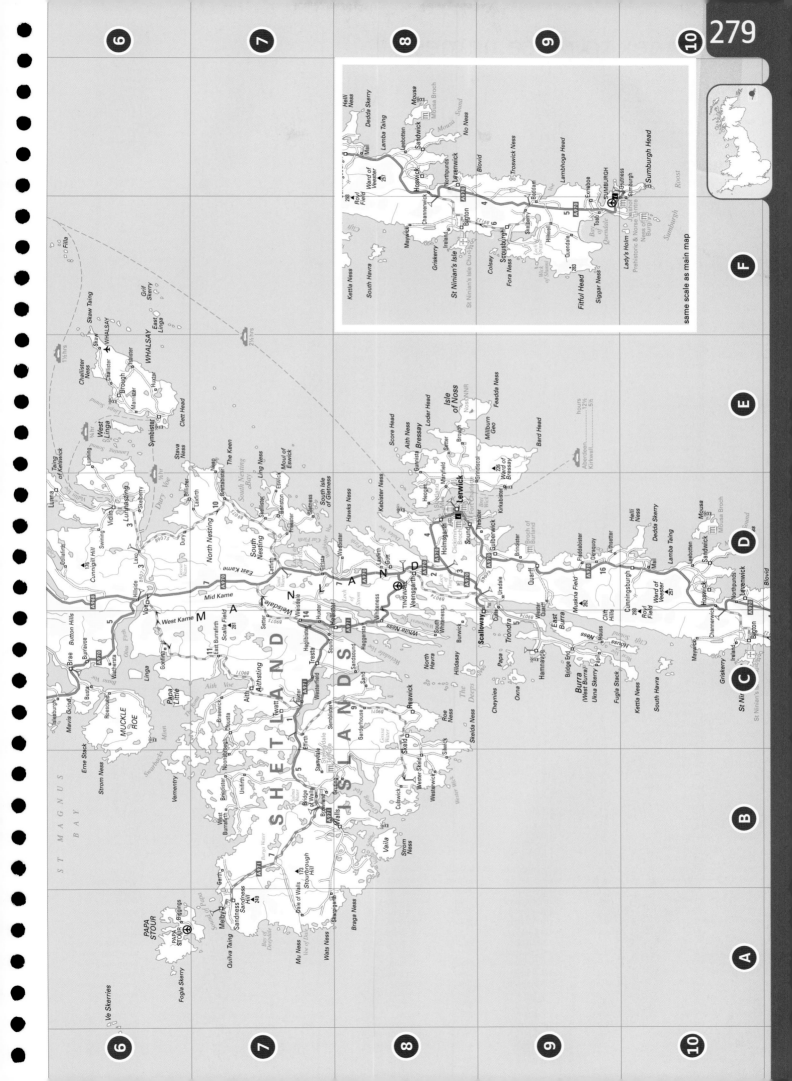

same scale as main map

Place and place of interest names are followed by a **page number** and a grid reference in black type. The feature can be found on the map somewhere within the grid square shown.

Where two or more places have the same name the abbreviated *county* or *unitary authority* names are shown to distinguish between them. A list of these abbreviated names appears below.

A selection of the most popular places of interest are shown within the index in blue type. Their postcode information is supplied after the county names to aid integration with satnav systems.

A&B	Argyll & Bute
Aber	Aberdeenshire
B&H	Brighton & Hove
B&NESom	Bath & North East Somerset
B'burn	Blackburn with Darwen
B'pool	Blackpool
BGwent	Blaenau Gwent
Bed	Bedford
Bourne	Bournemouth
BrackF	Bracknell Forest
Bucks	Buckinghamshire
Caerp	Caerphilly
Cambs	Cambridgeshire
Carmar	Carmarthenshire
CenBeds	Central Bedfordshire
Cere	Ceredigion
Chanl	Channel Islands
ChesE	Cheshire East
ChesW&C	Cheshire West & Chester
Corn	Cornwall
Cumb	Cumbria
D&G	Dumfries & Galloway
Darl	Darlington
Denb	Denbighshire
Derbys	Derbyshire
Dur	Durham
EAyr	East Ayrshire
EDun	East Dunbartonshire
ELoth	East Lothian
ERenf	East Renfrewshire
ERid	East Riding of Yorkshire
ESuss	East Sussex
Edin	Edinburgh
Falk	Falkirk
Flints	Flintshire
Glas	Glasgow
Glos	Gloucestershire
GtLon	Greater London
GtMan	Greater Manchester
Gwyn	Gwynedd
Hants	Hampshire
Hart	Hartlepool
Here	Herefordshire
Herts	Hertfordshire
High	Highland
Hull	Kingston upon Hull
Invcly	Inverclyde
IoA	Isle of Anglesey
IoM	Isle of Man
IoS	Isles of Scilly
IoW	Isle of Wight
Lancs	Lancashire
Leic	Leicester
Leics	Leicestershire
Lincs	Lincolnshire
MK	Milton Keynes
MTyd	Merthyr Tydfil
Med	Medway
Mersey	Merseyside
Middl	Middlesbrough
Midlo	Midlothian

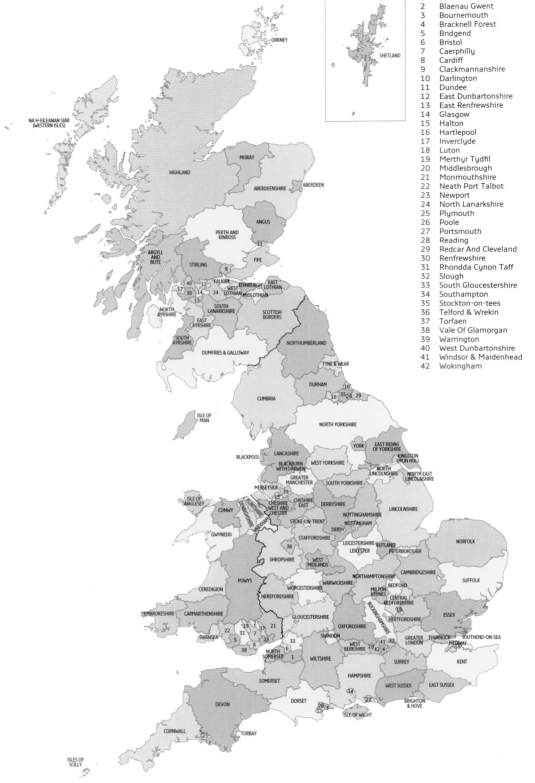

1	Bath & North East Somerset
2	Blaenau Gwent
3	Bournemouth
4	Bracknell Forest
5	Bridgend
6	Bristol
7	Caerphilly
8	Cardiff
9	Clackmannanshire
10	Darlington
11	Dundee
12	East Dunbartonshire
13	East Renfrewshire
14	Glasgow
15	Halton
16	Hartlepool
17	Inverclyde
18	Luton
19	Merthyr Tydfil
20	Middlesbrough
21	Monmouthshire
22	Neath Port Talbot
23	Newport
24	North Lanarkshire
25	Plymouth
26	Poole
27	Portsmouth
28	Reading
29	Redcar And Cleveland
30	Renfrewshire
31	Rhondda Cynon Taff
32	Slough
33	South Gloucestershire
34	Southampton
35	Stockton-on-tees
36	Telford & Wrekin
37	Torfaen
38	Vale Of Glamorgan
39	Warrington
40	West Dunbartonshire
41	Windsor & Maidenhead
42	Wokingham

Mon	Monmouthshire	*P&K*	Perth & Kinross	*ScBord*	Scottish Borders	*VGlam*	Vale of Glamorgan
Na H-E. Siar	Na H-Eileanan Siar (Western Isles)	*Pembs*	Pembrokeshire	*Shet*	Shetland	*W&M*	Windsor & Maidenhead
N'hants	Northamptonshire	*Peter*	Peterborough	*Shrop*	Shropshire		
N'umb	Northumberland	*Plym*	Plymouth	*Slo*	Slough	*W'ham*	Wokingham
NAyr	North Ayrshire	*Ports*	Portsmouth	*Som*	Somerset	*WBerks*	West Berkshire
NELincs	North East Lincolnshire	*R&C*	Redcar & Cleveland	*Soton*	Southampton	*WDun*	West Dunbartonshire
NLan	North Lanarkshire	*RCT*	Rhondda Cynon Taff	*Staffs*	Staffordshire		
NLincs	North Lincolnshire	*Read*	Reading	*Stir*	Stirling	*WLoth*	West Lothian
NPT	Neath Port Talbot	*Renf*	Renfrewshire	*Stock*	Stockton-on-Tees	*WMid*	West Midlands
NSom	North Somerset	*Rut*	Rutland	*Stoke*	Stoke-on-Trent	*WSuss*	West Sussex
NYorks	North Yorkshire	*S'end*	Southend-on-Sea	*Suff*	Suffolk	*WYorks*	West Yorkshire
Norf	Norfolk	*SAyr*	South Ayrshire	*Surr*	Surrey	*Warks*	Warwickshire
Nott	Nottingham	*SGlos*	South Gloucestershire	*Swan*	Swansea	*Warr*	Warrington
Notts	Nottinghamshire	*SLan*	South Lanarkshire	*Swin*	Swindon	*Wilts*	Wiltshire
Ork	Orkney	*SYorks*	South Yorkshire	*T&W*	Tyne & Wear	*Worcs*	Worcestershire
Oxon	Oxfordshire			*Tel&W*	Telford & Wrekin	*Wrex*	Wrexham
				Thur	Thurrock		

1853 Gallery WYorks BD18 3LA 26 C1

A

Ab Kettleby 174 C5
Ab Lench 146 C2
Abbas Combe 117 E5
Abberley 145 G1
Abberley Common 145 G1
Abberton Essex 138 C1
Abberton Worcs 146 B2
Abberwick 229 F5
Abbess Roding 137 E1
Abbey Dore 144 C4
Abbey Hulton 171 G3
Abbey St. Bathans 237 E3
Abbey Village 192 C5
Abbey Wood 137 D5
Abbeycwmhir 155 G5
Abbeydale 186 A4
Abbeystead 192 B2
Abbeytown 209 E1
Abbotrule 228 A5
Abbots Bickington 113 D4
Abbots Bromley 172 B5
Abbots Langley 135 F2
Abbots Leigh 131 E5
Abbots Morton 146 C2
Abbots Ripton 162 A5
Abbots Worthy 119 F4
Abbotsbury 104 B4
Abbotsbury Swannery, Subtropical Gardens & Children's Farm Dorset DT3 4JG 104 B4
Abbotsfield Farm 183 G3
Abbotsham 113 E3
Abbotskerswell 101 E1
Abbotsley 150 A2
Abbotstone 119 G4
Abbotts Ann 119 E3
Abbott's Barton 119 F4
Abbottswood 119 E5
Abdon 157 E4
Abdy 186 B3
Abenhall 131 F1
Aber 142 A1
Aber Village 144 A5
Aberaeron 142 A1
Aberaman 129 G2
Aberangell 155 E2
Aber-Arad 141 G3
Aberarder 249 E5
Aberarder House 258 D2
Aberargie 243 G3
Aberarth 142 A1
Aberavon 129 D3
Aber-banc 141 G3
Aberbargoed 130 A2
Aberbeeg 130 B2
Aberbowlan 142 C4
Aberbran 143 F5
Abercanaid 129 G2
Abercarn 130 B3
Abercastle 140 B4
Abercegir 155 E2
Aberchalder 257 K4
Aberchirder 268 E5
Abercorn 235 E2
Abercraf 129 E1
Abercregan 129 E3
Abercrombie 244 D4
Abercrychan 143 D4
Abercwmboi 129 G2
Abercych 141 F3
Abercynafon 129 G1
Abercynon 129 G3
Abercywarch 155 E1
Aberdalgie 243 F2
Aberdare 129 F2
Aberdaron 166 A5
Aberdeen (Obar Dheathain) 261 H4
Aberdeen Airport 261 G3
Aberdeen Art Gallery AB10 1FQ 63 Aberdeen
Aberdeen Exhibition & Conference Centre Aberdeen AB23 8BL 261 H3
Aberdesach 166 D2
Aberdour 235 F1
Aberdovey (Aberdyfi) 154 C3
Aberduhonw 143 G2
Aberdulais 129 D3
Aberedw 143 G3
Abereiddy 140 A4
Abererch 166 C4
Aberfan 129 G2
Aberfeldy 251 D5
Aberffraw 166 C1
Aberffrwd 154 C5
Aberford 194 D4
Aberfoyle 242 A4
Abergavenny (Y Fenni) 130 B1
Abergele 182 A5
Aber-Giâr 142 B3
Abergorlech 142 B4
Abergwesyn 143 E2
Abergwili 142 A5
Abergwydol 155 D2
Abergwynfi 129 E3
Abergwyngregyn 181 E5
Abergynolwyn 154 C2
Aberhafesp 155 G3
Aberhosan 155 E3
Aberkenfig 129 E4
Aberlady 236 B1
Aberlemno 252 D4
Aberllefenni 155 D2
Aber-Ilia 155 F5
Aberlour (Charlestown of Aberlour) 267 K7
Abermad 154 B5
Abermeurig 142 B2
Abermule (Aber-miwl) 156 A3
Abernaint 169 E5
Abernant Carmar 141 G5
Aber-nant RCT 129 G2
Abernethy 243 G3
Abernyte 244 A1
Aberporth 141 F2
Aberscross 266 E2

Abersky 258 C2
Abersoch 166 C5
Abersychan 130 B2
Aberthin 129 G5
Abertillery 130 B2
Abertridwr Caerp 130 A4
Abertridwr Powys 155 G1
Abertysswg 130 A2
Aberuthven 243 E3
Aberyscir 143 F5
Aberystwyth 154 B4
Aberystwyth Arts Centre Cere SY23 3DE 154 B4
Abhainnsuidhe 270 C7
Abingdon 133 G3
Abinger Common 121 G3
Abinger Hammer 121 F3
Abington 226 A3
Abington Pigotts 150 B3
Abingworth 108 D2
Ablington Glos 132 D2
Ablington Wilts 118 C3
Abney 185 F5
Above Church 172 B2
Aboyne 260 D5
Abram 184 A2
Abriachan (Obar Itheachan) 258 C1
Abridge 137 D3
Abronhill 234 B2
Abson 131 G5
Abthorpe 148 B3
Abune-the-Hill 276 B5
Aby 189 E5
Acaster Malbis 195 E3
Acaster Selby 195 E3
Accrington 193 D5
Accurrach 240 D2
Acha 246 A4
Achacha 248 B5
Achadacaie 231 G3
Achadh Mòr 271 F5
Achadh-chaorrunn 231 F4
Achadunan 241 E2
Achagavel 247 G4
Achaglass 231 F5
Achahoish 231 F2
Achalader 251 G5
Achallader 249 F5
Achamore 231 D2
Achanduin 248 A5
Achany 266 C1
Achaphubuil 248 C2
Acharacle 247 F3
Achargary 274 C3
Acharn A&B 240 D1
Acharn P&K 250 C5
Acharonich 239 D1
Acharosson 232 A2
Achateny 247 E2
Achath 261 F3
Achavanich 275 G4
Achddu 128 A2
Achduart 265 G1
Achentoul 274 D5
Achfary 272 E5
Achgarve 264 E2
Achiemore High 273 F2
Achiemore High 274 D3
Achies 275 G3
A'Chill 255 H4
Achiltibuie (Achd-'Ille-Bhuidhe) 265 G1
Achina 274 C2
Achindown 267 F7
Achinduich 266 C2
Achingills 275 G2
Achintee 265 F7
Achintee House (Achadh an t-Suidhe) 248 D2
Achintraid 256 E1
Achleanan 247 E4
Achleek 247 G4
Achlian 240 D2
Achlyness 272 E3
Achmelvich 272 C6
Achmony 258 C1
Achmore High 256 E1
Achmore High 265 G2
Achmore Stir 242 A1
Achnaba 232 A1
Achnabat 258 C1
Achnabourin 274 C3
Achnacairn 240 B1
Achnacarnin 272 C5
Achnacarry 249 D1
Achnaclerach 266 B5
Achnacloich A&B 240 B1
Achnacloich High 256 B4
Achnaclyth 275 F5
Achnacraig 247 D5
Achnacroish 248 A5
Achnadrish 248 A5
Achnafalnich 241 E2
Achnafauld 243 D1
Achnagarron 266 C7
Achnaha High 247 F5
Achnaha High 247 D3
Achnahanat 266 C2
Achnahannet 259 G2
Achnairn 273 H7
Achnalea 248 A3
Achnamara 231 F1
Achnanellan 247 G3
Achnasaul 249 D1
Achnasheen 265 H6
Achnashelloch 240 A5
Achnastank 259 K1
Achorn 275 G5
Achosnich High 266 E2
Achosnich High 246 D3
Achreamie 275 F2
Achriabhach 248 D3
Achriesgill 272 E3
Achtoty 273 J2
Achurch 161 F4
Achuvoldrach 273 H3
Achvaich 266 E2
Achvarasdal 274 E2
Achvlair 248 B4
Achvraie 265 G1
Ackenthwaite 199 G4
Ackergill 275 J3
Acklam Middl 203 D4
Acklam NYorks 195 G1
Ackleton 157 G3

Acklington 221 E1
Ackton 194 D5
Ackworth Moor Top 186 B1
Acle 179 F4
Acock's Green 158 D4
Acol 125 F2
Acomb N'umb 211 F1
Acomb York 195 E2
Aconbury 145 E4
Acre 193 D5
Acrefair 169 F3
Acrise Place 125 D4
Acton ChesE 170 D2
Acton Dorset 105 F5
Acton GtLon 136 A4
Acton Shrop 156 C4
Acton Staffs 171 F3
Acton Suff 151 G3
Acton Worcs 146 A1
Acton Beauchamp 145 F2
Acton Bridge 183 G5
Acton Burnell 157 E2
Acton Green 145 F2
Acton Pigott 157 E2
Acton Round 157 F3
Acton Scott 157 D4
Acton Trussell 158 B1
Acton Turville 132 A4
Adamhill 224 C2
Adbaston 171 E5
Adber 116 C5
Adderbury 147 G4
Adderley 171 D4
Adderstone 229 F3
Addiewell 235 D3
Addingham 193 G3
Addington Bucks 148 C5
Addington GtLon 122 C2
Addington Kent 123 F3
Addiscombe 122 C2
Addlestone 121 F1
Addlethorpe 176 D1
Adel 194 B4
Aden Country Park Aber AB42 5FQ 269 H6
Adeney 157 G1
Adeyfield 135 F2
Adfa 155 G2
Adforton 156 D5
Adisham 125 E3
Adlestrop 147 E5
Adlingfleet 196 A5
Adlington ChesE 184 D4
Adlington Lancs 183 G1
Admaston Staffs 172 B5
Admaston Tel&W 157 F1
Admington 147 E3
Adsborough 115 F5
Adscombe 115 E4
Adstock 148 C4
Adstone 148 A2
Adventure Island S'end SS1 1EE 138 B4
Adventure Wonderland Dorset BH23 6BA 3 D2
Adversane 121 F5
Advie 259 J1
Adwalton 194 B5
Adwell 134 B3
Adwick le Street 186 C2
Adwick upon Dearne 186 B2
Adziel 269 H5
Ae Village 217 D2
Afan Argoed Country Park NPT SA13 3HG 129 E3
Affetside 184 B1
Affleck 261 G2
Affpuddle 105 E3
Afon Wen 166 D4
Afon-wen 182 C5
Afonwen Craft & Antique Centre Flints CH7 5UB 182 C5
Africa Alive! Suff NR33 7TF 165 G3
Afton 106 C4
Afton Bridgend 225 E4
Agglethorpe 201 F4
Aigburth 183 E4
Aiginis 271 G4
Aike 196 C3
Aikerness 276 D2
Aikers 277 D8
Aiketgate 210 A3
Aikshaw 209 E2
Aikton 209 F1
Aikwood Tower 227 F3
Ailby 189 E5
Ailey 144 C3
Ailsworth 161 G3
Aimes Green 136 D2
Aimster 275 G2
Ainderby Quernhow 202 C4
Ainderby Steeple 202 C3
Aingers Green 152 C5
Ainsdale 183 E1
Ainsdale-on-Sea 183 E1
Ainstable 210 B3
Ainsworth 184 B1
Ainthorpe 203 G2
Aintree 183 E3
Aird Na H-E. Siar 262 C6
Aird Na H-E. Siar 271 H4
Aird a' Mhachair 262 C7
Aird a' Mhulaidh 270 D6
Aird Asaig 270 D7
Aird Dhail 271 G1
Aird Leimhe 263 G3
Aird Mhige 263 G2
Aird Mhighe 263 F3
Aird of Sleat 256 B4
Aird Thunga 271 G4
Aird Uig 270 C4
Airdrie Fife 245 D4
Airdrie NLan 234 B3
Aire View 193 F3
Airidh a' Bhruaich 270 D6
Aineland 216 B5
Aires 214 A4
Airgh-drishaig 256 D1
Airmyn 195 G5
Airntully 243 F1
Airor 256 D4
Airth 234 C1
Airton 193 F2

Airyhassen 207 D2
Aisby Lincs 187 F3
Aisby Lincs 175 F3
Aisgill 200 C3
Aish Devon 100 C1
Aish Devon 101 E2
Aisholt 115 E4
Aiskew 202 B4
Aislaby NYorks 204 B2
Aislaby NYorks 204 B1
Aislaby Stock 202 D1
Aisthorpe 187 G4
Aith Ork 277 B6
Aith Ork 276 F5
Aith Shet 279 C7
Aith Shet 278 F3
Aithsetter 279 D9
Aitnoch 259 G1
Akeld 228 D4
Akeley 148 C4
Akenham 152 C3
Albaston 99 E3
Albecq 101 E5
Alberbury 156 C1
Albert Park TS1 3LB 78 Middlesbrough
Albert Town 126 C1
Albourne 109 E2
Albourne Green 109 E2
Albrighton Shrop 158 A2
Albrighton Shrop 157 D1
Alburgh 165 D3
Albury Herts 150 C5
Albury Oxon 134 B2
Albury Surr 121 F3
Albury End 150 C5
Albury Heath 121 F3
Albyfield 210 B2
Alcaig 266 C6
Alcaston 157 D4
Alcester 146 C2
Alciston 110 A3
Alcombe 114 C3
Alconbury 161 G5
Alconbury Hill 161 G5
Alconbury Weston 161 G5
Aldborough Norf 178 C2
Aldborough NYorks 194 D1
Aldbourne 133 E5
Aldbrough 197 E4
Aldbrough St. John 202 B1
Aldbury 135 E1
Aldclune 251 E3
Aldeburgh 153 F2
Aldeby 165 F2
Aldenham 136 A3
Alderbury 118 C5
Alderford 178 C4
Alderholt 106 A1
Alderley 131 G3
Alderley Edge 184 C5
Aldermaston 119 G1
Aldermaston Wharf 120 B1
Alderminster 147 E3
Alderney 101 F4
Alderney Airport 101 F4
Alder's End 145 F4
Aldersey Green 170 B2
Aldershot 121 D2
Alderton Glos 146 B4
Alderton N'hants 148 C3
Alderton Shrop 157 D1
Alderton Suff 153 E3
Alderton Wilts 132 A4
Alderwasley 173 E2
Aldfield 194 B1
Aldford 170 B2
Aldham Essex 152 A5
Aldham Suff 152 B3
Aldie Aber 269 J6
Aldie High 266 E3
Aldingbourne 108 B3
Aldingham 199 D5
Aldington Kent 124 C5
Aldington Worcs 146 C3
Aldivalloch 260 B2
Aldochlay 241 F5
Aldons 214 C2
Aldous's Corner 165 E3
Aldreth 162 C5
Aldridge 158 C2
Aldringham 153 F1
Aldsworth Glos 133 D2
Aldsworth WSuss 107 G2
Aldunie 260 B2
Aldville 243 E1
Aldwark Derbys 172 D2
Aldwark NYorks 195 D1
Aldwick 108 B4
Aldwincle 161 F4
Aldworth 134 A5
Alexandra Palace GtLon N22 7AY 12 A1
Alexandria 233 E2
Aley 115 E4
Aley Green 135 F1
Alfardisworthy 112 C4
Alfington 103 E3
Alfold 121 F4
Alfold Crossways 121 F4
Alford Aber 260 D3
Alford Lincs 189 E5
Alford Som 116 C4
Alfreton 173 F2
Alfrick 145 G2
Alfrick Pound 145 G2
Alfriston 110 A3
Alhampton 116 C4
Alkborough 196 A5
Alkerton 147 F3
Alkham 125 E4
Alkington 170 C4
Alkmonton 172 C4
All Cannings 118 B1
All Saints South Elmham 165 E3
All Stretton 157 D3
Allaleigh 101 E2
Allanaquoich 259 J5
Allancreich 260 D5
Allanfearn 266 E7
Allangillfoot 218 A2
Allanton D&G 216 B3
Allanton EAyr 225 E2
Allanton NLan 234 C4

Allanton ScBord 237 F4
Allanton SLan 234 B4
Allardice 253 G2
Allathasdal 254 B4
Allbrook 119 F5
Allendale Town 211 G2
Allenheads 211 E3
Allen's Green 137 D1
Allensford 211 G3
Allensmore 145 D4
Allenton 173 E4
Aller 116 B5
Allerby 209 D3
Allercombe 102 C3
Allerford Devon 99 E2
Allerford Som 114 C3
Allerston 204 B4
Allerthorpe 195 G3
Allerton Mersey 183 F4
Allerton WYorks 194 A4
Allerton Bywater 194 D5
Allerton Mauleverer 194 D2
Allesley 159 E4
Allestree 173 E4
Allet Common 96 B5
Allexton 160 D2
Allgreave 171 G1
Allhallows 124 A1
Allhallows-on-Sea 124 A1
Alligin Shuas 264 E6
Allimore Green 158 A1
Allington Dorset 104 A3
Allington Lincs 175 D3
Allington Lincs 175 G4
Allington Wilts 118 B1
Allington Wilts 118 B1
Allington Wilts 132 A5
Allithwaite 199 E5
Allnabad 273 G3
Allonby 209 D2
Allostock 184 B5
Alloway 224 B4
Allowenshay 103 G1
Allscot 157 G2
Allscott 157 F1
Alltforgan 168 C3
Alltmawr 143 G3
Alltnacaillich 273 G4
Allt-nan-sùugh 257 F1
Alltsigh 258 B3
Alltwalis 142 A4
Alltwen 128 D2
Alltyblaca 142 B3
Allwood Green 164 B4
Almeley 144 C2
Almeley Wootton 144 C2
Almer 105 F3
Almington 171 E4
Almiston Cross 113 D3
Almondbank 243 F2
Almondbury 185 F1
Almondell & Calderwood Country Park WLoth EH52 5PE 235 F3
Almondsbury 131 F4
Alne 195 D1
Alness 266 D5
Alnham 229 D5
Alnmouth 229 G5
Alnwick 229 F5
Alnwick Garden, The N'umb NE66 1YU 229 F5
Alperton 136 A4
Alphamstone 151 G4
Alpheton 151 G2
Alphington 102 C3
Alport 172 D1
Alpraham 170 C2
Alresford 152 B5
Alrewas 159 D1
Alrick 251 G3
Alsager 171 E2
Alsagers Bank 171 F3
Alsop en le Dale 172 C2
Alston Cumb 210 D3
Alston Devon 103 G2
Alston Sutton 116 A2
Alstone Glos 146 B4
Alstone Som 116 A3
Alstone Staffs 158 A1
Alstonefield 172 C2
Alswear 114 A5
Alt 184 D2
Altandhu 272 B7
Altanduin 274 D6
Altarnun 97 G1
Altass 266 B2
Altens 261 H4
Alterwall 275 H2
Altham 193 D4
Althorne 138 C3
Althorp House N'hants NN7 4HQ 148 B1
Althorpe 187 F2
Alticry 215 D5
Altnafeadh 249 E4
Altnaharra 273 H5
Altofts 194 C5
Alton Derbys 173 E1
Alton Hants 120 C4
Alton Staffs 172 B3
Alton Barnes 118 C1
Alton Pancras 104 D2
Alton Priors 118 C1
Alton Towers Leisure Park Staffs ST10 4DB 172 B3
Alton Water Reservoir Suff IP9 2RY 152 C4
Altonside 267 K6
Altrincham 184 B4
Altura 257 J5
Alva 243 D5
Alvanley 183 F5
Alvaston 173 E4
Alvechurch 158 C5
Alvecote 159 E2
Alvediston 118 A5
Alveley 157 G4
Alverdiscott 113 F3
Alverstoke 107 F3
Alverstone 107 E4
Alverthorpe 194 C5
Alverton 174 C3

Alves 267 J5
Alvescot 133 E2
Alveston SGlos 131 F4
Alveston Warks 147 E2
Alvie 259 F4
Alvingham 189 D3
Alvington 131 F2
Alwalton 161 G3
Alweston 104 C1
Alwington 113 E3
Alwinton 220 B1
Alwoodley 194 B3
Alwoodley Gates 194 C3
Alyth 252 A5
Amalebra 94 B3
Ambaston 173 F4
Amber Hill 176 A3
Ambergate 173 E2
Amberley Glos 132 A2
Amberley WSuss 108 C2
Amble 221 E1
Amblecote 158 A4
Ambleside 199 E2
Ambleston 140 D5
Ambrismore 232 B4
Ambrosden 134 B1
Amcotts 187 F1
Amersham 135 E3
Amerton 171 G5
Amerton Farm Staffs ST18 0LA 171 G5
Amesbury 118 C3
Ameysford 105 G2
Amington 159 E2
Amisfield Town 217 E2
Amlwch 180 C3
Amlwch Port 180 C3
Ammanford (Rhydaman) 128 C1
Amotherby 203 G5
Ampfield 119 E5
Ampleforth 203 E5
Ampleforth College 203 E5
Ampney Crucis 132 C2
Ampney St. Mary 132 C2
Ampney St. Peter 132 C2
Amport 119 E3
Ampthill 149 F4
Ampton 163 G5
Amroth 127 E2
Amulree 243 D1
Anaboard 259 H1
Anaheilt 248 A3
Ancaster 175 E3
Ancroft 237 G5
Ancrum 228 A4
Ancton 108 B3
Anderby 189 F5
Anderby Creek 189 F5
Andersea 116 A4
Andersfield 115 F4
Anderson 105 E3
Anderton 184 A5
Andover 119 E3
Andover Down 119 E3
Andoversford 132 C1
Andreas 190 C2
Anelog 166 A5
Anfield 183 E3
Angarrack 94 C3
Angarrick 95 E3
Angelbank 157 E5
Angerton 209 F1
Angle 126 B2
Anglers Country Park WYorks WF4 2EB 186 A1
Angler's Retreat 154 D3
Anglesey (Ynys Môn) 180 B4
Anglesey Abbey Cambs CB25 9EJ 150 D1
Angmering 108 C3
Angmering-on-Sea 108 C3
Angram NYorks 195 E3
Angram NYorks 201 D3
Anick 211 F1
Anie 242 A3
Animal World & Butterfly House GtMan BL1 5UG 184 A1
Ankerville 267 F4
Anlaby 196 C5
Anmer 177 F5
Anmore 107 F1
Anna Valley 119 E3
Annan 217 F4
Annaside 198 B4
Annat A&B 240 C2
Annat High 264 E6
Annbank 224 C3
Anne Hathaway's Cottage Warks CV37 9HH 147 D2
Annesley 173 G2
Annesley Woodhouse 173 F2
Annfield Plain 212 A2
Anniesland 233 G3
Annscroft 157 D2
Ansdell 191 G5
Ansford 116 C4
Ansley 159 E3
Anslow 172 D5
Anslow Gate 172 C5
Anstey Herts 150 C4
Anstey Leics 160 A2
Anstruther 245 D4
Ansty Warks 159 F4
Ansty Wilts 118 A5
Ansty WSuss 109 E1
Ansty Coombe 118 A5
Ansty Cross 105 D2
Anthill Common 107 F1
Anthorn 209 E1
Antingham 179 D2
Anton's Gowt 176 A3
Antony 99 D5
Antrobus 184 A5
Anvil Corner 113 D5
Anvil Green 124 D4
Anwick 175 G2

Anwoth 215 G5
Aonach Mòr Mountain Gondola & Nevis Range Ski Centre High PH33 6SW 249 D2
Aoradh 230 A3
Apethorpe 161 F3
Apeton 158 A1
Apley 188 B5
Apperknowle 186 A5
Apperley 146 A5
Apperley Bridge 194 A4
Appersett 201 D3
Appin (An Apainn) 248 B5
Appin House 248 B5
Appleby 187 G1
Appleby Magna 159 F1
Appleby Parva 159 F2
Appleby-in-Westmorland 210 C5
Applecross 264 D7
Appledore Devon 113 E2
Appledore Devon 103 D1
Appledore Kent 111 E1
Appledore Heath 124 B5
Appleford 134 A3
Appleshaw 119 E3
Applethwaite 209 F4
Appleton Halton 183 G4
Appleton Oxon 133 G2
Appleton Roebuck 195 E3
Appleton Thorn 184 A4
Appleton Wiske 202 C2
Appleton-le-Moors 203 G4
Appleton-le-Street 203 G5
Appletreehall 227 G4
Appletreewick 193 G1
Appley 115 D5
Appley Bridge 183 G2
Apse Heath 107 E4
Apsey Green 153 D1
Apsley 135 F2
Apsley End 149 G4
Apuldram 108 A3
Arbeia Roman Fort & Museum T&W NE33 2BB 28 E1
Arbirlot 253 D5
Arborfield 120 C1
Arborfield Cross 120 C1
Arborfield Garrison 120 C1
Arbourthorne 186 A4
Arbroath 253 F2
Archdeacon Newton 202 B1
Archiestown 267 K7
Arclid 171 E2
Ard a' Chapuill 232 B1
Ardachearanbeg 232 B1
Ardacheranmor 232 B1
Ardachoil 239 G1
Ardachu 266 D1
Ardailly 231 E4
Ardalanish 238 C3
Ardallie 231 J1
Ardanaiseig 240 C2
Ardaneaskan 256 E1
Ardanstur 240 A3
Ardantiobairt 247 F4
Ardantrive 240 A2
Ardarroch 264 E7
Ardbeg A&B 232 B3
Ardbeg A&B 230 C5
Ardbeg A&B 232 C1
Ardblair 258 C1
Ardbrecknish 240 C2
Ardcharnich 265 H3
Ardchiavaig 238 C3
Ardchonnel 240 B1
Ardchonnell 240 B3
Ardchrishnish 238 D2
Ardchronie 266 D3
Ardchuilk 257 J1
Ardchullarie More 242 A3
Ardchyle 242 A2
Arddlin 156 B1
Ardchvie 257 H5
Ardeley 150 B5
Ardelve 256 E2
Arden 233 E1
Ardencaple House 239 G3
Ardens Grafton 146 D2
Ardentallen 240 A2
Ardentinny 232 C1
Ardeonaig 242 B1
Ardersier 266 E6
Ardery 247 G3
Ardessie 265 G3
Ardfad 239 G3
Ardfern 240 A4
Ardfin 230 C3
Ardgartan 241 E4
Ardgay A&B 240 C2
Ardgenavan 241 D3
Ardgour (Corran) 248 C3
Ardgowan 232 C2
Ardgowse 260 E3
Ardgye 267 J5
Ardhallow 232 C2
Ardheslaig 264 D6
Ardiecow 268 D4
Ardinamar 239 G3
Ardindrean 265 H3
Ardingly 109 F1
Ardington 133 G4
Ardington Wick 133 G4
Ardintoul 256 E2
Ardkinglas House 241 D3
Ardlair 260 D2
Ardlamont 232 A3
Ardleigh 152 B5
Ardleigh Green 137 E4
Ardleigh Heath 152 B4
Ardleish 241 F3
Ardler 252 A5
Ardley 148 A5
Ardley End 137 E1
Ardlui (Àird Laoigh) 241 F3
Ardlussa 231 E1
Ardmaddy 240 C1
Ardmair 265 H2
Ardmaleish 232 B3
Ardmay 241 E4
Ardmenish 231 D2
Ardmhòr 254 C4
Ardmolich 247 G2

Ardmore A&B 230 C4
Ardmore A&B 239 G2
Ardmore A&B 233 E2
Ardmore High 266 E3
Ardnackaig 239 G5
Ardnacross 247 E5
Ardnadam 232 C1
Ardnadrochit 239 G1
Ardnagoine 265 F1
Ardnagowan 240 D4
Ardnahein 241 D5
Ardnahoe 230 C2
Ardnarff 256 E1
Ardnastang 248 A3
Ardnave 230 A2
Ardno 241 D4
Ardo 261 G1
Ardoch D&G 225 G5
Ardoch Moray 267 J6
Ardoch P&K 243 F1
Ardochrig 234 A5
Ardoyne 260 E2
Ardpatrick 231 F3
Ardpeaton 232 D1
Ardradnaig 250 C5
Ardrishaig 231 G1
Ardroe 272 C6
Ardross 266 D4
Ardrossan 232 D5
Ardscalpsie 232 B4
Ardshave 266 E2
Ardshealach 247 F3
Ardshellach 239 G3
Ardsley 186 A2
Ardslignish 247 E3
Ardtalla 230 C4
Ardtalnaig 242 C1
Ardtaraig 232 B1
Ardteatle 240 D2
Ardtoe 247 F2
Ardtornish 247 G5
Ardtrostan 242 B2
Ardtur 248 B5
Arduaine 240 A3
Ardullie 266 C5
Ardura 239 F1
Ardvar 272 D5
Ardvasar 256 C4
Ardveenish 254 C4
Ardveich 242 B2
Ardverikie 250 A1
Ardvorlich A&B 241 F3
Ardvorlich P&K 242 B2
Ardwall 215 G5
Ardwell D&G 206 B2
Ardwell Moray 260 B1
Ardwell SAyr 214 C1
Ardwick 184 C3
Areley Kings 158 A5
Arford 120 D4
Argaty 242 C4
Argoed 130 A3
Argoed Mill 143 F1
Argos Hill 110 A1
Argrennan House 216 B5
Argyll & Sutherland Highlanders Museum Stir FK8 1EH 242 C5
Arichamish 240 B4
Arichastlich 241 E1
Arichonan 239 G5
Aridhglas 238 C2
Arienskill 247 G1
Arileod 246 A4
Arinacrinachd 264 D6
Arinafad Beg 231 F1
Arinagour 246 B4
Arinambane 254 C2
Arisaig (Àrasaig) 247 F1
Arivegaig 247 F3
Arkendale 194 C1
Arkesden 150 C4
Arkholme 199 G5
Arkle Town 201 F2
Arkleby 209 E3
Arkleside 201 F4
Arkleton 218 B2
Arkley 136 B3
Arksey 186 C2
Arkwright Town 186 B5
Arlary 243 G4
Arle 146 B5
Arlecdon 208 D5
Arlesey 149 G4
Arleston 157 F1
Arley 184 A4
Arlingham 131 G1
Arlington Devon 113 G1
Arlington ESuss 110 A3
Arlington Glos 132 D2
Arlington Beccott 113 G1
Armadale High 274 C2
Armadale High 256 C4
Armadale WLoth 234 D3
Armathwaite 210 B3
Arminghall 179 D5
Armitage 158 C1
Armitage Bridge 185 F1
Armley 194 B4
Armscote 147 E3
Armshead 171 G3
Armston 161 F4
Armthorpe 186 D2
Arnabost 246 B3
Arnaby 198 C4
Arncliffe 201 E5
Arncliffe Cote 201 E5
Arncroach 244 D4
Arne 105 F4
Arnesby 160 B3
Arngask 243 G3
Arngibbon 242 B5
Arngomery 242 B5
Arnhall 253 E3
Arnicle 222 C2
Arnipol 247 G1
Arnisdale (Arnasdal) 256 E3
Arnish 264 B7
Arniston Engine 236 A3
Arnol 271 F3
Arnold ERid 196 D3
Arnold Notts 173 G3
Arnolfini Gallery BS1 4QA 66 Bristol
Arnprior 242 B5
Arnside 199 F5
Aros Experience High IV51 9EU 263 K7
Arowry 170 B4
Arrad Foot 199 E4
Arradoul 268 C4
Arram 196 C3
Arran 223 E2
Arras 196 B3
Arrat 253 E4
Arrathorne 202 B3
Arreton 107 E4
Arrington 150 B2
Arrivain 241 E1
Arrochar 241 F4
Arrow 146 C2
Arscaig 273 H7
Arscott 156 D2
Arthington 194 B3
Arthingworth 160 C4
Arthog 154 C1
Arthrath 261 H1
Arthurstone 252 A5
Artrochie 261 J1
Aruadh 230 A3
Arundel 108 C3
Arundel Castle WSuss BN18 9AB 108 C3
Arundel Cathedral (R.C.) WSuss BN18 9AY 108 C3
Aryhoulan 248 C3
Asby 209 D4
Ascog 232 C3
Ascot 121 E1
Ascott 147 F4
Ascott d'Oyley 133 F1
Ascott Earl 133 E1
Ascott-under-Wychwood 133 F1
Ascreavie 252 B4
Asenby 202 D5
Asfordby 160 C1
Asfordby Hill 160 C1
Asgarby Lincs 176 B1
Asgarby Lincs 175 G3
Ash Dorset 105 E1
Ash Kent 125 E3
Ash Kent 123 F2
Ash Som 116 B5
Ash Surr 121 D2
Ash Barton 113 F5
Ash Bullayne 102 A2
Ash Green Surr 121 E3
Ash Green Warks 159 F4
Ash Magna 170 C4
Ash Mill 114 A5
Ash Parva 170 C4
Ash Priors 115 E5
Ash Street 152 B3
Ash Thomas 102 D1
Ash Vale 121 D2
Ashampstead 134 A5
Ashbocking 152 C2
Ashbourne 172 C3
Ashbrittle 115 D5
Ashburnham Place 110 B2
Ashburton 101 D1
Ashbury Devon 99 F1
Ashbury Oxon 133 E4
Ashby 187 F2
Ashby by Partney 176 C1
Ashby cum Fenby 188 C2
Ashby de la Launde 175 F2
Ashby de la Zouch 159 F1
Ashby Dell 165 G2
Ashby Folville 160 C1
Ashby Hill 188 C2
Ashby Magna 160 A3
Ashby Parva 160 A4
Ashby Puerorum 188 D5
Ashby St. Ledgers 148 A1
Ashby St. Mary 179 E5
Ashchurch 146 B4
Ashcombe Devon 102 C5
Ashcombe NSom 116 A1
Ashcott 116 B4
Ashdon 151 D3
Ashe 119 G3
Asheldham 138 C2
Ashen 151 F3
Ashenden 124 A5
Ashendon 134 C1
Ashens 231 G2
Ashfield A&B 231 F1
Ashfield Here 145 E5
Ashfield Stir 242 C4
Ashfield Suff 152 D1
Ashfield Green Suff 165 D4
Ashfield Green Suff 151 F2
Ashfold Crossways 109 E1
Ashford Devon 100 C3
Ashford Devon 113 F2
Ashford Hants 106 A1
Ashford Kent 124 C4
Ashford Surr 135 F5
Ashford Bowdler 157 E5
Ashford Carbonel 157 E5
Ashford Hill 119 G1
Ashford in the Water 185 F5
Ashgill 234 B4
Ashiestiel 227 F2
Ashill Devon 103 D1
Ashill Norf 163 G2
Ashill Som 103 G1
Ashingdon 138 B3
Ashington N'umb 221 E3
Ashington Som 116 C5
Ashington WSuss 108 D2
Ashkirk 227 F3
Ashlett 107 D2
Ashleworth 146 A5
Ashleworth Quay 146 A5
Ashley Cambs 151 E1
Ashley ChesE 184 B4
Ashley Devon 113 G4
Ashley Glos 132 B3
Ashley Hants 119 E4
Ashley Hants 106 B3
Ashley Kent 125 F4
Ashley N'hants 160 C3
Ashley Staffs 171 E4
Ashley Wilts 117 F1
Ashley Down 131 E5
Ashley Green 135 E2
Ashley Heath Dorset 106 A2
Ashley Heath Staffs 171 E4
Ashmanhaugh 179 E3
Ashmansworth 119 F2
Ashmansworthy 112 D4
Ashmolean Museum Oxon OX1 2PH 80 Oxford
Ashmore Dorset 105 F1
Ashmore P&K 251 G4
Ashmore Green 119 G1
Ashorne 147 F2
Ashover 173 E1
Ashover Hay 173 E1
Ashow 159 F5
Ashperton 145 F3
Ashprington 101 E2
Ashreigney 113 G4
Ashridge Estate Herts HP4 1LX 135 E1
Ashtead 121 G2
Ashton ChesW&C 170 C1
Ashton Corn 94 D4
Ashton Corn 99 D4
Ashton Hants 107 E1
Ashton Here 145 E1
Ashton Invcly 232 D2
Ashton N'hants 161 F4
Ashton N'hants 148 C3
Ashton Peter 161 G2
Ashton Common 117 F2
Ashton Court Estate NSom BS41 9JN 8 B3
Ashton Keynes 132 C3
Ashton under Hill 146 B4
Ashton upon Mersey 184 B3
Ashton-in-Makerfield 183 G3
Ashton-under-Lyne 184 D3
Ashurst Hants 106 C1
Ashurst Kent 123 E5
Ashurst WSuss 109 D2
Ashurst Bridge 106 C1
Ashurstwood 122 D5
Ashwater 99 D1
Ashwell Herts 150 A4
Ashwell Rut 161 D1
Ashwell End 150 A3
Ashwellthorpe 164 C2
Ashwick 116 D3
Ashwicken 163 F1
Ashybank 227 G4
Askam in Furness 198 D5
Askern 186 C1
Askernish (Aisgernis) 254 C2
Askerswell 104 B3
Askett 134 D2
Askham Cumb 210 B5
Askham Notts 187 E5
Askham Bryan 195 E3
Askham Richard 195 E3
Asknish 240 B5
Askrigg 201 E3
Askwith 194 A3
Aslackby 175 F4
Aslacton 164 C2
Aslockton 174 C3
Asloun 260 D3
Aspall 152 C1
Aspatria 209 E2
Aspenden 150 B5
Asperton 176 A4
Aspley Guise 149 E4
Aspley Heath 149 E4
Aspull 184 A2
Asselby 195 G5
Asserby 189 E5
Assington 152 A4
Assington Green 151 F2
Astbury 171 F1
Astcote 148 B2
Asterby 188 C5
Asterley 156 C2
Asterton 156 D3
Asthall 133 E1
Asthall Leigh 133 F1
Astle 184 C5
Astley GtMan 184 B2
Astley Shrop 157 E1
Astley Warks 159 F4
Astley Worcs 145 G1
Astley Abbotts 157 G3
Astley Bridge 184 B1
Astley Cross 146 A1
Astley Green 184 B3
Astley Lodge 157 E1
Aston ChesE 170 D3
Aston ChesW&C 183 G5
Aston Derbys 185 F4
Aston Derbys 172 C4
Aston Flints 170 A1
Aston Here 157 D5
Aston Here 145 D1
Aston Herts 150 A5
Aston Oxon 133 F2
Aston Shrop 170 C5
Aston Shrop 158 A3
Aston Staffs 171 E3
Aston SYorks 186 B4
Aston Tel&W 157 F2
Aston W'ham 134 C4
Aston WMid 158 C4
Aston Abbotts 148 D5
Aston Botterell 157 F4
Aston Cantlow 146 D2
Aston Clinton 135 D1
Aston Crews 145 F5
Aston Cross 146 B4
Aston End 150 A5
Aston Eyre 157 F3
Aston Fields 146 B1
Aston Flamville 159 G3
Aston Heath 183 G5
Aston Ingham 145 F5
Aston juxta Mondrum 171 D2
Aston le Walls 147 G2
Aston Magna 147 D4
Aston Munslow 157 E4
Aston on Carrant 146 B4
Aston on Clun 156 C4
Aston Pigott 156 C2
Aston Rogers 156 C2
Aston Rowant 134 C3
Aston Sandford 134 C2
Aston Somerville 146 C4
Aston Subedge 146 D3
Aston Tirrold 134 A4
Aston Upthorpe 134 A4
Aston-by-Stone 171 G4
Aston-on-Trent 173 F5
Astwick 150 A4
Astwood 149 E3
Astwood Bank 146 C1
Aswarby 175 F3
Aswardby 189 D5
Aswick Grange 162 B1
Atch Lench 146 C2
Atcham 157 E2
Ath Linne 270 D6
Athelhampton 105 D3
Athelington 164 D4
Athelney 116 A5
Athelstaneford 236 C2
Atherington Devon 113 F3
Atherington WSuss 108 C3
Athersley North 186 A2
Atherstone 159 F3
Atherstone on Stour 147 E2
Atherton 184 A2
Atlow 172 D3
Attadale 257 F1
Attenborough 173 G4
Attenborough Nature Reserve Nott NG9 6DY 174 A4
Atterby 187 G3
Attercliffe 186 A4
Atterley 157 F3
Atterton 159 F3
Attingham Park Shrop SY4 4TP 157 E1
Attleborough Norf 164 B2
Attleborough Warks 159 F3
Attlebridge 178 C4
Attleton Green 151 F2
Atwick 197 D2
Atworth 117 F1
Auberrow 145 D3
Aubourn 175 E1
Auch 241 F1
Auchairne 214 C2
Auchallater 251 G1
Auchameanach 231 G4
Auchamore 231 G5
Aucharnie 268 E6
Aucharrigill 266 B1
Auchattie 260 E5
Auchavan 251 G3
Auchbraad 231 G1
Auchbreck 259 K2
Auchenback 233 G4
Auchenblae 253 F2
Auchenbothie 233 E2
Auchenbrack 216 B1
Auchenbreck 232 B1
Auchencairn 216 B5
Auchencrow 237 F3
Auchendinny 235 G3
Auchendolly 216 B4
Auchenfoyle 233 E2
Auchengillan 233 G1
Auchengray 235 D4
Auchenhalrig 268 B4
Auchenheath 234 C5
Auchenhessnane 216 C1
Auchenlochan 232 A2
Auchenmalg 214 D5
Auchenrivock 218 B3
Auchentiber 233 E5
Auchenvennel 233 D1
Auchessan 241 G2
Auchgourish 259 G3
Auchinafaud 231 F4
Auchincruive 224 B3
Auchindarrach 231 G1
Auchindarroch 248 C4
Auchindrain 240 C4
Auchindrean 265 H3
Auchininna 268 E6
Auchinleck 224 D3
Auchinloch 234 A2
Auchinner 242 B3
Auchinroath 267 K6
Auchintoul Aber 260 D3
Auchintoul Aber 268 E5
Auchintoul High 266 C2
Auchiries 261 J1
Auchleven 260 E2
Auchlochan 225 G2
Auchlunachan 265 H3
Auchlunies 261 G5
Auchlunkart 268 B6
Auchlyne 242 A2
Auchmacoy 261 H1
Auchmair 260 B2
Auchmantle 214 C4
Auchmithie 253 E5
Auchmuirbridge 244 A4
Auchmull 253 D2
Auchnabony 208 A2
Auchnabreac 240 C4
Auchnacloich 242 D1
Auchnacraig 239 G1
Auchnacree 252 C3
Auchnafree 242 D1
Auchnagallin 259 H1
Auchnagatt 269 H6
Auchnaha 232 A1
Auchnangoul 240 C4
Aucholzie 260 B5
Auchorrie 260 E4
Auchrannie 252 A4
Auchraw 242 A2
Auchreoch 241 F2
Auchronie 252 C1
Auchterarder 243 E3
Auchtercairn 264 E4
Auchterderran 244 A5
Auchterhouse 244 B1
Auchtermuchty 244 A3
Auchterneed 266 B6
Auchtertool 244 A5
Auchtertyre Angus 252 A5
Auchtertyre (Uachdar Thire) High 256 E2
Auchtertyre Moray 267 J6
Auchtertyre Stir 241 F2
Auchtubh 242 A2
Auckengill 275 J2
Auckley 186 D2
Audenshaw 184 D3
Audlem 171 D3
Audley 171 E2
Audley End Essex 150 D4
Audley End Essex 151 G4
Audley End Suff 151 G2
Audmore 171 F5
Auds 268 E4
Aughton ERid 195 G4
Aughton Lancs 183 E2
Aughton Lancs 192 B1
Aughton SYorks 186 B4
Aughton Wilts 118 D2
Aughton Park 183 F2
Auldearn 267 G6
Aulden 145 D2
Auldgirth 216 D2
Auldhame 236 C1
Auldhouse 234 A4
Aulich 250 B4
Ault a'chruinn 257 F2
Ault Hucknall 173 F1
Aultanrynie 273 F5
Aultbea (An t-Allt Beithe) 264 E3
Aultgrishan 264 D3
Aultguish Inn 265 K4
Aultibea 275 F6
Aultiphurst 274 D2
Aultmore 268 C5
Ault-na-goire 258 C2
Aultnamain Inn 266 D3
Aultnapaddock 268 B6
Aulton 260 E2
Aultvaich 266 C7
Aultvoulin 256 D4
Aunby 161 F1
Aundorach 259 G3
Aunk 102 D2
Aunsby 175 F4
Auquhorthies 261 G2
Aust 131 E4
Austerfield 187 D3
Austrey 159 E2
Austwick 193 D1
Authorpe 189 E4
Authorpe Row 189 F5
Avebury 132 D5
Avebury Trusloe 118 B1
Aveley 137 E4
Avening 132 A3
Averham 174 C2
Avery Hill 136 D5
Aveton Gifford 100 C3
Aviation Viewing Park GtMan M90 1QX 25 E6
Avielochan 259 G3
Aviemore 259 F3
Avington Hants 119 G4
Avington WBerks 119 E1
Avoch 266 D6
Avon 106 A3
Avon Dassett 147 G2
Avon Heath Country Park Dorset BH24 2DA 3 E1
Avon Valley Railway SGlos BS30 6HD 8 E4
Avonbridge 234 D2
Avoncliff 117 F2
Avonmouth 131 E5
Avonwick 100 D2
Awbridge 119 E5
Awhirk 214 B5
Awkley 131 E4
Awliscombe 103 E2
Awre 131 G2
Awsworth 173 F3
Axbridge 116 B2
Axford Hants 120 B3
Axford Wilts 133 E5
Axminster 103 F3
Axmouth 103 F3
Axton 182 C4
Axtown 100 B1
Aycliffe 212 B5
Aydon 211 G1
Aylburton 131 F2
Ayle 210 D3
Aylesbeare 102 D3
Aylesbury 134 D1
Aylesby 188 C2
Aylesford 123 G3
Aylesham 125 E3
Aylestone 160 A2
Aylmerton 178 C2
Aylsham 178 C3
Aylton 145 F4
Aymestrey 144 D1
Aynho 148 A4
Ayot Green 136 B1
Ayot St. Lawrence 136 A1
Ayot St. Peter 136 B1
Ayr 224 B3
Aysgarth 201 F4
Aysgarth Falls & National Park Centre NYorks DL8 3TH 201 F4
Ayshford 102 D1
Ayside 199 E4
Ayston 161 D2
Aythorpe Roding 137 E1
Ayton P&K 243 G3
Ayton ScBord 237 G3
Aywick 278 E4
Azerley 202 B5

B

Babbacombe 101 F1
Babbacombe Model Village Torbay TQ1 3LA 101 F1
Babbinswood 170 A4
Babb's Green 136 C1
Babcary 116 C5
Babel 143 E4
Babell 182 C5
Babeny 99 G3
Bablock Hythe 133 G2
Babraham 150 D2
Babworth 187 D4
Baby's Hill 259 K1
Bac 271 G3
Bachau 180 C4
Back of Keppoch 247 F1
Back Street 151 F2
Backaland 276 E4
Backaskaill 276 D2
Backbarrow 199 E4
Backburn 260 D1
Backe 127 F1
Backfolds 269 J5
Backford 183 F5
Backhill 261 F1
Backhill of Clackriach 269 H6
Backhill of Trustach 260 E5
Backies High 267 F1
Backies Moray 268 D5
Backlass 275 H3
Backside 260 C1
Backwell 116 B1
Backworth 221 E4
Bacon End 137 E1
Baconend Green 137 E1
Baconsthorpe 178 C2
Bacton Here 144 C4
Bacton Norf 179 E2
Bacton Suff 152 B1
Bacton Green 152 B1
Bacup 193 E5
Badachro 264 D4
Badanloch Lodge 274 C5
Badavanich 265 H6
Badbea 275 F7
Badbury 133 D4
Badbury Wick 133 D4
Badby 148 A2
Badcall High 272 D4
Badcall High 272 E3
Badcaul 265 G2
Baddeley Green 171 G2
Badden 231 G1
Baddesley Clinton 159 D5
Baddesley Clinton Warks B93 0DQ 159 D5
Baddesley Ensor 159 E3
Baddidarach 272 C6
Badenscoth 261 F1
Badenyon 260 B3
Badgall 97 G1
Badger 157 G3
Badgerbank 184 C5
Badgers Mount 123 D2
Badgeworth 132 B1
Badgworth 116 A2
Badicaul 256 D2
Badingham 153 E1
Badintagairt 273 G7
Badlesmere 124 C3
Badley 152 B2
Badlipster 275 H4
Badluarach 265 F2
Badminton 132 A4
Badnaban 272 C6
Badnabay 272 E4
Badnafrave 259 K3
Badnagie 275 G5
Badnambiast 250 C2
Badninish 266 E2
Badrallach 265 G2
Badsey 146 C3
Badshot Lea 121 D3
Badsworth 186 B1
Badwell Ash 152 A1
Badworthy 100 C1
Badyo 251 E3
Bag Enderby 189 D5
Bagber 105 D1
Bagby 203 D4
Bagendon 132 C2
Baggeridge Country Park Staffs DY3 4HB 14 A2
Bagginswood 157 F4
Baggrave Hall 160 B2
Baggrow 209 E2
Bàgh Mòr 262 D6
Baghasdal 254 C3
Bagillt 182 D5
Baginton 159 F5
Baglan 128 D3
Bagley Shrop 170 B5
Bagley Som 116 B3
Bagmore 120 B3
Bagnall 171 G2
Bagnor 119 F1
Bagpath 132 A3
Bagshot Surr 121 E1
Bagshot Wilts 119 E1
Bagstone 131 F4
Bagthorpe Norf 177 F4
Bagthorpe Notts 173 F2
Baguley 184 C4
Bagworth 159 G2
Bagwyllydiart 144 D5
Baildon 194 A4
Baile an Truiseil 271 F2
Baile Boidheach 231 F2
Baile Gharbhaidh 262 C7
Baile Glas 262 D6
Baile Mhartainn 262 C4
Baile Mhic Phail 262 D4
Baile Mòr 238 B2
Baile nan Cailleach 262 C6
Baile Raghaill 262 C5
Bailebeag 258 C3
Baileguish 259 F5
Baile-na-Cille 262 D3
Bailetonach 247 F2
Bailiesward 260 C1
Bailiff Bridge 194 A5
Baillieston 234 A3
Bainbridge 201 E3
Bainsford 234 C1
Bainshole 260 E1
Bainton ERid 196 B2
Bainton Oxon 148 A5
Bainton Peter 161 F2
Bairnkine 228 A5
Bakebare 260 B1
Baker Street 137 F4
Baker's End 136 C1
Bakewell 172 D1
Bala (Y Bala) 168 C4
Balachuirn 264 B7
Balado 243 F4
Balafark 242 B5
Balaldie 267 F4
Balallan (Baile Ailein) 270 E5
Balavil 258 E4
Balbeg High 258 B1
Balbeg High 258 B2
Balbeggie 243 G2
Balbirnie 244 A4
Balbithan 261 F3
Balblair High 266 E5
Balblair High 266 C2
Balblair High 266 E3
Balby 186 C2
Balcharn 266 C1
Balcherry 267 F3
Balchers 269 F5
Balchladich 272 C5
Balchraggan High 266 C7
Balchraggan High 258 C1
Balchrick 272 D3
Balcombe 122 C5
Balcurvie 244 B4
Baldernock 233 G2
Baldersby 202 C5
Baldersby St. James 202 C5
Balderstone GtMan 184 D1
Balderstone Lancs 192 C4
Balderton ChesW&C 170 A1
Balderton Notts 174 D2
Baldhu 96 B5
Baldinnie 244 C3
Baldock 150 A4
Baldon Row 134 A2
Baldovan 244 B1
Baldovie Angus 252 B4
Baldovie Dundee 244 C1
Baldrine 190 C3
Baldslow 110 C2
Baldwin 190 B3
Baldwinholme 209 G1
Baldwin's Gate 171 E3
Baldwins Hill 122 C5
Bale 178 B2
Balelone (Baile Lion) 262 C4
Balemartine 246 A2
Balemore (Baile Mòr) 262 C5
Balendoch 252 A5
Balephuil 246 A2
Balerno 235 F3
Balernock 233 D1
Baleromindubh 238 C5
Balerominmore 238 C5
Baleshare (Bhaleshear) 262 C5
Balevulin 239 D2
Balfield 252 D3
Balfour Aber 260 D5
Balfour Ork 277 D6
Balfron 233 G1
Balfron Station 233 G1
Balgonar 243 F5
Balgove 261 G1
Balgowan D&G 206 B2
Balgowan High 258 D5
Balgown 263 J5
Balgreen 269 F5
Balgreggan 214 B5
Balgy 264 E6
Balhaldie 242 D4
Balhalgardy 261 F2
Balham 136 B5
Balhary 252 A5
Balhelvie 244 B2
Balhousie 244 C4
Baliasta 278 F2
Baligill 274 D2
Baligrundle 248 A5
Balindore 240 B1
Balintore Angus 252 A4
Balintore High 267 F4
Balintraid 266 E4
Balintyre 250 B5
Balivanich (Baile a'Mhanaich) 262 C6
Balkeerie 252 B5
Balkholme 195 G5
Balkissock 214 C2
Ball 170 A5
Ball Haye Green 171 G2
Ball Hill 119 F1
Balla 254 C3
Ballabeg 190 A4
Ballacannell 190 C3
Ballacarnane Beg 190 A3
Ballachulish (Baile a' Chaolais) 248 C4
Balladoole 190 A5
Ballafesson 190 A4
Ballagyr 190 A3
Ballajora 190 C2
Ballakilpheric 190 A4
Ballamodha 190 A4
Ballantrae 214 B2
Ballards Gore 138 C3
Ballasalla IoM 190 A4
Ballasalla IoM 190 B2
Ballater 260 B5
Ballaterach 260 C5
Ballaugh 190 B2
Ballaveare 190 B4
Ballchraggan 266 E4
Ballechin 251 E4
Balleich 242 A4
Ballencrieff 236 B2
Ballidon 172 D2
Balliekine 231 G5
Balliemeanoch 240 D4
Balliemore A&B 240 D5
Balliemore A&B 240 A2
Ballig 190 A3
Ballimeanoch 240 C3
Ballimore A&B 232 A1
Ballimore Stir 242 A3
Ballinaby 230 A3
Ballindean 244 A2
Ballingdon 151 G3
Ballinger Common 135 E2
Ballingham 145 E4
Ballingry 243 G5
Ballinlick 251 E5
Ballinluig P&K 251 E4
Ballinluig P&K 251 F4
Ballintuim 251 G4
Balloch Angus 252 B4
Balloch High 266 E7
Balloch NLan 234 B2
Balloch WDun 233 E1
Ballochan 260 D5
Ballochandrain 232 A1
Ballochford 260 B1
Ballochgair 222 C3
Ballochmartin 232 C4
Ballochmorrie 214 D2
Ballochmyle 224 D3
Ballochroy 231 F4

Ballogie 260 D5
Balls Cross 121 E5
Balls Green Essex 152 B5
Ball's Green Glos 132 A3
Balls Hill 158 B3
Ballyaurgan 231 F2
Ballygown 246 G5
Ballygrant 230 B3
Ballyhaugh 246 A4
Ballymeanoch 240 A5
Ballymichael 223 E2
Balmacara
(Baile Mac Ara) 256 E2
Balmaclellan 216 A3
Balmacneil 251 E4
Balmadies 253 D5
Balmae 207 G2
Balmaha 241 G5
Balmalcolm 244 B4
Balmaqueen 263 K4
Balmeanach A&B 247 F5
Balmeanach A&B 238 D1
Balmedie 261 H3
Balmedie Country Park
Aber AB23 8XG 261 H3
Balmer Heath 170 B4
Balmerino 244 B2
Balmerlawn 106 C2
Balminnoch 215 D4
Balmore EDun 234 A2
Balmore High 267 F7
Balmore High 257 K1
Balmore High 263 H7
Balmore P&K 250 C4
Balmullo 244 C2
Balmungie 266 E6
Balmyle 251 F4
Balnaboth 252 B3
Balnacra 265 F7
Balnagall 267 F3
Balnaguard 251 E4
Balnaguisich 266 D4
Balnain 258 B1
Balnaknock 263 K5
Balnamoon 252 D3
Balnapaling 266 E5
Balnespick 259 F4
Balsall 159 E5
Balsall Common 159 E5
Balsall Heath 158 C4
Balscote 147 F3
Balsham 151 D2
Baltasound 278 F2
Balterley 171 E2
Balterley Heath 171 E2
Baltersan 215 F4
Balthangie 269 G5
Balthayock 243 G2
Baluachraig 240 A5
Balulive 230 C3
Balure A&B 240 C1
Balure A&B 240 A1
Balvaird 266 C6
Balvarran 251 F3
Balvicar 239 G3
Balvraid High 256 E3
Balvraid High 259 F1
Bamber Bridge 192 B5
Bamber's Green 151 D5
Bamburgh 229 F3
Bamburgh Castle N'umb
NE69 7DF 229 F3
Bamff 252 A4
Bamford Derbys 185 G4
Bamford GtMan 184 C1
Bampton Cumb 199 G1
Bampton Devon 114 C5
Bampton Oxon 133 F2
Bampton Grange 199 G1
Banavie
(Banbhaidh) 248 D2
Banbury 147 G3
Banbury Museum Oxon
OX16 2PQ 147 G4
Bancffosfelen 128 A1
Banchor 267 G7
Banchory 261 F5
Banchory Devenick 261 H4
Bancycapel 128 A1
Bancyfelin 127 G1
Bancyffordd 142 A4
Bandon 244 A4
Bandrake Head 199 E4
Banff 268 E4
Bangor 181 D5
Bangor-on-Dee (Bangor-
is-y-coed) 170 A3
Bangor's Green 183 E2
Banham 164 B3
Banham Zoo Norf
NR16 2HE 164 B3
Bank 106 B2
Bank End 198 C4
Bank Newton 193 F2
Bank Street 145 F1
Bank Top Lancs 183 G2
Bank Top WYorks 194 A5
Bankend 217 E4
Bankfoot 243 F1
Bankglen 225 D4
Bankhead Aber 260 E3
Bankhead Aber 260 E4
Bankhead
Aberdeen 261 G3
Bankhead D&G 208 A2
Bankland 116 A5
Banknock 234 B2
Banks Cumb 210 B1
Banks Lancs 191 G5
Bankshill 217 F2
Banningham 178 D3
Bannister Green 151 E5
Bannockburn 242 D1
Banstead 122 B3
Bantam Grove 194 B5
Bantham 100 C3
Banton 234 B2
Banwell 116 A2
Banwen Pyrddin 129 E2
Banyard's Green 165 E4

Bapchild 124 B2
Baptiston 233 G1
Bapton 118 A4
Bar End 119 F5
Bar Hill 150 B4
Barachander 240 C2
Barassie 224 B2
Barbaraville 266 E4
Barber Booth 185 F4
Barber Green 199 E4
Barber's Moor 183 F1
Barbican Arts & Conference
Centre GtLon
EC2Y 8DS 45 J1
Barbon 200 B4
Barbridge 170 D2
Barbrook 114 A3
Barby 160 A5
Barcaldine (Am Barra
Calltainn) 248 B5
Barcaple 216 A5
Barcheston 147 E4
Barclose 210 A1
Barcombe 109 G2
Barcombe Cross 109 G2
Barden 202 A3
Barden Park 123 E4
Bardennoch 215 G1
Bardfield End Green 151 E4
Bardfield Saling 151 E5
Bardister 278 C5
Bardney 175 G1
Bardon Leics 159 G1
Bardon Moray 267 K6
Bardowie 233 G2
Bardsea 199 D5
Bardsey 194 C3
Bardsey Island
(Ynys Enlli) 166 A5
Bardwell 164 A4
Bare 192 A1
Barewood 144 C2
Barfad 231 G3
Barford Norf 178 C5
Barford Warks 147 E1
Barford St. John 147 G4
Barford St. Martin 118 B4
Barford St. Michael 147 G4
Barfrestone 125 E3
Bargaly 215 F4
Bargany Mains 224 A5
Bargeddie 234 A3
Bargoed 130 A3
Bargrennan 215 E3
Barham Cambs 161 G5
Barham Kent 125 E3
Barham Suff 152 C2
Barharrow 216 A5
Barholm 161 F1
Barholm Mains 215 F5
Barkby 160 B2
Barkby Thorpe 160 B2
Barkers Green 170 C5
Barkestone-le-Vale 174 C4
Barkham 120 C1
Barking GtLon 136 D4
Barking Suff 152 B2
Barking Tye 152 B2
Barkisland 193 G5
Barkston 175 E3
Barkston Ash 195 D4
Barkway 150 B4
Barlae 215 D4
Barland 144 B1
Barlaston 171 F4
Barlavington 108 B2
Barlborough 186 B5
Barlby 195 F4
Barlestone 159 G2
Barley Herts 150 B4
Barley Lancs 193 E3
Barley Green 164 D4
Barleycroft End 150 C5
Barleyhill 211 G2
Barleythorpe 160 D2
Barling 138 C4
Barlings 188 A5
Barlow Derbys 186 A5
Barlow NYorks 195 F5
Barlow T&W 212 A1
Barmby Moor 195 G3
Barmby on the
Marsh 195 F5
Barmer 177 G4
Barmollich 240 A5
Barmoor Lane End 229 E3
Barmouth
(Abermaw) 154 C1
Barmpton 202 C1
Barmston 197 D2
Barnaby Green 165 F4
Barnacabber 232 C1
Barnacarry 240 B5
Barnack 161 F2
Barnacle 159 F4
Barnamuc 248 C5
Barnard Castle 201 F1
Barnard Gate 133 G1
Barnardiston 151 F3
Barnard's Green 145 G3
Barnbarroch D&G 215 E5
Barnbarroch D&G 216 C5
Barnburgh 186 B2
Barnby 165 F3
Barnby Dun 186 D2
Barnby in
the Willows 175 D2
Barnby Moor 187 D4
Barndennoch 216 C2
Barne Barton 100 A2
Barnehurst 137 E5
Barnes 136 B5
Barnes Street 123 F4
Barnet 136 B3
Barnet Gate 136 B3
Barnetby le Wold 188 A2
Barney 178 A2
Barnham Suff 163 G5
Barnham WSuss 108 B3
Barnham Broom 178 B5
Barnhead 253 E4
Barnhill ChesW&C 170 B2
Barnhill Dundee 244 C1
Barnhill Moray 267 J6
Barnhills 214 A3
Barningham Dur 201 F1
Barningham Suff 164 A4

Barningham Green 178 C2
Barnoldby le Beck 188 C2
Barnoldswick 193 E3
Barns Green 121 G5
Barnsdale Bar 186 C1
Barnsley Glos 132 C2
Barnsley SYorks 186 A2
Barnsole 125 E3
Barnstaple 137 F1
Barnston Essex 137 F1
Barnston Mersey 183 D4
Barnstone 174 C4
Barnt Green 158 C5
Barnton ChesW&C 184 A5
Barnton Edin 235 F2
Barnwell All Saints 161 F4
Barnwell Country Park
N'hants
PE8 5PB 161 F4
Barnwell St. Andrew 161 F4
Barnwood 132 A1
Barons' Cross 145 D2
Barr A&B 230 B3
Barr High 247 F5
Barr SAyr 215 D1
Barr Som 115 E5
Barr Hall 151 F4
Barra (Barraigh) 254 B4
Barra (Tràigh Mhòr)
Airport 254 B4
Barrachan 207 D2
Barrackan 239 G4
Barraer 215 E4
Barraglom 270 D4
Barran 241 D2
Barrapoll 246 A2
Barrasford 220 B4
Barravullin 240 A4
Barregarrow 190 B3
Barrets Green 170 C2
Barrhead 233 F4
Barrhill 214 D2
Barrington Cambs 150 B3
Barrington Som 103 G1
Barripper 94 D3
Barrisdale 256 E3
Barrmill 233 E4
Barrnacarry 240 A2
Barrock 275 H1
Barrow Glos 146 A5
Barrow Lancs 192 D4
Barrow Rut 161 D1
Barrow Shrop 157 F2
Barrow Som 117 E4
Barrow Som 116 C3
Barrow Suff 151 F1
Barrow Gurney 116 C1
Barrow Hann 196 C5
Barrow Haven 196 C5
Barrow Hill 186 B5
Barrow Nook 183 F2
Barrow Street 117 F4
Barrow upon
Humber 196 C5
Barrow upon Soar 160 A1
Barrow upon Trent 173 E5
Barroway Drove 163 D2
Barrowby 175 D4
Barrowcliff 204 D4
Barrowden 161 E2
Barrowford 193 E4
Barrow-in-Furness 191 F1
Barrows Green 199 G4
Barry Angus 244 D1
Barry VGlam 115 E1
Barry Island Pleasure
Park VGlam
CF62 5TR 115 E1
Barsby 160 B1
Barsham 165 E3
Barskimming 224 C3
Barsloisnoch 240 A5
Barston 159 E5
Barter Books,
Alnwick N'umb
NE66 2NP 229 F5
Bartestree 145 E3
Barthol Chapel 261 G1
Bartholomew Green 151 F5
Barthomley 171 E2
Bartley 106 C1
Bartley Green 158 C4
Bartlow 151 D3
Barton Cambs 150 C2
Barton ChesW&C 170 B2
Barton Cumb 210 A5
Barton Glos 146 C5
Barton Lancs 192 B4
Barton Lancs 183 F2
Barton NYorks 202 B2
Barton Oxon 134 A2
Barton Torbay 101 F1
Barton Warks 146 D2
Barton Bendish 163 F2
Barton End 132 A3
Barton Green 159 D1
Barton Hartshorn 148 B4
Barton Hill 195 G1
Barton in Fabis 173 G4
Barton in the Beans 159 F2
Barton Mills 163 F5
Barton on Sea 106 B3
Barton St. David 116 C4
Barton Seagrave 148 D5
Barton Stacey 119 F3
Barton Town 113 G1
Barton Turf 179 E3
Bartongate 147 G5
Barton-le-Clay 149 F4
Barton-le-Street 203 G5
Barton-le-Willows 195 G1
Barton-
the-Heath 147 E4
Barton-under-
Needwood 159 D1
Barton-upon-
Humber 196 C5
Barvas
(Barabhas) 271 F3
Barway 162 D5
Barwell 159 G3
Barwick Herts 136 C1
Barwick Som 104 B1
Barwick in Elmet 194 C4
Barwinnock 207 E2
Baschurch 170 B5

Bascote 147 G1
Base Green 152 B1
Basford Green 171 G2
Bashall Eaves 192 C3
Bashall Town 192 D3
Bashley 106 B3
Basildon Essex 137 G4
Basildon WBerks 134 B5
Basingstoke 120 B2
Baslow 185 G5
Bason Bridge 116 A3
Bassaleg 130 B4
Bassenthwaite 209 F3
Basset's Cross 113 F5
Bassett 106 D1
Bassingbourn 150 B3
Bassingfield 174 B4
Bassingham 175 E2
Bassingthorpe 175 E5
Basta 278 E3
Baston 161 G1
Bastonford 146 A2
Bastwick 179 F4
Batavaime 241 G1
Batch 116 A2
Batchley 146 C1
Batchworth 135 F3
Batchworth Heath 135 F3
Batcombe
Dorset 104 C2
Batcombe Som 117 D4
Bate Heath 184 A5
Bath 117 E1
Bathampton 117 E1
Bathealton 115 D5
Batheaston 117 E1
Bathford 117 E1
Bathgate 235 D3
Bathley 174 C2
Bathpool Corn 97 G2
Bathpool Som 115 F5
Bathway 116 C2
Batley 194 B5
Batsford 147 D4
Batson 100 D4
Battersby 203 E2
Battersea 136 B5
Battersea Cats & Dogs
Home GtLon
SW8 4AA 13 A5
Battersea Park Children's
Zoo GtLon
SW11 4NJ 13 A5
Battisborough
Cross 100 C3
Battisford 152 B2
Battisford Tye 152 B2
Battle ESuss 110 C2
Battle Powys 143 G4
Battle Abbey ESuss
TN33 0AD 110 C2
Battledown 146 B5
Battlefield 157 E1
Battlesbridge 137 G3
Battlesden 149 E5
Battlesea Green 164 D4
Battleton 114 C5
Battlies Green 152 A1
Battramsley 106 C3
Batt's Corner 120 D3
Bauds of Cullen 268 C4
Baugh 246 B2
Baughton 146 A3
Baughurst 119 G1
Baulds 260 E5
Baulking 133 F3
Baumber 188 C5
Baunton 132 C2
Baveney Wood 157 F5
Baverstock 118 B4
Bawburgh 178 C5
Bawdeswell 178 B3
Bawdrip 116 A4
Bawdsey 153 E3
Bawdsey Manor 153 E4
Bawsey 163 E1
Bawtry 187 D3
Baxenden 192 D5
Baxterley 159 E3
Baxter's Green 151 F2
Baxters Highland
Village Moray
IV32 7LD 268 B4
Bay 263 H6
Baybridge 211 F3
Baycliff 199 D5
Baydon 133 E5
Bayford Herts 136 C2
Bayford Som 117 E5
Bayfordbury 136 C1
Bayham Abbey 123 F5
Bayles 210 D3
Baylham 152 C2
Baynards Green 148 A5
Baysham 145 E5
Bayston Hill 157 D2
Bayswater 136 B4
Baythorn End 151 F3
Bayton 157 F5
Bayworth 134 A2
Beach High 247 G4
Beach SGlos 131 G5
Beachampton 148 C4
Beachamwell 163 F2
Beachans 267 H7
Beacharr 231 E5
Beachley 131 E3
Beacon Devon 103 E2
Beacon Devon 103 E2
Beacon Fell Country
Park Lancs
PR3 2NL 192 B3
Beacon Hill Dorset 105 F3
Beacon Hill Essex 138 B1
Beacon Hill Surr 121 D4
Beacon Hill Country Park
Leics LE12 8SR 17 C2
Beacon Park,
Up Holland Lancs
WN8 7RU 183 G2
Beacon's Bottom 134 C3
Beaconsfield 135 E3
Beacravik 263 G2
Beadlam 203 F4
Beadlow 149 G4
Beadnell 229 G4
Beaford 113 F4

Beal N'umb 229 E2
Beal NYorks 195 E5
Bealach 248 B4
Beale Park WBerks
RG8 9NH 134 B5
Bealsmill 99 D3
Beambridge 170 D2
Beamhurst 172 B4
Beaminster 104 A2
Beamish 212 B2
Beamish, North of England
Open Air Museum
Dur DH9 0RG 29 A1
Beamsley 193 G2
Bean 137 E5
Beanacre 118 A1
Beanley 229 E5
Beaquoy 276 C5
Beardon 99 F2
Beardwood 192 C5
Beare 102 C2
Beare Green 121 G3
Bearley 147 D1
Bearnie 261 H1
Bearnock 258 B1
Bearnus 246 E5
Bearpark 212 B3
Bearsbridge 211 D2
Bearsden 233 G2
Bearsted 123 G3
Bearstone 171 E4
Bearwood Poole 105 G3
Bearwood WMid 158 C4
Beattock 226 B5
Beauchamp Roding 137 E1
Beauchief 186 A4
Beaudesert 147 D1
Beaufort 130 A1
Beaulieu 106 C3
Beaulieu: National Motor
Museum, Abbey & Palace
House Hants
SO42 7ZN 4 A5
Beauly (A' Mhanachainn)
266 C7
Beaumaris (Biwmares)
181 E5
Beaumont Chanl 100 C5
Beaumont Cumb 209 G1
Beaumont Essex 152 C5
Beaumont Hill 202 B1
Beaumont Leys 160 A2
Beausale 159 E5
Beauvale 173 F3
Beauworth 119 G5
Beaworthy 99 E1
Beazley End 151 F5
Bebington 183 E4
Bebside 221 E4
Beccles 165 F2
Beccles Heliport 165 F3
Becconsall 192 A5
Beck Foot 200 B3
Beck Hole 204 B2
Beck Row 163 E5
Beck Side Cumb 198 D4
Beck Side Cumb 199 E4
Beckbury 157 G2
Beckenham 122 C2
Beckering 188 B4
Beckermet 198 B2
Beckermonds 201 D4
Beckett End 163 F3
Beckfoot Cumb 198 C2
Beckfoot Cumb 209 D2
Beckford 146 B4
Beckhampton 118 B1
Beckingham Lincs 175 D2
Beckingham Notts 187 E4
Beckington 117 F2
Beckley ESuss 111 D1
Beckley Oxon 134 A1
Beck's Green 165 E2
Beckside 200 B4
Beckton 136 D4
Beckwithshaw 194 B2
Bedale 202 B4
Bedburn 211 G4
Bedchester 105 E1
Beddau 129 G4
Beddgelert 167 E3
Beddingham 109 G3
Beddington 122 B2
Beddington Corner 122 B2
Bedfield 152 D1
Bedford 149 F3
Bedford Little
Green 152 D1
Bedgebury Cross 123 G5
Bedgrove 134 D1
Bedham 121 F5
Bedhampton 107 G2
Bedingfield 152 C1
Bedingfield Green 152 C1
Bedingfield Street 152 C1
Bedingham Green 165 D2
Bedlam Lancs 193 D5
Bedlam NYorks 194 B1
Bedlar's Green 150 D5
Bedlington 221 E4
Bedlinog 129 G2
Bedminster 131 E5
Bedmond 135 F2
Bednall 158 B1
Bedrule 228 A5
Bedstone 156 C5
Bedwas 130 A4
Bedwell 150 A5
Bedwellty 130 A2
Bedworth 159 F4
Bedworth
Woodlands 159 F4
Beeby 160 B2
Beech Hants 120 B4
Beech Staffs 171 F4
Beech Hill 120 B1
Beechingstoke 118 B2
Beechwood 183 G4
Beecraigs Country
Park WLoth
EH49 6PL 235 D2
Beedon 133 G5
Beeford 196 D2

Beeley 173 D1
Beelsby 188 C2
Beenham 119 G1
Beeny 98 B1
Beer 103 F4
Beer Hackett 104 C1
Beercrocombe 116 A5
Beesands 101 E3
Beesby Lincs 189 E4
Beesby NELincs 188 C2
Beeson 101 E3
Beeston CenBeds 149 G3
Beeston ChesW&C 170 C2
Beeston Norf 178 A4
Beeston Notts 173 G4
Beeston WYorks 194 B4
Beeston Regis 178 C1
Beeston
St. Lawrence 179 E3
Beeswing 216 C4
Beetham Cumb 199 F5
Beetham Som 103 F1
Beetley 178 A4
Beffcote 158 A1
Began 130 B4
Begbroke 133 G1
Begdale 162 C2
Begelly 127 E2
Beggar's Bush 144 B1
Beggearn Huish 114 D4
Beggshill 260 D1
Beguildy (Bugeildy) 156 A5
Beighton Norf 179 E5
Beighton SYorks 186 B4
Beili-glas 130 C2
Beith 233 E4
Bekesbourne 125 D3
Belaugh 179 D4
Belbroughton 158 B5
Belchalwell 105 D2
Belchalwell Street 105 D2
Belchamp Otten 151 G3
Belchamp St. Paul 151 F3
Belchamp Walter 151 G3
Belchford 188 C5
Belfield 184 D1
Belford 229 F3
Belgrave 160 A2
Belhaven 237 D2
Belhelvie 261 H3
Belhinnie 260 C2
Bell Bar 136 B2
Bell Busk 193 F2
Bell End 158 B5
Bell Heath 158 B5
Bell Hill 120 C5
Bell o' th' Hill 170 C3
Bellabeg 260 B3
Belladrum 266 C7
Bellanoch 240 A5
Bellaty 252 A4
Belle Isle 194 C5
Belle Vue 209 G1
Belleau 189 E5
Bellehiglash 259 J1
Bellerby 202 A3
Bellever 99 G3
Bellfields 121 E2
Bellingdon 135 E2
Bellingham GtLon 136 C5
Bellingham N'umb 220 A3
Belloch 222 B2
Bellochantuy 222 B2
Bell's Cross 152 C2
Bells Yew Green 123 F5
Bellsbank 224 C5
Bellshill N'umb 229 F3
Bellshill NLan 234 B3
Bellside 234 C4
Bellsmyre 233 F2
Bellsquarry 235 E3
Belluton 116 D1
Belmaduthy 266 D6
Belmesthorpe 161 F1
Belmont B'burn 184 A1
Belmont GtLon 122 B2
Belmont GtLon 136 A4
Belmont Shet 278 E2
Belnie 176 A4
Belowda 97 D3
Belper 173 E3
Belper Lane End 173 E3
Belsay 220 D4
Belsize 135 F2
Belsford 101 D2
Belstead 152 C3
Belston 224 B3
Belstone 99 G1
Belstone Corner 99 G1
Belsyde 235 D2
Belthorn 192 D5
Beltinge 125 D2
Beltingham 211 D1
Beltoft 187 F2
Belton Leics 173 F5
Belton Lincs 175 E4
Belton NLincs 187 E2
Belton Norf 179 F5
Belton Rut 160 D2
Belton House Lincs
NG32 2LS 175 E4
Beltring 123 F4
Belvedere 137 D5
Belvoir 174 D4
Bembridge 107 F4
Bemersyde 227 G2
Bemerton 118 C4
Bempton 205 E5
Ben Alder Cottage 249 G3
Ben Alder Lodge 250 A2
Ben Rhydding 194 A3
Benacre 165 G3
Benbecula (Beinn na
Faoghla) 262 D6
Benbecula (Balivanich)
Airport 262 C6
Benbuie 216 B1
Benderloch
(Meadarloch) 240 B1
Bendish 149 G5
Benenden 124 A5
Benfield 215 E4
Benfieldside 211 G2
Bengate 179 D3
Bengeo 136 C1

Bengeworth 146 C3
Benhall 146 B5
Benhall Green 153 E1
Benhall Street 153 E1
Benholm 253 G3
Beningbrough 195 E2
Benington Herts 150 A5
Benington Lincs 176 B3
Benington Sea End 176 C3
Benllech 180 D4
Benmore A&B 232 C1
Benmore Stir 241 G2
Bennacott 98 C1
Bennan Cottage 216 A3
Bennett End 134 C3
Bennetts End 135 F2
Benniworth 188 C4
Benover 123 G4
Benson 134 B3
Benston 279 D7
Benthall N'umb 229 G5
Benthall Shrop 157 F2
Bentham 146 B1
Benthoul 261 G4
Bentlawnt 156 C2
Bentley ERid 196 C4
Bentley Essex 137 E3
Bentley Hants 120 C3
Bentley Suff 152 C4
Bentley SYorks 186 C2
Bentley Warks 159 E3
Bentley WMid 158 B3
Bentley WYorks 194 B4
Bentley Heath
Herts 136 B3
Bentley Heath
WMid 159 D5
Bentley Rise 186 C2
Benton 113 G2
Benton Square 221 F4
Bentpath 218 A2
Bentworth 120 B3
Benvie 244 B1
Benville Lane 104 B2
Benwell 212 B1
Benwick 162 B3
Beoley 146 C1
Beoraidbeg 256 C5
Bepton 108 A2
Berden 150 C5
Bere Alston 100 A1
Bere Ferrers 100 A1
Bere Regis 105 E3
Berea 140 A4
Berepper 95 D4
Bergh Apton 179 E5
Berinsfield 134 A3
Berkeley 131 F3
Berkhamsted 135 E2
Berkley 117 F3
Berkswell 159 E5
Bermondsey 136 C5
Bernera 256 E2
Berneray (Eilean
Bhearnaraigh) 262 E3
Berners Roding 137 F2
Bernice 240 D5
Bernisdale 263 K6
Berrick Prior 134 B3
Berrick Salome 134 B3
Berriedale 275 G6
Berriew (Aberriw) 156 A2
Berrington
N'umb 229 E2
Berrington Shrop 157 E2
Berrington Worcs 145 E1
Berrington Green 145 E1
Berriowbridge 97 G2
Berrow Som 115 F2
Berrow Worcs 145 G4
Berrow Green 145 G2
Berry Cross 113 E4
Berry Down Cross 113 F1
Berry Hill Glos 131 E1
Berry Hill Pembs 141 D3
Berry Pomeroy 101 E1
Berryhillock 268 D4
Berryhillock 268 D4
Berrynarbor 113 F1
Berry's Green 122 D3
Bersham 170 A3
Berstane 277 D6
Berthlŵyd 128 B3
Berwick 110 A3
Berwick Bassett 132 D5
Berwick Hill 221 D4
Berwick St. James 118 B4
Berwick St. John 118 A5
Berwick St. Leonard 118 A4
Berwick-upon-
Tweed 237 G4
Bescar 183 E1
Bescot 158 C3
Besford Shrop 170 C5
Besford Worcs 146 B3
Bessacarr 186 D2
Bessels Leigh 133 G2
Besses o' th' Barn 184 C2
Bessingby 197 D1
Bessingham 178 C2
Best Beech Hill 123 F5
Besthorpe Norf 164 B2
Besthorpe Notts 174 D1
Bestwood 173 G3
Bestwood Country Park
Notts NG6 8UF 19 G1
Beswick ERid 196 C3
Beswick GtMan 184 C3
Betchworth 122 B3
Bethania Cere 142 B1
Bethania Gwyn 168 A3
Bethania Gwyn 167 F3
Bethel Gwyn 167 E1
Bethel Gwyn 168 C4
Bethel IoA 180 B5
Bethersden 124 B5
Bethesda Gwyn 167 F1
Bethesda Pembs 127 D1
Bethlehem 142 C5
Bethnal Green 136 C4
Betley 171 E3
Betley Common 171 E3
Betsham 137 F5
Betteshanger 125 F3
Bettiscombe 103 G3
Bettisfield 170 B4
Betton Shrop 156 C2
Betton Shrop 171 D4
Betton Strange 157 E2
Bettws Bridgend 129 F4

Bettws Newport 130 B3
Bettws Bledrws 142 B2
Bettws Cedewain 156 A3
Bettws Gwerfil Goch 168 D3
Bettws Newydd 130 C2
Bettws-y-crwyn 156 B4
Bettyhill 274 C2
Betws 128 C1
Betws Disserth 144 A2
Betws Garmon 167 E2
Betws Ifan 141 G3
Betws-y-coed 168 A2
Betws-yn-Rhos 182 A5
Beulah Cere 141 F3
Beulah Powys 143 F2
Bevendean 109 F3
Bevercotes 187 D5
Beverley 196 C4
Beverston 132 A3
Bevington 131 F3
Bewaldeth 209 F3
Bewcastle 219 D4
Bewdley 157 G5
Bewerley 194 A1
Bewholme 197 D2
Bewl Water ESuss TN3 8JH 123 F5
Bewley Common 118 A1
Bexhill 110 C3
Bexley 137 D5
Bexleyheath 137 D5
Bexwell 163 E2
Beyton 152 A1
Beyton Green 152 A1
Bhalamus 270 E7
Bhaltos 270 C4
Biallaid 258 E5
Bibury 132 D2
Bicester 148 A5
Bickenhall 103 F1
Bickenhill 159 D4
Bicker 176 A4
Bickershaw 184 A2
Bickerstaffe 183 F2
Bickerton ChesW&C 170 C2
Bickerton Devon 101 E4
Bickerton N'umb 220 B1
Bickerton NYorks 195 D2
Bickford 158 A1
Bickham 114 C3
Bickham Bridge 100 D2
Bickham House 102 C4
Bickington Devon 113 F2
Bickington Devon 102 A5
Bickleigh Devon 100 B1
Bickleigh Devon 102 C2
Bickleton 113 F2
Bickley 122 D2
Bickley Moss 170 C3
Bickley Town 170 C3
Bicknacre 137 G2
Bicknoller 115 E4
Bicknor 124 A3
Bickton 106 A1
Bicton Here 145 D1
Bicton Shrop 156 D1
Bicton Shrop 156 B4
Bicton Heath 157 D1
Bicton Park Gardens Devon EX9 7BJ 103 D4
Bidborough 123 E4
Biddenden 124 A5
Biddenden Green 124 A4
Biddenham 149 F3
Biddestone 132 A5
Biddick 212 C2
Biddisham 116 A2
Biddlesden 148 B3
Biddlestone 220 B1
Biddulph 171 F2
Biddulph Moor 171 G2
Bideford 113 E3
Bidford-on-Avon 146 D2
Bidlake 99 E2
Bidston 183 D3
Bidwell 149 F5
Bielby 195 G3
Bieldside 261 G4
Bierley IoW 107 E5
Bierley WYorks 194 A4
Bierton 134 D1
Big Pit National Coal Museum Torfaen NP4 9XP 130 B2
Big Sand 264 D4
Big Sheep, The Devon EX39 5AP 113 E3
Big Sky Adventure Play Peter PE2 7BU 161 G3
Bigbury 100 C3
Bigbury-on-Sea 100 C3
Bigby 188 A2
Bigert Mire 198 C3
Biggar Cumb 191 E1
Biggar SLan 226 B2
Biggin Derbys 173 D3
Biggin Derbys 172 C2
Biggin NYorks 195 E4
Biggin Hill 122 D3
Biggin Hill Airport 122 D2
Biggings 279 A6
Biggleswade 149 G3
Bigholms 218 B3
Bighouse 274 D2
Bighton 120 B4
Biglands 209 F1
Bignor 108 B2
Bigrigg 208 D5
Bigton 279 C10
Bilberry 97 E4
Bilborough 173 G3
Bilbrook Som 114 D3
Bilbrook Staffs 158 A2
Bilbrough 195 E3
Bilbster 275 H3
Bilby 186 D4
Bildershaw 212 A5
Bildeston 152 A3
Billericay 137 F3
Billesdon 160 C2
Billesley 146 D2
Billholm 218 A2
Billingborough 175 G4
Billinge 183 G3
Billingford Norf 164 C4
Billingford Norf 178 B3
Billingham 213 D5
Billinghay 175 G2
Billingley 186 B2
Billingshurst 121 F5
Billingsley 157 G4
Billington CenBeds 149 E5
Billington Lancs 192 D4
Billington Staffs 171 F5
Billister 279 D6
Billockby 179 F4
Billy Row 212 A4
Bilsborrow 192 B4
Bilsby 189 E5
Bilsby Field 189 E5
Bilsdean 237 E2
Bilsham 108 B3
Bilsington 124 C5
Bilson Green 131 F1
Bilsthorpe 174 B1
Bilsthorpe Moor 174 B2
Bilston Midlo 235 G3
Bilston WMid 158 B3
Bilstone 159 F2
Bilting 124 C4
Bilton ERid 197 D4
Bilton N'umb 229 G5
Bilton NYorks 194 C2
Bilton Warks 159 G5
Bilton-in-Ainsty 195 D3
Bimbister 277 C6
Binbrook 188 C3
Bincombe 104 C4
Bindal 267 G3
Bindon 115 E5
Binegar 116 D3
Bines Green 109 D2
Binfield 134 D5
Binfield Heath 134 C5
Bingfield 220 B4
Bingham 174 C4
Bingham's Melcombe 105 D2
Bingley 194 A4
Bings Heath 157 E1
Binham 178 A2
Binley Hants 119 F2
Binley WMid 159 F5
Binniehill 234 C2
Binsoe 202 B5
Binstead 107 E3
Binsted Hants 120 C3
Binsted WSuss 108 B3
Binton 146 D2
Bintree 178 B3
Binweston 156 C2
Birch Essex 152 A5
Birch GtMan 184 C2
Birch Cross 172 C4
Birch Green Essex 138 C1
Birch Green Herts 136 B1
Birch Grove 109 G1
Birch Heath 170 C1
Birch Vale 185 E4
Birch Wood 103 F1
Bircham Newton 177 F4
Bircham Tofts 177 F4
Birchanger 150 D5
Bircher 145 D1
Bircher Common 145 D1
Birchfield 266 B2
Birchgrove Cardiff 130 A4
Birchgrove Swan 128 D3
Birchington 125 F2
Birchmoor 159 E2
Birchover 172 D1
Birchwood Lincs 175 E1
Birchwood Warr 184 A3
Bircotes 186 D3
Bird Street 152 B2
Birdbrook 151 F3
Birdbush 118 A5
Birdfield 240 B5
Birdforth 203 D5
Birdham 108 A3
Birdingbury 147 G1
Birdland, Bourton-on-the-Water Glos GL54 2BN 147 D5
Birdlip 132 B1
Birdoswald 210 C1
Birds Green 137 E2
Birdsall 196 A1
Birdsgreen 157 G4
Birdsmoor Gate 103 G2
Birdston 234 A2
Birdwell 186 A2
Birdwood 131 G1
Birdworld, Farnham Hants GU10 4LD 120 D3
Birgham 228 B3
Birichen 266 E2
Birkby Cumb 209 D3
Birkby NYorks 202 C2
Birkdale Mersey 183 E1
Birkdale NYorks 201 D2
Birkenhead 183 E4
Birkenhills 269 F6
Birkenshaw 194 B5
Birkhall 260 B5
Birkhill Angus 244 B1
Birkhill ScBord 236 C5
Birkhill ScBord 226 D4
Birkholme 175 E5
Birkin 195 E5
Birks 194 B5
Birkwood 225 G2
Birley 145 D2
Birley Carr 186 A3
Birling Kent 123 F2
Birling N'umb 221 E1
Birling Gap 110 A4
Birlingham 146 B3
Birmingham 158 C4
Birmingham Botanical Gardens WMid B15 3TR 34 B7
Birmingham City Museum & Art Gallery WMid B3 3DH 35 E4
Birmingham International Airport 159 D4
Birnam 251 F5
Birsay 276 B5 Birse 260 D5
Birsemore 260 D5
Birstall 160 A2
Birstall Smithies 194 B5
Birstwith 194 B2
Birthorpe 175 G4
Birtle 184 C1
Birtley Here 144 C1
Birtley N'umb 220 A4
Birtley T&W 212 B2
Birts Street 145 G4
Birtsmorton 146 A4
Bisbrooke 161 D3
Biscathorpe 188 C4
Bish Mill 114 A5
Bisham 135 D4
Bishampton 146 B2
Bishop Auckland 212 B5
Bishop Burton 196 B3
Bishop Middleham 212 C4
Bishop Monkton 194 C1
Bishop Norton 187 G3
Bishop Sutton 116 C2
Bishop Thornton 194 B1
Bishop Wilton 195 G2
Bishopbridge 188 A3
Bishopbriggs 234 A2
Bishopmill 267 K5
Bishops Cannings 118 B1
Bishop's Castle 156 C4
Bishop's Caundle 104 C1
Bishop's Cleeve 146 B5
Bishop's Frome 145 F3
Bishops Gate 135 E5
Bishop's Green Essex 137 F1
Bishop's Green Hants 119 G1
Bishop's Hull 115 F5
Bishop's Itchington 147 F2
Bishops Lydeard 115 E5
Bishop's Norton 146 A5
Bishops Nympton 114 A5
Bishop's Offley 171 E5
Bishop's Stortford 150 C5
Bishop's Sutton 120 B4
Bishop's Tachbrook 147 F1
Bishop's Tawton 113 F2
Bishop's Waltham 107 E1
Bishop's Wood 158 A2
Bishopsbourne 125 D3
Bishopsteignton 102 C5
Bishopstoke 107 D1
Bishopston Bristol 131 E5
Bishopston Swan 128 B4
Bishopstone Bucks 134 D1
Bishopstone ESuss 109 G3
Bishopstone Here 144 D3
Bishopstone Swin 133 E4
Bishopstone Wilts 118 B5
Bishopstrow 117 F3
Bishopswood 103 F1
Bishopsworth 116 C1
Bishopthorpe 195 E3
Bishopton Darl 212 C5
Bishopton NYorks 202 B5
Bishopton Renf 233 F2
Bishopton Warks 147 D2
Bishton 130 C4
Bisley Glos 132 B2
Bisley Surr 121 E2
Bispham 191 G4
Bispham Green 183 F1
Bissoe 96 B5
Bisterne 106 A2
Bisterne Close 106 B2
Bitchet Green 123 E3
Bitchfield 175 E5
Bittadon 113 F1
Bittaford 100 C2
Bittering 178 A4
Bitterley 157 E5
Bitterne 107 D1
Bitteswell 160 A4
Bitton 117 D1
Bix 134 C4
Bixter 279 C7
Blaby 160 A3
Black Bourton 133 E2
Black Bridge 126 C2
Black Callerton 212 A1
Black Carr 164 B2
Black Clauchrie 215 D2
Black Corries Lodge 249 E4
Black Country Living Museum WMid DY1 4SQ 14 B2
Black Crofts 240 B1
Black Cross 96 D3
Black Dog 102 B2
Black Heddon 220 C4
Black Hill 147 E2
Black Marsh 156 C3
Black Moor 194 B3
Black Mount 249 E5
Black Notley 151 F5
Black Park Country Park Bucks SL3 6DR 135 F4
Black Pill 128 C3
Black Sheep Brewery Visitor Centre NYorks HG4 4EN 202 B4
Black Street 165 G3
Black Swan Guild, Frome Som BA11 1BB 117 E3
Black Torrington 113 E5
Blackaburn 219 F4
Blackacre 217 E1
Blackadder 237 F4
Blackawton 101 E2
Blackborough Devon 103 D2
Blackborough Norf 163 E1
Blackborough End 163 E1
Blackboys 110 A1
Blackbraes Aber 261 G3
Blackbraes Falk 234 D2
Blackbrook Derbys 173 E3
Blackbrook Leics 159 G1
Blackbrook Mersey 183 G3
Blackbrook Staffs 171 E4
Blackburn Aber 261 G3
Blackburn B'burn 192 C5
Blackburn WLoth 235 D3
Blackbushe 120 C2
Blackcastle 267 F6
Blackchambers 261 F3
Blackcraig D&G 215 F4
Blackcraig D&G 216 B2
Blackden Heath 184 B5
Blackdog 261 H3
Blackdown Devon 99 F3
Blackdown Dorset 103 G2
Blackdown Warks 147 F1
Blacker Hill 186 A2
Blackfen 137 D5
Blackfield 106 D2
Blackford Aber 261 F1
Blackford Cumb 218 B5
Blackford P&K 243 D4
Blackford Som 117 D5
Blackford Som 116 B3
Blackford Bridge 184 C2
Blackfordby 159 F1
Blackgang 107 D5
Blackgang Chine IoW PO38 2HN 107 D5
Blackhall Edin 235 G2
Blackhall Renf 233 F3
Blackhall Colliery 213 D4
Blackhall Mill 212 A2
Blackhall Rocks 213 D4
Blackham 123 E5
Blackhaugh 227 F2
Blackheath Essex 152 B5
Blackheath GtLon 136 C5
Blackheath Suff 165 F4
Blackheath Surr 121 F3
Blackheath WMid 158 B4
Blackhill Aber 269 J5
Blackhill Aber 269 J6
Blackhillock 268 C6
Blackhills 267 K6
Blackland 118 B1
Blacklands 114 B4
Blackleach 192 A4
Blackley 184 C2
Blacklunans 251 G3
Blackmill 129 F4
Blackmoor Hants 120 C4
Blackmoor Som 103 E1
Blackmoor Gate 113 G1
Blackmoorfoot 185 E1
Blackmore 137 F2
Blackmore End Essex 151 F4
Blackmore End Herts 136 A1
Blackness Aber 260 E5
Blackness Falk 235 E2
Blackness High 275 H5
Blacknest 120 C3
Blackney 104 A3
Blacko 193 E3
Blackpole 146 A2
Blackpool B'pool 191 G4
Blackpool Devon 101 E3
Blackpool Bridge 127 D1
Blackpool Gate 218 D4
Blackpool Piers B'pool FY4 1BB 191 G4
Blackpool Pleasure Beach B'pool FY4 1PL 191 G4
Blackpool Tower FY1 4BJ 64 Blackpool
Blackpool Zoo B'pool FY3 8PP 191 G4
Blackridge 234 C3
Blackrock A&B 230 B3
Blackrock Mon 130 B1
Blackrod 184 A1
Blackshaw 217 E4
Blackshaw Head 193 F5
Blacksmith's Green 152 C1
Blacksnape 192 D5
Blackstone 109 E2
Blackthorn 134 B1
Blackthorpe 152 A1
Blacktoft 196 A5
Blacktop 261 G4
Blacktown 130 B4
Blackwater Corn 96 B5
Blackwater Hants 120 D2
Blackwater IoW 107 E4
Blackwater Norf 178 B3
Blackwater Som 103 F1
Blackwaterfoot 223 E3
Blackwell Darl 202 B1
Blackwell Derbys 185 F5
Blackwell Derbys 173 F2
Blackwell Warks 147 E3
Blackwell Worcs 158 B5
Blackwell WSuss 122 C5
Blackwells End 145 G5
Blackwood (Coed-duon) Caerp 130 A3
Blackwood D&G 216 D2
Blackwood SLan 234 B5
Blackwood Hill 171 G2
Blacon 170 A1
Bladbean 125 D4
Bladnoch 215 F5
Bladon 133 G1
Blaen Clydach 129 F3
Blaenannerch 141 F3
Blaenau Dolwyddelan 167 F2
Blaenau Ffestiniog 167 F3
Blaenavon 130 B2
Blaenawey 130 B1
Blaencelyn 141 G2
Blaencwm 129 F2
Blaendyryn 143 F4
Blaenffos 141 E4
Blaengarw 129 F3
Blaengeuffordd 154 C4
Blaengweche 128 C1
Blaengwrach 129 E2
Blaengwynfi 129 E3
Blaenllechau 129 G3
Blaenos 143 D4
Blaenpennal 142 C1
Blaenplwyf 154 B5
Blaenporth 141 F3
Blaenrhondda 129 F2
Blaenwaun 141 F5
Blaen-y-coed 141 G5
Blagdon NSom 116 B2
Blagdon Torbay 101 E1
Blagdon Hill 103 F1
Blaguegate 183 F2
Blaich 248 C2
Blaina 130 A2
Blair 233 E5
Blair Atholl 251 D3
Blair Castle P&K PH18 5TL 251 D3
Blair Drummond 242 C5
Blair Drummond Safari & Adventure Park Stir FK9 4UR 242 C5
Blairannaich 241 F4
Blairbuie 232 C2
Blairgowrie 251 G5
Blairhall 235 E1
Blairhoyle 242 B4
Blairhullichan 241 G4
Blairingone 243 E5
Blairkip 224 D2
Blairlogie 242 D5
Blairmore A&B 232 C1
Blairmore High 266 E1
Blairmore High 272 D3
Blairnairn 233 D1
Blairnamarrow 259 K3
Blairpark 232 D4
Blairquhan 224 B5
Blairquhosh 233 G1
Blair's Ferry 232 A3
Blairshinnoch 268 E4
Blairuskinmore 241 G4
Blairvadach 233 D1
Blairydryne 261 F5
Blairythan Cottage 261 H2
Blaisdon 131 G1
Blake End 151 F5
Blake House Craft Centre Essex CM77 6RA 151 F5
Blakebrook 158 A5
Blakedown 158 A5
Blakelaw ScBord 228 B3
Blakelaw T&W 212 B1
Blakeley 158 A3
Blakelow 171 D2
Blakemere 144 C3
Blakemere Shopping Experience ChesW&C CW8 2EB 183 G5
Blakeney Glos 131 F2
Blakeney Norf 178 B1
Blakenhall ChesE 171 E3
Blakenhall WMid 158 B3
Blakeshall 158 A4
Blakesley 148 B2
Blanchland 211 F2
Bland Hill 194 B2
Blandford Camp 105 F2
Blandford Forum 105 E2
Blandford St. Mary 105 E2
Blanefield 233 G2
Blanerne 237 F4
Blankney 175 F1
Blantyre 234 A4
Blar a' Chaorainn 248 D3
Blargie 258 D5
Blarglas 233 E1
Blarmachfoldach 248 C3
Blarnalearoch 265 H2
Blashford 106 A2
Blaston 160 D3
Blathaisbhal 262 D4
Blatherwycke 161 E3
Blawith 199 D4
Blaxhall 153 E2
Blaxton 187 D2
Blaydon 212 A1
Bleadney 116 B3
Bleadon 116 A2
Bleak Hey Nook 185 E2
Blean 124 D2
Bleasby Lincs 188 B4
Bleasby Notts 174 C3
Bleasby Moor 188 B4
Bleatarn 200 C1
Bleathwood Common 145 E1
Blebocraigs 244 C3
Bleddfa 144 B1
Bledington 147 E5
Bledlow 134 C2
Bledlow Ridge 134 C3
Blencarn 210 C4
Blencogo 209 E2
Blencow 210 A4
Blendworth 107 G1
Blenheim Palace Oxon OX20 1PX 133 G1
Blennerhasset 209 E2
Blervie Castle 267 H6
Bletchingdon 134 A1
Bletchingley 122 C3
Bletchley MK 149 D4
Bletchley Shrop 170 D4
Bletherston 141 D5
Bletsoe 149 F2
Blewbury 134 A4
Blickling 178 C3
Blickling Hall Norf NR11 6NF 178 C3
Blidworth 173 G2
Blidworth Bottoms 173 G2
Blindburn Aber 261 H1
Blindburn N'umb 228 C5
Blindcrake 209 E3
Blindley Heath 122 C4
Blisland 97 E2
Bliss Gate 157 G5
Blissford 106 A1
Blisworth 148 C2
Blithbury 172 B5
Blitterlees 209 E1
Blo' Norton 164 B4
Blockley 147 D4
Blofield 179 E5
Blofield Heath 179 E4
Blore 172 C3
Blossomfield 158 D5
Blount's Green 172 B4
Blowick 183 E1
Bloxham 147 G4
Bloxholm 175 F2
Bloxwich 158 B2
Bloxworth 105 E3
Blubberhouses 194 A2
Blue Anchor Corn 96 D4
Blue Anchor Som 114 D3
Blue Bell Hill 123 G2
Blue Planet Aquarium, Ellesmere Port ChesW&C CH65 9LF 183 F5
Blue Reef Aquarium ESuss TN34 3DW 75 Hastings
Blue Reef Aquarium, Newquay Corn TR7 1DU 96 C3
Blue Reef Aquarium, Southsea Ports PO5 3PB 5 G6
Blue Reef Aquarium, Tynemouth T&W NE30 4JF 28 E1
Bluebell Railway WSuss TN22 3QL 109 F1
Bluewater 137 E5
Blundellsands 183 E3
Blundeston 165 G2
Blunham 149 G2
Blunsdon St. Andrew 132 D4
Bluntington 158 A5
Bluntisham 162 B5
Blunts 98 D4
Blurton 171 F3
Blyborough 187 G3
Blyford 165 F4
Blymhill 158 A1
Blymhill Common 157 G1
Blymhill Lawn 158 A1
Blyth N'umb 221 F3
Blyth Notts 186 D4
Blyth Bridge 235 F5
Blyth End 159 E3
Blythburgh 165 F4
Blythe Bridge 171 G3
Blythe Marsh 171 G3
Blyton 187 F3
Boarhills 245 D3
Boarhunt 107 F2
Boars Hill 133 G2
Boarsgreave 193 E5
Boarshead 123 E5
Boarstall 134 B1
Boarzell 110 C1
Boasley Cross 99 F1
Boat o' Brig 268 B5
Boat of Garten 259 G3
Boath 266 C4
Bobbing 124 A2
Bobbington 158 A3
Bobbingworth 137 E2
Bocaddon 97 F4
Bochastle 242 B4
Bocketts Farm Park Surr KT22 9BS 121 G2
Bockhampton 133 F5
Bocking 151 F5
Bocking Churchstreet 151 F5
Bockleton 145 E1
Boconnoc 97 F3
Boddam Aber 269 K6
Boddam Shet 279 F9
Bodden 116 D3
Boddington 146 A5
Bodedern 180 B4
Bodelwyddan 182 B5
Bodenham Here 145 E2
Bodenham Wilts 118 C5
Bodenham Moor 145 E2
Bodesbeck 226 C5
Bodewryd 180 C3
Bodfari 182 B5
Bodffordd 180 C5
Bodfuan 166 C4
Bodham 178 C1
Bodiam 110 C1
Bodiam Castle ESuss TN32 5UA 110 C1
Bodicote 147 G4
Bodieve 97 D2
Bodinnick 97 F4
Bodior 180 A5
Bodle Street Green 110 B2
Bodleian Library Oxon OX1 3BG 80 Oxford
Bodmin 97 E3
Bodnant Garden Conwy LL28 5RE 181 G5
Bodney 163 G3
Bodorgan 166 C1
Bodrane 97 G3
Bodsham Green 124 D4
Bodwen 97 E3
Bodymoor Heath 159 D3
Bogallan 266 D6
Bogbain 266 E7
Bogbrae 261 J1
Bogbuie 266 C6
Bogend 224 B2
Bogfern 260 D4
Bogfields 260 D4
Bogfold 269 G5
Boghead Aber 268 E5
Boghead EAyr 225 E3
Boghead SLan 234 B5
Boghole Farm 267 G6
Bogmoor 268 B4
Bogniebrae 268 D6
Bognor Regis 108 B4
Bograxie 261 F3
Bogroy 259 G2
Bogside 243 E5
Bogston 260 B4
Bogton 268 E5
Bogue 216 A2
Bohemia 106 B1
Bohenie 249 E1
Bohetherick 100 A1
Bohortha 95 F3
Bohuntine 249 E1
Boirseam 263 F3
Bojewyan 94 A3
Bokiddick 97 E3
Bolam Dur 212 A5
Bolam N'umb 220 C3
Bolam Lake Country Park N'umb NE20 0HE 220 C3
Bolberry 100 C4
Bold Heath 183 G4
Bolderwood 106 B2
Boldon 212 C1
Boldon Colliery 212 C1
Boldre 106 C3
Boldron 201 F1
Bole 187 E4
Bolehill 173 D2
Boleigh 94 B4
Bolenowe 95 D3
Boleside 227 F2
Bolfracks 250 D5
Bolgoed 128 C2
Bolham Devon 102 C1
Bolham Notts 187 E4
Bolham Water 103 E1
Bolingey 96 B4
Bollington 184 D5
Bolney 109 E1
Bolnhurst 149 F2
Bolshan 253 E4
Bolsover 186 B5
Bolsterstone 185 G3
Bolstone 145 E4
Boltby 203 D4
Bolter End 134 C3
Bolton Cumb 210 C5
Bolton ELoth 236 C2
Bolton ERid 195 G2
Bolton GtMan 184 B2
Bolton N'umb 229 F5
Bolton Abbey 193 G2
Bolton Abbey Estate NYorks BD23 6EX 193 G2
Bolton Bridge 193 G2
Bolton by Bowland 193 D3
Bolton Houses 192 A4
Bolton Low Houses 209 F2
Bolton Museum & Art Gallery GtMan BL1 1SE 184 B2
Bolton Percy 195 E3
Bolton Priory NYorks BD23 6EX 193 G2
Bolton upon Dearne 186 B2
Bolton Wood Lane 209 F2
Boltonfellend 210 A1
Boltongate 209 F2
Bolton-le-Sands 192 A1
Bolton-on-Swale 202 B3
Bolventor 97 F2
Bombie 208 A2
Bomere Heath 157 D1
Bonar Bridge 266 D2
Bonawe (Bun Atha) 240 C1
Bonby 188 A1
Boncath 141 F4
Bonchester Bridge 227 G4
Bonchurch 107 E5
Bondleigh 113 G5
Bonds 192 A3
Bonehill 159 D2
Bo'ness 235 D1
Bonhill 233 E2
Boningale 158 A2
Bonjedward 228 A4
Bonkle 234 C4
Bonning Gate 199 F3
Bonnington Edin 235 F3
Bonnington Kent 124 C5
Bonnybank 244 B4
Bonnybridge 234 C1
Bonnykelly 269 G5
Bonnyrigg 236 A3
Bonnyton Aber 260 E1
Bonnyton Angus 245 D1
Bonnyton Angus 253 E4
Bonnyton Angus 244 B1
Bonsall 173 D2
Bont 130 C1
Bont Dolgadfan 155 E2
Bont Newydd 168 A5
Bontddu 154 C1
Bont-goch (Elerch) 154 C4
Bonthorpe 189 E5
Bont-newydd Conwy 182 B5
Bontnewydd Gwyn 167 D1
Bontuchel 169 D2
Bonvilston 129 G5
Bon-y-maen 128 C3
Boode 113 F2
Boohay 101 F2
Booker 134 D3
Booley 170 C5
Boor 264 E3
Boorley Green 107 E1
Boosbeck 203 F1
Boose's Green 151 G4
Boot 198 C2
Boot Street 152 D3
Booth 193 G5
Booth Bank 185 E1
Booth Green 184 D4
Booth Wood 185 E1
Boothby Graffoe 175 E2
Boothby Pagnell 175 E4
Boothstown 184 B2
Boothville 148 C1
Bootle Cumb 198 C4
Bootle Mersey 183 E3
Booton 178 C3
Boots Green 184 B5
Booze 201 F2
Boquhan 233 G1
Boraston 157 F5
Bordeaux 101 F4
Borden Kent 124 A2
Borden WSuss 120 D5
Bordley 193 F1
Bordon 120 C4
Boreham Essex 137 G2
Boreham Wilts 117 F3
Boreham Street 110 B2
Borehamwood 136 A3
Boreland D&G 217 F1
Boreland D&G 215 E4
Boreland Stir 242 A1
Boreley 146 A1
Boreraig 263 G6
Borgh Na H-E. Siar 262 E3
Borgh Na H-E. Siar 254 B4
Borghastan 270 D3
Borgie 273 J3
Borgue D&G 207 G2
Borgue High 275 G6
Borley 151 G3
Borley Green Essex 151 G3
Borley Green Suff 152 A1
Bornais 254 C2
Borness 207 G2
Bornisketaig 263 J4
Borough Green 123 F3

Boroughbridge 194 C1
Borras Head 170 A2
Borrowash 173 F4
Borrowby NYorks 203 G1
Borrowby NYorks 202 D4
Borrowdale 209 F5
Borrowfield 261 G5
Borstal 123 G2
Borth 154 C4
Borthwick 236 A4
Borthwickbrae 227 F4
Borthwickshiels 227 F4
Borth-y-Gest 167 G2
Borve (Borgh)
  Na H-E. Siar 271 G2
Borwick 199 G5
Borwick Rails 198 C5
Bosavern 94 A3
Bosbury 145 F3
Boscarne 97 E3
Boscastle 98 C1
Boscastle Pottery Corn
  PL35 0HE 98 B1
Boscombe Bourne 106 A3
Boscombe Wilts 118 D4
Bosham 108 A3
Bosham Hoe 108 A3
Bosherston 126 C3
Bosley 171 G1
Bossall 195 G1
Bossiney 97 E1
Bossingham 125 D4
Bossington Hants 119 E4
Bossington Som 114 B3
Bostadh 270 D4
Bostock Green 171 D1
Boston 176 B3
Boston Spa 194 D3
Boswarthan 94 B3
Boswinger 97 D5
Bosworth Battlefield
  Country Park Leics
  CV13 0AD 159 G2
Botallack 94 A3
Botanic Garden
  Oxon OX1 4AZ
  80 Oxford
Botany Bay 136 C3
Botany Bay Lancs
  PR6 9AF 184 A1
Botcheston 159 G2
Botesdale 164 B4
Bothal 221 E3
Bothamsall 187 D5
Bothel 209 E3
Bothenhampton 104 B3
Bothwell 234 B4
Botley Bucks 135 E2
Botley Hants 107 E1
Botley Oxon 133 G2
Botloe's Green 145 G5
Botolph Claydon 148 C5
Botolphs 109 D3
Botolph's Bridge 124 D5
Bottacks 266 B5
Bottesford Leics 174 D4
Bottesford NLincs 187 F2
Bottisham 150 D1
Bottlesford 118 C2
Bottom Boat 194 C5
Bottom of Hutton 192 A5
Bottom o'th'Moor 184 B1
Bottomcraig 244 B2
Bottoms 193 F5
Botton Head 192 C1
Botusfleming 100 A1
Botwnnog 166 B4
Bough Beech 123 D4
Boughrood 144 A4
Boughspring 131 E3
Boughton N'hants 148 C1
Boughton Norf 163 D2
Boughton Notts 174 B1
Boughton Aluph 124 C4
Boughton Lees 124 C4
Boughton Malherbe 124 A4
Boughton
  Monchelsea 123 G3
Boughton Street 124 C3
Boulby 203 G1
Bouldnor 106 C4
Bouldon 157 E4
Boulge 153 D2
Boulmer 229 G5
Boulston 126 C1
Boultenstone Hotel 260 C3
Boultham 175 E1
Boundary Derbys 159 F1
Boundary Staffs 171 G3
Bourn 150 B2
Bourne 175 F5
Bourne End Bucks 135 D4
Bourne End
  CenBeds 149 E3
Bourne End Herts 135 F2
Bournebridge 137 E3
Bournemouth 105 G3
Bournemouth
  Airport 106 A3
Bournemouth International
  Centre BH2 5BH 64
Bournemouth
Bournheath 158 B5
Bournmoor 212 C2
Bournville 158 C4
Bourton Bucks 148 C4
Bourton Dorset 117 E4
Bourton NSom 116 A1
Bourton Oxon 133 E4
Bourton Shrop 157 E3
Bourton Wilts 118 B1
Bourton on
  Dunsmore 159 G5
Bourton-on-the-Hill 147 D4
Bourton-on-
  the-Water 147 D5
Bousd 246 B2
Boustead Hill 209 F1
Bouth 199 E4
Bouthwaite 202 A5
Bovain 242 A1
Boveney 135 E5
Boveridge 105 G1
Boverton 114 C1
Bovey Tracey 102 B5
Bovingdon 135 F2
Bovinger 137 E2

Bovington Camp 105 E4
Bow Cumb 209 G1
Bow Devon 102 A2
Bow Devon 101 E2
Bow Ork 277 C8
Bow Brickhill 149 E4
Bow Fife 244 B3
Bow Street Cere 154 C4
Bow Street Norf 164 B2
Bowbank 211 F5
Bowburn 212 C1
Bowcombe 107 D4
Bowd 103 E3
Bowden Devon 101 E3
Bowden ScBord 227 G2
Bowden Hill 118 A1
Bowdon 184 B4
Bower 219 F3
Bower Hinton 104 A1
Bower House Tye 152 A3
Bowerchalke 118 B5
Bowerhill 118 A1
Bowermadden 275 H2
Bowers 171 F4
Bowers Gifford 137 G4
Bowershall 243 F5
Bowertower 275 H2
Bowes 201 E1
Bowgreave 192 A3
Bowhousebog 234 C4
Bowithick 97 F1
Bowker's Green 183 F2
Bowland Bridge 199 F4
Bowley 145 E2
Bowley Town 145 E2
Bowlhead Green 121 E4
Bowling WDun 233 F2
Bowling WYorks 194 A4
Bowling Bank 170 A3
Bowlish 116 D3
Bowmanstead 199 E3
Bowmore 230 B3
Bowness-on-
  Solway 218 A5
Bowness-on-
  Windermere 199 F3
Bowood House &
  Gardens Wilts
  SN11 0LZ 118 A1
Bowscale 209 G3
Bowsden 237 G5
Bowside Lodge 274 D2
Bowston 199 F3
Bowthorpe 178 C5
Box Glos 132 A2
Box Wilts 117 F1
Box End 149 F3
Boxbush Glos 131 G1
Boxbush Glos 145 F5
Boxford Suff 152 A3
Boxford WBerks 133 G5
Boxgrove 108 B3
Boxley 123 G3
Boxmoor 135 F2
Box's Shop 112 C5
Boxted Essex 152 A4
Boxted Suff 151 G2
Boxted Cross 152 A4
Boxwell 132 A3
Boxworth 150 B1
Boxworth End 150 B1
Boyden Gate 125 E2
Boydston 224 C2
Boylestone 172 C4
Boyndie 268 E4
Boynton 196 D1
Boys Hill 104 C2
Boysack 253 E5
Boyton Corn 98 D1
Boyton Suff 153 E3
Boyton Wilts 118 A4
Boyton Cross 137 F2
Boyton End 151 F3
Bozeat 149 E2
Braaid 190 B4
Braal Castle 275 G2
Brabling Green 153 D1
Brabourne 124 C4
Brabourne Lees 124 C4
Brabster 275 J2
Bracadale 255 J1
Braceborough 161 F1
Bracebridge Heath 175 E1
Braceby 175 F4
Bracewell 193 E3
Brachla 258 C1
Brackenber 200 C1
Brackenbottom 200 D5
Brackenfield 173 E2
Brackens 269 F5
Bracklach 260 B2
Bracklamore 269 G5
Bracklesham 108 A4
Brackletter (A' Bhreac-
  Leitir) 249 D1
Brackley A&B 231 G1
Brackley High 266 D5
Brackley N'hants 148 A4
Brackley Gate 173 E3
Brackley Hatch 148 B3
Bracknell 121 D1
Braco 242 D4
Bracobrae 268 D5
Bracon Ash 164 C2
Bracora 256 D5
Bracorina 256 D5
Bradbourne 172 D2
Bradbury 212 C5
Bradda 190 A4
Bradden 148 B3
Braddock 97 F3
Bradenham Bucks 134 D3
Bradenham Norf 178 A5
Bradenstoke 132 C5
Bradfield Devon 103 D2
Bradfield Essex 152 C4
Bradfield Norf 179 D2
Bradfield W'ham 134 B5
Bradfield Combust 151 G2
Bradfield Green 171 D2
Bradfield Heath 152 C5
Bradfield St. Clare 152 A2
Bradfield St. George 152 A1
Bradfield Southend
  (Southend) 134 A5
Bradford Corn 97 F2
Bradford Derbys 172 D1

Bradford Devon 113 E5
Bradford N'umb 229 F3
Bradford N'umb 220 C4
Bradford WYorks 194 A4
Bradford Abbas 104 B1
Bradford Cathedral
  Church of St. Peter
  WYorks BD1 4EH
  65 Bradford
Bradford Leigh 117 F1
Bradford Peverell 104 C3
Bradford-on-Avon 117 F1
Bradford-on-Tone 115 E5
Bradgate Park Leics
  LE6 0HE 17 B3
Bradiford 113 F2
Brading 107 F4
Bradley ChesW&C 183 G5
Bradley Derbys 172 D3
Bradley Hants 120 B3
Bradley NELincs 188 C2
Bradley Staffs 158 A1
Bradley WMid 158 B3
Bradley Fold 184 B2
Bradley (Low Bradley)
  NYorks 193 G3
Bradley Green
  Warks 159 E2
Bradley Green
  Worcs 146 B1
Bradley in the
  Moors 172 B3
Bradley Mills 185 F1
Bradley Stoke 131 F4
Bradmore Notts 173 G4
Bradmore WMid 158 A3
Bradney 116 A4
Bradninch 102 D2
Bradnop 172 B2
Bradnor Green 144 B2
Bradpole 104 A3
Bradshaw GtMan 184 B1
Bradshaw WYorks 193 G4
Bradstone 99 D2
Bradwall Green 171 E1
Bradwell Derbys 185 F4
Bradwell Devon 113 E1
Bradwell Essex 151 G5
Bradwell MK 148 D4
Bradwell Norf 179 G5
Bradwell Grove 133 E2
Bradwell Waterside 138 C2
Bradwell-on-Sea 138 D2
Bradworthy 112 D4
Brae D&G 216 C3
Brae High 266 E1
Brae Shet 279 C6
Brae of Achnahaird 272 C7
Braeantra 266 C2
Braedownie 252 A2
Braefoot 269 F6
Braegrum 243 F2
Braehead D&G 215 F5
Braehead Glas 233 G3
Braehead Moray 268 B6
Braehead Ork 277 E7
Braehead Ork 276 D3
Braehead SLan 225 G2
Braehead SLan 235 D4
Braehead of Lunan 253 E4
Braehoulland 278 B5
Braeleny 242 B3
Braemar 259 J5
Braemore High 266 C1
Braemore High 275 F5
Braemore High 265 H4
Braenaloin 259 K5
Braes of Enzie 268 B5
Braes of Foss 250 C4
Braes of Ullapool
  (Bruthaicheann Ullapuil)
  265 H2
Braeswick 276 F4
Braeval 242 A4
Braewick 279 C7
Brafferton Darl 212 B5
Brafferton NYorks 202 D5
Brafield-on-the-
  Green 148 D2
Bragar 270 E3
Bragbury End 150 A5
Bragenham 149 E5
Braichmelyn 167 F1
Braides 192 A2
Braidley 201 F4
Braidwood 234 C5
Braigo 230 A3
Brailsford 173 D3
Brain's Green 131 F2
Braintree 151 F5
Braiseworth 164 C4
Braishfield 119 E5
Braithwaite
  SYorks 186 D1
Braithwaite
  WYorks 193 G3
Braithwell 186 C3
Bramber 109 D2
Bramcote Notts 173 G4
Bramcote Warks 159 G4
Bramdean 120 B5
Bramerton 179 D5
Bramfield Herts 136 B1
Bramfield Suff 165 E4
Bramford 152 C3
Bramhall 184 C4
Bramham 194 D3
Bramhope 194 B3
Bramley Hants 120 B2
Bramley Surr 121 F3
Bramley SYorks 186 B3
Bramley Corner 120 B2
Bramley Head 194 A2
Bramley Vale 173 F1
Bramling 125 E3
Brampford Speke 102 C3
Brampton Cambs 162 A5
Brampton Cumb 210 B1
Brampton Cumb 210 C5
Brampton Derbys 186 A5
Brampton Lincs 187 F5
Brampton Norf 178 D3
Brampton Suff 165 F3
Brampton SYorks 186 B2

Brampton Abbotts 145 F5
Brampton Ash 160 C4
Brampton Bryan 156 C5
Brampton en le
  Morthen 186 B4
Brampton Street 165 F3
Brampton Valley Way
  Country Park N'hants
  NN6 9DG 160 C5
Bramshall 172 B4
Bramshaw 106 B1
Bramshill 120 C1
Bramshott 120 D4
Bramwell 116 B5
Bran End 151 E5
Branault 247 E3
Brancaster 177 F3
Brancaster Staithe 177 F3
Brancepeth 212 B4
Branch End 211 F1
Branchill 267 H6
Brand Green 145 G5
Brandelhow 209 F4
Branderburgh 267 K4
Brandesburton 196 D3
Brandeston 152 D1
Brandis Corner 113 E5
Brandiston 178 C3
Brandlingill 209 E4
Brandon Dur 212 B4
Brandon Lincs 175 E3
Brandon N'umb 229 E5
Brandon Suff 163 F4
Brandon Warks 159 G5
Brandon Bank 163 E4
Brandon Creek 163 E3
Brandon Park Suff
  IP27 0SU 163 F4
Brandon Parva 178 B5
Brandon to Bishop
  Auckland Walk Dur
  DH7 7RJ 212 B4
Brandsby 203 D5
Brandy Wharf 188 A3
Brane 94 B4
Branksome 105 G3
Branksome Park 105 G3
Bransbury 119 F3
Bransby 187 F5
Branscombe 103 E4
Bransford 146 A2
Bransgore 106 A3
Bransholme 196 D4
Branson's Cross 158 C5
Branston Leics 174 D5
Branston Lincs 175 F1
Branston Staffs 172 D5
Branston Booths 175 F1
Branstone 107 E4
Brant Broughton 175 E2
Brantham 152 C4
Branthwaite Cumb 209 F3
Branthwaite Cumb 209 D4
Brantingham 196 B5
Branton N'umb 229 E5
Branton SYorks 186 D2
Brantwood 199 E3
Branxholm
  Bridgend 227 F4
Branxholme 227 F4
Branxton 228 C3
Brassey Green 170 C1
Brassington 172 D2
Brasted 123 D3
Brasted Chart 123 D3
Brathens 260 E5
Bratoft 176 C1
Brattleby 187 G4
Bratton Som 114 C3
Bratton Tel&W 157 F1
Bratton Wilts 118 A3
Bratton Clovelly 99 E1
Bratton Fleming 113 G2
Bratton Seymour 117 D5
Braughing 150 B5
Brauncewell 175 F2
Braunston N'hants 148 A1
Braunston Rut 160 D2
Braunstone 160 A2
Braunton 113 E2
Brawby 203 G5
Brawdy 140 B5
Brawith 203 E2
Brawl 274 D2
Brawlbin 275 F3
Bray 135 E5
Bray Shop 98 D3
Bray Wick 135 D5
Braybrooke 160 C4
Braydon Side 132 C4
Brayford 113 G2
Brayshaw 193 D2
Braythorn 194 B3
Brayton 195 F4
Braywoodside 135 D5
Brazacott 98 C1
Brea 96 A5
Breach Kent 125 D4
Breach Kent 124 A2
Breachwood Green 149 G5
Breacleit 270 D4
Breaden Heath 170 B4
Breadsall 173 E3
Breadstone 131 G2
Breage 94 D4
Breakon 278 E2
Bream 131 F2
Breamore 106 A1
Brean 115 F2
Breanais 270 B5
Brearton 194 C1
Breascleit 270 E4
Breaston 173 F4
Brechfa 142 B4
Brechin 253 E3
Breck of Cruan 277 C6
Breckles 164 A2
Brecon
  (Aberhonddu) 143 G5
Brecon Beacons International
  Dark Sky Reserve
  Carmar./Powys 129 E1
Brecon Beacons Visitor
  Centre Powys
  LD3 8ER 143 F5
Breconside 225 G5
Bredbury 184 D3

Brede 110 D2
Bredenbury 145 F2
Bredfield 153 D2
Bredgar 124 A2
Bredhurst 123 G2
Bredon 146 B4
Bredon's Hardwick 146 B4
Bredon's Norton 146 B4
Bredwardine 144 C3
Breedon on the Hill 173 F5
Breibhig 271 G4
Breich 235 D3
Breightmet 184 B2
Breighton 195 G4
Breinton 145 D4
Breinton Common 145 D4
Bremhill 132 B5
Bremhill Wick 132 B5
Brenachoile 240 C4
Brenchley 123 F4
Brendon Devon 114 A3
Brendon Devon 113 D5
Brendon Devon 113 D5
Brenkley 221 E4
Brent Eleigh 152 A3
Brent Knoll 116 A2
Brent Pelham 150 C4
Brentford 136 A5
Brentingby 160 C1
Brentwood 137 E3
Brenzett 111 F1
Brenzett Green 111 F1
Breoch 216 B5
Brereton 158 C1
Brereton Green 171 E1
Brereton Heath 171 F1
Breretonhill 158 C1
Bressay 279 E8
Bressingham 164 B3
Bressingham Common 164 B3
Bressingham Steam
  Museum & Gardens
  Norf IP22 2AA 164 B3
Bretby 173 D5
Bretford 159 G5
Bretforton 146 C3
Bretherdale Head 199 G2
Bretherton 192 A5
Brettabister 279 D7
Brettenham Norf 164 A3
Brettenham Suff 152 A2
Bretton Derbys 185 F5
Bretton Flints 170 A1
Bretton Peter 161 G2
Brevig 254 B5
Brewood 158 A2
Briach 267 H6
Briantspuddle 105 E3
Brick End 151 D5
Brickendon 136 C2
Bricket Wood 136 A2
Brickfields Horse Country
  IoW PO33 3TH 107 E3
Brickkiln Green 151 F4
Bricklehampton 146 B3
Bride 190 C1
Bridekirk 209 E3
Bridell 141 E3
Bridestones 171 G1
Bridestowe 99 F2
Brideswell 260 D1
Bridford 102 B4
Bridge Corn 96 A5
Bridge Kent 125 D3
Bridge End Cumb 198 D4
Bridge End Devon 100 C3
Bridge End Essex 151 F4
Bridge End Lincs 175 G4
Bridge End Shet 279 C9
Bridge Hewick 202 C5
Bridge o'Ess 260 D5
Bridge of Alford 260 D3
Bridge of Allan 242 C5
Bridge of Avon 259 J1
Bridge of Awe
  (Drochaid Abha) 240 C1
Bridge of Balgie 250 A5
Bridge of
  Bogendreip 260 E5
Bridge of
  Brewlands 251 G3
Bridge of Brown 259 J2
Bridge of Cally 251 G4
Bridge of Canny 260 E5
Bridge of Craigisla 252 A4
Bridge of Dee Aber 259 J5
Bridge of Dee Aber 260 E5
Bridge of Dee D&G 216 B4
Bridge of Don 261 H4
Bridge of Dun 253 E4
Bridge of Dye 253 E1
Bridge of Earn 243 G3
Bridge of Ericht 250 A4
Bridge of Feugh 260 E5
Bridge of Forss 275 F2
Bridge of Gairn 260 B5
Bridge of Gaur 250 A4
Bridge of Muchalls 261 G5
Bridge of Muick 260 B5
Bridge of Orchy (Drochaid
  Urchaidh) 241 E1
Bridge of Tynet 268 B4
Bridge of Walls 279 B7
Bridge of Weir 233 E2
Bridge Reeve 113 G4
Bridge Sollers 144 D3
Bridge Street 151 G3
Bridge Trafford 183 F5
Bridgefoot Angus 244 B1
Bridgefoot Cambs 150 C3
Bridgefoot Cumb 209 D4
Bridgehampton 116 C5
Bridgehaugh 260 B1
Bridgehill 211 G2
Bridgemary 107 E2
Bridgemere 171 E3
Bridgend A&B 230 B3
Bridgend A&B 240 A5
Bridgend Aber 260 D1
Bridgend Aber 269 F6
Bridgend Angus 252 D3
Bridgend (Pen-y-bont ar
  Ogwr) Bridgend 129 F5
Bridgend Corn 97 F4
Bridgend Cumb 199 F1
Bridgend Fife 244 B3
Bridgend Moray 260 B1
Bridgend P&K 243 G2

Bridgend WLoth 235 E2
Bridgend of
  Lintrathen 252 A4
Bridgerule 112 C5
Bridges 156 C3
Bridgeton Aber 260 D3
Bridgeton Glas 234 A3
Bridgetown Corn 98 D2
Bridgetown Som 114 C4
Bridgeyate 131 F5
Bridgham 164 A3
Bridgnorth 157 G3
Bridgnorth Cliff
  Railway Shrop
  WV16 4AH 157 G3
Bridgtown 158 B2
Bridgwater 115 F4
Bridlington 197 D1
Bridport 104 A3
Bridstow 145 E5
Brierfield 193 E4
Brierley Glos 131 F1
Brierley Here 145 D2
Brierley SYorks 186 B1
Brierley Hill 158 B4
Brierton 213 D5
Briestfield 185 G1
Brig o'Turk 242 A4
Brigg 188 A2
Briggate 179 E3
Briggswath 204 B2
Brigham Cumb 209 D3
Brigham ERid 196 C2
Brighouse 194 A5
Brighstone 106 D4
Brightgate 173 D2
Brightholmlee 185 G3
Brightling 110 B1
Brightlingsea 139 D1
Brighton B&H 109 F3
Brighton Corn 96 D4
Brighton Centre, The
  B&H BN1 2GR
  65 Brighton
Brighton Museum &
  Art Gallery B&H
  BN1 1EE 65 Brighton
Brighton Pier B&H
  BN2 1TW 65 Brighton
Brightons 234 D2
Brightwalton 133 G5
Brightwalton Green 133 G5
Brightwell 152 D3
Brightwell Baldwin 134 B3
Brightwell
  Upperton 134 B3
Brightwell-cum-
  Sotwell 134 A3
Brignall 201 F1
Brigsley 188 C2
Brigsteer 199 F4
Brigstock 161 E4
Brill Bucks 134 B1
Brill Corn 95 E4
Brilley 144 B3
Brilley Mountain 144 B2
Brimaston 140 C5
Brimfield 145 E1
Brimington 186 B5
Brimington
  Common 186 B5
Brimley 102 B5
Brimpsfield 132 B1
Brimpton 119 G1
Brims 277 B9
Brimscombe 132 A2
Brimstage 183 E4
Brinacory 256 D5
Brindham 116 C3
Brindister Shet 279 D9
Brindister Shet 279 B7
Brindle 192 B5
Brindley Ford 171 F2
Brineton 158 A1
Bringhurst 160 D3
Brington 161 F5
Brinian 276 D5
Briningham 178 B2
Brinkhill 189 D5
Brinkley Cambs 151 E2
Brinkley Notts 174 C2
Brinklow 159 G5
Brinkworth 132 C4
Brinmore 258 D2
Brinscall 192 C5
Brinsea 116 B1
Brinsley 173 F3
Brinsop 144 D3
Brinsworth 186 B3
Brinton 178 B2
Brisco 210 A2
Brisley 178 A3
Brislington 131 F5
Brissenden Green 124 B5
Bristol 131 E5
Bristol Cathedral
  BS1 5TJ 66 Bristol
Bristol City Museum &
  Art Gallery Bristol
  BS8 1RL 8 B3
Bristol Filton
  Airport 131 E4
Bristol International
  Airport 116 C1
Bristol Zoo Bristol
  BS8 3HA 8 B3
Briston 178 B2
Britannia 193 E5
Britford 118 C5
Brithdir Caerp 130 A2
Brithdir Gwyn 155 D1
Brithem Bottom 102 D1
British Empire &
  Commonwealth Museum
  BS1 6QH 66 Bristol
British Library
  (St. Pancras) GtLon
  NW1 2DB 12 B2
British Museum GtLon
  WC1B 3DG 44 D1
Briton Ferry
  (Llansawel) 128 D3
Britwell 135 E4
Britwell Salome 134 B3

Brixham 101 F2
Brixton Devon 100 B3
Brixton GtLon 136 C5
Brixton Deverill 117 F4
Brixworth 160 C5
Brixworth Country Park
  N'hants
  NN6 9DG 160 C5
Brize Norton 133 E2
Broad Alley 146 A1
Broad Blunsdon 133 D3
Broad Campden 147 D4
Broad Carr 185 E1
Broad Chalke 118 B5
Broad Ford 123 G5
Broad Green
  Cambs 151 E2
Broad Green
  CenBeds 149 E3
Broad Green Essex 151 G5
Broad Green Essex 150 C4
Broad Green
  Mersey 183 F3
Broad Green Suff 152 B2
Broad Green Worcs 145 G2
Broad Haven 126 B1
Broad Hill 163 E5
Broad Hinton 132 D5
Broad Laying 119 F1
Broad Marston 146 D4
Broad Oak Carmar 142 B5
Broad Oak Cumb 198 C3
Broad Oak ESuss 110 B1
Broad Oak ESuss 110 B1
Broad Oak Here 145 D5
Broad Road 165 D4
Broad Street ESuss 111 D2
Broad Street Kent 124 A3
Broad Street Wilts 118 C2
Broad Street Green 138 B2
Broad Town 132 D5
Broadbottom 185 D3
Broadbridge 108 A3
Broadbridge Heath 121 G4
Broadclyst 102 C3
Broadfield Lancs 192 D5
Broadfield Lancs 192 B5
Broadford (An t-Ath
  Leathann) 256 C2
Broadford Airport 256 C2
Broadford Bridge 121 F5
Broadgate 198 C4
Broadhaugh 227 F5
Broadhaven 275 J3
Broadheath GtMan 184 B4
Broadheath Worcs 145 F1
Broadhembury 103 E2
Broadhempston 101 E1
Broadholme 187 F5
Broadland Row 110 D2
Broadlay 127 G2
Broadley Lancs 184 C1
Broadley Moray 268 B4
Broadley Common 136 D2
Broadmayne 104 D4
Broadmeadows 227 F2
Broadmere 120 B3
Broadmoor 127 D2
Broadnymett 102 A2
Broadoak Dorset 104 A3
Broadoak Glos 131 F1
Broadoak Kent 125 D2
Broadoak End 136 C1
Broadrashes 268 C5
Broad's Green 137 F1
Broadsea 269 H4
Broadstairs 125 F2
Broadstone Poole 105 G3
Broadstone Shrop 157 E4
Broadstreet
  Common 130 C4
Broadwas 145 G2
Broadwater Herts 150 A5
Broadwater WSuss 108 D3
Broadwater Down 123 E5
Broadwaters 158 A5
Broadway Carmar 127 G2
Broadway Carmar 127 F1
Broadway Pembs 126 B1
Broadway Som 103 G1
Broadway Suff 165 E4
Broadway Worcs 146 D4
Broadwell Glos 147 E5
Broadwell Glos 131 F1
Broadwell Oxon 133 E2
Broadwell Warks 147 G1
Broadwell House 211 F2
Broadway 104 C4
Broadwindsor 104 A2
Broadwood Kelly 113 G5
Broadwoodwidger 99 E2
Brobury 144 C3
Brocastle 129 F5
Brochel 264 B7
Brochloch 215 G3
Brock 246 B2
Brockamin 145 G2
Brockbridge 107 F1
Brockdish 164 D4
Brockenhurst 106 B2
Brockford Green 152 C1
Brockford Street 152 C1
Brockhall 148 B1
Brockham 121 G3
Brockhampton
  Glos 146 C5
Brockhampton
  Glos 146 B5
Brockhampton
  Here 145 E4
Brockhampton
  Here 145 E4
Brockhampton
  Green 104 C2
Brockholes 185 F1
Brockholes Lancs PR5 0AG
  192 B4
Brockhurst Hants 107 E2
Brockhurst WSuss 122 D5
Brocklebank 209 G2
Brocklesby 188 B1
Brockley NSom 116 B1
Brockley Suff 151 G2
Brockley Green 151 F3
Brock's Green 119 F1
Brockton Shrop 157 E3
Brockton Shrop 157 F2
Brockton Shrop 156 C3
Brockton Shrop 156 C4

Brockton Tel&W 157 G1
Brockweir 131 E2
Brockwood Park 120 B5
Brockworth 132 A1
Brocton 158 B1
Brodick 223 F2
Brodsworth 186 C2
Brogborough 149 E4
Brogden 193 E3
Brogyntyn 169 F4
Broken Cross ChesE 184 C5
Broken Cross ChesW&C 184 A5
Brokenborough 132 B4
Brokes 202 A3
Bromborough 183 E4
Brome 164 C4
Brome Street 164 C4
Bromeswell 153 E2
Bromfield Cumb 209 E2
Bromfield Shrop 157 D5
Bromham Bed 149 F2
Bromham Wilts 118 A1
Bromley GtLon 122 D2
Bromley SYorks 186 A3
Bromley Cross 184 B1
Bromley Green 124 B5
Brompton Med 123 G2
Brompton NYorks 202 C3
Brompton NYorks 204 C4
Brompton Shrop 157 E2
Brompton on Swale 202 B3
Brompton Ralph 115 D4
Brompton Regis 114 C4
Bromsash 145 F5
Bromsberrow 145 G4
Bromsberrow Heath 145 G4
Bromsgrove 158 B5
Bromstead Heath 158 A1
Bromyard 145 F2
Bromyard Downs 145 F2
Bronaber 168 A4
Brondesbury 136 B4
Brongest 141 G3
Bronington 170 B4
Bronllys 144 A4
Bronnant 142 C1
Brontë Weaving Shed WYorks BD22 8EP 193 G4
Bronwydd Arms 142 A5
Bronydd 144 B3
Bron-y-gaer 127 G1
Bronygarth 169 F4
Brook Carmar 127 F2
Brook Hants 106 B1
Brook Hants 119 E5
Brook IoW 106 C4
Brook Kent 124 C4
Brook Surr 121 E4
Brook Surr 121 F3
Brook Bottom 185 D2
Brook End Bed 149 F1
Brook End Herts 150 B5
Brook End MK 149 E3
Brook End Worcs 146 A3
Brook Hill 106 B1
Brook Street Essex 137 E3
Brook Street Kent 124 B5
Brook Street Suff 151 G3
Brook Street WSuss 109 F1
Brooke Norf 165 D2
Brooke Rut 160 D2
Brookend Glos 131 E3
Brookend Glos 131 F2
Brookfield 185 E3
Brookhampton 134 B3
Brookhouse ChesE 184 D5
Brookhouse Denb 169 D1
Brookhouse Lancs 192 B1
Brookhouse SYorks 186 C4
Brookhouse Green 171 F1
Brookhouses 171 G3
Brookland 111 E1
Brooklands D&G 216 C3
Brooklands Shrop 170 C3
Brooklands Museum Surr KT13 0QN 121 F1
Brookmans Park 136 B2
Brooks 156 A3
Brooks Green 121 G5
Brooksby 160 B1
Brookside Miniature Railway ChesE SK12 1BZ 25 G6
Brookthorpe 132 A1
Brookwood 121 E2
Broom CenBeds 149 G3
Broom Fife 244 B4
Broom Warks 146 C2
Broom Green 178 A3
Broom Hill Dorset 105 G2
Broom Hill Worcs 158 B5
Broom of Dalreach 243 F3
Broomcroft 157 E2
Broome Norf 165 E2
Broome Shrop 156 D4
Broome Worcs 158 B5
Broome Wood 229 F5
Broomedge 184 B4
Broomer's Corner 121 G5
Broomfield Aber 261 H1
Broomfield Essex 137 G1
Broomfield Kent 125 D2
Broomfield Kent 124 A3
Broomfield Som 115 F4
Broomfleet 196 A5
Broomhall Green 170 D3
Broomhaugh 211 G1
Broomhead 269 H4
Broomhill Bristol 131 F5
Broomhill N'umb 221 E1
Broomielaw 201 F1
Broomley 211 G1
Broompark 212 B3
Broom's Green 145 G4
Brora 267 G1
Broseley 157 F2
Brotherlee 211 F4
Brothertoft 176 A3
Brotherton 195 D5
Brotton 203 F1
Broubster 275 F2
Brough Cumb 200 C1
Brough Derbys 185 F4
Brough ERid 196 B5
Brough High 275 H1
Brough Notts 174 D2
Brough Ork 277 C6
Brough Shet 279 E8
Brough Shet 278 D5
Brough Shet 279 E6
Brough Shet 278 E5
Brough Lodge 278 E3
Brough Sowerby 200 C1
Broughall 170 C3
Brougham 210 B5
Brougham Hall Cumb CA10 2DE 210 B5
Broughton Bucks 134 D1
Broughton Cambs 162 A5
Broughton Flints 170 A1
Broughton Hants 119 E4
Broughton Lancs 192 B4
Broughton MK 149 D3
Broughton N'hants 160 D5
Broughton NLincs 187 G2
Broughton NYorks 203 G5
Broughton NYorks 193 F2
Broughton Ork 276 D3
Broughton Oxon 147 G4
Broughton ScBord 226 C2
Broughton VGlam 129 F5
Broughton Astley 160 A3
Broughton Beck 199 D4
Broughton Gifford 117 F1
Broughton Green 146 B1
Broughton Hackett 146 B2
Broughton in Furness 198 D4
Broughton Mills 198 D3
Broughton Moor 209 D3
Broughton Poggs 133 E2
Broughtown 276 F3
Broughty Ferry 244 C1
Browland 279 B7
Brown Candover 119 G4
Brown Edge Lancs 183 E1
Brown Edge Staffs 171 G2
Brown Heath 170 B1
Brown Lees 171 F2
Brown Street 152 B1
Brownber 200 C2
Browndown 107 E3
Brownheath 170 B5
Brownhill 269 G6
Brownhills Fife 244 D3
Brownhills WMid 158 C2
Brownieside 229 F4
Brownlow 171 F1
Brownlow Heath 171 F1
Brown's Bank 170 D3
Brownsea Island Dorset BH13 7EE 105 G4
Brownshill 132 A2
Brownshill Green 159 F4
Brownsover 160 A5
Brownston 100 C2
Browston Green 179 F5
Broxa 204 C3
Broxbourne 136 C2
Broxburn ELoth 237 D2
Broxburn WLoth 235 E2
Broxholme 187 G5
Broxted 151 D5
Broxton 170 B2
Broxwood 144 C2
Broyle Side 109 G2
Bruachmary 267 F7
Bruan 275 J5
Brue (Brù) 271 F3
Bruera 170 B1
Bruern 147 E5
Bruernish 254 C4
Bruichladdich 230 A3
Bruisyard 153 E1
Bruisyard Street 153 E1
Brumby 187 G1
Brund 172 C1
Brundall 179 E5
Brundish Norf 165 E2
Brundish Suff 153 D1
Brundish Street 165 D4
Brunstock 210 A2
Brunswick Village 221 E4
Bruntingthorpe 160 B3
Bruntland 260 C2
Brunton Fife 244 B2
Brunton N'umb 229 G4
Brunton Wilts 118 D2
Brushfield 185 F5
Brushford Devon 113 G5
Brushford Som 114 C5
Bruton 117 D4
Bryanston 105 E2
Bryant's Bottom 135 D3
Brydekirk 217 F3
Brymbo 169 F2
Brymor Ice Cream NYorks HG4 4PG 202 A4
Brympton 104 B1
Bryn Caerp 130 A3
Bryn Carmar 128 B2
Bryn ChesW&C 184 A5
Bryn GtMan 183 G2
Bryn NPT 129 E3
Bryn Shrop 156 B4
Bryn Bach Country Park BGwent NP22 3AY 130 A2
Bryn Bwbach 167 F4
Bryn Gates 183 G2
Bryn Pen-y-lan 170 A3
Brynamman 128 D1
Brynberian 141 E4
Bryncae 129 F4
Bryncethin 129 F4
Bryncir 167 D3
Bryncoch Bridgend 129 F4
Bryn-côch NPT 128 D3
Bryncroes 166 B4
Bryncrug 154 C2
Bryneglwys 169 E3
Brynford 182 C5
Bryngwran 180 B5
Bryngwyn Mon 130 C2
Bryngwyn Powys 144 A3
Bryn-henllan 140 D4
Brynhoffnant 141 G2
Bryning 192 A4
Brynithel 130 B2
Brynmawr BGwent 130 A1
Bryn-mawr Gwyn 166 B4
Brynmelyn 156 A5
Brynmenyn 129 F4
Brynna 129 F4
Brynnau Gwynion 129 F4
Brynog 142 B2
Bryn-penarth 156 A2
Brynrefail Gwyn 167 E1
Brynrefail IoA 180 C4
Brynsadler 129 G4
Brynsaithmarchog 169 D2
Brynsiencyn 167 D1
Bryn-teg IoA 180 C4
Brynteg Wrex 170 A2
Bryn-y-cochin 170 A4
Brynygwenin 130 C1
Bryn-y-maen 181 G5
Buaile nam Bodach 254 C4
Bualadubh 262 C7
Bualintur 255 K2
Bualnaluib 264 E2
Bubbenhall 159 F5
Bubnell 185 G5
Bubwith 195 G4
Buccleuch 227 E4
Buchan 216 B4
Buchanan Castle 233 F1
Buchanhaven 269 K6
Buchanty 243 E2
Buchlyvie 242 A5
Buckabank 209 G2
Buckby Wharf 148 B1
Buckden Cambs 149 G1
Buckden NYorks 201 E5
Buckenham 179 E5
Buckerell 103 E2
Buckfast 100 D1
Buckfast Abbey Devon TQ11 0EE 100 D1
Buckfastleigh 100 D1
Buckhaven 244 B5
Buckholm 227 F2
Buckholt 131 E1
Buckhorn Weston 117 E5
Buckhurst Hill 136 D3
Buckie 268 C4
Buckies 275 G2
Buckingham 148 B4
Buckingham Palace GtLon SW1A 1AA 44 B6
Buckland Bucks 135 D1
Buckland Devon 100 C3
Buckland Glos 146 C4
Buckland Hants 106 C3
Buckland Here 145 E2
Buckland Herts 150 B4
Buckland Kent 125 F4
Buckland Oxon 133 F3
Buckland Surr 122 B3
Buckland Brewer 113 E3
Buckland Common 135 E2
Buckland Dinham 117 E2
Buckland Filleigh 113 E5
Buckland in the Moor 102 A5
Buckland Monachorum 100 A1
Buckland Newton 104 C2
Buckland Ripers 104 C4
Buckland St. Mary 103 F1
Buckland-tout-Saints 101 D3
Bucklebury 134 A5
Bucklerheads 244 C1
Bucklers Hard 106 D3
Bucklesham 152 D3
Buckley (Bwcle) 169 F1
Buckley Green 147 D1
Bucklow Hill 184 B4
Buckman Corner 121 G5
Buckminster 175 D5
Bucknall 175 G1
Bucknell Oxon 148 A5
Bucknell Shrop 156 C5
Buckridge 157 G5
Buck's Cross 112 D3
Bucks Green 121 F4
Bucks Hill 135 F2
Bucks Horn Oak 120 D3
Buck's Mills 113 D3
Bucksburn 261 G4
Buckspool 126 C3
Buckton ERid 205 E5
Buckton Here 156 C5
Buckton N'umb 229 E3
Buckton Vale 185 D2
Buckworth 161 G5
Budbrooke 147 E1
Budby 186 D5
Buddon 244 D1
Bude 112 C5
Budge's Shop 98 D5
Budlake 102 C2
Budle 229 F3
Budleigh Salterton 103 D4
Budock Water 95 E3
Budworth Heath 184 A5
Buerton 171 D3
Bugbrooke 148 B2
Buglawton 171 F1
Bugle 97 E4
Bugthorpe 195 G2
Building End 150 C4
Buildwas 157 F2
Builth Road 143 G2
Builth Wells (Llanfair-ym-Muallt) 143 G2
Bulby 175 F5
Bulcote 174 B3
Buldoo 274 E2
Bulford 118 C3
Bulford Camp 118 C3
Bulkeley 170 C2
Bulkington Warks 159 F4
Bulkington Wilts 118 A2
Bulkworthy 113 D4
Bull Bay (Porth Llechog) 180 C3
Bull Green 124 B5
Bullbridge 173 E2
Bullbrook 121 D1
Bullen's Green 136 B2
Bulley 131 G1
Bullington 188 A5
Bullpot Farm 200 B4
Bulls Cross 136 C3
Bull's Green Herts 136 B1
Bull's Green Norf 165 F2
Bullwood 232 C2
Bulmer Essex 151 G3
Bulmer NYorks 195 F1
Bulmer Tye 151 G4
Bulphan 137 F4
Bulstone 103 E4
Bulverhythe 110 C3
Bulwark 269 H6
Bulwell 173 G3
Bulwick 161 E3
Bumble's Green 136 D2
Bun Abhainn Eadarra 270 D7
Bun Loyne 257 J4
Bunarkaig 249 D1
Bunbury 170 C2
Bunbury Heath 170 C2
Bunchrew 266 D7
Bundalloch 256 E2
Buness 278 F2
Bunessan 238 C2
Bungay 165 E3
Bunker's Hill 176 A2
Bunlarie 222 C2
Bunloit (Bun Leothaid) 258 C2
Bunmhullin 254 C3
Bunnahabhain 230 C2
Bunny 173 G5
Buntait 257 K1
Buntingford 150 B5
Bunwell 164 C2
Bunwell Street 164 C2
Burbage Derbys 185 E5
Burbage Leics 159 G3
Burbage Wilts 118 D1
Burbage Common Leics LE10 3DD 159 G3
Burchett's Green 134 D4
Burcombe 118 B4
Burcot Oxon 134 A3
Burcot Worcs 158 B5
Burcott 149 D5
Burdale 196 A1
Burdocks 121 F5
Burdon 212 C2
Burdrop 147 F4
Bure Valley Railway Norf NR11 6BW 178 D3
Bures 152 A4
Bures Green 152 A4
Burfa 144 B1
Burford Oxon 133 E1
Burford Shrop 145 E1
Burg 246 C5
Burgate 164 B4
Burgates 120 C5
Burge End 149 G4
Burgess Hill 109 F2
Burgh 152 D2
Burgh by Sands 209 G1
Burgh Castle 179 F5
Burgh Heath 122 B3
Burgh le Marsh 176 C1
Burgh next Aylsham 178 D3
Burgh on Bain 188 C4
Burgh St. Margaret (Fleggburgh) 179 F4
Burgh St. Peter 165 F2
Burghclere 119 F1
Burghead 267 J5
Burghfield 120 B1
Burghfield Common 120 B1
Burghfield Hill 120 B1
Burghill 145 D3
Burghwallis 186 C1
Burham 123 G2
Buriton 120 C5
Burland 170 D2
Burlawn 97 D3
Burleigh 121 E1
Burlescombe 103 D1
Burleston 105 D3
Burley Hants 106 B2
Burley Rut 161 D1
Burley WYorks 194 B4
Burley Gate 145 E3
Burley in Wharfedale 194 A3
Burley Street 106 B2
Burley Woodhead 194 A3
Burleydam 170 D3
Burlingjobb 144 B2
Burlow 110 A2
Burlton 170 B5
Burmarsh 124 D5
Burmington 147 E4
Burn 195 E5
Burn Farm 253 E2
Burn Naze 191 G3
Burn of Cambus 242 C4
Burnage 184 C3
Burnaston 173 D4
Burnby 196 A3
Burncross 186 A3
Burndell 108 B3
Burnden 184 B2
Burnedge 184 D1
Burnend 269 G6
Burneside 199 G3
Burness 276 F3
Burneston 202 C4
Burnett 117 D1
Burnfoot High 274 D6
Burnfoot P&K 243 E4
Burnfoot ScBord 227 G4
Burnfoot ScBord 227 F4
Burnham Bucks 135 E4
Burnham NLincs 188 A1
Burnham Deepdale 177 G3
Burnham Green 136 B1
Burnham Market 177 G3
Burnham Norton 177 G3
Burnham Overy Staithe 177 G3
Burnham Overy Town 177 G3
Burnham Thorpe 177 G3
Burnham-on-Crouch 138 C3
Burnham-on-Sea 116 A3
Burnhaven 269 K6
Burnhead D&G 215 G2
Burnhead D&G 216 C1
Burnhervie 261 F3
Burnhill Green 157 G2
Burnhope 212 A3
Burnhouse 233 E4
Burniston 204 D3
Burnley 193 E4
Burnmouth 237 G3
Burnopfield 212 A2
Burn's Green 150 B5
Burns National Heritage Park SAyr KA7 4PQ 224 B4
Burnsall 193 G1
Burnside Aber 261 F3
Burnside Angus 252 D4
Burnside EAyr 225 D4
Burnside Fife 243 G4
Burnside Shet 278 B5
Burnside WLoth 235 E2
Burnside of Duntrune 244 C1
Burnstones 210 C2
Burnswark 217 F3
Burnt Hill 134 A5
Burnt Houses 212 A5
Burnt Oak 136 B3
Burnt Yates 194 B1
Burntcliff Top 171 G1
Burntisland 235 G1
Burnton EAyr 224 C4
Burnton EAyr 224 C5
Burntwood 158 C2
Burntwood Green 158 C2
Burnworthy 103 E1
Burpham Surr 121 F2
Burpham WSuss 108 C3
Burra 279 C9
Burradon N'umb 220 B1
Burradon T&W 221 E4
Burrafirth 278 F1
Burraland 278 C5
Burras 95 D3
Burraton Corn 100 A1
Burraton Corn 100 A2
Burravoe Shet 278 E5
Burravoe Shet 279 C6
Burray 277 D8
Burrell Collection Glas G43 1AT 30 C4
Burrells 200 B1
Burrelton 244 A1
Burridge Devon 103 G2
Burridge Hants 107 E1
Burrill 202 B4
Burringham 187 F2
Burrington Devon 113 G4
Burrington Here 156 D5
Burrington NSom 116 B2
Burrough Green 151 E2
Burrough on the Hill 160 C1
Burrow Som 114 C3
Burrow Som 104 A1
Burrow Bridge 116 A4
Burrowhill 121 E1
Burrows Cross 121 F3
Burry 128 A3
Burry Green 128 A3
Burry Port 128 A2
Burscough 183 F1
Burscough Bridge 183 F1
Bursea 196 A4
Burshill 196 C3
Bursledon 107 D2
Burslem 171 F3
Burstall 152 C3
Burstock 104 A2
Burston Norf 164 C3
Burston Staffs 171 G4
Burstow 122 C4
Burstwick 197 E5
Burtersett 201 D4
Burthorpe 151 F1
Burthwaite 210 A3
Burtle 116 B3
Burtle Hill 116 A3
Burton ChesW&C 183 E5
Burton ChesW&C 170 C1
Burton Dorset 106 A3
Burton Lincs 187 G5
Burton N'umb 229 F3
Burton Pembs 126 C2
Burton Som 115 E3
Burton Wilts 132 A5
Burton Wilts 117 F4
Burton Agnes 196 D1
Burton Bradstock 104 A4
Burton Coggles 175 E5
Burton End 150 D5
Burton Ferry 126 C2
Burton Fleming 205 D5
Burton Green Warks 159 E5
Burton Green Wrex 170 A2
Burton Hastings 159 G4
Burton in Lonsdale 200 B5
Burton Joyce 174 B3
Burton Latimer 161 E5
Burton Lazars 160 C1
Burton Leonard 194 C1
Burton on the Wolds 173 G5
Burton Overy 160 B3
Burton Pedwardine 175 G3
Burton Pidsea 197 E4
Burton Salmon 195 D5
Burton Stather 187 F1
Burton upon Stather 187 F1
Burton upon Trent 172 D5
Burton-in-Kendal 199 G5
Burton's Green 151 G5
Burtonwood 183 G3
Burwardsley 170 C2
Burwarton 157 F4
Burwash 110 B1
Burwash Common 110 B1
Burwash Weald 110 B1
Burwell Cambs 151 D1
Burwell Lincs 189 D5
Burwen 180 C3
Burwick Ork 277 D9
Burwick Shet 279 C8
Bury Cambs 162 A4
Bury GtMan 184 C1
Bury Som 114 C5
Bury WSuss 108 C2
Bury End 146 C4
Bury Green 150 C5
Bury St. Edmunds 151 G1
Buryas Bridge 94 B4
Burythorpe 195 G1
Busbridge 121 E3
Busby ERenf 233 G4
Busby P&K 243 F2
Buscot 133 E3
Bush 112 C5
Bush Bank 145 D2
Bush Crathie 259 K5
Bush Green 164 D3
Bushbury 158 B2
Bushby 160 B2
Bushey 136 A3
Bushey Heath 136 A3
Bushley 146 A4
Bushley Green 146 A4
Bushton 132 C5
Bushy Common 178 A4
Business Design Centre, Islington GtLon N1 0QH 12 B3
Busk 210 C3
Buslingthorpe 188 A4
Bussage 132 A2
Busta 279 C6
Butcher's Common 179 E3
Butcher's Cross 110 A1
Butcher's Pasture 151 E5
Butcombe 116 C1
Bute 232 B3
Bute Town 130 A2
Buthill 267 J5
Butleigh 116 C4
Butleigh Wootton 116 C4
Butler's Cross 134 D2
Butler's Hill 173 G3
Butlers Marston 147 F3
Butlersbank 170 C5
Butley 153 E2
Butley Abbey 153 E3
Butley Low Corner 153 E3
Butley Mills 153 E2
Butley Town 184 D5
Butt Green 171 D2
Butt Lane 171 F2
Butterburn 219 E4
Buttercrambe 195 G2
Butterknowle 212 A5
Butterleigh 102 C2
Butterley 173 F2
Buttermere Cumb 209 E5
Buttermere Wilts 119 E1
Butters Green 171 F2
Buttershaw 194 A4
Butterstone 251 F5
Butterton Staffs 172 B2
Butterton Staffs 171 F3
Butterwick Dur 212 C5
Butterwick Lincs 176 B3
Butterwick NYorks 204 C5
Butterwick NYorks 203 G5
Buttington 156 B2
Buttonbridge 157 G5
Buttonoak 157 G5
Buttons' Green 152 A2
Butts 102 B4
Butt's Green Essex 137 G2
Butt's Green Hants 119 D5
Buttsash 106 D2
Buxhall 152 B2
Buxted 109 G1
Buxton Derbys 185 E5
Buxton Norf 178 D3
Buxton Heath 178 C3
Buxworth 185 E4
Bwlch 144 A5
Bwlch-clawdd 141 G4
Bwlch-derwin 167 D3
Bwlchgwyn 169 F2
Bwlch-llan 142 B2
Bwlchnewydd 141 G5
Bwlchtocyn 166 C5
Bwlch-y-cibau 156 A1
Bwlch-y-ddar 169 E5
Bwlchyfadfa 142 A3
Bwlch-y-ffridd 155 G3
Bwlch-y-groes 141 F4
Bwlchyllyn 167 E2
Bwlchymynydd 128 B3
Bwlch-y-sarnau 155 G5
Byers Green 212 B4
Byfield 148 A2
Byfleet 121 F1
Byford 144 C3
Bygrave 150 A4
Byker 212 B1
Byland Abbey 203 E5
Bylane End 97 G4
Bylchau 168 C1
Byley 171 E1
Bynea 128 B3
Byrness 219 F1
Bystock 102 D4
Bythorn 161 F5
Byton 144 C1
Bywell 211 G1
Byworth 121 E5

C

Cabharstadh 271 F5
Cabourne 188 B2
Cabourne Parva 188 B2
Cabrach A&B 230 C3
Cabrach Moray 260 B2
Cabus 192 A3
Cackle Street ESuss 110 D2
Cackle Street ESuss 109 G1
Cacrabank 227 E4
Cadboll 267 F4
Cadbury 102 C2
Cadbury Barton 113 G4
Cadbury Heath 131 F5
Cadbury World WMid B30 1JR 15 E5
Cadder 234 A2
Cadderlie 240 C1
Caddington 135 F1
Caddleton 239 G3
Caddonfoot 227 F2
Cade Street 110 B1
Cadeby Leics 159 G2
Cadeby SYorks 186 C2
Cadeleigh 102 C2
Cader 168 D1
Cadgwith 95 E5
Cadham 244 A4
Cadishead 184 B3
Cadle 128 C3
Cadley Lancs 192 B4
Cadley Wilts 118 D1
Cadmore End 134 C3
Cadnam 106 B1
Cadney 188 A2
Cadole 169 F1
Cadover Bridge 100 B1
Cadoxton 115 E1
Cadoxton-Juxta-Neath 129 D3
Cadwell 149 G4
Cadwst 168 D4
Cadzow 234 B4
Cae Ddafydd 167 F3
Caeathro 167 E1
Caehopkin 129 E1
Caen 275 F7
Caenby 188 A4
Caenby Corner 187 G4
Caer Llan 131 D2
Caerau Bridgend 129 E3
Caerau Cardiff 130 A5
Caerdeon 154 C1
Caerfarchell 140 A5
Caergeiliog 180 B5
Caergwrle 170 A2
Caerhun 181 F5
Caer-Lan 129 E1
Caerleon 130 C3
Caernarfon 167 D1
Caernarfon Castle Gwyn LL55 2AY 167 D1
Caerphilly 130 A4
Caersws 155 G3
Caerwedros 141 G2
Caerwent 131 D3
Caerwys 182 C5
Caethle Farm 154 C3
Caggan 259 F3
Caggle Street 130 C1
Caim High 247 E3
Caim IoA 181 E4
Caio 142 C4
Cairisiadar 270 C4
Cairminis 263 F3
Cairnargat 260 C1
Cairnbaan 240 A5
Cairnbeathie 260 D4
Cairnbrogie 261 G2
Cairnbulg 269 J4
Cairncross Angus 252 D2
Cairncross ScBord 237 F3
Cairncurran 233 E3
Cairndoon 207 D3
Cairndow 241 D3
Cairness 269 J4
Cairney Lodge 244 B3
Cairneyhill 235 E1
Cairngorm Mountain High PH22 1RB 259 G4
Cairnhill Aber 261 H2
Cairnhill Aber 260 E1
Cairnie Aber 261 G4
Cairnie Aber 268 C6
Cairnorrie 269 G6
Cairnryan 214 B4
Cairnsmore 215 F4
Caister-on-Sea 179 G4
Caistor 188 B2
Caistor St. Edmund 178 D5
Caistron 220 B1
Caithness Crystal Visitor Centre Norf PE30 4NE 163 E1
Cake Street 164 B2
Cakebole 158 A5
Calbost 271 G6
Calbourne 106 D4
Calceby 189 D5
Calcoed 182 C5
Calcot 134 B5
Calcott Kent 125 D2
Calcott Shrop 156 D1
Calcotts Green 131 G1
Calcutt 132 D3
Caldarvan 233 F1
Caldback 278 F2
Caldbeck 209 G3
Caldbergh 201 F4
Caldecote Cambs 150 B2
Caldecote Cambs 161 G4
Caldecote Herts 150 A4
Caldecote N'hants 148 B2
Caldecote Warks 159 F3
Caldecott N'hants 149 E1
Caldecott Oxon 133 G3
Caldecott Rut 161 D3
Calder Bridge 198 B2
Calder Grove 186 A1
Calder Mains 275 F3
Calder Vale 192 B3
Calderbank 234 B3
Calderbrook 184 D1
Caldercruix 234 C3
Calderglen 234 A4
Calderglen Country Park SLan G75 0QZ 31 E6
Caldermill 234 A5
Caldey Island 127 E3
Caldhame 252 C5
Caldicot 131 D4
Caldwell Derbys 159 E1
Caldwell ERenf 233 F4
Caldwell NYorks 202 A1
Caldy 182 D4
Calebreck 209 G3
Caledrhydiau 142 A2
Calford Green 151 E3
Calfsound 276 E4
Calgary 246 C4
Califer 267 H6
California Falk 234 D2
California Norf 179 G4
California Suff 152 D3
California Country Park W'ham RG40 4HT 120 C1
Calke 173 E5
Calke Abbey Derbys DE73 7LE 173 E5
Callakille 264 C6
Callaly 220 C1
Callander 242 B4
Callanish (Calanais) 270 E4
Callaughton 157 F3
Callerton Lane End 212 A1
Calliburn 222 C3

Calligarry 256 C4
Callington 99 D4
Callingwood 172 C5
Callisterhall 218 A3
Callow 145 D4
Callow End 146 A3
Callow Hill Wilts 132 C4
Callow Hill Worcs 157 G5
Callow Hill Worcs 146 C1
Callows Grave 145 E1
Calmore 106 C1
Calmsden 132 C2
Calow 186 B5
Calrossie 266 E4
Calshot 107 D2
Calstock 100 A1
Calstone
  Wellington 118 B1
Calthorpe 178 C2
Calthwaite 210 A3
Calton NYorks 193 F2
Calton Staffs 172 C2
Calveley 170 C2
Calver 185 G5
Calver Hill 144 C3
Calverhall 170 D4
Calverleigh 102 C1
Calverley 194 B4
Calvert 148 B2
Calverton MK 148 C4
Calverton Notts 174 B3
Calvine 250 C3
Calvo 209 E1
Cam 131 G3
Camasnacroise 248 A4
Camastianavaig 256 B1
Camasunary 256 B3
Camault Muir 266 C7
Camb 278 E3
Camber 111 E2
Camberley 121 D1
Camberwell 136 C5
Camblesforth 195 F5
Cambo 220 C3
Cambois 221 F3
Camborne 95 D3
Cambourne 150 B2
Cambridge Cambs 150 C2
Cambridge Glos 131 G2
Cambridge American
  Military Cemetery &
  Memorial Cambs
  CB23 7PH 150 B2
Cambridge City
  Airport 150 C2
Cambridge University
  Botanic Garden Cambs
  CB2 1JF 150 C2
Cambus 243 D5
Cambus o'May 260 C5
Cambusbarron 242 C5
Cambuslang 234 A3
Cambusnethan 234 C4
Camden Town 136 B4
Camel Hill 116 C5
Camel Trail Corn
  PL27 7AL 97 D2
Cameley 116 D2
Camelford 97 F1
Camelon 234 C1
Camelot Theme Park
  Lancs PR7 5LP 183 G1
Camelsdale 121 D4
Camer 123 F2
Cameron House 233 E1
Camerory 259 H1
Camer's Green 145 G4
Camerton
  B&NESom 117 D2
Camerton Cumb 208 D3
Camerton ERid 197 G5
Camghouran 250 A4
Camis Eskan 233 E1
Cammachmore 261 H5
Cammeringham 187 G4
Camore 266 E2
Camp Hill Pembs 127 E1
Camp Hill Warks 159 F3
Campbeltown (Ceann Loch
  Chille Chiarain) 222 C3
Campbeltown
  Airport 222 B3
Camperdown 221 E4
Camperdown Country
  Park Dundee
  DD2 4TF 244 B1
Campmuir 244 A1
Camps 235 F3
Camps End 151 E3
Camps Heath 165 G2
Campsall 186 C1
Campsea Ashe 153 E2
Campton 149 G4
Camptown 228 A5
Camquhart 232 A1
Camrose 140 C5
Camserney 250 C5
Camstraddan
  House 241 F5
Camus Croise 256 C3
Camus-luinie 257 F2
Camusnagaul High 248 C2
Camusnagaul High 265 G3
Camusrory 256 E5
Camusteel 264 D7
Camusterrach 264 D7
Camusurich 242 B1
Camusvrachan 250 B5
Canada 106 B1
Canaston Bridge 127 D1
Candacraig 260 B5
Candlesby 176 C1
Candy Mill 235 E5
Cane End 134 B5
Canewdon 138 B3
Canfield End 151 D5
Canford Bottom 105 G2
Canford Cliffs 105 G4
Canford Heath 105 G3
Canford Magna 105 G3
Canham's Green 152 B1
Canisbay 275 J1
Canley 159 F5
Cann 117 E5
Cann Common 117 F5
Canna 255 H4

Cannard's Grave 116 D3
Cannich (Canaich) 257 K1
Canning Town 136 C4
Cannington 115 F4
Cannock 158 B2
Cannock Wood 158 C1
Cannon Hall Country Park
  SYorks S75 4AT 185 G2
Cannon Hall Farm SYorks
  S75 4AT 185 G2
Cannon Hill Park WMid
  B13 8RD 15 E4
Cannop 131 F1
Canon Bridge 144 D3
Canon Frome 145 F3
Canon Pyon 145 D3
Canonbie 218 B4
Canons Ashby 148 A3
Canon's Town 94 C3
Canterbury Aber 268 D5
Canterbury Kent 124 D3
Canterbury Cathedral
  Kent CT1 2EH
  67 Canterbury
Canterbury Tales, The
  Kent CT1 2TG
  67 Canterbury
Cantley Norf 179 E5
Cantley SYorks 186 D2
Cantlop 157 E2
Canton 130 A5
Cantray 266 E7
Cantraydoune 266 E7
Cantraywood 266 E7
Cantsfield 200 B5
Canvey Island 137 G4
Canwell Hall 158 D2
Canwick 175 E1
Canworthy Water 98 C1
Caol 248 D2
Caolas A&B 246 B2
Caolas Na H-E. Siar 254 B5
Caolasnacon 248 D3
Capel Bed 149 E2
Capel Cambs 151 E2
Capel Kent 123 F4
Capel Surr 121 G3
Capel Bangor 154 C4
Capel Betws Lleucu 142 C2
Capel Carmel 166 A5
Capel Celyn 168 B3
Capel Coch 180 C4
Capel Curig 168 A2
Capel Cynon 141 G3
Capel Dewi Carmar 142 A5
Capel Dewi Cere 154 C4
Capel Dewi Cere 142 A3
Capel Garmon 168 B2
Capel Gwyn
  Carmar 142 A5
Capel Gwyn IoA 180 B5
Capel Gwynfe 142 B4
Capel Hendre 128 B1
Capel Isaac 142 B5
Capel le Ferne 125 E4
Capel Llanilltern 129 G4
Capel Mawr 180 C5
Capel Parc 180 C4
Capel St. Andrew 153 E3
Capel St. Mary 152 B3
Capel St. Silin 142 B2
Capel Seion 154 C5
Capel Tygwydd 141 F3
Capeluchaf 166 D3
Capelulo 181 F5
Capel-y-ffin 144 B4
Capel-y-graig 167 E1
Capenhurst 183 E5
Capernwray 199 G5
Capheaton 220 C3
Caplaw 233 F4
Capon's Green 153 D1
Cappercleuch 226 C3
Capplegill 226 C5
Capstone 123 G2
Capton Devon 101 E2
Capton Som 115 D4
Caputh 251 F5
Car Colston 174 C3
Caradon Town 97 G2
Carbellow 225 E3
Carberth 233 G2
Carbis Bay 94 C3
Carbost High 263 K7
Carbost High 255 J1
Carbrain 234 B2
Carbrooke 178 A5
Carburton 186 D5
Carcary 253 E4
Carco 225 F4
Carcroft 186 C1
Cardenden 244 A5
Cardeston 156 C1
Cardew 209 G2
Cardiff
  (Caerdydd) 130 A5
Cardiff Bay Visitor Centre
  Cardiff CF10 4PA 7 C4
Cardiff Castle & Museum
  CF10 3RB 67 Cardiff
Cardiff Airport 129 D1
Cardiff Millennium
  Stadium CF10 1GE
  67 Cardiff
Cardigan
  (Aberteifi) 141 E3
Cardinal's Green 151 E3
Cardington Bed 149 F3
Cardington Shrop 157 E3
Cardinham 97 F3
Cardno 269 H4
Cardonald 233 G3
Cardoness 215 G5
Cardow 267 J7
Cardrona 227 E3
Cardross 233 E2
Cardurnock 209 E1
Careby 161 F1
Careston 252 D4
Carew 126 D2
Carew Cheriton 126 D2
Carew Newton 126 D2
Carey 145 E4
Carfin 234 B4
Carfrae 236 C3
Carfraemill 236 C4
Cargate Green 179 E4
Cargen 217 D3
Cargenbridge 217 D3
Cargill 243 G1

Cargo 209 G1
Cargreen 100 A1
Carham 228 B3
Carhampton 114 D3
Carharrack 96 B5
Carie P&K 250 B4
Carie P&K 242 B1
Carines 96 B4
Carinish (Cairinis) 262 D5
Carisbrooke 107 D4
Carisbrooke Castle &
  Museum IoW
  PO30 1XY 107 D4
Cark 199 E5
Carkeel 100 A1
Carland Cross 96 C4
Carlatton 210 B2
Carlby 161 F1
Carlecotes 185 F2
Carleen 94 D4
Carleton Cumb 210 A2
Carleton Cumb 210 B5
Carleton Lancs 191 G3
Carleton NYorks 193 F3
Carleton WYorks 195 D5
Carleton Fishery 214 C2
Carleton Forehoe 178 B5
Carleton Rode 164 C2
Carleton St. Peter 179 E5
Carlin How 203 G1
Carlisle 210 A2
Carlisle Cathedral
  Cumb CA3 8TZ
  68 Carlisle
Carlisle Park,
  Morpeth N'umb
  NE61 1YD 221 D3
Carloggas 96 C3
Carlops 235 F4
Carloway
  (Càrlabhagh) 270 E3
Carlton Bed 149 E2
Carlton Cambs 151 E2
Carlton Leics 159 F2
Carlton Notts 174 B3
Carlton NYorks 195 F5
Carlton NYorks 201 F4
Carlton NYorks 203 F4
Carlton Stock 212 C5
Carlton Suff 153 E1
Carlton SYorks 186 A1
Carlton WYorks 194 C5
Carlton Colville 165 G2
Carlton Curlieu 160 B3
Carlton Green 151 E2
Carlton Husthwaite 203 D5
Carlton in Lindrick 186 C4
Carlton Miniott 202 C4
Carlton Scroop 175 E3
Carlton-in-
  Cleveland 203 E2
Carlton-le-
  Moorland 175 E2
Carlton-on-Trent 174 D1
Carluke 234 C4
Carlyon Bay 97 E4
Carmacoup 225 F3
Carmarthen
  (Caerfyrddin) 142 A5
Carmel Carmar 128 B1
Carmel Flints 182 C5
Carmel Gwyn 167 D2
Carmel IoA 180 B4
Carmichael 226 A2
Carmont 253 G1
Carmunnock 233 G4
Carmyle 234 A3
Carmyllie 253 D5
Carn 262 C7
Carn Dearg 264 C4
Carnaby 196 D1
Carnach High 257 G2
Carnach High 265 G2
Carnach Na H-E. Siar
  262 D5
Carnan 262 C7
Carnassarie 240 A4
Carnbee 244 D4
Carnbo 243 F4
Carnduff 234 A4
Carndu 256 E2
Carnduncan 230 A3
Carnforth 199 F5
Carnhedryn 140 B5
Carnhell Green 94 D3
Carnie 261 G4
Carnkie Corn 95 D3
Carnkie Corn 95 E3
Carnmore 230 B5
Carno 155 F3
Carnoch High 257 K1
Carnoch High 265 J6
Carnoch High 267 F7
Carnock 235 E1
Carnon Downs 96 C5
Carnousie 268 E5
Carnoustie 245 D1
Carntyne 234 A3
Carnwath 235 D5
Carnyorth 94 A3
Carol Green 159 E5
Carperby 201 F4
Carr 186 C3
Carr Hill 187 D3
Carr Houses 183 E1
Carr Shield 211 E3
Carr Vale 186 B5
Carradale 222 D2
Carragrich 263 G2
Carrbridge 259 G2
Carrefour Selous 100 C5
Carreglefn 180 B4
Carreg-wen 141 F3
Carrhouse 187 E2
Carrick 232 A1
Carrick Castle 241 D5
Carriden 235 E1
Carrine 222 B5
Carrington GtMan 184 B3
Carrington Lincs 176 B2
Carrington Midlo 236 A3
Carroch 216 A1
Carrog Conwy 168 A3
Carrog Denb 169 D3
Carroglen 242 C2
Carrol 267 F1
Carron A&B 240 B5
Carron Falk 234 C1

Carron Moray 267 K7
Carron Bridge 234 B1
Carronbridge 216 C1
Carronshore 234 C1
Carrot 252 C5
Carrow Hill 130 D3
Carruth 217 D3
Carrutherstown 217 F2
Carruthmuir 233 E3
Carrville 212 C3
Carry 232 A3
Carsaig 239 E2
Carscreugh 214 D4
Carse 231 F3
Carse of Ardersier 267 F6
Carsegowan 215 F5
Carseriggan 215 E4
Carsethorn 217 D5
Carsgoe 275 G2
Carshalton 122 B2
Carshalton Beeches 122 B2
Carsie 251 G5
Carsington 173 D2
Carsington Water Derbys
  DE6 1ST 173 D2
Carsluith 215 F5
Carsphairn 215 G1
Carstairs 235 D5
Carstairs Junction 235 D5
Carswell Marsh 133 F4
Carter's Clay 119 E5
Carterton 133 E2
Carterway Heads 211 G2
Carthew 97 E4
Carthorpe 202 C4
Cartington 220 C1
Cartland 234 C5
Cartmel 199 E5
Cartmel Fell 199 F4
Cartworth 185 F2
Carway 128 A2
Cascades Adventure
  Pool Devon
  EX33 1NZ 113 E2
Cascob 144 B1
Cashel Farm 241 G5
Cashes Green 132 A2
Cashlie 249 G5
Cashmoor 105 F1
Caskieberran 244 A4
Cassencarie 215 F5
Cassington 133 G1
Cassop 212 C4
Castell 168 A1
Castell Gorfod 141 F5
Castell Howell 142 A3
Castellau 129 G4
Castell-y-bwch 130 B3
Casterton 200 B5
Castle Acre 163 G1
Castle Ashby 149 E2
Castle Bolton 201 F3
Castle Bromwich 158 D4
Castle Bytham 161 F1
Castle Caereinion 156 A2
Castle Camps 151 E3
Castle Carrock 210 B2
Castle Cary 116 C4
Castle Combe 132 A5
Castle Donington 173 F5
Castle Douglas 216 B4
Castle Drogo Devon
  EX6 6PB 102 A3
Castle Eaton 132 D3
Castle Eden 212 D4
Castle Eden Dene National
  Nature Reserve Dur
  SR8 1NJ 212 D4
Castle End 159 E5
Castle Frome 145 F3
Castle Gate 94 B3
Castle Goring 108 D3
Castle Green 121 E1
Castle Gresley 159 E1
Castle Heaton 237 G5
Castle Hedingham 151 F4
Castle Hill Kent 123 F4
Castle Hill Suff 152 C3
Castle Howard NYorks
  YO60 7DA 195 G1
Castle Kennedy 214 C5
Castle Leod 266 B6
Castle Levan 232 D2
Castle Madoc 143 G4
Castle Morris 140 C4
Castle O'er 218 A2
Castle Rising 177 E5
Castle Semple Water
  Country Park Renf
  PA12 4HJ 233 E4
Castle Stuart 266 E7
Castlebay (Bàgh
  a'Chaisteil) 254 B5
Castlebythe 140 D5
Castlecary 234 B2
Castlecraig High 267 F5
Castlecraig ScBord 235 F5
Castlefairn 216 B2
Castleford 194 D5
Castlemartin 126 C3
Castlemilk D&G 217 F3
Castlemilk Glas 234 A4
Castlemorton 145 G4
Castleside 211 G3
Castlesteads 210 B1
Castleton A&B 231 G1
Castleton Aber 269 F5
Castleton Angus 252 B5
Castleton Derbys 185 F4
Castleton GtMan 184 C1
Castleton Newport 130 B4
Castleton NYorks 203 F2
Castleton ScBord 218 D2
Castletown Dorset 104 C5
Castletown High 275 G2
Castletown High 266 E7
Castletown IoM 190 A5
Castleweary 227 F5
Castlewigg 207 E2
Castley 194 B3
Caston 164 A2
Castor 161 G2
Castramont 215 G4
Caswell 128 B4
Cat & Fiddle Inn 185 E5
Catacol 232 A5

Catbrain 131 E4
Catbrook 131 E2
Catchall 94 B4
Catcleugh 219 F1
Catcliffe 186 B4
Catcott 116 A4
Caterham 122 C3
Catfield 179 E3
Catfirth 279 D7
Catford 136 C5
Catforth 192 A4
Cathays 130 A5
Cathcart 233 G3
Cathedine 144 A5
Catherine-de-
  Barnes 159 D4
Catherington 107 F1
Catherston
  Leweston 103 G3
Catherton 157 F5
Cathkin 234 A4
Catisfield 107 E2
Catlodge 258 D5
Catlowdy 218 C4
Catmere End 150 C4
Catmore 133 G4
Caton Devon 102 A5
Caton Lancs 192 B1
Caton Green 192 B1
Cator Court 99 G3
Catrine 224 D3
Catsfield 110 C2
Catsfield Stream 110 C2
Catshaw 185 G2
Catshill 158 B5
Cattadale 230 B3
Cattal 194 D2
Cattawade 152 B4
Catterall 192 B3
Catterick 202 B3
Catterick Bridge 202 B3
Catterick Garrison 202 A3
Catterlen 210 A4
Catterline 253 G2
Catterton 195 E3
Catteshall 121 E3
Catthorpe 160 A5
Cattishall 151 G1
Cattistock 104 B3
Catton N'umb 211 E2
Catton Norf 178 D4
Catton NYorks 202 C5
Catton Hall 159 E1
Catwick 196 D3
Catworth 161 F5
Caudle Green 132 B1
Caudwell's Mill & Craft
  Centre Derbys
  DE4 2EB 173 D1
Caulcott CenBeds 149 F3
Caulcott Oxon 148 A5
Cauldcots 253 E5
Cauldhame Stir 242 B5
Cauldhame Stir 242 D4
Cauldon 172 B3
Caulkerbush 216 D5
Caulside 218 C4
Caundle Marsh 104 C1
Caunsall 158 A4
Caunton 174 C1
Causeway End
  Cumb 209 E1
Causeway End
  Essex 137 F1
Causeway End
  Lancs 183 F1
Causewayhead
  Cumb 209 E1
Causewayhead Stir 242 D5
Causey 212 B2
Causey Arch Picnic Area
  Dur NE16 5EG 28 A4
Causey Park 221 D2
Causeyend 261 H3
Cautley 200 B3
Cavendish 151 G3
Cavendish Bridge 173 F5
Cavenham 151 F1
Cavens 217 D5
Cavers 227 G4
Caversfield 148 A5
Caversham 134 C5
Caverswall 171 G4
Cawdor 267 F6
Cawkeld 196 B2
Cawkwell 188 C4
Cawood 195 E4
Cawsand 100 A3
Cawston Norf 178 C3
Cawston Warks 159 G5
Cawthorn 203 F3
Cawthorne 185 G2
Cawthorpe 175 F5
Cawton 203 F5
Caxton 150 B2
Caxton Gibbet 150 A1
Caynham 157 E5
Caythorpe Lincs 175 E3
Caythorpe Notts 174 B3
Cayton 205 D4
Ceallan 262 D6
Ceann a' Bhàigh
  Na H-E. Siar 262 C5
Ceann a' Bhàigh
  Na H-E. Siar 263 F3
Ceann Loch
  Shiphoirt 270 E6
Ceannacroit 262 D6
Cearsiadar 271 F6
Cedig 168 C5
Cefn Berain 168 C1
Cefn Canol 169 F4
Cefn Cantref 143 G5
Cefn Coch Denb 169 E2
Cefn Coch Powys 155 G3
Cefn Cribwr 129 E4
Cefn Cross 129 E4
Cefn Einion 156 B4
Cefn Hengoed 130 A3
Cefn Llwyd 154 C4
Cefn Rhigos 129 F2
Cefn-brith 168 C2
Cefn-caer-Ferch 166 D3
Cefn-coch 169 E5
Cefn-coed-y-
  cymmer 129 G2

Cefn-ddwysarn 168 C4
Cefndeuddwr 168 A5
Cefneithin 128 B1
Cefn-gorwydd 143 F3
Cefn-gwyn 156 A4
Cefn-mawr 169 F3
Cefnpennar 129 G2
Cefn-y-bedd 170 A2
Cefn-y-pant 141 E5
Ceidio 180 C4
Ceidio Fawr 166 B3
Ceint 180 C5
Cellan 142 C3
Cellardyke 245 D4
Cellarhead 171 G3
Cemaes 180 B3
Cemmaes 155 E2
Cemmaes Road
  (Glantwymyn) 155 E2
Cenarth 141 F3
Cennin 167 D3
Centre for Life
  T&W NE1 4EP
  79 Newcastle upon Tyne
Ceramica Stoke
  ST6 3DS 20 C2
Ceres 244 C3
Cerist 155 F4
Cerne Abbas 104 C2
Cerney Wick 132 C3
Cerrigceinwen 180 C5
Cerrigydrudion 168 C3
Cessford 228 B4
Ceunant 167 E1
Chaceley 146 A4
Chacewater 96 B5
Chackmore 148 B4
Chacombe 147 G3
Chad Valley 158 C4
Chadderton 184 D2
Chadderton Fold 184 C2
Chaddesden 173 E4
Chaddesley Corbett 158 A5
Chaddleworth 133 G5
Chadlington 147 F5
Chadshunt 147 F2
Chadstone 149 D2
Chadwell Leics 174 C5
Chadwell St. Mary 137 F5
Chadwick End 159 E5
Chaffcombe 103 G1
Chafford Hundred 137 F5
Chagford 102 A4
Chailey 109 F2
Chainhurst 123 G4
Chalbury 105 G2
Chalbury Common 105 G2
Chaldon 122 C3
Chaldon Herring (East
  Chaldon) 105 D4
Chale 107 D5
Chale Green 107 D4
Chalfont Common 135 F3
Chalfont St. Giles 135 E2
Chalfont St. Peter 135 F3
Chalford Glos 132 A2
Chalford Wilts 117 F3
Chalgrove 134 B3
Chalk 137 F5
Chalk End 137 F1
Chalkhouse Green 134 B5
Challaborough 100 C3
Challacombe 113 G1
Challister 279 E6
Challoch 215 E4
Challock 124 C3
Chalmington 104 B2
Chalton CenBeds 149 F5
Chalton Hants 107 G1
Chalvey 135 E5
Chalvington 110 A3
Champany 235 E2
Chancery 154 B5
Chandler's Cross 135 F3
Chandler's Ford 119 F5
Channel Islands 100 A5
Channel's End 149 G2
Channerwick 279 D10
Chantry Som 117 E3
Chantry Suff 152 C3
Chapel 244 A5
Chapel Allerton
  Som 116 B2
Chapel Allerton
  WYorks 194 C4
Chapel Amble 97 D2
Chapel Brampton 148 C1
Chapel Chorlton 171 F4
Chapel Cleeve 114 D3
Chapel Cross 110 B1
Chapel End 149 F3
Chapel Green
  Warks 159 E4
Chapel Green
  Warks 147 G1
Chapel Haddlesey 195 E5
Chapel Hill Aber 261 J1
Chapel Hill Lincs 176 A2
Chapel Hill Mon 131 E2
Chapel Hill NYorks 194 C3
Chapel Knapp 117 F1
Chapel Lawn 156 C5
Chapel Leigh 115 E5
Chapel Milton 185 E4
Chapel of Garioch 261 F2
Chapel Rossan 206 B2
Chapel Row Essex 137 G2
Chapel Row
  WBerks 119 G1
Chapel St. Leonards 189 F5
Chapel Stile 199 E2
Chapel Town 96 C4
Chapelbank 243 F3
Chapeldonan 223 G5
Chapelend Way 151 F4
Chapel-en-le-Frith 185 E4
Chapelgate 176 C5
Chapelhall 234 B3
Chapelhill High 267 F4
Chapelhill P&K 244 A2
Chapelhill P&K 243 F1
Chapelknowe 218 B4
Chapel-le-Dale 200 C5
Chapelthorpe 186 A1
Chapelton Aber 253 G1
Chapelton Angus 253 E5
Chapelton Devon 113 F3
Chapelton SLan 234 A5

Chapeltown B'burn 184 B1
Chapeltown Cumb 218 C4
Chapeltown Moray 259 K2
Chapeltown SYorks 186 A3
Chapmans Well 99 D1
Chapmanslade 117 F3
Chapmore End 136 C1
Chappel 151 G5
Charaton 98 D4
Chard 103 G2
Chard Junction 103 G2
Chardleigh Green 103 G1
Chardstock 103 G2
Charfield 131 G3
Charing 124 B4
Charing Cross 106 A1
Charing Heath 124 B4
Charingworth 147 D4
Charlbury 133 F1
Charlcombe 117 E1
Charlecote 147 F2
Charles 113 G2
Charles Tye 152 B2
Charlesfield 227 G3
Charleshill 121 D3
Charleston 252 B5
Charlestown Aber 269 J4
Charlestown
  Aberdeen 261 H4
Charlestown Corn 97 E4
Charlestown
  Derbys 185 E3
Charlestown
  Dorset 104 C5
Charlestown Fife 235 E1
Charlestown
  GtMan 184 C2
Charlestown High 264 E4
Charlestown High 266 D7
Charlestown
  WYorks 194 A4
Charlestown
  WYorks 193 F5
Charlesworth of Aberlour
  (Aberlour) 267 K7
Charlesworth 185 E3
Charleton 244 C4
Charlinch 115 F4
Charlotteville 121 F3
Charlton GtLon 136 D5
Charlton Hants 119 E3
Charlton Herts 149 G5
Charlton N'hants 148 A4
Charlton N'umb 220 A3
Charlton Oxon 133 G4
Charlton Som 116 D3
Charlton Som 116 D3
Charlton Som 116 D3
Charlton Som 115 F5
Charlton Tel&W 157 E1
Charlton Wilts 118 A4
Charlton Wilts 132 B4
Charlton Wilts 118 C2
Charlton Worcs 146 C2
Charlton WSuss 108 A2
Charlton Abbots 146 C5
Charlton Adam 116 C5
Charlton Down 104 C3
Charlton
  Horethorne 117 D5
Charlton Kings 146 B5
Charlton Mackrell 116 C5
Charlton Marshall 105 E2
Charlton Musgrove 117 E5
Charlton on the Hill 105 E2
Charlton-All-Saints 118 C5
Charlton-on-
  Otmoor 134 A1
Charltons 203 F1
Charlwood 122 B4
Charminster 104 C3
Charmouth 103 G3
Charndon 148 B5
Charney Bassett 133 F3
Charnock Richard 183 G1
Charsfield 153 D2
Chart Corner 123 G4
Chart Sutton 124 A4
Charter Alley 119 G2
Charterhouse 116 B2
Charterville
  Allotments 133 F2
Chartham 124 D3
Chartham Hatch 124 D3
Chartridge 135 E2
Chartwell
  Kent TN16 1PS 123 D3
Charvil 134 C5
Charwelton 148 A2
Chase End Street 145 G4
Chase Terrace 158 C2
Chasetown 158 C2
Chastleton 147 E5
Chasty 112 D5
Chatburn 193 D3
Chatcull 171 E4
Chatelherault Country
  Park SLan
  ML3 7UE 31 G6
Chatham 123 G2
Chatham Green 137 G1
Chatham Historic
  Dockyard Med
  ME4 4TZ 123 G2
Chathill 229 F4
Chatsworth Farmyard &
  Adventure Playground
  Derbys
  DE45 1PP 185 G5
Chatsworth House Derbys
  DE45 1PP 185 G5
Chattenden 137 G5
Chatteris 162 B4
Chattisham 152 B3
Chatto 228 B5
Chatton 229 E4
Chaul End 149 F5
Chavey Down 121 D1
Chawleigh 102 A1
Chawley 133 G2
Chawston 149 G2
Chawton 120 C4
Chazey Heath 134 B5
Cheadle GtMan 184 C4
Cheadle Staffs 172 B3
Cheadle Heath 184 C4
Cheadle Hulme 184 C4
Cheam 122 B2
Cheapside 121 E1

287

Chearsley 134 C1
Chebsey 171 F5
Checkendon 134 B4
Checkley ChesE 171 E3
Checkley Here 145 E4
Checkley Staffs 172 B4
Checkley Green 171 E3
Chedburgh 151 F2
Cheddar 116 B2
Cheddar Caves & Gorge
  Som BS27 3QF 116 B2
Cheddington 135 E1
Cheddleton 171 G2
Cheddon Fitzpaine 115 F5
Chedglow 132 B3
Chedgrave 165 E2
Chedington 104 A2
Chediston 165 E4
Chediston Green 165 E4
Chedworth 132 C1
Chedzoy 116 A4
Cheesden 184 C1
Cheeseman's Green 124 C5
Cheetham Hill 184 C2
Cheglinch 113 F1
Cheldon 102 A1
Chelford 184 C5
Chellaston 173 E4
Chells 150 A5
Chelmarsh 157 G4
Chelmondiston 152 D4
Chelmsford 137 G2
Chelmsford Cathedral
  Essex CM1 1TY 137 G2
Chelmsley Wood 159 D4
Chelsea 136 B5
Chelsfield 123 D2
Chelsham 122 C3
Chelston Heath 115 E5
Chelsworth 152 A3
Cheltenham 146 B5
Chelveston 149 E1
Chelvey 116 B1
Chelwood 116 D1
Chelwood Common 109 G1
Chelwood Gate 109 G1
Chelworth 132 B3
Cheney Longville 156 D4
Chenies 135 F3
Chepstow
  (Cas-gwent) 131 E3
Cherhill 132 C5
Cherington Glos 132 B3
Cherington Warks 147 E4
Cheriton Devon 114 A3
Cheriton Hants 119 G5
Cheriton Kent 125 D5
Cheriton Pembs 126 C3
Cheriton Swan 128 A3
Cheriton Bishop 102 A3
Cheriton Cross 102 A3
Cheriton Fitzpaine 102 B2
Cherrington 171 D5
Cherry Burton 196 B3
Cherry Green 151 D5
Cherry Hinton 150 C2
Cherry Willingham 188 A5
Chertsey 121 F1
Cheselbourne 105 D3
Chesham 135 E2
Chesham Bois 135 E2
Cheshire Farm Ice Cream,
  Tattenhall ChesW&C
  CH3 9NE 170 B2
Cheshunt 136 C2
Cheslyn Hay 158 B2
Chessington 121 G1
Chessington World of
  Adventures GtLon
  KT9 2NE 121 G1
Chestall 158 C1
Chester 170 B1
Chester Cathedral
  ChesW&C CH1 2HU
  69 Chester
Chester Moor 212 B3
Chester Zoo ChesW&C
  CH2 1LH 183 F5
Chesterblade 117 D3
Chesterfield
  Derbys 186 A5
Chesterfield Staffs 158 D2
Chester-le-Street 212 B2
Chesters ScBord 228 B3
Chesters ScBord 228 A4
Chesterton Cambs 150 C1
Chesterton Cambs 161 G3
Chesterton Oxon 148 A5
Chesterton Shrop 157 G3
Chesterton Staffs 171 F3
Chesterton Warks 147 F2
Chesterton Green 147 F2
Chestfield 124 D2
Cheston 100 C2
Cheswardine 171 E5
Cheswick 229 E3
Cheswick Buildings 229 E2
Cheswick Green 158 D5
Chetnole 104 C2
Chettiscombe 102 C1
Chettisham 162 D4
Chettle 105 F1
Chetton 157 F3
Chetwode 148 B5
Chetwynd Aston 157 G1
Chetwynd Park 171 E5
Cheveley 151 E1
Chevening 123 D3
Cheverell's Green 135 F2
Chevin Forest Park WYorks
  LS21 3JL 194 B3
Chevington 151 F2
Chevithorne 102 C1
Chew Magna 116 C1
Chew Moor 184 A2
Chew Stoke 116 C1
Chewton
  Keynsham 116 D1
Chewton Mendip 116 C2
Chicacott 99 G1
Chicheley 149 E3
Chichester 108 A3
Chichester Cathedral WSuss
  PO19 1PX 108 A3
Chickerell 104 C4
Chickering 164 D4
Chicklade 118 A4

Chickney 151 D5
Chicksands 149 G4
Chidden 107 F1
Chiddingfold 121 E4
Chiddingly 110 A2
Chiddingstone 123 D4
Chiddingstone
  Causeway 123 E4
Chiddingstone
  Hoath 123 D4
Chideock 104 A3
Chidham 107 G2
Chidswell 194 B5
Chieveley 133 G5
Chignall St. James 137 F2
Chignall Smealy 137 F1
Chigwell 136 D3
Chigwell Row 137 D3
Chilbolton 119 E3
Chilcomb 119 G5
Chilcombe 104 B3
Chilcompton 117 D2
Chilcote 159 E1
Child Okeford 105 E1
Child's Ercall 171 D5
Childcote 153 E2
Childrey 133 F4
Children 229 E4
Chillington Som 103 G1
Chilmark 118 A4
Chilson Oxon 133 F1
Chilson Som 103 G2
Chilsworthy Corn 99 E3
Chilsworthy Devon 112 D5
Chilthorne Domer 104 B1
Chilton Bucks 134 B1
Chilton Devon 102 B2
Chilton Oxon 133 G4
Chilton Suff 151 G3
Chilton Candover 119 G4
Chilton Cantelo 116 C5
Chilton Foliat 133 F5
Chilton Polden 116 A4
Chilton Street 151 F3
Chilton Trinity 115 F4
Chilvers Coton 159 F3
Chilwell 173 G4
Chilworth Hants 106 D1
Chilworth Surr 121 F3
Chimney 133 F2
Chimney Street 151 F3
Chineham 120 B2
Chingford 136 C3
Chinley 185 E4
Chinley Head 185 E4
Chinnor 134 C2
Chipchase Castle 220 A4
Chipley 115 E5
Chipnall 171 E4
Chippenham
  Cambs 151 E1
Chippenham Wilts 132 B5
Chipperfield 135 F2
Chipping Herts 150 B4
Chipping Lancs 192 C3
Chipping Campden 147 D4
Chipping Hill 138 B1
Chipping Norton 147 F5
Chipping Ongar 137 E2
Chipping Sodbury 131 G4
Chipping Warden 147 G3
Chipstable 114 D5
Chipstead Kent 123 D3
Chipstead Surr 122 B3
Chirbury 156 B3
Chirk (Y Waun) 169 F4
Chirk Green 169 F4
Chirmorrie 214 D3
Chirnside 237 F4
Chirnsidebridge 237 F4
Chirton T&W 212 C1
Chirton Wilts 118 B2
Chisbury 119 D1
Chiscan 222 B4
Chiselborough 104 A1
Chiseldon 133 D5
Chiserley 193 G5
Chislehampton 134 A3
Chislehurst 136 D5
Chislet 125 E2
Chiswell Green 136 A2
Chiswick 136 B5
Chiswick End 150 B3
Chisworth 185 D3 Chithurst
  120 D5
Chittering 162 C5
Chitterne 118 A3
Chittlehamholt 113 G3
Chittlehampton 113 G3
Chittoe 118 A1
Chivelstone 101 D4
Chivenor 113 F2
Chobham 121 E1
Choicelee 237 E4
Cholderton 118 D3
Cholesbury 135 E2
Chollerford 220 B4
Chollerton 220 B4
Cholmondeston 170 D2
Cholsey 134 A4
Cholstrey 145 D2
Cholwell
  B&NESom 116 D2
Cholwell Devon 99 E3
Chop Gate 203 E3
Choppington 221 E4
Chopwell 212 A2
Chorley ChesE 170 C2
Chorley Lancs 183 G1
Chorley Shrop 157 F4

Chorley Staffs 158 C1
Chorleywood 135 F3
Chorlton 171 E2
Chorlton Lane 170 B3
Chorlton-cum-
  Hardy 184 C3
Chowley 170 B2
Chrishall 150 C4
Chrishall Grange 150 C3
Chriswell 232 D2
Christ Church Oxon
  OX1 1DP 80 Oxford
Christchurch
  Cambs 162 C3
Christchurch
  Dorset 106 A3
Christchurch Glos 131 E1
Christchurch
  Newport 130 C4
Christian Malford 132 B5
Christleton 170 B1
Christmas Common 134 C3
Christon 116 A2
Christon Bank 229 G4
Christow 102 B4
Chryston 234 A2
Chudleigh 102 B5
Chudleigh Knighton 102 B5
Chulmleigh 113 G4
Chunal 185 E3
Church 192 D5
Church Aston 157 G1
Church Brampton 148 C1
Church Brough 200 C1
Church Broughton 172 D4
Church Charwelton 148 A2
Church Common 153 E2
Church Crookham 120 D2
Church Eaton 158 A1
Church End Cambs 162 B2
Church End Cambs 162 B3
Church End Cambs 162 A4
Church End
  CenBeds 149 G4
Church End
  CenBeds 149 E5
Church End
  CenBeds 149 G2
Church End
  CenBeds 149 E4
Church End
  CenBeds 149 E4
Church End ERid 196 C2
Church End Essex 151 D3
Church End Essex 151 F5
Church End Glos 146 A4
Church End Hants 120 B2
Church End Herts 136 A1
Church End Herts 150 C5
Church End Lincs 176 A4
Church End Lincs 189 E3
Church End Warks 159 E3
Church End Wilts 132 C5
Church Enstone 147 F5
Church Fenton 195 E4
Church Green 103 E3
Church Gresley 159 E1
Church
  Hanborough 133 G1
Church Hill
  ChesW&C 170 D1
Church Hill Derbys 173 F1
Church Houses 203 F3
Church Knowle 105 F4
Church Laneham 187 F5
Church Langley 137 D2
Church Langton 160 C3
Church Lawford 159 F1
Church Lawton 171 F2
Church Leigh 172 B4
Church Lench 146 C2
Church Mayfield 172 C3
Church Minshull 171 D1
Church Norton 108 A4
Church Preen 157 E3
Church Pulverbatch 156 D2
Church Stoke 156 B3
Church Stowe 148 B2
Church Street
  Essex 151 E4
Church Street Kent 137 G5
Church Stretton 157 D3
Church Town Leics 159 F1
Church Town Surr 122 C3
Church Village 129 G4
Church Warsop 173 G1
Church Westcote 147 E5
Church Wilne 173 F4
Churcham 131 G1
Churchdown 132 A1
Churchend Essex 138 D3
Churchend Essex 151 E5
Churchend SGlos 131 G3
Churchfield 158 C2
Churchgate 136 C2
Churchgate Street 137 D1
Churchill Devon 113 F1
Churchill Devon 113 G1
Churchill NSom 116 B2
Churchill Oxon 147 E5
Churchill Worcs 146 B2
Churchill Worcs 158 A5
Churchill Museum &
  Cabinet War Rooms
  GtLon SW1A 2AQ 44 D5
Churchingford 103 F1
Churchover 160 A4
Churchstanton 103 E1
Churchstow 100 D3
Churchtown Devon 113 G1
Churchtown IoM 190 C2
Churchtown Lancs 192 A3
Churchtown
  Mersey 183 E1
Churnsike Lodge 219 E4
Churston Ferrers 101 F2
Churt 121 D4
Churton 170 B2
Churwell 194 B5
Chute Cadley 119 E2
Chute Standen 119 E2
Chwilog 166 D3
Chyandour 94 B3
Chysauster 94 B3

Cilan Uchaf 166 B5
Cilcain 169 E1
Cilcennin 142 B1
Cilcewydd 156 B2
Cilfrew 129 D2
Cilfynydd 129 G3
Cilgerran 141 E3
Cilgwyn Carmar 142 D4
Cilgwyn Pembs 141 D4
Ciliau Aeron 142 B2
Cille Bhrighde 254 C3
Cille Pheadair 254 C3
Cilmaengwyn 128 D2
Cilmery 143 G2
Cilrhedyn 141 F4
Cilrhedyn Bridge 140 D4
Cilsan 142 B5
Ciltalgarth 168 B3
Cilwendeg 141 F4
Cilybebyll 128 D2
Cilycwm 143 D3
Cimla 129 D3
Cinderford 131 F1
Cippenham 135 E4
Cippyn 141 E3
Cirbhig 270 D3
Cirencester 132 C2
City GtLon 136 C4
City VGlam 129 F5
City Airport 136 D4
City Dulas 180 C4
City of Coventry Stadium
  (Coventry City F.C.)
  WMid CV6 6GE 16 D2
Clabhach 246 A4
Clachaig 232 C1
Clachan A&B 241 D1
Clachan A&B 248 A5
Clachan A&B 231 F4
Clachan High 256 B1
Clachan
  Na H-E. Siar
  262 C7
Clachan Mòr 246 A2
Clachan of
  Campsie 234 A2
Clachan of
  Glendaruel 232 A1
Clachan-a-Luib 262 D1
Clachandhu 239 D1
Clachaneasy 215 E3
Clachanmore 206 A2
Clachan-Seil 239 G2
Clachanturn 259 K5
Clachbreck 231 F2
Clachnabrain 252 B3
Clachnaharry 266 D7
Clachtoll 272 C6
Cladach a Bhale
  Shear 262 D5
Cladach a' Chaolais 262 C5
Cladach Chircebost 262 C5
Cladach Chnoc a
  Lin 262 C5
Cladich
  (An Cladach) 240 C2
Cladswell 146 C2
Claggan (An Claigeann)
  High 248 D2
Claggan High 247 G5
Claigan 263 H6
Claines 146 A2
Clandown 117 D2
Clanfield Hants 107 G1
Clanfield Oxon 133 E2
Clannaborough
  Barton 102 A2
Clanville 119 E3
Claonaig 231 G4
Claonairigh 240 C4
Claonel 266 C1
Clapgate 150 C5
Clapham Bed 149 F2
Clapham Devon 102 B4
Clapham GtLon 136 B5
Clapham NYorks 192 D1
Clapham WSuss 108 C3
Clapham Green 149 F2
Clapham Hill 124 C2
Clappers 237 G4
Clappersgate 199 E2
Clapton Som 104 A2
Clapton Som 116 D2
Clapton-in-
  Gordano 131 D5
Clapton-on-the-Hill 133 D1
Clapworthy 113 G3
Clara Vale 212 A1
Clarach 154 C4
Clarbeston 141 D5
Clarbeston Road 140 D5
Clarborough 187 E4
Clardon 275 G2
Clare 151 F3
Clare Castle Country Park
  Suff CO10 8NJ 151 F3
Clarebrand 216 B4
Claremont Landscape
  Garden Surr
  KT10 9JG 121 G1
Clarencefield 217 E4
Clarilaw 227 G4
Clark's Green 121 G4
Clarkston 233 G4
Clashban 266 D2
Clashcoig 266 D2
Clashdorran 266 C7
Clashgour 249 E5
Clashindarroch 260 C1
Clashmore High 266 E3
Clashmore High 272 C5
Clashnessie 272 C5
Clashnoir 259 K2
Clatford 118 C1
Clatt 260 D2
Clatter 155 F3
Clatterford 107 D4
Clatterford End 137 E2
Clatterin Brig 253 E2

Clatteringshaws 215 G3
Clatworthy 115 D4
Claughton Lancs 192 A4
Claughton Lancs 192 B1
Claughton Lancs 192 B3
Clavelshay 115 F4
Claverdon 147 D1
Claverham 116 B1
Clavering 150 C4
Claverley 157 G3
Claverton 117 E1
Claverton Down 117 E1
Clawdd-côch 129 G5
Clawdd-newydd 169 D2
Clawfin 224 C5
Clawthorpe 199 G5
Clawton 99 D1
Claxby 188 B3
Claxby Pluckacre 176 B1
Claxby St. Andrew 189 E5
Claxton Norf 179 D5
Claxton NYorks 195 F1
Claxton Grange 213 D5
Clay Common 165 F3
Clay Coton 160 A5
Clay Cross 173 E1
Clay End 150 B5
Clay Hill 131 F5
Clay of Allan 267 F4
Claybrooke Magna 159 G4
Claybrooke Parva 159 G4
Claydene 123 D4
Claydon Oxon 147 G2
Claydon Suff 152 C3
Claygate Kent 123 G4
Claygate Surr 121 G1
Claygate Cross 123 F3
Clayhanger Devon 114 D5
Clayhanger WMid 158 C2
Clayhidon 103 E1
Clayhill ESuss 110 D1
Clayhill Hants 106 C2
Clayhithe 150 D1
Clayock 275 G3
Claypit Hill 150 B2
Claypits 131 G2
Claypole 174 D3
Claythorpe 189 E5
Clayton Staffs 171 F3
Clayton SYorks 186 B2
Clayton WSuss 109 E2
Clayton WYorks 194 A4
Clayton Green 192 B5
Clayton West 185 G1
Clayton-le-Moors 192 D4
Clayton-le-Woods 192 B5
Clayworth 187 E4
Cleadale 247 C4
Cleadon 212 C1
Clearbrook 100 B1
Clearwell 131 E2
Cleasby 202 B1
Cleat Ork 277 D9
Cleat Na H-E. Siar 254 B4
Cleatlam 202 A1
Cleatop 193 E2
Cleator 208 D5
Cleator Moor 208 D5
Cleckheaton 194 A5
Clee St. Margaret 157 E4
Cleedownton 157 E4
Cleehill 157 E5
Cleestanton 157 E5
Cleethorpes 188 D2
Cleethorpes Discovery
  Centre NELincs
  DN35 0AG 188 D2
Cleeton St. Mary 157 F5
Cleeve NSom 116 B1
Cleeve Oxon 134 B4
Cleeve Hill 146 B5
Cleeve Prior 146 C2
C3 Cleghorn 234 C5
Clehonger 145 D4
Cleigh 240 A2
Cleish 243 F5
Cleland 234 B4
Clement's End 135 F1
Clemsfold 121 G4
Clench Common 118 C1
Clenchwarton 177 D5
Clennell 220 B1
Clent 158 B5
Clent Hills
  Worcs DY9 9JR 14 B5
Cleobury Mortimer 157 F5
Cleobury North 157 F4
Clephanton 267 F6
Clerklands 227 G3
Clermiston 235 F2
Clestrain 277 C7
Cleuch Head 227 G4
Cleughbrae 217 E3
Clevancy 132 C5
Clevedon 130 D5
Cleveland Tontine
  Inn 202 D3
Cleveley 147 F5
Cleveleys 191 G3
Clevelode 146 A3
Cleverton 132 B4
Clewer 116 B2
Clewer Green 135 E5
Clewer Village 135 E5
Cley Marshes Norf
  NR25 7SA 178 B1
Cley next the Sea 178 B1
Cliburn 210 B5
Cliddesden 120 B3
Cliff Carmar 127 G2
Cliff High 247 F3
Cliff End 111 D2
Cliff Grange 170 D4
Cliffe Lancs 192 D4
Cliffe Med 137 G5
Cliffe NYorks 195 F4
Cliffe Woods 137 G5
Clifford Here 144 B3
Clifford WYorks 194 D3
Clifford Chambers 147 D2
Clifford's Mesne 145 F5
Clifford's Tower
  YO1 9SA 90 York
Cliffs End 125 F2
Clifton Bristol 131 E5
Clifton CenBeds 149 G4
Clifton Cumb 210 B5
Clifton Derbys 172 C3
Clifton Devon 113 F1

Clifton Lancs 192 A4
Clifton N'umb 221 E3
Clifton Nott 173 G4
Clifton NYorks 194 A3
Clifton Oxon 147 G4
Clifton Stir 241 F1
Clifton SYorks 186 C3
Clifton Worcs 146 A3
Clifton WYorks 194 A5
Clifton York 195 E2
Clifton Campville 159 E2
Clifton Hampden 134 A3
Clifton Maybank 104 B1
Clifton Park Museum
  SYorks S65 2AA 21 D1
Clifton Reynes 149 E2
Clifton upon
  Dunsmore 160 A5
Clifton upon Teme 145 G1
Cliftonville 125 F1
Climping 108 C3
Climpy 234 D1
Clink 117 E3
Clint 194 B2
Clint Green 178 B4
Clinterty 261 G3
Clintmains 228 A3
Clippesby 179 F4
Clippings Green 178 B4
Clipsham 161 E1
Clipston N'hants 160 C4
Clipston Notts 174 B4
Clipstone 173 G1
Clitheroe 192 D3
Clive 170 C5
Cliveden Garden & Maze
  Bucks SL6 0JA 135 E4
Clivocast 278 F2
Clixby 188 B2
Clocaenog 169 D2
Clochan 268 C4
Clochtow 261 J1
Clock Face 183 G3
Clockhill 269 G6
Cloddach 267 J6
Cloddiau 156 A2
Clodock 144 C5
Cloford 117 E3
Cloichran 242 B1
Clola 269 J6
Clonrae 216 C1
Clophill 149 F4
Clopton 161 F3
Clopton Corner 152 D2
Clopton Green Suff 151 F2
Clopton Green Suff 152 D2
Close Clark 190 A4
Closeburn 216 C1
Closworth 104 B1
Clothall 150 A4
Clothan 278 D4
Clotton 170 C1
Clough Cumb 200 C3
Clough GtMan 184 D1
Clough GtMan 184 D2
Clough WYorks 185 E1
Clough Foot 193 F5
Clough Head 193 G5
Cloughton 204 D3
Cloughton
  Newlands 204 D3
Clounlaid 247 G4
Clousta 279 C7
Clouston 277 C6
Clova Aber 260 C2
Clova Angus 252 B2
Clove Lodge 201 F3
Clovelly 112 D3
Clovelly Cross 112 D3
Clovelly Village Devon
  EX39 5TA 112 D3
Clovenfords 227 F2
Clovenstone 261 F3
Cloves 267 J5
Clovullin 248 C3
Clow Bridge 193 E5
Clowne 186 B5
Clows Top 157 G5
Cloyntie 224 B5
Cluanach 230 B4
Clubworthy 98 C1
Cluddley 157 F1
Cluer (Cliuthar) 263 G2
Clumber Country Park
  Notts S80 3AZ 186 D5
Clun 156 B4
Clunas 267 F7
Clunbury 156 C4
Clunderwen 127 E1
Clune High 258 E2
Clune Moray 268 D4
Clunes 249 E1
Clungunford 156 C5
Clunie Aber 268 E5
Clunie P&K 251 G5
Clunton 156 C4
Cluny 244 A5
Clutton B&NESom 116 D2
Clutton ChesW&C 170 B2
Clwt-y-bont 167 E1
Clwydyfagwyr 129 G2
Clydach Mon 130 B1
Clydach Swan 128 C2
Clydach Terrace 130 A1
Clydach Vale 129 F3
Clydebank 233 F2
Clydey 141 F4
Clyffe Pypard 132 C5
Clynder 232 D1
Clyne 129 E2
Clynelish 267 F1
Clynfyw 141 F4
Clynnog-fawr 166 D3
Clyro 144 B3
Clyst Honiton 102 C3
Clyst Hydon 102 D2
Clyst St. George 102 C4
Clyst St. Lawrence 102 D2
Clyst St. Mary 102 C3
Clyst William 103 D2
Cnewr 143 E5
Cnoc 271 G4
Cnwch Coch 154 C5
Coachford 268 C6
Coad's Green 97 G2
Coal Aston 186 A5
Coalbrookdale 157 F2
Coalbrookvale 130 A2

Coalburn 225 G2
Coalburns 212 A1
Coalcleugh 211 E3
Coaley 131 G2
Coalmoor 157 F2
Coalpit Heath 131 F4
Coalpit Hill 171 F2
Coalport 157 G2
Coalsnaughton 243 E5
Coaltown of
  Balgonie 244 B5
Coaltown of
  Wemyss 244 B5
Coalville 159 G1
Coalway 131 E1
Coanwood 210 C2
Coast 265 F2
Coat 116 B5
Coatbridge 234 B3
Coate Swin 133 D4
Coate Wilts 118 B1
Coates Cambs 162 B3
Coates Glos 132 B2
Coates Lincs 187 G4
Coates Notts 187 F4
Coates WSuss 108 B2
Coatham 213 E5
Coatham
  Mundeville 212 B5
Cobairdy 268 D6
Cobbaton 113 G3
Cobbler's Plain 131 D2
Cobby Syke 194 A2
Cobden 102 D3
Coberley 132 B1
Cobhall Common 145 D4
Cobham Kent 123 F2
Cobham Surr 121 G1
Cobleland 242 A5
Cobley Hill 158 C5
Cobnash 145 D1
Coburty 269 H4
Cochno 233 F2
Cock Alley 173 F1
Cock Bank 170 A3
Cock Bevington 146 C2
Cock Bridge 259 K4
Cock Clarks 138 B2
Cock Green 137 G1
Cock Marling 111 D2
Cockayne 203 F3
Cockayne Hatley 150 A3
Cockburnspath 237 E2
Cockenzie & Port
  Seton 236 B2
Cocker Bar 192 B5
Cockerham 192 A2
Cockermouth 209 E3
Cockernhoe 149 G5
Cockerton 202 B1
Cockett 128 C3
Cockfield Dur 212 A5
Cockfield Suff 152 A2
Cockfosters 136 B3
Cocking 108 A2
Cockington 101 E1
Cockington Country
  Park Torbay
  TQ2 6XA 101 E1
Cocklake 116 B3
Cocklaw 220 B4
Cockle Park 221 E3
Cockleford 132 B1
Cockley Beck 198 D2
Cockley Cley 163 F2
Cockpen 236 A3
Cockpole Green 134 C4
Cockshutt 170 B5
Cockthorpe 178 A1
Cockwood Devon 102 C4
Cockwood Som 115 F3
Cockyard 185 E4
Codda 97 F2
Coddenham 152 C2
Coddington
  ChesW&C 170 B2
Coddington Here 145 G3
Coddington N'hants 174 D2
Codford St. Mary 118 A4
Codford St. Peter 118 A4
Codicote 136 B1
Codmore Hill 108 C2
Codnor 173 F3
Codnor Park 173 F2
Codrington 131 G5
Codsall 158 A2
Codsall Wood 158 A2
Coed Morgan 130 C1
Coed Ystumgwern 167 E5
Coedcae 130 B2
Coedely 129 G4
Coedkernew 130 B4
Coedpoeth 169 F2
Coedway 156 C1
Coed-y-bryn 141 G3
Coed-y-caerau 130 C3
Coed-y-paen 130 C3
Coed-y-parc 167 F1
Coed-yr-ynys 144 A5
Coelbren 129 E1
Coffinswell 101 E1
Cofton 102 C4
Cofton Hackett 158 C5
Cogan 130 A5
Cogenhoe 148 D1
Cogges 133 F2
Coggeshall 151 G5
Coggeshall
  Hamlet 151 G5
Coggins Mill 110 A1
Cóig Peighinnean 271 H1
Coilantogle 242 A4
Coileitir 248 D5
Coilessan 241 E4
Coillaig 240 C2
Coille Mhorgil 257 G4
Coille-righ 257 F3
Coillore 255 J1
Coity 129 F4
Col 271 G4
Col Uarach 271 G4
Colaboll 273 H7
Colan 96 C4
Colaton Raleigh 103 D4
Colbost 263 H7
Colburn 202 B3
Colbury 106 C1

Colby *Cumb* 210 C5
Colby *IoM* 190 A4
Colby *Norf* 178 D2
Colchester 152 A5
Colchester Castle Museum *Essex* CO1 1TJ 152 A5
Colchester Green 152 A2
Colchester Zoo *Essex* CO3 0SL 152 A5
Colcot 115 E1
Cold Ash 119 G1
Cold Ashby 160 B5
Cold Ashton 131 G5
Cold Aston 132 D1
Cold Blow 127 E1
Cold Brayfield 149 E2
Cold Chapel 226 A3
Cold Cotes 200 C5
Cold Hanworth 188 A4
Cold Harbour 134 B4
Cold Hatton 170 D5
Cold Hatton Heath 170 D5
Cold Hesledon 212 D3
Cold Higham 148 B2
Cold Inn 127 E2
Cold Kirby 203 E4
Cold Newton 160 C2
Cold Northcott 97 G1
Cold Norton 138 B2
Cold Overton 160 D2
Cold Row 191 G3
Coldbackie 273 J2
Coldblow 137 E5
Coldean 109 F3
Coldeast 102 B5
Coldeaton 172 C2
Colden Common 119 F5
Coldfair Green 153 F1
Coldham 162 C2
Coldharbour *Glos* 131 E2
Coldharbour *Surr* 121 G3
Coldingham 237 G3
Coldrain 243 F4
Coldred 125 E4
Coldrey 120 C3
Coldridge 113 G5
Coldrife 220 C4
Coldstream 228 C3
Coldvreath 97 D4
Coldwaltham 108 C2
Coldwells 269 K6
Cole 117 D4
Cole End 159 D4
Cole Green 136 B1
Cole Henley 119 F2
Colebatch 156 C4
Colebrook 102 D2
Colebrooke 102 A2
Coleburn 267 K6
Coleby *Lincs* 175 E1
Coleby *NLincs* 187 F1
Coleford *Devon* 102 A2
Coleford *Glos* 131 E2
Coleford *Som* 117 D3
Colegate End 164 C3
Colehill 105 G2
Coleman Green 136 A1
Coleman's Hatch 122 D5
Colemere 170 B4
Colemore 120 C4
Colemore Green 157 G3
Colenden 243 G2
Coleorton 159 G1
Colerne 132 A2
Cole's Common 164 D3
Cole's Cross 101 D3
Cole's Green 153 D1
Colesbourne 132 C1
Colesden 149 G2
Coleshill *Bucks* 135 E3
Coleshill *Oxon* 133 E3
Coleshill *Warks* 159 E4
Colestocks 103 D2
Coley *B&NESom* 116 C2
Coley *Staffs* 172 B5
Colfin 214 B5
Colgate 122 B5
Colgrain 233 E2
Colindale 136 B4
Colinsburgh 244 C4
Colinton 235 G3
Colintraive 232 B2
Colkirk 178 A3
Coll 246 A4
Collace 244 A1
Collafirth 279 D6
Collamoor Head 98 B1
Collaton St. Mary 101 E1
Coll Dark Sky Island *Argyll & Bute* 246 B4
Collessie 244 A3
Colleton Mills 113 G4
Collett's Green 146 A2
Collier Row 137 E3
Collier Street 123 G4
Collier's End 150 B5
Collier's Wood 136 B5
Colliery Row 212 C3
Collieston 261 J2
Collin 217 E3
Collingbourne Ducis 118 D2
Collingbourne Kingston 118 D2
Collingham *Notts* 174 D1
Collingham *WYorks* 194 C3
Collington 145 F1
Collingtree 148 C2
Collins End 134 B5
Collins Green *Warr* 183 G3
Collins Green *Worcs* 145 G2
Colliston 253 E5
Colliton 103 D2
Collmuir 260 D4
Collycroft 159 F4
Collyhurst 184 C2
Collynie 261 G1
Collyweston 161 E2
Colmonell 214 C2
Colmworth 149 G2
Coln Rogers 132 C2
Coln St. Aldwyns 132 D2
Coln St. Dennis 132 C1
Colnabaichin 259 K4
Colnbrook 135 F5
Colne *Cambs* 162 B5

Colne *Lancs* 193 E4
Colne Engaine 151 G4
Colney 178 C5
Colney Heath 136 A2
Colney Street 136 A2
Colonsay 238 C5
Colonsay House 238 C5
Colony Gift Corporation *Cumb* LA12 0LD 199 D5
Colpy 260 E1
Colquhar 236 A3
Colsterdale 202 A4
Colsterworth 175 E5
Colston Bassett 174 C4
Colston Hall BS1 5AR 66 Bristol
Coltfield 267 J5
Colthouse 199 E3
Coltishall 179 D4
Coltness 234 C4
Colton *Cumb* 199 E4
Colton *Norf* 178 C5
Colton *NYorks* 195 E3
Colton *Staffs* 172 B5
Colton *WYorks* 194 C4
Colva 144 B2
Colvend 216 C5
Colvister 278 E3
Colwall 145 G3
Colwall Green 145 G3
Colwall Stone 145 G3
Colwell 220 B4
Colwich 172 B5
Colwick 174 B3
Colwinston 129 F5
Colworth 108 B3
Colwyn Bay (Bae Colwyn) 181 G5
Colyford 103 F3
Colyton 103 F3
Combe *Here* 144 C1
Combe *Oxon* 133 G1
Combe *Som* 116 B5
Combe *WBerks* 119 E1
Combe Common 121 E4
Combe Cross 102 A5
Combe Down 117 E1
Combe Florey 115 E4
Combe Hay 117 E2
Combe Martin 113 F1
Combe Martin Wildlife & Dinosaur Park *Devon* EX34 0NG 113 F1
Combe Pafford 101 F1
Combe Raleigh 103 E2
Combe St. Nicholas 103 J1
Combeinteignhead 102 B5
Comberbach 184 A5
Comberford 159 D2
Comberton *Cambs* 150 B2
Comberton *Here* 145 D1
Combpyne 103 F3
Combridge 172 B4
Combrook 147 F2
Combs *Derbys* 185 E5
Combs *Suff* 152 B2
Combs Ford 152 B2
Combwich 115 F3
Comer 241 F4
Comers 260 E4
Comhampton 146 A1
Comins Coch 154 C4
Commercial End 151 D1
Commins Coch 155 E2
Common Edge 191 G4
Common Moor 97 G2
Common Platt 132 D4
Common Side 186 A5
Common Square 188 A5
Commondale 203 F1
Commonside 172 D2
Compstall 185 D3
Compton *Devon* 101 E1
Compton *Hants* 119 F5
Compton *Plym* 100 A2
Compton *Staffs* 158 A4
Compton *Surr* 121 E3
Compton *WBerks* 134 A5
Compton *Wilts* 118 C3
Compton *WSuss* 107 G1
Compton *WYorks* 194 D3
Compton Abbas 105 E1
Compton Abdale 132 C1
Compton Bassett 132 C5
Compton Beauchamp 133 E4
Compton Bishop 116 A2
Compton Chamberlayne 118 B5
Compton Dando 116 D1
Compton Dundon 116 B4
Compton Martin 116 C2
Compton Pauncefoot 116 D5
Compton Valence 104 B3
Compton Verney 147 F2
Compton Wynyates 147 F3
Comra 258 C5
Comrie *Fife* 235 E1
Comrie *P&K* 242 C2
Conchra *A&B* 232 B1
Conchra *High* 256 E2
Concraigie 251 G5
Conder Green 192 A2
Conderton 146 B4
Condicote 146 D5
Condorrat 234 B2
Condover 157 D2
Coney Weston 164 A4
Coneyhurst 121 G5
Coneysthorpe 203 G5
Coneythorpe 194 C2
Conford 120 D4
Congash 259 H2
Congdon's Shop 97 G2
Congerstone 159 F2
Congham 177 F5
Congleton 171 F1
Congresbury 116 B1
Congreve 158 B1
Conicavel 267 G6
Coningsby 176 A2
Conington *Cambs* 161 G4
Conington *Cambs* 150 B1
Conisbrough 186 C3
Conisby 230 A3
Conisholme 189 E3

Coniston *Cumb* 199 E3
Coniston *ERid* 197 D4
Coniston Cold 193 F2
Conistone 193 F1
Conkers, Swadlincote *Leics* DE12 6GA 159 F1
Conland 260 E6
Connah's Quay 169 F1
Connel (A' Choingheal) 240 B1
Connel Park 225 E4
Connor Downs 94 C3
Conock 118 B2
Cononbie 193 E5
Cononley 193 F3
Cononsyth 253 D5
Consall 171 G3
Consett 212 A2
Constable Burton 202 A3
Constantine 95 E4
Constantine Bay 96 C2
Contin (Cunndainn) 266 B6
Contlaw 261 G4
Contullich 266 D4
Conwy 181 F5
Conwy Castle *Conwy* LL32 8LD 181 F5
Conyer 124 B2
Conyer's Green 151 G1
Cooden 110 C3
Coodham 224 C2
Cooil 190 B4
Cookbury 113 E5
Cookbury Wick 113 D5
Cookham 135 D4
Cookham Dean 135 D4
Cookham Rise 135 D4
Cookhill 146 C2
Cookley *Suff* 165 E4
Cookley *Worcs* 158 A4
Cookley Green *Oxon* 134 B3
Cookley Green *Suff* 165 E4
Cookney 261 G5
Cook's Green 152 A2
Cooksbridge 109 F2
Cooksey Green 146 B1
Cookshill 171 G3
Cooksmill Green 137 F2
Cookston 261 H1
Coolham 121 G5
Cooling 137 G5
Cooling Street 137 G5
Coombe 97 D4
Coombe *Corn* 112 C4
Coombe *Corn* 96 A5
Coombe *Corn* 96 C3
Coombe *Devon* 101 D3
Coombe *Devon* 102 B4
Coombe *Devon* 103 E3
Coombe *Som* 115 F5
Coombe *Som* 104 A2
Coombe *Wilts* 118 C2
Coombe Bissett 118 C5
Coombe Country Park *Warks* CV3 2AB 16 D3
Coombe End 114 D5
Coombe Hill 146 A5
Coombe Keynes 105 E4
Coombes 109 D3
Coombes Moor 144 C1
Cooper's Corner *ESuss* 110 C1
Cooper's Corner *Kent* 123 D4
Cooper's Green 136 A2
Coopersale 137 D2
Coopersale Street 137 D2
Cootham 108 C2
Cop Street 125 E3
Copdock 152 C3
Copford Green 152 A5
Copgrove 194 C1
Copister 278 D5
Cople 149 G3
Copley *Dur* 211 G5
Copley *WYorks* 193 G5
Coplow Dale 185 F5
Copmanthorpe 195 E3
Compere End 171 F5
Copp 192 A4
Coppathorne 112 C5
Coppenhall 158 B1
Coppenhall Moss 171 E2
Copperhouse 94 C3
Coppicegate 157 G4
Coppingford 161 G4
Coppleridge 117 F5
Copplestone 102 A2
Coppull 183 G1
Coppull Moor 183 G1
Copsale 121 G5
Copse Hill 122 B2
Copster Green 192 C4
Copston Magna 159 G4
Copt Heath 159 D5
Copt Hewick 202 C5
Copt Oak 159 G1
Copthall Green 136 D2
Copthorne 122 C5
Copy Lake 113 G4
Copythorne 106 C1
Corah 269 J4
Coralhill 269 J4
Corbets Tey 137 E4
Corbiegoe 275 J4
Corbridge 211 F1
Corby 161 D4
Corby Glen 175 F5
Cordach 260 E5
Cordorcan 215 E3
Coreley 157 F5
Corfcott Green 98 D1
Corfe 103 F1
Corfe Castle 105 F4
Corfe Castle *Dorset* BH20 5EZ 105 F4
Corfe Mullen 105 F3
Corfton 157 D4
Corgarff 259 K4
Corhampton 120 B5
Corley 159 F4
Corley Ash 159 E4
Corley Moor 159 E4
Corn Exchange *Cambs* CB2 3QB 66 Cambridge
Cornabus 230 B5

Cornard Tye 152 A3
Corndon 99 G2
Corney 198 C3
Cornforth 212 C4
Cornhill 268 E5
Cornhill on Tweed 228 C3
Cornholme 193 F5
Cornish Gold & Treasure Park *Corn* TR16 4HN 96 A5
Cornish Hall End 151 E4
Cornquoy 277 E7
Cornriggs 211 E3
Cornsay 212 A3
Cornsay Colliery 212 A3
Corntown *High* 266 C6
Corntown *VGlam* 129 F5
Cornwell 147 E5
Cornwood 100 C2
Cornworthy 101 E2
Corpach (A' Chorpaich) 248 D2
Corpusty 178 C3
Corrachree 260 C4
Corran *A&B* 241 E5
Corran *High* 256 E4
Corran (Ardgour) *High* 248 C3
Corranbuie 231 G3
Corranmore 239 G4
Corrany 190 C3
Corribeg 248 B2
Corrie 232 B5
Corrie Common 218 A3
Corriechrevie 231 F4
Corriecravie 223 E3
Corriedoo 216 A2
Corriekinloch 273 F6
Corrielorne 240 A3
Corrievorrie 258 E2
Corrimony 257 K1
Corringham *Lincs* 187 F3
Corringham *Thur* 137 G4
Corris 155 D2
Corris Uchaf 154 D2
Corrlarach 248 B2
Corrour Shooting Lodge 249 G3
Corrow 241 D4
Corry 256 C2
Corrychurrachan 248 C3
Corrylach 222 C2
Corrymuckloch 243 D1
Corsback 275 H1
Corscombe 104 B2
Corse *Aber* 268 E6
Corse *Glos* 145 G5
Corse Lawn 146 A4
Corsebank 225 G4
Corsegight 269 G5
Corsehill 217 F2
Corsewall 214 B4
Corsham 132 A5
Corsindae 260 E4
Corsley 117 F3
Corsley Heath 117 F3
Corsock 216 B3
Corston *B&NESom* 117 D1
Corston *Wilts* 132 B4
Corstorphine 235 F2
Cortachy 252 B4
Corton *Suff* 165 G2
Corton *Wilts* 118 A3
Corton Denham 116 D5
Corwar House 215 D2
Corwen 169 D3
Coryton *Devon* 99 E2
Coryton *Thur* 137 G4
Cosby 160 A3
Coscote 134 A4
Coseley 158 B3
Cosford *Shrop* 157 G2
Cosford *Warks* 160 A5
Cosgrove 148 C3
Cosham 107 F2
Cosheston 126 D2
Coshieville 250 C5
Coskills 188 A2
Cosmeston 115 E1
Cosmeston Lakes Country Park *VGlam* CF64 5UY 115 E1
Cossall 173 F3
Cossington *Leics* 160 B1
Cossington *Som* 116 A3
Costa 276 C5
Costessey 178 C4
Costock 173 G5
Coston *Leics* 174 D5
Coston *Norf* 178 B5
Cote *Oxon* 133 F2
Cote *Som* 116 A3
Cotebrook 170 C1
Cotehill 210 A2
Cotes *Cumb* 199 F4
Cotes *Leics* 173 G5
Cotes *Staffs* 171 F4
Cotesbach 160 A4
Cotford St. Luke 115 E4
Cotgrave 174 B4
Cothall 261 G3
Cotham 174 C3
Cothelstone 115 E4
Cotheridge 145 G2
Cotherstone 201 F1
Cothill 133 G3
Cotleigh 103 F2
Cotmanhay 173 F3
Coton *Cambs* 150 C2
Coton *N'hants* 160 B5
Coton *Staffs* 171 G4
Coton *Staffs* 171 F5
Coton *Staffs* 159 D2
Coton Clanford 171 F5
Coton Hill 171 G4
Coton in the Clay 172 C5
Coton in the Elms 159 E1
Cotonwood *Shrop* 170 C4
Cotonwood *Staffs* 171 F5
Cotswold Water Park *Glos* GL7 6DF 132 C3
Cotswold Wildlife Park *Oxon* OX18 4JP 133 E2
Cott *Oxon* 133 F2
Cott *Devon* 101 D1
Cottam *Lancs* 192 A4
Cottam *Notts* 187 F4

Cottartown 259 H1
Cottenham 150 C1
Cotterdale 200 D3
Cottered 150 B5
Cotteridge 158 C5
Cotterstock 161 F3
Cottesbrooke 160 C5
Cottesmore 161 E1
Cottingham *ERid* 196 C4
Cottingham *N'hants* 160 D3
Cottingley 194 A4
Cottisford 148 A4
Cotton *Staffs* 172 B3
Cotton *Suff* 152 B1
Cotton End 149 F3
Cottonworth 119 E4
Cottown *Aber* 260 D2
Cottown *Aber* 269 G6
Cottown *Aber* 261 F3
Cotts 100 A1
Cottwood 113 G4
Cotwall 171 F1
Cotwalton 171 G4
Couch's Mill 97 F4
Coughton *Here* 145 E5
Coughton *Warks* 146 C1
Cougie 257 J2
Coulaghailtro 231 F3
Coulags 265 F7
Coulby Newham 203 E1
Coulderton 198 A2
Coull 260 D4
Coulport 232 D1
Coulsdon 122 B3
Coulston 118 A2
Coulter 226 B2
Coultershaw Bridge 108 B2
Coultings 115 E3
Coulton 203 F5
Coultra 244 B2
Cound 157 E2
Coundlane 157 E2
Coundon *Dur* 212 B5
Coundon *WMid* 159 F4
Countersett 201 E4
Countess Wear 102 C3
Countesthorpe 160 A3
Countisbury 114 A3
Coup Green 192 B5
Coupar Angus 252 A5
Coupland *Cumb* 200 C1
Coupland *N'umb* 228 D3
Cour 231 G5
Court Colman 129 E4
Court Henry 142 B5
Court House Green 159 F4
Court-at-Street 124 C5
Courtauld Institute of Art Gallery *GtLon* WC2R 0RN 45 F3
Courteenhall 148 C2
Courtsend 138 D3
Courtway 115 E4
Cousland 236 A3
Cousley Wood 123 F5
Coustonn 232 B2
Cove *A&B* 232 D1
Cove *Devon* 102 C1
Cove *Hants* 120 D2
Cove *High* 264 E2
Cove *ScBord* 237 E2
Cove Bay 261 H4
Cove Bottom 165 G3
Covehithe 165 G3
Coven 158 B2
Coveney 162 C4
Covenham St. Bartholomew 188 D3
Covenham St. Mary 188 D3
Coventry 159 F5
Coventry Airport 159 F5
Coventry Cathedral *WMid* CV1 5AR 69 Coventry
Coventry Transport Museum *WMid* CV1 1JD 69 Coventry
Coverack 95 E5
Coverham 202 A4
Covesea 267 J4
Covingham 133 D4
Covington *Cambs* 161 F5
Covington *SLan* 226 A2
Cowan Bridge 200 B5
Cowbeech 110 B2
Cowbit 162 A1
Cowbridge *Som* 114 C3
Cowbridge *VGlam* 129 F5
Cowden 123 D4
Cowden Pound 123 D4
Cowdenbeath 243 F5
Cowdenburn 235 G4
Cowers Lane 173 E3
Cowes 107 D3
Cowesby 203 D4
Cowesfield Green 119 D5
Cowey Green 152 B5
Cowfold 109 E1
Cowgill 200 C4
Cowie *Aber* 253 C1
Cowie *Stir* 234 C1
Cowlam Manor 196 B3
Cowley *Devon* 102 C3
Cowley *Glos* 132 B1
Cowley *GtLon* 135 F4
Cowley *Oxon* 134 A2
Cowling *Lancs* 183 G1
Cowling *NYorks* 193 F3
Cowling *NYorks* 202 B4
Cowlinge 151 F2
Cowmes 185 F1
Cowpe 193 E5
Cowpen 221 E3
Cowpen Bewley 213 D5
Cowplain 107 F1
Cowsden 146 B2
Cowshill 211 E3
Cowthorpe 194 D2
Cox Common 165 E3
Coxbank 171 D3
Coxbench 173 E3
Coxbridge 116 C4
Coxford 177 G5
Coxheath 123 G3
Coxhoe 212 C4
Coxley 116 C3
Coxley Wick 116 C3
Coxpark 99 E3

Coxtie Green 137 E3
Coxwold 203 E5
Coychurch 129 F5
Coylton 224 C4
Coylumbridge 259 G3
Coynach 260 C4
Coynachie 260 C1
Coytrahen 129 E4
Crabbet Park 122 C5
Crabgate 178 B3
Crabtree *Plym* 100 B2
Crabtree *SYorks* 186 A4
Crabtree *WSuss* 109 E1
Crabtree Green 170 A3
Crackaig 230 C3
Crackenthorpe 210 C5
Crackington 98 B1
Crackington Haven 98 B1
Crackley 171 F2
Crackleybank 157 G1
Crackpot 201 E3
Crackthorn Corner 164 B3
Cracoe 193 F1
Craddock 103 D1
Cradhlastadh 270 C4
Cradley *Here* 145 G3
Cradley *WMid* 158 B4
Cradley Heath 158 B4
Crafthole 99 D5
Crafton 135 D1
Cragg 193 G5
Cragg Hill 194 B4
Craggan *Moray* 259 J1
Craggan *P&K* 242 D3
Cragganmore 259 J1
Cragganruar 250 B5
Craggie *High* 258 E1
Craggie *High* 274 D7
Craghead 212 B2
Cragside *N'umb* NE65 7PX 220 D1
Craibstone *Aberdeen* 261 G3
Craibstone *Moray* 268 C5
Craichie 252 D5
Craig *A&B* 240 C1
Craig *A&B* 239 F1
Craig *D&G* 216 A4
Craig *High* 265 F6
Craig *High* 265 G7
Craig *SAyr* 224 B5
Craig Berthlwyd 129 G3
Craigans 240 A5
Craigbeg 249 G1
Craig-cefn-parc 128 C2
Craigcleuch 218 B3
Craigculter 269 H5
Craigdallie 244 A2
Craigdam 261 G1
Craigdarroch *D&G* 216 B1
Craigdarroch *EAyr* 225 E5
Craigdhu *D&G* 207 D2
Craigdhu *High* 266 B7
Craigearn 261 F3
Craigellachie 267 K7
Craigellie 269 J4
Craigencallie 215 G3
Craigend *Moray* 267 J6
Craigend *P&K* 243 G2
Craigendive 232 B1
Craigendoran 233 E1
Craigengillan 224 C5
Craigenputtock 216 B2
Craigens 230 A3
Craigglas 240 A5
Craighall 244 A1
Craighat 233 F1
Craighead *Fife* 245 E3
Craighead *High* 266 E5
Craighlaw 215 E4
Craighouse 230 D3
Craigie *Aber* 261 H3
Craigie *Dundee* 244 C4
Craigie *P&K* 251 G5
Craigie *SAyr* 224 C2
Craigie Brae 261 G1
Craigieburn 226 C5
Craigieholm 243 G1
Craigielaw 236 B2
Craiglockhart 235 G2
Craiglug 261 G5
Craigmaud 269 G5
Craigmillar 235 G2
Craigmore 232 C3
Craigmyle House 260 E4
Craignafeoch 232 A2
Craignant 169 F4
Craigneil 214 C2
Craigneuk 234 B4
Craignure 239 G1
Craigo 253 E3
Craigoch 224 A5
Craigow 243 F4
Craigrothie 244 B3
Craigroy Farm 259 J1
Craigruie 241 G3
Craigsanquhar 244 B3
Craigton *Aberdeen* 261 G4
Craigton *Angus* 244 D1
Craigton *Angus* 252 B4
Craigton *High* 266 D7
Craigton *Stir* 234 A1
Craigtown 274 D3
Craig-y-nos 129 E1
Craik *Aber* 260 C2
Craik *ScBord* 227 E5
Crail 245 E4
Crailing 228 A4
Crailinghall 228 A4
Crakehill 202 D5
Crakemarsh 172 B4
Crambe 195 G1
Crambeck Village 195 G1
Cramlington 221 E4
Cramond 235 F2
Cramond Bridge 235 F2
Cranage 171 E1
Cranberry 171 F4
Cranborne 105 G1
Cranbourne 135 E5
Cranbrook *GtLon* 136 D4
Cranbrook *Kent* 123 G5
Cranbrook Common 123 G5
Crane Moor 186 A2
Crane Park Island *Gt Lon* N1C 4PW 11 A7

Cranfield 149 E3
Cranford *Devon* 112 D3
Cranford *GtLon* 136 A5
Cranford St. Andrew 161 E5
Cranford St. John 161 E5
Cranham *Glos* 132 A1
Cranham *GtLon* 137 E4
Crank 183 G3
Cranleigh 121 F4
Cranmer Green 164 B4
Cranmore *IoW* 106 C3
Cranmore *Som* 117 D3
Cranna 268 E5
Crannoch 268 C5
Cranoe 160 C3
Cransford 153 E1
Cranshaws 237 D3
Cranstal 190 C1
Crantock 96 B3
Cranwell 175 F3
Cranwich 163 F3
Cranworth 178 A5
Craobh Haven 239 G4
Crapstone 100 B1
Crarae 240 B5
Crask Inn 273 H6
Crask of Aigas 266 B7
Craskins 260 D4
Craster 229 G5
Craswall 144 B4
Crateford 158 B2
Cratfield 165 E4
Crathes 261 F5
Crathie *Aber* 259 K5
Crathie *High* 258 C5
Crathorne 202 D2
Craven Arms 156 D4
Craw 231 G5
Crawcrook 212 A1
Crawford *Lancs* 183 F2
Crawford *SLan* 226 A3
Crawfordjohn 225 G3
Crawfordton 216 B1
Crawick 225 F3
Crawley *Devon* 103 F2
Crawley *Hants* 119 F4
Crawley *Oxon* 133 F1
Crawley *WSuss* 122 B5
Crawley Down 122 C5
Crawleyside 211 F3
Crawshawbooth 193 E5
Crawton 253 G2
Crawyn 190 B2
Cray *NYorks* 201 E5
Cray *P&K* 251 G3
Cray *Powys* 143 E3
Crayford 137 E5
Crayke 203 E5
Crays Hill 137 G3
Cray's Pond 134 B4
Crazies Hill 134 C4
Creacombe 102 B1
Creagbheitheachain 248 B3
Creagorry (Creag Ghoraidh) 262 C7
Crealy Adventure Park *Devon* EX5 1DR 102 C3
Creamore Bank 170 C4
Creaton 160 C5
Creca 218 A4
Credenhill 145 D3
Crediton 102 B2
Creebridge 215 F4
Creech Heathfield 115 F5
Creech St. Michael 115 F5
Creed 96 D4
Creedy Park 102 B2
Creekmoor 105 F3
Creekmouth 137 D4
Creeting St. Mary 152 B2
Creeton 175 F5
Creetown 215 F5
Creggans 240 C4
Cregneash 190 A5
Cregrina 144 A2
Creich 244 B2
Creigau 131 D3
Creigiau 129 G4
Crelevan 257 K1
Crelly 95 D3
Cremyll 100 A2
Crendell 105 G1
Cressage 157 E2
Cressbrook 185 F5
Cresselly 127 D2
Cressing 151 F5
Cresswell *N'umb* 221 E2
Cresswell *Staffs* 171 G4
Cresswell Quay 127 D2
Creswell 186 C5
Cretingham 152 D2
Cretshengan 231 F3
Crewe *ChesE* 171 E2
Crewe *ChesW&C* 170 B2
Crewe Green 171 E2
Crewgreen 156 C1
Crewkerne 104 A2
Crew's Hole 131 F5
Crewton 173 E4
Crianlarich (A' Chrìon-Làraich) 241 F2
Cribbs Causeway 131 E4
Cribyn 142 B2
Criccieth 167 D4
Crich 173 E2
Crich Carr 173 E2
Crich Common 173 E2
Crich Tramway Village *Derbys* DE4 5DP 173 E2
Crichie 269 H6
Crichton 236 A3
Crick *Mon* 131 D3
Crick *N'hants* 160 A5
Crickadarn 143 G3
Cricket Hill 120 D1
Cricket St. Thomas 103 G2
Crickham 116 B3
Crickheath 169 F5
Crickhowell 130 B1
Cricklade 132 D3
Cricklewood 136 B4
Crickley Hill Country Park *Glos* GL4 8JY 132 B1
Crick's Green 145 F2
Criddlestyle 106 A1
Cridling Stubbs 195 E5

Crieff 243 D2
Crieff Visitor Centre & Caithness Glass P&K PH7 4HQ 243 D2
Criftins (Dudleston Heath) 170 A4
Criggan 97 E3
Criggion 156 B1
Crigglestone 186 A1
Crimble 184 C1
Crimchard 103 G2
Crimdon Park 213 D4
Crimond 269 J5
Crimonmogate 269 J5
Crimplesham 163 E2
Crinan 239 G5
Crinan Ferry 239 G5
Cringleford 178 C5
Cringletie 235 G5
Crinow 127 E1
Cripplestyle 105 G1
Cripp's Corner 110 C1
Crix 137 G1
Crizeley 144 D4
Croalchapel 216 D1
Croasdale 209 D5
Crock Street 103 G1
Crockenhill 123 E2
Crocker End 134 C4
Crockerhill 107 E2
Crockernwell 102 A3
Crockerton 117 F3
Crockerton Green 117 F3
Crocketford (Ninemile Bar) 216 C3
Crockey Hill 195 F3
Crockham Hill 122 D3
Crockhurst Street 123 F4
Crockleford Heath 152 B5
Croes Hywel 130 C1
Croesau Bach 169 F5
Croeserw 129 E3
Croesgoch 140 B4
Croes-lan 141 G3
Croesor 167 F3
Croespenmaen 130 A3
Croesyceiliog Carmar 128 A1
Croesyceiliog Torfaen 130 B2
Croes-y-mwyalch 130 C3
Croes-y-pant 130 C2
Croesywaun 167 E2
Croford 115 E5
Croft Here 145 D1
Croft Leics 160 A3
Croft Lincs 176 D1
Croft Warr 184 A3
Croftamie 233 F1
Crofthead 218 B4
Croftmore 251 D3
Crofton Wilts 119 E2
Crofton WYorks 186 A1
Croft-on-Tees 202 B2
Crofts 216 B3
Crofts of Benachielt 275 G5
Crofts of Buinach 267 J6
Crofts of Haddo 261 G1
Crofty 128 B3
Crogen 168 D4
Croggan 239 G2
Croglin 210 B3
Croick High 266 B2
Croick High 274 D3
Croig 246 D4
Crois Dughaill 254 C3
Croit e Caley 190 A5
Cromarty (Cromba) 266 E5
Crombie 235 E1
Crombie Country Park Angus DD5 3QL 252 D5
Crombie Mill 244 D1
Cromblet 261 F1
Cromdale 259 H2
Cromer Herts 150 A5
Cromer Norf 178 D1
Cromford 173 D2
Cromhall 131 F3
Cromhall Common 131 F4
Cromore 271 G5
Crompton Fold 185 D1
Cromwell 174 C1
Cronberry 225 E3
Crondall 120 C3
Cronk-y-Voddy 190 B3
Cronton 183 F4
Crook Cumb 199 F3
Crook Dur 212 A4
Crook of Devon 243 F4
Crooked Soley 133 F5
Crookedholm 224 C2
Crookham N'umb 228 D3
Crookham WBerks 119 G1
Crookham Eastfield 228 D3
Crookham Village 120 C2
Crooklands 199 G4
Cropredy 147 G3
Cropston 160 A1
Cropthorne 146 B3
Cropton 203 G4
Cropwell Bishop 174 B4
Cropwell Butler 174 B4
Crosbie 232 D5
Crosbost 271 G5
Crosby Cumb 209 D3
Crosby IoM 190 B4
Crosby Mersey 183 E3
Crosby NLincs 187 F1
Crosby Court 202 C3
Crosby Garrett 200 C3
Crosby Ravensworth 200 B1
Crosby Villa 209 D3
Crosby-on-Eden 210 A2
Croscombe 116 C3
Crosemere 170 B5
Crosland Hill 185 F1
Cross Som 116 B2
Cross (Cros) Na H-E. Siar 271 H1
Cross Ash 130 D1
Cross Bank 157 G5
Cross End Bed 149 F2
Cross End Essex 151 G4
Cross Foxes Inn 155 D1
Cross Gates 194 C4
Cross Green Devon 99 D2

Cross Green Staffs 158 B2
Cross Green Suff 152 A2
Cross Green Suff 151 G2
Cross Green Suff 151 G2
Cross Hands Carmar 128 B1
Cross Hands Pembs 127 D1
Cross Hill 173 F3
Cross Hills 193 G3
Cross Houses 157 E2
Cross in Hand 110 A1
Cross Inn Cere 141 G2
Cross Inn Cere 142 B1
Cross Inn RCT 129 G4
Cross Keys 132 A5
Cross Lane 107 E3
Cross Lane Head 157 G3
Cross Lanes Corn 96 B5
Cross Lanes Corn 95 D4
Cross Lanes NYorks 195 E1
Cross Lanes Wrex 170 A3
Cross of Jackston 261 F1
Cross o'th'hands 173 D3
Cross Street 164 C4
Crossaig 231 G3
Crossapol 246 A4
Crossapol 246 A2
Cross-at-Hand 123 G4
Crossbush 108 C3
Crosscanonby 209 D3
Crossdale Street 178 D2
Crossens 183 E1
Crossflatts 194 A3
Crossford D&G 216 C2
Crossford Fife 235 E1
Crossford SLan 234 C5
Crossgate Lincs 176 A5
Crossgate Staffs 171 G4
Crossgatehall 236 A3
Crossgates Fife 235 F1
Crossgates NYorks 204 D4
Crossgates P&K 243 F2
Crossgates Powys 143 G1
Crossgill 192 B1
Crosshands 123 E5
Crosshill Fife 243 G5
Crosshill SAyr 224 B5
Crosshouse 224 B2
Crosskeys 130 B3
Crosskirk 275 F1
Crosslanes 156 C1
Crosslee Renf 233 F3
Crosslee ScBord 227 E4
Crossmichael 216 C2
Crossmoor 192 A4
Crossroads Aber 261 F5
Crossroads EAyr 224 C2
Crossway Mon 130 D1
Crossway Powys 143 G2
Crossway Green Mon 131 E3
Crossway Green Worcs 146 A1
Crossways Dorset 105 D4
Crossways Glos 131 E1
Crosswell 141 E4
Crosthwaite 199 F3
Croston 183 F1
Crostwick 179 D4
Crostwight 179 E3
Crothair 270 D4
Crouch 123 F2
Crouch End 136 B4
Crouch Hill 104 D1
Croucheston 118 B5
Croughton 148 A4
Crovie 269 G4
Crow 106 A2
Crow Edge 185 F2
Crow Green 137 E3
Crow Hill 145 F5
Crowan 94 D3
Crowborough 123 E5
Crowborough Warren 123 E5
Crowcombe 115 E4
Crowdecote 172 C1
Crowden 185 E3
Crowdhill 119 F5
Crowell 134 C3
Crowfield N'hants 148 B3
Crowfield Suff 152 C2
Crowhurst ESuss 110 C2
Crowhurst Surr 122 C4
Crowhurst Lane End 122 C4
Crowland Lincs 162 A1
Crowland Suff 164 B4
Crowlas 94 B3
Crowle NLincs 187 E1
Crowle Worcs 146 B2
Crowle Green 146 B2
Crowmarsh Gifford 134 B4
Crown Corner 165 D4
Crownhill 100 A2
Crownthorpe 178 B5
Crowntown 94 D3
Crow's Nest 97 G3
Crows-an-wra 94 A4
Crowsnest 156 C2
Crowthorne 120 D1
Crowton 183 G5
Croxall 159 E1
Croxby 188 B3
Croxdale 212 B4
Croxden 172 B4
Croxley Green 135 F3
Croxteth Country Park Mersey L12 0HB 22 C1
Croxteth Hall Mersey L12 0HB 22 C1
Croxton Cambs 150 A2
Croxton NLincs 188 A1
Croxton Norf 163 G4
Croxton Staffs 171 E4
Croxton Green 170 C2
Croxton Kerrial 174 D5
Croy High 266 E7
Croy NLan 234 B2
Croyde 113 E2
Croyde Bay 113 E2
Croydon Cambs 150 B3
Croydon GtLon 122 C2
Cruach 268 D6
Cruchie 268 D6
Cruckmeole 156 D2
Cruckton 156 D1

Cruden Bay 261 J1
Crudgington 157 F1
Crudwell 132 B3
Crug 156 A5
Crugmeer 96 D2
Crugybar 142 C4
Crùlabhig 270 D4
Crumlin 130 B3
Crumpsall 184 C2
Crundale Kent 124 C4
Crundale Pembs 126 C1
Crunwere Farm 127 E1
Crutherland Farm 234 A4
Cruwys Morchard 102 B1
Crux Easton 119 F2
Crwbin 128 A1
Cryers Hill 135 D3
Crymlyn 181 E5
Crymych 141 E4
Crynant 129 D2
Crystal Palace 136 C5
Crystal Palace Park GtLon SE20 8DT 13 C7
Cuaig 264 D6
Cubbington 147 F1
Cubert 96 B4
Cubley 185 G2
Cublington Bucks 148 D5
Cublington Here 144 D4
Cuckfield 109 F1
Cucklington 117 E5
Cuckney 186 C5
Cuckold's Green 165 F3
Cuckoo Bridge 176 A5
Cuckoo's Corner 120 B3
Cuckoo's Nest 170 A1
Cuddesdon 134 A2
Cuddington Bucks 134 C1
Cuddington ChesW&C 183 G5
Cuddington Heath 170 B3
Cuddy Hill 192 A4
Cudham 122 D2
Cudliptown 99 F3
Cudworth Som 103 G1
Cudworth SYorks 186 A2
Cuerdley Cross 183 G4
Cuffley 136 C2
Cuidhaseadair 271 H2
Cuidhir 254 B4
Cuidrach 263 J6
Cuilmuich 241 D5
Cuil-uaine 240 B1
Culag 241 F5
Culbo 266 D5
Culbokie (Cùil Bhàicidh) 266 D6
Culbone 114 B3
Culburnie 266 B7
Culcabock 266 D7
Culcharan 240 B1
Culcharry 267 F6
Culcheth 184 A3
Culdrain 260 D1
Culduie 264 D7
Culford 151 G1
Culgaith 210 B5
Culgower 274 E7
Culham 134 A3
Culindrach 232 A4
Culkein 272 C5
Culkerton 132 B3
Cullachie 259 G2
Cullen 268 D4
Cullercoats 221 F4
Cullicudden 266 D5
Culligran 265 K7
Cullingworth 193 G4
Cullipool 239 G4
Cullivoe 278 E2
Culloch 242 C3
Culloden 266 E7
Cullompton 102 D2
Culmaily 267 F2
Culmalzie 215 E5
Culmington 157 D4
Culmstock 103 E2
Culnacraig 265 G1
Culnadalloch 240 B1
Culnaknock 264 B5
Culnamean 255 K2
Culpho 152 D3
Culquhirk 215 F5
Culrain 266 C2
Culross 235 D1
Culroy 224 B4
Culsh 260 B5
Culshabbin 215 E5
Culswick 279 B8
Culter Allers Farm 226 B2
Cultercullen 261 H2
Cults Aber 260 D1
Cults Aberdeen 261 G4
Cults D&G 207 G2
Culverhouse Cross 130 A5
Culverstone Green 123 F2
Culverthorpe 175 F3
Culvie 268 D5
Culworth 148 A3
Culzean Castle & Country Park SAyr KA19 8LE 224 A4
Cumberhead 225 F2
Cumberlow Green 150 B4
Cumbernauld 234 B2
Cumbernorth 189 F5
Cuminestown 269 G6
Cumloden 215 F4
Cummersdale 209 G1
Cummertrees 217 F4
Cummingstown 267 J5
Cumnock 225 D3
Cumnor 133 G2
Cumrew 210 B2
Cumrue 217 E2
Cumstoun 216 A5
Cumwhinton 210 A1
Cumwhitton 210 B2
Cundall 202 D5
Cunninghamhead 233 E5
Cunningsburgh 279 D10

Cunnister 278 E3
Cunnoquhie 244 B3
Cupar 244 B3
Cupar Muir 244 B3
Curbar 185 G5
Curborough 158 D1
Curbridge Hants 107 E1
Curbridge Oxon 133 F2
Curdridge 107 E1
Curdworth 159 D3
Curland 103 F1
Curlew Green 153 E1
Curling Tye Green 138 B2
Curload 116 A5
Curridge 133 G5
Currie 235 F3
Curry Mallet 116 A5
Curry Rivel 116 A5
Curteis' Corner 124 A5
Curtisden Green 123 G4
Curtisknowle 100 D2
Cury 95 D4
Cusgarne 96 B5
Cushnie 269 F4
Cushuish 115 E4
Cusop 144 B3
Cusworth 186 C2
Cutcloy 207 E3
Cutcombe 114 C4
Cutgate 184 C1
Cuthill 266 E3
Cutiau 154 C1
Cutlers Green 151 D4
Cutnall Green 146 A1
Cutsdean 146 C4
Cutsyke 194 D5
Cutthorpe 186 A5
Cutts 279 D9
Cuttyhill 269 J5
Cuxham 134 B3
Cuxton 123 G2
Cuxwold 188 B2
Cwm BGwent 130 A2
Cwm Denb 182 B5
Cwm Ffrwd-oer 130 B2
Cwm Gwaun 140 D4
Cwm Head 156 D4
Cwm Irfon 143 E3
Cwm Penmachno 168 A3
Cwm Plysgog 141 E3
Cwmafan 129 D3
Cwmaman 129 G3
Cwmann 142 B3
Cwmbach Carmar 141 F5
Cwmbach Carmar 128 A2
Cwmbach Powys 144 A4
Cwmbach Powys 143 G3
Cwmbach RCT 129 G2
Cwmbelan 155 F4
Cwmbrân 130 B3
Cwmbrwyno 154 D4
Cwmcarn 130 B3
Cwmcarvan 131 D2
Cwm-Cewydd 155 E1
Cwm-cou 141 F3
Cwmcrawnon 130 A1
Cwmdare 129 G2
Cwmdu Carmar 142 C4
Cwmdu Powys 144 A5
Cwmduad 141 G4
Cwmerfyn 154 D4
Cwmfelin 129 G2
Cwmfelin Boeth 127 E1
Cwmfelin Mynach 141 F5
Cwmfelinfach 130 A3
Cwmffrwd 128 A1
Cwmgiedd 129 D1
Cwmgors 128 D1
Cwmgwili 128 B1
Cwmgwrach 129 E2
Cwmgwyn 128 C3
Cwmhiraeth 141 G4
Cwmifor 142 C5
Cwmisfael 128 A1
Cwm-Llinau 155 E2
Cwmllyfri 127 G1
Cwmllynfell 128 D1
Cwm-mawr 128 B1
Cwm-miles 141 E5
Cwm-Morgan 141 F4
Cwm-parc 129 F3
Cwmpengraig 141 G4
Cwmpennar 129 G2
Cwmsychbant 142 A3
Cwmsymlog 154 C4
Cwm-twrch Isaf 129 D1
Cwm-twrch Uchaf 129 D1
Cwm-y-glo 167 E1
Cwmyoy 144 C5
Cwm-yr-Eglwys 140 D3
Cwmyrhaiadr 155 D5
Cwmystwyth 155 D5
Cwrt 154 C2
Cwrt-newydd 142 A3
Cwrt-y-cadno 142 C3
Cwrt-y-gollen 130 B1
Cyffylliog 169 D2
Cyfronydd 156 A2
Cymau 169 F2
Cymmer NPT 129 E3
Cymmer RCT 129 G3
Cyncoed 130 A4
Cynghordy 143 E4
Cynheidre 128 A2
Cynwyd 169 D3
Cynwyl Elfed 141 G5

D

Dabton 216 C1
Daccombe 101 F1
Dacre Cumb 210 A5
Dacre NYorks 194 A1
Dacre Banks 194 A1
Daddry Shield 211 E4
Dadford 148 B4
Dadlington 159 G3
Dafen 128 B2
Daffy Green 178 A5
Dagdale 172 B4
Dagenham 137 D4
Daggons 106 A1
Daglingworth 132 B2
Dagnall 135 E1
Dail 240 C1
Dail Beag 270 E3
Dail Mòr 270 E3
Dailly 224 A5

Dailnamac 240 B1
Dainton 101 E1
Dairsie (Osnaburgh) 244 C3
Dairy House 197 E5
Daisy Bank 158 C3
Daisy Green 152 B1
Dalabrog 254 C2
Dalavich 240 B3
Dalballoch 258 D5
Dalblair 225 E4
Dalbog 253 D2
Dalbreck 274 C7
Dalbury 173 D4
Dalby IoM 190 A4
Dalby Lincs 176 C1
Dalby NYorks 203 F5
Dalby Forest Drive NYorks YO18 7LT 204 B4
Dalcairnie 224 C5
Dalchalloch 250 C3
Dalchalm 267 G1
Dalchenna 240 C4
Dalchirach 259 J1
Dalchork 273 H7
Dalchreichart 257 J3
Dalchruin 242 C3
Dalcross 266 E7
Dalderby 176 A1
Daldownie 259 K4
Dale Cumb 210 B3
Dale GtMan 185 D2
Dale Pembs 126 B2
Dale Abbey 173 F4
Dale End Derbys 172 D1
Dale End NYorks 193 F3
Dale Head 199 F1
Dale of Walls 279 A7
Dale Park 108 B2
Dalehouse 203 G1
Dalelia 247 G3
Daless 259 F1
Dalestie 259 J2
Dalfad 260 B4
Dalganachan 275 F4
Dalgarven 233 D5
Dalgety Bay 235 F1
Dalgig 225 D4
Dalginross 242 C2
Dalguise 251 E5
Dalhalvaig 274 D3
Dalham 151 F1
Daligan 233 E1
Dalinlongart 232 C1
Dalivaddy 222 B3
Daljarroch 214 C2
Dalkeith 236 A3
Dallachulish 248 B5
Dallas 267 J6
Dallaschyle 267 F7
Dallash 215 F4
Dalleagles 225 D4
Dallinghoo 153 D2
Dallington ESuss 110 B2
Dallington N'hants 148 C1
Dallow 202 A5
Dalmadilly 261 F3
Dalmally (Dail Mhàilidh) 241 D2
Dalmarnock 251 F5
Dalmary 242 A5
Dalmellington 224 C5
Dalmeny 235 F2
Dalmichy 273 H7
Dalmigavie 258 E3
Dalmore 266 D5
Dalmuir 233 F2
Dalmunzie House Hotel 251 J2
Dalnabreck 247 G3
Dalnacarn 251 F3
Dalnaglar Castle 251 G3
Dalnaha 239 F2
Dalnahaitnach 259 F3
Dalnamain 266 E2
Dalnatrat (Dail na Tràghad) 248 B4
Dalnavert 259 F4
Dalnavie 266 D4
Dalness 249 D4
Dalnessie 273 J7
Dalnigap 214 C3
Dalqueich 243 F4
Dalreoch 214 C2
Dalriech 242 C1
Dalroy 266 E7
Dalrulzian 251 G3
Dalry 233 D5
Dalrymple 224 B4
Dalscote 148 B2
Dalserf 234 B5
Dalsetter 278 E3
Dalshangan 215 G2
Dalskairth 216 D3
Dalston 209 G1
Dalswinton 216 D2
Daltomach 258 E2
Dalton Cumb 199 G5
Dalton D&G 217 E3
Dalton Lancs 183 F2
Dalton N'umb 220 D4
Dalton N'umb 211 F2
Dalton NYorks 202 D5
Dalton NYorks 202 A2
Dalton SYorks 186 B3
Dalton Magna 186 B3
Dalton Piercy 213 D4
Dalton-in-Furness 198 D5
Dalton-le-Dale 212 D3
Dalton-on-Tees 202 B2
Daltote 231 F1
Daltra 267 G7
Dalveich 242 B2
Dalvennan 224 B4
Dalvourn 258 D1
Dalwood 103 F2
Dam Green 164 B3
Damask Green 150 A5
Damerham 106 A1
Damgate 179 F5
Damnaglaur 206 B3
Danaway 124 A2
Danby 203 G2

Danby Wiske 202 C3
Dancers Hill 136 B3
Dandaleith 267 K7
Danderhall 236 A3
Dane Bank 184 D3
Dane End 150 B5
Dane Hills 160 A2
Danebridge 171 G1
Danehill 109 G1
Danesmoor 173 E1
Danestone 261 H3
Daniel's Water 124 B4
Danskine 236 C3
Danthorpe 197 E4
Danzey Green 146 D1
Darby End 158 B4
Darby Green 120 D1
Darenth 137 E5
Daresbury 183 G4
Darfield 186 B2
Dargate 124 C2
Dargues 220 A2
Darite 97 G3
Darland 123 G2
Darlaston 158 B3
Darley 194 B2
Darley Bridge 173 D1
Darley Dale 173 D1
Darley Head 194 A2
Darley Hillside 173 D1
Darlingscott 147 E3
Darlington 202 B2
Darliston 170 C4
Darlton 187 E5
Darnabo 269 F6
Darnall 186 A4
Darnconner 225 D3
Darnford 261 F5
Darngarroch 216 A4
Darnick 227 G2
Darowen 155 E2
Darra 269 F6
Darracott 112 C4
Darras Hall 221 D4
Darrington 186 B1
Darrow Green 165 D3
Darsham 153 F1
Dartfield 269 J5
Dartford 137 E5
Dartington 101 D1
Dartington Cider Press Centre Devon TQ9 6TQ 101 D1
Dartington Crystal Ltd. Devon EX38 7AN 113 E4
Dartmeet 99 G3
Dartmouth 101 E2
Darton 186 A1
Darvel 225 D2
Darwell Hole 110 B2
Darwen 192 C5
Datchet 135 E5
Datchworth 136 B1
Datchworth Green 136 B1
Daubhill 184 A2
Daugh of Kinnermony 267 K7
Dauntsey 132 B4
Dauntsey Green 132 B4
Dauntsey Lock 132 B4
Dava 259 H1
Davaar 222 C4
Davan 260 C4
Davenham 184 A5
Davenport Green 184 C4
Daventry 148 A1
Daventry Country Park N'hants NN11 2JB 148 A1
David Marshall Lodge Stir FK8 3SX 242 A4
Davidstow 97 F1
Davington 226 D5
Daviot Aber 261 F2
Daviot High 258 E1
Davoch of Grange 268 C5
Davyhulme 184 B3
Dawley 157 F2
Dawlish 102 C5
Dawn 181 G5
Daws Heath 138 B4
Daw's House 98 D2
Dawsmere 176 C4
Day Green 171 E2
Dayhills 171 G4
Dayhouse Bank 158 B5
Daylesford 147 E5
Ddôl 182 C5
Deadman's Cross 149 G3
Deadwaters 234 B5
Deaf Hill 212 C4
Deal 125 F3
Deal Hall 138 D3
Dean Cumb 209 D4
Dean Devon 100 D1
Dean Dorset 105 F1
Dean Hants 107 E1
Dean Oxon 147 F5
Dean Som 117 D3
Dean Bank 212 B4
Dean Castle & Country Park EAyr KA3 1XB 224 C2
Dean Cross 113 F1
Dean Gallery Edin EH4 3DS 36 B4
Dean Head 185 G2
Dean Prior 100 D1
Dean Row 184 C4
Dean Street 123 G3
Deanburnhaugh 227 E4
Deane GtMan 184 A2
Deane Hants 119 G3
Deanland 105 F1
Deanlane End 107 G1
Deanscales 209 D4
Deansgreen 184 A4
Deanshanger 148 C4
Deanston 242 C4
Dearham 209 D3
Debach 152 D2
Debate 218 A3
Debden 151 D4
Debden Cross 151 D4
Debden Green Essex 51 D4

Debden Green Essex 136 D3
Debenham 152 C1
Deblin's Green 146 A3
Dechmont 235 E2
Decker Hill 157 G1
Deddington 147 G4
Dedham 152 B4
Dedham Heath 152 B4
Dedworth 135 E5
Deecastle 260 C5
Deene 161 E3
Deenethorpe 161 E3
Deep, The HU1 4DP 76 Kingston upon Hull
Deep Sea World, North Queensferry Fife KY11 1JR 235 F1
Deepcar 185 G3
Deepcut 121 E2
Deepdale Cumb 200 C4
Deepdale NYorks 201 D5
Deeping Gate 161 G2
Deeping St. James 161 G2
Deeping St. Nicholas 162 A1
Deepweir 131 D4
Deerhill 268 C5
Deerhurst 146 A5
Deerhurst Walton 146 A5
Deerness Valley Walk Dur DH7 7RJ 212 A3
Deerton Street 124 B2
Defford 146 B3
Defynnog 143 F5
Deganwy 181 F5
Degnish 239 G3
Deighton NYorks 202 C2
Deighton WYorks 185 F1
Deighton York 195 F3
Deiniolen 167 E1
Delabole 97 E1
Delamere 170 C1
Delabole 97 E1
Delamere 170 C1
Delavorar 259 J3
Delfrigs 261 H2
Dell Lodge 259 H3
Dell Quay 108 A3
Delliefure 259 H1
Delly End 133 F1
Delnabo 259 J3
Delny 266 E4
Delph 185 D2
Delphorrie 260 C3
Delves 212 A3
Delvine 251 G5
Dembleby 175 F4
Denaby 186 B3
Denaby Main 186 B3
Denbies Wine Estate Surr RH5 6AA 121 G2
Denbigh (Dinbych) 168 D1
Denbury 101 E1
Denby 173 E3
Denby Dale 185 G2
Denby Pottery Derbys DE5 8NX 18 C1
Denchworth 133 F3
Dendron 198 D5
Denend 260 E1
Denford 161 E5
Dengie 138 C2
Denham Bucks 135 F4
Denham Suff 164 C4
Denham Suff 151 F1
Denham Green 135 F4
Denham Street 164 C4
Denhead Aber 261 F3
Denhead Aber 269 J5
Denhead Fife 244 C3
Denhead of Arbirlot 253 D5
Denhead of Gray 244 B1
Denholm 227 G4
Denholme 193 G4
Denholme Clough 193 G4
Denio 166 C4
Denmead 107 F1
Denmill 261 G3
Denmoss 268 E6
Dennington 153 D1
Denny 234 C1
Dennyloanhead 234 C1
Denshaw 185 D1
Denside 261 G5
Densole 125 E4
Denston 151 F2
Denstone 172 B3
Dent 200 C4
Denton Cambs 161 G4
Denton Darl 202 B1
Denton ESuss 109 G3
Denton GtMan 184 D3
Denton Kent 125 E4
Denton Kent 137 F5
Denton Lincs 175 D4
Denton N'hants 148 D2
Denton Norf 165 D3
Denton NYorks 194 A3
Denton Oxon 134 A2
Denton's Green 183 F3
Denver 163 E2
Denville 178 B5
Denwick 229 G5
Deopham 178 B5
Deopham Green 164 B2
Depden 151 F2
Depden Green 151 F2
Deptford GtLon 136 C5
Deptford Wilts 118 B4
Derby 173 E4
Derby City Museum & Art Gallery DE1 1BS 70 Derby
Derbyhaven 190 A5
Dereham (East Dereham) 178 A4
Dererach 239 E2
Deri 130 A2
Derril 112 D5
Derringstone 125 E4
Derrington 171 F5
Derriton 112 D5
Derry 242 B2
Derry Hill 132 B5
Derrythorpe 187 F2
Dersingham 177 E4
Dervaig 246 D4
Derwen 169 D2

Derwenlas 154 D3
Derwent Walk Country Park
 Dur NE16 3BN 28 A3
Derwydd 128 C1
Derybruich 232 A2
Desborough 160 D4
Desford 159 G2
Detchant 229 E3
Dethick 173 E2
Detling 123 G3
Deuddwr 156 B1
Deuxhill 157 F4
Devauden 131 D3
Devil's Bridge
 (Pontarfynach) 154 D5
Devitts Green 159 E3
Devizes 118 B1
Devon Guild of Craftsmen
 Devon
 TQ13 9AF 102 B5
Devonport 100 A2
Devonside 243 E5
Devoran 95 E3
Dewar 236 A5
Dewlish 105 D3
Dewsall Court 145 D4
Dewsbury 194 B5
Dewsbury Moor 194 B5
Dhiseig 239 D1
Dhoon 190 C3
Dhoor 190 C2
Dhowin 190 C1
Dhuhallow 258 C2
Dial Green 121 E5
Dial Post 109 D2
Dibden 106 D2
Dibden Hill 135 E2
Dibden Purlieu 106 D2
Dick Institute EAyr
 KA1 3BU 224 C5
Dickleburgh 164 C3
Dickleburgh Moor 164 C3
Didbrook 146 C4
Didcot 134 A3
Diddington 149 G1
Diddlebury 157 E4
Didley 145 D4
Didling 108 A2
Didmarton 132 A4
Didsbury 184 C3
Didworthy 100 C1
Digby 175 F2
Digg 263 K5
Diggle 185 E2
Digmoor 183 F2
Digswell 136 B1
Dihewyd 142 A2
Dildawn 216 B5
Dilham 179 E3
Dilhorne 171 G4
Dillington 149 G1
Dilston 211 F1
Dilton 144 D2
Dilton Marsh 117 F3
Dilwyn 144 D2
Dilwyn Common 144 D2
Dimple 184 B1
Dinas Carmar 141 F4
Dinas Gwyn 167 D2
Dinas Gwyn 166 B4
Dinas Cross 140 D4
Dinas Dinlle 166 D2
Dinas Powys 130 A5
Dinas-Mawddwy 155 E1
Dinckley 192 C4
Dinder 116 C3
Dinedor 145 E4
Dingestow 131 D1
Dingley 160 C4
Dingwall (Inbhir
 Pheofharain) 266 C6
Dinlabyre 218 D2
Dinnet 260 C5
Dinnington Som 104 A1
Dinnington SYorks 186 C4
Dinnington T&W 221 E4
Dinorwig 167 E1
Dinosaur Adventure Park
 Norf NR9 5JW 178 C4
Dinosaur Museum,
 Dorchester Dorset
 DT1 1EW 104 C3
Dinton Bucks 134 C1
Dinton Wilts 118 B4
Dinton Pastures Country
 Park W'ham
 RG10 0TH 134 C5
Dinvin 214 B5
Dinwoodie Mains 217 F1
Dinworthy 112 D4
Dipford 115 F5
Dippen A&B 222 C2
Dippen NAyr 223 F3
Dippenhall 120 D3
Dipple Moray 268 B5
Dipple SAyr 224 A5
Diptford 100 D2
Dipton 212 A2
Dirdhu 259 H2
Dirleton 236 C1
Discoed 144 B1
Discovery Museum
 T&W NE1 4JA
 79 Newcastle upon Tyne
Diseworth 173 F5
Dishes 276 F5
Dishforth 202 C5
Dishley 173 G5
Disley 185 D4
Diss 164 C3
Disserth 143 G2
Distington 208 D4
Ditcheat 116 D4
Ditchingham 165 E2
Ditchley 147 F5
Ditchling 109 F2
Ditteridge 117 F1
Dittisham 101 E2
Ditton Halton 183 F4
Ditton Kent 123 G3
Ditton Green 151 E2
Ditton Priors 157 F4
Dixton Glos 146 B4
Dixton Mon 131 E1
Dobcross 185 D2
Dobwalls 97 G3
Doccombe 102 A4
Dochgarroch 258 D1

Dock Museum, Barrow-in-
 Furness Cumb
 LA14 2PW 191 E1
Dockenfield 120 D3
Docker Cumb 199 G3
Docker Lancs 199 G5
Docking 177 F4
Docklow 145 E2
Dockray Cumb 209 G4
Dockray Cumb 209 F1
Dodbrooke 100 D3
Dodbrooke 145 G2
Doddinghurst 137 E3
Doddington Cambs 162 C3
Doddington Kent 124 B3
Doddington Lincs 187 G5
Doddington
 N'umb 229 D3
Doddington Shrop 157 F5
Doddiscombsleigh 102 B4
Doddycross 98 D4
Dodford N'hants 148 B1
Dodford Worcs 158 B5
Dodington SGlos 131 G4
Dodington Som 115 E3
Dodington Ash 131 G5
Dodleston 170 A1
Dods Leigh 172 B4
Dodscott 113 F4
Dodworth 186 A2
Doehole 173 E2
Doffcocker 184 A1
Dog Village 102 C3
Dogdyke 176 A2
Dogmersfield 120 C2
Dogsthorpe 162 A2
Dol Fawr 155 E2
Dolanog 155 G1
Dolau Powys 144 A1
Dolau RCT 129 G4
Dolbenmaen 167 E3
Doley 171 E5
Dolfach 155 F5
Dolfor 156 A4
Dolgarreg 142 D4
Dolgarrog 168 A1
Dolgellau 154 D1
Dolgoch 154 C2
Dolgran 142 A4
Doll 267 F1
Dollar 243 E5
Dollarbeg 243 E5
Dolphin 182 C5
Dolphinholme 192 B2
Dolphinton 235 F5
Dolton 113 F4
Dolwen Conwy 181 G5
Dolwen Powys 155 F2
Dolwyddelan 168 A2
Dôl-y-bont 154 C4
Dol-y-cannau 144 A3
Dolyhir 144 B2
Dolwyern 169 F4
Domgay 156 B1
Doncaster 186 C2
Doncaster Racecourse
 Exhibition Centre
 SYorks DN2 6BB 186 D2
Donhead
 St. Andrew 118 A5
Donhead St. Mary 118 A5
Donibristle 235 F1
Doniford 115 D3
Donington Lincs 176 A4
Donington Shrop 158 A2
Donington le Heath 159 G1
Donington on Bain 188 C4
Donisthorpe 159 F1
Donkey Sanctuary,
 Salcombe Regis Devon
 EX10 0NU 103 E4
Donna Nook 189 E3
Donnington Glos 147 D5
Donnington Here 145 G4
Donnington Shrop 157 E2
Donnington Tel&W 157 G1
Donnington WBerks 119 F1
Donnington WSuss 108 A3
Donyatt 103 G1
Dorchester Dorset 104 C3
Dorchester Oxon 134 A3
Dorchester Abbey Oxon
 OX10 7HH 134 A3
Dordon 159 E2
Dore 186 A4
Dores (Duras) 258 C1
Dorket Head 173 G3
Dorking 121 G2
Dorley's Corner 153 E1
Dormans Park 122 C4
Dormansland 122 D4
Dormanstown 213 E5
Dormer's Wells 136 A4
Dormington 145 E3
Dormston 146 B2
Dorn 147 E4
Dorney 135 E5
Dorney Reach 135 E5
Dornie
 (An Dòrnaidh) 256 E2
Dornoch 266 E3
Dornock 218 A5
Dorrery 275 F3
Dorridge 159 D5
Dorrington Lincs 175 F2
Dorrington Shrop 157 D2
Dorsell 260 D3
Dorsington 146 D3
Dorstone 144 C3
Dorton 134 B1
Dorusduain 257 F2
Dosthill 159 E1
Dotland 211 F2
Dottery 104 A3
Doublebois 97 F3
Dougalston 233 G2
Dougarie 223 D2
Doughton 132 A3
Douglas IoM 190 B4
Douglas SLan 225 G2
Douglas & Angus 244 C1
Douglas Water 225 G2
Douglastown 252 C5
Doulting 116 D3
Dounby 276 B5
Doune A&B 241 F5
Doune A&B 241 F3
Doune High 259 F3

Doune High 266 B1
Doune Stir 242 C4
Dounepark 269 F4
Douneside 260 C4
Dounie High 266 D3
Dounie High 266 C2
Dounreay 274 E2
Dousland 100 B1
Dovaston 170 A5
Dove Holes 185 E5
Dovenby 209 D3
Dovendale 188 D4
Dover 122 D2
Dover Castle Kent
 CT16 1HU 70 Dover
Dovercourt 152 D4
Doverdale 146 A1
Doveridge 172 C4
Doversgreen 122 B4
Dowally 251 F5
Dowdeswell 146 C5
Dowhill 224 A5
Dowlais 129 G2
Dowland 113 F4
Dowlands 103 F3
Down Ampney 132 D3
Down End 116 A3
Down Hatherley 146 A5
Down St. Mary 102 A2
Down Thomas 100 B3
Downderry 98 D5
Downe 122 D2
Downend IoW 107 E4
Downend Essex 137 G3
Downham Lancs 193 D3
Downham N'umb 228 C3
Downham Market 163 E2
Downhead Corn 97 G5
Downhead Som 117 D3
Downhead Som 116 C5
Downholland Cross 183 E2
Downholme 202 A3
Downies 261 H5
Downley 135 D3
Downs 130 B1
Downside NSom 116 B1
Downside Som 116 D2
Downside Som 116 D2
Downside Surr 121 G2
Downton Devon 99 F2
Downton Devon 101 E2
Downton Hants 106 B3
Downton Wilts 118 C5
Downton on the
 Rock 156 D5
Dowsby 175 G5
Dowthwaitehead 209 G4
Doxey 171 G5
Doynton 131 G5
Drabblegate 178 D3
Draethen 130 B4
Draffan 234 B5
Dragley Beck 199 D5
Drakeland Corner 100 B2
Drakelow 158 A4
Drakemyre 233 D4
Drakes Broughton 146 B3
Drakes Cross 158 C5
Draughton N'hants 160 C5
Draughton NYorks 193 G2
Drax 195 F5
Draycot Foliat 133 D5
Draycote 147 G1
Draycott Derbys 173 F4
Draycott Glos 147 D4
Draycott Shrop 158 A3
Draycott Som 116 B2
Draycott Worcs 146 A3
Draycott in the
 Clay 172 C5
Draycott in the
 Moors 171 G4
Drayford 102 A1
Draynes 97 G3
Drayton Leics 160 D3
Drayton Lincs 176 A4
Drayton Norf 178 C4
Drayton Oxon 147 G3
Drayton Oxon 133 G3
Drayton Ports 107 F2
Drayton Som 116 B5
Drayton Warks 147 D2
Drayton Worcs 158 B5
Drayton Bassett 159 D2
Drayton Beauchamp
 135 E2
Drayton Manor Park Staffs
 B78 3TW 159 D2
Drayton Parslow 148 D5
Drayton
 St. Leonard 134 A3
Drebley 193 G2
Dreemskerry 190 C2
Dreenhill 126 C1
Drefach Carmar 141 G4
Drefach Carmar 128 B2
Dre-fach Cere 142 B3
Drefelin 141 G4
Dreghorn 224 B2
Drem 236 C2
Drewsteignton 102 A3
Driby 189 D5
Driffield ERid 196 C2
Driffield Glos 132 C3
Drigg 198 B3
Drighlington 194 B5
Drimfern 240 C3
Drimlee 240 D3
Drimnin 247 E4
Drimore 262 C7
Drimpton 104 A2
Drimsdale
 (Dreumasdal) 254 C1
Drimsynie 241 D4
Drimvore 240 A5
Drinan 256 B3
Dringhouses 195 E2
Drinisiader 263 G2
Drinkstone 152 A1
Drinkstone Green 152 A1
Drishaig 241 D3

Drissaig 240 B3
Drointon 172 B5
Droitwich Spa 146 A1
Dron 243 G3
Dronfield 186 A5
Dronfield
 Woodhouse 186 A5
Drongan 224 C4
Dronley 244 B1
Droop 105 D2
Dropmore 135 E4
Droxford 107 F1
Droylsden 184 D3
Druid 168 D3
Druidston 126 B1
Druimarbin 248 C2
Druimavuic 248 C5
Druimdrishaig 231 F2
Druimindarroch 247 F1
Druimkinnerras 258 B1
Drum A&B 232 B3
Drum P&K 243 F4
Druma-chlog 225 E2
Drumbeg 272 D5
Drumblade 268 D6
Drumblair 268 E6
Drumbuie D&G 225 F4
Drumbuie High 256 D1
Drumburgh 209 F1
Drumchapel 233 G2
Drumchardine 266 C7
Drumchork 264 E3
Drumclog 225 E2
Drumdelgie 268 C6
Drumderfit 266 D6
Drumeldrie 244 C4
Drumelzier 226 C2
Drumfearn 256 C3
Drumfern 248 B2
Drumgarve 222 C3
Drumgley 252 C4
Drumguish 258 E5
Drumhead 260 E5
Drumin 259 J1
Drumlamford
 House 215 D3
Drumlasie 260 E4
Drumlemble 222 B4
Drumlithie 253 F5
Drummond High 266 D5
Drummond Stir 242 B4
Drummore 206 B3
Drummuir 268 B6
Drumnadrochit (Druim na
 Drochaid) 258 C2
Drumnagorrach 268 D5
Drumnatorran 248 A3
Drumoak 261 F5
Drumore 222 C3
Drumour 243 F5
Drumrash 216 A3
Drumrunie 265 H1
Drumsturdy 244 C1
Drumuie 263 K7
Drumuillie 259 G2
Drumvaich 242 B4
Drumwhindle 261 H1
Drumwhirn 216 B2
Drunkendub 253 E5
Druridge 221 E2
Drury 169 F1
Drusillas Park ESuss
 BN26 5QS 110 A3
Drws-y-nant 168 B5
Dry Doddington 174 D3
Dry Drayton 150 B1
Dry Harbour 264 C6
Dry Sandford 133 G2
Dry Street 137 F4
Drybeck 200 B1
Drybridge Moray 268 C4
Drybridge NAyr 224 B2
Drybrook 131 F1
Dryburgh 227 G2
Drygrange 227 G2
Dryhope 227 D3
Drymen 233 F1
Drymuir 269 H6
Drynoch 255 K1
Dryton 157 E2
Duachy 240 A2
Dubford 269 F4
Dubhchladach 231 G3
Dubheads 243 E2
Dublin 152 C1
Dubton 253 D4
Duchal 233 E3
Duchally 273 F7
Duchray 241 G4
Duck Bay 233 E1
Duck End Bed 149 F3
Duck End Cambs 150 A1
Duck End Essex 151 E5
Duck Street 194 A1
Duckington 170 B2
Ducklington 133 F2
Duckmanton 186 B5
Duck's Cross 149 G2
Ducks Island 136 B3
Duddenhoe End 150 C4
Duddington 161 E2
Duddleswick 115 F5
Duddleswell 109 G1
Duddo 237 F5
Duddon 170 C1
Duddon Bridge 198 C4
Dudleston 170 A4
Dudleston Heath
 (Criftins) 170 A4
Dudley T&W 221 E4
Dudley WMid 158 B3
Dudley Port 158 B3
Dudley Zoo & Castle
 W/Mid DY1 4QB 14 B3
Dudlow's Green 184 A4
Dudsbury 105 G3
Duffield 173 E3

Duffryn 129 E3
Dufftown 260 B1
Duffus 267 J5
Dufton 210 C5
Duggleby 196 A1
Duiar 259 J1
Duible 274 E6
Duiletter 241 D2
Duinish 250 B3
Duirinish 256 D1
Duisdealmor 256 D3
Duisky 248 C2
Duke End 159 E4
Dukestown 130 A1
Dukinfield 184 D3
Dulas 180 C4
Dulax 260 B3
Dulcote 116 C3
Dulford 103 D2
Dull 250 D5
Dullatur 234 B2
Dullingham 151 E2
Dullingham Ley 151 E2
Dulnain Bridge 259 G2
Duloe Bed 149 G1
Duloe Corn 97 G4
Dulsie 267 G7
Dulverton 114 C5
Dulwich 136 C5
Dulwich Picture Gallery
 GtLon SE21 7AD 13 C7
Dumbarton 233 E2
Dumbleton 146 C4
Dumcrieff 226 C5
Dumeath 260 C1
Dumfin 233 E1
Dumfries 217 D3
Dumgoyne 233 G1
Dummer 119 G3
Dun 253 E4
Dunach 240 A2
Dunalastair 250 C4
Dunan A&B 232 C2
Dunan High 256 B2
Dunans 240 C5
Dunball 116 A3
Dunbar 237 D2
Dunbeath 275 G5
Dunbeg
 (An Dùn Beag) 240 A1
Dunblane 242 C4
Dunbog 244 A3
Dunbridge 119 E5
Duncanston Aber 260 D2
Duncanston High 266 C6
Dunchideock 102 B4
Dunchurch 159 G5
Duncote 148 B2
Duncow 217 D2
Duncraggan 242 A4
Duncrievie 243 G4
Duncroist 242 A1
Duncrub 243 F3
Duncryne 233 F1
Duncton 108 B2
Dundee 244 C1
Dundee Airport 244 B2
Dundee Contemporary Arts
 DD1 4DY 71 Dundee
Dundon 116 B4
Dundon Hayes 116 B4
Dundonald 224 B2
Dundonnell (Ach-Dà-
 Dhòmhnaill) 265 G3
Dundraw 209 F2
Dundreggan
 (Dul Dreagain) 257 K3
Dundrennan 208 A2
Dundridge 107 E1
Dundry 116 C1
Dunearn 235 G1
Dunecht 261 F4
Dunfermline 235 E1
Dunfield 132 D3
Dunford Bridge 185 F2
Dungate 124 B3
Dungavel 225 E2
Dungworth 185 G3
Dunham 187 F5
Dunham Massey Hall,
 Park & Gardens GtMan
 WA14 4SJ 24 C6
Dunham Town 184 B4
Dunham
 Woodhouses 184 B4
Dunham-on-the-
 Hill 183 F5
Dunhampton 146 A1
Dunholme 188 A5
Dunino 244 D3
Dunipace 234 C1
Dunira 242 B2
Dunkeld 251 F5
Dunkerton 117 E2
Dunkeswell 103 E2
Dunkeswick 194 C3
Dunkirk ChesW&C 183 E5
Dunkirk Kent 124 C3
Dunk's Green 123 F3
Dunlappie 253 D3
Dunley Hants 119 F2
Dunley Worcs 145 G1
Dunlop 233 F5
Dunloskin 232 C2
Dunmere 97 E3
Dunmore A&B 231 F3
Dunmore Falk 234 C1
Dunn 275 G3
Dunn Street 123 G2
Dunnabie 218 A3
Dunnet 275 H1
Dunnichen 252 D5
Dunning 243 F3
Dunnington ERid 197 D2
Dunnington Warks 146 C2
Dunnington York 195 F2
Dunnockshaw 193 E5
Dunoon 232 C2
Dunragit 214 C5
Dunrostan 231 F1
Duns 237 E4
Duns Tew 147 G5
Dunsa 185 G5
Dunsby 175 G5
Dunscore 216 C2
Dunscroft 187 D2
Dunsdale 203 F1
Dunsden Green 134 C5

Dunsfold 121 F4
Dunsford 102 B4
Dunshalt 244 A3
Dunshill 146 A4
Dunsinnan 243 G1
Dunsland Cross 113 E5
Dunsley NYorks 204 B1
Dunsley Staffs 158 A4
Dunsmore 135 D2
Dunsop Bridge 192 C2
Dunstable 149 F5
Dunstable Downs CenBeds
 LU6 2GY 149 F5
Dunstall 172 C5
Dunstall Green 151 F1
Dunstan 229 F5
Dunstan Steads 229 G4
Dunster 114 C3
Dunster Castle & Gardens
 Som TA24 6SL 114 C3
Dunston Lincs 175 F1
Dunston Norf 178 D5
Dunston Staffs 158 B1
Dunston Heath 158 B1
Dunston Hill 212 B1
Dunstone Devon 102 A5
Dunstone Devon 100 B2
Dunsville 187 D2
Dunswell 196 C4
Dunsyre 235 E5
Dunterton 99 D3
Duntisbourne
 Abbots 132 B2
Duntisbourne Leer 132 B2
Duntisbourne
 Rouse 132 B2
Duntish 104 C2
Duntocher 233 F2
Dunton Bucks 148 D5
Dunton CenBeds 150 A3
Dunton Norf 177 G4
Dunton Bassett 160 A3
Dunton Green 123 E3
Dunton Wayletts 137 F3
Duntulm 263 K4
Dunure 224 A4
Dunure Mains 224 A4
Dunvant 128 B3
Dunvegan 263 H7
Dunvegan Castle High
 IV55 8WF 263 H7
Dunwich 165 F4
Dura 244 C3
Durdar 210 A2
Durgan 95 E4
Durgates 123 F5
Durham 212 B2
Durham Cathedral
 DH1 3EH 71 Durham
Durham Dales Centre Dur
 DL13 2FJ 211 G4
Durham Tees Valley
 Airport 202 C1
Durinemast 247 F3
Durisdeer 225 G5
Durleigh 115 F4
Durley Hants 107 E1
Durley Wilts 118 D1
Durley Street 107 E1
Durlow Common 145 F4
Durlston Country
 Park Dorset
 BH19 2JL 105 G5
Durnamuck 265 G2
Durness 273 G2
Durno 261 F2
Duror 248 B4
Durran A&B 240 B4
Durran High 275 G2
Durrants 107 G2
Durrington Wilts 118 C3
Durrington WSuss 108 D3
Dursley 131 G3
Dursley Cross 131 F1
Durston 115 F5
Durweston 105 E2
Dury 279 D6
Duston 148 C1
Duthie Park & David Welch
 Winter Gardens Aberdeen
 AB11 7TH 261 H4
Duthil 259 G2
Dutlas 156 B5
Duton Hill 151 E5
Dutson 98 D2
Dutton 183 G5
Duxford 150 C3
Dwygyfylchi 181 F5
Dwyran 166 D1
Dyce 261 G3
Dyfatty 128 A2
Dyffryn Bridgend 129 E3
Dyffryn Pembs 140 C4
Dyffryn VGlam 129 G5
Dyffryn Ardudwy 167 E5
Dyffryn Castell 155 D4
Dyffryn Ceidrych 142 D5
Dyffryn Cellwen 129 E1
Dyke Devon 113 D3
Dyke Lincs 175 G5
Dyke Moray 267 G6
Dykehead Angus 252 B3
Dykehead NLan 234 C4
Dykehead Stir 242 A5
Dykelands 253 F3
Dykends 252 A4
Dykeside 269 F6
Dylan Thomas Centre
 SA1 1RR 86 Swansea
Dylife 155 E3
Dymchurch 111 G1
Dymock 145 G4
Dyrham 145 G1
Dyrham Park SGlos
 SN14 8ER 8 F2
Dysart 244 B5
Dyserth 182 B5

Eaglesfield Cumb 209 E4
Eaglesfield D&G 218 A4
Eaglesham 233 G4
Eaglethorpe 161 F3
Eagley 184 B1
Eairy 190 A4
Eakley 148 D2
Eakring 174 B1
Ealand 187 E1
Ealing 136 A4
Eamont Bridge 210 B5
Earby 193 F3
Earcroft 192 C5
Eardington 157 G3
Eardisland 144 D2
Eardisley 144 C3
Eardiston Shrop 170 A5
Eardiston Worcs 145 F1
Earith 162 B5
Earl Shilton 159 G3
Earl Soham 152 D1
Earl Sterndale 172 C5
Earl Stonham 152 C2
Earle 229 D4
Earlestown 183 G3
Earley 134 C5
Earlham 178 C5
Earlish 263 J5
Earls Barton 149 D1
Earls Colne 151 G5
Earl's Common 146 B2
Earl's Court 136 B5
Earl's Croome 146 A3
Earl's Green 152 B1
Earlsdon 159 F5
Earlsferry 244 C4
Earlsford 261 G1
Earlsheaton 194 B5
Earlston 227 G2
Earlswood Mon 131 D3
Earlswood Surr 122 B4
Earlswood Warks 158 D5
Earnley 108 A4
Earnshaw Bridge 192 B5
Earsairidh 254 C5
Earsdon 221 F4
Earsdon Moor 221 D2
Earsham 165 E3
Earsham Street 164 D4
Earswick 195 F2
Eartham 108 B3
Earthcott Green 131 F4
Easby 203 E2
Easdale 239 G3
Easebourne 121 D5
Easenhall 159 G5
Eashing 121 E3
Easington Bucks 134 B1
Easington Dur 212 D3
Easington ERid 189 D1
Easington N'umb 229 F3
Easington Oxon 134 B3
Easington Oxon 147 G4
Easington R&C 203 G1
Easington Colliery 212 D3
Easington Lane 212 C3
Easingwold 195 E1
Easole Street 125 E3
Eassie 252 B5
East Aberthaw 114 D1
East Acton 136 B4
East Allington 101 D3
East Anstey 114 B5
East Anton 119 E3
East Appleton 202 B3
East Ardsley 194 C5
East Ashey 107 E4
East Ashling 108 A3
East Ayton 204 C4
East Barkwith 188 B4
East Barming 123 G3
East Barnby 204 B1
East Barnet 136 B3
East Barsham 178 A2
East Beckham 178 C2
East Bedfont 135 F5
East Bergholt 152 B4
East Bierley 194 A5
East Bilney 178 A4
East Blatchington 109 G4
East Boldon 212 C1
East Boldre 106 C2
East Bolton 229 F5
East Bower 116 A4
East Brent 116 A2
East Bridge 153 F1
East Bridgford 174 B3
East Brora 267 G1
East Buckland 113 G2
East Budleigh 103 D4
East Burnham 135 E4
East Burra 279 C9
East Burrafirth 279 C7
East Burton 105 E4
East Butsfield 212 A3
East Butterleigh 102 C2
East Butterwick 187 F2
East Cairnbeg 253 F2
East Calder 235 E3
East Carleton 178 C5
East Carlton
 N'hants 160 D4
East Carlton
 WYorks 194 B3
East Carlton Countryside
 Park N'hants
 LE16 8YF 160 D4
East Chaldon (Chaldon
 Herring) 105 D4
East Challow 133 F4
East Charleton 101 D3
East Chelborough 104 B2
East Chiltington 109 F2
East Chinnock 104 A1
East Chisenbury 118 C2
East Clandon 121 F2
East Claydon 148 C5
East Clyne 267 G1
East Clyth 275 H5
East Coker 104 B1
East Compton
 Dorset 105 E1
East Compton
 Som 116 D3
East Coombe 102 B2
East Cornworthy 101 E2
East Cottingwith 195 G3

East Cowes 107 E3
East Cowick 195 F5
East Cowton 202 C2
East Cramlington 221 E4
East Cranmore 117 D3
East Creech 105 F4
East Croachy 258 D2
East Darlochan 222 B3
East Davoch 260 C4
East Dean ESuss 110 A4
East Dean Hants 107 E2
East Dean WSuss 108 B2
East Dereham
  (Dereham) 178 A4
East Down 113 F1
East Drayton 187 E5
East Dundry 116 C2
East Ella 196 C5
East End ERid 197 D4
East End ERid 197 E5
East End Essex 138 D2
East End Hants 119 F1
East End Hants 106 C3
East End Herts 150 C5
East End Kent 124 A5
East End Kent 124 B1
East End MK 149 E3
East End NSom 131 D5
East End Oxon 133 G2
East End Poole 105 F3
East End Som 116 C2
East End Suff 152 C4
East End Suff 152 C2
East Farleigh 123 G3
East Farndon 160 C4
East Ferry 187 F3
East Firsby 188 A4
East Fleetham 229 G4
East Fortune 236 C2
East Garston 133 F5
East Ginge 133 G4
East Goscote 160 B1
East Grafton 119 D1
East Green Suff 153 F1
East Green Suff 151 F1
East Grimstead 118 D5
East Grinstead 122 C5
East Guldeford 111 E1
East Haddon 148 B1
East Hagbourne 134 A4
East Halton 188 B4
East Ham 136 D4
East Hanney 133 G3
East Hanningfield 137 G2
East Hardwick 186 B1
East Harling 164 A3
East Harlsey 202 D3
East Harnham 118 C5
East Harptree 116 C2
East Hartford 221 E4
East Harting 107 G1
East Hatch 118 A5
East Hatley 150 A2
East Hauxwell 202 A3
East Haven 245 D1
East Heckington 175 G3
East Hedleyhope 212 A4
East Helmsdale 275 F7
East Hendred 133 G4
East Herrington 212 C2
East Heslerton 204 C5
East Hewish 116 B1
East Hoathly 110 A2
East Holme 105 E4
East Horndon 137 F4
East Horrington 116 C3
East Horsley 121 F2
East Horton 229 E3
East Howe 105 G3
East Huntspill 116 A3
East Hyde 136 A1
East Ilsley 133 G4
East Keal 176 B1
East Kennett 118 C1
East Keswick 194 C3
East Kilbride 234 A4
East Kimber 99 E1
East Kirkby 176 B1
East Knapton 204 B5
East Knighton 105 E4
East Knowstone 114 B5
East Knoyle 117 F4
East Kyloe 229 E3
East Lambrook 104 A1
East Lancashire Railway
  Lancs BL9 0EY 193 E5
East Langdon 125 E4
East Langton 160 C3
East Langwell 266 E1
East Lavant 108 A3
East Lavington 108 B2
East Layton 202 A1
East Leake 173 G5
East Learmouth 228 C3
East Learney 260 E4
East Leigh Devon 102 A2
East Leigh Devon 102 A1
East Leigh Devon 101 D2
East Leigh Devon 100 C2
East Lexham 163 G1
East Lilburn 229 E4
East Linton 236 C2
East Liss 120 C5
East Lockinge 133 G4
East Looe 97 G4
East Lound 187 E2
East Lulworth 105 E4
East Lutton 196 B1
East Lydford 116 C4
East Lyn 114 A3
East Lyng 116 A5
East Mains 260 E5
East Malling 123 G3
East Malling Heath 123 F3
East March 244 C1
East Marden 108 A2
East Markham 187 E5
East Martin 105 G1
East Marton 193 F2
East Meon 120 B5
East Mere 102 C1
East Mersea 139 D1
East Mey 275 J1
East Midlands
  Airport 173 F5
East Molesey 121 G1
East Moor 194 C5
East Morden 105 F3

East Morriston 236 D5
East Morton 194 A3
East Ness 203 F5
East Newton 197 E4
East Norton 160 C2
East Oakley 119 G2
East Ogwell 102 B5
East Orchard 105 E1
East Ord 237 G4
East Panson 99 D1
East Parley 106 A3
East Peckham 123 F4
East Pennard 116 C4
East Point Pavilion,
  Lowestoft Suff
  NR33 0AP 165 G2
East Portlemouth 100 D4
East Prawle 101 D4
East Preston 108 C3
East Pulham 104 D2
East Putford 113 D4
East Quantoxhead 115 E3
East Rainton 212 C3
East Ravendale 188 C3
East Raynham 177 G5
East Retford
  (Retford) 187 E4
East Rigton 194 C3
East Rolstone 116 A1
East Rounton 202 D2
East Row 204 B1
East Rudham 177 D1
East Runton 178 D1
East Ruston 179 E3
East Saltoun 236 B3
East Shefford 133 F5
East Sleekburn 221 E3
East Somerton 179 F4
East Stockwith 187 F3
East Stoke Dorset 105 E4
East Stoke Notts 174 C3
East Stour 117 F5
East Stourmouth 125 E2
East Stratton 119 G3
East Street 116 C4
East Studdal 125 F4
East Suisnish 256 B1
East Taphouse 97 F3
East Thirston 221 D2
East Tilbury 137 F5
East Tisted 120 C4
East Torrington 188 B4
East Town 116 D3
East Tuddenham 178 B4
East Tytherley 119 D5
East Tytherton 132 B5
East Village 102 B2
East Wall 157 E3
East Wellow 119 E5
East Walton 163 F1
East Wemyss 244 B5
East Whitburn 235 D3
East Wickham 137 D5
East Williamston 127 D2
East Winch 163 E1
East Winterslow 118 D4
East Wittering 107 G3
East Witton 202 A4
East Woodburn 220 B3
East Woodhay 119 F1
East Woodlands 117 E3
East Worldham 120 C4
East Worlington 102 A1
East Youlstone 112 C4
Eastacott 113 G3
Eastbourne 110 B4
Eastbourne Pier ESuss
  BN21 3EL 72 Eastbourne
Eastbrook 130 A5
Eastburn ERid 196 B2
Eastburn WYorks 193 G3
Eastbury Herts 136 A3
Eastbury WBerks 133 F5
Eastby 193 G2
Eastchurch 124 B1
Eastcombe Glos 132 A2
Eastcombe Som 115 E4
Eastcote GtLon 136 A4
Eastcote N'hants 148 B2
Eastcote WMid 159 D5
Eastcott Corn 112 C4
Eastcott Wilts 118 B2
Eastcourt 132 B3
Eastdown 101 E3
Eastend 147 F5
Easter Ardross 266 D4
Easter Balgedie 243 G4
Easter Balmoral 259 K5
Easter Boleskine 258 C2
Easter Borland 242 B4
Easter Brae 266 D5
Easter Buckieburn 234 B1
Easter Compton 131 E4
Easter Drummond 258 B3
Easter Dullater 242 B4
Easter Ellister 230 A4
Easter Fearn 266 D3
Easter Galcantray 267 F7
Easter Howlaws 237 E5
Easter Kinkell 266 C6
Easter Knox 253 D5
Easter Lednathie 252 B3
Easter Moniack 266 C7
Easter Ord 261 G4
Easter Poldar 242 B5
Easter Skeld (Skeld) 279 C8
Easter Suddie 266 D6
Easter Tulloch 253 F2
Easter Whyntie 268 E4
Eastergate 108 B3
Easterhouse 234 A3
Easterton 118 B2
Easterton Sands 118 B2
Eastertown 116 A2
Eastfield Bristol 131 E5
Eastfield NLan 234 C3
Eastfield NYorks 204 D4
Eastfield Hall 221 E1
Eastgate Dur 211 E4
Eastgate Lincs 161 G1
Eastgate Norf 178 C3
Easthall 150 A5
Eastham Mersey 183 E4
Easthampstead 121 D1
Easthampton 144 D1
Easthaugh 178 B4
Eastheath 120 D1

Easthope 157 E3
Easthorpe Essex 152 A5
Easthorpe Leics 174 D4
Easthorpe Notts 174 C2
Easthouses 236 A3
Eastington Devon 102 A2
Eastington Glos 132 B1
Eastington Glos 131 G2
Eastleach Martin 133 E2
Eastleach Turville 133 E2
Eastleigh Devon 113 E3
Eastleigh Hants 106 D1
Eastling 124 B3
Eastmoor Derbys 186 A5
Eastmoor Norf 163 F2
Eastnor 145 G4
Eastoft 187 F1
Eastoke 107 G3
Easton Cambs 161 G5
Easton Cumb 218 C4
Easton Cumb 209 F1
Easton Devon 102 A4
Easton Dorset 104 C5
Easton Hants 119 G4
Easton IoW 106 C4
Easton Lincs 175 E5
Easton Norf 178 C4
Easton Som 116 C3
Easton Suff 153 D2
Easton Wilts 132 A5
Easton Grey 132 A4
Easton Maudit 149 D2
Easton on the Hill 161 F2
Easton Royal 118 D1
Easton-in-Gordano 131 E5
Eastrea 162 A3
Eastriggs 218 A5
Eastrington 195 G4
Eastry 125 F3
Eastside 277 D8
East-the-Water 113 E3
Eastville 131 F5
Eastwell 174 C5
Eastwick 136 D1
Eastwood Notts 173 F3
Eastwood S'end 138 B4
Eastwood SYorks 186 B3
Eastwood
  WYorks 193 F5
Eastwood End 162 C3
Eathorpe 147 F1
Eaton ChesE 171 F1
Eaton ChesW&C 170 C1
Eaton Leics 174 C5
Eaton Norf 178 D5
Eaton Norf 177 E4
Eaton Notts 187 E5
Eaton Oxon 133 G2
Eaton Shrop 157 E3
Eaton Shrop 156 C4
Eaton Bishop 144 D4
Eaton Bray 149 E5
Eaton Constantine 157 F2
Eaton Ford 149 G2
Eaton Hall 170 B1
Eaton Hastings 133 E3
Eaton Socon 149 G2
Eaton upon Tern 171 D5
Eaves Green 159 E4
Eavestone 194 B1
Ebberston 204 B4
Ebbesborne Wake 118 A5
Ebbw Vale
  (Glynebwy) 130 A2
Ebchester 212 A2
Ebdon 116 A1
Ebford 102 C4
Ebley 132 A2
Ebnal 170 B3
Ebost 255 J1
Ebrington 147 D3
Ebsworthy Town 99 F1
Ecchinswell 119 F2
Ecclaw 237 E3
Ecclefechan 217 F3
Eccles GtMan 184 B3
Eccles Kent 123 G2
Eccles ScBord 237 E5
Eccles Green 144 C3
Eccles Road 164 B2
Ecclesfield 186 A3
Ecclesgreig 253 F3
Eccleshall 171 F5
Eccleshill 194 A4
Ecclesmachan 235 E2
Eccles-on-Sea 179 F3
Eccleston
  ChesW&C 170 B1
Eccleston Lancs 183 G1
Eccleston Mersey 183 F3
Eccup 194 B3
Echt 261 F4
Eckford 228 B4
Eckington Derbys 186 B5
Eckington Worcs 146 B3
Ecton N'hants 148 D1
Ecton Staffs 172 B2
Edale 185 F4
Eday 276 E4
Eday Airfield 276 E4
Edburton 109 E2
Edderside 209 E2
Edderton 266 E3
Eddington 119 E1
Eddleston 235 G5
Eden Camp NYorks
  YO17 6RT 204 B5
Eden Park 122 C2
Eden Project Corn
  PL24 2SG 97 E4
Eden Vale 212 D4
Edenbridge 122 D4
Edendonich 241 D2
Edenfield 184 B1
Edenhall 210 B4
Edenham 175 F5
Edensor 185 G5
Edentaggart 241 G5
Edenthorpe 186 D2
Edern 166 B4
Edgarley 116 C4
Edgbaston 158 C4
Edgcote 148 A3
Edgcott Bucks 148 B5
Edgcott Som 114 B4
Edgcumbe 95 E3
Edge Glos 132 A2
Edge Shrop 156 C2

Edge End 131 E1
Edge Green
  ChesW&C 170 B2
Edge Green GtMan 183 G3
Edge Green Norf 164 B3
Edgebolton 170 C5
Edgefield 178 B2
Edgehead 236 A3
Edgeley 170 C3
Edgerton 185 F1
Edgeworth 132 B2
Edgmond 157 G1
Edgmond Marsh 171 E5
Edgton 156 C4
Edgware 136 B3
Edgworth 184 B1
Edinample 242 B2
Edinbanchory 260 C3
Edinbane 263 J6
Edinbarnet 233 G2
Edinburgh 235 G2
Edinburgh Airport 235 F2
Edinburgh Castle Edin
  EH1 2NG 37 E4
Edinburgh Zoo Edin
  EH12 6TS 32 B1
Edinchip 242 A2
Edingale 159 E1
Edingley 174 B2
Edingthorpe 179 E2
Edingthorpe Green 179 E2
Edington Som 116 A4
Edington Wilts 118 A2
Edintore 268 C6
Edinvale 267 J6
Edistone 112 C3
Edith Weston 161 E2
Edithmead 116 A3
Edlaston 172 C3
Edlesborough 135 E1
Edlington 188 B5
Edmondsham 105 G1
Edmondsley 212 B3
Edmondthorpe 161 D1
Edmonstone 276 E5
Edmonton Corn 97 D2
Edmonton GtLon 136 C3
Edmundbyers 211 G2
Ednam 228 B3
Ednaston 172 D3
Edney Common 137 F2
Edra 241 G3
Edradynate 251 D4
Edrom 237 F4
Edstaston 170 C4
Edstone 147 D1
Edvin Loach 145 F2
Edwalton 173 G4
Edwardstone 152 A3
Edwardsville 129 G3
Edwinsford 142 C4
Edwinstowe 174 B1
Edworth 150 A3
Edwyn Ralph 145 F2
Edzell 253 E3
Efail Isaf 129 G4
Efail-fâch 129 D3
Efailnewydd 166 C4
Efailwen 141 E5
Efenechtyd 169 E2
Effingham 121 G2
Effirth 279 C7
Efflinch 159 D1
Efford 102 B2
Egbury 119 F2
Egdean 121 E5
Egdon 146 B2
Egerton GtMan 184 B1
Egerton Kent 124 A4
Egerton Forstal 124 A4
Egerton Green 170 C2
Egg Buckland 100 A2
Eggborough 195 E5
Eggerness 207 E2
Eggesford Barton 113 G4
Eggington 149 E5
Egginton 173 D5
Egglescliffe 202 D1
Eggleston 211 F5
Egham 135 F5
Egham Wick 135 E5
Egilsay 276 D5
Egleton 161 D2
Eglingham 229 E5
Eglinton 233 E5
Egloshayle 97 E2
Egloskerry 97 G1
Eglwys Cross 170 B3
Eglwys Fach 154 C3
Eglwys Nunydd 129 E4
Eglwysbach 181 G5
Eglwys-Brewis 114 D1
Eglwyswrw 141 E4
Egmanton 174 C1
Egmere 178 A2
Egremont 208 D5
Egton 204 B2
Egton Bridge 204 B2
Egypt 119 G2
Eiamoor Back 131 E5
Eignaig 247 G5
Eil 259 F3
Eilanreach 256 E3
Eildon 227 G2
Eilean Darach 265 H3
Eilean Donan Castle High
  IV40 8DX 256 E2
Eilean Shona 247 F2
Eisgean 271 F6
Eisingrug 167 F2
Eisteddfa Gurig 155 D4
Elan Valley Visitor Centre
  Powys LD6 5HP 143 F1
Elan Village 143 F2
Elberton 131 F4
Elborough 116 A2
Elburton 100 B2
Elcho 243 G2
Elcombe 132 D4
Elder Street 151 E4
Eldernell 162 B3
Eldersfield 145 G4

Elderslie 233 F3
Eldon 212 B5
Eldrick 215 D2
Eldroth 193 D1
Eldwick 194 A3
Elemore Vale 212 C3
Elford N'umb 229 F4
Elford Staffs 159 D1
Elford Closes 162 D5
Elgin 267 K5
Elgol 256 B3
Elham 125 D4
Elie 244 C4
Elilaw 220 B1
Elim 180 B4
Eling Hants 106 C1
Eling WBerks 134 A5
Eling Tide Mill Hants
  SO40 9HF 4 A3
Eliock 225 G4
Elishader 263 K5
Elishaw 220 A1
Elkesley 187 D5
Elkington 160 B5
Elkstone 132 B1
Elland 194 A5
Elland Upper Edge 194 A5
Ellary 231 F2
Ellastone 172 C3
Ellbridge 100 A1
Ellel 192 A2
Ellemford 237 E3
Ellenabeich 239 G3
Ellenborough 208 D3
Ellenhall 171 F5
Ellen's Green 121 F4
Ellerbeck 202 D3
Ellerburn 204 B4
Ellerby 203 G1
Ellerdine 170 D5
Ellerdine Heath 170 D5
Elleric (Eileinig) 248 C5
Ellerker 196 B5
Ellerton ERid 195 G3
Ellerton NYorks 202 B3
Ellerton Shrop 171 E5
Ellerton Abbey 201 F3
Ellesborough 134 D2
Ellesmere 170 A4
Ellesmere Park 184 B3
Ellesmere Port 183 F5
Ellingham Hants 106 A2
Ellingham N'umb 229 F5
Ellingham Norf 165 E2
Ellingstring 202 A4
Ellington Cambs 161 G5
Ellington N'umb 221 E2
Ellington Thorpe 161 G5
Elliot 245 E1
Elliot's Green 117 E3
Ellisfield 120 B3
Ellistown 159 G1
Ellon Aber 261 H1
Ellonby 210 A4
Ellough 165 F3
Ellough Moor 165 F3
Elloughton 196 B5
Ellwood 131 E2
Elm 162 C2
Elm Park 137 E4
Elmbridge 146 B1
Elmdon Essex 150 C4
Elmdon WMid 159 D4
Elmdon Heath 159 D4
Elmers End 122 C2
Elmer's Green 183 F2
Elmesthorpe 159 G3
Elmhurst 158 D1
Elmley Castle 146 B3
Elmley Lovett 146 A1
Elmore 131 G1
Elmore Back 131 G1
Elmscott 112 C3
Elmsett 152 B3
Elmstead Essex 152 B5
Elmstead GtLon 136 D5
Elmstead Market 152 B5
Elmstone 125 E2
Elmstone
  Hardwicke 146 B5
Elmswell ERid 196 B2
Elmswell Suff 152 A1
Elmton 186 C5
Elphin 272 E7
Elphinstone 236 A2
Elrick Aber 261 G4
Elrick Moray 260 C2
Elrig 206 D2
Elrigbeag 240 D3
Elsdon 220 B2
Elsecar 186 A3
Elsecar Heritage Centre
  SYorks S74 8HJ 186 A3
Elsenham 150 D5
Elsfield 134 A1
Elsham 188 A1
Elsing 178 B4
Elslack 193 F3
Elson Hants 107 F2
Elson Shrop 170 A4
Elsrickle 235 E5
Elstead 121 E3
Elsted 108 A2
Elsthorpe 175 F5
Elstob 212 C5
Elston Lancs 192 B4
Elston Notts 174 C3
Elstone 113 G4
Elstow 149 F3
Elstree 136 A3
Elstronwick 197 E4
Elswick 192 A4
Elsworth 150 B1
Elterwater 199 E2
Eltham 136 D5
Eltisley 150 A2
Elton Cambs 161 F3
Elton ChesW&C 183 F5
Elton Derbys 172 D1
Elton Glos 131 G1
Elton GtMan 184 B1
Elton Here 157 D5
Elton Notts 174 D5
Elton Stock 202 D1
Elton Green 183 F5
Elvanfoot 226 A4
Elvaston 173 F4
Elvaston Castle Country Park
  Derbys DE72 3EP 18 C4

Elveden 163 G5
Elvingston 236 B2
Elvington Kent 125 E3
Elvington York 195 G3
Elwick Hart 213 D4
Elwick N'umb 229 F3
Elworth 171 E1
Elworthy 115 D4
Ely Cambs 162 D5
Ely Cardiff 130 A5
Emberton 149 D3
Emberton Country Park
  MK MK46 5FJ 149 D2
Embleton Cumb 209 E3
Embleton Hart 212 D5
Embleton N'umb 229 G4
Embo 267 F2
Embo Street 267 F2
Emborough 116 D2
Embsay 193 G2
Embsay Steam Railway
  NYorks
  BD23 6AF 193 G2
Emerson Park 137 E4
Emery Down 106 B2
Emley 185 G1
Emmington 134 C2
Emneth 162 C2
Emneth Hungate 162 D2
Empingham 161 E2
Empshott 120 C4
Empshott Green 120 C4
Emsworth 107 G2
Enborne 119 F1
Enborne Row 119 F1
Enchmarsh 157 E3
Enderby 160 A3
Endmoor 199 G4
Endon 171 G2
Endon Bank 171 G2
Enfield 136 C3
Enfield Wash 136 C3
Enford 118 C2
Engine Common 131 F4
Englefield 134 B5
Englefield Green 135 E5
Englesea-brook 171 E2
Elenaberch 239 G3
English Bicknor 131 E1
English Frankton 170 B5
Englishcombe 117 E1
Enham Alamein 119 E3
Enmore 115 F4
Ennerdale
  Bridge 209 D3
Enniscaven 97 D4
Ennochdhu 251 F3
Ensay 246 C5
Ensdon 156 D1
Ensis 113 F3
Enson 171 G5
Enstone 147 F5
Enterkinfoot 225 G3
Enterpen 203 D2
Enton Green 121 E3
Enville 158 A4
Eolaigearraidh 254 C4
Eorabus 238 C2
Eorodal 271 H1
Eoropaidh 271 H1
Epney 131 G2
Epperstone 174 B3
Epping 137 D3
Epping Green
  Essex 136 D2
Epping Green
  Herts 136 B2
Epping Upland 136 D2
Eppleby 202 B1
Eppleworth 196 C4
Epsom 122 B2
Epwell 147 F3
Epworth 187 E2
Epworth Turbary 187 E2
Erbistock 170 A3
Erbusaig 256 D2
Erchless Castle 266 B7
Erdington 158 D3
Eredine 240 B4
Eriboll 273 G3
Ericstane 226 B4
Eridge Green 123 E5
Eriff 224 D5
Erines 231 G2
Erisey Barton 95 E5
Eriswell 163 F5
Erith 137 E5
Erlestoke 118 A2
Ermington 100 C2
Ernesettle 100 A1
Erpingham 178 C2
Erringden Grange 193 F5
Errogie (Earagaidh) 258 C2
Errol 244 A2
Errollston 261 J1
Erskine 233 F2
Ervie 214 A4
Erwarton 152 D4
Erwood 143 G3
Eryholme 202 C2
Eryrys 169 F2
Escart 231 G3
Escart Farm 231 G4
Escomb 212 A5
Escrick 195 F3
Esgair 141 G5
Esgairgeiliog 155 D2
Esgyryn 181 G5
Esh 212 A3
Esh Winning 212 A3
Esher 121 G1
Eshott 221 E2
Eshton 193 F2
Eskadale 258 B1
Eskbank 236 A3
Eskdale Green 198 C2
Eskdalemuir 218 A2
Eskham 189 D3
Esknish 230 B3
Esperley Lane Ends 212 A5
Espley Hall 221 D2
Esprick 192 A4
Essendine 161 F1
Essendon 136 B2
Essich 258 D1
Essington 158 B2
Esslemont 261 H2

Eston 203 E1
Eswick 279 D7
Etal 228 D3
Etchilhampton 118 B1
Etchingham 110 C1
Etchinghill Kent 125 D5
Etchinghill Staffs 158 C1
Etherdwick Grange 197 E4
Etherley Dene 212 A5
Etherow Country Park
  GtMan SK6 5JQ 25 H5
Ethie Mains 253 E5
Eton 135 E5
Eton Wick 135 E5
Etteridge 258 D5
Ettiley Heath 171 E1
Ettington 147 E3
Etton ERid 196 B3
Etton Peter 161 G2
Ettrick 227 D4
Ettrickbridge 227 E3
Ettrickhill 227 D4
Etwall 173 D4
Eudon George 157 F4
Eurach 240 A4
Eureka! Museum for
  Children WYorks
  HX1 2NE 26 B4
Euston 163 G5
Euxton 183 G1
Evanstown 129 F4
Evanton 266 D5
Evedon 175 F3
Evelix 266 E2
Evenjobb 144 B1
Evenley 148 A4
Evenlode 147 E5
Evenwood 212 A5
Evenwood Gate 212 A5
Everbay 276 F5
Evercreech 116 D4
Everdon 148 A2
Everleigh 118 D2
Everley High 275 J2
Everley NYorks 204 C4
Eversholt 149 E4
Evershot 104 B2
Eversley 120 C1
Eversley Cross 120 C1
Everthorpe 196 B4
Everton CenBeds 150 A2
Everton Hants 106 A4
Everton Mersey 183 E3
Everton Notts 187 D3
Evertown 218 B4
Eves Corner 138 C3
Evesbatch 145 F3
Evesham 146 C3
Evesham Country Park
  Shopping & Garden
  Centre Worcs
  WR11 4TP 146 C3
Evie 276 C5
Evington 160 B2
Ewart Newtown 229 D3
Ewden Village 185 G3
Ewell 122 B2
Ewell Minnis 125 E4
Ewelme 134 B3
Ewen 132 C3
Ewenny 129 F5
Ewerby 175 G3
Ewerby Thorpe 175 G3
Ewhurst 121 F3
Ewhurst Green
  ESuss 110 C1
Ewhurst Green Surr 121 F4
Ewloe 170 A1
Ewloe Green 169 F1
Ewood 192 C5
Ewood Bridge 193 D5
Eworthy 99 E1
Ewshot 120 D3
Ewyas Harold 144 C5
Exbourne 113 G5
Exbury 106 D2
Exbury Gardens Hants
  SO45 1AZ 4 B6
Exceat 110 A4
Exebridge 114 C5
Exelby 202 B4
Exeter 102 C3
Exeter Cathedral Devon
  EX1 1HS 72 Exeter
Exeter International
  Airport 102 C3
Exford 114 B4
Exfords Green 157 D2
Exhall Warks 146 D2
Exhall Warks 159 F4
Exlade Street 134 B4
Exminster 102 C4
Exmoor International Dark
  Sky Reserve Devon/Som.
  114 A3
Exmouth 102 D4
Exnaboe 279 F9
Exning 151 E1
Explore-At-Bristol
  BS1 5DB 66 Bristol
Exton Devon 102 C4
Exton Hants 120 B5
Exton Rut 161 E1
Exton Som 114 C4
Exwick 102 C3
Eyam 185 G5
Eydon 148 A3
Eye Here 145 D1
Eye Peter 162 A2
Eye Suff 164 C4
Eye Green 162 A2
Eyeworth 150 A3
Eyhorne Street 124 A3
Eyke 153 E2
Eynesbury 149 G2
Eynort 255 J2
Eynsford 123 E2
Eynsham 133 G2
Eype 104 A3
Eyre 263 K6
Eythorne 125 E4
Eyton Here 145 D1
Eyton Shrop 156 C4
Eyton on Severn 157 E2
Eyton upon the Weald
  Moors 157 F1

F

Faccombe 119 E2
Fachwen 167 E1
Facit 184 E1
Faddiley 170 C2
Fadmoor 203 F4
Faebait 266 B6
Faifley 233 G2
Fail 224 C3
Failand 131 E5
Failford 224 C3
Failsworth 184 C2
Fain 265 H4
Fair Isle 278 A1
Fair Isle Airstrip 278 A1
Fair Oak Devon 102 D1
Fair Oak Hants 107 D1
Fair Oak Hants 119 G1
Fair Oak Green 120 B1
Fairbourne 154 C1
Fairburn 195 D5
Fairfield Derbys 185 E5
Fairfield GtMan 184 D3
Fairfield Kent 111 E1
Fairfield Mersey 183 D4
Fairfield Stock 202 D1
Fairfield Worcs 158 B5
Fairfield Halls, Croydon
    GtLon CR9 1DG 122 C3
Fairford 132 D2
Fairgirth 216 C5
Fairhaven 191 G5
Fairhill 234 B4
Fairholm 234 B4
Fairley 261 G4
Fairlie 232 D4
Fairlight 111 D2
Fairlight Cove 111 D2
Fairmile Devon 103 D3
Fairmile Surr 121 G1
Fairmilehead 235 G3
Fairnington 228 A4
Fairoak 171 E4
Fairseat 123 F2
Fairstead 137 G1
Fairwarp 109 G1
Fairwater 130 A5
Fairy Cross 113 E3
Fairyhill 128 A3
Fakenham 178 A3
Fakenham Magna 164 A4
Fala 236 B3
Fala Dam 236 B3
Falahill 236 A4
Faldingworth 188 A4
Falfield Fife 244 C4
Falfield SGlos 131 F3
Falin-Wnda 141 G3
Falkenham 153 D4
Falkirk 234 C2
Falkirk Wheel Falk
    FK1 4RS 234 C1
Falkland 244 A4
Falla 228 B5
Fallgate 173 E1
Fallin 242 D5
Falmer 109 F3
Falmouth 95 F3
Falsgrave 204 D4
Falstone 219 F3
Famous Grouse Experience,
    Glenturret Distillery
    P&K PH7 4HA 243 D2
Fanagmore 272 D4
Fanans 240 C2
Fancott 149 F5
Fangdale Beck 203 E3
Fangfoss 195 G2
Fankerton 234 B1
Fanmore 246 D5
Fanner's Green 137 F1
Fans 236 D5
Fantasy Island Lincs
    PE25 1RH 177 D1
Far Cotton 148 C2
Far Forest 157 G5
Far Gearstones 200 C4
Far Green 131 G2
Far Moor 183 G2
Far Oakridge 132 B2
Far Royds 194 B4
Far Sawrey 199 E3
Farcet 162 A3
Farden 157 E5
Fareham 107 E2
Farewell 158 C1
Farforth 188 D5
Faringdon 133 E3
Farington 192 B5
Farlam 210 B2
Farlary 266 E1
Farleigh NSom 116 C1
Farleigh Surr 122 C2
Farleigh Hungerford
    117 F2
Farleigh Wallop 120 B3
Farlesthorpe 189 E5
Farleton Cumb 199 G4
Farleton Lancs 192 B1
Farley Derbys 173 D1
Farley Shrop 156 C2
Farley Staffs 172 B3
Farley Wilts 118 D5
Farley Green Suff 151 G2
Farley Green Surr 121 F3
Farley Hill 120 C1
Farleys End 131 G1
Farlington 195 F1
Farlow 157 F4
Farm Town 159 F4
Farmborough 117 D1
Farmcote 146 C5
Farmington 132 D1
Farmoor 133 G2
Farmtown 268 D5
Farnborough
    GtLon 122 D2
Farnborough
    Hants 121 D2
Farnborough
    Warks 147 G3
Farnborough
    WBerks 133 G4

Farnborough Street 121 D2
Farncombe 121 E3
Farndish 149 E1
Farndon ChesW&C 170 B2
Farndon Notts 174 C2
Farne Islands 229 G3
Farnell 253 E4
Farnham Dorset 105 F1
Farnham Essex 150 C5
Farnham NYorks 194 C1
Farnham Suff 153 E1
Farnham Surr 120 D3
Farnham Common 135 E4
Farnham Green 150 C5
Farnham Royal 135 E4
Farningham 123 E2
Farnley NYorks 194 B3
Farnley WYorks 194 B4
Farnley Tyas 185 F1
Farnsfield 174 B2
Farnworth GtMan 184 B2
Farnworth Halton 183 G4
Farr High 274 C2
Farr High 258 D1
Farr High 259 F4
Farr House 258 D1
Farraline 258 C2
Farringdon 102 D3
Farrington Gurney 116 D2
Farsley 194 B4
Farthing Corner 124 A2
Farthing Green 124 A4
Farthinghoe 148 A4
Farthingstone 148 B2
Farthorpe 188 C5
Fartown 185 F1
Farway 103 E3
Fasag 264 E6
Fasagrianach 265 H3
Fascadale 247 E2
Faslane 232 D1
Fasnacloich 248 C5
Fasnakyle 257 K2
Fassfern 248 C2
Fatfield 212 C2
Fattahead 268 E5
Faugh 210 B2
Fauldhouse 234 D4
Faulkbourne 137 G1
Faulkland 117 E2
Fauls 170 C4
Faulston 118 B5
Faversham 124 C2
Favillar 259 K1
Fawdington 202 D5
Fawdon 212 B1
Fawfieldhead 172 B1
Fawkham Green 123 E2
Fawler 133 F1
Fawley Bucks 134 C4
Fawley Hants 107 D2
Fawley WBerks 133 F4
Fawley Chapel 145 E5
Fawsyde 253 G2
Faxfleet 196 A5
Faxton 160 C5
Faygate 122 B5
Fazeley 159 E2
Fearby 202 A4
Fearn 267 F4
Fearnan 250 C5
Fearnbeg 264 D6
Fearnhead 184 A3
Fearnmore 264 D5
Fearnoch A&B 232 B2
Fearnoch A&B 232 A1
Featherstone
    Staffs 158 B2
Featherstone
    WYorks 194 D5
Featherstone Castle 210 C1
Feckenham 146 C1
Feering 151 G1
Feetham 201 E3
Feith-hill 268 E6
Feizor 193 D1
Felbridge 122 C5
Felbrigg 178 D2
Felcourt 122 C4
Felden 135 F2
Felhampton 156 D4
Felindre Carmar 142 D5
Felindre Carmar 142 B5
Felindre Carmar 141 G4
Felindre Carmar 142 C4
Felindre Cere 142 B2
Felindre Powys 156 A4
Felindre Powys 144 A5
Felindre Swan 128 B2
Felinfach Cere 142 B2
Felinfach Powys 143 G4
Felinfoel 128 B2
Felingwmisaf 142 B5
Felingwmuchaf 142 B5
Felixkirk 203 D4
Felixstowe 153 E4
Felixstowe Ferry 153 E4
Felkington 237 G5
Felldownhead 99 D2
Felling 212 B1
Fellonmore 239 F2
Felmersham 149 E2
Felmingham 179 D3
Felpham 108 B4
Felsham 152 A2
Felsted 151 E5
Feltham 136 A5
Felthamhill 136 A5
Felthorpe 178 C4
Felton N'umb 221 D1
Felton NSom 116 C1
Felton Butler 156 C1
Feltwell 163 F3
Fen Ditton 150 C1
Fen Drayton 150 B1
Fen End 159 E5
Fen Street Norf 164 A2
Fen Street Norf 164 B4
Fen Street Suff 164 B5
Fen Street Suff 152 C1
Fenay Bridge 185 F1
Fence 193 E4
Fence Houses 212 C2
Fencott 134 A1

Fendike Corner 176 C1
Fenham 229 E2
Fenhouses 176 A3
Feniscowles 192 C5
Feniton 103 E3
Fenn Street 137 G5
Fenni-fach 143 G3
Fenny Bentley 172 C2
Fenny Bridges 103 E3
Fenny Compton 147 G2
Fenny Drayton 159 F3
Fenny Stratford 149 D4
Fenrother 221 D2
Fenstanton 150 B1
Fenton Cambs 162 B5
Fenton Lincs 187 F5
Fenton Lincs 175 D2
Fenton N'umb 229 D3
Fenton Notts 187 E4
Fenton Stoke 171 F3
Fenton Barns 236 C1
Fenwick EAyr 233 F5
Fenwick N'umb 220 C4
Fenwick N'umb 229 E3
Fenwick SYorks 186 C1
Feochaig 222 C4
Feock 95 F3
Feolin 230 D3
Feolin Ferry 230 C3
Feorlan 222 B5
Feorlin 230 B1
Ferens Art Gallery
    HU1 3RA
    76 Kingston upon Hull
Ferguslie Park 233 F3
Feriniquarrie 263 G6
Fern 252 C3
Ferndale 129 F3
Ferndown 105 G2
Fernham 133 E3
Fernhill Heath 146 A2
Fernhurst 121 D5
Fernie 244 B3
Fernilea 255 J1
Fernilee 185 E5
Fernybank 252 D2
Ferrensby 194 C1
Ferrindonald 256 C4
Ferring 108 C3
Ferry Hill 162 B4
Ferrybridge 195 D5
Ferryden 253 F4
Ferryhill 212 B4
Ferryside
    (Glanyferi) 127 G1
Fersfield 164 B3
Fersit 249 E1
Ferwig 141 E3
Feshiebridge 259 F4
Festival Park BGwent
    NP23 8FP 130 A2
Fetcham 121 G2
Fetlar 278 F3
Fetlar Airport 278 F3
Fetterangus 269 H5
Fettercairn 253 E2
Fetternear House 261 F3
Feus of Caldhame 253 E3
Fewcott 148 A5
Fewston 194 A2
Ffairfach 142 C5
Ffaldybrenin 142 C3
Ffarmers 142 C3
Ffawyddog 130 B1
Ffestiniog
    (Llan Ffestiniog) 168 A3
Ffestiniog Railway Gwyn
    LL49 9NF 167 F3
Fforddlas Denb 169 E1
Fforddlas Powys 144 B4
Fforest 128 B2
Fforest-fach 128 C3
Ffostrasol 141 G3
Ffos-y-ffin 142 A1
Ffridd Uchaf 167 E2
Ffrith Denb 182 B4
Ffrith Flints 169 F2
Ffrwdgrech 143 G5
Ffynnon 127 G1
Ffynnongroyw 182 C4
Fibhig 270 E3
Fichlie 260 C3
Fidden 238 C2
Fiddington Glos 146 B4
Fiddington Som 115 F3
Fiddleford 105 E1
Fiddler's Green
    Glos 146 B5
Fiddler's Green
    Here 145 E4
Fiddler's Green
    Norf 163 G1
Fiddler's Green
    Norf 164 B2
Fiddlers Hamlet 137 D2
Field 172 B4
Field Broughton 199 E4
Field Dalling 178 B2
Field Head 159 G2
Fife Keith 268 C5
Fifehead Magdalen 117 E5
Fifehead Neville 105 D1
Fifehead
    St. Quintin 105 D1
Fifield Oxon 133 E1
Fifield W&M 135 E5
Fifield Bavant 118 B5
Figheldean 118 C3
Filby 179 F4
Filey 205 E4
Filgrave 149 D3
Filham 100 C2
Filkins 133 E3
Filleigh Devon 113 G3
Filleigh Devon 102 A1
Fillingham 187 G4
Fillongley 159 E4
Filmore Hill 120 B5
Filton 131 F5
Fimber 196 A1
Finavon 252 C4
Fincham 163 E2
Finchampstead 120 C1

Finchdean 107 G1
Finchingfield 151 E4
Finchley 136 B3
Findern 173 E4
Findhorn 267 H5
Findhorn Bridge 259 F2
Findo Gask 243 F2
Findochty 268 C4
Findon Aber 261 H5
Findon WSuss 108 D3
Findon Mains 266 D5
Findon Valley 108 D3
Findrassie 267 J5
Findron 259 J3
Finedon 161 E5
Finegand 251 G3
Fingal Street 164 D4
Fingask 261 F2
Fingerpost 157 G5
Fingest 134 C3
Finghall 202 A4
Fingland Cumb 209 F1
Fingland D&G 226 A3
Fingland D&G 225 F4
Finglesham 125 F3
Fingringhoe 152 B5
Finkle Street 186 A3
Finlarig 242 A1
Finmere 148 B4
Finnart A&B 241 E5
Finnart P&K 250 A4
Finney Hill 159 G1
Finningham 152 B1
Finningley 187 D3
Finnygaud 268 E5
Finsbury
    (Fionnsbhagh) 263 F3
Finsbury 136 C4
Finstall 158 B5
Finsthwaite 199 E4
Finstock 133 F1
Finstown 277 C6
Fintry Aber 269 F5
Fintry Stir 234 A1
Finwood 147 D1
Finzean 260 D5
Fir Tree 212 A4
Firbank 200 B3
Firbeck 186 C4
Firby NYorks 203 F5
Firby NYorks 195 G1
Firgrove 184 D1
Firs Lane 184 A2
Firsby 176 C1
Firsdown 118 D4
Firth 278 D5
Fishbourne IoW 107 E3
Fishbourne WSuss
    108 A1
Fishburn 212 C4
Fishcross 243 E5
Fisherford 261 F1
Fishers Farm Park WSuss
    RH14 0EG 121 F5
Fisher's Pond 119 F5
Fisher's Row 191 G3
Fishersgate 109 E3
Fisherstreet 121 E4
Fisherton High 266 E6
Fisherton SAyr 224 A4
Fisherton de la
    Mere 118 A4
Fishguard
    (Abergwaun) 140 C4
Fishlake 187 D1
Fishleigh Barton 113 F3
Fishley 179 F4
Fishnish 247 F5
Fishpond Bottom 103 G3
Fishponds 131 F5
Fishpool 184 C2
Fishtoft 176 B3
Fishtoft Drove 176 B3
Fishtown of Usan 253 F4
Fishwick 237 G4
Fiskavaig 255 J1
Fiskerton Lincs 188 A5
Fiskerton Notts 174 C2
Fitling 197 E4
Fittleton 118 C3
Fittleworth 108 C2
Fitton End 162 C1
Fitz 156 D1
Fitzhead 115 E5
Fitzroy 115 E5
Fitzwilliam 186 B1
Fitzwilliam Museum
    Cambs CB2 1RB
    66 Cambridge
Fiunary 247 F5
Five Acres 131 E1
Five Ash Down 109 G1
Five Ashes 110 A1
Five Bridges 145 F3
Five Houses 106 D4
Five Lanes 130 C4
Five Oak Green 123 F4
Five Oaks Chanl 100 C5
Five Oaks WSuss 121 F5
Five Roads 128 A2
Five Turnings 156 B5
Five Wents 124 A3
Fivehead 116 A5
Fivelanes 97 G1
Flack's Green 137 G1
Flackwell Heath 135 D4
Fladbury 146 B3
Fladdabister 279 D9
Flagg 172 C1
Flambards Experience, The
    Corn TR13 0QA 95 D4
Flamborough 205 F4
Flamborough Cliffs Nature
    Reserve ERid YO15 1BJ
    205 F5
Flamingo Land Theme
    Park NYorks
    YO17 6UX 203 G4
Flamingo Park,
    Hastings ESuss
    TN34 3AR 110 D3
Flamstead 135 F1
Flamstead End 136 C2
Flansham 108 B3
Flanshaw 194 C5
Flasby 193 F2
Flash 172 B1

Flashader 263 J6
Flask Inn 204 C2
Flatts Lane Woodland
    Country Park R&C
    TS6 0NN 29 D4
Flaunden 135 F2
Flawborough 174 C3
Flawith 195 D1
Flax Bourton 116 C1
Flax Moss 193 D5
Flaxby 194 C2
Flaxholme 173 E3
Flaxlands 164 C2
Flaxley 131 G1
Flaxpool 115 E4
Flaxton 195 F1
Fleckney 160 B3
Flecknoe 148 A1
Fledborough 187 F5
Fleet Hants 120 D2
Fleet Hants 107 G2
Fleet Lincs 176 B5
Fleet Air Arm Museum
    Som BA22 8HT 116 C5
Fleet Hargate 176 B5
Fleetville 136 B5
Fleetwood 191 G3
Fleggburgh (Burgh St.
    Margaret) 179 F4
Flemingston 129 G5
Flemington 234 A4
Flempton 151 G1
Fleoideabhagh 263 F3
Flesherin 271 H4
Fletchersbridge 97 F3
Fletchertown 209 F2
Fletching 109 G1
Fleuchats 260 B4
Fleur-de-lis 130 A3
Flexbury 112 C5
Flexford 121 E2
Flimby 208 D3
Flimwell 123 G5
Flint (Y Fflint) 182 D5
Flint Cross 150 C3
Flint Mountain 182 D5
Flintham 174 C3
Flinton 197 E4
Flint's Green 159 E4
Flishinghurst 123 G5
Flitcham 177 F5
Flitholme 200 C1
Flitton 149 F4
Flitwick 149 F4
Flixborough 187 F1
Flixton GtMan 184 B3
Flixton NYorks 204 D5
Flixton Suff 165 E3
Flockton 185 G1
Flockton Green 185 G1
Flodden 228 D3
Flodigarry 263 K4
Flood's Ferry 162 B3
Flookburgh 199 E5
Floors 268 C5
Flordon 164 C2
Flore 148 B1
Flotta 277 C8
Flotterton 220 C1
Flowton 152 B3
Flushdyke 194 B5
Flushing Aber 269 J6
Flushing Corn 95 F3
Flushing Corn 95 H5
Fluxton 103 D3
Flyford Flavell 146 B2
Foals Green 165 D4
Fobbing 137 G4
Fochabers 268 B5
Fochriw 130 A2
Fockerby 187 F1
Fodderletter 259 J2
Fodderty 266 C6
Foddington 116 C5
Foel 155 F1
Foelgastell 128 B1
Foffarty 252 C5
Fogg 237 E5
Fogorig 237 E5
Fogwatt 267 K6
Foindle 272 D4
Folda 251 G3
Fole 172 B4
Foleshill 159 F4
Folke 104 C1
Folkestone 125 E5
Folkingham 175 F4
Folkington 110 A3
Folksworth 161 G4
Folkton 205 D5
Folla Rule 261 F1
Follifoot 194 C2
Folly Dorset 104 D2
Folly Pembs 140 C5
Folly Farm, Begelly Pembs
    SA68 0XA 127 E2
Folly Gate 99 F1
Fonmon 115 D1
Fonthill Bishop 118 A4
Fonthill Gifford 118 A4
Fontmell Magna 105 E1
Fontmell Parva 105 E1
Fontwell 108 B3
Font-y-gary 115 D1
Foolow 185 F5
Footherley 158 D2
Foots Cray 137 D5
Forbestown 260 B3
Force Forge 199 E3
Force Green 122 D3
Forcett 202 A1
Forches Cross 102 A2
Ford A&B 240 A4
Ford Bucks 134 C1
Ford Devon 100 C3
Ford Devon 113 E3
Ford Devon 101 D5
Ford Glos 146 C5
Ford Mersey 183 E3
Ford Midlo 236 A3
Ford N'umb 229 D3
Ford Pembs 140 C5
Ford Plym 100 C5
Ford Shrop 156 D1
Ford Som 115 D5
Ford Staffs 172 B2
Ford Wilts 132 A5
Ford WSuss 108 B3

Ford End 137 F1
Ford Green 192 A3
Ford Heath 156 D1
Ford Street 103 E1
Forda 99 F1
Fordbridge 159 D4
Fordcombe 123 E4
Fordell 235 F1
Forden (Fforddun) 156 B2
Forder Green 101 D1
Fordgate 116 A4
Fordham Cambs 163 E5
Fordham Essex 152 A5
Fordham Norf 163 E3
Fordham Abbey 163 E5
Fordham Heath 152 A5
Fordhouses 158 B2
Fordon 205 D5
Fordoun 253 F2
Fordstreet 152 A5
Fordwells 133 F1
Fordwich 125 D3
Fordyce 268 D4
Forebrae 243 E2
Forebridge 171 G5
Foredale 193 E1
Foreland 230 A3
Foremark 173 E5
Foremark Reservoir Derbys
    DE65 6EG 173 E5
Forest 202 B2
Forest Coal Pit 144 B5
Forest Gate 136 D4
Forest Green 121 G3
Forest Hall Cumb 199 G2
Forest Hall T&W 212 B1
Forest Head 210 B2
Forest Hill GtLon 136 C5
Forest Hill Oxon 134 A2
Forest Lane Head 194 C2
Forest Lodge (Taigh na
    Frithe) A&B 249 E5
Forest Lodge P&K 251 E2
Forest Row 122 D5
Forest Side 107 D4
Forest Town 173 G1
Forestburn Gate 220 D2
Forest-in-Teesdale 211 E3
Forestmill 243 E5
Forestside 107 G1
Forfar 252 C4
Forfar Loch Country Park
    Angus DD8 1BT 252 C4
Forgandenny 243 F3
Forge 155 D3
Forgie 268 B5
Forhill 158 C5
Formby 183 D2
Forncett End 164 C2
Forncett St. Mary 164 C2
Forncett St. Peter 164 C2
Forneth 251 F5
Fornham All Saints 151 G1
Fornham St. Martin
    151 G1
Fornighty 267 G6
Forres 267 H6
Forrest 234 C3
Forrest Lodge 215 G2
Forsbrook 171 G3
Forse 275 H5
Forse 275 F2
Forsinain 274 E4
Forsinard 274 D4
Forston 104 C3
Fort Augustus (Cille
    Chuimein) 257 K4
Fort Fun, Eastbourne
    ESuss BN22 7LQ 110 B3
Fort George 266 E6
Fort William
    (An Gearasdan) 248 D2
Forter 251 G3
Forteviot 243 F3
Forth 234 D4
Forthampton 146 A4
Fortingall 250 C5
Fortis Green 136 B4
Forton Hants 119 F3
Forton Lancs 192 A2
Forton Shrop 156 D1
Forton Som 103 G2
Forton Staffs 171 E5
Fortrie 268 E6
Fortrose
    (A'Chananaich) 266 E6
Fortuneswell 104 C5
Forty Green 135 E3
Forty Hill 136 C3
Forward Green 152 B2
Fosbury 119 E2
Foscot 147 E5
Fosdyke 176 B4
Foss 250 C4
Foss Cross 132 C2
Fossdale 201 D3
Fossebridge 132 C1
Foster Street 137 D2
Fosterhouses 186 D1
Foster's Booth 148 B2
Foston Derbys 172 C4
Foston Leics 160 B3
Foston Lincs 175 D3
Foston NYorks 195 F1
Foston on the
    Wolds 196 D2
Fotherby 188 D3
Fotheringhay 161 F3
Foubister 277 E7
Foul Mile 110 B2
Foula 278 A4
Foula Airstrip 278 B1
Foulden Norf 163 F3
Foulden ScBord 237 G4
Foulness Island 138 D3
Foulsham 178 B3
Foulstone 199 G4
Foulzie 269 F4
Fountainhall 236 B5
Four Ashes Staffs 158 B2
Four Ashes Staffs 158 B4
Four Ashes Suff 164 A4
Four Crosses
    Denb 168 D3

Four Crosses
    Powys 156 B1
Four Crosses
    Powys 155 G2
Four Crosses
    Staffs 158 B2
Four Elms 123 D4
Four Forks 115 F4
Four Gotes 162 C1
Four Lane Ends
    B'burn 192 C5
Four Lane Ends
    ChesW&C 170 C1
Four Lane Ends
    York 195 F2
Four Lanes 95 D3
Four Marks 120 B4
Four Mile Bridge 180 A5
Four Oaks ESuss 111 D1
Four Oaks Glos 145 F5
Four Oaks WMid 159 E4
Four Oaks WMid 158 D5
Four Oaks Park 158 D3
Four Roads 128 A2
Four Throws 110 C1
Fourlane Ends 173 E1
Fourlanes End 171 F2
Fourpenny 267 F2
Fourstones 211 E1
Fovant 118 B5
Foveran House 261 H2
Fowey 97 F4
Fowlis 244 B1
Fowlis Wester 243 E2
Fowlmere 150 C3
Fownhope 145 E4
Fox Hatch 137 E3
Fox Lane 121 D2
Fox Street 152 B5
Fox Up 201 D5
Foxbar 233 F3
Foxcombe Hill 133 G2
Foxcote Glos 132 C1
Foxcote Som 117 E2
Foxdale 190 A4
Foxearth 151 G3
Foxfield 198 D4
Foxham 132 B5
Foxhole Corn 97 D4
Foxhole High 258 C1
Foxholes 204 D5
Foxhunt Green 110 A2
Foxley Here 144 D3
Foxley N'hants 148 B2
Foxley Norf 178 B3
Foxley Wilts 132 A4
Foxt 172 B3
Foxton Cambs 150 C3
Foxton Dur 212 C4
Foxton Leics 160 B3
Foxton Locks Leics
    LE16 7RA 160 B4
Foxwist Green 170 C1
Foy 145 E5
Foyers (Foithir) 258 C2
Frachadil 246 C4
Fraddam 94 C3
Fraddon 96 D4
Fradley 159 D1
Fradswell 171 G4
Fraisthorpe 197 D1
Framfield 109 G1
Framingham Earl 179 D5
Framingham Pigot 179 D5
Framlingham 153 D1
Frampton Dorset 104 C3
Frampton Lincs 176 B3
Frampton Cotterell 131 F4
Frampton Mansell 132 B2
Frampton on
    Severn 131 G2
Frampton West
    End 176 A3
Framsden 152 D2
Framwellgate Moor 212 B3
France Lynch 132 B2
Frances Green 192 C4
Franche 158 A5
Frandley 184 A5
Frankby 182 D4
Frankfort 179 E3
Frankley 158 B4
Franksbridge 144 A2
Frankton 159 G5
Frant 123 E5
Fraserburgh 269 H4
Frating 152 B5
Fratton 107 F2
Freasley 159 E3
Freathy 99 D5
Freckenham 163 E5
Freckleton 192 A5
Freeby 174 D5
Freefolk 119 F3
Freehay 172 B3
Freeland 133 G1
Freester 279 D7
Freethorpe
    Common 179 F5
Freiston 176 B3
Freiston Shore 176 B3
Fremington Devon 113 F2
Fremington NYorks 201 F3
French Brothers Cruises
    W&M SL4 5JH 135 E5
Frenchay 131 F5
Frenchbeer 99 G2
Frendraught 268 E6
Frenich 241 G4
Frensham 120 D3
Fresgoe 274 E2
Freshbrook 132 D4
Freshfield 183 D2
Freshford 117 E2
Freshwater 106 C4
Freshwater Bay 106 C4
Freshwater East 126 D3
Fressingfield 165 D4
Freston 152 C4
Freswick 275 J2
Fretherne 131 G2
Frettenham 178 D4
Freuchie 244 A4
Freystrop Cross 126 C1
Friars, The, Aylesford Kent
    ME20 7BX 123 G3
Friars Carse 216 D2

Friar's Gate 123 D5
Friarton 243 G2
Friday Bridge 162 C2
Friday Street ESuss 110 B3
Friday Street Suff 152 D2
Friday Street Suff 153 E2
Friday Street Surr 121 G3
Fridaythorpe 196 A2
Friern Barnet 136 B3
Frieston 175 E3
Frieth 134 C3
Frilford 133 G3
Frilsham 134 A5
Frimley 121 D2
Frimley Green 121 D2
Frindsbury 123 G2
Fring 177 F4
Fringford 148 B5
Friningham 124 A3
Frinsted 124 A3
Frinton-on-Sea 139 F1
Friockheim 253 D5
Friog 154 C1
Frisby on the
   Wreake 160 B1
Friskney 176 C2
Friskney
   Eaudyke 176 C2
Friston ESuss 110 A4
Friston Suff 153 F1
Fritchley 173 E2
Frith 124 B3
Frith Bank 176 B3
Frith Common 145 F1
Fritham 106 B1
Frithelstock 113 E4
Frithelstock
   Stone 113 E4
Frithville 176 B2
Frittenden 124 A4
Frittiscombe 101 E3
Fritton Norf 164 D2
Fritton Norf 179 F5
Fritwell 148 A5
Frizinghall 194 A4
Frizington 208 D5
Frocester 131 G2
Frochas 156 B2
Frodesley 157 E2
Frodesley Lane 157 E2
Frodingham 187 F1
Frodsham 183 G5
Frog End 150 C2
Frog Pool 145 G1
Frogden 228 B4
Froggatt 185 G5
Froghall 172 B3
Frogham 106 A1
Frogland Cross 131 F4
Frogmore Devon 101 D3
Frogmore Hants 120 D2
Frogmore Herts 136 A2
Frogwell 98 D4
Frolesworth 160 A3
Frome 117 E3
Frome Market 117 F2
Frome St. Quintin 104 B2
Frome Whitfield 104 C3
Fromes Hill 145 F3
Fron Gwyn 166 C4
Fron Powys 156 B2
Fron Powys 143 G1
Fron Powys 156 A3
Fron Isaf 169 F3
Froncysyllte 169 F3
Fron-goch 168 C4
Frostenden 165 F3
Frosterley 211 G4
Froxfield 119 E1
Froxfield Green 120 C5
Fruitmarket Gallery Edin
   EH1 1DF 37 G4
Fryerning 137 F2
Fugglestone
   St. Peter 118 C4
Fulbeck 175 E2
Fulbourn 150 D2
Fulbrook 133 E1
Fulflood 119 F5
Fulford Som 115 F5
Fulford Staffs 171 G4
Fulford York 195 F3
Fulham 136 B5
Fulking 109 E2
Full Sutton 195 G2
Fullaford 113 G2
Fuller Street 137 G1
Fuller's Moor 170 B2
Fullerton 119 E4
Fulletby 188 C5
Fullwood 233 F4
Fulmer 135 F4
Fulmodeston 178 A2
Fulnetby 188 B5
Fulready 147 E3
Fulstone 185 F2
Fulstow 188 D3
Fulwell Oxon 147 F5
Fulwell T&W 212 C2
Fulwood Lancs 192 B4
Fulwood SYorks 186 A4
Fun Farm, Spalding Lincs
   PE12 6JU 176 A5
Fundenhall 164 C2
Fundenhall
   Street 164 C2
Funtington 108 A3
Funtley 107 F2
Funzie 278 F3
Furley 103 F2
Furnace A&B 240 C4
Furnace Carmar 128 B2
Furnace Cere 154 C4
Furnace High 265 F4
Furner's Green 109 G1
Furneux Pelham 150 C5
Furnham 103 G2
Further Quarter 124 A5
Furtho 148 C3
Furze Green 164 D3
Furze Platt 135 D4
Furzehill Devon 114 A3
Furzehill Dorset 105 G2
Furzeley Corner 107 F1
Furzey Lodge 106 C2

Furzley 106 B1
Fyfett 103 F1
Fyfield Essex 137 E2
Fyfield Glos 133 E2
Fyfield Hants 119 D3
Fyfield Oxon 133 G3
Fyfield Wilts 118 C1
Fyfield Wilts 118 C1
Fylingthorpe 204 C2
Fyning 120 D5
Fyvie 261 F1

G
Gabalfa 130 A5
Gabhsunn Bho
   Dheas 271 G2
Gabhsunn Bho
   Thuath 271 G2
Gablon 266 C2
Gabroc Hill 233 F4
Gaddesby 160 B1
Gaddesden Row 135 F1
Gadebridge 135 F2
Gadshill 137 G5
Gaer Newport 130 B4
Gaer Powys 144 A5
Gaer-fawr 130 D3
Gaerllwyd 130 D3
Gaerwen 180 C5
Gagingwell 147 G5
Gaich High 259 H2
Gaich High 258 D1
Gaick Lodge 250 C1
Gailes 224 B2
Gailey 158 B1
Gainford 202 A1
Gainsborough 187 F3
Gainsford End 151 F4
Gairloch
   (Geàrrloch) 264 D4
Gairlochy (Geàrr
   Lòchaidh) 249 D1
Gairney Bank 243 G5
Gairnshiel Lodge 259 K4
Gaitsgill 209 G2
Galabank 236 B5
Galashiels 227 F2
Galdenoch 214 C4
Gale 184 D1
Galgate 192 A2
Galhampton 116 D5
Gallanach 240 A2
Gallantry Bank 170 C2
Gallatown 244 A5
Gallchoille 239 G5
Gallery 253 E2
Gallery of Modern Art,
   Glasgow Glas
   G1 3AH 39 F4
Galley Common 159 F3
Galleyend 137 G2
Galleywood 137 G2
Galloway Forest Dark Sky
   Park D & G 215 F2
Gallowfauld 252 C5
Gallowhill 233 F3
Gallows Green 172 B3
Gallowstree
   Common 134 B4
Gallowstree Elm 158 A4
Galltair 252 E3
Gallt-y-foel 167 E1
Gallypot Street 123 D5
Galmington 115 F5
Galmisdale 247 D1
Galmpton Devon 100 C3
Galmpton Torbay 101 E2
Galmpton
   Warborough 101 E2
Galphay 202 B5
Galston 224 C2
Galtrigill 263 G6
Gamble's Green 137 G1
Gamblesby 210 C4
Gamelsby 209 F1
Gamesley 185 E3
Gamlingay 150 A2
Gamlingay Cinques 150 A2
Gamlingay Great
   Heath 150 A2
Gammaton 113 E3
Gammaton Moor 113 E3
Gammersgill 201 F4
Gamrie 269 F4
Gamston Notts 187 E5
Gamston Notts 174 B4
Ganarew 131 E1
Gang 98 D4
Ganllwyd 168 A5
Gannochy 253 E2
Ganstead 197 D4
Ganthorpe 203 F5
Ganton 204 C5
Ganwick Corner 136 B3
Gaodhail 239 F1
Gappah 102 B5
Gara Bridge 100 D2
Garabal 241 F3
Garadheancal 265 F1
Garbat 266 B5
Garbhallt 240 C5
Garboldisham 164 B3
Garden 242 A5
Garden City 170 A1
Garden Village 185 G3
Gardeners Green 120 D1
Gardenstown 269 F4
Garderhouse 279 C8
Gardham 196 B3
Gare Hill 117 E3
Garford 133 G3
Garforth 194 D4
Gargrave 193 F2
Gargunnock 242 C5
Gariob 231 F1
Garlic Street 164 D3
Garlies Castle 215 F4
Garlieston 207 E2
Garlinge Green 124 D3
Garlogie 261 F4
Garmelow 171 F5
Garmond 269 G5
Garmony 247 F5
Garmouth 268 B4
Garmston 157 F2
Garnant 128 C1

Garndolbenmaen 167 D3
Garneddwen 155 D2
Garnett Bridge 199 G3
Garnfadryn 166 B4
Garnswllt 128 C2
Garrabost 271 H4
Garrachra 232 B1
Garralburn 268 C5
Garras 95 E4
Garreg 167 E3
Garreg Bank 156 B1
Garrick 242 D3
Garrigill 210 D3
Garriston 202 A3
Garroch 215 G2
Garrochty 232 B4
Garros 263 K5
Garrow 242 D1
Garryhorn 215 G1
Garrynahine (Gearraidh na
   h-Aibhne) 270 D4
Garsdale 200 C4
Garsdale Head 200 C3
Garsdon 132 B4
Garshall Green 171 G4
Garsington 134 A2
Garstang 192 A3
Garston 183 F4
Garswood 183 G3
Gartachoil 242 A5
Gartally 258 B1
Gartavaich 231 G4
Gartbreck 230 A4
Gartcosh 234 A3
Garth Bridgend 129 E3
Garth Cere 154 C4
Garth Gwyn 181 D5
Garth IoM 190 B4
Garth Powys 143 F3
Garth Shet 279 B7
Garth Wrex 169 F3
Garth Row 199 G3
Garthbrengy 143 G4
Garthdee 261 H4
Gartheli 142 B2
Garthmyl 156 A3
Garthorpe Leics 174 D5
Garthorpe NLincs 187 F1
Garths 199 G3
Garthynty 142 D3
Gartincaber 242 B4
Gartly 260 D1
Gartmore 242 A4
Gartnagrenach 231 F4
Gartnatra 230 B3
Gartness 233 G1
Gartocharn 233 F1
Garton 197 E4
Garton-on-the-
   Wolds 196 B1
Gartymore 275 F7
Garvald 236 C2
Garvamore 258 C5
Garvan 248 B2
Garvard 238 C5
Garve (Clachan
   Ghairbh) 265 K5
Garveld 222 B5
Garvestone 178 B5
Garvie 232 B1
Garvock Aber 253 F2
Garvock Invcly 233 D2
Garvock P&K 243 F3
Garwald 226 D5
Garwaldwaterfoot 226 D5
Garway 145 D5
Garway Hill 144 D5
Gask Aber 269 J6
Gask Aber 269 F6
Gask P&K 243 E3
Gaskan 248 A2
Gass 224 C5
Gastard 117 F1
Gasthorpe 164 A3
Gaston Green 137 E1
Gatcombe 107 D4
Gate Burton 187 F4
Gate Helmsley 195 F2
Gateacre 183 F4
Gateford 186 C4
Gateforth 195 E5
Gatehead 224 B2
Gatehouse 251 D5
Gatehouse of Fleet 216 A5
Gatelawbridge 216 D1
Gateley 178 B3
Gatenby 202 C4
Gatesgarth 209 E5
Gateshaw 228 B4
Gateshead 212 B1
Gatesheath 170 B1
Gateside Aber 260 E3
Gateside Angus 252 C5
Gateside Fife 243 G4
Gateside NAyr 233 E4
Gateslack 225 G5
Gathurst 183 G2
Gatley 184 C4
Gattonside 227 G2
Gatwick Airport 122 B4
Gaufron 143 F1
Gaulby 160 B2
Gauldry 244 B2
Gauntons Bank 170 C3
Gaunt's Common 105 G2
Gaunt's Earthcott 131 F4
Gautby 188 B5
Gavinton 237 D3
Gawber 186 A2
Gawcott 148 B4
Gawsworth 184 C5
Gawthrop 200 B4
Gawthwaite 199 D4
Gay Bowers 137 G2
Gay Street 121 F5
Gaydon 147 F2
Gayhurst 148 D3
Gayle 201 E4
Gayles 202 A2
Gayton Mersey 183 D4
Gayton N'hants 148 C2
Gayton Norf 163 F1
Gayton Staffs 171 G5
Gayton le Marsh 189 E4
Gayton le Wold 188 C4
Gayton Thorpe 163 F1

Gaywood 177 E5
Gazeley 151 F1
Geanies House 267 F4
Gearach 230 A4
Gearnsary 274 C3
Gearradh 248 B3
Gearraidh Bhailteas
   254 C2
Gearraidh Bhaird 271 F5
Gearraidh na
   Monadh 254 C3
Gearrannan 270 D3
Geary 263 H5
Gedding 152 A2
Geddington 161 D4
Gedgrave Hall 153 F3
Gedintailor 256 B1
Gedling 174 B3
Gedney 176 C5
Gedney Broadgate 176 C5
Gedney Drove End 176 C5
Gedney Dyke 176 C5
Gedney Hill 162 B1
Gee Cross 185 D3
Geilston 233 E2
Geirinis 262 C7
Geisiadar 270 D4
Geldeston 165 E2
Gell Conwy 168 B1
Gell Gwyn 167 D4
Gelli Conwy 168 B1
Gelli Gwyn 167 D4
Gelli Aur Country
   Park Carmar
   SA32 8LR 142 C5
Gelli Gynan 169 E2
Gellideg 129 G2
Gellifor 169 E1
Gelligaer 130 A3
Gellilydan 167 F4
Gellioedd 168 C3
Gelly 127 D1
Gellyburn 243 F1
Gelston D&G 216 B5
Gelston Lincs 175 E3
Gembling 196 D2
Genoch 214 C5
Genoch Square 214 C5
Gentleshaw 158 C1
Geocrab 263 G2
George Green 135 F4
George Nympton 114 A5
Georgeham 113 E2
Georgetown 233 F3
Gerlan 167 F1
Germansweek 99 E1
Germoe 94 C4
Gerrans 95 E4
Gerrards Cross 135 F4
Gerston 275 G3
Gestingthorpe 151 G4
Geufron 155 E4
Gibbet Hill 117 E3
Gibbshill 216 B3
Gibraltar Lincs 177 D2
Gibraltar Suff 152 C2
Gibraltar Point National
   Nature Reserve Lincs
   PE24 4SU 177 D2
Gibside T&W
   NE16 6BG 212 A2
Giddeahall 132 A5
Giddy Green 105 E4
Gidea Park 137 E4
Gidleigh 99 G2
Gifford 236 C3
Giffordland 233 D5
Giffordtown 244 A3
Giggleswick 193 E1
Gigha 231 E5
Gilberdyke 196 A5
Gilbert's End 146 A3
Gilchriston 236 B3
Gilcrux 209 E3
Gildersome 194 B5
Gildingwells 186 C4
Gileston 115 D1
Gilfach 130 A3
Gilfach Goch 129 F4
Gilfachrheda 142 A2
Gilgarran 208 D4
Gill 210 A5
Gillamoor 203 F4
Gillen 263 H5
Gillenbie 217 F2
Gillfoot 217 D3
Gilling East 203 F5
Gilling West 202 A2
Gillingham Dorset 117 F5
Gillingham Med 123 G2
Gillingham Norf 165 F2
Gillivoan 275 G5
Gillock 275 H3
Gillow Heath 171 F2
Gills 275 J1
Gill's Green 123 G5
Gilmanscleuch 227 E3
Gilmerton Edin 235 G3
Gilmerton P&K 243 D2
Gilmilnscroft 225 D3
Gilmonby 201 E1
Gilmorton 160 A4
Gilsland 210 C1
Gilsland Spa 210 C1
Gilson 159 D3
Gilstead 194 A4
Gilston 236 B4
Gilston Park 136 D1
Giltbrook 173 F3
Gilwern 130 B1
Gimingham 179 D2
Gin Pit 184 A2
Ginclough 185 D5
Ginger's Green 110 B2
Giosla 270 D5
Gipping 152 B1
Gipsey Bridge 176 A3
Girlsta 279 D7
Girsby 202 C2
Girtford 149 G3
Girthon 216 A5
Girton Cambs 150 C1
Girton Notts 174 D1
Girvan 214 C1

Gisburn 193 E3
Gisburn Cotes 193 E3
Gisleham 165 G3
Gislingham 164 B4
Gissing 164 C3
Gittisham 103 E3
Givons Grove 121 G2
Glackour 265 H3
Gladestry 144 B2
Gladsmuir 236 B2
Glaic 232 B2
Glais 128 D2
Glaisdale 203 G2
Glaister 223 E2
Glame 264 B7
Glamis 252 B5
Glamis Castle Angus
   DD8 1QJ 252 B5
Glan Conwy 168 B2
Glanaber Terrace 168 A3
Glanaman 128 C1
Glanbran 143 E2
Glan-Denys 142 B2
Glanderston 260 D2
Glandford 178 B1
Glan-Duar 142 B3
Glandwr 141 E5
Glan-Dwyfach 167 D3
Glangrwyney 130 B1
Glanllynfi 129 E3
Glanmule 156 A3
Glan-rhyd NPT 129 D2
Glanrhyd Pembs 141 E3
Glanton 229 E5
Glanton Pyke 229 E5
Glanvilles Wootton 104 C2
Glanwern 154 C4
Glan-y-don 182 C5
Glan-y-llyn 130 A4
Glan-y-nant 155 F4
Glan-yr-afon
   Gwyn 168 C3
Glan-yr-afon
   Gwyn 168 D3
Glan-yr-afon IoA 181 E4
Glan-y-Wern 167 F4
Glapthorn 161 F3
Glapwell 173 F5
Glasahoile 241 G4
Glasbury 144 A4
Glaschoil 259 H1
Glascoed Mon 130 C2
Glascoed Wrex 169 F2
Glascorrie 260 C5
Glascote 159 E2
Glascwm 144 A2
Glasdrum 248 C5
Glasfryn 168 C2
Glasgow (Glaschu) 233 G3
Glasgow Airport 233 F3
Glasgow Botanic
   Garden Glas
   G12 0UE 30 C3
Glasgow Prestwick
   Airport 224 B3
Glasgow Royal Concert Hall
   Glas G2 3NY 39 F3
Glasgow Science Centre
   Glas G51 1EA 38 A4
Glashmore 261 F4
Glasinfryn 167 E1
Glasnacardoch 256 C5
Glasnakille 256 B3
Glaspant 141 F4
Glaspwll 154 D3
Glass Studio, Eastbourne
   Pier ESuss
   BN21 3EL 110 B4
Glassburn 257 K1
Glassel 260 E5
Glassenbury 123 G5
Glasserton 207 E3
Glassford 234 B5
Glasshouse 145 G5
Glasshouses 194 A1
Glassingall 242 C4
Glasslie 244 A4
Glasson Cumb 218 A5
Glasson Lancs 192 A3
Glasson Dock 192 A2
Glassonby 210 B4
Glasterlaw 253 D4
Glaston 161 D2
Glastonbury 116 B4
Glastonbury Abbey Som
   BA6 9EL 116 C4
Glatton 161 G4
Glazebrook 184 A3
Glazebury 184 A3
Glazeley 157 G4
Gleadless 186 A4
Gleadsmoss 171 F1
Gleann Tholastaidh 271 H3
Gleaston 199 D5
Glecknabae 232 B3
Gledhow 194 C4
Gledrid 169 F4
Glemsford 151 G3
Glen D&G 216 C3
Glen D&G 215 G5
Glen Auldyn 190 C2
Glen Mona 190 C3
Glen Parva 160 A3
Glen Trool Lodge 215 F2
Glen Village 234 C2
Glen Vine 190 B4
Glenae 217 D2
Glenaladale 248 A2
Glenald 241 E5
Glenamachrie 240 B2
Glenapp Castle 214 B2
Glenarm 252 B3
Glenbar 222 B2
Glenbatrick 230 D2
Glenbeg High 265 K3
Glenbeg High 259 H2
Glenbeg High 247 E3
Glenbeich 242 A2
Glenbervie Aber 253 F1
Glenbervie Falk 234 C1
Glenboig 234 A3
Glenborrodale 247 F3
Glenbranter 240 D5
Glenbreck 226 B3
Glenbrittle 255 K2
Glenburn 233 F3
Glenbyre 239 E2

Glynarthen 141 G3
Glyncoch 129 G3
Glyncorrwg 129 E3
Glyn-Cywarch 167 F4
Glynde 109 G3
Glyndebourne 109 G2
Glyndyfrdwy 169 E3
Glynneath
   (Glyn-Nedd) 129 E2
Glynogwr 129 F4
Glyntaff 129 G4
Gnosall 171 F5
Gnosall Heath 171 F5
Go Bananas, Colchester
   Essex CO1 1BX 152 A5
Goadby 160 C3
Goadby Marwood 174 C5
Goatacre 132 C5
Goatfield 240 C4
Goathill 104 C1
Goathland 204 B2
Goathurst 115 F4
Gobernuisgeach 274 E5
Gobhaig 270 C7
Gobowen 170 A4
Godalming 121 E3
Goddard's Corner 153 D1
Goddards Green 109 E1
Godden Green 123 E3
Goddington 123 D2
Godford Cross 103 E2
Godington 148 B5
Godleybrook 171 G3
Godmanchester 162 A5
Godmanstone 104 C3
Godmersham 124 C3
Godney 116 B3
Godolphin Cross 94 D3
Godor 156 B1
Godre'r-graig 129 D2
Godshill Hants 106 A1
Godshill IoW 107 E4
Godstone 122 C3
Godstone Farm Surr
   RH9 8LX 122 C3
Godwick 178 A3
Goetre 130 C2
Goff's Oak 136 C2
Gogar 235 F2
Gogarth 181 F4
Goginan 154 C4
Goirtean a'
   Chladaich 248 C2
Goirtein 232 A1
Golan 167 E3
Golant 97 F4
Golberdon 98 D3
Golborne 184 A3
Golcar 185 F1
Gold Hill Cambs 162 D3
Gold Hill Dorset 105 E1
Goldcliff 130 C4
Golden Acre Park
   WYorks
   LS16 8BQ 194 B3
Golden Cross 110 A2
Golden Green 123 F4
Golden Grove 128 B1
Golden Pot 120 C3
Golden Valley
   Derbys 173 F2
Golden Valley Glos 146 B5
Goldenhill 171 F2
Golders Green 136 B4
Goldhanger 138 C2
Goldielea 216 D2
Golding 157 E2
Goldington 149 F2
Goldsborough
   NYorks 204 B1
Goldsborough
   NYorks 194 C2
Goldsithney 94 C3
Goldstone 171 E5
Goldthorn Park 158 B3
Goldthorpe 186 B2
Goldworthy 113 E3
Goleulong 2000 Lightship,
   Cardiff Cardiff
   CF10 4PA 7 C4
Golford 123 G5
Gollanfield 267 F6
Gollinglith Foot 202 A4
Golspie 267 F2
Golval 274 D2
Gomeldon 118 C4
Gomersal 194 B5
Gometra 246 C5
Gometra House 246 C5
Gomshall 121 F3
Gonachan Cottage 234 A1
Gonalston 174 B3
Gonerby Hill Foot 175 E4
Gonfirth 279 C6
Good Easter 137 F1
Gooderstone 163 F2
Goodleigh 113 G2
Goodmanham 196 A3
Goodmayes 137 D4
Goodnestone Kent 125 E3
Goodnestone Kent 124 C2
Goodrich 131 E1
Goodrington 101 E2
Goodshaw 193 E5
Goodshaw Fold 193 E5
Goodwick (Wdig) 140 C4
Goodworth Clatford 119 E3
Goodyers End 159 F4
Goole 195 G5
Goom's Hill 146 C2
Goonbell 96 B5
Goonhavern 96 B4
Goonvrea 96 B5
Goose Green Essex 152 C5
Goose Green Essex 152 C5
Goose Green
   GtMan 183 G2
Goose Green Kent 123 F3
Goose Green SGlos 131 F5
Goose Pool 145 D4
Gooseham 112 C4
Goosehill Green 146 B1
Goosewell 100 B2
Goosey 133 F3
Goosnargh 192 B4
Goostrey 184 B5
Gorcott Hill 146 C1
Gorddinog 181 E5

Gordon **236** D5
Gordonbush **267** F1
Gordonstoun **267** J5
Gordonstown *Aber* **268** D5
Gordonstown *Aber* **261** F1
Gore Cross **118** B2
Gore End **119** F1
Gore Pit **138** B1
Gore Street **125** E2
Gorebridge **236** A3
Gorefield **162** C1
Gorey **100** D5
Gorgie **235** G2
Gorgie City Farm *Edin* EH11 2LA **36** B7
Goring **134** B4
Goring Heath **134** B5
Goring-by-Sea **108** D3
Gorleston-on-Sea **179** G5
Gorllwyn **141** G4
Gornalwood **158** B3
Gorrachie **269** F5
Gorran Churchtown **97** D5
Gorran Haven **97** E5
Gors **154** C5
Gorsedd **182** C5
Gorseinon **128** B3
Gorseness **277** D6
Gorseybank **173** D2
Gorsgoch **142** A2
Gorslas **128** B1
Gorsley **145** F5
Gorsley Common **145** F5
Gorstage **184** A5
Gorstan **265** K5
Gorstanvorran **248** A2
Gorsty Hill **172** C5
Gorten **239** G1
Gortenbuie **239** E1
Gorteneorn **247** F3
Gorton *A&B* **246** A4
Gorton *GtMan* **184** C3
Gosbeck **152** C2
Gosberton **176** A4
Gosberton Clough **175** G5
Goseley Dale **173** E5
Gosfield **151** F5
Gosford *Here* **145** E1
Gosford *Oxon* **134** A1
Gosforth *Cumb* **198** B2
Gosforth *T&W* **212** B1
Gosland Green **170** C2
Gosmore **149** G5
Gospel End **158** A3
Gosport **107** F3
Gossabrough **278** E4
Gossington **131** G2
Gossops Green **122** B5
Goswick **229** E2
Gotham **173** G4
Gotherington **146** B5
Gothers **97** D4
Gott **279** D8
Gotton **115** F5
Goudhurst **123** G5
Goulceby **188** C5
Gourdas **269** F6
Gourdon **253** G2
Gourock **232** D2
Govan **233** G3
Goverton **174** C2
Goveton **101** D3
Govilon **130** B1
Gowanhill **269** J4
Gowdall **195** F5
Gowerton **128** B3
Gowkhall **235** E1
Gowkthrapple **234** B4
Gowthorpe **195** G2
Goxhill *ERid* **197** D3
Goxhill *NLincs* **196** D5
Goytre **129** D4
Gozzard's Ford **133** G3
Grabhair **271** F6
Graby **175** F5
Gradbach **171** G1
Grade **95** E5
Gradeley Green **170** C2
Graffham **108** B2
Grafham *Cambs* **149** G1
Grafham *Surr* **121** F3
Grafham Water *Cambs* PE28 0BH **149** G1
Grafton *Here* **145** D4
Grafton *NYorks* **194** D1
Grafton *Oxon* **133** E2
Grafton *Shrop* **156** D1
Grafton *Worcs* **145** E1
Grafton *Worcs* **146** B4
Grafton Flyford **146** B2
Grafton Regis **148** C3
Grafton Underwood **161** E4
Grafty Green **124** A4
Graianrhyd **169** F2
Graig *Carmar* **128** A2
Graig *Conwy* **181** G5
Graig *Denb* **182** B5
Graig-fechan **169** E2
Grain **124** A1
Grainel **230** A3
Grainhow **269** G6
Grains Bar **185** D2
Grainsby **188** C3
Grainthorpe **189** D3
Graizelound **187** E3
Gramisdale (Gramsdal) **262** D6
Grampound **96** D5
Grampound Road **96** D4
Granborough **148** C5
Granby **174** C4
Grand Pier, Teignmouth *Devon* TQ14 8BB **102** C5
Grandborough **147** G1
Grandes Rocques **101** F4
Grandtully **251** E4
Grange *Cumb* **209** F5
Grange *EAyr* **224** C2
Grange *High* **257** K1
Grange *Med* **123** G2
Grange *Mersey* **182** D4
Grange *P&K* **244** A2
Grange Crossroads **268** C5
Grange de Lings **187** G5
Grange Hall **267** H5
Grange Hill **136** D3
Grange Moor **185** G1
Grange of Lindores **244** A3
Grange Villa **212** B2
Grangemill **172** D2
Grangemouth **234** D1
Grangemuir **244** D4
Grange-over-Sands **199** F5
Grangeston **214** D1
Grangetown *Cardiff* **130** A5
Grangetown *R&C* **213** E5
Granish **259** G3
Gransmoor **196** D2
Granston **140** B4
Grantchester **150** C2
Grantham **175** E4
Grantley **202** B5
Grantlodge **261** F3
Granton **235** G2
Granton House **226** B5
Grantown-on-Spey **259** H2
Grantsfield **145** E1
Grantshouse **237** F3
Grappenhall **184** A4
Grasby **188** A2
Grasmere **199** E2
Grass Green **151** F4
Grasscroft **185** D2
Grassendale **183** E4
Grassgarth **199** F3
Grassholme **211** F5
Grassington **193** G1
Grassmoor **173** F1
Grassthorpe **174** C1
Grateley **119** D3
Gratwich **172** B4
Gravel Hill **135** F3
Graveley *Cambs* **150** A1
Graveley *Herts* **150** A5
Gravelly Hill **158** D3
Gravels **156** C2
Graven **278** D5
Graveney **124** C2
Gravesend **137** F5
Grayingham **187** G3
Grayrigg **199** G3
Grays **137** F5
Grayshott **121** D4
Grayswood **121** E4
Grazeley **120** B1
Greasbrough **186** B3
Greasby **183** D4
Great Aberystwyth Camera Obscura *Cere* SY23 2DN **154** B4
Great Abington **150** D3
Great Addington **161** E5
Great Alne **146** D2
Great Altcar **183** E2
Great Amwell **136** C1
Great Asby **200** B1
Great Ashfield **152** A1
Great Ayton **203** E1
Great Baddow **137** G2
Great Bardfield **151** E4
Great Barford **149** G2
Great Barr **158** C3
Great Barrington **133** E1
Great Barrow **170** B1
Great Barton **151** G1
Great Barugh **203** G5
Great Bavington **220** B3
Great Bealings **152** D3
Great Bedwyn **119** D1
Great Bentley **152** C5
Great Bernera **270** D4
Great Billing **148** D1
Great Bircham **177** F4
Great Blakenham **152** C2
Great Bolas **170** D5
Great Bookham **121** G2
Great Bourton **147** G3
Great Bowden **160** C4
Great Bradley **151** E2
Great Braxted **138** B1
Great Bricett **152** B2
Great Brickhill **149** E4
Great Bridgeford **171** F5
Great Brington **148** B1
Great Bromley **152** B5
Great Broughton *Cumb* **209** D3
Great Broughton *NYorks* **203** E2
Great Buckland **123** F2
Great Budworth **184** A5
Great Burdon **202** C1
Great Burstead **137** F3
Great Busby **203** E2
Great Cambourne **150** B2
Great Canfield **137** E1
Great Canney **138** B2
Great Carlton **189** E4
Great Casterton **161** F2
Great Chalfield **117** F1
Great Chart **124** B4
Great Chatwell **157** G1
Great Chell **171** F2
Great Chesterford **150** D3
Great Cheverell **118** A2
Great Chishill **150** C4
Great Clacton **139** E1
Great Clifton **208** D4
Great Coates **188** C2
Great Comberton **146** B3
Great Corby **210** A2
Great Cornard **151** G3
Great Cowden **197** E3
Great Coxwell **133** E3
Great Crakehall **202** B4
Great Cransley **160** D5
Great Cressingham **163** G2
Great Crosby **183** E2
Great Crosthwaite **209** F4
Great Cubley **172** C4
Great Cumbrae **232** C4
Great Dalby **160** C1
Great Doddington **149** D1
Great Doward **131** E1
Great Dunham **163** G1
Great Dunmow **151** E5
Great Durnford **118** C4
Great Easton *Essex* **151** E5
Great Easton *Leics* **160** D3
Great Eccleston **192** A3
Great Edstone **203** G4
Great Ellingham **164** B2
Great Elm **117** E3
Great Eversden **150** B2
Great Fencote **202** B3
Great Finborough **152** B2
Great Fransham **163** G1
Great Gaddesden **135** F1
Great Gidding **161** G4
Great Givendale **196** A2
Great Glemham **153** E1
Great Glen **160** B3
Great Gonerby **175** D4
Great Gransden **150** A2
Great Green *Cambs* **150** A3
Great Green *Norf* **165** D3
Great Green *Suff* **152** A2
Great Green *Suff* **164** C4
Great Green *Suff* **164** B4
Great Habton **203** G5
Great Hale **175** G3
Great Hall *Hants* SO23 8UJ **89** Winchester
Great Hallingbury **137** E1
Great Hampden **134** D2
Great Harrowden **161** D5
Great Harwood **192** D4
Great Haseley **134** B2
Great Hatfield **197** D3
Great Haywood **172** B5
Great Heath **159** F4
Great Heck **195** E5
Great Henny **151** G4
Great Hinton **118** A2
Great Hockham **164** A2
Great Holland **139** F1
Great Horkesley **152** A4
Great Hormead **150** C4
Great Horton **194** A4
Great Horwood **148** C4
Great Houghton *N'hants* **148** C2
Great Houghton *SYorks* **186** B2
Great Hucklow **185** F5
Great Kelk **196** D2
Great Kimble **134** D2
Great Kingshill **135** D3
Great Langton **202** B3
Great Leighs **137** G1
Great Limber **188** B2
Great Linford **148** D3
Great Livermere **163** G5
Great Longstone **185** G5
Great Lumley **212** B3
Great Lyth **157** D2
Great Malvern **145** G3
Great Maplestead **151** G4
Great Marton **191** G4
Great Massingham **177** F5
Great Melton **178** C5
Great Milton **134** B2
Great Missenden **135** D2
Great Mitton **192** D4
Great Mongeham **125** F3
Great Moulton **164** C2
Great Munden **150** B5
Great Musgrave **200** C1
Great Ness **156** D1
Great Notley **151** F5
Great Nurcot **114** C4
Great Oak **130** C2
Great Oakley *Essex* **152** C5
Great Oakley *N'hants* **161** D4
Great Offley **149** G5
Great Orme Tramway *Conwy* LL30 2HG **181** F4
Great Ormside **200** C1
Great Orton **209** G1
Great Ouseburn **194** D1
Great Oxendon **160** C4
Great Oxney Green **137** F2
Great Palgrave **163** G1
Great Parndon **136** D2
Great Paxton **150** A1
Great Plumpton **191** G4
Great Plumstead **179** E5
Great Ponton **175** E4
Great Potheridge **113** F4
Great Preston **194** C5
Great Purston **148** A4
Great Raveley **162** A4
Great Rissington **133** D1
Great Rollright **147** F4
Great Ryburgh **178** A3
Great Ryle **229** E5
Great Ryton **157** D2
Great St. Mary's Church *Cambs* CB2 3PQ **66** Cambridge
Great Saling **151** F5
Great Salkeld **210** B4
Great Sampford **151** E4
Great Sankey **183** G4
Great Saredon **158** B2
Great Saxham **151** F1
Great Shefford **133** F5
Great Shelford **150** C2
Great Smeaton **202** C2
Great Snoring **178** A2
Great Somerford **132** B4
Great Stainton **212** C5
Great Stambridge **138** C3
Great Staughton **149** G1
Great Steeping **176** C1
Great Stonar **125** F3
Great Strickland **210** B5
Great Stukeley **162** A5
Great Sturton **188** C5
Great Sutton *ChesW&C* **183** E5
Great Sutton *Shrop* **157** E4
Great Swinburne **220** B4
Great Tew **147** F5
Great Tey **151** G5
Great Thorness **107** D3
Great Thurlow **151** E3
Great Torr **100** C3
Great Torrington **113** E4
Great Tosson **220** C1
Great Totham *Essex* **138** B1
Great Totham *Essex* **138** B1
Great Tows **188** C3
Great Urswick **199** D5
Great Wakering **138** C4
Great Waldingfield **152** A3
Great Walsingham **178** A2
Great Waltham **137** F1
Great Warley **137** E3
Great Washbourne **146** B4
Great Weeke **102** A4
Great Welnetham **151** G2
Great Wenham **152** B4
Great Whittington **220** C4
Great Wigborough **138** C1
Great Wigsell **110** C1
Great Wilbraham **150** D2
Great Wilne **173** F4
Great Wishford **118** B4
Great Witcombe **132** B1
Great Witley **145** G1
Great Wolford **147** E4
Great Wratting **151** E3
Great Wymondley **150** A5
Great Wyrley **158** B2
Great Wytheford **157** E1
Great Yarmouth **179** G5
Great Yeldham **151** F4
Greatford **161** F1
Greatgate **172** B3
Greatham *Hants* **120** C4
Greatham *Hart* **213** D5
Greatham *WSuss* **108** C2
Greatness **123** E3
Greatstone-on-Sea **111** F1
Greatworth **148** A3
Green **169** D1
Green Cross **121** D4
Green End *Bed* **149** G2
Green End *Bucks* **149** E4
Green End *Cambs* **162** A5
Green End *Cambs* **162** B5
Green End *Herts* **150** B5
Green End *Herts* **150** B4
Green End *Warks* **159** E4
Green Hammerton **195** D2
Green Hill **132** C4
Green Lane **146** C1
Green Moor **185** G3
Green Ore **116** C2
Green Quarter **199** F2
Green Street *ESuss* **110** C2
Green Street *Herts* **136** A3
Green Street *Herts* **150** C5
Green Street *Worcs* **146** A3
Green Street *WSuss* **121** G5
Green Street Green *GtLon* **123** D2
Green Street Green *Kent* **137** E5
Green Tye **136** D1
Greenburn **252** C5
Greencroft **212** A3
Greendams **253** E1
Greendykes **229** E4
Greenend **147** F5
Greenfaulds **234** B2
Greenfield *CenBeds* **149** F4
Greenfield (Maes-Glas) *Flints* **182** C5
Greenfield *GtMan* **185** E2
Greenfield *High* **257** J4
Greenfield *Lincs* **189** E5
Greenfield *Oxon* **134** C3
Greenford **136** A4
Greengairs **234** B2
Greengates **194** A4
Greengill **209** E3
Greenhalgh **192** A4
Greenhall **260** E2
Greenham **119** F1
Greenhaugh **219** F3
Greenhead **210** C1
Greenheads **261** J1
Greenheys **184** B2
Greenhill *GtLon* **136** A4
Greenhill *High* **267** G1
Greenhill *SYorks* **186** A4
Greenhithe **137** E5
Greenholm **224** D2
Greenholme **199** G2
Greenhow Hill **194** A1
Greenigo **277** D7
Greenland **275** H2
Greenlands **134** C4
Greenlaw *Aber* **268** E5
Greenlaw *ScBord* **237** E5
Greenloaning **242** D4
Greenmeadow **130** B3
Greenmoor Hill **134** B4
Greenmount **184** B1
Greenmyre **261** G1
Greenock **233** D2
Greenodd **199** E4
Greens Norton **148** B3
Greenscares **242** C3
Greenside *T&W* **212** A1
Greenside *WYorks* **185** F1
Greenstead **152** B5
Greenstead Green **151** G5
Greensted **137** E2
Greensted Green **137** E2
Greenway *Pembs* **141** D4
Greenway *Som* **116** A5
Greenwell **210** B2
Greenwich **136** C5
Greenwood Forest Park, Y Felinheli *Gwyn* LL56 4QN **167** E1
Greet **146** C4
Greete **157** E5
Greetham *Lincs* **188** D5
Greetham *Rut* **161** E1
Greetland **193** G5
Gregson Lane **192** B5
Greinton **116** B4
Grenaby **190** A4
Grendon *N'hants* **149** D1
Grendon *Warks* **159** E3
Grendon Common **159** E3
Grendon Green **145** E2
Grendon Underwood **148** B5
Grenitote (Greinetobht) **262** D4
Grenofen **99** E3
Grenoside **186** A3
Greosabhagh **263** G2
Gresford **170** A2
Gresham **178** C2
Greshornish **263** J6
Gress (Griais) **271** G3
Gressenhall **178** A4
Gressingham **192** B1
Greta Bridge **201** F1
Gretna **218** B5
Gretna Green **218** B5
Gretton *Glos* **146** C4
Gretton *N'hants* **161** E3
Gretton *Shrop* **157** E3
Grewelthorpe **202** B5
Greygarth **202** A5
Greylake **116** A4
Greys Green **134** C4
Greysouthen **209** D4
Greystead **219** F3
Greystoke **210** A4
Greystone *Aber* **259** K5
Greystone *Angus* **252** D5
Greystone *Lancs* **193** E3
Greystones **186** A4
Greywell **120** C2
Gribthorpe **195** G4
Gribton **216** D2
Griff **159** F4
Griffithstown **130** B3
Grigadale **246** D3
Grigghall **199** F3
Grimeford Village **184** A1
Grimesthorpe **186** A3
Grimethorpe **186** B2
Griminish (Griminis) **262** C6
Grimister **278** D3
Grimley **146** A1
Grimmet **224** B4
Grimness **277** D8
Grimoldby **189** D4
Grimpo **170** A5
Grimsargh **192** B4
Grimsay (Griomasaigh) **262** D6
Grimsbury **147** G3
Grimsby **188** C2
Grimscote **148** B2
Grimscott **112** C5
Grimshader (Griomsiadar) **271** G5
Grimsthorpe **175** F5
Grimston *ERid* **197** E4
Grimston *Leics* **174** B5
Grimston *Norf* **177** F5
Grimstone **104** C3
Grimstone End **152** A1
Grindale **205** E5
Grindiscol **279** D9
Grindle **157** G2
Grindleford **185** G5
Grindleton **193** D3
Grindley **172** B5
Grindley Brook **170** C3
Grindlow **185** F5
Grindon *N'umb* **237** G5
Grindon *Staffs* **172** B2
Grindon *Stock* **212** C5
Grindon *T&W* **212** C2
Gringley on the Hill **187** E3
Grinsdale **209** G1
Grinshill **170** C5
Grinton **201** F3
Griomarstaidh **270** E4
Grisdale **200** C3
Grishipoll **246** A4
Gristhorpe **205** D4
Griston **164** A2
Gritley **277** E7
Grittenham **132** C4
Grittleton **132** A5
Grizebeck **198** D4
Grizedale **199** E3
Grizedale Forest Park *Cumb* LA22 0QJ **199** E3
Grobister **276** F5
Groby **160** A2
Groes **168** D1
Groes-faen **129** G4
Groesffordd **166** B4
Groesffordd Marli **182** B5
Groeslon *Gwyn* **167** D2
Groeslon *Gwyn* **167** E1
Groes-lwyd **156** B1
Groes-wen **130** A4
Grogport **231** G5
Groigearraidh **254** C1
Gromford **153** E2
Gronant **182** B4
Groombridge **123** E5
Groombridge Place Gardens *Kent* TN3 9QG **123** E5
Grosmont *Mon* **144** D5
Grosmont *NYorks* **204** B2
Grotaig **258** B2
Groton **152** A3
Groundistone Heights **227** F4
Grouville **100** C5
Grove *Bucks* **149** E5
Grove *Dorset* **104** C5
Grove *Kent* **125** E2
Grove *Notts* **187** E5
Grove *Oxon* **133** G3
Grove End **124** A2
Grove Green **123** G3
Grove Park **136** D5
Grove Town **195** D5
Grovehill **135** F2
Grovesend *SGlos* **131** F4
Grovesend *Swan* **128** B2
Gruids **266** C1
Grula **255** J2
Gruline **247** E5
Grumbla **94** B4
Grundcruie **243** F2
Grundisburgh **152** D2
Gruting **279** B8
Grutness **279** G10
Gualachulain **248** D5
Guardbridge **244** C3
Guarlford **146** A3
Guay **251** F5
Gubbergill **198** B3
Gubblecote **135** E1
Guernsey **101** F5
Guernsey Airport **101** E5
Guestling Green **111** D2
Guestling Thorn **111** D2
Guestwick **178** B3
Guestwick Green **178** B3
Guide **192** D5
Guide Post **221** E3
Guilden Down **156** C4
Guilden Morden **150** A3
Guilden Sutton **170** B1
Guildford **121** E3
Guildford House Gallery *Surr* GU1 3AJ **74** Guildford
Guildtown **243** G1
Guilsborough **160** B5
Guilsfield (Cegidfa) **156** B1
Guilthwaite **186** B4
Guisborough **203** F1
Guiseley **194** A3
Guist **178** B3
Guith **276** E4
Guiting Power **146** C5
Gulberwick **279** D9
Gullane **236** B1
Gullane Bents *ELoth* EH31 2AZ **236** B1
Gulval **94** B3
Gulworthy **99** E3
Gumfreston **127** E2
Gumley **160** B3
Gunby *Lincs* **175** E5
Gunby *Lincs* **176** C1
Gundleton **120** B4
Gunn **113** G2
Gunnersbury **136** A5
Gunnerside **201** E3
Gunnerton **220** B4
Gunness **187** F1
Gunnislake **99** E3
Gunnista **279** E8
Gunnister **278** C5
Gunstone **158** A2
Gunter's Bridge **121** E5
Gunthorpe *Norf* **178** B2
Gunthorpe *Notts* **174** B3
Gunthorpe *Rut* **161** D2
Gunville **107** D4
Gunwalloe **95** D4
Gupworthy **114** C4
Gurnard **107** D3
Gurnett **184** D5
Gurney Slade **116** D3
Gurnos *MTyd* **129** G2
Gurnos *Powys* **129** D2
Gushmere **124** C3
Gussage All Saints **105** G1
Gussage St. Andrew **105** F1
Gussage St. Michael **105** F1
Guston **125** F4
Gutcher **278** E3
Guthram Gowt **175** G5
Guthrie **253** D4
Guyhirn **162** B2
Guynd **253** D5
Guy's Head **176** C5
Guy's Marsh **117** F5
Guyzance **221** E1
Gwaelod-y-garth **130** A4
Gwaenysgor **182** B4
Gwaithla **144** B2
Gwalchmai **180** B5
Gwastad **140** D5
Gwastadnant **167** F2
Gwaun-Cae-Gurwen **128** D1
Gwaynynog **168** D1
Gwbert **141** E3
Gweek **95** E4
Gwehelog **130** C2
Gwenddwr **143** G3
Gwendreath **95** E5
Gwennap **96** B5
Gwenter **95** E5
Gwernaffield **169** F1
Gwernesney **130** D2
Gwernogle **142** B4
Gwernymynydd **169** F1
Gwern-y-Steeple **129** G5
Gwersyllt **170** A2
Gwespyr **182** C4
Gwinear **94** C3
Gwithian **94** C2
Gwredog **180** C4
Gwrhay **130** A3
Gwyddelwern **169** D3
Gwyddgrug **142** A4
Gwynfryn **169** F2
Gwystre **143** G1
Gwytherin **168** B1
Gyfelia **170** A3
Gyre **277** C7
Gyrn Goch **166** D3

H

H.M.S. Belfast *GtLon* SE1 2JH **12** C4
H.M.S. Victory PO1 3PX **82** Portsmouth
H.M.S. Warrior PO1 3QX **82** Portsmouth
Habberley **156** C2
Habin **120** D5
Habrough **188** B1
Haccombe **102** B5
Hacconby **175** G5
Haceby **175** F4
Hacheston **153** E2
Hackbridge **122** B2
Hackenthorpe **186** B4
Hackford **178** B5
Hackforth **202** B3
Hackland **276** C5
Hacklet (Haclait) **262** D7
Hacklete (Tacleit) **270** D4
Hackleton **148** D2
Hacklinge **125** F3
Hackness *NYorks* **204** C3
Hackness *Ork* **277** C8
Hackney **136** C4
Hackthorn **187** G4
Hackthorpe **210** B5
Hacton **137** E4
Hadden **228** B3
Haddenham *Bucks* **134** C2
Haddenham *Cambs* **162** C5
Haddington *ELoth* **236** C2
Haddington *Lincs* **175** E1
Haddiscoe **165** F2
Haddo Country Park *Aber* AB41 7EQ **261** G1
Haddon **161** G3
Hade Edge **185** F2
Hademore **159** D2
Hadfield **185** E3
Hadham Cross **136** D1
Hadham Ford **150** C5
Hadleigh *Essex* **138** B4
Hadleigh *Suff* **152** B3
Hadleigh Castle Country Park *Essex* SS7 2PP **138** B4
Hadleigh Farm *Essex* SS7 2AP **138** B4
Hadleigh Heath **152** A3
Hadley *Tel&W* **157** F1
Hadley *Worcs* **146** A1
Hadley End **172** C5
Hadley Wood **136** B3
Hadlow **123** F4
Hadlow Down **110** A1
Hadnall **170** C5
Hadspen **117** D4
Hadstock **151** D3
Hadston **221** E2
Hadzor **146** B1
Haffenden Quarter **124** A4
Hafod Bridge **142** C4
Hafod-Dinbych **168** B2
Hafodunos **168** B1
Hafodyrynys **130** B3
Haggate **193** E4
Haggbeck **218** C4
Haggersta **279** C8
Haggerston *GtLon* **136** C4
Haggerston *N'umb* **229** E2
Haggrister **278** C5
Haggs **234** B2
Hagley *Here* **145** E3
Hagley *Worcs* **158** B4
Hagnaby *Lincs* **176** B1
Hagnaby *Lincs* **189** E5
Hague Bar **185** D4
Hagworthingham **176** B1
Haigh **184** A2
Haigh Hall Country Park *GtMan* WN2 1PE **183** G2
Haighton Green **192** B4
Hail Weston **149** G1
Haile **198** B2
Hailes **146** C4
Hailey *Herts* **136** C1
Hailey *Oxon* **134** B4
Hailey *Oxon* **133** F1
Hailsham **110** A3
Haimer **275** G2
Hainault **137** D3
Hainault Forest Country Park *Essex* IG7 4QN **137** D3
Haine **125** F2
Hainford **178** D4
Hainton **188** B4
Haisthorpe **196** D1
Hakin **126** B2
Halam **174** B2
Halbeath **235** F1
Halberton **102** D1
Halcro **275** H2
Hale *Cumb* **199** G5
Hale *GtMan* **184** B4
Hale *Halton* **183** F4
Hale *Hants* **106** A1
Hale *Surr* **120** D3
Hale Bank **183** F4
Hale Barns **184** B4
Hale Nook **191** G3
Hale Street **123** F4
Hales *Norf* **165** E2
Hales *Staffs* **171** E4
Hales Green **172** C3
Hales Place **124** D3
Halesgate **176** B5
Halesowen **158** B4
Halesworth **165** E4
Halewood **183** F4
Half Way Inn **102** D3
Halford *Devon* **102** B5
Halford *Shrop* **156** D4
Halford *Warks* **147** E3
Halfpenny **199** G4
Halfpenny Green **158** A3
Halfway *Carmar* **142** C4
Halfway *Carmar* **128** B2
Halfway *Powys* **143** E4
Halfway *SYorks* **186** B4
Halfway *WBerks* **119** F1
Halfway Bridge **121** E5
Halfway House **156** C1
Halfway Houses *Kent* **124** B1
Halfway Houses *Lincs* **175** D1
Halghton Mill **170** B3
Halifax **193** G5
Halistra **263** H6
Halket **233** F4
Halkirk **275** G3
Halkyn **182** D5
Hall **233** F4
Hall Cross **192** A5
Hall Dunnerdale **198** D3
Hall Green *ChesE* **171** F2
Hall Green *Lancs* **192** A5
Hall Green *WMid* **158** D4
Hall Grove **136** B1
Hall of the Forest **156** B4
Halland **110** A2
Hallaton **160** C3
Hallatrow **116** D2
Hallbankgate **210** B2
Hallen **131** E4
Hallfield Gate **173** E2
Hallglen **234** C2
Hallin **263** H6
Halling **123** G2
Hallington *Lincs* **188** D4
Hallington *N'umb* **220** B4
Halliwell **184** A1
Halloughton **174** B2
Hallow **146** A2
Hallow Heath **146** A2
Hallrule **227** G4
Halls **237** D2
Halls Green *Essex* **136** D2
Hall's Green *Herts* **150** A5
Hallsands **101** E4
Hallthwaites **198** C4
Hallwood Green **145** F4
Hallworthy **97** F1
Hallyne **235** F5
Halmer End **171** E3
Halmond's Frome **145** F3

Halmore 131 F2
Halmyre Mains 235 F5
Halnaker 108 B3
Halsall 183 E1
Halse N'hants 148 A3
Halse Som 115 E5
Halsetown 94 C3
Halsham 197 E5
Halsinger 113 F2
Halstead Essex 151 G4
Halstead Kent 123 D2
Halstead Leics 160 C2
Halstock 104 B2
Halsway 179 F5
Halterprice Farm 196 C4
Haltham 176 A1
Haltoft End 176 B3
Halton Bucks 135 D1
Halton Halton 183 G4
Halton Lancs 192 B1
Halton N'umb 211 F1
Halton Wrex 170 A4
Halton East 193 G2
Halton Green 193 F1
Halton Gill 201 D5
Halton Holegate 176 C1
Halton Lea Gate 210 C2
Halton Park 192 B1
Halton West 193 E2
Haltwhistle 210 D1
Halvergate 179 F5
Halwell 101 D2
Halwill 99 E1
Halwill Junction 99 E1
Ham Devon 103 F2
Ham Glos 131 F3
Ham Glos 146 B5
Ham GtLon 136 A5
Ham High 275 H1
Ham Kent 125 F3
Ham Plym 100 A2
Ham Shet 278 B1
Ham Som 115 E5
Ham Som 103 F1
Ham Wilts 119 E1
Ham Common 117 F5
Ham Green Here 145 G3
Ham Green Kent 124 A2
Ham Green Kent 111 D1
Ham Green NSom 131 E5
Ham Green Worcs 146 C1
Ham Hill 123 F2
Ham Hill Country Park
    Som TA14 6RW 104 A1
Ham Street 116 C4
Hambleden 134 C4
Hambledon Hants 107 F1
Hambledon Surr 121 E4
Hambleton Lancs 191 G3
Hambleton NYorks 195 E4
Hambridge 116 A5
Hambrook SGlos 131 F5
Hambrook WSuss 107 G2
Hameringham 176 B1
Hamerton 161 G5
Hamilton 234 B4
Hamlet Devon 103 E3
Hamlet Dorset 104 B2
Hammer 121 D4
Hammerpot 108 C3
Hammersmith 135 B5
Hammersmith Apollo
    GtLon W6 9QH 11 E5
Hammerwich 158 C2
Hammerwood 122 D5
Hammond Street 136 C5
Hammoon 105 E1
Hamnavoe Shet 279 C9
Hamnavoe Shet 278 D4
Hamnavoe Shet 278 B4
Hamnavoe Shet 278 D5
Hamnish Clifford 145 E2
Hamp 115 F4
Hampden Park 116 B3
Hampden Park Stadium
    Glas G42 9BA 30 D4
Hampnett 132 D1
Hampole 186 C2
Hampreston 105 G3
Hampstead 136 B4
Hampstead
    Norreys 134 A5
Hampsthwaite 194 B2
Hampton Devon 103 F3
Hampton GtLon 121 G1
Hampton Kent 125 D4
Hampton Peter 161 G3
Hampton Shrop 157 G4
Hampton Swin 133 D3
Hampton Worcs 146 C3
Hampton Bishop 145 E4
Hampton Court Palace &
    Garden GtLon
    KT8 9AU 11 B8
Hampton Fields 132 A3
Hampton Heath 170 B3
Hampton in Arden 159 E4
Hampton Loade 157 G4
Hampton Lovett 146 A1
Hampton Lucy 147 E2
Hampton on the
    Hill 147 E1
Hampton Poyle 134 A1
Hampton Wick 121 G1
Hamptworth 106 B1
Hamsey 109 G2
Hamstall Ridware 158 D1
Hamstead 106 D4
Hamstead Marshall 119 F1
Hamsteels 212 A4
Hamsterley Dur 212 A4
Hamsterley Dur 212 A2
Hamsterley Forest Dur
    DL13 3NL 211 G5
Hamworthy 105 F3
Hanbury Staffs 172 C5
Hanbury Worcs 146 B1
Hanbury Woodend 172 C5
Hanby 175 F4
Hanchurch 171 F3
Handa Island 272 D4
Handbridge 170 B1
Handcross 122 B5
Handforth 184 C4

Handley ChesW&C 170 B2
Handley Derbys 173 E1
Handley Green 137 F2
Handsacre 158 C1
Handside 136 B1
Handsworth SYorks 186 B4
Handsworth WMid 158 C4
Handwoodbank 156 D1
Handy Cross 135 D3
Hanford Dorset 105 E1
Hanford Stoke 171 F3
Hanging Bridge 172 C3
Hanging Houghton 160 C5
Hanging Langford 118 B4
Hangingshaw 217 F2
Hanham 131 F5
Hankelow 171 D3
Hankerton 132 B3
Hankham 110 B3
Hanley 171 F3
Hanley Castle 146 A3
Hanley Child 145 F1
Hanley Swan 146 A3
Hanley William 145 F1
Hanlith 193 F1
Hanmer 170 B4
Hannah 189 E5
Hannington Hants 119 G2
Hannington
    N'hants 160 D5
Hannington Swin 133 D3
Hannington Wick 133 D3
Hanslope 148 D3
Hanthorpe 175 F5
Hanwell GtLon 136 A4
Hanwell Oxon 147 G3
Hanwood 156 D2
Hanworth GtLon 136 A5
Hanworth Norf 178 C2
Happisburgh 179 E2
Happisburgh
    Common 179 E3
Hapsford 183 F5
Hapton Lancs 193 D4
Hapton Norf 164 C2
Harberton 101 D2
Harbertonford 101 D2
Harbledown 124 D3
Harborne 158 C4
Harborough Magna 159 G5
Harbost (Tabost) 271 H1
Harbottle 220 B1
Harbour Park Amusements,
    Littlehampton WSuss
    BN17 5LL 108 C3
Harbourneford 100 D1
Harbridge 106 A1
Harbridge Green 106 A1
Harburn 235 E3
Harbury 147 F2
Harby Leics 174 C4
Harby Notts 187 F5
Harcombe 103 E3
Harcombe Bottom 103 G3
Harden WMid 158 C4
Harden WYorks 193 G4
Hardendale 199 G1
Hardenhuish 132 B5
Hardgate Aber 261 F4
Hardgate NYorks 194 B1
Hardham 108 C2
Hardhorn 191 G4
Hardingham 178 B5
Hardingstone 148 C2
Hardington 117 E2
Hardington
    Mandeville 104 B1
Hardington Marsh 104 B2
Hardington Moor 104 B1
Hardley 106 D2
Hardley Street 179 E5
Hardmead 149 E3
Hardraw 201 D3
Hardstoft 173 F1
Hardway Hants 107 F2
Hardway Som 117 E4
Hardwick Bucks 134 D1
Hardwick Cambs 150 B2
Hardwick Lincs 187 F5
Hardwick N'hants 149 D1
Hardwick Norf 164 D2
Hardwick Oxon 133 F2
Hardwick Oxon 148 A5
Hardwick SYorks 186 B4
Hardwick WMid 158 C3
Hardwick Hall Derbys
    S44 5QJ 173 F1
Hardwick Hall Country Park,
    Sedgefield Dur
    TS21 2EH 212 C5
Hardwick Village 186 D5
Hardwicke Glos 146 B5
Hardwicke Glos 131 G1
Hardwicke Here 144 B3
Hardy's Green 152 A5
Hare Green 152 B5
Hare Hatch 134 C5
Hare Street Herts 150 B5
Hare Street Herts 150 B5
Hareby 176 B1
Harecroft 193 G4
Hareden 192 C2
Harefield 135 F3
Harehill 172 C4
Harehills 194 C4
Harehope 229 E4
Harelaw 234 D5
Hareplain 124 A5
Haresceugh 210 C3
Harescombe 132 A1
Haresfield 132 A1
Hareshaw NLan 234 C3
Hareshaw SLan 234 A5
Harestock 119 F4
Harewood 194 C3
Harewood End 145 E5
Harewood House WYorks
    LS17 9LG 194 C3
Harford Devon 100 C2
Harford Devon 102 B3
Hargate 164 C2
Hargatewall 185 F5
Hargrave ChesW&C 170 B1
Hargrave N'hants 161 F5
Hargrave Suff 151 F2
Hargrave Green 151 F2
Harker 218 B5
Harkstead 152 C4

Harlaston 159 E1
Harlaxton 175 E4
Harle Syke 193 E4
Harlech 167 E4
Harlech Castle Gwyn
    LL46 2YH 167 E4
Harlequin 174 B4
Harlescott 157 E1
Harlesden 136 B4
Harleston Devon 101 D3
Harleston Norf 164 D3
Harleston Suff 152 B1
Harlestone 148 C1
Harley Shrop 157 E2
Harley SYorks 186 A3
Harleyholm 226 A2
Harlington
    CenBeds 149 F4
Harlington GtLon 135 F5
Harlosh 263 H7
Harlow 136 D2
Harlow Hill 211 G1
Harlthorpe 195 G4
Harlton 150 B2
Harlyn 96 C2
Harman's Cross 105 F4
Harmby 202 A4
Harmer Green 136 B1
Harmer Hill 170 B5
Harmondsworth 135 F5
Harmston 175 E1
Harnage 157 E2
Harnham 118 C5
Harnhill 132 C2
Harold Hill 137 E3
Harold Park 137 E3
Harold Wood 137 E3
Haroldston West 126 B1
Haroldswick 278 F1
Harome 203 F4
Harpenden 136 A1
Harpford 103 D3
Harpham 196 C1
Harpley Norf 177 F5
Harpley Worcs 145 F1
Harpole 148 B1
Harpsdale 275 G3
Harpsden 134 C4
Harpswell 187 G4
Harpur Hill 185 E5
Harpurhey 184 C2
Harracott 113 F3
Harrapool 256 C2
Harrietfield 243 E2
Harrietsham 124 A3
Harringay 136 C4
Harrington Cumb 208 C4
Harrington Lincs 189 D5
Harrington N'hants 160 C5
Harringworth 161 E3
Harris 255 J5
Harris Green 164 D2
Harris Museum & Art
    Gallery, Preston Lancs
    PR1 2PP 192 B5
Harriseahead 171 F2
Harriston 209 E2
Harrogate 194 C2
Harrogate International
    Centre NYorks HG1 5LA
    74 Harrogate
Harrold 149 E2
Harrold-Odell Country Park
    Bed MK43 7DS 149 E2
Harrop Fold 192 D3
Harrow GtLon 136 A4
Harrow High 275 H1
Harrow Green 151 G2
Harrow Museum GtLon
    HA2 6PX 10 B1
Harrow on the Hill 136 A4
Harrow Weald 136 A3
Harrowbarrow 99 E3
Harrowden 149 F3
Harrowgate Hill 202 B1
Harry Stoke 131 F5
Harston Cambs 150 C2
Harston Leics 174 D4
Harswell 196 A3
Hart 213 D4
Hartburn 220 C3
Hartest 151 G2
Hartfield ESuss 123 D5
Hartfield High 264 D7
Hartford Cambs 162 A5
Hartford
    ChesW&C 184 A5
Hartford Som 114 C5
Hartford End 137 F1
Hartfordbridge 120 C2
Hartforth 202 A2
Hartgrove 105 E1
Harthill ChesW&C 170 C2
Harthill NLan 234 D3
Harthill SYorks 186 B4
Hartington 172 C1
Hartington Hall 220 C3
Hartland 112 C3
Hartland Quay 112 C3
Hartlebury 158 A5
Hartlepool 213 E4
Hartlepool's Maritime
    Experience Hart
    TS24 0XZ 213 D4
Hartley Cumb 200 C2
Hartley Kent 123 F2
Hartley Kent 123 G5
Hartley N'umb 221 F4
Hartley Green 171 G5
Hartley Mauditt 120 C4
Hartley Wespall 120 B2
Hartley Wintney 120 C2
Hartlington 193 G1
Hartlip 124 A2
Hartoft End 203 G3
Harton NYorks 195 G1
Harton Shrop 157 D4
Harton T&W 212 C1
Hartpury 146 A5
Hartrigge 228 A4
Hartshead 194 A5
Harthill 159 F3
Hartsholme Country Park
    Lincs LN6 0EY 175 E1
Hartshorne 173 E5
Hartsop 199 F1
Hartwell Bucks 134 C1

Hartwell ESuss 123 D5
Hartwell N'hants 148 C2
Hartwith 194 B1
Hartwood 234 C4
Harvel 123 F2
Harvington Worcs 146 C3
Harvington Worcs 158 A5
Harwell Notts 187 E3
Harwell Oxon 133 G4
Harwich 152 D4
Harwood Dur 211 E4
Harwood GtMan 184 B1
Harwood N'umb 220 C1
Harwood Dale 204 C3
Harwood on
    Teviot 227 F5
Harworth 186 D3
Hasbury 158 B4
Hascombe 121 E3
Haselbech 160 C5
Haselbury
    Plucknett 104 A1
Haseley 147 E1
Haseley Knob 159 E5
Haselor 146 D2
Hasfield 146 A5
Hasguard 126 B2
Haskayne 183 E2
Hasketon 153 D2
Hasland 173 E1
Hasland Green 173 E1
Haslemere 121 E4
Haslingden 193 D5
Haslingden Grane 193 D5
Haslingfield 150 C2
Haslington 171 E2
Hassall 171 E2
Hassall Green 171 E2
Hassall Street 124 C4
Hassendean 227 G3
Hassingham 179 E5
Hassocks 109 F2
Hassop 185 G5
Haster 275 J3
Hasthorpe 176 C1
Hastigrow 275 H2
Hastingleigh 124 C4
Hastings ESuss 110 D3
Hastings Som 103 G1
Hastings Fisherman's
    Museum ESuss
    TN34 3DW 75 Hastings
Hastingwood 137 D2
Hastoe 135 E2
Haswell 212 C3
Haswell Plough 212 C3
Hatch CenBeds 149 G3
Hatch Hants 120 B2
Hatch Beauchamp 116 A5
Hatch End 136 A3
Hatch Green 103 G1
Hatching Green 136 A1
Hatchmere 183 G5
Hatcliffe 188 C2
Hatfield Here 145 E2
Hatfield Herts 136 B2
Hatfield SYorks 187 D2
Hatfield Broad Oak 137 E1
Hatfield Heath 137 E1
Hatfield House Herts
    AL9 5NF 136 B2
Hatfield Peverel 137 G1
Hatfield
    Woodhouse 187 D2
Hatford 133 F3
Hatherden 119 E2
Hatherleigh 113 F5
Hathern 173 F5
Hatherop 132 D1
Hathersage 185 G4
Hathersage Booths 185 G4
Hathershaw 184 D2
Hatherton ChesE 171 D3
Hatherton Staffs 158 B1
Hatley St. George 150 A2
Hatt 99 D4
Hattingley 120 B4
Hatton Aber 261 J1
Hatton Derbys 172 D5
Hatton GtLon 136 A5
Hatton Lincs 188 B5
Hatton Shrop 157 D3
Hatton Warks 147 E1
Hatton Warr 183 G4
Hatton Castle 269 F6
Hatton Country World
    Warks
    CV35 8XA 147 E1
Hatton Heath 170 B1
Hatton of Fintray 261 G3
Hattoncrook 261 G2
Haugh 189 E5
Haugh Head 229 E4
Haugh of Glass 260 C1
Haugh of Urr 216 C4
Haugham 188 D4
Haughhead 234 A2
Haughley 152 B1
Haughley Green 152 B1
Haughley New
    Street 152 B1
Haughs 268 D6
Haughton ChesE 170 C2
Haughton Notts 187 D5
Haughton Powys 156 C1
Haughton Shrop 157 F3
Haughton Shrop 157 F1
Haughton Shrop 170 A5
Haughton Staffs 171 F5
Haughton Le Skerne 202 C1
Haultwick 150 B5
Haunn 254 B5
Haunton 159 E1
Hauxton 150 C2
Havannah 171 F1
Havant 107 G2
Haven 144 D2
Havenstreet 107 E3
Havercroft 186 A1
Haverfordwest
    (Hwlffordd) 126 C1
Haverhill 151 E3
Haverigg 198 C5
Havering Park 137 D3
Havering-atte-
    Bower 137 E3
Haversham 148 D3

Haverthwaite 199 E4
Heads Nook 210 A2
Heady Hill 184 C1
Heage 178 E2
Healaugh NYorks 201 F3
Healaugh NYorks 195 E3
Heald Green 184 C4
Heale Devon 113 G1
Heale Som 116 A4
Healey Lancs 184 C1
Healey N'umb 211 G2
Healey WYorks 194 A4
Healey WYorks 194 B5
Healey's Cornish Cyder Farm
    Corn TR4 9LW 96 A3
Healing 188 C1
Heamoor 94 B3
Heaning 199 F3
Heanish 246 B2
Heanor 173 F3
Heanton
    Punchardon 113 F2
Heanton Satchville 113 F4
Heap Bridge 184 C1
Heapey 192 C5
Heapham 187 F4
Hearn 120 D4
Heart of the Country
    Centre Staffs
    WS14 9QR 158 D2
Hearthstane 226 C3
Heasley Mill 114 A4
Heast 256 C3
Heath Cardiff 130 A4
Heath Derbys 173 F1
Heath WYorks 186 A1
Heath & Reach 149 E5
Heath End Derbys 173 E5
Heath End Hants 119 G1
Heath End Hants 119 F1
Heath End Surr 120 D3
Heath Hayes 158 C1
Heath Hill 157 G1
Heath House 116 B3
Heath Town 158 B3
Heathbrook 170 D5
Heathcot 261 G4
Heathcote Derbys 172 C1
Heathcote Shrop 171 D5
Heathencote 148 C3
Heather 159 F1
Heatherton Activity Park
    Pembs
    SA70 8RJ 127 D2
Heathfield Devon 102 B5
Heathfield ESuss 110 A1
Heathfield NYorks 194 A1
Heathfield Som 115 E5
Heathrow Airport 135 F5
Heathton 158 A3
Heatley 184 B4
Heaton Lancs 192 A1
Heaton Staffs 171 G1
Heaton T&W 212 B1
Heaton WYorks 194 A4
Heaton Moor 184 C3
Heaton Park GtMan
    M25 2SW 25 C7
Heaton's Bridge 183 F1
Heaverham 123 E3
Heaviley 184 D4
Heavitree 102 C3
Hebburn 212 C1
Hebden 193 G1
Hebden Bridge 193 F5
Hebden Green 170 D1
Hebing End 150 B5
Hebron Carmar 141 E5
Hebron N'umb 221 D3
Heck 217 E2
Heckfield 120 C1
Heckfield Green 164 C4
Heckfordbridge 152 A5
Heckingham 165 E2
Heckington 175 G3
Heckmondwike 194 B5
Heddington 118 A1
Heddle 277 C6
Heddon-on-the-
    Wall 212 A1
Hedenham 165 E2
Hedge End 107 D1
Hedgerley 135 E4
Hedging 116 A5
Hedley on the Hill 211 G2
Hednesford 158 C1
Hedon 197 D5
Hedsor 135 E4
Heeley 186 A4
Heglibister 279 C7
Heighington Darl 212 B5
Heighington Lincs 175 F1
Heightington 157 G5
Heights of Brae 266 C5
Heilam 273 G2
Heisker Islands (Monach
    Islands) 262 B5
Heithat 217 F2
Heiton 228 B3
Hele Devon 113 F1
Hele Devon 102 C5
Hele Devon 98 D1
Hele Devon 102 A5
Hele Som 115 E5
Hele Torbay 101 F1
Hele Bridge 113 F5
Hele Lane 102 A1
Helebridge 112 C5
Helensburgh 233 D1
Helford 95 E4
Helhoughton 177 G5
Helions Bumpstead 151 E3
Hell Corner 119 E1
Hellaby 186 C3
Helland Corn 97 E2
Helland Som 116 A5
Hellandbridge 97 E2
Hellesdon 178 D4
Hellidon 148 A2
Hellifield 193 E2
Hellingly 110 A2
Hellington 179 E5
Hellister 279 C8
Helmdon 148 A3
Helmingham 152 C2
Helmington Row 212 A4
Helmsdale 275 F7

Helmshore 193 D5
Helmsley 203 F4
Helperby 194 D1
Helperthorpe 204 C5
Helpringham 175 G3
Helpston 161 G2
Helsby 183 F5
Helsey 189 F5
Helston 95 D4
Helstone 97 E1
Helton 210 B5
Helwith 201 F2
Helwith Bridge 193 E1
Hem 156 B2
Hemborough Post 101 E2
Hemel Hempstead 135 F2
Hemerdon 100 B2
Hemingbrough 195 F4
Hemingby 188 C5
Hemingfield 186 A2
Hemingford Abbots 162 A5
Hemingford Grey 162 A5
Hemingstone 152 C2
Hemington Leics 173 F5
Hemington
    N'hants 161 F4
Hemington Som 117 E2
Hemley 153 D3
Hemlington 203 D1
Hemp Green 153 E1
Hempholme 196 C2
Hempnall 164 D2
Hempnall Green 164 D2
Hempriggs 267 J5
Hempriggs House 275 J4
Hempstead Essex 151 E4
Hempstead Med 123 G2
Hempstead Norf 179 F3
Hempstead Norf 178 C2
Hempsted 132 A1
Hempton Norf 178 A3
Hempton Oxon 147 G4
Hemsby 179 F4
Hemswell 187 G3
Hemswell Cliff 187 G4
Hemsworth 186 B1
Hemyock 103 E2
Henbury Bristol 131 E5
Henbury ChesE 184 C5
Henderland 216 C3
Hendersyde Park 228 B3
Hendham 100 D2
Hendon GtLon 136 B4
Hendon T&W 212 C2
Hendraburnick 97 F1
Hendre Bridgend 129 F4
Hendre Gwyn 166 C2
Hendreforgan 129 F4
Hendy 128 B2
Heneglwys 180 C5
Henfield SGlos 131 F5
Henfield WSuss 109 E2
Henford 99 D1
Hengherst 124 B5
Hengoed Caerp 130 A3
Hengoed Powys 144 B3
Hengoed Shrop 169 F4
Hengrave 151 G1
Henham 150 D5
Heniarth 156 A2
Henlade 115 F5
Henley Dorset 104 C2
Henley Shrop 157 E5
Henley Som 116 B4
Henley Som 104 A2
Henley Suff 152 C2
Henley WSuss 121 D5
Henley Corner 116 B4
Henley Park 121 E2
Henley-in-Arden 147 D1
Henley-on-Thames 134 C4
Henley's Down 110 C2
Henllan Carmar 141 G3
Henllan Denb 168 C1
Henllan Amgoed 141 E5
Henllys 130 B3
Henlow 149 G4
Hennock 102 B4
Henny Street 151 G4
Henryd 181 F5
Henry's Moat 140 D5
Hensall 195 E5
Henshaw 211 D1
Hensingham 208 C5
Henstead 165 F3
Hensting 119 F5
Henstridge 104 D1
Henstridge Ash 104 D1
Henstridge
    Bowden 117 D5
Henstridge Marsh 117 E5
Henton Oxon 134 C2
Henton Som 116 B3
Henwood 97 G2
Heogan 279 D8
Heol Senni 143 F5
Heolgerrig 129 G2
Heol-y-Cyw 129 F4
Hepburn 229 E4
Hepburn Bell 229 E4
Hepple 220 B1
Hepscott 221 E3
Hepthorne Lane 173 F1
Heptonstall 193 F5
Hepworth Suff 164 A4
Hepworth WYorks 185 F2
Hepworth South
    Common 164 A4
Herbrandston 126 B2
Hereford 145 E3
Hereford Cathedral
    Here HR1 2NG
    75 Hereford
Heriot 236 A4
Heritage Motor Centre,
    Gaydon Warks
    CV35 0BJ 147 F2
Herm 101 C5
Hermiston 235 F2
Hermitage D&G 216 B4
Hermitage Dorset 104 C2
Hermitage ScBord 218 D2
Hermitage WBerks 134 A5
Hermitage WSuss 107 G2
Hermon Aberd 184 A3
Hermon Carmar 141 G4
Hermon IoA 166 C1
Hermon Pembs 141 F4

Her - Hou

Herne 125 D2
Herne Bay 125 D2
Herne Common 125 D2
Herne Pound 123 F3
Herner 113 F3
Hernhill 124 C2
Herodsfoot 97 G3
Herongate 137 F3
Heron's Ghyll 109 G1
Heronsgate 135 F3
Herriard 120 B3
Herringfleet 165 F2
Herring's Green 149 F3
Herringswell 151 F1
Herringthorpe 186 B3
Hersden 125 D2
Hersham Corn 112 C5
Hersham Surr 121 G1
Herstmonceux 110 B2
Herston 277 D8
Hertford 136 C1
Hertford Heath 136 C1
Hertingfordbury 136 C1
Hesket Newmarket 209 G3
Hesketh Bank 192 A5
Hesketh Lane 192 C3
Heskin Green 183 G1
Hesleden 212 D4
Hesleyside 220 A3
Heslington 195 F2
Hessay 195 E2
Hessenford 98 D5
Hessett 152 A1
Hessle 196 C5
Hest Bank 192 A1
Hester's Way 146 B5
Hestley Green 152 C1
Heston 136 A5
Heswall 183 D4
Hethe 148 A5
Hethelpit Cross 145 G5
Hetherington 220 A4
Hethersett 178 C5
Hethersgill 210 A1
Hethpool 228 C4
Hett 212 B4
Hetton 193 F2
Hetton-le-Hole 212 C3
Heugh 220 C4
Heugh-head Aber 260 B3
Heugh-head Aber 260 D5
Heveningham 165 E4
Hever 123 D4
Hever Castle & Gardens Kent TN8 7NG 123 D4
Heversham 199 F4
Hevingham 178 C3
Hewas Water 97 D5
Hewell Grange 146 C1
Hewell Lane 146 C1
Hewelsfield 131 E2
Hewelsfield Common 131 E2
Hewish NSom 116 B1
Hewish Som 104 A2
Hewood 103 G2
Heworth 195 F2
Hewton 99 F1
Hexham 211 F1
Hexham Abbey N'umb NE46 3NB 211 F1
Hextable 137 E5
Hexthorpe 186 C2
Hexton 149 G4
Hexworthy 99 G3
Hey 193 E3
Hey Houses 191 G5
Heybridge Essex 137 F3
Heybridge Essex 138 B2
Heybridge Basin 138 B2
Heybrook Bay 100 A3
Heydon Cambs 150 C3
Heydon Norf 178 C3
Heydour 175 F4
Heylipoll 246 A2
Heylor 278 B4
Heyop 156 B5
Heysham 192 A1
Heyshaw 194 A1
Heyshott 108 A2
Heyside 184 D2
Heytesbury 118 A3
Heythrop 147 F5
Heywood GtMan 184 C1
Heywood Wilts 117 F2
Hibaldstow 187 G2
Hibb's Green 151 G2
Hickleton 186 B2
Hickling Norf 179 F3
Hickling Notts 174 B5
Hickling Green 179 F3
Hickling Heath 179 F3
Hickstead 109 E1
Hidcote Bartrim 147 D3
Hidcote Boyce 147 D3
Hidcote Manor Garden Glos GL55 6LR 147 D3
High Ackworth 186 B1
High Angerton 220 C3
High Balantyre 240 C3
High Bankhill 210 B3
High Beach 136 D3
High Bentham (Higher Bentham) 192 C1
High Bickington 113 F3
High Birkwith 200 C5
High Blantyre 234 A4
High Bonnybridge 234 C2
High Borgue 216 A5
High Borve 271 G2
High Bradfield 185 G3
High Bradley 193 G3
High Bransholme 196 D4
High Bray 113 G2
High Bridge 209 G2
High Brooms 123 E4
High Bullen 113 F3
High Burton 202 B4
High Buston 221 E1
High Callerton 221 D4
High Casterton 200 B5
High Catton 195 G2
High Close 202 A1
High Cogges 133 F2
High Common 164 C3
High Coniscliffe 202 B1
High Crompton 184 D2
High Cross Hants 120 C5
High Cross Herts 136 C1
High Cross WSuss 109 E2
High Easter 137 F1
High Ellington 202 A4
High Entercommon 202 C2
High Ercall 157 E1
High Etherley 212 A5
High Ferry 176 B3
High Flatts 185 G2
High Garrett 151 F5
High Gate 193 F5
High Grange 212 A4
High Green Norf 178 C5
High Green Norf 178 A4
High Green Norf 178 A5
High Green Suff 151 G1
High Green SYorks 186 A3
High Green Worcs 146 A3
High Halden 124 A5
High Halstow 137 G5
High Ham 116 B4
High Harrington 208 D4
High Harrogate 194 C2
High Hatton 170 D5
High Hauxley 221 E1
High Hawsker 204 C2
High Heath Shrop 171 D5
High Heath WMid 158 C2
High Hesket 210 A3
High Hesleden 213 D4
High Hoyland 185 G1
High Hunsley 196 B4
High Hurstwood 109 G1
High Hutton 195 G1
High Ireby 209 F3
High Kelling 178 B2
High Kilburn 203 E5
High Kingthorpe 204 B4
High Knipe 199 G1
High Lane Derbys 173 F3
High Lane GtMan 185 D4
High Lane Worcs 145 F1
High Laver 137 E2
High Legh 184 B4
High Leven 203 D1
High Littleton 116 D2
High Lodge Forest Centre Suff IP27 0AF 163 G4
High Lorton 209 E4
High Marishes 204 B5
High Marnham 187 F5
High Melton 186 C2
High Moor 186 B4
High Moorland Visitor Centre, Princetown Devon PL20 6QF 99 F3
High Newton 199 F4
High Newton-by-the-Sea 229 G4
High Nibthwaite 199 D3
High Offley 171 E5
High Ongar 137 E2
High Onn 158 A1
High Park Corner 152 B5
High Roding 137 F1
High Shaw 201 D3
High Spen 212 A1
High Stoop 212 A3
High Street Corn 97 D4
High Street Kent 123 G5
High Street Suff 153 F2
High Street Suff 165 E3
High Street Suff 165 F4
High Street Suff 151 G3
High Street Green 152 B2
High Throston 213 D4
High Town 158 B1
High Toynton 176 A1
High Trewhitt 220 C1
High Wham 212 A5
High Wigsell 110 C1
High Woods Country Park Essex CO4 5JR 152 B5
High Woolaston 131 E3
High Worsall 202 C2
High Wray 199 E3
High Wych 137 D1
High Wycombe 135 D3
Higham Derbys 173 E2
Higham Kent 137 G5
Higham Lancs 193 E4
Higham Suff 151 F1
Higham Suff 152 B4
Higham SYorks 186 A2
Higham Dykes 220 D4
Higham Ferrers 149 E1
Higham Gobian 149 G4
Higham on the Hill 159 F3
Higham Wood 123 F4
Highampton 113 E5
Highams Park 136 C3
Highbridge Hants 119 F5
Highbridge Som 116 A3
Highbrook 122 C5
Highburton 185 F1
Highbury 117 D3
Highclere 119 F1
Highcliffe 106 B3
Higher Alham 117 D3
Higher Ansty 105 D2
Higher Ashton 102 B4
Higher Ballam 191 G4
Higher Bentham (High Bentham) 192 C1
Higher Blackley 184 C2
Higher Brixham 101 F2
Higher Cheriton 103 E2
Higher Combe 114 C4
Higher Folds 184 A2
Higher Gabwell 101 F1
Higher Green 184 B3
Higher Halstock Leigh 104 B2
Higher Kingcombe 104 B3
Higher Kinnerton 170 A1
Higher Muddiford 113 F2
Higher Nyland 117 E5
Higher Prestacott 99 D1
Higher Standen 193 D3
Higher Tale 103 D2
Higher Thrushgill 192 C1
Higher Town Corn 97 E3
Higher Town IoS 96 B1
Higher Walreddon 99 E3
Higher Walton Lancs 192 B5
Higher Walton Warr 183 G4
Higher Wambrook 103 F2
Higher Whatcombe 105 E2
Higher Wheelton 192 C5
Higher Whiteleigh 98 C1
Higher Whitley 184 A4
Higher Wincham 184 A5
Higher Woodhill 184 B1
Higher Woodsford 105 D4
Higher Wraxall 104 B2
Higher Wych 170 B3
Highfield ERid 195 G4
Highfield NAyr 233 E4
Highfield Oxon 148 A5
Highfield SYorks 186 A4
Highfield T&W 212 A2
Highfields Cambs 150 B2
Highfields N'umb 237 G4
Highgate ESuss 122 D5
Highgate GtLon 136 B4
Highgreen Manor 220 A2
Highlane ChesE 171 F1
Highlane Derbys 186 B4
Highlaws 209 E2
Highleadon 145 G5
Highleigh Devon 114 C5
Highleigh WSuss 108 A4
Highley 157 G4
Highmead 142 B3
Highmoor Cross 134 B4
Highmoor Hill 131 D4
Highnam 131 G1
Highstead 125 E2
Highsted 124 B2
Highstreet 124 C2
Highstreet Green Essex 151 F4
Highstreet Green Surr 121 E4
Hightae 217 E3
Highter's Heath 158 C5
Hightown Hants 106 A2
Hightown Mersey 183 D2
Hightown Green 152 A2
Highway 132 C5
Highweek 102 B5
Highwood 145 F1
Highwood Hill 136 B3
Highworth 133 E3
Hilborough 163 G2
Hilcote 173 F2
Hilcott 118 C2
Hilden Park 123 E4
Hildenborough 123 E4
Hildenley 203 G5
Hildersham 150 D3
Hilderstone 171 G4
Hilderthorpe 197 D1
Hilfield 104 C2
Hilgay 163 E3
Hill SGlos 131 F3
Hill Warks 147 G1
Hill Worcs 146 B3
Hill Brow 120 C5
Hill Chorlton 171 E4
Hill Common 179 F3
Hill Cottages 203 G3
Hill Croome 146 A3
Hill Deverill 117 F3
Hill Dyke 176 B3
Hill End Dur 211 G4
Hill End Fife 243 F5
Hill End Glos 146 A4
Hill End GtLon 135 F3
Hill End NYorks 193 G2
Hill Green 150 C4
Hill Head 107 E2
Hill Houses 157 F5
Hill Mountain 126 C2
Hill of Beath 235 F1
Hill of Fearn 267 F4
Hill Ridware 158 C1
Hill Row 162 C5
Hill Side 185 F1
Hill Street 106 C1
Hill Top Hants 106 D2
Hill Top SYorks 186 B3
Hill Top SYorks 185 G4
Hill View 105 F3
Hill Wootton 147 F1
Hillam 195 E5
Hillbeck 200 C1
Hillberry 190 B4
Hillborough 125 E2
Hillbrae Aber 268 E6
Hillbrae Aber 261 F2
Hillbrae Aber 261 G1
Hillbutts 105 F2
Hillclifflane 173 D3
Hillend Aber 268 C6
Hillend Fife 235 F1
Hillend Midlo 235 G3
Hillend NLan 234 C3
Hillend Swan 128 A3
Hillend Green 145 G5
Hillersland 131 E1
Hillesden 148 B5
Hillesley 131 G4
Hillfarrance 115 E5
Hillfoot End 149 G4
Hillhead Devon 101 F2
Hillhead SAyr 224 C3
Hillhead of Auchentumb 269 H5
Hillhead of Cocklaw 269 J6
Hilliard's Cross 159 D1
Hilliclay 275 G2
Hillingdon 135 F4
Hillington Glas 233 G3
Hillington Norf 177 F5
Hillmorton 160 A5
Hillockhead Aber 260 B4
Hillockhead Aber 260 C3
Hillowton 216 B4
Hillpound 107 E1
Hill's End 149 E4
Hills Town 173 F1
Hillsborough 186 A3
Hillsford Bridge 114 A3
Hillside Aber 261 H5
Hillside Angus 253 F3
Hillside Moray 267 J5
Hillside Shet 279 D6
Hillside Worcs 145 G1
Hillswick 278 B5
Hillway 107 F4
Hillwell 279 F9
Hillyfields 106 C1
Hilmarton 132 C5
Hilperton 117 F2
Hilsea 107 F2
Hilston 197 E4
Hilton Cambs 150 A1
Hilton Cumb 210 D5
Hilton Derbys 172 D4
Hilton Dorset 105 D2
Hilton Dur 212 A5
Hilton High 267 G3
Hilton Shrop 157 G3
Hilton Staffs 158 C2
Hilton Stock 203 D1
Hilton Croft 261 H1
Hilton of Cadboll 267 F4
Hilton of Delnies 267 F6
Himbleton 146 B2
Himley 158 A3
Himley Hall & Park WMid DY3 4DF 14 A2
Hincaster 199 G4
Hinchley Wood 121 G1
Hinckley 159 G3
Hinderclay 164 B4
Hinderton 183 E5
Hinderwell 203 G1
Hindford 170 A4
Hindhead 121 D4
Hindley GtMan 184 A2
Hindley N'umb 211 G2
Hindley Green 184 A2
Hindlip 146 A2
Hindolveston 178 B3
Hindon Som 114 C3
Hindon Wilts 118 A4
Hindringham 178 A2
Hingham 178 B5
Hinksford 158 A4
Hinstock 171 D5
Hintlesham 152 B3
Hinton Glos 131 F2
Hinton Hants 106 B3
Hinton Here 144 C4
Hinton N'hants 148 A2
Hinton SGlos 131 G5
Hinton Shrop 156 D2
Hinton Admiral 106 B3
Hinton Ampner 119 G5
Hinton Blewett 116 C2
Hinton Charterhouse 117 E2
Hinton Martell 105 G2
Hinton on the Green 146 C3
Hinton Parva Dorset 105 F2
Hinton Parva Swin 133 E4
Hinton St. George 104 A1
Hinton St. Mary 105 D1
Hinton Waldrist 133 F3
Hinton-in-the-Hedges 148 A4
Hints Shrop 157 F5
Hints Staffs 159 D2
Hinwick 149 E1
Hinxhill 124 C4
Hinxton 150 C3
Hinxworth 150 A3
Hipperholme 194 A5
Hipsburn 229 G5
Hipswell 202 A3
Hirn 261 F4
Hirnant 169 D5
Hirst 221 E3
Hirst Courtney 195 F5
Hirwaen 169 E1
Hirwaun 129 F2
Hiscott 113 F3
Histon 150 C1
Hitcham Bucks 135 E4
Hitcham Suff 152 A2
Hitchin 149 G5
Hither Green 136 C5
Hittisleigh 102 A3
Hittisleigh Barton 102 A3
Hive 196 A4
Hixon 172 B5
Hoaden 125 E3
Hoaldalbert 144 C5
Hoar Cross 172 C5
Hoar Park Craft Centre Warks CV10 0QU 159 E3
Hoarwithy 145 E5
Hoath 125 E2
Hobarris 156 C5
Hobbister 277 C7
Hobbles Green 151 F2
Hobbs Cross 137 D3
Hobbs Lots Bridge 162 B2
Hobkirk 227 G4
Hobland Hall 179 G5
Hobson 212 A2
Hoby 160 B1
Hockerill 150 C5
Hockering 178 B4
Hockerton 174 C2
Hockley 138 B3
Hockley Heath 159 D5
Hockliffe 149 E5
Hockwold cum Wilton 163 F4
Hockworthy 102 D1
Hoddesdon 136 C2
Hoddlesden 192 D5
Hodgehill 171 F1
Hodgeston 126 D3
Hodnet 170 D5
Hodnetheath 170 D5
Hodsoll Street 123 F2
Hodson 133 D4
Hodthorpe 186 C5
Hoe 178 A4
Hoe Gate 107 F1
Hoff 200 B1
Hoffleet Stow 176 A4
Hoggard's Green 151 G2
Hoggeston 148 D5
Hoggie 268 D5
Hoggrill's End 159 E3
Hogha Gearraidh 262 C4
Hoghton 192 C5
Hognaston 172 D2
Hogsthorpe 189 F5
Holbeach 176 B5
Holbeach Bank 176 B5
Holbeach Clough 176 B5
Holbeach Drove 162 B1
Holbeach Hurn 176 B5
Holbeach St. Johns 162 B1
Holbeach St. Marks 176 B4
Holbeach St. Matthew 176 C4
Holbeck 186 C5
Holbeck Woodhouse 186 C5
Holberrow Green 146 C2
Holbeton 100 C2
Holborough 123 G2
Holbrook Derbys 173 E3
Holbrook Suff 152 C4
Holbrooks 159 F4
Holburn 229 E3
Holbury 106 D2
Holcombe Devon 102 C5
Holcombe GtMan 184 B1
Holcombe Som 117 D3
Holcombe Burnell Barton 102 B3
Holcombe Rogus 103 D1
Holcot 148 C1
Holden 193 D3
Holden Gate 193 E5
Holdenby 148 B1
Holdenhurst 106 A3
Holder's Green 151 E5
Holders Hill 136 B4
Holdgate 157 E4
Holdingham 175 F3
Holditch 103 G2
Hole 103 E1
Hole Park 124 A5
Holehouse 185 E3
Hole-in-the-Wall 145 F5
Holford 115 E3
Holgate 195 E2
Holker 199 E5
Holkham 177 G3
Hollacombe Devon 113 D5
Hollacombe Devon 102 B2
Hollacombe Town 113 G4
Holland Ork 276 D2
Holland Ork 276 F5
Holland Surr 122 D3
Holland Fen 176 A3
Holland-on-Sea 139 E1
Hollandstoun 276 G2
Hollee 218 A5
Hollesley 153 E3
Hollicombe 101 F1
Hollingbourne 124 A3
Hollingbury 109 F3
Hollingrove 110 B1
Hollington Derbys 172 D4
Hollington ESuss 110 C2
Hollington Staffs 172 B4
Hollingworth 185 E3
Hollins 186 A5
Hollins Green 184 A3
Hollins Lane 192 A2
Hollinsclough 172 B1
Hollinwood GtMan 184 D2
Hollinwood Shrop 170 C4
Hollocombe 113 G4
Hollow Meadows 185 G4
Holloway 173 E2
Hollowell 160 B5
Holly Bush 170 B3
Holly End 162 C2
Holly Green 134 C2
Hollybush Caerp 130 A2
Hollybush EAyr 224 B4
Hollybush Worcs 145 G4
Hollyhurst 170 C3
Hollym 197 F5
Hollywater 120 D4
Hollywood 158 C5
Holm D&G 218 A2
Holm (Tolm) Na H-E. Siar 271 G4
Holm of Drumlanrig 216 C1
Holmbridge 185 F2
Holmbury St. Mary 121 G3
Holmbush 122 B5
Holme Cambs 161 G4
Holme Cumb 199 G5
Holme NLincs 187 G2
Holme Notts 174 D2
Holme NYorks 202 C4
Holme WYorks 185 F2
Holme Chapel 193 E5
Holme Hale 163 G2
Holme Lacy 145 E4
Holme Marsh 144 C2
Holme next the Sea 177 F3
Holme on the Wolds 196 B3
Holme Pierrepont 174 B4
Holme St. Cuthbert 209 E2
Holme-on-Spalding-Moor 196 A4
Holmer 145 E3
Holmer Green 135 E3
Holmes 183 F1
Holmes Chapel 171 E1
Holme's Hill 110 A2
Holmesfield 186 A5
Holmeswood 183 F1
Holmewood 173 F1
Holmfield 193 G5
Holmfirth 185 F2
Holmhead D&G 216 B2
Holmhead EAyr 225 D3
Holmpton 197 F5
Holmrook 198 B2
Holmsgarth 279 D8
Holmside 212 B3
Holmsleigh Green 103 F2
Holmston 224 B3
Holmwrangle 210 B3
Holne 100 D1
Holnest 104 C2
Holnicote 114 C3
Holsworthy 112 D5
Holsworthy Beacon 113 D5
Holt Dorset 105 G2
Holt Norf 178 B2
Holt Wilts 117 F1
Holt Worcs 146 A1
Holt Wrex 170 B2
Holt End Hants 120 B4
Holt End Worcs 146 C1
Holt Fleet 146 A1
Holt Heath Dorset 105 G2
Holt Heath Worcs 146 A1
Holt Wood 105 G2
Holtby 195 F2
Holton Oxon 134 B2
Holton Som 117 D5
Holton Suff 165 F4
Holton cum Beckering 188 B4
Holton Heath 105 F3
Holton le Clay 188 C2
Holton le Moor 188 A3
Holton St. Mary 152 B4
Holtspur 135 E4
Holtye 123 D5
Holtye Common 123 D5
Holway 115 F5
Holwell Dorset 104 C1
Holwell Herts 149 G4
Holwell Leics 174 C5
Holwell Oxon 133 E2
Holwell Som 117 E3
Holwick 211 F5
Holworth 105 D4
Holy Cross 158 B5
Holy Island IoA 180 A5
Holy Island (Lindisfarne) N'umb 229 F2
Holy Trinity Church, Skipton NYorks BD23 1NJ 193 F2
Holy Trinity Church, Stratford-upon-Avon Warks CV37 6BG 85 Stratford-upon-Avon
Holybourne 120 C3
Holyfield 136 C2
Holyhead (Caergybi) 180 A4
Holymoorside 173 E1
Holyport 135 D5
Holystone 220 B1
Holytown 234 B3
Holywell Cambs 162 B5
Holywell Corn 96 B4
Holywell Dorset 104 B2
Holywell ESuss 110 B4
Holywell (Treffynnon) Flints 182 C5
Holywell N'umb 221 F4
Holywell Bay Fun Park Corn TR8 5PW 96 B4
Holywell Green 185 E1
Holywell Lake 115 E5
Holywell Row 163 F5
Holywood 216 D2
Hom Green 145 E5
Homer 157 F2
Homersfield 165 D3
Homington 118 C5
Homore (Tobha Mòr) 254 C1
Honey Hill 124 D2
Honey Street 118 C1
Honey Tye 152 A4
Honeyborough 126 C2
Honeybourne 146 D3
Honeychurch 113 G5
Honicknowle 100 A2
Honiley 159 E5
Honing 179 E3
Honingham 178 C4
Honington Lincs 175 E3
Honington Suff 164 A4
Honington Warks 147 E3
Honiton 103 E2
Honkley 170 A2
Honley 185 F1
Hoo Med 137 G5
Hoo Suff 153 D2
Hoo Green 184 B4
Hoo Meavy 100 B1
Hood Green 186 A2
Hood Hill 186 A3
Hooe ESuss 110 B3
Hooe Plym 100 B2
Hooe Common 110 B2
Hook Cambs 162 C3
Hook ERid 195 G5
Hook GtLon 121 G1
Hook Hants 120 C2
Hook Hants 107 E2
Hook Pembs 126 C1
Hook Wilts 132 C4
Hook Green Kent 123 F5
Hook Green Kent 123 F2
Hook Green Kent 137 F5
Hook Green Kent 137 E5
Hook Norton 147 F4
Hook-a-Gate 157 D2
Hooke 104 B2
Hookgate 171 E4
Hookway 102 B3
Hookwood 122 B4
Hoole 170 B1
Hooley 122 B3
Hoop 131 E2
Hooton 183 E5
Hooton Levitt 186 C3
Hooton Pagnell 186 B2
Hooton Roberts 186 B3
Hop Farm, The Kent TN12 6PY 123 F4
Hop Pocket, The Here WR6 5BT 145 F3
Hop Pole 161 G1
Hopcrofts Holt 147 G5
Hope Derbys 185 F4
Hope Devon 100 C4
Hope Flints 170 A2
Hope Powys 156 B2
Hope Shrop 156 C2
Hope Staffs 172 C2
Hope Bagot 157 E5
Hope Bowdler 157 D3
Hope End Green 151 D5
Hope Mansell 131 F1
Hope under Dinmore 145 E2
Hopehouse 227 D4
Hopeman 267 J5
Hope's Green 137 G4
Hopesay 156 C4
Hopkinstown 129 G3
Hopley's Green 144 C2
Hopperton 194 D2
Hopsford 159 G4
Hopstone 157 G3
Hopton Derbys 173 D2
Hopton Norf 165 G2
Hopton Shrop 170 C5
Hopton Shrop 170 A5
Hopton Staffs 171 G5
Hopton Suff 164 A4
Hopton Cangeford 157 E4
Hopton Castle 156 C5
Hopton Wafers 157 F5
Hoptonheath 156 C5
Hopwas 159 D2
Hopwood 158 C5
Horam 110 A2
Horbling 175 G4
Horbury 185 G1
Horden 212 D3
Horderley 156 D4
Hordle 106 B3
Hordley 170 A4
Horeb Carmar 128 A2
Horeb Cere 141 G3
Horeb Flints 169 F2
Horfield 131 E5
Horham 164 D4
Horkesley Heath 152 A5
Horkstow 187 G1
Horley Oxon 147 G3
Horley Surr 122 B4
Horn Hill 135 F3
Hornblotton 116 C4
Hornblotton Green 116 C4
Hornby Lancs 192 B1
Hornby NYorks 202 B3
Hornby NYorks 202 C2
Horncastle 176 A1
Hornchurch 137 E4
Horncliffe 237 G5
Horndean Hants 107 G1
Horndean ScBord 237 G5
Horndon 99 F2
Horndon on the Hill 137 F4
Horne 122 C4
Horne Row 137 G2
Horner 114 B3
Horniehaugh 252 C3
Horniman Museum GtLon SE23 3PQ 13 C7
Horning 179 E4
Horninghold 160 D3
Horninglow 172 D5
Horningsea 150 C1
Horningsham 117 F3
Horningtoft 178 A3
Horningtops 97 G3
Horns Cross Devon 113 D3
Horns Cross ESuss 110 D1
Horns Green 123 D3
Hornsbury 103 G1
Hornsby 210 B3
Hornsby Gate 210 B2
Hornsea 197 E3
Hornsea Freeport ERid HU18 1UT 197 E3
Hornsey 136 C4
Hornton 147 F3
Horrabridge 100 B1
Horridge 102 A5
Horringer 151 G1
Horrocks Fold 184 B1
Horse Bridge 171 G2
Horsebridge Devon 99 E3
Horsebridge Hants 119 E4
Horsebrook 158 A1
Horsecastle 116 B1
Horsehay 157 F2
Horseheath 151 E3
Horsehouse 201 F4
Horsell 121 E2
Horseman's Green 170 B3
Horsenden 134 C2
Horseshoe Green 123 D4
Horseway 162 C4
Horsey 179 F3
Horsey Corner 179 F3
Horsford 178 C4
Horsforth 194 B4
Horsham Worcs 145 G2
Horsham WSuss 121 G4
Horsham St. Faith 178 D4
Horsington Lincs 175 G1
Horsington Som 117 E5
Horsington Marsh 117 E5
Horsley Derbys 173 E3
Horsley Glos 132 A3
Horsley N'umb 211 G1
Horsley N'umb 220 A2
Horsley Cross 152 C5
Horsley Woodhouse 173 E3
Horsleycross Street 152 C5
Horsleygate 186 A5
Horsleyhill 227 G4
Horsmonden 123 F4
Horspath 134 A2
Horstead 179 D4
Horsted Keynes 109 F1
Horton Bucks 135 E1
Horton Dorset 105 G2
Horton Lancs 193 E2
Horton N'hants 148 D2
Horton SGlos 131 G4
Horton Shrop 170 B5
Horton Som 103 G1
Horton Staffs 171 G2
Horton Swan 128 A4
Horton Tel&W 157 F1
Horton W&M 135 F5
Horton Wilts 118 B1
Horton Cross 103 G1
Horton Grange 221 E4
Horton Green 170 B3
Horton Heath 107 D1
Horton in Ribblesdale 200 D5
Horton Inn 105 G2
Horton Kirby 123 E2
Horton Park Farm Surr KT19 8PT 121 G1
Horton-cum-Studley 134 B1
Horwich 184 A1
Horwich End 185 E4
Horwood 113 F3
Hoscar 183 F1
Hose 174 C5
Hoses 198 D3
Hosh 243 D2
Hosta 262 C4
Hoswick 279 D10
Hotham 196 A4
Hothfield 124 B4
Hoton 173 G5
Houbie 278 F3
Houdston 214 C1

Hough 171 E2
Hough Green 183 F4
Hougham 175 D3
Hough-on-the-Hill 175 E3
Houghton Cambs 162 A5
Houghton Cumb 210 A2
Houghton Devon 100 C3
Houghton Hants 119 E4
Houghton Pembs 126 C2
Houghton WSuss 108 C2
Houghton Bank 212 B5
Houghton Conquest 149 F3
Houghton le Spring 212 C3
Houghton on the
  Hill 160 B2
Houghton Regis 149 F5
Houghton St. Giles 178 A2
Houghton-le-Side 212 B5
Houlsyke 203 G2
Hound 107 D2
Hound Green 120 C2
Houndslow 236 D5
Houndsmoor 115 E5
Houndwood 237 F3
Hounsdown 106 C1
Hounslow 136 A5
House of Marbles & Teign
  Valley Glass Devon
  TQ13 9DS 102 B5
Housebay 276 D5
Househill 267 F6
Houses Hill 185 F1
Housesteads Roman
  Fort N'umb
  NE47 6NN 211 D1
Houssetter 278 C4
Housham Tye 137 E1
Houss 279 C9
Houston 233 F3
Houstry 275 G5
Houstry of Dunn 275 H3
Houton 277 C7
Hove 109 E4
Hove Edge 194 A5
Hoveringham 174 B3
Hoveton 179 E4
Hovingham 203 F5
How 210 B2
How Caple 145 F4
How End 149 F3
How Green 123 D4
How Man 208 C5
Howbrook 186 A3
Howden 195 G5
Howden Clough 194 B5
Howden-le-Wear 212 A4
Howe Cumb 199 F4
Howe High 275 J2
Howe Norf 165 D2
Howe NYorks 202 C4
Howe Green 137 G2
Howe of Teuchar 269 F6
Howe Street Essex 137 F1
Howe Street Essex 151 E4
Howegreen 138 B2
Howell 175 G3
Howey 143 G2
Howgate Cumb 208 C4
Howgate Midlo 235 G4
Howgill Lancs 193 E3
Howgill NYorks 193 G2
Howick 229 G5
Howle 171 D5
Howle Hill 145 F5
Howlett End 151 D4
Howletts Wild Animal Park
  Kent CT4 5EL 125 D3
Howley 103 F2
Hownam 228 B5
Hownam Mains 228 B4
Howpasley 227 E5
Howsham NLincs 188 A2
Howsham NYorks 195 G1
Howt Green 124 A2
Howtel 228 C3
Howton 144 D5
Howwood 233 F3
Hoxa 277 D8
Hoxne 164 C4
Hoy High 275 H2
Hoy Ork 277 B8
Hoylake 182 D4
Hoyland 186 A2
Hoylandswaine 185 G2
Hoyle 108 B2
Hubberholme 201 E5
Hubberston 126 B2
Hubbert's Bridge 176 A3
Huby NYorks 195 E1
Huby NYorks 194 B3
Hucclecote 132 A1
Hucking 124 A3
Hucknall 173 G3
Huddersfield 185 F1
Huddington 146 B2
Huddlesford 158 D2
Hudnall 135 F1
Hudscott 113 G3
Hudswell 202 A3
Huggate 196 A2
Hugglescote 159 G1
Hugh Town 96 B1
Hughenden Valley 135 D3
Hughley 157 E3
Hugmore 170 A2
Hugus 96 B5
Huish Devon 113 F4
Huish Wilts 118 C1
Huish Champflower 114 D5
Huish Episcopi 116 B5
Huisinis 270 B6
Hulcote 149 E4
Hulcott 135 D1
Hull 196 D5
Hulland 172 D3
Hulland Ward 173 D3
Hullavington 132 A4
Hullbridge 138 B3
Hulme 173 G2
Hulme End 172 C2
Hulme Walfield 171 F1
Hulver Street 165 F3
Hulverstone 106 C4
Humber Devon 102 B5
Humber Here 145 E2
Humber Bridge Country
  Park ERid
  HU13 0LN 196 C5

Humberside Airport 188 A1
Humberston 188 D2
Humberstone 160 B2
Humberton 194 D1
Humbie 236 B3
Humbleton Dur 201 F1
Humbleton ERid 197 E4
Humbleton N'umb 229 D4
Humby 175 F4
Hume 237 E5
Humehall 237 E5
Hummer 104 B1
Humshaugh 220 B4
Huna 275 J1
Huncoat 193 D4
Huncote 160 A3
Hundalee 228 A5
Hundall 186 A5
Hunderthwaite 211 E5
Hundleby 176 B1
Hundleton 126 C2
Hundon 151 F3
Hundred Acres 107 E1
Hundred End 192 A5
Hundred House 144 A2
Hungarton 160 B2
Hungate End 148 C3
Hungerford Hants 106 A1
Hungerford Shrop 157 E4
Hungerford WBerks 119 E1
Hungerford
  Newtown 133 F5
Hungerton 175 D5
Hunglader 263 J4
Hunmanby 205 D5
Hunningham 147 F1
Hunningham Hill 147 F1
Hunny Hill 107 D4
Hunsdon 136 D1
Hunsingore 194 D2
Hunslet 194 C4
Hunsonby 210 B4
Hunspow 275 H1
Hunstanton 177 E3
Hunstanworth 211 F3
Hunston Suff 152 A1
Hunston WSuss 108 A3
Hunsworth 194 A5
Hunt End 146 C1
Hunt House 204 B3
Huntercombe End 134 B4
Hunters Forstal 125 D2
Hunter's Inn 113 G1
Hunter's Quay 232 C2
Hunterston 232 C4
Huntford 219 E1
Huntham 116 A5
Huntingdon 162 A5
Huntingfield 165 E4
Huntingford 157 F4
Huntington Here 144 B2
Huntington Here 145 D3
Huntington Staffs 158 B1
Huntington Tel&W 157 F2
Huntington York 195 F2
Huntingtower 243 F2
Huntley 131 G1
Huntly 260 D1
Huntlywood 236 D5
Hunton Hants 119 F3
Hunton Kent 123 G4
Hunton NYorks 202 A3
Hunton Bridge 135 F2
Hunt's Cross 183 F4
Huntscott 114 C3
Huntsham 114 D5
Huntshaw 113 F3
Huntshaw Cross 113 F3
Huntshaw Water 113 F3
Huntspill 116 A3
Huntworth 116 A4
Hunwick 212 A4
Hunworth 178 B2
Hurcott Som 116 C5
Hurcott Som 103 G1
Hurdley 156 B3
Hurdsfield 184 D5
Hurley W&M 134 D4
Hurley Warks 159 E3
Hurley Bottom 134 D4
Hurlford 224 C2
Hurliness 277 B9
Hurlston Green 183 E1
Hurn 106 A3
Hursley 119 F5
Hurst NYorks 201 F2
Hurst W'ham 134 C5
Hurst Green Essex 139 D1
Hurst Green ESuss 110 C1
Hurst Green Lancs 192 C4
Hurst Green Surr 122 C3
Hurst Wickham 109 E2
Hurstbourne Priors 119 F3
Hurstbourne
  Tarrant 119 E2
Hurstpierpoint 109 E2
Hurstwood 193 E4
Hurtmore 121 E3
Hurworth-on-Tees 202 C1
Hury 211 F5
Husabost 263 G6
Husbands
  Bosworth 160 B4
Husborne Crawley 149 E4
Husthwaite 203 E5
Hutcherleigh 101 D2
Huthwaite 173 F2
Huttoft 189 F5
Hutton Cumb 210 A5
Hutton Essex 137 F3
Hutton Lancs 192 A5
Hutton NSom 116 A2
Hutton ScBord 237 G4
Hutton Bonville 202 C2
Hutton Buscel 204 C4
Hutton Conyers 202 C5
Hutton Cranswick 196 C2
Hutton End 210 A4
Hutton Hang 202 A4
Hutton Henry 212 D4
Hutton Magna 202 A1
Hutton Mount 137 F3
Hutton Mulgrave 204 B2
Hutton Roof Cumb 199 G5
Hutton Roof Cumb 209 G3
Hutton Rudby 203 D2
Hutton Sessay 203 D5
Hutton Wandesley 195 E2

Hutton-le-Hole 203 G3
Huxham 102 C3
Huxham Green 116 C4
Huxley 170 C1
Huxter Shet 279 C7
Huxter Shet 279 E6
Huyton 183 F3
Hycemoor 198 B4
Hyde Glos 132 A2
Hyde GtMan 184 D3
Hyde End W'ham 120 C1
Hyde End WBerks 119 G1
Hyde Heath 135 E2
Hyde Lea 158 B1
Hydestile 121 E3
Hylands Park Essex
  CM2 8WQ 137 F2
Hyndford Bridge 234 D5
Hyndlee 227 G5
Hynish 246 A3
Hyssington 156 C3
Hythe Hants 106 D2
Hythe Kent 125 D5
Hythe End 135 F5
Hythie 269 J5
Hyton 198 B4

I

Ianstown 268 C4
Iarsiadar 270 D4
Ibberton 105 D2
Ible 172 D2
Ibsley 106 A2
Ibstock 159 G1
Ibstone 134 C3
Ibthorpe 119 E2
Ibworth 119 G2
Icelton 116 A1
Ickburgh 163 G3
Ickenham 135 F4
Ickford 134 B2
Ickham 125 E3
Ickleford 149 G4
Icklesham 111 D2
Ickleton 150 C3
Icklingham 163 F5
Ickwell Green 149 G3
Icomb 147 E5
Idbury 147 E5
Iddesleigh 113 F5
Ide 102 C3
Ide Hill 123 D3
Ideford 102 B5
Iden 111 E1
Iden Green Kent 123 G5
Iden Green Kent 124 A5
Idle 194 A4
Idless 96 C5
Idlicote 147 E3
Idmiston 118 C4
Idridgehay 173 D3
Idridgehay Green 173 D3
Idrigil 263 J5
Idstone 133 E4
Idvies 252 D5
Iffley 134 A2
Ifield 122 B5
Ifieldwood 122 B5
Ifold 121 F4
Iford Bourne 106 A3
Iford ESuss 109 G3
Ifton 131 D4
Ifton Heath 170 A4
Ightfield 170 C4
Ightham 123 E3
Ightham Mote Kent
  TN15 0NT 123 E3
Iken 153 F2
Ilam 172 C2
Ilchester 116 C5
Ilderton 229 E4
Ilford 136 D4
Ilfracombe 113 F1
Ilkeston 173 F3
Ilketshall
  St. Andrew 165 E3
Ilketshall
  St. Lawrence 165 E3
Ilketshall
  St. Margaret 165 E3
Ilkley 194 A3
Illey 158 B4
Illidge Green 171 E1
Illington 164 A3
Illingworth 193 G5
Illogan 96 A5
Illston on the Hill 160 C3
Ilmer 134 C2
Ilmington 147 E3
Ilminster 103 G1
Ilsington Devon 102 A5
Ilsington Dorset 105 D3
Ilston 128 B3
Ilton NYorks 202 A5
Ilton Som 103 G1
Imachar 231 G5
Imber 118 A3
Immeroin 242 A3
Immingham 188 B1
Immingham Dock 188 C1
Imperial War Museum,
  Duxford Cambs
  CB22 4QR 150 C3
Imperial War Museum,
  London GtLon
  SE1 6HZ 45 G7
Imperial War Museum
  North GtMan
  M17 1TZ 24 D3
Impington 150 C1
Ince 183 F5
Ince Blundell 183 E2
Ince-in-Makerfield 183 G2
Inch Kenneth 238 D1
Inch of Arnhall 253 E2
Inchbae Lodge 266 B5
Inchbare 253 E3
Inchberry 268 B5
Inchbraoch 253 F4
Inchgrundle 252 C2
Inchindown 266 D4
Inchinnan 233 F3
Inchkinloch 273 J4
Inchlumpie 266 C4
Inchmarlo 260 E5
Inchmarnock 232 B4
Inchnabobart 252 B1

Inchnacardoch
  Hotel 257 K3
Inchnadamph 272 E6
Inchock 253 E5
Inchree 248 C3
Inchrory 259 J4
Inchture 244 A2
Inchvuilt 257 J1
Inchyra 243 G2
Indian Queens 96 D4
Ineval 230 B5
Ingatestone 137 F3
Ingbirchworth 185 G2
Ingerthorpe 194 B1
Ingestre 171 G5
Ingham Lincs 187 G4
Ingham Norf 179 E3
Ingham Suff 163 G5
Ingham Corner 179 E3
Ingleborough 162 C1
Ingleby Derbys 158 D3
Ingleby Lincs 187 F5
Ingleby Barwick 202 D1
Ingleby Greenhow 203 E2
Ingleigh Green 113 G5
Inglesbatch 117 E1
Inglesham 133 E3
Ingleton Dur 212 A5
Ingleton NYorks 200 B5
Inglewhite 192 B4
Ingliston 235 F2
Ingmire Hall 200 B3
Ingoe 220 C4
Ingoldisthorpe 177 E4
Ingoldmells 177 D1
Ingoldsby 175 F4
Ingon 147 E2
Ingram 229 E5
Ingrave 137 F3
Ingrow 193 G4
Ings 199 F3
Ingst 131 E4
Ingworth 178 C3
Inhurst 119 G1
Iniston 240 D2
Injebreck 190 B3
Inkberrow 146 C2
Inkersall 186 B5
Inkersall Green 186 B5
Inkhorn 261 H1
Inkpen 119 E1
Inkstack 275 H1
Inmarsh 118 A1
Innellan 232 C3
Innerhadden 250 B4
Innerleithen 227 E2
Innerleven 244 B4
Innermessan 214 B4
Innerwick ELoth 237 E2
Innerwick P&K 250 A5
Inninbeg 247 F5
Innsworth 146 A5
Insch 260 E2
Insh 259 F4
Inshore 273 F2
Inskip 192 A4
Instow 113 E2
Intake 186 C2
Intech, Winchester Hants
  SO21 1HX 119 G5
International Centre, The,
  Telford Tel&W
  TF3 4JH 157 G2
Intwood 178 C5
Inver A&B 248 B5
Inver Aber 259 K5
Inver High 267 F3
Inver High 275 G5
Inver Mallie 248 C1
Inverailort 247 G1
Inveralligin 264 E6
Inverallochy 269 J4
Inveran 266 C2
Inveraray
  (Inbhir Aora) 240 C4
Inverardoch Mains 242 C4
Inverardran 242 F2
Inverarish 256 B1
Inverarity 252 C5
Inverarnan
  (Inbhir Àirnein) 241 F3
Inverasdale 264 E3
Inverbain 264 D6
Inverbeg 241 F5
Inverbervie 253 G2
Inverbroom 265 H3
Inverbrough 259 F2
Invercassley 266 B1
Invercharnan 248 D5
Inverchaolain 232 B2
Invercharnan 248 D5
Invercharron 266 C2
Inverchorachan 241 E3
Invercreran 248 C5
Inverdruie 259 G3
Inverebrie 261 H1
Invereen 258 E1
Invererne 267 H5
Inveresk 236 A2
Inverey 251 F2
Inverfarigaig 258 C2
Invergarry
  (Inbhir Garadh) 257 K4
Invergelder 259 K5
Invergeldie 242 C2
Invergloy 249 E1
Invergordon 266 E5
Invergowrie 244 B2
Inverguseran 256 D4
Inverharroch Farm 260 B1
Inverherive 241 F2
Inverhope 273 G2
Inverie 256 D4
Inverinan 240 B3
Inverinate 257 F2
Inverkeilor 253 E5
Inverkeithing 235 F1
Inverkeithny 268 E6
Inverkip 232 D2
Inverkirkaig 272 C7
Inverlael 265 H3
Inverlauren 233 E1
Inverliever 240 A4
Inverliver 240 C1
Inverlochlarig 241 G3

Inverlochy 241 D2
Inverlussa 231 E1
Invermay 243 F3
Invermoriston (Inbhir
  Moireasdan) 258 B3
Invernaver 274 C2
Inverneil 231 G1
Inverness
  (Inbhir Nis) 266 D7
Inverness Airport 266 E6
Invernettie 269 K6
Invernoaden 240 D5
Inveroran Hotel (Inbhir
  Orain) 249 E5
Inverquharity 252 C4
Inverquhomery 269 J6
Inverroy 249 E1
Inversanda 248 B4
Invershiel 257 F3
Invershore 275 H5
Inversnaid Hotel 241 F4
Invertrossachs 242 A4
Inveruglas 269 K6
Inveruglas (Inbhir
  Dhubhghlais) 241 F4
Inveruglass 259 F4
Inverurie 261 F2
Invervar 250 B5
Invervegain 232 B2
Invery House 260 E5
Inverythan 269 F6
Inwardleigh 99 F1
Inworth 138 B1
Iochdar 262 C7
Iona 238 B2
Iping 121 D5
Ipplepen 101 E1
Ipsden 134 B4
Ipstones 172 B3
Ipswich 152 C3
Irby 183 D4
Irby Hill 183 D4
Irby in the Marsh 176 C1
Irby upon Humber 188 B2
Irchester 149 E1
Irchester Country Park
  N'hants NN29 7DL 149 E1
Ireby Cumb 209 F3
Ireby Lancs 200 B5
Ireland Ork 277 C7
Ireland Shet 279 C10
Ireland's Cross 171 E3
Ireleth 198 D5
Ireshopeburn 211 E4
Irlam 184 B3
Irnham 175 F5
Iron Acton 131 F4
Iron Cross 146 C2
Ironbridge 157 F2
Irons Bottom 122 B4
Ironside 269 G5
Ironville 173 F2
Irstead 179 E3
Irthington 210 A1
Irthlingborough 161 E5
Irton 204 D4
Irvine 224 B2
Isauld 274 E2
Isbister Ork 277 C6
Isbister Ork 276 B5
Isbister Shet 279 E6
Isbister Shet 278 C3
Isfield 109 G2
Isham 161 D5
Ishriff 239 F1
Isington 120 C3
Island of Stroma 275 J1
Islawr-dref 154 C1
Islay 230 A3
Islay Airport 230 B4
Islay House 230 B3
Isle Abbotts 116 A5
Isle Brewers 116 A5
Isle of Bute Discovery Centre
  A&B PA20 0AH 232 B3
Isle of Lewis (Eilean
  Leodhais) 271 F3
Isle of Man 190 B3
Isle of Man Airport 190 A5
Isle of May 245 E4
Isle of Noss 279 E8
Isle of Sheppey 124 B1
Isle of Walney 191 E1
Isle of Whithorn 207 E3
Isle of Wight 107 D4
Isle of Wight Pearl IoW
  PO30 4DD 106 D4
Isle of Wight (Sandown)
  Airport 107 E4
Isle of Wight Zoo IoW
  PO36 8QB 107 F4
Isleham 163 E5
Isleornsay (Eilean
  Iarmain) 256 C3
Isles of Scilly
  (Scilly Isles) 96 B1
Islesburgh 279 C6
Islesteps 217 D3
Isley Walton 173 F5
Islibhig 270 B5
Islip N'hants 161 E5
Islip Oxon 134 A1
Isombridge 157 F1
Istead Rise 137 F5
Itchen 106 D1
Itchen Abbas 119 G4
Itchen Stoke 119 G4
Itchen Valley Country Park
  Hants SO30 3HQ 4 C2
Itchingfield 121 G5
Itchington 131 F4
Itteringham 178 C2
Itton Devon 99 G1
Itton Mon 131 D3
Itton Common 131 D3
Ivegill 210 A3
Ivelet 201 E3
Iver 135 F4
Iver Heath 135 F4
Iveston 212 A2
Ivetsey Bank 158 A1
Ivinghoe 135 E1
Ivinghoe Aston 135 E1
Ivington 145 D2
Ivington Green 145 D2
Ivy Hatch 123 E3

Ivy Todd 163 G2
Ivybridge 100 C2
Ivychurch 111 F1
Iwade 124 B2
Iwerne Courtney
  (Shroton) 105 E1
Iwerne Minster 105 E1
Ixworth 164 A4
Ixworth Thorpe 164 A4

J

Jack Hill 194 A2
Jackfield 157 F2
Jacksdale 173 F2
Jackstown 261 F1
Jackton 233 G4
Jacobstow 98 B1
Jacobstowe 113 F5
Jacobswell 121 E2
James Hamilton
  Heritage Park SLan
  G74 5LB 31 E5
James Pringle Weavers
  of Inverness High
  IV2 4RB 266 D7
Jameston 127 D3
Jamestown D&G 218 B2
Jamestown High 266 B6
Jamestown WDun 233 E1
Janefield 266 E6
Janetstown High 275 F2
Janetstown High 275 J3
Jarrow 212 C1
Jarvis Brook 123 E5
Jasper's Green 151 F5
Jawcraig 234 C2
Jayes Park 121 G3
Jaywick 139 E1
Jealott's Hill 135 D5
Jeater Houses 202 D3
Jedburgh 228 A4
Jeffreyston 127 D2
Jemimaville 266 E5
Jephson Gardens Warks
  CV32 4ER 16 B6
Jericho 184 C1
Jersay 234 C3
Jersey 100 C5
Jersey Airport 100 B5
Jersey Marine 128 C3
Jerviswood 234 C5
Jesmond 212 B1
Jevington 110 A3
Jinney Ring Craft Centre,
  The Worcs
  B60 4BU 16 A5
Jockey End 135 F1
Jodrell Bank 184 B5
Jodrell Bank Observatory &
  Arboretum ChesE
  SK11 9DL 184 B5
John Muir Country Park
  ELoth
  EH42 1UW 236 D2
John o' Groats 275 J1
Johnby 210 A4
John's Cross 110 C1
Johnshaven 253 F3
Johnson Street 179 E4
Johnston 126 C1
Johnston Mains 253 F2
Johnstone 233 F3
Johnstone Castle 233 F3
Johnstonebridge 217 E1
Johnstons Cashmere Visitor
  Centre Moray
  IV30 4AF 267 K5
Johnstown
  Carmar 127 G1
Johnstown Wrex 170 A3
Joppa 224 C4
Jordans 135 E3
Jordanston 140 C4
Jordanstone 252 A5
Jorvik YO1 9WT 90 York
Jorvik Glass NYorks
  YO60 7DA 195 G1
Joy's Green 131 F1
Jumpers Common 106 A3
Juniper Green 235 F3
Juniper Hill 148 A4
Jura 231 E1
Jura House 230 C3
Jurby East 190 B2
Jurby West 190 B2

K

Kaber 200 C1
Kaimes 235 G3
Kames A&B 232 A2
Kames A&B 240 A3
Kames EAyr 225 E3
Kathellan Fife
  KY4 0JR 243 G5
Kea 96 C5
Keadby 187 F1
Keal Cotes 176 B1
Kearsley 184 B2
Kearstwick 200 B5
Kearton 201 F3
Kearvaig 272 E1
Keasden 192 D1
Kebholes 268 E5
Keckwick 183 G4
Keddington 188 D4
Keddington Corner 189 D4
Kedington 151 F3
Kedleston 173 E3
Keelby 188 B1
Keele 171 F3
Keeley Green 149 F3
Keelham 193 G4
Keenthorne 115 F4
Keeres Green 137 E1
Keeston 126 B1
Keevil 118 A2
Kegworth 173 F5
Kehelland 96 A5
Keig 260 E3
Keighley 193 G3
Keighley & Worth Valley
  Railway WYorks
  BD22 8NJ 193 G3
Keil A&B 222 B5
Keil High 248 B4
Keilhill 269 F5
Keillmore 231 E1
Keillor 252 A5

Keillour 243 E2
Keills 230 C3
Keils 230 D3
Keinton Mandeville 116 C4
Keir House 242 C5
Keir Mill 216 C1
Keisby 175 F5
Keisley 210 C5
Keiss 275 J2
Keith 268 C5
Keithick 244 A1
Keithmore 260 B1
Keithock 253 E3
Kelbrook 193 F3
Kelby 175 F3
Keld Cumb 199 G1
Keld NYorks 201 D2
Keldholme 203 G4
Keldy Castle 203 G3
Kelfield NLincs 187 F2
Kelfield NYorks 195 E4
Kelham 174 C2
Kella 190 B2
Kellacott 99 E2
Kellan 247 E5
Kellas Angus 244 C1
Kellas Moray 267 J6
Kellaton 101 E4
Kellaways 132 B5
Kelleth 200 B2
Kelleythorpe 196 C2
Kelling 178 B1
Kellington 195 E5
Kelloe 212 C4
Kellolm 225 F4
Kelly Corn 97 G2
Kelly Devon 99 D2
Kelly Bray 99 D3
Kelmarsh 160 C5
Kelmscott 133 E3
Kelsale 153 E1
Kelsall 170 C1
Kelsay 230 A4
Kelshall 150 B4
Kelsick 209 F1
Kelso 228 B3
Kelstedge 173 E1
Kelstern 188 C3
Kelston 117 E1
Keltneyburn 250 C5
Kelton 217 D3
Kelton Hill
  (Rhonehouse) 216 B5
Kelty 243 G5
Kelvedon 138 B1
Kelvedon Hatch 137 E3
Kelvingrove Art Gallery &
  Museum Glas
  G3 8AG 38 D2
Kelvinside 233 G3
Kelynack 94 A4
Kemacott 113 G1
Kemback 244 C3
Kemberton 157 G2
Kemble 132 B3
Kemerton 146 B4
Kemeys
  Commander 130 C2
Kemeys Inferior 130 C3
Kemnay 261 F3
Kemp Town 109 F3
Kempe's Corner 124 C4
Kempley 145 F5
Kempley Green 145 F5
Kemps Green 158 D5
Kempsey 146 A2
Kempsford 133 D3
Kempshott 119 G3
Kempston 149 F3
Kempston Hardwick 149 F3
Kempston West End 149 E3
Kempton 156 C4
Kemsing 123 E3
Kemsley 124 B2
Kenardington 124 B5
Kenchester 144 B5
Kencot 133 E2
Kendal 199 G3
Kenderchurch 144 D5
Kendleshire 131 F5
Kenfig 129 D4
Kenfig Hill 129 D4
Kenidjack 94 A3
Kenilworth 159 E5
Kenilworth Castle Warks
  CV8 1NE 16 A1
Kenknock P&K 250 A5
Kenknock Stir 241 G1
Kenley GtLon 122 C2
Kenley Shrop 157 E2
Kenmore A&B 240 C4
Kenmore High 264 D6
Kenmore P&K 250 C5
Kenmore Na H-E. Siar
  270 E7
Kenn Devon 102 C4
Kenn NSom 116 B1
Kennacley 263 G2
Kennacraig 231 G3
Kennards House 97 G1
Kennavay 263 H2
Kenneggy Downs 94 C4
Kennerleigh 102 B2
Kennet 243 E5
Kennethmont 260 D2
Kennett 151 E1
Kennford 102 C4
Kenninghall 164 B3
Kennington Kent 124 C4
Kennington Oxon 134 A2
Kennoway 244 B4
Kenny 103 G1
Kennyhill 163 E5
Kennythorpe 195 G1
Kenovay 246 A2
Kensaleyre 263 K6
Kensington 136 B4
Kensington Palace GtLon
  W8 4PX 10 E4
Kenstone 170 C5
Kensworth 135 F1
Kent & East Sussex Railway
  Kent TN30 6HE 124 A5
Kent Street ESuss 110 C2
Kent Street Kent 123 F3
Kentallen (Ceann an t-
  Sàilein) 248 C4

Kentchurch 144 D5
Kentford 151 F1
Kentisbeare 103 D2
Kentisbury 113 G1
Kentisbury Ford 113 G1
Kentish Town 136 B4
Kentmere 199 F2
Kenton Devon 102 C4
Kenton Suff 152 C1
Kenton T&W 212 B1
Kenton Corner 152 D1
Kentra 247 F3
Kents Bank 199 E5
Kent's Green 145 G5
Kent's Oak 119 E5
Kenwick 170 B4
Kenwood House GtLon
   NW3 7JR 10 F2
Kenwyn 96 C5
Kenyon 184 A3
Keoldale 273 F2
Keose (Ceòs) 271 F5
Keppanach 248 C3
Keppoch A&B 233 E2
Keppoch High 256 E2
Keprigan 222 B4
Kepwick 203 D3
Keresley 159 F4
Kernborough 101 D3
Kerrera 240 A2
Kerridge 184 D5
Kerris 94 B4
Kerry (Ceri) 156 A3
Kerry's Gate 144 C4
Kerrycroy 232 C3
Kerrysdale 264 E4
Kersall 174 C1
Kersey 152 B3
Kersey Vale 152 B3
Kershopefoot 218 C3
Kerswell 103 D2
Kerswell Green 146 A3
Kerthen Wood 94 C3
Kesgrave 152 D3
Kessingland 165 G3
Kessingland Beach 165 G3
Kestle 97 D5
Kestle Mill 96 C4
Keston 122 C2
Keswick Cumb 209 F4
Keswick Norf 178 D5
Keswick Norf 179 E2
Ketley Bank 157 F1
Ketsby 189 D5
Kettering 161 D5
Ketteringham 178 C5
Kettins 244 A1
Kettle Corner 123 G3
Kettlebaston 152 A2
Kettlebridge 244 B4
Kettlebrook 159 E2
Kettleburgh 153 D1
Kettlehill 244 B4
Kettleholm 217 F3
Kettleness 204 B1
Kettleshulme 185 D5
Kettlesing 184 A2
Kettlesing Bottom 194 B2
Kettlesing Head 194 B2
Kettlestone 178 A2
Kettlethorpe 187 F5
Kettletoft 276 F4
Kettlewell 201 E5
Ketton 161 E2
Kevingtown 123 D2
Kew 136 A5
Kewstoke 114 A1
Kexbrough 186 A2
Kexby Lincs 187 F4
Kexby York 195 G2
Key Green 171 F1
Keyham 160 B2
Keyhaven 106 C3
Keyingham 197 F5
Keymer 109 F2
Keynsham 117 D1
Key's Toft 176 C2
Keysoe 149 F1
Keysoe Row 149 F1
Keyston 161 F5
Keyworth 174 B4
Kibblesworth 212 B2
Kibworth
   Beauchamp 160 B3
Kibworth Harcourt 160 B3
Kidbrooke 136 D5
Kiddemore Green 158 A2
Kidderminster 158 A5
Kiddington 147 F5
Kidlington 133 G1
Kidmore End 134 B5
Kidnal 170 B3
Kidsdale 207 E3
Kidsgrove 171 F2
Kidstones 201 E4
Kidwelly (Cydweli) 128 A2
Kiel Crofts 240 A1
Kielder 219 E2
Kielder Forest N'umb
   NE48 1ER 219 F3
Kielder Water N'umb
   NE48 1BX 219 F3
Kilbarchan 233 F3
Kilbeg 256 C4
Kilberry 231 F3
Kilbirnie 233 E4
Kilblaan 240 D3
Kilbraur 274 D7
Kilbrennan 246 D5
Kilbride A&B 240 A2
Kilbride A&B 232 B3
Kilbride High 256 B2
Kilbride Farm 232 A3
Kilbridemore 240 C5
Kilburn Derbys 173 E3
Kilburn GtLon 136 B4
Kilburn NYorks 203 E5
Kilby 160 B3
Kilchattan Bay 232 C4
Kilcheran 240 A1
Kilchiaran 230 A3
Kilchoan A&B 239 G3
Kilchoan High 247 D5
Kilchoman 230 A3
Kilchrenan
   (Cill Chrèanain) 240 C2
Kilchrist 222 B4

Kilconquhar 244 C4
Kilcot 145 G5
Kilcoy 266 C6
Kilcreggan 232 D1
Kildale 203 F2
Kildary 266 E4
Kildavie 222 C4
Kildermorie Lodge 266 C4
Kildonan NAyr 223 F3
Kildonan (Cilldonnain)
   Na H-E. Siar 254 C2
Kildonan Lodge 274 E6
Kildonnan 247 D1
Kildrochet House 214 B5
Kildrummy 260 C3
Kildwick 193 G3
Kilfinan 232 A2
Kilfinnan 257 J5
Kilgetty 127 E2
Kilgwrrwg Common 131 D3
Kilham ERid 196 C1
Kilham N'umb 228 C3
Kilkenneth 246 A2
Kilkenny 132 C1
Kilkerran A&B 222 C4
Kilkerran SAyr 224 B5
Kilkhampton 112 C4
Killamarsh 186 B4
Killay 128 C3
Killbeg 247 F5
Killean A&B 221 F1
Killean A&B 240 C4
Killearn 233 G1
Killellan 222 B4
Killen 266 D6
Killerby 212 A5
Killerton 102 C2
Killerton Devon
   EX5 3LE 102 C2
Killichonate 249 E1
Killichonate 249 E1
Killiechonan 247 E5
Killiecrankie 251 E3
Killiehuntly 258 E5
Killiemor 239 D1
Killilan 257 F3
Killimster 275 J3
Killin High 267 F1
Killin Stir 242 A1
Killinallan 230 B2
Killinghall 194 B2
Killington Cumb 200 B4
Killington Devon 113 G1
Killingworth 221 E4
Killochyett 236 B5
Killocraw 222 B2
Killunaig 239 D2
Killundine 247 E5
Kilmaha 240 B4
Kilmahog 242 B4
Kilmalieu 248 A4
Kilmaluag 263 K4
Kilmany 244 B2
Kilmarie 256 B3
Kilmarnock 224 C2
Kilmartin 240 A5
Kilmaurs 233 F5
Kilmelford 240 A3
Kilmeny 230 B3
Kilmersdon 117 D2
Kilmeston 119 G5
Kilmichael 222 B3
Kilmichael
   Glassary 240 A5
Kilmichael of
   Inverlussa 231 F1
Kilmington Devon 103 F3
Kilmington Wilts 117 E4
Kilmington
   Common 117 E4
Kilmorack 266 B7
Kilmore (A' Chille Mhòr)
   A&B 240 A1
Kilmore High 256 C4
Kilmory A&B 231 F3
Kilmory A&B 231 F3
Kilmory High 255 J4
Kilmory High 247 E2
Kilmory NAyr 223 E3
Kilmote 274 E7
Kilmuir High 263 H7
Kilmuir High 266 D7
Kilmuir High 266 E4
Kilmuir High 263 J4
Kilmun 232 C1
Kilmux 244 B4
Kiln Green Here 131 F1
Kiln Green W'ham 134 D5
Kiln Pit Hill 211 G2
Kilnave 230 A2
Kilncadzow 234 C5
Kilndown 123 G5
Kilnhurst 186 B3
Kilninian 246 D5
Kilninver 240 A2
Kilnsea 189 E1
Kilnsey 193 F1
Kilnwick 196 B3
Kilnwick Percy 196 A2
Kiloran 238 C5
Kilpatrick 223 F3
Kilpeck 144 D4
Kilphedir 274 E7
Kilpin 195 G5
Kilpin Pike 195 G5
Kilrenny 245 D4
Kilsby 160 A5
Kilspindie 244 A2
Kilstay 206 B3
Kilsyth 234 B2
Kiltarlity 266 C7
Kilton Notts 186 C5
Kilton R&C 203 F1
Kilton Som 115 E3
Kilton Thorpe 203 F1
Kiltyrie 242 A1
Kilve 115 E3
Kilverstone 163 G4
Kilvington 174 D3
Kilwinning 233 E5
Kimberley Norf 178 B5
Kimberley Notts 173 G3
Kimberworth 186 B3
Kimble Wick 134 D2
Kimbolton Cambs 149 F1

Kimbolton Here 145 E1
Kimbridge 119 E5
Kimcote 160 A4
Kimmeridge 105 F5
Kimmerston 229 D3
Kimpton Hants 119 D3
Kimpton Herts 136 A1
Kinaldy 244 D4
Kinblethmont 253 E5
Kinbrace 274 D5
Kinbreack 257 G5
Kinbuck 242 C4
Kincaldrum 252 C5
Kincaple 244 C3
Kincardine Fife 234 D1
Kincardine High 266 D3
Kincardine O'Neil 260 D5
Kinclaven 243 G1
Kincorth 261 H4
Kincraig Aber 261 H2
Kincraig High 259 F4
Kincraigie 251 E5
Kindallachan 251 E4
Kindrogan Field
   Centre 251 F3
Kinellar 261 G3
Kineton Glos 146 C5
Kineton Warks 147 F2
Kineton Green 158 D4
Kinfauns 243 G2
King Sterndale 185 E5
Kingarth 232 B4
Kingcoed 130 D2
Kingerby 188 A3
Kingham 147 E5
Kingholm Quay 217 D3
Kinghorn 235 G1
Kinglassie 244 A5
Kingoodie 244 B2
King's Acre 145 D3
King's Bank 111 D1
King's Bromley 158 D1
Kings Caple 145 E5
Kingscavil 235 D2
Kingsclere 119 G2
Kingscote 132 A3
Kingscott 113 F4
Kingsdale 244 B4
Kingsdon 116 C5
Kingsdown Kent 125 F4
Kingsdown Swin 133 D4
Kingsdown Wilts 117 F1
Kingseat 243 G5
Kingsey 134 C2
Kingsfold Pembs 126 C3
Kingsfold WSuss 121 G4
Kingsford Aber 269 F6
Kingsford Aber 260 D3
Kingsford
   Aberdeen 261 G4
Kingsford EAyr 233 F5
Kingsford Worcs 158 A4
Kingsgate 125 F1
Kingshall Street 152 A1
Kingsheanton 113 F2
Kingshouse 242 A2
Kingshouse Hotel 249 E4
Kingshurst 159 D4
Kingskerswell 101 E1
Kingskettle 244 B4
Kingsland Here 144 D1
Kingsland IoA 180 A4
Kingsley ChesW&C 183 G5
Kingsley Hants 120 C4
Kingsley Staffs 172 B3
Kingsley Green 121 D4
Kingsley Holt 172 B3
Kingslow 157 G3
Kingsmoor 136 D2
Kingsmuir Angus 252 C5
Kingsmuir Fife 244 D4
Kingsnorth 124 C5
Kingsnorth Power
   Station 124 A1
Kingstanding 158 C3
Kingsteignton 102 B5
Kingsteps 267 G6
Kingsthorne 145 D4
Kingsthorpe 148 C1
Kingston Cambs 150 B2
Kingston Corn 99 D3
Kingston Devon 100 D4
Kingston Devon 100 D4
Kingston Dorset 104 D2
Kingston Dorset 105 F5
Kingston ELoth 236 C1

Kingston GtMan 184 D3
Kingston Hants 106 A2
Kingston IoW 107 D4
Kingston Kent 125 E3
Kingston Moray 268 B4
Kingston WSuss 108 A3
Kingston Bagpuize 133 G3
Kingston by Sea 109 E3
Kingston Gorse 108 A3
Kingston Lacy Dorset
   BH21 4EA 3 A1
Kingston Lisle 133 F4
Kingston Maurward 104 D3
Kingston near
   Lewes 109 F3
Kingston on Soar 173 G5
Kingston Russell 104 B3
Kingston St. Mary 115 F5
Kingston Seymour 116 B1
Kingston Stert 134 C2
Kingston upon Hull 196 D5
Kingston upon
   Thames 121 G1
Kingston Warren 133 F4
Kingstone Here 144 D4
Kingstone Here 145 F5
Kingstone Som 103 G1
Kingstone Staffs 172 B5
Kingston Winslow 133 E4
Kingstown 209 G1
Kingswear 101 E2
Kingswells 261 G4
Kingswinford 158 A4
Kingswood Bucks 134 B1
Kingswood Glos 131 G3
Kingswood Here 144 B2
Kingswood Kent 124 A3
Kingswood Powys 156 B2
Kingswood SGlos 131 F5
Kingswood Som 115 E4
Kingswood Surr 122 B3
Kingswood Warks 159 D5
Kingthorpe 188 B5
Kington Here 144 B2
Kington Worcs 146 B2
Kington Langley 132 B5
Kington Magna 117 E5
Kington St. Michael 132 B5
Kingussie 258 E4
Kingweston 116 C4
Kinharrachie 261 H1
Kinharvie 216 D4
Kinkell 234 A2
Kinkell Bridge 243 D3
Kinknockie 269 J6
Kinlet 157 G4
Kinloch Fife 244 A3
Kinloch High 273 F5
Kinloch High 247 F4
Kinloch High 255 K5
Kinloch High 266 C4
Kinloch P&K 252 A5
Kinloch P&K 251 G5
Kinloch Hourn (Ceann Loch
   Shubhairne) 257 F4
Kinloch Laggan 250 A1
Kinloch Rannoch 250 B4
Kinlochan 248 A3
Kinlochard 241 G4
Kinlocharkaig 257 F5
Kinlochbeoraid 248 A1
Kinlochbervie 272 E3
Kinlocheil 248 B2
Kinlochetive 248 D5
Kinlochewe 265 G5
Kinlochlaich 248 B5
Kinlochleven (Ceann Loch
   Liobhann) 249 D3
Kinlochmoidart 247 G2
Kinlochmorar 256 E5
Kinlochmore 249 D3
Kinlochroag (Ceann
   Lochroag) 270 D5
Kinlochspelve 239 D2
Kinloss 267 H5
Kinmel Bay
   (Bae Cinmel) 182 A4
Kinmuck 261 G3
Kinnaber 253 F3
Kinnadie 269 H6
Kinnaird 243 G2
Kinneff 253 G2
Kinnelhead 226 B5
Kinnell Angus 253 E4
Kinnell Stir 242 A1
Kinnerley 170 A5
Kinnersley Here 144 C3
Kinnersley Worcs 146 A3
Kinnerton 144 B1
Kinnerton Green 170 A1
Kinnesswood 243 G4
Kinnettles 252 C5
Kinninvie 211 G5
Kinnordy 252 B4
Kinoulton 174 B4
Kinrara 259 F4
Kinross 243 G4
Kinrossie 243 G1
Kinsbourne Green 136 A1
Kinsham Here 144 C1
Kinsham Worcs 146 B4
Kinsley 186 B1
Kinson 105 G3
Kintarvie 270 E6
Kintbury 119 E1
Kintessack 267 G5
Kintillo 243 G3
Kintocher 260 D4
Kinton Here 156 D5
Kinton Shrop 156 C1
Kintore 261 F3
Kintour 230 C4
Kintra A&B 238 C2
Kintra A&B 238 C2
Kintraw 240 A4
Kinuachdrachd 239 G5
Kinver 158 A4
Kinwarton 146 D2
Kiplaw Croft 261 J1
Kipp 242 A1
Kippax 194 D4
Kippen P&K 243 F3

Kippen Stir 242 B5
Kippenross House 242 C4
Kippford (Scaur) 216 C5
Kipping's Cross 123 F4
Kippington 123 E3
Kirbister Ork 277 C7
Kirbister Ork 276 C7
Kirbuster 276 B5
Kirby Bedon 179 D5
Kirby Bellars 160 C1
Kirby Cane 165 E2
Kirby Corner 159 E5
Kirby Cross 152 D5
Kirby Fields 160 A2
Kirby Green 165 E2
Kirby Grindalythe 196 B1
Kirby Hill NYorks 202 A2
Kirby Hill NYorks 194 C1
Kirby Knowle 203 D5
Kirby le Soken 152 D5
Kirby Misperton 203 G5
Kirby Muxloe 160 A2
Kirby Row 165 E2
Kirby Sigston 202 D3
Kirby Underdale 196 A2
Kirby Wiske 202 C4
Kirdford 121 F5
Kirk 275 H3
Kirk Bramwith 186 D1
Kirk Deighton 194 C2
Kirk Ella 196 C5
Kirk Hallam 173 F3
Kirk Hammerton 195 D2
Kirk Ireton 173 D2
Kirk Langley 173 D4
Kirk Merrington 212 B4
Kirk Michael 190 B2
Kirk of Shotts 234 C3
Kirk Sandall 186 D2
Kirk Smeaton 186 C1
Kirk Yetholm 228 C4
Kirkabister 279 D9
Kirkandrews 207 G2
Kirkandrews-upon-
   Eden 209 G1
Kirkbampton 209 G1
Kirkbean 217 D5
Kirkbride 209 F1
Kirkbuddo 252 D5
Kirkburn ERid 196 B2
Kirkburn ScBord 227 D2
Kirkburton 185 F1
Kirkby Lincs 188 A3
Kirkby Mersey 183 F3
Kirkby NYorks 203 E2
Kirkby Fleetham 202 B3
Kirkby Green 175 F2
Kirkby in Ashfield 173 F2
Kirkby la Thorpe 175 F3
Kirkby Lonsdale 200 B5
Kirkby Malham 193 E1
Kirkby Mallory 159 G2
Kirkby Malzeard 202 B5
Kirkby on Bain 176 A1
Kirkby Overblow 194 C3
Kirkby Stephen 200 C2
Kirkby Thore 210 C5
Kirkby Underwood 175 F5
Kirkby Wharfe 195 E3
Kirkby Woodhouse 173 F2
Kirkby-in-Furness 198 D4
Kirkbymoorside 203 F4
Kirkcaldy 244 A5
Kirkcambeck 210 B1
Kirkcolm 214 B4
Kirkconnel 225 F4
Kirkconnell 217 D4
Kirkcowan 215 E4
Kirkcudbright 216 A5
Kirkdale House 215 G5
Kirkdean 235 F5
Kirkfieldbank 234 C5
Kirkgunzeon 216 C4
Kirkham Lancs 192 A4
Kirkham NYorks 195 G1
Kirkhamgate 194 C5
Kirkharle 220 C3
Kirkhaugh 210 C3
Kirkheaton N'umb 220 C4
Kirkheaton WYorks 185 F1
Kirkhill Angus 253 E3
Kirkhill High 266 C7
Kirkhill Moray 268 B5
Kirkhope 227 E3
Kirkibost Here 256 B3
Kirkibost (Circebost)
   Na H-E. Siar 270 D4
Kirkinch 252 B5
Kirkinner 215 F5
Kirkintilloch 234 A2
Kirkland Cumb 210 C4
Kirkland Cumb 209 D5
Kirkland D&G 216 C1
Kirkland D&G 225 F4
Kirkland D&G 217 E2
Kirkland of
   Longcastle 207 D2
Kirklebham 207 D2
Kirklevington 202 D1
Kirkley 165 G2
Kirklington Notts 174 B2
Kirklington NYorks 202 C4
Kirklinton 210 A1
Kirkliston 235 F2
Kirkmaiden 206 B3
Kirkmichael P&K 251 F3
Kirkmichael SAyr 224 B5
Kirkmuirhill 234 B5
Kirknewton N'umb 228 D3
Kirknewton WLoth 235 F3
Kirkney 260 D1
Kirkoswald Cumb 210 B3
Kirkoswald SAyr 224 A5
Kirkpatrick Durham 216 B3
Kirkpatrick-Fleming 218 A4
Kirksanton 198 C4
Kirkstall 194 B4
Kirkstead 175 G1
Kirkstile Aber 260 D1
Kirkstile D&G 218 B2
Kirkstyle 275 J1
Kirkthorpe 194 C5
Kirkton Aber 260 E2
Kirkton Aber 260 E2
Kirkton Aber 268 E5
Kirkton Angus 252 C5
Kirkton D&G 217 D2

Kirkton Fife 244 B2
Kirkton High 258 D1
Kirkton High 266 E1
Kirkton High 266 E6
Kirkton High 274 D2
Kirkton High 256 E2
Kirkton P&K 243 D2
Kirkton ScBord 227 G4
Kirkton Manor 226 D2
Kirkton of Airlie 252 B4
Kirkton of
   Auchterhouse 244 B1
Kirkton of Barevan 267 F7
Kirkton of Bourtie 261 G2
Kirkton of Collace 243 G1
Kirkton of Craig 253 F4
Kirkton of
   Culsalmond 260 E1
Kirkton of Durris 261 F5
Kirkton of
   Glenbuchat 260 B3
Kirkton of Glenisla 252 A3
Kirkton of
   Kingoldrum 252 B4
Kirkton of Lethendy 251 G5
Kirkton of Logie
   Buchan 261 H2
Kirkton of
   Maryculter 261 G5
Kirkton of Menmuir 252 D3
Kirkton of Monikie 244 D1
Kirkton of Rayne 260 E1
Kirkton of Skene 261 G4
Kirkton of Tealing 244 C1
Kirktonhill Aber 253 E3
Kirktonhill WDun 233 E2
Kirktown 269 J5
Kirktown of Alvah 268 E4
Kirktown of
   Auchterless 269 F6
Kirktown of
   Deskford 268 D4
Kirktown of
   Fetteresso 253 G1
Kirktown of Slains 261 J2
Kirkwall 277 D6
Kirkwall Airport 277 D7
Kirkwhelpington 220 B3
Kirmington 188 B3
Kirmond le Mire 188 B3
Kirn 232 C2
Kirriemuir 252 B4
Kirstead Green 165 D2
Kirtlebridge 218 A3
Kirtleton 218 A3
Kirtling 151 E2
Kirtling Green 151 E2
Kirtlington 134 A1
Kirtomy 274 C2
Kirton Lincs 176 B3
Kirton Notts 174 B1
Kirton Suff 153 D4
Kirton End 176 A3
Kirton Holme 176 A3
Kirton in Lindsey 187 G3
Kiscadale 223 F3
Kislingbury 148 B2
Kismeldon Bridge 113 D4
Kit Hill Country Park
   Corn PL17 8AX 99 D3
Kites Hardwick 147 G1
Kitley 100 B2
Kittisford 115 D5
Kittisford Barton 115 D5
Kittle 128 B4
Kitt's End 136 B3
Kitt's Green 159 D4
Kitwood 120 B4
Kivernoll 145 D4
Kiveton Park 186 B4
Klibreck 273 H5
Knabbygates 268 D5
Knaith 187 F4
Knaith Park 187 F4
Knap Corner 117 F5
Knaphill 121 E2
Knaplock 114 B4
Knapp P&K 244 A1
Knapp Som 116 A5
Knapthorpe 174 C2
Knaptoft 160 B4
Knapton Norf 179 E2
Knapton York 195 E2
Knapton Green 144 D2
Knapwell 150 B1
Knaresborough 194 C2
Knarsdale 210 C2
Knarston 276 C5
Knaven 269 G6
Knayton 202 D4
Knebworth 150 A5
Knebworth House Herts
   SG3 6PY 150 A5
Knedlington 195 G5
Kneesall 174 C1
Kneesworth 150 B3
Kneeton 174 C3
Knelston 128 A4
Knenhall 171 G4
Knettishall 164 A3
Knettishall Heath Country
   Park Suff
   IP22 2TQ 164 A3
Knightacott 113 G2
Knightcote 147 G2
Knightley 171 F5
Knightley Dale 171 F5
Knighton Devon 100 B3
Knighton Dorset 104 C1
Knighton Leic 160 A2
Knighton Poole 105 G3
Knighton (Tref-y-clawdd)
   Powys 156 B5
Knighton Som 115 E3
Knighton Staffs 171 E5
Knighton Staffs 171 E3
Knighton Wilts 133 E5
Knighton on Teme 157 F5
Knightswood 233 G3
Knightwick 145 G2
Knill 144 B1
Knipoch 240 A2
Knipton 174 D4
Knitsley 212 A3
Kniveton 172 D2
Knock A&B 239 E1
Knock Cumb 210 C5
Knock High 256 C4

Knock Moray 268 D5
Knock of
   Auchnahannet 259 H1
Knockalava 240 B5
Knockally 275 G6
Knockaloe Moar 190 A3
Knockan 272 E7
Knockandhu 259 K2
Knockandu 267 J7
Knockarthur 266 E1
Knockbain 266 D6
Knockban 265 J5
Knockbreck 266 C5
Knockbrex 207 F2
Knockdamph 265 J2
Knockdee 275 G2
Knockdow 232 C2
Knockdown 132 A4
Knockenkelly 223 F3
Knockentiber 224 B2
Knockfin 257 K2
Knockgray 215 G3
Knockholt 123 D3
Knockholt Pound 123 D3
Knockin 170 A5
Knockinlaw 224 C2
Knockintorran (Cnoc an
   Torrain) 262 C5
Knocklearn 216 B3
Knockmill 123 E3
Knocknaha 222 B4
Knocknain 214 A4
Knocknalling 215 G2
Knockrome 231 D2
Knocksharry 190 A3
Knockville 215 E3
Knockvologan 238 C3
Knodishall 153 F1
Knodishall
   Common 153 F1
Knodishall Green 153 F1
Knole 116 B5
Knolls Green 184 C5
Knolton 170 A4
Knook 118 A3
Knossington 160 D2
Knott End-on-Sea 191 G3
Knotting 149 F1
Knotting Green 149 F1
Knottingley 195 E5
Knotts 193 D2
Knotty Green 135 E3
Knowbury 157 E5
Knowe 215 E3
Knowes of Elrick 268 E5
Knowesgate 220 B3
Knoweside 224 A4
Knowetownhead 227 G4
Knowhead 269 H5
Knowl Green 151 F3
Knowl Hill 134 D5
Knowl Wall 171 F4
Knowle Bristol 131 F5
Knowle Devon 113 E2
Knowle Devon 103 E2
Knowle Devon 103 E4
Knowle Shrop 157 E5
Knowle Som 114 C3
Knowle WMid 159 D5
Knowle Cross 102 D3
Knowle Green 192 C4
Knowle Hall 116 A3
Knowle St. Giles 103 G1
Knowlton Dorset 105 G1
Knowlton Kent 125 E3
Knowsley 183 F3
Knowsley Safari Park
   Mersey L34 4AN 23 E2
Knowstone 114 B5
Knox Bridge 123 G4
Knucklas (Cnwclas)
   156 B5
Knutsford 184 B5
Knypersley 171 F2
Krumlin 185 E1
Kuggar 95 E5
Kyle of Lochalsh (Caol
   Loch Aillse) 256 D2
Kyleakin
   (Caol Acain) 256 D2
Kylerhea
   (Ceol Reatha) 256 D2
Kyles Scalpay (Caolas
   Scalpaigh) 263 H2
Kylesbeg 247 F2
Kylesknoydart 256 E5
Kylesku 272 E5
Kylesmorar 256 E5
Kylestrome 272 E5
Kyloag 266 D2
Kynaston 170 A5
Kynnersley 157 F1
Kyre Park 145 F1

L

Labost 270 E3
Lacasaigh 271 F5
Lace Market Centre
   NG1 1HF 80 Nottingham
Laceby 188 C2
Lacey Green 134 D2
Lach Dennis 184 B5
Lackford 163 F5
Lacklee
   (Leac a' Li) 263 G2
Lacock 118 A1
Ladbroke 147 G2
Laddingford 123 F4
Lade Bank 176 B2
Ladies Hill 192 A3
Ladock 96 C4
Lady Hall 198 C4
Lady Lever Art Gallery
   Mersey
   CH62 5EQ 22 B4
Ladybank 244 B3
Ladycross 98 D2
Ladyfield 240 C3
Ladykirk 237 F5
Ladywood Worcs 146 A1
Laga 247 F3
Lagalochan 240 A3
Lagavulin 230 C5
Lagg A&B 231 D2
Lagg NAyr 223 E3
Lagg SAyr 224 A4
Laggan A&B 230 A4

Laggan (An Lagan) High 257 J5
Laggan High 258 D5
Laggan Moray 260 B1
Laggan Stir 242 A3
Lagganulva 247 D5
Lagganvoulin 259 J3
Laglingarten 240 D4
Lagnalean 266 D7
Lagrae 225 F4
Laguna 243 G1
Laid 273 G3
Laide 265 F2
Laig 247 D1
Laight 225 E4
Lainchoil 259 H3
Laindon 137 F4
Laing Art Gallery T&W NE1 8AG 79 Newcastle upon Tyne
Lair 251 G3
Lairg 266 C1
Lairg Lodge 266 C1
Lairigmor 248 D3
Laisterdyke 194 A4
Laithes 210 A4
Lake Devon 113 F2
Lake Devon 100 B1
Lake IoW 107 E4
Lake Wilts 118 C4
Lake District Visitor Centre at Brockhole LA23 1LJ 199 E2
Lakenham 178 D5
Lakenheath 163 F4
Lakes Aquarium Cumb LA12 8AS 199 E4
Lakes End 162 D3
Lakes Glass Centre, Ulverston Cumb LA12 7LY 199 D5
Lakeside Cumb 199 E4
Lakeside Thur 137 E5
Lakeside & Haverthwaite Railway Cumb LA12 8AL 199 E4
Laleham 121 F1
Laleston 129 E5
Lamancha 235 G4
Lamarsh 151 G4
Lamas 178 D3
Lamb Corner 152 B4
Lamb Roe 192 D4
Lambden 237 E5
Lamberhurst 123 F5
Lamberhurst Quarter 123 F5
Lamberton 237 E5
Lambfell Moar 190 A3
Lambley N'umb 210 C2
Lambley Notts 174 B3
Lambourn 133 F5
Lambourn Woodlands 133 F5
Lambourne End 137 D3
Lambs Green 122 B5
Lambston 126 C1
Lambton 212 B2
Lamellion 97 G3
Lamerton 99 E3
Lamesley 212 B2
Lamington High 266 E4
Lamington SLan 226 A2
Lamlash 223 F2
Lamloch 215 G1
Lamonby 210 A4
Lamorna 94 B4
Lamorran 96 C5
Lampert 219 E4
Lampeter (Llanbedr Pont Steffan) 142 B3
Lampeter Velfrey 127 E1
Lamphey 126 D2
Lamplugh 209 D4
Lamport 160 C5
Lamyatt 117 D4
Lana Devon 98 D1
Lana Devon 112 D5
Lanark 234 A4
Lanarth 95 E4
Lancaster 192 A1
Lancaster Leisure Park Lancs LA1 3LA 192 A1
Lancaster Priory Lancs LA1 1YZ 192 A1
Lanchester 212 A3
Lancing 109 D3
Landbeach 150 C1
Landcross 113 E3
Landerberry 261 F4
Landewednack 95 E5
Landford 106 B1
Landhallow 275 G5
Landican 183 D4
Landimore 128 A3
Landkey 113 F2
Landmoth 202 D3
Landore 128 C3
Landrake 99 D4
Land's End Corn TR19 7AA 94 A4
Landscove 101 D1
Landshipping 126 D1
Landulph 100 A1
Landwade 151 E1
Landywood 158 B2
Lane Bottom 193 E4
Lane End Bucks 134 D3
Lane End Cumb 198 C3
Lane End Derbys 173 F1
Lane End Dorset 105 E3
Lane End Hants 119 G5
Lane End Here 145 E3
Lane End Kent 137 E5
Lane End Wilts 117 F4
Lane Ends Derbys 172 D4
Lane Ends Lancs 193 D4
Lane Ends NYorks 193 F3
Lane Green 158 A2
Lane Head Dur 202 A1
Lane Head Dur 211 G5
Lane Head GtMan 185 D3
Lane Head WYorks 185 F2
Lane Heads 192 A4
Lane Side 193 D5

Laneast 97 G1
Lane-end 97 E3
Laneham 187 F5
Lanehead Dur 211 E3
Lanehead N'umb 219 F3
Lanesend 127 D2
Lanesfield 158 B3
Laneshawbridge 193 F3
Langais 262 D1
Langamull 246 C4
Langar 174 C4
Langbank 233 E2
Langbar 193 G2
Langbaurgh 203 E1
Langcliffe 193 E1
Langdale End 204 C3
Langdon Corn 98 C1
Langdon Corn 98 D2
Langdon Beck 211 E4
Langdon Hills 137 F4
Langdon Hills Country Park Essex SS17 9NH 137 F4
Langdon House 101 E4
Langdyke 244 B4
Langford CenBeds 149 G3
Langford Essex 138 B2
Langford Notts 174 D2
Langford Oxon 133 E2
Langford Budville 115 E5
Langham Essex 152 B4
Langham Norf 178 B1
Langham Rut 160 D1
Langham Suff 152 A1
Langham Moor 152 B4
Langho 192 C4
Langholm 218 B3
Langland 128 C4
Langlands 216 A5
Langlee 228 A3
Langleeford 228 D4
Langley ChesE 184 D5
Langley Derbys 173 F3
Langley Essex 150 C4
Langley Glos 146 C5
Langley GtMan 184 C2
Langley Hants 106 D2
Langley Herts 150 A5
Langley Kent 123 G3
Langley N'umb 211 E1
Langley Oxon 133 F1
Langley Slo 135 F2
Langley Som 115 D5
Langley Warks 147 D1
Langley WSuss 120 D5
Langley Burrell 132 B5
Langley Corner 135 F4
Langley Green Derbys 173 D4
Langley Green Works 147 E1
Langley Green WSuss 122 B5
Langley Heath 124 A3
Langley Marsh 115 D5
Langley Mill 173 F3
Langley Moor 212 B3
Langley Park 212 B3
Langley Park Bucks SL3 6DW 135 F4
Langley Street 179 E5
Langney 110 B3
Langold 186 C4
Langore 97 G1
Langport 116 B5
Langrick 176 A3
Langrick Bridge 176 A3
Langridge B&NESom 117 E1
Langridge Devon 113 F3
Langridgeford 113 F3
Langrigg 209 E2
Langrish 120 C5
Langsett 185 G2
Langshaw 227 G2
Langshawburn 227 D5
Langside Glas 233 G3
Langside P&K 242 C3
Langskaill 276 D3
Langstone Newport 130 C3
Langthorne 202 B3
Langthorpe 194 C1
Langthwaite 201 F3
Langtoft ERid 196 C1
Langtoft Lincs 161 G1
Langton Dur 202 A1
Langton Lincs 189 D5
Langton Lincs 176 A1
Langton NYorks 195 G1
Langton by Wragby 188 B5
Langton Green Kent 123 E5
Langton Green Suff 164 C4
Langton Herring 104 C4
Langton Long Blandford 105 E2
Langton Matravers 105 F5
Langtree 113 E4
Langtree Week 113 E4
Langwathby 210 B4
Langwell 266 B1
Langwell House 275 G6
Langwith 186 C5
Langworth 188 A5
Lanhydrock Corn PL30 5AD 97 E3
Lanivet 97 E3
Lank 97 E2
Lanlivery 97 E4
Lanner 96 B5
Lanoy 97 G2
Lanreath 97 F4
Lansallos 97 F4
Lansdown 117 E1
Lanteglos 97 E2
Lanteglos Highway 97 F4
Lanton N'umb 228 D3
Lanton ScBord 228 A4
Lanvean 96 C3
Lapford 102 A2
Laphroaig 230 B5
Lapley 158 A1
Lapworth 159 D5
Larach na Gaibhre 231 F2
Larachbeag 247 F5
Larbert 234 C1
Larden Green 170 C2

Larg 215 E3
Largie 260 E1
Largiemore 232 A1
Largoward 244 C4
Largs 232 D4
Largue 268 E6
Largybaan 222 B4
Largybeg 223 F3
Largymore 223 F3
Lark Hall 151 D2
Larkfield 232 D2
Larkhall 234 B4
Larkhill 118 C3
Larklands 173 F3
Larling 164 A3
Larriston 218 D2
Lartington 201 F1
Lary 260 B3
Lasborough 132 A3
Lasham 120 B3
Lashbrook 113 E5
Lashenden 124 A4
Lassington 145 G5
Lassodie 243 G5
Lastingham 203 G3
Latchford 184 A4
Latchingdon 138 B2
Latchley 99 E3
Lately Common 184 A3
Lathbury 149 D3
Latheron 275 G5
Latheronwheel 275 G5
Lathockar 244 C3
Lathones 244 C4
Lathrisk 244 A4
Latimer 135 F3
Latteridge 131 F4
Lattiford 117 D5
Latton 132 C3
Lauchentyre 215 G5
Lauchintilly 261 F3
Lauder 236 C5
Laugharne (Lacharn) 127 G1
Laughterton 187 F5
Laughton ESuss 110 A2
Laughton Leics 160 B4
Laughton Lincs 175 F4
Laughton Lincs 187 F3
Laughton en le Morthen 186 C4
Launcells 112 C5
Launcells Cross 112 C5
Launceston 98 D2
Launde Abbey 160 C2
Launton 148 B5
Laurencekirk 253 F2
Laurieston D&G 216 A4
Laurieston Falk 234 D2
Lavendon 149 E2
Lavenham 152 A3
Laverhay 217 F1
Lavernock 115 E1
Laversdale 210 A1
Laverstock 118 C4
Laverstoke 119 F3
Laverton Glos 146 C4
Laverton NYorks 202 B5
Laverton Som 117 E2
Lavister 170 A2
Law 234 C4
Lawers P&K 242 C1
Lawers P&K 242 B1
Lawford Essex 152 B4
Lawford Som 115 E4
Lawhitton 99 D2
Lawkland 193 D1
Lawkland Green 193 D1
Lawley 157 F2
Lawnhead 171 F5
Lawrence Weston 131 E5
Lawrenny 126 D2
Laws 244 C1
Lawshall 151 G2
Lawshall Green 151 G2
Lawton 144 D2
Laxdale (Lacasdal) 271 G4
Laxey 190 C3
Laxfield 165 D4
Laxfirth Shet 279 D7
Laxfirth Shet 279 D8
Laxford Bridge 272 E4
Laxo 279 D6
Laxton ERid 195 G5
Laxton N'hants 161 E3
Laxton Notts 174 C1
Laycock 193 G3
Layer Breton 138 C1
Layer de la Haye 138 C1
Layer Marney 138 C1
Layham 152 B3
Laymore 103 G2
Layter's Green 135 E3
Laytham 195 G4
Layton 191 G4
Lazenby 213 E5
Lazonby 210 B4
Lea Derbys 173 E2
Lea Here 145 F5
Lea Lincs 187 F4
Lea Shrop 156 C4
Lea Shrop 156 D2
Lea Wilts 132 B4
Lea Bridge 173 E2
Lea Green 145 F1
Lea Marston 159 E3
Lea Town 192 A4
Lea Yeat 200 C4
Leachd 240 C5
Leachkin (An Leacainn) 266 D7
Leadburn 235 G4
Leaden Roding 137 E1
Leadenham 175 E2
Leaderfoot 227 G2
Leadgate Cumb 210 D3
Leadgate Dur 212 A2
Leadgate N'umb 212 A2
Leadhills 225 G4
Leadingcross Green 124 A3
Leafield 133 F1
Leagrave 149 F5
Leake Commonside 176 B2
Leake Hurn's End 176 C3
Lealands 110 A2

Lealholm 203 G2
Lealt A&B 230 B1
Lealt High 264 B5
Leam 185 G5
Leamington Hastings 147 G1
Leamington Spa 147 F1
Leamington Spa Art Gallery & Museum Works CV32 4AA 16 B6
Leamoor Common 156 D4
Leanach A&B 240 C5
Leanach High 266 E7
Leanaig 266 C6
Leanoch 267 J6
Leargybreck 230 D2
Leasgill 199 F4
Leasingham 175 F3
Leason 128 A3
Leasowe 183 D3
Leat 98 D2
Leatherhead 121 G2
Leathley 194 B3
Leaton Shrop 157 D1
Leaton Tel&W 157 F1
Leaveland 124 C3
Leavenheath 152 A4
Leavening 195 G1
Leaves Green 122 D2
Leavesden Green 136 A2
Lebberston 205 D4
Lechlade-on-Thames 133 E3
Leck 200 B5
Leckford 119 E4
Leckfurin 274 C3
Leckgruinart 230 A3
Leckhampstead Bucks 148 C4
Leckhampstead WBerks 133 G5
Leckhampstead Thicket 133 G5
Leckhampton 132 B1
Leckie High 265 G5
Leckie Stir 242 B5
Leckmelm (Leac Mailm) 265 H3
Leckroy 257 K5
Leckuary 240 A5
Leckwith 130 A5
Leconfield 196 C3
Ledaig (Leideag) 240 B1
Ledard 241 G4
Ledbeg 272 E7
Ledburn 149 D5
Ledbury 145 G4
Ledcharrie 242 A2
Ledgemoor 144 D1
Ledicot 144 D1
Ledmore A&B 247 E5
Ledmore High 272 E7
Lednagullin 274 D2
Ledsham ChesW&C 183 E5
Ledsham WYorks 195 D5
Ledston 194 D5
Ledstone 100 D3
Ledwell 147 G5
Lee A&B 238 D2
Lee Devon 113 E1
Lee Hants 106 C1
Lee Lancs 192 B3
Lee Shrop 170 B4
Lee Brockhurst 170 C5
Lee Chapel 137 F4
Lee Clump 135 E2
Lee Mill Bridge 100 B2
Lee Moor 100 B1
Lee Valley Park Essex EN9 1XQ 136 C2
Leebotten 279 D10
Leebotwood 157 D3
Leece 191 F1
Leeds Kent 124 A3
Leeds WYorks 194 B4
Leeds Art Gallery WYorks LS1 3AA 40 E3
Leeds Bradford International Airport 194 B3
Leeds Castle & Gardens Kent ME17 1PL 124 A3
Leedstown 94 D3
Leegomery 157 F1
Leek 171 G2
Leek Wootton 147 E1
Leekbrook 171 G2
Leeming NYorks 202 B4
Leeming WYorks 193 G4
Leeming Bar 202 B4
Lees Derbys 173 D4
Lees GtMan 185 D2
Leeswood 169 F2
Leftwich 184 A5
Legars 237 E5
Legbourne 189 D4
Legerwood 236 C5
Legoland Windsor W&M SL4 4AY 135 F5
Legsby 188 B4
Leicester 160 A2
Leicester Forest East 160 A2
Leideag 254 B5
Leigh Dorset 104 C2
Leigh Dorset 105 G3
Leigh GtMan 184 A2
Leigh Kent 123 E4
Leigh Shrop 156 C2
Leigh Surr 122 B4
Leigh Wilts 132 C3
Leigh Worcs 145 G2
Leigh Beck 138 B4
Leigh Common 117 E5
Leigh Delamere 132 A5
Leigh Green 124 B5
Leigh Park 107 G2
Leigh Sinton 145 G2
Leigh upon Mendip 117 D3
Leigh Woods 131 E5
Leigham 100 E5
Leighland Chapel 114 D4
Leigh-on-Sea 138 B4
Leighterton 132 A3
Leighton NYorks 202 A5

Leighton (Tre'r Llai) Powys 156 B2
Leighton Shrop 157 F2
Leighton Som 117 E3
Leighton Bromswold 161 G5
Leighton Buzzard 149 E5
Leinthall Earls 144 D1
Leinthall Starkes 144 D1
Leintwardine 156 D5
Leire 160 A4
Leirinmore 273 G2
Leiston 153 F1
Leith 235 G2
Leitholm 237 E5
Lelant 94 C3
Lelley 197 E4
Lem Hill 157 G5
Lemington 212 A1
Lemnas 269 G4
Lempitlaw 228 B3
Lemsford 136 B1
Lenchwick 146 C3
Lendalfoot 214 C1
Lendrick Lodge 242 A4
Lenham 124 A3
Lenham Heath 124 B4
Lenie 258 C2
Lenimore 231 G5
Lennel 237 F5
Lennox Plunton 216 A5
Lennoxtown 234 A2
Lent Rise 135 E4
Lenton Lincs 175 F4
Lenton Nott 173 G4
Lenton Abbey 173 G4
Lenwade 178 B4
Lenzie 234 A2
Leoch 244 B1
Leochel-Cushnie 260 D3
Leominster 145 D2
Leonard Stanley 132 A2
Leorin 230 B5
Lepe 106 D3
Lephin 263 G7
Lephinchapel 240 B5
Lephinmore 240 B5
Leppington 195 G1
Lepton 185 G1
Lerags 240 B2
Lerryn 97 F4
Lerwick 279 D8
Lesbury 229 G5
Leschangie 261 F3
Leslie Aber 260 D2
Leslie Fife 244 A4
Lesmahagow 225 G2
Lesnewth 98 B1
Lessendrum 268 D6
Lessingham 179 E3
Lessness Heath 137 D5
Lessonhall 209 F1
Leswalt 214 B4
Letchmore Heath 136 A3
Letchworth Garden City 150 A4
Letcombe Bassett 133 F4
Letcombe Regis 133 F4
Leth Meadhanach 254 C3
Letham Angus 252 D5
Letham Falk 234 C1
Letham Fife 244 B3
Lethanhill 224 C4
Lethenty 269 G6
Letheringham 153 D2
Letheringsett 178 B2
Lettaford 102 A4
Letter Finlay 257 J5
Letterewe 265 F4
Letterfearn (Leitir Fheàrna) 256 C2
Lettermorar 247 G1
Lettermore A&B 247 D5
Lettermore High 273 J4
Letters 265 H3
Lettershaws 225 G3
Letterston 140 C5
Lettoch High 259 H3
Lettoch High 259 J1
Letton Here 156 C5
Letton Here 144 C3
Letty Green 136 B1
Letwell 186 C4
Leuchars 244 C2
Leumrabhagh 271 F6
Leurbost (Liurbost) 271 F5
Leusdon 102 A5
Levedale 158 A1
Level's Green 150 C5
Leven ERid 196 D3
Leven Fife 244 B4
Levencorroch 223 F3
Levenhall 236 A2
Levens 199 F4
Levens Green 150 B5
Levenshulme 184 C3
Levenwick 279 D10
Leverburgh (An T-Òb) 263 F3
Leverington 162 C1
Leverstock Green 135 F2
Leverton 176 B3
Leverton Lucasgate 176 C3
Leverton Outgate 176 C3
Levington 152 D4
Levisham 204 B3
Levishie 258 B3
Lew 133 F2
Lewannick 97 G1
Lewcombe 104 B2
Lewdown 99 E2
Lewes 109 G2
Leweston 140 C5
Lewisham 136 C5
Lewiston (Blàr na Maigh) 258 C2
Lewistown 129 F4
Lewknor 134 C3
Leworthy 113 G2
Lewson Street 124 B2
Lewth 192 A4
Lewtrenchard 99 E2
Ley Aber 260 D3
Ley Corn 97 F3
Ley Green 149 G5
Leybourne 123 F3
Leyburn 202 A3
Leyland 192 B5

Leylodge 261 F3
Leymoor 185 F1
Leys Aber 269 J5
Leys Aber 260 C4
Leys P&K 244 A1
Leys of Cossans 252 B5
Leysdown-on-Sea 124 C1
Leysmill 253 E5
Leyton 136 C4
Leytonstone 136 C4
Lezant 98 D3
Lezerea 95 D3
Lhanbryde 267 K5
Liatrie 257 J1
Libanus 143 F5
Libberton 235 D5
Libbery 146 B2
Liberton 235 G3
Liceasto 263 G2
Lichfield 158 D2
Lichfield Cathedral Staffs WS13 7LD 158 D2
Lickey 158 B5
Lickey End 158 B5
Lickey Hills Country Park Worcs B45 8ER 14 C6
Lickfold 121 E5
Liddaton Green 99 E2
Liddel 277 D9
Liddesdale 247 G4
Liddington 133 E4
Lidgate Derbys 186 A5
Lidgate Suff 151 F2
Lidget 174 B1
Lidgett 174 B1
Lidlington 149 E4
Lidsey 108 B3
Lidsing 123 G2
Lidstone 147 G5
Lienassie 257 F2
Lieurary 275 F2
Liff 244 B1
Lifton 99 D2
Liftondown 99 D2
Lightcliffe 194 A5
Lighthorne 147 F2
Lighthorne Heath 147 F2
Lighthouse, The, Glasgow Glas G1 3NU 39 F4
Lighthouse, The - Poole's Centre for the Arts Poole BH15 1UG 3 B4
Lightwater 121 E1
Lightwater Valley Park NYorks HG4 3HT 202 B5
Lightwood 171 G3
Lightwood Green ChesE 170 D3
Lightwood Green Wrex 170 A3
Lilbourne 160 A5
Lilburn Tower 229 E4
Lilleshall 157 G1
Lilley Herts 149 G5
Lilley WBerks 133 G5
Lilliesleaf 227 G3
Lilling Green 195 F1
Lillingstone Dayrell 148 C4
Lillingstone Lovell 148 C3
Lillington Dorset 104 C1
Lillington Warks 147 F1
Lilliput 105 G4
Lilstock 115 E3
Lilyhurst 157 G1
Lilybank 233 E2
Limbury 149 F5
Lime Side 184 D2
Limefield 184 C1
Limehillock 268 D5
Limehurst 184 D2
Limekilnburn 234 B4
Limekilns 235 E1
Limerigg 234 C2
Limerstone 106 D4
Limington 116 C5
Limpenhoe 179 E5
Limpley Stoke 117 E1
Limpsfield 122 D3
Limpsfield Chart 122 D3
Linaclate (Lionacleit) 262 C7
Linacre Reservoirs Derbys S42 7JW 186 A5
Linbriggs 220 A1
Linby 173 G2
Linchmere 121 D4
Lincluden 217 D3
Lincoln 187 G5
Lincoln Castle Lincs LN1 3AA 77 Lincoln
Lincoln Cathedral Lincs LN2 1PL 77 Lincoln
Lincomb 146 A1
Lincombe Devon 100 D2
Lincombe Devon 100 D3
Lindal in Furness 199 D5
Lindale 199 F4
Lindean 227 F2
Lindertis 252 B4
Lindfield 109 F1
Lindford 120 D4
Lindifferon 244 B3
Lindisfarne (Holy Island) 229 F2
Lindley 194 B3
Lindores 244 A3
Lindow End 184 C5
Lindridge 145 F1
Lindsaig 232 A2
Lindsell 151 E4
Lindsey 152 A3
Lindsey Tye 152 A3
Linfitts 185 D2
Linford Hants 106 A2
Linford Thur 137 F5
Linford Wood 148 D3
Lingague 190 A4
Lingards Wood 185 E1
Lingdale 203 F1
Lingen 144 C1
Lingfield 122 C4
Lingley Green 183 G4
Lingwood 179 E5
Linhead 268 E5
Linhope 227 F5
Linicro 263 J5

Linkend 146 A4
Linkenholt 119 E2
Linkhill 110 D1
Linkinhorne 98 D3
Linklater 277 D9
Linksness Ork 277 B7
Linksness Ork 277 E6
Linktown 244 A5
Linley Shrop 156 C3
Linley Shrop 157 F3
Linley Green 145 F2
Linlithgow 235 E2
Linlithgow Bridge 235 D2
Linn of Muick Cottage 252 B1
Linnels 211 F1
Linney 126 B3
Linshiels 220 A1
Linsiadar 270 E4
Linsidemore 266 C2
Linslade 149 E5
Linstead Parva 165 E4
Linstock 210 A2
Linthwaite 185 F1
Lintlaw 237 F4
Lintmill 268 D4
Linton Cambs 151 D3
Linton Derbys 159 E1
Linton Here 145 F5
Linton Kent 123 G3
Linton NYorks 193 F1
Linton ScBord 228 B4
Linton WYorks 194 C3
Linton-on-Ouse 195 D1
Lintzford 212 A2
Linwood Hants 106 A2
Linwood Lincs 188 B4
Linwood Renf 233 F3
Lionel (Lional) 271 H1
Liphook 120 D4
Lipley 171 E4
Liscard 183 E3
Liscombe 114 B4
Liskeard 97 G3
L'islet 101 F4
Lismore 240 A1
Liss 120 C5
Liss Forest 120 C5
Lissett 196 D2
Lissington 188 B4
Liston 151 G3
Lisvane 130 A4
Liswerry 130 C4
Litcham 163 G1
Litchborough 148 B2
Litchfield 119 F2
Litherland 183 E3
Litlington Cambs 150 B3
Litlington ESuss 110 A3
Little Abington 150 D3
Little Addington 161 E5
Little Alne 146 D1
Little Altcar 183 E2
Little Amwell 136 C1
Little Ann 119 E3
Little Asby 200 B2
Little Assynt 272 D6
Little Aston 158 C3
Little Atherfield 107 D5
Little Ayton 203 E1
Little Baddow 137 G2
Little Badminton 132 A4
Little Ballinluig 251 E4
Little Bampton 209 F1
Little Bardfield 151 E4
Little Barford 149 G2
Little Barningham 178 C2
Little Barrington 133 E1
Little Barrow 170 B1
Little Barugh 203 G5
Little Bavington 220 B4
Little Bealings 152 D3
Little Bedwyn 119 D1
Little Beeby 160 B2
Little Bentley 152 C5
Little Berkhamsted 136 B2
Little Billing 148 D1
Little Birch 145 E4
Little Bispham 191 G3
Little Blakenham 152 C3
Little Bloxwich 158 C2
Little Bollington 184 B4
Little Bookham 121 G2
Little Bourton 147 G3
Little Bowden 160 C4
Little Bradley 151 E2
Little Brampton 156 C4
Little Braxted 138 B1
Little Brechin 253 D3
Little Brickhill 149 E4
Little Bridgeford 171 F5
Little Brington 148 B1
Little Bromley 152 B5
Little Broughton 209 D3
Little Budworth 170 C1
Little Burdon 202 C1
Little Burstead 137 F3
Little Burton 196 D3
Little Bytham 161 F1
Little Canfield 151 D5
Little Carlton Lincs 189 D4
Little Carlton Notts 174 C2
Little Casterton 161 F1
Little Catwick 196 D3
Little Catworth 161 F5
Little Cawthorpe 189 D4
Little Chalfield 117 F1
Little Chalfont 135 E3
Little Chart 124 B4
Little Chesterford 150 D3
Little Chesterton 148 A5
Little Cheverell 118 A2
Little Clacton 139 E1
Little Clanfield 133 E2
Little Clifton 209 D4
Little Coates 188 C2
Little Comberton 146 B3
Little Common 110 C3
Little Compton 147 E4
Little Corby 210 A2
Little Cornard 151 G4
Little Cowarne 145 F2
Little Coxwell 133 E3
Little Crakehall 202 B3
Little Cransley 160 D5
Little Crawley 149 E3
Little Creaton 160 C5
Little Creich 266 D3

Little Cressingham 163 G3
Little Crosby 183 E2
Little Crosthwaite 209 F4
Little Cubley 172 C4
Little Dalby 160 C1
Little Dens 269 J6
Little Dewchurch 145 E4
Little Ditton 151 E2
Little Doward 131 E1
Little Down 119 E2
Little Downham 162 D4
Little Drayton 171 D4
Little Driffield 196 C2
Little Dunkeld 251 E1
Little Dunham 163 G1
Little Dunmow 151 E5
Little Durnford 118 C4
Little Easton 151 E5
Little Eaton 173 E3
Little Eccleston 192 A4
Little Ellingham 164 B2
Little End 137 E2
Little Everdon 148 A2
Little Eversden 150 B2
Little Faringdon 133 E2
Little Fencote 202 B3
Little Fenton 195 E4
Little Finborough 152 B2
Little Fransham 178 A4
Little Gaddesden 135 E1
Little Garway 144 D5
Little Gidding 161 G4
Little Glemham 153 E2
Little Glenshee 243 E1
Little Gorsley 145 F5
Little Gransden 150 A2
Little Green Cambs 150 A3
Little Green Notts 174 C3
Little Green Suff 164 B4
Little Green Suff 164 B4
Little Green Wrex 170 B3
Little Grimsby 188 D3
Little Gringley 187 E4
Little Gruinard 265 F3
Little Habton 203 G5
Little Hadham 150 C5
Little Hale 175 G3
Little Hallingbury 137 D1
Little Hampden 135 E1
Little Haresfield 132 A2
Little Harrowden 161 D5
Little Haseley 134 B2
Little Hatfield 197 D3
Little Hautbois 179 D3
Little Haven
        Pembs 126 B1
Little Haven WSuss 121 G4
Little Hay 158 D2
Little Hayfield 185 E4
Little Haywood 172 B5
Little Heath 159 F4
Little Hereford 145 E1
Little Hockham 164 A2
Little Horkesley 152 A4
Little Hormead 150 C5
Little Horsted 109 G2
Little Horton 118 B1
Little Horwood 148 C4
Little Houghton 148 D2
Little Hucklow 185 F5
Little Hulton 184 B2
Little Hungerford 134 A5
Little Hutton 203 D5
Little Irchester 149 E1
Little Keyford 117 E3
Little Kimble 134 D2
Little Kineton 147 F2
Little Kingshill 135 D3
Little Langdale 199 E2
Little Langford 118 B4
Little Laver 137 E2
Little Lawford 159 G5
Little Leigh 184 A5
Little Leighs 137 G1
Little Lever 184 B2
Little Ley 260 E3
Little Linford 148 D3
Little Linton 151 D3
Little London
        Bucks 134 B1
Little London
        Essex 150 C5
Little London
        ESuss 110 A2
Little London
        Hants 119 E3
Little London
        Hants 120 B2
Little London IoM 190 B3
Little London Lincs 176 C5
Little London Lincs 176 A5
Little London Lincs 188 D5
Little London Lincs 188 B4
Little London Norf 177 D5
Little London Norf 163 F3
Little London Oxon 134 A2
Little London
        Powys 155 G4
Little London Suff 152 B2
Little London
        WYorks 194 B4
Little Longstone 185 F5
Little Lyth 157 D2
Little Malvern 145 G3
Little Maplestead 151 E4
Little Marcle 145 F4
Little Marland 113 F4
Little Marlow 135 D4
Little Marsden 193 E4
Little Massingham 177 F5
Little Melton 178 C5
Little Milford 126 C1
Little Mill 130 C2
Little Milton 134 B2
Little Missenden 135 E3
Little Musgrave 200 C1
Little Ness 156 C1
Little Neston 183 D5
Little Newcastle 140 C5
Little Newsham 202 A1
Little Oakley
        Essex 152 D5
Little Oakley
        N'hants 161 D4
Little Odell 149 E2
Little Offley 149 G5
Little Onn 158 A1
Little Orton Cumb 209 G1

Little Orton Leics 159 F2
Little Ouse 163 E4
Little Ouseburn 194 D1
Little Overton 170 A3
Little Packington 159 E4
Little Parndon 136 D1
Little Paxton 149 G1
Little Petherick 96 D2
Little Plumpton 191 G4
Little Plumstead 179 E4
Little Ponton 175 E4
Little Posbrook 107 E2
Little Potheridge 113 F4
Little Preston 148 A1
Little Raveley 162 A4
Little Ribston 194 C2
Little Rissington 133 E1
Little Rogart 266 E1
Little Rollright 147 E4
Little Ryburgh 178 A3
Little Ryle 229 E5
Little Ryton 157 D2
Little Salkeld 210 B4
Little Sampford 151 E4
Little Saxham 151 G1
Little Scatwell 265 K6
Little Shelford 150 C2
Little Shrawardine 156 C1
Little Silver 102 C2
Little Singleton 191 G4
Little Smeaton
        NYorks 186 C1
Little Smeaton
        NYorks 202 C2
Little Snoring 178 A2
Little Sodbury 131 G4
Little Sodbury End 131 G4
Little Somborne 119 E4
Little Somerford 132 B4
Little Soudley 171 E5
Little Stainforth 193 E1
Little Stainton 202 C1
Little Stanney 183 F5
Little Staughton 149 G1
Little Steeping 176 C1
Little Stoke 171 G4
Little Stonham 152 C2
Little Street 162 D4
Little Stretton Leics 160 B2
Little Stretton
        Shrop 156 D3
Little Strickland 199 G1
Little Stukeley 162 A5
Little Sugnall 171 F4
Little Sutton 183 E5
Little Swinburne 220 B4
Little Tarrington 145 F3
Little Tew 147 F5
Little Tey 151 G5
Little Thetford 162 D5
Little Thornage 178 B2
Little Thornton 191 G3
Little Thorpe 212 D3
Little Thurlow 151 E2
Little Thurlow
        Green 151 E2
Little Thurrock 137 F5
Little Torboll 266 E2
Little Torrington 113 E4
Little Tosson 220 C1
Little Totham 138 B1
Little Twycross 159 F2
Little Urswick 199 D5
Little Wakering 138 C4
Little Walden 150 D3
Little Waldingfield 152 A3
Little Walsingham 178 A2
Little Waltham 137 G1
Little Warley 137 F3
Little Washbourne 146 B4
Little Weighton 196 B4
Little Welland 146 A4
Little Welnetham 151 G1
Little Wenham 152 B4
Little Wenlock 157 F2
Little Whittington 211 F1
Little Wilbraham 150 D2
Little Wishford 118 B4
Little Witcombe 132 B1
Little Witley 145 G1
Little Wittenham 134 A3
Little Wittingham
        Green 165 D4
Little Wolford 147 E4
Little Woodcote 122 B2
Little Wratting 151 E3
Little Wymington 149 E1
Little
        Wymondley 150 A5
Little Wyrley 158 C2
Little Wytheford 157 E1
Little Yeldham 151 F4
Littlebeck 204 B2
Littleborough
        Devon 102 B1
Littleborough
        GtMan 184 D1
Littleborough
        Notts 187 F5
Littlebourne 125 E3
Littlebredy 104 B4
Littlebury 150 D4
Littlebury Green 150 C4
Littledean 131 F1
Littleferry 267 F2
Littleham Devon 113 E3
Littleham Devon 102 D4
Littlehampton 108 C3
Littlehempston 101 E1
Littlehoughton 229 G5
Littlemill EAyr 224 C4
Littlemill High 267 G6
Littlemoor Derbys 173 E1
Littlemoor Dorset 104 C4
Littlemore 134 A2
Littlemoss 184 D3
Littleover 173 E4
Littleport 163 D4
Littlestead Green 134 C5
Littlestone-on-Sea 111 F1
Littlethorpe 194 C1
Littleton ChesW&C 170 B1
Littleton Hants 119 F4
Littleton P&K 244 A1
Littleton Som 116 B4

Littleton Surr 121 F1
Littleton Drew 132 A4
Littleton Panell 118 B2
Littleton-on-Severn 131 E3
Littletown Dur 212 C3
Littletown IoW 107 E4
Littlewick Green 134 D5
Littlewindsor 104 A2
Littleworth Glos 146 D4
Littleworth Oxon 133 F3
Littleworth Staffs 158 C1
Littleworth SYorks 186 D3
Littleworth Worcs 146 A3
Littley Green 137 F1
Litton Derbys 185 F5
Litton NYorks 201 E5
Litton Som 116 C2
Litton Cheney 104 B3
Liverpool 183 E4
Liverpool Cathedral
        Mersey L1 7AZ 42 E6
Liverpool John Lennon
        Airport 183 F4
Liverpool Metropolitan
        Cathedral (RC) Mersey
        L3 5TQ 43 M4
Liversedge 194 B5
Liverton Devon 102 B5
Liverton R&C 203 G1
Liverton Street 124 A4
Living Coasts, Torquay
        Torbay TQ1 2BG 101 F1
Livingston 235 E3
Livingston Village 235 E3
Lixwm 182 C5
Lizard 95 E5
Llaingarreglwyd 142 A2
Llaingoch 180 A4
Llaithddu 155 G4
Llampha 129 F5
Llan 155 E2
Llanaber 154 C1
Llanaelhaearn 166 C3
Llanaeron 142 A1
Llanafan 154 C5
Llanafan-fawr 143 F2
Llanafan-fechan 143 F2
Llanallgo 180 C4
Llanarmon 166 D4
Llanarmon Dyffryn
        Ceiriog 169 E4
Llanarmon-yn-Ial 169 E2
Llanarth Cere 142 A2
Llanarth Mon 130 C1
Llanarthney 142 B5
Llanasa 182 C4
Llanbabo 180 B4
Llanbadarn Fawr 154 B4
Llanbadarn Fynydd 155 G5
Llanbadarn-y-
        garreg 144 A3
Llanbadoc 130 C2
Llanbadrig 180 B3
Llanbeder 130 C3
Llanbedr Gwyn 167 E5
Llanbedr Powys 144 B5
Llanbedr Powys 144 A3
Llanbedr-Dyffryn-
        Clwyd 169 E2
Llanbedrgoch 180 D4
Llanbedrog 166 C4
Llanbedr-y-cennin 168 A1
Llanberis 167 E2
Llanbethery 114 D1
Llanbister 156 A5
Llanblethian 129 F5
Llanboidy 141 F5
Llanbradach 130 A3
Llanbryn-mair 155 E2
Llancadle 114 D1
Llancarfan 129 G5
Llancayo 130 C2
Llancynfelyn 154 C3
Llandafal 130 A2
Llandaff 130 A5
Llandaff North 130 A5
Llandanwg 167 E5
Llandawke 127 F1
Llanddaniel Fab 180 C5
Llanddarog 128 A1
Llanddeiniol 154 B5
Llanddeiniolen 167 E1
Llanderfel 168 C4
Llanddeusant
        Carmar 143 D4
Llanddeusant IoA 180 B4
Llanddew 143 G4
Llanddewi 128 A4
Llanddewi
        Rhydderch 130 C1
Llanddewi
        Skirrid 130 C1
Llanddewi Velfrey 127 E1
Llanddewi
        Ystradenni 144 A1
Llanddewi-Brefi 142 C2
Llanddewi'r Cwm 143 G3
Llanddoged 168 B1
Llanddona 181 D5
Llanddowror 127 F1
Llanddulas 182 A5
Llanddwywe 167 E5
Llanddyfnan 180 C5
Llandefaelog Fach 143 G4
Llandefaelog-
        tre'r-graig 144 A5
Llandefalle 144 A4
Llandegfan 181 D5
Llandegfedd Reservoir
        Mon NP4 0TA 130 C3
Llandegla 169 E2
Llandegley 144 A1
Llandegveth 130 C3
Llandegwning 166 B4
Llandeilo 142 C5
Llandeilo
        Abercywyn 127 G1
Llandeilo Graban 143 G3
Llandeilo'r-Fan 143 E4
Llandeloy 140 B5
Llandenny 130 D2
Llandevenny 130 D4
Llandinabo 145 E5
Llandinam 155 F4
Llandissilio 141 E5
Llandogo 131 E2
Llandough VGlam 129 F5
Llandough VGlam 130 A5

Llandough VGlam 129 F5
Llandovery
        (Llanymddyfri) 143 D4
Llandow 129 F5
Llandre Carmar 142 C3
Llandre Carmar 141 G5
Llandre Cere 154 C4
Llandrillo 168 D4
Llandrindod Wells 143 G1
Llandrinio 156 B1
Llandudno 181 F4
Llandudno Junction 181 F5
Llandwrog 167 D2
Llandybie 128 C1
Llandyfaelog 128 A1
Llandyfan 128 C1
Llandyfriog 141 G3
Llandyfrydog 180 C4
Llandygai 181 E5
Llandygwydd 141 F3
Llandynog 169 E1
Llandysilio 156 B1
Llandyssil 156 A3
Llandysul 142 A3
Llanedeyrn 130 B4
Llanedy 128 B2
Llaneglwys 143 G3
Llanegryn 154 C2
Llanegwad 142 B5
Llaneilian 180 C3
Llanelian-yn-Rhos 181 G5
Llanelidan 169 E2
Llanelieu 144 A4
Llanellen 144 A4
Llanellen 130 C1
Llanelli 128 B2
Llanelli Millennium Coastal
        Park Carmar
        SA15 2LF 128 A3
Llanelltyd 154 D1
Llanelly 130 B1
Llanelly Hill 130 B1
Llanelwedd 143 G2
Llanenddwyn 167 E5
Llanengan 166 B5
Llanerfyl 155 G2
Llaneuddog 180 C4
Llanfachraeth 180 B4
Llanfachreth 168 A5
Llanfaelog 180 B5
Llanfaelrhys 166 B5
Llanfaenor 130 C1
Llan-faes IoA 181 E5
Llanfaes Powys 143 G5
Llanfaethlu 180 B4
Llanfaglan 167 D1
Llanfair 167 E5
Llanfair Caereinion 156 A2
Llanfair Clydogau 142 C2
Llanfair Dyffryn
        Clwyd 169 E2
Llanfair Talhaiarn 182 A5
Llanfair Waterdine 156 B5
Llanfairfechan 181 E5
Llanfair-Nant-Gwyn 141 E4
Llanfair-Orllwyn 141 G3
Llanfairpwllgwyngyll
        180 D5
Llanfairynghornwy 180 B3
Llanfair-yn-neubwll 180 B5
Llanfallteg 127 E1
Llanfaredd 143 G2
Llanfarian 154 B5
Llanfechain 156 A1
Llanfechell 180 B3
Llanfendigaid 154 B2
Llanferres 169 E1
Llanfflewyn 180 B4
Llanfigael 180 B4
Llanfihangel Glyn
        Myfyr 168 C3
Llanfihangel Nant
        Bran 143 F4
Llanfihangel
        Rhydithon 144 A1
Llanfihangel Rogiet 130 D4
Llanfihangel
        Tal-y-llyn 144 A5
Llanfihangel-
        ar-arth 142 A3
Llanfihangel-nant-
        Melan 144 A2
Llanfihangel-uwch-
        Gwili 142 A5
Llanfihangel-y-
        Creuddyn 154 C5
Llanfihangel-yng-
        Ngwynfa 155 G1
Llanfihangel-y-
        Nhywn 180 B5
Llanfihangel-y-pennant
        Gwyn 167 E3
Llanfihangel-y-pennant
        Gwyn 154 C2
Llanfilo 144 A4
Llanfoist 130 B1
Llanfor 168 C4
Llanfrechfa 130 C3
Llanfrothen 167 F3
Llanfrynach 143 G5
Llanfwrog Denb 169 E2
Llanfwrog IoA 180 B4
Llanfyllin 156 A1
Llanfynydd Carmar 142 B5
Llanfynydd Flints 169 F2
Llanfyrnach 141 F4
Llangadfan 155 G1
Llangadog 142 D5
Llangadwaladr IoA 166 C1
Llangadwaladr
        Powys 169 E4
Llangaffo 166 D1
Llangain 127 G1
Llangammarch
        Wells 143 F3
Llangan 129 F5
Llangasty-Talyllyn 144 A5
Llangathen 142 C5
Llangattock 130 B1
Llangattock
        Lingoed 130 C1
Llangattock-Vibon-
        Avel 131 D1
Llangedwyn 169 E5
Llangefni 180 C5
Llangeinor 129 F4
Llangeitho 142 C2

Llangeler 141 G4
Llangelynin 154 B2
Llangendeirne 128 A1
Llangennech 128 B2
Llangennith 128 A3
Llangenny 130 B1
Llangernyw 168 B1
Llangian 166 B5
Llangiwg 128 D2
Llangloffan 140 C4
Llanglydwen 141 E5
Llangoed 181 E5
Llangoedmor 141 E2
Llangollen 169 F3
Llangollen Railway Denb
        LL20 8SN 169 F3
Llangolman 141 E5
Llangorse 144 A5
Llangorwen 154 C4
Llangovan 131 D2
Llangower 168 C4
Llangrannog 141 G2
Llangristiolus 180 C5
Llangrove 131 E1
Llangua 144 C5
Llangunllo 156 B5
Llangunnor 142 A5
Llangurig 155 F5
Llangwm Conwy 168 C3
Llangwm Mon 130 D2
Llangwm Pembs 126 C2
Llangwnnadl 166 B4
Llangwyfan 169 E1
Llangwyllog 180 C5
Llangwyryfon 154 C5
Llangybi Cere 142 C2
Llangybi Gwyn 166 D3
Llangybi Mon 130 C3
Llangyfelach 128 C3
Llangynhafal 169 E1
Llangynidr 130 A1
Llangyniew 156 A2
Llangynin 127 F1
Llangynllo 141 G3
Llangynog Carmar 127 G1
Llangynog Powys 169 D5
Llangynwyd 129 E4
Llanhamlach 143 G5
Llanharan 129 G4
Llanharry 129 G4
Llanhennock 130 C3
Llanhilleth 130 B2
Llanidloes 155 F4
Llaniestyn 166 B4
Llanigon 144 B4
Llanilar 154 C5
Llanilid 129 F4
Llanishen Cardiff 130 A4
Llanishen Mon 131 D2
Llanllawddog 142 A5
Llanllechid 167 F1
Llanlleonfel 143 F2
Llanllugan 155 G2
Llanllwch 127 G1
Llanllwchaiarn 156 A3
Llanllwni 142 A3
Llanllyfni 167 D2
Llanllywel 130 C3
Llanmadoc 128 A3
Llanmaes 114 C1
Llanmartin 130 C4
Llanmerewig 156 A3
Llanmihangel 129 F5
Llan-mill 127 E1
Llanmiloe 127 F2
Llanmorlais 128 B3
Llannefydd 182 A5
Llannerch Hall 182 B5
Llannerch-y-medd 180 C4
Llannerch-y-Môr 182 C5
Llannon Carmar 128 B2
Llan-non Cere 142 B1
Llannor 166 C4
Llanover 130 C2
Llanpumsaint 142 A5
Llanreithan 140 B5
Llanrhaeadr 169 E1
Llanrhaeadr-ym-
        Mochnant 169 E5
Llanrhian 140 B4
Llanrhidian 128 A3
Llanrhyddlad 180 B4
Llanrhystud 142 B1
Llanrothal 131 D1
Llanrug 167 E1
Llanrumney 130 B4
Llanrwst 168 A1
Llansadurnen 127 F1
Llansadwrn Carmar 142 C4
Llansadwrn IoA 181 D5
Llansaint 127 G2
Llansamlet 128 C3
Llansanffraid 142 B1
Llansanffraid Glan
        Conwy 181 G5
Llansannan 168 C1
Llansannor 129 F5
Llansantffraed 144 A5
Llansantffraed-
        Cwmdeuddwr 143 F1
Llansantffraed-in-
        Elwel 143 G2
Llansantffraid-ym-
        Mechain 169 F5
Llansawel 142 C4
Llansilin 169 F5
Llansoy 130 D2
Llanspyddid 143 G5
Llanstadwell 126 C2
Llansteffan 127 G1
Llanstephan 144 A3
Llantarnam 130 C3
Llanteg 127 E1
Llanthony 144 B5
Llantilio Crossenny 130 C1
Llantilio Pertholey 130 C1
Llantood 141 E3
Llantrisant IoA 180 B4
Llantrisant Mon 130 C3
Llantrisant RCT 129 G4
Llantrithyd 129 G5
Llantwit Fardre 129 G4
Llantwit Major 114 C1
Llantysilio 169 E3
Llanuwchllyn 168 B5
Llanvaches 130 D4
Llanvair-Discoed 130 D3
Llanvapley 130 C1

Llanvetherine 130 C1
Llanveynoe 144 C4
Llanvihangel Crucorney
        (Llanfihangel Crucornau)
        144 C5
Llanvihangel
        Gobion 130 C2
Llanvihangel-Ystern-
        Llewern 130 C1
Llanwddyn 155 G1
Llanwarne 145 E5
Llanwddyn 142 A3
Llanwenog 142 A3
Llanwern 130 C4
Llanwinio 141 F5
Llanwnda Gwyn 167 D2
Llanwnda Pembs 140 C4
Llanwnnen 142 B3
Llanwnog 155 G3
Llanwonno 129 G3
Llanwrda 142 D4
Llanwrin 155 D2
Llanwrthwl 143 F1
Llanwrtyd 143 E3
Llanwrtyd Wells 143 E3
Llanwyddelan 155 G2
Llanyblodwel 169 F5
Llanybri 127 G1
Llanybydder 142 B3
Llanycefn 141 D5
Llanychaer
        Bridge 140 C4
Llanycil 168 C4
Llanycrwys 142 C3
Llanymawddwy 155 E1
Llanymynech 169 F5
Llanynghenedl 180 B4
Llanynys 169 E1
Llan-y-pwll 170 A2
Llanyre 143 G1
Llanystumdwy 167 D4
Llanywern 144 A5
Llawhaden 127 D1
Llawndy 182 C4
Llawnt 169 F4
Llawr-y-dref 166 B5
Llawryglyn 155 F3
Llay 170 A2
Llechcynfarwy 180 B4
Llechfaen 143 G5
Llechfaen 143 G5
Llechryd Caerp 130 A2
Llechryd Cere 141 F3
Llechrydau 169 F4
Llechwedd Slate Caverns
        Gwyn LL41 3NB 168 A3
Lledrod Cere 154 C5
Lledrod Powys 169 F5
Llethryd 128 B3
Llidiardau 168 B4
Llidiat-Nenog 142 B4
Llithfaen 166 C3
Lloc 182 C5
Llong 169 F1
Llowes 144 A3
Lloyney 156 B5
Llundain-fach 142 B2
Llwydcoed 129 F2
Llwydiarth 155 G1
Llwyn 156 B5
Llwyncelyn 142 A2
Llwyn-croes 142 A5
Llwyndafydd 141 G2
Llwynderw 156 B2
Llwyndyrys 166 C3
Llwyneinion 169 F3
Llwyngwril 154 B2
Llwynhendy 128 B3
Llwyn-Madoc 143 F2
Llwyn-onn Cere 142 A2
Llwyn-onn MTyd 129 G2
Llwyn-y-brain
        Carmar 127 E1
Llwyn-y-brain
        Carmar 142 D4
Llwyn-y-groes 142 B2
Llwynypia 129 F3
Llyn Brenig Conwy
        LL21 9TT 168 C2
Llyn Llech Owain Country
        Park Carmar
        SA14 7NF 128 B1
Llynclys 169 F5
Llynfaes 180 C5
Llysfaen 181 G5
Llyswen 144 A4
Llysworney 129 F5
Llys-y-frân 140 D5
Llywel 143 E4
Load Brook 185 G4
Loandhu 267 F4
Loanhead Aber 261 H1
Loanhead Midlo 235 G3
Loans 224 B3
Lobb 113 E2
Loch a Charnain 262 D7
Loch an Eilein Visitor Centre
        & Forest Trail High
        PH22 1QT 259 F4
Loch Choire Lodge 273 J5
Loch Eil Outward
        Bound 248 C2
Loch Head D&G 206 A2
Loch Head D&G 215 F1
Loch Lomond Shores &
        Gateway Centre WDun
        G83 8QL 233 E1
Loch Ness Exhibition Centre
        High IV63 6TU 258 C2
Loch of the Lowes P&K
        PH8 0HH 251 F5
Loch Sgioport 254 D1
Lochailort (Ceann Loch
        Ailleart) 247 F5
Lochaline
        (Loch Àlainn) 247 F5
Lochans 214 B5
Locharbriggs 217 D2
Lochawe
        (Loch Obha) 240 D2
Lochboisdale (Loch
        Baghasdail) 254 C3
Lochbuie 239 F2
Lochcarron
        (Loch Carrann) 264 E7
Lochdhu Hotel 275 F4

Lochdon 239 G1
Lochdrum 265 J4
Lochearnhead (Ceann Loch
        Èireann) 242 A2
Lochee 244 B1
Lochend High 275 H2
Lochend (Ceann Loch)
        High 258 C1
Lochend
        (Locheuphort) 262 D5
Lochfoot 216 D3
Lochgair 240 B5
Lochgarthside 258 C3
Lochgelly 243 G5
Lochgilphead (Ceann Loch
        Gilb) 231 G1
Lochgoilhead 241 E4
Lochgoyn 233 G3
Lochhill EAyr 225 D4
Lochhill Moray 267 K5
Lochinch Castle 214 C4
Lochinver
        (Loch an Inbhir) 272 C6
Lochlair 252 D5
Lochlane 242 C2
Lochlea 224 C3
Lochluichart 265 K5
Lochmaben 217 E2
Lochmaddy (Loch na
        Madadh) 262 E5
Lochore 243 G5
Lochore Meadows Country
        Park Fife
        KY5 8BA 243 G5
Lochportain 262 E4
Lochranza 232 B5
Lochside Aber 253 F3
Lochside High 273 G3
Lochside High 274 D5
Lochside High 275 H2
Lochslin 267 F3
Lochton 215 D2
Lochty 244 D4
Lochuisge 247 G4
Lochurr 216 B2
Lochussie 266 B6
Lochwinnoch 233 E4
Lockengate 97 E3
Lockerbie 217 F2
Lockeridge 118 C1
Lockerley 119 D5
Lockhills 210 B3
Locking 116 A2
Lockington ERid 196 B3
Lockington Leics 173 F5
Lockleywood 171 D5
Locks Heath 107 E2
Locksbottom 122 D2
Locksgreen 106 D3
Lockton 204 B4
Locomotion: The National
        Railway Museum at
        Shildon Dur
        DL4 1PQ 212 B5
Loddington Leics 160 C2
Loddington
        N'hants 160 D5
Loddiswell 100 D3
Loddon 165 E2
Lode 150 D1
Loders 104 A3
Lodsworth 121 E5
Lofthouse NYorks 202 A5
Lofthouse WYorks 194 C5
Loftus 203 G1
Logan D&G 206 A2
Logan EAyr 225 D3
Loganlea 235 E3
Loggerheads 171 E4
Loggerheads Country Park
        Denb CH7 5LH 169 E1
Loggie (An Lagaidh) 265 H2
Logie Angus 253 E3
Logie Angus 252 B4
Logie Fife 244 C2
Logie Moray 267 H6
Logie Coldstone 260 C4
Logie Hill 266 E4
Logie Newton 260 E1
Logie Pert 253 E3
Logierait 251 E4
Login 141 E5
Lolworth 150 B1
Lonbain 264 C6
Londesborough 196 A3
London 136 C4
London Apprentice 97 E5
London Ashford
        Airport 111 F1
London Beach 124 A5
London Biggin Hill
        Airport 122 D2
London City
        Airport 136 D4
London Colney 136 A2
London Eye GtLon
        SE1 7PB 45 M4
London Gatwick
        Airport 122 B4
London Heathrow
        Airport 135 F4
London Luton
        Airport 149 G5
London Minstead 106 B1
London Southend
        Airport 138 B4
London Stansted
        Airport 150 D5
London Transport Museum
        GtLon WC2E 7BB 45 E3
Londonderry 202 B4
Londonthorpe 175 E4
Londubh 264 E3
Lonemore 266 E3
Long Bank 157 G5
Long Bennington 174 D3
Long Bredy 104 B3
Long Buckby 148 B1
Long Clawson 174 C5
Long Compton
        Staffs 171 F5
Long Compton
        Warks 147 E4
Long Crendon 134 B2
Long Crichel 105 F1
Long Dean 132 A5
Long Downs 95 E3

Lon - Mar

Long Drax 195 F5
Long Duckmanton 186 B5
Long Eaton 173 F4
Long Gill 193 D2
Long Green
ChesW&C 183 F5
Long Green *Essex* 152 A5
Long Green *Worcs* 146 A4
Long Hanborough 133 G1
Long Itchington 147 G1
Long Lane 157 F1
Long Lawford 159 G5
Long Load 116 B5
Long Marston *Herts* 135 D1
Long Marston
NYorks 195 E2
Long Marston
Warks 147 D3
Long Marton 210 C5
Long Meadowend 156 D4
Long Melford 151 G3
Long Newnton 132 B3
Long Preston 193 E2
Long Riston 196 D3
Long Stratton 164 C2
Long Street 148 C3
Long Sutton *Hants* 120 C3
Long Sutton *Lincs* 176 C5
Long Sutton *Som* 116 B5
Long Thurlow 152 B1
Long Whatton 173 F5
Long Wittenham 134 A3
Longbenton 212 B1
Longborough 147 D5
Longbridge *Plym* 100 B2
Longbridge *Warks* 147 E1
Longbridge *WMid* 158 C5
Longbridge Deverill 117 F3
Longburgh 209 G1
Longburton 104 C1
Longcliffe 172 D2
Longcombe 101 E2
Longcot 133 E3
Longcroft 234 B2
Longcross *Devon* 99 E3
Longcross *Surr* 121 E1
Longden 156 D2
Longdon *Staffs* 158 C1
Longdon *Worcs* 146 A4
Longdon Green 158 C1
Longdon upon Tern 157 F1
Longdown 102 B3
Longdrum 261 H3
Longfield 123 F2
Longfield Hill 123 F2
Longfleet 105 G3
Longford *Derbys* 172 D4
Longford *Glos* 146 A5
Longford *GtLon* 135 F5
Longford *Shrop* 170 D4
Longford *Tel&W* 157 G1
Longford *WMid* 159 F4
Longforgan 244 B2
Longformacus 237 D4
Longframlington 220 D1
Longham *Dorset* 105 G3
Longham *Norf* 178 A4
Longhill 269 H5
Longhirst 221 E3
Longhope *Glos* 131 F1
Longhope *Ork* 277 C8
Longhorsley 220 D2
Longhoughton 229 G5
Longlands *Aber* 260 C2
Longlands *Cumb* 209 F3
Longlands *GtLon* 136 D5
Longlane *Derbys* 173 D4
Longlane *WBerks* 133 G5
Longleat House *Wilts*
BA12 7NW 117 F3
Longleat Safari Park *Wilts*
BA12 7NW 117 F3
Longlevens 132 A1
Longley 185 F2
Longley Green 145 G2
Longmanhill 269 F4
Longmoor Camp 120 C4
Longmorn 267 K6
Longnewton *ScBord* 227 G3
Longnewton *Stock* 202 C1
Longney 131 G1
Longniddry 236 B2
Longniddry Bents *ELoth*
EH32 0PX 236 B2
Longnor *Shrop* 157 D2
Longnor *Staffs* 172 B1
Longparish 119 F3
Longridge *Lancs* 192 C4
Longridge *Staffs* 158 B1
Longridge *WLoth* 235 D3
Longridge End 146 A5
Longridge Towers 237 G4
Longriggend 234 C2
Longrock 94 C3
Longsdon 171 G2
Longshaw 183 G2
Longside 269 J6
Longslow 171 D4
Longsowerby 209 G1
Longstanton 150 C1
Longstock 119 E4
Longstone 94 C3
Longstowe 150 B2
Longstreet 118 C2
Longthorpe 161 G3
Longton *Lancs* 192 A5
Longton *Stoke* 171 G3
Longtown *Cumb* 218 B5
Longtown *Here* 144 C5
Longville in the
Dale 157 E3
Longwell Green 131 F5
Longwick 134 C2
Longwitton 220 C3
Longworth 133 F3
Longyester 236 C3
Lonmay 269 J5
Lonmore 263 H7
Looe 97 G4
Look Out Discovery Park,
Bracknell *BrackF*
RG12 7QW 121 D1
Loose 123 G3
Loosebeare 102 A2
Loosegate 176 B5
Loosley Row 134 D2
Lopcombe Corner 119 D4
Lopen 104 A1
Loppington 170 B5
Lorbottle 220 C1
Lorbottle Hall 220 C1
Lordington 107 G2
Lord's Cricket Ground &
Museum *GtLon*
NW8 8QN 10 F4
Lord's Hill 106 C1
Lorgill 263 G7
Lorn 233 E1
Lornty 251 G5
Loscoe 173 F3
Loscombe 104 A3
Losgaintir 263 F2
Lossiemouth 267 K4
Lossit 230 A4
Lost Gardens of Heligan
Corn PL26 6EN 97 D5
Lostock Gralam 184 A5
Lostock Green 184 A5
Lostock
Junction 184 A2
Lostwithiel 97 F4
Loth 276 F4
Lothbeg 274 E7
Lothersdale 193 F3
Lotherton Hall Estate
WYorks
LS25 3EB 195 D4
Lothmore 274 E7
Loudwater 135 E3
Loughborough 160 A1
Loughor 128 B3
Loughton *Essex* 136 D3
Loughton *MK* 148 D4
Loughton *Shrop* 157 F4
Louis Tussaud's Waxworks
FY1 5AA 64 Blackpool
Lound *Lincs* 161 F1
Lound *Notts* 187 D4
Lound *Suff* 165 G2
Lount 159 F1
Lour 252 C5
Louth 188 D4
Love Clough 193 E5
Lovedean 107 F1
Lover 106 B1
Loversall 186 C3
Loves Green 137 F2
Lovesome Hill 202 C3
Loveston 127 D2
Lovington 116 C4
Low Ackworth 186 B1
Low Angerton 220 C3
Low Ballevain 222 B3
Low Barlay 215 G5
Low Barlings 188 A5
Low Bentham (Lower
Bentham) 192 C1
Low Bolton 201 F3
Low Bradfield 185 G3
Low Bradley
(Bradley) 193 G3
Low Braithwaite 210 A3
Low Brunton 220 B4
Low Burnham 187 E2
Low Burton 202 B4
Low Buston 221 E1
Low Catton 195 G2
Low Coniscliffe 202 B1
Low Craighead 224 A5
Low Dinsdale 202 C1
Low Ellington 202 B4
Low Entercommon 202 C2
Low Etherley 212 A5
Low Fell 212 B2
Low Gate 211 F1
Low Grantley 202 B5
Low Green 151 G1
Low Habberley 158 A5
Low Ham 116 B5
Low Hawsker 204 C2
Low Haygarth 200 B3
Low Hesket 210 A3
Low Hesleyhurst 220 C2
Low Hutton 195 G1
Low Kingthorpe 204 B4
Low Laithe 194 A1
Low Langton 188 B5
Low Leighton 185 E4
Low Lorton 209 E4
Low Marishes 204 B5
Low Marnham 174 D1
Low Middleton 229 F3
Low Mill 203 F3
Low Moor *Lancs* 192 D3
Low Moor *WYorks* 194 A5
Low Moorsley 212 C3
Low Moresby 208 C4
Low Newton-by-
the-Sea 229 G4
Low Row *Cumb* 210 B1
Low Row *NYorks* 201 E3
Low Stillaig 232 A3
Low Street 178 B5
Low Tharston 164 C2
Low Torry 235 E1
Low Town 220 D1
Low Toynton 188 C5
Low Wood 199 E4
Low Worsall 202 C2
Lowbands 145 G4
Lowdham 174 B3
Lowe 170 C4
Lowe Hill 171 G2
Lower Achachenna 240 C2
Lower Aisholt 115 F4
Lower Apperley 146 A5
Lower Arncott 134 B1
Lower Ashtead 121 G2
Lower Ashton 102 B4
Lower Assendon 134 C4
Lower Auchalick 232 A2
Lower Ballam 191 G4
Lower Barewood 144 C2
Lower Bartle 192 A4
Lower Bayble
(Pabail Iarach) 271 H4
Lower Beeding 109 E1
Lower Benefield 161 E4
Lower Bentham (Low
Bentham) 192 C1
Lower Bentley 146 B1
Lower Berry Hill 131 E1
Lower Birchwood 173 F2
Lower Boddington 147 G2
Lower Boscaswell 94 A3
Lower Bourne 120 D3
Lower Brailes 147 F4
Lower Breakish 256 C2
Lower Bredbury 184 D3
Lower Broadheath 146 A2
Lower Brynamman 128 D1
Lower Bullingham 145 E4
Lower Bullington 119 F3
Lower Burgate 106 A1
Lower Burrow 116 B5
Lower Burton 144 D2
Lower Caldecote 149 G3
Lower Cam 131 G2
Lower Cambourne 150 B2
Lower Camster 275 H4
Lower Chapel 143 G4
Lower Cheriton 103 E2
Lower Chicksgrove 118 A4
Lower Chute 119 E2
Lower Clent 158 B4
Lower Creedy 102 B2
Lower
Cumberworth 185 G2
Lower Darwen 192 C5
Lower Dean 149 F1
Lower Diabaig 264 D5
Lower Dicker 110 A2
Lower Dinchope 157 D4
Lower Down 156 C4
Lower Drift 94 B4
Lower Dunsforth 194 D1
Lower Earley 134 C5
Lower Edmonton 136 C3
Lower Elkstone 172 B2
Lower End *Bucks* 134 B2
Lower End *MK* 149 E4
Lower End *N'hants* 149 D1
Lower Everleigh 118 C2
Lower Eythorne 125 E4
Lower Failand 131 E5
Lower Farringdon 120 C4
Lower Fittleworth 108 C2
Lower Foxdale 190 A4
Lower Freystrop 126 C1
Lower Froyle 120 C3
Lower Gabwell 101 F1
Lower Gledfield 266 C2
Lower Godney 116 B3
Lower Gravenhurst 149 G4
Lower Green *Essex* 150 C4
Lower Green *Herts* 149 G4
Lower Green *Kent* 123 F4
Lower Green *Norf* 178 A2
Lower Green *Staffs* 158 B2
Lower Green Bank 192 B2
Lower Halstock
Leigh 104 B2
Lower Halstow 124 A2
Lower Hardres 124 D3
Lower Harpton 144 B1
Lower Hartshay 173 E2
Lower Hawthwaite 198 D4
Lower Haysden 123 E4
Lower Hayton 157 E4
Lower Heath 171 F1
Lower Hergest 144 B2
Lower Heyford 147 G5
Lower Higham 137 G5
Lower Holbrook 152 C4
Lower Hopton 185 G1
Lower Hordley 170 A5
Lower Horncroft 108 C2
Lower Horsebridge 110 A2
Lower Houses 185 F1
Lower Howsell 145 G3
Lower Kersal 184 C2
Lower Kilchattan 238 C5
Lower Kilcott 131 G4
Lower Killeyan 230 A5
Lower Kingcombe 104 B3
Lower Kingswood 122 B3
Lower Kinnerton 170 A1
Lower Langford 116 B1
Lower Largo 244 C4
Lower Leigh 172 B4
Lower Lemington 147 E4
Lower Lovacott 113 F3
Lower Loxhore 113 G2
Lower Lydbrook 131 E1
Lower Lye 144 D1
Lower Machen 130 B4
Lower Maes-coed 144 C4
Lower Mannington 105 G2
Lower Middleton
Cheney 148 A3
Lower Milton 116 C3
Lower Moor 146 B3
Lower Morton 131 F3
Lower Nash 126 D2
Lower Nazeing 136 C2
Lower Netchwood 157 F3
Lower Nyland 117 E5
Lower Oddington 147 E5
Lower Ollach 256 B1
Lower Penarth 130 A5
Lower Penn 158 A3
Lower Pennington 106 C3
Lower Peover 184 B5
Lower Pollicott 134 C1
Lower Quinton 147 D3
Lower Race 130 B2
Lower Rainham 124 A2
Lower Roadwater 114 D4
Lower Sapey 145 F1
Lower Seagry 132 B4
Lower Shelton 149 E3
Lower Shiplake 134 C5
Lower Shuckburgh 147 G1
Lower Slaughter 147 D5
Lower Soothill 194 B5
Lower Stanton
St. Quintin 132 B4
Lower Stoke 124 A1
Lower Stondon 149 G4
Lower Stone 131 F3
Lower Stonnall 158 C2
Lower Stow Bedon 164 A2
Lower Street *Dorset* 105 E3
Lower Street *ESuss* 110 C2
Lower Street *Norf* 179 D2
Lower Street *Norf* 178 C2
Lower Street *Suff* 152 C2
Lower Stretton 184 A4
Lower Sundon 149 F5
Lower Swanwick 107 D2
Lower Swell 147 D5
Lower Tadmarton 147 G4
Lower Tale 103 D2
Lower Tean 172 B4
Lower Thurlton 165 F2
Lower Thurnham 192 A2
Lower Town *Corn* 95 D4
Lower Town *Devon* 102 A5
Lower Town *IoS* 96 B1
Lower Town *Pembs* 140 C4
Lower Trebullett 98 D3
Lower Tysoe 147 F3
Lower Upcott 102 B4
Lower Upham 107 E1
Lower Upnor 137 G5
Lower Vexford 115 E4
Lower Wallop 156 C2
Lower Walton 184 A4
Lower Waterhay 132 C3
Lower Weald 148 C4
Lower Wear 102 C4
Lower Weare 116 B2
Lower Welson 144 B2
Lower Whatley 117 E3
Lower Whitley 184 A5
Lower Wick 146 A2
Lower Wield 120 B3
Lower Winchendon (Nether
Winchendon) 134 C1
Lower Withington 171 F1
Lower Woodend 134 D4
Lower Woodford 118 C4
Lower Wyche 145 G3
Lowerhouse 193 E4
Lowertown 277 D8
Lowesby 160 C2
Lowestoft 165 G2
Loweswater 209 E4
Lowfield Heath 122 B4
Lowgill *Cumb* 200 B3
Lowgill *Lancs* 192 C1
Lowick *Cumb* 199 D4
Lowick *N'hants* 161 E4
Lowick *N'umb* 229 E3
Lowick Bridge 199 D4
Lowick Green 199 D4
Lownie Moor 252 C5
Lowry, The *GtMan*
M50 3AZ 24 D3
Lowsonford 147 D1
Lowther 210 B5
Lowther Castle 210 B5
Lowthorpe 196 C1
Lowton *Devon* 113 G5
Lowton *GtMan* 184 A3
Lowton *Som* 103 E1
Lowton Common 184 A3
Loxbeare 102 C1
Loxhill 121 F4
Loxhore 113 G2
Loxley 147 E2
Loxley Green 172 B4
Loxton 116 A2
Loxwood 121 F4
Lubachoinnich 266 B2
Lubcroy 265 K1
Lubenham 160 C4
Lubfearn 265 K4
Lubmore 265 G6
Lubreoch 249 G5
Luccombe 114 C3
Luccombe Village 107 E4
Lucker 229 F3
Luckett 99 D3
Luckington 132 A4
Lucklawhill 244 C2
Luckwell Bridge 114 C4
Lucton 144 D1
Lucy Cross 202 B1
Ludag 254 C3
Ludborough 188 C3
Ludbrook 100 C2
Ludchurch 127 E1
Luddenden 193 G5
Luddenden Foot 193 G5
Luddenham Court 124 B2
Luddesdown 123 F2
Luddington *NLincs* 187 F1
Luddington *Warks* 147 D2
Luddington in the
Brook 161 G4
Ludford *Lincs* 188 B4
Ludford *Shrop* 157 E5
Ludgershall *Bucks* 134 B1
Ludgershall *Wilts* 119 D2
Ludgvan 94 C3
Ludham 179 E4
Ludlow 157 E5
Ludney 189 D3
Ludstock 145 F4
Ludstone 158 A3
Ludwell 118 A5
Ludworth 212 C3
Luffincott 98 D1
Luffness 236 B1
Lufton 104 B1
Lugar 225 D3
Luggate 236 C2
Luggate Burn 236 D2
Luggiebank 234 B2
Lugton 233 F4
Lugwardine 145 E3
Luib 256 B2
Luibeilt 249 E3
Luing 239 G3
Lulham 144 D3
Lullington *Derbys* 159 E1
Lullington *Som* 117 E2
Lulsgate Bottom 116 C1
Lulsley 145 G2
Lulworth Camp 105 E4
Lulworth Cove & Heritage
Centre *Dorset*
BH20 5RQ 105 E5
Lumb *Lancs* 193 E5
Lumb *WYorks* 193 G5
Lumbutts 193 F5
Lumby 195 D4
Lumphanan 260 D4
Lumphinnans 243 G5
Lumsdaine 237 F3
Lumsdale 173 E1
Lumsden 260 C2
Lunan 253 E4
Lunanhead 252 C4
Luncarty 243 F2
Lund *ERid* 196 B3
Lund *NYorks* 195 F4
Lund *Shet* 278 E2
Lundale 270 D4
Lundavra 248 C3
Lunderston Bay *Invcly*
PA16 0DN 232 D2
Lunderton 269 K6
Lundie *Angus* 244 A1
Lundie *High* 257 H3
Lundin Links 244 C4
Lundwood 186 A2
Lundy 112 B1
Lunga 240 A4
Lunna 279 D6
Lunning 279 E6
Lunnon 128 B4
Lunsford's Cross 110 C2
Lunt 183 E2
Luntley 144 C2
Luppitt 103 E2
Lupset 186 A1
Lupton 199 G4
Lurgashall 121 E5
Lurignich 248 B4
Lusby 176 B1
Luss 241 F5
Lussagiven 231 E1
Lusta 263 H6
Lustleigh 102 A4
Luston 145 D1
Luthermuir 253 E3
Luthrie 244 B3
Luton *Devon* 103 D2
Luton *Devon* 102 C5
Luton *Luton* 149 F5
Luton *Med* 123 G2
Luton Airport 149 G5
Lutterworth 160 A4
Lutton *Devon* 100 B2
Lutton *Dorset* 105 F4
Lutton *Lincs* 176 C5
Lutton *N'hants* 161 G4
Luxborough 114 C4
Luxulyan 97 E4
Lybster *High* 275 F2
Lybster *High* 275 H5
Lydacott 113 E5
Lydbury North 156 C4
Lydcott 113 G2
Lydd 111 F1
Lydden 125 E4
Lyddington 161 D3
Lydd-on-Sea 111 F1
Lyde Green 131 F5
Lydeard
St. Lawrence 115 E4
Lydford 99 F2
Lydford-on-Fosse 116 C4
Lydgate *GtMan* 185 D1
Lydgate *GtMan* 185 D2
Lydgate *WYorks* 193 F5
Lydham 156 C3
Lydiard Millicent 132 C4
Lydiard Tregoze 132 D4
Lydiate 183 E2
Lydlinch 104 D1
Lydney 131 F2
Lydstep 127 D3
Lye 158 B4
Lye Cross 116 B1
Lye Green *Bucks* 135 E2
Lye Green *ESuss* 123 E5
Lye Green *Warks* 147 D1
Lye's Green 117 F3
Lyford 133 F3
Lymbridge Green 124 D4
Lyme Regis 103 G3
Lymekilns 234 A4
Lyminge 125 D4
Lymington 106 C3
Lyminster 108 C3
Lymm 184 A4
Lymore 106 B3
Lympne 124 D5
Lympsham 116 A2
Lympstone 102 C4
Lynaberack 258 E5
Lynch 114 B3
Lynch Green 178 C5
Lynchat 258 E4
Lyndale House 263 J6
Lyndhurst 106 B2
Lyndon 161 E2
Lyne *Aber* 261 F4
Lyne *ScBord* 235 G5
Lyne *Surr* 121 F1
Lyne Down 145 F4
Lyne of Gorthleck 258 C2
Lyne of Skene 261 F3
Lyne Station 235 G5
Lyneal 170 B4
Lynegar 275 H3
Lyneham *Oxon* 147 E5
Lyneham *Wilts* 132 C5
Lyneholmeford 218 D4
Lynemore *High* 259 H2
Lynemore *Moray* 259 J1
Lynemouth 221 E2
Lyness 277 C8
Lynford 163 G3
Lyng 178 B4
Lyngate 179 E3
Lynmouth 114 A3
Lynn 157 G1
Lynsted 124 B2
Lynstone 112 C5
Lynton 114 A3
Lynton & Lynmouth Cliff
Railway *Devon*
EX35 6EP 114 A3
Lyon's Gate 104 C2
Lyonshall 144 C2
Lyrabus 230 A3
Lytchett Matravers 105 F3
Lytchett Minster 105 F3
Lyth 275 H2
Lytham 191 G5
Lytham St. Anne's 191 G5
Lythe 204 B1
Lythe Hill 121 E4
Lythes 277 D9
Lythmore 275 F2

M

M.V. Princess Pocahontas
Kent DA11 0BS 137 F5
Mabe Burnthouse 95 E3
Mabie 217 D3
Mablethorpe 189 F4
Macclesfield 184 D5
Macclesfield Forest 185 D5
Macduff 269 F4
Macedonia 244 A4
Machan 234 B4
Machany 243 D3
Macharioch 222 C5
Machen 130 B4
Machrie *A&B* 230 A3
Machrie *A&B* 230 B5
Machrie *NAyr* 223 D2
Machrihanish 222 B3
Machrins 238 C5
Machynlleth 154 D2
McInroy's Point 232 D2
Mackerye End 136 A1
Mackworth 173 E4
Macmerry 236 B2
Macterry 269 F6
Madame Tussauds *GtLon*
NW1 5LR 12 A4
Madderty 243 E2
Maddiston 234 D2
Madehurst 108 B2
Madeley *Staffs* 171 E3
Madeley *Tel&W* 157 G2
Madeley Heath 171 E3
Maders 98 D3
Madford 103 E1
Madingley 150 B1
Madjeston 117 F5
Madley 144 D4
Madresfield 146 A3
Madron 94 B3
Maenaddwyn 180 C4
Maenclochog 141 D5
Maendy *Cardiff* 130 A5
Maendy *VGlam* 129 G5
Maenporth 95 E4
Maentwrog 167 F3
Maen-y-groes 141 G2
Maer *Corn* 112 C5
Maer *Staffs* 171 E4
Maerdy *Carmar* 142 C5
Maerdy *Carmar* 142 C5
Maerdy *Conwy* 168 D3
Maerdy *RCT* 129 F3
Maesbrook 169 F5
Maesbury Marsh 170 A5
Maes-glas 130 B4
Maesgwynne 141 F5
Maeshafn 169 F1
Maesllyn 141 G3
Maesmynis 143 G3
Maesteg 129 E3
Maes-Treylow 144 B1
Maesybont 128 B1
Maesycrugiau 142 A3
Maesycwmmer 130 A3
Magdalen Laver 137 E2
Maggieknockater 268 B6
Maggots End 150 C5
Magham Down 110 B2
Maghull 183 E2
Magna Centre, Rotherham
SYorks S60 1DX 21 C1
Magna Park 160 A4
Magor 130 D4
Magpie Green 164 B4
Maiden Bradley 117 E4
Maiden Head 116 C1
Maiden Law 212 A3
Maiden Newton 104 B3
Maiden Wells 126 C3
Maidencombe 101 F1
Maidenhayne 103 F3
Maidenhead 135 D4
Maidens 224 A5
Maiden's Green 135 D5
Maidensgrove 134 C4
Maidenwell *Corn* 97 F2
Maidenwell *Lincs* 188 D5
Maidford 148 B2
Maids' Moreton 148 C4
Maidstone 123 G3
Maidwell 160 C5
Mail 279 D10
Maindee 130 C4
Mainland *Ork* 277 B6
Mainland *Shet* 279 C7
Mains of Ardestie 244 D1
Mains of Balgavies 252 D4
Mains of Balhall 252 D3
Mains of Ballindarg 252 C4
Mains of Burgie 267 H6
Mains of Culsh 269 G6
Mains of Dillavaird 253 F1
Mains of Drum 261 G4
Mains of Dudwick 261 H1
Mains of Faillie 258 E1
Mains of Fedderate 269 G6
Mains of Glack 261 F2
Mains of Glassaugh 268 D4
Mains of
Glenbuchat 260 B3
Mains of Linton 261 F3
Mains of Melgund 252 D4
Mains of Pitfour 269 H6
Mains of Pittrichie 261 G2
Mains of Sluie 267 H6
Mains of Tannachy 268 B4
Mains of Thornton 253 E2
Mains of Tig 214 C2
Mains of Watten 275 H3
Mainsforth 212 C4
Mainsriddle 216 D5
Mainstone 156 B4
Maisemore 146 A5
Major's Green 158 D5
Makendon 220 A1
Makeney 173 E3
Makerstoun 228 A3
Malacleit 262 C4
Malborough 100 D4
Malden Rushett 121 G1
Maldon 138 B2
Malham 193 F1
Maligar 263 K5
Malin Bridge 186 A4
Mallaig (Malaig) 256 C5
Mallaigmore 256 C5
Mallaigvaig 256 C5
Malleny Mills 235 F3
Malletsheugh 233 G4
Malling 242 A4
Mallows Green 150 C5
Malltraeth 166 D1
Mallwyd 155 E1
Malmesbury 132 B4
Malmsmead 114 A3
Malpas *ChesW&C* 170 B3
Malpas *Corn* 96 C5
Malpas *Newport* 130 C3
Maltby *Lincs* 188 D4
Maltby *Stock* 203 D1
Maltby *SYorks* 186 C3
Maltby le Marsh 189 E4
Malting End 151 F2
Malting Green 138 C1
Maltman's Hill 124 A4
Malton 203 G5
Malvern Link 145 G3
Malvern Wells 145 G3
Mambeg 232 D1
Mamble 157 F5
Mamhead 102 C4
Mamhilad 130 C2
Manaccan 95 E4
Manadon 100 A2
Manafon 156 A2
Manaton 102 A4
Manby 189 D4
Mancetter 159 F3
Manchester 184 C3
Manchester Airport 184 C4
Manchester Apollo *GtMan*
M12 6AP 47 H6
Manchester Art Gallery
GtMan M2 3JL 47 E4
Manchester Central *GtMan*
M2 3GX 46 D5
Manchester Craft & Design
Centre *GtMan*
M4 5JD 47 F3
Manchester Museum
GtMan M13 9PL 47 F7
Manchester United Museum
& Stadium Tour Centre
GtMan M16 0RA 24 D3
Mancot Royal 170 A1
Mandally
(Manndalaidh) 257 J4
Manea 162 C4
Maneight 224 D5
Manfield 202 B1
Mangaster 278 C5
Mangerton 104 A3
Mangotsfield 131 F5
Mangrove Green 149 G5
Mangurstadh 270 C4
Manish (Manais) 263 G3
Mankinholes 193 F5
Manley 183 G5
Manmoel 130 A2
Mannal 246 A2
Manningford
Abbots 118 C2
Manningford
Bohune 118 C2
Manningford Bruce 118 C2
Mannings Amusement Park
Suff IP11 2DW 153 D4
Mannings Heath 109 E1
Mannington 105 G2
Manningtree 152 C4
Mannofield 261 H4
Manor Farm Country Park
Hants SO30 2ER 4 D3
Manor Park 135 E4
Manorbier 127 D3
Manorbier Newton 126 D2
Manordeifi 141 F3
Manordeilo 142 C5
Manorowen 140 C4
Mansell Gamage 144 C3
Mansell Lacy 144 D3
Mansergh 200 B4
Mansfield 173 G1
Mansfield
Woodhouse 173 G1
Manson Green 178 B5
Mansriggs 199 D4
Manston *Dorset* 105 E1
Manston *Kent* 125 F2
Manston *WYorks* 194 C4
Manswood 105 F2
Manthorpe *Lincs* 161 F1
Manthorpe *Lincs* 175 E4
Manton *NLincs* 187 G2
Manton *Notts* 186 C5
Manton *Rut* 161 D2
Manton *Wilts* 118 C1
Manuden 150 C5
Manwood Green 137 E1
Maolachy 240 A3
Maperton 117 D5
Maple Cross 135 F3
Maplebeck 174 C1
Mapledurham 134 B5
Mapledurwell 120 B2
Maplehurst 121 G5
Maplescombe 123 E2
Mapleton 172 C3
Mapperley *Derbys* 173 F3
Mapperley *Notts* 173 G3
Mapperton *Dorset* 104 B3
Mapperton *Dorset* 105 F3
Mappleborough
Green 146 C1
Mappleton 197 E3
Mapplewell 186 A2
Mappowder 104 D2
Mar Lodge 259 H5
Maraig (Maaruig) 270 E7
Marazion 94 C3
Marbhig 271 G6
Marbury 170 C3
Marbury Country Park
ChesW&C
CW9 6AT 184 A5
March 162 C3
Marcham 133 G3
Marchamley 170 C5
Marchamley Wood 170 C4
Marchington 172 C4
Marchington
Woodlands 172 C5
Marchwiel 170 A3
Marchwood 106 C1
Marcross 114 C1
Marcus 252 D4
Marden *Here* 145 E3
Marden *Kent* 123 G4
Marden *T&W* 221 F4
Marden *Wilts* 118 B2
Marden Ash 137 E2
Marden Beech 123 G4
Marden Thorn 123 G4

Marden's Hill **123** D5
Mardon **228** D3
Mardy **130** C1
Mare Green **116** A5
Marefield **160** C2
Mareham le Fen **176** A1
Mareham on
the Hill **176** A1
Maresfield **109** G1
Marfleet **196** D4
Marford **170** A2
Margam **129** D4
Margam Country Park
NPT SA13 2TJ **129** E4
Margaret Marsh **105** D1
Margaret Roding **137** E1
Margaretting **137** F2
Margaretting Tye **137** F2
Margate **125** F1
Margnaheglish **223** F2
Margreig **216** C3
Margrove Park **203** F1
Marham **163** F2
Marhamchurch **112** C5
Marholm **161** G2
Marian Cwm **182** B5
Mariandyrys **181** E4
Marianglas **180** D4
Mariansleigh **114** A5
Marishader **263** K5
Maristow House **100** A1
Mark **116** A3
Mark Causeway **116** A3
Mark Cross **123** E5
Markbeech **123** D4
Markby **189** E5
Markdhu **214** C3
Markeaton **173** E4
Markeaton Park Craft Village
Derby DE22 3BG **18** A3
Market Bosworth **159** G2
Market Bosworth Country
Park Leics
CV13 0LP **159** G2
Market Deeping **161** G2
Market Drayton **171** D4
Market Harborough **160** C4
Market Lavington **118** B2
Market Overton **161** D1
Market Rasen **188** B4
Market Stainton **188** C5
Market Street **179** D3
Market Warsop **173** G1
Market Weighton **196** A3
Market Weston **164** A4
Markethill **244** A1
Markfield **159** G1
Markham **130** A2
Markham Moor **187** E5
Markinch **244** A4
Markington **194** B1
Marks Tey **152** A5
Marksbury **117** D1
Markwell **99** D5
Markyate **135** F1
Marl Bank **145** G3
Marland **184** C1
Marlborough **118** C1
Marlbrook **158** B5
Marlcliff **146** C2
Marldon **101** E1
Marle Green **110** A2
Marlesford **153** E2
Marley Green **170** C3
Marley Hill **212** B2
Marlingford **178** C5
Marloes **126** A2
Marlow *Bucks* **135** D4
Marlow *Here* **156** D5
Marlpit Hill **122** D4
Marlpool **173** F3
Marnhull **105** D1
Marnoch **268** D5
Marple **185** D4
Marple Bridge **185** D4
Marr **186** C2
Marrel **275** F7
Marrick **201** F3
Marrister **279** E6
Marros **127** F2
Marsden *T&W* **212** C1
Marsden *WYorks* **185** E1
Marsett **201** E4
Marsh **103** F1
Marsh Baldon **134** A3
Marsh Benham **119** F1
Marsh Farm Country Park
Essex CM3 5WP **138** B3
Marsh Gibbon **148** B5
Marsh Green
Devon **102** D3
Marsh Green
GtMan **183** G2
Marsh Green
Kent **122** D4
Marsh Green
Tel&W **157** F1
Marsh Lane **186** B5
Marsh Street **114** C3
Marshall Meadows **237** G4
Marshalsea **103** G2
Marshalswick **136** A2
Marsham **178** C4
Marshaw **192** B2
Marshborough **125** F3
Marshbrook **156** D4
Marshchapel **189** D3
Marshfield
Newport **130** B4
Marshfield
SGlos **131** G5
Marshgate **98** B1
Marshland
St. James **162** D2
Marshside **183** E1
Marshwood **103** G3
Marske **202** A2
Marske-by-the-Sea **213** F5
Marsland Green **184** A3
Marston *ChesW&C* **184** A5
Marston *Here* **144** C2
Marston *Lincs* **175** D3
Marston *Oxon* **134** A2
Marston *Staffs* **171** G5
Marston *Staffs* **158** A1
Marston *Warks* **159** E3
Marston *Wilts* **118** A2

Marston Doles **147** G2
Marston Green **159** D4
Marston Magna **116** C5
Marston Meysey **132** D3
Marston
Montgomery **172** C4
Marston Moretaine **149** E3
Marston on Dove **172** D5
Marston
St. Lawrence **148** A3
Marston Stannett **145** E2
Marston Trussell **160** B4
Marston Vale Millennium
Country Park CenBeds
MK43 0PR **149** F3
Marstow **131** E1
Marsworth **135** E1
Marten **119** D1
Marthall **184** B5
Martham **179** F4
Martin *Hants* **105** G1
Martin *Lincs* **175** G2
Martin *Lincs* **176** A1
Martin Drove End **118** B5
Martin Hussingtree **146** A1
Martin Mere Lancs
L40 0TA **183** F1
Martinhoe **113** G1
Martinscroft **184** A4
Martinstown **104** C4
Martlesham **152** D3
Martlesham Heath **152** D3
Martletwy **126** D1
Martley **145** G1
Martock **104** A1
Marton *ChesE* **171** F1
Marton *Cumb* **198** D5
Marton *Cumb* **199** D1
Marton *ERid* **197** D4
Marton *ERid* **197** E1
Marton *Lincs* **187** F4
Marton *Middl* **203** E1
Marton *NYorks* **194** D1
Marton *NYorks* **203** G4
Marton *Shrop* **156** B2
Marton *Shrop* **170** B5
Marton *Warks* **195** E1
Marton Abbey **195** E1
Marton-in-the-
Forest **195** E1
Marton-le-Moor **202** C5
Martyr Worthy **119** G4
Martyr's Green **121** F2
Marwell Zoo Hants
SO21 1JH **4** D1
Marwick **276** B5
Marwood **113** F2
Mary Rose PO1 3LX
82 Portsmouth
Mary Tavy **99** F3
Marybank (An Lagaidh)
High **266** B6
Marybank *Na H-E. Siar*
271 F4
Maryburgh
(Baile Màiri) **266** C6
Maryfield *Corn* **100** A2
Maryfield *Shet* **279** D8
Marygold **237** F4
Maryhill *Aber* **269** G6
Maryhill *Glas* **233** G3
Marykirk **253** E3
Marylebone *GtLon* **136** B4
Marylebone *GtMan* **183** G2
Marypark **259** J1
Maryport *Cumb* **208** D3
Maryport *D&G* **206** B3
Marystow **99** E2
Maryton **253** E4
Marywell *Aber* **261** H5
Marywell *Aber* **260** D5
Marywell *Angus* **253** E5
Masham **202** B4
Mashbury **137** F1
Masongill **200** B5
Mastin Moor **186** B5
Mastrick **261** H4
Matchborough **146** C1
Matching **137** E1
Matching Green **137** E1
Matching Tye **137** E1
Matfen **220** C4
Matfield **123** F4
Mathern **131** E3
Mathon **145** G3
Mathry **140** B4
Matlaske **178** C2
Matlock **173** E1
Matlock Bank **173** E1
Matlock Bath **173** D2
Matson **132** A1
Matterdale End **209** G4
Mattersey **187** D4
Mattersey Thorpe **187** D4
Mattingley **120** C2
Mattishall **178** B4
Mattishall Burgh **178** B4
Mauchline **224** C3
Maud **269** H6
Maufant **100** C3
Maugersbury **147** D5
Maughold **190** C2
Mauld **257** K1
Maulden **149** F4
Maulds Meaburn **200** B1
Maunby **202** C4
Maund Bryan **145** E2
Maundown **115** D5
Mautby **179** F4
Mavesyn Ridware **158** C1
Mavis Enderby **176** B1
Maw Green **171** E2
Mawbray **209** D2
Mawdesley **183** F1
Mawdlam **129** E4
Mawgan **95** E4
Mawgan Porth **96** C3
Mawla **96** B5
Mawnan **95** E4
Mawnan Smith **95** E4
Mawsley **160** D5
Mawthorpe **189** E5
Maxey **161** G2
Maxstoke **159** E4
Maxted Street **124** D4
Maxton *Kent* **125** F4
Maxton *ScBord* **228** A3
Maxwellheugh **228** B3
Maxwelltown **217** D3

Maxworthy **98** C1
May Hill **145** G5
Mayals **128** C3
Maybole **224** B5
Maybury **121** F2
Mayen **268** D6
Mayfair **136** B4
Mayfield *ESuss* **110** A1
Mayfield *Midlo* **236** A3
Mayfield *Staffs* **172** C3
Mayford **121** E2
Mayland **138** C2
Maylandsea **138** C2
Maynard's Green **110** A2
Maypole *IoS* **96** B1
Maypole *Kent* **125** D2
Maypole *Mon* **131** D1
Maypole Green
Essex **152** A5
Maypole Green
Norf **165** F2
Maypole Green
Suff **153** D1
Maypole Green
Suff **152** C2
May's Green *NSom* **116** A1
Mays Green *Oxon* **134** C4
Maywick **279** C10
Mead **112** C4
Mead End **118** B5
Meadgate **117** D2
Meadle **134** D2
Meadow Green **145** G2
Meadowhall **186** A3
Meadowmill **236** B2
Meadowtown **156** C2
Meadwell **99** E2
Meaford **171** F4
Meal Bank **199** G3
Mealasta **270** B5
Meals **189** E3
Mealsgate **209** F2
Meanley **192** D3
Meanwood **194** B4
Mearbeck **193** E1
Meare **116** B3
Meare Green **115** F5
Mearns **233** G4
Mears Ashby **148** D1
Measham **159** F1
Meathop **199** F4
Meavy **100** B1
Medbourne **160** D3
Meddon **112** C4
Meden Vale **173** G1
Medlar **192** A4
Medmenham **134** D4
Medomsley **212** A2
Medstead **120** B4
Meer Common **144** C2
Meer End **159** E5
Meerbrook **171** G1
Meesden **150** C4
Meeson **171** D5
Meeth **113** F5
Meeting House Hill **179** E3
Meggethead **226** C3
Meidrim **141** F5
Meifod *Denb* **168** D2
Meifod *Powys* **156** A1
Meigle **252** A5
Meikle Earnock **234** B4
Meikle Grenach **232** B3
Meikle Kilmory **232** B3
Meikle Rahane **232** D1
Meikle Strath **253** E2
Meikle Tarty **261** H2
Meikle Wartle **261** F1
Meikleour **243** G1
Meikleyard **224** D2
Meinciau **128** A1
Meir **171** G3
Meirheath **171** G3
Melbost **271** G4
Melbost Borve
(Mealabost) **271** G2
Melbourn **150** B3
Melbourne *Derbys* **173** E5
Melbourne *ERid* **195** G3
Melbury **113** D4
Melbury Abbas **105** E1
Melbury Bubb **104** B2
Melbury Osmond **104** B2
Melbury Sampford **104** B2
Melby **279** A7
Melchbourne **149** F1
Melcombe
Bingham **105** D2
Melcombe Regis **104** C4
Meldon *Devon* **99** F1
Meldon *N'umb* **220** D3
Meldreth **150** B3
Meledor **96** D4
Melfort **240** A3
Melgarve **258** B5
Melgum **260** C4
Meliden
(Gallt Melyd) **182** B4
Melincourt **129** E2
Melin-y-coed **168** B1
Melin-y-ddol **155** G2
Melin-y-grug **155** G2
Melin-y-Wig **168** D3
Melkinthorpe **210** B5
Melkridge **210** D1
Melksham **118** A1
Melksham Forest **118** A1
Melldalloch **232** A2
Melling *Lancs* **199** G5
Melling *Mersey* **183** E2
Melling Mount **183** F2
Mellis **164** B4
Mellon Charles **264** E2
Mellon Udrigle **264** E2
Mellor *GtMan* **185** D4
Mellor *Lancs* **192** C4
Mellor Brook **192** C4
Mells **117** E3
Melmerby *Cumb* **210** C4
Melmerby *NYorks* **201** F4
Melmerby *NYorks* **202** C5
Melplash **104** A3
Melrose *Aber* **269** F3
Melrose *ScBord* **227** G2
Melsetter **277** B9
Melsonby **202** A2
Meltham **185** E1
Melton *ERid* **196** B5

Melton *Suff* **153** D2
Melton Constable **178** B2
Melton Mowbray **160** C1
Melton Ross **188** A1
Meltonby **195** G2
Melvaig **264** D3
Melverley **156** C1
Melverley Green **156** C1
Melvich **274** D2
Membury **103** F2
Memsie **269** H4
Memus **252** C4
Menabilly **97** E4
Menai Bridge
(Porthaethwy) **181** D5
Mendham **165** D3
Mendlesham **152** C1
Mendlesham Green **152** B1
Menethorpe **195** G1
Menheniot **97** G3
Menie House **261** H2
Menithwood **145** G1
Mennock **225** G5
Menston **194** A3
Menstrie **242** D5
Mentmore **135** E1
Meoble **247** G1
Meole Brace **157** D1
Meols **182** D3
Meon **107** E2
Meonstoke **107** F1
Meopham **123** F2
Meopham Green **123** F2
Mepal **162** C4
Meppershall **149** G4
Merbach **144** C3
Mercaston **173** D3
Mere *ChesE* **184** B4
Mere *Wilts* **117** F4
Mere Brow **183** F1
Mere Green *Suff* **152** A1
Mere Green **158** D3
Mere Heath **184** A5
Mereclough **193** E4
Mereside **191** G4
Meretown **171** E5
Mereworth **123** F3
Mergie **253** F1
Meriden **159** E4
Merkadale **252** J1
Merkland **216** B3
Merley **105** G3
Merlin's Bridge **126** C1
Merridge **115** F4
Merrifield **101** E3
Merrington **170** B5
Merrion **126** C3
Merriott **104** A1
Merrivale **99** F3
Merrow **121** F2
Merry Hill *Herts* **136** A3
Merry Hill *WMid* **158** A3
Merry Hill *WMid* **158** B4
Merrymeet **97** G3
Mersea Island **138** D1
Mersey Ferries *Mersey*
CH44 6QY **42** A4
Merseyside Maritime
Museum Mersey
L3 4AQ **42** B5
Mersham **124** C5
Merstham **122** B3
Merston **108** A3
Merstone **107** E4
Merther **96** C5
Merthyr **141** G5
Merthyr Cynog **143** F4
Merthyr Dyfan **115** E1
Merthyr Mawr **129** E5
Merthyr Tydfil **129** G2
Merthyr Vale **129** G3
Merton *Devon* **113** F4
Merton *Norf* **164** A2
Merton *Oxon* **134** A1
Merton *GtLon* **136** B5
Mervinslaw **228** A5
Meshaw **102** A1
Messing **138** C1
Messingham **187** F2
Metcombe **103** D3
Metfield **165** D3
Metherell **100** A1
Metheringham **175** F1
Methil **244** B5
Methlem **166** A4
Methley **194** C5
Methley Junction **194** C5
Methlick **261** G1
Methven **243** F2
Methwold **163** F3
Methwold Hythe **163** F3
MetroCentre **212** B1
Mettingham **165** E3
Metton **178** C2
Mevagissey **97** E5
Mewith Head **192** D1
Mexborough **186** B3
Mey **275** H1
Meysey Hampton **132** D2
Miabhag *Na H-E. Siar*
263 G2
Miabhag *Na H-E. Siar*
270 C7
Mial **264** D2
Miavaig (Miabhaig) **270** C4
Michaelchurch **145** E5
Michaelchurch
Escley **144** C4
Michaelchurch-on-
Arrow **144** B2
Michaelston-le-Pit **130** A5
Michaelston-super-
Ely **130** A5
Michaelston-y-
Fedw **130** B4
Michaelstow **97** E2
Michelcombe **100** C1
Micheldever **119** G4
Michelmersh **119** E5
Mickfield **152** C1
Mickle Trafford **170** B1
Micklebring **186** C3
Mickleby **204** B1
Micklefield **194** D4
Micklefield Green **135** F3
Mickleham **121** G3
Micklehurst **185** D2
Mickleover **173** E4
Micklethwaite
Cumb **209** F1

Micklethwaite
WYorks **193** G3
Midhurst **121** D5
Mickleton *Dur* **211** F5
Mickleton *Glos* **147** D3
Mickletown **194** C5
Mickley *Derbys* **186** A5
Mickley *NYorks* **202** B5
Mickley Green **151** G2
Mickley Square **211** G1
Mid Ardlaw **269** H4
Mid Beltie **260** E4
Mid Calder **235** E3
Mid Clyth **275** H5
Mid Lambrook **104** A1
Mid Lavant **108** A3
Mid Letter **240** C4
Mid Lix **242** A1
Mid Mossdale **200** D3
Mid Yell **278** E3
Midbea **276** D3
Middle Assendon **134** C4
Middle Aston **147** G5
Middle Barton **147** G5
Middle Bickenhill **159** E4
Middle
Bockhampton **106** A3
Middle Claydon **148** C5
Middle Drift **97** F3
Middle Drums **253** D4
Middle
Duntisbourne **132** B2
Middle Handley **186** B5
Middle Harling **164** A3
Middle Kames **232** A1
Middle Littleton **146** C3
Middle Maes-coed **144** C4
Middle Marwood **113** F2
Middle Mill **140** B5
Middle Quarter **124** A5
Middle Rasen **188** A4
Middle Rigg **243** F4
Middle Salter **192** C1
Middle Sontley **170** A3
Middle Stoford **115** E5
Middle Taphouse **97** F3
Middle Town **96** B1
Middle Tysoe **147** F3
Middle Wallop **119** D4
Middle Winterslow **118** D4
Middle Woodford **118** C4
Middlebie **218** A4
Middlecliff **186** B2
Middlecott **113** E5
Middleham **202** A4
Middlehill *Aber* **269** G6
Middlehill *Corn* **97** G3
Middlehope **157** E4
Middlemarsh **104** C2
Middlemoor **99** E3
Middlequarter (Ceathramh
Meadhanach) **262** D4
Middlesbrough **213** D5
Middlesceugh **210** A3
Middleshaw **199** G4
Middlesmoor **201** F5
Middlestone **212** B4
Middlestone Moor **212** B4
Middlestown **185** G1
Middleton *Aber* **261** G3
Middleton *Angus* **253** D5
Middleton *Cumb* **200** B4
Middleton *Derbys* **173** D2
Middleton *Derbys* **172** C1
Middleton *Essex* **151** G4
Middleton *GtMan* **184** C2
Middleton *Hants* **119** F3
Middleton *Here* **145** E1
Middleton *Lancs* **192** A2
Middleton *Midlo* **236** A4
Middleton *N'hants* **160** D4
Middleton *N'umb* **220** C3
Middleton *N'umb* **229** E3
Middleton *Norf* **163** E1
Middleton *NYorks* **203** G4
Middleton *P&K* **243** G4
Middleton *P&K* **251** G5
Middleton *Shrop* **156** B3
Middleton *Shrop* **157** E5
Middleton *Shrop* **170** C5
Middleton *Suff* **153** F1
Middleton *Swan* **128** A4
Middleton *Warks* **159** D3
Middleton *WYorks* **194** B5
Middleton *WYorks* **194** C5
Middleton Baggot **157** F3
Middleton Bank Top **220** C3
Middleton Cheney **147** G3
Middleton Green **171** G4
Middleton Hall **229** D4
Middleton Moor **153** F1
Middleton of
Potterton **261** H3
Middleton on the
Hill **145** E1
Middleton One Row **202** C1
Middleton Park **261** H3
Middleton Priors **157** F4
Middleton
Quernhow **202** C5
Middleton
St. George **202** C1
Middleton Scriven **157** F4
Middleton Stoney **148** A5
Middleton Tyas **202** B2
Middleton-in-
Teesdale **211** F5
Middleton-on-
Leven **203** D2
Middleton-on-Sea **108** B3
Middleton-on-the-
Wolds **196** B3
Middletown *Cumb* **198** A2
Middletown *Powys* **156** C1
Middlewich **171** E1
Middlewood *ChesE* **184** D4
Middlewood *SYorks* **186** A3
Middlewood Green **152** B1
Middlezoy **116** A4
Middridge **212** B5
Midfield **273** H2
Midford **117** E1
Midge Hall **192** B5
Midgeholme **210** C2
Midgham **119** G1
Midgley *WYorks* **185** G1
Midgley *WYorks* **193** G5

Micklethwaite **185** G3
Midhopestones **185** G3
Midhurst **121** D5
Midland Railway Centre
Derbys DE5 3QZ **173** F2
Midlem **227** G3
Midloe Grange **149** G1
Midpark **232** B3
Midsomer Norton **117** D2
Midthorpe **188** C5
Midtown *High* **273** H2
Midtown *High* **264** E3
Midtown of Barras **253** G1
Midville **176** B2
Midway **173** E5
Migdale **266** D2
Migvie **260** C4
Milarrochy **241** G5
Milber **102** B5
Milbethill **268** E5
Milborne
St. Andrew **105** D3
Milborne Wick **117** D5
Milbourne
N'umb **220** D4
Milbourne *Wilts* **132** B4
Milburn **210** C5
Milbury Heath **131** F3
Milcombe **147** G4
Milden **152** A2
Mildenhall *Suff* **163** F5
Mildenhall *Wilts* **118** D1
Mile Elm **118** A1
Mile End *Essex* **152** A5
Mile End *Glos* **131** E1
Mile End Park GtLon
E3 4HL **12** D4
Mile Oak **123** F4
Mile Town **124** B1
Milebrook **156** C5
Milebush **123** G4
Mileham **178** A4
Miles Green **171** F3
Miles Hope **145** E1
Miles's Green **119** G1
Milfield **228** D3
Milford *Derbys* **173** E3
Milford *Devon* **112** C3
Milford *Shrop* **170** B5
Milford *Staffs* **171** G5
Milford *Surr* **121** E3
Milford Haven
(Aberdaugleddau)
126 B2
Milford on Sea **106** B3
Milkwall **131** E2
Milky Way Adventure
Park Devon
EX39 5RY **112** D3
Mill Bank **193** G5
Mill Brow **185** D4
Mill End *Bucks* **134** C4
Mill End *Cambs* **151** E2
Mill End *Herts* **150** B4
Mill End Green **151** E5
Mill Green *Cambs* **151** E3
Mill Green *Essex* **137** F2
Mill Green *Herts* **136** B1
Mill Green *Norf* **164** C3
Mill Green *Shrop* **171** D5
Mill Green *Staffs* **172** B5
Mill Green *Suff* **153** E1
Mill Green *Suff* **152** C1
Mill Green *Suff* **152** C2
Mill Green *WMid* **158** C2
Mill Hill *B'burn* **192** C5
Mill Hill *Cambs* **150** A2
Mill Hill *GtLon* **136** B3
Mill Houses **192** C1
Mill Lane **120** C2
Mill of Camsail **233** D1
Mill of Colp **269** F6
Mill of Elrick **269** H6
Mill of Fortune **242** C2
Mill of Kingoodie **261** G2
Mill of Monquich **261** G5
Mill of Uras **253** G1
Mill Side **199** F4
Mill Street *Kent* **123** F3
Mill Street *Norf* **178** B4
Milland **120** D5
Millbank **269** J6
Millbeck **209** F4
Millbounds **276** E4
Millbreck **269** J6
Millbridge **120** D3
Millbrook *CenBeds* **149** F4
Millbrook *Corn* **100** A2
Millbrook *Devon* **103** G3
Millbrook *Soton* **106** C1
Millburn *Aber* **260** D2
Millburn *Aber* **260** E1
Millcombe **101** E3
Millcorner **110** D1
Milldale **172** C2
Millden **261** H3
Milldens **252** D4
Millearne **243** E3
Millend **147** F1
Millenheath **170** C4
Millennium Seed Bank,
Wakehurst Place WSuss
RH17 6TN **122** C5
Millerhill **236** A3
Miller's Dale **185** F5
Millers Green
Derbys **173** D2
Miller's Green
Essex **137** E2
Millgate **193** E5
Millhalf **144** B3
Millhayes *Devon* **103** E1
Millhayes *Devon* **103** F2
Millholme **199** G3
Millhouse *A&B* **232** A2
Millhouse *Cumb* **209** G3
Millhouse Green **185** G2
Millhousebridge **217** F2
Millin Cross **126** C1
Millington **196** A2
Millington Green **173** D3
Millmeece **171** F4
Millness **257** K1
Millom **198** C4
Millow **150** A3
Millpool **97** F2

Millport **232** C4
Millthorpe **186** A5
Millthrop **200** B3
Milltimber **261** G4
Milltown *Aber* **259** K4
Milltown *Corn* **97** F4
Milltown *D&G* **218** A4
Milltown *Derbys* **173** E1
Milltown *Devon* **113** F2
Milltown *High* **267** G7
Milltown of
Aberdalgie **243** F2
Milltown of
Auchindoun **260** B1
Milltown of
Craigston **269** F5
Milltown of
Edinville **267** K7
Milltown of
Kildrummy **260** C3
Milltown of
Rothiemay **268** D6
Milltown of Towie **260** C3
Milnathort **243** G4
Milners Heath **170** B1
Milngavie **233** G2
Milnrow **184** D1
Milnsbridge **185** F1
Milnthorpe **199** F4
Milovaig **263** G6
Milrig **224** D2
Milson **157** F5
Milstead **124** B3
Milston **118** C3
Milton *Angus* **252** B5
Milton *Cambs* **150** C1
Milton *Cumb* **210** C2
Milton *D&G* **216** C2
Milton *D&G* **216** C3
Milton *D&G* **214** D5
Milton *Derbys* **173** E5
Milton *High* **265** K6
Milton *High* **266** C4
Milton *High* **267** G6
Milton *High* **264** D7
Milton *High* **266** C7
Milton *High* **275** J3
Milton (Baile a' Mhuilinn)
High **258** B1
Milton *Moray* **268** D4
Milton *Newport* **130** C4
Milton *Notts* **187** E5
Milton *NSom* **116** A1
Milton *Oxon* **147** G4
Milton *Oxon* **133** G3
Milton *P&K* **243** E1
Milton *Pembs* **126** D2
Milton *Ports* **107** F3
Milton *Som* **116** B5
Milton *Stir* **242** A4
Milton *Stoke* **171** G2
Milton *WDun* **233** F2
Milton Abbas **105** E2
Milton Abbot **99** E3
Milton Bridge **235** G3
Milton Bryan **149** E4
Milton Clevedon **117** D4
Milton Combe **100** A1
Milton Country Park Cambs
CB24 6AZ **150** C1
Milton Damerel **113** D4
Milton End **131** G1
Milton Ernest **149** F2
Milton Green **170** B2
Milton Hill **133** G3
Milton Keynes **149** D4
Milton Keynes
Village **149** D4
Milton Lilbourne **118** C1
Milton Malsor **148** C2
Milton Morenish **242** B1
Milton of
Auchinhove **260** D4
Milton of Balgonie **244** B4
Milton of Buchanan **241** G5
Milton of
Cairnborrow **268** C6
Milton of Callander **242** A4
Milton of Campfield **260** E4
Milton of Campsie **234** A2
Milton of Coldwells **261** H1
Milton of Cullerlie **261** F4
Milton of Cushnie **260** D3
Milton of Dalcapon **251** E4
Milton of
Inveramsay **261** F2
Milton of Noth **260** D2
Milton of Tullich **260** B5
Milton on Stour **117** E5
Milton Regis **124** A2
Milton Street **110** A3
Miltonduff **267** J5
Miltonhill **267** H5
Miltonise **214** C3
Milton-Lockhart **234** C5
Milton-under-
Wychwood **133** E1
Milverton *Som* **115** E5
Milverton *Warks* **147** F1
Milwich **171** G4
Mimbridge **121** E1
Minack Theatre Corn
TR19 6JU **94** A4
Minard **240** B5
Minard Castle **240** B5
Minchinhampton **132** A2
Minchington **105** F1
Mindrum **228** C3
Mindrummill **228** C3
Minehead **114** C3
Minera **169** F2
Minety **132** C3
Minety Lower Moor **132** C3
Minffordd *Gwyn* **154** D1
Minffordd *Gwyn* **167** E4
Minffordd *Gwyn* **181** D5
Miningsby **176** B1
Minions **97** G2
Minishant **224** B4
Minley Manor **120** D2
Minllyn **155** E1
Minnes **261** H2
Minngearrarbh **254** C2
Minnigaff **215** F4
Minnonie **269** F4
Minskip **194** C1
Minstead **106** B1
Minsted **121** D5

Minster *Kent* 124 B1
Minster *Kent* 125 F2
Minsteracres 211 G2
Minsterworth 131 G1
Minterne Magna 104 C2
Minterne Parva 104 C2
Minting 188 B5
Mintlaw 269 J6
Minto 227 G3
Minton 156 B3
Minwear 126 D1
Minworth 159 D3
Miodar 246 B1
Mirehouse 208 C5
Mireland 275 J2
Mirfield 194 B5
Miserden 132 B2
Miskin *RCT* 129 G4
Miskin *RCT* 129 G3
Misselfore 118 B5
Misson 187 E3
Misterton *Leics* 160 A4
Misterton *Notts* 187 E3
Misterton *Som* 104 A2
Mistley 152 C4
Mitcham 122 B2
Mitcheldean 131 F1
Mitchell 96 C4
Mitchelland 199 F3
Mitcheltroy
  Common 131 D2
Mithian 96 B4
Mitford 221 D3
Mithian 98 B4
Mitton 158 A1
Mixbury 148 B4
Mixenden 193 G5
Moar 250 A5
Moat 218 C4
Moats Tye 152 B2
Mobberley *ChesE* 184 B5
Mobberley *Staffs* 172 B3
Moccas 144 C3
Mochdre *Conwy* 181 G5
Mochdre *Powys* 155 G4
Mochrum 206 C5
Mockbeggar *Hants* 106 A2
Mockbeggar *Kent* 123 G4
Mockerkin 209 D4
Modbury 100 C2
Moddershall 171 G4
Modern Art Oxford *Oxon*
  OX1 1BP 80 Oxford
Modsarie 273 J2
Moel Famau Country Park
  Denb LL15 1US 169 E1
Moelfre *IoA* 180 D4
Moelfre *Powys* 169 E5
Moffat 226 B5
Mogerhanger 149 G3
Moin'a'choire 230 B3
Moine House 273 H3
Moira 159 F1
Molash 124 C3
Mol-chlach 255 K3
Mold (Yr Wyddgrug) 169 F1
Molehill Green
  Essex 151 D5
Molehill Green
  Essex 151 F5
Molescroft 196 C3
Molesden 220 D3
Molesworth 161 F5
Mollance 216 B4
Molland 114 B5
Mollington
  ChesW&C 183 E5
Mollington *Oxon* 147 G3
Mollinsburn 234 B2
Monach Islands (Heisker
  Islands) 262 B5
Monachty 142 B1
Monachyle 241 G3
Monevechadan 241 D4
Monewden 152 D2
Moneydie 243 F2
Moneyrow Green 135 D5
Moniaive 216 B1
Monifieth 244 D1
Monikie 244 D1
Monikie Country Park
  Angus DD5 3QN 244 C1
Monimail 244 A3
Monington 141 E3
Monk Bretton 186 A2
Monk Fryston 195 E1
Monk Hesleden 213 D4
Monk Sherborne 120 B2
Monk Soham 152 D1
Monk Soham
  Green 152 D1
Monken Hadley 136 B3
Monkerton 102 C3
Monkey Mates *W'ham*
  RG41 1JA 134 C5
Monkey World, Wareham
  Dorset
  BH20 6HH 105 E4
Monkhide 145 F3
Monkhill 209 G1
Monkhopton 157 F3
Monkland 145 D2
Monkleigh 113 E3
Monknash 129 F5
Monkokehampton 113 F5
Monks Eleigh 152 A3
Monks Eleigh Tye 152 A3
Monk's Gate 109 E1
Monk's Heath 184 C5
Monk's Hill 124 A4
Monks Horton 124 D5
Monks Kirby 159 G4
Monks Risborough 134 D2
Monkscross 99 D3
Monkseaton 221 F4
Monkshill 269 F6
Monksilver 115 D4
Monkswood 130 C1
Monkton *Devon* 103 E2
Monkton *Kent* 125 E2
Monkton *Pembs* 126 C2
Monkton *SAyr* 224 B3
Monkton *T&W* 212 C1

Monkton *VGlam* 129 F5
Monkton Combe 117 E1
Monkton Deverill 117 F4
Monkton Farleigh 117 F1
Monkton Heathfield 115 F5
Monkton Up
  Wimborne 105 G1
Monkton Wyld 103 G3
Monkwearmouth 212 C2
Monkwood 120 B4
Monmouth
  (Trefynwy) 131 E1
Monnington Court 144 C4
Monnington on
  Wye 144 C3
Monreith 207 D2
Montacute 104 B1
Montacute House *Som*
  TA15 6XP 104 B1
Montford 156 D1
Montford Bridge 156 D1
Montgarrie 260 D3
Montgomery
  (Trefaldwyn) 156 B3
Montgreenan 233 E5
Montpellier Gallery *Warks*
  CV37 6EP
  85 Stratford-upon-Avon
Montrave 244 A4
Montrose 253 F4
Monxton 119 E3
Monyash 172 C1
Monymusk 260 E3
Monzie 243 E2
Moodiesburn 234 A2
Moons Moat North 146 C1
Moonzie 244 B3
Moor Allerton 194 C4
Moor Cock 192 C1
Moor Crichel 105 F2
Moor End *Bed* 149 F2
Moor End *CenBeds* 149 E5
Moor End *Cumb* 199 G5
Moor End *ERid* 196 A4
Moor End *Lancs* 191 G3
Moor End *NYorks* 195 E4
Moor End *WYorks* 193 G5
Moor Green *WMid* 158 C4
Moor Green *Wilts* 117 F1
Moor Head 194 A4
Moor Monkton 195 E2
Moor Row 208 D5
Moor Side *Cumb* 198 D5
Moor Side *Lancs* 192 A4
Moor Side *Lancs* 192 A4
Moor Side *Lincs* 176 A2
Moor Street 124 A2
Moorby 176 A1
Moorcot 144 C2
Moordown 105 G3
Moore 183 G4
Moorend 209 G1
Moorends 187 D1
Moorfield 185 E3
Moorgreen 173 F3
Moorhall 186 A5
Moorhampton 144 C3
Moorhouse *Cumb* 209 G1
Moorhouse *Notts* 174 C1
Moorland (Northmoor
  Green) 116 A4
Moorlinch 116 A4
Moors Centre, Danby
  NYorks
  YO21 2NB 203 G2
Moors Valley Country Park
  Dorset
  BH24 2ET 106 A2
Moors Valley Railway
  Dorset
  BH24 2ET 105 G2
Moorsholm 203 F1
Moorside *Dorset* 105 D1
Moorside *GtMan* 185 D2
Moorside *WYorks* 194 B4
Moorthorpe 186 B1
Moortown *IoW* 106 D4
Moortown *Lincs* 188 A3
Moortown *Tel&W* 157 F1
Morangie 266 E3
Morar 256 C5
Morborne 161 G4
Morchard Bishop 102 A2
Morcombelake 104 A3
Morcott 161 F2
Morda 169 F5
Morden *Dorset* 105 F3
Morden *GtLon* 122 B2
Morden Hall Park *GtLon*
  SM4 5JD 11 F8
Morden Park 122 B2
Mordiford 145 E4
Mordington
  Holdings 237 G4
Mordon 212 C5
More 156 C3
Morebath 114 C5
Morebattle 228 B4
Morecambe 192 A1
Morefield 265 H2
Moreleigh 101 D2
Morenish 242 B1
Moresby Parks 208 C5
Morestead 119 G5
Moreton *Dorset* 105 E4
Moreton *Essex* 137 E2
Moreton *Here* 145 E1
Moreton *Mersey* 183 D4
Moreton *Oxon* 134 B2
Moreton *Staffs* 172 C4
Moreton *Staffs* 171 G1
Moreton Corbet 170 C5
Moreton Jeffries 145 F3
Moreton Mill 170 C5
Moreton Morrell 147 F2
Moreton on Lugg 145 E3
Moreton Paddox 147 F2
Moreton Pinkney 148 A3
Moreton Say 170 D4
Moreton Valence 131 G2
Moretonhampstead 102 A4
Moreton-in-Marsh 147 E4
Morfa *Carmar* 128 B1
Morfa *Cere* 141 G2
Morfa Bychan 167 E4
Morfa Glas 129 E2
Morfa Nefyn 166 B3

Morgan's Vale 118 C5
Morganstown 130 A4
Mork 131 E2
Morland 210 B5
Morley *Derbys* 173 E3
Morley *Dur* 212 A5
Morley *WYorks* 194 B5
Morley Green 184 C4
Morley St. Botolph 164 B2
Mornick 98 D3
Morningside *Edin* 235 G2
Morningside *NLan* 234 C4
Morningthorpe 164 D2
Morpeth 221 E3
Morphie 253 F3
Morrey 158 D1
Morridge Side 172 B2
Morrilow Heath 171 G4
Morriston *SAyr* 224 A5
Morriston *Swan* 128 C3
Morristown 130 A5
Morroch 247 F1
Morston 178 B1
Mortehoe 113 E1
Morthen 186 B4
Mortimer 120 B1
Mortimer West End 120 B1
Mortimer's Cross 144 D1
Mortlake 136 B5
Morton *Derbys* 173 F1
Morton *Lincs* 175 F5
Morton *Lincs* 187 F3
Morton *Lincs* 175 D1
Morton *Notts* 174 C2
Morton *SGlos* 131 F3
Morton *Shrop* 169 F5
Morton Bagot 146 D1
Morton on the Hill 178 C4
Morton Tinmouth 212 A5
Morton-on-Swale 202 C3
Morvah 94 B3
Morval 97 G4
Morvich (A'Mhormhaich)
  High 257 F2
Morvich *High* 266 E1
Morvil 140 D4
Morville 157 F3
Morwellham 100 A1
Morwellham Quay Museum
  Devon PL19 8JL 99 E3
Morwenstow 112 C4
Morwick Hall 221 E1
Mosborough 186 B4
Moscow 233 F5
Mosedale 209 G3
Moseley Heath 185 E1
Moseley *WMid* 158 B3
Moseley *Worcs* 146 A2
Moses Gate 184 B2
Moss *A&B* 246 A2
Moss *SYorks* 186 C1
Moss *Wrex* 170 A2
Moss Bank 183 G3
Moss Houses 184 C5
Moss Nook 184 C4
Moss of
  Barmuckity 267 K5
Moss Side *GtMan* 184 C3
Moss Side *Lancs* 191 G4
Moss Side *Mersey* 183 E2
Mossat 260 C3
Mossbank 278 D5
Mossblown 224 C3
Mossburnford 228 A5
Mossdale 216 A3
Mossend 234 B3
Mosser 209 E4
Mossgiel 224 C3
Mosshead 260 D1
Mosside of
  Ballinshoe 252 C4
Mossley *ChesE* 171 F1
Mossley *GtMan* 185 D2
Mossley Hill 183 E4
Mosspaul Hotel 218 B2
Moss-side *High* 267 F6
Moss-side *Moray* 268 D5
Mosstodloch 268 B4
Mosston 252 D5
Mossy Lea 183 G1
Mosterton 104 A2
Moston *GtMan* 184 C2
Moston *Shrop* 170 C5
Moston Green 171 E1
Mostyn 182 C4
Motcombe 117 F5
Mothecombe 100 C3
Mother Shipton's Cave
  NYorks
  HG5 8DD 194 C2
Motherby 210 A5
Motherwell 234 B4
Mottingham 136
  D5 Mottisfont 119 E5
Mottisfont Abbey *Hants*
  SO51 0LP 119 E5
Mottistone 106 D4
Mottram in
  Longdendale 185 D3
Mottram
  St. Andrew 184 C5
Moulin 251 E4
Mouldsworth 183 G5
Moulsecoomb 109 F3
Moulsford 134 A4
Moulsham 137 G2
Moulsoe 149 E3
Moulton *ChesW&C* 171 D1
Moulton *Lincs* 176 B5
Moulton *N'hants* 148 C1
Moulton *NYorks* 202 B2
Moulton *Suff* 151 E1
Moulton *VGlam* 129 G5
Moulton Chapel 162 A1
Moulton St. Mary 179 F5
Moulton Seas End 176 B5
Mounie Castle 261 F2
Mount *Corn* 96 B4
Mount *Corn* 97 F3
Mount *High* 267 G7
Mount *Kent* 125 D4
Mount *WYorks* 185 F1
Mount Ambrose 96 B5
Mount Bures 152 A4
Mount Charles 97 E4
Mount Edgcumbe Country
  Park *Corn*
  PL10 1HZ 2 B3

Mount Hawke 96 B5
Mount Manisty 183 E5
Mount Oliphant 224 B4
Mount Pleasant
  ChesE 171 F2
Mount Pleasant
  Derbys 173 E3
Mount Pleasant
  Derbys 159 E1
Mount Pleasant
  ESuss 109 G1
Mount Pleasant
  Flints 182 D5
Mount Pleasant
  GtLon 135 F4
Mount Pleasant
  Hants 106 C3
Mount Pleasant
  Norf 164 A2
Mount Pleasant
  Suff 151 F3
Mount Sorrel 118 B5
Mount Tabor 193 G5
Mountain 193 G4
Mountain Ash
  (Aberpennar) 129 G3
Mountain Cross 235 F5
Mountain Water 140 C5
Mountbenger 227 E3
Mountblairy 268 E5
Mountblow 233 F2
Mountfield 110 C1
Mountgerald 266 C5
Mountjoy 96 C3
Mountnessing 137 F3
Mountsorrel 160 A1
Mousa 279 D10
Mousehole 94 B4
Mouswald 217 E3
Mow Cop 171 F2
Mowden 202 B1
Mowhaugh 228 C4
Mowsley 160 B4
Moxley 158 B3
Moy *High* 249 D1
Moy *High* 249 G1
Moy *High* 258 E1
Moy House 267 H6
Moylgrove 141 E2
Muasdale 231 E5
Much Birch 145 E4
Much Cowarne 145 F3
Much Dewchurch 145 D4
Much Hadham 136 D1
Much Hoole 192 A5
Much Hoole Town 192 A5
Much Marcle 145 F4
Much Wenlock 157 F2
Muchalls 261 H5
Muchelney 116 B5
Muchelney Ham 116 B5
Muchlarnick 97 G4
Muchra 226 D4
Muchrachd 257 J1
Muck 246 D2
Mucking 137 F4
Muckle Roe 279 C6
Muckleford 104 C3
Muckleton 170 C5
Muckletown 260 D2
Muckley 157 F3
Muckley Corner 158 C2
Muckton 189 D4
Mudale 273 H5
Muddiford 113 F2
Muddles Green 110 A2
Muddleswood 109 E2
Mudeford 106 A3
Mudford 104 B1
Mudgley 116 B3
Mugdock 233 G2
Mugeary 255 K1
Muggintonlane
  End 173 D3
Mugginton 173 D3
Muggleswick 211 G3
Mugswell 122 B3
Muie 266 D1
Muir 251 F1
Muir of Fowlis 260 D3
Muir of Lochs 268 B4
Muir of Ord
  (Am Blàr Dubh) 266 C6
Muiravonside Country Park
  Falk EH49 6LW 235 D2
Muirden 269 F5
Muirdrum 245 D1
Muiredge 244 B5
Muirhead *Aber* 260 D3
Muirhead *Angus* 244 B1
Muirhead *Fife* 244 A4
Muirhead *Moray* 267 H5
Muirhead *NLan* 234 A3
Muirhouses 235 E1
Muirkirk 225 D3
Muirmill 234 B1
Muirtack *Aber* 261 H1
Muirtack *Aber* 269 G6
Muirton *High* 266 E5
Muirton *P&K* 243 E3
Muirton *P&K* 243 G2
Muirton of Ardblair 251 G5
Muirton of Ballochy 253 E3
Muirtown 267 G6
Muiryfold 269 F5
Muker 201 F3
Mulbarton 178 C5
Mulben 268 B5
Mulhagery 271 F7
Mull 239 F1
Mullach
  Chàrlabhaigh 270 E3
Mullacott Cross 113 F1
Mullion 95 D5
Mullion Cove 95 D5
Mumby 189 E5
Munderfield Row 145 F2
Munderfield Stocks 145 F2
Mundesley 179 E2
Mundford 163 G3
Mundham 165 E2
Mundon 138 B2
Mundurno 261 H3

Munerigie 257 J4
Mungasdale 265 F4
Mungoswells 236 B2
Mungrisdale 209 G3
Munnoch 232 D5
Munsley 145 F3
Munslow 157 E4
Murchington 99 G2
Murcott *Oxon* 134 A1
Murcott *Wilts* 132 B3
Murdostoun 234 C4
Murieston 235 E3
Murkle 275 G2
Murlaganmore 242 A1
Murlaggan *High* 257 G5
Murlaggan *High* 249 F1
Murra 277 B7
Murrell Green 120 C2
Murrow 162 B2
Mursley 148 D5
Murston 124 B2
Murthill 252 C4
Murthly 243 F1
Murton *Cumb* 210 D5
Murton *Dur* 212 C3
Murton *N'umb* 237 G5
Murton *Swan* 128 B4
Murton *York* 195 F2
Musbury 103 F3
Muscliff 105 G3
Musdale (Musdàl) 240 B2
Museum in Docklands
  GtLon E14 4AL 12 D4
Museum of Childhood,
  Edinburgh *Edin*
  EH1 1TG 37 H4
Museum of Childhood,
  London *GtLon*
  E2 9PA 12 C4
Museum of Flight *ELoth*
  EH39 5LF 236 C2
Museum of Garden History,
  London *GtLon*
  SE1 7LB 45 F7
Museum of London *GtLon*
  EC2Y 5HN 45 J2
Museum of Science &
  Industry, Manchester
  GtMan M3 4FP 46 C4
Museum of Transport,
  Glasgow *Glas*
  G3 8DP 38 A2
Musselburgh 236 A2
Mustard Hyrn 179 F4
Mustard Shop *Norf*
  NR2 1NQ 79 Norwich
Muston *Leics* 174 D4
Muston *NYorks* 205 D5
Mustow Green 158 A5
Mutford 165 F3
Muthill 243 D3
Mutley 100 A2
Mutterton 102 D2
Muxton 157 G1
Mybster 275 G3
Myddfai 143 D5
Myddle 170 B5
Myddlewood 170 B5
Mydroilyn 142 A2
Myerscough
  College 192 A4
Myerscough Smithy 192 C4
Mylor 95 F3
Mylor Bridge 95 F3
Mynachdy 130 A5
Mynachlog-ddu 141 E4
Myndtown 156 C4
Mynydd Llandygai 167 F1
Mynydd Mechell 180 B4
Mynydd-bach *Mon* 131 D3
Mynydd-bach
  Swan 128 C3
Mynyddygarreg 128 A2
Mynytho 166 C4
Myrebird 261 F5
Mytchett 121 D2
Mytholm 193 F5
Mytholmroyd 193 G5
Mythop 191 G4
Myton-on-Swale 194 D1
Mytton 156 D1

N

Naast 264 E3
Nab's Head 192 C5
Na-Buirgh 263 F2
Naburn 195 E3
Nackington 125 D3
Nacton 152 D3
Nadderwater 102 B3
Nafferton 196 C2
Nailbridge 131 F1
Nailsbourne 115 F5
Nailsea 131 D5
Nailstone 159 G2
Nailsworth 132 A3
Nairn 267 F6
Nancegollan 94 D3
Nancekuke 96 A5
Nancledra 94 B3
Nanhoron 166 B4
Nannau 168 A5
Nannerch 169 E1
Nanpantan 160 A1
Nanpean 97 D4
Nanstallon 97 E3
Nant Peris 167 F2
Nant-ddu 129 G1
Nanternis 141 G2
Nantgarw 130 A4
Nant-glas 143 F2
Nantgaredig 142 A5
Nantgarw 130 A4
Nant-glas 143 F2
Nantglyn 168 C1
Nantgwyn 155 F5
Nantlle 167 E2
Nantmawr 169 F5
Nantmel 143 G1
Nantmor 167 F3
Nantwich 170 D2
Nantycaws 128 A1
Nant-y-derry 130 C2
Nant-y-dugoed 155 F1
Nantyffyllon 129 E3
Nantyglo 130 A1
Nant-y-Gollen 169 F5
Nant-y-groes 143 G1

Nant-y-moel 129 F3
Nant-y-Pandy 181 E5
Naphill 135 D2
Napley Heath 171 E4
Napton on the Hill
  147 G1
Narberth (Arberth) 127 E1
Narborough
  Leics 160 A3
Narborough *Norf* 163 F1
Narkurs 98 D5
Narrachan 240 B3
Nasareth 167 D3
Naseby 160 B5
Nash *Bucks* 148 C4
Nash *Here* 144 C1
Nash *Newport* 130 C4
Nash *Shrop* 157 F5
Nash *VGlam* 129 F5
Nash Street 123 F2
Nassington 161 F3
Nasty 160 C5
Nateby *Cumb* 200 C2
Nateby *Lancs* 192 A3
Nately Scures 120 C2
National Agricultural Centre,
  Stoneleigh *Warks*
  CV8 2LZ 16 B5
National Army Museum
  GtLon SW3 4HT 13 A5
National Botanic Garden
  of Wales *Carmar*
  SA32 8HG 128 B1
National Coal Mining
  Museum for England
  WYorks
  WF4 4RH 27 F6
National Exhibition Centre
  WMid B40 1NT 15 H4
National Fishing Heritage
  Centre, Grimsby *NELincs*
  DN31 1UZ 188 C2
National Gallery *GtLon*
  WC2N 5DN 44 D4
National Gallery of Scotland
  Edin EH2 2EL 37 H4
National Indoor Arena,
  Birmingham
  WMid B1 2AA 34 D4
National Marine Aquarium
  PL4 0LF 81 Plymouth
National Maritime Museum
  TR11 3QY 95 F3
National Maritime Museum,
  Greenwich *GtLon*
  SE10 9NF 13 D5
National Media Museum
  WYorks BD1 1NQ
  65 Bradford
National Memorial
  Arboretum, Alrewas
  Staffs
  DE13 7AR 159 D1
National Motorcycle
  Museum, Solihull *WMid*
  B92 0EJ 159 E4
National Museum Cardiff
  CF10 3NP
  67 Cardiff
National Museum of
  Scotland *Edin*
  EH1 1JF 37 G5
National Portrait Gallery
  GtLon
  WC2H 0HE 44 D4
National Railway Museum
  YO26 4XJ 90 York
National Sea Life Centre,
  Birmingham
  WMid B1 2JB 34 D4
National Slate Museum,
  Llanberis *Gwyn*
  LL55 4TY 167 G2
National Space Centre,
  Leicester *Leic*
  LE4 5NS 17 C4
National Wallace Monument
  Stir FK9 5LF 242 D5
National War Museum,
  Edinburgh *Edin*
  EH1 2NG 37 G4
National Waterfront
  Museum SA1 3RD
  86 Swansea
National Wildflower Centre,
  Liverpool *Mersey*
  L16 3NA 22 D3
Natland 199 G4
Natural History Museum
  at Tring *Herts*
  HP23 6AP 135 E1
Natural History Museum,
  London *GtLon*
  SW7 5BD 11 D5
Natureland Seal
  Sanctuary *Lincs*
  PE25 1DB 177 D1
Naughton 152 B3
Naunton *Glos* 146 D5
Naunton *Worcs* 146 A4
Naunton
  Beauchamp 146 B2
Navenby 175 E2
Navestock *ESuss* 110 C2
Navestock Side 137 E3
Navidale 275 F7
Navity 266 E5
Nawton 203 F4
Nayland 152 A4
Nazeing 136 D2
Neacroft 106 A3
Neal's Green 159 F4
Neap 279 E7
Neap House 187 F1
Near Sawrey 199 E3
Nearton End 148 D5
Neasden 136 B4
Neasham 202 C1
Neat Enstone 147 F5
Neath
  (Castell-nedd) 129 D3
Neatham 120 C3
Neatishead 179 E3
Nebo *Cere* 142 B1

Nebo *Conwy* 168 B2
Nebo *Gwyn* 167 D2
Nebo *IoA* 180 C3
Necton 163 G2
Nedd 272 D5
Nedderton 221 E3
Nedging 152 A3
Nedging Tye 152 B3
Needham 164 D3
Needham Lake *Suff*
  IP6 8NU 152 B2
Needham Market 152 B2
Needham Street 151 F1
Needingworth 162 B5
Needles Pleasure Park *IoW*
  PO39 0JD 106 C4
Needwood 172 C5
Neen Savage 157 F5
Neen Sollars 157 F5
Neenton 157 F4
Nefyn 166 C3
Neighbourne 116 D3
Neilston 233 F4
Neithrop 147 G3
Nelson *Caerp* 130 A3
Nelson *Lancs* 193 E4
Nelson Village 221 E4
Nemphlar 234 C5
Nempnett
  Thrubwell 116 C1
Nenthall 211 D3
Nenthead 211 D3
Nenthorn 228 A3
Neopardy 102 A3
Nerabus 230 A4
Nercwys 169 F1
Neriby 230 B3
Nerston 234 A4
Nesbit 229 D3
Nesfield 193 G3
Ness 183 E5
Ness Botanic Gardens
  ChesW&C
  CH64 4AY 183 E5
Ness of Tenston 277 B6
Nesscliffe 156 C1
Neston *ChesW&C* 183 D5
Neston *Wilts* 117 F1
Nether Alderley 184 C5
Nether
  Auchendrane 224 B4
Nether Barr 215 F4
Nether Blainslie 236 C5
Nether Broughton 174 B5
Nether Burrow 200 C4
Nether Cerne 104 C3
Nether Compton 104 B1
Nether Crimond 261 G2
Nether Dalgliesh 227 D5
Nether Dallachy 268 B4
Nether Edge 186 A4
Nether End 185 G5
Nether Exe 102 C3
Nether Glasslaw 269 G5
Nether Handwick 252 B5
Nether Haugh 186 B3
Nether Heselden 201 D5
Nether Heyford 148 B2
Nether Kellet 192 B1
Nether Kinmundy 269 J6
Nether Langwith 186 C5
Nether Lenshie 268 E6
Nether Loads 173 E1
Nether Moor 173 E1
Nether Padley 185 G5
Nether Pitforthie 253 G2
Nether Poppleton 195 E2
Nether Silton 203 D3
Nether Skyborry 156 B5
Nether Stowey 115 E4
Nether Urquhart 243 G4
Nether Wallop 119 E4
Nether Wasdale 198 C2
Nether Wellwood 225 E3
Nether Welton 209 G2
Nether Westcote 147 E5
Nether Whitacre 159 E3
Nether Winchendon (Lower
  Winchendon) 134 C1
Nether Worton 147 G5
Netheravon 118 C3
Netherbrae 269 F5
Netherbrough 277 C6
Netherburn 234 C5
Netherbury 104 A3
Netherby *Cumb* 218 B4
Netherby *NYorks* 194 C3
Nethercott 147 G5
Netherend *ESuss* 110 C2
Netherfield *Notts* 174 B3
Netherfield *SLan* 234 B5
Netherhall 232 D3
Netherhampton 118 C5
Netherhay 104 A2
Netherland Green 172 C4
Netherley 261 G5
Nethermill 217 E2
Nethermuir 269 H6
Netherseal 159 E1
Nethershield 225 D3
Netherstreet 118 A1
Netherthird *D&G* 216 B5
Netherthird *EAyr* 225 D4
Netherthong 185 F2
Netherthorpe 186 C4
Netherton *Angus* 252 D4
Netherton
  ChesW&C 183 G5
Netherton *Devon* 102 B5
Netherton *Hants* 119 E2
Netherton *Mersey* 183 E2
Netherton *N'umb* 220 B1
Netherton *NLan* 234 B4
Netherton *Oxon* 133 G2
Netherton *P&K* 251 G4
Netherton *SLan* 234 D4
Netherton *WMid* 158 B4
Netherton *Worcs* 146 B3
Netherton *WYorks* 185 G1
Netherton *WYorks* 185 F1
Netherton
  Burnfoot 220 B1
Netherton
  Northside 220 B1
Nethertown *Cumb* 198 A3
Nethertown *Ork* 275 J1
Nethertown *Staffs* 158 D1

Netherwitton 220 D2
Netherwood D&G 217 D3
Netherwood EAyr 225 E3
Nethy Bridge 259 H2
Netley Abbey 107 D2
Netley Marsh 106 C1
Nettlebed 134 B4
Nettlebridge 116 D3
Nettlecombe Dorset 104 B3
Nettlecombe IoW 107 E5
Nettlecombe Som 115 D4
Nettleden 135 F1
Nettleham 188 A5
Nettlestead Kent 123 F3
Nettlestead Suff 152 B3
Nettlestead Green 123 F3
Nettlestone 107 F3
Nettlesworth 212 B3
Nettleton Lincs 188 B2
Nettleton Wilts 132 A5
Nettleton Hill 185 E1
Netton Devon 100 B3
Netton Wilts 118 C4
Neuadd Cere 142 A2
Neuadd IoA 180 B3
Neuadd Powys 143 F3
Nevendon 137 G3
Nevern 141 D4
Nevill Holt 160 D3
New Abbey 217 D4
New Aberdour 269 G4
New Addington 122 C2
New Alresford 119 G4
New Alyth 252 A5
New Arley 159 E3
New Arram 196 C3
New Ash Green 123 F2
New Balderton 174 D2
New Barn 123 F2
New Belses 227 G3
New Bewick 229 E4
New Bolingbroke 176 B2
New Boultham 187 G5
New Bradwell 148 D3
New Brancepeth 212 B3
New Bridge D&G 216 D3
New Bridge Devon 102 A5
New Brighton Flints 169 F1
New Brighton Hants 107 G2
New Brighton Mersey 183 E3
New Brighton Wrex 169 F2
New Brighton WYorks 194 B5
New Brinsley 173 F2
New Broughton 170 A2
New Buckenham 164 B2
New Byth 269 G5
New Cheriton 119 G5
New Cross Cere 154 C5
New Cross GtLon 136 C5
New Cumnock 225 E4
New Deer 269 G6
New Duston 148 C1
New Earswick 195 F2
New Edlington 186 C3
New Elgin 267 K5
New Ellerby 197 D4
New Eltham 136 D5
New End 146 C1
New England 161 G2
New Farnley 194 B4
New Ferry 183 E4
New Galloway 216 A3
New Gilston 244 C4
New Greens 136 A2
New Grimsby 96 A1
New Hartley 221 F4
New Haw 121 F1
New Heaton 228 C3
New Hedges 127 E2
New Herrington 212 C2
New Hinksey 134 A2
New Holland 196 C5
New Houghton Derbys 173 G1
New Houghton Norf 177 F5
New Houses 200 D5
New Hunwick 212 A4
New Hutton 199 G3
New Hythe 123 G3
New Inn Carmar 142 A4
New Inn Fife 244 A4
New Inn Mon 131 D2
New Inn Torfaen 130 B3
New Invention Shrop 156 B5
New Invention WMid 158 B2
New Kelso 265 F7
New Lanark 234 C5
New Lanark World Heritage Site SLan ML11 9DB 234 C5
New Lane 183 F1
New Lane End 184 A3
New Leake 176 C2
New Leeds 269 H5
New Leslie 260 D2
New Lodge 186 A2
New Longton 192 B5
New Luce 214 C4
New Mains 225 G2
New Mains of Ury 253 G1
New Malden 122 B2
New Marske 213 F5
New Marton 170 A4
New Mill Corn 94 B3
New Mill Herts 135 E1
New Mill WYorks 185 F2
New Mill End 136 A1
New Mills Corn 96 C4
New Mills Derbys 185 E4
New Mills Glos 131 F2
New Mills Mon 131 E2
New Mills (Y Felin Newydd) Powys 155 G2
New Milton 106 B3
New Mistley 152 C4
New Moat 141 D5
New Ollerton 174 B1
New Orleans 222 C4
New Oscott 158 C3
New Palace & Adventureland, New Brighton Mersey CH45 2JX 22 A2
New Park Corn 97 F1
New Park NYorks 194 B2
New Pitsligo 269 G5
New Polzeath 96 D2
New Quay (Ceinewydd) 141 G1
New Rackheath 179 D4
New Radnor (Maesyfed) 144 B1
New Rent 210 A4
New Ridley 211 G1
New Road Side 193 F3
New Romney 111 F1
New Rossington 186 D3
New Row Cere 154 D5
New Row Lancs 192 C4
New Sawley 173 F4
New Shoreston 229 F3
New Silksworth 212 C2
New Stevenston 234 B4
New Swannington 159 G1
New Totley 186 A5
New Town CenBeds 149 G3
New Town Cere 141 E3
New Town Dorset 105 F1
New Town Dorset 105 F2
New Town ELoth 236 B2
New Town ESuss 109 G1
New Town Glos 146 C4
New Tredegar 130 A2
New Tupton 173 E1
New Ulva 231 F1
New Valley 271 G4
New Village 186 C2
New Walk Museum & Art Gallery LE1 7EA 77 Leicester
New Walsoken 162 C2
New Waltham 188 C2
New Walton Pier Essex CO14 8ES 153 D5
New Winton 236 B2
New World 162 B3
New Yatt 133 F1
New York Lincs 176 A2
New York T&W 221 F4
Newall 194 B3
Newark Ork 276 G3
Newark Peter 162 A2
Newark Castle, Newark-on-Trent Notts NG24 1BG 174 C2
Newark-on-Trent 174 D2
Newarthill 234 B4
Newball 188 A5
Newbarn 125 D5
Newbarns 198 D5
Newbattle 236 A3
Newbiggin Cumb 210 A5
Newbiggin Cumb 210 C5
Newbiggin Cumb 210 B3
Newbiggin Cumb 191 F1
Newbiggin Cumb 198 B3
Newbiggin Dur 211 F5
Newbiggin N'umb 211 F1
Newbiggin NYorks 201 F4
Newbiggin NYorks 201 E3
Newbiggin-by-the-Sea 221 F3
Newbigging Aber 261 G5
Newbigging Aber 251 G1
Newbigging Angus 244 C1
Newbigging Angus 244 C1
Newbigging Angus 252 A5
Newbigging SLan 235 E5
Newbiggin-on-Lune 200 C2
Newbold Derbys 186 A5
Newbold Leics 159 G1
Newbold on Avon 159 G5
Newbold on Stour 147 E3
Newbold Pacey 147 E2
Newbold Verdon 159 G2
Newborough (Niwbwrch) IoA 166 D1
Newborough Peter 162 A2
Newborough Staffs 172 C5
Newbottle N'hants 148 A4
Newbottle T&W 212 C2
Newbourne 153 D3
Newbridge (Cefn Bychan) Caerp 130 B3
Newbridge Corn 94 B3
Newbridge Corn 98 D4
Newbridge Edin 235 F2
Newbridge ESuss 123 D5
Newbridge Hants 106 B1
Newbridge IoW 106 D4
Newbridge NYorks 204 B4
Newbridge Oxon 133 G2
Newbridge Pembs 140 C4
Newbridge Wrex 169 F3
Newbridge Green 146 A4
Newbridge on Wye 143 G2
Newbridge-on-Usk 130 C3
Newbrough 211 E1
Newbuildings 102 A2
Newburgh Aber 269 H5
Newburgh Aber 261 H2
Newburgh Fife 244 A3
Newburgh Lancs 183 F1
Newburgh ScBord 227 E3
Newburn 212 A1
Newbury Som 117 D2
Newbury WBerks 119 F1
Newbury Wilts 117 F3
Newbury Park 136 D4
Newby Cumb 210 B5
Newby Lancs 193 E3
Newby NYorks 203 E1
Newby NYorks 192 D1
Newby NYorks 204 D4
Newby Bridge 199 E4
Newby Cote 200 C5
Newby Cross 209 G1
Newby East 210 A2
Newby Hall NYorks HG4 5AE 194 C1
Newby West 209 G1
Newby Wiske 202 C4
Newcastle Bridgend 129 E5
Newcastle Mon 130 D1
Newcastle Shrop 156 B4
Newcastle Emlyn (Castell Newydd Emlyn) 141 G3
Newcastle International Airport 221 D4
Newcastle upon Tyne 212 B1
Newcastleton 218 C3
Newcastle-under-Lyme 171 F3
Newchapel Pembs 141 F4
Newchapel Staffs 171 F2
Newchapel Surr 122 C4
Newchurch Carmar 141 G5
Newchurch IoW 107 E4
Newchurch Kent 124 C5
Newchurch Lancs 193 E5
Newchurch Lancs 193 E4
Newchurch Mon 131 D3
Newchurch Powys 144 B2
Newchurch Staffs 172 C5
Newcott 103 F2
Newcraighall 236 A2
Newdigate 121 G3
Newell Green 135 D5
Newenden 110 D1
Newent 145 G5
Newerne 131 F2
Newfield Dur 212 B4
Newfield Dur 212 B2
Newfield High 266 E4
Newfound 119 G2
Newgale 140 B5
Newgate 178 B1
Newgate Street 136 C2
Newgord 278 E2
Newhall ChesE 170 D3
Newhall Derbys 173 D5
Newham 229 F4
Newham Hall 229 F4
Newhaven 109 G3
Newhey 184 D1
Newholm 204 B1
Newhouse 234 B3
Newick 109 G1
Newingreen 124 D5
Newington Edin 235 G2
Newington Kent 125 D5
Newington Kent 124 A2
Newington Notts 187 D3
Newington Oxon 134 B3
Newington Bagpath 132 A3
Newland Cumb 199 E5
Newland Glos 131 E2
Newland Hull 196 C4
Newland NYorks 195 F5
Newland Oxon 133 F1
Newland Worcs 145 G3
Newlandrig 236 A3
Newlands Cumb 209 G3
Newlands Essex 138 B4
Newlands N'umb 211 G2
Newlands ScBord 218 D2
Newland's Corner 121 F3
Newlands of Geise 275 F2
Newlands of Tynet 268 B4
Newlyn 94 B4
Newmachar 261 G3
Newmains 234 C4
Newman's End 137 E1
Newman's Green 151 G3
Newmarket Suff 151 E1
Newmarket Na H-E. Siar 271 G4
Newmill Aber 253 F1
Newmill Aber 269 G6
Newmill Aber 261 G2
Newmill Moray 268 C5
Newmill ScBord 227 F4
Newmill of Inshewan 252 C3
Newmillerdam 186 A1
Newmillerdam Country Park WYorks WF2 6QP 27 H6
Newmills 266 D5
Newmiln P&K 243 G1
Newmiln P&K 243 F2
Newmilns 224 D2
Newney Green 137 F2
Newnham Glos 131 F1
Newnham Hants 120 C2
Newnham Herts 150 A4
Newnham Kent 124 B3
Newnham N'hants 148 A2
Newnham Bridge 145 F1
Newnham Paddox 159 G4
Newnoth 260 D1
Newport Corn 98 D2
Newport Devon 113 F2
Newport ERid 196 A4
Newport Essex 150 D4
Newport Glos 131 F3
Newport High 275 G6
Newport IoW 107 E4
Newport (Casnewydd) Newport 130 C4
Newport Norf 179 G4
Newport (Trefdraeth) Pembs 141 D4
Newport Som 116 A5
Newport Tel&W 157 G1
Newport Pagnell 149 D3
Newport-on-Tay 244 C2
Newpound Common 121 F5
Newquay 96 C3
Newquay Cornwall International Airport 96 C3
Newquay Zoo Corn TR7 2LZ 96 C3
Newsbank 171 F1
Newseat 261 F1
Newsells 150 B4
Newsham Lancs 192 B4
Newsham N'umb 221 E4
Newsham NYorks 202 A1
Newsham NYorks 202 C4
Newsholme ERid 195 G5
Newsholme Lancs 193 E2
Newsome 185 F1
Newstead N'umb 229 F4
Newstead Notts 173 G2
Newstead ScBord 227 G2
Newstead Abbey Notts NG15 8NA 173 G2
Newthorpe Notts 173 F3
Newthorpe NYorks 195 D4
Newtoft 188 A4
Newton A&B 240 C5
Newton Aber 268 C6
Newton Aber 269 J6
Newton Bridgend 129 E5
Newton Cambs 162 C1
Newton Cambs 150 C3
Newton Cardiff 130 B5
Newton ChesW&C 170 C2
Newton ChesW&C 183 G5
Newton Cumb 198 D5
Newton D&G 217 F1
Newton Derbys 173 F2
Newton GtMan 185 D3
Newton Here 144 C1
Newton Here 145 E2
Newton Here 144 C4
Newton High 275 J3
Newton High 266 E7
Newton High 275 H5
Newton High 272 E5
Newton High 266 C6
Newton High 266 E5
Newton Lancs 192 C2
Newton Lancs 199 G5
Newton Lancs 191 G4
Newton Lincs 175 F4
Newton Moray 268 B4
Newton N'hants 161 D4
Newton N'umb 211 G1
Newton N'umb 220 B1
Newton NAyr 232 A4
Newton Norf 163 G1
Newton Notts 174 B3
Newton P&K 243 D1
Newton Pembs 140 B5
Newton Pembs 126 C2
Newton ScBord 228 A4
Newton SGlos 131 F3
Newton Shrop 170 B4
Newton SLan 226 A2
Newton Som 115 E4
Newton Staffs 172 B5
Newton Suff 152 A3
Newton Swan 128 C4
Newton Warks 160 A5
Newton Wilts 118 D5
Newton WLoth 235 E2
Newton WYorks 194 D5
Newton Abbot 102 B5
Newton Arlosh 209 F1
Newton Aycliffe 212 B5
Newton Bewley 213 D5
Newton Blossomville 149 E2
Newton Bromswold 149 E1
Newton Burgoland 159 F2
Newton by Toft 188 A4
Newton Ferrers 100 B3
Newton Flotman 164 D2
Newton Green 131 E3
Newton Harcourt 160 B3
Newton Kyme 195 D3
Newton Longville 148 D4
Newton Mearns 233 G4
Newton Morrell NYorks 202 B2
Newton Morrell Oxon 148 B5
Newton Mountain 126 C2
Newton Mulgrave 203 G1
Newton of Affleck 244 C1
Newton of Ardtoe 247 F2
Newton of Balcanquhal 243 G3
Newton of Dalvey 267 H6
Newton of Falkland 244 A4
Newton of Leys 258 D1
Newton on the Hill 170 B5
Newton on Trent 187 F5
Newton Poppleford 103 D4
Newton Purcell 148 B4
Newton Regis 159 E2
Newton Reigny 210 A4
Newton St. Cyres 102 B3
Newton St. Faith 178 D4
Newton St. Loe 117 E1
Newton St. Petrock 113 E4
Newton Solney 173 D5
Newton Stacey 119 F3
Newton Stewart 215 F4
Newton Tony 118 D3
Newton Tracey 113 F3
Newton under Roseberry 203 E1
Newton Underwood 221 D3
Newton upon Derwent 195 G3
Newton Valence 120 C4
Newton with Scales 192 A4
Newtonairds 216 C2
Newtongrange 236 A3
Newtonhill 261 H5
Newton-le-Willows Mersey 183 G3
Newton-le-Willows NYorks 202 B4
Newtonmill 253 E3
Newtonmore (Baile Ùr an t-Slèibh) 258 E5
Newton-on-Ouse 195 E2
Newton-on-Rawcliffe 204 B3
Newton-on-the-Moor 221 D1
Newtown Bucks 135 E2
Newtown ChesW&C 170 C2
Newtown Corn 97 G2
Newtown Corn 94 C4
Newtown Cumb 210 B1
Newtown Derbys 185 D4
Newtown Devon 114 A5
Newtown Devon 103 D3
Newtown Dorset 104 A2
Newtown Glos 131 F2
Newtown GtMan 183 G2
Newtown GtMan 184 B2
Newtown Hants 107 F1
Newtown Hants 119 F1
Newtown Hants 106 B1
Newtown Hants 119 E5
Newtown Hants 107 E1
Newtown Here 145 F3
Newtown Here 145 D2
Newtown High 257 K4
Newtown IoM 190 B4
Newtown IoW 106 D3
Newtown N'umb 220 C1
Newtown N'umb 229 E4
Newtown Oxon 134 C4
Newtown (Y Drenewydd) Powys 156 A3
Newtown RCT 129 G3
Newtown Shrop 170 B4
Newtown Som 115 F4
Newtown Som 103 F1
Newtown Staffs 171 G1
Newtown Staffs 172 B1
Newtown Staffs 158 B2
Newtown Wilts 118 A5
Newtown Wilts 119 E1
Newtown Linford 160 A2
Newtown St. Boswells 227 G2
Newtown Unthank 159 G2
Newtown-in-Saint-Martin 95 E4
Newtyle 252 A5
Newyears Green 135 F4
Neyland 126 C2
Nibley Glos 131 F2
Nibley SGlos 131 F4
Nibley Green 131 G3
Nicholashayne 103 E1
Nicholaston 128 B4
Nidd 194 C1
Nigg Aberdeen 261 H4
Nigg High 267 F4
Nightcott 114 B5
Nilig 168 D2
Nilston Rigg 211 E1
Nimlet 131 G5
Nine Ashes 137 E2
Nine Elms 132 D4
Nine Mile Burn 235 F4
Ninebanks 211 D2
Ninemile Bar (Crocketford) 216 C3
Nineveh 145 F1
Ninfield 110 C2
Ningwood 106 D4
Nisbet 228 A4
Niton 107 E5
Nitshill 233 G3
Nizels 123 E3
No Man's Heath ChesW&C 170 C3
No Man's Heath Warks 159 E2
No Man's Land 97 G4
Noah's Ark 123 E3
Noak Hill 137 E3
Noblehill 217 D3
Noblethorpe 185 G2
Nobottle 148 B1
Nocton 175 F1
Noddsdale 232 D3
Nogdam End 179 E5
Noke 134 A1
Nolton 126 B1
Nolton Haven 126 B1
Nomansland Devon 102 B1
Nomansland Wilts 106 B1
Noneley 170 B5
Nonington 125 E3
Nook Cumb 218 C4
Nook Cumb 199 G4
Noonsbrough 279 B7
Noranside 252 C3
Norbreck 191 G3
Norbury ChesE 170 C3
Norbury Derbys 172 C3
Norbury GtLon 136 C5
Norbury Shrop 156 C3
Norbury Staffs 171 E5
Norbury Common 170 C3
Norbury Junction 171 E5
Norchard 127 D3
Norcott Brook 184 A4
Nordelph 163 D2
Norden Dorset 105 F4
Norden GtMan 184 C1
Nordley 157 F3
Norfolk Lavender, Heacham Norf PE31 7JE 177 E4
Norham 237 G5
Norland Town 193 G5
Norley 183 G5
Norleywood 106 C3
Norlington 109 G2
Norman Cross 161 G3
Normanby NLincs 187 F1
Normanby NYorks 203 G4
Normanby R&C 203 E1
Normanby by Stow 187 F4
Normanby Hall Country Park NLincs DN15 9HU 187 F1
Normanby le Wold 188 B3
Normanby-by-Spital 188 A4
Normandy 121 E2
Normann's Ruh 246 D5
Norman's Bay 110 B3
Norman's Green 103 D2
Normanston 165 G2
Normanton Derby 173 E4
Normanton Leics 174 D3
Normanton Lincs 175 E3
Normanton Notts 174 C2
Normanton Rut 161 E2
Normanton WYorks 194 C5
Normanton le Heath 159 F1
Normanton on Soar 173 G5
Normanton on Trent 174 C1
Normanton-on-the-Wolds 174 B4
Normoss 191 G4
Norrington Common 117 F1
Norris Green 100 A1
Norris Hill 159 F1
Norristhorpe 194 B5
North Acton 136 B4
North Anston 186 C4
North Ascot 121 E1
North Aston 147 G5
North Baddesley 106 C1
North Ballachulish (Baile a' Chaolais a Tuath) 248 C3
North Balloch 215 E1
North Barrow 116 D5
North Barsham 178 A2
North Bay Miniature Railway NYorks YO12 6PF 204 D3
North Benfleet 137 G4
North Bersted 108 B3
North Berwick 236 C1
North Boarhunt 107 F1
North Bogbain 268 B5
North Bovey 102 A4
North Bradley 117 F2
North Brentor 99 E2
North Brewham 117 E4
North Bridge 121 E4
North Buckland 113 E1
North Burlingham 179 E4
North Cadbury 116 D5
North Cairn 214 A3
North Camp 121 D2
North Carlton Lincs 187 G5
North Carlton Notts 186 C4
North Cave 196 A4
North Cerney 132 C2
North Chailey 109 F1
North Charford 106 A1
North Charlton 229 F4
North Cheriton 117 D5
North Chideock 104 A3
North Cliffe 196 A4
North Clifton 187 F5
North Cockerington 189 D3
North Coker 104 B1
North Collafirth 278 C4
North Common SGlos 131 F5
North Common Suff 164 A4
North Commonty 269 G6
North Connel 240 B1
North Coombe 102 B2
North Cornelly 129 E4
North Corner 131 F4
North Cotes 188 D2
North Cove 165 F3
North Cowton 202 B2
North Crawley 149 E3
North Cray 137 D5
North Creake 177 G4
North Curry 116 A5
North Dallens 248 B5
North Dalton 196 B2
North Dawn 277 D7
North Deighton 194 C2
North Dell (Dail Bho Thuath) 271 G1
North Duffield 195 F4
North Elkington 188 C3
North Elmham 178 A3
North Elmsall 186 B1
North End Bucks 148 D5
North End Dorset 117 F5
North End ERid 197 D2
North End ERid 197 D3
North End ERid 197 E4
North End Essex 137 F1
North End Hants 119 G5
North End Hants 106 A1
North End Leics 160 A1
North End N'umb 220 D1
North End Norf 164 B2
North End NSom 116 B1
North End Ports 107 F2
North End WSuss 108 D2
North End WSuss 108 B3
North Erradale 264 D3
North Essie 269 J5
North Fambridge 138 B3
North Ferriby 196 B5
North Frodingham 196 D2
North Gluss 278 C5
North Gorley 106 A1
North Green Norf 164 D3
North Green Suff 165 E4
North Green Suff 153 E1
North Green Suff 153 E1
North Grimston 196 A1
North Halling 123 G2
North Harby 187 F5
North Hayling 107 G2
North Hazelrigg 229 E3
North Heasley 114 A4
North Heath WBerks 133 G5
North Heath WSuss 121 F5
North Hill 97 G2
North Hillingdon 135 F4
North Hinksey 133 G2
North Holmwood 121 G3
North Houghton 119 E4
North Huish 100 D2
North Hykeham 175 E1
North Johnston 126 C1
North Kelsey 188 A2
North Kessock 266 D7
North Killingholme 188 B1
North Kilvington 202 D4
North Kilworth 160 B4
North Kingston 106 A2
North Kyme 175 G2
North Lancing 109 D3
North Lee 134 D2
North Lees 202 C5
North Leigh 133 F1
North Leverton with Habblesthorpe 187 E4
North Littleton 146 C3
North Lopham 164 B3
North Luffenham 161 E2
North Marden 108 A2
North Marston 148 C5
North Middleton Midlo 236 A4
North Middleton N'umb 229 E4
North Millbrex 269 G6
North Molton 114 A5
North Moreton 134 A4
North Mundham 108 A3
North Muskham 174 C2
North Newbald 196 B4
North Newington 147 G4
North Newnton 118 C2
North Newton 115 F4
North Nibley 131 G3
North Norfolk Railway Norf NR26 8RA 178 C1
North Oakley 119 G2
North Ockendon 137 E4
North Ormesby 203 E1
North Ormsby 188 C3
North Otterington 202 C4
North Owersby 188 A3
North Perrott 104 A2
North Petherton 115 F4
North Petherwin 97 G1
North Pickenham 163 G2
North Piddle 146 B2
North Plain 217 F4
North Pool 101 D3
North Poorton 104 B3
North Quarme 114 C4
North Queensferry 235 F1
North Radworthy 114 A4
North Rauceby 175 F3
North Reston 189 D4
North Riding Forest Park NYorks YO18 7LT 204 B3
North Rigton 194 B3
North Rode 171 F1
North Roe 278 C4
North Ronaldsay 276 G2
North Ronaldsay Airfield 276 G2
North Runcton 163 E1
North Sandwick 278 E3
North Scale 191 E1
North Scarle 175 D1
North Seaton 221 E3
North Shian (Sithean a Tuath) 248 B5
North Shields 212 C1
North Shoebury 138 C4
North Side 162 A3
North Skelton 203 F1
North Somercotes 189 E3
North Stainley 202 B5
North Stainmore 200 D1
North Stifford 137 F4
North Stoke B&NESom 117 E1
North Stoke Oxon 134 B4
North Stoke WSuss 108 C2
North Stoneham 106 D1
North Street Hants 120 B4
North Street Kent 124 C3
North Street Med 124 A1
North Street WBerks 134 B5
North Sunderland 229 G3
North Tamerton 98 D1
North Tarbothill 261 H3
North Tawton 113 G5
North Third 234 B1
North Thoresby 188 C3
North Tidworth 118 D3
North Togston 221 E1
North Town Devon 113 F5
North Town Hants 121 D2
North Town W&M 135 D4
North Tuddenham 178 B4
North Uist (Uibhist a Tuath) 262 D4
North Walsham 179 D2
North Waltham 119 G3
North Warnborough 120 C2
North Water Bridge 253 E3
North Watten 275 H3
North Weald Bassett 137 D2
North Wembley 136 A4
North Wheatley 187 E4
North Whilborough 101 E1
North Wick 116 C1
North Widcombe 116 C2
North Willingham 188 B4
North Wingfield 173 F1
North Witham 175 E5
North Wootton Dorset 104 C1
North Wootton Norf 177 E5
North Wootton Som 116 C3
North Wraxall 132 A5
North Wroughton 132 D4
North Yardhope 220 B1
North Yorkshire Moors Railway NYorks YO18 7AJ 204 B4
Northacre 164 A2
Northall 149 E5
Northall Green 178 A4
Northallerton 202 C3
Northam Devon 113 E3
Northam Soton 106 D1
Northam Burrows Country Park Devon EX39 1XR 113 E2
Northampton 148 C1
Northaw 136 B2
Northay Devon 103 G2
Northay Som 103 F1
Northbay 254 C4
Northbeck 175 F3
Northborough 161 G2
Northbourne Kent 125 F3
Northbourne Oxon 134 A4
Northbridge Street 110 C1
Northbrook Hants 119 G4
Northbrook Oxon 147 G5
Northburnhill 269 G6
Northchapel 121 E5
Northchurch 135 E2
Northcote Manor 113 G4
Northcott 98 D1
Northcourt 134 A3
Northdyke 276 B5
Northedge 173 E1
Northend B&NESom 117 E1
Northend Bucks 134 C3
Northend Warks 147 F2
Northfield Aber 269 G4
Northfield Aberdeen 261 H4
Northfield High 275 J4

Northfield Hull 196 C5
Northfield ScBord 237 G3
Northfield Som 115 F4
Northfield WMid 158 C5
Northfields 161 F2
Northfleet 137 F5
Northhouse 227 F5
Northiam 110 D1
Northill 149 G3
Northington Glos 131 G2
Northington
   Hants 119 G4
Northlands 176 B2
Northleach 132 D1
Northleigh Devon 103 E3
Northleigh Devon 113 G2
Northlew 99 F1
Northmoor 133 G2
Northmoor Green
   (Moorland) 116 A4
Northmuir 252 B4
Northney 107 G2
Northolt 136 A4
Northop
   (Llaneurgain) 169 F1
Northop Hall 169 F1
Northorpe Lincs 176 A4
Northorpe Lincs 187 F3
Northorpe Lincs 161 F1
Northover Som 116 B4
Northover Som 116 B4
Northowram 194 A5
Northport 105 F4
Northpunds 279 D10
Northrepps 178 D2
Northton
   (Taobh Tuath) 262 E3
Northtown 277 D8
Northumberland Dark Sky
   Park N'umb 219 F4
Northumbria Craft Centre,
   Morpeth N'umb
   NE61 1PD 221 E3
Northway Glos 146 B4
Northway Som 115 E5
Northwich 184 A5
Northwick SGlos 131 E4
Northwick Worcs 146 A2
Northwold 163 F3
Northwood GtLon 135 F3
Northwood IoW 107 D3
Northwood Kent 125 F2
Northwood Mersey 183 F3
Northwood Shrop 170 B4
Northwood Green 131 G1
Northwood Hills 136 A3
Norton Glos 146 A5
Norton Halton 183 G4
Norton Herts 150 A4
Norton IoW 106 C4
Norton Mon 144 D5
Norton N'hants 148 B1
Norton Notts 186 C5
Norton NSom 116 B1
Norton NYorks 203 G5
Norton Powys 144 C1
Norton Shrop 157 E2
Norton Shrop 157 G2
Norton Shrop 157 D4
Norton Stock 212 D5
Norton Suff 152 A1
Norton Swan 128 C4
Norton SYorks 186 C1
Norton SYorks 186 A5
Norton VGlam 129 E5
Norton Wilts 132 B4
Norton WMid 158 A4
Norton Worcs 146 A2
Norton Worcs 146 C3
Norton WSuss 108 B3
Norton WSuss 108 A4
Norton Bavant 118 A3
Norton Bridge 171 F4
Norton Canes 158 C2
Norton Canon 144 C3
Norton Disney 175 D2
Norton Ferris 117 E4
Norton Fitzwarren 115 E5
Norton Green
   Herts 150 A5
Norton Green IoW 106 C4
Norton Green
   Stoke 171 G2
Norton Hawkfield 116 C1
Norton Heath 137 F2
Norton in Hales 171 E4
Norton in the
   Moors 171 F2
Norton Lindsey 147 E1
Norton Little Green 152 A1
Norton Malreward 116 D1
Norton Mandeville 137 F2
Norton St. Philip 117 E2
Norton Subcourse 165 F2
Norton Wood 144 C3
Norton Woodseats 186 A4
Norton-Juxta-
   Twycross 159 F2
Norton-le-Clay 202 D5
Norton-sub-
   Hamdon 104 A1
Norwell 174 C1
Norwell Woodhouse 174 C1
Norwich 178 D5
Norwich Castle Museum &
   Art Gallery Norf
   NR1 3JU 79 Norwich
Norwich Cathedral Norf
   NR1 4DH 79 Norwich
Norwich International
   Airport 178 D4
Norwick 278 F1
Norwood End 137 E2
Norwood Green
   GtLon 136 A5
Norwood Green
   WYorks 194 A5
Norwood Hill 122 B4
Norwood Park 116 C4
Noseley 160 C3
Noss Mayo 100 B3
Nosterfield 202 B4
Nosterfield End 151 E3
Noste 256 E2
Notgrove 146 D5
Nottage 129 E5
Notting Hill 136 B4

Nottingham High 275 H5
Nottingham Nott 173 G3
Nottingham Castle Museum
   & Art Gallery NG1 6EL
   80 Nottingham
Nottington 104 C3
Notton Wilts 118 A1
Notton WYorks 186 A1
Nottswood Hill 131 G1
Nounsley 137 G1
Noutard's Green 145 G1
Nowton 151 G1
Nowton Park Suff
   IP29 5LU 151 G1
Nox 156 D1
Noyadd Trefawr 141 F3
Nuffield 134 B4
Nun Monkton 195 E2
Nunburnholme 196 A3
Nuneaton 159 F3
Nuneham
   Courtenay 134 A3
Nunney 117 E3
Nunnington Here 145 E3
Nunnington
   NYorks 203 F5
Nunnington Park 115 D5
Nunnykirk 220 C2
Nunsthorpe 188 C2
Nunthorpe Middl 203 E1
Nunthorpe York 195 E2
Nunton 118 C5
Nunwick N'umb 220 A4
Nunwick NYorks 202 C5
Nup End 136 B1
Nupend 131 G2
Nursling 106 C1
Nursted 120 C5
Nurton 158 A3
Nuthampstead 150 C4
Nuthurst Warks 159 D5
Nuthurst WSuss 121 G5
Nutley ESuss 109 G1
Nutley Hants 120 B3
Nutwell 186 D2
Nyadd 242 C5
Nybster 275 J2
Nyetimber 108 A4
Nyewood 120 C5
Nymans WSuss
   RH17 6EB 109 E1
Nymet Rowland 102 A2
Nymet Tracey 102 A2
Nympsfield 132 A2
Nynehead 115 E5
Nythe 116 B4
Nyton 108 B3

O
O2, The GtLon
   SE10 0BB 13 E5
Oad Street 124 A2
Oadby 160 B2
Oak Cross 99 F1
Oak Tree 202 C1
Oakamoor 172 B3
Oakbank A&B 239 G1
Oakbank WLoth 235 E3
Oakdale Caerp 130 A3
Oakdale Poole 105 G3
Oake 115 E5
Oaken 158 A2
Oakenclough 192 B3
Oakengates 157 G1
Oakenhead 267 K5
Oakenholt 183 D5
Oakenshaw Dur 212 B4
Oakenshaw
   WYorks 194 A5
Oakerthorpe 173 E2
Oakes 185 F1
Oakfield IoW 107 E3
Oakford Cere 142 A2
Oakford Devon 114 C5
Oakfordbridge 114 C5
Oakgrove 171 G2
Oakham 161 D2
Oakhanger 120 C4
Oakhill 116 D3
Oakington 150 C1
Oaklands Conwy 168 B2
Oaklands Herts 136 B1
Oakle Street 131 G1
Oakley Bed 149 F2
Oakley Bucks 134 B1
Oakley Fife 235 E1
Oakley Hants 119 G3
Oakley Oxon 134 C2
Oakley Poole 105 G3
Oakley Suff 164 C4
Oakley Green 135 E5
Oakley Park 155 F4
Oakridge Lynch 132 B2
Oaks 156 D2
Oaks Green 172 C4
Oaksey 132 B3
Oakshaw Ford 218 D4
Oakshott 120 C5
Oakthorpe 159 F1
Oaktree Hill 202 C3
Oakwell Hall & Country Park
   WYorks
   WF17 9LG 27 E4
Oakwood Leisure Park
   Pembs
   SA67 8DE 127 D1
Oakwoodhill 121 G4
Oakworth 193 G4
Oare Kent 124 C2
Oare Som 114 B3
Oare Wilts 118 C1
Oasby 175 F4
Oatfield 222 B4
Oath 116 A5
Oathlaw 252 C4
Oatlands 194 C2
Oban
   (An t-Òban) 240 A2
Obley 156 C5
Oborne 104 C1
Obthorpe 161 F1
Occlestone Green 171 D1
Occold 164 C4

Occumster 275 H5
Oceanarium BH2 5AA
   64 Bournemouth
Ochiltree 224 D3
Ochr-y-foel 182 B5
Ochtermuthill 242 D3
Ochtertyre P&K 242 D2
Ochtertyre Stir 242 C5
Ockbrook 173 F4
Ockeridge 145 G1
Ockham 121 F2
Ockle 247 E2
Ockley 121 G4
Ocle Pychard 145 E3
Octon 204 D5
Odcombe 104 B1
Odd Down 117 E1
Oddendale 200 B1
Oddingley 146 B2
Oddington 134 A1
Odds Farm Park Bucks
   HP10 0LX 135 E4
Oddsta 278 E3
Odell 149 E2
Odie 276 F5
Odiham 120 C2
Odsey 150 A4
Odstock 118 C5
Odstone 159 F2
Offchurch 147 F1
Offenham 146 C3
Offerton 184 C2
Offham ESuss 109 F2
Offham Kent 123 F3
Offham WSuss 108 C3
Offley Hoo 149 G5
Offleymarsh 171 E5
Offord Cluny 150 A1
Offord D'Arcy 150 A1
Offton 152 B3
Offwell 103 E3
Ogbourne Maizey 133 D5
Ogbourne
   St. Andrew 133 D5
Ogbourne
   St. George 133 D5
Ogden Water WYorks
   HX2 8YA 26 A3
Ogil 252 C3
Ogle 220 D4
Oglet 183 F4
Ogmore 129 E5
Ogmore Vale 129 F3
Ogmore-by-Sea 129 E5
Ogston Reservoir Derbys
   DE55 6EL 173 E1
Oil Terminal 277 C8
Okeford Fitzpaine 105 E1
Okehampton 99 F1
Okehampton Camp 99 F1
Okraquoy 279 D9
Olchard 102 B5
Olchfa 128 C3
Old 160 C5
Old Aberdeen 261 H4
Old Alresford 119 G4
Old Arley 159 E3
Old Basford 173 G3
Old Basing 120 B2
Old Belses 227 G3
Old Bewick 229 E4
Old Bolingbroke 176 B1
Old Bramhope 194 B3
Old Brampton 186 A5
Old Bridge of Urr 216 B4
Old Buckenham 164 B2
Old Burdon 212 C2
Old Burghclere 119 F2
Old Byland 203 E4
Old Cassop 212 C4
Old Church Stoke 156 B3
Old Cleeve 114 D3
Old Clipstone 174 B4
Old Colwyn 181 G5
Old Craig 261 H2
Old Craighall 236 A2
Old Crombie 268 D5
Old Dailly 214 D1
Old Dalby 174 B5
Old Dam 185 F5
Old Deer 269 H6
Old Dilton 117 F3
Old Down SGlos 131 F4
Old Down Som 116 D2
Old Edlington 186 C3
Old Eldon 212 B5
Old Ellerby 197 D4
Old Felixstowe 153 E4
Old Fletton 161 G3
Old Ford 136 C4
Old Glossop 185 E3
Old Goginan 154 C4
Old Goole 195 G5
Old Gore 145 F5
Old Grimsby 96 A1
Old Hall 188 C1
Old Hall Green 150 B5
Old Hall Street 179 E2
Old Harlow 137 D1
Old Heath 152 B5
Old Heathfield 110 A1
Old Hill 158 B4
Old Hurst 162 B5
Old Hutton 199 G4
Old Kea 96 C5
Old Kilpatrick 233 F2
Old Kinnernie 261 F4
Old Knebworth 150 A5
Old Leake 176 C1
Old Leslie 260 D2
Old Malton 204 B5
Old Milton 106 B3
Old Milverton 147 E1
Old Montsale 138 D3
Old Netley 107 D1
Old Newton 152 B1
Old Philpstoun 235 E2
Old Poltalloch 240 A4
Old Radnor
   (Pencraig) 144 B2
Old Rattray 269 J5
Old Rayne 260 E2
Old Romney 111 F1

Old Royal Naval College,
   Greenwich GtLon
   SE10 9LW 13 D5
Old Scone 243 G2
Old Shields 234 C2
Old Sodbury 131 G4
Old Somerby 175 E4
Old Station, The, Tintern
   Parva Mon
   NP16 7NX 131 E2
Old Stratford 148 C3
Old Sunderlandwick 196 C2
Old Swarland 221 D1
Old Swinford 158 B4
Old Thirsk 202 D4
Old Town Cumb 199 G4
Old Town IoS 96 B1
Old Town Farm 220 A2
Old Tupton 173 E1
Old Warden 149 G3
Old Weston 161 F5
Old Windsor 135 E5
Old Wives Lees 124 C3
Old Woking 121 F2
Old Woodhall 176 A1
Old Woods 170 B5
Oldberrow 146 D1
Oldborough 102 A2
Oldbury Kent 123 E3
Oldbury Shrop 157 G3
Oldbury Warks 159 F3
Oldbury WMid 158 B4
Oldbury Court Estate
   Bristol BS16 2JH 8 D2
Oldbury Naite 131 F3
Oldbury on the Hill 132 A4
Oldbury-on-Severn 131 F3
Oldcastle Bridgend 129 F5
Oldcastle Mon 144 C5
Oldcastle Heath 170 B3
Oldcotes 186 C4
Oldcroft 131 F2
Oldeamere 162 B3
Oldfield 146 A1
Oldford 117 E2
Oldhall Aber 260 C5
Oldham High 275 H3
Oldham 184 D2
Oldham Edge 184 D2
Oldhamstocks 237 E2
Oldland 131 F5
Oldmeldrum 261 G2
Oldmill 260 D4
Oldpark 157 F2
Oldridge 102 B3
Oldshore Beg 272 D3
Oldshoremore 272 E3
Oldstead 203 E5
Oldtown 266 C3
Oldtown of Aigas 266 B7
Oldtown of Ord 268 E5
Oldwalls 128 A3
Oldways End 114 B5
Oldwhat 269 G5
Oldwich Lane 159 E5
Olgrinmore 275 G3
Oliver 226 B2
Oliver's Battery 119 F5
Ollaberry 278 C4
Ollerton ChesE 184 B5
Ollerton Notts 174 B1
Ollerton Shrop 170 D5
Olmstead Green 151 E3
Olney 149 D2
Olrig House 275 G2
Olton 158 D4
Olveston 131 F4
Olympia GtLon
   W14 8UX 11 A6
Ombersley 146 A1
Ompton 174 B1
Onchan 190 B4
Onecote 172 B2
Onehouse 152 B2
Ongar Hill 177 D5
Ongar Street 144 C1
Onibury 157 D5
Onich
   (Omhanaich) 248 C3
Onllwyn 129 E1
Onneley 171 E3
Onslow Green 137 F1
Onslow Village 121 E3
Opinan High 264 E2
Opinan High 264 D4
Orange Lane 237 E5
Orasaigh 271 F6
Orbliston 268 B5
Orbost 263 H7
Orby 176 C1
Orcadia 232 C3
Orchard 232 C1
Orchard Portman 115 F5
Orcheston 118 B3
Orcop 145 D5
Orcop Hill 145 D5
Ord 256 C3
Ordhead 260 E3
Ordie 260 C4
Ordiequish 268 B5
Ordsall 187 D5
Ore 110 D2
Oreham Common 109 E2
Oreston 100 B2
Oreton 157 F5
Orford Suff 153 F3
Orford Warr 184 A3
Organford 105 F3
Orgreave 158 D1
Orkney Islands 276 C5
Orleton Here 145 D1
Orleton Worcs 145 F1
Orleton Common 145 D1
Orlingbury 161 D5
Ormacleit 254 C1
Ormesby 203 E1
Ormesby
   St. Margaret 179 F4
Ormesby
   St. Michael 179 F4
Ormidale 232 B1
Ormiscaig 264 E2
Ormiston 236 B3
Ormlie 275 G2
Ormsaigmore 247 D3
Ormsary 231 F2
Ormskirk 183 F2

Oronsay 230 B1
Orphir 277 C7
Orpington 123 D2
Orrell GtMan 183 G2
Orrell Mersey 183 E3
Orrisdale 190 B2
Orrok House 261 H3
Orroland 208 A2
Orsett 137 F4
Orsett Heath 137 F4
Orslow 158 A1
Orston 174 C3
Orton Cumb 200 B2
Orton N'hants 160 D5
Orton Longueville 161 G3
Orton Rigg 209 G1
Orton Waterville 161 G3
Orton-on-the-Hill 159 F2
Orwell 150 B2
Osbaldeston 192 C4
Osbaldwick 195 F2
Osbaston Leics 159 G2
Osbaston Shrop 170 A5
Osbaston Tel&W 157 F1
Osbaston Hollow 159 G2
Osborne 107 E3
Osborne House IoW
   PO32 6JX 107 E3
Osbournby 175 F4
Oscroft 170 C1
Ose 263 J7
Osgathorpe 159 G1
Osgodby Lincs 188 A3
Osgodby NYorks 195 F4
Osgodby NYorks 205 D4
Oskaig 256 B1
Osleston 172 D4
Osmaston Derby 173 E4
Osmaston Derbys 172 C3
Osmington 104 D4
Osmington Mills 104 D4
Osmondthorpe 194 C4
Osmotherley 203 D3
Osnaburgh (Dairsie) 244 C3
Ospringe 124 C2
Ossett 194 B5
Ossett Street Side 194 B5
Ossington 174 C1
Ostend 138 C3
Osterley 135 G5
Osterley Park & House
   GtLon TW7 4RB 11 B5
Oswaldkirk 203 F5
Oswaldtwistle 192 D5
Oswestry 169 F5
Oteley 170 B4
Otford 123 E3
Otham 123 G3
Otherton 158 B1
Othery 116 A4
Otley Suff 152 D2
Otley WYorks 194 B3
Otter 232 A1
Otter Ferry 232 A1
Otterbourne 119 F5
Otterburn N'umb 220 A2
Otterburn NYorks 193 F2
Otterburn Camp 220 A2
Otterden Place 124 B3
Otterham 98 B1
Otterham Quay 124 A2
Otterhampton 115 F3
Otternish 262 E4
Ottershaw 121 F1
Otterswick 278 E4
Otterton 103 E4
Otterwood 107 D2
Ottery St. Mary 103 D3
Ottinge 125 D4
Ottringham 197 E5
Oughterby 209 F1
Oughtershaw 201 D4
Oughterside 209 E2
Oughtibridge 186 A3
Oulston 203 E5
Oulton Cumb 209 F1
Oulton Norf 178 C3
Oulton Staffs 171 G4
Oulton Staffs 171 E5
Oulton Suff 165 G2
Oulton WYorks 194 C4
Oulton Broad 165 G2
Oulton Grange 171 G4
Oulton Street 178 C3
Oultoncross 171 G4
Oundle 161 F4
Our Dynamic Earth Edin
   EH8 8AS 37 J4
Ousby 210 C4
Ousdale 275 F6
Ousden 151 F2
Ousefleet 196 A5
Ouston Dur 212 B2
Ouston N'umb 220 C4
Out Newton 197 F5
Out Rawcliffe 192 A3
Out Skerries
   Airstrip 278 F5
Outcast 199 E5
Outchester 229 F3
Outertown 277 B7
Outgate 199 E3
Outhgill 200 C2
Outlands 171 E5
Outlane 185 E1
Outwell 162 D2
Outwood Surr 122 C4
Outwood WYorks 194 C5
Outwoods 157 G1
Ouzlewell Green 194 C5
Ovenden 193 G5
Over Cambs 162 B5
Over ChesW&C 170 D1
Over Glos 132 A1
Over SGlos 131 E4
Over Burrows 173 D4
Over Compton 104 B1
Over Dinsdale 202 C1
Over End 185 G5
Over Green 159 D3
Over Haddon 172 D1
Over Hulton 184 A2
Over Kellet 192 B1
Over Kiddington 147 G5
Over Monnow 131 D1
Over Norton 147 F5

Over Peover 184 B5
Over Rankeilour 244 B3
Over Silton 203 D3
Over Stowey 115 E4
Over Stratton 104 A1
Over Tabley 184 B4
Over Wallop 119 D3
Over Whitacre 159 E3
Over Winchendon (Upper
   Winchendon) 134 C1
Over Worton 147 G5
Overbister 276 F3
Overbrae 269 G5
Overbury 146 B4
Overcombe 104 C4
Overgreen 186 A5
Overleigh 116 B4
Overpool 183 E5
Overscaig Hotel 273 G6
Overseal 159 E1
Overslade 159 G5
Oversland 124 C3
Oversley Green 146 C2
Overstone 148 D1
Overstrand 178 D1
Overthorpe 147 G3
Overton Aber 261 F3
Overton Aberdeen 261 G3
Overton
   ChesW&C 183 G5
Overton Hants 119 G3
Overton Lancs 192 A2
Overton NYorks 195 E2
Overton Shrop 157 E5
Overton Swan 128 A4
Overton (Owrtyn)
   Wrex 170 A3
Overton WYorks 185 G1
Overton Bridge 170 A3
Overtown Lancs 200 B5
Overtown NLan 234 C4
Overtown Swin 133 D5
Overy 134 A3
Oving Bucks 148 C5
Oving WSuss 108 B3
Ovingdean 109 F3
Ovingham 211 G1
Ovington Dur 202 A1
Ovington Essex 151 F3
Ovington Hants 119 G4
Ovington N'umb 211 G1
Ovington Norf 178 A5
Ower Hants 106 C1
Ower Hants 107 D2
Owermoigne 105 D4
Owler Bar 185 G5
Owlpen 131 G3
Owl's Green 153 D1
Owlswick 134 C2
Owmby 188 C2
Owmby-by-Spital 188 A4
Owrslebury 119 G5
Owston 160 C2
Owston Ferry 187 F2
Owstwick 197 E4
Owthorne 197 F5
Owthorpe 174 B4
Oxborough 163 F2
Oxcombe 188 D5
Oxen End 151 E5
Oxen Park 199 E4
Oxencombe 102 B4
Oxenhall 145 G5
Oxenholme 199 G3
Oxenhope 193 G4
Oxenpill 116 B3
Oxenton 146 B4
Oxenwood 119 E2
Oxford 134 A2
Oxford Cathedral Oxon
   OX1 1AB 80 Oxford
Oxford Story Oxon
   OX1 3AJ 80 Oxford
Oxford University Museum
   of Natural History
   Oxon OX1 3PW
   80 Oxford
Oxhey 136 A3
Oxhill 147 F3
Oxley 158 B2
Oxley Green 138 C1
Oxley's Green 110 B1
Oxnam 228 B5
Oxnead 178 D4
Oxnop Ghyll 201 E3
Oxshott 121 G1
Oxspring 185 G2
Oxted 122 C3
Oxton Mersey 183 E4
Oxton Notts 174 B2
Oxton ScBord 236 B3
Oxwich 128 A4
Oxwich Green 128 A4
Oxwick 178 A3
Oykel Bridge 265 K1
Oyne 260 E2
Ozleworth 131 G3

P
Pabbay 262 D3
Packington 159 F1
Packwood 159 D5
Padanaram 252 C4
Padarn Country Park
   Gwyn
   LL55 4TY 167 E1
Padbury 148 C4
Paddington 136 B4
Paddlesworth 125 D4
Paddock 124 B3
Paddock Wood 123 F4
Paddockhaugh 267 K6
Paddockhole 218 A3
Paddolgreen 170 C4
Padeswood 169 F1
Padfield 185 E3
Padiham 193 D4
Padside 194 A2
Padstow 96 D2
Padworth 120 B1
Paganhill 132 A2
Pagham 108 A4
Paglesham
   Churchend 138 C3
Paglesham Eastend
   138 C3
Paible 263 F2
Paignton 101 E1

Paignton & Dartmouth
   Steam Railway
   Torbay
   TQ4 6AF 101 E2
Paignton Pier
   Torbay
   TQ4 6BW 101 E1
Paignton Zoo
   Torbay
   TQ4 7EU 101 E2
Pailton 159 G4
Paine's Corner 110 B1
Painscastle 144 A3
Painshawfield 211 G1
Painswick 132 A2
Pairc 270 E5
Paisley 233 F3
Pakefield 165 G2
Pakenham 152 A1
Palace of Holyroodhouse
   Edin EH8 8DX 37 J4
Palacerigg Country Park
   NLan G67 3HU 234 B2
Pale 168 C3
Palehouse
   Common 109 G2
Palestine 119 D3
Paley Street 135 D5
Palgowan 215 E3
Palgrave 164 C4
Pallinsburn House 228 C3
Palmarsh 124 D5
Palmers Cross 121 F3
Palmers Green 136 C3
Palmerscross 267 K5
Palmerstown 130 A5
Palnackie 216 C5
Palnure 215 F4
Palterton 173 F1
Pamber End 120 B2
Pamber Green 120 B2
Pamber Heath 120 B1
Pamington 146 B4
Pamphill 105 F2
Pampisford 150 C3
Pan 107 E4
Panborough 116 B3
Panbride 245 D1
Pancrasweek 112 C5
Pancross 114 D1
Pandy Gwyn 154 C2
Pandy Mon 144 C4
Pandy Powys 155 F2
Pandy Wrex 169 E4
Pandy Gwyn 168 B5
Pandy Tudur 168 B1
Pandy'r Capel 169 D2
Panfield 151 F5
Pangbourne 134 B5
Pannal 194 C2
Pannal Ash 194 C2
Panshanger 136 B1
Pant 169 F5
Pant Glas 167 D3
Pant Gwyn 168 B5
Pant Mawr 155 E4
Pantasaph 182 C5
Panteg 130 C3
Pantglas 155 D3
Pantgwyn Carmar 142 B5
Pantgwyn Cere 141 F3
Pant-lasau 128 C2
Panton 188 B5
Pantperthog 154 D2
Pant-y-dwr 155 F5
Pantyffordd 169 F2
Pant-y-ffridd 156 A2
Pantyffynnon 128 C1
Pantygasseg 130 B3
Pantygelli 130 C1
Pantymwyn 169 E1
Panxworth 179 E4
Papa Stour 279 A6
Papa Stour Airstrip 279 A6
Papa Westray 276 D2
Papa Westray
   Airfield 276 D2
Papcastle 209 E3
Papil 279 C9
Papple 236 C2
Papplewick 173 G2
Papworth Everard 150 A1
Papworth St. Agnes 150 A1
Par 97 E4
Paradise Park, Newhaven
   ESuss BN9 0DH 109 G3
Paradise Wildlife Park,
   Broxbourne Herts
   EN10 7QA 136 C2
Parbold 183 F1
Parbrook Som 116 C4
Parbrook WSuss 121 F5
Parc 168 C3
Parciau 130 C3
Parc-Seymour 130 D3
Parc-y-rhôs 142 B3
Pardshaw 209 D4
Parham 153 E1
Parish Holm 225 F3
Park 268 D5
Park Close 193 E3
Park Corner ESuss 123 E5
Park Corner Oxon 134 B4
Park End N'umb 220 A4
Park End Staffs 171 E2
Park End Worcs 157 G5
Park Gate Hants 107 E2
Park Gate Worcs 158 B5
Park Gate WYorks 194 A3
Park Gate WYorks 185 G1
Park Green 152 C1
Park Hill 186 A4
Park Lane 170 B4
Park Langley 122 C1
Park Rose Pottery & Leisure
   Park ERid
   YO15 3QF 196 D1
Park Street 136 A2
Parkend Cumb 209 G3
Parkend Glos 131 F2
Parker's Green 123 F4
Parkeston 152 D4
Parkfield Cornw 98 D4
Parkfield SGlos 131 F5
Parkfield WMid 158 B3
Parkford 252 C4
Parkgate ChesW&C 183 D5

Parkgate D&G 217 E2
Parkgate Kent 124 A5
Parkgate Surr 122 B4
Parkgate SYorks 186 B3
Parkham 113 D3
Parkham Ash 113 D3
Parkhead 234 A3
Parkhill Angus 253 E5
Parkhill P&K 251 G5
Parkhouse 131 D2
Parkhurst 107 D3
Parkmill 128 B4
Parkmore 268 B6
Parkneuk 253 F2
Parkside 170 A2
Parkstone 105 G3
Parkway 116 C5
Parley Cross 105 G3
Parley Green 106 A3
Parlington 194 D4
Parracombe 113 G1
Parrog 140 D4
Parson Cross 186 A3
Parson Drove 162 B2
Parsonage Green 137 F1
Parsonby 209 E3
Partick 233 G3
Partington 184 B3
Partney 176 C1
Parton Cumb 208 C4
Parton D&G 216 A3
Partridge Green 109 D2
Parwich 172 C2
Paslow Wood Common 137 E2
Passenham 148 C4
Passfield 120 D4
Passingford Bridge 137 E3
Paston 179 E2
Paston Street 179 E2
Pasturefields 171 G5
Patchacott 99 E1
Patcham 109 F3
Patchetts Green 136 A3
Patching 108 C3
Patchole 113 G1
Patchway 131 F4
Pateley Bridge 194 A1
Path of Condie 243 F3
Pathe 116 A4
Pathfinder Village 102 B3
Pathhead Aber 253 F3
Pathhead EAyr 225 E4
Pathhead Fife 244 A5
Pathhead Midlo 236 A3
Pathlow 147 D2
Patmore Heath 150 C5
Patna 224 C4
Patney 118 B2
Patrick 190 A3
Patrick Brompton 202 B3
Patrington 197 F5
Patrington Haven 197 F5
Patrishow 144 B5
Patrixbourne 125 D3
Patterdale 209 G5
Pattingham 158 A3
Pattishall 148 B2
Pattiswick 151 G5
Paul 94 B4
Paulerspury 148 C3
Paull 197 D5
Paull Holme 197 D5
Paul's Green 94 D3
Paulton 117 D2
Paultons Park Hants SO51 6AL 106 C1
Pauperhaugh 220 C2
Pave Lane 157 G1
Pavenham 149 E2
Pavilion Gardens, Buxton Derbys SK17 6XN 185 E5
Pawlett 116 A3
Pawston 228 C3
Paxford 147 D4
Paxhill Park 109 F1
Paxton 237 G4
Payden Street 124 B3
Payhembury 103 D2
Paythorne 193 E2
Peacehaven 109 G3
Peacemarsh 117 F5
Peachley 146 A2
Peak Dale 185 E5
Peak Forest 185 F5
Peakirk 161 G2
Pean Hill 124 D2
Pear Tree 173 E4
Pearsie 252 B4
Pearson's Green 123 F4
Peartree 136 B1
Peartree Green Essex 137 E3
Peartree Green Here 145 F4
Pease Pottage 122 B5
Peasedown St. John 117 E2
Peasehill 173 F3
Peaseland Green 178 B4
Peasemore 133 G5
Peasenhall 153 E1
Peaslake 121 F3
Peasley Cross 183 G3
Peasmarsh ESuss 111 D1
Peasmarsh Surr 121 E3
Peaston 236 B3
Peastonbank 236 B3
Peat Inn 244 C4
Peathill 269 H4
Peathrow 212 A5
Peatling Magna 160 A3
Peatling Parva 160 A4
Peaton 157 E4
Pebble Coombe 122 B3
Pebmarsh 151 G4
Pebworth 146 D3
Pecket Well 193 F5
Peckforton 170 C2
Peckham 136 C5
Peckleton 159 G2
Pedham 179 E4
Pedmore 158 B4
Pedwell 116 B4
Peebles 235 G5
Peel IoM 190 A3
Peel Lancs 191 G4
Peening Quarter 111 D1
Peggs Green 159 G1
Pegsdon 149 G4
Pegswood 221 E3
Pegwell 125 F2
Peighinn nan Aoireann 254 C1
Peinchorran 256 B1
Peinlich 263 K6
Pelaw 212 B1
Pelcomb 126 C1
Pelcomb Bridge 126 C1
Pelcomb Cross 126 C1
Peldon 138 C1
Pellon 193 G5
Pelsall 158 C2
Pelton 212 B2
Pelutho 209 E2
Pelynt 97 G4
Pemberton 183 G2
Pembrey (Pen-bre) 128 A2
Pembrey Country Park Carmar SA16 0EJ 128 A2
Pembridge 144 C2
Pembroke (Penfro) 126 C2
Pembroke Dock (Doc Penfro) 126 C2
Pembury 123 F4
Penallt 131 E1
Penally 127 E3
Penalt 145 E5
Penare 97 D5
Penarran 156 A4
Penarth 130 A5
Pen-bont Rhydybeddau 154 C4
Penboyr 141 G4
Penbryn 141 F2
Pencader 142 A4
Pen-cae 142 A2
Pen-cae-cwm 168 C1
Pencaenewydd 166 D3
Pencaitland 236 B3
Pencarnisiog 180 B5
Pencarreg 142 B3
Pencarrow 97 F1
Pencelli 143 G5
Pen-clawdd 128 B3
Pencoed 129 F4
Pencombe 145 E2
Pencoyd 145 E5
Pencraig Here 145 E5
Pencraig Powys 168 D5
Pendeen 94 A3
Penderyn 129 F2
Pendine (Pentywyn) 127 F2
Pendlebury 184 B2
Pendleton 193 D4
Pendock 145 G4
Pendoggett 97 E2
Pendomer 104 B1
Pendoylan 129 G5
Penegoes 155 D2
Penelewey 96 C5
Pen-ffordd 141 D5
Pengam 130 A3
Penge 136 C5
Pengenffordd 144 A5
Pengorffwysfa 180 C3
Pengover Green 97 G3
Pen-groes-oped 130 C2
Pengwern 182 B5
Penhale 95 D5
Penhallow 96 B4
Penhalvean 95 E3
Penhelig 154 C3
Penhill 133 D4
Penhow 130 D3
Penhurst 110 B2
Peniarth 154 C2
Penicuik 235 G3
Peniel 142 A5
Penifiler 263 K7
Peninver 222 C3
Penisa'r Waun 167 E1
Penisarcwm 155 G1
Penishawain 143 G4
Penistone 185 G2
Penjerrick 95 E3
Penketh 183 G4
Penkill 214 D1
Penkridge 158 B1
Penlean 98 C1
Penley 170 B4
Penllech 166 B4
Penllergaer 128 C3
Pen-llyn IoA 180 B4
Penllyn VGlam 129 F5
Pen-lôn 166 D1
Penmachno 168 A2
Penmaen 128 B4
Penmaenan 181 F5
Penmaenmawr 181 F5
Penmaenpool (Llyn Penmaen) 154 C1
Penmaen-Rhôs 181 G5
Penmark 115 D1
Penmon 181 E4
Penmorfa 167 E3
Penmynydd 180 D5
Penn Bucks 135 E3
Penn WMid 158 A3
Penn Street 135 E3
Pennal 154 C2
Pennal-isaf 154 D2
Pennan 269 G4
Pennance 96 B5
Pennant Cere 142 B1
Pennant Powys 155 E3
Pennant Melangell 168 D5
Pennar 126 C2
Pennard 128 B4
Pennerley 156 C3
Penninghame 215 E4
Pennington Cumb 199 D5
Pennington Hants 106 C3
Pennington Flash Country Park GtMan WN7 3PA 184 A3
Pennington Green 184 A2
Pennorth 144 A5
Pennsylvania 131 G5
Penny Bridge 199 E4
Pennycross 100 A2
Pennyfuir 240 A1
Pennygate 179 E3
Pennyghael 239 E2
Pennyglen 224 A4
Pennygown 247 F5
Pennymoor 102 B1
Penny's Green 164 C2
Pennyvenie 224 C5
Penparc Cere 141 F3
Penparc Pembs 140 B4
Penparcau 154 B4
Penpedairheol 130 C2
Penpethy 97 E1
Penpillick 97 E4
Penpol 95 F3
Penpoll 97 F4
Penponds 94 D3
Penpont D&G 216 C1
Penpont Powys 143 F5
Penprysg 129 F4
Penquit 100 C2
Penrherber 141 F4
Penrhiw 141 F3
Penrhiwceiber 129 G3
Penrhiwgoch 128 B1
Penrhiw-llan 141 G3
Penrhiw-pâl 141 G3
Penrhiwtyn 128 D3
Penrhos Gwyn 166 C4
Penrhos IoA 180 A4
Penrhos Mon 130 D1
Penrhos Powys 129 E1
Penrhos-garnedd 181 D5
Penrhyn Bay (Bae Penrhyn) 181 G4
Penrhyn Castle Gwyn LL57 4HN 181 E5
Penrhyn-coch 154 C4
Penrhyndeudraeth 167 F4
Penrhyn-side 181 G4
Penrhys 129 G3
Penrice 128 A4
Penrith 210 B5
Penrose Corn 96 C2
Penrose Corn 97 G1
Penruddock 210 A5
Penryn 95 E3
Pensarn Carmar 128 A1
Pensarn Conwy 182 A5
Pen-sarn Gwyn 167 E5
Pen-sarn Gwyn 166 D3
Pensax 145 G1
Pensby 183 D4
Penselwood 117 E4
Pensford 116 D1
Pensham 146 B3
Penshaw 212 C2
Penshurst 123 E4
Pensilva 97 G3
Pensnett 158 B4
Penston 236 B2
Pentewan 97 E5
Pentir 167 E1
Pentire 96 B3
Pentireglaze 96 D2
Pentlepoir 127 E2
Pentlow 151 G3
Pentlow Street 151 G3
Pentney 163 F1
Penton Mewsey 119 E3
Pentonville 136 C4
Pentraeth 180 D5
Pentre Powys 169 D5
Pentre Powys 155 G4
Pentre Powys 144 B1
Pentre Powys 156 B3
Pentre Powys 156 A4
Pentre RCT 129 F3
Pentre Shrop 156 C1
Pentre Shrop 156 C5
Pentre Wrex 169 F3
Pentre Wrex 170 A3
Pentre Berw 180 C5
Pentre Ffwrndan 183 D5
Pentre Galar 141 E4
Pentre Gwenlais 128 C1
Pentre Gwynfryn 167 E5
Pentre Halkyn 182 D5
Pentre Isaf 168 B1
Pentre Llanrhaeadr 169 D1
Pentre Maelor 170 A3
Pentre Meyrick 129 F5
Pentre Poeth 128 C3
Pentre Saron 168 D1
Pentre-bach Cere 142 B3
Pentrebach MTyd 129 G2
Pentre-bach Powys 143 F4
Pentrebach RCT 129 G4
Pentrebach Swan 128 B2
Pentre-bont 168 A2
Pentre-bwlch 169 E3
Pentrecagal 141 G3
Pentre-celyn Denb 169 E2
Pentre-celyn Powys 155 E2
Pentre-chwyth 128 C3
Pentreclwydau 129 E2
Pentre-cwrt 141 G4
Pentre-Dolau-Honddu 143 F3
Pentredwr Denb 169 E3
Pentre-dwr Swan 128 C3
Pentrefelin Carmar 142 C5
Pentrefelin Cere 142 C3
Pentrefelin Conwy 181 G5
Pentrefelin Gwyn 167 E4
Pentrefelin Powys 169 E5
Pentrefoelas 168 B2
Pentregat 141 G2
Pentreheyling 156 B3
Pentre-llwyn-llwyd 143 F2
Pentre-llyn 154 C5
Pentre-llyn-cymmer 168 C2
Pentre-piod 168 B4
Pentre-poeth 130 B4
Pentre'r beirdd 156 A1
Pentre'r Felin 168 B1
Pentre'r-felin 143 F4
Pentre-tafarn-y-fedw 168 B1
Pentre-ty-gwyn 143 E4
Pentrich 173 E2
Pentridge 105 G1
Pentwyn Caerp 130 A2
Pen-twyn Caerp 130 B2
Pentwyn Cardiff 130 B4
Pen-twyn Mon 131 E2
Pentwyn-mawr 130 A3
Pentyrch 130 A4
Penuwch 142 B1
Penwithick 97 E4
Penwood 119 F1
Penwortham 192 B5
Penwortham Lane 192 B5
Penwyllt 129 E1
Pen-y-banc 142 C5
Pen-y-bont Carmar 143 D4
Pen-y-bont Carmar 141 G5
Pen-y-bont Powys 155 G1
Pen-y-bont Powys 169 F5
Penybont Powys 144 A1
Penybontfawr 169 D5
Penybryn Caerp 130 A3
Pen-y-bryn Gwyn 154 C1
Pen-y-bryn Pembs 141 E3
Pen-y-bryn Wrex 169 F3
Pen-y-cae Powys 129 E1
Penycae Wrex 169 F3
Pen-y-cae-mawr 130 D3
Pen-y-cefn 182 C5
Pen-y-clawdd 130 D2
Pen-y-coedcae 129 G4
Penycwm 140 B5
Pen-y-Darren 129 G2
Pen-y-fai 129 E4
Penyffordd Flints 170 A1
Pen-y-ffordd Flints 182 C4
Penyffridd 167 E2
Pen-y-gaer 144 A5
Pen-y-garn Carmar 142 B4
Pen-y-garn Cere 154 C4
Penygarn Torfaen 130 B2
Penygarnedd 169 E5
Pen-y-garreg 143 G3
Pen-y-Graig Gwyn 166 B4
Penygraig RCT 129 G3
Penygroes Carmar 128 B1
Penygroes Gwyn 167 D2
Pen-y-Gwryd Hotel 167 F2
Pen-y-lan 130 A5
Pen-y-Mynydd Carmar 128 A2
Penymynydd Flints 170 A1
Pen-y-parc 169 F1
Pen-y-Park 144 B3
Pen-yr-englyn 129 F3
Pen-yr-heol Mon 130 D1
Penyrheol Swan 128 B3
Pen-y-sarn 180 C3
Pen-y-stryt 169 E2
Penywaun 129 F2
Penzance 94 B3
Penzance Heliport 94 B3
People's Palace & Winter Gardens Glas G40 1AT 39 H6
Peopleton 146 B2
Peover Heath 184 B5
Peper Harow 121 E3
Peplow 170 D5
Pepper Arden 202 B2
Pepper's Green 137 F1
Perceton 233 E5
Percie 260 D5
Percyhorner 269 H4
Perham Down 119 D3
Periton 114 C3
Perivale 136 A4
Perkhill 260 D4
Perkins Beach 156 C2
Perkin's Village 102 D3
Perlethorpe 186 D5
Perran Downs 94 C3
Perranarworthal 95 E3
Perranporth 96 B4
Perranuthnoe 94 C4
Perranzabuloe 96 B4
Perrott's Brook 132 C2
Perry Barr 158 C3
Perry Crofts 159 E2
Perry Green Essex 151 G5
Perry Green Herts 136 D1
Perry Green Wilts 132 B4
Perry Street 137 F5
Perrymead 117 E1
Pershall 171 F5
Pershore 146 B3
Persie House 251 G4
Pert 253 E3
Pertenhall 149 F1
Perth (Peairt) 243 G2
Perthcelyn 129 G3
Perthy 170 A4
Perton 158 A3
Pestalozzi Children's Village 110 C2
Peter Tavy 99 F3
Peterborough 161 G3
Peterburn 264 D3
Peterchurch 144 C4
Peterculter 261 G4
Peterhead 269 K6
Peterlee 212 D3
Peter's Green 136 A1
Peters Marland 113 E4
Peters Port (Port Pheadair) 262 D7
Petersfield 120 C5
Petersfinger 118 C5
Peterstone Wentlooge 130 B4
Peterston-super-Ely 129 G5
Peterstow 145 E5
Petham 124 D3
Petrockstowe 113 F5
Pett 111 D2
Pettaugh 152 C2
Petteril Green 210 A3
Pettinain 235 D5
Pettistree 153 D2
Petton Devon 114 D5
Petton Shrop 170 B5
Petts Wood 122 D2
Petty 261 F1
Petty France 131 G4
Pettycur 235 G1
Pettymuick 261 H2
Petworth 121 E5
Pevensey 110 B3
Pevensey Bay 110 B3
Peverell 100 A2
Pewsey 118 C1
Pheasant's Hill 134 C4
Phesdo 253 E2
Philham 112 C3
Philharmonic Hall, Liverpool Mersey L1 9BP 43 E5
Philiphaugh 227 F3
Phillack 94 C3
Philleigh 95 F3
Philpstoun 235 E2
Phocle Green 145 F5
Phoenix Green 120 C2
Phones 258 E5
Phorp 267 H6
Photographer's Gallery, The, London GtLon WC2H 7HY 44 E3
Pibsbury 116 B5
Pica 208 D4
Piccadilly Corner 165 D3
Pickerells 137 E2
Pickering 203 G4
Pickering Nook 212 A2
Picket Piece 119 E3
Picket Post 106 A2
Pickford Green 159 E4
Pickhill 202 C4
Picklescott 156 D3
Pickletillem 244 C2
Pickmere 184 A5
Pickney 115 E5
Pickstock 171 E5
Pickston 243 E2
Pickup Bank 192 D5
Pickwell Devon 113 E1
Pickwell Leics 160 C1
Pickworth Lincs 175 F4
Pickworth Rut 161 E1
Picton ChesW&C 183 F5
Picton NYorks 202 D2
Piddinghoe 109 G3
Piddington Bucks 134 D3
Piddington N'hants 148 D2
Piddington Oxon 134 B1
Piddlehinton 104 D3
Piddletrenthide 104 D3
Pidley 162 B5
Piece Hall, Halifax WYorks HX1 1RE 26 B4
Piercebridge 202 B1
Pierowall 276 D3
Pigdon 221 D3
Pike Hill 193 E4
Pikehall 172 C2
Pikeshill 106 B2
Pilgrims Hatch 137 E3
Pilham 187 F3
Pill 131 E5
Pillaton Corn 99 D4
Pillaton Staffs 158 B1
Pillerton Hersey 147 E3
Pillerton Priors 147 E3
Pilleth 144 B1
Pilley Hants 106 C3
Pilley SYorks 186 A2
Pilling 192 A3
Pilling Lane 191 G3
Pillowell 131 F2
Pilning 131 E4
Pilsbury 172 C1
Pilsdon 104 A3
Pilsgate 161 F2
Pilsley Derbys 173 F1
Pilsley Derbys 185 G5
Pilson Green 179 E4
Piltdown 109 G1
Pilton Devon 113 F2
Pilton N'hants 161 F4
Pilton Rut 161 E2
Pilton Som 116 C3
Pilton Swan 128 A4
Pilton Green 128 A4
Pimhole 184 C1
Pimlico 135 F2
Pimperne 105 F2
Pin Mill 152 D4
Pinchbeck 176 A5
Pinchbeck Bars 176 A5
Pinchbeck West 176 A5
Pincheon Green 187 D1
Pinchinthorpe 203 E1
Pindon End 148 C3
Pinehurst 132 D4
Pinfold 183 E1
Pinged 128 A2
Pinhay 103 G3
Pinhoe 102 C3
Pinkneys Green 135 D4
Pinley Green 147 E1
Pinminnoch 214 C1
Pinmore 214 D1
Pinn 103 E4
Pinner 136 A4
Pinner Green 136 A3
Pinvin 146 B3
Pinwherry 214 C2
Pinxton 173 F2
Pipe & Lyde 145 E3
Pipe Gate 171 E3
Pipe Ridware 158 C1
Pipehill 158 C2
Piperhall 232 B4
Piperhill 267 F6
Pipers Pool 97 G1
Pipewell 160 D4
Pippacott 113 F2
Pipton 144 A4
Pirbright 121 E2
Pirnmill 231 G5
Pirton Herts 149 G4
Pirton Worcs 146 A3
Pisgah 242 C4
Pishill 134 C4
Pistyll 166 C3
Pitagowan 250 D3
Pitblae 269 H4
Pitcairngreen 243 F2
Pitcairns 243 F3
Pitcaple 261 F2
Pitch Green 134 C2
Pitch Place Surr 121 E2
Pitch Place Surr 121 D4
Pitchcombe 132 A2
Pitchcott 148 C5
Pitchford 157 E2
Pitcombe 117 D4
Pitcot 129 E5
Pitcox 236 D2
Pitcur 244 A1
Pitfichie 260 E3
Pitgrudy 266 E2
Pitinnan 261 F1
Pitkennedy 252 D4
Pitkevy 244 A4
Pitlessie 244 B4
Pitlochry 251 E4
Pitman's Corner 152 C1
Pitmedden 261 G2
Pitminster 103 F1
Pitmuies 253 D5
Pitmunie 260 E3
Pitnacree 251 E4
Pitney 116 B5
Pitroddie 244 A2
Pitscottie 244 C3
Pitsea 137 G4
Pitsford 148 C1
Pitsford Hill 115 D4
Pitstone 135 E1
Pitt Devon 102 D1
Pitt Hants 119 F5
Pitt Rivers Museum Oxon OX1 3PP 80 Oxford
Pittendreich 267 J5
Pittentrail 266 E1
Pittenweem 244 D4
Pitteuchar 244 A5
Pittington 212 C3
Pittodrie House 260 E2
Pitton Swan 128 A4
Pitton Wilts 118 D4
Pittulie 269 H4
Pittville 146 B5
Pity Me 212 B3
Pityme 96 D2
Pixey Green 164 D4
Pixley 145 F4
Place Newton 204 B5
Plaidy 269 F5
Plain Dealings 127 D1
Plainfield 220 B1
Plains 234 B3
Plainsfield 115 E4
Plaish 157 E3
Plaistow GtLon 136 C4
Plaistow WSuss 121 F4
Plaitford 106 B1
Plaitford Green 119 D5
Plas 142 A5
Plas Gwynant 167 F2
Plas Isaf 169 D3
Plas Llwyd 182 A5
Plas Llwyngwern 155 D2
Plas Llysyn 155 F3
Plas Nantyr 169 E4
Plashett 127 F2
Plasisaf 168 C1
Plas-rhiw-Saeson 155 F2
Plastow Green 119 G1
Plas-yn-Cefn 182 B5
Platt 123 F3
Platt Bridge 184 A2
Platt Lane 170 C4
Platt's Heath 124 A3
Plawsworth 212 B3
Plaxtol 123 F3
Play Hatch 134 C5
Playden 111 E1
Playford 152 D3
Playing Place 96 C5
Playley Green 145 G4
Plealey 156 D2
Plean 234 C1
Pleasance 244 A3
Pleasant Valley 150 D4
Pleasington 192 C5
Pleasley 173 G1
Pleasleyhill 173 G1
Pleasure Beach, Great Yarmouth Norf NR30 3EH 179 G5
Pleasure Island Theme Park NELincs DN35 0PL 188 D2
Pleasurewood Hills Theme Park Suff NR32 5DZ 165 G2
Pleck Dorset 104 D1
Pleck WMid 158 B3
Pledgdon Green 151 D5
Pledwick 186 A1
Plemstall 183 F5
Plenmeller 210 D1
Pleshey 137 F1
Plessey Woods Country Park N'umb NE22 6AN 221 E3
Plockton (Am Ploc) 256 E1
Plocropol 263 G2
Plomer's Hill 135 D3
Plot Gate 116 C4
Plough Hill 159 F3
Plowden 156 C4
Ploxgreen 156 C2
Pluckley 124 B4
Pluckley Thorne 124 B4
Plucks Gutter 125 E2
Plumbland 209 E3
Plumbley 186 B4
Plumley 184 B5
Plumpton Cumb 210 A4
Plumpton ESuss 109 F2
Plumpton N'hants 148 B3
Plumpton Green 109 F2
Plumpton Head 210 B4
Plumstead GtLon 137 D5
Plumstead Norf 178 C2
Plumtree 174 B4
Plungar 174 C4
Plush 104 D2
Plusha 97 G1
Plushabridge 98 D3
Plwmp 141 G2
Plym Bridge 100 B2
Plymouth 100 A2
Plymouth Pavilions PL1 3LF 81 Plymouth
Plympton 100 B2
Plymstock 100 B2
Plymtree 103 D2
Pockley 203 F4
Pocklington 196 A3
Pockthorpe 178 B3
Pocombe Bridge 102 B3
Pode Hole 176 A5
Podimore 116 C5
Podington 149 E1
Podmore 171 E4
Podsmead 132 A1
Poffley End 133 F1
Point Clear 139 D1
Pointon 175 G4
Polanach 248 B4
Polapit Tamar 98 D2
Polbae 215 D3
Polbain 272 B7
Polbathic 98 D5
Polbeth 235 E3
Poldean 217 F1
Pole Moor 185 E1
Polebrook 161 F4
Polegate 110 A3
Poles 266 E2
Polesden Lacey Surr RH5 6BD 121 G2
Polesworth 159 E2
Polglass 265 G1
Polgooth 97 D4
Polgown 225 F5
Poling 108 C3
Poling Corner 108 C3
Polkemmet Country Park WLoth EH47 0AD 234 D3
Polkerris 97 E4
Poll a' Charra 254 C3
Polla 273 F3
Pollardras 94 D3
Polldubh 248 D3
Pollie 274 C7
Pollington 186 D1
Polloch 247 G3
Pollok 233 G3
Pollokshaws 233 G3
Pollokshields 233 G3
Polmassick 97 D5
Polmont 234 D2
Polnoon 233 G4
Polperro 97 G4
Polruan 97 F4
Polsham 116 C3
Polstead 152 A4
Polstead Heath 152 A3
Poltalloch 240 A5
Poltimore 102 C3
Polton 235 G3
Polwarth 237 E4
Polyphant 97 G1
Polzeath 96 D2
Pomphlett 100 B2
Pond Street 150 C4
Ponders End 136 C3
Pondersbridge 162 A3
Ponsanooth 95 E3
Ponsonby 198 B2
Ponsongath 95 E5
Ponsworthy 102 A5
Pont Aber 142 D5
Pont Aberglaslyn 167 E3
Pont ar Hydfer 143 E5
Pont Crugnant 155 E3
Pont Cyfyng 168 A2
Pont Dolgarrog 168 A1
Pont Pen-y-benglog 167 F1
Pont Rhyd-sarn 168 B5
Pont Rhyd-y-cyff 129 E4
Pont Walby 129 E2
Pont yr Alwen 168 C2
Pontamman 128 C1
Pontantwn 128 A1
Pontardawe 128 D2
Pontarddulais 128 B2
Pontargothi 142 B5
Pont-ar-llechau 142 D5
Pontarsais 142 A5
Pontblyddyn 169 F1
Pontbren Llwyd 129 F2
Pontefract 195 D5
Ponteland 221 D4
Ponterwyd 154 D4
Pontesbury 156 D2
Pontesbury Hill 156 C2
Pontesford 156 D2
Pontfadog 169 F4
Pontfaen Pembs 140 D4
Pont-faen Powys 143 F4
Pontgarreg 141 G2
Pont-Henri 128 A2
Ponthir 130 C3
Ponthirwaun 141 F3
Pontllanfraith 130 A3
Pontlliw 128 C2
Pontllyfni 166 D2
Pontlottyn 130 A2
Pontneddfechan 129 F2
Pontrhydfendigaid 142 D1
Pontrhydyfen 129 D3
Pont-rhyd-y-groes 154 D5
Pontrhydyrun 130 B3
Pontrilas 144 C5
Pontrobert 156 A1
Pont-rug 167 E1
Ponts Green 110 B2
Pontshill 145 F5
Pont-siân 142 A3
Pontsticill 129 G1
Pontwelly 142 A4
Pontyates (Pont-iets) 128 A2
Pontyberem 128 B1
Pont-y-blew 170 A4
Pontybodkin 169 F2
Pontyclun 129 G4
Pontycymer 129 F3
Pontygwaith 129 G3
Pontymister 130 B3
Pontymoel 130 B2
Pont-y-pant 168 A2
Pontypool 130 B2
Pontypridd 129 G3
Pont-y-rhyl 129 F4
Pontywaun 130 B3
Pooksgreen 106 C1
Pool Corn 96 A5
Pool WYorks 194 B3
Pool Bank 199 F4
Pool Green 158 C2
Pool Head 145 E2
Pool of Muckhart 243 F4
Pool Quay 156 B1
Pool Street 151 F4
Poole 105 G3
Poole Keynes 132 B3

Poole Pottery *Poole*
  BH15 1HJ **3** B4
Poolend **171** G2
Poolewe **264** E3
Pooley Bridge **210** A5
Pooley Street **164** B3
Poolfold **171** F2
Poolhill **145** G5
Poolsbrook **186** B5
Poolthorne Farm **188** A2
Pope Hill **126** C1
Popeswood **120** D1
Popham **119** G3
Poplar **136** C4
Porchfield **106** D3
Porin **265** K6
Poringland **179** D5
Porlock **114** B3
Porlock Weir **114** B3
Port Allen **244** A2
Port Appin (Port na
  h-Apainn) **248** B5
Port Askaig **230** C3
Port Bannatyne **232** B3
Port Carlisle **218** A5
Port Charlotte **230** A4
Port Clarence **213** E5
Port Driseach **232** A2
Port e Vullen **190** C2
Port Ellen **230** B5
Port Elphinstone **261** F3
Port Erin **190** A5
Porth **175** G2
Port Gaverne **97** E1
Port Glasgow **233** E2
Port Henderson **264** D4
Port Isaac **97** D1
Port Logan **206** A2
Port Lympne Wild Animal
  Park *Kent*
  CT21 4PD **124** D5
Port Mòr **246** D2
Port Mulgrave **203** G1
Port na Craig **251** E4
Port of Menteith **242** A4
Port of Ness
  (Port Nis) **271** H1
Port o'Warren **216** C5
Port Penrhyn **181** D5
Port Quin **97** D1
Port Ramsay **248** A5
Port St. Mary **190** A5
Port Solent **107** F2
Port Sunlight **183** E4
Port Talbot **129** D4
Port Tennant **128** C3
Port Wemyss **230** A4
Port William **206** D2
Portachoillan **231** F4
Portavadie **232** A3
Portbury **131** E5
Portchester **107** F2
Portencross **232** C5
Portesham **104** C4
Portessie **268** C4
Portfield *A&B* **239** G2
Portfield *WSuss* **108** A3
Portfield Gate **126** C1
Portgate **99** E2
Portgordon **268** B4
Portgower **275** F7
Porth *Corn* **96** C3
Porth *RCT* **129** G3
Porth Colmon **166** A4
Porth Navas **95** E4
Porthallow *Corn* **95** E4
Porthallow *Corn* **97** G4
Porthcawl **129** E5
Porthcothan **96** C2
Porthcurno **94** A4
Porthgain **140** B4
Porthill **171** F3
Porthkerry **115** D1
Porthkerry Country Park
  VGlam
  CF62 3BY **115** D1
Porthleven **94** D3
Porthmadog **167** E4
Porthmeor **94** B3
Portholland **97** D5
Porthoustock **95** F4
Porthpean **97** E4
Porthtowan **96** A5
Porthyrhyd
  Carmar **142** D4
Porthyrhyd
  Carmar **128** B1
Porth-y-waen **169** F5
Portincaple **241** E5
Portington **195** G4
Portinnisherrich **240** B3
Portinscale **209** F4
Portishead **131** D5
Portknockie **268** C4
Portland Basin Museum
  GtMan
  OL7 0QA **25** H3
Portlethen **261** H5
Portlethen Village **261** H5
Portloe **95** G3
Portlooe **97** G4
Portmahomack **267** G3
Portmeirion **167** E4
Portmeirion Village *Gwyn*
  LL48 6ET **167** E4
Portmellon **97** E5
Portmore **106** C3
Port-na-Con **273** G2
Portnacroish
  (Port na Croise) **248** B5
Portnaguran (Port nan
  Giúran) **271** H4
Portnahaven **230** A4
Portnalong **255** J1
Portnaluchaig **247** G2
Portobello **236** A2
Porton **118** C4
Portpatrick **214** B5
Portreath **96** A5
Portree (Port Righ) **263** K7
Portscatho **95** F4
Portsea **107** F2
Portskerra **274** D2
Portskewett **131** E4
Portslade **109** E3

Portslade-by-Sea **109** E3
Portslogan **214** A5
Portsmouth **107** F3
Portsmouth Guildhall
  PO1 2AB
  82 Portsmouth
Portsmouth Historic
  Dockyard PO1 3LJ
  82 Portsmouth
Portsonachan **240** C2
Portsoy **268** D4
Portuairk **246** D3
Portvoller **271** H4
Portway *Here* **144** C3
Portway *Here* **145** D3
Portway *Here* **145** D4
Portway *Worcs* **158** C5
Portwrinkle **99** G1
Portyerrock **207** F3
Posenhall **157** F2
Poslingford **151** F3
Postbridge **99** G3
Postcombe **134** C3
Postling **124** D5
Postwick **179** D5
Potarch **260** E5
Potsgrove **149** E5
Pott Row **177** F5
Pott Shrigley **184** D5
Potten End **135** F2
Potter Brompton **204** C5
Potter Heigham **179** F4
Potter Street **137** D2
Pottergate Street **164** C2
Potterhanworth **175** F1
Potterhanworth
  Booths **175** F1
Potteries Museum & Art
  Gallery ST1 3DW
  85 Stoke-on-Trent
Potterne **118** A2
Potterne Wick **118** B2
Potternewton **194** C4
Potters Bar **136** B2
Potters Crouch **136** A2
Potter's Green **159** F4
Potters Marston **159** G3
Potterspury **148** C3
Potterton *Aber* **261** H3
Potterton *WYorks* **194** D4
Pottle Street **117** F3
Potto **203** D2
Potton **150** A3
Pott's Green **152** A5
Poughill *Corn* **112** C5
Poughill *Devon* **102** B2
Poulshot **118** A2
Poulton **132** D2
Poulton-le-Fylde **191** G4
Pound Bank **145** G3
Pound Green *ESuss* **110** A1
Pound Green *Suff* **151** F2
Pound Green
  Worcs **157** G5
Pound Hill **122** B2
Pound Street **119** F1
Poundbury **104** C3
Poundffald **128** B3
Poundfield **123** E5
Poundgate **109** G1
Poundland **214** C2
Poundon **148** B5
Poundsbridge **123** E4
Poundsgate **102** A5
Poundstock **98** C1
Povey Cross **122** B4
Pow Green **145** G3
Powburn **229** E5
Powderham **102** C4
Powderham Castle *Devon*
  EX6 8JQ **102** C4
Powerstock **104** B3
Powfoot **217** F4
Powick **146** A2
Powis Castle & Garden
  Powys
  SY21 8RG **156** B2
Powler's Piece **113** D4
Powmill **243** F5
Poxwell **104** D4
Poyle **135** F5
Poynings **109** E2
Poyntington **117** D5
Poynton *ChesE* **184** D4
Poynton *Tel&W* **157** E1
Poynton Green **157** E1
Poyntzfield **266** E3
Poys Street **165** E4
Poyston **126** C1
Poyston Cross **126** C1
Poystreet Green **152** A2
Praa Sands **94** C4
Pratis **244** B4
Pratt's Bottom **123** D2
Praze-an-Beeble **94** D3
Predannack Wollas **95** D5
Prees **170** C4
Prees Green **170** C4
Prees Heath **170** C4
Prees Higher Heath **170** C4
Prees Lower Heath **170** C4
Preesall **191** G3
Preesgweene **169** F4
Prenbrigog **169** F1
Prendergast **126** C1
Prendwick **229** E5
Pren-gwyn **142** A3
Prenteg **167** E3
Prenton **183** E4
Prescot **183** F3
Prescott *Devon* **103** D1
Prescott *Shrop* **170** B5
Presley **267** H6
Pressen **228** C3
Prestatyn **182** B4
Prestbury *ChesE* **184** D5
Prestbury *Glos* **146** B5
Presteigne
  (Llanandras) **144** C1
Presthope **157** E3
Prestleigh **116** D3
Prestolee **184** B2
Preston *B&H* **109** E3
Preston *Devon* **102** B5
Preston *Dorset* **104** D4
Preston *ELoth* **236** C2
Preston *ERid* **197** D4
Preston *Glos* **145** F4

Preston *Glos* **132** C2
Preston *Herts* **149** G5
Preston *Kent* **124** C2
Preston *Kent* **125** E4
Preston *Lancs* **192** B5
Preston *N'umb* **229** F4
Preston *Rut* **161** D2
Preston *ScBord* **237** E4
Preston *Shrop* **157** E1
Preston *Som* **115** D4
Preston *Suff* **152** A2
Preston *Torbay* **101** E1
Preston *Wilts* **132** C5
Preston Bagot **147** E1
Preston Bissett **148** B4
Preston Bowyer **115** E5
Preston Brockhurst **170** C5
Preston Brook **183** G4
Preston Candover **120** B3
Preston Capes **148** A2
Preston Deanery **148** C2
Preston Gubbals **157** D1
Preston Guildhall *Lancs*
  PR1 1HT **192** B5
Preston on Stour **147** E3
Preston on the Hill **183** G4
Preston on Wye **144** C3
Preston Plucknett **104** B1
Preston upon the Weald
  Moors **157** F1
Preston Wynne **145** E3
Preston-le-Skerne **212** C5
Prestonpans **236** A2
Preston-under-Scar **201** F3
Prestwich **184** C2
Prestwick *N'umb* **221** E4
Prestwick *SAyr* **224** B3
Prestwold **173** G5
Prestwood *Bucks* **135** D2
Prestwood *Staffs* **172** C3
Price Town **129** F3
Prickly Ball Farm &
  Hedgehog Hospital
  Devon
  TQ12 6BZ **101** E1
Prickwillow **163** D4
Priddy **116** C2
Priest Hill **192** C4
Priest Hutton **199** G4
Priest Weston **156** B3
Priestcliffe **185** F5
Priestland **225** D2
Priestwood **123** F2
Primethorpe **160** A3
Primrose Green **178** B4
Primrose Hill **136** B4
Princes End **158** B3
Princes Gate **127** E1
Princes Risborough **134** D2
Princethorpe **159** G5
Princetown *Caerp* **130** A1
Princetown *Devon* **99** F3
Prior Muir **244** D3
Prior's Frome **145** E4
Priors Halton **157** D5
Priors Hardwick **147** G2
Priors Marston **147** G2
Prior's Norton **146** A5
Priors Park **146** A4
Priorslee **157** G1
Priory Country Park *Bed*
  MK41 9SH **149** E2
Priory Wood **144** B3
Priston **117** D1
Pristow Green **164** C3
Prittlewell **138** B4
Privett **120** B5
Prixford **113** F2
Proaig **230** C4
Probus **96** C5
Protstonhill **269** G4
Prudhoe **211** G1
Prussia Cove **94** C4
Pubil **249** G5
Publow **116** D1
Puckeridge **150** B5
Puckington **103** G1
Pucklechurch **131** F5
Pucknall **119** E5
Puckrup **146** A4
Puddinglake **171** E1
Puddington
  ChesW&C **183** E5
Puddington
  Devon **102** B1
Puddlebrook **131** F1
Puddledock **164** B2
Puddletown **105** D3
Pudleston **145** E2
Pudsey **194** B4
Pugneys Country Park
  WYorks
  WF2 7EQ **27** G6
Pulborough **108** C2
Pulborough Brooks RSPB
  Nature Reserve *WSuss*
  RH20 2EL **108** C2
Puldagon **275** J4
Puleston **171** E5
Pulford **170** A2
Pulham **104** C2
Pulham Market **164** C3
Pulham St. Mary **164** D3
Pulley **157** D2
Pulloxhill **149** F4
Pulrossie **266** E3
Pulverbatch **156** D2
Pumpherston **235** E3
Pumsaint **142** C3
Puncheston **140** D5
Puncknowle **104** B4
Punnett's Town **110** B1
Purbrook **107** F2
Purewell **106** A3
Purfleet **137** E5
Puriton **116** A3
Purleigh **138** B2
Purley **122** C2
Purley on Thames **134** B5
Purlogue **156** B5
Purlpit **117** F1
Purls Bridge **162** C4
Purse Caundle **104** C1
Purslow **156** C4
Purston Jaglin **186** B1
Purtington **103** G2

Purton *Glos* **131** F2
Purton *Glos* **131** F2
Purton *Wilts* **132** C3
Purton Stoke **132** C3
Purves Hall **237** E5
Pury End **148** C3
Pusey **133** F3
Putley **145** F4
Putley Green **145** F4
Putney **136** C4
Putsborough **113** E1
Puttenham *Herts* **135** D1
Puttenham *Surr* **121** E3
Puttock End **151** G3
Putts Corner **103** E3
Puxton **116** B1
Pwll **128** A2
Pwllcrochan **126** C2
Pwlldefaid **166** A5
Pwll-glas **169** E2
Pwllgloyw **143** G4
Pwllheli **166** C4
Pwll-Mawr **130** B5
Pwllmeyric **131** E3
Pwll-trap **127** F1
Pwll-y-glaw **129** D3
Pye Corner *Herts* **137** D1
Pye Corner *Kent* **124** A4
Pye Corner
  Newport **130** C4
Pye Green **158** B1
Pyecombe **109** E2
Pyle *Bridgend* **129** E4
Pyle *IoW* **107** D5
Pyleigh **115** E4
Pylle **116** D3
Pymoor (Pymore) **162** C4
Pymore (Pymoor)
  Cambs **162** C4
Pymore *Dorset* **104** A3
Pyrford **121** F2
Pyrford Green **121** F2
Pyrton **134** B3
Pytchley **161** D5
Pyworthy **112** D5

Q

Quabbs **156** B4
Quadring **176** A4
Quadring Eaudike **176** A4
Quainton **148** C5
Quarley **119** D3
Quarndon **173** E3
Quarr Hill **107** E3
Quarrier's Village **233** E3
Quarrington **175** F3
Quarrington Hill **212** C4
Quarry Bank **158** B4
Quarry Bank Mill & Styal
  Estate *ChesE*
  SK9 4LA **184** C4
Quarrybank **170** C1
Quarrywood **267** J5
Quarter **234** B4
Quatford **157** G3
Quatt **157** G3
Quebec **212** A3
Quedgeley **132** A1
Queen Adelaide **163** D4
Queen Camel **116** C5
Queen Charlton **116** D1
Queen Dart **102** B1
Queen Elizabeth Country
  Park, Petersfield *Hants*
  PO8 0QE **107** G1
Queen Elizabeth Forest Park
  Stir FK8 3SX **241** G5
Queen Elizabeth Hall
  GtLon SE1 8XX **45** F4
Queen Elizabeth Olympic
  Park *GtLon*
  E20 2ST **12** D3
Queen Elizabeth II
  Conference Centre *GtLon*
  SW1P 3EE **44** D6
Queen Elizabeth II Country
  Park, Ashington *N'umb*
  NE63 9YF **221** E1
Queen Oak **117** E4
Queen Street **123** F4
Queenborough **124** B1
Queen's Bower **107** E4
Queen's Gallery,
  Buckingham Palace
  GtLon SW1A 1AA **44** B6
Queen's Hall, Edinburgh
  Edin EH8 9JG **37** H6
Queen's Head **170** A5
Queen's View Centre *P&K*
  PH16 5NR **251** E2
Queensbury *GtLon* **136** A4
Queensbury
  WYorks **194** A4
Queensferry (South
  Queensferry)
  Edin **235** F2
Queensferry *Flints* **170** A1
Queenswood Country Park
  Here HR6 0PY **145** D2
Queenzieburn **234** A2
Quemerford **118** B1
Quendale **279** F9
Quendon **150** D4
Queniborough **160** B1
Quenington **132** C2
Quernmore **192** B1
Queslett **158** C3
Quethiock **98** D4
Quick's Green **134** A5
Quidenham **164** B3
Quidhampton **119** G2
Quidinish
  (Cuidhtinis) **263** F3
Quilquox **261** H1
Quina Brook **170** C4
Quindry **277** D8
Quine's Hill **190** B4
Quinhill **231** F4
Quinton *N'hants* **148** C2
Quinton *WMid* **158** B4
Quinton Green **148** C2
Quintrell Downs **96** C3
Quixhill **172** C3
Quoditch **99** E1
Quoig **242** D2
Quoiggs House **242** D4

Quoisley **170** C3
Quorn (Quorndon) **160** A1
Quorndon (Quorn) **160** A1
Quothquan **226** A2
Quoyloo **276** B5
Quoys **278** F1
Quoys of Reiss **275** J3

R

R.A.F. Museum, Cosford
  Shrop TF11 8UP **157** G2
R.A.F. Museum, Hendon
  GtLon
  NW9 5LL **10** D1
R.H.S. Garden Harlow Carr
  NYorks
  HG3 1QB **194** B2
R.H.S. Garden Hyde Hall
  Essex
  CM3 8ET **137** G3
R.H.S. Garden Rosemoor
  Devon EX38 8PH **113** F4
R.H.S. Garden Wisley *Surr*
  GU23 6QB **121** F2
Raasay **264** B7
Raby **183** E5
Rachan **226** C2
Rachub **167** F1
Rackenford **102** B1
Rackham **108** C2
Rackheath **179** D4
Racks **217** E3
Rackwick *Ork* **277** B8
Rackwick *Ork* **276** D3
Radbourne **173** E4
Radcliffe *N'umb* **221** E1
Radcliffe on Trent **174** B4
Radclive **148** B4
Radcot **133** E3
Raddington **114** D5
Radernie **244** C4
Radford *B&NESom* **117** D2
Radford *Nott* **173** G3
Radford *Oxon* **147** G5
Radford *WMid* **159** F4
Radford Semele **147** F1
Radipole **104** C4
Radlett **136** A2
Radley **134** A3
Radley Green **137** F2
Radmore Green **170** C2
Radnage **134** C3
Radstock **117** D2
Radstone **148** A3
Radway **147** F3
Radway Green **171** E2
Radwell *Bed* **149** F2
Radwell *Herts* **150** A4
Radwinter **151** E4
Radyr **130** A4
Raechester **220** B3
Raemoir House **260** E5
Raffin **272** C5
Rafford **267** H6
Ragdale **160** B1
Ragged Appleshaw **119** E3
Raglan **131** D2
Ragnall **187** F5
Rahoy **247** F4
Rain Shore **184** C1
Rainford **183** F3
Rainham *GtLon* **137** E4
Rainham *Med* **124** A2
Rainhill **183** F3
Rainhill Stoops **183** G3
Rainow **185** D5
Rainsough **184** C2
Rainton **202** C5
Rainworth **173** G2
Raisbeck **200** B2
Raise **210** C3
Rait **244** A2
Raithby *Lincs* **176** B1
Raithby *Lincs* **188** D4
Rake **120** D5
Raleigh's Cross **114** D4
Ram **142** B3
Ram Alley **118** D1
Ram Lane **124** B4
Ramasaig **263** G7
Rame *Corn* **95** E3
Rame *Corn* **100** A3
Rampisham **104** B2
Rampside **191** F4
Rampton *Cambs* **150** C1
Rampton *Notts* **187** F5
Ramsbottom **184** B1
Ramsbury **133** E5
Ramscraigs **275** G6
Ramsdean **120** C5
Ramsdell **119** G2
Ramsden **133** F1
Ramsden Bellhouse **137** G3
Ramsden Heath **137** G3
Ramsey *Cambs* **162** A4
Ramsey *Essex* **152** D4
Ramsey *IoM* **190** C2
Ramsey Forty Foot **162** B4
Ramsey Heights **162** A4
Ramsey Island
  Essex **138** C2
Ramsey Island
  Pembs **140** A5
Ramsey Mereside **162** A4
Ramsey St. Mary's **162** A4
Ramsgate **125** F2
Ramsgate Street **178** B2
Ramsgill **202** A5
Ramshorn **172** C3
Ramsnest Common **121** E4
Ranachan **247** G3
Ranby *Lincs* **188** C5
Ranby *Notts* **187** D4
Rand **188** B5
Randwick **132** A2
Rangemore **172** C5
Rangeworthy **131** F4
Ranish (Ranais) **271** G5
Rankinston **224** C4
Rank's Green **137** G1
Ranmoor **186** A4
Rannoch School **250** A4
Ranochan **248** A1
Ranscombe **114** C4

Ranskill **187** D4
Ranton **171** F5
Ranton Green **171** F5
Ranworth **179** E4
Rapness **276** D3
Rapps **103** G1
Rascarrel **208** B2
Rash **200** B4
Rashwood **146** B1
Raskelf **203** E5
Rassau **130** A1
Rastrick **194** A5
Ratagan **257** F2
Ratby **160** A2
Ratcliffe Culey **159** F3
Ratcliffe on Soar **173** F5
Ratcliffe on the
  Wreake **160** B1
Ratford Bridge **126** B1
Ratfyn **118** C3
Rathen **269** H4
Rathillet **244** B2
Rathliesbeag **249** E1
Rathmell **193** E1
Ratho **235** F2
Ratho Station **235** F2
Rathven **268** C4
Ratley **147** F3
Ratling **125** E3
Ratlinghope **156** D3
Ratsloe **102** C3
Rattar **275** H1
Ratten Row *Cumb* **209** G2
Ratten Row *Lancs* **192** A3
Rattery **100** C1
Rattlesden **152** A2
Rattray **251** F4
Raughton Head **209** G2
Raunds **161** E5
Ravenfield **186** B3
Ravenglass **198** B3
Ravenglass & Eskdale
  Railway *Cumb*
  CA18 1SW **198** C3
Raveningham **165** E2
Raven's Green **152** C5
Ravenscar **204** C2
Ravensdale **190** B2
Ravensden **149** F2
Ravenshaw **193** F3
Ravenshayes **102** C2
Ravenshead **173** G2
Ravensmoor **170** D2
Ravensthorpe
  N'hants **160** B5
Ravensthorpe
  WYorks **194** B5
Ravenstone *Leics* **159** G1
Ravenstone *MK* **149** D2
Ravenstonedale **200** C2
Ravenstruther **234** D5
Ravensworth **202** A2
Raw **204** C2
Rawcliffe *ERid* **195** F5
Rawcliffe *York* **195** E2
Rawcliffe Bridge **195** F5
Rawdon **194** B4
Rawmarsh **186** B3
Rawnsley **158** C1
Rawreth **137** G3
Rawridge **103** F2
Rawson Green **173** E3
Rawtenstall **193** E5
Rawyards **234** B3
Raxton **261** G1
Raydon **152** B4
Raylees **220** B3
Rayleigh **138** B3
Raymond's Hill **103** G3
Rayne **151** F5
Rayners Lane **136** A4
Raynes Park **122** B2
Reach **151** D2
Read **193** D4
Reading **134** C5
Reading Green **164** C4
Reading Street **124** B5
Reagill **200** B1
Real Mary King's Close, The
  Edin EH1 1PG **37** F4
Rearquhar **266** E2
Rearsby **160** B1
Rease Heath **170** C2
Reaster **275** H2
Reaveley **229** E5
Reawick **279** C8
Reay **274** E2
Reculver **125** E2
Red Ball **103** D1
Red Bull **171** F2
Red Dial **209** F2
Red Hill *Hants* **107** G1
Red Hill *Warks* **146** D2
Red Lodge **163** E5
Red Lumb **184** C1
Red Oaks Hill **151** D4
Red Point **264** D5
Red Post *Corn* **112** C5
Red Post *Devon* **101** E1
Red Rail **145** E5
Red Rock **183** G2
Red Roses **127** F1
Red Row **221** E1
Red Street **171** F2
Red Wharf Bay
  (Traeth Coch) **180** D4
Redberth **127** D2
Redbourn **136** A1
Redbourne **187** G3
Redbrook *Glos* **131** E1
Redbrook Street **124** B5
Redburn *High* **266** C5
Redburn *High* **267** G6
Redburn *N'umb* **211** D1
Redcar **213** F5
Redcastle *Angus* **253** E4
Redcastle *High* **266** C7
Redcliff Bay **130** D5
Redcloak **253** G1
Reddingmuirhead **234** D2
Reddish **184** D3
Redditch **146** C1
Rede **151** G2
Redenhall **165** D3
Redesmouth **220** A3
Redford *Aber* **253** F2
Redford *Angus* **253** D5

Redford *Dur* **211** G4
Redford *WSuss* **121** D5
Redgrave **164** B4
Redheugh **252** C3
Redhill *Aber* **260** E1
Redhill *Aber* **261** G4
Redhill *Moray* **268** B5
Redhill *Notts* **173** G3
Redhill *N'som* **116** B1
Redhill *Surr* **122** B3
Redhill Aerodrome &
  Heliport **122** B3
Redhouse *A&B* **231** G3
Redhouse *Aber* **260** D2
Redhouses **230** B3
Redisham **165** F3
Redland *Bristol* **131** E5
Redland *Ork* **276** C5
Redlingfield **164** C4
Redlynch *Som* **117** E4
Redlynch *Wilts* **118** C5
Redmarley D'Abitot **145** G4
Redmarshall **212** C5
Redmile **174** C4
Redmire **201** F3
Redmoor **97** E3
Rednal **170** A5
Redpath **227** G2
Redruth **96** A5
Redscarhead **235** G5
Redshaw **225** G3
Redstone Bank **127** E1
Redwick *Newport* **130** D4
Redwick *SGlos* **131** E4
Redworth **212** B5
Reed **150** B4
Reed End **150** B4
Reedham **179** F5
Reedley **193** E4
Reedness **195** G5
Reef (Riof) **270** D4
Reepham *Lincs* **188** A5
Reepham *Norf* **178** B3
Reeth **201** F3
Regaby **190** C2
Regil **116** C1
Regoul **267** F6
Reiff **272** B7
Reigate **122** B3
Reighton **205** E5
Reisgill **275** H5
Reiss **275** J3
Rejerrah **96** C4
Releath **95** D3
Relubbus **94** C3
Relugas **267** G7
Remenham **134** C4
Remenham Hill **134** C4
Remony **250** C5
Rempstone **173** G5
Rendcomb **132** C1
Rendham **153** E1
Rendlesham **153** E2
Renfrew **233** G3
Renhold **149** F2
Renishaw **186** B5
Rennington **229** G5
Renton **233** E2
Renwick **210** B3
Repps **179** F4
Repton **173** E5
Rescobie **252** D4
Rescorla **97** E4
Resipole **247** G3
Resolis **266** D5
Resolven **129** E2
Resourie **248** A2
Respryn **97** F3
Reston **237** F3
Restormel **97** F3
Reswallie **252** D4
Reterth **96** D4
Retew **96** D4
Retford
  (East Retford) **187** E4
Rettendon **137** G3
Rettendon Place **137** G3
Retyn **96** C4
Revesby **176** A1
Revesby Bridge **176** B1
Rew **102** A5
Rew Street **107** D3
Rewe *Devon* **102** C3
Rewe *Devon* **102** B3
Reybridge **118** A1
Reydon **165** F4
Reydon Smear **165** G4
Reymerston **178** B5
Reynalton **127** D2
Reynoldston **128** A4
Rezare **99** D3
Rhadyr **130** C2
Rhandirmwyn **143** D3
Rhaoine **266** D1
Rhayader
  (Rhaeadr Gwy) **143** F1
Rhedyn **166** B4
Rheged - the Village in the
  Hill *Cumb*
  CA11 0DQ **210** A5
Rhegreanoch **272** C7
Rheindown **266** C7
Rhelonie **266** C2
Rhemore **247** E4
Rheniglade
  (Reinigeadal) **270** E7
Rheola **129** E2
Rhes-y-cae **169** E1
Rhewl *Denb* **169** E3
Rhewl *Denb* **169** E1
Rhewl *Shrop* **170** A4
Rhian **273** H7
Rhicarn **272** C6
Rhiconich **272** E3
Rhicullen **266** D4
Rhidorroch **265** H2
Rhifail **274** C4
Rhigos **129** F2
Rhilochan **266** E1
Rhinduie **266** C7
Rhireavoch **265** G2
Rhiroy **265** H3
Rhiston **156** B3
Rhiw **166** B5
Rhiwargor **168** C5
Rhiwbina **130** A4
Rhiwbryfdir **167** F3
Rhiwderin **130** B4

Rhiwinder 129 G4
Rhiwlas Gwyn 167 E1
Rhiwlas Gwyn 168 C4
Rhiwlas Powys 169 F4
Rhode 115 F4
Rhodes Minnis 124 D4
Rhodesia 186 C5
Rhodiad-y-brenin 140 A5
Rhodmad 154 B5
Rhonadale 222 C2
Rhonehouse
   (Kelton Hill) 216 B5
Rhoose 115 D1
Rhos Carmar 141 G4
Rhos NPT 128 D2
Rhos Common 156 B1
Rhoscolyn 180 A5
Rhoscrowther 126 C2
Rhosesmor 169 F1
Rhos-fawr 166 C4
Rhosgadfan 167 E2
Rhos-goch IoA 180 C4
Rhosgoch Powys 144 A3
Rhos-hill 141 E3
Rhoshirwaun 166 A5
Rhoslan 167 D3
Rhoslefain 154 B2
Rhosllanerchrugog 169 F3
Rhoslligwy 180 C4
Rhosmaen 142 C5
Rhosmeirch 180 C5
Rhosneigr 180 A5
Rhosnesni 170 A2
Rhôs-on-Sea 181 G4
Rhossili 128 A4
Rhosson 140 A5
Rhostrehwfa 180 C5
Rhostryfan 167 D2
Rhostyllen 170 A2
Rhos-y-bol 180 C4
Rhos-y-brithdir 169 E5
Rhosycaerau 140 C4
Rhos-y-garth 154 C5
Rhos-y-gwaliau 168 C5
Rhos-y-llan 166 B4
Rhos-y-mawn 168 B1
Rhos-y-Meirch 144 B1
Rhu 233 D1
Rhuallt 182 B5
Rhubodach 232 B2
Rhuddall Heath 170 C1
Rhuddlan 182 B5
Rhue 265 H2
Rhulen 144 A3
Rhumach 247 F1
Rhyd Gwyn 167 F3
Rhyd Powys 155 F2
Rhydargaeau 142 A5
Rhydcymerau 142 B4
Rhyd-Ddu 167 E2
Rhydding 128 D3
Rhydgaled 168 C1
Rhydlanfair 168 B2
Rhydlewis 141 G3
Rhydlios 166 A4
Rhydlydan Conwy 168 B2
Rhydlydan Powys 155 G3
Rhydolion 166 B5
Rhydowen 142 A3
Rhyd-Rosser 142 B1
Rhydspence 144 B3
Rhydtalog 169 F2
Rhyd-uchaf 168 B4
Rhyd-wen 168 C5
Rhyd-wyn 180 B4
Rhyd-y-ceirw 169 F2
Rhyd-y-clafdy 166 C4
Rhydycroesau 169 F4
Rhyd-y-felin Cere 154 B5
Rhydyfelin RCT 129 G4
Rhyd-y-foel 182 A5
Rhyd-y-fro 128 D2
Rhyd-y-groes 167 E1
Rhydymain 168 B5
Rhydymwyn 169 F1
Rhyd-yr-onnen 154 C2
Rhyd-y-sarn 167 F3
Rhydywrach 127 E1
Rhyl 182 B4
Rhyl Sun Centre Denb
   LL18 3AQ 182 B4
Rhymney 130 A2
Rhyn 170 A4
Rhynd 243 G2
Rhynie Aber 260 C2
Rhynie High 267 F4
Ribbesford 157 G5
Ribchester 192 C4
Ribigill 273 H3
Riby 188 B3
Riccall 195 F4
Richards Castle 145 D1
Richings Park 135 F5
Richmond GtLon 136 A5
Richmond NYorks 202 A2
Richmond SYorks 186 B4
Rich's Holford 115 E4
Rickarton 253 G1
Rickerscote 171 G5
Rickford 116 B2
Rickinghall 164 B4
Rickleton 212 B2
Rickling 150 C4
Rickling Green 150 D5
Rickmansworth 135 F3
Riddell 227 G3
Riddings 173 F2
Riddlecombe 113 G4
Riddlesden 193 G3
Ridge Dorset 105 F4
Ridge Herts 136 B2
Ridge Wilts 118 A4
Ridge Green 122 C4
Ridge Lane 159 E3
Ridgebourne 143 G2
Ridgeway Cross 145 G3
Ridgeway Moor 186 B4
Ridgewell 151 F3
Ridgewood 109 G1
Ridgmont 149 E4
Ridham Dock 124 B2
Riding Gate 117 E5
Riding Mill 211 G1
Ridley 123 F2

Ridleywood 170 A2
Ridlington Norf 179 E2
Ridlington Rut 160 D2
Ridsdale 220 B3
Riechip 251 F5
Rievaulx 203 F4
Rift House 213 D4
Rigg D&G 218 A5
Rigg High 264 B6
Riggend 234 B3
Rigifa 275 J1
Rigmaden Park 200 B4
Rigsby 189 E5
Rigside 225 G2
Riley Green 192 C5
Rileyhill 158 D1
Rillaton 97 G2
Rillington 204 B5
Rimington 193 E3
Rimpton 116 D5
Rimswell 197 F5
Rinaston 140 C5
Ring o' Bells 183 F1
Ringford 216 A5
Ringinglow 185 G4
Ringland 178 C4
Ringles Cross 109 G1
Ringmer 109 G2
Ringmore Devon 100 C3
Ringmore Devon 102 C5
Ringorm 267 K7
Ring's End 162 B1
Ringsfield 165 F3
Ringsfield Corner 165 F3
Ringshall Herts 135 E1
Ringshall Suff 152 B2
Ringshall Stocks 152 B2
Ringstead
   N'hants 161 E5
Ringstead Norf 177 F3
Ringwood 106 A2
Ringwould 125 F4
Rinloan 259 K4
Rinmore 260 C3
Rinnigill 277 C8
Rinsey 94 C4
Ripe 110 A3
Ripley Derbys 173 E2
Ripley Hants 106 A3
Ripley NYorks 194 B1
Ripley Surr 121 F2
Riplingham 196 B4
Ripon 202 C5
Rippingale 175 G5
Ripple Kent 125 F4
Ripple Worcs 146 A4
Ripponden 185 E1
Risabus 230 B5
Risbury 145 E2
Risby ERid 196 C3
Risby Suff 151 F1
Risca 130 B3
Rise 197 D3
Riseden 123 E5
Risegate 176 A5
Riseholme 187 G5
Riseley Bed 149 F1
Riseley W'ham 120 C1
Rishangles 152 C1
Rishton 192 D4
Rishworth 185 E1
Risinghurst 134 A2
Risley Derbys 173 F4
Risley Warr 184 A3
Risplith 194 B1
Rispond 273 G2
Rivar 119 E1
Rivenhall 138 B1
Rivenhall End 138 B1
River Kent 125 E4
River WSuss 121 E5
River Bank 150 D1
River Bridge 116 A3

Robinswood Hill Country
   Park Glos
   GL4 6SX 132 A1
Roborough Devon 113 F4
Roborough Plym 100 B1
Roby 183 F3
Roby Mill 183 G2
Rocester 172 C4
Roch 140 B5
Roch Bridge 140 B5
Roch Gate 140 B5
Rochallie 251 G4
Rochdale 184 C1
Roche 97 D3
Rochester Med 123 G2
Rochester N'umb 220 A2
Rochester Cathedral Med
   ME1 1SX 123 G2
Rochford Essex 138 B3
Rochford Worcs 145 F1
Rock Corn 96 D2
Rock N'umb 229 G5
Rock Worcs 157 G5
Rock Ferry 183 E4
Rockbeare 102 D3
Rockbourne 106 A1
Rockcliffe Cumb 218 B5
Rockcliffe D&G 216 C5
Rockcliffe Cross 218 B5
Rockfield A&B 231 G4
Rockfield High 267 G3
Rockfield Mon 131 D1
Rockford 106 A2
Rockhampton 131 F3
Rockhead 97 E1
Rockingham 161 D3
Rockland All Saints 164 A2
Rockland St. Mary 179 E5
Rockland St. Peter 164 A2
Rockley 133 D5
Rockside 230 A3
Rockwell End 134 C4
Rockwell Green 103 E1
Rodborough 132 A2
Rodbourne 132 B4
Rodbridge Corner 151 G3
Rodd 144 C1
Roddam 229 E4
Rodden 104 C4
Rode 117 F2
Rode Heath 171 F2
Rodel (Roghadal) 263 F3
Roden 157 E1
Rodhuish 114 D4
Rodington 157 E1
Rodington Heath 157 E1
Rodley 131 G1
Rodmarton 132 B3
Rodmell 109 G3
Rodmersham 124 B2
Rodmersham Green 124 B2
Rodney Stoke 116 B2
Rodsley 172 D3
Rodway 115 F3
Roe Cross 185 D3
Roe Green 150 B4
Roecliffe 194 C1
Roehampton 136 B5
Roesound 279 C6
Roffey 121 G4
Rogart 266 E1
Rogate 120 D5
Rogerstone 130 B4
Rogiet 131 D4
Rokemarsh 134 B3
Roker 212 D2
Rollesby 179 F4
Rolleston Leics 160 C2
Rolleston Notts 174 C2
Rollestone 118 B3
Rolleston-on-Dove 172 D5
Rolston 197 E3
Rolstone 116 A3
Rolvenden 124 A5
Rolvenden Layne 124 A5
Romaldkirk 211 F5
Romanby 202 C3
Romanno Bridge 235 F5
Romansleigh 114 A5
Romesdal 263 K6
Romford Dorset 105 G2
Romford GtLon 137 E4
Romiley 184 D3
Romney, Hythe &
   Dymchurch Railway
   Kent TN28 8PL 124 D5
Romney Street 123 E2
Romsey 119 E5
Romsley Shrop 157 G4
Romsley Worcs 158 B5
Rona 264 C6
Ronachan 231 F4
Ronague 190 A4
Ronnachmore 230 B4
Rood End 158 C4
Rookhope 211 F3
Rookley 107 E4
Rookley Green 107 E4
Rooks Bridge 116 A2
Rook's Nest 115 D4
Rookwith 202 B4
Roos 197 E4
Roose 191 F1
Roosebeck 191 F1
Roosecote 191 F1
Rootham's Green 149 F2
Rootpark 235 D4
Ropley 120 B4
Ropley Dean 120 B4
Ropley Soke 120 B4
Ropsley 175 E4
Rora 269 J5
Rorandle 260 E3
Rorrington 156 C2
Rosarie 268 B6
Rose 96 B4
Rose Ash 114 A5
Rose Green Essex 152 A5
Rose Green WSuss 108 B4
Rose Hill 109 G2
Roseacre Kent 123 G3
Roseacre Lancs 192 A4
Rosebank 234 C5
Rosebrough 229 F4

Rosebush 141 D5
Rosecare 98 B1
Rosecliston 96 C4
Rosedale Abbey 203 G3
Roseden 229 E4
Rosehall 266 B1
Rosehearty 269 H4
Rosehill Aber 260 D5
Rosehill Shrop 157 D1
Roseisle 267 J5
Roselands 110 B3
Rosemarket 126 C2
Rosemarkie 266 E6
Rosemary Lane 103 E1
Rosemount P&K 251 G5
Rosemount SAyr 224 B3
Rosenannon 97 D3
Rosenithon 95 F4
Rosepool 126 B1
Rosevean 97 E4
Roseville 158 B3
Rosewell 235 G3
Roseworth 212 D5
Rosgill 199 G1
Roshven 247 F2
Roskhill 263 H7
Roskorwell 95 E4
Rosley 209 G2
Roslin 235 G3
Rosliston 159 E1
Rosneath 233 D1
Ross D&G 207 G2
Ross N'umb 229 F2
Ross P&K 242 C2
Ross Priory 233 F1
Rossdhu House 233 E1
Rossett 170 A2
Rossett Green 194 C2
Rosside 199 F1
Rossie Farm School 253 E4
Rossie Ochill 243 F3
Rossie Priory 244 A1
Rossington 186 D3
Rosskeen 266 D5
Rosslyn Chapel Midlo
   EH25 9PU 32 D4
Rossmore 105 G3
Ross-on-Wye 145 F5
Roster 275 H5
Rostherne 184 B4
Rosthwaite Cumb 209 F5
Rosthwaite Cumb 198 D4
Roston 172 C3
Rosudgeon 94 C4
Rosyth 235 F1
Rothbury 220 D1
Rotherby 160 B1
Rotherfield 123 E5
Rotherfield Greys 134 C4
Rotherfield Peppard 134 C4
Rotherham 186 B3
Rotherthorpe 148 B2
Rotherwick 120 C2
Rothes 267 K7
Rothesay 232 B3
Rothiebrisbane 261 F1
Rothiemurchus High
   PH22 1QH 259 G4
Rothienorman 261 F1
Rothiesholm 276 F5
Rothley Leics 160 A1
Rothley N'umb 220 C3
Rothney 260 E2
Rothwell Lincs 188 B3
Rothwell N'hants 160 D4
Rothwell WYorks 194 C5
Rotsea 196 C2
Rottal 252 B3
Rotten Row Bucks 134 C4
Rotten Row WMid 159 D5
Rottingdean 109 F3
Rottington 208 C5
Roud 107 E4
Roudham 164 A3
Rough Close 171 G4
Rough Common 124 D3
Rougham Norf 177 G5
Rougham Suff 152 A1
Rougham Green 152 A1
Roughburn 249 E1
Roughlee 193 E3
Roughley 158 D5
Roughton Lincs 176 A1
Roughton Norf 178 D2
Roughton Shrop 157 G3
Round Bush 136 A3
Roundbush Green 137 E1
Roundham 104 A2
Roundhay 194 C4
Roundstreet
   Common 121 F5
Roundway 118 B1
Rous Lench 146 C2
Rousay 276 D4
Rousdon 103 F3
Rousham 147 G5
Rousham Gap 147 G5
Routenburn 232 C3
Routh 196 C3
Rout's Green 134 C3
Row Corn 97 E2
Row Cumb 199 F4
Row Cumb 210 C4
Row Heath 139 E1
Row Town 121 F1
Rowanburn 218 C4
Rowardennan
   Lodge 241 F5
Rowarth 185 E4
Rowbarton 115 F5
Rowberrow 116 B2
Rowchoish 241 F4
Rowde 118 A1
Rowden 99 G1
Rowen 181 F5
Rowfields 172 C3
Rowfoot 210 C1
Rowhedge 152 B5
Rowhook 121 G4
Rowington 147 E1
Rowland 185 G5
Rowland's Castle 107 G1
Rowlands Gill 212 A2

Rowledge 120 D3
Rowlestone 144 C5
Rowley Devon 102 A1
Rowley Dur 211 G2
Rowley Shrop 156 C2
Rowley Park 171 G5
Rowley Regis 158 B4
Rowly 121 F3
Rowner 107 E2
Rowney Green 158 C5
Rownhams 106 C1
Rowrah 209 D5
Rowsham 135 D1
Rowstock 133 G4
Rowston 175 F2
Rowthorne 173 F1
Rowton
   ChesW&C 170 B1
Rowton Shrop 156 C1
Rowton Tel&W 157 F1
Roxburgh 228 B3
Roxby NLincs 187 G1
Roxby NYorks 203 G5
Roxton 149 G2
Roxwell 137 F2
Royal Academy of Arts
   GtLon W1J OBD 44 C4
Royal Albert Hall GtLon
   SW7 2AP 11 F5
Royal Albert Memorial
   Museum & Art Gallery
   Devon EX4 3RX
   72 Exeter
Royal Armouries Museum,
   Leeds GtLon
   LS10 1LT 41 G5
Royal Artillery Barracks
   GtLon SE18 5DP 13 F5
Royal Bath & West
   Showground Som
   BA4 6QN 116 D4
Royal Botanic Garden,
   Edinburgh Edin
   EH3 5LR 36 D4
Royal Botanic Gardens,
   Kew GtLon
   TW9 3AB 11 C6
Royal British Legion
   Village 123 G3
Royal Centre NG1 5ND
   80 Nottingham
Royal Cornwall Museum
   Corn TR1 2SJ 96 C5
Royal Festival Hall GtLon
   SE1 8XX 45 E3
Royal Highland Showground
   Edin EH28 8NB 32 A2
Royal Horticultural Halls
   GtLon SW1P 2PB 44 D7
Royal Hospital Chelsea
   GtLon SW3 4SR 13 A5
Royal Leamington
   Spa 147 F1
Royal Mews, Buckingham
   Palace GtLon
   SW1W 0QH 44 B6
Royal Naval Museum
   PO1 3NH
   82 Portsmouth
Royal Oak 183 F2
Royal Observatory
   Greenwich GtLon
   SE10 8XJ 13 D5
Royal Opera House GtLon
   WC2E 9DD 45 E3
Royal Pavilion B&H
   BN1 1EE 65 Brighton
Royal Scots Regimental
   Museum, The Edin
   EH1 2YT 37 F5
Royal Scottish Academy
   Edin EH2 2EL 37 F4
Royal Tunbridge
   Wells 123 E5
Royal Victoria Country Park
   Hants SO31 5GA 4 C4
Royal Welch Fusiliers
   Regimental Museum
   Gwyn LL55 2AY 167 D1
Royal Wootton
   Bassett 132 C4
Royal Yacht Britannia
   Edin EH6 6JJ 32 C1
Roybridge (Drochaid
   Ruaidh) 249 E1
Roydon Essex 136 D1
Roydon Norf 164 B3
Roydon Norf 177 F5
Roydon Hamlet 136 D2
Royston Herts 150 B3
Royston SYorks 186 A1
Royton 184 D2
Ruabon (Rhiwabon) 170 A3
Ruaig 246 B2
Ruan Lanihorne 96 C5
Ruan Major 95 D5
Ruan Minor 95 E5
Ruanaich 238 B2
Ruardean 131 F1
Ruardean Hill 131 F1
Ruardean Woodside 131 F1
Rubery 158 B5
Ruckcroft 210 B3
Ruckinge 124 C5
Ruckland 188 D5
Rucklers Lane 135 F2
Ruckley 157 E2
Rudbaxton 140 C5
Rudchester 212 A1
Ruddington 173 G4
Ruddlemoor 97 E4
Rudford 145 G5
Rudge 117 F2
Rudgeway 131 F4
Rudgwick 121 F4
Rudhall 145 F5
Rudheath 184 A5
Rudley Green 138 B2
Rudloe 117 F1
Rudry 130 A4
Rudston 196 C1
Rudyard 171 G2
Rudyard Lake Staffs
   ST13 8RT 171 G2

Rufford Country Park Notts
   NG22 9DF 174 B1
Rufforth 195 E2
Ruffside 211 F2
Rugby 160 A5
Rugby Football Union,
   Twickenham GtLon
   TW1 1DZ 11 B6
Rugeley 158 C1
Ruilick 266 C7
Ruishton 115 F5
Ruisigearraidh 262 E3
Ruislip 135 F4
Ruislip Gardens 135 F4
Ruislip Manor 136 A4
Rum 255 J5
Rumbling Bridge 243 F5
Rumburgh 165 E3
Rumford 96 C2
Rumleigh 100 A1
Rumney 130 B5
Rumwell 115 E5
Runacraig 242 A3
Runcorn 183 G4
Runcton 108 A3
Runcton Holme 163 E2
Rundlestone 99 F3
Runfold 121 D3
Runhall 178 B5
Runham Norf 179 F4
Runham Norf 179 G5
Runnington 115 E5
Runsell Green 137 G2
Runshaw Moor 183 G1
Runswick Bay 204 B1
Runtaleave 252 A3
Runwell 137 G3
Ruscombe Glos 132 A2
Ruscombe
   W'ham 134 C5
Rush Green
   GtLon 137 E4
Rush Green Herts 150 A5
Rushall Here 145 F4
Rushall Norf 164 C3
Rushall Wilts 118 C2
Rushall WMid 158 C2
Rushbrooke 151 G1
Rushbury 157 E3
Rushden Herts 150 B4
Rushden N'hants 149 E1
Rushford Devon 99 E3
Rushford Norf 164 A3
Rushgreen 184 A4
Rushlake Green 110 B2
Rushmere 165 F3
Rushmere
   St. Andrew 152 D3
Rushmoor 121 D3
Rushock 158 A5
Rusholme 184 C3
Rushton ChesW&C
   170 C1
Rushton N'hants 160 D4
Rushton Shrop 157 F2
Rushton Spencer 171 G1
Rushwick 146 A2
Rushy Green 109 G2
Rushyford 212 B5
Ruskie 242 B4
Ruskington 175 F2
Rusko 215 G5
Rusland 199 E4
Rusper 122 B5
Ruspidge 131 F1
Russ Hill 122 B4
Russel 264 E7
Russell Green 137 G1
Russell's Green 110 C2
Russell's Water 134 C4
Russel's Green 165 D4
Rusthall 123 E5
Rustington 108 C3
Ruston 204 C4
Ruston Parva 196 C1
Ruswarp 204 B2
Rutherend 234 B4
Rutherford 228 A3
Rutherglen 234 A3
Ruthernbridge 97 E3
Ruthers of Howe 275 J2
Ruthin (Rhuthun)
   Denb 169 E2
Ruthin VGlam 129 F5
Ruthrieston 261 H4
Ruthven Aber 268 D6
Ruthven Angus 252 A5
Ruthven High 259 F5
Ruthven High 258 E5
Ruthvoes 96 D3
Ruthwaite 209 F3
Ruthwell 217 D4
Rutland Water Rut
   LE15 8QL 161 D2
Ryal 220 C4
Ryal Fold 192 C5
Ryall Dorset 104 A3
Ryall Worcs 146 A3
Ryarsh 123 F3
Rydal 199 E2
Ryde 107 E3
Rydon 112 D5
Rye 111 E1
Rye Foreign 111 D1
Rye Harbour 111 E2
Rye Harbour ESuss
   TN31 7TX 111 E2
Rye Park 136 C2
Rye Street 145 G4
Ryebank 170 C3
Ryeford 145 F5
Ryehill Aber 260 E2
Ryehill ERid 197 E5
Ryehill 161 F1
Ryeland 186 A1
Ryhall 161 F1
Ryhope 212 D2
Rylands 173 G4
Rylstone 193 F2
Ryme Intrinseca 104 B3
Ryther 195 E4
Ryton Glos 145 G4
Ryton NYorks 203 G5
Ryton Shrop 157 G2
Ryton T&W 212 A1
Ryton-
   Dunsmore 159 F5

S

S.S. Great Britain Bristol
   BS1 6TY 8 B3
Saasaig 256 C4
Sabden 193 D4
Sabden Fold 193 E4
Sackers Green 152 A4
Sacombe 136 C1
Sacombe Green 136 C1
Sacriston 212 B3
Sadberge 202 C2
Saddell 222 C2
Saddington 160 B3
Saddle Bow 163 E1
Sadgill 199 F2
Saffron Walden 150 D4
Sageston 127 D2
Saham Hills 178 A5
Saham Toney 163 G5
Saighdinis 262 D5
Saighton 170 B1
St. Abbs 237 G3
St. Agnes 96 B4
St. Aidan's Winery N'umb
   TD15 2RX 229 F2
St. Albans 136 A2
St. Albans Cathedral Herts
   AL1 1BY 136 A2
St. Allen 96 C4
St. Andrews 244 C3
St. Andrew's & Blackfriars
   Halls Norf NR3 1AU
   79 Norwich
St. Andrews Major 130 A5
St. Anne 101 G4
St. Anne's 191 G5
St. Ann's 217 E1
St. Ann's Chapel
   Corn 99 E3
St. Ann's Chapel
   Devon 100 C3
St. Anthony 95 F3
St. Anthony-in-
   Meneage 95 E4
St. Anthony's Hill 110 B3
St. Arvans 131 E3
St. Asaph
   (Llanelwy) 182 B5
St. Athan 114 D1
St. Aubin 100 C5
St. Audries 115 E3
St. Austell 97 E4
St. Bees 208 C5
St. Blazey 97 E4
St. Blazey Gate 97 E4
St. Boswells 227 G2
St. Botolph's Church, Boston
   Lincs PE21 6NP 176 B3
St. Brelade 100 B5
St. Breock 97 D2
St. Breward 97 E2
St. Briavels 131 E2
St. Brides 126 B1
St. Brides Major 129 E5
St. Bride's
   Netherwent 130 D4
St. Brides
   Wentlooge 130 B4
St. Bride's-super-
   Ely 129 G5
St. Budeaux 100 A2
St. Buryan 94 B4
St. Catherine 117 E1
St. Catherines 240 D4
St. Clears (Sanclêr) 127 E1
St. Cleer 97 G3
St. Clement Chanl 100 C5
St. Clement Corn 96 C5
St. Clether 97 G1
St. Colmac 232 B3
St. Columb Major 96 D3
St. Columb Minor 96 C3
St. Columb Road 96 D3
St. Combs 269 J4
St. Cross South
   Elmham 165 D3
St. Cyrus 253 F3
St. Davids Fife 235 F1
St. David's P&K 243 E2
St. David's (Tyddewi)
   Pembs 140 A5
St. David's Hall CF10 1AH
   67 Cardiff
St. Day 96 B5
St. Decumans 115 D3
St. Dennis 97 D4
St. Denys 106 D1
St. Dogmaels
   (Llandudoch) 141 E3
St. Dogwells 140 C5
St. Dominick 99 E4
St. Donats 114 C1
St. Edith's Marsh 118 A1
St. Endellion 97 D1
St. Enoder 96 C4
St. Erme 96 C5
St. Erney 99 E5
St. Erth 94 C3
St. Erth Praze 94 C3
St. Ervan 96 C2
St. Eval 96 C3
St. Ewe 97 D5
St. Fagans 130 A5
St. Fagans National History
   Museum Cardiff
   CF5 6XB 7 A4
St. Fergus 269 J5
St. Fillans 242 B2
St. Florence 127 D2
St. Gennys 98 B1
St. George Bristol 131 F5
St. George Conwy 182 A5
St. Georges NSom 116 A1
St. George's Tel&W 157 F1
St. George's VGlam 129 G5
St. George's Hall, Liverpool
   Mersey L1 1JJ 42 D4
St. Germans 99 E5
St. Giles' Cathedral,
   Edinburgh Edin
   EH1 1RE 37 F4
St. Giles in the
   Wood 113 F4
St. Giles on the
   Heath 99 D1
St. Harmon 155 F5
St. Helen Auckland 212 A5

St. Helena 178 C4
St. Helen's ESuss 110 D2
St. Helens IoW 107 F4
St. Helens Mersey 183 G3
St. Helier Chanl 100 C5
St. Helier GtLon 122 B3
St. Hilary Corn 94 C3
St. Hilary VGlam 129 G5
St. Hill 122 C5
St. Ibbs 149 G5
St. Illtyd 130 B2
St. Ippollitts 149 G5
St. Ishmael 127 G2
St. Ishmael's 126 B2
St. Issey 96 D2
St. Ive 98 D4
St. Ives Cambs 162 B5
St. Ives Corn 94 C2
St. Ives Dorset 106 A2
St. James South
  Elmham 165 E3
St. John Chanl 100 C4
St. John Corn 100 A1
St. John the Baptist Church,
  Cirencester Glos
  GL7 2NX 132 C2
St. John's GtLon 136 C5
St. John's IoM 190 B3
St. John's Surr 121 E2
St. John's Worcs 146 A2
St. John's Chapel
  Devon 113 F3
St. John's Chapel
  Dur 211 E4
St. John's Fen End 162 D1
St. John's Hall 211 G4
St. John's Highway 162 D1
St. John's Kirk 226 A2
St. John's Town of
  Dalry 216 A2
St. Judes 190 B2
St. Just 94 A3
St. Just in Roseland 95 F3
St. Katherines 261 F1
St. Keverne 95 E4
St. Kew 97 E2
St. Kew Highway 97 E2
St. Keyne 97 G3
St. Lawrence Corn 97 E3
St. Lawrence Essex 138 C2
St. Lawrence IoW 107 E5
St. Lawrence's Church,
  Eyam Derbys
  S32 5QH 185 G5
St. Leonards
  Bucks 135 E2
St. Leonards
  Dorset 106 A2
St. Leonards
  ESuss 110 D3
St. Leonards
  Grange 106 D3
St. Leonard's Street
  123 F3
St. Levan 94 A4
St. Lythans 130 A5
St. Mabyn 97 E2
St. Madoes 243 G2
St. Margaret South
  Elmham 165 E3
St. Margarets
  Here 144 C4
St. Margarets
  Herts 136 C1
St. Margarets
  Wilts 118 D1
St. Margaret's at
  Cliffe 125 F4
St. Margaret's Hope 277 D8
St. Mark's 190 A4
St. Martin Chanl 101 F5
St. Martin Chanl 100 C5
St. Martin Corn 97 G4
St. Martin Corn 95 E4
St. Martin-in-the-Fields
  Church GtLon
  WC2N 4JH 44 E4
St. Martin's IoS 96 B1
St. Martins P&K 243 G1
St. Martin's Shrop 170 A4
St. Mary 100 C5
St. Mary Bourne 119 F2
St. Mary Church 129 G5
St. Mary Cray 123 D2
St. Mary Hill 129 F5
St. Mary Hoo 137 G5
St. Mary in the
  Marsh 111 F1
St. Mary Magdalene Chapel,
  Sandringham Norf
  PE35 6EH 177 G3
St. Mary the Virgin Church,
  Holy Island N'umb
  TD15 2RX 229 F2
St. Mary the Virgin Church,
  Oxford Oxon
  OX1 4AH 134 A2
St. Mary the Virgin Church,
  Rye ESuss
  TN31 7HE 111 E2
St. Marychurch 101 F1
St. Mary's IoS 96 B1
St. Mary's Ork 277 D7
St. Mary's Airport 96 B1
St. Mary's Bay 111 F1
St. Mary's Church, Whitby
  NYorks
  YO22 4JT 204 C1
St. Mary's Grove 116 B1
St. Maughans
  Green 131 D1
St. Mawes 95 F3
St. Mawgan 96 C3
St. Mellion 99 D4
St. Mellons 130 B4
St. Merryn 96 C5
St. Mewan 97 D4
St. Michael Caerhays 97 D5
St. Michael Church 116 A4
St. Michael Penkevil 96 C5
St. Michael South
  Elmham 165 E3
St. Michaels Fife 244 C2
St. Michaels Kent 124 A5
St. Michaels Worcs 145 G4
St. Michael's Church,
  Hathersage Derbys
  S32 1AJ 185 G4

St. Michael's Mount Corn
  TR17 0HT 94 C3
St. Michael's on
  Wyre 192 A3
St. Mildred's Church,
  Whippingham IoW
  PO32 6LP 107 E3
St. Minver 97 D3
St. Monans 244 D4
St. Mungo Museum of
  Religious Life & Art
  Glas G4 0RH 39 H3
St. Mungo's Cathedral,
  Glasgow Glas
  G4 0QZ 39 J3
St. Neot 97 F3
St. Neots 149 G1
St. Newlyn East 96 C4
St. Nicholas Pembs 140 C4
St. Nicholas VGlam 129 G5
St. Nicholas at
  Wade 125 D4
St. Ninians 242 C5
St. Osyth 139 E1
St. Ouen 100 B5
St. Owen's Cross 145 E5
St. Paul's Cathedral,
  London GtLon
  EC4M 8AD 45 J3
St. Paul's Cray 123 D2
St. Paul's Walden 149 G5
St. Peter 100 C5
St. Peter Port 101 F5
St. Peter's 125 F2
St. Petrox 126 C3
St. Pinnock 97 G3
St. Quivox 224 B3
St. Ruan 95 E5
St. Sampson 101 F4
St. Saviour Chanl 101 E5
St. Saviour Chanl 100 C5
St. Stephen 96 D4
St. Stephens Corn 100 A2
St. Stephens Corn 98 D2
St. Stephens Herts 136 A2
St. Teath 97 E1
St. Tudy 97 E2
St. Twynnells 126 C3
St. Veep 97 F4
St. Vigeans 253 E5
St. Wenn 97 D3
St. Weonards 145 D5
St. Winnow 97 F4
St. Winwaloe's Church,
  Gunwalloe Corn
  TR12 7QE 95 D4
Saintbury 146 D4
Salachail 248 C4
Salcombe 100 D4
Salcombe Regis 103 E4
Salcott 138 C1
Sale 184 B3
Sale Green 146 B2
Saleby 189 E5
Salehurst 110 C1
Salem Carmar 142 C5
Salem Cere 154 C4
Salem Gwyn 167 E2
Salen A&B 247 E3
Salen High 247 F3
Salendine Nook 185 F1
Salesbury 192 C4
Saleway 146 B2
Salford CenBeds 149 E4
Salford GtMan 184 C3
Salford Oxon 147 E5
Salford Priors 146 C2
Salfords 122 B4
Salhouse 179 E4
Saline 243 F5
Salisbury 118 C5
Salisbury Cathedral
  Wilts SP1 2EF
  83 Salisbury
Salkeld Dykes 210 B4
Sallachan 248 B3
Sallachy 240 C3
Sallachy High 266 C1
Sallachy High 257 F1
Salle 178 C3
Sally Lunn's House
  B&NESom BA1 1NX
  63 Bath
Salmonby 188 D5
Salmond's Muir 245 D1
Salperton 146 C5
Salph End 149 F2
Salsburgh 234 C3
Salt 171 G5
Salt Hill 135 E4
Salt Holme 213 D5
Saltaire 194 A4
Saltash 100 A2
Saltburn 266 E4
Saltburn-by-the-
  Sea 213 F5
Saltburn's Inclined
  Tramway R&C
  TS12 1DP 213 F5
Saltby 175 D5
Saltcoats Cumb 198 B3
Saltcoats NAyr 232 D5
Saltcotes 191 G5
Saltdean 109 F3
Salter 192 B1
Salterbeck 208 C4
Salterforth 193 E3
Saltergate 204 B3
Salterhill 267 K5
Salters Lode 163 E2
Saltfleet 189 E3
Saltfleetby All
  Saints 189 E3
Saltfleetby
  St. Clements 189 E3
Saltfleetby St. Peter 189 E4
Saltford 117 D1
Salthaugh Grange 197 E5
Salthouse 178 B1
Saltley 158 C4
Saltmarshe 195 G5
Saltness 277 B8
Saltney 170 A1
Salton 203 G4
Saltrens 113 E3
Saltwell Park, Gateshead
  T&W NE9 5AX 28 B3
Saltwick 221 D4

Saltwood 125 D5
Salum 246 A2
Salvington 108 D3
Salwarpe 146 A1
Salwayash 104 A3
Sambourne 146 C1
Sambrook 171 E5
Samhla 262 C5
Samlesbury 192 C4
Sampford Arundel 103 E1
Sampford Brett 115 D3
Sampford
  Courtenay 113 G5
Sampford Moor 103 E1
Sampford Peverell 102 D1
Sampford Spiney 99 F3
Samuelston 236 B2
Sanaigmore 230 A2
Sancreed 94 B4
Sancton 196 B4
Sand Shr 279 C8
Sand Som 116 B3
Sand Hutton 195 F2
Sandaig A&B 246 A2
Sandaig High 256 D4
Sandaig High 256 D4
Sandal Magna 186 A1
Sanday 279 F3
Sanday Airfield 276 F3
Sandbach 171 E1
Sandbank 232 C1
Sandbanks 105 G4
Sandend 268 D4
Sanderstead 122 C2
Sandford Cumb 200 C1
Sandford Devon 102 B2
Sandford Dorset 105 F4
Sandford IoW 107 E5
Sandford NSom 116 B2
Sandford Shrop 170 C4
Sandford Shrop 170 A5
Sandford SLan 234 B5
Sandford Orcas 116 D5
Sandford St. Martin 147 G5
Sandfordhill 269 K6
Sandford-on-
  Thames 134 A2
Sandgarth 277 E6
Sandgate 125 E5
Sandgreen 215 G5
Sandhaven 269 H4
Sandhead 214 B5
Sandhills Dorset 104 C1
Sandhills Dorset 104 B2
Sandhills Surr 121 E4
Sandhills WYorks 194 C4
Sandhoe 211 F1
Sandholme ERid 196 A4
Sandholme Lincs 176 B4
Sandhurst BrackF 120 D1
Sandhurst Glos 146 A5
Sandhurst Kent 110 C1
Sandhurst Cross 110 C1
Sandhutton 202 C4
Sandiacre 173 F4
Sandilands 189 F4
Sandiway 184 A5
Sandleheath 106 A1
Sandleigh 133 G2
Sandling 123 G3
Sandlow Green 171 E1
Sandness 279 A7
Sandon Essex 137 G2
Sandon Herts 150 B4
Sandon Staffs 171 G5
Sandown 107 F4
Sandplace 97 G4
Sandquoy 276 F2
Sandridge Devon 101 E2
Sandridge Herts 136 A1
Sandridge Wilts 118 A1
Sandringham 177 E5
Sandrocks 109 F1
Sandsend 204 B1
Sandside 199 F4
Sandside House 274 E2
Sandsound 279 C8
Sandtoft 187 E2
Sanduck 102 A4
Sandway 124 A3
Sandwell 158 C4
Sandwell Park Farm WMid
  B71 4BG 14 C2
Sandwell Valley Country
  Park WMid
  B71 4BG 14 C2
Sandwich 125 F5
Sandwick Cumb 199 F1
Sandwick Shet 279 D10
Sandwick (Sanndabhaig)
  Na H-E. Siar 271 G4
Sandwith 208 C5
Sandy Carmar 128 A2
Sandy CenBeds 149 G3
Sandy Bank 176 A2
Sandy Haven 126 B2
Sandy Lane Wilts 118 A1
Sandy Lane Wrex 170 B3
Sandy Lane
  WYorks 194 A4
Sandy Way 107 D4
Sandycroft 170 A1
Sandygate Devon 102 B5
Sandygate IoM 190 B2
Sandyhills 216 C5
Sandylands 192 A1
Sandypark 102 A4
Sandyway 145 D5
Sangobeg 273 G2
Sankyn's Green 145 G1
Sanna 247 D3
Sannaig 230 D3
Sannox 232 B5
Sanquhar 225 F5
Santon Bridge 198 C2
Santon Downham 163 G4
Sant-y-Nyll 129 G5
Sapcote 159 G3
Sapey Common 145 G1
Sapiston 164 A4
Sapperton Derbys 172 C4
Sapperton Glos 132 B2
Sapperton Lincs 175 F4
Saracen's Head 176 B5
Sarclet 275 J4
Sardis 126 C2
Sarisbury 107 E2
Sark 101 G5

Sark Dark Sky Island 101 G5
Sarn Bridgend 129 F4
Sarn Powys 156 B3
Sarn Bach 166 C5
Sarnau Carmar 127 G1
Sarnau Cere 141 G2
Sarnau Gwyn 168 C4
Sarnau Powys 156 B3
Sarnau Powys 143 G4
Sarnesfield 144 C2
Saron Carmar 128 C1
Saron Carmar 141 G4
Saron Gwyn 167 E1
Saron Gwyn 167 D2
Sarratt 135 F3
Sarre 125 E2
Sarsden 147 E5
Sarsgrum 273 F2
Sartfield 190 B2
Satley 212 A3
Satron 201 E3
Satterleigh 113 G3
Satterthwaite 199 E3
Sauchen 260 E3
Saucher 243 G1
Sauchie 243 D5
Sauchieburn 253 E3
Saughall 183 E5
Saughall Massie 183 D4
Saughtree 219 D2
Saul 131 G2
Saundby 187 E4
Saundersfoot 127 E2
Saunderton 134 C2
Saunton 113 E2
Sausthorpe 176 B1
Saval 266 C1
Savalbeg 266 C1
Saverley Green 171 G4
Savile Town 194 B5
Sawbridge 148 A1
Sawbridgeworth 137 D1
Sawdon 204 C4
Sawley Derbys 173 F4
Sawley Lancs 193 D3
Sawley NYorks 194 B1
Sawston 150 C3
Sawtry 161 G4
Saxby Leics 160 D1
Saxby Lincs 188 A4
Saxby All Saints 187 G1
Saxelby 174 B5
Saxham Street 152 B1
Saxilby 187 F5
Saxlingham 178 B2
Saxlingham Green 164 D2
Saxlingham
  Nethergate 164 D2
Saxlingham
  Thorpe 164 D2
Saxmundham 153 E1
Saxon Street 151 E2
Saxondale 174 B4
Saxtead 153 D1
Saxtead Green 153 D1
Saxtead Little
  Green 153 D1
Saxthorpe 178 C2
Saxton 195 D4
Sayers Common 109 E2
Scackleton 203 F5
Scadabhagh 263 G2
Scaftworth 187 D3
Scagglethorpe 204 B5
Scaitcliffe 193 D5
Scalasaig 238 C5
Scalby ERid 196 A5
Scalby NYorks 204 D3
Scaldwell 160 C5
Scale Houses 210 B3
Scaleby 210 A1
Scalebyhill 210 A1
Scales Cumb 209 G4
Scales Cumb 199 D5
Scalford 174 C5
Scaling 203 G1
Scallasaig 256 E3
Scallastle 239 G1
Scalloway 279 C9
Scalpay (Eilean
  Scalpaigh) 263 H2
Scamblesby 188 C5
Scammadale 240 A2
Scamodale 248 A2
Scampston 204 B5
Scampton 187 G5
Scaniport 258 D1
Scapa 277 D7
Scapegoat Hill 185 E1
Scar 276 F2
Scarborough 204 D4
Scarborough Sea Life &
  Marine Sanctuary
  NYorks
  YO12 6RP 204 D4
Scarcewater 96 D4
Scarcliffe 173 F1
Scarcroft 194 C3
Scardroy 265 J6
Scarff 278 B4
Scarfskerry 275 H1
Scargill 201 F1
Scarinish 246 B2
Scarisbrick 183 E1
Scarning 178 A4
Scarrington 174 C3
Scarrowhill 210 B2
Scarth Hill 183 F2
Scarthingwell 195 D4
Scartho 188 C2
Scarwell 276 B5
Scatraig 258 E1
Scaur (Kippford)
  D&G 216 C5
Scaur D&G 216 C3
Scawby 187 G2
Scawby Brook 187 G2
Scawton 203 E4
Scayne's Hill 109 F1
Scealascro 270 D5
Scethrog 144 A5
Schaw 224 C3
Scholar Green 171 F2
Scholes SYorks 186 A3
Scholes WYorks 194 C4
Scholes WYorks 185 F2

Scholes WYorks 194 A5
School Green 170 D1
School House 103 G2
Schoose 208 B5
Sciberscross 266 E1
Science Museum GtLon
  SW7 2DD 11 F5
Scilly Isles
  (Isles of Scilly) 96 B1
Scissett 185 G1
Scleddau 140 C4
Sco Ruston 179 D3
Scofton 186 D4
Scole 164 C4
Scolpaig 262 C4
Scone 243 G2
Scones Lethendy 243 G2
Sconser 256 B1
Scoor 238 D3
Scopwick 175 F2
Scoraig 265 G2
Scorborough 196 C3
Scorrier 96 B5
Scorriton 100 D1
Scorton Lancs 192 B3
Scorton NYorks 202 B2
Scot Hay 171 E3
Scotby 210 A2
Scotch Corner 202 B2
Scotch Whisky Heritage
  Centre Edin
  EH1 2NE 37 F4
Scotforth 192 A2
Scothern 188 A5
Scotland 175 F4
Scotland End 147 F4
Scotland Street 152 A4
Scotland Street School
  Museum of Education
  Glas G5 8QB 38 C6
Scotlandwell 243 G4
Scotnish 231 F1
Scots' Gap 220 C3
Scotsburn 266 E4
Scotston Aber 253 F2
Scotston P&K 251 E5
Scotstoun 233 G3
Scotstown 248 A3
Scott Willoughby 175 F4
Scotter 187 F2
Scotterthorpe 187 F2
Scottish Exhibition &
  Conference Centre
  (S.E.C.C.) Glas
  G3 8YW 38 B4
Scottish National Gallery
  of Modern Art Edin
  EH4 3DR 36 A1
Scottish National Portrait
  Gallery Edin
  EH2 1JD 37 F3
Scottish Parliament Edin
  EH99 1SP 37 H4
Scottish Seabird Centre,
  North Berwick ELoth
  EH39 4SS 236 C1
Scottish Wool Centre,
  Aberfoyle Stir
  FK8 3UQ 242 A4
Scottlethorpe 175 F5
Scotton Lincs 187 F3
Scotton NYorks 202 A3
Scotton NYorks 194 C2
Scottow 179 D3
Scoughall 236 D1
Scoulton 178 A5
Scounslow Green 172 B5
Scourie 272 D4
Scourie More 272 D4
Scousburgh 279 F9
Scouthead 185 D2
Scrabster 275 G1
Scrafield 176 B1
Scrainwood 220 B1
Scrane End 176 B3
Scraptoft 160 B2
Scratby 179 F4
Scrayingham 195 G2
Scredington 175 F3
Scremby 176 C1
Scremerston 229 E2
Screveton 174 C3
Scriven 194 C2
Scronkey 192 A3
Scrooby 187 D3
Scropton 172 C4
Scrub Hill 176 A2
Scruton 202 C3
Sculcoates 177 G4
Scunthorpe 187 F1
Scurlage 128 A4
Sea 103 G1
Sea Life Centre, Blackpool
  FY1 5AA
  64 Blackpool
Sea Life Centre, Brighton
  B&H BN2 1TB
  65 Brighton
Sea Life Centre, Great
  Yarmouth Norf
  NR30 3AH 179 G5
Sea Life London Aquarium
  GtLon SE1 7PD 45 F5
Sea Life Sanctuary,
  Hunstanton Norf
  PE36 5BH 177 E4
Sea Mills 131 E5
Sea Palling 179 F3
Seabank 248 B5
Seaborough 104 A2
Seaburn 212 D1
Seacombe 183 E3
Seacroft Lincs 176 D1
Seacroft WYorks 194 C4
Seadyke 176 B4
Seafield A&B 231 F1
Seafield SAyr 224 B3
Seafield WLoth 235 E3
Seaford 109 G4
Seaforth 183 E3
Seagrave 160 B1
Seagry Heath 132 B4
Seaham 212 D3
Seaham Grange 212 D2
Seahouses 229 G3
Seal 123 E3
Sealand 170 A1
Seale 121 D3

Sea-Life Adventure,
  Southend-on-Sea S'end
  SS1 2ER 138 B4
Sealyham 140 C5
Seamer NYorks 203 D1
Seamer NYorks 204 D4
Seamill 232 C5
SeaQuarium, Rhyl Denb
  LL18 3AF 182 B4
Searby 188 B2
Seasalter 124 C2
Seascale 198 B2
Seathorne 177 D1
Seathwaite Cumb 209 F5
Seathwaite Cumb 198 D3
Seatle 199 E4
Seatoller 199 E3
Seaton Corn 98 D5
Seaton Cumb 208 B3
Seaton Devon 103 F3
Seaton Dur 212 C2
Seaton ERid 197 D3
Seaton N'umb 221 F4
Seaton Rut 161 E3
Seaton Burn 221 E4
Seaton Carew 213 E5
Seaton Delaval 221 F4
Seaton Junction 103 F3
Seaton Ross 195 G3
Seaton Sluice 221 F4
Seaton Tramway Devon
  EX12 2NQ 103 F3
Seatown Aber 269 J5
Seatown Dorset 104 A3
Seatown Moray 268 D4
Seave Green 203 E2
Seaview 107 F3
Seaville 209 E1
Seavington
  St. Mary 104 A1
Seavington
  St. Michael 104 A1
Seawick 139 E1
Sebastopol 130 B3
Sebergham 209 G2
Seckington 159 E2
Second Coast 265 F2
Sedbergh 200 B3
Sedbury 131 E3
Sedbusk 201 D3
Seddington 149 G3
Sedgeberrow 146 C4
Sedgebrook 175 D4
Sedgefield 212 C5
Sedgeford 177 F4
Sedgehill 117 F5
Sedgemere 159 E5
Sedgley 158 B3
Sedgwick 199 G4
Sedlescombe 110 C2
Sedlescombe
  Street 110 C2
Seend 118 A1
Seend Cleeve 118 A1
Seer Green 135 E3
Seething 165 E2
Sefton 183 E2
Sefton Park 183 E4
Seghill 221 E4
Seighford 171 F5
Seil 239 G3
Seilebost 263 F2
Seion 167 E1
Seisdon 158 A3
Seisiadar 271 H4
Seized! Revenue &
  Customs Uncovered
  Mersey L3 4AQ
  42 B5
Selattyn 169 F3
Selborne 120 C4
Selby 195 F4
Selham 121 E5
Selhurst 122 C2
Selkirk 227 F3
Sellack 145 E5
Sellafield 198 B2
Sellafield Visitors Centre
  Cumb CA20 1PG 198 B2
Sellafirth 278 E3
Sellindge 124 D5
Selling 124 C3
Sells Green 118 A1
Selly Oak 158 C4
Selmeston 110 A3
Selsdon 122 C2
Selsey 108 A4
Selsfield Common 122 C5
Selside Cumb 199 G3
Selside NYorks 200 C5
Selsley 132 A2
Selstead 125 E4
Selston 173 F2
Selworthy 114 C3
Semblister 279 C7
Semer 152 A3
Semington 117 F1
Semley 117 F5
Send 121 F2
Send Marsh 121 F2
Senghenydd 130 A3
Sennen 94 A4
Sennen Cove 94 A4
Sennybridge 143 F5
Senwick 207 G2
Sequer's Bridge 100 C2
Serlby 186 D4
Serpentine Gallery GtLon
  W2 3XA 11 F5
Serrington 118 B4
Sessay 203 D5
Setchey 163 E1
Setley 106 C2
Setter Shet 279 E8
Setter Shet 279 C7
Settiscarth 277 C6
Settle 193 E1
Settrington 204 B5
Seven Ash 115 E4
Seven Bridges 132 D3
Seven Kings 137 D4
Seven Sisters 129 E3
Seven Springs 132 B1
Sevenhampton
  Glos 146 C5
Sevenhampton
  Swin 133 E3
Sevenoaks 123 E3

Sevenoaks Weald 123 E3
Severn Beach 131 E4
Severn Stoke 146 A3
Severn Valley Railway
  Shrop
  DY12 1BG 157 G4
Sevick End 149 F2
Sevington 124 C4
Sewards End 151 E4
Sewardstone 136 C3
Sewerby 197 E1
Sewerby Hall & Gardens
  ERid
  YO15 1EA 197 E1
Seworgan 95 E3
Sewstern 175 D5
Seymour Villas 113 E1
Sezincote 147 D4
Sgarasta Mhòr 263 F2
Sgiogarstaigh 271 H1
Sgodachail 266 B2
Shabbington 134 B2
Shackerley 158 A2
Shackerstone 159 F2
Shackleford 121 E3
Shadfen 221 E3
Shadforth 212 C3
Shadingfield 165 F3
Shadoxhurst 124 B5
Shadsworth 192 D5
Shadwell Norf 164 A3
Shadwell WYorks 194 C3
Shaftenhoe End 150 C4
Shaftesbury 117 F5
Shafton 186 A1
Shakespeare's Birthplace
  Warks CV37 6QW
  85 Stratford-upon-Avon
Shakespeare's Globe Theatre
  GtLon SE1 9DT 45 J4
Shalbourne 119 E1
Shalcombe 106 C4
Shalden 120 B3
Shalden Green 120 C3
Shaldon 102 C5
Shalfleet 106 D4
Shalford Essex 151 F5
Shalford Surr 121 F3
Shalford Green 151 F5
Shallowford Devon 114 A3
Shallowford Staffs 171 F5
Shalmsford Street 124 C3
Shalmstry 275 G2
Shalstone 148 B4
Shalunt 232 B2
Shambellie 217 D4
Shamley Green 121 F3
Shandon 233 D1
Shandwick 267 F4
Shangton 160 C3
Shankend 227 G5
Shankhouse 221 E4
Shanklin 107 E4
Shanklin Chine IoW
  PO37 6BW 107 E4
Shannochie 223 E3
Shantron 233 E1
Shantullich 266 D6
Shanzie 252 A4
Shap 199 G1
Shapinsay 277 E6
Shapwick Dorset 105 F2
Shapwick Som 116 B4
Sharcott 118 C2
Shard End 159 D4
Shardlow 173 F4
Shareshill 158 B2
Sharlston 186 A1
Sharlston Common 186 A1
Sharnal Street 137 G5
Sharnbrook 149 E2
Sharneyford 193 E5
Sharnford 159 G3
Sharnhill Green 104 D2
Sharow 202 C5
Sharp Street 179 E3
Sharpenhoe 149 F4
Sharperton 220 B1
Sharpham House 101 E2
Sharpness 131 F2
Sharpthorne 122 C5
Sharrington 178 B2
Shatterford 157 G4
Shattering 125 E3
Shaugh Prior 100 B1
Shave Cross 104 A3
Shavington 171 E2
Shaw GtMan 184 D2
Shaw Swin 132 D3
Shaw WBerks 119 F1
Shaw Wilts 117 F1
Shaw Green Herts 150 A4
Shaw Green NYorks 194 B2
Shaw Mills 194 B1
Shaw Side 184 D2
Shawbost
  (Siabost) 270 E3
Shawbury 170 C5
Shawell 160 A4
Shawfield GtMan 184 C1
Shawfield Staffs 172 B1
Shawford 119 F5
Shawforth 193 E5
Shawhead 216 C3
Shawtonhill 234 A5
Sheanachie 222 C4
Sheandow 259 K1
Shearington 217 E4
Shearsby 160 B3
Shebbear 113 E5
Shebdon 171 E5
Shebster 275 F2
Shedfield 107 E1
Sheen 172 C1
Sheepridge 185 F1
Sheepscombe 132 A1
Sheepstor 100 B1
Sheepwash Devon 113 E5
Sheepwash N'umb 221 E3
Sheepway 131 D5
Sheepy Magna 159 F2
Sheepy Parva 159 F2
Sheering 137 E1
Sheerness 124 B1
Sheet 120 C5
Sheffield 186 A4
Sheffield Botanic Gardens
  SYorks S10 2LN 21 B3

Sheffield Bottom 120 B1
Sheffield Green 109 G1
Sheffield Park Garden ESuss TN22 3QX 109 G1
Shefford 149 G4
Shefford Woodlands 133 F5
Sheigra 272 D2
Sheinton 157 F2
Shelderton 156 D5
Sheldon Derbys 172 C1
Sheldon Devon 103 E2
Sheldon WMid 158 D4
Sheldwich 124 C3
Sheldwich Lees 124 C3
Shelf Bridgend 129 F4
Shelf WYorks 194 A5
Shelfanger 164 C3
Shelfield Warks 146 D1
Shelfield WMid 158 C2
Shelfield Green 146 D1
Shelford 174 B3
Shellachan A&B 240 A2
Shellachan A&B 240 C2
Shellbrook 159 F1
Shellbrook Hill 170 A3
Shelley Essex 137 E2
Shelley Suff 152 B4
Shelley WYorks 185 G1
Shellingford 133 F3
Shellow Bowells 137 F2
Shelsley Beauchamp 145 G1
Shelsley Walsh 145 G1
Shelswell 148 B4
Shelthorpe 160 A1
Shelton Bed 149 F1
Shelton Norf 164 D2
Shelton Notts 174 C3
Shelton Shrop 157 D1
Shelve 156 C3
Shelwick 145 E3
Shelwick Green 145 E3
Shenfield 137 F3
Shenington 147 F3
Shenley 136 A2
Shenley Brook End 148 D4
Shenley Church End 148 D4
Shenleybury 136 A2
Shenmore 144 C4
Shennanton 215 E4
Shenstone Staffs 158 D2
Shenstone Worcs 158 A5
Shenstone Woodend 158 D2
Shenton 159 F2
Shenval 259 K2
Shepeau Stow 162 B1
Shephall 150 A5
Shepherd's Bush 136 B5
Shepherd's Green 134 C4
Shepherd's Patch 131 G2
Shepherdswell (Sibertswold) 125 E4
Shepley 185 F2
Sheppardstown 275 H5
Shepperdine 131 F3
Shepperton 121 F1
Shepreth 150 B3
Shepreth Wildlife Park Cambs SG8 6PZ 150 B3
Shepshed 159 G1
Shepton Beauchamp 104 A1
Shepton Mallet 116 D3
Shepton Montague 117 D4
Shepway 123 G3
Sheraton 212 D4
Sherborne Dorset 104 C1
Sherborne Glos 133 D1
Sherborne St. John 120 B2
Sherbourne 147 E1
Sherbourne Street 152 A3
Sherburn Dur 212 C3
Sherburn NYorks 204 C5
Sherburn Hill 212 C3
Sherburn in Elmet 195 D4
Shere 121 F3
Shereford 177 G5
Sherfield English 119 D5
Sherfield on oddon 120 B2
Sherford Devon 101 D3
Sherford Som 115 F5
Sheriff Hutton 195 F1
Sheriffhales 157 G1
Sheringham 178 C1
Sheringham Park Norf NR26 8TL 178 C1
Sherington 149 D3
Shernal Green 146 B1
Shernborne 177 F4
Sherramore 258 C5
Sherrington 118 A4
Sherston 132 A4
Sherwood 173 G3
Sherwood Forest Country Park Notts NG21 9HN 174 B1
Sherwood Forest Fun Park Notts NG21 9QA 174 B1
Sherwood Green 113 F3
Sherwood Pines Forest Park Notts NG21 9JL 174 B1
Shetland Islands 279 B7
Shevington 183 G2
Shevington Moor 183 G1
Sheviock 99 D5
Shide 107 E4
Shiel Bridge (Drochaid Sheile) 257 F3
Shieldaig High 264 E6
Shieldaig High 264 E4
Shieldhill 234 C2
Shielfoot 247 F2
Shielhill 252 C4
Shiels 260 E4
Shifford 133 F2
Shifnal 157 G2
Shilbottle 221 D1
Shildon 212 B5
Shillingford Devon 114 C5
Shillingford Oxon 134 A3
Shillingford Abbot 102 C4
Shillingford St. George 102 C4
Shillingstone 105 E1
Shillington 149 G4
Shillmoor 220 A1
Shilstone 113 F5
Shilton Oxon 133 E2
Shilton Warks 159 G4
Shimpling Norf 164 C3
Shimpling Suff 151 G2
Shimpling Street 151 G2
Shincliffe 212 B3
Shiney Row 212 C2
Shinfield 120 C1
Shingay 150 B3
Shingham 163 F2
Shingle Street 153 E3
Shinness Lodge 273 H7
Shipbourne 123 E3
Shipbrookhill 184 A5
Shipdham 178 A5
Shipham 116 B2
Shiphay 101 E1
Shiplake 134 C5
Shiplake Row 134 C5
Shipley N'umb 229 F5
Shipley Shrop 158 A3
Shipley WSuss 121 G5
Shipley WYorks 194 A4
Shipley Bridge Devon 100 C1
Shipley Bridge Surr 122 C4
Shipley Common 173 F3
Shipley Country Park Derbys DE75 7GX 18 D2
Shipmeadow 165 E2
Shippea Hill 163 E4
Shippon 133 G3
Shipston on Stour 147 E3
Shipton Glos 132 C1
Shipton NYorks 195 E2
Shipton Shrop 157 E3
Shipton Bellinger 118 D3
Shipton Gorge 104 A3
Shipton Green 108 A3
Shipton Moyne 132 A4
Shipton Oliffe 132 C1
Shipton Solers 132 C1
Shipton-on-Cherwell 133 G1
Shiptonthorpe 196 A3
Shipton-under-Wychwood 133 E1
Shira 241 D3
Shirburn 134 B3
Shirdley Hill 183 E1
Shire Hall Gallery, Stafford Staffs ST16 2LD 171 G5
Shire Oak 158 C2
Shirebrook 173 G1
Shirecliffe 186 A3
Shiregreen 186 A3
Shirehampton 131 E5
Shiremoor 221 F4
Shirenewton 131 D3
Shireoaks 186 C4
Shirl Heath 144 D2
Shirland 173 E2
Shirley Derbys 172 D3
Shirley GtLon 122 C2
Shirley Hants 106 A3
Shirley Soton 106 D1
Shirley WMid 158 D5
Shirley Heath 158 D5
Shirley Warren 106 C1
Shirleywich 171 G5
Shirrell Heath 107 E1
Shirwell 113 F2
Shirwell Cross 113 F2
Shiskine 223 E3
Shittlehope 211 G4
Shobdon 144 C1
Shobley 106 A2
Shobrooke 102 B2
Shocklach 170 B3
Shocklach Green 170 B3
Shoeburyness 138 C4
Sholden 125 F3
Sholing 107 D1
Shoot Hill 156 D1
Shooter's Hill 136 D5
Shop Corn 96 C2
Shop Corn 112 C4
Shop Corner 152 D4
Shopnoller 115 E4
Shore 184 D1
Shoreditch 136 C4
Shoreham 123 E2
Shoreham Airport 109 D3
Shoreham-by-Sea 109 E3
Shoremill 266 E5
Shoresdean 237 G5
Shoreswood 237 G5
Shoreton 266 D5
Shorley 119 G5
Shorncote 132 C3
Shorne 137 F5
Shorne Ridgeway 137 F5
Short Cross 156 B2
Short Green 164 B3
Short Heath Derbys 159 F1
Short Heath WMid 158 C3
Shortacombe 99 F2
Shortbridge 109 G1
Shortfield Common 120 D3
Shortgate 109 G2
Shortgrove 150 D4
Shorthampton 147 F5
Shortlands 122 C2
Shortlanesend 96 C5
Shorton 101 E1
Shorwell 107 D4
Shoscombe 117 E2
Shotatton 170 A5
Shotesham 164 D2
Shotgate 137 G3
Shotley N'hants 161 E3
Shotley Suff 152 D4
Shotley Bridge 211 G2
Shotley Gate 152 D4
Shotleyfield 211 G2
Shottenden 124 C3
Shottermill 121 D4
Shottery 147 D2
Shotteswell 147 G3
Shottisham 153 E3
Shottle 173 E2
Shottlegate 173 E3
Shotton Dur 212 D4
Shotton Dur 212 C5
Shotton Flints 170 A1
Shotton N'umb 221 E4
Shotton Colliery 212 C3
Shotts 234 C3
Shotwick 183 E5
Shouldham 163 E2
Shouldham Thorpe 163 E2
Shoulton 146 A2
Shover's Green 123 F5
Shrawardine 156 C1
Shrawley 146 A1
Shreding Green 135 F4
Shrewley 147 E1
Shrewsbury 157 D1
Shrewton 118 B3
Shri Venkateswara (Balaji) Temple of the United Kingdom WMid B69 3DU 14 C3
Shrine of Our Lady of Walsingham (Anglican) Norf NR22 6EF 178 A2
Shripney 108 B3
Shrivenham 133 E4
Shropham 164 A2
Shroton (Iwerne Courtney) 105 E1
Shrub End 152 A5
Shucknall 145 E3
Shudy Camps 151 E3
Shugborough Estate Staffs ST17 0XB 171 G5
Shurdington 132 B1
Shurlock Row 134 D5
Shurnock 146 C1
Shurrery 275 F3
Shurrery Lodge 275 F3
Shurton 115 F3
Shustoke 159 E3
Shut Heath 171 F5
Shute Devon 103 F3
Shute Devon 102 B2
Shutford 147 F3
Shuthonger 146 A4
Shutlanger 148 C3
Shutt Green 158 A2
Shuttington 159 E2
Shuttlewood 186 B5
Shuttleworth 184 B1
Siabost Bho Dheas 270 E3
Siabost Bho Thuath 270 E3
Siadar Iarach 271 F2
Siadar Uarach 271 F2
Sibbaldbie 217 F2
Sibbertoft 160 B4
Sibdon Carwood 156 D4
Sibertswold (Shepherdswell) 125 E4
Sibford Ferris 147 F4
Sibford Gower 147 F4
Sible Hedingham 151 F4
Sibley's Green 151 E5
Sibsey 176 B2
Sibson Cambs 161 F3
Sibson Leics 159 F2
Sibster 275 J3
Sibthorpe 174 C3
Sibton 153 E1
Sibton Green 165 E4
Sicklesmere 151 G1
Sicklinghall 194 C3
Sidbury Devon 103 E3
Sidbury Shrop 157 F4
Sidcot 116 B2
Sidcup 137 D5
Siddal 194 A5
Siddington ChesE 184 C5
Siddington Glos 132 C3
Sidemoor 158 B5
Sidestrand 179 D2
Sidford 103 E3
Sidlesham 108 A4
Sidley 110 C3
Sidlow 122 B4
Sidmouth 103 E4
Sigford 102 A5
Sigglesthorne 197 D3
Sigingstone 129 F5
Signet 133 E1
Silchester 120 B1
Sildinis 270 E6
Sileby 160 B1
Silecroft 198 C4
Silfield 164 C2
Silian 142 B2
Silk Willoughby 175 F3
Silkstead 119 F5
Silkstone 185 G2
Silkstone Common 185 G2
Sill Field 199 G4
Silloth 209 E1
Sills 220 A1
Sillyearn 268 D5
Silpho 204 C3
Silsden 193 G3
Silsoe 149 F4
Silver End CenBeds 149 G3
Silver End Essex 151 G5
Silver Green 165 D2
Silver Street Kent 124 A2
Silver Street Som 116 C4
Silverburn 235 G3
Silvercraigs 231 G1
Silverdale Lancs 199 F5
Silverdale Staffs 171 F3
Silvergate 178 C3
Silverhill 110 C2
Silverlace Green 153 E2
Silverley's Green 165 D4
Silvermoss 261 G1
Silverstone 148 B3
Silverton 102 C2
Silvington 157 F5
Silwick 279 B8
Simister 184 C2
Simmondley 185 E3
Simonburn 220 A4
Simonsbath 114 A4
Simonside 212 C1
Simonstone Bridgend 129 F4
Simonstone Lancs 193 D4
Simprim 237 F5
Simpson 149 D4
Sinclair's Hill 237 F4
Sinclairston 224 C4
Sinderby 202 C4
Sinderhope 211 E2
Sindlesham 120 C1
Sinfin 173 E4
Singdean 227 G5
Singleton Lancs 191 G4
Singleton WSuss 108 A2
Singlewell 137 F5
Singret 170 A2
Sinkhurst Green 124 A4
Sinnahard 260 C3
Sinnington 203 G4
Sinton Green 146 A1
Sipson 135 F5
Sirhowy 130 A1
Sirhowy Valley Country Park Caerp NP11 7BD 130 A3
Sisland 165 E2
Sissinghurst 123 G5
Sissinghurst Castle Garden Kent TN17 2AB 124 A5
Siston 131 F5
Sithney 94 D4
Sittingbourne 124 B2
Siulaisiadar 271 H4
Six Ashes 157 G4
Six Hills 174 B5
Six Mile Bottom 151 D2
Six Roads End 172 C5
Sixhills 188 B4
Sixmile 124 D4
Sixpenny Handley 105 G1
Sizewell 153 F1
Skail 274 C4
Skaill Ork 277 B6
Skaill Ork 277 E7
Skaill Ork 276 D4
Skares Aber 260 E1
Skares EAyr 224 D4
Skarpigarth 279 A7
Skateraw 237 E2
Skaw 279 E6
Skeabost 263 K7
Skeabrae 276 B5
Skeeby 202 B2
Skeffington 160 C2
Skeffling 189 D1
Skegby 173 G1
Skegness 177 D1
Skegness Water Leisure Park Lincs PE25 1JF 177 D1
Skelberry Shet 279 F9
Skelberry Shet 279 D6
Skelbo 266 E2
Skelbo Street 266 E2
Skelbrooke 186 C1
Skeld (Easter Skeld) 279 C8
Skeldon 224 B4
Skeldyke 176 B4
Skellingthorpe 187 G5
Skellister 279 D7
Skellow 186 C1
Skelmanthorpe 185 G1
Skelmersdale 183 F2
Skelmonae 261 G1
Skelmorlie 232 C3
Skelmuir 269 H6
Skelpick 274 C3
Skelton Cumb 210 A4
Skelton ERid 195 G5
Skelton NYorks 201 F2
Skelton (Skelton-in-Cleveland) R&C 203 F1
Skelton York 195 E2
Skelton-in-Cleveland (Skelton) 203 F1
Skelton-on-Ure 194 C1
Skelwick 276 D3
Skelwith Bridge 199 E2
Skendleby 176 C1
Skendleby Psalter 189 E5
Skenfrith 145 D5
Skerne 196 C2
Skeroblingarry 222 C3
Skerray 273 J2
Skerton 192 A1
Sketchley 159 G3
Sketty 128 C3
Skewen 128 D3
Skewsby 203 F5
Skeyton 178 D3
Skeyton Corner 179 D3
Skidbrooke 189 E3
Skidbrooke North End 189 E3
Skidby 196 C4
Skilgate 114 C5
Skillington 175 D5
Skinburness 209 E1
Skinflats 234 D1
Skinidin 263 H7
Skinnet 275 G2
Skinningrove 203 G1
Skipness 231 G4
Skippool 191 G3
Skipsea 197 D2
Skipsea Brough 197 D2
Skipton 193 F2
Skipton Castle NYorks BD23 1AW 193 F2
Skipton-on-Swale 202 C5
Skipwith 195 F4
Skirbeck 176 B3
Skirbeck Quarter 176 B3
Skirethorns 193 F1
Skirlaugh 196 D4
Skirling 226 B2
Skirmett 134 C4
Skirpenbeck 195 G2
Skirwith Cumb 210 C4
Skirwith NYorks 200 C5
Skirza 275 J2
Skittle Green 134 C2
Skomer Island 126 A2
Skulamus 256 C2
Skullomie 273 J2
Skyborry Green 156 B5
Skye 255 K1
Skye Green 151 G5
Skye of Curr 259 G2
Skyreholme 193 G1
Slack Aber 260 D1
Slack Derbys 173 E1
Slack WYorks 193 F5
Slackhall 185 E4
Slackhead 268 C4
Slad 132 A2
Slade Devon 113 F1
Slade Devon 103 E2
Slade Pembs 126 C1
Slade Swan 128 A4
Slade Green 137 E5
Slade Hooton 186 C4
Sladesbridge 97 E2
Slaggyford 210 C2
Slaidburn 192 D2
Slains Park 253 G2
Slaithwaite 185 E1
Slaley 211 F2
Slamannan 234 C2
Slapton Bucks 149 E5
Slapton Devon 101 E3
Slapton N'hants 148 B3
Slate Haugh 268 C4
Slatepit Dale 173 E1
Slattadale 264 E4
Slaugham 109 E1
Slaughden 153 F2
Slaughterford 132 A5
Slawston 160 C3
Sleaford Hants 120 D4
Sleaford Lincs 175 F3
Sleagill 199 G1
Sleap 170 B5
Sledge Green 146 A4
Sledmere 196 B1
Sleights 204 B2
Slepe 105 F3
Slerra 112 D3
Slickly 275 H2
Sliddery 223 E3
Sliemore 259 H2
Sligachan 255 K2
Slimbridge 131 G2
Slimbridge Wildfowl & Wetlands Trust Glos GL2 7BT 131 G2
Slindon Staffs 171 F4
Slindon WSuss 108 B3
Slinfold 121 G4
Sling 131 E2
Slingsby 203 F5
Slioch 260 D1
Slip End CenBeds 135 F1
Slip End Herts 150 A4
Slipper Chapel, Houghton St. Giles Norf NR22 6AL 178 A2
Slipton 161 E5
Slitting Mill 158 C1
Slochd 259 F2
Slockavullin 240 A5
Slogarie 216 A4
Sloley 179 D3
Slongaber 216 C3
Sloothby 189 E5
Slough 135 E4
Slough Green Som 115 F5
Slough Green WSuss 109 E1
Sluggan 259 F2
Slyne 192 A1
Smailholm 228 A3
Small Dole 109 E2
Small Hythe 124 A5
Smallbridge 184 D1
Smallbrook 102 B3
Smallburgh 179 E3
Smallburn Aber 269 J6
Smallburn EAyr 225 E3
Smalldale 185 E5
Smalley 173 F3
Smallfield 122 C4
Smallford 136 A2
Smallridge 103 F2
Smallthorne 171 F2
Smallworth 164 B3
Smannell 119 E3
Smardale 200 C2
Smarden 124 A4
Smaull 230 A3
Smeatharpe 103 E1
Smeeth 124 C5
Smeeton Westerby 160 B3
Smerclet 254 C3
Smerral 275 G5
Smestow 158 A3
Smethwick 158 C4
Smethwick Green 171 F1
Smirisary 247 F2
Smisby 159 F1
Smith End Green 145 G2
Smithfield 210 A1
Smithies 186 A2
Smithincott 103 D1
Smith's End 150 B4
Smith's Green Essex 151 D5
Smith's Green Essex 151 E3
Smithstown 264 D4
Smithton 266 E7
Smithy Green 184 B5
Smockington 159 G4
Smugglers Adventure ESuss TN34 3HY 75 Hastings
Smyrton 214 C2
Smythe's Green 138 C1
Snailbeach 156 C2
Snailwell 151 E1
Snainton 204 C4
Snaith 195 F5
Snape NYorks 202 B4
Snape Suff 153 E2
Snape Green 183 E1
Snape Watering 153 E2
Snarestone 159 F2
Snarford 188 A4
Snargate 111 E1
Snave 111 F1
Sneachill 146 B2
Snead 156 C3
Snead's Green 146 A1
Sneath Common 164 C3
Sneaton 204 B2
Sneatonthorpe 204 C2
Snelland 188 A4
Snellings 198 A2
Snelston 172 C3
Snetterton 164 A2
Snettisham 177 E4
Snipeshill 124 B2
Snishival (Sniseabhal) 254 C1
Snitter 220 C1
Snitterby 187 G3
Snitterfield 147 E2
Snitterton 173 D1
Snittlegarth 209 F3
Snitton 157 E5
Snodhill 144 C3
Snodland 123 G2
Snow End 150 C4
Snow Street 164 B3
Snowden Hill 185 G2
Snowdon Mountain Railway Gwyn LL55 4TY 167 E2
Snowshill 146 C4
Snowshill Manor Glos WR12 7JU 146 C4
Soar Cardiff 129 G4
Soar Carmar 142 C5
Soar Devon 100 D4
Soay 255 K3
Soberton 107 F1
Soberton Heath 107 F1
Sockbridge 210 B5
Sockburn 202 C2
Sodom 182 B5
Sodylt Bank 170 A4
Softley 211 G5
Soham 163 D5
Soham Cotes 163 D5
Soldon 112 D4
Soldon Cross 112 D4
Soldridge 120 B4
Sole Street Kent 124 C4
Sole Street Kent 123 F2
Soleburn 214 B4
Solihull 159 D5
Solihull Lodge 158 C5
Sollas (Solas) 262 D4
Sollers Dilwyn 144 D2
Sollers Hope 145 F4
Sollom 183 F1
Solomon's Tump 131 G1
Solsgirth 243 E5
Solva 140 A5
Solwaybank 218 B4
Somerby Leics 160 C1
Somerby Lincs 188 A2
Somercotes 173 F2
Somerford 158 B2
Somerford Keynes 132 C3
Somerley 108 A4
Somerleyton 165 F2
Somersal Herbert 172 C4
Somersby 188 D5
Somerset House GtLon WC2R 1LA 45 F3
Somersham Cambs 162 B5
Somersham Suff 152 B3
Somerton Newport 130 C4
Somerton Oxon 147 G5
Somerton Som 116 B5
Somerton Suff 151 G2
Sompting 109 D3
Sompting Abbotts 109 D3
Sonning 134 C5
Sonning Common 134 C4
Sonning Eye 134 C5
Sontley 170 A3
Sookholme 173 G1
Sopley 106 A3
Sopworth 132 A4
Sorbie 207 E2
Sordale 275 G2
Sorisdale 246 B3
Sorn 225 D3
Sornhill 224 D2
Soroba 240 A2
Sortat 275 H2
Sotby 188 C5
Sots Hole 175 G1
Sotterley 165 F3
Soudley 171 E5
Soughton 169 F1
Soulbury 149 D5
Soulby 200 C1
Souldern 148 A4
Souldrop 149 E1
Sound ChesE 170 D3
Sound Shet 279 D8
Sound Shet 279 C7
Sourhope 228 C4
Sourin 276 D4
Sourton 99 F1
Soutergate 198 D4
South Acre 163 G1
South Acton 136 A5
South Alkham 125 E4
South Allington 101 D4
South Alloa 243 D5
South Ambersham 121 E5
South Anston 186 C4
South Ascot 121 E1
South Baddesley 106 C3
South Ballachulish (Baile a' Chaolais a Deas) 248 C4
South Balloch 215 E1
South Bank 213 E5
South Barrow 116 D5
South Bellsdyke 234 D1
South Benfleet 137 G4
South Bersted 108 B3
South Blackbog 261 F1
South Bockhampton 106 A3
South Bowood 104 A3
South Brent 100 C1
South Brentor 99 E2
South Brewham 117 E4
South Broomhill 221 E2
South Burlingham 179 E5
South Cadbury 116 D5
South Cairn 214 A4
South Carlton 187 G5
South Cave 196 B4
South Cerney 132 C3
South Chard 103 G2
South Charlton 229 F4
South Cheriton 117 D5
South Church 212 B5
South Cliffe 196 A4
South Clifton 187 F5
South Cockerington 189 D4
South Collafirth 278 C4
South Common 109 F2
South Cornelly 129 E4
South Corriegills 223 F2
South Cove 165 F3
South Creagan 248 B5
South Creake 177 G4
South Crosland 185 F1
South Croxton 160 B1
South Croydon 122 C2
South Dalton 196 B3
South Darenth 137 E5
South Dell (Dail Bho Dheas) 271 G1
South Duffield 195 F4
South Elkington 188 C4
South Elmsall 186 B1
South End Bucks 149 D5
South End Cumb 191 F1
South End Hants 106 A1
South End NLincs 196 D5
South Erradale 264 D4
South Fambridge 138 B3
South Fawley 133 F4
South Ferriby 196 B5
South Field 196 C5
South Flobbets 261 F1
South Garth 278 E3
South Godstone 122 C4
South Gorley 106 A1
South Green Essex 137 F3
South Green Essex 138 D1
South Green Norf 178 B4
South Green Suff 164 C4
South Gyle 235 F2
South Hall 232 B2
South Hanningfield 137 G3
South Harefield 135 F4
South Harting 107 G1
South Hayling 107 G3
South Hazelrigg 229 E3
South Heath 135 E2
South Heighton 109 G3
South Hetton 212 C3
South Hiendley 186 A1
South Hill 98 D3
South Hinksey 134 A2
South Hole 112 C4
South Holme 203 F5
South Holmwood 121 G3
South Hornchurch 137 E4
South Hourat 233 D4
South Huish 100 C3
South Hykeham 175 E1
South Hylton 212 C2
South Kelsey 188 A3
South Kessock (Ceasag a Deas) 266 D7
South Killingholme 188 B1
South Kilvington 202 D4
South Kilworth 160 B4
South Kirkby 186 B1
South Kirkton 261 F4
South Knighton 102 B5
South Kyme 175 G3
South Lakes Wild Animal Park Cumb LA15 8JR 198 D5
South Lancing 109 D3
South Ledaig 240 B1
South Leigh 133 F2
South Leverton 187 E4
South Littleton 146 C3
South Lopham 164 B3
South Luffenham 161 E2
South Malling 109 G2
South Marston 133 D4
South Middleton 229 D4
South Milford 195 D4
South Milton 100 C3
South Mimms 136 B2
South Molton 114 A5
South Moor 212 A2
South Moreton 134 A4
South Mundham 108 A3
South Muskham 174 C2
South Newbald 196 B4
South Newington 147 G4
South Newton 118 B4
South Normanton 173 F2
South Norwood 122 C2
South Nutfield 122 C4
South Ockendon 137 E4
South Ormsby 189 D5
South Ossett 185 G1
South Otterington 202 C4
South Owersby 188 A3
South Oxhey 136 A3
South Park 122 B4
South Parks 244 A4
South Perrott 104 A2
South Petherton 104 A1
South Petherwin 98 D2
South Pickenham 163 G2
South Pool 101 D3
South Queensferry (Queensferry) 235 F2
South Radworthy 114 A4
South Rauceby 175 F3
South Raynham 177 G5
South Redbriggs 269 F6
South Reston 189 E4
South Ronaldsay 277 D9
South Ruislip 136 A4
South Runcton 163 E2
South Scarle 174 D1
South Shian (Sithean a Deas) 248 B5
South Shields 212 C1
South Shields Museum & Art Gallery T&W NE33 2JA 28 E2
South Somercotes 189 E3
South Somercotes Fen Houses 189 E3
South Stainley 194 C1
South Stoke B&NESom 117 E1
South Stoke Oxon 134 B4
South Stoke WSuss 108 C3
South Street ESuss 109 F2
South Street GtLon 122 D3
South Street Kent 123 F2
South Street Kent 124 D2
South Street Kent 124 A2
South Tawton 99 G1
South Thoresby 189 E5
South Tidworth 118 D3

South Tottenham 136 C4
South Town Devon 102 C4
South Town Hants 120 B4
South Uist (Uibhist a Deas) 254 C1
South Upper Barrack 269 H6
South View 120 B2
South Walsham 179 E4
South Warnborough 120 C3
South Weald 137 E3
South Weston 134 C3
South Wheatley Corn 98 C1
South Wheatley Notts 187 E4
South Whiteness 279 C8
South Wigston 160 A3
South Willingham 188 B4
South Wingfield 173 E2
South Witham 161 E1
South Wonston 119 F4
South Woodham Ferrers 138 B3
South Wootton 177 E5
South Wraxall 117 F1
South Yardle 158 D4
South Zeal 99 G1
Southall 136 A4
Southam Glos 146 B5
Southam Warks 147 G1
Southampton 106 D1
Southampton Airport 107 D1
Southbar 233 F3
Southborough GtLon 122 D2
Southborough Kent 123 E4
Southbourne Bourne 106 A3
Southbourne WSuss 107 G2
Southbrook 102 D3
Southburgh 178 B5
Southburn 196 B2
Southchurch 138 C4
Southcott Devon 99 F1
Southcott Wilts 118 C2
Southcourt 134 D1
Southdean 219 E1
Southdene 183 F3
Southease 109 G3
Southend A&B 222 B5
Southend Aber 269 F6
Southend Bucks 134 C4
Southend (Bradfield Southend) WBerks 134 A5
Southend Wilts 133 D5
Southend Airport 138 B4
Southend Pier S'end SS1 1EE 138 B4
Southend-on-Sea 138 B4
Southerfield 209 E2
Southerly 99 F2
Southern Green 150 B4
Southerndown 129 E5
Southerness 217 D5
Southery 163 E3
Southfield 244 A5
Southfields 136 B5
Southfleet 137 F5
Southgate Cere 154 B4
Southgate GtLon 136 C3
Southgate Norf 178 C3
Southgate Norf 177 E4
Southgate Swan 128 B4
Southill 149 G3
Southington 119 G3
Southleigh 103 F3
Southmarsh 117 E4
Southminster 138 C3
Southmoor 133 F3
Southmuir 252 B4
Southoe 149 G1
Southolt 152 C1
Southorpe 161 F2
Southowram 194 A5
Southport 183 E1
Southport Pier Mersey PR8 1QX 183 E1
Southrepps 179 D2
Southrey 175 G1
Southrop 133 D2
Southrope 120 B3
Southsea Ports 107 F3
Southsea Wrex 169 F2
Southtown Norf 179 G5
Southtown Ork 277 D8
Southwaite Cumb 200 C2
Southwaite Cumb 210 A3
Southwark Cathedral GtLon SE1 9DA 12 B4
Southwater 121 G5
Southwater Street 121 G5
Southway 116 C3
Southwell Dorset 104 C5
Southwell Notts 174 B2
Southwell Minster Notts NG25 0HD 174 C2
Southwick D&G 216 D5
Southwick Hants 107 F2
Southwick N'hants 161 F3
Southwick Som 116 A3
Southwick T&W 212 C2
Southwick Wilts 117 F2
Southwick WSuss 109 E3
Southwold 165 G4
Southwood 116 C4
Sowden 102 C4
Sower Carr 191 G3
Sowerby NYorks 202 D4
Sowerby WYorks 193 G5
Sowerby Bridge 193 G5
Sowerby Row 209 G2
Sowerhill 114 B5
Sowley Green 151 F2
Sowood 185 E1
Sowton 102 C3
Soyal 266 C2
Spa Common 179 D2
Spa Complex NYorks YO11 2HD 83 Scarborough
Spadeadam 219 D4
Spalding 176 A5
Spaldington 195 G4
Spaldwick 161 G5
Spalefield 245 D4
Spalford 174 D1
Spanby 175 F4
Sparham 178 B4
Spark Bridge 199 E4
Sparkford 116 D5
Sparkhill 158 C4
Sparkwell 100 B2
Sparrow Green 178 A4
Sparrowpit 185 E4
Sparrow's Green 123 F5
Sparsholt Hants 119 F4
Sparsholt Oxon 133 F4
Spartylea 211 E3
Spath 172 B4
Spaunton 203 G4
Spaxton 115 F4
Spean Bridge (Drochaid an Aonachain) 249 E1
Spean Bridge Woollen Mill High PH34 4EP 249 E1
Spear Hill 108 D2
Speddoch 216 C2
Speedwell 131 F5
Speen Bucks 134 D2
Speen WBerks 119 F1
Speeton 205 E5
Speke 183 F4
Speldhurst 123 E4
Spellbrook 137 D1
Spelsbury 147 F5
Spen Green 171 F1
Spencers Wood 120 C1
Spennithorne 202 A4
Spennymoor 212 B4
Spernall 146 C1
Spetchley 146 A2
Spetisbury 105 F2
Spexhall 165 E3
Spey Bay 268 B4
Speybridge 259 H2
Speyview 267 K7
Spilsby 176 B1
Spindlestone 229 F3
Spinkhill 186 B5
Spinnaker Tower PO1 3TN 82 Portsmouth
Spinningdale 266 D3
Spirthill 132 B5
Spital High 275 G3
Spital W&M 135 E5
Spital in the Street 187 G3
Spitalbrook 136 C2
Spitfire & Hurricane Memorial, R.A.F. Manston Kent CT12 5DF 125 F2
Spithurst 109 G2
Spittal D&G 215 F4
Spittal D&G 215 E5
Spittal ELoth 236 B2
Spittal N'umb 229 E1
Spittal Pembs 140 C5
Spittal of Glenmuick 252 B1
Spittal of Glenshee 251 G3
Spittalfield 251 G5
Spixworth 178 D4
Splayne's Green 109 G1
Splott 130 B5
Spofforth 194 C2
Spondon 173 F4
Spooner Row 164 B2
Spoonley 171 D4
Sporle 163 G1
Sportsman's Arms 168 C2
Spott 237 D2
Spratton 160 C5
Spreakley 120 D3
Spreyton 99 G1
Spriddlestone 100 B2
Spridlington 188 A4
Spring Grove 136 A5
Spring Vale 107 F3
Springburn 234 A3
Springfield A&B 232 B2
Springfield D&G 218 B5
Springfield Fife 244 B3
Springfield Moray 267 H6
Springfield P&K 243 G1
Springfield WMid 158 C4
Springhill Staffs 158 C2
Springhill Staffs 158 B2
Springholm 216 C4
Springkell 218 A4
Springleys 261 F1
Springside 224 B2
Springthorpe 187 F4
Springwell 212 B2
Sproatley 197 D4
Sproston Green 171 E1
Sprotbrough 186 C2
Sproughton 152 C3
Sprouston 228 B3
Sprowston 178 D4
Sproxton Leics 175 D5
Sproxton NYorks 203 F4
Sprytown 99 E2
Spurlands End 135 D3
Spurstow 170 C2
Spyway 104 B3
Square Point 216 B3
Squires Gate 191 G4
Sròndoire 231 G2
Sronphadruig Lodge 250 C2
Stableford Shrop 157 G3
Stableford Staffs 171 F4
Stacey Bank 185 G3
Stackhouse 193 E1
Stackpole 126 C3
Stacksteads 193 E5
Staddiscombe 100 B2
Staddlethorpe 196 A5
Staden 185 E5
Stadhampton 134 B3
Staffield 210 B3
Staffin 263 K5
Stafford 171 G5
Stagden Cross 137 F1
Stagsden 149 E3
Stagshaw Bank 211 F1
Stain 275 J2
Stainburn Cumb 208 D4
Stainburn NYorks 194 B3
Stainby 175 E5
Staincross 186 A1
Staindrop 212 A5
Staines-upon-Thames 135 F5
Stainfield Lincs 175 F5
Stainfield Lincs 188 B5
Stainforth NYorks 193 E1
Stainforth SYorks 186 D1
Staining 191 G4
Stainland 185 E1
Stainsacre 204 C2
Stainsby Derbys 173 F1
Stainsby Lincs 188 D5
Stainton Cumb 199 G4
Stainton Cumb 210 A5
Stainton Dur 201 F1
Stainton Middl 203 D1
Stainton NYorks 202 A3
Stainton SYorks 186 C3
Stainton by Langworth 188 A5
Stainton le Vale 188 B3
Stainton with Adgarley 198 D5
Staintondale 204 C3
Stair Cumb 209 F4
Stair EAyr 224 C3
Stairfoot 186 A2
Staithes 203 G1
Stake Pool 192 A3
Stakeford 221 E3
Stakes 107 F2
Stalbridge 104 D1
Stalbridge Weston 104 D1
Stalham 179 E3
Stalham Green 179 E3
Stalisfield Green 124 B3
Stalling Busk 201 E4
Stallingborough 188 B1
Stallington 171 G4
Stalmine 191 G3
Stalybridge 185 D3
Stambourne 151 F4
Stamford Lincs 161 F2
Stamford N'umb 229 G5
Stamford Bridge ChesW&C 170 B1
Stamford Bridge ERid 195 G2
Stamfordham 220 C4
Stanah 191 G3
Stanborough 136 B1
Stanborough Park Herts AL8 6XF 136 B1
Stanbridge CenBeds 149 E5
Stanbridge Dorset 105 G2
Stanbridge Earls 119 E5
Stanbury 193 G4
Stand 234 B3
Standalone Farm, Letchworth Garden City Herts SG6 4JN 150 A4
Standburn 234 D2
Standedge Tunnel & Visitor Centre WYorks HD7 6NQ 185 E1
Standeford 158 B2
Standen 124 A5
Standen Street 124 A5
Standerwick 117 F2
Standford 120 D4
Standford Bridge 171 E5
Standish Glos 132 A2
Standish GtMan 183 G1
Standlake 133 F2
Standon Hants 119 F5
Standon Herts 150 B5
Standon Staffs 171 F4
Standon Green End 136 C1
Stane 234 C4
Stanecastle 224 B2
Stanfield 178 A3
Stanford CenBeds 149 G3
Stanford Kent 124 D5
Stanford Shrop 156 C1
Stanford Bishop 145 F2
Stanford Bridge 145 G1
Stanford Dingley 134 A5
Stanford End 120 C1
Stanford in the Vale 133 F3
Stanford on Avon 160 A5
Stanford on Soar 173 G5
Stanford on Teme 145 G1
Stanford Rivers 137 E2
Stanford-le-Hope 137 F4
Stanfree 186 B5
Stanghow 203 F1
Stanground 162 A3
Stanhoe 177 G4
Stanhope Dur 211 F4
Stanhope ScBord 226 C3
Stanion 161 E4
Stanklyn 158 A5
Stanley Derbys 173 F3
Stanley Dur 212 A2
Stanley Notts 173 F1
Stanley P&K 243 G1
Stanley Staffs 171 G2
Stanley Wilts 132 B5
Stanley WYorks 194 C5
Stanley Common 173 F3
Stanley Crook 212 A4
Stanley Gate 183 F2
Stanley Hill 145 F3
Stanleygreen 170 C4
Stanlow ChesW&C 183 F5
Stanlow Shrop 157 G3
Stanmer 109 F2
Stanmore GtLon 136 A3
Stanmore WBerks 133 G5
Stannersburn 219 F3
Stanningfield 151 G2
Stannington N'umb 221 E4
Stannington SYorks 186 A4
Stansbatch 144 C1
Stansfield 151 F2
Stanshope 172 C2
Stanstead 151 G3
Stanstead Abbotts 136 C1
Stansted 123 F2
Stansted Airport 150 D5
Stansted Mountfitchet 150 D5
Stanton Derbys 159 E1
Stanton Glos 146 C4
Stanton N'umb 220 D2
Stanton Staffs 172 C3
Stanton Suff 164 A4
Stanton by Bridge 173 E5
Stanton by Dale 173 F4
Stanton Drew 116 C1
Stanton Fitzwarren 133 D3
Stanton Harcourt 133 G2
Stanton Hill 173 F1
Stanton in Peak 172 D1
Stanton Lacy 157 D5
Stanton Lees 173 D1
Stanton Long 157 E3
Stanton Prior 117 D1
Stanton St. Bernard 118 B1
Stanton St. John 134 A2
Stanton St. Quintin 132 B5
Stanton Street 152 A1
Stanton under Bardon 159 G1
Stanton upon Hine Heath 170 C5
Stanton Wick 116 D1
Stanton-on-the-Wolds 174 B4
Stanwardine in the Fields 170 B5
Stanwardine in the Wood 170 B5
Stanway Essex 152 A5
Stanway Glos 146 C4
Stanway Green Essex 152 A5
Stanway Green Suff 164 D4
Stanwell 135 F5
Stanwell Moor 135 F5
Stanwick 161 E5
Stanwix 210 A2
Stanydale 279 B7
Staoinebrig 254 C1
Stapeley 171 D3
Stapenhill 173 D5
Staple Kent 125 E3
Staple Som 115 E3
Staple Cross 114 D5
Staple Fitzpaine 103 F1
Staplecross 110 C1
Staplefield 109 E1
Stapleford Cambs 150 C2
Stapleford Herts 136 C1
Stapleford Leics 160 D1
Stapleford Lincs 175 D2
Stapleford Notts 173 F4
Stapleford Wilts 118 B4
Stapleford Abbotts 137 D3
Stapleford Tawney 137 E3
Staplegrove 115 F5
Staplehay 115 F5
Staplehurst 123 G4
Staplers 107 E4
Staplestreet 124 C2
Stapleton Cumb 218 D4
Stapleton Here 144 C1
Stapleton Leics 159 G3
Stapleton NYorks 202 B1
Stapleton Shrop 157 D2
Stapleton Som 116 B5
Stapley 103 E1
Staploe 149 G1
Staplow 145 F3
Star Fife 244 B4
Star Pembs 141 F4
Star Som 116 B2
Starbotton 201 E5
Starcross 102 C4
Stareton 159 F5
Starkholmes 173 E2
Starling 184 B1
Starling's Green 150 C4
Starr 215 F1
Starston 164 D3
Startforth 201 F1
Startley 132 B4
Statham 184 A4
Stathe 116 A5
Stathern 174 C4
Station Town 212 D4
Staughton Green 149 G1
Staughton Highway 149 G1
Staunton Glos 131 E1
Staunton Glos 145 G5
Staunton Harold Hall 173 E5
Staunton Harold Reservoir Derbys DE73 8DN 173 E5
Staunton in the Vale 174 D3
Staunton on Arrow 144 C1
Staunton on Wye 144 C3
Staveley Cumb 199 F3
Staveley Derbys 186 B5
Staveley NYorks 194 C1
Staveley-in-Cartmel 199 E4
Staverton Devon 101 D1
Staverton Glos 146 A5
Staverton N'hants 148 A1
Staverton Wilts 117 F1
Staverton Bridge 146 A5
Stawell 116 A4
Stawley 115 D5
Staxigoe 275 J3
Staxton 204 D5
Staylittle (Penffordd-las) 155 E3
Staynall 191 G3
Staythorpe 174 C2
Stean 201 F5
Steane 148 A4
Stearsby 203 F5
Steart 115 F3
Stebbing 151 E5
Stebbing Green 151 E5
Stechford 158 D4
Stedham 121 D5
Steel Cross 123 E5
Steel Green 198 C5
Steele Road 218 D2
Steen's Bridge 145 E2
Steep 120 C5
Steep Marsh 120 C5
Steeple Dorset 105 F4
Steeple Essex 138 C2
Steeple Ashton 118 A2
Steeple Aston 147 G5
Steeple Barton 147 G5
Steeple Bumpstead 151 E3
Steeple Claydon 148 B5
Steeple Gidding 161 G4
Steeple Langford 118 B4
Steeple Morden 150 A3
Steeraway 157 F2
Steeton 193 G3
Stein 263 H6
Steinis 271 G4
Steinmanhill 269 F6
Stella 212 A1
Stelling Minnis 124 D4
Stembridge 116 B5
Stemster High 275 G2
Stemster High 275 G4
Stemster House 275 G2
Stenalees 97 E4
Stenhill 103 D1
Stenhousemuir 234 C1
Stenigot 188 C4
Stenness 278 B5
Stenscholl 263 K5
Stenson 173 E5
Stenton ELoth 236 D2
Stenton P&K 251 F5
Stepaside Pembs 127 E2
Stepaside Powys 155 G4
Stepney 136 C4
Steppingley 149 F4
Stepps 234 A3
Sternfield 153 E1
Sterridge 113 F1
Stert 118 B2
Stetchworth 151 E2
Stevenage 150 A5
Stevenston 233 D5
Steventon Hants 119 G3
Steventon Oxon 133 G3
Steventon End 151 E3
Stevington 149 F2
Stewart Park, Middlesbrough Middl TS7 8AR 29 C4
Stewartby 149 F3
Stewarton D&G 207 E2
Stewarton EAyr 233 F5
Stewkley 149 D5
Stewley 103 G1
Stewton 189 D4
Steyning 109 D2
Steynton 126 C2
Stibb 112 C4
Stibb Cross 113 E4
Stibb Green 118 D1
Stibbard 178 A3
Stibbington 161 F3
Stichill 228 B3
Sticker 97 D4
Stickford 176 B1
Sticklepath Devon 99 G1
Sticklepath Som 103 G1
Stickling Green 150 C4
Stickney 176 B2
Stiff Street 124 A2
Stiffkey 178 A1
Stifford's Bridge 145 G3
Stileway 116 B3
Stilligarry (Stadhlaigearraidh) 254 C1
Stillingfleet 195 E3
Stillington NYorks 195 E1
Stillington Stock 212 C5
Stilton 161 G4
Stinchcombe 131 G3
Stinsford 104 D3
Stirchley Tel&W 157 G2
Stirchley WMid 158 C4
Stirkoke House 275 J3
Stirling Aber 269 K6
Stirling (Sruighlea) Stir 242 C5
Stirling Castle Stir FK8 1EJ 242 C5
Stirling Visitor Centre Stir FK8 1EH 242 C5
Stirton 193 F2
Stisted 151 G5
Stitchcombe 118 D1
Stithians 95 E3
Stittenham 266 D4
Stivichall 159 F5
Stix 250 C5
Stixwould 175 G1
Stoak 183 F5
Stobo 226 C2
Stoborough 105 F4
Stoborough Green 105 F4
Stobwood 235 D4
Stock 137 F3
Stock Green 146 B2
Stock Lane 133 E5
Stock Wood 146 C2
Stockbridge Hants 119 E4
Stockbridge Stir 242 C4
Stockbridge WSuss 108 A3
Stockbury 124 A2
Stockcross 119 F1
Stockdale 95 E3
Stockdalewath 209 G2
Stockerston 160 D3
Stockgrove Country Park CenBeds LU7 0BA 149 E5
Stocking Green Essex 151 D4
Stocking Green MK 148 D3
Stocking Pelham 150 C5
Stockingford 159 F3
Stockinish (Stocinis) 263 G2
Stockland Cardiff 130 A5
Stockland Devon 103 F2
Stockland Bristol 115 F3
Stockleigh English 102 B2
Stockleigh Pomeroy 102 B2
Stockley 118 B1
Stocklinch 103 G1
Stockport 184 C3
Stocksbridge 185 G3
Stocksfield 211 G1
Stockton Here 145 E1
Stockton Norf 165 E2
Stockton Shrop 157 G3
Stockton Shrop 156 B2
Stockton Tel&W 157 G1
Stockton Warks 147 G1
Stockton Wilts 118 A4
Stockton Heath 184 A4
Stockton on Teme 145 G1
Stockton on the Forest 195 F2
Stockton-on-Tees 202 D1
Stockwell 132 B1
Stockwell Heath 172 B5
Stockwood Bristol 116 D1
Stockwood Dorset 104 B2
Stodday 192 A2
Stodmarsh 125 E2
Stody 178 B2
Stoer 272 C6
Stoford Som 104 B1
Stoford Wilts 118 B4
Stogumber 115 D4
Stogursey 115 F3
Stoke Devon 112 C3
Stoke Hants 119 F2
Stoke Hants 107 G2
Stoke Med 124 A1
Stoke Plym 100 A2
Stoke WMid 159 F5
Stoke Abbott 104 A2
Stoke Albany 160 D4
Stoke Ash 164 C4
Stoke Bardolph 174 B3
Stoke Bishop 131 E5
Stoke Bliss 145 F1
Stoke Bruerne 148 C2
Stoke by Clare 151 F3
Stoke Canon 102 C3
Stoke Charity 119 F4
Stoke Climsland 99 D3
Stoke D'Abernon 121 G2
Stoke Doyle 161 F4
Stoke Dry 161 D3
Stoke Edith 145 F3
Stoke Farthing 118 B5
Stoke Ferry 163 F3
Stoke Fleming 101 E3
Stoke Gabriel 101 E2
Stoke Gifford 131 F5
Stoke Golding 159 F3
Stoke Goldington 148 D3
Stoke Green 135 E4
Stoke Hammond 149 D5
Stoke Heath Shrop 171 D5
Stoke Heath Worcs 146 B1
Stoke Holy Cross 178 D5
Stoke Lacy 145 F3
Stoke Lyne 148 A5
Stoke Mandeville 134 D1
Stoke Newington 136 C4
Stoke on Tern 170 D5
Stoke Orchard 146 B5
Stoke Pero 114 B3
Stoke Poges 135 E4
Stoke Pound 146 B1
Stoke Prior Here 145 E2
Stoke Prior Worcs 146 B1
Stoke Rivers 113 G2
Stoke Rochford 175 E5
Stoke Row 134 B4
Stoke St. Gregory 116 A5
Stoke St. Mary 115 F5
Stoke St. Michael 117 D3
Stoke St. Milborough 157 E4
Stoke sub Hamdon 104 A1
Stoke Talmage 134 B3
Stoke Trister 117 E5
Stoke Villice 116 C1
Stoke Wake 105 D2
Stoke-by-Nayland 152 A4
Stokeford 105 E4
Stokeham 187 E5
Stokeinteignhead 102 C5
Stokenchurch 134 C3
Stokenham 101 E3
Stoke-on-Trent 171 F3
Stokesay 156 D4
Stokesby 179 F4
Stokesley 203 E2
Stolford 115 F3
Ston Easton 116 D2
Stonar Cut 125 F2
Stondon Massey 137 E2
Stone Bucks 134 C1
Stone Glos 131 F3
Stone Kent 137 E5
Stone Kent 111 E1
Stone Som 116 C4
Stone Staffs 171 G4
Stone SYorks 186 C4
Stone Worcs 158 A5
Stone Allerton 116 B2
Stone Cross Dur 201 F1
Stone Cross ESuss 110 B3
Stone Cross ESuss 110 A1
Stone Cross Kent 124 C5
Stone Cross Kent 123 E5
Stone House 200 C4
Stone Street Kent 123 E3
Stone Street Suff 165 E3
Stone Street Suff 152 A4
Stonea 162 C3
Stonebridge ESuss 110 A1
Stonebridge NSom 116 A2
Stonebridge Warks 159 E4
Stonebroom 173 F2
Stonecross Green 151 G2
Stonefield A&B 231 G2
Stonefield Staffs 171 G4
Stonegate ESuss 110 B1
Stonegate NYorks 203 G2
Stonegrave 203 F5
Stonehaugh 219 F4
Stonehaven 253 G1
Stonehenge Wilts SP4 7DE 118 C3
Stonehill 121 E1
Stonehouse ChesW&C 183 G5
Stonehouse D&G 216 C4
Stonehouse Glos 132 A2
Stonehouse N'umb 210 C2
Stonehouse Plym 100 A2
Stonehouse SLan 234 B5
Stoneleigh Surr 122 B2
Stoneleigh Warks 159 F5
Stoneley Green 170 D2
Stonely 149 G1
Stoner Hill 120 C5
Stones 193 F5
Stones Green 152 C5
Stonesby 174 D5
Stonesfield 133 F1
Stonestreet Green 124 C5
Stonethwaite 209 F5
Stoney Cross 106 B1
Stoney Middleton 185 G5
Stoney Stanton 159 G3
Stoney Stoke 117 E4
Stoney Stratton 117 D4
Stoney Stretton 156 C2
Stoneyburn 235 D3
Stoneyford 103 D4
Stoneygate 160 B2
Stoneyhills 138 C3
Stoneykirk 214 B5
Stoneywood 261 G3
Stonganess 278 E2
Stonham Aspal 152 C2
Stonham Barns Suff IP14 6AT 152 C2
Stonnall 158 C2
Stonor 134 C4
Stonton Wyville 160 C3
Stony Houghton 173 F1
Stony Stratford 148 C3
Stonybreck 278 A1
Stoodleigh Devon 102 C1
Stoodleigh Devon 113 G2
Stopham 108 C2
Stopsley 149 G5
Stoptide 96 D2
Storeton 183 E4
Stormontfield 243 G2
Stornoway (Steornabhagh) 271 G4
Stornoway Airport 271 G4
Storridge 145 G3
Storrington 108 C2
Storrs 185 G4
Storth 199 F4
Storwood 195 G3
Storybook Glen Aber AB12 5FT 261 G5
Stotfield 267 K4
Stotfold 150 A4
Stottesdon 157 F4
Stoughton Leics 160 B2
Stoughton Surr 121 E2
Stoughton WSuss 107 G1
Stoughton Cross 116 B3
Stoul 256 D5
Stoulton 146 B3
Stour Provost 117 E5
Stour Row 117 F5
Stourbridge 158 A4
Stourhead Wilts BA12 6QD 117 E4
Stourpaine 105 E2
Stourport-on-Severn 158 A5
Stourton Staffs 158 A4
Stourton Warks 147 E4
Stourton Wilts 117 E4
Stourton Caundle 104 D1
Stove 276 F4
Stoven 165 F3
Stow Lincs 187 F4
Stow ScBord 236 B5
Stow Bardolph 163 E2
Stow Bedon 164 A2
Stow cum Quy 150 D1
Stow Longa 161 G5
Stow Maries 138 B3
Stow Pasture 187 F4
Stowbridge 163 D2
Stowe Glos 131 E2
Stowe Shrop 156 C5
Stowe Staffs 158 D1
Stowe Landscape Gardens Bucks MK18 5DQ 148 B4
Stowe-by-Chartley 172 B5
Stowehill 148 B2
Stowell Glos 132 C1
Stowell Som 117 D5
Stowey 116 C2
Stowford Devon 99 E2
Stowford Devon 113 G3
Stowford Devon 103 E4
Stowlangtoft 152 A1
Stowmarket 152 B2
Stow-on-the-Wold 147 D5
Stowting 124 D4
Stowupland 152 B2
Straad 232 B3
Stracathro 253 E3
Strachan 260 E5
Strachur (Clachan Strachur) 240 C4
Stradbroke 164 D4
Stradishall 151 F2
Stradsett 163 E2
Stragglethorpe 175 E2
Straight Soley 133 F5
Straiton Edin 235 G3
Straiton SAyr 224 B5
Straloch Aber 261 G2
Straloch P&K 251 F3
Stramshall 172 B4
Strands 198 C4
Strang 190 B4
Strangford 145 E5
Strannda 263 F3
Stranraer 214 B4
Strata Florida 142 D1
Stratfield Mortimer 120 B1
Stratfield Saye 120 B1
Stratfield Turgis 120 B2
Stratford CenBeds 149 G3
Stratford Glos 146 A4
Stratford GtLon 136 C4
Stratford St. Andrew 153 E2
Stratford St. Mary 152 B4
Stratford sub Castle 118 C4
Stratford Tony 118 B5
Stratford-upon-Avon 147 E2
Stratford-upon-Avon Butterfly Farm Warks CV37 7LS 85 Stratford-upon-Avon
Strath 275 H3
Strathan High 272 C6
Strathan High 257 F5
Strathaven 234 B5
Strathblane 233 G2
Strathcanaird 265 H1
Strathcarron 265 F7
Strathclyde Country Park NLan ML1 3ED 31 G5
Strathdon 260 B3
Strathgirnock 260 B5
Strathkinness 244 C3
Strathmiglo 244 A3
Strathpeffer (Strath Pheofhair) 266 B6

Strathrannoch 265 K4
Strathtay 251 E4
Strathwhillan 223 F2
Strathy 274 D2
Strathyre 242 A1
Stratton Corn 112 C5
Stratton Dorset 104 C3
Stratton Glos 132 C4
Stratton Audley 148 B5
Stratton Hall 152 E4
Stratton St.
  Margaret 133 D4
Stratton St. Michael 164 D2
Stratton Strawless 178 D3
Stratton-on-the-Fosse
  117 D2
Stravanan 232 B4
Stravithie 244 D3
Strawberry Hill 136 A5
Stream 115 D4
Streat 109 F2
Streatham 136 B5
Streatham Ice and Leisure
  Centre GtLon
  SW16 6HX 13 B7
Streatham Vale 136 B5
Streatley CenBeds 149 F5
Streatley WBerks 134 A4
Street Devon 103 E4
Street Lancs 192 B2
Street NYorks 203 G2
Street Som 116 B4
Street Som 103 E4
Street Ashton 159 G4
Street Dinas 170 A4
Street End 108 A4
Street Gate 212 B2
Street Houses 195 E3
Street Lane 173 E3
Street on the Fosse 116 D4
Streethay 158 D1
Streethouse 194 C5
Streetlam 202 C2
Streetly 158 C3
Streetly End 151 E3
Strefford 156 D4
Strelley 173 G3
Strensall 195 F1
Strensham 146 B3
Stretcholt 115 F3
Strete 101 E3
Stretford GtMan 184 B3
Stretford Here 144 D2
Stretford Here 145 E2
Strethall 150 C4
Stretham 162 D5
Strettington 108 A3
Stretton ChesW&C 170 B2
Stretton Derbys 173 E1
Stretton Rut 161 E1
Stretton Staffs 158 A1
Stretton Staffs 173 E1
Stretton Warr 184 A4
Stretton en le Field 159 F1
Stretton Grandison 145 F3
Stretton Heath 156 C1
Stretton Sugwas 145 D3
Stretton under
  Fosse 159 G4
Stretton Westwood 157 E3
Stretton-on-
  Dunsmore 159 G5
Stretton-on-Fosse 147 E4
Stribers 199 E4
Strichen 269 H5
Strines 185 D4
Strinesdale Countryside
  Area GtMan
  OL4 2JJ 25 H1
Stringston 115 E3
Strixton 149 E1
Stroat 131 E3
Stromeferry 256 E1
Stromemore 256 E1
Stromness 277 B7
Stronaba 249 E1
Stronachlachar 241 G3
Strone A&B 241 G4
Strone High 258 C2
Strone High 248 D1
Strone Stir 241 G3
Stronechrubie 272 E7
Stronlonag 232 C1
Stronmilchan (Sròn nam
  Mialchon) 241 D1
Stronsay 276 F5
Stronsay Airfield 276 F5
Strontian (Sròn an
  t-Sithein) 248 A3
Strontoiller 240 B2
Stronvar 242 A2
Strood 123 G2
Strood Green Surr 122 B4
Strood Green WSuss 121 F5
Strood Green
  WSuss 121 G4
Stroquhan 216 C2
Stroud Glos 132 A2
Stroud Hants 120 C5
Stroud Common 121 F3
Stroud Green Essex 138 B3
Stroud Green Glos 132 A2
Stroude 121 F1
Stroul 232 D1
Stroxton 175 E4
Struan High 255 J1
Struan P&K 250 C3
Strubby Lincs 189 E4
Strubby Lincs 188 B5
Strumpshaw 179 E5
Struthers 244 B4
Struy 258 B1
Stryd y Facsen 180 B4
Stryt-cae-rhedyn 169 F1
Stryt-issa 169 F3

Stubshaw Cross 183 G2
Stubton 175 D3
Stuck A&B 232 B3
Stuck A&B 240 D5
Stuckbeg 241 E5
Stuckgowan 241 F4
Stuckindroin 241 F3
Stuckton 106 A1
Stud Green 135 D5
Studdon 211 E2
Studfold 200 D5
Studham 135 F1
Studholme 209 F1
Studland 105 G4
Studland & Godlingston
  Heath NNR Dorset
  BH19 3AX 105 G4
Studley Warks 146 C1
Studley Wilts 132 B5
Studley Common 146 C1
Studley Green 134 C3
Studley Roger 202 B1
Studley Royal Park & ruins of
  Fountains Abbey NYorks
  HG4 3DY 194 B1
Stuggadhoo 190 B4
Stump Cross Essex 150 D3
Stump Cross Lancs 192 B4
Stuntney 163 D5
Stunts Green 110 B2
Sturbridge 171 F4
Sturgate 187 F4
Sturmer 151 E3
Sturminster
  Common 105 D1
Sturminster
  Marshall 105 F2
Sturminster
  Newton 105 D1
Sturry 125 D2
Sturton by Stow 187 F4
Sturton le Steeple 187 E4
Stuston 164 C4
Stutton NYorks 195 D3
Stutton Suff 152 C4
Styal 184 C4
Styrrup 186 D3
Suardail 271 G4
Succoth A&B 241 E4
Succoth Aber 260 C1
Succothmore 240 D4
Suckley 145 G2
Suckley Green 145 G2
Suckley Knowl 145 G2
Sudborough 161 E4
Sudbourne 153 F2
Sudbrook Lincs 175 E3
Sudbrook Mon 131 E4
Sudbrooke 188 B5
Sudbury Derbys 172 C4
Sudbury GtLon 136 A4
Sudbury Suff 152 A3
Sudbury Hall Derbys
  DE6 5HT 172 C4
Sudden 184 C1
Sudgrove 132 B2
Suffield Norf 178 D2
Suffield NYorks 204 C3
Sugarloaf 124 B5
Sugnall 171 F5
Sugwas Pool 145 D3
Suie Lodge Hotel 241 G2
Suisnish 256 B3
Sulby IoM 190 B3
Sulby IoM 190 B4
Sulgrave 148 A3
Sulham 134 B5
Sulhamstead 120 B1
Sullington 108 C3
Sullom 278 C5
Sullom Voe Oil
  Terminal 278 C5
Sully 115 E1
Sumburgh 279 F10
Sumburgh Airport 279 F9
Summer Bridge 194 B1
Summer Isles 265 F1
Summer Lodge 201 E3
Summercourt 96 C4
Summerfield Norf 177 F4
Summerfield Worcs 158 A5
Summerhill 170 A2
Summerhouse 202 B1
Summerlands 199 G4
Summerleaze 130 D4
Summertown 134 A2
Summit 184 D1
Sun Green 185 D3
Sunadale 231 G5
Sunbiggin 200 B2
Sunbury 121 G1
Sundaywell 216 C2
Sunderland Cumb 209 E3
Sunderland Lancs 192 A3
Sunderland T&W 212 C2
Sunderland Bridge 212 B4
Sunderland Museum &
  Winter Gardens
  T&W SR1 1PP
  86 Sunderland
Sundhope 227 E3
Sundon Park 149 F5
Sundown Adventure Land
  Notts
  DN22 0HX 187 E5
Sundridge 123 D3
Sundrum Mains 224 C3
Sunhill 132 D2
Sunipol 246 C4
Sunk Island 197 E5
Sunningdale 121 E1
Sunninghill 121 E1
Sunningwell 133 G2
Sunniside Dur 212 A4
Sunniside T&W 212 B4
Sunny Bank 199 D3
Sunny Brow 212 A4
Sunnylaw 242 C5
Sunnyside Aber 261 G5
Sunnyside N'umb 211 F1
Sunnyside SYorks 186 B3
Sunnyside WSuss 122 C5
Sunton 118 D2
Sunwick 237 F4
Surbiton 121 G1
Surfleet 176 A4
Surfleet Seas End 176 A5

Surlingham 179 E5
Sustead 178 C2
Susworth 187 F2
Sutcombe 112 D4
Sutcombemill 112 D4
Suton 164 B2
Sutterton 176 A4
Sutton Cambs 162 C5
Sutton CenBeds 150 A3
Sutton Devon 102 A2
Sutton Devon 100 D3
Sutton GtLon 122 B2
Sutton Kent 125 F4
Sutton Lincs 175 D2
Sutton Norf 179 E3
Sutton Notts 174 C4
Sutton Notts 187 D4
Sutton Oxon 133 G2
Sutton Pembs 126 C1
Sutton Peter 161 F3
Sutton Shrop 157 G4
Sutton Shrop 171 D4
Sutton Shrop 157 E1
Sutton Shrop 170 A5
Sutton Staffs 171 E5
Sutton Suff 153 E3
Sutton SYorks 186 C1
Sutton WSuss 108 B2
Sutton Abinger 121 G3
Sutton at Hone 137 E5
Sutton Bank National Park
  Centre NYorks
  YO7 2EH 203 E4
Sutton Bassett 160 C4
Sutton Benger 132 B5
Sutton Bingham 104 B1
Sutton Bonington 173 G5
Sutton Bridge 176 C5
Sutton Cheney 159 G2
Sutton Coldfield 158 D3
Sutton Courtenay 134 A3
Sutton Crosses 176 C5
Sutton Grange 202 B5
Sutton Green Oxon 133 G2
Sutton Green Surr 121 F2
Sutton Green Wrex 170 B3
Sutton Holms 105 G2
Sutton Howgrave 202 C5
Sutton in Ashfield 173 F2
Sutton in the Elms 160 A3
Sutton Ings 196 C4
Sutton Lane Ends 184 D5
Sutton le Marsh 189 F4
Sutton Leach 183 G3
Sutton Maddock 157 G2
Sutton Mallet 116 A4
Sutton Mandeville 118 A5
Sutton Montis 116 D5
Sutton on Sea 189 F4
Sutton on the Hill 172 D4
Sutton on Trent 174 C1
Sutton Poyntz 104 D4
Sutton St. Edmund 162 B1
Sutton St. James 162 C1
Sutton St. Nicholas 145 E3
Sutton Scarsdale 173 F1
Sutton Scotney 119 F4
Sutton upon Derwent
  195 G3
Sutton Valence 124 A4
Sutton Veny 117 F3
Sutton Waldron 105 E1
Sutton Weaver 183 G5
Sutton Wick
  B&NESom 116 C2
Sutton Wick Oxon 133 G3
Sutton-in-Craven 193 G3
Sutton-on-Hull 196 C4
Sutton-on-the-Forest
  195 E1
Sutton-under-Braies
  147 F4
Sutton-under-
  Whitestonecliffe 203 D4
Swaby 189 D5
Swadlincote 159 F1
Swaffham 163 G2
Swaffham Bulbeck 151 D1
Swaffham Prior 151 D1
Swafield 179 D2
Swainbost
  (Suaineabost) 271 H1
Swainby 203 D2
Swainshill 145 D3
Swainsthorpe 178 D5
Swainswick 117 E1
Swalcliffe 147 F4
Swalecliffe 124 D2
Swallow 188 B2
Swallow Beck 175 E1
Swallow Falls Conwy
  LL24 0DW 168 A2
Swallowcliffe 118 A5
Swallowfield 120 C1
Swallows Cross 137 F3
Swampton 119 F2
Swan Green
  ChesW&C 184 B5
Swan Green Suff 165 D4
Swan Street 151 G5
Swanage 105 G5
Swanage Railway Dorset
  BH19 1HB 105 G5
Swanbach 171 D3
Swanbourne 148 D5
Swanbridge 115 E1
Swancote 157 G3
Swanland 196 B5
Swanlaws 228 B5
Swanley 123 E2
Swanley Village 123 E2
Swanmore Hants 107 E1
Swanmore IoW 107 E3
Swannington Leics 159 G1
Swannington Norf 178 C4
Swanscombe 137 F5
Swansea
  (Abertawe) 128 C3
Swansea Museum SA1 1SN
  86 Swansea
Swanston 235 G2
Swanton Abbot 179 D3
Swanton Morley 178 B4
Swanton Novers 178 B2
Swanton Street 124 A3
Swanwick Derbys 173 F2

Swanwick Hants 107 E2
Swanwick Green 170 C3
Swarby 175 F3
Swardeston 178 D5
Swarkestone 173 E5
Swarland 221 D1
Swarraton 119 G4
Swarthmoor 199 D5
Swaton 175 G4
Swavesey 150 B1
Sway 106 B3
Swayfield 175 E5
Swaythling 106 D1
Swaythorpe 196 C1
Sweetham 102 B3
Sweetham 115 F5
Sweetshouse 97 E3
Swell 116 A5
Swepstone 159 F1
Swerford 147 F4
Swettenham 171 F1
Swffryd 130 B3
Swift's Green 124 A4
Swiftsden 110 C1
Swilland 152 C2
Swillington 194 C4
Swimbridge 113 G3
Swimbridge Newland
  113 F2
Swinbrook 133 E1
Swincliffe 194 B2
Swincombe 113 G1
Swinden 193 F1
Swinderby 175 D1
Swindon Staffs 158 A3
Swindon Swin 133 D4
Swindon Village 146 B5
Swine 196 D4
Swinefleet 195 G5
Swineford 117 D1
Swineshead Bed 149 F1
Swineshead Lincs 176 A3
Swineshead Bridge 176 A3
Swineside 201 F4
Swiney 275 H5
Swinford Leics 160 A5
Swinford Oxon 133 G2
Swingate 173 G3
Swingfield Minnis 125 E4
Swingleton Green 152 A3
Swinhoe 229 G3
Swinhope 188 C3
Swining 279 D6
Swinithwaite 201 F4
Swinscoe 172 C3
Swinside Hall 228 B5
Swinstead 175 E5
Swinton GtMan 184 B2
Swinton NYorks 203 G5
Swinton NYorks 202 B5
Swinton ScBord 237 F5
Swinton SYorks 186 B3
Swinton Quarter 237 F5
Swintonmill 237 F5
Swithland 160 A1
Swordale 256 C5
Swordland 256 D5
Swordle 247 E2
Sworton Heath 184 A4
Swyddffynnon 142 C1
Swyncombe 134 B3
Swynnerton 171 F4
Swyre 104 B4
Sychnant 155 F5
Syde 132 B1
Sydenham GtLon 136 C5
Sydenham Devon 99 E3
Syderstone 177 G4
Sydling St. Nicholas 104 C3
Sydmonton 119 F2
Sydney 171 E2
Syerston 174 C3
Sykehouse 186 D1
Sykes 192 C2
Sylen 128 B2
Symbister 279 E6
Symington SAyr 224 B2
Symington SLan 226 A2
Symonds Yat 131 E1
Symondsbury 104 A3
Synod Inn
  (Post-mawr) 142 A2
Syre 273 J3
Syreford 146 C5
Syresham 148 B3
Syston Leics 160 B1
Syston Lincs 175 E3
Sytchampton 146 A1
Sywell 148 D1
Sywell Country Park N'hants
  NN6 0QX 148 D1

T
Taagan 265 G5
Tableyhill 184 B5
Tabost 271 F6
Tachbrook Mallory 147 F1
Tacher 275 G4
Tackley 147 G5
Tacolneston 164 C2
Tadcaster 195 D3
Tadden 105 F2
Taddington Derbys 185 F5
Taddington Glos 146 C4
Taddiport 113 E4
Tadley 120 B1
Tadlow 150 A3
Tadmarton 147 F4
Tadpole Bridge 133 F2
Tadworth 122 B3
Tafarnaubach 130 A1
Tafarn-y-bwlch 141 D4
Tafarn-y-Gelyn 169 E1
Taff Merthyr Garden
  Village 130 A3
Taff's Well
  (Ffynnon Taf) 130 A4
Tafolwern 155 E2
Taibach NPT 129 D4
Tai-bach Powys 169 E5
Taicynhaeaf 154 C1
Tain High 275 H2
Tain High 266 E3
Tai'n Lôn 166 D3
Tai'r Bull 143 F5

Tairgwaith 128 D1
Tai'r-heol 130 A3
Tairlaw 224 C5
Tair-ysgol 128 C3
Takeley 151 D5
Takeley Street 150 D5
Talachddu 143 G4
Talacre 182 C3
Talardd 168 B5
Talaton 103 D3
Talbenny 126 B1
Talbot Green 129 G4
Talbot Village 105 G3
Talerddig 155 F2
Talgarreg 142 A2
Talgarth 144 A4
Taliesin 154 C3
Talisker 255 J1
Talke 171 F2
Talke Pits 171 F2
Talkin 210 B2
Talkin Tarn Country Park
  Cumb CA8 1HN 210 B2
Talla Linnfoots 226 C3
Talladale 265 F4
Talladh-a-Bheithe 250 A4
Talland 97 G4
Tallarn Green 170 B3
Tallentire 209 E3
Talley (Talyllychau) 142 C4
Tallington 161 F2
Talmine 273 H2
Talog 141 G5
Tal-sarn 142 B2
Talsarnau 167 F4
Talskiddy 96 D3
Talwrn IoA 180 C5
Talwrn Wrex 169 F3
Talwrn Wrex 170 A3
Talybont Cere 154 C4
Tal-y-bont Conwy 168 A1
Tal-y-bont Gwyn 167 E3
Tal-y-bont Gwyn 181 E5
Talybont-on-Usk 144 A5
Tal-y-Cae 167 E1
Tal-y-cafn 181 F5
Tal-y-coed 130 D1
Talygarn 129 G4
Tal-y-llyn Gwyn 154 D2
Talyllyn Powys 144 A5
Talysarn 167 D2
Tal-y-wern 155 E2
Tamavoid 242 A5
Tamerton Foliot 100 A1
Tamworth 159 E2
Tamworth Green 176 B3
Tan Office Green 151 F2
Tandem 185 F1
Tandridge 122 C3
Tanerdy 142 A5
Tanfield 212 A2
Tanfield Lea 212 A2
Tang 194 B2
Tang Hall 195 F2
Tangiers 126 C1
Tanglandford 261 G1
Tangley 119 E2
Tangmere 108 B3
Tangwick 278 B5
Tangy 222 C3
Tankerness 277 E7
Tankersley 186 A2
Tankerton 124 D2
Tan-lan 167 F3
Tannach 275 J4
Tannachie 253 F1
Tannachy 266 E1
Tannadice 252 C4
Tannington 152 D1
Tannochside 234 A3
Tansley 173 E2
Tansley Knoll 173 E2
Tansor 161 F3
Tantobie 212 A2
Tanton 203 E2
Tanworth in Arden 158 D5
Tan-y-fron 168 C1
Tan-y-graig 166 C3
Tanygrisiau 167 F3
Tan-y-groes 141 F3
Tan-y-pistyll 169 D5
Tan-yr-allt 182 B4
Taobh a' Deas Loch
  Baghasdail 254 C3
Taobh Siar 270 C5
Tapeley 113 E3
Taplow 135 E4
Tapton Grove 186 B5
Taransay
  (Tarasaigh) 270 C7
Taraphocain 248 C5
Tarbat House 266 E4
Tarbert A&B 231 G3
Tarbert A&B 231 E4
Tarbert A&B 231 E1
Tarbert (Tairbeart)
  Na H-E. Siar 270 D7
Tarbet (An Tairbeart)
  A&B 241 F4
Tarbet High 256 D5
Tarbet High 272 D4
Tarbock Green 183 F4
Tarbolton 224 C3
Tarbrax 235 E4
Tardebigge 146 B1
Tardy Gate 192 B5
Tarfside 252 C2
Tarland 260 C4
Tarleton 192 A5
Tarlscough 183 F1
Tarlton 132 B3
Tarnbrook 192 B2
Tarnock 116 A2
Tarporley 170 C1
Tarr 115 E4
Tarrant Crawford 105 F2
Tarrant Gunville 105 F1
Tarrant Hinton 105 F1
Tarrant Keyneston
  105 F2
Tarrant
  Launceston 105 F2
Tarrant Monkton 105 F2
Tarrant Rawston 105 F2
Tarrant Rushton 105 F2
Tarrel 267 F3

Tarring Neville 109 G3
Tarrington 145 F3
Tarrnacraig 223 E2
Tarsappie 243 G2
Tarskavaig 256 B4
Tarves 261 G1
Tarvie (Tairbhidh)
  High 266 B6
Tarvin 170 B1
Tarvin Sands 170 B1
Tasburgh 164 D2
Tasley 157 F3
Taston 147 F5
Tate Britain GtLon
  SW1P 4RG 13 B5
Tate Liverpool
  Mersey L3 4BB 42 B5
Tate Modern GtLon
  SE1 9TG 45 H4
Tate St. Ives Corn
  TR26 1TG 94 C3
Tatenhill 172 D5
Tathall End 148 D3
Tatham 192 C1
Tathwell 188 D4
Tatsfield 122 D3
Tattenhall 170 B2
Tattenhoe 148 D4
Tatterford 177 G5
Tattersett 177 G4
Tattershall 176 A2
Tattershall Bridge 175 G2
Tattershall
  Thorpe 176 A2
Tattingstone 152 C4
Tatton Park ChesE
  WA16 6QN 184 B4
Tatworth 103 G2
Tauchers 268 B6
Taunton 115 F5
Tavelty 261 F3
Taverham 178 C4
Tavernspite 127 E1
Tavistock 99 E3
Taw Bridge 113 G2
Taw Green 99 G1
Tawstock 113 F3
Taxal 185 E5
Tayburn 233 G5
Taychreggan 240 C2
Tayinloan 231 E5
Taylors Cross 112 C4
Taynafead 240 C3
Taynish 231 F1
Taynton Glos 145 G5
Taynton Oxon 133 E1
Taynuilt
  (Taigh an Uillt) 240 C1
Tayock 253 E4
Tayovullin 230 A2
Tayport 244 C2
Teala 183 B3
Tealing 244 C1
Team Valley 212 B1
Teangue 256 C4
Teasses 244 C4
Tebay 200 B2
Tebworth 149 E5
Techniquest, Cardiff Cardiff
  CF10 5BW 7 B4
Tedburn St. Mary 102 B3
Teddington Glos 146 B4
Teddington Kent 124 C5
Tedstone Delamere 145 F2
Tedstone Wafre 145 F2
Teeton 160 B5
Teffont Evias 118 A4
Teffont Magna 118 A4
Tegryn 141 F4
Teigh 161 D1
Teign Village 102 B4
Teigncombe 102 B5
Teigngrace 102 B5
Teignmouth 102 C5
Telford 157 F2
Telford Wonderland Tel&W
  TF3 4AY 157 G2
Telham 110 C2
Tellisford 117 F2
Telscombe 109 G3
Telscombe Cliffs 109 G3
Tempar 250 B4
Templand 217 E2
Temple Corn 97 F2
Temple Midlo 236 A4
Temple Balsall 159 E5
Temple Bar 142 B2
Temple Cloud 116 D2
Temple End 151 E2
Temple Ewell 125 E4
Temple Grafton 146 D2
Temple Guiting 146 C5
Temple Herdewyke 147 F2
Temple Hirst 195 F5
Temple Newsam WYorks
  LS15 0AE 27 H2
Temple Normanton 173 F1
Temple Sowerby 210 C5
Templecombe 117 E5
Templeton Devon 102 B1
Templeton Pembs 127 E1
Templeton Bridge 102 B1
Templewood 253 E3
Tempsford 149 G2
Ten Mile Bank 163 E3
Tenbury Wells 145 E1
Tenby (Dinbych-y-
  pysgod) 127 E2
Tendring 152 C5
Tendring Green 152 C5
Tenga 247 E5
Tenterden 124 A5
Tepersie Castle 260 D2
Terally 214 B2
Terling 137 G1
Tern 157 E2
Ternhill 170 D4
Terregles 216 D3
Terriers 135 D3
Terrington 203 F5

Terrington
  St. Clement 177 D5
Terrington St. John 162 D1
Terry's Green 158 D5
Terwick 158 D5
Terwick 259 K1
Teston 123 G3
Testwood 106 C1
Tetbury 132 A3
Tetbury Upton 132 A3
Tetchill 170 A4
Tetcott 98 D1
Tetford 188 D5
Tetney 188 D2
Tetney Lock 188 D2
Tetsworth 134 B2
Tettenhall 158 A2
Tettenhall Wood 158 A3
Tetworth 150 A2
Teuchan 261 J1
Teversal 173 F1
Teversham 150 C2
Teviot Water Gardens
  ScBord TD5 8LE 228 B4
Teviothead 227 F5
Tewel 253 G1
Tewin 136 B1
Tewkesbury 146 A4
Tewkesbury Abbey Glos
  GL20 5RZ 146 A4
Teynham 124 B2
Thackley 194 A4
Thainston 253 E2
Thainstone 261 F3
Thakeham 108 D2
Thame 134 C2
Thames Ditton 121 G1
Thames Haven 137 G4
Thamesmead 137 D4
Thanington 124 D3
Thankerton 226 A2
Tharston 164 C2
Thatcham 119 G1
Thatto Heath 183 G3
Thaxted 151 E4
The Apes Hall 163 D3
The Bage 144 B3
The Balloch 242 D3
The Banking 261 F1
The Bar 121 G5
The Birks 261 F4
The Bog 156 C3
The Bourne 120 D3
The Bratch 158 A3
The Broad 145 D1
The Bryn 130 C2
The Burf 146 A1
The Burn 253 D2
The Butts 117 E3
The Camp 132 B2
The Chequer 170 B3
The City Bucks 134 C3
The City Suff 165 E3
The Common Wilts 118 C4
The Common Wilts 132 C4
The Craigs 266 B2
The Cronk 190 B2
The Delves 158 C3
The Den 233 E4
The Dicker 110 A3
The Down 157 F3
The Drums 252 B3
The Eaves 131 F2
The Flatt 219 D4
The Folly 136 A1
The Forge 144 C2
The Forstal ESuss 123 E5
The Forstal Kent 124 C5
The Grange Lincs 189 F5
The Grange Shrop 170 B3
The Grange Surr 122 C4
The Green A&B 246 A2
The Green Cumb 198 C4
The Green Essex 137 G1
The Green Flints 169 F1
The Green Wilts 117 F4
The Grove 146 B3
The Haven 121 F4
The Headland 213 E4
The Heath 172 B4
The Herberts 129 F5
The Hermitage 122 B3
The Hill 198 C4
The Holme 194 B2
The Howe 190 A5
The Isle 157 D1
The Laurels 165 E2
The Leacon 124 B5
The Lee 135 D2
The Leigh 146 A5
The Lhen 190 B1
The Lodge 241 D5
The Marsh 156 C3
The Moor ESuss 110 D2
The Moor Kent 110 C1
The Mumbles 128 C4
The Murray 234 A4
The Mythe 146 A4
The Narth 131 E2
The Neuk 261 F5
The Node 136 B1
The Oval 117 E1
The Polchar 259 G4
The Quarter 124 A4
The Reddings 146 B5
The Rhos 126 D1
The Rookery 171 F2
The Rowe 171 F4
The Sale 159 D1
The Sands 120 D3
The Shoe 132 A5
The Slade 134 A5
The Smithies 157 F3
The Stocks 111 E1
The Swillett 135 F3
The Thrift 150 B4
The Vauld 145 E3
The Wern 169 F2
The Wyke 157 G2
Theakston 202 C4
Thealby 187 F1
Theale Som 116 B3
Theale WBerks 134 B5
Thearne 196 C4
Theberton 153 F1
Thedden Grange 120 B4
Theddingworth 160 B4
Theddlethorpe
  All Saints 189 F4

Theddlethorpe
    St. Helen 189 E4
Thelbridge Barton 102 A1
Thelbridge Cross 102 A1
Thelnetham 164 B4
Thelveton 164 C3
Thelwall 184 A4
Themelthorpe 178 B3
Thenford 148 A3
Therfield 150 B4
Thermae Bath Spa B&NESom
    BA1 1SJ 63 Bath
Thetford Lincs 161 G1
Thetford Norf 163 G4
Thetford Forest Park Norf
    IP27 0TJ 163 G4
Thethwaite 209 G2
Theydon Bois 136 D3
Theydon Garnon 137 D3
Theydon Mount 137 D3
Thickwood 132 A5
Thimbleby Lincs 176 A1
Thimbleby NYorks 202 D3
Thingley 117 F1
Thirkleby 203 D5
Thirlby 203 D4
Thirlestane 236 C5
Thirn 202 B4
Thirsk 202 D4
Thirston New
    Houses 221 D2
Thirtleby 197 D4
Thistleton Lancs 192 A4
Thistleton Rut 161 E1
Thistley Green 163 E5
Thixendale 196 A1
Thockrington 220 B4
Tholomas Drove 162 B2
Tholthorpe 195 D1
Thomas Chapel 127 E2
Thomas Close 210 A3
Thomastown 260 D1
Thompson 164 A2
Thomshill 267 K6
Thong 137 F5
Thongsbridge 185 F1
Thoralby 201 F4
Thoresby 186 D5
Thoresthorpe 189 E5
Thoresway 188 B3
Thorganby Lincs 188 C3
Thorganby NYorks 195 F3
Thorgill 203 G3
Thorington 165 F4
Thorington Street 152 B4
Thorley 137 D1
Thorley Houses 150 C5
Thorley Street Herts 137 D1
Thorley Street IoW 106 C4
Thormanby 203 D5
Thornaby-on-Tees 203 D1
Thornage 178 B2
Thornborough
    Bucks 148 C4
Thornborough
    NYorks 202 B5
Thornbury Devon 113 D5
Thornbury Here 145 F2
Thornbury SGlos 131 E3
Thornbury WYorks 194 A4
Thornby 160 B5
Thorncliff 185 G1
Thorncliffe 185 D5
Thorncombe 103 G2
Thorncombe Street 121 F3
Thorncote Green 149 G3
Thorncross 106 D4
Thorndon 152 C4
Thorndon Country Park Essex
    CM13 3RZ 137 F3
Thorndon Cross 99 F1
Thorne 187 D1
Thorne St. Margaret 115 D5
Thorner 194 C4
Thorney Bucks 135 F5
Thorney Notts 187 F5
Thorney Peter 162 A2
Thorney Som 116 B5
Thorney Close 212 C2
Thorney Hill 106 B3
Thornfalcon 115 F5
Thornford 104 C1
Thorngrafton 211 D1
Thorngrove 116 A4
Thorngumbald 197 E5
Thornham 177 F3
Thornham Magna 164 C4
Thornham Parva 164 C4
Thornhaugh 161 F2
Thornhill Cardiff 130 A4
Thornhill Cumb 198 B2
Thornhill D&G 216 C1
Thornhill Derbys 185 F4
Thornhill Soton 107 D1
Thornhill Stir 242 B4
Thornhill WYorks 185 G1
Thornhill Lees 185 G1
Thornholme 196 D1
Thornicombe 105 E2
Thornley Dur 212 B4
Thornley Dur 212 A4
Thornley Gate 211 E2
Thornliebank 233 G4
Thornroan 261 G1
Thorns 151 F2
Thorns Green 184 B4
Thornsett 185 E4
Thornthwaite Cumb 209 F4
Thornthwaite NYorks 194 A2
Thornton Angus 252 B5
Thornton Bucks 148 C4
Thornton ERid 195 G3
Thornton Fife 244 A5
Thornton Lancs 191 G3
Thornton Leics 159 G2
Thornton Lincs 176 A1
Thornton Mersey 183 E2
Thornton Middl 203 D1
Thornton N'umb 237 G5
Thornton P&K 251 F5
Thornton Pembs 126 C2
Thornton WYorks 194 A4
Thornton Bridge 202 D5
Thornton Curtis 188 A1
Thornton Heath 122 C2
Thornton Hough 183 E4
Thornton in Lonsdale 200 B5
Thornton le Moor 188 A3

Thornton Park 237 G5
Thornton Rust 201 E4
Thornton Steward 202 A4
Thornton Watlass 202 B4
Thorntonhall 233 G4
Thornton-in-Craven 193 F3
Thornton-le-Beans 202 D3
Thornton-le-Dale 204 B4
Thornton-le-Moor 202 C4
Thornton-le-Moors 183 F5
Thornton-le-Street 202 D4
Thorntonloch 237 E2
Thornwood 137 D2
Thornyhill 253 E2
Thornylee 227 F2
Thoroton 174 C3
Thorp Arch 194 D3
Thorpe Derbys 172 C2
Thorpe ERid 196 B3
Thorpe Lincs 189 E4
Thorpe Norf 165 F2
Thorpe Notts 174 C2
Thorpe NYorks 193 G1
Thorpe Surr 121 F1
Thorpe Abbotts 164 C3
Thorpe Acre 173 G5
Thorpe Arnold 174 C5
Thorpe Audlin 186 B1
Thorpe Bassett 204 B5
Thorpe Bay 138 C4
Thorpe by Water 161 D3
Thorpe Common 179 D4
Thorpe Constantine 159 E2
Thorpe Culvert 176 C1
Thorpe End 179 D4
Thorpe Green Essex 152 C5
Thorpe Green Lancs 192 B5
Thorpe Green Suff 152 A2
Thorpe Hall 203 E5
Thorpe Hesley 186 A3
Thorpe in Balne 186 C1
Thorpe in the Fallows 187 G4
Thorpe Langton 160 C3
Thorpe Larches 212 C5
Thorpe le Street 196 A3
Thorpe Malsor 160 D5
Thorpe Mandeville 148 A3
Thorpe Market 178 D2
Thorpe Morieux 152 A2
Thorpe on the Hill
    Lincs 175 E1
Thorpe on the Hill
    WYorks 194 C5
Thorpe Park Surr
    KT16 8PN 121 F1
Thorpe Row 178 A5
Thorpe St. Andrew 179 D5
Thorpe St. Peter 176 C1
Thorpe Salvin 186 C4
Thorpe Satchville 160 C1
Thorpe Street 164 B4
Thorpe Thewles 212 D5
Thorpe Tilney Dales 175 G2
Thorpe Underwood
    N'hants 160 C4
Thorpe Underwood
    NYorks 195 D2
Thorpe Waterville 161 F4
Thorpe Willoughby 195 E4
Thorpefield 202 D5
Thorpe-le-Soken 152 C5
Thorpeness 153 F1
Thorpland 163 E2
Thorrington 152 B5
Thorverton 102 C2
Thrandeston 164 C4
Thrapston 161 E5
Threapland 193 F1
Threapwood 170 B3
Threapwood Head 172 B3
Three Ashes 117 D3
Three Bridges 122 B5
Three Burrows 96 B5
Three Chimneys 124 A5
Three Cocks
    (Aberllynfi) 144 A4
Three Counties Showground
    Worcs WR13 6NW 145 G3
Three Crosses 128 B3
Three Cups Corner 110 B1
Three Hammers 97 G1
Three Holes 162 D2
Three Leg Cross 123 F5
Three Legged Cross 105 G2
Three Mile Cross 120 C1
Three Oaks 110 D2
Threehammer
    Common 179 E4
Threekingham 175 F4
Threemilestone 96 B5
Threlkeld 209 G4
Threshfield 193 F1
Threxton Hill 163 G2
Thriepley 244 B1
Thrigby 179 F4
Thringarth 211 F5
Thringstone 159 G1
Thrintoft 202 C3
Thriplow 150 C3
Throapham 186 C4
Throckenholt 162 B2
Throcking 150 B4
Throckley 212 A1
Throckmorton 146 B3
Throop 105 E3
Throphill 220 D3
Thropton 220 C1
Througham 132 A2
Throwleigh 99 G1
Throwley 124 B3
Throws 151 E5
Thrumpton Notts 173 G4
Thrumpton Notts 187 E5
Thrumster 275 J4
Thruscross 194 A2
Thrushelton 99 E2
Thrussington 160 B1
Thruxton Hants 119 D3
Thruxton Here 144 D4
Thrybergh 186 B3
Thrybergh Country Park
    SYorks S65 4NU 186 B3

Thulston 173 F4
Thunder Bridge 185 F1
Thundergay 231 G5
Thundersley 138 B4
Thunderton 269 J6
Thundridge 136 C1
Thurcaston 160 A1
Thurcroft 186 B4
Thurdistoft 275 H2
Thurdon 112 C4
Thurgarton Norf 178 C2
Thurgarton Notts 174 B3
Thurgoland 185 G2
Thurlaston Leics 160 A3
Thurlaston Warks 159 G5
Thurlbear 115 F5
Thurlby Lincs 161 G1
Thurlby Lincs 175 E1
Thurlby Lincs 189 E5
Thurleigh 149 F2
Thurlestone 100 C3
Thurloxton 115 F4
Thurlstone 185 G2
Thurlton 165 F2
Thurlwood 171 F2
Thurnby 160 B2
Thurne 179 F4
Thurnham 124 A3
Thurning N'hants 161 F4
Thurning Norf 178 B3
Thurnscoe 186 B2
Thursby 209 G1
Thursden 193 F4
Thursford 178 A2
Thursford Collection Norf
    NR21 0AS 178 A2
Thursley 121 E4
Thurso (Inbhir
    Theòrsa) 275 G2
Thurso (Inbhir
    Theòrsa) 275 G2
Thurstaston 182 D4
Thurston 152 A1
Thurston Clough 185 D2
Thurstonfield 209 G1
Thurstonland 185 F1
Thurton 179 E5
Thurvaston Derbys 172 D4
Thurvaston Derbys 172 C4
Thuster 275 H3
Thuxton 178 B5
Thwaite NYorks 201 D3
Thwaite Suff 152 C1
Thwaite Head 199 E3
Thwaite St. Mary 165 E2
Thwaites 193 G3
Thwaites Brow 193 G3
Thwing 205 D5
Tibbermore 243 F2
Tibberton Glos 145 G5
Tibberton Tel&W 171 D5
Tibberton Worcs 146 B2
Tibbie Shiels Inn 226 D3
Tibenham 164 C2
Tibertich 240 A4
Tibshelf 173 F1
Tibthorpe 196 B2
Ticehurst 123 F5
Tichborne 119 G4
Tickencote 161 E2
Tickenham 131 D5
Tickford End 149 D3
Tickhill 186 C3
Ticklerton 157 D3
Tickton 196 C3
Tidbury Green 158 C5
Tidcombe 119 D2
Tiddington Oxon 134 B2
Tiddington Warks 147 E2
Tiddleywink 132 A5
Tidebrook 110 B1
Tideford 98 D5
Tideford Cross 98 D4
Tidenham 131 E3
Tidenham Chase 131 E3
Tideswell 185 F5
Tidmarsh 134 B5
Tidmington 147 E4
Tidpit 105 G1
Tidworth 118 D3
Tiers Cross 126 C1
Tiffield 148 B2
Tifty 269 F6
Tigerton 252 D3
Tigh a' Gearraidh 262 C4
Tighachnoic 247 F5
Tighnablair 242 C3
Tighnabruaich 232 A2
Tighnacomaire 248 B3
Tigley 101 D1
Tilbrook 149 F1
Tilbury 137 F5
Tilbury Green 151 F3
Tile Hill 159 E5
Tilehurst 134 B5
Tilford 121 D3
Tilgate 122 B5
Tilgate Forest Row 122 B5
Tilgate Park WSuss
    RH10 5PQ 122 B5
Tillathrowie 260 C1
Tillers' Green 145 F4
Tillery 261 H2
Tilley 170 C5
Tillicoultry 243 E5
Tillietudlem 225 G1
Tillingham 138 C2
Tillington Here 145 D3
Tillington WSuss 121 E5
Tillington Common 145 D3
Tillyarblet 252 D3
Tillybirloch 260 E4
Tillycairn Castle 260 E3
Tillycorthie 261 H2
Tillydrine 260 E5
Tillyfar 269 G6
Tillyfour 260 D3
Tillyfourie 260 E3
Tillygarmond 260 E5
Tillygreig 261 G2
Tillypronie 260 C4
Tilmanstone 125 F3
Tiln 187 E4
Tilney All Saints 163 E1
Tilney Fen End 162 D1
Tilney High End 163 D1
Tilney St. Lawrence 162 D1
Tilshead 118 B3
Tilstock 170 C4

Tilston 170 B2
Tilstone Fearnall 170 C1
Tilsworth 149 E5
Tilton on the Hill 160 C2
Tiltups End 132 A3
Timberland 175 G2
Timberland Dales 175 G1
Timbersbrook 171 F1
Timberscombe 114 C3
Timble 194 A2
Timewell 114 C5
Timperley 184 B4
Timsbury
    B&NESom 117 D2
Timsbury Hants 119 E5
Timsgearraidh 270 C4
Timworth 151 G1
Timworth Green 151 G1
Tincleton 105 D3
Tindale 210 C2
Tindon End 151 E4
Tingewick 148 B4
Tingley 194 B5
Tingrith 149 F4
Tingwall 276 D5
Tingwall (Lerwick)
    Airport 279 D8
Tinhay 99 D2
Tinney 98 C1
Tinshill 194 B4
Tinsley 186 B3
Tinsley Green 122 B5
Tintagel 97 E1
Tintagel Castle Corn
    PL34 0HE 97 E1
Tintern Parva 131 E2
Tintinhull 104 A1
Tintwistle 185 E3
Tinwald 217 E2
Tinwell 161 F2
Tippacott 114 A3
Tipperty Aber 253 F1
Tipperty Aber 261 H2
Tipps End 162 C3
Tiptoe 106 B3
Tipton 158 B3
Tipton St. John 103 D3
Tiptree 138 C1
Tiptree Heath 138 C1
Tiptree Museum Essex
    CO5 0RF 138 C1
Tirabad 143 E3
Tiree 246 A2
Tiree Airport 246 A2
Tirindrish 249 E1
Tirley 146 A5
Tirphil 130 A2
Tir-y-dail 128 C1
Tisbury 118 A5
Tisman's Common 121 F4
Tissington 172 C2
Tister 275 G2
Titchberry 112 C3
Titchfield 107 E2
Titchmarsh 161 F5
Titchwell 177 F3
Titchwell Marsh Norf
    PE31 8BB 177 F3
Tithby 174 B4
Titley 144 C1
Titlington 229 F5
Titmore Green 150 A5
Titsey 122 D3
Titson 112 C5
Tittensor 171 F4
Tittesworth Reservoir & Visitor
    Centre Staffs
    ST13 8TQ 171 G2
Tittleshall 177 G5
Tiverton ChesW&C 170 C1
Tiverton Devon 102 C1
Tivetshall
    St. Margaret 164 C3
Tivetshall St. Mary 164 C3
Tivington 114 C3
Tixall 171 G5
Tixover 161 E2
Toab Ork 277 E7
Toab Shet 279 F9
Tobermory 247 E4
Toberonochy 239 G4
Tobson 270 D4
Tocher 260 E1
Tockenham 132 C5
Tockenham Wick 132 C4
Tockholes 192 C5
Tockington 131 F4
Tockwith 195 D2
Todber 117 E5
Toddington CenBeds 149 F5
Toddington Glos 146 C4
Todenham 147 E4
Todhills Angus 244 C1
Todhills Cumb 218 B5
Todlachie 260 E3
Todmorden 193 F5
Todwick 186 B4
Toft Cambs 150 B2
Toft Lincs 161 F1
Toft Shet 278 D5
Toft Hill 212 A5
Toft Monks 165 F2
Toft next Newton 188 A4
Toftcarl 275 J4
Toftrees 177 G4
Tofts 275 J2
Toftwood 178 A4
Togston 221 E1
Tokavaig 256 C3
Tokers Green 134 B5
Tolastadh 271 H3
Tolastadh a' Chaolais 270 D4
Tolastadh Ur 271 H3
Toll Bar 186 C2
Toll Down Gate 104 B2
Tolland 115 E4
Tollard Farnham 105 F1
Tollard Royal 105 F1
Tollcross 234 A3
Toller Down Gate 104 B2
Toller Fratrum 104 B3
Toller Porcorum 104 B3
Toller Whelme 104 B2
Tollerton Notts 174 B4
Tollerton NYorks 195 E1
Tollesbury 138 C1
Tollesby 203 E1

Tolleshunt D'Arcy 138 C1
Tolleshunt Knights 138 C1
Tolleshunt Major 138 B1
Tolmachan 270 C7
Tolpuddle 105 D3
Tolvah 259 F5
Tolworth 121 G1
Tom an Fhuadain 271 F6
Tomatin 259 F2
Tombreck 258 D1
Tomchrasky 257 J3
Tom Chrasgaidh
    (Tom Chrasgaidh) 257 J3
Tomdoun 257 H4
Tomdow 267 H7
Tomich High 257 K2
Tomich High 266 E4
Tomich High 266 D1
Tomintoul 259 J3
Tomnacross 266 C7
Tomnamoon 267 H6
Tomnaven 260 C1
Tomnavoulin 259 K2
Tomvaich 259 H1
Ton Pentre 129 F3
Tonbridge 123 E4
Tondu 129 E4
Tonedale 115 E5
Tonfanau 154 B2
Tong Kent 124 A4
Tong Shrop 157 G2
Tong WYorks 194 B4
Tong Norton 157 G2
Tong Street 194 B4
Tonge 173 F5
Tongham 121 D3
Tongland 216 A5
Tongue 273 H3
Tongue House 273 H3
Tongwynlais 130 A4
Tonmawr 129 E3
Tonna 129 D3
Tonwell 136 C1
Tonypandy 129 F3
Tonyrefail 129 G4
Toot Baldon 134 B2
Toot Hill 137 E2
Toothill Hants 106 C1
Toothill Swin 132 D4
Top End 149 F1
Top of Hebers 184 C2
Topcliffe 202 D5
Topcroft 165 D2
Topcroft Street 165 D2
Toppesfield 151 F4
Toppings 184 B1
Toprow 164 C2
Topsham 102 C4
Topsham Bridge 100 D2
Torastan 246 B3
Torbain 259 J3
Torbeg Aber 260 B5
Torbeg NAyr 223 E3
Torbothie 234 C4
Torbryan 101 E1
Torcastle 248 D2
Torcross 101 E3
Tordarroch 258 D1
Tore (An Todhar) 266 D6
Toredurff 267 J5
Toremore High 259 J1
Toremore High 275 G3
Torfrey 97 F4
Torgyle 257 K3
Torksey 187 F5
Torlum 262 C6
Torlundy
    (Tòrr Lunndaidh) 248 D2
Tormarton 131 G5
Tormisdale 230 A4
Tormore 223 D2
Tornagrain 266 E6
Tornahaish 259 K4
Tornaveen 260 E4
Torness 258 C2
Toronto 212 A4
Torpenhow 209 F3
Torphichen 235 D2
Torphins 260 E4
Torpoint 100 A2
Torquay 101 F1
Torquhan 236 B5
Torr 100 B2
Torran A&B 240 A4
Torran High 266 E4
Torran High 264 B7
Torrance 234 A2
Torrance House 234 A4
Torrancroy 260 B3
Torre Som 114 C4
Torre Torbay 101 F1
Torrich 267 F6
Torridon 264 E6
Torrin 256 B2
Torrisdale A&B 222 C2
Torrisdale High 273 J2
Torrish 274 D2
Torrisholme 192 A1
Torroble 266 C1
Torry Aber 268 C6
Torry Aberdeen 261 H4
Torryburn 235 E1
Torsonce 236 B5
Torterston 269 J6
Torthorwald 217 E3
Tortington 108 B3
Torton 158 A5
Tortworth 131 G3
Torvaig 263 K7
Torver 199 D3
Torwood 234 C1
Torworth 187 D4
Tosberry 112 C3
Toscaig 256 D1
Toseland 150 A1
Tosside 193 D2
Tostarie 246 C5
Tostock 152 A1
Totaig 263 G6
Totamore 246 A4
Tote 263 K7
Tote Hill 121 D5
Totegan 274 D2
Totford 119 G4
Totham Hill 138 B1
Tothill 189 E4
Totland 106 C4

Totley 186 A5
Toton 173 G4
Toton 173 G4
Totronald 246 A4
Totscore 263 J5
Tottenham 136 C3
Tottenhill 163 E1
Tottenhill Row 163 E1
Totteridge Bucks 135 D3
Totteridge GtLon 136 B3
Totternhoe 149 E5
Tottington GtMan 184 B1
Tottington Norf 163 G3
Totton 106 C1
Toulton 115 E4
Tournaig 264 E3
Toux 269 H5
Tovil 123 G3
Tow Law 212 A4
Towan Cross 96 B5
Toward 232 C3
Towcester 148 B3
Towednack 94 B3
Tower Bridge Exhibition
    GtLon SE1 2UP 12 C4
Tower End 163 E1
Tower of London GtLon
    EC3N 4AB 12 C4
Towersey 134 C2
Towie Aber 269 G4
Towie Aber 260 D2
Towie Aber 260 C3
Towiemore 268 B6
Town End Cambs 162 C3
Town End Cumb 199 F4
Town End Mersey 183 F4
Town End Norf 199 E4
Town Green Lancs 183 F2
Town Green Norf 179 E4
Town Row 123 E5
Town Street 163 F4
Town Yetholm 228 C4
Town of Lowton 184 A3
Towneley Hall Art Gallery &
    Museum Lancs
    BB11 3RQ 193 E4
Townend 211 F3
Townhead D&G 207 G2
Townhead SYorks 185 F2
Townhead of
    Greenlaw 216 B4
Townhill Fife 235 F1
Townhill Swan 128 C3
Towns End 119 G2
Towns Green 170 D1
Townshend 94 C3
Towthorpe ERid 196 B1
Towthorpe York 195 F2
Towton 195 D4
Towyn 182 A5
Toynton All Saints 176 B1
Toynton Fen Side 176 B1
Toynton St. Peter 176 C1
Toy's Hill 123 D3
Trabboch 224 C3
Traboe 95 E4
Tradespark High 267 F6
Tradespark Ork 277 D7
Trafford Centre 184 B3
Trafford Park 184 B3
Trago Mills, Newton Abbot
    Devon TQ12 6JD 102 B5
Trallong 143 F5
Trallwn 128 C3
Tram Inn 145 D4
Tranent 236 B2
Tranmere 183 E4
Trantlebeg 274 D3
Trantlemore 274 D3
Tranwell 221 D3
Trap 128 C1
Trap Street 171 F1
Trapp 128 C1
Traprain 236 C2
Traquair 227 E2
Trawden 193 F4
Trawscoed
    (Crosswood) 154 C5
Trawsfynydd 168 A4
Trealaw 129 G3
Treales 192 A4
Trearddur 180 A5
Treaslane 263 J6
Tre-Aubrey 129 G5
Trebah Garden Corn
    TR11 5JZ 95 E4
Trebanog 129 G3
Trebanos 128 D2
Trebarrow 98 C1
Trebartha 97 G2
Trebarvah 95 E3
Trebarwith 97 E1
Trebeath 97 G1
Trebetherick 96 D2
Trebister 279 D9
Treborough 114 D4
Trebudannon 96 C3
Trebullett 98 D3
Treburley 98 D3
Treburrick 96 C2
Trebyan 97 E3
Trecastle 143 E5
Trecott 113 G5
Trecrogo 98 D2
Trecwn 140 C4
Trecynon 129 F2
Tredaule 97 G1
Tredavoe 94 B4
Treddiog 140 B5
Tredegar 130 A2
Tredington Glos 146 B5
Tredington Warks 147 E3
Tredinnick Corn 96 D3
Tredinnick Corn 97 G4
Tredogan 115 D1
Tredomen 144 A4
Tredrissi 141 D3
Tredunnock 130 C3
Tredustan 144 A4
Tredworth 132 A1
Treen Corn 94 A4
Treen Corn 94 B3
Treesmill 97 E4
Treeton 186 B4
Trefasser 140 B4
Trefdraeth 180 C5
Trefecca 144 A4
Trefechan 129 G2

Trefeglwys 155 F3
Trefenter 142 C1
Treffgarne 140 C5
Treffynnon 140 B5
Trefgarn Owen 140 B5
Trefil 130 A1
Trefilan 142 B2
Trefin 140 B4
Treflach 169 F5
Trefnanney 156 B1
Trefnant 182 B5
Trefonen 169 F5
Trefor Gwyn 166 D2
Trefor IoA 180 B4
Treforest 130 A4
Treforest Industrial
    Estate 130 A4
Trefriw 168 A1
Tregadillett 97 G1
Tregaian 180 C5
Tregare 130 D1
Tregarland 97 G4
Tregarne 95 E4
Tregaron 142 C2
Tregarth 167 F1
Tregaswith 96 C3
Tregavethan 96 B5
Tregear 96 C3
Tregeare 97 G1
Tregeiriog 169 E4
Tregele 180 B3
Tregidden 95 E4
Tregiskey 97 E5
Treglemais 140 B5
Tregolds 96 C2
Tregole 98 B1
Tregonetha 97 D3
Tregony 96 D5
Tregoodwell 97 F1
Tregoss 97 D3
Tregowris 95 E4
Tregoyd 144 A4
Tregrehan Mills 97 E4
Tre-groes 142 A3
Treguff 129 G5
Tregullon 97 E3
Tregunnon 97 G1
Tregurrian 96 C3
Tregynon 155 G3
Trehafod 129 G3
Trehan 100 A4
Treharris 129 G3
Treherbert 129 F3
Tre-hill 129 G5
Trekenner 98 D3
Treknow 97 E1
Trelan 95 E5
Trelash 98 B1
Trelassick 96 C4
Trelawnyd 182 B5
Trelech 141 F4
Treleddyd-fawr 140 A5
Trelewis 130 A3
Treligga 97 E1
Trelights 97 D2
Trelill 97 E2
Trelissick 95 F3
Trelissick Corn
    TR3 6QL 95 F3
Trelleck 131 E2
Trelleck Grange 131 D2
Trelogan 182 C4
Trelowla 97 G4
Trelystan 156 B2
Tremadog 167 E3
Tremail 97 F1
Tremain 141 F3
Tremaine 97 G1
Tremar 97 G3
Trematon 99 D5
Tremeirchion 182 B5
Tremethick Cross 94 B3
Tremore 97 E3
Trenance Corn 96 C3
Trenance Corn 96 D2
Trenarren 97 E5
Trench Tel&W 157 F1
Trench Wrex 170 A4
Trencreek 96 C3
Trenear 95 D3
Treneglos 97 G1
Trenewan 97 F4
Trengune 98 B1
Trent 104 B1
Trent Port 187 F4
Trent Vale 171 F3
Trentham 171 F3
Trentishoe 113 G1
Trenwheal 94 C3
Treoes 129 F5
Treorchy 129 F3
Treowen 130 B3
Trequite 97 E2
Tre'r-ddol 154 C3
Trerhyngyll 129 G5
Tre-Rhys 141 E3
Tresaith 141 F2
Tresco 96 A1
Trescott 158 A3
Trescowe 94 C3
Tresean 96 B4
Tresham 131 G3
Treshnish 246 C5
Tresillian 96 C5
Tresinney 97 F1
Tresinwen 140 B3
Treskinnick Cross 98 C1
Treslea 97 F3
Tresmeer 97 G1
Tresowes Green 94 D4
Tresparrett 98 B1
Tresparrett Posts 98 B1
Tressait 250 D3
Tresta Shet 278 F3
Tresta Shet 279 C7
Treswell 187 E5
Trethewey 94 A4
Trethomas 130 A4
Trethurgy 97 E4
Tretio 140 A5
Tretire 145 E5
Tretower 144 A5
Treuddyn 169 F2
Trevadlock 97 G2
Trevalga 97 E1
Trevalyn 170 A2
Trevanson 97 D2

314

Trevarnon 94 C3
Trevarrack 94 B3
Trevarren 96 D3
Trevarrian 96 C3
Trevarrick 97 D5
Tre-vaughan Carmar 141 G5
Trevaughan Carmar 127 E1
Treveighan 97 G3
Trevellas 96 B4
Trevelmond 97 G3
Trevenen 95 D4
Treverva 95 E3
Trevescan 94 A4
Trevethin 130 B4
Trevigro 98 B4
Treviscoe 96 D4
Trevivian 97 F1
Trevone 96 C2
Trevor 169 F3
Trewalder 97 E1
Trewarmett 97 E1
Trewarthenick 96 D5
Trewassa 97 F1
Trewellard 94 A3
Trewen Corn 97 G1
Trewen Here 131 E1
Trewennack 95 D4
Trewent 126 D3
Trewern 156 B1
Trewethern 97 E2
Trewidland 97 G4
Trewilym 141 E3
Trewint Corn 98 B3
Trewint Corn 97 G1
Trewithian 95 F3
Trewoon 97 D4
Treworga 96 C5
Treworlas 95 F3
Trewornan 97 D2
Treworthal 95 F3
Tre-wyn 144 C5
Treyarnon 96 C2
Treyford 108 A2
Trezaise 97 D4
Triangle 193 G5
Trickett's Cross 105 G2
Triermain 210 B1
Trimdon 212 C4
Trimdon Colliery 212 C4
Trimdon Grange 212 C4
Trimingham 179 D2
Trimley Lower Street 153 D4
Trimley St. Martin 153 D4
Trimley St. Mary 153 D4
Trimpley 157 G5
Trimsaran 128 A3
Trimstone 113 E1
Trinafour 250 C3
Trinant 130 B3
Tring 135 E1
Trinity Angus 253 E3
Trinity Chanl 100 C5
Trinity Edin 235 G2
Trisant 154 D5
Triscombe Som 114 C4
Triscombe Som 115 E4
Trislaig 248 C2
Trispen 96 C4
Tritlington 221 E2
Trochry 243 E1
Troedyraur 141 G3
Troedyrhiw 129 G2
Trofarth 181 D5
Trondavoe 278 C3
Troon Corn 95 D3
Troon SAyr 224 B2
Tropical Butterfly House,
    Wildlife & Falconry Centre
    SYorks S25 4EQ 21 F3
Tropical World, Roundhay
    WYorks LS8 2ER 27 G1
Trosairidh 254 C3
Troston 163 G5
Troswell 98 C1
Trottick 244 C1
Trottiscliffe 123 F2
Trotton 120 D5
Trough Gate 193 E5
Troughend 220 A2
Troustan 232 B2
Troutbeck Cumb 199 F2
Troutbeck Cumb 209 G4
Troutbeck Bridge 199 F2
Trow Green 131 E2
Troway 186 A5
Trowbridge Cardiff 130 B4
Trowbridge Wilts 117 F2
Trowell 173 F4
Trowle Common 117 F2
Trowley Bottom 135 F1
Trows 228 A3
Trowse Newton 178 D5
Troy 194 B4
Trudernish 230 C4
Trudoxhill 117 E3
Trull 115 F5
Trumaisgearraidh 262 D4
Trumpan 263 H5
Trumpet 145 F4
Trumpington 150 C2
Trumps Green 121 E1
Trunch 179 D2
Trunnah 191 G3
Truro 96 C5
Truro Cathedral Corn
    TR1 2AF 96 C5
Truscott 98 C1
Trusham 102 B4
Trusley 173 D4
Trusthorpe 189 F4
Truthan 96 C4
Trysull 158 A3
Tubney 193 G3
Tuckenhay 101 E2
Tuckhill 157 G4
Tuckingmill 96 A5
Tuddenham Suff 162 C3
Tuddenham Suff 163 F5
Tudeley 123 F4
Tudeley Hale 123 F4
Tudhoe 212 B4
Tudweiliog 166 B4
Tuesley 121 E3
Tuffley 132 A1
Tufton Hants 119 F3
Tufton Pembs 140 D5
Tugby 160 C2

Tugford 157 E4
Tughall 229 G4
Tulchan 243 E2
Tulleys Farm WSuss
    RH10 4PE 122 C5
Tullibardine Distillery P&K
    PH4 1QG 243 E4
Tullibody 243 D5
Tullich A&B 240 C3
Tullich A&B 240 A3
Tullich High 267 H4
Tullich High 258 D2
Tullich Moray 268 B6
Tullich Muir 266 E4
Tullie House Museum & Art
    Gallery Cumb CA3 8TP
    68 Carlisle
Tulliemet 251 F4
Tulloch Aber 261 G1
Tulloch High 266 D2
Tulloch Moray 267 H6
Tullochgorm 240 B5
Tullochgribban High 259 G2
Tullochvenus 260 D4
Tulloes 252 D5
Tullybannocher 242 C2
Tullybelton 243 F1
Tullyfergus 252 A5
Tullymurdoch 251 G4
Tullynessle 260 D3
Tulse Hill 136 C5
Tumble (Y Tymbl) 128 B1
Tumby 176 A2
Tumby Woodside 176 A2
Tummel Bridge 250 C4
Tundergarth Mains 217 F2
Tunga 271 G2
Tungate 179 D3
Tunley 117 D2
Tunstall ERid 197 F4
Tunstall Kent 124 A2
Tunstall Lancs 200 B5
Tunstall Norf 179 F5
Tunstall NYorks 202 B3
Tunstall Stoke 171 F4
Tunstall Suff 153 E2
Tunstall T&W 212 C2
Tunstead GtMan 185 E2
Tunstead Norf 179 E3
Tunstead Milton 185 E4
Tunworth 120 B3
Tupholme 175 G1
Tupsley 145 E4
Tupton 173 E1
Tur Langton 160 C3
Turbiskill 231 F1
Turclossie 269 G5
Turgis Green 120 B5
Turin 252 D4
Turkdean 132 D1
Turleigh 117 F1
Turn 184 C1
Turnastone 144 C4
Turnberry 224 A5
Turnchapel 100 A2
Turnditch 173 D3
Turner's Green 147 D1
Turners Hill 122 C5
Turners Puddle 105 E3
Turnford 136 C2
Turnworth 105 E2
Turret Bridge 257 K5
Turriff 269 F6
Turton Bottoms 184 B1
Turvey 149 E2
Turville 134 C3
Turville Heath 134 C3
Turweston 148 B4
Tutankhamun Exhibition,
    Dorchester Dorset
    DT1 1UW 104 C3
Tutbury 172 D5
Tutbury Castle Staffs DE13
    9JF 172 D5
Tutnall 158 B5
Tutshill 131 E3
Tuttington 178 D3
Tutts Clump 134 A5
Tutwell 99 D3
Tuxford 187 E5
Twatt Ork 276 B5
Twatt Shet 279 C7
Twechar 234 B2
Tweedbank 227 G2
Tweedmouth 237 G4
Tweedsmuir 226 B3
Twelve Oaks 110 B1
Twelveheads 96 B5
Twemlow Green 171 E1
Twenty 175 G5
Twickenham 136 A5
Twigworth 146 A5
Twineham 109 E1
Twineham Green 109 E1
Twinhoe 117 E2
Twinstead 151 G4
Twiss Green 184 A3
Twiston 193 E3
Twitchen Devon 114 A4
Twitchen Shrop 156 C5
Twitton 123 E3
Twizell House 229 F4
Two Bridges Devon 99 G3
Two Bridges Glos 131 F2
Two Dales 173 D1
Two Gates 159 E2
Two Mills 183 E5
Twycross 159 F2
Twycross Zoo Leics
    CV9 3PX 159 F2
Twyford Bucks 148 B5
Twyford Derbys 173 E5
Twyford Dorset 105 E1
Twyford Hants 119 F5
Twyford Leics 160 C1
Twyford Norf 178 B3
Twyford Oxon 147 G4
Twyford Common 145 E4
Twyn Shôn-Ifan 130 A3
Twyning 146 A4
Twynllanan 143 D5
Twyn-yr-odyn 130 A5
Twyn-y-Sheriff 130 D2
Twywell 161 E5

Ty Croes 180 B5
Tyberton 144 C4
Tycroes 128 C1
Tycrwyn 156 A1
Tydd Gote 162 C1
Tydd St. Giles 162 C1
Tydd St. Mary 162 C1
Tye Common 137 F3
Tye Green Essex 151 F1
Tye Green Essex 150 D5
Tye Green Essex 137 F1
Tye Green Essex 136 D2
Tyersal 194 A4
Ty-hen 166 A4
Tyldesley 184 A2
Tyle-garw 129 G4
Tyler Hill 124 D2
Tylers Green Bucks 135 E3
Tyler's Green Essex 137 E2
Tylorstown 129 G3
Tylwch 155 F5
Ty-Mawr Conwy 168 C3
Ty-mawr Denb 169 E3
Ty-nant Conwy 168 C3
Ty-nant Gwyn 168 C5
Tyndrum
    (Taigh an Droma) 241 F1
Tyneham 105 E4
Tynehead 236 A4
Tynemouth 212 C1
Tynewydd 129 F3
Tyninghame 236 D2
Tynron 216 C1
Tyn-y-cefn 169 D3
Ty'n-y-coedcae 130 A4
Tyn-y-cwm 155 E4
Tyn-y-ffridd 169 E4
Ty'n-y-garn 129 E4
Tyn-y-gongl 180 D4
Tynygraig Cere 142 C1
Tyn-y-graig
    Powys 143 G3
Ty'n-y-groes 181 F5
Tyrie 269 H4
Tyringham 149 D3
Tyseley 158 D4
Tythegston 129 E5
Tytherington ChesE 184 D5
Tytherington SGlos 131 F4
Tytherington Som 117 E3
Tytherington Wilts 118 A3
Tytherton Lucas 132 B5
Tythenhanger 136 A2
Ty-uchaf 168 C5
Tywardreath 97 E4
Tywardreath Highway 97 E4
Tywyn 154 B2

U

Uachdar 262 D6
Uags 256 D1
Ubberley 171 G3
Ubbeston Green 165 E4
Ubley 116 C2
Uckerby 202 B2
Uckfield 109 G1
Uckinghall 146 A4
Uckington 146 B5
Uddingston 234 A3
Uddington 225 G2
Udley 116 B1
Udny Green 261 G2
Udny Station 261 H2
Udston 234 B4
Udstonhead 234 B5
Uffcott 132 D5
Uffculme 103 D1
Uffington Lincs 161 F2
Uffington Oxon 133 F4
Uffington Shrop 157 E1
Ufford Peter 161 F2
Ufford Suff 153 D2
Ufton 147 F1
Ufton Green 120 B1
Ufton Nervet 120 B1
Ugborough 100 C2
Ugford 118 B4
Uggeshall 165 F3
Ugglebarnby 204 B2
Ugley 150 D5
Ugley Green 150 D5
Ugthorpe 203 G1
Uidh 254 B5
Uig A&B 246 A4
Uig A&B 232 C1
Uig (Uige) High 263 J5
Uig High 263 G6
Uigen 270 C4
Uiginish 263 H7
Uigshader 263 K7
Uisken 238 C2
Uiskevagh
    (Uisgebhagh) 262 D6
Ulbster 275 J4
Ulcat Row 210 A5
Ulceby Lincs 189 E5
Ulceby NLincs 188 B1
Ulceby Cross 189 E5
Ulceby Skitter 188 B1
Ulcombe 124 A4
Uldale 209 F3
Uldale House 200 B3
Uley 131 G3
Ulgham 221 E2
Ullapool (Ullapol) 265 H2
Ullenhall 146 D1
Ullenwood 132 B1
Ulleskelf 195 E4
Ulley 186 B4
Ullingswick 145 E3
Ullinish 255 J1
Ullock 209 F4
Ulpha Cumb 198 C3
Ulpha Cumb 199 F4
Ulrome 197 D2
Ulsta 278 D4
Ulting 138 B2
Uluvalt 239 E1
Ulva 238 D1

Ulverston 199 D5
Ulwell 105 G4
Ulzieside 225 F5
Umberleigh 113 G3
Unapool 272 E5
Underbarrow 199 F3
Undercliffe 194 A4
Underhill 136 B3
Underhoull 278 E2
Underling Green 123 G4
Underriver 123 E3
Underwood Newport 130 C4
Underwood Notts 173 F2
Underwood Plym 100 B2
Undley 163 E4
Undy 130 D4
Ungisiadar 270 D5
Unifirth 279 B7
Union Croft 261 G5
Union Mills 190 B4
Union Street 123 G5
University of Glasgow Visitor
    Centre Glas
    G12 8QQ 38 B1
Unst 278 F1
Unst Airport 278 F2
Unstone 186 A5
Unstone Green 186 A5
Unsworth 184 C2
Unthank Cumb 210 A4
Unthank Derbys 186 A5
Up Cerne 104 C2
Up Exe 102 C2
Up Hatherley 146 B5
Up Holland 183 G2
Up Marden 107 G1
Up Mudford 104 B1
Up Nately 120 B2
Up Somborne 119 E4
Up Sydling 104 C2
Upavon 118 C2
Upchurch 124 A2
Upcott Devon 99 E1
Upcott Devon 113 F2
Upcott Here 144 C2
Upcott Som 114 C5
Upend 151 F2
Upgate 178 C4
Upgate Street Norf 164 B2
Upgate Street Norf 165 D2
Uphall Dorset 104 B2
Uphall WLoth 235 E2
Uphall Station 235 E3
Upham Devon 102 B2
Upham Hants 119 G5
Uphampton Here 144 C1
Uphampton Worcs 146 A1
Uphempston 101 E2
Uphill 116 A2
Uplands Glos 132 A2
Uplands Swan 128 C3
Uplawmoor 233 F4
Upleadon 145 G5
Upleatham 203 F1
Uplees 124 C2
Uploders 104 B3
Uplowman 102 D1
Uplyme 103 G3
Upminster 137 E4
Upottery 103 F2
Upper Affcot 156 D4
Upper Ardroscadale 232 B3
Upper Arley 157 G4
Upper Arncott 134 B1
Upper Astley 157 E1
Upper Aston 158 A3
Upper Astrop 148 A4
Upper Barvas 271 F2
Upper Basildon 134 B5
Upper Bayble
    (Pabail Uarach) 271 H4
Upper Beeding 109 D2
Upper Benefield 161 E4
Upper Bentley 146 B1
Upper Berwick 157 D1
Upper Bighouse 274 D3
Upper Boat 130 A4
Upper Boddam 260 E1
Upper Boddington 147 G2
Upper Borth 154 C4
Upper Boyndlie 269 H4
Upper Brailes 147 G4
Upper Breakish 256 C2
Upper Breinton 145 D3
Upper Broadheath 146 A2
Upper Broughton 174 B5
Upper Brynamman 128 D1
Upper Bucklebury 119 G1
Upper Burgate 106 A1
Upper Burnhaugh 261 G5
Upper Caldecote 149 G3
Upper Camster 275 H4
Upper Canada 116 A2
Upper Catesby 148 A2
Upper Catshill 158 B5
Upper Chapel 143 G3
Upper Cheddon 115 F5
Upper Chicksgrove 118 A4
Upper Chute 119 E2
Upper Clatford 119 E3
Upper Coberley 132 B1
Upper Colwall 145 G3
Upper Cotton 172 B3
Upper Cound 157 E2
Upper Cumberworth 185 G2
Upper Cwmbran 130 B3
Upper Dallachy 268 B4
Upper Dean 149 F1
Upper Denby 185 G2
Upper Denton 210 C1
Upper Derraid 259 H1
Upper Derwent Reservoirs
    Derbys S33 0AQ 185 F4
Upper Diabaig 264 D3
Upper Dicker 110 A2
Upper Dovercourt 152 D4
Upper Dunsley 135 E1
Upper Dunsforth 194 D1
Upper Eashing 121 E3
Upper Eastern Green 159 E4
Upper Eathie 266 E5
Upper Egleton 145 F3
Upper Elkstone 172 B2
Upper End 185 E5
Upper Enham 119 E3
Upper Farringdon 120 C4
Upper Framilode 131 G1
Upper Froyle 120 C3
Upper Gills 275 J1

Upper Glendessarry 257 F5
Upper Godney 116 B3
Upper Gornal 158 B3
Upper Gravenhurst 149 G4
Upper Green Essex 150 C4
Upper Green Essex 151 D4
Upper Green Mon 130 C1
Upper Green WBerks 119 E1
Upper Grove Common 145 E5
Upper Gylen 240 A2
Upper Hackney 173 D1
Upper Halliford 121 F1
Upper Halling 123 F2
Upper Hambleton 161 E2
Upper Hardres Court 125 D3
Upper Harbledown 124 D3
Upper Hartfield 123 D5
Upper Hatton 171 F4
Upper Hawkhillock 261 J1
Upper Hayesden 123 E4
Upper Hayton 157 E4
Upper Heath 157 E4
Upper Heaton 185 F1
Upper Hellesdon 178 D4
Upper Helmsley 195 F2
Upper Hengoed 169 F4
Upper Hergest 144 B2
Upper Heyford
    N'hants 148 B2
Upper Heyford
    Oxon 147 G5
Upper Hill Here 145 D2
Upper Hill SGlos 131 F3
Upper Horsebridge 110 A2
Upper Howsell 145 G3
Upper Hulme 172 B1
Upper Inglesham 133 E3
Upper Kilchattan 238 C5
Upper Killay 128 B3
Upper Knockando 267 J7
Upper Lambourn 133 F4
Upper Langford 116 B2
Upper Langwith 173 G1
Upper Largo 244 C4
Upper Leigh 172 B4
Upper Ley 131 G1
Upper Loads 173 E1
Upper Lochton 260 E5
Upper Longdon 158 C1
Upper Longwood 157 F2
Upper Ludstone 158 A3
Upper Lybster 275 H5
Upper Lydbrook 131 F1
Upper Lyde 145 D3
Upper Lye 144 C1
Upper Maes-coed 144 C4
Upper Midhope 185 G3
Upper Milovaig 263 G7
Upper Milton 133 E1
Upper Minety 132 C3
Upper Moor 146 B3
Upper Morton 131 F3
Upper Muirskie 261 G5
Upper Nash 126 D2
Upper Newbold 186 A5
Upper North Dean 135 D3
Upper Norwood 136 C5
Upper Obney 243 F1
Upper Oddington 147 E5
Upper Ollach 256 B1
Upper Padley 185 G5
Upper Pennington 106 B3
Upper Pollicott 134 C1
Upper Poppleton 195 E2
Upper Quinton 147 D3
Upper Ratley 119 E5
Upper Ridinghill 269 J5
Upper Rissington 147 E5
Upper Rochford 145 F1
Upper Sanday 277 E7
Upper Sapey 145 F1
Upper Scolton 140 C5
Upper Seagry 132 B4
Upper Shelton 149 E3
Upper Sheringham 178 C1
Upper Shuckburgh 147 G1
Upper Siddington 132 C3
Upper Skelmorlie 232 D3
Upper Slaughter 147 D5
Upper Sonachan 240 C2
Upper Soudley 131 F1
Upper Staploe 149 G2
Upper Stoke 179 D5
Upper Stondon 149 G4
Upper Stowe 148 B2
Upper Street Hants 106 A1
Upper Street Norf 179 E4
Upper Street Norf 164 C4
Upper Street Suff 152 C4
Upper Street Suff 152 C4
Upper Strensham 146 B4
Upper Sundon 149 F5
Upper Swanmore 107 E1
Upper Swell 147 D5
Upper Tean 172 B4
Upper Thurnham 192 A2
Upper Tillyrie 243 F4
Upper Tooting 136 B5
Upper Town Derbys 172 D2
Upper Town Derbys 173 D2
Upper Town Derbys 172 D2
Upper Town Here 145 E3
Upper Town NSom 116 C1
Upper Tysoe 147 F3
Upper Upham 133 E5
Upper Upnor 137 G5
Upper Victoria 244 D1
Upper Vobster 117 E3
Upper Wardington 147 G3
Upper Waterhay 132 C3
Upper Weald 148 B2
Upper Weedon 148 B2
Upper Welson 144 B2
Upper Weston 117 E1
Upper Whiston 186 B4
Upper Wick 146 A2
Upper Wield 120 A3
Upper Winchendon (Over
    Winchendon) 134 C1
Upper Witton 158 C3
Upper Woodford 118 C4
Upper Woolhampton 119 G1
Upper Wootton 119 G2
Upper Wraxall 132 A5
Upper Wyche 145 G3
Upperby 210 A2
Uppermill 185 D2
Upperthong 185 F2

Upperton 121 E5
Uppertown Derbys 173 E1
Uppertown Ork 275 J1
Uppingham 161 D2
Uppington 157 E2
Upsall 203 D4
Upsettlington 237 F5
Upshire 136 D2
Upstreet 125 E2
Upthorpe 164 A4
Upton Bucks 134 C1
Upton Cambs 161 G5
Upton ChesW&C 170 B1
Upton Corn 97 G2
Upton Corn 112 C5
Upton Devon 103 D2
Upton Devon 100 B3
Upton Dorset 105 F3
Upton Dorset 104 D4
Upton ERid 196 D2
Upton Hants 119 E2
Upton Hants 106 C1
Upton Leics 159 F3
Upton Lincs 187 F4
Upton Mersey 183 D4
Upton N'hants 148 B2
Upton Norf 179 E4
Upton Notts 187 E5
Upton Notts 174 C2
Upton Oxon 134 A4
Upton Oxon 133 E1
Upton Pembs 126 D2
Upton Peter 161 G2
Upton Slo 135 E5
Upton Som 114 C5
Upton Som 116 B5
Upton Wilts 117 F4
Upton WYorks 186 B1
Upton Bishop 145 F5
Upton Cheyney 117 D1
Upton Country Park Poole
    BH17 7BJ 3 A3
Upton Cressett 157 F3
Upton Crews 145 F5
Upton Cross 97 G2
Upton End 149 G4
Upton Grey 120 B3
Upton Hellions 102 B2
Upton Lovell 118 A3
Upton Magna 157 E1
Upton Noble 117 E4
Upton Park 136 D4
Upton Pyne 102 C2
Upton St. Leonards 132 A1
Upton Scudamore 117 F3
Upton Snodsbury 146 B2
Upton upon Severn 146 A3
Upton Warren 146 B1
Upwaltham 108 B2
Upware 162 D5
Upwell 162 D2
Upwey 104 C4
Upwick Green 150 C5
Upwood 162 A4
Uradale 279 D9
Urafirth 278 C5
Urbis, Manchester GtMan
    M4 3BG 47 C3
Urchany 267 F7
Urchfont 118 B2
Urdimarsh 145 E3
Ure 278 B5
Urgha 263 G2
Urlay Nook 202 D1
Urmston 184 B3
Urpeth 212 B2
Urquhart High 266 C6
Urquhart Moray 267 K5
Urquhart Castle High
    IV63 6XJ 258 C2
Urra 203 E2
Urray 266 C6
Ushaw Moor 212 B3
Usher Hall, Edinburgh Edin
    EH1 2EA 36 E5
Usk (Brynbuga) 130 C2
Usselby 188 A3
Usworth 212 C2
Utley 193 G3
Uton 102 B3
Utterby 188 D3
Uttoxeter 172 B4
Uwchmynydd 166 A5
Uxbridge 135 F4
Uyeasound 278 E2
Uzmaston 126 C1

V

Valley (Y Fali) 180 A5
Valley Truckle 97 F1
Valleyfield D&G 216 A5
Valleyfield Fife 235 E1
Valsgarth 278 F1
Vange 137 G4
Vardre 128 C2
Varteg 130 B2
Vatersay (Bhatarsaigh)
    254 B5
Vatsetter 278 E4
Vatten 263 H7
Vaul 246 B2
Vaynor 129 G1
Vaynor Park 156 A2
Veaullt 144 A2
Veensgarth 279 D8
Velindre Pembs 141 D4
Velindre Powys 144 A4
Vellow 115 D4
Velly 112 C3
Venn 100 D3
Venn Ottery 103 D3
Venngreen 113 D4
Vennington 156 C2
Venny Tedburn 102 B3
Venterdon 99 D3
Ventnor 107 E5
Ventnor Botanic Gardens IoW
    PO38 1UL 107 E5
Venton 100 B2
Venue Cymru, Llandudno
    Conwy LL30 1BB 181 F4
Vernham Dean 119 E2
Vernham Street 119 E2
Vernolds Common 157 D4
Verwood 105 G2
Veryan 96 D5
Veryan Green 96 D5
Vickerstown 191 E1

Victoria 97 D3
Victoria & Albert Museum
    GtLon SW7 2RL 11 F5
Victoria Art Gallery B&NESom
    BA2 4AT 63 Bath
Vidlin 279 D6
Viewfield 275 F2
Viewpark 234 B3
Vigo 158 C2
Vigo Village 123 F2
Villavin 113 F4
Vinehall Street 110 C1
Vine's Cross 110 A1
Viney Hill 131 F2
Virginia Water 121 E1
Virginstow 99 D1
Virley 138 C1
Vobster 117 E3
Voe Shet 279 D6
Voe Shet 278 C4
Vogrie Country Park Midlo
    EH23 4NU 32 B1
Voirrey Embroidery Mersey
    CH63 6JA 22 A5
Volks Electric Railway B&H
    BN2 1EN 109 F3
Vowchurch 144 C4
Voy 277 B6
Vron Gate 156 C2

W

W.R. Outhwaite & Son
    Ropemakers NYorks
    DL8 3NT 201 D4
Waberthwaite 198 C3
Wackerfield 212 A5
Wacton 164 C2
Wadbister 279 D8
Wadborough 146 B3
Waddesdon 134 C1
Waddesdon Manor Bucks
    HP18 0JH 134 C1
Waddeton 101 E2
Waddicar 183 E3
Waddingham 187 F3
Waddington Lancs 192 D3
Waddington Lincs 175 E1
Waddingworth 188 C5
Waddon Devon 102 B5
Waddon GtLon 122 C2
Wadebridge 97 D3
Wadeford 103 G1
Wadenhoe 161 F4
Wadesmill 136 C1
Wadhurst 123 F5
Wadshelf 186 A5
Wadworth 186 C3
Wadworth Hill 197 E5
Waen Denb 169 F1
Waen Denb 168 C1
Waen Aberwheeler 169 D1
Waen-fach 156 B1
Waen-wen 167 E1
Wag 275 F6
Wainfleet All Saints 176 C2
Wainfleet Bank 176 C2
Wainfleet St. Mary 176 C2
Wainford 165 E2
Waingroves 173 F3
Wainhouse Corner 98 B1
Wainscott 137 G5
Wainstalls 193 G5
Waitby 200 C2
Wakefield 194 C4
Wakehurst Place WSuss
    RH17 6TN 122 C5
Wakerley 161 E3
Wakes Colne 151 G5
Walberswick 165 F4
Walberton 108 B4
Walbottle 212 A1
Walcot Lincs 175 F4
Walcot Lincs 175 F2
Walcot NLincs 196 A5
Walcot Shrop 156 C4
Walcot Tel&W 157 E1
Walcot Green 164 C3
Walcote Leics 160 A4
Walcote Warks 146 D2
Walcott 179 E2
Walcott Dales 175 G2
Walden 201 F4
Walden Head 201 E4
Walden Stubbs 186 C1
Walderslade 123 G2
Walderton 107 G1
Walditch 104 A3
Waldley 172 C4
Waldridge 212 B3
Waldringfield 153 D3
Waldron 110 A2
Wales 186 B4
Wales Millennium Centre,
    Cardiff Cardiff
    CF10 5AL 130 A5
Walesby Lincs 188 B3
Walesby Notts 187 D5
Waleswood 186 B4
Walford Here 156 C5
Walford Here 145 E5
Walford Shrop 170 B5
Walford Staffs 171 F4
Walford Heath 156 D1
Walgherton 171 D3
Walgrave 160 D5
Walhampton 106 C3
Walk Mill 193 E4
Walkden 184 B2
Walker 212 B1
Walker Art Gallery, Liverpool
    Mersey L3 8EL 42 D3
Walker Fold 192 C3
Walkerburn 227 E2
Walkeringham 187 E3
Walkerith 187 E3
Walkern 150 A5
Walker's Green 145 E3
Walkford 106 B3
Walkhampton 100 B1
Walkingham Hill 194 C1
Walkington 196 B4
Walkwood 146 C1
Wall Corn 94 D3
Wall N'umb 211 F1
Wall Staffs 158 D2
Wall End 198 D4
Wall Heath 158 A4
Wall Houses 211 G1

315

Wal - Wes

Wall under Heywood 157 E3
Wallace Collection, London GtLon W1U 3BN 44 A2
Wallacehall 218 A4
Wallacetown 224 A5
Wallasey 183 D3
Wallaston Green 126 C2
Wallend 124 A1
Waller's Green 145 F4
Wallingford 134 B4
Wallington GtLon 122 B2
Wallington Hants 107 E2
Wallington Herts 150 A4
Wallington Wrex 170 B3
Wallingwells 186 C4
Wallis 140 D5
Wallisdown 105 G3
Walliswood 121 G4
Walls 279 B8
Wallsend 212 C1
Wallyford 236 A2
Walmer 125 F3
Walmer Bridge 192 A5
Walmersley 184 C1
Walmley 158 D3
Walmsgate 189 D5
Walpole 165 E4
Walpole Cross Keys 162 D1
Walpole Highway 162 D1
Walpole Marsh 162 C1
Walpole St. Andrew 162 D1
Walpole St. Peter 162 D1
Walrond's Park 116 A5
Walrow 116 A3
Walsall 158 C3
Walsall Arboretum Illuminations WMid WS1 2AB 14 D1
Walsall Wood 158 C2
Walsden 193 F5
Walsgrave on Sowe 159 F4
Walsham le Willows 164 B4
Walshford 194 D2
Walsoken 162 C1
Walston 235 E5
Walsworth 149 G4
Walter's Ash 134 D3
Walterston 129 G5
Walterstone 144 C5
Waltham Kent 124 D4
Waltham NELincs 188 C2
Waltham Abbey 136 C2
Waltham Chase 107 E1
Waltham Cross 136 C2
Waltham on the Wolds 174 C5
Waltham St. Lawrence 134 D5
Walthamstow 136 C4
Walton Bucks 134 D1
Walton Cumb 210 B1
Walton Derbys 173 E1
Walton Leics 160 A4
Walton Mersey 183 E3
Walton MK 149 D4
Walton Peter 161 G2
Walton Powys 144 B2
Walton Shrop 157 D5
Walton Som 116 B4
Walton Staffs 171 F4
Walton Suff 153 E4
Walton Tel&W 157 E1
Walton Warks 147 E2
Walton WYorks 186 A1
Walton WYorks 194 D3
Walton Cardiff 146 B4
Walton East 140 D5
Walton Elm 105 D1
Walton Hall Gardens Warr WA4 6SN 23 H4
Walton Highway 162 C1
Walton Lower Street 153 D4
Walton on the Hill 122 B3
Walton on the Naze 153 D5
Walton on the Wolds 160 A1
Walton Park D&G 216 B3
Walton Park NSom 130 D5
Walton West 126 B1
Walton-in-Gordano 130 D5
Walton-le-Dale 192 B5
Walton-on-Thames 121 G1
Walton-on-the-Hill 171 G5
Walton-on-Trent 159 E1
Walwen Flints 182 C5
Walwen Flints 182 D5
Walwick 220 B4
Walworth 202 B1
Walworth Gate 212 B5
Walwyn's Castle 126 B1
Wambrook 103 F2
Wanborough Surr 121 E3
Wanborough Swin 133 E4
Wandel 226 A3
Wandon 229 E4
Wandon End 149 G5
Wandsworth 136 B5
Wandylaw 229 F4
Wangford Suff 165 F4
Wangford Suff 163 F4
Wanlip 160 A1
Wanlockhead 225 G4
Wannock 110 A3
Wansbeck Riverside Park N'umb NE63 8TX 221 E3
Wansford ERid 196 C2
Wansford Peter 161 F3
Wanshurst Green 123 G4
Wanstrow 117 E3
Wanswell 131 F2
Wantage 133 F4
Wapley 131 G5
Wappenbury 147 F1
Wappenham 148 B3
Warblebank 209 F2
Warbleton 110 B2
Warblington 107 G2
Warborough 134 A3
Warboys 162 B4
Warbreck 191 G4
Warbstow 98 C1
Warburton 184 A4
Warcop 200 C1
Ward End 158 D4
Ward Green 152 B1
Warden Kent 124 C1
Warden N'umb 211 F1
Warden Hill 146 B5
Warden Street 149 G3
Wardhouse 260 D1
Wardington 147 G3
Wardle ChesE 170 D2
Wardle GtMan 184 D1
Wardley GtMan 184 B2
Wardley Rut 160 D2
Wardley T&W 212 C1
Wardlow 185 F5
Wardsend 184 D4
Wardy Hill 162 C4
Ware Herts 136 C1
Ware Kent 125 E2
Wareham 105 F4
Warehorne 124 B5
Waren Mill 229 F3
Warenford 229 F4
Warenton 229 F3
Wareside 136 C1
Waresley Cambs 150 A2
Waresley Worcs 158 A5
Warfield 135 D5
Wargrave Mersey 183 G3
Wargrave W'ham 134 C5
Warham Here 145 D4
Warham Norf 178 A1
Wark N'umb 220 A4
Wark N'umb 228 C3
Warkleigh 113 G3
Warkton 161 D5
Warkworth N'hants 147 G3
Warkworth N'umb 221 E1
Warland 193 F5
Warleggan 97 F3
Warley Essex 137 E3
Warley WMid 158 C4
Warley Town 193 G5
Warlingham 122 C3
Warmfield 194 C5
Warmingham 171 E1
Warminghurst 108 D2
Warmington N'hants 161 F3
Warmington Warks 147 G3
Warminster 117 F3
Warmlake 124 A4
Warmley 131 F5
Warmley Hill 131 F5
Warmsworth 186 C2
Warmwell 105 D4
Warndon 146 A2
Warners End 135 F2
Warnford 120 B5
Warnham 121 G4
Warningcamp 108 C3
Warninglid 109 E1
Warren ChesE 184 C5
Warren Pembs 126 C3
Warren House 99 G2
Warren Row 134 D4
Warren Street 124 B3
Warrenby 213 E5
Warren's Green 150 A5
Warrington MK 149 D2
Warrington Warr 184 A4
Warroch 243 F4
Warsash 107 D2
Warslow 172 B2
Warsop Vale 173 G1
Warter 196 A2
Warthill 195 F2
Wartle 260 D4
Wartling 110 B3
Wartnaby 174 C5
Warton Lancs 199 G5
Warton Lancs 192 A5
Warton N'umb 220 C1
Warton Warks 159 E2
Warton Bank 192 A5
Warwick 147 E1
Warwick Bridge 210 A2
Warwick Castle Warks CV34 4QU 16 A6
Warwick Wold 122 C3
Warwick-on-Eden 210 A2
Wasbister 276 C4
Wasdale Head 198 C2
Waseley Hills Country Park Worcs B45 9AT 14 C6
Wash 185 E4
Wash Common 119 F1
Washall Green 150 C4
Washaway 97 E3
Washbourne 101 D2
Washbrook 116 B3
Washfield 102 C1
Washfold 201 F2
Washford Som 114 D3
Washford Warks 146 C1
Washford Pyne 102 B1
Washingborough 188 A5
Washington T&W 212 C2
Washington WSuss 108 D2
Washmere Green 152 A3
Wasing 119 G1
Waskerley 211 G3
Wasperton 147 E2
Wasps Nest 175 F1
Wass 203 E5
Wat Tyler Country Park Essex SS16 4UH 137 G4
Watchet 115 D3
Watchfield Oxon 133 E3
Watchfield Som 116 A3
Watchgate 199 G3
Watcombe 101 F1
Watendlath 209 F5
Water 193 E5
Water Eaton MK 149 D4
Water Eaton Oxon 134 A1
Water End Bed 149 G3
Water End CenBeds 149 F4
Water End ERid 195 G4
Water End Essex 151 D3
Water End Herts 136 B2
Water End Herts 135 F1
Water Newton 161 G3
Water Orton 159 D3
Water Stratford 148 B4
Water Yeat 199 D4
Waterbeach 150 C1
Waterbeck 218 A4
Watercombe 105 D4
Waterend 134 C3
Waterfall 172 B2
Waterfoot ERenf 233 G4
Waterfoot Lancs 193 E5
Waterford 136 C1
Watergate 97 F1
Waterhead Cumb 199 E2
Waterhead D&G 216 B2
Waterheath 165 F2
Waterhill of Bruxie 269 H6
Waterhouses Dur 212 A3
Waterhouses Staffs 172 B2
Wateringbury 123 F3
Waterlane 132 B2
Waterloo Aber 261 J1
Waterloo Derbys 173 F1
Waterloo GtMan 184 D2
Waterloo High 256 C2
Waterloo Mersey 183 E3
Waterloo NLan 234 C4
Waterloo Norf 178 D4
Waterloo P&K 243 F1
Waterloo Pembs 126 C2
Waterloo Poole 105 G3
Waterloo Cross 103 D1
Waterloo Port 167 D1
Waterlooville 107 F1
Watermead Country Park Leics LE7 4PF 17 C3
Watermeetings 226 A4
Watermillock 210 A5
Watermouth Castle Devon EX34 9SL 113 F1
Waterperry 134 B2
Waterperry Oxon OX33 1JZ 134 B2
Waterrow 115 D5
Waters Upton 157 F1
Watersfield 108 C2
Watershed Mill Visitor Centre, Settle NYorks BD24 9LR 193 E1
Watersheddings 184 D2
Waterside Aber 260 B3
Waterside Aber 261 J2
Waterside B'burn 192 D5
Waterside Bucks 135 E2
Waterside EAyr 224 C5
Waterside EAyr 233 F5
Waterside EDun 234 A2
Watersmeet House Devon EX35 6NT 114 A3
Waterstock 134 B2
Waterston 126 C2
Waterthorpe 186 B4
Waterworld, Hanley ST1 5PU 85 Stoke-on-Trent
Watford Herts 136 A3
Watford N'hants 148 B1
Watford Park 130 A4
Wath NYorks 202 C5
Wath NYorks 194 A1
Wath Brow 208 D5
Wath upon Dearne 186 B2
Watley's End 131 F4
Watlington Norf 163 E1
Watlington Oxon 134 B3
Watnall 173 G3
Watten 275 H3
Wattisfield 164 B4
Wattisham 152 B2
Watton Dorset 104 A3
Watton ERid 196 C3
Watton Norf 178 A5
Watton at Stone 136 C1
Watton Green 178 A5
Watton's Green 137 E3
Wattston 234 B3
Wattstown 129 G3
Wattsville 130 B3
Waughtonhill 269 H5
Waun Fawr 154 C4
Waun y Clyn 128 A2
Waunarlwydd 128 C3
Waunclunda 142 C4
Waunfawr 167 E2
Waun-Lwyd 130 A2
Wavendon 149 E4
Waverbridge 209 F2
Waverton ChesW&C 170 B1
Waverton Cumb 209 F2
Wavertree 183 E4
Wawne 196 C4
Waxham 179 F3
Waxholme 197 F5
Way Gill 193 F1
Way Village 102 B1
Way Wick 116 A1
Wayford 104 A2
Waytown 104 A3
Weachyburn 268 E5
Weacombe 115 E3
Weald 133 F2
Weald & Downland Open Air Museum WSuss PO18 0EU 108 A2
Weald Country Park Essex CM14 5QS 137 E3
Wealdstone 136 A3
Weardley 194 B3
Weare 116 B2
Weare Giffard 113 E3
Wearhead 211 E4
Wearne 116 B5
Weasenham All Saints 177 G5
Weasenham St. Peter 177 G5
Weathercote 200 C5
Weatheroak Hill 158 C5
Weaverham 184 A5
Weaverthorpe 204 C5
Webheath 146 C1
Webton 144 D4
Wedderlairs 261 G1
Weddington 159 F3
Wedhampton 118 B2
Wedmore 116 B3
Wednesbury 158 B3
Wednesfield 158 B3
Weedon 134 D1
Weedon Bec 148 B2
Weedon Lois 148 B3
Weeford 158 D2
Week Devon 102 A1
Week Devon 101 D1
Week Som 114 C4
Week Orchard 112 C5
Week St. Mary 98 C1
Weeke 119 F4
Weekley 161 D4
Weel 196 C4
Weeley 152 C5
Weeley Heath 152 C5
Weem 250 D4
Weeping Cross 171 G5
Weethley 146 C2
Weeting 163 F4
Weeton ERid 197 F5
Weeton Lancs 191 G4
Weeton NYorks 194 B3
Wetwood 194 B4
Weir Essex 138 B4
Weir Lancs 193 E5
Weir Quay 100 A1
Weirbrook 170 A5
Weisdale 279 C7
Welbeck Abbey 186 C5
Welborne 178 B5
Welbourn 175 E2
Welburn NYorks 195 G1
Welburn NYorks 203 F4
Welbury 202 C2
Welby 175 E4
Welches Dam 162 C4
Welcombe 112 C4
Weldon 161 E4
Welford N'hants 160 B4
Welford WBerks 133 G5
Welford-on-Avon 146 D2
Welham Leics 160 C3
Welham Notts 187 E4
Welham Green 136 B2
Well Hants 120 C3
Well Lincs 189 E5
Well NYorks 202 B4
Well End Bucks 135 D4
Well End Herts 136 B3
Well Hill 123 D2
Well Street 123 F3
Well Town 102 C2
Welland 145 G3
Wellbank 244 C1
Wellesbourne 147 E2
Wellhill 267 G5
Wellhouse WBerks 134 A5
Wellhouse WYorks 185 E1
Welling 137 D5
Wellingborough 149 D1
Wellingham 177 G5
Wellingore 175 E2
Wellington Cumb 198 B2
Wellington Here 145 D3
Wellington Som 115 E5
Wellington Tel&W 157 F1
Wellington Heath 145 G3
Wellington Marsh 145 D3
Wellow B&NESom 117 E2
Wellow IoW 106 C4
Wellow Notts 174 B1
Wells 116 C3
Wells Cathedral Som BA5 2UE 116 C3
Wells Green 158 D4
Wellsborough 159 F2
Wells-next-the-Sea 178 A1
Wellstyle Green 137 F1
Wellwood 235 E1
Welney 162 D3
Welsh Bicknor 131 E1
Welsh End 170 C4
Welsh Frankton 170 A4
Welsh Hook 140 C5
Welsh Mountain Zoo Conwy LL28 5UY 181 G5
Welsh Newton 131 D1
Welsh St. Donats 129 G5
Welshampton 170 B4
Welshpool (Y Trallwng) 156 B2
Welton B&NESom 117 D2
Welton Cumb 209 G2
Welton ERid 196 B5
Welton Lincs 188 A4
Welton N'hants 148 A1
Welton le Marsh 176 C1
Welton le Wold 188 C4
Welwick 197 F5
Welwyn 136 B1
Welwyn Garden City 136 B1
Wem 170 C5
Wembdon 115 F4
Wembley 136 A4
Wembley GtLon HA9 0WS 10 C3
Wembley Park 136 A4
Wembury 100 B3
Wembworthy 113 G4
Wemyss Bay 232 C3
Wenallt Cere 154 C5
Wenallt Gwyn 168 C3
Wendens Ambo 150 D4
Wendlebury 134 A1
Wendling 178 A4
Wendover 135 D2
Wendover Dean 135 D2
Wendron 95 D3
Wendy 150 B3
Wenfordbridge 97 E2
Wenhaston 165 F4
Wenlli 168 B1
Wennington Cambs 162 A5
Wennington GtLon 137 E4
Wennington Lancs 200 B5
Wensley Derbys 173 D1
Wensley NYorks 201 F4
Wensleydale Cheese Visitor Centre, Hawes NYorks DL8 3RN 201 D4
Wentbridge 186 B1
Wentnor 156 C3
Wentworth Cambs 162 C5
Wentworth SYorks 186 A3
Wenvoe 130 A5
Weobley 144 C2
Weobley Marsh 144 D2
Weoley Castle 158 C4
Wepham 108 C3
Wepre 169 F1
Wepre Country Park Flints CH5 4HL 169 F1
Wereham 163 E2
Wergs 158 A2
Wern Gwyn 167 E4
Wern Powys 156 B1
Wern Powys 130 A1
Wern Shrop 169 F4
Wernffrwd 128 B3
Wern-olau 128 B3
Wernrheolydd 130 C1
Wern-y-cwrt 130 C2
Werrington Corn 98 D2
Werrington Peter 161 G2
Werrington Staffs 171 G3
Wervil Grange 141 G2
Wervin 183 F5
Wesham 192 A4
Wessington 173 E2
West Aberthaw 114 D1
West Acre 163 F1
West Acton 136 A4
West Allerdean 237 G5
West Alvington 100 D3
West Amesbury 118 C3
West Anstey 114 B5
West Ashby 188 C5
West Ashford 113 F2
West Ashling 108 A3
West Ashton 117 F2
West Auckland 212 A5
West Ayton 204 C4
West Bagborough 115 E4
West Barkwith 188 B4
West Barnby 204 B1
West Barns 237 D2
West Barsham 178 A2
West Bay 104 A3
West Beckham 178 C2
West Benhar 234 C3
West Bergholt 152 A5
West Bexington 104 B4
West Bilney 163 F1
West Blatchington 109 E3
West Boldon 212 C1
West Bourton 117 E5
West Bowling 194 A4
West Brabourne 124 C4
West Bradford 192 D3
West Bradley 116 C4
West Bretton 185 G1
West Bridgford 173 G4
West Bromwich 158 C3
West Buckland Devon 113 G2
West Buckland Som 115 E5
West Burrafirth 279 B7
West Burton NYorks 201 F4
West Burton WSuss 108 B2
West Butsfield 211 G3
West Butterwick 187 F2
West Byfleet 121 F1
West Cairncake 269 G6
West Caister 179 G4
West Calder 235 E3
West Camel 116 C5
West Carbeth 233 G2
West Carr Houses 187 E2
West Cauldcoats 234 A5
West Chaldon 105 D4
West Challow 133 F4
West Charleton 101 D3
West Chevington 221 E2
West Chiltington 108 C2
West Chiltington Common 108 C2
West Chinnock 104 A1
West Chisenbury 118 C2
West Clandon 121 F2
West Cliffe 125 F4
West Clyne 267 F1
West Coker 104 B1
West Compton Dorset 104 B3
West Compton Som 116 C3
West Cowick 195 F5
West Cross 128 C4
West Crudwell 132 B3
West Curry 98 C1
West Curthwaite 209 G2
West Dean Wilts 119 D5
West Dean WSuss 108 A2
West Deeping 161 G2
West Derby 183 E3
West Dereham 163 E2
West Ditchburn 229 F4
West Down 113 F1
West Drayton GtLon 135 F5
West Drayton Notts 187 E5
West Dullater 242 A4
West Dunnet 275 H1
West Edington 221 D3
West Ella 196 C5
West End Bed 149 E2
West End BrackF 135 D5
West End Caerp 130 B3
West End Cambs 162 C3
West End ERid 196 C1
West End Hants 107 D1
West End Herts 136 B2
West End Kent 125 D2
West End Lancs 192 A1
West End Lincs 189 D3
West End Norf 179 F4
West End Norf 178 A5
West End NSom 116 B1
West End NYorks 194 A2
West End Oxon 133 G2
West End Oxon 134 A4
West End SLan 235 D5
West End Suff 165 F3
West End Surr 121 G1
West End Surr 121 E1
West End Wilts 132 B5
West End Wilts 118 A5
West End Wilts 118 A5
West End Green 120 B1
West Farleigh 123 G3
West Farndon 148 A2
West Felton 170 A5
West Firle 109 G3
West Fleetham 229 F4
West Flotmanby 205 D5
West Garforth 194 C4
West Ginge 133 G4
West Glen 232 A2
West Grafton 118 D1
West Green GtLon 136 C4
West Green Hants 120 C2
West Grimstead 118 D5
West Grinstead 121 G5
West Haddlesey 195 E5
West Haddon 160 B5
West Hagbourne 134 A4
West Hagley 158 B4
West Hall 210 B1
West Hallam 173 F3
West Halton 196 B5
West Ham 136 C4
West Handley 186 A5
West Hanney 133 G3
West Hanningfield 137 G3
West Hardwick 186 B1
West Harnham 118 C5
West Harptree 116 C2
West Harrow 136 A4
West Harting 120 C5
West Hatch Som 115 F5
West Hatch Wilts 118 A5
West Head 163 D2
West Heath ChesE 171 F1
West Heath GtLon 137 D5
West Heath Hants 121 D2
West Heath Hants 119 G2
West Heath WMid 158 C5
West Helmsdale 275 F7
West Hendon 136 B4
West Hendred 133 G4
West Heslerton 204 C5
West Hewish 116 A1
West Hill Devon 103 D3
West Hill ERid 197 D1
West Hill NSom 131 D5
West Hoathly 122 C5
West Holme 105 E4
West Horndon 137 F4
West Horrington 116 C3
West Horsley 121 F2
West Horton 229 E3
West Hougham 125 E5
West Howe 105 G3
West Howetown 114 C4
West Huntspill 116 A3
West Hyde 135 F3
West Hythe 124 D5
West Ilsley 133 G4
West Itchenor 107 G2
West Keal 176 B1
West Kennett 118 C1
West Kilbride 232 D5
West Kingsdown 123 E2
West Kington 132 A5
West Kington Wick 132 A5
West Kirby 182 D4
West Knapton 204 B5
West Knighton 104 D4
West Knoyle 117 F4
West Kyloe 229 E2
West Lambrook 104 A1
West Langdon 125 F4
West Langwell 266 D1
West Lavington Wilts 118 B2
West Lavington WSuss 121 D5
West Layton 202 A2
West Leake 173 G5
West Learmouth 228 C3
West Lees 203 D2
West Leigh Devon 113 G5
West Leigh Devon 101 D2
West Leigh Som 115 E4
West Leith 135 E1
West Lexham 163 G1
West Lilling 195 F1
West Lingo 244 C4
West Linton 235 F4
West Liss 120 C5
West Littleton 131 G5
West Lockinge 133 G4
West Looe 97 G4
West Lulworth 105 E4
West Lutton 196 B1
West Lydford 116 C4
West Lyn 114 A3
West Lyng 116 A5
West Lynn 163 E1
West Mains 229 E2
West Malling 123 F3
West Malvern 145 G3
West Marden 107 G1
West Markham 187 E5
West Marsh 188 C2
West Marton 193 E2
West Melbury 117 F5
West Melton 186 B2
West Meon 120 B5
West Meon Hut 120 B5
West Mersea 138 D1
West Midland Safari Park & Leisure Park Worcs DY12 1LF 158 A5
West Milton 104 A3
West Minster 124 B1
West Molesey 121 G1
West Monkton 115 F5
West Moors 105 G2
West Morden 105 F3
West Morriston 236 D5
West Morton 193 G3
West Mostard 200 C3
West Mudford 116 C5
West Muir 253 D3
West Ness 203 F5
West Newbiggin 202 C1
West Newton ERid 197 D4
West Newton Norf 177 E5
West Norwood 136 C5
West Ogwell 101 E1
West Orchard 105 E1
West Overton 118 C1
West Panson 98 D1
West Park Aber 261 F5
West Park Mersey 183 G3
West Parley 105 G3
West Peckham 123 F3
West Pelton 212 B2
West Pennard 116 C4
West Pentire 96 B3
West Perry 149 G1
West Porlock 114 B3
West Prawle 101 D4
West Preston 108 C3
West Pulham 104 D2
West Putford 113 D4
West Quantoxhead 115 E3
West Raddon 102 B2
West Rainton 212 C3
West Rasen 188 A4
West Raynham 177 G5
West Retford 187 D4
West Rounton 202 D2
West Row 163 E5
West Rudham 177 G5
West Runton 178 C1
West Saltoun 236 B3
West Sandford 102 B2
West Sandwick 278 D4
West Scrafton 201 F4
West Shepton 116 D3
West Shinness Lodge 273 H7
West Somerset Railway Som TA24 5BG 115 E4
West Somerton 179 F4
West Stafford 104 D4
West Stockwith 187 E3
West Stoke 108 A3
West Stonesdale 201 D2
West Stoughton 116 B3
West Stour 117 E5
West Stourmouth 125 E2
West Stow 163 G5
West Stow Country Park Suff IP28 6HG 163 F5
West Stowell 118 C1
West Stratton 119 G3
West Street Kent 124 B3
West Street Med 137 G5
West Street Suff 164 A4
West Tanfield 202 B5
West Taphouse 97 F3
West Tarbert 231 G3
West Tarring 108 D3
West Thirston 221 D1
West Thorney 107 G2
West Thurrock 137 E5
West Tilbury 137 F5
West Tisted 120 B5
West Tofts Norf 163 G3
West Tofts P&K 243 G1
West Torrington 188 B4
West Town B&NESom 116 C1
West Town Hants 107 G3
West Town NSom 116 B1
West Town Som 116 C4
West Tytherley 119 D5
West Walton 162 C1
West Wellow 106 B1
West Wembury 100 B3
West Wemyss 244 B5
West Wick 116 A1
West Wickham Cambs 151 E3
West Wickham GtLon 122 C2
West Williamston 126 D2
West Winch 163 E1
West Winterslow 118 D4
West Wittering 107 G3
West Witton 201 F4
West Woodburn 220 A3
West Woodhay 119 E1
West Woodlands 117 E3
West Worldham 120 C4
West Worlington 102 A1
West Worthing 108 D3
West Wratting 151 E2
West Wycombe 134 D3
West Yatton 132 A5
West Yell 278 D4
West Youlstone 112 C4
Westbere 125 D2
Westborough 174 D3
Westbourne Bourne 105 G3
Westbourne WSuss 107 G2
Westbourne Green 136 B4
Westbrook Kent 125 F1
Westbrook WBerks 133 G5
Westbrook Wilts 118 A1
Westbury Bucks 148 B4
Westbury Shrop 156 C2
Westbury Wilts 117 F2
Westbury Leigh 117 F2
Westbury on Trym 131 E5
Westbury-on-Severn 131 G1
Westbury-sub-Mendip 116 C3
Westby Lancs 191 G4
Westby Lincs 175 E5
Westcliff-on-Sea 138 B4
Westcombe 117 D4
Westcot 133 F4
Westcott Bucks 134 C1
Westcott Devon 102 D2
Westcott Surr 121 G3
Westcott Barton 147 G5
Westcourt 118 D1
Westcroft 148 D4
Westdean 110 A4
Westdowns 97 E1
Westend Town 131 G5
Wester Aberchalder 258 C2
Wester Badentyre 269 F5
Wester Balgedie 243 G4
Wester Culbeuchly 268 E4
Wester Dechmont 235 E2
Wester Fintray 261 G3
Wester Foffarty 252 C5
Wester Greenskares 269 F4
Wester Gruinards 266 C2
Wester Hailes 235 G3
Wester Lealty 266 D4
Wester Lonvine 266 E4
Wester Newburn 244 C4
Wester Ord 261 G4
Wester Quarff 279 D9
Wester Skeld 279 B8
Westerdale High 275 G3
Westerdale NYorks 203 F2
Westerfield Shet 279 C7
Westerfield Suff 152 C3
Westergate 108 B3
Westerham 122 D3
Westerhope 212 A1
Westerleigh 131 F5
Westerloch 275 J3
Westerton Aber 261 F5
Westerton Angus 253 E4
Westerton Dur 212 B4
Westerton P&K 243 D3
Westerwick 279 B8
Westfield Cumb 208 C4
Westfield ESuss 110 D2
Westfield High 275 F2
Westfield NLan 234 B2
Westfield Norf 178 A5
Westfield WLoth 234 D2
Westfield WYorks 194 B5
Westfield Sole 123 G2
Westgate Dur 211 F4
Westgate N'umb 220 D4
Westgate NLincs 187 E2
Westgate Norf 178 A1
Westgate Hill 194 B5
Westgate on Sea 125 F1
Westhall Aber 260 E2
Westhall Suff 165 F3
Westham Dorset 104 C5
Westham ESuss 110 B3
Westham Som 116 B3
Westhampnett 108 A3

Westhay Devon 103 G2
Westhay Som 116 B3
Westhead 183 F2
Westhide 145 E3
Westhill Aber 261 G4
Westhill High 266 E7
Westhope Here 145 D2
Westhope Shrop 157 D4
Westhorp 148 A2
Westhorpe Lincs 176 A4
Westhorpe Notts 174 B2
Westhorpe Suff 152 B1
Westhoughton 184 A2
Westhouse 200 B5
Westhouses 173 F2
Westhumble 121 G2
Westing 278 E2
Westlake 100 C2
Westlands 171 F3
Westlea 132 D4
Westleigh Devon 113 E3
Westleigh Devon 103 D1
Westleigh GtMan 184 A2
Westleton 153 F1
Westley Shrop 156 C2
Westley Suff 151 G1
Westley Heights 137 F4
Westley Waterless 151 E2
Westlington 134 C1
Westlinton 218 B5
Westloch 235 G4
Westmancote 146 B4
Westmarsh 125 E2
Westmeston 109 F2
Westmill 150 B5
Westminster 136 B5
Westminster Abbey GtLon SW1P 3PA 44 E6
Westminster Abbey - Chapter House & Pyx Chamber GtLon SW1P 3PA 44 E6
Westminster Cathedral GtLon SW1P 2QW 44 C7
Westmuir 252 B4
Westness 276 C5
Westnewton Cumb 209 E2
Westnewton N'umb 228 D3
Westoe 212 C1
Weston B&NESom 117 E1
Weston ChesE 171 E2
Weston Devon 103 E4
Weston Devon 103 E2
Weston Dorset 104 C5
Weston Halton 183 G4
Weston Hants 120 C5
Weston Here 144 C2
Weston Herts 150 A4
Weston Lincs 176 A5
Weston Moray 268 C4
Weston N'hants 148 A3
Weston Notts 174 C1
Weston NYorks 194 A3
Weston Shrop 170 C5
Weston Shrop 157 E3
Weston Shrop 156 C5
Weston Soton 107 D1
Weston Staffs 171 G5
Weston WBerks 133 G5
Weston Bampfylde 116 D5
Weston Beggard 145 E3
Weston by Welland 160 C3
Weston Colville 151 E2
Weston Corbett 120 B3
Weston Coyney 171 G3
Weston Favell 148 C1
Weston Green Cambs 151 E2
Weston Green Norf 178 C4
Weston Heath 157 G1
Weston Hills 176 A5
Weston in Arden 159 F4
Weston Jones 171 E5
Weston Longville 178 C4
Weston Lullingfields 170 B5
Weston Park Staffs TF11 8LE 158 A1
Weston Patrick 120 B3
Weston Point 183 F4
Weston Rhyn 169 F4
Weston Subedge 146 D3
Weston Town 117 E3
Weston Turville 135 D1
Weston under Penyard 145 F5
Weston under Wetherley 147 F1
Weston Underwood Derbys 173 D3
Weston Underwood MK 149 D2
Westonbirt 132 A4
Westonbirt - The National Arboretum Glos GL8 8QS 132 A4
Westoning 149 F4
Weston-in-Gordano 131 D5
Weston-on-Avon 147 D2
Weston-on-the-Green 134 A1
Weston-on-Trent 173 F5
Weston-super-Mare 116 A1
Weston-under-Lizard 158 A1
Westonzoyland 116 A4
Westow 195 G1
Westpoint Arena, Clyst St. Mary Devon EX5 1DJ 102 C3
Westport A&B 222 B3
Westport Som 116 A5
Westra 130 A5
Westray 276 D3
Westray Airfield 276 D2
Westridge Green 134 A5
Westrigg 234 D3
Westruther 236 D5
Westry 162 B3
Westside 261 G5
Westvale 183 F3
Westville 173 G3
Westward 209 F2
Westward Ho! 113 E3
Westwell Kent 124 B4
Westwell Oxon 133 E2
Westwell Leacon 124 B4
Westwick Cambs 150 C1
Westwick Dur 201 F1
Westwick Norf 179 D3
Westwick NYorks 194 C1
Westwood Devon 102 D3
Westwood Peter 161 G3
Westwood SLan 234 A4
Westwood Wilts 117 F2
Westwood Heath 159 E5
Westwoodside 187 E3
Wetham Green 124 A2
Wetheral 210 A2
Wetherby 194 D3
Wetherden 152 B1
Wetherden Upper Town 152 B1
Wetheringsett 152 C1
Wethersfield 151 F4
Wethersta 279 C6
Wetherup Street 152 C1
Wetley Abbey 171 G3
Wetley Rocks 171 G3
Wettenhall 170 D1
Wettenhall Green 170 D1
Wetton 172 C2
Wetwang 196 B2
Wetwood 171 E4
Wexcombe 119 D2
Wexham Street 135 E4
Weybourne Norf 178 C1
Weybourne Surr 121 D3
Weybread 164 D3
Weybread Street 165 D4
Weybridge 121 F1
Weycroft 103 G2
Weydale 275 G2
Weyhill 119 E3
Weymouth 104 C5
Weymouth Sea Life Adventure Park & Marine Sanctuary Dorset DT4 7SX 104 C4
Whaddon Bucks 148 D4
Whaddon Cambs 150 B3
Whaddon Glos 132 A1
Whaddon Glos 146 B5
Whaddon Wilts 118 C5
Whaddon Wilts 117 F1
Whaddon Gap 150 B3
Whale 210 B5
Whaley 186 C5
Whaley Bridge 185 E4
Whaley Thorns 186 C5
Whaligoe 275 J4
Whalley 192 D4
Whalsay 279 E6
Whalsay Airport 279 E6
Whalton 220 D3
Wham 193 D1
Whaplode 176 B5
Whaplode Drove 162 B1
Whaplode St. Catherine 162 B1
Wharfe 193 D1
Wharles 192 A4
Wharley End 149 E3
Wharncliffe Side 185 G3
Wharram le Street 196 A1
Wharram Percy 196 A1
Wharton ChesW&C 171 D1
Wharton Here 145 E2
Whashton 202 A2
Whatcote 147 F3
Whateley 159 E3
Whatfield 152 B3
Whatley 117 E3
Whatlington 110 C2
Whatsole Street 124 D4
Whatstandwell 173 E2
Whatton 174 C4
Whauphill 207 E2
Whaw 201 E2
Wheatacre 165 F2
Wheatcroft 173 E2
Wheatenhurst 131 G2
Wheatfield 134 B3
Wheathampstead 136 A1
Wheathill Shrop 157 F4
Wheathill Som 116 C4
Wheatley Hants 120 C4
Wheatley Oxon 134 B2
Wheatley WYorks 193 G5
Wheatley Hill 212 C4
Wheatley Lane 193 E4
Wheatley Park 186 C2
Wheaton Aston 158 A1
Wheddon Cross 114 C4
Wheedlemont 260 C2
Wheelerstreet 121 E3
Wheelock 171 E2
Wheelock Heath 171 E2
Wheelton 192 C5
Wheen 252 B2
Wheldale 195 D5
Wheldrake 195 F3
Whelford 133 D3
Whelley 183 G2
Whelpley Hill 135 E2
Whelpo 209 G3
Whelston 182 D5
Whenby 195 F1
Whepstead 151 G2
Wherstead 152 C3
Wherwell 119 E3
Wheston 185 F5
Whetley Cross 104 A2
Whetsted 123 F4
Whetstone GtLon 136 B3
Whetstone Leics 160 A3
Whicham 198 C4
Whichford 147 F4
Whickham 212 B1
Whiddon 113 E5
Whiddon Down 99 G1
Whifflet 234 B3
Whigstreet 252 C5
Whilton 148 B1
Whim 235 G4
Whimble 112 D5
Whimple 102 D3
Whimpwell Green 179 E3
Whin Lane End 192 A3
Whinburgh 178 B5
Whinlatter Forest Cumb CA12 5TW 209 E4
Whinny Hill 202 C1
Whinnyfold 261 J1
Whippingham 107 E3
Whipsnade 135 F1
Whipsnade Zoo CenBeds LU6 2LF 135 F1
Whipton 102 C3
Whirlow 186 A4
Whisby 175 E1
Whissendine 160 D1
Whissonsett 178 A3
Whisterfield 184 C5
Whistley Green 134 C5
Whiston Mersey 183 F3
Whiston N'hants 148 D1
Whiston Staffs 172 B3
Whiston Staffs 158 A1
Whiston SYorks 186 B3
Whiston Cross 157 G2
Whiston Eaves 172 B3
Whitacre Fields 159 E3
Whitacre Heath 159 E3
Whitbeck 198 C4
Whitbourne 145 G2
Whitburn T&W 212 D1
Whitburn WLoth 234 D3
Whitby ChesW&C 183 E5
Whitby NYorks 204 B1
Whitby Abbey NYorks YO22 4JT 204 C1
Whitby Lifeboat Museum NYorks YO21 3PU 204 B1
Whitbyheath 183 E5
Whitchurch B&NESom 116 D1
Whitchurch Bucks 148 D5
Whitchurch Cardiff 130 A4
Whitchurch Devon 99 E3
Whitchurch Hants 119 F3
Whitchurch Here 131 E1
Whitchurch Pembs 140 A5
Whitchurch Shrop 170 C3
Whitchurch Warks 147 E3
Whitchurch Canonicorum 103 G3
Whitchurch Hill 134 B5
Whitchurch-on-Thames 134 B5
Whitcombe 104 D4
Whitcott Keysett 156 B4
White Ball 103 D1
White Colne 151 G5
White Coppice 184 A1
White Cross Corn 96 C4
White Cross Devon 102 D3
White Cross Here 145 D3
White Cross Wilts 117 E4
White Cube GtLon N1 6PB 12 C4
White End 146 A5
White Hill 117 F4
White Houses 187 E5
White Kirkley 211 G4
White Lackington 104 D3
White Ladies Aston 146 B2
White Lund 192 A1
White Mill 142 A5
White Moor 173 E3
White Notley 137 G1
White Ox Mead 117 E2
White Pit 189 D5
White Post Farm Centre, Farnsfield Notts NG22 8HL 174 B2
White Rocks 144 D5
White Roding 137 E1
White Waltham 134 D5
Whiteacen 267 K7
Whiteash Green 151 F4
Whitebirk 192 D5
Whitebog 269 H5
Whitebridge High 275 H1
Whitebridge (An Drochaid Bhàn) High 258 B3
Whitebrook 131 E2
Whiteburn 236 C5
Whitecairn 214 D5
Whitecairns 261 H3
Whitecastle 235 E5
Whitechapel 192 B3
Whitechurch 141 E4
Whitecote 194 B4
Whitecraig 236 A2
Whitecroft 131 F2
Whitecrook 214 C5
Whitecross Corn 94 C3
Whitecross Corn 97 D2
Whitecross Dorset 104 A3
Whitecross Falk 235 D2
Whiteface 266 E3
Whitefield Aber 261 F2
Whitefield Devon 114 A4
Whitefield Dorset 105 F3
Whitefield GtMan 184 C2
Whitefield High 258 C2
Whitefield High 275 H3
Whitefield P&K 243 G1
Whiteford 261 F2
Whitegate 170 D1
Whitehall Devon 103 E1
Whitehall Hants 120 C2
Whitehall Ork 276 F5
Whitehall WSuss 121 G5
Whitehaven 208 C5
Whitehill Aber 269 H5
Whitehill Hants 120 C4
Whitehill Kent 124 B3
Whitehill Midlo 236 A3
Whitehill NAyr 233 D4
Whitehills 268 E4
Whitehouse A&B 231 G3
Whitehouse Aber 260 E3
Whitehouse Common 158 D3
Whitekirk 236 C1
Whitelackington 103 G1
Whitelaw 237 F4
Whiteleen 275 J4
Whitelees 224 B2
Whiteley 107 E2
Whiteley Bank 107 E4
Whiteley Green 184 D5
Whiteley Village 121 F1
Whiteleys 214 B5
Whitemans Green 109 F1
Whitemire 267 G6
Whitemoor 97 D4
Whiteness 279 C8
Whiteoak Green 133 F1
Whiteparish 118 D5
Whiterashes 261 G2
Whiterow 275 J4
Whiteshill 132 A2
Whiteside N'umb 210 D1
Whiteside WLoth 235 D3
Whitesmith 110 A2
Whitestaunton 103 F1
Whitestone A&B 222 C2
Whitestone Aber 260 E5
Whitestone Devon 102 B3
Whitestreet Green 152 A4
Whitestripe 269 H5
Whiteway 132 B1
Whitewell Aber 269 H4
Whitewell Lancs 192 C3
Whitewell Wrex 170 B3
Whiteworks 99 G3
Whitewreath 267 K6
Whitfield Here 144 D4
Whitfield Kent 125 F4
Whitfield N'hants 148 B4
Whitfield N'umb 211 D2
Whitfield SGlos 131 F3
Whitford Devon 103 F3
Whitford (Chwitffordd) Flints 182 C5
Whitgift 196 A5
Whitgreave 171 F5
Whithorn 207 E2
Whiting Bay 223 F3
Whitkirk 194 C4
Whitlam 261 G2
Whitland (Hendy-Gwyn) 127 F1
Whitland Abbey 127 F1
Whitleigh 100 A1
Whitletts 224 B3
Whitley NYorks 195 E5
Whitley Read 120 C1
Whitley Wilts 117 F1
Whitley WMid 159 F5
Whitley Bay 221 F4
Whitley Chapel 211 F2
Whitley Heath 171 F5
Whitley Lower 185 G1
Whitley Row 123 D3
Whitlock's End 158 D5
Whitminster 131 G2
Whitmore Dorset 105 G2
Whitmore Staffs 171 F3
Whitnage 102 D1
Whitnash 147 F1
Whitnell 115 F3
Whitney-on-Wye 144 B3
Whitrigg Cumb 209 F1
Whitrigg Cumb 209 F3
Whitsbury 106 A1
Whitsome 237 F4
Whitson 130 C4
Whitstable 124 D2
Whitstone 98 C1
Whittingham 229 E5
Whittingslow 156 D4
Whittington Derbys 186 A5
Whittington Glos 146 C5
Whittington Lancs 200 B5
Whittington Norf 163 F3
Whittington Shrop 170 A4
Whittington Staffs 158 A4
Whittington Staffs 159 D2
Whittington Worcs 146 A2
Whittlebury 148 B3
Whittle-le-Woods 192 B5
Whittlesey 162 A3
Whittlesford 150 C3
Whittlestone Head 184 B1
Whitton GtLon 136 A5
Whitton N'umb 220 C1
Whitton NLincs 196 B5
Whitton Powys 144 B1
Whitton Shrop 157 E5
Whitton Stock 212 C5
Whitton Suff 152 C3
Whittonditch 133 E5
Whittonstall 211 G2
Whitway 119 F2
Whitwell Derbys 186 C5
Whitwell Herts 149 G5
Whitwell IoW 107 E5
Whitwell NYorks 202 B3
Whitwell Rut 161 E2
Whitwell Street 178 C3
Whitwell-on-the-Hill 195 G1
Whitwick 159 G1
Whitwood 194 D5
Whitworth 184 C1
Whitworth Art Gallery, Manchester GtMan M15 6ER 25 E4
Whixall 170 C4
Whixley 194 D2
Whorlton Dur 202 A1
Whorlton NYorks 203 D2
Whygate 219 F4
Whyle 145 E1
Whyteleafe 122 C3
Wibdon 131 E3
Wibsey 194 A4
Wibtoft 159 G4
Wichenford 145 G1
Wichling 124 B3
Wick Bourne 106 A3
Wick Devon 103 E2
Wick (Inbhir Ùige) High 275 J3
Wick SGlos 131 G5
Wick Som 115 F3
Wick Som 116 C4
Wick VGlam 129 F5
Wick Wilts 118 C5
Wick Worcs 146 B3
Wick WSuss 108 C3
Wick John O'Groats Airport 275 J3
Wick Hill Kent 124 A4
Wick Hill W'ham 120 C1
Wick St. Lawrence 116 A1
Wicken Cambs 163 D5
Wicken N'hants 148 C4
Wicken Bonhunt 150 C4
Wickenby 188 A4
Wicker Street Green 152 A3
Wickerslack 200 B1
Wickersley 186 B3
Wicketwood Hill 174 B3
Wickford 137 G3
Wickham Hants 107 E1
Wickham WBerks 133 F5
Wickham Bishops 138 B1
Wickham Heath 119 F1
Wickham Market 153 E2
Wickham St. Paul 151 G4
Wickham Skeith 152 B1
Wickham Street Suff 151 F2
Wickham Street Suff 152 B1
Wickhambreaux 125 E3
Wickhambrook 151 F2
Wickhamford 146 C3
Wickhampton 179 F5
Wicklewood 178 B5
Wickmere 178 C2
Wicksteed Park N'hants NN15 6NJ 161 D5
Wickstreet 110 A3
Wickwar 131 G4
Widcombe 117 E1
Widdington 150 D4
Widdop 193 F4
Widdrington 221 E2
Widdrington Station 221 E2
Wide Open 221 E4
Widecombe in the Moor 102 A5
Widegates 97 G4
Widemouth Bay 112 C5
Widewall 277 D8
Widford Essex 137 F2
Widford Herts 136 D1
Widford Oxon 133 E1
Widgham Green 151 E2
Widmer End 135 D3
Widmerpool 174 B5
Widnes 183 G4
Widworthy 103 F3
Wigan 183 G2
Wigan Pier GtMan WN3 4EU 183 G2
Wiganthorpe 203 F5
Wigborough 104 A1
Wiggaton 103 E3
Wiggenhall St. Germans 163 D1
Wiggenhall St. Mary Magdalen 163 D1
Wiggenhall St. Mary the Virgin 163 D1
Wiggenhall St. Peter 163 E1
Wiggens Green 151 E3
Wigginton Herts 135 E1
Wigginton Oxon 147 F4
Wigginton Shrop 170 A4
Wigginton Staffs 159 E2
Wigginton York 195 F2
Wigglesworth 193 E2
Wiggonby 209 G1
Wiggonholt 108 C2
Wighill 195 D3
Wighton 178 A2
Wightwizzle 185 G3
Wigley 106 C1
Wigmore Here 144 D1
Wigmore Med 124 A2
Wigsley 187 F5
Wigsthorpe 161 F4
Wigston 160 B3
Wigston Parva 159 G4
Wigthorpe 186 C4
Wigtoft 176 A4
Wigton 209 F2
Wigtown 215 F5
Wike 194 C3
Wilbarston 160 D4
Wilberfoss 195 G2
Wilburton 162 C5
Wilby N'hants 149 D1
Wilby Norf 164 B2
Wilby Suff 164 D4
Wilcot 118 C1
Wilcott 156 C1
Wilcrick 130 D4
Wilday Green 186 A5
Wildboarclough 171 G1
Wilde Street 163 F5
Wilden Bed 149 F2
Wilden Worcs 158 A5
Wildhern 119 E2
Wildhill 136 B2
Wildmoor 158 B5
Wildsworth 187 F3
Wilford 173 G4
Wilkesley 170 D3
Wilkhaven 267 G3
Wilkieston 235 F3
Wilksby 176 A1
Willand Devon 102 D1
Willand Som 103 E1
Willaston ChesE 171 D2
Willaston ChesW&C 183 E5
Willaston Shrop 170 C4
Willen 149 D3
Willen Lakeside Park MK MK15 9HQ 9 D2
Willenhall WMid 158 B3
Willenhall WMid 159 F5
Willerby ERid 196 C5
Willerby NYorks 204 D5
Willersey 146 D4
Willersley 144 C3
Willesborough 124 C4
Willesborough Lees 124 C4
Willesden 136 B4
Willesleigh 113 F2
Willesley 132 A4
Willett 115 E4
Willey Shrop 157 F3
Willey Warks 159 G4
Willey Green 121 E2
William's Green 152 A3
Williamscot 147 G3
Williamson Park, Lancaster Lancs LA1 1UX 192 A1
Williamthorpe 173 F1
Willian 150 A4
Willimontswick 211 D1
Willingale 137 E2
Willingdon 110 A3
Willingham 162 C5
Willingham by Stow 187 F4
Willingham Green 151 E2
Willington Bed 149 G2
Willington Derbys 173 D5
Willington Dur 212 A4
Willington Kent 123 G3
Willington T&W 212 C1
Willington Warks 147 E4
Willington Corner 170 C1
Willisham 152 B2
Willitoft 195 G4
Williton 115 D3
Willoughbridge 171 E3
Willoughby Lincs 189 E5
Willoughby Warks 148 A1
Willoughby Waterleys 160 A3
Willoughby-on-the-Wolds 174 B5
Willoughton 187 G3
Willow Green 184 A5
Willows Farm Village Herts AL2 1BB 136 A2
Willows Green 137 G1
Willsbridge 131 F5
Willslock 172 B4
Willsworthy 99 F2
Willtown 116 A5
Wilmcote 147 D2
Wilmington B&NESom 117 D1
Wilmington Devon 103 F2
Wilmington ESuss 110 A3
Wilmington Kent 137 E5
Wilmslow 184 C4
Wilnecote 159 E2
Wilney Green 164 B3
Wilpshire 192 C4
Wilsden 193 G4
Wilsford Lincs 175 F3
Wilsford Wilts 118 C4
Wilsford Wilts 118 C2
Wilsham 114 A3
Wilshaw 185 F2
Wilsill 194 A1
Wilsley Green 123 G5
Wilsley Pound 123 G5
Wilson 173 F5
Wilstead 149 F3
Wilsthorpe ERid 197 D1
Wilsthorpe Lincs 161 F1
Wilstone 135 E1
Wilton Cumb 208 D5
Wilton Here 145 E5
Wilton NYorks 204 B4
Wilton R&C 203 E1
Wilton ScBord 227 F4
Wilton Wilts 119 D1
Wilton Wilts 118 B4
Wilton House Wilts SP2 0BJ 118 B4
Wiltown 103 E1
Wimbish 151 D4
Wimbish Green 151 E4
Wimblebury 158 C1
Wimbledon 136 B5
Wimbledon All England Lawn Tennis & Croquet Club GtLon SW19 5AG 11 E7
Wimblington 162 C3
Wimborne Minster 105 G2
Wimborne Minster Dorset BH21 1HT 3 B2
Wimborne St. Giles 105 G1
Wimbotsham 163 E2
Wimpole 150 B2
Wimpole Home Farm Cambs SG8 0BW 150 B3
Wimpole Lodge 150 B3
Wimpstone 147 E3
Wincanton 117 E5
Winceby 176 B1
Wincham 184 A5
Winchburgh 235 E2
Winchcombe 146 C5
Winchelsea 111 E2
Winchelsea Beach 111 E2
Winchester 119 F5
Winchester Cathedral Hants SO23 9LS 89 Winchester
Winchet Hill 123 G4
Winchfield 120 C2
Winchmore Hill Bucks 135 E3
Winchmore Hill GtLon 136 C3
Wincle 171 G1
Wincobank 186 A3
Windermere 199 F3
Windermere Lake Cruises Cumb LA12 8AS 199 E3
Winderton 147 F3
Windhill 266 C7
Windle Hill 183 E5
Windlehurst 185 D4
Windlesham 121 E1
Windley 173 E3
Windmill 185 F5
Windmill Hill ESuss 110 B2
Windmill Hill Som 103 G1
Windmill Hill Worcs 146 B3
Windrush 133 D1
Windsor 135 E5
Windsor Castle W&M SL4 1NJ 89 Windsor
Windsor Green 151 G2
Windy Nook 212 B1
Windygates 244 B4
Windy-Yett 233 F4
Wineham 109 E1
Winestead 197 E5
Winewall 193 F4
Winfarthing 164 C3
Winford IoW 107 E4
Winford NSom 116 C1
Winforton 144 B3
Winfrith Newburgh 105 E4
Wing Bucks 149 D5
Wing Rut 161 D2
Wingate 212 C4
Wingates GtMan 184 A2
Wingates N'umb 220 C2
Wingerworth 173 E1
Wingfield CenBeds 149 F5
Wingfield Suff 164 D4
Wingfield Wilts 117 F2
Wingfield Green 164 D4
Wingham 125 E3
Wingham Well 125 E3
Wingmore 125 D4
Wingrave 135 D1
Winkburn 174 C2
Winkfield 135 E5
Winkfield Row 135 D5
Winkhill 172 B2
Winkleigh 113 G5
Winksley 202 B5
Winkton 106 A3
Winlaton 212 A1
Winlaton Mill 212 A1
Winless 275 J3
Winmarleigh 192 A3
Winnard's Perch 96 D3
Winnersh 134 C5
Winnington 184 A5
Winscombe 116 B2
Winsford ChesW&C 171 D1
Winsford Som 114 C4
Winsham Devon 113 E2
Winsham Som 103 G2
Winshill 173 D5
Winsh-wen 128 C3
Winskill 210 B4
Winslade 120 B3
Winsley 117 F1
Winslow 148 C5
Winson 132 C2
Winsor 106 C1
Winster Cumb 199 F3
Winster Derbys 172 D1
Winston Dur 202 A1
Winston Suff 152 C1
Winston Green 152 C1
Winstone 132 B2
Winswell 113 E4
Winter Gardens FY1 1HW 64 Blackpool
Winter Gardens NSom BS23 1AJ 88 Weston-super-Mare
Winterborne Came 104 D4
Winterborne Clenston 105 E2
Winterborne Herrington 104 C4
Winterborne Houghton 105 E2
Winterborne Kingston 105 E3
Winterborne Monkton 104 C4
Winterborne Stickland 105 E2
Winterborne Whitechurch 105 E2
Winterborne Zelston 105 E3
Winterbourne SGlos 131 F4
Winterbourne WBerks 133 G5
Winterbourne Abbas 104 C3
Winterbourne Bassett 132 D5
Winterbourne Dauntsey 118 C4
Winterbourne Earls 118 C4
Winterbourne Gunner 118 C4
Winterbourne Monkton 132 D5
Winterbourne Steepleton 104 C4
Winterbourne Stoke 118 B3
Winterbrook 134 B4
Winterburn 193 F2
Wintercleugh 226 A4
Winteringham 196 B5
Winterley 171 E2
Wintersett 186 A1
Wintershill 107 E1
Winterslow 118 D4
Winterton 187 G1
Winterton-on-Sea 179 F4
Winthorpe Lincs 177 D1
Winthorpe Notts 174 D2
Winton Bourne 105 G3
Winton Cumb 200 C1
Wintringham 204 B5
Winwick Cambs 161 G4
Winwick N'hants 160 B5
Winwick Warr 184 A3
Wirksworth 173 D2
Wirksworth Moor 173 E2
Wirral Country Park Mersey CH61 0HN 182 D4
Wirswall 170 C3
Wisbech 162 C2
Wisbech St. Mary 162 C2
Wisborough Green 121 F5
Wiseton 187 E4
Wishaw NLan 234 B4
Wishaw Warks 159 D3
Wisley 121 F2
Wispington 188 C5
Wissett 165 E4
Wissington 152 A4
Wistanstow 156 D4
Wistanswick 171 D5
Wistaston 171 D2
Wiston Pembs 126 D1
Wiston SLan 226 A2
Wiston WSuss 108 D2
Wistow Cambs 162 A4
Wistow NYorks 195 E4
Wiswell 192 D4
Witcham 162 C5
Witchampton 105 F2
Witchburn 222 C3
Witchford 162 D5
Witcombe 116 B5
Witham 138 B1
Witham Friary 117 E3
Witham on the Hill 161 F1
Withcall 188 C4
Withcote 160 C2
Withdean 109 F3
Witherenden Hill 110 B1
Witherhurst 110 B1
Witheridge 102 B1
Witherley 159 F3
Withern 189 E4
Withernsea 197 F5
Withernwick 197 D3
Withersdale Street 165 D3
Withersfield 151 E3
Witherslack 199 F4
Witherslack Hall 199 F4
Withiel 97 D3
Withiel Florey 114 C4
Withielgoose 97 E3
Withington Glos 132 C1
Withington GtMan 184 C3
Withington Here 145 E3
Withington Shrop 157 E1
Withington Staffs 172 B4
Withington Green 184 C5
Withington Marsh 145 E3
Withleigh 102 C1
Withnell 192 C5
Withnell Fold 192 C5
Withybrook Som 117 D3
Withybrook Warks 159 G4
Withycombe 114 D3
Withycombe Raleigh 102 D4
Withyham 123 D5
Withypool 114 B4
Witley 121 E4
Witnesham 152 C2
Witney 133 F2

Wittering 161 F2
Wittersham 111 D1
Witton Angus 253 D2
Witton Norf 179 E5
Witton Worcs 146 A1
Witton Bridge 179 E2
Witton Gilbert 212 B3
Witton Park 212 A4
Witton-le-Wear 212 A4
Wiveliscombe 115 D5
Wivelsfield 109 F1
Wivelsfield Green 109 F2
Wivenhoe 152 B5
Wiveton 178 B1
Wix 152 C5
Wixford 146 C2
Wixhill 170 C5
Wixoe 151 F3
Woburn 149 E4
Woburn Safari Park CenBeds
    MK17 9QN 9 F3
Woburn Sands 149 E4
Wokefield Park 120 B1
Woking 121 F2
Wokingham 120 D1
Wolborough 102 B5
Wold Newton ERid 204 D5
Wold Newton NELincs 188 C3
Woldingham 122 C3
Wolds Village, Bainton ERid
    YO25 9EF 196 B2
Wolfelee 227 G5
Wolferlow 145 F1
Wolferton 177 E5
Wolfhampcote 148 A1
Wolfhill 243 G1
Wolfpits 144 B2
Wolf's Castle 140 C5
Wolfsdale 140 C5
Woll 227 F3
Wollaston N'hants 149 E1
Wollaston Shrop 156 C1
Wollaston WMid 158 A4
Wollaton 173 G4
Wollerton 170 D5
Wollescote 158 B4
Wolsingham 211 G4
Wolston 159 G5
Wolsty 209 E1
Wolvercote 134 A2
Wolverhampton 158 B3
Wolverhampton Art Gallery
    WMid WV1 1DU 14 A1
Wolverley Shrop 170 B4
Wolverley Worcs 158 A5
Wolvers Hill 116 A1
Wolverton Hants 119 G2
Wolverton MK 148 D3
Wolverton Warks 147 E1
Wolverton Wilts 117 E4
Wolverton Common 119 G2
Wolvesnewton 131 D3
Wolvey 159 G4
Wolvey Heath 159 G4
Wolviston 213 D5
Womaston 144 B1
Wombleton 203 F4
Wombourne 158 A3
Wombwell 186 A2
Womenswold 125 E3
Womersley 186 C1
Wonastow 131 D1
Wonersh 121 F3
Wonford 102 C3
Wonson 99 G2
Wonston 119 F4
Wooburn 135 E4
Wooburn Green 135 E4
Wood Bevington 146 C2
Wood Burcote 148 B3
Wood Dalling 178 B3
Wood Eaton 158 A1
Wood End Bed 149 F3
Wood End Bed 149 F1
Wood End Bucks 148 C4
Wood End Herts 150 B5
Wood End Warks 159 E3
Wood End Warks 158 D5
Wood End Warks 159 E4
Wood End WMid 158 B2
Wood Enderby 176 A1
Wood Green GtLon 136 C3
Wood Green Norf 164 D2
Wood Green Animal Shelter,
    Godmanchester Cambs
    PE29 2NH 150 A1
Wood Lane 170 B4
Wood Norton 178 B3
Wood Seats 186 A3
Wood Stanway 146 C4
Wood Street 179 E3
Wood Street Village 121 E2
Woodacott 113 D5
Woodale 201 F5
Woodall 186 B4
Woodbastwick 179 E4
Woodbeck 187 E5
Woodborough Notts 174 B3
Woodborough Wilts 118 C2
Woodbridge Devon 103 E3
Woodbridge Dorset 104 D1
Woodbridge Suff 153 D2
Woodbury Devon 102 D4
Woodbury Som 116 C3
Woodbury Salterton 102 D4
Woodchester 132 A2
Woodchurch Kent 124 B5
Woodchurch Mersey 183 D4
Woodcombe 114 C3
Woodcote Oxon 134 B4
Woodcote Tel&W 157 G1
Woodcote Green 158 B5
Woodcott 119 F2
Woodcroft 131 E3
Woodcutts 105 F1
Wooddington 113 E3
Woodeaton 134 A1
Woodend Aber 260 E3
Woodend Cumb 198 C3
Woodend High 258 E2
Woodend High 247 G2
Woodend N'hants 148 B3
Woodend P&K 250 C5
Woodend WSuss 108 A3
Woodend Green 151 D5
Woodfalls 118 C5
Woodfield Oxon 148 A5
Woodfield SAyr 224 B3
Woodfoot 200 B1
Woodford Corn 112 C4
Woodford Devon 101 D2
Woodford Glos 131 F3
Woodford GtLon 136 D3
Woodford GtMan 184 C4
Woodford N'hants 161 E5
Woodford Som 115 D4
Woodford Bridge 136 D3
Woodford Green 136 D3
Woodford Halse 148 A2
Woodgate Devon 103 E1
Woodgate Norf 178 B4
Woodgate Worcs 146 B1
Woodgate WSuss 108 B3
Woodgreen 106 A1
Woodhall Invclyd 233 E2
Woodhall NYorks 201 E3
Woodhall Hills 194 A4
Woodhall Spa 175 G1
Woodham Bucks 134 B1
Woodham Dur 212 B5
Woodham Surr 121 F1
Woodham Ferrers 137 G3
Woodham Mortimer 138 B3
Woodham Walter 138 B2
Woodhaven 244 C2
Woodhead Aber 261 F1
Woodhead Staffs 172 B3
Woodhey 183 E4
Woodhey Green 170 C2
Woodhill Shrop 157 G4
Woodhill Som 116 A5
Woodhorn 221 E3
Woodhouse Cumb 199 G4
Woodhouse Leics 160 A1
Woodhouse SYorks 186 B4
Woodhouse WYorks 194 B4
Woodhouse WYorks 194 C5
Woodhouse WYorks 194 A5
Woodhouse Down 131 F4
Woodhouse Eaves 160 A1
Woodhouse Green 171 G1
Woodhouses GtMan 184 C2
Woodhouses Staffs 159 D1
Woodhouses Staffs 158 C2
Woodhuish 101 F2
Woodhurst 162 B5
Woodingdean 109 F3
Woodington 119 E5
Woodland Devon 101 D1
Woodland Dur 211 G5
Woodland Kent 124 D4
Woodland Head 102 A3
Woodlands Dorset 105 G2
Woodlands Hants 106 C1
Woodlands NYorks 194 C2
Woodlands Shrop 157 G5
Woodlands Som 115 E3
Woodlands Leisure Park,
    Dartmouth Devon
    TQ9 7DQ 101 E2
Woodlands Park 135 D5
Woodlands St. Mary 133 F5
Woodlane 172 C5
Woodleigh 100 D3
Woodlesford 194 C5
Woodley GtMan 184 D3
Woodley W'ham 134 C5
Woodmancote Glos 132 C2
Woodmancote Glos 146 B5
Woodmancote Glos 131 G3
Woodmancote
    WSuss 109 E2
Woodmancote
    WSuss 107 G2
Woodmancott 119 G3
Woodmansey 196 C4
Woodmansterne 122 B3
Woodmanton 102 D4
Woodmill 172 C5
Woodminton 118 B5
Woodmoor 156 B2
Woodnesborough 125 E3
Woodnewton 161 F3
Woodperry 134 A1
Woodplumpton 192 B4
Woodrising 178 A5
Woodrow 105 D1
Wood's Corner 110 B2
Woods Eaves 144 B3
Wood's Green 123 F5
Woodseaves Shrop 171 D4
Woodseaves Staffs 171 E5
Woodsend 133 E5
Woodsetts 186 C4
Woodsford 105 D3
Woodside Aberdeen 261 H4
Woodside BrackF 135 E5
Woodside CenBeds 135 F1
Woodside Cumb 208 D3
Woodside D&G 217 E3
Woodside Fife 244 C4
Woodside Fife 244 A4
Woodside GtLon 122 C2
Woodside Hants 106 C3
Woodside Herts 136 B2
Woodside NAyr 233 E4
Woodside P&K 243 G1
Woodside Shrop 156 C4
Woodside WMid 158 B4
Woodside Animal Farm &
    Leisure Park CenBeds
    LU1 4DG 135 F1
Woodside Green 124 B3
Woodstock Oxon 133 G1
Woodstock Pembs 140 D5
Woodthorpe Derbys 186 B5
Woodthorpe Leics 160 A1
Woodthorpe Lincs 189 E4
Woodthorpe SYorks 186 A4
Woodthorpe York 195 E3
Woodton 165 D2
Woodtown 113 E3
Woodvale 183 E1
Woodville 159 F4
Woodwall Green 171 E4
Woodwalton 162 A4
Woodwick 276 C5
Woodworth Green 170 C2
Woodyates 105 G1
Woofferton 145 E1
Wookey 116 C3
Wookey Hole 116 C3
Wookey Hole Caves &
    Papermill Som
    BA5 1BB 116 C3
Wool 105 E4
Woolacombe 113 E1
Woolage Green 125 E4
Woolage Village 125 E3
Woolaston 131 E2
Woolaston Slade 131 E2
Woolavington 116 A3
Woolbeding 121 D4
Woolcotts 114 C4
Wooldale 185 F2
Wooler 229 E4
Woolfardisworthy
    Devon 102 B2
Woolfardisworthy
    Devon 113 D3
Woolfold 184 B1
Woolfords Cottages 235 E4
Woolgarston 105 F4
Woolgreaves 186 A1
Woolhampton 119 G1
Woolhope 145 F4
Woolland 105 D2
Woollard 116 D1
Woollaton 113 E4
Woollensbrook 136 C2
Woolley B&NESom 117 E1
Woolley Cambs 161 G5
Woolley Corn 112 C4
Woolley Derbys 173 E1
Woolley WYorks 186 A1
Woolley Green W&M 135 D5
Woolley Green Wilts 117 F1
Woolmer Green 136 B1
Woolmere Green 146 B1
Woolmersdon 115 F4
Woolpit 152 A1
Woolpit Green 152 A1
Woolscott 147 G1
Woolsgrove 102 A2
Woolstaston 157 D3
Woolsthorpe 174 D4
Woolsthorpe by
    Colsterworth 175 E5
Woolston Devon 100 D3
Woolston Shrop 170 A5
Woolston Shrop 156 D2
Woolston Soton 106 D1
Woolston Warr 184 A4
Woolston Green 101 D1
Woolstone Glos 146 B5
Woolstone MK 149 D4
Woolstone Oxon 133 E4
Woolton 183 F4
Woolton Hill 119 F1
Woolverstone 152 C4
Woolverton 117 E2
Woolwich 136 D5
Woonton 144 C2
Wooperton 229 E5
Woore 171 E3
Wootten Green 164 D4
Wootton Bed 149 F3
Wootton Hants 106 B3
Wootton IoW 107 E3
Wootton Kent 125 E4
Wootton N'hants 148 C2
Wootton NLincs 188 A1
Wootton Oxon 133 G1
Wootton Oxon 133 G2
Wootton Shrop 157 D5
Wootton Shrop 156 D2
Wootton Staffs 171 F5
Wootton Staffs 172 C3
Wootton Bassett 132 C4
Wootton Bridge 107 E3
Wootton Common 107 E3
Wootton Courtenay 114 C3
Wootton Fitzpaine 103 G3
Wootton Green 149 F3
Wootton Rivers 118 C1
Wootton St. Lawrence 119 G2
Wootton Wawen 147 D1
Worcester 146 A2
Worcester Cathedral Worcs
    WR1 2LH 90 Worcester
Worcester Park 122 B2
Worcester Woods Country Park
    Worcs WR5 2LG 146 A2
Wordsley 158 A4
Wordwell 163 E5
Worfield 157 G3
Worgret 105 F4
Work 277 D6
Workhouse End 149 G2
Workington 208 D4
Worksop 186 C5
Worlaby Lincs 188 D5
Worlaby NLincs 188 A1
World Museum Liverpool
    Mersey L3 8EN 42 D1
World of Beatrix Potter
    Attraction Cumb
    LA23 3BX 199 F3
World of James Herriot, Thirsk
    NYorks YO7 1PL 202 D4
World's End Bucks 135 D2
Worlds End Hants 107 F1
World's End
    WBerks 133 G5
Worlds End WMid 158 D4
Worle 116 A1
Worleston 171 D2
Worlingham 165 F3
Worlington 163 E5
Worlingworth 152 D1
Wormald Green 194 C1
Wormbridge 144 D4
Wormegay 163 E1
Wormelow Tump 145 D4
Wormhill 185 F5
Worminghall 134 B2
Wormington 146 C4
Worminster 116 C3
Wormiston 245 E1
Wormit 244 B2
Wormleighton 147 G2
Wormley Herts 136 C2
Wormley Surr 121 E4
Wormley West End 136 C2
Wormshill 124 A3
Wormsley 144 D3
Worplesdon 121 E2
Worrall 186 A3
Worsbrough 186 A2
Worsley 184 B2
Worstead 179 E3
Worsted Lodge 150 D2
Worsthorne 193 E4
Worston 193 D3
Worswell 100 B3
Worth Kent 125 F3
Worth WSuss 122 B5
Worth Matravers 105 F5
Wortham 164 B4
Worthen 156 C2
Worthenbury 170 B3
Worthing Norf 178 A4
Worthing WSuss 108 D3
Worthington 173 F5
Worting 120 B2
Wortley Glos 131 G3
Wortley SYorks 186 A3
Wortley WYorks 194 B4
Worton NYorks 201 E4
Worton Wilts 118 A2
Wortwell 165 D3
Wothersome 194 D3
Wotherton 156 B2
Wotter 100 B1
Wotton 121 G3
Wotton Underwood 134 B2
Wotton-under-Edge 131 G3
Woughton on the
    Green 149 D4
Wouldham 123 G2
Wrabness 152 C4
Wrae 269 F5
Wrafton 113 E2
Wragby 188 B5
Wragholme 189 D3
Wramplingham 178 C5
Wrangaton 100 C2
Wrangham 260 E1
Wrangle 176 C2
Wrangle Lowgate 176 C2
Wrangway 103 E1
Wrantage 116 A5
Wrawby 188 A2
Wraxall NSom 131 D5
Wraxall Som 116 D4
Wray 192 C1
Wray Castle 199 E2
Wrays 182 B4
Wraysbury 135 F5
Wrayton 200 B5
Wrea Green 191 G4
Wreay Cumb 210 A5
Wreay Cumb 210 A3
Wrecclesham 120 D3
Wrekenton 212 B2
Wrelton 203 G4
Wrenbury 170 C3
Wreningham 164 C2
Wrentham 165 F3
Wrenthorpe 194 C5
Wrentnall 156 D2
Wressle ERid 195 G4
Wressle NLincs 187 G2
Wrestlingworth 150 A3
Wretham 164 A2
Wretton 163 E2
Wrexham (Wrecsam) 170 A3
Wrexham Arts Centre Wrex
    LL11 1AU 170 A3
Wrexham Industrial
    Estate 170 A3
Wribbenhall 157 G5
Wrightington Bar 183 G1
Wrightpark 242 B5
Wright's Green 137 E1
Wrinehill 171 E3
Wrington 116 B1
Writhlington 117 D2
Writtle 137 F2
Wrockwardine 157 F1
Wroot 187 E2
Wrose 194 A4
Wrotham 123 F3
Wrotham Heath 123 F3
Wrotham Hill Park 123 F2
Wrottesley 158 A2
Wroughton 132 D4
Wroxall IoW 107 E5
Wroxall Warks 159 E5
Wroxeter 157 E2
Wroxham 179 E4
Wroxham Barns Norf
    NR12 8QU 179 E3
Wroxton 147 G3
Wstrws 141 G3
Wyaston 172 C3
Wyberton 176 B3
Wyboston 149 G2
Wybunbury 171 D3
Wych Cross 122 D5
Wychbold 146 B1
Wychnor 159 D1
Wychnor Bridges 159 D1
Wyck 120 C4
Wyck Rissington 147 D5
Wycliffe 202 A1
Wycoller 193 F4
Wycoller Country Park
    Lancs BB8 8SY 193 F4
Wycomb 174 C5
Wycombe Marsh 135 D3
Wyddial 150 B4
Wye 124 C4
Wyesham 131 E1
Wyfordby 160 C1
Wyke Devon 102 B3
Wyke Dorset 117 E5
Wyke Shrop 157 F2
Wyke Surr 121 E2
Wyke WYorks 194 A5
Wyke Champflower 117 D4
Wyke Regis 104 C5
Wykeham NYorks 204 C4
Wykeham NYorks 204 B5
Wyken Shrop 157 G3
Wyken WMid 159 F4
Wykey 170 A5
Wylam 212 A1
Wylde Green 158 D3
Wyllie 130 A3
Wylye 118 B4
Wymering 107 F2
Wymeswold 174 B5
Wymington 149 E1
Wymondham Leics 161 D1
Wymondham Norf 178 C5
Wyndham 129 F3
Wynford Eagle 104 B3
Wynnstay Park 170 A3
Wynyard 212 D1
Wynyard Woodland Park
    Stock TS21 3JG 212 C5
Wyre Forest Worcs
    DY14 9XQ 157 G5
Wyre Piddle 146 B3
Wyresdale Tower 192 C2
Wysall 174 B5
Wyson 145 E1
Wythall 158 C5
Wytham 133 G2
Wythburn 209 G5
Wythenshawe 184 C4
Wyton Cambs 162 A5
Wyton ERid 197 D4
Wyverstone 152 B1
Wyverstone Street 152 B1
Wyville 175 D5
Wyvis Lodge 266 B4

X
Xscape Castleford WYorks
    WF10 4DA 194 D5

Y
Y Bryn 168 B5
Y Fan 155 F4
Y Felinheli 167 E1
Y Ffôr 166 C4
Y Fron (Upper
    Llandwrog) 167 E2
Yaddlethorpe 187 F2
Yafford 106 D4
Yafforth 202 C3
Yalberton 101 E2
Yalding 123 F4
Yanley 116 C1
Yanwath 210 B5
Yanworth 132 C1
Yapham 195 G2
Yapton 108 B3
Yarburgh 188 D3
Yarcombe 103 F2
Yardley 158 D4
Yardley Gobion 148 C3
Yardley Hastings 149 D2
Yardro 144 B2
Yarford 115 F5
Yarkhill 145 F3
Yarley 116 C3
Yarlington 117 D5
Yarm 202 D1
Yarmouth 106 C4
Yarnacott 113 G2
Yarnbrook 117 F2
Yarnfield 171 F4
Yarnscombe 113 F3
Yarnton 133 G2
Yarpole 145 D1
Yarrow ScBord 227 E3
Yarrow Som 116 A3
Yarrow Feus 227 E3
Yarrowford 227 F3
Yarsop 144 D3
Yarwell 161 F3
Yate 131 G4
Yatehouse Green 171 E1
Yateley 120 D1
Yatesbury 132 C5
Yattendon 134 A5
Yatton Here 144 D1
Yatton NSom 116 B1
Yatton Keynell 132 A5
Yaverland 107 F4
Yawl 103 G3
Yaxham 178 B4
Yaxley Cambs 161 G3
Yaxley Suff 164 C4
Yazor 144 D3
Ye Olde Pork Pie Shoppe,
    Melton Mowbray Leics
    LE13 1NW 160 C1
Yeabridge 104 A1
Yeading 136 A4
Yeadon 194 B3
Yealand Conyers 199 G5
Yealand Redmayne 199 G5
Yealand Storrs 199 G5
Yealmbridge 100 B2
Yealmpton 100 B2
Yearby 213 F5
Yearsley 203 E5
Yeaton 156 D1
Yeaveley 172 C3
Yeavering 228 D3
Yedingham 204 B5
Yelford 133 F2
Yell 278 D4
Yelland Devon 113 E2
Yelland Devon 99 F1
Yelling 150 A1
Yellowcraig ELoth
    EH39 5DS 236 C1
Yelvertoft 160 A5
Yelverton Devon 100 B1
Yelverton Norf 179 D5
Yenston 117 E5
Yeo Mill 114 B5
Yeo Vale 113 E3
Yeoford 102 A3
Yeolmbridge 98 D2
Yeomadon 112 D5
Yeovil 104 B1
Yeovil Country Park Som
    BA20 1QZ 104 B1
Yeovil Marsh 104 B1
Yeovilton 116 C5
Yerbeston 127 D2
Yesnaby 277 B6
Yesterday's World, Battle
    ESuss TN33 0AQ 110 C2
Yetholm Mains 228 C4
Yetlington 229 E5
Yetminster 104 B1
Yettington 103 D4
Yetts o'Muckhart 243 F4
Yew Green 147 E1
Yielden 149 F1
Yieldshields 234 C4
Ynys 167 E4
Ynys Tachwedd 154 C3
Ynysboeth 129 G3
Ynysddu 130 A3
Ynyshir 129 G3
Ynyslas 154 C3
Ynysmaerdy 129 G4
Ynysmeudwy 128 D2
Ynystawe 128 C2
Ynyswen 129 F3
Ynysybwl 129 G3
Yockenthwaite 201 E5
Yockleton 156 C1
Yokefleet 196 A5
Yoker 233 G3
Yonder Bognie 268 E6
York 195 F2
York Castle Museum
    YO1 9SA 90 York
York Dungeon
    YO1 9RD 90 York
York Minster
    YO1 7HH 90 York
Yorkletts 124 C2
Yorkley 131 F2
Yorkshire Museum
    YO1 7FR 90 York
Yorkshire Sculpture Park
    WYorks WF4 4LG 185 G1
Yorton 170 C5
Yorton Heath 170 C5
Youldon 112 D5
Youldonmoor Cross 112 D5
Youlgreave 172 D1
Youlthorpe 195 G2
Youlton 195 D1
Young's End 137 G1
Yoxall 158 D1
Yoxford 153 E1
Ysbyty Cynfyn 155 D5
Ysbyty Ifan 168 B3
Ysbyty Ystwyth 154 D5
Ysceifiog 182 C5
Ysgubor-y-coed 154 C3
Ystalyfera 129 D2
Ystrad 129 F3
Ystrad Aeron 142 B2
Ystrad Meurig 142 D1
Ystrad Mynach 130 A3
Ystradfellte 129 F1
Ystradffin 143 D3
Ystradgynlais 129 D1
Ystradowen Carmar 128 D1
Ystradowen VGlam 129 G5
Ystumtuen 154 D5
Ythanwells 260 E1
Ythsie 261 G1

Z
Zeal Monachorum 102 A2
Zeals 117 E4
Zelah 96 C4
Zennor 94 B3
Zouch 173 G5
ZSL London Zoo GtLon
    NW1 4RY 12 A3

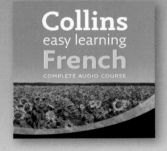

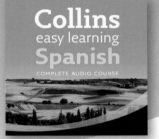

i-SPY

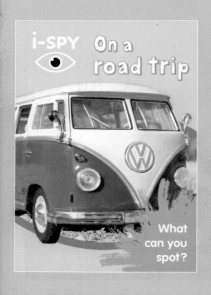

Look around you and discover the world with i-SPY

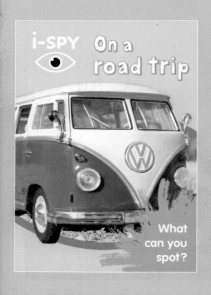
i-SPY On a road trip — What can you spot?

i-SPY Nature — What can you spot?

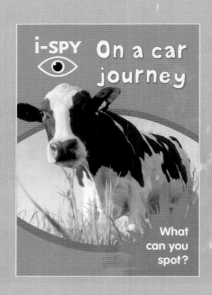
i-SPY On a car journey — What can you spot?

Spy it
up to 200 fun things to spot around you

Spot it
tick off what you see as you go

Score it
score points for each spot and receive your super-spotter certificate and badge!

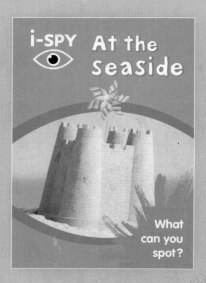
i-SPY At the seaside — What can you spot?

collins.co.uk/i-SPY

@Collins4Parents f facebook.com/collins4parents

MICHELIN

What can you spot?